CONSUMER LAW AND POLICY: TEXT AND MATERIALS ON REGULATING CONSUMER MARKETS

This new edition continues to provide a critical introduction to the legal regulation of consumer markets, situating it within the context of broader debates about rationales for regulation, the role of the state and the growth of neo-liberalism. It draws on interdisciplinary sources, assessing, for example, the increased influence of behavioural economics on consumer law. It analyses the Europeanisation of consumer law and the tensions between neo-liberalism and the social market, consumer protection and consumer choice, in the establishment of the single market ground rules. The book also assesses national, regional and international responses to the world financial crisis as reflected in the regulation of consumer credit markets.

This edition incorporates recent legislative and judicial developments of the law, blending substantial extracts from primary UK, EU and international legal materials.

Consumer Law and Policy:
Text and Materials on
Regulating Consumer Markets

Third Edition

Iain Ramsay

Professor, Kent Law School
University of Kent

·HART·
PUBLISHING

OXFORD AND PORTLAND, OREGON
2012

Published in the United Kingdom by Hart Publishing Ltd
16C Worcester Place, Oxford, OX1 2JW
Telephone: +44 (0)1865 517530
Fax: +44 (0)1865 510710
E-mail: mail@hartpub.co.uk
Website: http://www.hartpub.co.uk

Published in North America (US and Canada) by
Hart Publishing
c/o International Specialized Book Services
920 NE 58th Avenue, Suite 300
Portland, OR 97213-3786
USA
Tel: +1 503 287 3093 or toll-free: (1) 800 944 6190
Fax: +1 503 280 8832
E-mail: orders@isbs.com
Website: http://www.isbs.com

British Library Cataloguing in Publication Data

Data Available

ISBN: 978-1-84946-262-4

Typeset by Forewords, Oxford
Printed and bound in Great Britain by
TJ International Ltd, Padstow, Cornwall

Preface to the Third Edition

This edition continues to provide a critical and interdisciplinary introduction to consumer law and policy. The chapter on consumer credit has expanded substantially in the light of the international, regional and national developments in response to the Great Recession. As a consequence the chapter on the Office of Fair Trading has not been carried forward to this edition but other chapters include material on the OFT's approaches to regulation .

I would like to acknowledge the assistance of the Department of Law at the University of Kent which provided financial support for completing this edition and to Virginia Torrie for valuable research assistance on Chapter 6. I also thank Hart Publishing for their excellent work in preparing the manuscript for publication. As always, thanks to Toni Williams.

Canterbury, Kent
September 2012

Acknowledgements

Grateful acknowledgement is made to all the authors and publishers of copyright material which appears in this book, and in particular to the following for permission to reprint material from the sources indicated:

ABTA – The Travel Association: for the notice detailing their scheme for protection against the financial failure of ABTA members.

Bloomsbury Publishing and Rogers, Coleridge & White Ltd: for an extract from Polly Toynbee, *Hard Work Life in Low-Pay Britain* (2003). Reproduced by permission of the author c/o Rogers, Coleridge & White Ltd, 20 Powis Mews, London W11 1JN.

Columbia Law Review: for an extract from Friedrich Kessler, 'Contracts of Adhesion: Some Thoughts about Freedom of Contract' (1943) 43 *Columbia Law Review* 629, 631–32, 640.

Competition Commission: for extracts from the *Home Credit Inquiry* (2006) and *Extended Warranties on Domestic Electrical Goods: A Report on the Supply of Extended Warranties on Domestic Electrical Goods within the UK*, vols 1, 2 and 3 (2003).

Democracy: A Journal of Ideas, Inc: for an extract from Elizabeth Warren, 'Unsafe at Any Rate' (Summer 2007) *Democracy Journal* 8–9.

Edward Elgar Publishing: for an extract from Iain Ramsay and Toni Williams, 'The Crash that Launched a Thousand Fixes: Regulation of Consumer Credit after the Lending Revolution and the Credit Crunch', in K Alexander and N Moloney (eds), *Law Reform and Financial Markets* (2011).

Financial Stability Board: for an extract from *Consumer Finance Protection with Particular Focus on Credit* (2011).

Harvard Law Review: for extracts from 'Developments in the Law: Corporate Crime' (1978–79) 92 *Harvard Law Review* 1227, 1231; and Todd Rakoff, 'Contracts of Adhesion: An Essay in Reconstruction' (1983) 96 *Harvard Law Review* 1174, 1222.

Incorporated Council of Law Reporting: for extracts from the Law Reports: *Appeal Cases* (AC), *Queen's Bench Division* (QB) and *Weekly Law Reports* (WLR).

Macmillan Publishers Ltd: for an extract from Ross Cranston, *Regulating Business: Law and Consumer Agencies* (Palgrave, 1979).

Minnesota Law Review: for an extract from William Prosser, 'The Implied Warranty of Merchantable Quality' (1943), 27 *Minnesota Law Review* 117, 122–25.

Mulheron, Rachel: for an extract from *Reform of Collective Redress in England and Wales: A Perspective of Need* (2009).

National Audit Office: for an extract from the National Audit Office Report by the Comptroller and Auditor General, *The Office of Fair Trading: Protecting the Consumer from Unfair Trading Practices* (HC 57 1999/00).

OECD: for a figure from *OECD Factbook 2010: Economic, Environmental and Social Statistics,*

OECD Publishing http://dx.doi.org/10.1787/factbook-2010-en, and an extract from *Consumer Dispute Resolution and Redress in the Global Marketplace* (2006) www.oecd.org/internet/consumerpolicy/36456184.pdf.

Osgoode Hall Law Journal and the authors: for extracts from Michael Trebilcock, 'Winners and Losers in the Modern Regulatory System: Must the Consumer Always Lose?' (1975) 13 *Osgoode Hall Law Journal* 618, 620–25; and Sinai Deutch, 'Are Consumer Rights, Human Rights?' (1994) 32 *Osgoode Hall Law Journal* 537, 551–53, 576.

Springer: for an extract from Iain Ramsay, 'Consumer Credit Regulation After the Fall: International Dimensions' (2011) 1 *Zeitschrift für Europäisches Unternehmens- und Verbraucherrecht*. With kind permission from Springer Science+Business Media BV.

Sweet & Maxwell: for an extract from the *European Human Rights Reports*.

Thomson Reuters: for extracts from the *Pacific Reporter 2d* and Iain Ramsay, 'Regulation and the Constitution of the Single Market; The Role of Consumer Law' (2010) 50 *Canadian Business Law Journal* 322; and an extract from the *Dominion Law Reports*, reproduced by permission of Canada Law Book, a division of Thomson Reuters Canada Limited.

University of Chicago Press and the authors: for extracts from V Goldberg, 'Institutional Change and the Quasi-Invisible Hand' (1974) 17 *Journal of Law and Economics* 461, 483–87; H Beales, R Craswell and S Salop, 'The Efficient Regulation of Consumer Information' (1981) 24 *Journal of Law and Economics*, 491, 513–14, 516, 521–23, 527, 529–31, 532; and Ben-Shahar and Posner, 'The Right to Withdraw in Contract Law' (2011) 40 *Journal of Legal Studies* 115.

University of Pennsylvania Law Review: for an extract from O Ben-Shahar and C Schneider, 'The Failure of Mandated Disclosure' (2011) 159 *University of Pennsylvania Law Review* 647.

University of Toronto Press: for an extract from Iain Ramsay, 'To Heap Distress upon Distress: Comparative Reflections on Interest Rate Ceilings' (2010) 60 *University of Toronto Law Journal* 707. Reprinted with permission from University of Toronto Press (www.utpjournals.com).

Perseus Books: for an extract from James Q Wilson, 'The Politics of Regulation' in James Q Wilson (ed), *The Politics of Regulation* (Basic Books, 1980).

Wiley-Blackwell Publishing Ltd: for extracts from Colin Scott, 'Regulatory Innovation and the Online Consumer' (2004) 26 *Law and Policy* 476, 479, 480; and Iain Ramsay, 'A Tale of Two Debtors: Responding to the Shock of Overindebtedness in France and England—A Story from the Trente Piteuses' (2012) 75 *MLR* 212 at 246.

Yale Law Journal: from an extract from G Priest, 'A Theory of the Consumer Product Warranty' (1980–81) 90 *Yale Law Journal* 1297, 1343–46.

All extracts printed without footnotes.

Every effort has been made to trace and contact copyright holders prior to publication but this has not been possible in every case. If notified, the publisher will undertake to rectify any errors or omissions at the earliest opportunity.

Contents

8   QUALITY REGULATION AND POST-PURCHASE QUALITY
    PROBLEMS   505

9   PRODUCT SAFETY REGULATION   581

Table of Cases

Table of Legislation

National

Australia

Brazil

Canada

France

Germany

Israel

United Kingdom

United States

1

Setting the Context

This book is about contemporary regulation of consumer markets. It analyses the reasons for consumer law and policy and the different approaches to regulation of the price, quality and terms of consumer products and services. It provides an opportunity to assess the role and limits of consumer law and policy in addressing the pathologies of affluent consumer societies such as overindebtedness and to assess whether consumer law is a progressive form of law or merely a subaltern in the onwards march of neo-liberalism. The growth of a regulatory state in the UK and the EU provides the backdrop to current consumer law and we explore the ideas and institutions associated with this new form of state and their effects on consumer law and policy. Regional (EU) and international developments and institutions increasingly structure consumer law and policy. Consumer law is part of the establishment of the ground rules of the EU internal market and the development of transnational private regulation (Cafaggi, 2011).

'Consumer law' could be understood as all laws and regulations affecting consumption and the structuring of consumer markets. This would include most of the legal system—competition law, intellectual property, etc, and we focus primarily on traditional areas of consumer law. However, we use these areas—consumer credit, advertising, product safety—to illustrate some of the difficult economic, political and institutional choices that are embedded in choices of legal framework for markets. Consumer law is an instrumental form of law and requires reflection on the relationship of law to behavioural norms in markets, and the complexities of the relationship between these norms.

1. The development of consumer law and policy

Many assume that the 'consumer society' is a recent phenomenon, which developed after the Second World War. For the past two decades historians have, however, argued over the 'birth' of the consumer society which may date from at least the eighteenth century (Stearns, 1997; Brewer, 2003; Trentmann, 2006). While this should make us wary of associating the consumer society with the contemporary era, this is the focus of this text. But what is a consumer society? Benson offers the following starting point:

> [T]hey are societies ... in which choice and credit are readily available, in which social value is defined in terms of purchasing power and material possessions, and in which there is a desire, above all, for that which is new, modern, exciting and fashionable. (Benson, 1994: 5)

Avner Offer locates 'affluent' societies in the post-Second World War period, noting that since that time 'the markets of Western Europe and the United States have delivered a flow of novel and compelling opportunities, services and goods. North America and Europe are about three times as rich as they were in 1950. I call that affluence' (Offer, 2006:1). The changing nature of consumption and consumer markets since the Second World War provides the context for understanding present-day consumer regulation in the United Kingdom. During this period, the consumption of durable goods increased enormously, continuing the growth of the mass consumer markets which had developed during the interwar years (Atiyah, 1979; Stevenson, 1984). Margaret Hall, an economist, wrote in 1960 that the consumer sector during the 1950s was marked by several features, including (Hall in Warswick and Ady, 1962: 429, 457)

> growth in consumers' real income and the emergence of mass 'middle class' purchasing power ... a rapid growth in the demand for consumer durable goods, such as motorcars, radios and television sets ...the development of hire-purchase ... [and] an explicit recognition of the consumer's interest, evidenced, for example, by the formation of consumers' associations and by legislation against restrictive practices. ...[She concluded that] consumption is becoming more of a social force than production.

The growing affluence of the population during this period, coupled with changes in occupational structure, provided a large and stable consumer market which seemed to presage the development of a 'consumer society' similar to that which existed in North America. The development of a large middle group of technical and administrative occupations, a characteristic of advanced capitalism, might, it was thought, break down traditional class barriers (Halsey, 1986: 32). Some sociologists developed an 'embourgeoisement' argument—that the working class was gradually being assimilated, through consumption of products similar to those of the middle class, to the style and manners of that class (compare Goldthorpe et al, 1969, 1987). Antony Crosland had argued in *The Future of Socialism* that 'the sociological significance of the spread of high consumption ... must weaken the sense, as of course it lessens the fact, of inferior or unequal standards of life, and of class inequality generally' (Crosland, 1956: 286), and Michael Young, a founder of the Consumers Association, argued in 1960 that 'class based on production is slowly giving way to status based on consumption as the centre of social gravity'.

The harnessing of technological developments to large-scale production methods made much more widely available a broad range of relatively sophisticated products which were increasingly marketed through national distribution and retail chains. The growth of nationally branded products advertised through the new mass medium of television changed the nature of traditional consumer markets. The role of the small retailer declined as retailing and distribution became organised in large bureaucratic units in order to take advantage of scale economies. Industry became increasingly concentrated (Hannah, 1976). During this period, a general thrust of government economic policy was to dismantle wartime controls and trade-protection legislation. It was argued that such restrictions hampered the competitiveness of British industry and jeopardised the central post-war goal of full employment (Craig, 1987: 204–05). The Restrictive Trade Practices Act 1956 was a major assault on the traditions of cartelisation which pervaded much of UK industry. These measures aided the transformation of the market into an effective mechanism for meeting consumer demand.

These developments formed the background to the establishment, in 1959, of the Molony Committee on Consumer Protection. The terms of reference of the Committee included the broad mandate 'to consider and report what changes if any in the law and what other measures, if any, are desirable for the further protection of the consuming public'. The Committee restricted its focus, however, to the situation of 'one who purchases (or hire-purchases) goods for private use or consumption', excluding from its purview the interests both of the ultimate user and of the service sector.

Although the Committee's report was greeted as being 'not quite sufficiently radically pro-consumer' (*The Economist*, 1962: 326), and although its legal recommendations were described as 'good hearted … unimaginative' and 'insular' (Diamond, 1963: 66; and see Hilton below at 20), it provides an appropriate historical point of entry to present-day consumer regulation. The report, intended to provide 'a foundation for policy making for the next twenty years', stands at the beginning of a series of measures that were taken to protect consumers. It provided, for example, the model for the regulation of advertising and for trade descriptions legislation, and was the source for most of the consumer-protection initiatives of the 1960s. The general philosophy of the Committee was that competition and market forces were the best protections for consumer interests. The Committee members were sensitive, however, to the potential dangers of changes in the structure of the marketplace. In the following extract, they outline the arguments expressed to them concerning the potentially detrimental impact of these changes.

Board of Trade, *Final Report of the Committee on Consumer Protection* (Molony Committee), Cmnd 1781/1962, paras 40–43, 403, 820–21, 869, 891

Alleged inadequacy of system

40. The essence of the views which many have expressed to us is that the old-established balance between buyer and seller has been seriously disturbed in recent years by the emergence of radically different methods of manufacture, of distribution and of merchandising; and that as a result, the existing system of consumer protection has become inadequate in various respects. …

Consumer's shopping problems

41. The contention that the consumer now stands in need of greater protection is put forward in this way. Whereas the consumer of fifty years ago needed only a reasonable modicum of skill and knowledge to recognise the composition of the goods on offer and their manner of production, and to assess their quality and fitness for his particular purpose, the consumer of today finds it difficult if not impossible to do so because of the development of complicated production techniques. … The job of ascertaining and soundly assessing the wide range of alternative choices open to him is more, his supporters aver, than the consumer can possibly be expected to do. It is further argued that the increased sale of branded and nationally

advertised goods has tended to reduce the retailer's function to that of handing over what the customer has already been persuaded to buy before entering the shop; and that partly for this reason, partly because it is almost as difficult for him as for his customer to sort out the merits and shortcomings of the goods he stocks, the retailer is far less able to perform his special and essential function of giving expert advice to the individual customer. This trend is seen in its most advanced form in self-service retailing. For all these reasons, it is said, the further protection of the consumer has become at once more necessary and more difficult to achieve.

Complexity of goods

42. Moreover, the ordinary consumer now spends a good deal of money on appliances and equipment of types unknown, or known only to a favoured few, thirty years ago. His car or his motor-scooter, his radio or television set, his vacuum cleaner, washing machine or refrigerator are relatively expensive and complicated assemblies of components, the precise working of which is imperfectly understood by the vast majority of buyers. The quality and relative merit of each can be assessed (if at all) only by a qualified expert using special equipment. Their useful life will depend, to marked extent, on the manner in which they are used and serviced, as well as on their initial quality. The failure of a single small component may put the whole machine out of action. When confronted with the need to make a choice between different models of such goods the consumer is incapable of intelligent discrimination; even price will not provide a sure signpost to the degree of satisfaction he is likely to achieve.

Vulnerability of consumer

43. In such a maze, the contention runs, the consumer finds it beyond his power to make a wise and informed choice and is vulnerable to exploitation and deception. On the extent to which the consumer is in fact exploited or deceived, witnesses have expressed or implied divergent views, ranging from those who think such an occurrence to be disgracefully widespread to those who see it as little more than a potential danger. Even if no advantage is taken of his ignorance, his ill-informed approach to the shopping problems arising in an era of plenty and prosperity is likely, it is said, to lead him into purchases unsuited to his needs. At the hands of the advertiser, the artful shop assistant or the ingratiating door-to-door caller, he is liable, it is suggested, to fall victim to the wiles of salesmanship. ...

Reluctance to pursue claims

403. There was widespread recognition that the ordinary consumer—devoid of technical knowledge, lacking ready access to independent technical advice, uncertain of the strength of his case, a stranger to the law and its ways—must be reluctant to incur the considerable trouble and appreciable cost of pursuing what he regards as his legitimate complaint. This reluctance is deepened if the outlay on expert investigation and legal proceedings is disproportionate to the price paid for the goods, and especially if satisfaction cannot be obtained short of bringing his case to trial. The consequences are that the less reputable retailer, knowing that the challenge is not likely to be maintained, is not disposed to canvass the idea of a settlement. In the result, it is, said, the rights which the law give[s] to the consumer too often go by default. ...

Consumer unorganised

891. The business of making and selling is highly organised, often in large units, and calls to its aid at every step complex and highly expert skills. The business of buying is conducted by the smallest unit, the individual consumer, relying on the guidance afforded by experience, if he possesses it, and, if not, on instinctive but not always rational thought processes. The capacity of sales staff in shops to help the consumer has deteriorated. The manufacturer and the distributor, in a country dependent on exports, speak with a well-organised and powerful

voice in national affairs. The interests of the consumer are sometimes overlooked because he is voiceless. The need for consumers to organise themselves was first expressed in the genesis of the Co-operative movement. When traders combine, or a single trader buys on a large scale, there is no doubt about the capacity of the purchaser to protect himself....

Call for redesign

820. ... through many of the submissions reaching us there ran the theme that piecemeal improvement would not ensure that a proper balance between buyer and seller would be wholly restored and permanently maintained; and that this purpose could only be achieved by a fundamental alteration in the structure of the system.

Argument for redesign

821. The argument supporting this theme was, in broad terms, that there existed on the side of the manufacturers and distributors effective organisation, providing mutual assistance and potent representation. Their approach to the difficulties of the consumer was one of indifference. The idea of a 'consumers' sovereignty' was fallacious. In truth, it was said, the producer easily prevailed over the welfare of the consumer; and would continue to do so until the consumer was provided with an organisation of equal weight to protect and represent him. ...

Attention to enforcement

869. Acts and regulations are of little value unless they are observed. A major cause of consumer weakness in the past has lain in the inadequate enforcement of the many laws in his favour. ...

A major thrust of consumer policies during the early 1970s was to redress the apparent imbalance of power between producers and consumers through the introduction of public regulation and the subsidisation of consumer organisations. These initiatives drew on such documents as the Crowther Committee's report on consumer credit (1971) and on the broad political support for consumer protection that existed in the early 1970s. Public regulation to protect consumers against economic losses was often justified by the diffuse nature of such losses, which although very large in total, were such that any one individual found it uneconomical to seek to redress her own loss through traditional methods. New agencies such as the Office of Fair Trading (1973) and the National Consumer Council (1975) were created. According to Lord Borrie, 'during the main period of advance in consumer protection in the 1960s and 1970s, the common law did not contribute very much' apart from cases such as *Jarvis v Swans Tours Holidays* (1973) which seemed to recognise the distinct nature of experiential loss in consumer contracts for services (Borrie, 1984: 7, 9).

In the area of health and safety, public regulation had existed since Victorian times to protect consumers against adulterated food (Paulus, 1974). The use of complex new technology in the production and distribution process posed new and uncharted risks. The Thalidomide disaster in the early 1960s symbolised the potential dangers of technology and drew attention to the limited public regulation of drug distribution in the United Kingdom. In addition, scientists were beginning to discover the long-term carcinogenic effects of certain food additives, and smoking was being clearly linked with lung cancer. The reduction in Western countries of the risks of being affected by natural diseases and disasters focused greater interest on potential man-made health-and-safety risks.

The period from 1964 to 1979 is viewed by many as the 'heyday' of consumer legislation throughout the Western capitalist world (Reich and Micklitz, 1980: 1–12). Lizabeth Cohen described the postwar US economy as a 'consumer's republic' where exanded access to credit for male wage-earners, along with substantial government subsidies to the housing industry, promised the democratic ideal of equal citizenship through greater equality of consumption—rather than through an increased welfare state. This focus on consumption, including equal access to safe consumption, created a growing political constituency (see also Aaker and Day, 1971; Nadel, 1971). In 1960 John F Kennedy made a promise during his presidential campaign that 'the consumer is the only man [*sic*] in our economy without a high-powered lobbyist. I intend to be that lobbyist' (quoted in Cohen, 2004: 345). In 1962 Kennedy introduced to Congress a consumer bill of rights (the right to know, to be safe, to choose and to be heard) and a (modest) agenda of consumer bills. This 'consumer rights' agenda was an inspiration for developments in other parts of the world and the later international principles of consumer protection (see below at 39).

Cohen (2003) argues that consumerism during this period in the US had three demands: the passage of laws that protected consumers better in the marketplace; a reorientation of regulators towards the public interest rather than industry, reviving the New Deal model of the independent regulatory agency serving the public interest; and giving consumers a permanent voice in government. Public agencies such as the Federal Trade Commission were revitalised, and new social regulatory agencies such as the Consumer Product Safety Commission were created (1972). She comments that least progress was made on the goal of consumer representation in government and that 'all … levels of consumer advocacy assumed the viability and desirability of capitalist private enterprise and markets … overall this was a politics of Americans who bandied together as consumers to protest the practice not the ideal of advanced capitalism' (Cohen 2003: 358–59). It provided the possibility for a populist critique that transcended divisions of class, gender and race; concerns with poverty were translated into ensuring that the poor had access to the same products and services as the middle classes. The US courts, through the development of strict liability in tort, the creation of a law of products liability, and the growth of class actions, were increasingly regarded as a regulator of the marketplace 'another existing arm of government retooled to curb the influence of exploitative corporations and empower consumers' (ibid: 361).

US developments are referred to throughout this book because UK capitalism is often viewed as having characteristics closer to the US model than other European countries, and its problems, policies and approaches have often influenced the UK. US ideas (such as class action, strict product liability and a fresh start for consumer bankrupts) have also influenced European developments (see Wiegand, 1991, on early influences) although increasingly the EU has developed a distinctive and competing model of regulation.

Consumer law and regulation during this period was only one example of government response to problems originating in the economic system. There was also a significant growth in environmental protection and in health and safety regulation of the workplace. It was regarded as a legitimate and proper role for government in a mixed economy to protect consumers and others against threats to their quality of life. This could be viewed as part of a movement to protect the new 'social rights' in modern society—rights to health and material security (Cappelletti and Garth, 1978: 7–8). This quest for security is reflected in loss-distribution and risk-spreading policies in several areas of consumer protection, eg consumer credit and products liability and the use of standards and licensing in relation to health-and-safety risks. Such developments reflected a transition in modern law from an emphasis on private rights to an acceptance of public regulation. It would be dangerous, however, to view this period of consumer law as identified with the welfare state or welfarism. Most consumer legislation in the UK was introduced by a Conservative government and was intended to make markets work better.

---

2. Consumer law, neo-liberalism and the social market

A transformation in ideas about the role of the state and the market has taken place since the 1970s. First, there has been in the UK a transition from producerism to consumerism—from policies being primarily concerned with their impact on the individual as a producer to a pervasive concern about the impact on consumer choice (Whitman, 2009). By 1999 it could be stated that: 'Old Labour used to champion producers. New Labour crusades for consumers' (*New Statesman*: 10 January 2000: iv). Contrast the following comments:

> From a social perspective, work not only occupies a large proportion of most peoples days, but also provides one of the principal sites where we can construct social relationships and seek meaning for our lives. The consequence of unemployment is often described as 'social exclusion'. (Collins et al, Labour Law 1)

> We are all consumers now, consumers first and foremost, consumers by right and by duty. The day after the 11/9 outrage George W Bush, when calling Americans to get over the trauma and go back to normal, found no better words than 'go back shopping'. It is the level of our shopping activity and the ease with which we dispose of one object of consumption in order to replace it with a 'new and improved' one which serves us as the prime measure of our social standing and the score in the life-success competition. To all problems we encounter on the road away from trouble and towards satisfaction we seek solutions in shops.

> From cradle to coffin we are trained and drilled to treat shops as pharmacies filled with drugs to cure or at least mitigate all illnesses and afflictions of our lives and lives in common. Shops and shopping acquire thereby a fully and truly eschatological dimension. ... The fullness of consumer enjoyment means fullness of life. I shop, therefore I am. To shop or not to shop, this is the question.

> For defective consumers, those contemporary have-nots, non-shopping is the jarring and festering stigma of a life un-fulfilled—and of own nonentity and good-for-nothingness. Not just the absence of pleasure: absence of human dignity. Of life meaning. Ultimately, of humanity and any other ground for self-respect and respect of the others around. (Bauman, 2011)

These contrasting viewpoints on the relative dominance of our identity as consumers or producers should be kept in mind in discussion of the importance of 'consumer choice' and 'empowerment' in policymaking. This may result in greater pressure on and regulation of our lives as producers. It also draws attention to the links between consumption and production regimes in society.

Second, it is an era identified with the dominance of neo-liberalism and finance capitalism. These phenomena are associated with the breakdown of trade barriers, and capital controls, increased competition at national, regional and international level and a consequent reduction in labour power. Although sometimes identified with a minimal state, there is often a need for re-regulation of markets and the co-ordination of the international financial system. The state becomes a regulatory state. David Harvey (Harvey, 2005) argues that it is primarily a class phenomenon (Harvey does note the complexity here of identifying class), a reassertion of class hegemony and the restoration of power to a narrow upper class. He identifies the following characteristics: the fusion of the privileges of ownership and management in capitalist enterprises (eg through stock options); and the reduction of the historical gap between finance capital and production and manufacturing. Large corporations become dependent on financial dealings to sustain a profit rather than through production. The increased volatility in the international economy makes the regulation of the integrity of the financial system a central concern.

Harvey argues that 'freedom' has become associated with 'mindless consumerism' and a discourse that constructs a 'neo-liberal market based popular culture of differentiated consumerism and individual libertarianism'. Neo-liberalism constructs freedom and liberty as pitted against the stifling bureaucracy of the state and state regulation. In relation to the UK he argues that

> Thatcher forged consent through the cultivation of a middle class that relished the joys of home ownership, private property, individualism and the liberation of entrepreneurial opportunities ... middle class values spread more widely to encompass many of those who had once had a firm working-class identity. The opening of Britain to freer trade allowed a consumer culture to flourish, and the proliferation of financial institutions brought more and more of a debt culture into the centre of a formerly staid British life. (Harvey, 2005: 61–62).

The neo-liberal state views competition as a primary virtue.

> Privatization and deregulation combined with competition ... increase productivity, improve quality and reduce costs. ... The neo-liberal state should persistently seek out internal reorganizations and new institutional arrangements that improve its competitive position vis a vis other states in the global market...While personal and individual freedom in the marketplace is guaranteed, each individual is held responsible and accountable for his or her own actions and well being. This principle extends into the realms of welfare, education, health care and even pensions.

In terms of governance

> neo-liberals are however, profoundly suspicious of democracy. Governance by majority rule is seen as a potential threat to individual rights and constitutional liberties. ... Neo-liberals therefore tend to favour governance by experts and elites. ... Given that neo-liberal theory centres on the rule of law ... it follows conflicts and opposition must be mediated through the courts. (ibid: 65–66)

Harvey points, however, to contradictions in the role of the state under neo-liberalism, with the need to regulate market failures and ensure the smooth operation of institutions such as the international financial system: the distaste for democratic control leads to 'the paradox of intense state interventions and government by elites and "experts"' (eg the IMF) 'in a world where the state is supposed not to be interventionist'.

To what extent do the developments in regulation of consumer markets at the national, regional and international level which we consider throughout this book reflect these themes of neo-liberalism? Is regulation of consumer markets primarily an exercise in making the world safe for market capitalism? By assuring the conditions for capitalist accumulation, legitimating it through the idea of consumer sovereignty—does the market provide individuals with 'what they want'—but not subject it to democratic control?

Third, inequality increased during this period. "[F]rom the 1980s onwards, inequalities in British and American societies increased sharply, especially in comparison with Europe (Offer, 2006: 273). There is a paradox therefore that in these affluent societies many individuals experienced a relative decline in their economic position. This was also a period when there was a rise in the two-income earner family in order to maintain the status associated with the earlier model of the single male wage earner. Offer argues that during this period, the US and UK traded off security and equality for greater consumption choices. In his view "the Thatcher Project deliberately set out to emulate the American model, and has been pursued with similar ardor by new Labour" (ibid: 357). He also argues that these societies have developed significant pathologies such as overindebtedness and obesity as a consequence of a general myopic tendency to favour short-term interests so that individual choices sacrifice the future to the present and do not lead to overall social welfare.

Fourth, the Thatcher government generally saw competition as the best consumer policy and did not favour extensive consumer regulation. To the extent that there were consumer law developments during this period (1979–97) they were generally stimulated by the need to give effect to European directives, for example, in the area of unfair terms in consumer contracts.

The emergence of a regulatory state spawned the growth of regulation as an academic area of study. Much initial economic analysis drew attention to the potential failures of government regulation including burdensome compliance costs, and to such potential anticompetitive effects of regulation as the creation of barriers to market entry and the stifling of innovation (Peltzman, 1975). Others argued that governments had often failed to 'think through' the rationales for intervention, thus causing a 'mismatch' between mischief and remedy (Breyer, 1982: 184). Political theorists argued that the attempt by governments to bring about substantive social objectives through legal regulation—instrumental law—could only be made at the cost of the 'overlegalization' (Offe, 1984: 280) of social relations and would be ultimately ineffective. Gunther Teubner articulated his regulatory 'trilemma' of 'circumvention, perversity and negative feedback' that resulted in a pathology of increasingly elaborate and legalised regulation that was ultimately ineffective (Teubner, 1987; and see Habermas 1998).

Julia Black summarizes these critiques of regulation:

> [T]he instruments used (laws backed by sanctions) are inappropriate and unsophisticated (instrument failure), that government has insufficient knowledge to be able to identify the causes of the problems, to design solutions that are appropriate, and to identify non-compliance (information failure), that implementation of the regulation is inadequate (implementation

failure) and/or that those being regulated are insufficiently inclined to comply (motivation failure). (Black, 2001: 106)

These developments stimulated a great deal of rethinking of the role and nature of regulation of markets. These included the idea of 'responsive regulation' where regulation would reflect a mix of instruments (reflecting the 'hybridity' of regulation), and the resources of the regulated would be harnessed to achieve compliance (see below Chapters 2 and 3). At a higher level of abstraction there was a focus on what appeared to be new forms of governance in neo-liberalism which attempt to manage the subject of consumption—the consumer—through education, expert advice and knowledge (eg Rose, 1999). Deregulation and privatisation often imposed greater choices on individuals (eg pensions). Forced to make choices, individuals were invited to regulate themselves according to particular norms of behaviour. Thus in consumer finance markets individuals must learn the appropriate norms of credit and savings behavior and become financially literate. More recently insights from behavioural economics have been harnessed to 'nudge' individuals to change their behavior. Whether these strategies of 'mobilising' or 'responsibilising' the consumer are likely to be successful—consumers seem often to be unmanageable—it draws attention to the very significant role of information as a tool of consumer policy 'and its explicit recognition as a regulatory tool' (Black, 2002).

The arrival of 'New Labour' in government in 1997 in the UK resulted in a new interest in the role of consumer policy as part of a 'The Third Way' approach to rejuvenating civil society and social democracy and as a response to the phenomenon of globalisation. Globalisation was viewed both as a 'challenge and opportunity' by the Blair government (Grant, 2002: 6). The government viewed efficient consumer markets with demanding consumers as a method for achieving global competitiveness for the UK economy. There was a role for the state as a regulator based on market failures (see below Chapter 2). Anthony Giddens, a primary intellectual architect of the Third Way, argued for a new model of welfare that would go beyond traditional approaches of direct transfers and embrace educational, preventive and regulatory measures (Giddens, 1994: 155). Giddens recognises the need for a social market model that shares risks widely, protects the most vulnerable and cultivates social cohesion (Giddens, 2007: ch 1). Greater individual responsibility and risk-taking could take place against a background of social solidarity.

The influences of these general ideas are found in consumer law and policy. In *Modern Markets, Confident Consumers* (1999) the aim of policy is to reinforce the 'virtuous cycle of strong consumers and strong business' and consumer and competition policy are viewed as contributing to national competitiveness in a globalised world. There is the adoption of Porter's thesis developed in *The Competitive Advantage of Nations* (1990) of competitive advantage in a globalised world through continuous upgrading of quality and the idea that demanding consumers in a home market make businesses more competitive internationally There is also the increasing use of 'international benchmarking' to compare the effectiveness of regulatory regimes. Consider in the following extract the emphasis on increased individual choice in a wide array of public and private services and the need for informed choice.

Modern Markets, Confident Consumers (1999)

1.1 "A Stiff upper lip is not good for upgrading an economy" says Michael Porter in his analysis of international competitiveness, pointing out that the British are reluctant to complain and are less demanding as consumers than many other nations. He links demanding consumers in the home market with the competitiveness of a nation's suppliers. ... The more informed and demanding we are, the more likely business is to respond, improving its competitiveness in the process and leading to better value for everybody

1.2 [Past measures] ... overlooked the contribution that consumers can make to competitiveness. The Government will put consumers at the heart of policy-making to ensure such mistakes are not repeated.

1.3 The aim of this White Paper is to reinforce this virtuous circle of strong consumers and strong businesses.

Opportunity and Challenge

1.4 New technologies and the opening of global markets are delivering more choice than ever before as well as falling prices in real terms for many goods and services. The spread of electronic commerce will speed up these trends ...

... The opening up of utility markets has brought choice but requires more judgement by the individual. People are taking more responsibility for pensions, health and care in old age, involving them in important but complex choices, the success of which may not be known for many years.

Information

Information on the price and quality of products and services abounds, with IT enabling more and more to be made available. But two-thirds of consumers find the amount of information too hard to handle. A similar proportion do not understand their rights. ...

The information revolution enables business to meet the needs of their customers more precisely. But this creates concerns about privacy and some may lose out if business moves out of less profitable markets.

Consumers are increasingly concerned about health, safety, and the environmental impact of products. They have a vital role to play in tackling these major issues. ...

Social Exclusion

More complex markets and the growing amount of information needed to make good choices bear particularly hard on those who have low levels of education and skills and on the socially excluded who get limited help from the community. They are particularly vulnerable to the most unscrupulous trader. The poorest in society are least able to afford the consequences of bad purchases.

A Strategic Approach

1.6 This White Paper ... establishes a policy framework. ... The Government will look first for opportunities to make markets work, including through better information and self-regulation, but will not hesitate to regulate when other options have failed to solve problems or the risks to public health and safety are unacceptable. And it will ensure consumers' concerns are heard in Government ...

These ideas were reiterated by the Department of Trade and Industry (DTI) in 2005 with comments that constitute the New Labour view on the future of consumer policy:

> The Government wants Britain's consumer regime to be as good as any in the world. [We want] a regime that will empower and protect consumers, support open, competitive and innovative markets, that is as fair to business as it is to consumers and that has the minimum regulation necessary to achieve these goals. ...
>
> The Government is committed to improving Britain's consumer regime. We want a regime that delivers social justice, economic and environmental progress, and which is as fair to business as it is to consumers. We have set ourselves the target of raising our consumer regime to the level of the best in the world. (DTI, 2005)

In 2003 the DTI conducted an international benchmarking study of UK consumer law and policy, which concluded that

> the UK was amongst the best in terms of: consumer rights in regard to sale of goods and services; small claims court procedures; maintaining Product Safety; provision of consumer advice; strength of consumer advocacy at policy making level and sponsoring advocacy; investigating markets that are not working well for consumers.
>
> The UK appears to be behind the best in not having a duty to trade fairly, fragmentation of enforcement and poor consumer information about good and bad traders. (DTI, 2003)

Several of the issues highlighted as weaknesses are addressed in current policies. The implementation of the Unfair Commercial Practices Directive through the Consumer Protection from Unfair Trading Regulations 2008 introduces a duty not to trade unfairly.

There is continuity between *Modern Markets* and the Molony Committee report. Both identify problems of new technology (in the latter the Internet), information deficits and consumer redress as potential problems. They also emphasise the importance of the consumer voice being heard in government. *Modern Markets* introduces the issue of social exclusion (discussed in Chapter 2 below), a term that is wider than traditional definitions of poverty and that emerged in France in the early 1970s to replace Marxist concepts of exploitation (see Boltanski and Chiapello, 2011). *Modern Markets* indicates also that the focus of consumer policy has widened since the Molony Committee report. That report adopted a relatively limited interpretation of the consumer relationship: it excluded both the ultimate user of products and the supply of services, and restricted its focus to the private sector. The growth of services markets is significant in areas such as financial services, leisure and tourism as well as 'services of general interest'. There is increasingly a knowledge and services society with a greater 'individualisation' of life choices for example in relation to pensions.

The most recent coalition government statement on consumer policy (2011) concludes that:

> The Government's prime objective for consumer policy is to empower consumers to make wise decisions when purchasing goods and services. Empowered consumers demand choice and by exercising it, stimulate competition and innovation as well as high standards of consumer care ... Empowerment depends upon an underpinning framework of competition and consumer law so that choices are offered fairly. And the law needs to be properly enforced. But it is vital that the law is not too prescriptive otherwise it runs the risk of dampening competition and innovation and of loading costs onto businesses which are then passed on to consumers in the form of higher prices. Excessive regulation may limit consumer

choice and, even if intended to protect consumers, can end up costing them more than the benefit it brings. (www.bis.gov.uk/assets/biscore/consumer-issues/docs/e/11-970-empowering-protecting-consumers-consultation-on-institutional-changes.pdf)

Note the emphasis on choice, fairness and a concern about the costs of regulation. The reduction of social exclusion is not included as a prominent goal. There is a contrast here between general consumer policy and policymaking in financial markets (see below Chapter 7) where the world financial crisis has simulated greater interest in protecting consumers from the market, rather than merely facilitating choice.

A significant change from Molony is the growth of powerful retailers and super-markets that have challenged the apparent dominance of manufacturers documented by the Molony Committee. Consumer markets no longer fit the arresting description of one US judge who commented that 'the manufacturer is the father of the transac-tion ... the dealer is simply a way station, a conduit on its trip from manufacturer to consumer' (Francis J in *Santor v A & M Karagheusian, Inc*, 1965: 309). Indeed, it has been argued that the leading supermarket retailers dominate suppliers, resulting in an investigation by the Competition Commission of the competitive nature of the grocery supermarket business. Competition policy and the desirability of vigorous competition are also highlighted in *Modern Markets* and a theme in contemporary policy analysis is drawing the links between competition and consumer policy.

The reference to health, safety and environmental risks in *Modern Markets* reflects the increasing preoccupation with issues of risk in contemporary society. Several writers have argued that although many societies are much richer than in the past there is a much greater concern with risks and the management of risk in society. These risks may often be generated by science and technology . They are also increasingly transnational so that 'unlike the factory-related or occupational hazards of the nine-teenth century and the first half of the twentieth century, these can no longer be limited to certain localities or groups but rather exhibit a tendency to globalization which spans ... national borders', and in this sense brings into being '*supra*-national and *non*-class specific *global hazards*' with a new type of social and political dynamism' (Beck, 1992: 13; see below Chapter 9). These global risks may include health risks, environmental risks, financial crises and economic destabilization (King and Narliker, 2003: 337). The sub-prime mortgage débâcle in the US in the late 2000s triggered the worldwide financial panic and subsequent recession. The management of risk is a central theme in contemporary regulation.

Changes in approaches to consumer law have often been a response to scandal and disaster. The Thalidomide disaster in Europe drove the international development of pharmaceutical regulation in the late 1960s; in the 1990s the BSE scare and con-cerns about genetically modified organisms stimulated the creation of new regulatory agencies (Food Standards Agency) in both in the UK and the EU; the current credit crunch is stimulating new approaches to credit regulation. These scandals may become national and sometimes transnational political demands for action as well as prompting a search for new forms of regulation . When scandals create a 'crisis consciousness' (Habermas, 1996: 442) the loss of trust in politicians creates pressures for regulation and better oversight of regulation that will maintain public trust. Perceptions of govern-ment and regulatory failure during the 1990s (see below Chapter 9) resulted in demands for higher and more effective levels of regulation in the area of regulation of health and safety risks in the UK and Europe. The accompanying decline of trust in expertise also resulted in greater opportunities for consumer representation on utility or financial services regulators.

The relationship between consumerism and citizenship is central to much contemporary work on consumer policy. Consumers are concerned about the processes by which products are made (eg fair trade initiatives) and one question is whether market choices might contribute to social justice and sustainable consumption. This collapse of the public and private sphere is mirrored in government policies that wish to bring the values of the private market—choice—into the public services and welfare state. However, commentators have raised problems with such a strategy. These include the pervasive problems of defining the consumer interest since different groups of consumers may have different interests and demands, and ensuring that services do not simply respond to the voices of the articulate. Moreover the concept of choice may need some probing. There is also the danger that the infusion of consumer values becomes very much a 'top-down' affair that is not responsive to the potentially complex needs of individuals in relation to public service. It is, however, equally dangerous to assume that the insertion of consumer values will result in a dystopic consumerisation of life where individuals conceive of all relationships in market terms. Research suggests that individuals conceive of their relationship to the NHS in a different manner to their relationship with a supermarket. Given the permeability of the public/private distinction there may be possibilities of greater cross-fertilisation of ideas between the two sectors.

3. Consumer influence in contemporary society: the politics of consumer protection

Several themes appear to underlie contemporary consumerism: an increasing desire for economic security and for protection from technological risks; a concern about corporate power, and the need to control it and make it accountable; and ideas of participation in social decision-making and of self-determination. Given these themes, a market model of consumerism may not always be appropriate, or effective, in providing real consumer influence over producer decision-making. This belief underlies the argument for greater consumer participation, and a greater consumer 'voice' (Hirschman, 1970), in producer and service-provider decision-making, and increased partnership between providers and users. This aspect of consumerism links it to the general societal problem of how to control and make accountable large bureaucratic organisations in both the public and private sector. Notwithstanding the embourgeoisement thesis, there remain large differences between the resources, aspirations and problems of rich and poor consumers, and issues of gender and race may also structure individual's opportunities and choices. Consumerism has, in part, been concerned with the problems of the poor in the market-place, and a theme running throughout this book is the extent to which it may be part of social policy shaping and correcting market outcomes.

3.1 Explaining the existence of patterns of consumer regulation

This seems a simple question. Consumer protection may be conceptualised as a response to countervailing consumer power within a pluralist model of democracy. However, economic and political theorists have suggested that this is an overly simple explanation.

Economists, drawing on the analogy of the competitive market implicit in the pluralistic model, point to certain pervasive 'failures' in the political marketplace which undermine the effectiveness of the consumer interest. Michael Trebilcock summarizes these problems.

M Trebilcock, 'Winners and Losers in the Modern Regulatory System: Must the Consumer Always Lose?' (1975) 13 *Osgoode Hall LJ* 618 at 620–25

In a heavily regulated society, the doctrine of pluralism envisages competition amongst groups as a self-corrective mechanism analogous to Adam Smith's 'invisible hand' in an unregulated marketplace. Unless consumers as an interest group can find mechanisms for counting themselves in on this process of political decision-making by competition amongst groups, they are likely to have minimal impact on the political process or its regulatory arms. However, some formidable obstacles stand in the way of consumerism sustaining itself as, or developing itself into, a major political force.

1. Diffusion of the Consumer Interest

Consumer concerns are diffused across the 50,000 or so products and services that each of us typically consumes in our life-time. An individual consumer's interest in anyone product or service will usually be so small that it will not be worth his while registering his dissatisfaction with the item to business, government, or a government's regulatory agencies. At the same time, business interests concerned with the manufacturing or merchandising of that product have a sufficiently concentrated stake in any prospective regulation of it to make their views known very forcefully to government. …

2. The Fragmentation of the Consumer Interest

Unlike the position generally with highly concentrated producer interests, the consumer interest is not homogeneous. Most consumers are also producers, and as producers we will often see things differently from the way we see them as consumers. … If we work on an automobile production line, we may see questions of public transit, pollution and safety standards, and lower tariffs on imported cars differently from other consumers. As environmentalists, we may favour underground wires but as consumers we may not be prepared to pay the cost. A higher-income consumer may be prepared to pay $500 for a safer, cleaner car but a lower-income consumer may not be able to afford the 'luxury' of more safety and less pollution. …

There is also a range of ideological issues pertaining ultimately to questions of life-style, such as the role and regulation of advertising, rules governing the availability of credit and product proliferation, and the relationship between expenditures in the private and public sectors about which wide consensus is unlikely to be forthcoming.

The non-materialist ethic upon which the writings of many critics of the modern consumer marketplace, such as Galbraith and Packard, are premised is reflected in Packard's dedication to his book, The Waste-Makers: 'To my mother and father who have never confused the possession of goods with the good life', and his idolizing, in the same book, of the life-style of an old woman in a lonely New England coastal cottage, without worldly possessions, who spends her time making greeting cards out of sea-weed. It is not clear that most consumers share these life-style ambitions, or that if they do they would be prepared to see them imposed on everyone by state fiat, which of course, would call into question the very nature of our existing social and economic order. ...

All of these considerations bear on the fragmentation of the consumer interest and increase the difficulty of achieving a substantial, on-going coalition of consumer support around basic consumer issues. ...

3. The 'Free Rider Problem

Even if a group of concerned consumers concert their efforts in order to promote their collective interests, the movement will never be as strong as the number of its potential beneficiaries would imply it should, because a number of potential contributors of money, time and expertise either need, or are able, to take a 'free ride' at the expense of existing members.

Olson points out that the nation state, as the extreme example of a large, latent group, cannot survive on voluntary dues or payments but must resort to coercive taxes. His central thesis is that unless the number of individuals in a group is quite small, or unless there is some other special device or incentive to make individuals act in their common interest, rational, self-interested individuals will not act to achieve their common or group interests. Olson suggests that, in the absence of coercion, the explanation for membership in existing large pressure group organizations lies not primarily in the collective goods these organizations provide to their members but rather in the non-collective goods they provide to members. The pursuit of collective goods, ie common or group interests, is merely a by-product of the provision of non-collective goods.

The analysis and assumptions made by Trebilcock are similar to those of public choice analysis, a branch of economics which attempts to explain the origins and growth of existing patterns of government regulation in terms of competition among private, self-interested groups. The basic thrust of this theory is that government regulation is not a response to the public interest. Rather, it is a 'commodity' supplied to private interest groups, who therefore 'buy' regulatory protection. The thesis was first developed in relation to the regulation of prices in, and of entry into, a single industry or profession. It was argued that this regulation served industry's interests, rather than those of the public, through the creation of barriers to market entry and monopoly rents for producers. This economic theory of regulation was related to other current theories in political science, which argued that regulators become 'captured' by the regulated industry (Bernstein, 1955).

The economic theory of regulation was generalised to cover all forms of government regulation by Peltzman (1976), who conceptualized the role of government as distributing regulatory benefits to the highest bidders in the political marketplace. Developments of this model suggest that there are a variety of players in the political market—politicians, bureaucrats, interest groups, the media—each pursuing their own self-interest. Thus, bureaucrats are assumed to be maximising their budgets or seeking further powers, and politicians may be assumed to be maximising their chances of re-election. Success for one group may depend upon building temporary coalitions with other groups. It was argued that the information and organisation costs facing diffuse groups such as consumers place them at a disadvantage in this regulatory game, and that, in consequence, politicians tend to bestow merely symbolic benefits on consumers (eg unenforced legislation), while providing more tangible benefits for small, concentrated groups (see further Mclean, 1996; Ogus,1994: ch 4; Symposium, 2002).

The economic theory of regulation is a powerful, if somewhat cynical, lens for viewing regulation. However, it fails to explain adequately the fact that there are in existence a broad variety of consumer-protection measures which do not seem to be a product of the power of narrow, private-interest groups (Posner, 1974: 535). Nor does it explain deregulation.

Partly in response to the limitations of the economic approach, JQ Wilson has developed a political theory of regulation (Wilson, 1980: 357). He distinguishes between a variety of policies in terms of the distribution of burdens and benefits: (i) where both the benefits and costs are widely distributed; (ii) where both the benefits and costs are concentrated; (iii) where the benefits are concentrated and the costs widely distributed; (iv) where the benefits are widely distributed and the costs concentrated (eg automobile safety).

James Q Wilson, 'The Politics of Regulation' in James Q Wilson (ed), *The Politics of Regulation* (1980) 366–70

When both costs and benefits are widely distributed, we expect to find *majoritarian* politics. All or most of society expects to gain; all or most of society expects to pay. Interest groups have little incentive to form around such issues because no small, definable segment of society (an industry, an occupation, a locality) can expect to capture a disproportionate share of the benefits or avoid a disproportionate share of the burdens. Not all measures that seem to offer a net gain to popular majorities are passed: proposals must first get onto the political agenda, people must agree that it is legitimate for the government to take action, and ideological objections to the propriety or feasibility of the measures must be overcome. ...

When both costs and benefits are narrowly concentrated, conditions are ripe for *interest-group politics*. A subsidy or regulation will often benefit a relatively small group at the expense of another comparable small group. Each side has a strong incentive to organize and exercise political influence. The public does not believe it will be much affected one way or another; though it may sympathize more with one side than the other, its voice is likely to be heard in only weak or general terms. ...

When the benefits of a prospective policy are concentrated but the costs widely distributed, *client politics* is likely to result. Some small, easily organized group will benefit and thus has a powerful incentive to organize and lobby; the costs of the benefit are distributed at a low per capita rate over a large number of people, and hence they have little incentive to organize in opposition—if, indeed, they even hear of the policy. As we shall see, however, an important organizational change has occurred that has altered the normal advantage enjoyed by the client group in these circumstances—the emergence of 'watchdog' or 'public interest' associations that have devised ways of maintaining themselves without having to recruit and organize the people who will be affected by a policy. Absent such watchdog organizations, however, client politics produces regulatory legislation that most nearly approximates the producer-dominance model. ...

Finally, a policy may be proposed that will confer general (though perhaps small) benefits at a cost to be borne chiefly by a small segment of society. When this is attempted, we are witnessing entrepreneurial politics. Antipollution and auto-safety bills were proposed to make air cleaner or cars safer for everyone at an expense that was imposed, at least initially, on particular segments of industry. Since the incentive to organize is strong for opponents of the policy but weak for the beneficiaries, and since the political system provides many points at which opposition can be registered, it may seem astonishing that regulatory legislation of this sort is ever passed. It is, and with growing frequency in recent years—but it requires the efforts of a skilled entrepreneur who can mobilize latent public sentiment (by revealing a scandal or capitalizing on a crisis), put the opponents of the plan publicly on the defensive (by accusing them of deforming babies or killing motorists), and associate the legislation with widely shared values (clean air, pure water, health, and safety). The entrepreneur serves as the vicarious representative of groups not directly part of the legislative process.

Consumer law and policy may fall into several of Wilson's categories. For example, given the power of financial interests, entrepreneurial politics may be necessary in the areas of consumer finance, whereas a general law on unfair commercial practices might fit majoritarian politics. It is also necessary to separate the enactment from the implementation of a law. Even if an entrepreneur or a coalition succeeds in achieving legislation by using the media to generate awareness of an issue, this success may be undermined in the day-to-day implementation and enforcement of it. Or a highly symbolic 'crackdown' may be promised that wanes in effectiveness over time as groups lose interest and the media moves on to another issue. Producer groups will have incentives to undermine enforcement, and consumer groups may lack the resources to monitor, on a continuing basis, the enforcement process. Consumer groups may exploit the media to create 'information cascades' which create moral panics or 'mass delusions' around issues, particularly those associated with health and safety, with politicians reacting by regulation even though these are minor risks or alternatives to regulation would be more effective (see below Chapter 9).

The insights of public choice and Wilson's theory have informed policymaking. Thus greater efforts (through subsidies and other techniques) have been made to ensure consumer representation in all facets of the policy and implementation process. The supercomplaint process is one example (see below at 109) of policy facilitating consumer groups to insert an issue on the policy agenda. In addition, the fear that agencies would be 'captured' or not be responsive to external goals has stimulated a wide variety of accountability measures in regulation.

These interest-group analyses above are used throughout the text. For example, why are cooling-off periods such a popular form of consumer policy (see below at Chapter 4). Are they primarily symbolic responses? What explains the exceptions to the scope of cooling-off periods where certain transactions are excluded? Which groups will benefit from the implementation of the Consumer Protection from Unfair Trading Regulations?

While most consumer organisations accept what might loosely be termed a 'social-market economy' ideology, in which governments are justified in protecting consumers where they are unable to protect themselves in the market, as Trebilcock indicates there are, potentially, significant ideological divisions within the consumer movement. For example, the political agenda of 'green consumerists' has traditionally differed significantly from organisations concerned to obtain 'value for money' in the market. These groups may also challenge dominant values of the consumer society and may be understood as partly fitting within the model of 'new social movements' (see Tilly, 2004; Touraine, 1974) which emerged in the 1970s. These are movements that in post-industrial societies with the decline of the traditional politics of class, focus on issues of identity and autonomy in the face of the increasing domination by a 'consumer society'. These social movements, such as environmentalism and feminism, may aim for social transformation. They may also defend 'traditional' values or norms that seem threatened by the encroachment of the market. Middle-class parents may view television advertising to children as threatening middle-class child-rearing values. Ethical consumerism elides the division between consumerism and citizenship. There are also groups organised around single issues such as 'Debt on our Doorstep' or the impact of food advertising on children.

Writers of both the left and the right often seem to suggest that government ultimately serves powerful producer interests. This conclusion gains credence from arguments that business is, of necessity, the most powerful interest group, because governments depend on it to sustain economic growth (Lindblom, 1977: 170) and because of its influence on the media through corporate advertising and so on. Lindblom, for example, argues that business is able to ensure that certain core issues—private enterprise, private property and a high degree of corporate autonomy—are beyond serious public debate (Lindblom, 1977: 205). However, as I have already noted, it is difficult to conceptualise all consumer legislation as simply the product of producer interests or of those of narrow, private-interest groups. Moreover, it is misleading to conceive of producers as a monolithic force. There may be clear conflicts of interest between manufacturers and retailers, and between small and large businesses.

Trumbull argues (Trumbull, 2010) that public choice and existing interest-group theories do not adequately explain consumer policy. He argues that there is substantial consumer protection legislation, 'capture' of agencies is rare, and consumers have been influential in the development of consumer laws. Consumer groups provide legitimacy to the regulatory process and this has driven government subsidies of consumer representation. He also argues that the particular structure of consumer representation and consumer groups in different countries has an impact on regulation. Thus labour groups have been influential in consumer NGOs in France and this is reflected in some skepticism towards the benefits of consumer credit, viewed as undermining the working person's wage. In contrast, consumer groups in the UK, such as Which?, in general supported the extension of consumer credit, a model of informed consumer choice, and opposed measures such as interest rate ceilings which might reduce access to credit.

Recent historical studies argue that construction and promotion of the 'consumer interest' is often dependent on wider national and international interests and ideologies Hilton, in discussing the relationship of consumerism to other interests argues that it has often been hitched to the star of other, more powerful, interests that have constructed 'the consumer' and the consumer interest according to their own agenda and ideology, while Maclachlan and Trentmann (2004) suggest that the success of consumer politics depends on the conjunctures of specific interests and ideologies which may provide opportunities for consumer groups. The New Labour interest in promoting the consumer interest as a means of achieving global competitiveness and perhaps reinvigorating democracy is an example. Although this renewal of interest was not a response to consumer groups, it provided an opportunity for consumer groups to promote an agenda that fitted with the prevailing ideology. Roberts (1975) suggested that many of the postwar measures protecting the economic interests of consumers in the United Kingdom were introduced because they also served the interests of powerful government players who wished to break down trade restrictions, and that consumer-protection legislation essentially 'piggy-backed' on the achievement of these goals. Thus, where consumer-protection reforms were concerned with social goals unrelated to these economic goals success was less likely to be achieved. Certainly, this explanation appears plausible in regard to some measures, eg the creation of the Office of Fair Trading in 1973. Roberts denies that consumer protection may be explained as a response to consumerism in the same way that, for example, labour legislation was a response to the labour movement.

Mathew Hilton (2003) has charted the development of consumerism in the UK in the twentieth century and suggests a continuing tension between consumerism as a limited force for getting more from the existing market and a movement for social transformation that might be associated with a broader conception of citizenship. He argues that consumer influence in the UK after the Second World War was increasingly dominated by a 'value for money' consumerism represented by the professional middle classes and the 'informed paternalism' of the best-buy testing instituted by professionals at the Consumers' Association (Which?) (see below). This ethic appealed to a significant portion of the middle classes where consumption was also becoming more of a male domain as it related more to major durables such as cars and appliances. It is no coincidence that this transition was accompanied by a conception of the consumer as a rational chooser rather than the historical figure of the impulsive and irrational female shopper. The Cooperative movement, which promised an alternative vision of consumer–producer relationships, had meantime fallen by the wayside having failed to engage with the politics of affluence.

Most mainstream consumer-protection measures have, unlike labour legislation, not been associated either with a major attempt to bring about a fundamental redistribution of resources in society or with the conflict inherent in capital–labour relations. Consumer interests may often coincide with government interests or with certain producer interests or with both sets of interests.

3.1.1 The structure of UK consumer representation

In the United Kingdom, mainstream consumer representation was provided by Which? (formerly the Consumers' Association), a private organisation, and by the National Consumer Council, created in 1975. The former has a mainly middle-class membership of approximately 700,000. It campaigned extensively on a variety of issues, including unfair contract terms, the introduction of Consumer Advice Centres and the abolition of the solicitors' conveyancing monopoly. It has operated primarily through lobbying (rather than litigation) and the use of the Private Members' Bill procedure. According to *The Times*, it 'can claim to have filled more pages of the statute book than any other pressure group this century'.

Its relative success appears attributable partly to its relatively thorough research and professional approach to campaigning, combined with its effective political skills (Gray, 1978: 262). These characteristics have endowed it with legitimacy in the eyes of bureaucrats and politicians, who view it as a 'responsible' voice for consumers. Like many interest groups, it is only able to provide the 'collective goods' from campaigning as a by-product of the revenues from its commercial operation—selling a variety of information to its members. The Consumers' Association separated clearly its campaigning wing from its commercial operations in the late 1980s through the creation of a separate charitable trust. The following extract is from Which's application to the DTI to be designated as a specified body empowered to bring proceedings comprising claims for damages before the Competition Appeal Tribunal (CAT) under section 19 of the Enterprise Act 2002 and section 47B of the Competition Act 1998:

CA does not receive funding from government as CA wishes to operate independently of government influence. CA needs funds to conduct its work and these come from the trading company. The profits or surplus of the trading company are only used to further the stated objectives of the charity. Which? Limited incurs the physical production costs of the magazine print run, associated salary expenses and so on and earns revenue from the sale of information material of interest to consumers such as the magazine. Which? Limited gift-aids all of its profits to CA so that CA can conduct its campaigns work. ...

CA actively campaigns on markets, personal finance, consumer markets and trade and competition. In all its campaigns, CA is committed to getting the best deal for consumers. Our campaigns have attracted extensive publicity and led directly to considerable improvements in the rights of consumers. Our biggest successes include ending rip-off car prices, winning compensation for missold endowment holders, getting the Food Standards Agency off the ground, strengthening the Financial Services Authority by lobbying for its additional powers, making inroads into CAP reform and persuading the OFT to investigate and take action on private dentistry, care homes and banking.

CA is invited to consult on hundreds of governmental consultations, steering groups and international forums each year and as such, has played a role in policy formation, draft legislation and information exchange at national and international levels. CA is an active member of BEUC- the Brussels based federation of 38 independent national consumer organisations; ECLG (European Consumer Law Group) within BEUC; the newly formed OECD joint working group on competition and consumer law and various academic networks.

In the United Kingdom CA has sponsored various successful private members' Bills including the Property Misdescriptions Act 1991, Cheques Act 1992, Sale and Supply of Goods Act 1994, Private Hire Vehicles (London) Act 1998 and Health Services Commissioner (Amendment) Act 2000.

CA's legitimate interest in protecting the collective interests of consumers is well recognised by the courts.

In R v Secretary of State for Trade and Industry ex-p Consumers' Association and Which? Ltd (Case C-82/96) CA complained that UK legislation implementing the Directive deprived consumer organisations, such as ours, of the right to take action in respect of unfair contract terms. The law was subsequently changed to reflect this. ...

... CA's Council is ultimately responsible for any decisions involving risk and cost assessment.

CA has demonstrated that it is prepared to commence litigation where circumstances point to the necessity of this being done for consumers. CA has also demonstrated that it uses the full spectrum of its range of legal powers. Since 1 October 1999, CA has been a qualifying body entitled to take action under the Unfair Terms in Consumer Contracts Regulations 1999. Indeed, CA promoted the private member's Bill that became the Unfair Contract Terms Act 1977. CA raises concerns about unfair contract terms with companies in various sectors. CA does not have the power to compel the provision of information hence tends to foster contractual improvements by issuing recommendations for modification and emphasising best practice. CA enjoys an open and co-operative relationship with the Office of Fair Trading and other bodies qualified to enforce the Regulations. CA helps contribute to consumer education worldwide by accepting overseas delegations and explaining how UK consumer law works.

Which? runs a Legal Service consisting of 12 lawyers based in Hertford (and four administrative assistants) who provide general consumer law advice to members. CA has two staff responsible for and familiar with administration of the Consumer Regulations Webpage. (www.dti.gov.uk/files11956.pdf)

The National Consumer Council (NCC) was established during the era of corporatism to act as a counterpart to the representation of producer and labour interests. It was given a broad mandate to act as a partisan body to promote action for furthering and safeguarding consumers' interests—in particular those of the disadvantaged (see Department of Prices and Consumer Protection, 1974). Hilton notes that:

[M]ajor successes for the National Consumer Council included its contribution to the opening up of the banking system and air transport, the expansion of shop trading hours, and its criticisms of the legal system that saw further developments in the small claims courts … and in alternative dispute resolutions, such the introduction of the ombudsman to the private sector. … Today, despite some uncertainties as to its role in the mid to late 90s, the NCC continues to work to educate consumers, regulate markets in the consumer interest, tackle issues of exclusion for those on low incomes, increase consumer representation and develop consumer protection measures. (Hilton, 2003: 294–95)

The NCC was replaced by Consumer Focus in 2007 with a mandate similar to that of the NCC. Citizens Advice is the third primary consumer body in the UK. In addition to supporting the work of individual Citizens Advice Bureaux it includes as its aim 'to exercise a responsible influence on the development of social policies and services, both locally and nationally'. It is funded largely by the DBIS with local CABx funded by local authorities. It also may bring supercomplaints (and has done so on payment protection insurance and door-to-door selling). It highlighted the topic of overindebtedness in the late 1990s.

The UK coalition government proposes to make Citizens Advice the central advocacy and representation body for consumers (DBIS, 2012), conferring on it the existing powers and role of Consumer Focus. Citizens Advice will 'become the publicly-funded voice of consumers, championing their needs and empowering them to make the right choices for themselves … their role will include research and horizon-scanning about issues that become important in the future' (DBIS, 2012, para 2).

The deregulation and privatisation of services such as gas, electricity and telecommunications posed questions as to consumer accountability for the new regulators in these industries. Privatisation was an attempt to substitute the discipline of the market and market efficiency which should make consumers better off. However, to the extent that industries were natural monopolies and often provided essential services, issues of consumer voice in these industries were raised. Demand for representation for individual consumers was underlined by the apparently high profits and compensation being paid to executives of privatised industries (see Moran, 2003: 112–13). Writing in 1999, Baldwin and Cave document research demonstrating that 'the consumer voice has been said to be weak in British regulation because information and expertise may be limited and because access to important processes [eg license modification negotiations in the utilities] may be incomplete' (Baldwin and Cave, 1999: 303). They outline several models of 'voice' in regulation: (1) institutionalising representation within the regulator. This is the model of the Financial Services Authority which has a Financial Services Consumer Panel. (2) Independent individual consumer councils for particular industries. This was adopted in the creation of Energywatch established under the Utilities Act 2000 to represent the interests of electricity and gas consumers (but subsequently abolished and folded into Consumer Focus, and to be included within the new role of Citizens Advice). (3) Increasing the resources of existing consumer bodies. (4) Appointment of consumer advocates to regulatory boards.

Established consumer groups have an increasingly important role in the UK.

First, designated groups such as Which? and Citizens Advice may make 'supercomplaints' under section 11 of the Enterprise Act to the Office of Fair Trading which must provide a reasoned response within 90 days concerning the action which it will take. This 'right of initiation' permits a consumer group to have a role in agenda setting (see below discussion Chapter 3 at 109). Second, consumer bodies may be designated enforcers under Part 8 of the Enterprise Act 2002, the Unfair Terms in Consumer Contracts regulations 1999, and bring claims for compensation on behalf of consumers under the Competition Act 1998. Several of these initiatives represent the influence of European directives which, based on practice in several European countries, conceived of private groups as playing an important role in consumer enforcement and implementation.

The institutionalisation of mainstream consumer representation in the UK draws attention to a second model for viewing contemporary consumer representation. This is corporatism. Discussion of corporatism is hampered by a lack of agreement on the meaning of the concept (Grant and Nath, 1984: 21; Schmitter,1974: 93–94). Corporatism may profitably be viewed as an approach towards policymaking. A feature of corporatism is the lack of a clear distinction between the public and private sphere, the private sphere performing what traditionally have been public functions.

Burgess comments on the incipient corporatist nature of contemporary consumer representation in the UK:

> Heading the UK offensive against overpricing and other consumer causes lies a 'movement' of advocacy groups drawn into intimate embrace with the state, most importantly, the influential Consumers Association (CA). ... The CA has frequently set the news agenda in recent years ... representatives of the CA are consulted on a wide array of issues and have influenced government policies in areas as diverse as pensions, health care, legal reform and financial services. Government demand for the consumer group perspective is such that it threatens to outstrip the CA's capacity to provide such advice. ... Organizations like the CA have achieved a semi-official status through participating in government in this way. (Burgess, 2001: 99)

Although corporatism was repudiated by the Thatcher government, "responsible" consumer groups play an important role in contemporary policymaking. In addition to issues of constitutional legitimacy, a danger with a corporatist approach is that it may confine effective policymaking input to established representatives of interest groups.

Much consumer law and policy takes place now at the EU level, providing a further dimension to the politics of consumer lawmaking and implementation. Few studies exist of the political economy of consumer law and policy in the EU. Several writers argue that business interests have a privileged position partly because the complexity of policymaking at the European level requires a heavy investment in monitoring resources and expertise and the need for the Commission, particularly in areas of specialist expertise to rely on sectoral expertise (see Moran, 2003: 167). Grant comments that 'Business interests have a close and mutually beneficial relationship with EU institutions. There are few environments that are more conducive to the political expression of the structural power of capital' (Grant, 2000: 105). ALTER-EU argued that expert committees in financial services are dominated by industry (ALTER-EU, 2009). The need to achieve legitimacy for community policies and to avoid continuing criticisms of the democratic deficit have resulted in significant subsidisation of consumer groups by the EU and perhaps a greater attention to the consumer interest than might be expected.

4. Markets, consumption and ideology

Beliefs about the role of markets and consumption in modern society affect both general policymaking and individual regulatory decisions. The resurgence of belief in the value of the market may be contrasted with a widespread assumption of the 1960s and 1970s of the need to tame 'the violence of the market' (Schonfield, 1965: 66) and of the importance of regulation and planning. Basic assumptions about the value of technology and the media to the quality of life may also influence regulatory decisions. A judge's 'inarticulate premises' on the nature and power of advertising may clinch a decision about whether a 'mere puff' gives rise to legal liability. It is impossible ultimately to avoid these issues and it is best, therefore, to face them at the outset.

An initial model of the relative role of markets and government is the market system coupled with natural liberty (Smith, 1904: 184; Nozick, 1974; Friedman, 1962: 7; Friedman, 1979). Within this libertarian model, government has a very modest role—a role limited to defining initial property rights, enforcing contracts, exercising a police power and dealing with the few situations where the market system fails. This view draws a close connection between economic and political freedom. A classic statement of this is chapter 1 of *Capitalism and Freedom* by Milton Friedman (1962). In that chapter, Friedman stresses the following virtues of the impersonal market system: (i) it separates economic from political power—the decentralisation of power implicit in the market model limits the ability of one person to coerce another; (ii) in it, unpopular individuals do not have to convince any central authority of the value of their talents or ideas; (iii) it promotes diversity and innovation, and no individuals or institutions are able to impede progress; (iv) the voluntary nature of private market transactions is likely to enhance the welfare of the participants; and (v) potential coercion of one individual by another is reduced by the presence of market alternatives. Friedman notes that the mutually beneficial nature of markets depends on the transaction being 'voluntary and informed' and that markets may need to be regulated in the case of monopoly and third party effects that are not priced in the exchange (Friedman, 1962: 8–9).

Friedrich von Hayek underlined the importance of local knowledge in a market system that it would be impossible for government planners to duplicate.

Friedrich von Hayek, 'The Use of Knowledge in Society' (1945) 35 *American Economic Review* 519

> If we can agree that the economic problem of society is mainly one of rapid adaptation to changes in the particular circumstances of time and place, it would seem to follow that the ultimate decisions must be left to the people who are familiar with these circumstances, who know directly of the relevant changes and of the resources immediately available to meet them. We cannot expect that this problem will be solved by first communicating all this knowledge to a central board which, after integrating all knowledge, issues its orders. We must solve it by some form of decentralization. … Fundamentally, in a system in which the knowledge of the relevant facts is dispersed among many people, prices can act to coordinate the separate actions of different people in the same way as subjective values help the individual to coordinate the parts of his plan.

Hayek and Friedman were important influences on the resurgence of neo-liberalism since the 1970s. But should we accept the argument that economic freedom is in itself important? Friedman's position on the issue should be compared with an earlier liberal—John Stuart Mill's views on trade regulation:

> [T]rade is a social act. Whoever undertakes to sell any description of goods to the public does what affects the interests of other persons, and of society in general; and thus his conduct, in principle, comes within the jurisdiction of society. … Restrictions on trade, or on production for purposes of trade, are indeed restraints; and all restraint, qua restraint, is an evil; but the restraints in question affect only that part of conduct which society is competent to restrain, and are wrong solely because they do not really produce the results which it is desired to produce by them. As the principle of individual liberty is not involved in the doctrine of free trade, so neither is it in most of the questions which arise respecting the limits of that doctrine, as, for example, what amount of public control is admissible for the prevention of fraud by adulteration. … Such questions involve considerations of liberty only in so far as leaving people to themselves is always better *caeteris paribus*, than controlling them; but that they may be legitimately controlled for these ends is in principle undeniable. (John Stuart Mill 1974: 164–65)

A consistent economic critique of Friedman's position may be found in the work of JK Galbraith (see discussion below Chapter 4). The main thrust of his work is to argue that, in certain sectors of the modern consumer economy, large corporations have, through the use of advertising, managed to gain power over the market. This undermines the idea of the market as responding to individual preferences—giving individuals what they want. Producer power replaces consumer sovereignty. The major goal of private producers is to sustain continued demand for new forms of private consumption, often at the expense of the provision of public services. This led to Galbraith's description of the USA as a land of 'private affluence and public squalor'. Galbraith's thesis is controversial; however, many economists do agree that corporations operating in oligopolistic markets are less subject to the disciplines of the market than the Friedman model presumes (Williamson, 1985). In addition, the economist Tibor Scitovsky has argued that the modern mass consumer market does not necessarily provide the diversity and choice espoused by Friedman. He argues that economies of scale in production and the continuing need to expand markets lead to the production of items which appeal to the lowest common denominator in public taste (Scitovsky, 1976: 1–11).

In a major restatement of liberalism, John Rawls (1971) rejected the system of natural liberty and free markets. Market outcomes depend, in his view, on arbitrary factors such as natural talents and abilities. Governments, therefore, have a duty to rectify market failures and to redistribute income. The outcomes of markets are only justified to the extent that they benefit the least-advantaged group in society in the long run (Rawls, 1971: 100–08). In addition, Anthony Kronman has pointed out that in setting the 'rules of the game' for voluntary economic exchange, it is impossible to avoid distributional judgements on the extent to which it is legitimate for one person to take advantage of another. For example, should a company with superior information be required to disclose it to a consumer? Rules which regulate the exchange of information between contracting parties will almost invariably have a significant distributional impact (Kronman, 1979).

At a more general level, Kronman's argument is that there is 'no natural state of *laissez-faire*' to be contrasted with state 'intervention'. The free market is a creation of the state. This point is emphasized in Karl Polanyi's description of the growth of capitalism in the nineteenth century:

> [The] introduction of free markets, far from doing away with the need for control, regulation, and intervention, enormously increased their range. Administrators had to be constantly on the watch to ensure the free working of the system. (Polanyi, 1957: 140–41)

Compare Polanyi's comments with Harvey's (above at 8). Both indicate the need for market ground rules. The particular ground rules may shape the nature of the market (see Ramsay, 1995). Markets are not, therefore, simply a neutral mechanism responding to individual demands. This point is underlined both by Edwin Baker (1975–76: 37) and by Rawls (1971: 259):

> The starkest failure of the ethical defense results from its necessary assumption of the neutrality of the market vis-a-vis individual values. The supposed freedom exists only if all choices are made by individuals while the structure imposes no values. However, no structure is value neutral; all social structures affect both what people get and also how they interact; that is, affect both end results and processes. Any structure, but more specifically the market and consumer sovereignty, shapes tastes and distributions, organizes the processes of realizing values, and embodies a concept of value and of man.

> [A]n economic system is not only an institutional device for satisfying existing wants and needs but a way of creating and fashioning wants in the future. How men work together now to satisfy their present desires affects the desires they will have later on, the kind of persons they will be.

From this perspective, the issue of markets versus regulation is transformed into a question of what kind of society we desire and what kinds of influence and shaping we wish to be subjected to.

Some historians argue that consumerism is primarily an exercise in social control. Stuart Ewen argues that a major role of advertising in the early days of mass production was to educate the masses into viewing consumption as a desirable way of life (Ewen, 1976).

Stuart Ewen, *Captains of Consciousness: Advertising and the Social Roots of Consumer Culture* (1976)

Industrialization, then, was more than a question of producing more goods in a new way. It also entailed a process of socialization which aimed at stabilizing and inculcating fidelity among those whose labor was being conscripted. ... In the early years of the twentieth century, there was widespread working class resistance to industrial capitalism. ... It was within this context that American industry began to produce a cultural apparatus aimed at defusing and neutralizing potential unrest. ... As the notion of control expanded, the ways in which working people might be involved in the industrial process beyond their factory role became increasingly explored. The studies of early twentieth-century social scientists and Progressive social critics began to create a general understanding that the social control of workers must stretch beyond the realm of the factory and into the very communities and structures within which they lived. ...

It was within such a context that the advertising industry began to assume modern proportions and that the institution of a mass consumer market began to arise. Up to that point, much of indigenous working-class culture had resisted capitalist growth in general, and the invasion of capitalism into their work and lifestyles in particular ... advertising was to develop as a tool of social order [to] ... break down the barriers of individual habits. It defined itself as at once the destroyer and creator in the process of the ever-evolving new. Its constructive effort [was] ... to superimpose new conceptions of individual attainment and community desire; to solidify the productive process while at the same time parrying anticorporate feeling. [B]usinessmen ... looked to move beyond their nineteenth-century characterization as captains of industry toward a position in which they could control the entire social realm. They aspired to become captains of consciousness.

Ramsay outlines the development of this critical theme:

Iain Ramsay, 'Consumer Law and The Search for Empowerment' (1991) 19 *Canadian Business Law Journal* 405

The starting points in this approach are: (1) consumption and consumption policy are an attempted form of social integration and control in contemporary capitalist societies. They are associated with processes of 'normalization'—of particular forms of social relations. However, this process has never been completely successful in producing 'passive consumers' so that (2) consumption relations may be important sites for political struggle. This extends arenas of conflict beyond capital/labour relations and (3) conflict may often be around differing visions of consumption relations ...

The consumer society did not therefore lead to the end of ideology, the classless or homogenous society. ... In fact, there have developed a large number of 'new social movements' organized around issues of consumption and the relationship of consumption to production. These include urban movements (tenants groups, etc.), ecological, feminist, ethnic and radical media groups and so on. They do not fit the concept of the traditional working class movement and the site for struggle is not the workplace. Their challenge is to an oppressive form of social relations rather than merely to a lack of bargaining power in the market. ...

Consumer politics becomes the politics of consumption—a topic both richer and more complex than existing understanding. Consumerism is a contradictory discourse of oppression and liberation. In its right-wing guise, it promised liberation from traditional class structures and the equation of empowerment with freedom to choose material goods. This is radically different from consumer power as political participation and greater democratic accountability.

Sheila Rowbotham outlines starkly the critique of consumerism in the US:

> [I]t was never just a matter of selling goods; advertisers promoted the good life. During
> the Cold War the superiority of American society in terms of individual consumption was
> an important ideological weapon. ... The particular pattern of consumption set by this era
> of optimistic faith in the capacity of the commodity to fulfil human needs was to have
> an international impact economically, socially and culturally. It has both met needs and
> generated new wants; made many aspects of life—including housework—more convenient,
> while creating new forms of inequality and deprivation. On the whole, this approach to
> consumption has been better at providing things for those who can afford to buy than meeting
> needs which require social reorganization. It has neglected the well-being and social rights
> of the poor, devastated the environment and failed to attend to the importance of care and
> nurture. (Rowbotham, 1999: 189)

A different approach which links consumerism to feminist and sexual politics is outlined by Mica Nava.

M Nava, 'Consumerism and its Contradictions' (1987) 1 *Cultural Studies* 204

Conventionally consumerism has been seen to confirm women in their subordination. A good
deal of feminist intellectual work has documented the ways in which women have both
been targeted as consumers and done a major part of the labour involved (approximately
80 percent of purchasing power in the Western world is wielded by women). ... Rather less
attention has been paid to the contradictory way in which the relative status and power of
women has paradoxically been enhanced by consumer society. Consumption (as a feature of
modern capitalism) has offered women new areas of authority and expertise, new sources of
income, a new sense of consumer rights; and one of the consequences of these developments
has been a heightened awareness of entitlement outside the sphere of consumption (which
may well have contributed to the conditions for the emergence of modern feminism. ... Thus
the buying of commodities and images can be understood both as a source of power and
pleasure for women (it has indeed given them a 'sense of identity, purpose and creativity')
and simultaneously as an instrument which secures their subordination.

I think it is possible to argue that these disparate theories and practices constitute an advance
on the cruder certainties of the immediate past precisely because of their more nuanced,
complex and contradictory nature. Consumerism is here split from its historic one-to-one
relation with production. ...

Consumerism does not simply mirror production. Cultural forms and meanings are not
reducible to class and the economic. Consumerism is far more than just economic activity: it
is also about dreams and consolation, communication and confrontation, image and identity.
Like sexuality, it consists of a multiplicity of fragmented and contradictory discourses.
Consumerism is a discourse through which disciplinary power is both exercised and contested.
While not negating its relation to capitalism, we must refuse to return it always to questions
of production.

5. The regional and global dimension

5.1 European consumer law and policy: establishing the ground rules of the internal market

Consumer law is increasingly Europeanised as part of the ground rules of the single market; there are the many directives on consumer law that continue to reshape UK consumer law and that we consider throughout the book (see eg below Chapters 4, 6, 7) (for specialized texts see Weatherill, 2005: Micklitz, Reich and Rott, 2009; Stuyck et al, 2010). Several reasons underline the significance of contemporary EU consumer law.

First, the EU is an important contributor to a variety of techniques of regulation and governance, as it faces the challenge of regulation in transnational space. It provided the 'new approach' to standards setting in the area of product safety (see below Chapter 9) and has developed policymaking and enforcement networks. The new approach to standards developed in the 1980s harnesses both private and public actors and creates a system of governance by committees. The increasing role of networks of enforcers and experts in the implementation of EU consumer policy poses the question of the extent to which there is a nascent network governance of consumer policy at the European level. This raises questions of legitimacy and effectiveness concerning the process of European consumer policy making (see eg Scott, 2002: Poncibo, 2011).

Second, there is the question of the vision of social relations embodied in EU consumer law. Two models vie for dominance. There is on one hand a market-oriented vision of consumer law where consumer law is limited to responding to information failures in markets and where the state plays little role in shaping standards in the market. On the other is a vision of consumer protection as recognising norms of fairness, risk spreading and protection of the vulnerable. It may thus from this perspective be viewed as part of the European 'social market model' within the Lisbon Treaty vision of a 'competitive social market economy'.

Iain Ramsay, 'Regulation and the Constitution of the Single Market; The Role of Consumer Law' (2010) 50 *Canadian Business Law Journal* 322

This topic [of EU consumer law] embraces two central themes: the search for better governance in the EU, recognizing the challenges of transnational, multi-level governance; and the tensions between different visions of the ground rules for the internal market— questions of the extent to which one party should look out for the interests of the other, and fairness and risk spreading.

EU developments have relevance beyond the EU. First, they illustrate issues concerning optimal levels of regulation (local, national, regional, international) in supra-national and transnational space. Second, regulation of consumer markets in the EU raises questions about the role of public and private actors in implementation and enforcement. ... Third, the EU provides an international model of consumer regulation, which attempts to balance consumer choice and consumer protection. As consumer protection is internationalized as part of international economic regulation, there will be increased competition and benchmarking among regional models of consumer protection. The EU, not surprisingly, hopes that exporting its model will provide 'a World competitive advantage to the EU community.'

I. CONTEXT: CONSTITUTING THE MARKET

Consumer law and policy are almost always framed and developed as part of broader political projects. These include attempts to make economies more competitive, free trade, social solidarity, or the demands of international agencies for 'modernization.' The EU hitches the development of consumer law to the objectives of driving competitive markets while at the same time providing a human face to the internal market, demonstrating citizen responsiveness and perhaps reducing the 'chasm between political elites and citizens.' The EU Commission argues that 'the 493 million EU consumers are central to the three main challenges facing the EU: growth, jobs, and the need to re-connect with our citizens. ... Confident, informed and empowered consumers are the motor of economic change.' To these goals has been added recently the speculation that a consumer contract code, by reducing transaction costs and stimulating consumer confidence, will help Europe to emerge from the current economic crisis. The consumer is therefore an important regulatory subject for these EU wide aspirations.

Consumer law often reflects tensions between the distinct ideas of consumer protection and consumer choice. Lady Hale claimed recently that, '[a]s a very general proposition, consumer law in this country aims to give the consumer an informed choice rather than to protect the consumer from making an unwise choice.'

[After discussing Whitman's distinctions between producerism and consumerism] ... These distinctions may be situated within 'the four clusters' of capitalism in member states: continental social market economy countries, Anglo-Saxon neo-liberal countries, Central and Eastern European countries (neo-liberal), and Nordic (liberal with safety nets) countries. Monti identifies the Anglo-Saxon member states as the 'driving force for the single market, competition policy, encouragement of economic reforms ... and light regulation.' The distinctions between these models of capitalism are finessed in The Lisbon Treaty's reference to the creation of 'a highly competitive social market economy,' a distinction recognized by the Commission in consumer policy where 'consumer interests cannot be exclusively defined in terms of economic efficiency. Citizens expect single market policy to deliver socially acceptable outcomes, sometimes at the expense of economic efficiency. For example, concern for human health, the environment and safety means that consumer products are strictly regulated. There is also a consensus that affordable access to certain essential commercially provided services, vital for economic and social inclusion, should be guaranteed to all, wherever they live.'

This quotation underlines the breadth of consumer policy which includes services of general interest, such as privatized public utilities, where universal access for all at reasonable prices is an important goal. This value may also be significant for aspects of financial services which are necessaries in contemporary society.

The distinctions above frame debates within the EU about the extent to which consumer policy reflects neo-liberal rather than social market goals. The concept of a social market should not be equated with socialism, but rather the idea of protection against market risks and insecurity, possibly social solidarity, along with the benefits of a competitive market place. The most significant clashes between neo-liberalism and the social market are in labour law rather than consumer law. However, EU initiatives in consumer contracts and credit regulation do raise contested issues of fairness and 'images of society' implicit in consumer law. It should be added that social democratic governments in Europe have furthered neo-liberal policies through the mechanism of the EU, transferring unpopular or contentious decisions—and responsibility for these decisions—to the EU level. A study of EU consumer law is primarily a study of the varieties of liberalism.

Consumer law in the EU is best conceptualized as a form of market regulation. This instrumental conceptualization of consumer law cuts across existing boundaries of public and private law as well as distinctions between legal and non-legal norms. Indeed the growth of consumer law in the 1970s symbolized the differentiation, fragmentation and possible disintegration of private law. Private law is a form of market regulation: it establishes and alters bargaining power and may have a patterning effect on risk allocation between

consumers and producers. It may also have an expressive effect as a model of social relationships. Consumer law is also pluralistic, ranging from hard law, through co-regulation, self-regulation and market norms and practices which may exceed the requirements of the law, a theme developed recently by Calliess and Zumbansen where Calliess outlines a nascent transnational lex consumeria in online b to c commerce.

There are limits on the resources and formal powers of the EU Commission to act in relation to consumer law, heightening the importance and attractiveness of achieving regulatory objectives through soft law methods of self-regulation, recommendations, moral suasion, benchmarking, naming and shaming, academic common frames of reference, or harnessing private actors in rulemaking. These forms of regulation raise issues of legitimacy, effectiveness and accountability. Legitimacy and accountability are important questions in the EU, the subject of a separate study.The study of EU consumer law, its forms and effects, is inevitably interdisciplinary. Lawyers played an important role in the early development of the EU, but increasingly policy making draws on economic and social science. Behavioural economics dominates contemporary analysis at DG Consumer Policy within the EU Commission.

There was no discrete focus on the consumer in the Treaty of Rome although it was assumed that consumers would benefit from a reduction in trade barriers and increased competition. A preliminary consumer programme was outlined in 1975 which imported the Kennedy principles of the right to protection of health and safety, the right to protection of economic interests, the right of redress, the right to information and education, and the right of representation. The Council resolution seemed to view the consumer as more than merely a market purchaser:

> [T]he consumer is no longer seen merely as a purchaser and user of goods and services for personal, family or group purposes but also as a person concerned with the various facets of society which might affect him directly or indirectly as a consumer.

The Treaty of Maastricht (1992) recognised consumer protection as one of the aims of the Community. Weatherill notes that 'it was as late as 1995 when a separate Directorate General (now known as DG Sanco) within the Commission was created to take charge of consumer policy; and as late as 1997 when the new DG gained sufficient staff to wield real clout, in the wake of the BSE "mad cow" crisis' (Weatherill, 1999: 695). The Treaty of Amsterdam (1999) incorporated changes to Article 153 (now 169) which recognise the concept of consumers' rights—to information, education and to organize themselves in order to safeguard their interests. The combination of Article 153 (now 169) and Article 114 (old 95) underline how completing the internal market and a high level of consumer protection are linked so that writers describe the 'Janus-faced' nature of EU consumer policy 'on the one hand aiming at creating a common internal market, on the other hand striving at some protective goals as well' (Wilhelmsson, 2004: 319, citing Reich, 1996).

The European Court of Justice has played an important political role in the development of consumer law and policy. This was initially through negative integration where it took an aggressive position on non-tariff trade barriers, such as product standards, partly because of political gridlock in other community institutions. In the famous *Cassis de Dijon* case (*REWE-Zentral-AG Bundesmonopolverwaltung fur Branntwein* (1979)) the plaintiff, a French company, wished to import into Germany a liqueur, Cassis de Dijon, and applied to the German Federal Monopoly Administration of Spirits for a licence to do so. This was refused on the basis that the liqueur was not suitable to be marketed in Germany because of its insufficient alcoholic strength. German regulations stipulated a minimum alcoholic strength for specified categories of liqueurs and fruit liqueurs such as Cassis de Dijon required an alcoholic strength of 25 per cent. The alcohol content of the French liqueur was only 15–20 per cent. The plaintiff argued that the German regulations were a measure having equivalent effect to a trade barrier under Article 28 (now 34) of the Treaty. The European Court of Justice held the German regulation to contravene Article 28.

REWE-Zentral-AG Bundesmonopolverwaltung fur Branntwein [1979] ECR 649

8. In the absence of common rules relating to the production and marketing of alcohol—a proposal for a regulation submitted to the Council by the Commission on 7 December 1976 (Official Journal C 309/ 2) not yet having received the Council's approval—it is for the Member States to regulate all matters relating to the production and marketing of alcohol and alcoholic beverages on their own territory. Obstacles to movement within the Community resulting from disparities between the national laws relating to the marketing of the products in question must be accepted in so far as those provisions may be recognized as being necessary in order to satisfy mandatory requirements relating in particular to the effectiveness of fiscal supervision, the protection of public health, the fairness of commercial transactions and the defense of the consumer.

...

12. The German Government also claims that the fixing of a lower limit for the alcohol content of certain liqueurs is designed to protect the consumer against unfair practices on the part of producers and distributors of alcoholic beverages. This argument is based on the consideration that the lowering of the alcohol content secures a competitive advantage in relation to beverages with a higher alcohol content, since alcohol constitutes by far the most expensive constituent of beverages by reason of the high rate of tax to which it is subject. ...

13. As the Commission rightly observed, the fixing of limits in relation to the alcohol content of beverages may lead to the standardization of products placed on the market and of their designations, in the interests of a greater transparency of commercial transactions and offers for sale to the public. However, this line of argument cannot be taken so far as to regard the mandatory fixing of minimum alcohol contents as being an essential guarantee of the fairness of commercial transactions, since it is a simple matter to ensure that suitable information is conveyed to the purchaser by requiring the display of an indication of origin and of the alcohol content on the packaging of products.

14. It is clear from the foregoing that the requirements relating to the minimum alcohol content of alcoholic beverages do not serve a purpose which is in the general interest and

such as to take precedence over the requirements of the free movement of goods, which constitutes one of the fundamental rules of the Community.

Cassis de Dijon was important in deregulating national consumer protection measures that could not be justified as serving a valid public objective. The Court of Justice adopted an approach not dissimilar to that of economic market failure analysis (see below Chapter 2). Protective rules could be justified if they were a proportionate response to a genuine consumer problem. Consumer protection could not be used to mask protectionism in trade.

A consequence of the generally deregulatory strategy of the court was the need for harmonisation of standards. Moreover by the mid-1980s the development of the internal market had reached somewhat of an impasse with many trade barriers still in existence and there was a sense that the EU as a concept had little broad political appeal. The 'new approach' to standards was adopted in 1985 as an approach to the logjam on standards. We discuss it in Chapter 9 below. A second approach was through a positive harmonisation programme of consumer law that could also be marketed as promoting the benefits of the common market to consumer-citizens.

5.2 Conceptions of the consumer in EU law

A recurring theme in consumer law concerns the image of the consumer who is to be protected in consumer law. Is it that of the reasonable consumer or a consumer who makes impulsive judgements? We explore this issue in greater depth in discussion of the Unfair Commercial Practices Directive in Chapter 4. The European Court of Justice addressed this issue in challenges to unfair competition regulations in several states that were argued to constitute barriers to trade under Article 28. The challenged regulations were often justified by the state in terms of consumer protection. Germany, for example, had strict rules on advertising, prohibiting 'eye-catching' price claims even if they were true (see *Yves Rocher*). The Court often had to address the question whether consumers might be deceived or otherwise harmed if the regulation was lifted. Given the political desire to break down trade barriers, the Court often adopted in these cases a relatively robust model of the consumer and a standard of deception of 'an average consumer who is reasonably well informed and reasonably observant and circumspect' (see *Gut Springenheide*, 1998, below). It also used a consumer's 'right' to information as a technique for striking down limits on comparative price advertising (*GB-Inno*, 1990). These techniques helped to justify deregulation of laws which appeared to the Court to be primarily designed to protect competitors and small businesses (viewing the legislation through a public choice lens) rather than consumers. However, the Court, given the differing political pressures on it and concerned to retain legitimacy, has attempted to balance this neo-liberal construction, for example, by limiting the attempts of business to attack national regulations on marketing practices (see *Keck*, 1993), by recognising national 'social and cultural interests' in misleading advertising, and the need to protect the 'vulnerable' (*Buet*, see below 174) and weaker consumer, and limiting the application of Article 28 in the case of Sunday shopping (see generally Everson, 2006: 112). Writers have also noted that the European Court of Justice has often interpreted Directives in a manner furthering consumer protection objectives, restricting any attempts by states to derogate from a Directive (Heininger, 2001), and that this seems to contrast with the often deregulatory approach in the line of cases starting from *Cassis de Dijon* (Unberath and Johnston, 2010). In addition, the Court has made reference to the fundamental nature of consumer protection in the Community 'compensating for the imbalance which exists between the consumer and the supplier' (*Claro*, ECJ C168-05). The implementation of the Unfair Commercial Practices Directive (below Chapter 4) raises squarely the issue of the image of the consumer in European consumer law.

5.3 The competence of the EU in consumer policy

Weatherill argues that a generous reading of the ability to harmonise laws under Article 114 permitted the development of EU consumer protection directives. The extent of this power was challenged by the decision of the Court of Justice in 2000 in a case brought by Germany to challenge the competence of the EU under Article 114 to ban all forms of tobacco advertising. The Court held that while certain aspects of the directive could be upheld, such as prohibitions on advertising in periodicals and magazines, other prohibitions, for example on advertising on parasols and ashtrays, could not be justified as facilitating trade in the products concerned. The Court required that a measure adopted on the basis of Article 114 must do more than be based on 'disparities beween national rules and of the abstract risk of obstacles to the exercise of fundamental freedoms or of distortions to competition' but must actually 'contribute to eliminating obstacles to the free movement of goods and services'. The Court will verify whether the distortion of competition which the measure purports to eliminate is appreciable. 'In the absence of such a requirement, the powers of the Community legislature would be practically unlimited (*Germany v European Parliament* [2000] Case C-376/98).

Weatherill argues that 'consumer confidence'—a demand-side argument—has become significant in Commission documentation on consumer protection and suggests that this might be an argument for harmonisation in a similar manner to attacking supply-side barriers.

Commission of the European Communities Green Paper on European Union Consumer Protection, Brussels COM(2001) 531 final

> It is the cross border movement of goods and services that allows consumers to search out bargains and innovative products and services and thus ensures that they optimize their consumption decisions. This cross-border demand increases competitive pressure within the internal market and allows for a more efficient and competitively priced supply of goods and services. This virtuous circle can only be achieved if the regulatory framework in place encourages consumers and businesses to engage in cross-border trade.

European Commission, *Consumer Policy Strategy 2002–2006*, Brussels, European Commission. COM(2002) 208 final at 7

> Barriers to cross-border trade should therefore be overcome in order that the consumer dimension of the internal market can develop in parallel with its business dimension. EU

consumer policy therefore aims at setting a *coherent and common environment ensuring that consumers are confident in shopping across borders throughout the EU.* (emphasis in original)

Consumer Policy 2007–2013

EU Health and Consumer policies have three core joint objectives:

1. Protect citizens from risks and threats which are beyond the control of individuals and that cannot be effectively tackled by individual Member States alone (eg health threats, unsafe products, unfair commercial practices).

2. Increase the ability of citizens to take better decisions about their health and consumer interests.

3. Mainstream health and consumer policy objectives across all Community policies in order to put health and consumer issues at the centre of policymaking.

… two priority areas:

*   ensuring a common high level of protection for all EU consumers, wherever they live, travel to or buy from in the EU, from risks and threats to their safety and economic interests.

*   increasing consumers' capacity to promote their own interests, ie helping consumers help themselves.

Four strands of actions are foreseen:

4.2.1. Better understanding of consumers and markets

This includes:

*   Developing and updating its scientific knowledge base and assessment tools on consumer exposure to chemicals, including with respect to general product safety. …

4.2.2. Better consumer protection regulation

This includes:

*   Completing the review of consumer law directives, developing a Common Frame of Reference for European contract law.

*   Analysis of the safety aspects of the growing cross-border market in services, full analysis of he General Product Safety directive,and more systematic use of standards.

*   Understand better national consumer policies: identify and promote best practice; setting benchmarks and recommendations; training policy makers and enforcers.

*   Examining how consumer interests are taken into account in standardisation, identify improvement needs.

*   Ensuring consumers are heard in EU policy-making, support effective consumer organisations at EU level and their participation in consultative bodies, forum groups, and specialist panels.

4.2.3. Better enforcement, monitoring and redress

This includes:

*   Strengthening cross-border enforcement: implementation of relevant legislation and

coordinating the work of all actors, and in particular customs, including on General Product Safety, RAPEX, and taking into account the international dimension.

- Improving transposition and implementation of EU directives, focusing more resources on monitoring transposition and implementation, to ensure consistent interpretation.

- Improving consumer organisations' ability to assist consumers, act as an early warning system to identify rogue traders, and monitor national policies.

- Improve consumers' means of redress, notably in cross-border cases, including access to Alternative Dispute Resolution; developing the network of European Consumer Centres.

4.2.4. Better informed and educated consumers

This includes:

- Ensuring that consumers, through better information, are able to make informed, environmentally and socially responsible choices on food, the most advantageous products and services, and those that correspond most to their lifestyle objectives thus building up trust and confidence.

To what extent are these goals similar to those outlined in the material on UK policy? Several commentators argue that the current foundations of Community consumer policy primarily construct the consumer as a means to achieving a more competitive market based on the model of the active information seeking consumer who is reasonably circumspect in making shopping decisions (Reich, 1992; Stuyck, 2000; Micklitz, 2002; Howells and Wilhelmsson, 2003).

5.4 The move to maximal harmonisation; framework directives

A central issue is when rulemaking at the European level pre-empts national measures. Minimal harmonisation clauses in EU directives permit countries to provide a higher protection than is required by a directive (see Howells, 2006). Minimal harmonisation does not mean, however, that individual states are completely free to establish their own level of consumer protection. It is possible that any measure might be challenged under the *Cassis de Dijon* principle that the measure acts as a non-tariff trade barrier. A maximal directive means that a state may not have a higher or lower level of protection within the area covered by the directive. In recent years there has been a tendency towards the idea of maximal harmonisation for Directives with 'targeted harmonisation' as a variation where some aspects of law are fully harmonised. The Court of Justice has also interpreted the Product Liability directive as maximal (below Chapter 9) so that states may not provide more generous protection in relation to issues covered by the directive. Maximal harmonisation is part of a policy shift in regulatory style within the EU.

Iain Ramsay, 'Regulation and the Constitution of the Single Market: The Contribution of Consumer Law' (2010) 50 *Canadian Business Law Journal* 322 at 331–35

III. BETTER REGULATION: FRAMEWORK DIRECTIVES, FULL HARMONIZATION, COMMON FRAMES OF REFERENCE

The 'Better regulation' agenda, developed by the EU in the early 2000s influences consumer policy making. The Commission indicates in 2008 that consumer policy making should shift from a legalistic perspective to one which focused on identifying problems in markets and assessing the most effective method of addressing the problem. In assessing the contribution of consumer policies to the creation of the single market "more attention needs to be paid to the final outcomes affecting EU citizens and not just to the legal tools. Policies need to be more evidence-based and outcome-oriented. Better monitoring and evaluation of outcomes for citizens is a priority for the Commission to move to the next stage of the single market... better monitoring is also essential in itself as a way of demonstrating to citizens that their concerns are taken into account."

The Commission has developed a markets "scoreboard" to identify problems in markets as a prelude to more in-depth study, proposing alternative policies and monitoring their effectiveness. Benchmarking the extent of retail integration and national enforcement might include 'naming and shaming' those states with poor enforcement records.

... Many of the better regulation approaches in consumer policy are hardly novel to Anglo-Saxon policy makers, for example the use of impact analysis, evidence based policy, and recourse to self-regulation. However the shift to this model of lawmaking within the EU is viewed as signaling an Anglo-Saxon shift (coup?) at the Commission where economic analysis may be replacing the hegemony of lawyers in consumer law reform and eroding the concept of a community founded on law.

Framework directives, full harmonization and increased use of varieties of self-regulation, are examples of the application of better regulation in consumer law. Framework directives, a development from the new approach to standards, uses general principles determined at a political level but harnesses experts in elaborating detailed norms and adjusting norms to new developments. A common approach is the creation of a committee of experts which could offer guidelines on interpretation. The objectives were more responsive regulation that can adapt quickly to changing market conditions and avoid the limits of detailed sector specific legislation. ...

The change from minimal harmonization, where member states may have higher national protections, to full harmonization, where a member state may not adopt a higher or lower level of protection, is a significant policy change. Full harmonization was adopted in the Unfair Commercial Practices Directive, and a variant—'targeted full harmonization'—in the Consumer Credit Directive and the proposed Consumer Rights Directive. The strategy of full harmonization is inevitably controversial, and moves the decisive political decision making to Brussels. Business groups generally favour full harmonization while consumer groups oppose. The Commission justify full harmonization by the reduction of transaction costs for business and the creation of consumer confidence in cross border shopping , leading to greater competition and productivity. The development of this ideological image of the confident consumer is attributed by Micklitz to the 1992 Sutherland report of an 'integrated market' with 'confident consumers.' Everson describes it pithily as 'the frontier consumer, the active moulder of the European market.'

Critics of full harmonization argue that (1) the empirical evidence to support the legal transactions cost argument does not exist. Language and culture are more important costs.

(2) The actual measures proposed are unlikely to have much impact on consumer confidence in cross-border transactions. (3) The EU Directives create a false sense of full harmonization because (a) there will inevitably be distinct interpretations of general clauses such as 'good faith' (b) directives will be parachuted into a landscape of existing private law rights and remedies. Unless these are harmonized there will remain substantial differences between countries. (c) Directives will be implemented and enforced by a variety of institutions— Ministries, independent agencies etc. Since the law takes shape through implementation there will still be substantial differences. (4) Recognising the heterogeneity of consumer preferences throughout member states consumer law should reflect national preferences. (5) Full harmonization undermines the possibility of learning through diversity and regulatory competition within a market which ensures minimum protections. (6) A regulation rather than a Directive would be a more effective instrument.

This article is not the forum to discuss fully these arguments. There is some evidence that different national regulations do create barriers to trade … [However] The impact analysis for the Directive on Consumer Rights had difficulty in linking low levels of consumer confidence in cross border shopping to legal regulations. There is unfortunately little empirical study of the effects, if any, of consumer law on consumer behaviour and the relationship of consumer law to other non-legal pressures on market behaviour. This was one critique of the Commission's impact study for the consumer rights Directive. The confident consumer rationale remains therefore less compelling, convincing some writers to suspect that harmonization is primarily an exercise favouring business interests: a thinly disguised measure of neo-liberalism.

In 2011 the EU adopted a modest Consumer Rights Directive and the Commission introduced a proposal for a Regulation on a common European sales law which would apply to cross-border transactions (2011).

---

6. International consumer law

Consumer law is increasingly an aspect of international economic regulation. The world financial crisis triggered by problems in US sub-prime mortgage financing illustrated the international significance of weak national consumer protection. The World Bank and the Financial Stability Board have developed best practices for consumer protection in financial services, and the World Bank is addressing issues of personal insolvency. Other international bodies such as the OECD develop influential guidelines (see eg guidelines on electronic commerce) and provide an information exchange and site for networks of experts and regulators (eg ICPEN) which often develop best practices and enforcement norms. There is the increased influence of 'modelling' at the international level where particular models of regulation become diffused internationally. International standards in health and safety (see below Chapter 9) are established by a combination of public and private actors which raise starkly issues of 'expert' knowledge and democratic accountability. Regions compete for adoption of their model of consumer protection. The EU model of products liability seems to have triumphed as a model in terms of its rate of adoption throughout the world. NGOs operate internationally and may use the media to promote models of regulation. The primary consumer organisation is Consumers International established in 1960. Braithwaite and Drahos (2000) argue that international NGOs can run campaigns promoting new models of consumer protection since they can be distributed at low cost throughout the international media. These groups function as 'model mongers'. It is not clear what is the overall distributional impact of this increased globalisation. Braithwaite and Drahos conclude that: '[O]ur story of the globalization of business regulation is a story of domination ... the global lawmakers today are the men who run the largest corporations, the US and the EC' (Braithwaite and Drahos, 2000: 629), while David Levi-Faur argues that international 'regulatory capitalism is much more open to collective action' and that 'the growing reliance on regulation as a mode of governance reopens the field for a more balanced approach to the distribution of power and resources' (Levi-Faur, 2005: 28).

The UN Guidelines for Consumer Protection were introduced in 1985 and expanded in 1999 to include principles of sustainable consumption.

United Nations Guidelines for Consumer Protection (as expanded in 1999)

I. Objectives

1. Taking into account the interests and needs of consumers in all countries, particularly those in developing countries; recognizing that consumers often face imbalances in economic terms, educational levels and bargaining power; and bearing in mind that consumers should have the right of access to non-hazardous products, as well as the right to promote just, equitable and sustainable economic and social development and environmental protection, these guidelines for consumer protection have the following objectives:

(a) To assist countries in achieving or maintaining adequate protection for their population as consumers;

(b) To facilitate production and distribution patterns responsive to the needs and desires of consumers;

(c) To encourage high levels of ethic al conduct for those engaged in the production and distribution of goods and services to consumers;

(d) To assist countries in curbing abusive business practices by all enterprises at the national and international levels which adversely affect consumers;

(e) To facilitate the development of independent consumer groups; (f) To further international cooperation in the field of consumer protection; (g) To encourage the development of market conditions which provide consumers with greater choice at lower prices;

(h) To promote sustainable consumption.

II. General principles

2. Governments should develop or maintain a strong consumer protection policy, taking into account the guidelines set out below and relevant international agreements. In so doing, each Government should set its own priorities for the protection of consumers in accordance with the economic, social and environmental circumstances of the country and the needs of its population, bearing in mind the costs and benefits of proposed measures.

3. The legitimate needs which the guidelines are intended to meet are the following:

(a) The protection of consumers from hazards to their health and safety;

(b) The promotion and protection of the economic interests of consumers

(c)   Access of consumers to adequate information to enable them to make informed choices according to individual wishes and needs;

(d)   Consumer education, including education on the environmental, social and economic impacts of consumer choice;

(e)   Availability of effective consumer redress;

(f)   Freedom to form consumer and other relevant groups or organizations and the opportunity of such organizations to present their views in decision-making processes affecting them;

(g)   The promotion of sustainable consumption patterns.

4. Unsustainable patterns of production and consumption, particularly in industrialized countries, are the major cause of the continued deterioration of the global environment. All countries should strive to promote sustainable consumption patterns; developed countries should take the lead in achieving sustainable consumption patterns; developing countries should seek to achieve sustainable consumption patterns in their development process, having due regard to the principle of common but differentiated responsibilities. The special situation and needs of developing countries in this regard should be fully taken into account.

5. Policies for promoting sustainable consumption should take into account the goals of eradicating poverty, satisfying the basic human needs of all members of society, and reducing inequality within and between countries.

6. Governments should provide or maintain adequate infrastructure to develop, implement and monitor consumer protection policies. Special care should be taken to ensure that measures for consumer protection are implemented for the benefit of all sectors of the population, particularly the rural population and people living in poverty.

7. All enterprises should obey the relevant laws and regulations of the countries in which they do business. They should also conform to the appropriate provisions of international standards for consumer protection to which the competent authorities of the country in question have agreed. (Hereinafter references to international standards in the guidelines should be viewed in the context of this paragraph.)

8. The potential positive role of universities and public and private enterprises in research should be considered when developing consumer protection policies. Consumers International (CI) is the only independent global campaigning voice for consumers. With over 220 member organisations in 115 countries, we are building a powerful international consumer movement to help protect and empower consumers everywhere.

III. Guidelines

9. The following guidelines should apply both to home-produced goods and services and to imports.

10. In applying any procedures or regulations for consumer protection, due regard should be given to ensuring that they do not become barriers to international trade and that they are consistent with international trade obligations.

David Harland argued in 1999 that the guidelines had 'a significant influence on consumer policy actions by both governments and consumer organizations in many countries with widely varying social, cultural and political traditions' (Harland, 1999: 16). They influenced the development of consumer laws in Latin America and Central and Eastern Europe and have 'been especially useful in many countries where consumer law and policy was previously little developed' (ibid: 17).

Rationales for Consumer Law and Policy

The purpose of this chapter is to outline the major rationales for consumer policy-making. Many official and unofficial reports during the 1960s and 1970s stressed the idea that inequality of bargaining power is the primary rationale for consumer law. For example, this concept appeared both in the Molony Report and in the influential Crowther Report on consumer credit, which formed the basis for the Consumer Credit Act 1974. In 1973, a Canadian commentator wrote:

> I believe it will be found that every consumer problem exhibits one or more of the following characteristic. First, a disparity of bargaining power between the supplier of goods or services and the consumer to whom they are being offered; secondly, a growing and frequently total disparity of knowledge concerning the characteristics and technical components of the goods or services; and, thirdly, a no less striking disparity of resources between the two sides, whether that disparity reflects itself in a consumer's difficulty to obtain redress unaided for a legitimate grievance or in a supplier's ability to absorb the cost of a defective product as part of his general overhead as compared to the consumer to whom its malfunctioning may represent the loss of a considerable capital investment. (Ziegel, 1973: 193)

The general impression gained from reading this extract is of the disparity in power between producers and consumers. This chapter explores systematically the sources of this apparent disparity and the specific public policy reasons for consumer policy. The subsequent sections outline two influential contemporary paradigms for regulation. These are: (1) neo-classical market failure; and (2) behavioural economics. I then examine equitable goals such as addressing social exclusion and paternalism. Finally, I briefly outline the relationship of sustainable consumption to consumer policy.

1. Neo-classical rationales: market failure

Market failure is the central economic rationale for government regulation of the marketplace. The general value of an economic approach to consumer protection is its ability to focus clearly on the objectives of consumer-protection measures, to identify the sources of consumer problems and to analyse the potential consequences of alternative policies in terms of their costs and benefits and direct and indirect effects on market behaviour.

The following extract outlines the economic approach to intervention, the role of cost–benefit analysis and the assumptions upon which the analysis is based.

IDC Ramsay, *Rationales for Intervention in the Consumer Marketplace* **(1984) 15–24**

3. EFFICIENCY-BASED RATIONALES

Market failure analysis

3.1 The central economic rationale for government intervention is that of 'market failure'. A potential market failure occurs when there is a failure of one of the conditions for the optimal operation of a competitive market. This provides a necessary but not sufficient reason for government intervention. It is not sufficient because it is necessary to estimate the effect of the failure on the price, quality and quantity of goods or services provided in a market and to identify the costs of remedying the failure. Government intervention is not costless and an estimate must be made of the costs and benefits of intervention and the potential impact of a remedy on the market and the behaviour of those affected.

3.2 A primary purpose of market failure analysis is to diagnose the source of efficiency problems in markets. It is the initial step in policy analysis.

3.3 The conditions for the optimal operation of a competitive market are:

(i)   there are numerous buyers and sellers in the market, such that the activities of any one economic actor will have only minimal impact on the output or price in the market;

(ii)   there is free entry into and exit from the market;

(iii) the commodity sold in the market is homogeneous; that is, essentially the same product is sold by each seller in the particular market;

(iv)   all economic actors in the market have perfect information about the nature and value of the commodities traded;

(v)   all the costs of producing a commodity are borne by the producer and all the benefits of a commodity accrue to the consumer—that is, there are no externalities.

3.4 The perfectly competitive market model has been criticised by some economists as a basis for policy-making and theories of 'workable competition' have been developed to appraise the complex nature of oligopolistic markets. The assumptions of the perfectly competitive model are invaluable however for focusing clearly on potential market failures in the area of consumer protection. ...

3.5 There are therefore initially a number of potential market failures in consumer markets:

(i)   there may be a lack of competition (monopoly, oligopoly);

(ii) there may be barriers to entry;

(iii) there may be problems with product differentiation where there are qualitative differences within a product market (and thus a lack of product homogeneity);

(iv) there may be information gaps between buyer and seller, or certain market signals, eg seller reputation may be imperfect;

(v)   there may be third-party effects which are not costed in the market price. This is the classic problem of externalities; two examples are pollution and the effect of one consumer's use of his automobile on other road users and the environment.

3.8 Two potential failures are of fundamental importance in consumer protection policymaking concerned with the economic interests of consumers. Firstly, markets need adequate information on prices, quality and terms if they are to function efficiently. The perception that consumers are imperfectly informed as to the nature and consequence of their purchasing decisions has justified many consumer protection measures. Although it might seem trite to some readers to stress the importance of information to consumer markets and to point in a general way to 'information failures' as a rationale for government regulation, it is only in recent years that scholars have become sensitive to the complexities involved in regulating market information.

3.9 Secondly, the overall efficiency of the market depends upon the institutional framework which secures the performance of market exchanges. The private law system of individual enforcement of rights was traditionally regarded as the counterpart to the market system of economic exchange. A major issue in consumer protection has been the perceived inadequacy of this system of individual private law litigation to secure performance in a massconsumption economy where the impact of harm is large in the aggregate but small for any one individual. Since the transaction costs (information, time and trouble, uncertainty of outcome) of enforcing individual consumer claims may often outweigh the 'expected recovery, the private law system may fail either to deter socially wasteful activity or to compensate for violations of rights. The growth of public regulation, for example, by the Office of Fair Trading, is partly a reaction to this particular failure.

3.10 Public regulation is not, however, the only method of addressing this failure. Class actions and actions by consumer groups are another alternative and, attempts might be made through, for example, the introduction of small claims courts and trade association arbitration schemes to reduce the costs of private enforcement. An important contemporary issue is the appropriate balance between public and private enforcement.

...

3.12 The externality category recognises that the purchaser may not be the only person affected by a purchasing decision. An unsafe product, for example a dangerous automobile, may affect other road users. These social costs of a market transaction may not be costed in the market price and one objective of consumer protection is to minimise these externalities and thus the social costs of these private activities.

...

3.14 Finally, it is relevant to mention the idea of 'public goods'. A public good is a commodity from which individuals may benefit without having contributed to the cost of its provision. There is consequently liable to be an underprovision of such goods by the private market.

The classic economic example is the lighthouse from which all ships will benefit whether or not their owners contribute to its costs. They would be able to free ride on the efforts of others. This tendency to free ride means that individuals may hide their true willingness to pay for public goods. Information, a central topic in consumer protection, has some of the characteristics of a public good implying that there will generally be an underprovision of product information in consumer markets.

3.15 Certain consumers are more vigilant in complaining and seeking out information in the marketplace. The activities of this group of marginal consumers may have significant effects on general market conditions. There is therefore a public good dimension to the work of this group which ought to be taken into account in consumer protection policy-making.

3.16 A market failure may lead to potential inefficiencies in the price, quality or quantity of goods and services produced in the particular market. Since almost all real world markets will be imperfect, it is important to diagnose the extent of any particular market failure and its effects on these three aspects. Minor imperfections may not justify corrective action, since such corrective action will itself entail costs and may have unintended side effects.

3.17 Any decision to intervene must be made therefore in the light of both the costs and benefits of intervention, comparing imperfect markets with imperfect government intervention. There are two interrelated issues involved in this process. An attempt must be made to predict:

(i)   the costs and benefits of the policy and its impact on the behaviour of those affected by it; and

(ii) the distribution (equitable effect) of the costs and benefits among different groups of consumers and producers.

3.18 The second aspect is a key question in consumer protection since measures are often designed to protect particular groups of consumers, eg low income or vulnerable individuals. It is important to assess whether these measures will attain their objectives and the costs to other consumers and producers. Such questions as what groups of consumers will benefit from mandatory guarantees on used cars? what will be the effect of requiring such guarantees on different sales outlets? must be answered. A traditional approach of economists to cost–benefit analysis has been to ignore these distributional effects and simply to assess the aggregate benefits to society. If aggregate benefits exceeded costs then (subject to various compensating criteria) a policy was socially beneficial, ie efficient. However, a policy that disproportionately benefited middle class consumers might be regarded as undesirable and it is therefore important to isolate this distributional impact.

3.19 Cost–benefit analysis is the subsequent step after identifying a market failure. It envisages the following stages of analysis:

(i)   identification of source (s) of problem(s) in market;

(ii) analysis of alternative responses in terms of—

       (a) benefits to consumers and sellers;

       (b) compliance costs to affected firms;

       (c) costs of rule formulation;

       (d) costs of enforcement; and

       (e) costs to buyers and sellers of any unintended side effects.

3.20 A calculus which minimises these costs and requires that economic benefits exceed costs will result in *efficient* legal interventions. Economists have shown a preference for choosing those remedies which harness market incentives arguing that the benefit/cost ratio will in general be increased by this approach . .

3.22 What ought to be the role of cost–benefit analysis in consumer protection policymaking? Its attraction is primarily that it *appears* to offer a relatively value free approach and quantitative answers to policy questions. It fits also the commonsense intuition that policies ought only to be adopted where their social benefits exceed their costs.

3.23 The following reasons suggest caution however in any use of cost–benefit analysis:

(i)   there may be equitable reasons for overriding the economic calculus, eg the protection of vulnerable or low-income groups;

(ii) it is a difficult and costly task to carry out a methodologically sound cost benefit analysis, and to identify correctly the efficiency rather than purely financial costs and benefits of regulation;

(iii) it is difficult to quantify the benefits of consumer regulation—it is, for example, notoriously difficult to measure either the benefits of the provision of information or intangible effects such as greater confidence in consumer markets;

(iv) there is always the danger that the more measurable costs (eg compliance costs) to directly affected groups will be regarded as outweighing the intangible benefits to a large and diffuse consumer group;

(v)   there will be difficulties in obtaining data to make any precise measurements of costs and benefits—for example, reliable data necessary to calculate the compliance costs of an industry may not be readily available and assumptions will have to be made about what level of compliance may be expected;

(vi) if policy making is based on an economic cost–benefit analysis, then it will be in the interests of pressure groups (eg the Confederation of British Industry) to demonstrate through their own analysis the benefits or costs of particular policies—to the extent that certain concentrated producer groups have greater access to information and expertise this may cause policy-making to be skewed in their interest, and there is always the danger therefore that cost–benefit analysis will simply become another technique to be abused to promote particular interests;

(vii) the economic calculus is based on certain assumptions and potentially controversial value judgements. …

(viii) a concentration on cost–benefit analysis may divert attention from the important issues of process, concerning the appropriate institutional structure for making decisions affecting consumers.

3.24 Notwithstanding these defects, cost–benefit analysis may be a significant aid to policymaking. Firstly, the cost–benefit framework does at least force decision-makers to make explicit, and quantify in a rough manner, all the potential consequences of a policy. Second, it may aid in matching policies to particular market failures, avoiding excessively expensive rules. Third, it may be possible to make valuable use of it in those areas affecting consumers' economic interests where there are fewer intangibles than in the areas of health and safety. Finally, the discipline of the requirement that one thinks through systematically the potential impact (including distributional impact) of a policy is invaluable.

Since 1998 a Regulatory Impact Assessment (RIA) is required where any regulatory proposal has an expected effect on business, charities or voluntary associations. Regulators should outline the purpose of regulation, the problem, benefits, costs, including those of securing compliance, the impact on small businesses, and competition. A race impact statement is required. There should also be public consultation, monitoring and evaluation of recommendations (see Ogus, 1994; Baldwin, 2005).

RIAs evolved from cost–benefit analysis and are justified as providing a more rigorous and transparent approach to policymaking. The current RIA process does address some of the issues raised in Ramsay's paper (eg process) and consultation is now institutionalised through, for example, consumer panels under the Financial Services Authority. However, in relation to consumer economic losses there remains the danger that the more measurable direct costs will be viewed as outweighing the more diffuse and intangible (eg greater market confidence) consumer benefits. The issue of equity may partly be addressed by constructing different utility functions for lower-income consumers based on the diminishing marginal utility of money. Thus there is a higher consumer detriment where an individual earning £1,000 a week suffers a loss of £100 than the same loss suffered by an individual earning £10,000 a week (see OFT, 1999: 10).

A review of the use of regulatory impact analysis in 2004 by the National Audit Office concluded that 'Regulatory Impact Assessments (RIAs) can improve the regulatory process when undertaken thoroughly, although the RIAs themselves could be improved in some cases' (National Audit Office, 2004). Continuing issues in the use of RIAs are the difficulties of quantification of benefits of a policy (many RIAs do not quantify these); the assumptions that must be made about compliance (since it is unlikely that there will be full compliance); the use of consistent assumptions and methodologies; and distinguishing between direct financial costs of a proposal (a distributional question) and the efficiency costs. Assumptions about consumer behaviour in response to regulatory proposals are often based on rational actor models rather than more realistic behavioural models. Robert Baldwin argues that the use of RIA by policymakers who are familiar with traditional command and control regulation often results in a failure to consider more imaginative or softer approaches to regulation, and that RIAs focus on policymaking at a single point in time and fail to conceptualise regulation as a continuous process (Baldwin, 2005).

The RIA seems to fit uneasily into the current 'joined-up' process of government. For example, the over-indebtedness action plan (see below Chapter 7 at 376) depends on several interlocking policy initiatives including information disclosure, regulation and greater access to insolvency procedures. These involve different government departments and it will be difficult to disentangle the effects of individual policies. The Annual Report on Over-indebtedness notes that 'evaluation of the whole strategy will be complex due to the number of policy interventions, the influence of external variables and the complexity of the drivers of over-indebtedness' (DTI, 2005: 58).

In summary, there are advantages to the RIA as an opportunity to consider the effects of alternative policies. At the same time there is a broader question of the extent to which RIAs privilege technocratic accountability over citizen accountability in policymaking (see Bronwen Morgan, 2003) notwithstanding the requirement of public consultation.

1.1 Assumptions of market failure analysis

Ramsay, *Rationales for Intervention in the Consumer Marketplace* **(1984)**

Assumptions of market failure analysis and the economic approach

3.26 The market model of efficiency takes as given several factors:

(i)   the existing technology of production;

(ii) the stability of individual tastes and preferences; and

(iii) the existing distribution of wealth and resources.

Each individual in the market is assumed to be the best judge of his own interests and to act rationally, maximising his utility (or personal satisfaction) within the constraints of his economic resources. Firms maximise profits. A further, sometimes unstated, assumption is that the consumer is ultimately in control of the market since it responds to demand generated by consumers (consumer sovereignty).

3.27 It is important to remember these background assumptions of the market approach, eg the individual as the best judge of his own interest ... and the existing distribution of wealth and rights taken as given. If these assumptions are thought to fail significantly, then there may be a prima facie case for intervention. For example, the law modifies the preferences of certain groups (eg the insane, infants) because of a distrust of their ability to make rational decisions. One controversial issue concerns the extent to which 'lifestyle' and other forms of psychological advertising may affect the rationality of ordinary decision-making, moulding consumer preferences and undermining the concept of consumer sovereignty. We may also be concerned about the effect of existing patterns of distribution of income on consumer protection. The ability to purchase goods or consumer protection may depend on one's income and certain groups may be unable to purchase as much as others. Equitable intervention may therefore be desirable in these situations. Even in this case, however, economic analysis may be able to suggest the potential impact and side effects of different methods of redistribution.

3.28 There is no doubt that the model of the competitive market place has attracted many adherents because of the political arguments in its favour. The decentralization of power implied by an atomistic structure of individual sellers and buyers, the ability of markets to allocate resources impersonally through the price mechanism and freedom of opportunity are often cited as its virtues. However, the primary reason for using market failure analysis in this paper is that it provides a useful model for diagnosing the source of problems in markets and suggesting policy responses. It is important to stress that the model and its assumptions are not intended to be a description of the reality of any particular real-life market. For example, the rational consumer who consistently maximises his utility is a scientific abstraction. Its stylization of behaviour is intended to capture the idea that a certain proportion of individuals (sometimes referred to as 'the marginal consumer') act as if they are attempting to maximise their satisfactions from the use of their resources. The use of this and other theoretical assumptions lies primarily in their ability to generate a sharp understanding of problems for regulation, to provide a rigorous grid to impose on a problem, and to supply hypotheses which may be tested by empirical data.

Economic market failure analysis takes the existing distribution of rights and resources for granted and prefers redistribution to be carried out through the tax and transfer system. It envisages little redistributive role for consumer protection rules that alter the ground rules of the marketplace. There are several reasons which are put forward for this position. First, there is the futility argument. This argument assumes that so long as individuals remain free to contract, businesses will *pass along* the increased costs of any redistributive measure to consumers, and that if businesses are prevented from doing so, then they may be unwilling to deal with consumers. In short, the measure intended to protect consumers will *backfire*. In the context of credit markets this could mean that regulation of the price of low-income credit might lead to suppliers being unwilling to continue to provide the service. As a consequence individual consumers might be forced to use illegal forms of lending such as loan sharks. The neo-classical approach argues that the more effective and fair method of addressing the problems of lower-income individuals is through the tax and transfer system which would address directly what is perceived as the basic problem—insufficiency of resources—and not place the burdens of redistribution solely on those who supply services to lower income consumers (see further discussion below Chapter 7 at 10).

The above argument is often found in policy debates over such issues as credit card interest-rate ceilings, restrictions on creditor remedies or quality regulation. There is undoubtedly some truth in the 'pass-along' argument. There are, however, several questions concerning the argument. First, all laws have a distributional impact that advantages or disadvantages particular individuals or groups. The extent to which any advantage will be undercut by market forces is an empirical question depending on the conditions of the particular market. The pass-along argument is often stated in a priori terms without much serious investigation of the nature of particular markets. Cass Sunstein claims that 'efforts to redistribute resources through regulation end up harming the most vulnerable members of society' (Sunstein, 1990: 106 and see Hillman, 2002) but provides remarkably thin documentation (one law review article) for this assertion. When the distributional effects are studied carefully the potential detrimental effects may be much more modest and need to be balanced against the benefits of the legislation and other social values which might be furthered by the regulation. Second, there is the reality that the tax and transfer system is increasingly under pressure and that there must be concern about progressive measures of redistribution being undercut by a regressive market system where, for example, consumer credit is being used to purchase the necessities of life. Third, tax and transfer redistributions may give rise to unintended side effects to those attributed above to consumer protection measures.

The role of the welfare state is being rethought in many countries. Anthony Giddens has argued that we should conceptualise approaches to risk in the welfare state based on a model of 'positive welfare' (Giddens, 1994). This recognises that welfare policy must combine a mix of approaches which are not merely reactive but which attempt to address all facets of a problem. This might involve educational, regulatory and material components, and would go beyond a view of welfare as solely comprising income transfer. Giddens has also argued that a social market model requires risk sharing and the cultivation of social cohesion (Giddens, 2007: ch 1). Consumer policy might be viewed as part of an overall regulatory mix of regulation, education and institutional initiatives which are intended to achieve both economic and social goals.

The assumption that individuals are the best judge of their own interests raises issues of paternalism and market manipulation. It is assumed that certain groups, eg children, may have difficulty in making rational choices. Taking tastes and preferences as stable raises issues concerning the influence of advertising and the commercial media in shaping preferences. The general role of advertising in creating wants and exploiting interdependent utilities ('keeping up with the Joneses') has been a much-studied topic in economics in terms of the optimal level of product differentiation in product markets, and the role of trademarks as barriers to entry. It also implicates the more general issues of sustainable consumption, consumerism and citizenship.

One point should be emphasised. The language of market failure is that of 'intervention' in the market, suggesting that before intervention the market was 'unregulated'. This is, of course, a false dichotomy. All markets have ground rules such as the common law of contract and property that specify the extent to which individuals are able to take advantage of others in the market. We cannot assume that such rules are necessarily efficient or equitable since the concept of efficiency is relative to the initial distribution of rights. Both private and public law rules may facilitate and compensate for risk taking in society. We cannot assume that they are a natural and pre-political set of rules. Policymaking in consumer law often therefore involves a comparative institutional analysis of different regulatory frameworks for markets where the uncertainties of efficiency analysis may highlight issues of fairness and distributional values.

1.1.1 Market failure as a policy discourse

A further objection to market failure is to its dominance in policy discourse. This means that those who wish to be taken seriously by governments must frame their proposals within this discourse. Thus rather than argue that it is unfair that the poor pay more (see below), the argument should be made that there are information failures in low-income markets which result in the poor paying more. Bronwen Morgan argues that although consumer groups may achieve successes by harnessing the discourse of economic market failure analysis, the silencing of other forms of argument, eg appeals to shared values of citizenship, is a significant cost of this approach (Morgan, 2003; Mcvea, 2006: 413). There is also the argument that technocratic accountability—the cost–benefit state (Sunstein, 2002)—dominates discourse and prevents a serious democratic conversation over issues of risk in society. Certainly Harvey associates the abhorrence of democracy and governance by experts with neo-liberalism (above Chapter 1 at 4.1).

---

2. Information failures in consumer markets

> Information economics has made us realize that much of standard economics is based on foundations resting on quicksand. (Stiglitz, 2000: 1461)

Imperfect consumer information has been identified as a fundamental rationale for consumer measures, such as truth in lending (below Chapter 7), controls on misleading advertising (below Chapter 4), and implied warranties (below Chapter 8). All address imperfections either in the provision of market information or in a consumer's ability to process complex information. The criterion of imperfect information is, however, relatively vague and might justify intervention in almost any consumer market. The development of the economics of information literature provides hypotheses concerning those market situations where information failures are likely to lead to significant consumer injuries. The following extract provides an early synthesis of some of the findings of this literature (see Schwartz and Wilde, 1979; Federal Trade Commission, 1979; Reich, 1979; Beales, Crasswell and Salop, 1981; Hadfield, Howse and Trebilcock, 1998; London Economics, 1997).

Ramsay, *Rationales for Intervention in the Consumer Marketplace* (1984) 25–35

INFORMATION RATIONALES

4.3 Consumers will rarely possess the perfect information of the textbook market model, and differing consumer markets will vary in the amount and quality of information provided. The criterion of 'imperfect information' or 'the uninformed consumer' might therefore, without further precision, justify almost any intervention in consumer markets. A decision-maker with limited resources is concerned, however, to identify more particularly those market conditions where intervention is justified. An approach which attempted to remedy every informational deficiency would be extremely costly and have possible detrimental side effects. The question of intervention must be answered therefore in the light of both the costs and benefits of any proposed intervention. The appropriate goal ought to be 'adequate' rather than 'perfect' information.

Information and the market

4.4 Information on price, quality and terms permits buyers to make efficient choices in the marketplace. By using information, consumers transmit to sellers their preferred alternatives, providing sellers with an incentive to compete by producing goods and services which consumers value highly. Without such information the incentive to compete on price, quality and terms will be weakened.

4.5 Obtaining information is a cost of engaging in market transactions (transaction cost). A consumer faces several costs in determining his information needs. These include obtaining diagnosis (what do I need?) and testing information (will the qualities of this car meet my needs?). He may also face processing costs (what does 'APR' mean?). In order to obtain information a consumer must often search for it. This is therefore a further cost. A rational consumer, in allocating his resources to searching for information, will be assumed to make a cost–benefit calculation concerning the amount of search. The best buy will be therefore relative to the costs of diagnosis, product testing, search and processing.

4.6 Consumers may obtain information not only through search but also from experience. Many low-cost products may only be tested through experience (hence the general 'try me' formula of most advertising for chocolate bars, etc) and this may be a sufficient guide in the case of low-priced frequently-purchased products without any hidden costs (eg physical danger). However, with infrequently-purchased high-price products qualities of these products or services may be relatively complex and may only be tested through experience (eg the comfort of a car). Consumers may however have no fund of experience to draw on. They may therefore have difficulties in assessing the probability of a breakdown in product performance. In this situation they may seek information provided by third parties, ranging from friends and family to *Which?* or specialised agents, for example, department stores.

4.7 Sellers also have incentives to provide consumers with information in order to distinguish themselves from their competitors. They might provide warranties or service contracts and their market reputation will provide to consumers a 'signal' of reliability. In addition, they may be able to generate information on their products more efficiently than consumers or third parties. Given this variety of sources of information what are the potential failures in markets for information?

Information failure as a rationale for intervention

4.8 There are two general considerations which are central to an understanding of potential information failures. Firstly, information has the properties of a public good. Since it is difficult for a person producing information to prevent non-paying customers from gaining access to it there will be a tendency for individuals to free ride on the efforts of others. This suggests that in consumer markets there will be an underprovision of information and a shortage of fully informed consumers. The public good characteristic of information might provide a prima facie rationale for government subsidisation of the provision of consumer information.

4.9 Second, information has a 'market perfecting' effect. This qualifies the public good conclusion since it describes the fact that information need only be used by a small number of individuals in a market for business to respond. Thus the small group of individuals who search for information and complain about defective products (the marginal consumers) provide benefits to other consumers by keeping producers in line.

4.10 An important point which follows from this observation is that it is not necessary for all consumers to be well informed in order for markets to be behaving competitively. The focus in policy-making ought not to be therefore on whether individuals are uninformed but rather whether this lack of information has produced non-competitive prices and terms. ...

Effects of information failures on markets

4.15 Imperfect consumer information might result in the following potential market failures:

(i)   misallocation of consumer resources;

(ii)   informational market power;

(iii) artificial product differentiation; and

(iv)   informational inefficiencies—providing misleading signals to consumers.

Misallocation of consumer resources

False and misleading claims

4.16 This is perhaps the best known, most obvious and oldest reason for intervention. However, the regulation of this area is not as simple as might appear at first glance.

4. 17 Literally false claims offer consumers no benefits and ought therefore not to be tolerated. If a market is riddled with false claims, then consumers may lose confidence in the truth of all seller claims. However, we may still wish to discriminate among different types of false claims in allocating enforcement resources. The most serious case for intervention will be situations where consumers are unable easily to verify through experience the performance of the relevant attribute. False claims ought to be of greatest concern, therefore, in relation to relatively expensive and infrequently purchased experience goods and markets where sellers are not dependent on repeat purchasers.

4.18 Claims are generally misleading rather than false. The problem with misleading claims is that they are often ambiguous, depend on consumers drawing incorrect inferences and are consequently misleading to some but not to all consumers. A programme of regulation which is not sensitive to these facts and which seeks 'truth' at all costs may restrict unnecessarily the flow of market information. There may be equitable reasons for protecting a minority of deceived consumers against misleading claims but the costs of such a policy ought to be clearly articulated.

Hidden costs

4.19 A basic problem under this heading is that experience of a product or service will not reveal clearly either performance deficiencies or the source of the deficiencies. Examples include the installation of home insulation where it may be difficult to detect savings from the electricity bill or to know whether performance deficiencies are attributable to the insulation or installation. Similarly if consumers buy 'health' food or vitamins without nutritional information it may be difficult to know whether the consumption of the product is associated with changes in health. A further example is the carcinogenic properties of, for example, food, drugs or cosmetics where these costs of using the product may not become apparent until years after use by which time it is difficult to attribute them to a particular product or brand. Given the difficulties consumers face in appraising these costs, sellers may lack incentives to provide information on these issues, or to provide superior products.

4.20 An important area of hidden costs concerns the situation where diagnosis and treatment of a consumer problem are bundled together, for example, home and car repairs, legal and medical services. The consumer may have difficulty in judging the quality of the diagnosis, the quality of the treatment, and whether the services are necessary. Consumers may be unsure as to the value of a 'second opinion' and the potential risks of not obtaining a second opinion. The seller, unfortunately, may not have an incentive to disclose this information. This bundling problem may be particularly acute with professional services which are purchased infrequently and where there may be significant information gaps between consumers and producers. The bundling problem is a major justification for the fiduciary duty of solicitors to their clients, The economic assumption of rational self-interested behaviour suggests, however, that the diagnosis function may not always function efficiently and that there may be inappropriate levels of quality in these markets, Even after legal services have been performed, a consumer may be unsure as to whether the particular level of quality provided matches his needs.

4.21 Consumers buying infrequently-purchased products may have difficulty in estimating post-purchase running costs, repairs and servicing costs. These costs are all part of 'the price' of the product, a study at Massachusetts Institute of Technology indicating that in the case of refrigerators the purchase price is a mere 40 per cent of the product's overall life-cycle costs.

4.22 Consumers may rely on producer reputation or warranties as a signal of these life-cycle costs and journals such as *Which?* provide rough guides to the average repair costs of major durables. There is however the danger that consumers will misestimate the value of a guarantee or service contract as a signal of reliability, and purchase either too much or too little protection, Consumers' reliance on these signals may also provide incentives to producers to overinvest or distort them rather than provide detailed information on product reliability.

4.23 There may also be problems with hidden costs where the individual purchasing the services is not the beneficiary and the beneficiary has difficulty in complaining. In this situation the seller may have little incentive to maintain adequate performance. Examples of this might include children's services or nursing home facilities for the elderly. ...

Information and market structure

Non-repeat sales

4.25 If a seller is unconcerned about a potential consumer as a 'repeat player', then he will have little incentive to provide him with accurate information or to disclose costs. The tourist trap and the fly-by-night are obvious examples, Others may include some types of door-todoor sales, certain mail order firms, and home improvement companies, There is often a connection between this type of market structure and high pressure sales techniques. Since a seller will be unconcerned about future sales he will invest his resources in overcoming consumer resistance—for example through aggressive sales tactics and false and misleading claims.

Information and oligopoly

4.26 It is argued that in oligopolistic markets sellers may avoid disclosing certain product characteristics for fear of triggering mutually disadvantageous competition. This tendency may be reinforced by the legal and 'gentlemanly' restrictions on comparative advertising. Where all products in a market have the same defect (eg cigarettes) no seller is likely to disclose this fact. In addition, if a company is in a monopolistic or near monopolistic position, then it may concentrate on public image advertising rather than discussing product qualities.

Informational market power

4.28 If consumers are imperfectly informed and face high search costs then even small sellers in unconcentrated markets may achieve 'informational market power. ... The fact that in the USA the bereaved face high search costs (economic and psychic) in shopping for funerals was reflected in the Federal Trade Commission's findings of industry fragmentation and excessively high prices throughout the funeral industry.

...

Price/quality relationships and information inefficiencies

4.30 The inability of consumers to observe product quality characteristics (eg the mechanical reliability of a car) may channel competition in a market towards more easily observed attributes (eg price). This may lead to a general depression of quality below the level which would operate in a perfectly functioning market. It is possible that consumers may come to accept this lower level of quality—there is not necessarily any deception involved. They might however be willing to pay a slightly higher price if quality was easier to observe. This argument was first deployed in a famous article by Akerlof who indicated that the above conditions fitted the private used car market and resulted in the dominance of 'lemons' in that market. ...

4.31 This tendency towards the 'lemons' state may be counteracted by consumers using signals other than price as a guide to quality. For example, warranties, trademarks and sellers' advertising may perform this role. If however signals are misleading, then there may be misallocation of resources. There is always a danger of signals being manipulated. ...

Problems in information processing

4.32 Information processing costs represent the costs to a consumer of comprehending information and applying it to his situation. They are additional to the initial costs of acquiring information. If processing costs are high, for example, in relation to technical data or professional services, then efforts at increasing the supply of information may not be effective. A suitable policy response to high processing costs as a cause of market failure might therefore be a product standard, quality certification or licensing.

Developments in the information literature since Ramsay's article raise the following issues.

First, the existence of search costs means that the 'law of a single price' may not apply—there may not be a stable equilibrium price. Sellers as profit maximisers who know that consumers face search costs may have incentives to increase consumer search costs (eg through increasing the costs of comparison shopping, bundling together different aspects of a product or service and/or discriminating between consumers with low and high search costs—see Salop and Stiglitz, 1977; Bar-Gill, 2006; Gabaix and Laibson, 2006). This literature also challenges the assumption that the marginal consumers who search the market police it on behalf of the non-searchers. Sellers might be able to charge different prices to searching and non-searching consumers. A slightly different phenomenon is that of 'switching costs' (Klemperer, 1995), discussed below, which may result in consumers being potentially open to price exploitation.

Second, the literature on adverse selection and moral hazard has grown enormously. Adverse selection is reflected in Akerlof's findings that information asymmetry may lead to failures in a product market where one party does not have a credible method of signalling quality and the other party cannot readily assess quality. We consider this further in relation to product quality (below Chapter 8) and credit contracts (below Chapter 7). Adverse selection in credit markets may result in credit rationing. Moral hazard was originally used in the context of insurance contracts to describe the situation where one party might have reduced incentives to protect against a risk but it might be difficult for the other party (insurance company) to monitor the other party's behaviour.

A further characteristic of goods and services not mentioned in the Ramsay extract is a 'credence' quality. These are characteristics of goods and services which cannot be easily evaluated by consumers even after their experience of the service. These include some professional and financial services. They may also be situations where consumers face difficulties in assessing their needs.

2.1 Market structure and information failures

There may be connections between market structures and consumer protection problems. A market that has the characteristics of the competitive ideal (low barriers to entry/exit, many sellers) may also be one with significant consumer problems since sellers may have little interest in investing in consumer goodwill and may be focused on short-term profit.

Several writers have noted the connection between particular market structures and information failures (see eg Ramsay, 1984; London Economics, 1996; Hadfield, Howse and Trebilcock, 1998: 155–56), and have outlined the following characteristics of markets where there was potential for significant consumer detriment.

1. Repeat transactions are rare, and consequently the performance incentives created by the possibility of repeat business from satisfied customers are blunted.
2. Entry and exit costs in the industry are low, leading to the possibility of a large number of fly-by-night operators with few sunk costs and only modest investments in reputational capital.
3. Many sellers or producers are extrajurisdictional, making redress through private law more difficult for consumers.
4. Sellers characteristically have few assets against which a judgment may be enforced.

5. The costs to consumers of a 'bad' transaction are delayed or potentially catastrophic, making ex post relief an inadequate or unsatisfactory solution.
6. The small size of a typical transaction creates a significant disincentive to seeking ex post relief through the courts.

2.1.1 Doorstep sales

Some types of doorstep selling of home improvements fit many of the characteristics outlined above. This form of sale also often includes the use of commissions that create an incentive for salespersons to engage in high-pressure selling. An OFT study of doorstep selling (see below Chapter 6 at 7.1) noted that many consumers who had bought from door-to-door sellers 'find that they have made an inappropriate choice, often as a result of pressure selling, that the prices they have paid were too high and/or that the product they have bought is not suitable for the intended purpose. Subsequently they can find themselves inadvertently locked into a contract with no option to cancel.'

The study drew a distinction between doorstep sales of low-value products where the consumer was often a repeat purchaser and doorstep selling of high-value products. Consumer satisfaction was much higher in the former case and most complaints related to high-value products. In the case of high-value products, eg home improvements, the study identified a number of common psychological techniques employed by sellers, usually working on commission, that were highly effective in securing sales. Consumers paid significantly more for such products and there was substantial price dispersion in prices of double-glazing products sold door to door. Even where a visit was solicited, consumers were often likely to regret a purchase. These findings underline the fact that in relation to an infrequently purchased product such as double glazing, consumers will often be price ignorant in the context of door-to-door sales. The study also indicated that there is a significant subcategory of fraudulent door to door selling of primarily home improvements (roofing, etc) that targets vulnerable populations.

2.1.2 Why are mainstream lenders uninterested in low-income lending? The Community Reinvestment Act as a response to information asymmetry

Information asymmetry may be one reason for the reluctance of mainstream financial institutions such as banks to enter the sub-prime lending market (see the discussion of home credit below, Chapter 7 at 372) or to develop products for low-income consumers. Mainstream lenders currently lack knowledge of the needs of individuals in these markets as well as the characteristics of good and bad payers. This was one of the points made by the banks to the Competition Commission in its home shopping inquiry (see below Chapter 7). The advantage of existing home shopping suppliers is that by employing local suppliers who live and work in the community they have substantial information on their clients, can adjust the credit to their needs and know how to maximise profitability. Established firms in the home credit market therefore have a substantial information advantage over new entrants. Mainstream lenders may also be deterred by information externalities—if they invest in developing the market they may have to share information on borrowers with other lenders who will be able to obtain the information from credit bureaux (see Barr, 2005). This may increase the perceived costs of entering what might be regarded as a relatively thin market. A third barrier to entry by mainstream lenders is the perceived reputational effects if it becomes known that they are lending to lower-income individuals at higher rates than to other individuals. These barriers to entry may result in less than full competition in such markets.

One policy would therefore be to stimulate mainstream financial institutions to develop knowledge of these markets. This has been one effect in the US of the Community Reinvestment Act enacted in 1977 to address redlining, ie drawing a red line around an area and refusing to provide credit or financial services within that area. The Act requires that banks meet 'the credit needs of its entire community, including low and moderate income neighbourhoods, consistent with the sound and safe operation of a bank'. Banks are evaluated by banking agencies on their performance in achieving this goal. The ultimate sanction for an unsatisfactory performance is that a financial institution may be prevented from expansion through merger or acquisition. Recent research concludes that the Act has on balance been beneficial (Barr, 2005 and see below Chapter 7 at 14.3). An important result of the Act was that it created groups within banks that have developed knowledge of lower-income credit markets, overcoming some of the information asymmetries that mainstream institutions face in lending to lower-income consumers.

---

3. The new policy paradigm: behavioural economics

Behavioural economics has become an influential source for policymaking in consumer law and policy. Government agencies often adopt this framework. The EU Commission recommends its use in the interpretation of the EU Unfair Commercial Practices Directive (see below) (see for further references (2011) 34 *Journal of Consumer Policy*, no 3 Special Issue on Behavioural Economics, Consumer Policy and Consumer Law):

> The main contention of behavioral research, is that many of the basic assumptions in standard economic models are not based on how people actually make economic decisions, and that they therefore lead to a descriptively worse theory than one based on more behaviorally correct assumptions. (Weber and Dawes, 2005: 91)

Behavioural economics challenges three aspects of neo-classical economics: unbounded rationality, unbounded willpower and unbounded self-interest (see eg Mullainathan and Thaler, 2005). Behavioural economics also challenges two further assumptions in neo-classical economics: (1) that markets inevitably have a learning effect because individuals learn from their mistakes; (2) that markets will reduce irrational behaviour because only rational actors will survive in the market. Mullainathan and Thaler point out that individuals may continue to make mistakes and survive at a lower equilibrium and that in some cases there is no opportunity for learning. The example of pension decision-making is a case where the opportunities for learning from mistakes may be zero.

Behavioural economics is now a large subdiscipline in economics and the following provides a summary of certain well-established findings in the literature.

3.1 Hyperbolic discounting

[T]here is no quality in human nature, which causes more fatal errors in our conduct, than that which leads us to prefer whatever is present to the distant and remote. (David Hume, *Treatise of Human Nature* (1739) Bk III, pt ii, s vii, quoted in Offer, 2006: 42)

[A]t the very time of acting, at the moment in which passion mounts the highest, he hesitates and trembles at the thought of what he is about to do: he is secretly conscious to himself that he is breaking through those measures of conduct which, in all his cool hours, he had resolved never to infringe, which he had never seen infringed by others without the highest disapprobation, and of which the infringement, his own mind forebodes, must soon render him the object of the same disagreeable sentiments. (Adam Smith, *The Theory of Moral Sentiments* (1759) 227, quoted in Weber and Dawes, 2005: 97)

The concept of hyperbolic discounting means that consumers may have present regarding preferences, and preferences are not consistent over time.

Consumer decisions often require intertemporal comparisons. Should I save now and consume later? Neo-classical economic analysis assumes that individuals in making these decisions act 'rationally', ie they can weigh present and future costs and benefits using appropriate and consistent discount rates. For example, in deciding whether to receive money now or later, they would discount money streams at the market rate of interest and this discounting would be consistent over time. Both of these assumptions appear to be 'importantly wrong' (see Frederick, Loewenstein and O'Donoghue, 2002). Richard Thaler, in a well-known experiment, asked individuals how much money they would require in one month, one year and ten years to make them indifferent to receiving $15 now. The median responses, $20, $50 and $100, represent discount rates of 345%, 120% and 19%, respectively (see Thaler, 1981: 201). Discount rates declined sharply over time with individuals being willing to pay a higher discount rate to receive cash within a short period of time.

Hyperbolic discounting may also result in preference reversals. Individuals may prefer $110 in 31 days over $100 in 30 days, but also prefer $100 now over $110 tomorrow (see Frederick et al, 2002: 360). This preference reversal suggests the proposition that 'it is always harder to delay gratification for one day when that date is now'. At a more general level it suggests that individuals may be myopic in the short term, but more rational in the long term. There is, in short, a conflict between these two selves. This conflict suggests that we cannot assume that consumer choice always reflects consumer preferences.

Thaler also found two further patterns in addition to the general finding of a short-term perspective by consumers. Discount rates varied with the amount at stake—with individuals being willing to pay a higher amount in relation to small amounts (under $100). Individuals were more willing to wait for $150 in one year rather than receive $100 now, than they were willing to wait for $15 dollars in one year than $10 now. They explained this difference by suggesting that individuals have different methods of mental accounting. Small windfalls are checked into the consumption account and larger amounts into a mental savings account. The cost of waiting for the small amount is viewed as forgoing consumption, and to the extent that consumption is more tempting than forgoing interest, individuals will take the small amount for immediate consumption. These findings are relevant to credit markets where there has been concern about individuals paying high interest rates on short-term consumption loans (so-called 'payday loans', see below Chapter 7 at 370).

Individuals may develop commitment devices to overcome their myopia, through, for example, automatic deductions to locked-in savings accounts. Society might also provide these devices by influencing consumer behaviour, developing social norms, and legal regulation through cooling-off periods, or mandatory rules such as compulsory pension plans. One question is the ability of different social groups to develop commitment and self-control devices. Offer argues that 'if self-control is difficult to achieve, if it is easier for those with education, assets, and access to institutions like banks and insurance companies, then the well-off are in a better position to achieve it than those who are not' (Offer, 2006: 3).

3.2 Over-optimism

Repeated experiments indicate that individuals are over-optimistic. Ninety per cent of people, for example, think that they are above-average drivers. In a review of the literature Christine Jolls refers to over 200 studies demonstrating over-optimism (Jolls, 2005: 7). Individuals may overestimate their future use of a service such as a health or fitness club (particularly in January!) and consequently enter into a suboptimal contract (see below Chapter 6 at 1.3, discussing Della Vigna and Malmender, 2006: 695). Over-optimism is relevant to the design of regulations. For example, generic warnings may be discounted because individuals will assume that the problem will not affect them.

3.3 Framing effects and status quo bias

Individuals respond to the same problem with differing decisions depending on how the problem is framed. For example, individuals are loss averse and therefore more averse to a choice framed as a loss than one framed as forgoing a gain. Framing is related to the endowment effect, where individuals demand more to give up an object than they are willing to pay to obtain it. In a famous experiment, one group of people were given a mug and asked how much they would want to give up the mug. A second group was not given a mug, but was instead shown the same mug as the first group, and asked the price they would pay to purchase the mug. The first group consistently priced the mug higher than the second (Kahneman et al, 1990: 1325; Tversky and Kahneman, 1991).

Framing underlines the importance of default rules since different default rules will affect the choices that individuals make. Thus programmes that require an individual to 'opt in' will result in a much smaller take up than programmes where the default rule includes all consumers in the programme but permits them to 'opt out'. An offer that states 'surcharge for credit' rather than 'discount for cash' will result in very different patterns of consumer decisions. The framing effect seems to be one of the most robust findings of behavioural economics. It is also well known in the marketing literature.

For example, it appears that labelling a food product '75 per cent non-fat' rather than '25 per cent fat' substantially increases sales (Sutherland and Sylvester, 1993: 384).

3.4 Availability and anchoring

Individuals are poor statisticians and use heuristics (short cuts) to assess risk. One of these is the availability heuristic whereby individuals estimate the probability of a risk by the ease with which the particular risk comes to mind. This leads to over-estimation of risks that can be vividly recalled such as airline accidents, and under-estimation of less well-reported and less vivid risks. An example here is credit markets where individuals may underestimate the risk of default and be over-optimistic about their ability to repay (see below Chapter 7 at 3).

The availability heuristic underlines the role of the media in affecting individual perceptions of risk. Vivid coverage in the media of issues (eg airline disasters, 'mad cow' disease) may contribute to individuals' misperceptions of risks. They may also create a political demand to respond in a high-profile manner to such risks even though (i) the risk may be less significant than lower visibility risks and (ii) a less dramatic response might be more effective (see Ogus, 2005). In relation to credit, one might speculate on the relative influence of media stories about the perils of debt over-commitment compared with the high-visibility advertising of credit that connects credit to the good things in life.

Individuals seem to use a variety of heuristics in decision-making in consumer markets. Writers suggest, for example, that these include a belief that the unit price of goods packaged in larger quantities is lower than that of goods packaged in smaller quantities, and that large stores offer better prices than small stores. Marketing literature often draws on these insights when developing marketing strategies.

Anchoring describes the situation where individuals focus on a convenient or easily accessible number in decision-making. This may be an internal number generated from previous shopping experience or it may be provided by a supplier or third party. The initial selection of a number will skew decision making towards that number. Rachlinski (2003: 1171) cites a study that found that students asked to estimate the average price of textbooks in the college bookstore provided a higher price when they were provided with a ludicrous anchor, namely was the price 'greater or lesser than $7,137.30'. Thus, notwithstanding that an initial price may be high ('sticker shock'), it will be used by a consumer as a reference in reaching the ultimate selling price. Anchoring is relevant to regulation of such practices as 'hi-lo' pricing (see below Chapter 4 at 7.2).

3.5 Information overload

Although information overload is not necessarily an aspect of behavioural economics it is useful to include it here. Studies suggests that as the number of attributes and choices of products faced by a consumer rises, there will be a reduction in the quality of consumer decision-making. Thus a variation in the number of alternatives from 4 to 8, 12 and 16 resulted in poorer-quality decisions (Jacoby, Speller and Berning, 1974: 1). Some of the potential negative effects are that: (i) consumers make poorer decisions;

(ii) consumers faced with too many choices may be more likely to respond to price promotions that provide a simple method of justifying their choice; and (iii) consumers may avoid making decisions where they have a wealth of alternatives and show greater satisfaction when purchasing from a smaller choice set (see Matthews, 2006). A study of consumer choice in relation to pre-packaged foodstuffs found that the majority of consumers thought that there was too much information on pre-packaged foodstuffs and ignored much of it (see Lennard et al, 2001: 177). This overload may cause consumers to rely on misleading heuristics such as the 'volume discount heuristic'—the belief that the unit price of goods packaged in larger quantities is lower than that of goods package in smaller quantities.

Information overload is also relevant to disclosure policies where regulations often require detailed disclosures (eg as in consumer credit, see below Chapter 7 at 6). One study suggests that individuals cannot deal simultaneously with more than seven pieces of significant information (see Miller, 1956: 81).

3.6 Fairness

Neo-classical economics assumes a norm of individual self-interest, but experiments in psychology show that individuals care about how others are treated in the market and are willing to punish firms that act unfairly. Individuals have a sense of fairness that they bring to market transactions. For example, assume that there is an excess demand for a children's toy at Christmas. Most respondents in studies conclude that it would be unfair for the store to auction the toy to the highest bidder. This type of finding is used to support the proposition that 'it is unfair for a firm to exploit an increase in its market power to alter the terms of the reference transaction at the direct expense of a customer' (Kahneman, Knetsch and Thaler, 1986: 296): 'the opposition to exploitation of market power also entails a strong rejection of excessive monopoly gains ... and of price discrimination'.

Individuals seem to regard prices as unfair if there is a significant departure from the reference transaction, that is to say the usual terms of trade for that particular good (see Kahneman, Knetsch and Thaler, 1986: 297). It is possible that interest-rate ceilings on credit are best explained as responding to fairness concerns that transactions are a substantial departure from the reference transaction. The continued criticism of the interest rates charged by credit cards seems partly based on this perception that there is a substantial difference between the interest charged and the normal interest on loans. The appropriate 'reference price' is of course crucial. For certain forms of short-term credit or risky credit the reference price may not be the interest payable on a mainstream bank loan.

3.7 Emotions and the economy

Behavioural economics was a modest step beyond the analytic simplicity of neo-classical approaches. There has also been a return to the study of the role of emotions in decision-making. Berzein argues that this is partly 'an attempt to counter the growing salience of rational choice and formal economic models' (Berzein, 2005: 109). Shiller's study of the stock market suggested that it was subject to 'irrational exuberance' where 'investors, or more precisely small investors continued to pour money into the market, even when it became clear that a bubble was forming' (Berzein, 2005: 118). Shop-aholics are an extreme example of emotions swamping reason, but intuitively we would argue that much consumption is emotional, often based on status and 'bandwagon' effects (Leibenstein, 1950). This poses two questions for policy: (i) when should policy attempt to regulate these emotions? And (ii) how should it regulate them?

3.8 Behavioural economics and regulators

Some studies argue that regulators, like consumers, may be subject to behavioural biases. Choi et al suggest that examination of the performance of the US Securities and Exchange Commission indicates that it demonstrated overconfidence, was bounded in the search for regulatory alternatives and subject to the availability bias, ie it responded to high-profile media coverage of issues (Choi et al, 2003). Many regulatory develop-ments in the UK during the past decade have been responses to these perceived biases in regulators (see below Chapter 3).

3.9 Implications of behavioural economics for consumer law and policy

> Behavioural economics suggests that individuals often lack clear, stable or well ordered preferences: choices are influenced by context for example by default rules, and framing. (Sunstein and Thaler, 2003: 1159)

Offer concludes that:

> the thrust of empirical work since the 1960s in a variety of approaches is that the rational consumer is a fiction, and that choice is often fallible. The choices people make do not always accord with what, from a different temporal viewpoint, they would judge as being good for themselves. (Offer, 2006: 70)

The behavioural literature has philosophical and practical implications for thinking about consumer policy. Policymakers should consider carefully the role of policies in providing 'debiasing interventions' that might counteract the biases identified by the literature of behavioural economics (eg financial literacy programmes, and see below Chapter 3 at 2.3). This may require a significant re-evaluation of traditional policies such as information disclosure that are often premised on the assumption of rational consumer decision-making. Until recently much of EU consumer policy was based on an 'information paradigm' with directives imposing extensive information obligations on suppliers (see eg Distance Selling Directive, Unfair Commercial Practices Direc-tive). Behavioural analysis indicates that more careful analysis of the potential and effects of disclosure programmes is necessary. Sunstein and Thaler comment that:

> because framing effects are inevitable, it is hopelessly inadequate to say that when people lack relevant information the best response is to provide it. In order to be effective, any effort to inform people must be rooted in an understanding of how people actually think. Presentation

makes a great deal of difference: the behavioral consequences of otherwise identical pieces of information depend on how they are framed. (Sunstein and Thaler, 2003: 1182)

A basic question in disclosure regulation relates to the assumptions policymakers hold about consumer behaviour. Do they assume consumers act 'rationally' (ie that they can weigh present and future costs and benefits using appropriate and consistent discount rates), or do they assume consumers are subject to costly behavioural biases (particularly the bias of myopia or 'hyperbolic discounting')? If their decisions are subject to costly biases, what interventions can policymakers use to reduce their influence?

Framing is also central to the establishment of default rules in consumer transactions, given the significance of default rules on choice. The concept of a default rule might be interpreted widely to include not only legal default rules but also 'what most people do' or 'what the right people do'. It is also relevant to regulation of standard form contracts. Requiring producers to offer consumers a choice of terms may not be sufficient if the choice is framed in such a manner that few consumers will be interested in the alternative offered (see the discussion below of *Woodman v Photo Trade Processing* and unfair terms; see Howells, 2005).

Second, writers argue that firms are aware of many of the findings of behavioural economics and may exploit consumer irrationalities. Hanson and Kysar argue that:

because individuals exhibit systematic and persistent cognitive processes that depart from axioms of rationality they are susceptible to manipulation by those actors in a position to influence the decision-making context. Moreover, the actors in the dominant position *must* capitalize on this manipulation or eventually be displaced from the market. (Hanson and Kysar, 1999:1424–25)

Amos Tversky, the economist who won the Nobel Prize for economics for his work in behavioural economics, once stated that the findings of behavioural economics would be well known to 'advertisers and used-car salesmen' (Hanson and Kysar, 1999: 1439).

Markets may be competitive without excess profits being made, but not be optimal from a consumer welfare point of view, given behavioural biases that are exploited by suppliers (see eg credit card pricing below, cell phones). Indeed as we shall see in the case of credit markets, the argument is that firms *must* exploit these irrationalities in order to remain competitive. This provides perhaps a deeper explanation of the common comment by businesses that they would like to avoid using certain practices but must adopt them because 'everybody does it' and that they would be disadvantaged if they did not. Collective and credible 'hands-tying' might be required by businesses to shift the structure of competition.

Third, the difficulties that individuals face in making accurate risk assessments suggest that in areas such as product safety a relatively bright-line rule, eg a duty to supply safe goods, may be socially optimal even if the consequence is a reduction in consumer choice.

Fourth, the findings of behavioural economics pose philosophical questions about regulation. The neo-classical approach is based on the assumption of consumer sovereignty and a distrust of paternalism. A commonplace argument is that it is not the role of government to protect individuals against making 'foolish' choices. Provided consumers have adequate information and there are no substantial market failures, then there is no reason to 'intervene' in the market. Behavioural economics suggests that this is an overly simple dichotomy although it has a strong rhetorical appeal. If consumers do not have well-formed preferences, then consumer policy becomes more complex. To argue that the goal of policy is 'consumer sovereignty' must prompt the question: which consumer? The consumer with short-term or long-term preferences? The preferences that are most easily stimulated but which the individual may regret following? Moreover since preferences are not distinct from their context, this includes existing government rules (or the absence of rules).

Consider the following example. James Whitman suggests that retail trading laws in France and Germany are more 'producerist' than the US (and UK) 'consumerist' laws (Whitman, 2007). By this he means that there are greater controls on shop hours, on forms of selling (prohibition on retail at loss, the *zone de chalandage*), and so on. These laws may be part of a larger architecture of regulation that protects small businesses against being put to the wall by large price cutters. An economic approach might view these regulations from a public choice perspective: they reflect the lobbying power of small business. And US policy has favoured price cutting as a competitive method of furthering consumer sovereignty in being offered low prices. But what if these distinctions in laws result in a different market structure with greater choice in France and Germany of quality artisanal products but more sticky prices? Is the US or European consumer being provided with 'what they want'? French policy may say that the consumer is being provided with greater choice, ie the maintenance of small stores alongside supermarkets, but fewer price-cutting alternatives (see further discussion of Unfair Commercial Practices Directive).

Current policymaking in many areas (see eg below Chapter 4 on unfair commercial practices) does justify more intrusive regulation to protect 'vulnerable' consumers who are sometimes distinguished from more rational consumers by their inability to make rational decisions. Behavioural economics suggests that this distinction needs rethinking given the systematic nature of the findings in relation to consumers generally. Legal standards are based on images of consumers in the marketplace, and a continuing issue in European and US consumer law is whether the 'reasonable' or 'credulous' consumer should be protected (see below, Unfair Commercial Practices Directive). Behavioural economics underlines the importance of the context and framing of particular consumer decisions which make it difficult to make a priori judgements as to whether or not consumers are vulnerable.

Finally, similar caveats might be raised concerning the discourse of behavioural economics and legal discourse. The law is itself an important discourse in society so that legal images of the consumer may be influential in shaping norms. The law is unlikely to follow the latest trend in policy science, even if the latter provides a useful normative critique.

3.9.1 The case of credit card interest rates

There are many points throughout this book where we consider the relevance of behavioural analysis. The following example shows the relevance of the analysis and the interaction of several factors (eg time-inconsistent preferences, over-optimism and under-estimation) in credit card pricing. It also indicates the tension between behavioural and neo-classical accounts as well as increased incorporation of behavioural analysis within mainstream economics.

Why are interest rates for borrowing on credit cards generally so high compared with other forms of borrowing? High interest rates and late payment fees associated with credit cards have been subject to criticism. Critics have argued that the use of practices such as automatic increases in borrowing limits, reductions in minimum payments, the use of credit card cheques and low-interest introductory offers encourage over-indebtedness (see House of Commons Treasury Committee, 2003: 34). Credit card companies make the bulk of their profits from individuals who do not pay off the balance on their card every month.

A credit card provides a consumer with a bundle of services including a method of payment, an interest-free period between purchases and payment, the possibility of borrowing on the card and, increasingly, other services such as frequent flyer points. A basic question is how these services should be priced—eg through transaction fees, annual fees or the interest on overdue balances. The credit card market in the UK and the US appears to be competitive with a large number of providers. Data show that almost no regular credit cards in the UK have annual or transaction fees and most only required a minimum repayment of 2% of outstanding balance in 2006 (Which?, 2006). Almost all cards have late-payment fees and over-limit fees.

Research during the past decade suggests that there may be failures in the credit card market caused by consumer behavioural biases. Initial work by Ausubel (1991, 1997) concluded that credit card companies in the US earned supra-normal profits because individuals under-estimate the future extent of their borrowing on the card. Since they did not intend to use the card as a borrowing mechanism from the outset (reflecting also over-optimism) they paid little attention to the interest rate charged on the card but were concerned about the immediate costs of the annual fee (see Ausubel, 1991; Bar-Gill, 2004). Since competition will focus on the annual fee, this will result in pressure to reduce the annual fee but maintain a high interest rate and increase late payment charges and fees. Research on low-interest introductory offers also indicates that consumers under-estimate the amount of their future borrowing on the new card and over-estimate the benefits of switching cards (Ausubel, 1999). Neo-classical economists countered Ausubel's explanation with the argument that consumers borrowed on credit cards because of the lower transaction costs of doing so, compared with other forms of short-term borrowing (Brito and Hartley, 1995).

Bar-Gill (2004) argues that a combination of hyperbolic discounting, under-estimation and over-optimism result in welfare failures in credit card markets.

Oren Bar-Gill, 'Seduction by Plastic' (2004) 98 *Northwestern University Law Review* 1373 at 1395

'Many consumers overestimate their ability to resist the temptation to finance consumption by borrowing, and consequently underestimate future borrowing. ...' When a hyperbolic discounter is naïve about the nature of her time preferences, she will overestimate her willpower, and consequently underestimate her future borrowing. ...Credit cards opened the door to the 'the seductiveness of incremental irresponsibility', as manifested in a-little-at-a-time borrowing.

Underestimation of future borrowing may also result from an optimism bias that might lead consumers to underestimate the likelihood of contingencies bearing economic hardship. Specifically, consumers might underestimate the likelihood of adverse events that might generate a need to borrow. ...

Individuals tend to underestimate the likelihood that they will lose their job or underestimate the length of time it would take them to find a new job.

These biases have resulted in a structure of credit card pricing that over-prices long-term contingencies, such as the need to borrow on a card or miss a payment, and under-prices non-contingent short-term prices, such as annual fees or transaction fees. While this structure does not necessarily result in excess profits—there may be intense competition over balance transfer rates, frequent flyer miles, etc—it does increase the costs of financial distress since the interest payments made when a consumer has suffered an income decrease will, given the decreasing marginal utility of money, out-weigh any savings from the absence of an annual fee at the outset when the consumer has a higher income. To this must be added the social costs of financial distress and over-indebtedness. This structure of pricing also results in cross-subsidisation of trans-actors (those who pay their bill in full) by borrowers, a cross-subsidisation that may be regressive. Given consumers' preferences (eg dislike of annual fees), businesses that wish to compete successfully in the credit card market must exploit these behavioural biases. The conclusion therefore it is that the current structure of credit card pricing may be regressive from a consumer viewpoint notwithstanding the fact that the market is competitive.

Studies show that consumers are aware of the interest rates (APR) on their credit cards (Durkin, 2002; DTI, 2004) but this does not seem to prevent the behavioural biases outlined by Bar-Gill.

Several studies (see Sullivan, Warren and Westbrook, 2000; Warren, 2003) have shown that consumers who experience a job loss or other shock to their finances often use credit cards to maintain a lifestyle. Individuals expect that their problems will be temporary and some continue to borrow past a time when any rational individual would do so. Borrowing on a credit card is, however, very costly and in the event that the problem is not temporary an individual may become over-indebted. This behaviour seems to fit phenomena identified by behavioural economics, namely that individuals have a status quo bias, are averse to losses and are over-optimistic.

Finally, other economic studies suggest that individuals borrow at high interest rates on credit cards while maintaining at the same time a stock of illiquid assets. These assets may be regarded as a form of hand tying, a commitment device to ensure that individuals will have assets for retirement. This suggests that individuals are attempting to balance the conflict between the rational and myopic self (Laibson et al, 2003; and for survey see Bertaut and Haliassos, 2006). However, these individuals also had liquid assets that could have been used to pay down the credit card debt but which remained in low-interest accounts. The ability to use a commitment device such as a stock of illiquid assets raises distributional issues, since not all consumers would possess the funds to make the commitment.

What are the possible policy responses to these findings?

1. Disclosure regulation

Since there is a separation between the time when the consumer obtains a card and the time when she borrows, additional disclosures at the time of borrowing may be more effective than disclosure at the time of obtaining the card. Ronald Mann suggests that individuals should be able to view the balance on their card every time they make a purchase (Mann, 2006: 163). If this was technologically feasible, then this might be an effective policy.

One current policy initiative is to disclose the dangers of making the minimum payment on a credit card. UK regulations (see 2007 regulations enacted under section 78(4)(a) Consumer Credit Act 1974) require the following disclosure:

> Minimum repayments
>
> If you make only the minimum payment each month, it will take you longer and cost you more to clear your balance.

A more specific warning is provided under section 1301 of the US Bankruptcy Abuse Prevention and Consumer Protection Act 2005:

> Minimum Payment Warning: making only the minimum payment will increase the interest you pay in the time it takes to repay your balance. For example, making only the typical 2% minimum monthly payment on a balance of $1000 at an interest rate of 17% would take 88 months to repay the balance in full. For an estimate of the time it would take to repay your balance, making only minimum payments, call this toll-free number.

The effectiveness of the UK disclosure will be undercut by the fact that it is a generic disclosure. Since many people are over-optimistic, they will discount its application to their situation. Moreover the general knowledge that making minimum payments will require longer to pay off the debt and cost more is not necessarily something that people are unaware of.

The second disclosure is more specific, but using a hypothetical example makes it difficult for an individual to relate it to his own situation.

A further possibility therefore is a customised disclosure. This might state: 'Your balance of xxx will take xxx month to pay off ... at a total cost of xxx in principal, and xxx in interest, if only the minimum monthly payments are made up.'

The US General Accounting Office (2006) concludes that customised disclosures would provide more information to consumers and that consumers who typically carry balances found customised disclosures very useful. Credit card issuers indicated that providing cardholders with customised information is feasible. The primary increased costs would be that of increased postage costs. Ronald Mann suggests a disclosure that would indicate to the consumer how long it will take to pay off the balance if a consumer continues to make the same payments as they are currently making.

The Competition Commission in the UK, after concluding an investigation that found the store card credit industry (which charges higher interest rates than regular cards) to be uncompetitive, required a warning that store cards may charge higher interest rates (see Competition Commission, store card investigation, 2006).

2. Providing annual statements on the costs of credit card use

3. Changing default rules

A further possibility is to change the default rule in credit card transactions. For example, minimum payments might be set at a higher rate than current. If a consumer wished to make a lower minimum payment, he or she could request this from a card issuer. Automatic increases in the credit limits might be prohibited without the express consent of the consumer at the time of the proposed change to the credit limit. The UK financial institutions have agreed to a protocol which implements this requirement. See also in the US the Credit Card Accountability Responsibility and Disclosure Act 2009.

4. Encouraging pre-commitment strategies

Encouraging pre-commitment strategies might include encouraging individuals to establish a direct debit for their credit card payments to avoid late fees, and to make a commitment to pay a substantial amount on the card every month. This would have the effect off making a credit card more like a debit card. Increased use of debit cards might be in carriage through the provision of similar legal protections for debit card holders as currently exist for credit card holders. The Competition Commission requires store card providers to provide consumers with the option of establishing and paying their card by direct debit.

5. Price controls

Regulators might control the interest charged or the price for late payment. This would change the pricing structure of cards by requiring credit card companies to increase the short-term costs of the card. The Office of Fair Trading, in effect, controlled the price of penalty fees in its threatened action in 2006 against major credit card companies, all of whom responded by reducing their fees from approximately £25 to £12.

---

4. Competition, information failures, bundling and switching costs

> Competition is increasingly being recognized as a core consumer issue. (Sir John Vickers, 'Competition is for Consumers', speech to the Social Market Foundation, 21 February 2002)

Competition law and policy is a large subject with its own literature. Competition policy has traditionally focused on the supply side of markets and the effects of market structure and supplier conduct on competition in a market. Within this paradigm, competition policy ensures that consumer choice is not restricted and consumer policy ensures consumers are able to choose freely and make rational market choices.

Competition policy must now pay greater attention to the demand side of markets and the behaviour of consumers (Waterson, 2003). Three facts support this observation in the UK: (i) the privatisation and deregulation of services previously supplied by one supplier; (ii) the large literature on switching costs; and (iii) the literature of behavioural economics.

First, it is not sufficient to open markets to competition if consumers do not take advantage of market choices. Real and perceived switching costs may reduce the effectiveness of competition. Switching costs incude exit fees, the costs of learning about an alternative provider, the costs of comparing the alternative terms and such issues as the paperwork necessary to effect the change. Consumers may also have a status quo bias and inertia that inhibits switching (see Farrell and Klemperer, 2006). Waterson argues that the substantial difference in switching costs between the UK insurance and banking industry may account for the supra-normal profits made by the latter (Waterson, 2003). Waterson notes that the motor insurance industry is characterised by: (i) a standard contract length of one year; (ii) the ability to change insurer by telephone; and (iii) a general practice in the insurance industry of accepting an individual's claims history from another insurer. In contrast, the standard bank contract is indefinite in duration, goodwill developed with one provider may not be transferable to another, direct debits may not be easy to change, and bank charges are not always easily comparable between suppliers.

Waterson concludes that policy might focus not only on traditional methods of reducing search costs through greater price transparency and standardisation but also on contract terms (eg using fixed-term contracts rather than automatically renewable contracts). Waterson also suggests that this form of regulation will be most desirable in industries that are 'relatively mature … where performance is habitually a long way short of competitive … a particular instance is where the industry has traditionally been in state hands, so that consumers are not very used to exercising choice' (Waterson, 2003: 147). Governments might respond to switching costs with information programmes and by supplying comparative standardised information on the relative costs of different providers. The costs of switching might be reduced through a reduction in the notice period for cancellation of contracts (see below the OFT and unfair terms, Chapter 6) and the methods of cancellation might be expanded (eg any method—telephone, in person, fax, email—as long as an individual can prove cancellation).

Firms may have incentives to create switching costs that will result in consumers being locked in and subject to potential 'monopoly rents'. Examples include 'frequent flyer plans' (where consumers over-estimate the benefits from the plan) or 'lock-ins' to long-term contracts. If suppliers are able to do so, they may price discriminate between existing consumers of the product and new consumers, charging higher prices to the former group.

Secondly, competition policy assumes that consumers will respond to competition in a rational manner, whereas much of behavioural economics indicates that consumers often respond irrationally. A recent study of consumer switching decisions in the electricity market argues that consumer mistakes in relation to switching (either under- or over-estimating) were more common where there were a large number of competitors and this seemed to be explained by information overload (Wilson and Waddams-Price, 2006). Consumers were paradoxically harmed by an increase in choice.

The case of 'aftermarkets' (eg maintenance and servicing costs) associated with the

purchase of products illustrates the interplay of competition policy and behavioural economics. This is the situation where a product or service may have a low initial cost and
then high subsequent costs such as replacement of printer cartridges or car servicing.
Competition may focus on the primary cost of the product. This has been described as
a 'bargain then rip-off' pattern of pricing (Farrell and Klemperer, 2006). A neo-classical
economist might argue that this equilibrium is not sustainable because a new firm will
enter the market offering a different balance of pricing. It is possible, however, that
new entrants may not respond to this problem by offering more balanced pricing given
individuals' focus on the purchase of the product and the under-estimation of future
usage costs. The provision of lifecycle cost information to consumers might reduce this
tendency but may not be effective if consumers have a persistent bias towards focusing
on the immediate costs (see Gans, 2005; Sylvan, 2005).

Ireland (2004) suggests that competition policy should consider the issue of search
costs in merger policy. Ireland considers the situation where a firm is sending multiple
signals concerning the same product to the market either because it (i) operates from
outlets with different names; or (ii) markets the same product under different brand
names. In these situations consumers searching these products are sampling from the
same source and therefore engaging in wasteful search activity. Ireland concludes that
this results in higher than average prices and that a firm supplying the same product
through multiple trade names is engaging in a practice similar to price fixing among a
subset of suppliers.

Ireland provides the example of the OFT decision (2001) approving the exclusive
dealer status of DSG Retail (which includes Dixons, Currys and Price World) in
relation to Compaq and Packard Bell. The OFT concluded that the status should be
confirmed because (i) market shares were not dominant (less than 40 per cent); and (ii)
customers were not attracted to particular brands since price was the main reason for
competition. However, Ireland points out that: (i) retailers needed prominent brands in
order to compete; (ii) the ability of DSG to sell through three different retail chains
may mislead consumers who are unaware of the connection; and (iii) consumers will
find it difficult to compare with independent retailers because other chains do not sell
these particular products.

There is also the role of consumer influence over the development of competition policy. Competition policy is a relatively complex and low-visibility area and it
may be difficult for consumers to see clearly the effects of international cartels in raw
materials on their pocketbook. The ability of consumer groups to make supercomplaints (see below Chapter 3) is therefore an important method of ensuring that the
consumer voice has an input into competition policy. Two further issues are the ability
of consumer groups to bring class actions for damages under competition law and for
public enforcement to secure compensation for individuals affected by anticompetitive
activity. Section 47B of the Competition Act 1998 provides that recognised consumer
groups may bring a representative action for damages on behalf of named consumers
against firms that have been convicted of cartel activity or other anticompetitive practices.

Given the significance of competition policy in public policy at the national,
regional and international level, the challenge for consumer interests is to harness it
for the benefit of consumers. Braithwaite and Drahos argue that a 'great attraction of

competition law is that it recruits business to do the consumer movement's work …
anti-competitive practices usually have business as well as consumer victims; the business victims normally have more resources and incentive to launch court cases against
monopolistic practices' (Braithwaite and Drahos, 2000: 621). The example of WalMart
and other retailers challenging the charging practices of the international credit card
networks might be cited here. However, actions by competitors will not always benefit
consumers and may dampen competition (see below Chapter 4 at 3).

---

5. Equity

How extremely expensive it is to be poor. (James Baldwin quoted in Cohen, 2003: 355)

Consumer law and policy may be viewed as a general attempt to redistribute power
and resources (eg rights) from producers to consumers, and changing producer markets
to consumer markets. This might not merely involve low prices but also policies of
loss-spreading which shift risks from consumer to producer. This will be a progressive
measure if one accepts, together with the premise mentioned above, the assumption
that consumers are in general poorer or less able to protect themselves than producers.
Even if some of these costs are passed along to consumers through the price mechanism, the assumption is that consumers are willing to pay for this insurance. This
is particularly true in the case of product safety and threats to health. Although few
consumer-protection measures have specifically identified the poor consumer as the
intended beneficiary of legislation, the alleviation of the problems of poverty and of the
disadvantaged (the elderly, the young) has been a continuing undercurrent in consumer
protection. Consumer policy might therefore be part of a general policy of 'positive
welfare' designed to establish minimum standards in the marketplace, provide equal
access to consumption opportunities and enforce rights.

The special problems facing low-income consumers in the United States were documented by the Federal Trade Commission, which found that consumers purchasing
from retailers catering mainly for those with low incomes pay significantly higher
prices than those charged by general-market retailers for identical products (FTC,
1968). These findings were corroborated in David Caplovitz's study *The Poor Pay
More* and Alan Andreasen's *Disadvantaged Consumer*. In the United Kingdom the
National Consumer Council (NCC), established with the specific mandate to represent
the 'inarticulate and the disadvantaged', conducted several studies on the problems of
low-income consumers. In *Why the Poor Pay More*, it documented in 1977 the concept
of 'consumer detriment'. In 2004 the NCC updated its 1977 study by publishing *Paying
More: Getting Less*:

> We live in an era of inequality. Poverty has become a focus of policy, with significant effort
> focused on public services—for example, through work on social exclusion—and on people's
> income—for example, through expanding employment. There has been a welcome focus on
> the needs of particular groups, such as elderly people and families with children. But the

NCC's research, set out in this consultation pack, suggests that there are issues that are not resolved with these approaches.

The NCC's findings focus on essential services for consumers, in particular those who are disadvantaged. What we have found to be true across a range of services is that the poor pay more … or get less. At present, there is no consensus about which goods and services are essential to meet consumers' basic needs, and therefore what policies are needed to ensure inclusion. More fundamentally, there is poor understanding of consumers' real needs; often disadvantaged consumers are left to choose from services that are inappropriate.

Changing nature of service provision

Many of the essential goods and services that people need to get by are provided by the market. Everyday essential goods and services such as energy for heating, nutritious food, clean water, healthcare, access to financial advice, are clearly basic needs. We need them for health and well-being, and for active and meaningful participation in society. And yet there is little consistency or focus in government policy towards the increasingly important role of the private sector—from water and telecommunications through to services such as transport

Barriers to access

Definitions of 'essential' will change over time. For example, in the last five years we have seen an increasing need to access mobile phones and the internet. The more dynamic and innovative a society is, the more creative its response to social inclusion needs to be. But disadvantaged consumers face many barriers gaining access to essentials, and contend with fewer resources (such as money and transport) and skills (such as numeracy).

…There are four reasons why the poor pay more:

- How you pay—life on cash is more expensive.

- How you buy—if you can't buy in bulk, or afford a weekly shop, you pay more.

- How you access services—if you can't get around, because of a disability or limited transport, you can't shop around.

- Who you are—in some cases, such as credit, markets may not be competitive for those on a low income. In others, such as financial advice, there are regulatory barriers standing in the way of innovation.

Absent, inappropriate and expensive services

Disadvantaged consumers' lives are taken up with relentless daily struggles to access essential goods and services while avoiding debt. Money is spent on bills or loan repayments first. There is never enough money to go around, so they get into debt, go without, or develop other coping strategies.

… Lack of money is not the only problem. Some services are either unsuitable or nonexistent for disadvantaged consumers.

Many disadvantaged consumers feel they are targets for irresponsible provision—for example, promotions for items from fashionable children's trainers to 'two-for-one' convenience dinners, or unaffordable loans.

Changing nature of service provision

The nature of poverty and social exclusion

Increasingly government has encouraged the private sector in the supply of essentials. This can be seen in the privatisation of national industries and the introduction of competition, mixed models of provision in public services and the withdrawal of public subsidies from public services. But competition is not serving the needs of the most disadvantaged. Public service rationing increasingly bars those with greatest need. Disadvantaged consumers are excluded either because they lack the skills to negotiate complex markets and systems, they are too costly to serve or they lack purchasing power.

Market-based exclusion is therefore the problem to be tackled if the government is to be successful in eliminating poverty and social exclusion.

Cherry-picking

Competition can help bring prices down, but providers 'cherry-pick' the most profitable consumers using increasingly sophisticated marketing techniques. Inadequate market intervention has meant that some socio-economic groups benefit less from price competition than others. Consumers who are costly to supply are charged in excess of their ability to pay or denied services altogether. The increasing reduction of socially motivated consumer crosssubsidies has compounded this problem.

Regulation for social goals

Regulation for the achievement of social objectives and the protection of vulnerable consumer groups (such as disabled people, those on low-income, or in rural areas) is frequently a poor 'rival' for economic (primarily pro-competition) and environmental regulation. This is particularly the case in the utilities and financial services.

Barriers to access

Extra support needed

Many people lack the skills and confidence to get the services they need. The consumers in our research varied greatly in their degree of confidence and ability to tackle providers. Consumers with basic skills difficulties have trouble with most consumer transactions. They experience the greatest access problems, yet are the least catered for. Independent help is highly valued, but in short supply. All relied heavily on community centres, friends and family for dealing with providers—even for basics such as understanding bills.

Compounding exclusion

Access to some services—such as financial services, transport and telephone—depends on having access to other essentials. For example, electronic salary payments make bank accounts a precursor to legitimate paid employment. Some services can only be paid for with direct debit or debit cards and, without these facilities, access to the capital necessary for purchasing expensive household items, such as fridges, may be out of reach.

Technology

The technology harnessed by many providers to minimise costs and reduce prices (such as internet banking) may be welcomed by many, but for disadvantaged consumers, this distancing from suppliers causes further barriers to access—for example, call centres for the utilities and welfare benefits, or prepayment meters which help consumers to budget but impose additional costs.

5.1 Assuring consumer access to markets at reasonable prices: social exclusion and consumer markets

Social exclusion 'is a broader concept than poverty, encompassing not only low material means but the inability to participate effectively in economic, social, political and cultural life, and, in some characterizations, alienation and distance from the mainstream society' (Duffy, 1995).

Financial Services Authority, *In or Out? Financial Exclusion: A Literature and Research Review* (2000) 7–8

1.4 Social exclusion is a term that is much used in European policy debates, but which has only relatively recently gained currency in the UK. Although it has clear links with earlier debates about poverty, disadvantage and deprivation, social exclusion is a much broader concept, which is a shorthand term for what can happen when people or areas suffer from a combination of linked problems such as unemployment, poor skills, low incomes, poor housing, high crime environments, bad health, poverty and family breakdown.

(From website, http://www.cabinet-office.gov.uk/seu/index/faqs.html)

1.5 As these dimensions of social exclusion are typically interrelated, each one increases the likelihood of the others (see, for example, Rogaly et al, 1999).

1.6 Three core elements of social exclusion are commonly identified, although the analysis of them differs between commentators. They are:

- Low income related to employment status, for example lack of employment opportunities and low levels of benefit among people not in work.

- Lack of access to services such as education, vocational training, health care and financial services.

- Poor environment, including poor housing, deprived neighbourhoods and difficult family life.

Together, these factors can lead to social exclusion, or what the government describes as a 'cycle of disadvantage', the effects of which can persist throughout people's lives and be passed between generations (Department of Social Services, 1999).

1.7 Burchardt et al (1999), using panel data from the British Household Panel Survey 1991–1995, concluded that there is no distinct group of completely excluded individuals. Their study tracked a range of possible outcomes, one of which was savings, and they found few individuals who were excluded on all dimensions in any one year. Even fewer experienced multiple exclusion for all five years. The researchers concluded that it is preferable to treat the different dimensions of social exclusion separately rather than thinking about social exclusion in terms of a single homogeneous group. (Burchardt et al, 1999)

Being relatively poor in a rich country may be a significant handicap even though one's financial income is high in terms of world standards. The need to take part in the life of the community may result in a demand for televisions, DVD recorders, cell phones, etc, that places a burden on the finances of those who are relatively poor and that may result in difficulties in paying for what may on another index be classified as necessities such as fuel and food (Sen, 1999).

The Poverty and Social Exclusion Survey of Great Britain defines poverty in terms of lack of access to a list of goods and services that 50 per cent or more of a representative sample of the population believe no one should be without.

One study concludes that it is important to understand issues of social exclusion in relation to the *methods* that consumers use to obtain goods and services. Williams and Windebank (2002: 502), using a definition by Philo (2000) of social exclusion that describes the situation 'in which members of a society are, or become, separated from much that comprises the normal "round" of living and working within that society' introduce the notion of the 'excluded consumer'. Based on a study of 400 households in lower income urban neighbourhoods in England, they conclude that:

> [H]ouseholds define themselves as separated from the rest of society not just when they cannot afford to buy goods but also by their goods acquisition practices. They perceive their inability to buy new goods from formal retail outlets and their reliance on alternative retail channels (eg family, car boot sales, second-hand shops) when most people do not have to use such sources as a mark of their exclusion from mainstream consumption practices.

Williams and Windebank argue that although the majority of the population studied have acquired all the items that are viewed as necessities this 'does not mean that all such persons are "included consumers". Many who acquired these goods from alternative retail sites will still view themselves as excluded from participating in mainstream consumption practices.' Williams and Windebank propose greater regulation of the quality of goods sold in the alternative retailing sector.

Financial exclusion is a major concern in the United Kingdom. We have already considered it in discussing cost–benefit analysis and we explore it further in Chapter 7.

A major change since the 1977 NCC report is the privatisation of utility services (gas, 1984; electricity generation and supply, 1989; water, 1991) that initially resulted in the transfer of 'public property to private interests at concessionary prices' (Moran, 2003: 103) and which changed the relationship of providers to consumers. Although regulators in these industries were often initially conceptualised as merely concerned with efficiency or mimicking a competitive market through price control, the Utilities Act 2000 introduced greater input for stakeholders through the establishment of an independent consumer watchdog (eg Energywatch) and also the requirement for electricity and gas regulators to have regard to the following interests in regulation:

(a)   individuals who are disabled or chronically sick;

(b)   individuals of pensionable age;

(c)   individuals with low incomes; and

(d)   individuals residing in rural areas;

> but that is not to be taken as implying that regard may not be had to the interests of other descriptions of consumer. (s 13, Utilities Act 2000 inserting s 3A(3) amending Electricity Act 1989)

Graham (2006) notes that privatisation of utilities has not resulted in a worse outcome for disadvantaged consumers than existed under the nationalised industries. This may be for several reasons including the change of government in 1997, consumer activism and a political climate that pushed regulators to respond. The privatised utilities now operate within 'an increasingly complex web of public service obligations, covering issues like guarantees of universal service and safeguards against disconnection of services' (Moran, 2003: 111) and an institutionalised structure of consumer voice. Regulation of utilities in the UK provides an interesting experiment in attempting to blend efficiency, equity and citizenship values (see further Wilhelmsson, 2003: 149). An important question will be whether the new voice for consumer interests through a regulated industries unit outlined in Chapter 1 will be as effective as the more focused Energywatch.

The importance of so-called 'services of general interest' within the EU which covers traditional public utilities has resulted in a White Paper on this topic. Consider the implications of the values expressed in the White Paper for the privatised utilities in the UK. Should financial services be included within the definition below?

Commission of the European Communities, *Green Paper on Services of General Economic Interest*, COM(2003) 270

The term 'services of general economic interest' is used in Articles 16 and 86(2) of the Treaty. It is not defined in the Treaty or in secondary legislation. However, in Community practice there is broad agreement that the term refers to services of an economic nature which the Member States or the Community subject to specific public service obligations by virtue of a general interest criterion. The concept of services of general economic interest thus covers in particular certain services provided by the big network industries such as transport, postal services, energy and communications. However, the term also extends to any other economic activity subject to public service obligations.

Commission of the European Communities, *White Paper on Services of General Economic Interest*, COM(2004) 374

2.1 An essential component of the European model

The debate on the Green Paper has strongly confirmed the importance of services of general interest as one of the pillars of the European model of society. In spite of sometimes substantial differences in the views and perspectives of the various participants in the debate, the consultation has shown a broad consensus on the need to ensure the provision of high-quality and affordable services of general interest to all citizens and enterprises in the European Union. It has also confirmed the existence of a common concept of services of general interest in the Union. This concept reflects Community values and goals and is based on a set of common elements, including: universal service, continuity, quality of service, affordability, as well as user and consumer protection.

In the Union, services of general interest remain essential for ensuring social and territorial cohesion and for the competitiveness of the European economy. ...

3.3 Ensuring cohesion and universal access

...[U]niversal service is a key concept the Community has developed in order to ensure effective accessibility of essential services. It establishes the right of everyone to access certain services considered as essential and imposes obligations on service providers to offer defined services according to specified conditions, including complete territorial coverage and at an affordable price. Universal service is a dynamic and flexible concept and has proven to be an effective safety net provision for those who could otherwise not buy essential services for themselves.... The concept allows common principles to be defined at Community level and the implementation of these principles to be left to the Member States, thus making it possible to take account of specific situations in each country, in line with the principle of subsidiarity.

...

3.5 Ensuring consumer and user rights

The consultation on the Green Paper has shown that there is broad agreement that the provision of services of general interest must be organised in such a way that a high level of consumer and user rights is ensured. ...These include in particular the access to services, including to cross-border services, throughout the territory of the Union and for all groups of the population, affordability of services, including special schemes for persons with low income, physical safety, security and reliability, continuity, high quality, choice, transparency and access to information from providers and regulators.

The implementation of these principles generally requires the existence of independent regulators with clearly defined powers and duties. These include powers of sanction (means to monitor the transposition and enforcement of universal service provisions) and should include provisions for the representation and active participation of consumers and users in the definition and the evaluation of services, the availability of appropriate redress and compensation mechanisms and the existence of an evolutionary clause allowing requirements to be adapted in accordance with changing user and consumer needs and concerns, and with changes in the economic and technological environment. Regulators should also monitor market developments and provide data for evaluation purposes.

A further aspect of social exclusion is the 'digital divide': the extent to which information and communication technology (ICT) increases or reduces social divisions and contributes to social exclusion. A review of the literature and policy on the digital divide notes the danger of conceptualising the divide purely in terms of formal physical access. How an individual is able to use ICT is just as important (at home, in a public library) in terms of the types of activities that may be carried out on the Web. Effective use of ICT may relate to an individual's economic, cultural and social capital. This includes ease of access to expert advice and the extent of an individual's socialisation into the technoculture. If an individual can easily draw on others' (families, friends, neighbours and relatives) knowledge and encouragement in navigating ICT, then this will result in very different access from that of an isolated individual (Selwyn, 2004: 341).

An absence of social and cultural capital and the ability to draw on social and professional contacts may often be an aspect of consumer detriment. Writing in 1986, Golding summarised these aspects of consumer detriment (Golding: 1986: x–xi) and the extent to which poverty limits autonomy:

[P]overty is not just about money but about powerlessness. ... In so many ways active citizenship requires the capacity to confront the institutions, public and private, which frame people's lives. Tackling the town hall, getting to see and challenge your child's teacher, battling with the shop which sold you faulty goods, seeking advice in an unexpected run-in with the law, all demand that easy access to time, telephones, transport, and the soft terrorism of middle-class articulacy which are denied to so many.

[P]overty curtails freedom of choice. The freedom to eat as you wish, to go where and when you like, to seek the leisure pursuits or political activities which others expect, all are denied to those without the resources to buy their entry ticket through the many turnstiles our society sets up at the entry points to social activity. To be excluded by poverty is to be denied the full freedom of choice which is supposed to be the pivot of a modern industrial society.

It has been argued that low-income consumers are less rational in their market behaviour and may be less able to process market information or voice complaints about defective products (Best and Andreasen, 1977). For example, Caplovitz suggested that low-income consumers may engage in 'compensatory consumption'—impulse buying —to compensate for their disadvantages. Other studies deny that lower-income groups display a lower level of rationality and argue that low-income consumers act rationally given the general insecurities that they face (Alwitt and Donley, 1998). There is always the danger, as illustrated by Paul Johnson's historical study of working-class savings and credit, of not understanding low-income behaviour from the perspective of low-income consumers:

> In their comments, these individualists [who advocated self-help] never took proper account of the precarious economic circumstances of working-class life, and so, despite all the detailed and well meaning investigation, they failed to understand the life of mean streets from the perspective of mean streets. … The insecurity of working-class income prevented the adoption of long-term savings plans that might conform to middle-class models of saving over the life-cycle. (Johnson, 1985: 218–19)

It is obviously important for policymaking to clarify these competing hypotheses. For example, information policies in credit markets will be of little relevance to low-income consumers if they cannot adequately process information or if they have limited sources of credit (see below Chapter 7).

Finally, if consumer protection has been an attempt to redistribute resources (eg income or rights) from producers to consumers, then this draws attention again to regulation as an attempt by competing interest groups to harness the power of the state to serve their interests. LeGrand and others have shown how many aspects of the welfare state (education, health services) benefited primarily middle-income groups (LeGrand, 1982; LeGrand and Robinson, 1984). Given the difficulties outlined earlier concerning consumer representation, there is the danger that consumer policy will benefit well-organised, middle-income consumers and consumer groups at the expense of poorly organised, low-income groups. For example, extension of the right to obtain damages for disappointment through a failed holiday (see *Jarvis v Swans Tours Ltd* (1973)) may be little help to the minority of the population who cannot afford an annual holiday.

5.2 Consumer entitlements: a rights approach?

The concept of a right to regulatory protection contrasts with the utilitarian approach of market-failure analysis, denying the legitimacy of the trade-offs implicit in the utilitarian calculus. For example, a right to safety removes the issue of safety from the marketplace and cost–benefit analysis (Okun, 1975: 20). Rights 'trump' competing considerations. A rights approach draws ultimately on the Kantian idea of personal autonomy—that an individual may not be used as a means to social ends. For example, Hugh Collins views consumer protection as designed to protect the individual right to be treated with dignity and in a way that will not damage self-respect (Collins, 1986: 136; Machan and Den Uyl, 1987: 119).

A rights approach was important symbolically in the political development of consumerism and in the staking of consumers' claims to a redistribution of power in society . Consumer rights were and are part of the new range of social rights claimed in modern society (Scheingold, 1974; Stewart and Sunstein, 1982). The United Nations Guidelines on Consumer Protection adopt a rights approach and the EU treaty refers to consumers' rights to information, education and organisation. The connection between human rights and consumer rights is highlighted in access to necessities such as water where the UN has articulated a human right to water (see Morgan, 2006). Human rights are often divided into three 'generations'. First-generation rights include civil and political rights, second-generation rights are economic and social rights—such as a right to a minimum standard of living—and third-generation rights are those not yet recognized as human rights but that may have been approved by international organisations such as the UN—eg the right to development and environmental rights (see Benöhr and Micklitz, 2010).

Sinai Deutch has argued that consumer rights should be treated as a third-generation form of human rights.

Sinai Deutch, 'Are Consumer Rights, Human Rights?' (1994) 32 *Osgoode Hall LJ* 537 at 551–53, 576

Consumer rights are rights of the individual and not rights of a group. Consumers are not a separate group of people, since every person is a consumer from time to time. With respect to products and services needed for private use, every vendor is also a consumer.

Consumer rights focus on the individual to whom basic rights to fair trade and safe products are granted. One of the main ideas behind consumer protection is that the individual is entitled to protection notwithstanding that, on the basis of a cost–benefit analysis, the economy might benefit if the individual consumer receives defective goods or hazardous products. Similarly, one of the main features of human rights is an emphasis on the individual as opposed to the collective. The acknowledgement that human rights protect the individual's prosperity, honour, and development makes consumer rights suitable to be declared as human rights.

In a consumer society, protection of the individual consumer is part of maintaining human dignity. If not given the right to fair trade, the right to a fair contract, and the right of access to courts, a person's dignity is disregarded. At the end of the day, these rights are no less important than other human rights.

Consumer rights are similar to other accepted human rights in other aspects as well. Human rights are intended to protect the individual from arbitrary infringements by government. In the same way, the individual consumer is entitled to protection against big business organizations, monopolies, cartels, and multinational corporations. The big business organization should be considered less like an individual, who bargains on equal terms, and more like a government, which controls the private consumer.

There is a school of thought that considers standard contracts as private lawmaking by large economic corporations. The inequality of bargaining power leads to contracts of adhesion and to the erosion of the basic right to negotiate. Where an individual consumer is one party and a strong economic organization is the other party, the organization can impose its will on the consumer on 'a take it or leave it' basis, thereby disregarding the consumer's honour and dignity. Since every person is a consumer from time to time, it is a common problem. In order to introduce equality and justice into the market, the inequality must be alleviated by consumer protection legislation. Consumer rights are intended to prevent abuse of power and, in this sense as well, are similar to other well-defined economic human rights, which protect the individual against abuse of power by governments.

It is also necessary today to regulate consumer protection on an international level. More and more transactions are conducted by transnational corporations. Commerce has become increasingly international and the problem of hazardous goods and defective products is not merely a national concern. These developments have already led to some international recognition of consumer rights by the United Nations and other international organizations.

Another phase in the establishment of consumer rights as human rights is their inclusion in the constitutions of several countries.

In Brazil, the comprehensive 1990 code of consumer protection states that it is based on articles 5 XXXII and 170 V of the federal Constitution. Article 5 is part of Title II—Fundamental Rights and Guarantees and is also part of Chapter I—Individual and Collective Rights and Duties. Article 170 delineates the general principles of economic activities. In each article, consumer rights are part of the basic human rights to life, liberty, equality, security, and property. The comprehensive code of consumer protection declares basic consumer rights and is based on the principles and the rules of the UNGCP in both structure and content.

The Charter of Fundamental Rights of the European Union includes a guarantee of a high level of consumer protection, suggesting a 'commitment of the European Union to human values and not only to market integration' (Benöhr and Micklitz, 2010: 29). Many countries have included consumer protection in their constitutions.

Critics of a rights approach argue that consumer rights to safety or information are impossible to protect, and hopelessly vague as guides to decision-makers, who must often make difficult trade-offs with limited resources. They argue, in addition, that there would be difficulties in balancing these rights against other, perhaps more fundamental, rights and that it would be necessary to decide whether consumers should be able to trade away these consumer rights. A view that such rights are inalienable would, for example, prevent individuals buying at below the particular level of safety set to protect the right to safety.

The concept of consumer rights may, however, still draw on the idea of personal autonomy and be interpreted as requiring that consumers have a right to self-development, and equal representation with other groups in the process of deciding what level of information or product risk is adopted by society. If society today is deeply divided on common substantive goals, then procedural elements of the right to be heard in social and economic decision-making become crucial. Regulation of consumer markets becomes therefore a dialogue about the nature of risks and the role of regulation. This right might extend not only to government decisions, but also to decisions emanating from other centres of power, eg large private corporations. Only through such a process are consumers treated with equal concern and respect.

5.3 Community values

The concept of community values in consumer protection refers to values such as honesty, fair-dealing and loss-sharing which are not simply reducible to individual self-interest, to their contribution to economic efficiency or to the protection of individual rights (Stewart and Sunstein, 1982: 1238). Yet can we be certain that there are shared 'community values' on the appropriate levels of honesty and fairness to be respected in the marketplace? To what extent ought the consumer market to be regarded as a game in which the players bargain, bluff and sometimes lie?

An important theme in economic and sociological works is that the rational self-interested behaviour associated with markets can only flourish where there exist mutual trust and confidence. George Simmel (Simmel, 1908, cited in Dingwall and Fenn, 1987: 57; Arrow, 1974; Schumpeter, 1947) noted that:

> Our modern life is based to a much larger extent than is usually realized upon the faith in the honesty of the other. Examples are our economy which becomes more and more a credit economy. ...[W]e base our gravest decisions on a complex system of conceptions most of which presuppose the confidence that we will not be betrayed.

Kenneth Arrow has also drawn attention to the importance of these values to social life:

> Consider what is thought of as a higher or more elusive value ... trust among people. Now trust has a very important pragmatic value, if nothing else. Trust is an important lubricant of a social system. It is extremely efficient; it saves a lot of trouble to have a fair degree of reliance on other people's word. Unfortunately, this is not a commodity which can be bought very easily. If you have to buy it, you already have some doubts about what you've bought. Trust and similar values. ... have real, practical, economic value; they increase the efficiency of the system, enable you to produce more goods or more of whatever values you hold in high esteem. But they are not commodities for which trade on the open market is technically possible or even meaningful.

> It follows from these remarks that from the point of view of efficiency as well as from the point of view of distributive justice, something more than the market is called for. The government may indeed perform somewhat better than the private sector in realizing social feelings, trust, and empathy, but within limits. (Arrow, 1974: 23)

Consumer policy may be conceived as contributing to this background security for market transactions, and as providing a source for the development of social norms of trust and confidence. The EU Commission partly appeals to this value in promoting its harmonisation programme for consumer law in the EU. Debate over consumer regulation is not, therefore, simply a matter of counting economic costs and benefits or dealing with consumer entitlements but 'part of a continuing process of deciding what sort of society ours shall be—how risk averse, how solicitous of the vulnerable and how willing to allocate resources through markets or public control' (Stewart and Sunstein, 1982: 1238). This issue is posed by the competing conceptions of consumer law in the test of the average consumer under the Unfair Commercial Practices Directive (see below Chapter 4).

6. Paternalism

Paternalistic measures override individual preferences, substituting government judgement for that of the individual. These interventions are often based either on distrust
of the consumer's ability to evaluate information or on the fear that individuals, even
with accurate information, will act irrationally, misestimating product risks. It is associated with regulation where mistakes by consumers might have costly consequences (eg
physical injury or major economic losses) or where consumers' short-term preferences
appear to need to be overruled in favour of their long-term interests. The behavioural
literature has underlined the slippery nature of paternalism for it may not be easy
to distinguish between situations where intervention accords with an individual's real
preferences (where these are blocked by, for example, problems of bounded rationality)
and those where government overrules an individual's real preferences, substituting its
own judgement. The analysis is complicated by the fact that certain consumers may
want to be protected from themselves. The meeting of such desires may be described as
'rational paternalism', with individuals delegating to government the task of protecting
them from succumbing to impulsive buying or from making costly mistakes (Barry,
1965: 226–27).

   Paternalism is an important concept in discussions of consumer policy. It is frowned
upon by economists who make the assumptions of market economics since it assumes
that government knows better than an individual what he or she wants or what is good
for him or her. Yet the growth of the pejorative connotation of the term 'paternalism'
is relatively recent, coinciding with the dominance of liberal individualism (Kleinig,
1983: 3). Paternalism is viewed by some as both compassionate and humanitarian—as
an attempt to overcome the alienation of individualism and to show sympathy for
others (Kennedy 1976; 1982). Kleinig comments (1984: 38) that:

> Paternalists after all, are not generally or at least obviously out to advance their own interests,
> except in so far as they have the interests of others as one of their interests. And that would
> appear to be a morally commendable interest. (Kleinig, 1984: 38)

Paternalism also invites us to question the assumptions of the market model (and liberal
individualism?) that individuals are the best judge of their own interests and that they
prefer what they choose in the marketplace (Offer, 2006: ch 2). Economists have traditionally considered preference and choice as synonymous—reinforcing the doctrine
of consumer sovereignty. In the following extract HLA Hart criticises what he views
as the 'extravagance' of John Stuart Mill's protests against paternalism and relates the
issues raised by paternalism to changing views of the limits of individual autonomy.
His comments reflect, perhaps, the values underlying much of the consumer-protection
legislation of the 1960s and 1970s.

> No doubt if we no longer sympathise with this criticism this is due, in part, to a general
> decline in the belief that individuals know their own interests best, and to an increased
> awareness of a great range of factors which diminish the significance to be attached to an
> apparently free choice or to consent. Choices may be made or consent given without adequate
> reflection or appreciation of the consequences; or in pursuit of merely transitory desires; or in

various predicaments when the judgment is likely to be clouded; or under inner psychological compulsion; or under pressure by others of a kind too subtle to be susceptible of proof in a law court. Underlying Mill's extreme fear of paternalism there perhaps is a concept of what a normal human being is like which now seems not to correspond to the facts. Mill, in fact, endows him with too much of the psychology of a middle-aged man whose desires are relatively fixed, not liable to be artificially stimulated by external influences; who knows what he wants and what gives him satisfaction or happiness; and who pursues these things when he can. (Hart, 1962: 32–33)

7. Sustainable consumption: ethical and fair trade

Sustainable consumption is now recognised as an aspect of consumer policy. It is included in the UN Guidelines on consumer protection, and the 2005 DTI framework document expects individuals to act as reflective consumers who consider the impact of their consumption decisions on the environment (DTI, 2005). Economists conceptualise environmental effects as an externality (third-party effect) that is not costed in the price of consumer products and there is much written on the most effective techniques for minimising environmental effects (eg Ogus, 1994: 204–13). It is not possible in this text to discuss all of the many approaches to addressing environmental degradation but I focus on the role of the consumer in environmental policy.

Sustainable consumption has made modest gains in countries of the North. However, commentators suggest that this is primarily in terms of 'weak' sustainable consumption (driving a car that uses less fuel) rather than 'strong' sustainable consumption (going by train rather than car). Fuchs and Lorek comment that although 'there is some indication of the willingness of consumers to move towards green consumption … there is little evidence that consumers are willing to change fundamentally or to reduce consumption for sustainability objectives' (Fuchs and Lorek, 2005: 261, 279) . While 30 per cent of people claim to care about companies' environmental and social record, only 3 per cent reflect this in their purchases (Coop Bank, cited in Defra, 2005: 24).

Intermediaries such as large retailers might be convinced to respond to consumer claims to care about environmentalism by making it easy to identify environmentally friendly products. The availability of transparent and trustworthy information is a key since it is difficult for consumers to assess claims that products or services are environmentally friendly. Thus the development of corporate social responsibility reporting and institutions such as the FTSE4GoodIndex are important factors in the information environment.

The limits of individual choice in addressing sustainable consumption have been pointed out by Seyfang:

> [W]hile consumers can choose from a range of more-or-less energy efficient cars using several different fuels, there is little scope to choose public transport, or to live close enough to work and shops to be able to walk and cycle. In these ways, consumers are effectively locked in to particular consumption patterns by the overarching social structures of market, business, working patterns, urban planning and development. (Seyfang, 2004: 323)

Sustainable consumption seems also to be in conflict with the general deregulation of consumer markets (eg permitting Sunday shopping) and promotion of credit for further consumption. The behavioural findings on consumer behaviour (hyperbolic discounting) also suggest that consumers will generally not take into account the future effects of their present consumption preferences. Moreover, governments may be unwilling to impose unpopular measures such as high taxes on travel.

Sustainable consumption is also related to global competitiveness. Porter argues that firms with good environmental records will be more successful globally, and Braithwaite and Drahos argue that consumer groups should at the international level attempt to ratchet up standards by persuading individual firms to 'lead the pack', and by pressing for the adoption of 'continuous improvement' in management practices. Whatever the actual strategy adopted, their argument underlines the important role of international standard setting in the area of sustainable consumption.

Consumers are also concerned about the processes by which products are made and consumers may have, as Kysar argues, 'preferences for processes'—for products that are produced in accordance with particular processes (Kysar, 2005). Fair trade and green consumer initiatives are naturally connected to a study of corporate social responsibility and the recognition that many large transnational corporations are as powerful actors as nation states. The Fair Trademark is an international certification that must meet standards set by the international certification body Fairtrade Labelling Organisations International established in 1997, which is an association of 20 national labelling initiatives that promote and market the Fairtrade label in their countries. Fair trading principles require that the following factors should be followed: payment of a fair price, a safe and healthy working environment for producers, conformity to the UN Convention on the Rights of the Child, gender equity, responsible methods of production including good environmental practices, and long-term relationships based on trust (www.ifat.org/index.php?option=com_frontpage&Itemid=1).

The increasing salience of issues of sustainable consumption and fair trade pose the question of the role of market instruments, such as greater information on the sourcing of products and their environmental effects, in achieving greater social responsibility or environmental friendliness. Do consumers have a right to this information—not merely so that they can make more informed shopping decisions but as a recognition of the new role of the 'citizen consumer'?

Frameworks and Forms of Regulation of Consumer Markets

1. The new regulation

The creation of a regulatory state (see Braithwaite, 2000; Moran, 2003) in the UK and the EU during the last thirty years has been accompanied by innovation in regulatory forms, principles and initiatives (OECD, 2002: 7). 'Better regulation' is a theme in these initiatives. The world financial crisis of 2008 has also caused a rethinking of regulatory assumptions, for example that market forces and informed consumers will constrain bad practices, or that regulation should be a last resort. At the same time the influence of behavioural economics advocates 'libertarian paternalism' (see below) that will 'nudge' consumers to make better decisions. No new overarching paradigm has evolved in regulation, however, and therefore this chapter outlines some of the general themes that are explored in more detail in subsequent chapters.

David Levi-Faur identifies the following characteristics associated with the 'new regulation':

(1) increased delegation of regulation through varieties of self-regulation; accompanied by
(2) greater regulation within government to prevent the classic problem of regulatory 'capture' and to maintain public trust;
(3) the rise of new instruments of regulation that involve increased internal monitoring by corporations;
(4) increased international regulation through technical standards;
(5) the diffusion of regulatory ideas worldwide through regulatory networks and international regulatory competition through increased international benchmarking. (Levi-Faur, 2005)

Varieties of self-regulation and soft law (guidelines, guidance, codes of conduct) have always been an aspect of consumer law and policy in the UK. An intriguing question is the extent to which these forms have been affected by aspects of the 'new public management' which has developed over recent decades where the focus is on 'account-ability, explicit standards and measures of performance' (Rose, 1999: 150; and see Moran, 2003) (see eg discussion of advertising self-regulation below). Measures have been adopted to ensure that government agencies are not 'captured' (RIAs, review by the National Audit Office, etc), do not respond to 'atrocity stories' in the media, develop meaningful standards for measuring success and provide transparent and accountable regulation. Hood et al (1999) note the doubling of the budgets of government oversight bodies during the 1990s. An example of Levi-Faur's third heading is the attempt by the Financial Services Authority to change the corporate culture of financial institutions to ensure that they 'treat customers fairly' (below Chapter 7). Internationalisation is a characteristic of contemporary consumer law with the development of transnational networks of regulators within the EU (see eg Regulation 2006/2004).

There has also been a search for 'smart' regulation since the 1980s (see Baldwin, 2005) and this has often involved mixing differing regulatory instruments (eg informa-tion and regulation), and harnessing non-state actors to achieve regulatory goals. The Better Regulation Task Force in 2003 classified regulation into four categories: classic regulation, ie no intervention; incentive-based systems; information and education; self-regulation and co-regulation. Classic regulation is 'where a law is passed to tell people what to do or what not to do'. This may be primary legislation—where there is an Act of Parliament—or secondary legislation, often (confusingly) known as 'regulations'.

Better Regulation Task Force, *Imaginative Thinking for Better Regulation* (2003)

Classic regulation is the traditional way for the State to seek to change behaviour. If there seems to be a need to intervene in a market; a new health risk needs to be addressed; there has been an accident or disaster and 'something must be done', the first thought is usually 'we need to regulate'. We want to stop this from being the first thought. Too often this first thought becomes the only option. We want Departments to choose the best way of solving their problem. Classic regulation may prove to be the best way; but equally it may not. There are advantages. Classic regulation can make it clear how people have to behave, and sometimes this can be easier for them than having to work out what to do each time. It applies to everyone within scope—not just those who choose to opt in—so it can deliver a level-playing field. This can have business benefits. However, there are disadvantages too. Although a piece of legislation may apply to someone, they may not know they are within its scope; or know what to do. Legislation has to be promoted, explained and, importantly, enforced, if it is to have an impact. People may not comply through ignorance; or they may try to avoid or break the rules if they get in the way of what they want to do. As a result, compliance may be a problem, and costly policing may be necessary. This in turn may mean more bureaucracy. Proving that you comply may mean form-filling and recordkeeping.

In order to close all the loopholes, classic regulation can become complex. Classic regulation generally only makes sense if those regulated are able to comply with it. And compliance with a new piece of classic regulation can involve a big change in behaviour, which can be burdensome and costly. ...Sometimes demonstrating compliance with regulations requires recordkeeping and other administration. These take time, and can be disproportionately burdensome to small firms.

Enforcement can be expensive. The Government has to pay the people to do it, train them, and provide any equipment they may need.

The Better Regulation model may be an exaggerated picture of 'traditional' regula-tion in the UK, whereas the OECD indicates there is a long tradition in consumer policy of the use of informal measures, industry self-regulation and a compliance rather than sanctioning approach to enforcement (OECD, 2002). There is, however, now a rediscovery of 'alternatives to classic regulation' and the role of self-regulation and co-regulation play an important role. The Task Force also drew attention to alterna-tive methods of achieving policy goals, eg through government providing information, advice and persuasion—running campaigns such as those against drink driving.

The Better Regulation Task Force also proposed the following principles of regula-tion.

Better Regulation Task Force, *Principles of Good Regulation* (2006) 1

Proportionate: Regulators should only intervene when necessary. Remedies should be appropriate to the risk posed, and costs identified and minimised.

Accountable: Regulators must be able to justify decisions, and be subject to public scrutiny.

Consistent: Government rules and standards must be joined up and implemented fairly.

Transparent: Regulators should be open, and keep regulations simple and user friendly.

Targeted: Regulation should be focused on the problem, and minimise side effects.

In terms of regulatory theory, contemporary policy approaches in UK regulation may be seen against the background of two models of regulation: the public interest and the public choice (see Ogus, 1994). The public-interest rationale for regulation stresses a technocratic model of government responding to market failures with agencies such as the Office of Fair Trading (OFT) providing the expertise and continuity of administra-tion that contrast with the limitations of the legislative and judicial process in these regards (Landis, 1938; Belobaba, 1977: 383; Baldwin and Cave, 1999).

The public-interest rationale was challenged by public choice which conceived of regulation as serving private rather than public interests (see above Chapter 1). The most famous private-interest theory is the amorphous 'capture model'. This theory views agencies as initially vigorous policemen who gradually become captured by the regulated industry, a process described in Bernstein's lifecycle metaphor (Bernstein, 1955). This is summarised by Galbraith:

[R]egulatory bodies, like the people who comprise them, have a marked life cycle. In youth they are vigorous, aggressive, evangelistic, and even intolerant. Later they mellow, and in old age—after a matter often of fifteen years—they become with some exceptions, either an arm of the industry they are regulating or senile. (Galbraith, 1955: 171)

Yet the capture theory always had several limitations. First, it lacks empirical backing. Although some agencies have appeared to represent the interests of the regulated industry, others have remained relatively vigorous (Breyer, 1982: 9; Ogus, 1994: 57–58). Second, it seems to provide little explanation of the behaviour of agencies in the field of social regulation, whose 'mandates span many industries. It becomes more difficult to identify the particular industry or group which will capture it' (see Posner, 1974: 342) However, the capture theory did draw attention to the potential for self-interested behaviour by regulators and bureaucrats. Rephrased in terms of principal-agent theory—the problem of devising methods for ensuring accountability by regulators—this theory may be viewed as one influence on the variety of contemporary control mechanisms in government (see Wintrobe, 1997).

A more recent perspective on regulatory failure is provided by behavioural analysis which argues that just as consumers may be prone to behavioural biases, so may regulators. Thus Choi et al (2003) argue that regulators may be subject to overconfidence, may be subject to bounded searching in terms of regulatory alternatives and are subject to availability bias, ie they respond to high-profile media coverage of issues.

If we turn our focus to the characteristics of public regulatory bodies, we find that they share certain common characteristics (Breyer, 1982: 6): they are bureaucracies; their discretion is subject to the control of administrative law; and they face significant information problems in identifying problems, fashioning remedies and measuring success.

It is a truism that regulators will generally have some discretion both in general policy choices and in individual decision-making. The limited resources of an agency, and the generally over-inclusive nature of regulation, make this inevitable. For example, trading standards officers must make difficult discretionary decisions in determining whether to prosecute breaches of consumer legislation (see below Chapter 5) and in deciding which sectors of industry to target with their limited resources.

Administrative law places a variety of constraints on the operation of public regulation (see Scott, 2000). Rule-making is subject to parliamentary scrutiny and requires consultation with affected groups. Enforcement must respect due process values and enforcement policy may be subject to judicial review. There are also the requirements of a regulatory impact assessment, the use of risk-assessment guidelines in enforcement, controls through Treasury contracts with agencies and potential review by the National Audit Agency. The 'new public management' imposes increased transparency and performance measures on regulators. In addition, regulation must respect the Human Rights Act 1998.

The problem of assembling accurate and full information on market problems is particularly acute for an agency such as the OFT whose mandate spans many industries. Stigler draws attention to this problem in the context of the enforcement of the US antitrust laws. After rejecting the 'popular view that bureaucrats are inherently incompetent or lazy or timid in the conduct of public affairs', he notes:

> Consider the enforcement of the Sherman Act. Presently it is enforced by a troop of lawyers, aided by some FBI agents and occasionally a stray economist—all, let us assume, of the highest quality. How can this collection of people, removed from commerce and largely concentrated in the nation's capital, know whether company W in industry X is violating the Act in state Y with respect to commodity Z? The only way in which the Antitrust Division could possibly learn of this violation is if it received a letter of complaint from an aggrieved party. Many such letters are received, but there is surely no serious presumption that the most serious violations call forth the first and the most helpful complaints—that would be fortuitous in the extreme. ...

> The argument can be generalized: very seldom, indeed, will the regulators be well situated in experience and knowledge to detect and prove violations. A dozen people are more likely than the IRS to know whether X is cheating on his tax, and a score of truckers know better than

the ICC whether firm Y is violating its certificate restrictions. Professional competence and integrity are not sufficient to qualify one as a superior enforcer. (Stigler, 1975: 170)

Stigler's comments also draw attention to the limitations of using surrogates (eg letters of complaint) for providing information. The European Union has developed a 'Market Scoreboard' to attempt to identify potential markets for regulation. The high cost of obtaining information on, and expertise for dealing with, a regulatory problem (eg drug safety or anticompetitive practices) means that, in practice, a variety of private groups play an important role in supplementing a regulator's limited resources (see, for example, below, Chapter 9, in regard to product safety standards). This need for information, coupled with a desire to obtain voluntary compliance (thereby reducing enforcement costs), may lead to a co-operative approach by the regulator to the regulated.

Information is also relevant to a second problem facing agencies: the measurement of success. Unlike private industry, an agency will rarely have the ultimate goal of a measurable profit or loss to use as a criterion of success. For example, how is a consumer agency, entrusted with regulating 'unfair trade practices', to measure its success? This is a problem which permeates all levels of the agency. For example, the individual inspector must have some measure of success for his day-to-day activities. Bureaucracies will, therefore, seek some concrete measure of success, particularly since they must compete with other departments in an annual budgetary allocation process. These measures are often surrogates for success, for example the number of convictions. There is a danger that too close attention to the surrogates may allow sight to be lost of the overall objectives. Annual reports of consumer agencies will often state how many convictions have been obtained and how much money has been recovered for consumers. But this tells us little about whether these agencies have identified and attacked the most significant consumer problems in the marketplace. The pressure to provide a measure of success is also partly a response to political pressures. Agencies fighting for scarce resources in a potentially hostile political climate must demonstrate a continuing need for their services. There is the danger, therefore, that in such an environment there will be too much emphasis on activities which can be easily measured. Stigler again (1975: 171):

[V]ery often the regulators proudly tell us how many cases they have won: how many adulterators they have apprehended, how many false advertisements they have challenged, how many thieves they have jailed. This is as if General Electric told us proudly how many items it had produced last year, counting aircraft engines equally with turbines and refrigerators and light bulbs. Such a report would properly cause General Electric to be ridiculed, but each year the FTC gravely reports the number of cease and desist orders it has mailed out. We should demand measures of performance which take account of importance. (Stigler, 1975: 171)

The Macrory Report on regulatory enforcement (Macrory Report, 2006) echoes Stigler's critique:

I have found that most regulators, when talking about enforcement activity or compliance, report on the number of prosecutions or the number of enforcement notices that they have issued. However, there is very little evidence of what the actual outcomes of these enforcement actions are. I therefore propose that regulators should measure outcomes and not just outputs. I appreciate that this is not an easy exercise. (Regulatory Justice, 2006:21)

Underlying the information limitation of regulators is the argument made from several different traditions that 'the state could not acquire the local knowledge to intervene effectively' (Braithwaite, 2000: 231).

---

2. Regulation and governance

Julia Black argued in the early 2000s that regulation was increasingly 'decentered'. This approach recognises:

(1) the complexity of causal interactions and unintended consequences in regulation;
(2) the fragmentation of knowledge ie no single actor has sufficient knowledge 'to solve a social problem: it is not a question of industry having and government needing';
(3) the fragmentation of power with 'power and control dispersed between social actors and between actors and the state';
(4) interdependence recognises the autonomy of different actors and sub systems in regulation so that 'no single actor can hope to dominate the regulatory process unilaterally …' a clear counterpoint to the assumptions of theories of 'regulatory capture';
(5) a clear rejection of the public/private distinction … regulation is 'the product of interactions not of the exercise of the formal constitutionally recognized authority of government'. (Black, 2002)

This approach may be linked to other writing that describes contemporary regulation in terms of 'governmentality' where government embraces 'all endeavours to shape, guide direct the conduct of others … and it also embraces the ways in which one might be urged and educated to bridle one's passions, to control one's instincts and to govern oneself' (Rose, 1999: 3). Rose views this form of governance as characteristic of neoliberalism.

Decentred regulation will be, according to Black, 'hybrid, combining governmental and non- governmental actors, multifaceted—the use of different strategies of regulation sequentially and simultaneously' and often indirect where regulation is a 'process of coordinating, steering, influencing and balancing interactions between actors/systems to organize themselves' (Black, 2002). In this approach government is:

coordinating, steering, influencing, and balancing interactions between actors … and … creating new patterns of interaction which enable social actors/systems to organize themselves … the normative aspect of the new understanding of regulation is that intervention in the selfregulation of social actors … has to be indirect. (Black, 2001: 126)

The decentred approach should make us sensitive to the complexity of regulation of consumer markets and also expand our horizons. For example, we might see credit market regulation as a combination of measures informed by several objectives such as market failure, access to justice, fairness and social justice (see Chapter 7). This may involve a variety of approaches to regulation that attempt to harness consumers as 'responsible borrowers' and lenders as 'responsible lenders'. Within this market private 'gatekeepers' such as credit card companies may perform a screening function in the market. Decentred regulation draws attention to the role of non-state actors in regulation—a phenomenon that has a relatively long pedigree in regulation of consumer markets in the UK (see Hutter and O'Mahony, 2004; Hutter, 2006).

The focus on 'self-regulation' in a decentred approach includes harnessing internal bureaucracies of corporations to achieve compliance with consumer regulation (see eg the strategy of the Financial Services Authority below, Chapter 7): this approach is linked therefore to policies concerned with corporate social responsibility and corporate governance. Attempting to harness internal corporate bureaucracies to achieve public policy goals has been described by Christine Parker as 'meta-regulation':

> This is concerned with the way in which law could (and sometimes does) seek to hold businesses accountable for taking their responsibilities seriously by using various mechanisms to encourage or enforce businesses to put in place internal governance structures, management systems and corporate cultures aimed at achieving responsible outcomes. Law attempts to constitute corporate 'consciences'—getting companies 'to want to do what they should do'—not just compliant outcomes and actions. …

> [Citing Selznick, 2002: 101] A corporate conscience is created when values that transcend narrow self-interest are built into the practice and structure of the enterprise. This can be done in several ways; by clarifying policies and making them public;by practicing sensitive recruitment of staff; by inculcating appropriate attitudes and habits; by establishing special units to implement policies affecting the well-being of employees, or environmental and consumer protection; and by cooperating with relevant outside groups, such as trade unions and public agencies. All this becomes an 'organizational culture,' a framework within which the main goals of the enterprise are pursued. (Parker, 2007)

The idea of meta-regulation may be traced to Ian Ayres and John Braithwaite's influential book *Responsive Regulation* which argued that:

> Good policy analysis is not about choosing between the free market and government regulation. Nor is it simply deciding what the law should proscribe. If we accept that sound policy analysis is about understanding private regulation—by industry associations, by firms, by peers, and by individual consciences—and how it is interdependent with state regulation, then interesting possibilities open up to steer the mix of private and public regulation. It is this mix, this interplay, that works to assist or impede solution of the policy problem. (Ayres and Braithwaite, 1992: 1)

They advocated several new approaches to regulation including ideas such as tripartism—'empowering citizen associations' as a solution to the dilemma of regulatory capture. The 'supercomplaint' procedure under the Enterprise Act 2002 (see below 5.2) is one technique.

Much writing also argues that markets are embedded phenomena. This means that there may be a structure of expectations and trust that provide the background glue and trust for market transactions (see eg Granovetter, 1985). We might view regulation as attempting to shape or change the social norms or ground rules of a marketplace. If we adopt a ground rules approach we can view many rules as altering the ground rules of consumer markets. For example, reforms to the substantive rights and remedies of consumers in relation to the sale and supply of goods alter the bargaining power between the parties (see below, discussion of the Unfair Terms in Consumer Contracts regulations and quality regulation). This is intended to have a distributional effect, changing the market from a sellers' to a buyers' market and altering the distribution of risks in the market.

2.1 Self-regulation, guidance, best practices and benchmarking

A characteristic of contemporary regulation is a focus on varieties of self-regulation that range from corporate codes of practice to forms of co-regulation (see eg Bartle and Vass, 2007). Thus we encounter the codes of practice associated with the OFT, co-regulation of advertising by the ASA, private groups and standards in consumer safety (Chapter 9) and Internet codes. European directives (partly in response to UK pressures) refer to the potential of self-regulation and consumer policy has been a significant site for the development of self-regulation (see eg advertising, privacy (Directive 95/46, Article 3), electronic commerce (Directive 2000/31, Article 16) and unfair commercial practices (Unfair Commercial Practices Directive, Articles 10,11)).

Self-regulation may be linked to the use of 'soft law' where governments use guidance, best practices and benchmarking as methods of governance. The OFT, for example, makes extensive use of guidance under the Consumer Credit Act 1974 and the EU increasingly relies on soft law forms in areas which may be difficult to regulate through 'hard law'. According to the Lex Fori study for the European Commission on Soft Law (1999) (www.lexfori.net/soft_law_en.htm):

> The United Kingdom is without doubt the country that has conducted the fullest studies of soft law. In Europe, it has a virtual monopoly on the analysis of, and reflection on, soft law. The concept of soft law, the related vocabulary and the reports of various bodies are highly developed there. And yet, specialists consider that these experiments have produced mixed results.

Non-state actors often play an important role in policy through 'information gathering, standard setting and behaviour modification aspects of regulatory control' (Hutter, 2006: 1). The importance of the private sector in policy implementation is exemplified by the role of trade associations (see below, on trade association codes of practice) and institutions such as the British Standards Association. Trade associations have a long historical pedigree in the United Kingdom (Atiyah, 1979: 597–98; Cousins and Pickering, 1981). According to Cousins and Pickering, they have traditionally performed four roles:

> First, there is a representational role in which they represent their industry to government, the media and other interest groups. Secondly, they exercise a data collection and dissemination function on behalf of their members. This role also covers the provision of advisory and consultancy services, trade publications, the preparation of standards and general assistance with sales promotion activities. ... Finally, where the law has allowed, schemes to control prices and outputs through various forms of cartel have been operated. (Cousins and Pickering, 1981)

Atiyah traces the growth of trade associations to the protective goals of small and less-efficient enterprises concerned with the threat of international competition (Atiyah, 1979: 700).

The major economic arguments in favour of industry self-regulation are that information, rule-making and enforcement costs may be reduced; over-inclusive statutory rules may be fine-tuned to a particular industry; regulation by trade associations may secure greater voluntary compliance than will government regulation; and industry or professional expertise may be brought to bear to determine standards of competence. The factors most favourable to effective industry self-regulation are a low cost of compliance, small in-group conflict, a cohesive group, minimal third-party effects, low costs of detection, effective sanctions and credible threats. Ironically, these characteristics are similar to those which favour the development of a cartel. The quotation above from Adam Smith on the historical origins of trade associations underlines this danger in self-regulation.

Governments may also have political reasons for preferring self-regulation. It does not involve a commitment of government funds, and may permit a government to create the appearance of protecting a diffuse group (eg consumers) while conferring tangible benefits on a narrow industry group (Trebilcock in Dewees (ed), 1983: 103). It may also allow government to avoid responsibility for regulatory mistakes. In addition, writers on corporatism have suggested that governments may use self-regulation as a means of extending state control, either to avoid traditional forms of accountability (Winkler, 1975: 123) or where direct regulation has proved difficult (Blankenburg, 1984: 287).

How ought we to evaluate the role of self-regulation? Two points are crucial. First, there is a danger of viewing self-regulation as an imperfect substitute for government regulation. This view of self-regulation may often draw on an idealised model of public regulation. In our second-best world, imperfect self-regulation must be compared with imperfect government regulation. In addition, a pluralist model of law would not necessarily assume the hierarchical inferiority of self-regulation. In this model, self-regulation 'is no longer necessarily seen as an alternative to state regulation' (Schepel, 2005: 31) but part of an overall approach to governance where central issues become those of expertise, efficiency, accountability and legitimacy.

Forms of 'soft law' are important internationally. The EU, for example, through the Open Method of Co-ordination uses a variety of techniques, including best practices, benchmarking and guidance, to stimulate a learning process of regulation and increased harmonisation particularly in areas where the EU does not have formal powers (see below Chapter 7 in relation to over-indebtedness).

2.2 Market norms and default rules

Consumer markets have often been the site of economic and social studies of the role of private ordering, eg the role of complaints as a problem-solving mechanism (Ross and Littlefield, 1977; Ramsay, 1981). Consumer law was often a critique of formalist understandings of the role of law. It was also an instrumental form of law that recognised the pluralistic nature of law in contemporary society. Market actors may have incentives to develop practices that provide more protection than the law. Two examples are returns policies on goods and chargeback practices. The question is what the role of the law should be in relation to such practices. Should it recognise them as a required norm for all businesses?—or merely a default rule which can be contracted out of by the consumer (but not by the supplier)? Given the heterogeneity of consumer preferences and the increased individualisation of many service contracts, 'one contractual size may not fit all consumers'.

Businesses may exploit default rules. Two examples are inertia selling and the use of automatic tick boxes in contracting on the Internet (now regulated by the 2011 EU Consumer Rights Directive) exploiting consumer inertia. The attempt to achieve transnational norms of European consumer law highlights the potential of harnessing market norms of international standard terms in consumer transactions.

The choice of default rules may be significant in consumer markets. For example, Sunstein and Thaler provide the following US example:

> In the context of insurance, an unplanned, natural experiment showed that the default rule can be very 'sticky.' New Jersey created a system in which the default insurance program for motorists included a relatively low premium and no right to sue; purchasers were allowed to deviate from the default program and to purchase the right to sue by choosing a program with that right and also a higher premium. By contrast, Pennsylvania offered a default program containing a full right to sue and a relatively high premium; purchasers could elect to switch to a new plan by 'selling' the more ample right to sue and paying a lower premium. In both cases, the default rule tended to stick. A strong majority accepted the default rule in both states, with only about 20% of New Jersey drivers acquiring the full right to sue, and 75% of Pennsylvanians retaining that right. There is no reason to think that the citizens of Pennsylvania have systematically different preferences from the citizens of New Jersey. The default plan is what produced the ultimate effects. And indeed controlled experiments find the same results, showing that the value of the right to sue is much higher when it is presented as part of the default package. (Sunstein and Thaler, 2003: 1175)

Explanations for the persistence of default rules include inertia, ill-formed preferences and the endowment effect. Individuals may prefer to do what they think others do (which may be associated with the default) and what is right to do. We noted in Chapter 2 that the framing of a default rule may be important: there is a large difference in responses to choices framed as 'opting in' or 'opting out'. Individuals react differently to choices framed as 'surcharge for credit' than 'discount for cash'. Sunstein and Thaler outline when defaults might reduce decision-making costs:

> In some domains, consumers and workers are highly informed—so much so that they will not even be influenced by default rules. Most adults have experimented enough over the course of their lives to have a good sense of what flavors of ice cream they like. They can do a decent job of picking even in a shop offering dozens of flavors. If the default option is asparagus flavored ice cream, they will be unlikely to choose it, and might well be annoyed. But when faced with a menu listing many unfamiliar foods in a foreign country, people might not be benefited by being asked to choose among them, and they might prefer a small list or ask the waiter for a default suggestion (eg, what do other tourists like?). Clever restaurants catering to tourists often offer a default 'tourist menu.' Many actual choices fall between the poles of ice cream flavors and foreign menus. (Sunstein and Thaler, 2003: 1197)

We might argue that many consumer contract terms often resemble 'unfamiliar foods in a foreign country' to consumers. Consumers focus on a limited number of terms when purchasing a good or service and may have difficulty in assessing their future use of a contractual service (eg a gym contract: see below at 302). There may be an argument therefore either for (i) standardisation of subsidiary terms based on the reasonable expectations of consumers; (ii) an agent for consumers that could negotiate with businesses to establish terms that met consumers' reasonable expectations (see below the role of the OFT); or (iii) a default rule that provides a contracting-out option for consumers. These measures might be accompanied by better information on alternatives. Where consumers have particular expectations about the nature of a service the law might require firms that deviated from these expectations in a way that was not obviously beneficial to consumers to signal this fact. This approach is adopted in the Unfair Commercial Practices Directive where firms that have arrangements for payment, delivery, performance and complaint handling that depart from accepted norms (the requirements of professional diligence) must disclose this fact to potential buyers (see below Chapter 4).

2.3 The consumer as a regulatory subject

Economic analysis identified consumer sovereignty as a goal of market regulation and certain theorists of consumer law identify autonomy and self-determination as goals of consumer law (see Drexl, 1998). The emphasis within contemporary policy on the empowered consumer is, however, slightly more complex. Consumers are to be active, responsible citizens policing private and public bureaucracies. The consumer is viewed as an important agent of consumer policy, contributing to achieving a high quality and competitive business climate as well as reflecting on the consequences of their choices on the environment. Consumer policy therefore increasingly involves a variety of techniques—education, information, guidance, intended to upskill consumers so that once 'responsibilized and entrepreneurialized [individuals] would govern themselves' (Rose, 1999: 139) based on their own life plan. This conceives of the consumer as an active chooser rather than a victim who needs to be protected. Consumer 'education' is increasingly viewed as a significant (and complex) role for government agencies and is included in the new mandate of the OFT under the Enterprise Act 2002. A dedicated money advice and financial education body exists under the Financial Services and Markets Act 2000. Williams quotes an OECD report as stating that 'higher levels of financial literacy will improve economic growth and help to reduce poverty in all economies' (Williams, 2007: 229).

This new role for the consumer as an empowered subject raises issues of practicality (is it possible given the large literature on behavioural economics in consumer decision-making?) and how manageable consumers are given the importance of local knowledge (Gabriel and Lang, 2006). It also raises the consumer/citizen dichotomy raised in Chapter 1—the critique that a focus on the consumer and individual choice undercuts social engagement and communal citizenship.

2.3.1 'Nudging' the consumer

The behavioural economics literature, as represented by Richard Thaler and Cass Sunstein's book *Nudge*, advocates a variety of measures to get consumers to 'do the right thing'. These include improving individuals' 'choice architectures' through better disclosures, or the strategic use of default rules. Nudging includes

any aspect of the choice architecture that alters people's behaviour in a predictable way without forbidding any options or significantly changing their economic incentives. To count as a mere nudge, the intervention must be easy and cheap to avoid. Nudges are not mandates. Putting the fruit at eye level counts as a nudge. Banning junk food does not.

Nudge is informed by the concept of libertarian paternalism, 'a relatively weak, soft, and nonintrusive type of paternalism because choices are not blocked, fenced off, or significantly burdened (Nudge, 2008: 5).

The House of Lords Committee on Science and Technology Committee reviewed the role of nudging interventions in its *Second Report Behaviour Change* (2011). It commented:

> The currently influential book *Nudge* by Richard Thaler and Cass Sunstein advocates a range of non-regulatory interventions that seek to influence behaviour by altering the context or environment in which people choose, and seek to influence behaviour in ways which people often do not notice. This approach differs from more traditional government attempts to change behaviour, which have either used regulatory interventions or relied on overt persuasion. The current Government have taken a considerable interest in the use of 'nudge interventions'. Consequently, one aim of this inquiry was to assess the evidence-base for the effectiveness of 'nudges'. However, we also examined evidence for the effectiveness of other types of policy intervention, regulatory and non-regulatory, and asked whether the Government make good use of the full range of available evidence when seeking to change behaviour.
>
> We heard evidence that, although much was understood about human behaviour from basic research, there was relatively little evidence about how this understanding could be applied in practice to change the behaviour of populations ('applied research at a population level'). We make some recommendations to address this issue.
>
> Although we acknowledge that further applied research at a population level is needed, we also found that the available evidence supports a number of conclusions. Our central finding is that non-regulatory measures used in isolation, including 'nudges', are less likely to be effective. Effective policies often use a range of interventions.
>
> We concluded that it is important to consider the whole range of possible interventions when policy interventions are designed. We place particular emphasis on this conclusion because the evidence we received indicated that the Government's preference for non-regulatory interventions has encouraged officials to exclude consideration of regulatory measures when thinking about behaviour change. Though there is a lack of applied research on changing behaviour at a population level, there is other available evidence that the Government need to use to better effect. We were therefore disappointed to find that, although we received some examples of evidence-based policies, such as policies on energy-efficient products and smoking cessation services, we were also given many examples of policies that had not taken account of available evidence, including policies on food labelling and alcohol pricing.
>
> We also found that a lot more could, and should, be done to improve the evaluation of interventions. This is not only good practice but would help to build a body of research that could inform effective policies targeting population-level behaviour change.

2.4 Transnational consumer regulation

If decentred regulation seeks to harness individuals in civil society as part of the regulatory project—essentially a move downwards from direct state regulation—another product of the 'new learning' on regulation highlights the influence of transnational and international norms and institutions over domestic consumer protection policy, and in this section I discuss briefly networks and epistemic communities in consumer law. Braithwaite and Drahos define an epistemic community as 'loose collections of knowledge-based experts who share certain attitudes and values and substantive knowledge, as well as ways of thinking about how to use this knowledge' (Braithwaite and Drahos, 2000: 501, citing Haas, 1989). While the idea of an epistemic community seems particularly applicable to networks of regulators who share values, it may also bring together adversaries. Thus business, consumers and regulators meet within the umbrella of the OECD. Epistemic communities may be significant in constructing global norms or a shared 'common sense' about methods of regulating consumer markets, a common sense that influences national norms.

Writers on competition policy argue that networks provide the potential for development of uniformity without centralisation as well as facilitating the export of models of regulation used by more-developed countries. Imelda Maher underlines the central role of the OECD as the locus for the interaction of technocrats and policymakers from developed countries in formulating international competition law norms and co-ordinating enforcement (Maher, 2002: 111). In addition, the 'outreach' programmes developed by the International Competition Network attempt to harness business and consumer constituencies by convincing them of the benefits of competition policy.

There is a marked growth in networks of regulators in consumer policy (see also Slaughter, 2004: 37–64; Poncibo, 2011). The International Consumer Protection Enforcement Network (ICPEN) is a global network of national consumer agencies formed in 1992. The agencies share information and best practice, assist each other in investigations to the extent permitted by national law, maintain a database of case materials, and organise co-ordinated global sweeps against false and misleading claims on the Internet.

Within the EU, networking is promoted by the EU Regulation on Consumer Protection Cooperation (Regulation 2006/2004) that requires national agencies to have common investigative and enforcement powers, to share information, and to have the power to seek and obtain action from their counterparts in other Member States. The monitoring and development of policy in such areas as unfair trade practices and consumer safety increases the density of networks of regulators, committees and experts. Everson and Joerges refer to this as the growth of 'flexible expert governance' (Everson and Joerges, 2006). Product and service standards are established at the regional and international level in areas such as consumer safety, food and financial services through private standard-setting bodies with a public mandate (CEN, ISO, etc). European standards now represent 90 per cent of the output of national standards institutions within the EU. These developments raise issues of effectiveness and legitimacy.

The OECD consumer policy group provides a forum for the diffusion of policy initiatives and possibly the export of models of regulation from influential countries. The Federal Trade Commission, for example, in its Annual Report under the heading 'Promoting Market-Oriented Policies' comments:

> The FTC promotes consumer protection policies abroad to ensure that consumer protection rules focus on practices that distort consumer choice and threaten the proper functioning of markets. The American approach to consumer protection generally involves flexible, marketoriented standards backed by aggressive enforcement. ... FTC staff has led efforts

within the OECD Committee on Consumer Policy to encourage countries to adopt an economics-based approach to consumer protection. (Federal Trade Commission, 2006: 49)

and comments that:

> The FTC works to promote competition and convergence towards best practices with competition and consumer protection agencies around the world. The FTC ... plays a lead role in key multilateral fora. (ibid: 45)

Imelda Maher underlines the central role of the OECD as the locus for the interaction of technocrats and policymakers from the developed countries in formulating international competition law norms and co-ordinating enforcement (Maher, 2002: 111).

There is also increased international 'benchmarking' of the performance of agencies. For example, the World Bank has developed best practices in financial consumer protection and the world financial crisis stimulated increased efforts at developing common standards for financial consumer protection (below Chapter 7 at 4.1).

---

3. Techniques of regulation

The economic, market-failure approach attempts initially to 'match' the proposed instrument of regulation to the market failure. For example, an information policy ought to be adopted to cure an information failure. This approach also will prefer the least interventionist policy consistent with achieving the desired objective. Although this approach appears relatively straightforward, there will be a considerable degree of empirical uncertainty in using it. Analysis is further complicated if there are important distributional or ethical concerns. For example, information policies might be rejected for certain safety risks from dangerous goods on the basis that the choices that would be involved are ones to which an individual ought not to be subjected (Dewees, Mathewson and Trebilcock, 1983: 31). The effectiveness of a regulatory instrument will also depend on the particular institutional framework. Thus, controlling misleading information through broad judicial standards will have a different impact from doing so through administrative regulation. The following section outlines the main techniques of regulation, which are considered in greater detail throughout the book.

3.1 Information remedies

The following extract outlines an economic perspective on this type of remedy and argues that it might often be superior to direct regulation through product standards or bans. It provides a valuable outline of the variety of available information remedies and indicates the assumptions underlying this approach to regulation.

H Beales, R Craswell and S Salop, 'The Efficient Regulation of Consumer Information' (1981) 24 *Journal of Law and Economics*, 491 at 513–14, 516, 521–23, 527, 529–31, 532

Most government information remedies are attempts to respond to ... problems in the consumer information market. However, it should be noted that information remedies are not the only possible response to these problems. A more common regulatory response has been to attempt to correct the resulting failure in the product market by setting product standards or by directly regulating the production process or the terms of trade. Bans on untested drugs, automobile fuel economy standards, and judicial refusals to enforce certain harsh contract clauses—all can be viewed as attempts to correct, by direct regulation, market performances that may well be due to deficiencies in buyers' information.

The focus on information remedies in this paper reflects the belief that, where inefficient outcomes are the result of inadequate consumer information, information remedies will usually be the preferable solution. Remedies which simply adjust the information available to consumers still leave consumers free to make their own choices, thus introducing less rigidity into the market. Such remedies leave the market free to respond as consumer preferences and production technologies change over time. For the same reason, information remedies pose less risk of serious harm if the regulator turns out to have been mistaken. For example, if consumers are not really interested in increasing the quality or safety of certain product attributes, an information remedy will not force the market to make an inefficient change (where a mandatory product standard would). Similarly, information remedies allow different consumers to strike different balances between price and product quality, while direct quality regulation almost necessarily imposes a single choice on all consumers.

In short, information remedies allow consumers to protect themselves according to personal preferences rather than place on regulators the difficult task of compromising diverse preferences with a common standard. ...

However, remedying deficiencies in the information market is in some ways a more complex and subtle task than regulating product markets directly ... information remedies can be classed into three general categories: (a) removing restraints on information; (b) correcting misleading information; and (c) encouraging additional information.

A. Removing Information Restraints

Perhaps the information remedy most compatible with the interests of individual sellers (if not their collective interest) is the removal of private or governmental restraints on the free flow of information. Such restrictions often tend to inhibit competition, with consequent efficiency losses.

Most notorious of the restraints on the flow of information are bans on advertising by professionals. ...

B. Prohibiting Misleading Claims

Remedies which prohibit misleading claims, unlike the other remedies discussed here, work by reducing the amount of information available to consumers. The rationale for such remedies, obviously, is that misleading claims do more harm than good, and that consumers are therefore made better off by their prohibition. However, because such prohibitions do work to restrict the information communicated to consumers, the prohibitions should be treated with some care . . .

C. Increasing Consumer Information

Most common are remedies designed to increase consumers' information about competing products. As discussed above, the disclosure of additional information may often be the most efficient remedy for correcting advertising claims that generate inaccurate consumer expectations. ...

Traditionally, this has usually taken the form of a requirement that sellers disclose certain standardized information to consumers. Cigarette manufacturers are required to disclose on packages and in advertising the general warning that smoking may be hazardous to health. ... This form of required disclosure is not the only method of increasing consumer information. Two additional methods which are also considered are: (a) stopping at the establishment of a standardized scoring system for measuring product attributes; and (b) consumer education efforts. Depending on the circumstances, any of these three techniques (or some combination of them) may represent the most efficient remedy . . .

... [T]here is usually an advantage in designing disclosure remedies that leave as large a role as possible to normal market forces, to restrict the market as little as possible. The goal should be not to specify the exact information to be disclosed and the exact manner in which it will be disclosed but to give sellers the proper incentives to make these decisions on their own. This reduces the consequences of a bad decision by the government since it avoids forcing sellers to disclose information in an ineffective manner or to disclose information which, because of a change in circumstances, is no longer desired by consumers. It also increases the effectiveness of the remedy by harnessing sellers' own incentives to develop the most effective ways of informing consumers. Thus, innovation should be encouraged by leaving sellers latitude to experiment. . . .

1. *Establishing a Scoring System.* A scoring system measures the quantity of one or more product attributes across brands. The score may be dichotomous, as with a definition (for example, 'walnut' means solid walnut, as opposed to veneer), or it may be continuous (for example, gasoline mileage ratings).

However devised, scoring systems are intended to reduce the costs of communicating about measured attributes ...

Two factors may limit the emergence of scoring systems in the absence of government intervention. First, when an attribute is relatively complex, there frequently is no unambiguously best measure of it. As a result, nearly any measure can be challenged as false or misleading, at least by competitors ...

Second, informational measures may be particularly vulnerable to deceptive usage. If cigarette 'tar' measurements were not standardized, a manufacturer could generate a lower measured tar content for his cigarette by basing the measure on fewer or smaller puffs of smoke without being discovered by most consumers. ... Competing firms might counter by explaining the differences in the scores, but the firm that does must thereby bear costs for free-riding competitors. Because of this free-rider problem, a voluntary system may not be viable. ...

2. *Required Disclosures.* Once a scoring system is available, it is tempting for governmental agencies to require that each brand's score be disclosed on product labels or in advertising. Disclosures may be triggered whenever a particular claim is made (for example, any claim about gas mileage triggers a requirement to disclose the EPA mileage estimate), or they may be across-the-board (for example, all cigarette advertisements must include a health warning).

The need for requiring disclosure, in general, depends on the completeness of the total information environment and sellers' incentives to disclose voluntarily. If information is readily available from another source, or if firms have their own incentives to disclose whenever disclosure would be useful, required disclosure is unnecessary. ...

... [T]he effective communication of required disclosures must always be carefully considered. Although advertisers can be relied upon to deliver the disclosure message to the same target audience as the main message of the advertisement, they have an obvious incentive to minimize the effectiveness of any disclosure which reflects unfavorably on their products ... [See below Chapter 8 at 3.2 concerning corrective advertising.]

Clearly, writing effective advertising copy is a subtle and complex business. Legislatures and governmental agencies are generally inexpert as it requires specialized skills and knowledge which public bodies seldom possess. As an alternative to mastering the art and science of producing effective communications, courts or agencies could impose standards of performance and leave the design of the most cost-effective message and media strategy to the affected firms. ...

3. *Consumer Education.* Consumer education is often overlooked as a means of dealing with incomplete information. ...

One ... advantage of consumer education over a disclosure approach is that an education campaign can be targeted more precisely to those who need the information. ...

... One important implication of the analysis presented here is that it is extremely difficult to develop many hard-and-fast rules and that the proper policy to be followed will depend heavily on the facts of each case.

Experience of disclosure regulation indicates significant challenges in achieving a successful policy. Indeed Ben Shahar and Schneider argue that in general mandated disclosures have been a failure (see below Chapter 7).

There is the general problem of 'information overload' (see above Chapter 2 at 3.5) and Howells and others have been critical of European directives 'which pile on the information requirements with little regard to their impact' (Howells, 2005: 363). Regulators in some jurisdictions have responded by providing 'key information' or 'key facts' (see below Chapter 7) , providing both 'summary' and 'full disclosures'.

The information approach may be inappropriate where consumers face high processing costs (eg in relation to complex, technical information) or where consumers, even with perfect information, systematically underestimate the risks of low-probability events. The difficulties in consumer risk assessment identified by the behavioural economics literature suggest that a simple standard such as that 'products must be safe' (see below Chapter 9) or simple warnings may be optimal. There is the danger that a heightened focus on one attribute (eg APR) may lead consumers to pay less attention to other aspects of the purchase.

Behavioural analysis suggests that the framing of disclosures is a key policy issue. Exploiting consumer loss aversion and the endowment effect may be one technique (see below, the use of wealth warnings in consumer credit). Targeting individualised disclosures may be more effective than a generic disclosure since individuals (who are over-optimistic) will discount its application to them. Sunstein argues that

a good rule of thumb is that disclosure should be concrete, straightforward, simple, meaningful, timely and salient. If the goal is to inform people how to avoid risks or to obtain benefits, disclosure should avoid abstract statements ... and instead clearly identify the steps that might be taken to obtain the relevant goal. (Sunstein, 2011: 1369–70)

There is an argument that lower-income groups may benefit least from information policies and may be locked into particular patterns of shopping (see eg McNeil et al, 1979: 719). Little systematic empirical evidence substantiates this argument. Advertising of information on the potential health benefits of certain products seems to have been most beneficial to lower-income consumers in the US (Ippolito and Mathios, 1991). Whether lower-income consumers benefit from information remedies underlines the fact that the costs and benefits of information remedies will vary among consumers so that it is worthwhile to identify which groups are likely to benefit most. In addition, since it is not necessary for all consumers to be informed for businesses to respond, a key question is whether there is a sufficient margin of sophisticated consumers in a market who will protect other consumers or whether suppliers are able to discriminate between different groups of consumers. The increased individualisation of products and services may undermine the effects of this market policing. Howells (2005: 353) underlines the importance of providing consumers with information on the negative aspects of a trader such as records of adjudications by the Advertising Standards Authority and county court judgments. Government is often in the best position to pool this information and make it available.

Comparative price and term may be a powerful remedy (see Schwartz and Wilde, 1979: 662) and Howells notes that this has not been stressed by the UK government. The UK Competition Commission recently emphasised the importance of easily accessible price information to low-income consumers of home credit. It implemented a remedy requiring a website be established, funded by the large providers of home credit, with comparative price information.

Cooling-off periods which permit a consumer a limited period to change his mind and rescind a contract have become ubiquitous in consumer policymaking. They are a form of information remedy since they provide an individual with an opportunity to search for more information on a product or service (see discussion below Chapter 4).

3.1.1 Disclosures and social goals

Disclosures might be an approach to achieving social goals. For example, corporations in the US must disclose under the Home Mortgage Disclosure Act the geographic distribution of their loans as well as the ethnicity of borrowers. This is intended to discourage red-lining and racial discrimination. In 2003 Which? published its first comparative rating on the ethical performance of manufacturers of sports shoes. Disclosure of the process of production (eg GMO) or the labour conditions under which a product is made may respond to consumers' rights to information, and Kysar argues that if consumers are to play an important citizenship role then they should have access to relevant information (Kysar, 2005). Critics of such disclosures argue that consumers' behavioural biases will lead them to overstate the dangers from labels indicating that a product contains GMOs and that interest groups can exploit this to create irrational panics. There are certainly difficult practical issues in developing such schemes (see Doorey, 2006: 1). Critics also argue that well-intentioned consumer actions in countries of the North may have unintended detrimental consequences on workers in countries of the South. Fair-trade disclosures underline the international dimension of consumer policy and the role of international NGOs such as Consumers International.

From a political economy perspective, information policies 'do not necessarily impose great costs on concentrated interests such as individual producers, and therefore may meet less resistance than direct regulation. On the other hand, an information policy may be seen by consumers or consumer groups as a weak response to a problem' (Dewees, Mathewson and Trebilcock, 1983: 31).

3.2 Reducing enforcement costs

Within a market system, two major objectives of private-law litigation are to protect individual entitlements and to secure an efficient level of market performance where other social or market sanctions fail. The failure of private law litigation to achieve these goals was and is a major rationale for public regulation which is intended to provide ex ante protection.

Several further policies might be adopted to reduce the costs to the consumer of enforcement via private-law litigation:

1. the reduction of the ambiguity of the relevant legal doctrines;
2. the provision of alternative, low-cost forms of dispute settlement (see Financial Ombudsman Service, Chapter 7) and more accessible judicial institutions ;
3. class actions (see below Chapter 5);
4. minimum damage clauses irrespective of the actual damage suffered;
5. the provision of greater standing to sue for consumer groups;
6. harnessing market actors as gatekeepers (see below Chapter 8); and
7. permitting public agencies to recover compensation on behalf of a group of consumers.

The *sanction of nullity* is a common form of regulation in consumer transactions and might be mentioned under the heading of reducing enforcement costs. This sanction is usually attached to a supplier's obligations to provide consumers with information and/ or ensure that the correct formalities have been met. It will provide that if a supplier does not meet these obligations, then the contract is unenforceable or unenforceable without a court order.

The sanction of nullity is intended to achieve a high level of compliance and is usually used in industries where there have been significant patterns of consumer detriment (see discussion below on consumer credit at Chapter 7). It recognises that consumers are unlikely to litigate an issue where the likelihood of success is dependent on an 'all the circumstances of the case' finding by a court and provides a 'bright-line' rule that is intended to be self-enforceable. Given the limited resources of public agencies to enforce consumer protection legislation, there is the need for additional, automatic 'self-enforcing' legislation. If the sanction is restricted to a particular industry the costs of compliance should not be high for a business which engages in repeat transactions.

3.3 Encouraging pre-commitment strategies

We noted this approach in the case study on credit card charges. The Competition Commission used this strategy in their study of store credit cards.

3.4 Standards

Standards are a 'classical method for regulating industry's behaviour' (Breyer, 1982: 96). They are 'a dominant form of social regulation' (Ogus, 1994: 150; Baldwin and Cave, 1999; Schepel, 2005). They may be aimed at many objectives (eg increasing product safety, providing consumers with better information), enforced through a variety of sanctions and 'written broadly or narrowly, with widespread or narrow application' (Breyer, 1982: 96).

The establishment and implementation of standards is both a technical and political process: there is a need for both scientific expertise and the participation of affected political groups. Government's need for technical information and its desire to secure voluntary compliance result in industry groups playing a central role in standard-setting (see, for example, below in relation to consumer safety, Chapter 9), and government may delegate standard-setting to private bodies, as in the case of professional self-regulation. In the United Kingdom there are often a number of agencies involved in standard-setting in relation to consumer protection. The general issues relating to the establishment and implementation of standards are discussed below, in relation to commercial trade practices and consumer safety (Chapters 4 and 9), standard form consumer contracts (Chapter 6) and the question of the competence of courts as standard-setters is also raised in the discussion of standard-form contracts.

A recurring issue in consumer law is the optimal precision of a law and the use of detailed rules or standards (see discussion of unfair commercial practices). Detailed rules reduce compliance costs for business, particularly small business, and consumers (see Ehrlich and Posner, 1974; Whitford, 1981). If it is intended that consumers should be involved in implementing or enforcing a rule, then a precise rule that is easy to communicate and use in market interactions should be adopted. Detailed rules will be both over- and under-inclusive. For example, setting a rule on capacity to contract at the age of 16 will include some individuals capable of understanding the implications of contracts and exclude others who do not. A detailed rule also invites the Holmesian 'bad man' to circumvent the rules. Detailed rules may also not be transparent in terms of their purpose.

A standard such as that of 'unfair practices' will be more costly to administer and require a decision-maker to exercise discretion to determine whether conduct falls within the standard. While a standard addresses the problem of the Holmesian 'bad man', it may chill desirable behaviour at the margins or conversely be treated by businesses as an unpredictable possibility that cannot be planned for. In the latter case it is unlikely to have significant impact on business behaviour. Many regulatory programmes now combine the use of standards with more detailed rules that can be altered to changing circumstances. A regulation should state its purpose in general terms so that individuals and decision-makers may apply it to novel situations. English consumer law often uses codes of practice and guidance by agencies, essentially forms of soft law, to achieve these objectives. This has benefits but also renders regulation less transparent because of the overlapping layers of hard and soft law.

3.5 Individualised screening: licensing

Licensing screens out from the market individual products or persons who do not meet the regulatory standards (Breyer, 1982: 575–76: Ogus, 1994: 214). It is generally justified by the difficulties which consumers face in assessing products and services before purchase and by the severe consequences of an error of judgement. Examples in the United Kingdom are the licensing of food additives and drugs, and credit and financial services licensing (Consumer Credit Act 1974, Financial Services and Markets Act 2000). The global financial crisis has stimulated greater interest in the use of *ex ante* measures such as licensing to ensure that 'toxic' or dangerous credit products are not placed on the market.

3.6 Price controls

A variety of justifications have been put forward for price controls in consumer markets. These include the need to regulate prices in industries characterised as 'natural monopolies'—ie industries where only one firm can operate efficiently—the need to restrain windfall or monopoly profits and the need to control inflation. A primary motive in consumer protection has often been redistributive: to restrict price levels in order to protect the weak and vulnerable, and in order to make available to them a commodity at a reasonable price. Two examples of this are rent controls and interest-rate ceilings on the cost of credit. The desirability and effectiveness of these controls is a controversial issue; it is explored below in relation to interest-rate ceilings (Chapter 7).

---

4. Competition policy, economic regulation and consumer policy

We discussed briefly the role of competition policy in Chapter 2 but it is impossible within the scope of this book to explore in detail competition law and policies or the issues associated with the economic regulation of specific industries (for further reading see eg Baldwin and Cave, 1999: ch 16; Whish, 2003; Cseres, 2005; Prosser, 2005; Stuyck, 2005;).

---

5. Adjudication and the regulatory role of the courts

Adjudication has often been a central institution in reforms intended to provide consumer protection, and the adjudicative process is an important model for administrative decision-making. In this book, the role of adjudication is analysed specifically in relation to such issues as the regulation of standard-form contracts (below Chapter 6).

Horowitz has suggested the following characteristics of adjudication which differentiate it from the legislative and administrative process (Horowitz, 1977: 34–56):

1. Adjudication is focused, that is to say, it is concerned with individual rights and duties rather than canvassing a broad range of alternative policy issues.
2. Courts have a limited framework of remedies—damages, injunctions, fines, imprisonment—compared with the broader range of alternatives open to a legislator or administrative agency.
3. Adjudication is piecemeal—'the supreme example of incremental decision making' (p 35). It is therefore more appropriate to step-by-step adjustments.
4. Courts are passive and reactive—'they must act when litigants call' (p 38). Litigation is therefore *ex post facto* 'after the grievance has crystallized … and it is too late to plan to avert the unwanted occurrence' (p 39). The random nature of adjudication means that cases are not necessarily representative of an underlying pattern of social problems. Indeed, plaintiffs or prosecutors will tend to bring the most extreme cases.
5. Fact finding in adjudication is ill-suited to ascertaining broad social facts concerning the general policy issues raised in an individual case. There are difficulties in assembling and presenting behavioural science data in the context of an individual suit.
6. Adjudication makes no provision for policy review or monitoring of compliance and the unintended behavioural impact of decisions. 'The courts are mainly dependent for their impact information on a single feedback mechanism: the follow- up lawsuit' (p 55).

The problems of monitoring compliance are particularly acute in relation to decisions with a major redistributive effect between different social groups since the groups who lose out will strongly resist and will attempt to undercut the impact of the decision.

Horowitz argues that these limitations are more or less significant depending on judicial familiarity with the regulatory area in question. Thus, he comments that:

> [I]f, for example, the question is how to persuade or compel corporate organizations to include environmental impact in their calculations … courts are not likely to possess expertise in the incentive structure of complex organizations. The adjudicative process is not likely to throw up sufficient material to enlighten them, and both lawyers and judges are likely to fill in the interstices with some highly stereotyped notions of 'bureaucracy'. (Horowitz, 1977: 58)

Finally, an important factor in regulating through adjudication is the precision of regulatory standards developed in judicial decision-making. There is often a need for clear standards which can be administered over a broad range of transactions by non-specialist decision-makers. Compliance by private bureaucracies is also likely to be higher where there are precise rules. Judicial decision-making is, however, often discursive, and rulings generally have furry edges. It is difficult to know how far a given ruling will apply beyond the situation in question. In addition, in order to fully understand a judicial rule it may be necessary to be aware of a background of legal doctrines and practices. Although this limitation may be overcome, to a certain degree, by the introduction of specific legislation, there will still be a certain level of uncertainty if adjudication is the primary method of developing regulatory policy.

These factors suggest that courts might best fulfil a central role in those areas of consumer policy where an incremental approach to policymaking is most appropriate, where there is no major attempt to redistribute resources and where no specialised knowledge is necessary.

There is a contrasting view of the role of adjudication in a regulatory state, first articulated by Chayes (1976). He argues that courts may have advantages because: (1) judges are insulated from 'narrow political pressures'; (2) procedures can permit 'a relatively high level of participation by representatives of those affected'; (3) it permits focused application and a learning process through experience; (4) it provides a focus for information on a topic that will be subject to adversarial review; (5) it may be able to balance more effectively than the legislature competing policy issues in a specific situation; (6) it can function like a 'smallish representative task force, assembled ad hoc, and easily dismantled when the problem is finally solved'.

In a world where local knowledge may be important and where there is a loss of trust in the ability of governments to regulate systematically all risk, there is greater interest in the role of courts applying private liability rules. This may also reflect US influence as models of class actions (see below Chapter 5) are increasingly advocated in Europe. The role of litigation as a form of regulation and its relationship to public regulation is complex. Thomas Wilhelmsson (2007) notes that:

> The private law solutions do not remove, however, the demands for more regulation. On the contrary, every private law case may be seen as a failure of regulation. It may give rise to debate in the media and to demands for new regulation. Put in the language of a learning law: by the sanctioning of new forms of risk behaviour private law 'discovers' possible objects for administrative action.

> This is important to stress, in order to avoid the picture that private law only would be an adequate solution to the uncertainty of the risk society. On the contrary, for the purpose of steering of behaviour detailed regulatory norms are often more efficient than general clauses concretised in a few cases. In addition, nothing of course guarantees that the courts learn from experience. (Wilhelmsson, 2007)

A private law decision may often be a signal, providing information to public agencies of a problem, that may become translated into action, particularly if it is covered in the media (see the case of *London North Securities v Meadows* (below Chapter 7). It may be part of a continuing political battle (eg overdraft charges – *OFT v Abbey National*). Public regulation may also highlight an issue, such as the payment protection insurance (PPI) scandal, that stimulated many private claims.

One might hypothesise that private law litigation is the arena of wealthier consumers. Litigation over product or service quality often involves high-priced automobiles, yachts or properties (*Farley v Skinner: Ruxley*, below Chapter 8). The plaintiff in *Jarvis v Swans Tours* (1973) was a solicitor. Baldwin's study of the small claims court suggest that they are dominated by professionals and a relatively narrow range of consumers as plaintiffs. Such litigation may have externalities in protecting ordinary consumers who bargain over problems with businesses, but empirical studies raise questions as to the relationship between legal and market norms. Experience with unfair terms in consumer contracts (Chapter 6) suggests substantial limitations on private litigation affecting market behaviour.

Private law adjudication does seem to be of significance in consumer credit markets.

Hugh Collins describes the reaction of the UK banks to the holding in *Barclays Bank v O'Brien* (1994) where the House of Lords suggested that banks should in circumstances similar to those in *O'Brien* hold a private meeting with the spouse to explain the risks of the transaction:

> Following this defeat, the banks engaged in extensive strategic litigation to challenge this ruling. Although the doctrine of constructive notice was conceded, the banks insisted that the private meeting with the wife should not be necessary. ... Eventually, in a consolidated appeal of eight cases, the House of Lords bowed to pressure from the banks and accepted a watered down version of the requirement of taking reasonable steps. ...

> This history of strategic litigation, with large companies acting as repeat players, in order to obtain more favorable legal determinations could be reported in many other instances. The pattern reveals how the courts do not operate in a vacuum ... but have to face repeated attempts to persuade them to modify their decisions in the light of powerful business interests. Although these repeat players do not always succeed, they rarely give up without a long and expensive fight, during which time they can use the threat of litigation to obtain more favorable settlements. (Collins, 2004: 21)

Trade associations often act as repeat players in credit litigation, and have often sponsored such litigation, at least since *Helby v Matthews*, which approved the structure of hire-purchase as the dominant form of consumer credit (Ramsay, 1995). Geraint Howells argues that there has been an explosion of consumer credit litigation during the 2000s, partly through the existence of the entrepreneurial activity of intermediaries (Howells, 2010). The overall impact of this on the normative landscape of credit law remains unclear.

From a public choice perspective it may always be tempting for government to provide consumers with rights that are exercised ex post by adjudication since this is a form of off-budget regulation of a problem. Trebilcock notes that:

> Given the fiscal constraints on government resources, there is likely to be a tendency to seek to provide relief to constituencies in an off-budget fashion, for example, through civil redress mechanisms, even though in principle it may be more efficient to deal with these concerns through publicly enforced sanctions or regulatory requirements. ... In general a large volume of consumer civil claims should raise a presumption that other features of consumer protection policy are not working effectively, rather than being a source of policy satisfaction. In other words, consumer civil claims should be the residual, not primary response to a consumer protection problem. (Trebilcock, 2003: 84)

5.1 The balance of public and private enforcement of consumer law

Some of the general benefits claimed to accrue from extending private enforcement rights of consumer law are that they compensate for 'regulatory failure', develop valuable precedents and may act as a catalyst for political change. In addition, legal actions by private groups may more accurately reflect consumer preferences than does government action, and provide a valuable addition to democratic participation and the opportunity for the development of public values.

There are dangers involved in extending public-interest interventions. For example, can we expect private groups to be more successful in setting priorities, identifying regulatory targets and implementing strategies than are public agencies? Are there not dangers in allowing unaccountable and potentially unrepresentative consumer groups to determine when an intervention is to be made to defend the 'consumer interest'? The following extract summarises the advantages and disadvantages of private action in enforcement:

> [T]he benefits of private decision of the question of whether judicial action should be initiated are the benefits of individuality, of entrepreneurial decision-making: the possibility of iconoclastic challenges to the conventional hierarchy of competing interests, resource constraints which are a function not of extrinsic facts but of the prospects of a particular case and thus likely to impose a discipline which mirrors a statute's own judgment of the merits of a case, and a capacity for innovation. But the defects of individuality are present also: the risk of intolerance manifest in actions brought to vindicate specific interests, a cognate risk that evaluation of the desirability of a case which looks only to the governing statute will ignore the perhaps constraining values of other statutes, a tendency towards disorganized or uneven enforcement practices. (*Harvard Law Review*, 1978: 1631)

The debate over private enforcement in the UK is tied also to arguments concerning the potential introduction of class actions (see discussion below Chapter 5), concerns about a supposed compensation culture (which do not seem to be substantiated: Lewis, 2011), and the role of ADR mechanisms such as Financial Ombudsmen.

5.2 Public interest groups and agenda setting: supercomplaints

The recognition that both markets and government might fail to provide adequate consumer protection has led to interest in a 'third force' in consumer protection, that of public-interest groups (see Cooper and Dhavaan, 1986). Trebilcock, Prichard and Waverman provide the following reasons for promoting representation by public interest groups:

> [T]he theoretical case for state sponsorship of interest group representation in public decision-making involves the following elements: first, theories of pluralism as principally explaining the outcome of political processes; second, a recognition that thinly spread groups such as consumers, cannot, unaided, rationally afford to participate extensively in those processes; third, a recognition that vigorous competition in ideas, in a modern and increasingly complex society where good ideas are always in short supply, is a virtue worth promoting in itself; and fourth, a 'process' value attached by the community to enhanced public participation in collective decision-making. (Trebilcock, Prichard and Waverman, 1982: 267)

Several developments in the UK envisage greater formal input into policymaking by recognised consumer groups:

1. the supercomplaint process under the Enterprise Act 2002;
2. the possibility of bringing damage actions under section 47B of the Competition Act 1998 where there has been a successful competition law prosecution;
3. the possibility of being a designated enforcer under Part 8 of the Enterprise Act; and
4. the possibility of consumer groups bringing representative actions on behalf of consumers under consumer legislation (see below Chapter 5).

The Enterprise Act 2002 section 11 introduced the possibility of supercomplaints by designated consumer groups to the OFT and sectoral regulators. This pursued the objective of 'strengthening the voice of the consumer in competition' (Competition White Paper, para 4.25). A regulator must respond within 90 days to a supercomplaint, and provide at that point a reasoned explanation of the action it intends to take.

Productivity and Enterprise—A World Class Competition Regime, Cmnd 5233 (2001)

> 4.25 Anti-competitive behaviour in consumer markets can be particularly difficult to detect. Where there are a large number of consumers, and most firms operate in a similar way, consumers will often not know whether they are getting a raw deal. Individual consumers rarely have access to the information necessary to put together a cogent complaint.
>
> 4.26 In this situation, consumer groups have a crucial role to play. Through them the interests and power of large numbers of consumers can be articulated.
>
> 4.27 The Government wishes to strengthen the voice of the consumer in competition. It therefore proposes to give consumer groups the right to bring super-complaints to the OFT where they suspect there are market structures or practices which are working against the interest of consumers.

Consumer groups welcomed the initiative. The CBI was more cautious, arguing that 'in order for the power not to be brought into disrepute, it must be used sparingly and only where the consumer organization has a reasoned, justifiable prima facie case of competition law infringement' (CBI, position paper 28 September, 2001). The criteria for becoming a 'designated consumer group' are:

1. The body is so constituted, managed and controlled as to be expected to act independently, impartially and with complete integrity.
2. The body can demonstrate considerable experience and competence in representing the interests of consumers of any description.
3. The body has the capability to put together reasoned supercomplaints on a range of issues.
4. The body is ready and willing to co-operate with the OFT, and/or with any other authority, body or person having responsibility for responding to supercomplaints. In particular, the body agrees to take account of any guidance issued by the OFT on the making of supercomplaints.
5. The fact that a body has a trading arm will not disqualify it from being designated provided that the trading arm does not control the body; any profits of the trading arm are only used to further the stated objectives of the body; and the body has established procedures to ensure that any potential conflicts of interest are properly dealt with.

Groups currently designated are: The Consumers' Association (Which?), National Consumer Council and Citizens Advice, Postwatch, CAMRA and the General Consumer Council of Northern Ireland. The OFT provides guidance on making supercomplaints and indicates that the possible outcomes may include the following:

- enforcement action by the OFT's competition or consumer regulation divisions;

- finding that another authority with concurrent duties is better placed to deal with the complaint;
- launching a market study into the issue;
- making a market investigation reference to the Competition Commission (CC) if there is a competition problem;
- action by a sectoral regulator with concurrent duties;
- referring the complaint to a sectoral regulator without concurrent duties;
- referring the complaint to the OFT for action (if the complaint was sent to a regulator with concurrent duties);
- referring the complaint to another consumer enforcement body;
- finding the complaint requires no action;
- finding the complaint to be unfounded;
- dismissing the complaint as frivolous or vexatious.

Phil Evans of Which? argues that

> The advantages of super-complaints are many, they allow an issue to be publicly discussed, they provide competition authorities with a formal route for dealing with consumers' organisations, they impose some discipline on bodies that may wish to raise matters with the OFT, and they provide a clear process for making competition meaningful for consumers. (Evans, 2005: 188)

The following extract outlines the views of executives of the National Consumer Council on the costs and benefits of a supercomplaint strategy.

Philip Cullum and Claire Whyley, Supercomplaint Strategy (2005)

> Our experience with home credit has reinforced our view that the power to make a supercomplaint is a tool rather than an end in itself. They can also be resource-intensive, not least because our involvement does not end when the complaint has been submitted: we devoted significant amount of time to discussions with the OFT, and we are now working with the Competition Commission as it conducts its home credit inquiry. We should therefore investigate and submit supercomplaints only when they can help us achieve our objectives in particular markets—we should not do them lightly. This includes ensuring that we explore potential remedies before submitting any supercomplaint, so that we are at least reasonably confident that the issues raised could be resolved by some form of action by the OFT, Competition Commission or one of the other regulators.

> 12. Nevertheless, we should remain alive to the potential for supercomplaints in all areas of our work; and we should also recognise the power of threatening as well as actually submitting a supercomplaint. Such threats have value only if the people we are trying to put pressure on—whether an individual business, an entire industry or in some instances the regulator itself—genuinely believe that we might submit a supercomplaint. There is therefore probably a need to submit a supercomplaint at least occasionally, to keep the threat real.

> One of the main attractions of the supercomplaint procedure is that it allows us to achieve high impact with limited investment, by using modest NCC spending to leverage the much greater resources of the OFT and other regulators. We should not seek to replicate the OFT's role in the process.

As noted in 2002 and 2003, on occasion it will be worth exploring with other organisations (including those who possess expertise in a particular market but do not have supercomplainant status) the opportunity to collaborate on a supercomplaint. This would obviously be subject to safeguards on quality of work, and any proposed collaboration would have to be consistent with our workplan and mission

Each supercomplaint is a valuable opportunity to change companies' behaviour and market structures, not only through the formal legal process but also by drawing public attention to issues of concern.

Each one is also a chance to enhance NCC's reputation and relationships, and to create a real sense of purpose within our organization.

We are of course consumer advocates and exist to stand up for the consumer interest. So our stance on supercomplaints will unashamedly be partisan, making the case when appropriate for action to promote consumers' interests. But in doing this, we need to live up to our value of 'Fair: We tell it how it is', positioning ourselves as objective analysts of a market rather than looking for issues to raise for their own sake. This also governs how we relate to regulators, industry representatives and other organisations: we will so far as possible seek to work on supercomplaints in a straightforward, open and collaborative way.

As noted above, submitting a supercomplaint does have considerable resource implications, especially with regard to policy, communications and corporate functinion
What has been the experience of supercomplaints? The following are the complaints made to the OFT since the introduction of the procedure:

- CAMRA: supply of beer in UK pubs, 24 July 2009
- Consumers' Association: care homes, 5 December 2003
- Consumer Focus: cash ISAs, 31 March 2010
- Which?: credit card interest rates - 1 April 2007
- CAB: doorstep selling, 3 September 2002
- NCC: home credit, 14 June 2004
- Postwatch: mail consolidation, 17 March 2003
- Which?: Northern Ireland banking, 15 November 2004
- CAB: PPI, 13 September 2005
- Consumers' Association: private dentistry, 25 October 2001
- Which?: Scottish legal profession, 9 May 2007
- CAB: sub-prime credit brokerage, 3 March 2011:
- Which?: travel money card surcharges, 30 March 2011.

Credit and financial services dominate the complaints. There is no study of the overall success of the supercomplaints policy. The PPI and home credit complaints resulted in references to the Competition Commission and extensive, high-quality analyses of these markets. In both these cases legislative orders were introduced by the Competition Commission to regulate these markets. The firms subject to supercomplaints have complained about the excessive length of inquiries. Measuring success of the process would need to consider not only the outcomes but also their contribution to public debate and their stimulation of private action as occurred with PPI. The Financial Services and Markets Act 2012 will permit the new Financial Conduct Authority to make supercomplaints to the new Competition and Markets Authority.

The Competition Commision may not be convinced that its priorities should be determined by supercomplaints. In its evidence to the Select Committee on Regulators (2006) it states:

> The Enterprise Act was predicated on the expectation that strong independent competition authorities would make decisions that would lead to improvements in UK productivity, and hence improve UK competitiveness. To date however none of the completed market investigations has involved a sector of sufficient scale or importance for increased competition to have a significant effect on UK productivity, nor have they involved competitive effects with a direct negative effect on productivity. They have generally been about harm to consumers arising from a lack of competition in relatively small markets. Indeed several of them have derived from 'super complaints' from consumer bodies. This is not to say that the investigations have not been worthwhile, but it is hard to believe that they are quite what Ministers had in mind when taking the Enterprise Bill through Parliament.

6. Transnational regulation, the Internet and cross-border transactions

> [The Internet] … will carry us into a new world of low-friction, low-overhead capitalism, in which market information will be plentiful and transaction costs low. It will be a shopper's heaven. (Bill Gates, *The Road Ahead* (1995))

> Thanks to the Internet, the consumer is finally seizing power. (*The Economist*, 2 April 2005)

The growth of a 'knowledge-based economy' is often associated with developments on the Internet and its potential both to empower consumers in their market purchases and to influence policy. At the end of the twentieth century the European Commission suggested that:

> the twin forces of globalization of markets and wide dissemination of new communication and information processing technologies have set in train significant social and economic changes. They have revolutionized the way markets serve consumers. At the same time, these changes have transformed consumer expectations. Consumer policy has to adapt to these new developments. (EU, 1999: 1)

The technological and cross-border characteristics of the Internet have driven searches for regulatory innovation. Early discussion of the Internet suggested that it would reduce consumer search costs and stimulate price competition. The existence of free price comparison sites such as shopper.com, 'shopbots', and online buying services (such as autobytel.com) might be predicted to lead markets closer to the textbook model of perfect competition.

A review of research on the effects of the Internet on consumer markets suggests that in certain markets, such as term insurance, travel and new cars, the Internet has lowered consumer prices. Consumers are able, for example, to obtain the invoice price paid by car dealers, a valuable bargaining tool. Use of the Internet may reduce the potential for price discrimination which results from face-to-face negotiations, benefiting in particular consumers who have a high disutility for bargaining or whose characteristics may disadvantage them in bargaining. US studies have found that African American and Hispanic consumers pay an offline premium for automobiles that is partly explicable by income, education and search costs. It was also found that minority buyers using an Internet referral service for the purchase of automobiles paid the same price as Whites, irrespective of their income, education or search costs (Morton, Zettelmeyer, Silva-Risso, 2003: 65). This suggests also that the Internet will benefit most those groups who are least likely to use it, thus contributing to the regressive effects of the digital divide.

There continues to be significant price dispersion for homogeneous products (eg books) on the Internet (as evidenced through price comparison sites). This may be partly accounted for by consumer interest in non-price attributes such as shipping, branding and other non-price factors that may be relevant even for homogeneous goods. One study (Brynjolfsson, Dick and Smith, 2003) found continuing price dispersion over time for electronic products sold online. Differences in price dispersion depended on market structure, with greater price dispersion associated with a small number of firms listing prices (ibid: 463).

Given the reduction of consumer search costs on the Internet, suppliers as profit maximisers have incentives to raise consumer search costs or devise methods to discriminate between shoppers. Ellison and Ellison outline several methods whereby suppliers may raise consumers' search costs on the Internet including:

1. 'bait and switch': offline this requires sales personnel but this can be automated on the Web. Retailers offer a low-quality product at an inferior price on a price comparison site and try to convince consumers who visit the site to buy a higher-priced item. The incentives for this practice are that if firms advertise a higher-quality price with good terms, their offering will be lost behind the dozens of other offers on the price comparison screen (Ellison and Ellison, 2004).
2. e-purchases are bundled with shipping costs permitting variations in pricing.
3. e-retailers gather information on consumers and discriminate between consumers.

The authors found that (2) was ubiquitous. Other research draws attention to the ability of firms to use information gathered on consumers to use differential (higher) pricing for loyal consumers through e-mail targeting (Chen and Sudhir, 2002). Janet Bush, referring to analysis by Peter Swann, concludes that the Internet works both for and against consumers. It reduces search costs but also 'allows sellers to judge with a high degree of accuracy what any particular individual consumer is prepared to pay for a particular product and price accordingly. There is considerable evidence of "differential pricing" or "price discrimination" on the Internet' (Bush, 2004: 14).

Can the Internet through online information and discussion groups empower consumers in their interactions with suppliers in markets traditionally associated with substantial information asymmetry? Markets for professional services have traditionally been characterised by significant information asymmetry between providers and consumers based on professional knowledge. The Internet promises consumers access to both a large amount of information on these services as well as the possibility of exchanging information with other consumers through online discussion groups and communities. Research on the interaction between 'high involvement' consumers, (defined as individuals who had consulted a qualified professional within the last twelve months and who had made use of the Internet in one of the sectors studied—legal, medical and financial) and professional service providers indicates that there is not a simple relationship between the use of the Internet and consumer empowerment in these relationships. The consumer–professional relationship continues to exhibit a variety of patterns described as 'compliant, collaborative, confirmatory, and consumerist' (see Laing, Newholm and Hogg, 2005).

Colin Scott summarises the advantages and disadvantages of online purchasing by consumers:

Colin Scott, 'Regulatory Innovation and the Online Consumer' (2004) 26 *Law and Policy* 476 at 479, 480

First, there are potential price savings, accruing from: reduced costs for traders who do not have to maintain costly shop-front premises and/or who can buy in bulk; the potential for avoiding local taxes ... the creation of new markets for highly perishable services (such as flights and hotel accommodation), which service providers are willing to offload at substantial discounts provided they can charge above marginal cost. ... Second, online transacting might reduce search costs by enabling comparison of products and prices from the comfort of a computer screen. Third, consumers may be able to purchase goods and services with (at least a perception of) greater privacy. Fourth, and relatedly, they may be able to acquire products the supply of which is prohibited within their own jurisdiction either by public law or by licensing or other agreements made by producers. A central example of this is online gambling. Fifth, consumers may be able to benefit from greater immediacy with highly time-sensitive transactions (such as stock purchases). Sixth, the Internet may enable consumers to find sellers (and indeed buyers) for goods and services that can readily be supplied to a remote location but where it might otherwise be difficult to locate such persons (www.ebay.com provides a key example of the Internet providing intermediation for this kind of service, though it applies also to niche market e-tailers such as sellers of rare books and maps). Seventh, and relatedly, the Internet may create markets in transactions for which payments are very small.

The peculiar problems faced by consumers in online transactions are largely related to information. On the one hand, the space provided by the Internet for describing products and supplying images, and the potential for comparing the offerings of different traders, or locating independent product reviews, may reduce search costs and enhance the information available to consumers about the product (whether goods or services) to be supplied. On the other hand, online consumers may have informational disadvantages as compared with their bricks-and-mortar counterparts, for example in respect of reliability and quality. As with goods and services ordered by telephone or post, consumers can rarely try before they buy. Products may meet their specification but still disappoint their new owner. Even where traders offer no-quibble money-back guarantees (as with many suppliers of goods) some of the cost of returning products often falls on the consumer. With services there is less potential for such guarantees. An online bet is consumed before the consumer is liable to become disappointed. It is in the nature of online investing that there can be few guarantees. There are good reasons why consumers have historically relied on trusted intermediaries in their transacting behavior, and stripping them out of transactions creates risks.

The greater the expertise required to assess the wisdom of a transaction, the greater the risks. For this reason, online investing presents particularly accentuated risks.

Where consumers can acquire good information about the product to be supplied, they may lack key information about the transaction. First, they may not know who they are dealing with. This is of little consequence when the product is supplied in conformity with expectations. But where things go wrong it may be fundamental. A traditional consumer can visit the premises of the supplier, and if necessary cause a lawyer's letter or legal claim to be delivered. Most traditional businesses value their reputations sufficiently that they have incentives to seek solutions to problems that are acceptable to consumers, often in excess of legal rights, or offering remedies not provided for by law. These informational problems are perhaps most acute in the case of fraud—for example, where money is taken with no intent to supply the product or no intent to supply a product that conforms to expectations. Even in the absence of fraud, such problems as non-delivery, defective products, and overcharging can be far from straightforward. When the consumer has full information about the supplier, they are unlikely to be aware of which legal rules govern the transaction or what remedies are available. Securing the remedies that are, in theory, available, may be difficult where the trader is located in a different jurisdiction.

6.1 Establishing the ground rule of consumer Internet transactions

A distinction is sometimes drawn between regulation that facilitates the development of markets (that will make everyone better off) and measures that regulate a market (and that are intended to benefit a particular group). Much of the regulation of the Internet is justified under the former category. However, consider the comments of Hal Scott:

> [T]he need to provide rational ordering is not a sufficient explanation for statutory development. Statutory commercial law rules are instead understood as largely regulatory in import. ... They reflect concern with the ability of various transactors, whether merchants or consumers to protect themselves in the marketplace, and they are ultimately distributional in character. (Scott, 1978: 739)

We described in Chapter 1 the argument that European consumer law was being driven by the imperatives of the internal market rather than consumer needs. Consider to what extent this criticism is legitimate in the context of Internet regulation and the extent to which Internet regulation is animated by distributional ideas of risk and loss spreading.

Commission of the European Communities SEC(2004) 1390 Commission Staff Working Document, Consumer Confidence in E-Commerce: Lessons Learned from the e-Confidence Initiative

1. Introduction

The European Union has made the competitiveness of the European economy one of its priorities as the work in the context of the Lisbon Reform Agenda witnesses. Consumer protection, and its contribution to this agenda, is one of the essential elements that contribute to competitiveness. Good consumer protection rules and systems strengthen consumer confidence in the functioning of the market. This strengthens demand and, ultimately, competitiveness. ... Reports on the structure of the e-commerce market in Europe suggest that consumers still lack this confidence in the e-commerce market. Practically 90% of the e-commerce market consists of business-to-business transactions, and the development of the consumer market continues to lag behind. Even though most analysts believe that growth is picking up (reported market growth in B2C e-commerce, depending on the sector, is in two digit figures, but remains low in absolute terms), this information shows that the full potential of the market is not being realised for consumers. ... Payment security ranks as issue number one, but product delivery, and information to consumers, as well as issues such as refunds and withdrawal conditions, are of equally serious concern. Consumers are, in general, much more concerned about losing their money, or not obtaining what they ordered, when buying over the Internet, than they would be on the high street. ... Spam, or unsolicited commercial e-mail, is a major issue.

R Brownsword and G Howells, 'When Surfers Start to Shop: Internet Commerce and Contract Law' (1999) 19 *Legal Studies* 287

Given that electronic commerce is set to cross borders both regionally and beyond, the need for enabling legal frameworks is urgent. There is, however, every indication that, where legal systems address the matter, the spirit of facilitation will drive the agenda.

... In 1996 UNCITRAL published its Model Law on Electronic Commerce ... the entire thrust of the model law is one of facilitation coupled with flexibility.

6.2 Formalities, information disclosure, cooling off and Internet consumer contracts

Transactions in electronic commerce raise questions about the role of formalities in consumer transactions. The requirement of a written document for consumer trans-actions is intended to perform both a cautionary or warning function—making the consumer aware of the nature of the legal obligation being entered into—and an evi-dentiary function—providing an objective source of information on key aspects of the transaction. In the latter role they may protect against fraud and also reduce dispute settlement costs.

Many jurisdictions have been eager to facilitate electronic transactions by reducing writing formalities, although an e-mail probably already satisfies the requirement of a writing, and a 'click' a signature in English law (see Law Commission, 2001). There may be a concern that permitting the use of electronic communications in consumer transactions will reduce consumer protection. Jean Braucher comments that:

Use of electronic communications for required consumer protection disclosures and notices is cause for concern that the result will be to diminish effective communication and the cautionary function of these notices ... the biggest potential problem with moving consumer protection notices online is that standard form contracts might be used to 'agree' to electronic notice, even though the consumer does not have a computer, does not have an Internet connection, or does not regularly use it. (Braucher, 2001: 538–39)

Amendments to the Consumer Credit Act 1974 permit a person to agree to receive copies of an agreement and other statutory notices and documents by electronic com-munication. The documents so transmitted must be stored by the sender 'for future reference for an appropriate period in a way which allows the information to be repro-duced without change' (section 176A(1)(c) Consumer Credit Act 1974 (Electronic Communications) Order 2004). However, cancellation and default notices are still required to be sent by post.

The Electronic Commerce Directive (see Electronic Commerce (EC Directive) Reg-ulations 2002) and the Distance Selling Directive (now replaced by the 2011 Consumer

Rights Directive) regulate the process of entering Internet contracts. In addition the Consumer Protection from Unfair Trading Regulations 2008 apply to Internet trans-actions and a failure to provide the information required by a Community Directive such as the Distance Selling Directive will be an unfair commercial practice (see below Chapter 4). The Electronic Commerce (EC Directive) Regulations 2002 are prima-rily a facilitative regulation intended to stimulate electronic commerce. According to the EU Commission, the Directive 'provides a light and flexible legal framework for e-commerce and addresses only those elements which are strictly necessary in order to ensure the proper functioning of the Internal Market in e-commerce' (EU Commission, 2003).

The primary focus of the Directive is informational but it also outlines the proce-dures for concluding Internet contracts. The regulations require that information service providers provide 'in a form and manner which is easily, directly and permanently accessible' to recipients of the service information on such issues as the identity, and address of the service (regulation 6). Commercial communications must be clearly identified (regulation 7) and any unsolicited commercial communication must be 'clearly and unambiguously identifiable as such as soon as it is received' (regulation 8). Before the conclusion of a consumer transaction by electronic means, a service provider must provide in a 'clear comprehensible and unambiguous manner' informa-tion on the technical steps to conclude an order and the means of correcting mistakes (regulation 9). The service provider must acknowledge receipt of the order (regulation 11) and make available to the recipient of the service 'effective and accessible technical means' to identify and correct input errors prior to the placing of the order (regulation 11). A service provider must also make available the terms of the transaction 'in a way that allows him to store and reproduce them' (regulation 9(3)) and indicate whether he subscribes to any codes of conduct and how these codes may be consulted electroni-cally (regulation 9(2)). Failure to provide any of the above information is actionable as a breach of statutory duty (regulation 13). A person may rescind the contract if the service provider has not made available means of allowing him to identify and correct input errors (regulation 15).

The Electronic Commerce Regulations provide that a service provider must comply only with its home state regulations concerning requirements applicable to information society service providers covered by the 'co-ordinated field' (regulation 4(4)). This provision, intended to facilitate the internal market, does not apply to contractual obli-gations concerning consumer contracts (Schedule 3) and a state may take enforcement action against an information society service in order to protect consumers where the service prejudices or represents a 'serious and grave risk of prejudice to the protection of consumers and the measures are proportionate'(regulations 5(1)(d) and 5(3)).

The Distance Selling Regulations established a battery of pre-contractual and con-tractual information requirements, create a default rule of performance of the contract within 30 days, and provide protection against fraudulent use of a credit card and inertia sales. A central protection is the 7-day (now 14 days under the Consumer Rights Directive) cooling-off period which we discuss in greater detail below (Chapter 4). The Privacy and Electronic Communications (EC Directive) Regulations 2003 also require the consumer to be provided with clear and comprehensible information on the use of any information provided and the use of cookies (regulation 6).

There is no cooling-off period in Internet sales in the US or Canada, although many companies offer 30-day return policies. Some US commentators doubt the efficacy of a cooling-off period since 'consumers are unlikely to find the time or make the effort to return' the goods (Hillman, 2006: 299). Hillman argues that a cooling-off period 'could make Internet contracting prohibitively expensive for e-businesses and for little gain' (Hillman, 2006: 299). There is no evidence that the cooling-off period has had this impact in Europe although it is also possible that many consumers are not aware of it or do not exercise their rights. Moreover some of those businesses that might be substantially affected have secured exemption. We do not know the role of these laws in contributing to 'consumer confidence'. A study in Ireland indicated, however, that although consumers were not well informed about their rights they felt confident in shopping on the Internet. Other factors such as brand recognition may have been important (Donnelly and White, 2005). Hillman found in a US study that few consumers read e-standard forms beyond the price and description of the goods but that a significant number (one-third) do read beyond this when the value of the contract is high or the vendor unknown (Hillman, 2006). The application of the EU unfair contract terms directive in the EU means that many unfair terms on the Internet (eg mandatory arbitration in foreign jurisdictions) will be prohibited.

6.2 Consumer redress and the Internet

Consumer redress for an Internet transaction may pose problems for consumers particularly since it may often raise cross-border issues. The EU, in a review of ecommerce (EU, 2004: 3), refers to a study which indicates that 'delivery is a real issue for consumers: the Report of the European Consumer Centres about the e-commerce market in the EU comments that 33% of ordered goods were not delivered'. Traditional legal remedies through courts are not a serious option for many consumer transactions on the Internet. Questions of jurisdiction, appropriate law and the ability to enforce a judgment across jurisdictions pose significant costs for a consumer. The EU has been active in promoting consumer-friendly jurisdiction and choice-of-law rules (see discussion in Micklitz, Reich and Rott, 2009) and a specific cross-border small-claims procedure (Regulation 861/2007). In this section, however, we consider the potential of non-state and market norms in protecting the consumer in transnational consumer transactions.

6.2.1 Harnessing gatekeepers to protect consumers: chargebacks

Harnessing credit card companies to protect consumers is one example of using intermediaries on the Internet as a method of protecting consumers. The fundamental rationale is that intermediaries may be the least cost loss avoider and risk spreader (see further eg Scott, 2004; Mann and Belzley, 2005).

OECD, *Consumer Dispute Resolution and Redress in the Global Marketplace* (2006) 12, 14, 15, 16

> Payment cardholder protections, sometimes referred to as 'chargebacks,' are remedies provided by payment card issuers to consumers for unauthorised or disputed charges on their

payment cards. The protections currently available to cardholders vary considerably among OECD member countries [for UK protection see below Chapter 10.9]. ... These payment card networks have global reach, thereby considerably reducing redress challenges for consumers shopping across national borders. When provided in a transparent and effective manner, cardholder protections can increase consumer confidence in the use of payment cards for online purchases, and in the global marketplace more generally.

Protections set out in international and regional instruments

The OECD E-commerce Guidelines highlight the important role of payment cardholder protections and enhanced consumer education in the development of the online global marketplace. The Guidelines provide that '[l]imitations of liability for unauthorised or fraudulent use of payment systems, and chargeback mechanisms offer powerful tools to enhance consumer confidence and their development and use should be encouraged in the context of electronic commerce.' The importance of protections for payment cardholders, especially for unauthorised and fraudulent payments in cross-border transactions is echoed in the OECD Cross-Border Fraud Guidelines, which call on member countries to jointly study 'approaches to developing additional safeguards against the abuse of payment systems and redress for consumer victims of such abuse.'

...

Different protections for different payment schemes.

One key question as new payment methods, such as prepaid cards, mobile and online payment schemes, evolve is whether current legal and regulatory regimes cover all payment mechanisms and not only the more traditional credit and debit cards. These new payment mechanisms may eventually be a major component of the online business-to-consumer marketplace. Consumers may wish to use other systems to avoid the disclosure of their credit card information. However, in doing so, they may relinquish consumer protections unless these laws and regulatory regimes apply to the new payment systems.

Currently a number of countries limit consumer protections to users of credit cards as opposed to other types of payment cards or emerging payment systems [for UK see below Chapter 10. 9]. ...

Protections mandated by industry practice

In addition to laws and regulations, important protections are also provided by industry practice through such means as industry codes, card network requirements and individual issuer initiatives.

Industry codes

In a number of countries the card industry has implemented self-regulatory codes that contain provisions relevant to card-related protections and the rights and responsibilities of the parties to the card system. ...

... The major card networks impose obligations on their issuers to provide protections that may exceed those required by national laws. Such measures can provide important benefits to cardholders. The three largest card networks, Visa, MasterCard, and American Express, recommend that issuers of its cards abide by a number of policies aimed at protecting cardholders. For example, Visa USA advertises a 'zero liability' policy for US cardholders, which promises protection against liability for certain unauthorised credit or debit charges. Visa International has a global policy that requires issuers to implement the chargeback process for certain kinds of complaints. Visa Canada has issued a voluntary "epromise" initiative to provide consumers recourse in most situations ... (see above) for all forms of distance sales (eg Internet, mail and telephone order). MasterCard also advertises a 'zero liability' policy for certain unauthorised uses of US-issued credit and debit cards.

American Express has implemented a programme through which US cardholder disputes regarding charges for electronically delivered goods or services will result in an immediate chargeback.

Individual card issuers

In some cases, individual issuers supplement the requirements imposed by the card networks to provide additional protections for consumers. For example, some US-based issuers opted to go to the zero-liability policy for Internet purchases prior to being required to do so by the payment card networks. Some of these protections are marketed specifically to allay fears of online shopping, providing protections like 'purchase insurance' and 'extended warranty' or 'purchase replacement protection'. Issuers in various other member countries provide similar reassurances.

Cross-border considerations

Some legal and regulatory regimes differentiate between domestic and cross-border transactions. In an era where cross-border transactions are breaking down barriers between national jurisdictions, this issue can be especially important. A lack of resolution could leave consumers either confused as to when protections apply in one case or over-confident in their protections in another.

... Due to the limitations of legal protections in some countries, policies instituted by the card networks can be particularly useful because they can standardise protective measures across national borders. However, where they are optional, their use is left to the discretion of the individual issuer.

The application of the protection provided by section 75 of the Consumer Credit Act 1974 to foreign purchases is discussed in Chapter 8. The protection of section 75 does not, however, extend to payment by debit card or other payment mechanisms such as Paypal that may be used on the Internet.

The OECD article emphasises the role of the card network rules on chargebacks. These chargeback rules are developed by the card networks but are not publicly available and represent the outcome of a 'private government'. Ramsay comments:

Iain Ramsay, 'Consumer Law, Regulatory Capitalism and the New Regulation' (2006) 28 *Sydney Law Review* 9 at 26

The credit card networks are an important conduit for the diffusion of international standards of protection. At present, however, little is known about the dynamics of this private rulemaking. Braithwaite and Drahos argue that an important strategy for consumer groups should be to ratchet up standards by targeting gatekeepers in global webs of regulation. There are several sites of regulation here: national, where regulators such as the OFT may press for high levels of consumer protection; the EU level, where the European Commission has proposed a legal framework for payment arrangements that would provide for the possibility of chargebacks for goods that are not delivered or non-conforming goods irrespective of the form of electronic payment. Finally, there is the role of the OECD. The OECD has played an active role as a forum for developing standards in relation to chargeback liability. The challenge for consumer interests in this area is to harness 'best practices' within one global region and develop it as a global standard that is subject to continuous improvement. This may require consumer groups to bypass national governments and work with credit card companies within an international site such as the OECD.

The argument for extending chargebacks to all forms of payment (debit, Paypal, etc) is to provide a level playing field and regulatory transparency. On the issue of increased costs if chargeback procedures were applied to debit cards, Arnold Rosenberg quotes Ronald Mann:

> One obvious concern is that the extension of the reversibility rule to the debit card context will increase the costs of debit cards to those that use them. If so, the reform might alter the relative desirability of the products in significant ways. From one perspective, that is not a reason for concern. The only reason that it might alter the costs significantly is if there is a significant volume of chargeback activity, which suggests that there are a significant number of transactions in which consumers currently lack effective recourse. On the other hand, as discussed above, there is the empirical possibility that a significant level of chargebacks might reflect abusive consumer conduct rather than dishonest merchant conduct. For the reasons discussed above, however, I think it unlikely that there will be a sufficiently large volume of chargebacks to affect pricing significantly, largely because the volume of payment-reversing charge-backs in the credit-card system now is quite small. (Rosenberg, 2005: 591)

Card networks may also make greater use of the architecture of computer codes to protect against mistakes, fraud or foolishness by consumers (automatic limits on maximum expenditures on online gambling; the development of 'Verified by Visa'). Governments might persuade intermediaries to regulate transactions that may be difficult to regulate through traditional techniques, for example by refusing credit to transactions identified as online gambling.

6.3 Enhancing reputational devices: trustmarks and reputation intermediaries

Reputation is particularly important in transactions where the high enforcement costs facing consumers make it unlikely that they will take any action should there be a problem with a purchase. The significance of reputation is reflected in the importance of brand names on the Internet and the greater willingness of many consumers to deal with such brand names. Indeed this may create difficulties for small companies entering the electronic marketplace.

Trustmarks may provide a signal that traders subscribe to certain standards. Trustmarks have not as yet been very successful at the pan-European level. The EU Commission reported on this failure in 2004 in relation to their e-confidence initiative to establish an EU trustmark:

Commission of the European Communities, *Consumer Confidence in E-Commerce: Lessons Learned from the e-Confidence Initiative*, SEC (2004) 1390.

6.2 The e-confidence initiative

In 2000, the European Commission launched the 'e-confidence initiative'. At the time, the European Commission felt that consumer confidence could be enhanced by identifying a set of common principles for codes of conduct aimed at gaining consumer trust, particularly since rapid proliferation of trustmarks and codes at the time was considered as potentially confusing for consumers. The initiative involved a large number of the concerned business and consumer stakeholders. Ultimately,this led to the joint drafting by BEUC and UNICE of the European Trustmark Requirements.

7. THE EUROPEAN TRUSTMARK REQUIREMENTS (ETR)

The ETR developed by BEUC and UNICE aim at providing guidance to anyone seeking to set up a trustmark scheme. The initial idea behind the ETR was that any trustmark could have its organisation and code certified as conforming with the ETR, and obtain an EU 'logo'.

The European Trustmark Requirements include independent monitoring and certification process, and provide a model for how this process could be organised. In particular, they foresee the certification of trustmark codes through an independent third party, and the monitoring of their performance against the ETR on the basis of annual reports. They also foresee the establishment of an e-confidence committee which would oversee the certification and monitoring process, and, in particular, assess the Independent Third Party itself against specific criteria to ensure overall trustworthiness of the scheme.

Despite initial hopes for a speedy implementation, it became clear, after the ETR had been presented to the European Commission, at the end of 2001, that the momentum behind the initiative had faded. Repeated efforts by the Commission Services to marshal financial backing from industry for the setting-up of the certification and monitoring scheme were not successful. Even though this was disappointing, it was perhaps not surprising, given the slower than expected evolution of the e-commerce market and the collapse of the 'dot.com bubble'. In the view of the Commission services it is important to test the effectiveness of self-regulation at EU level—for example, through efforts such as the joint development of codes between business and consumers, and their effective implementation. A lack of success in this area would augur badly for the concept of self-regulation, resulting in a need for greater reliance on legislation to adequately protect consumers' interests.

7.1. Overall assessment of the ETR

… [A] major weakness of the ETR is that it provides no business plan explaining how the mechanism proposed in the ETR will be financed and maintained over time.

8. LESSONS LEARNED

It is the experience of the Commission Services that involvement of all relevant stakeholders in the development of codes is important. In the case of the ETR, which is intended to boost consumer confidence, the input and support of consumer (as well as business) organisations has been essential. The Commission's Services also believe that it is not the Commission's role to participate in the structures set up by private operators to implement their own codes of best practice.

A global trustmark alliance organising committee was established in 2004 comprising self-regulatory organisations from America, Asia and Europe, but it has not yet produced a trustmark (www.globaltrustmarkalliance.org/members.asp).

The Internet might also permit the growth of 'reputational intermediaries'. Consumers are able to post their reviews of products or services on websites. Amazon.com invites individuals to review books. Travel sites include information on the experience of consumers with hotels. A sophisticated system is that of eBay where sellers are rated according to stars based on feedback from buyers, and buyers may assess the validity of comments posted by buyers by cross-checking all comments made by a buyer. However, in an analysis of the eBay system Clayton Gillette argues that the reputational signal of eBay comments was limited. The informational content of comments was not always high, and there were significant incentives against posting negative information. He speculates that the threat of defamation actions deterred useful negative feedback (see Gillette, 2002: 1165).

6.4 Online dispute resolution

Online dispute resolution (ODR) includes mechanisms which address online disputes as well as those which also settle offline disputes. It is part of the increased interest in the role of alternative dispute resolution as a means of providing accessible consumer redress.

***Consumer Dispute Resolution and Redress in the Global Marketplace,* OECD (2006) 17, 18, 19**

> While some online ADR services may only be used to resolve disputes arising from online or ecommerce transactions, more commonly they may be used for all forms of disputes, whether online or offline. … Online ADR services for business to consumer disputes exist in a variety of contexts, including within a particular online marketplace (eg online auction sites), as part of a trustmark or seal programme, or on an independent basis. These differences may have an effect on consumer access to ADR and on business compliance with the outcome.

> Principles for ADR procedural rules

> To date there are no legally binding international principles setting out procedural safeguards governing the accessibility, independence, transparency, and cost, among other issues for ADR services in business to consumer cases. On the other hand, there have been a number of initiatives to develop voluntary or 'soft-law' principles.

> At the international level, the OECD E-Commerce Guidelines set out that alternative dispute resolution mechanisms should provide 'effective resolution of the dispute in a fair and timely manner and without undue cost or burden to the consumer.' The International Standards Organisation (ISO) is also currently developing an international standard on external dispute resolution which is expected to be completed in 2006. … At the regional level, the European Commission has issued two recommendations to guide the implementation of ADR services for consumer disputes. [See below Chapter 5.]

> In the last few years there have also been a number of private sector initiatives setting out principles for business to consumer ADR schemes operating in the global marketplace. … The International Chamber of Commerce has also issued best practices for online dispute resolution (ODR) in business to consumer and consumer to consumer transactions (ICC, 2003). The best practices include guidance for businesses engaging in online transactions with consumers and for online dispute resolution providers. They encourage businesses to use ODR wherever practicable when disputes with consumers cannot be resolved internally and set out recommendations for ODR providers relating to the accessibility, convenience, privacy and confidentiality, user information, representation, and choice and qualification of dispute resolution professionals. …

With respect to online ADR, Consumers International has recommended that to be 'useful to consumers' mechanisms need to cover all types of B2C disputes; be free or low cost; be available for initiation by consumers; be visible, accessible and easy to use; and operate in a timely fashion. Furthermore, they state, in order to be 'optimally effective,' online ADR mechanisms need to accommodate linguistic diversity; be scaleable and coordinated with each other; and offer appropriate levels of security. (Consumers International, 2001: 15)

ODR sites vary significantly in their caseloads. Square Trade, originally associated with eBay, indicates that it has handled over 2 million disputes across 120 countries in five languages. Conley-Tyler concluded in 2004 that 'there is little data on settlement rates for the sites surveyed', but Square Trade, for example, reported a settlement rate of 85 per cent through facilitated negotiation and reported a user satisfaction rate of 80 per cent. International surveys of online ADR user satisfaction is rarely tracked; however, one site that collects this information has positive data (see Callies, 2006: 749).

The EU has proposed a regulation on ODR and ADR (COM(2011) 794 final). This will establish a European ODR platform.

The present proposal aims at establishing a European online dispute resolution platform ('ODR platform'). This ODR platform takes the form of an interactive website which offers a single point of entry to consumers and traders who seek to resolve out-of-court a dispute which has arisen from a cross-border e-commerce transaction. The platform can be accessed in all official languages of the EU and its use is free of charge. ADR schemes established in the Member States which have been notified to the Commission in accordance with the 'Directive on consumer ADR' will be registered electronically with the ODR platform.

Consumers and traders will be able to submit their complaints through an electronic complaint form which will be available on the platform's website in all official languages of the EU. The platform will check if a complaint can be processed and seek the agreement of the parties to transmit it to the ADR scheme which is competent to deal with the dispute. The competent ADR scheme will seek the resolution of the dispute in accordance with its own rules of procedure within 30 days from the date of receipt of the complaint. The ADR scheme will have to notify to the platform some data in relation to the development of the dispute (date when the complaint was notified to the parties; date when the dispute was resolved; outcome of the dispute).

Under the proposal, a network of online dispute resolution facilitators ('ODR facilitators' network') will be established which will consist of one contact point for online dispute resolution in each Member State. The ODR facilitators' network will provide support to the resolution of disputes submitted via the ODR platform.'

The EU proposal establishes procedures for expeditious resolution of disputes and in a companion Regulation on ADR, COM(2011) 793 final, it establishes standards of expertise and impartiality (Article 6), transparency, effectiveness and fairness for ADR bodies. Member States must designate a competent authority to monitor these standards and establish a list of competent authorities. The EU provides therefore a set of constitutional norms that could be used by private ADR mechanisms.

Calliess and Zumbansen (2010) argue that electronic marketplaces such as eBay may function as private systems of legal ordering linking 'private rule making (codes of conduct) with online dispute resolution procedures, mechanisms of socio-economic sanctioning (reputation, loss of trustmark, exclusion) and private enforcement (money-back guarantee, charge back)'. The 'eBay market order' is established by the 'user agreement' which may be revised in the light of users' comments. The online reputation mechanism is used to assess the reliability of sellers and buyers. They conclude that 'private ordering has proven to be a valuable alternative to state law' (2010: 180). They recognize, however, the need for substantive ground rules for this private ordering that may be developed through 'co-regulatory efforts between states, industry and civil society actors'. This might include the OECD, the EU, ICC and international consumer organisations.

This example demonstrates that private ordering can play a role in international consumer transactions just as it does under the *lex mercatoria*. Legal norms such as the EU rules on ODR may provide background legal ground rules that facilitate this new *lex consumeria*. (For a more critical view see Reich, 2009: 310–13.)

4

The Regulation of Deceptive and Unfair Commercial Practices

I think one must voice his disapproval of unfair and deceptive practices precisely as he would voice his disapproval of sin, for instance, but I should be very much more comfortable if I knew just what acts or practices we are making unlawful … (80 Congressional Record 6597 (1936) Senator Wallace H White discussing the introduction of the Federal Trade Commission's power to regulate 'unfair acts or practices', quoted in Craswell, 1981: 107)

This chapter discusses the 'ground rules' of marketing and advertising in consumer markets. This involves both substantive and institutional questions. Substantive issues concern the extent to which one party must consider the interests of the other contracting party, determined by reference to conceptions of market fairness and information disclosure. Institutional issues include the role of general standards and specific rules, as well as the extent to which the law might restructure contract default rules, for example by providing a right to withdraw. Introduction of this right raises the relationship between consumer law and marketplace norms and practices. Themes raised in this chapter are explored in further detail in analysis of credit advertising and credit market regulation.

---

1. Constituting the market

1.1 The role of advertising

Advertising is a central symbol of the consumer society, so that it is hardly surprising that regulation of advertising raises fundamental questions concerning the objectives and techniques of consumer protection. The pervasiveness and high visibility of media advertising, and its use of sophisticated psychological techniques, have made its economic, social and cultural impact a topic of continuing interest in consumer protection. Avner Offer summarises the arguments about the effects of advertising:

> Advertising ... engages the senses, stimulates novelty, broadens the range of experience and choice. ... It presents information about products and services. It pays for a good part of the media, and underwrites sporting and cultural activity. ... There is a widespread sense that advertising is a mixed blessing. ... Critics assail it in two different ways: it promotes the wrong kind of goods, and is also a bad in itself. ... Advertising, it is argued, supports the spurious differentiation of identical goods, and thus makes them more expensive. ... It undermines rational choice. It conveys seductive but misleading information, making it harder to compare quality and prices. ... Some economists argue that the use of advertising to establish a market presence raises barriers to entry. ... Scholars and laypersons have blamed it for degrading women with its use of sex. Environmentalists and urbanists deplore its visual impact. (Offer, 2006: 103–05)

It is difficult to be ideologically neutral about the value or power of advertising. Approaches to specific issues, eg manufacturers' liability for advertising messages, may often reflect 'inarticulate major premises' of the decision-maker on the general power of advertising in society.

Economists recognise that advertising may provide information or change tastes. As discussed in Chapter 2, advertising can lower consumer search costs. An inability to advertise prices may increase consumer search costs and lead to higher prices (see Benham, 1972). Advertising might be a signal of quality for goods subject to repeat purchase (Nelson, 1974), but empirical research does not find a correlation between product quality and advertising (Caves and Greene, 1996). Advertising may, as Offner indicates, create artificial product differentiation in certain industries creating brand loyalty and leading to a barrier to entry. (For a review of the economics of advertising, see Bagwell, 2005.) Stigler and Becker rationalise image advertising as responding to consumers' desire for status (Stigler and Becker, 1977). Economists are uncomfortable with the idea that advertising changes tastes since this undermines the predictive nature of economic modelling. However, Ronald Coase comments that:

> Advertisements may also change people's tastes. ... Given that an individual's tastes will usually be determined by a large number of factors other than advertising—by family influences, religion, education, genetic factors, and the particular individuals' experiences one would not expect the effect of advertising on taste normally to be great. ... But this does not mean that the effect of advertising on taste is negligible, even if its only consequence is to speed up a change in taste which is occurring for some other reason.

> The generality of economists seem to have thought that advertising which brings about a change in tastes is necessarily bad—either because it tends to corrupt tastes or because, if it does not do this but produces a new set of demands no better than the old, advertising expenditures clearly represent a waste of resources. The possibility that advertising might elevate tastes, even to a small degree, never seems to be considered. Yet, once we decide to take into account changes in tastes into account in assessing the worth of advertising (and I think we should) we need to decide whether the new tastes are better or worse than the old ones. (Coase, 1977: 9)

The relatively thin theory of consumer behaviour evident in the neo-classical economic model of consumer sovereignty—that people prefer what they choose—has never completely dominated the economic literature. The conception of preferences as socially conditioned goes back at least to the work of Thorstein Veblen. Veblen argued in *The Theory of the Leisure Class* (1899) that all consumption was embedded in social and cultural norms, and the idea of the consumer as Robinson Crusoe neglected the interdependent nature of consumption decisions that might often be based on status competition. In the 1920s, Chamberlin stressed the importance of 'selling costs' in his theory of monopolistic competition. He argued that advertising might manipulate preferences through taste transfer:

> Selling methods which play upon the buyer's susceptibilities, which use against him the laws of psychology with which he is unfamiliar and therefore against which he cannot defend himself ... all of these have nothing to do with his knowledge. They are not informative; they are manipulative. They create a new scheme of wants. (Chamberlin, 1950: 119–20)

Galbraith's concept of the 'dependence effect', where producers use advertising to create wants rather than respond to consumer needs, is probably the best-known modern statement of the preference manipulation thesis in relation to those consumer markets dominated by large corporations operating in oligopolistic markets. Galbraith argued that:

> The even more direct link between production and wants is provided by the institutions of modem advertising and salesmanship. These cannot be reconciled with the notion of independently determined desires, for their central function is to create desires-to bring into being wants that previously did not exist. (Galbraith, 1984: 129)

Advertising aids in consolidating producer power over the market, and undermining consumer sovereignty. Galbraith also argued that advertising by corporations sustains and stimulates increasingly wasteful levels of private consumption at the expense of public services, contributing to a picture of the United States as a land of 'private affluence and public squalor'.

> As a society becomes increasingly affluent, wants are increasingly created by the process by which they are satisfied. This may operate passively. Increases in consumption, the counterpart of increases in production, act by suggestion or emulation to create wants. Expectation rises with attainment. Or producers may proceed actively to create wants through advertising and salesmanship. Wants thus come to depend on output. In technical terms, it can no longer be assumed that welfare is greater at an all-round higher level of production than at a lower one. It may be the same. The higher level of production has, merely, a higher level of want creation, necessitating a higher level of want satisfaction. (Galbraith, 1984: 127, 129–31)

If Galbraith is correct and advertising does undermine consumer sovereignty, then intervention to 'correct' consumer preferences need not be regarded as paternalistic. Advertising may ensure that consumers remain 'locked in' to a consumer culture. Thus Jon Hanson and Douglas Kysar comment that:

> Each day, eighteen billion display ads appear in newspapers and magazines throughout the United States; each year fourteen billion shopping catalogues are mailed to consumers' homes. Inflation-adjusted per capita expenditures on advertising have increased eightfold since 1935. Even if these 'pervasive' advertising efforts do not artificially 'create' consumer needs, they almost certainly do much more than merely convey information about products that consumers already desire. (Hanson and Kysar, 1999: 1438)

Behavioural economics suggests that advertising is not merely information. Amos

Tversky, winner of the Nobel Prize for Economics for his work in behavioural economics, stated that the findings of behavioural economics would be well known to 'advertisers and used-car salesmen' (Tversky, quoted in Hanson and Kysar, 1999).

Galbraith's arguments have been challenged by many economists. They point out that very few wants are 'innate' and that many desires, for example, for artistic or cultural experience, are learnt, but that this does not mean that, since individuals do not have 'independently determined desires' for art or literature, the artistic process of production creates the wants (see, for example, Hayek, 1961). Milton Friedman also drew attention to the fact that many products (approximately 80 per cent of new products) fail to attract consumer patronage, notwithstanding expensive advertising campaigns. He comments that:

> [A]dvertising is a cost of doing business Surely it will be generally cheaper to sell them something that meets wants they already have than to create an artificial want. ... The real objection of most critics of advertising is not that advertising manipulates tastes but that the public at large has meretricious tastes—that is, tastes that do not agree with the critics. (Friedman, 1980: 266)

Galbraith's work probably stimulated economists to study taste formation and change (see Scitovsky, 1976; Marschak, 1978; and, for a statement of the traditional orthodoxy, Becker and Stigler, 1977: 76). Moreover, Galbraith's work can be related to the broader theme of the role of advertising in developing a culture of consumption (see above Chapter 1).

1.2 Commercial speech: a constitutional right to advertise?

Freedom of expression is regarded as part of the foundations of a democratic society, and in many jurisdictions state interference with this freedom is heavily circumscribed by constitutional protections. The Human Rights Act 1998 incorporates the European Convention on Human Rights into UK law and Article 10 of the Convention states:

> Article 10 Freedom of Expression
>
> 1. Everyone has the right to freedom of expression. This right shall include freedom to hold opinions and to receive and impart information and ideas without interference by public authority and regardless of frontiers. This Article shall not prevent States from requiring the licensing of broadcasting, television or cinema enterprises.
>
> 2. The exercise of these freedoms, since it carries with it duties and responsibilities, may be subject to such formalities, conditions, restrictions or penalties as are prescribed by law and are necessary in a democratic society, in the interests of national security, territorial integrity or public safety, for the prevention of disorder or crime, for the protection of health or morals, for the protection of the reputation or rights of others, for preventing the disclosure of information received in confidence, or for maintaining the authority and impartiality of the judiciary.

The justification for protection of freedom of expression has traditionally rested on three grounds: (i) the importance of free expression to intelligent self-government; (ii) the marketplace of ideas rationale; and (iii) freedom of expression as an aspect of individual autonomy, necessary to personal growth and self-fulfilment. The idea that 'commercial speech' should be protected is associated with the decision of the US Supreme Court in *Virginia State Board of Pharmacy et al v Virginia Citizens Consumer Council Inc et al* (1976). In this case, the Supreme Court struck down restrictions on the advertising of pharmaceutical prices by a state regulatory body. As you read the majority and dissenting opinions in the following extracts, consider how far the justices justify their positions in terms of the traditional arguments for freedom of expression.

Virginia State Board of Pharmacy et al v Virginia Citizens Consumer Council Inc et al (1976) 425 US 748

Mr Justice Blackmun: ... The question first arises whether, even assuming that First Amendment protection attaches to the flow of drug price information, it is a protection enjoyed by the appellees as recipients of the information, and not solely, if at all, by the advertisers themselves who seek to disseminate that information.

... Freedom of speech presupposes a willing speaker. But where a speaker exists, as is the case here, the protection afforded is to the communication, to its source and to its recipients both. ... Our question is whether speech which does 'no more than propose a commercial transaction' ... is so removed from any 'exposition of ideas' ... that it lacks all protection. Our answer is that it is not.

... Focusing first on the individual parties to the transaction that is proposed in the commercial advertisement, we may assume that the advertiser's interest is a purely economic one. That hardly disqualifies him from protection under the First Amendment. ...

As to the particular consumer's interest in the free flow of commercial information, that interest may be as keen, if not keener by far, than his interest in the day's most urgent political debate. Appellees' case in this respect is a convincing one. Those whom the suppression of prescription drug price information hits the hardest are the poor, the sick, and particularly the aged. A disproportionate amount of their income tends to be spent on prescription drugs; yet they are the least able to learn, by shopping from pharmacist to pharmacist, where their scarce dollars are best spent. ...

Generalizing, society also may have a strong interest in the free flow of commercial information. Even an individual advertisement, though entirely 'commercial' may be of general public interest. ...

Obviously, not all commercial messages contain the same or even a very great public interest element. There are few to which such an element, however, could not be added. ...

Moreover, there is another consideration that suggests no line between publicly 'interesting' or 'important' commercial advertising and the opposite kind could ever be drawn. Advertising, however tasteless and excessive it sometimes may seem, is nonetheless dissemination of information as to who is producing and selling what product, for what reason and at what price. So long as we preserve a predominantly free enterprise economy, the allocation of our resources in large measure will be made through numerous' private economic decisions. It is a matter of public interest that those decisions, in the aggregate, be intelligent and well informed. To this end, the free flow of commercial information is indispensable. ...

... And if it is indispensable to the proper allocation of resources in a free enterprise system, it is also indispensable to the formation of intelligent opinions as to how that system ought to be regulated or altered. Therefore, even if the First Amendment were thought to be primarily an instrument to enlighten public decision making in a democracy, we could not say that the free flow of information does not serve that goal. ...

[MR JUSTICE REHNQUIST, dissenting] The logical consequences of the Court's decision in this case, a decision which elevates commercial intercourse between a seller hawking his wares and a buyer seeking to strike a bargain to the same plane as has been previously reserved for the free marketplace of ideas, are far reaching indeed. …

The Court insists that the rule it lays down is consistent even with the view that the First Amendment is 'primarily an instrument to enlighten public decisionmaking in a democracy.'

I had understood this view to relate to public decisionmaking as to political, social, and other public issues, rather than the decision of a particular individual as to whether to purchase one or another kind of shampoo. It is undoubtedly arguable that many people in the country regard the choice of shampoo as just as important as who may be elected to local state, or national political office, but that does not automatically bring information about competing shampoos within the protection of the First Amendment. It is one thing to say that the line between strictly ideological and political commentaries and other kinds of commentary is difficult to draw, and that the mere fact that the former may have in it an element of commercialism does not strip it of First Amendment protection . . . But it is another thing to say that because that line is difficult to draw, we will stand at the other end of the spectrum and reject out of hand the observation of so dedicated a champion of the First Amendment as Mr. Justice Black that the protections of the Amendment do not apply to a '"merchant" who goes from door to door "selling pots".'

Although the category of commercial speech has not been extensively discussed in English law (see Munro, 2003: 134), the issue of commercial speech is increasingly raised in regulation of advertising in Europe (Randall, 2006: 530) and we note below challenges to ASA adjudications on this ground (see also challenge to tobacco regulations in the UK (*British American Tobacco UK Ltd, R (on the application of) v Secretary of State for Health* (2004)). The European Court of Human Rights has indicated that Article 10 ECHR applies to advertising (see, for example, *Casado Coca* (1994) 18 EHRR 1, which addressed restrictions on advertising by lawyers in Spain) noting that any restrictions on truthful advertising must 'be closely scrutinized'. In the *British American Tobacco* litigation, in which the tobacco companies challenged regulations limiting advertising at point of sale as being overbroad, the court applied the test of whether the restrictions were necessary in a democratic society—ie they responded to a pressing social need and were proportionate to the legitimate aim pursued by the legislation.

The court noted that commercial speech was further from the core values of freedom of expression than other forms of speech, that important public health issues were at stake and that:

there are areas where the courts must be wary of imposing its own value judgments on a legislative scheme. The protection of health is a far-reaching social policy. The right to commercial free speech while less fundamental than political or artistic speech, is protected by the Convention and restrictions must be justified. However, it will be principally for the decision maker to resolve how best the aim can be achieved by restricting promotion of extremely harmful but historically lawful products.

Determining proportionality may raise difficult questions of expert evidence, requiring the government to have a coherent rationale for adopting the particular strategy.

The following extract is the report of the Advocate General in the tobacco litigation where Germany challenged the competence of the EU to ban all forms of tobacco sponsorship and advertising (*Germany v European Parliament*, Case C-376/98 2000). Although it was not necessary to address the commercial speech issue because the European Court of Justice held that the EU had exceeded its competence, the opinion of the Advocate General provides a useful guide to the interpretation of Article 10(2) of the European Convention on Human Rights.

Joined opinion of Mr Advocate General Fennelly, *Federal Republic of Germany v European Parliament and Council of the European Union*, (2000) Directive 98/43/EC

(vi) Freedom of expression ...

153. The case-law of the European Court of Human Rights indicates that all forms of expression merit protection by virtue of Article 10(1) of the Convention. This includes what is commonly known as commercial expression, that is, the provision of information, expression of ideas or communication of images as part of the promotion of a commercial activity and the concomitant right to receive such communications.

154. Commercial expression should also be protected in Community law. Commercial expression does not contribute in the same way as political, journalistic, literary or artistic expression do, in a liberal democratic society, to the achievement of social goods such as, for example, the enhancement of democratic debate and accountability or the questioning of current orthodoxies with a view to furthering tolerance or change. However, in my view, personal rights are recognised as being fundamental in character, not merely because of their instrumental, social functions, but also because they are necessary for the autonomy, dignity and personal development of individuals. Thus, individuals' freedom to promote commercial activities derives not only from their right to engage in economic activities and the general commitment, in the Community context, to a market economy based upon free competition, but also from their inherent entitlement as human beings freely to express and receive views on any topic, including the merits of the goods or services which they market or purchase.

155. On the other hand, it is clear that the exercise of freedom of expression, like that of other rights and freedoms,may be subject to proportionate restrictions in order to secure the enjoyment of rights by others or the achievement of certain objectives in the common good. The protection of health is one of the grounds on which Article 10(2) of the European Convention on Human Rights permits the imposition of restrictions on freedom of expression.

156. None the less, given the fundamental character of freedom of expression, the public interest in limiting its exercise in specified circumstances or for specified purposes must be demonstrated by the public authority which proposes or enacts such a limitation. In particular, it must show compliance with the three-part test of proportionality. The Court set out the following three-part test of proportionality in BSE:

> [T]he principle of proportionality ... requires that measures adopted by Community institutions do not exceed the limits of what is appropriate and necessary in order to attain the objectives legitimately pursued by the legislation in question; when there is a choice between several appropriate measures recourse must be had to the least onerous, and the disadvantages caused must not be disproportionate to the aims pursued.

The case made for the Advertising Directive is that consumption of tobacco products is dangerous for the health of smokers, that advertising and sponsorship promote such consumption and that the comprehensive prohibition of those forms of expression will result in a reduction in tobacco consumption and, thus, improved public health. The damage caused to health by smoking has not been disputed in the present cases and Germany underlined its own desire to reduce consumption. There has, however, been considerable debate over whether the prohibition of most forms of promotion of tobacco products will achieve its aim of reduction in consumption of tobacco, rather than simply affecting competition between tobacco brands.

158. The European Court of Human Rights normally requires that Contracting Parties present convincing evidence of a pressing social need for a restriction on expression. That Court has apparently adopted a different approach in the case of commercial expression: limits thereon are acceptable where the competent authorities, on reasonable grounds, had considered the restrictions to be necessary. Such a difference in treatment is justified, in my view, because of the different manner in which commercial expression and, for example, political expression interact with more general public interests.

159. I would advocate, therefore, that a similar approach be adopted in the Community legal order. Where it is established that a Community measure restricts freedom of commercial expression, as the Advertising Directive clearly does, the Community legislator should also be obliged to satisfy the Court that it had reasonable grounds for adopting the measure in question in the public interest. In concrete terms, it should supply coherent evidence that the measure will be effective in achieving the public interest objective invoked—in these cases, a reduction in tobacco consumption relative to the level which would otherwise have obtained—and that less restrictive measures would not have been equally effective.

160. The evidence required to justify a restriction will depend on the nature of the claim made. We are here largely concerned with the objective assessment of the likely effects of the Advertising Directive. The legislator should not enjoy as wide a margin of appreciation as in the case, for example, of the protection of morals. However, the Community should not be prevented from acting in the public interest simply because justification of its action necessarily depends, not on hard scientific studies, but on evidence of a social scientific character, which predicts, on the basis of past behaviour, the future responses of consumers to changes in their level of exposure to promotional material. Furthermore, where the Community legislator can show that it acted upon the basis of reputable specialist studies in the field, the fact that other apparently reputable studies have reached a contrary conclusion does not, in itself, show that the legislator did not have reasonable grounds for acting.

161. Evidentiary requirements may be less strict where public health is at stake. The Court stated in BSE that [w]here there is uncertainty as to the existence or extent of risks to human health, the institutions may take protective measures without having to wait until the reality and seriousness of those risks become fully apparent. However, the present cases do not concern a prohibition of the marketing of tobacco products themselves, whose harmful effects on health have not been disputed, but rather a comprehensive ban on promotion of such products. The scientific debate at issue relates to the effects of such promotion on overall consumption levels (as opposed to the mere choice of brands by existing smokers), which is at one remove from the assessment of the health risks actually posed by such consumption. Furthermore, the ban at issue in BSE was temporary in nature and was subject to review after a further examination of the situation. Differences of opinion regarding the effect of tobacco advertising are of long standing and are unlikely to be resolved quickly. The standard proposed in the immediately preceding paragraph makes allowance for the lack of unanimity in scientific circles; it would, in my view, be insufficiently respectful of freedom of expression to go beyond that and to permit the legislator to restrict the exercise of that right

without any clear evidence that such a restriction is likely to result in changes in behaviour which, in turn, were likely to benefit public health.

164. As regards the requirement that restrictions imposed be no more burdensome than necessary, I would accept the point that a nearly total ban on advertising an economic activity is a particularly grave intrusion on the exercise of the right of free expression. The more restrictive the effects, the greater is the onus on the legislator to show that a less burdensome measure would not have sufficed. However, I conclude that the legislator has discharged that onus in the present cases, by demonstrating that it had reasonable grounds to consider that limited restrictions on tobacco promotion are ineffective. The fact that other, positive measures, such as information campaigns, might also have an effect does not in itself show a comprehensive advertising ban to be over-restrictive, as (subject to the division of competence between the Community and the Member States) one option does not exclude the other and there is no evidence that their effects entirely overlap.

165. I now turn to the third stage of analysis, regarding whether or not the Advertising Directive imposes restrictions on freedom of commercial expression which are disproportionate having regard to the public interest gains envisaged, no matter how efficiently pursued. Given the massive role of tobacco consumption as a mortality factor and as a cause of grievous health problems in the Community, I consider that a potential reduction in consumption levels of 6.9% would be a significant gain for public health, probably corresponding to the saving of thousands of lives.

166. I would take the view that, in principle, where the requirements of effectiveness and minimal necessary burden are satisfied, rights such as freedom of commercial expression are not unacceptably impaired by a ban on the promotion of dangerous products, where exchanges of scientific and other information and of political views about the regulation of the trade in question remain unrestricted. Tobacco producers remain free to market their products, to which the expression rights invoked ultimately relate, and may even engage in point of sale advertising if national rules permit this.

167. The fact that the Advertising Directive prohibits the promotion of products which are lawfully marketed in the Community is not conclusive, although it is not irrelevant either. The European Court of Human Rights observed in Open Door Counselling v Ireland that the contested national rules required careful scrutiny because the prohibited information in that case related to an activity which was lawful in the place it was performed, implying that the supply of information about lawful activities may be justifiably restricted in some circumstances. I suggest that the Court take judicial notice of the enforcement and other problems which could attend on banning outright an addictive activity such as smoking (as well as the restriction of the personal freedom of smokers that this would entail). The lawfulness of an activity (and the impracticability of prohibiting it) does not, therefore, imply that it is without deleterious effects which the legislator may seek to control in the public interest. Moreover, it is not necessarily consistent with the requirement that the least restrictive means be used to achieve legitimate objectives to require that an activity itself be banned in order to permit restrictions to be placed on its promotion.

I conclude, therefore, that the Advertising Directive does not constitute a disproportionate restriction on freedom of expression in so far as it imposes a comprehensive prohibition on the advertising of tobacco products.

176. I do not, however, take the same view regarding the prohibition of the advertising of diversification products. It is by no means self-evident that the advertising of non-tobacco goods and services which bear brands or other distinguishing features associated with tobacco products has an effect on consumption levels of the latter products, taken as

a whole. No evidence has been presented on behalf of the Community legislator to suggest that such a link exists. In these circumstances, I conclude that it has not discharged the onus of showing that it had reasonable grounds to adopt the restrictions on such advertising contained in Article 3(3)(b) of the Directive and that that provision should be annulled.

Roger Shiner, after reviewing European decisions on commercial speech, concludes that where the speech is primarily commercial as with product advertising the courts have 'invariably upheld the restriction on advertising as justified under Article 10'. The courts 'have not shown the kind of willingness to tinker, enthusiasm for tinkering even, with government restrictions on advertising displayed by courts in Canada and the United States' (Shiner, 2003: 107). The rise of commercial speech coincides with the dominance of neo-liberalism. Should we view the distinct US and European approaches as representing different ideologies about the role of the state and the market?

Commercial speech was developed in the US as a pro-consumer measure in *Virginia Pharmacy* by striking down controls on advertising of prices of pharmaceuticals. The US Supreme Court stressed the importance of 'listener's rights to information'. An expansive interpretation of this right could be used to require greater disclosures by corporations.

---

2. The common law ground rules

Consumer law norms are sometimes constructed as an exception to the common law, a special form of law designed for the protection of consumers. The common law, it is argued, also represents a more *laissez-faire* approach to contract than civilian systems. Judges sometimes adopt this position. In *OFT v Purely Creative Industries* Briggs J indicated that 'The starting point under English common law in relation to pre-contractual negotiations is *caveat emptor*' (paragraph 73). But is this true? Hugh Collins, for example, argues that, taking together a variety of doctrines, there is a general principle in English law to take care in negotiation. Consumer law is merely an example of this phenomenon. Consider in this context Article 28 of the Proposal for a Regulation of the European Parliament and of the Council on a Common European Sales Law (COM(2011) 635 final)

> A party who supplies information before or at the time a contract is concluded ... has a duty to take reasonable care to ensure that the information supplied is correct and not misleading

This section focuses on the question of when statements of value or opinion—often the stock in trade of marketing and advertising—will be regarded as constituting actionable misrepresentations or terms rather than 'mere puffs'. This is considered in relation to the general liability for manufacturers' advertising. In addition, the general desirability of private regulation of advertising by competitors' actions is briefly canvassed.

Two reasons suggest the value of considering private law doctrines in this area. First, the relevant theories of recovery, and standards of deception, reflect value judgements as to the respective responsibilities of producers (manufacturers, retailers) and consumers for the collection and provision of accurate market information. It is valuable not only to understand these judgements but also to compare them with those that underlie statutory (CPUT regulations) and self-regulatory standards (Advertising Standards Authority). Second, the focus on private law responses to manufacturers' advertising permits an evaluation of the extent to which judicial doctrines have been modified to reflect the market structure of the consumer economy—to reflect the importance therein of manufacturers' advertising and the relative dominance of manufacturers in several sectors.

2.1 Puffing and its limits

The law has historically drawn a distinction between the 'mere puff' for which there is no liability and statements making factual claims which might give rise to liability if they are false and misleading. The modern rationales for the puffing doctrine are that no reasonable person would take puffs seriously and they are too vague and subjective to represent any factual product claim. With characteristic confidence Mr Justice Holmes stated in 1889 that:

> It is settled that the law does not exact good faith from a seller in those vague commendations of his wares which manifestly are open to difference of opinion,—which do not imply untrue assertions concerning matters of direct observation ... and as to which it always has been understood, the world over, that such statements are to be distrusted. (*Deming v Darling* 20 NE 107 (1889))

And Justice Learned Hand commented that:

> There are some kinds of talk which no sensible man takes seriously, and if he does he suffers from his own credulity. If we were all scrupulously honest it would not be so; but, as it is, neither party usually believes what the seller says about his own opinions and each knows it. (*Vulcan Metals Co v Simmons Mfg Co* 248 F 853 (2d cir 1918) 856)

Jacobs J comments in *British Airways plc v Ryanair* (2000) that:

> It is of course the case that the average consumer has been exposed from birth to advertising. People get case hardened by it. They expect hyperbole and puff. One can almost say no advertisement is complete without them.

The puffing defence is recognised in the EU Unfair Commercial Practices Directive (UCPD) in relation to the protection of 'vulnerable' consumers against unfair commercial practices.

> Commercial practices which are likely to materially distort the economic behaviour only of a clearly identifiable group of consumers who are particularly vulnerable to the practice or the underlying product because of their mental or physical infirmity, age or credulity in a way which the trader could reasonably be expected to foresee, shall be assessed from the perspective of the average member of that group. This is without prejudice to the common and legitimate advertising practice of making exaggerated statements or statements which are not meant to be taken literally.

A common example of a claim that no one takes seriously is that a Vienna roll comes from Vienna or a Danish pastry from Denmark. However, the issue of puffing may raise more complex questions. Consider the following report of a US case:

> In May, Michigan Court of Appeals affirmed a lower court decision dismissing Richard Overton's $10,000 lawsuit against Anheuser Busch for false advertising. Overton said he suffered physical and mental injury and emotional distress because the implicit promises in the company's advertisements, especially of success with women, did not come true for him when he drank their product, and that besides that he sometimes got sick when he drank. (*Toronto Star*, 23 July 1994)

Mr Overton's suit is not another apocryphal example of the supposed US litigation explosion (the full report of this case is *Overton v Anheuser Busch* 517 NW 2d 308 (1994)). He had claimed that television advertising for the beer Bud Light misled the public because they were based on fantasies coming to life, 'fantasies involving tropical settings, and beautiful women and men engaged in unrestricted merriment'. One might initially conclude, as did the court, that these claims are merely sales puffs. No one would believe the literal truth of these advertisements. Susan Bordo comments that 'any fool knows that advertisers manipulate reality in the service of selling their product' (Bordo, 1993: 104). But she continues 'I agree that on some level we "know" [that the advertisements are just images].' However, Bordo recognises that we may still 'buy in' to the images and the relationships portrayed in the images even though we are aware that they are just images. Returning to Mr Overton's case, advertisements for beer are not just selling beer, but images of men, women and social relationships. The product is an appendage to these images so that the puff or image is the core of the advertisement. Research has suggested that 'harmless puffery' may have a significant impact on buying decisions (Preston, 1975; Oliver, 1979).

Avner Offer comments that 'puffs, like anchoring, are effective even when known to be untrue. What else could account for their widespread use? Hence the legal attitude is misconceived; it applies the test of reason to claims that are designed to bypass the filter of reason' (Offer, 2006: 109; see also Hoffman, 2006). If we accept the criticism that the existing legal attitude is misconceived, then how should the law develop? Should it attempt to draw on social science—eg the findings of behavioural economics and other disciplines—in determining the effects of advertising? Are judges likely to be in a good position to assess when puffs are harmful and what would be the remedies? Trzaskowski argues that studies suggest that claims that products are 'the best in the world' do have an influence on consumers and could be argued to be 'aggressive' commercial practices (Trzaskowski, 2011: 388).

Does the material on the power of advertising images and behavioural economics suggest that the legal dichotomy of the rational and credulous consumer is a meaningful distinction? To the extent that the law is an important form of discourse in society, does it contribute to images of the consumer as a generally rational actor by sustaining the puffing doctrine?

There are clearly conflicting visions of advertising as information and advertising as manipulation. A neo-classical economic perspective would suggest that the courts ought to assess liability for manufacturers' advertising in terms of the adequacy of information in the market and the costs to consumers of checking the reliability of advertising. This could provide a guide for applying the 'average consumer' test to different product markets. Since an advertisement concerning the performance qualities of a complex product might be difficult for a consumer to check or test, it might be assumed for the purpose of assessing such liability that a manufacturer has substantiation for a claim that, for example, a car is 'reliable', and that a consumer is justified in relying on this information. The reason for not including the technical details in the advertisements would be the high cost of communicating such information in a comprehensible manner. On the other hand, against vague claims for low-priced products with no hidden costs (eg chocolate bars or razor blades), which may often be of the 'try me' type, consumer experience may be a sufficient protection (Nelson, 1974; Grady, 1981: 222). To some extent this approach is adopted in the EU Commission guidance on the 'average consumer' (see below 171).

2.2 Theories of recovery for manufacturers' advertising claims

A user's or purchaser's ability to recover against a manufacturer is constrained by the doctrine of privity of contract, which prevents a direct contractual action by a purchaser against a manufacturer. This means that there are two principal theories of recovery: (i) the collateral contract; and (ii) negligent misrepresentation at common law and under the Misrepresentation Act 1967. A leading consumer case which anticipates the collateral contract theory is *Carlill v Carbolic Smoke Ball Co* where the defendant manufacturer had offered £100 to anyone who contracted influenza after using the smoke ball as directed. The advertisement indicated that £1,000 had been deposited with a bank to indicate the sincerity of the promise. Mrs Carlill contracted influenza after using the smoke ball and sued for £100. In relation to the argument that no one would take the promise seriously, Bowen LJ commented:

Carlill v Carbolic Smoke Ball Co [1893] 1 QB 256

Bowen LJ: In order to arrive at a right conclusion we must read this advertisement in its plain meaning, as the public would understand it. It was intended to be issued to the public and to be read by the public. How would an ordinary person reading this document construe it? It was intended unquestionably to have some effect and I think that the effect which it was intended to have, was to make people use the smoke ball. … It did not follow that the smoke ball was to be purchased from the defendants directly, or even from agents of theirs directly. The intention was that the circulation of the smoke ball should be promoted and that the use of it should be increased. …

But it was said there was no check on the part of the persons who issued the advertisement, and that it would be an insensate thing to promise £100 to a person who used the smoke ball unless you could check or superintend his manner of using it. The answer to that argument seems to me to be that if a person chooses to make extravagant promises of this kind he probably does so because it pays him to make them, and if he has made them, the extravagance of the promises is no reason in law why he should not be bound by them. …

[The advertisement] is an offer to become liable to anyone who, before it is retracted, performs the condition, and although the offer is made to the world, the contract is made with that limited portion of the public who come forward and perform the condition on the faith of the advertisement.

English courts have been unwilling to hold manufacturers liable to ultimate purchasers or consumers based on a collateral contract (or unilateral contract) theory outlined by Bowen in *Carlill*. Although the courts have been willing to cut down 'opinion immunity' in relation to marketing statements made personally to a potential purchaser (see eg *Andrews v Hopkinson* (1957)) there has been a reluctance to extend liability to general advertising statements made by producers or manufacturers. In contrast, many US cases have recognised actions against manufacturers based on an express warranty theory of liability (see eg *Baxter v Ford Motor Co* and discussion by Trebilcock (1972: 3–4, 6–10; see cases in Miller and Goldberg, 2004: 47). The policy arguments underlying the US cases is articulated in the following extract where the defendants were held liable for misleading advertising concerning the shrink-proof nature of their fabric.

Randy Knitwear Inc v American Cyanamid Co (1962) 181 NE 2d 399, Court of Appeals of New York

> The world of merchandising is, in brief, no longer a world of direct contract; it is, rather, a world of advertising and, when representations expressed and disseminated in the mass communications media and on labels (attached to the goods themselves) prove false and the user or consumer is damaged by reason of his reliance on those representations, it is difficult to justify the manufacturer's denial of liability on the sole ground of the absence of technical privity. Manufacturers make extensive use of newspapers, periodicals and other media to call attention, in glowing terms, to the qualities and virtues of their products, and this advertising is directed at the ultimate consumer or at some manufacturer or supplier who is not in privity with them. Equally sanguine representations on packages and labels frequently accompany the article throughout its journey to the ultimate consumer and, as intended, are relied upon by remote purchasers. Under these circumstances, it is highly unrealistic to limit a purchaser's protection to warranties made directly to him by his immediate seller. The protection he really needs is against the manufacturer whose published representations caused him to make the purchase.
>
> The manufacturer places his product upon the market and, by advertising and labeling it, represents its quality to the public in such a way as to induce reliance upon his representations. He unquestionably intends and expects that the product will be purchased and used in reliance upon his express assurance of its quality and, in fact, it is so purchased and used. Having invited and solicited the use, the manufacturer should not be permitted to avoid responsibility, when the expected use leads to injury and loss, by claiming that he made no contract directly with the user.

The distinction between an actionable representation and a collateral contract or binding promise is often difficult to draw in English law as is the underlying distinction in these actions between statements of present fact, opinion and future intention. Underlying the distinctions is the concept of reasonable reliance (Chitty, 2004: 434), but English courts have shown a marked reluctance to regard the consumer as acting in reasonable reliance upon advertising by a manufacturer. To admit that consumers act in reliance upon manufacturers' advertising might be a prelude to a general recognition of direct action in negligence by consumers against manufacturers for economic loss, which is currently not possible in England.

The reluctance to impose liability on manufacturers for advertising statements was reflected in *Lambert v Lewis* (1981). In this complex product-liability case, the supplier of a defectively designed Land Rover coupling attempted to pass liability for damage caused by it to the coupling's manufacturer. Since the suppliers were not in contractual relations with the manufacturer, they relied on collateral warranty and common law negligent misrepresentation as theories of recovery. The facts disclosed that the manufacturer, which had a generally good reputation for quality and safety, had stated specifically in its advertising to the trade and public that the coupling required 'no maintenance', was 'foolproof' and 'locked positively and automatically' with 'no metallic springs to break or rust'. The suppliers argued that these claims were clearly intended to be taken seriously, that they had relied upon them and that consequently they constituted either collateral warranties or negligent misrepresentations. The Court of Appeal, however, rejected both these arguments.

Lambert v Lewis (1981) 2 WLR 713

STEPHENSON LJ ... Turner relied before the, judge, and also before us, on the evidence of Mr Dixon-Bate himself that the manufacturers intended these claims to be taken seriously and on the decisions of this court in *Carlill v Carbolic Smoke Ball Co* [1893] I QB 256 and of McNair J in *Shanklin Pier Ltd v Detel Products Ltd* [1951] 2 KB 854.

We accept Mr Turner's submission that not much is needed to conclude that when a warranty of suitability for a particular purpose is expressed or implied in a contract of sale that warranty has been relied on by the purchaser: *Hardwick Game Farm v Suffolk Agricultural Poultry Producers Association* [1969] 2 AC 3 I, *per* Lord Reid at p 84 and per Lord Pearce at p 115; *Christopher Hill Ltd v Ashington Piggeries Ltd* [1972] AC 441, 495, *per* Lord Wilberforce. But the difficulty is to show that what the manufacturers stated in the literature advertising and accompanying their products as to their safety and suitability was intended to be a contractual warranty or binding promise. It is one thing to express or imply it in a contract of sale, another to treat it as expressed or implied as a contract, or a term of a contract, collateral to a contract of sale. There may be cases where the purchase from an intermediate seller may be regarded as fortuitous and the original supplier or seller can properly be held liable for breaches of warranty given by the intermediate seller as well as for those given by him: *Wells (Merstham) Ltd v Buckland Sand and Silica Ltd* [1965] 2 QB 170. But that is not, in our judgment, this case.

... *Carlill v Carbolic Smoke Ball Co* [1893] I QB 256 ... is no authority for holding that the manufacturers were saying to the retailers: 'If you acquire our product we promise it is safe and merchantable and if it is not we will pay you such damages as the law requires.'

[W]hether the statement is oral or written, made contemporaneously with the contract or earlier, the question is whether it is intended to be binding. ... The construction of these documents in the circumstances of this case leads us to the same conclusion as the judge at p 94, that the claims in them 'were not intended to be, nor were they acted upon as being express warranties, and' (though this further finding, if it adds anything, is not strictly necessary) 'the retailers did not purchase the coupling in reliance on such warranties.'

Nor do we think that the development of the law in the *Shanklin Pier Ltd v Detel Products Ltd* [1951] 2 KB 854—and it may be in the unreported case of *Independent Broadcasting Authority v EMI Electronics Ltd*, Court of Appeal (Civil Division) Transcript No 670 of 1978—helps the retailers to a different result. The effect and ratio of the former decision are correctly stated by the judge in these terms [1979] RTR 61, 93:

'In that case the defendant paint company made certain express representations as to the quality of its paint and its suitability for use on the plaintiffs' pier which was then to be repaired by contractors. On the strength of that representation the plaintiffs caused the specification for their works to be carried out by contractors to be amended by substituting the defendants' paint for that previously specified. The contractors bought and used the paint, which was unsatisfactory and unsuitable for use on the pier. It was held that the plaintiff company could recover damages on the warranty from the defendant paint company despite the fact that there was no contract other than a collateral one between the plaintiff pier company and the defendant paint company. In my judgment the basis of this decision was that consideration for the representation was the procurement by the plaintiffs of a contract sale by their contractors with the defendants.'

There the express representation was clearly an express warranty, for which the consideration was the procurement of a particular contract, as the judge pointed out; but here was no warranty and we find it unnecessary to consider whether that decision could be extended to the contract of purchase made by the retailers, or the contract of resale made by them, and to hold that in consideration of either of those contracts, both in fact unknown to the manufacturers, they are promising or warranting, either expressly or by implication, that their claims for their hitch are true, and they are prepared to stand by their warranties and pay the retailers and any other distributors in their position damages for breach of them—as long (Mr Turner was constrained to add) as the user of the hitch is reasonable.

The judge went on to hold that this finding that the manufacturers' claims were not warranted precluded the retailers from recovering damages from the manufacturers in tort for negligent misrepresentation. The basis of his finding against Mr Turner's second submission was that the House of Lords in *Hedley Byrne & Co Ltd v Heller & Partners Ltd* [1964] AC 465 had 'limited the ambit of those entitled to sue in respect of negligent mis-statement to the person to whom'—we add the words 'the answer to'—'the inquiry was directed and for the purposes for which the inquiry was made': see [1979] RTR 61, 94. And the judge appears to have held that even if the ambit could have been extended to the retailers they would be defeated by the fact that they did not rely on the manufacturers' mis-statements.

Mr Turner does not dispute that a special relationship is necessary between the maker of the mis-statement and the person who suffers damage by acting on it before the former can be liable for the damage to the latter on the Hedley Byrne principle. He concedes also that it is easier to prove that relationship and the consequent duty of care if the information or advice contained in the statement is asked for. But he submits that if the statement is made seriously, not casually, and is intended to be acted upon and is in fact acted upon and it is negligent, it is actionable at the suit of him who acts upon it notwithstanding the maker has forestalled an inquiry for the information or advice it contains by volunteering the one or the other.

This may sometimes be so. ... But we cannot regard the manufacturer and supplier of an article as putting himself into a special relationship with every distributor who obtains his product and reads what he says or prints about it and so owing him a duty to take reasonable care to give him true information or good advice.

While the rejection of negligent misrepresentation as a ground of recovery is con-sistent with the later case of *Caparo Industries v Dickson* (1990), the arguments and assumptions made here by Stephenson LJ have been criticised by several writers (see Atiyah, 1983: 429; Borrie, 1984: 31). Also, it contrasts with the approach taken by Lord Simon of Glaisdale in *Esso Petroleum Ltd v Commissioners of Customs and Excise* (1976), where he stated that 'it seems to me in general undesirable to allow a commercial promoter to claim that what he has done is a mere puff, not intended to create legal relations' (at 121–22).

Bowerman v ABTA (1995) concerned a school skiing holiday in 1991. The booking for the holiday was made with the tour operator by Mr Wallace, a teacher, on behalf of pupils from Nower School in Pinner, London. The tour operator became insolvent and ceased to trade. Since the operator was a member of ABTA the group was entitled to a refund under the ABTA compensation scheme. ABTA paid the refund except for £10. This represented holiday insurance premiums paid by the group. It was excluded from coverage by a statement of published ABTA policy that had not been seen by the teacher. The cost of the tour was £350. The action was brought by Wallace, described by Waite J as 'a seasoned organizer of school trips', as agent for Emma Bowerman, a schoolgirl who was a member of the ski party. The case was regarded as a test case in relation to other consumers who had booked with Adventure Express and other companies that had failed at about the same time.

All ABTA tour operators were required to display prominently the following notice in their offices:

THE ASSOCIATION OF BRITISH TRAVEL AGENTS LIMITED

Notice describing ABTA's scheme of protection against the financial failure of ABTA members

SCHEME OF PROTECTION

(1) To protect you their customers, all ABTA Tour Operators are required to provide bonds, guarantees or other securities to ABTA.*

(2) Similarly to protect you, some ABTA Travel Agents provide bonds to ABTA which in addition has an insurance indemnity scheme and fund known as the Travel Agents' Fund to supplement this protection.

(3) The Scheme of protection for customers is for your benefit in respect of holidays and other travel arrangements which are yet to commence or are in progress at the time of the financial failure of an ABTA Tour Operator or ABTA Travel Agent. If an ABTA member ceases to belong to ABTA and thereafter fails financially, ABTA still protects you if you made the booking before the time when ABTA membership ceased.

THE PROTECTION IS THAT

(4) When holidays or other travel arrangements are in progress at the time of the failure of an ABTA members, ABTA sees to arrange for you to continue with the booked arrangement as far as possible and ensures that if you are abroad you will be able to return to the United Kingdom.

(5) Where holidays or other travel arrangements have not yet commenced at the time of failure, ABTA arranges for you to be reimbursed the money you have paid in respect of your holidays arrangements. In some instances ABTA may however be able to arrange for the existing arrangements to proceed as planned or offer similar alternative arrangements.

LIMITATIONS

(6) Whilst the travel arrangements of some non-ABTA companies (eg scheduled airlines) may be booked through an ABTA Travel Agent, ABTA's protection scheme regrettably cannot cover the financial failure of these non-ABTA companies even if the booking was made through an ABTA agent.

(7) Where travel arrangements are not subject to protection, customers should consider taking out their own insurance against the risk of financial failure. Protection may however be provided by way of the bonds which some non-ABTA companies provide to other organisations.

(8) ABTA's financial protection does not apply where the claim is in respect of any

arrangement which has been completed, or contracts which have been terminated or broken at the time of the financial failure.

(9) Where credit cards have been used for payment the card company may be liable to reimburse customers.Where this is so ABTA may require you to claim against the card company before having recourse to ABTA's scheme of protection.

*In the case of travel arrangements covered by Air Travel Organiser Licences there is additionally protection against the financial failure of the ATOL holder available through the Air Travel Trust.

Bowerman v Association of British Travel Agents Ltd, **Court of Appeal Civil Division**, *The Times*, **24 November 1995**, *The Independent*, **23 November 1995**, **145 NLJ 1815**

Waite LJ: ...[I]t is common ground that the question of whether or not ABTA is liable to reimburse the £10 insurance ... rests upon the view that would be taken of ABTA's published statements by a hypothetical figure—namely the ordinary member of the public. For the purposes of this appeal there has only been one such statement to consider from that perspective.

Before analysing the detail in that Notice, it may be helpful to stand aside and look for a moment at the attributes which need to be given to the ordinary member of the public as he or she steps down from the Clapham omnibus, enters the Travel Agency in which the Notice is displayed, and reads it. Such a reader would be aware of the vulnerability of agents and operators in a highly competitive market where failures are not uncommon, and of the disappointment and financial loss which members of the public have experienced in the past as a result of sudden cancellations following financial collapse. The reader would appreciate, too, that ABTA is not a charity or a friendly society, but (as its full name makes clear) an association, for the purposes of trade, of persons and firms carrying on the business of travel agent. He or she would, further, be aware that it is in the interests of such an association to win business for its constituent members by inspiring public confidence. There should also be imputed to the reader common knowledge that those who wish to disclaim legal liability for public representations frequently say so—in large print or in small. Finally it is to be assumed that such a person would read the whole notice—neither cursorily nor with pedantic analysis of every nuance of its wording, but with the ordinary care to be expected of the average customer who is applying money they could not easily afford to lose in buying a holiday which it would be a serious disappointment to forego.

The central issue in this appeal is whether the ordinary member of the public, reading the Notice as a whole, would regard it as intended to create legal relations between ABTA and those who buy tours or holidays through its members. ...[T]he issue in this case arises from the equivocation resulting from the introduction of words capable of bearing a promissory or representational meaning into a varied textual context in which words of obligation appear side by side with words of lesser commitment.

In the end this case depends, as with so many questions involving construction of a document, upon impression—in this instance an impression gained by the court at one remove the eyes of the hypothetical member of the public. My own view is that the Notice—notwithstanding the bewildering miscellany it contains of information, promise, disclaimer and reassurance—would be understood by the ordinary member of the public as importing an intention to create legal relations with customers of ABTA members. The words that are crucial to the present case:

'Where holidays or other travel arrangements have not yet commenced at the time of failure, ABTA arranges for you to be reimbursed the money you have paid in respect of your holiday arrangements'

would in my judgment be understood by the ordinary reader as words of clear promise which do not lose their significance or their promissory character through being associated in the same context with words connoting a lesser degree of commitment.

...

I would allow the appeal and substitute for the order made by the judge a declaration in the terms prayed that ABTA is obliged to reimburse to the plaintiffs the cost of providing insurance cover for the lost holiday with Adventure Express.

Hobhouse LJ: Over one hundred years ago, in December 1892, this Court had to consider the appeal of the defendants in *Carlill v Carbolic Smoke Ball Company* [1893] 1 QB 256.

In the present case we have listened to arguments advanced on behalf of the Defendants, the Association of British Travel Agents Limited (ABTA), which echo in almost every respect those rejected by the Court of Appeal more than a century ago. The main question in the present case is whether those arguments have a greater validity in relation to the differently worded document which ABTA caused to be published and which Mr Wallace, the Second Plaintiff, read and relied on.

The members of ABTA are travel agents and tour operators. One of the features of this industry is that the agents and operators deal with members of the public, very often holiday makers, who pay money to travel agents and tour operators in advance in the faith of the various travel and holiday arrangements being fulfilled as booked. However, the nature of the business being as it is, there is always a risk that the agent or operator may get into financial difficulties or become insolvent. Such situations are both a matter of public concern and of very critical concern to those who are booking holidays and choosing the agent or operator through whom they should book. ABTA recognise this and have made it a cornerstone of the promotion of their members to publish how ABTA protects the travelling and holiday making public from these risks.

The position of Mr Wallace was summarised by the Judge (p 4):

'Mr Wallace by early 1990 had very considerable experience (over a period of some ten years), in booking holidays of this nature. The local authority for the area in which his school is situated is the London Borough of Harrow. That local authority required all overseas school trips which involved the reservation of accommodation to be booked through operators who were members of either ABTA or SAGTA. Furthermore, says Mr Wallace, parents will not agree to make funds available for such purposes unless the holiday is, as he put it, "ABTA backed". These attitudes are not surprising because ABTA have in recent years gone to very considerable lengths to publicise (and instill public confidence in) the fact of and the worth of their policy and practice in relation of members of the public who having booked and paid for a holiday with an ABTA member, face the prospect of losing their holiday by virtue of the financial failure of their tour operator.'

Mr Wallace's sources of information about the existence and the extent of what has become known as the 'ABTA promise' are primarily television holiday programmes and reading about the 'ABTA promise' in travel agents' premises. He emphasised that he had seen such a notice in certainly two such premises before making the booking with Adventure Express. This holiday was booked in 1990—not in a travel agents' premises but at the

Bracknell Ski Centre. Adventure Express had invited a number of teachers to that location in order to promote their own holidays. The Adventure Express representatives were not slow to point out that Adventure Express was an ABTA member and that in consequence, in the event of financial collapse, the money would be refunded or an alternative holiday would be provided. He negotiated a discount and made a firm booking.

It is under these circumstances that Mr Wallace and those for whom he was acting contend that they were entitled to rely upon the relevant document, that issued in 1988, as constituting a contractual offer which he was entitled contractually to accept by booking with, and paying his and their money to, an ABTA member, that is to say, to Adventure Express.

…Turning to the document itself, it is accepted that the words of Bowen LJ are apt:

> 'It was intended to be issued to the public and to be read by the public. How would an ordinary person reading this document construe it?'

The rival contentions … are whether the document is simply telling the public about a scheme which ABTA has for its own members or whether it goes further than this and contains an offer which a member of the public can take up and hold ABTA to should the ABTA member with whom the member of the public is dealing fail financially.

I prefer the latter view. I recognise that the document is headed 'Notice Describing ABTA's Scheme of Protection' and that in paras 4 and 5 the present tense is used—'ABTA seeks'— 'ABTA ensures'—'ABTA arranges'—and not the future tense—'ABTA will ensure' or 'ABTA will arrange'. These points undoubtedly support the view of the Judge and the Defendants' argument. But the document has to be read as a whole. It is clearly intended to have an effect on the reader and to lead him to believe that he is getting something of value. The scheme is an ABTA scheme in relation to its members but it is a scheme of protection of the customers of ABTA members. It emphasises that it is 'to protect you their customers' and is 'for your benefit'.

ABTA is offering to protect the reader of the notice, the prospective customer. It is an inevitable inference that what ABTA is saying is that it, ABTA, will do something for the customer if the member should fail financially.

What ABTA is to do is set out in the next section: 'THE PROTECTION IS THAT'. It is not a scheme which reduces the risk of financial failure or bolsters the finances of the member. It is a scheme whereby ABTA is going to step in if the member fails and deal directly with the customer. What ABTA is to do in that contingency is coherently stated. If the holiday is already in progress then ABTA seeks to arrange the continuation of the booked holiday or travel as far as possible. In my judgment the member of the public reading this document would understand, and this Court should hold, that ABTA is undertaking to use its best endeavours, free of further expense to the customer, to procure that the customer is able to enjoy the rest of the holiday for which he has booked. Similarly it says that 'ABTA ensures that if you are abroad you will be able to return to the United Kingdom'. This wording is unqualified and again, in my judgment, is to be understood as a promise that ABTA will see that the traveller is brought back to the United Kingdom. I wholly reject the submission made by counsel on behalf of ABTA that this simply amounted to making arrangements at the expense of the traveller; it is clearly an undertaking with a financial content.

…

In my judgment this document is intended to be read and would reasonably be read by a member of the public as containing an offer of a promise which the customer is entitled to accept by choosing to do business with an ABTA member. A member of the public would not analyse his situation in legal terms but he would clearly understand that this notice would only apply to him if he should choose to do business with an ABTA member and he would also understand that if he did do so he would be entitled to hold ABTA to what he understood ABTA to be promising in this document. In my judgment it satisfies the criteria for a unilateral contract and contains promises which are sufficiently clear to be capable of legal enforcement.

This conclusion also covers ABTA's further argument that it had no intention to create legal relations. The document as reasonably read by a member of the public would be taken to be an offer of a legally enforceable promise. Given that this is the effect of the document which ABTA has chosen to publish, it does not advance ABTA's case to say that ABTA privately did not intend to expose itself to any legal liability to the public. A contracting party cannot escape liability by saying that he had his fingers crossed behind his back.

… Like in the Carbolic Smoke Ball case, we have had urged on us the potential size of the obligations which ABTA would be accepting should a number of its members fail and the difficulty of meeting all the claims which might be made on ABTA. This was a matter for the judgment of ABTA before it chose to issue the notice. It is the job of ABTA and no concern of the customer to see that its bonding and mutual and external insurance arrangements suffice. The argument has no more merit than the equivalent argument which was advanced in the Carbolic Smoke Ball case.

The existence of consideration to support the contractual obligation of ABTA is clear. A picture was presented to us, wholly unrealistically, of ABTA as some benevolent body which gained no benefit from and had no interest in travellers choosing to deal with ABTA members. The function of ABTA is to promote its members. It was also argued that as Mr Wallace was required by the local Education Authority and by the children's parents to buy only ABTA backed holidays that meant that Mr Wallace and those on whose behalf he was acting gave no consideration because, so it was argued, Mr Wallace was already under an obligation to buy an ABTA backed holiday. Mr Wallace was under no obligation to buy any holiday at all nor were the parents. …[A]nybody who chooses to do business with them is certainly giving consideration to ABTA for any contract or 'collateral' contract which may ensue.

I therefore cannot agree with the judgment of Mr Justice Mitchell and consider that this appeal should be allowed. The Plaintiffs were entitled to and did accept the offer contained in the document issued by ABTA and it fills one with disquiet that any organisation in the position of ABTA should after the event, when it finds that its liabilities are greater than it had anticipated, seek to contend otherwise. As counsel pointed out, if ABTA had wished to deny that it was accepting any legal obligation to the traveller or wished to say that it was not making any promises, nothing would have been simpler than for it to have said so in the document. For obvious commercial reasons ABTA did not choose this course. To have included such words would have destroyed the value of the document in the eyes of the public and nullified the very effect which ABTA intended it to, and which it did, achieve—to induce the public to book with and entrust their money to ABTA members.

I would allow the appeal.

Gerard McMeel comments that:

Bowerman v ABTA is to be welcomed as confirming that the collateral contract device can confer direct rights upon consumers as against manufacturers, trade associations or related companies who offer inducements to the public to purchase goods and services from their retailers, members or associates. … Clearly issues of construction of the particular words will remain important. However, manufacturers' warranties and the like are very influential in people's market choices and should generally be a matter of obligation not discretion for those who issue them. (McMeel, 1997: 49)

Canadian jurisprudence has recognised private law actions against manufacturers based on brochures and advertising. See, for example, *Murray v Sperry Rand Corporation et al* (1979), *cf* the earlier pre-consumer era Australian case, *International Harvester Co of Australia Pty Ltd v Carrigan's Hazeldene Pastoral Co* (1958), where the plaintiff farmer failed to recover against the manufacturer. Other cases in Canada have held manufacturers directly liable to consumers based on guarantees in manufacturers' brochures (*Hallmark Pool Corpn v Storey* (1983)). In this case the Storeys had purchased a pool after seeing an advertisement in a magazine for a pool that stated:

HALLMARK FIBERGLASS POOLS

Beat the heat without bucking the crowd. A Hallmark Pool is easy to own, in any shape or size, with terms up to 7 years. Hallmark Pools always look new; you get a no-nonsense 15-year FIBERGLASS guarantee against chipping, cracking, peeling, mildew, rust, tearing apart. And installation is complete with all equipment and accessories. Have the best, a glamorous in-ground pool that's weatherproof, from 50 below in Canada to searing heat in the Southwest. No 1 Selling FIBERGLASS Pool in the World.

WRITE FOR FREE COLOR BROCHURE AND NAME OF YOUR NEAREST HALLMARK POOL BUILDER . . .

The Storeys were also provided with a brochure by the authorised builder for the pools. The following description of the brochure is from the judgment of Laforest J:

The inside of the brochure began with a large caption:

ENJOYMENT IS YOURS FOR A LIFETIME WITH A QUALITY HALLMARK FIBERGLASS FAMILY POOL

Under this caption, it was stated:

Protect your investment by building a pool that is beautiful, durable, easy to maintain, practical, functional and efficient. Have a quality pool built for you ... a Hallmark FIBERGLASS Pool. The pool with a proven record of performance gained from thousands of installations from 50 below zero in Canada to the searing desert heat of the Southwest. Build Hallmark, the lifetime pool, as in all probability you will build one pool in your lifetime. AVAILABLE IN ANY SIZE OR SHAPE.

There followed statements about the reinforced fibreglass construction, ease of maintenance ('A Hallmark FIBERGLASS Pool always looks new'), and special safety features; the pool, it added, was completely equipped, with no extras to buy. Then at the bottom of the page, under a heading that announced that the pool could be installed in a week or less, was the statement:

Because of the minimum time it takes to build a Hallmark Pool, your Hallmark Pool builder can offer quality, beauty and design at a price competitive to pools of inferior quality and construction materials.

On the back of the brochure, surrounded by a description and a picture of a family using the pool as a skating rink and by pictures of the covers of a number of national magazines where Hallmark advertisements could be found, was the information about the guarantee. Under the heading '15 year guarantee', it read as follows:

> Guaranteed durability … in writing for 15 years. Hallmark's amazing and generous 15 year FIBERGLASS Guarantee has made Hallmark one of the world's most acceptable pools. It is why Hallmark is a better investment!

Above this was an illustration or reproduction of a guarantee entitled '15 year guarantee'. It looked impressive with borders rather like Canada Savings Bonds and other security instruments. Mrs Storey read the material describing the guarantee, but she did not read the writing in the illustration of the guarantee. That was in exceedingly fine print. As she stated 'I couldn't read it … I haven't the eyesight to read something that small.'

The pool had many defects and ultimately was a write-off. The Storeys sued the dealer and builder but also sued Hallmark based on the 15-year guarantee. The New Brunswick Court of Appeal held Hallmark liable on a theory of collateral contract. Hallmark defended partly on the basis of a limitation of liability in the small print on the guarantee.

Hallmark Pools v Storey et al (1983) 144 DLR (3d) 56

New Brunswick Court of Appeal

La Forest JA: … I think the Storeys are entitled to recover on the basis of the representations and guarantee described in the advertisements and the brochure. That liability rests on a collateral contract created with Hallmark when the Storeys accepted its offer of guarantee by entering into the contract with Price.

Such an approach goes at least as far back as the well-known case of *Carlill v Carbolic Smoke Ball Co*, [1893] 1 QB 256 …

As in the Carbolic Smoke Ball case, supra, the representations in the present case were not of a kind the reasonable consumer shucks off as 'mere puff' or laudatory commendation. In both cases, the advertisers showed proof of their sincerity in the Smoke Ball case by stating that they had deposited £ 1,000 in a bank as security, and in the present case, by offering a 15-year durability guarantee. A guarantee can scarcely be considered mere puffery.

In some respects, the present case is stronger than the Smoke Ball case. In the latter case, the language was in several respects 'vague and uncertain' but the court found no difficulty in giving it a reasonable business construction. Here there is little difficulty in understanding what is meant by a 15-year durability guarantee when it is effectively alleged that pools built by Hallmark builders have a proven record of performance in 50° below zero temperature in Canada.

The present case is stronger in other ways. The advertisement in the Smoke Ball case was simply published in a newspaper. Here the original advertisement was followed by a brochure supplied directly by Hallmark through its authorized builder and discussed with Mrs Storey by the builder's representative in planning and negotiating for the sale of her pool. I am satisfied that Mr Price and his companies and Mr Evans had ostensible authority to act as agents for Hallmark vis-a-vis Mrs Storey during the negotiations even though the contract between Hallmark and Mr Price's companies defined the relationship of these companies to Hallmark as that of an independent contractor. But though it fortifies my view, this is not really necessary to the conclusion to which I have come. The simple fact is that Hallmark itself made the representations to Mrs. Storey in a manner and in accordance with an arrangement it had itself set up.

Were this all, I would have no difficulty under the circumstances in holding Hallmark liable to the Storeys under the guarantee described in the advertisements and the brochure. Its representation that a pool built by a Hallmark dealer carried a 15 year durability guarantee constituted an offer which was accepted by the Storeys when they entered into a contract with the Hallmark dealer to have a pool built. That offer and acceptance constituted a collateral contract consisting of the representations and guarantee described in Hallmark's literature.

[Commenting on Hallmark's defence] ... The essence of this argument is that Hallmark's guarantee was not the guarantee as it was understood by Mrs Storey from the words she read in the brochure, but as it appeared on the formal guarantee which was reproduced in fine print in the illustration in the brochure.

Like Mrs Storey, I was at first unable to read the words in the illustration of the guarantee in the brochure. However, with the aid of a magnifying glass and by comparing it with a copy of an original guarantee mercifully submitted in evidence by counsel for the defendants, I was able to make it out. ...

If these words govern the transaction, I am prepared to concede that the Storeys have no case. This document is a far cry from what the advertisement and the brochure would lead the ordinary person to believe was guaranteed. It hardly fits the description of a 'no-nonsense' guarantee; if the matter was not so serious I would have thought it was the reverse. It is not altogether inaccurate, I suppose, to speak of this alleged guarantee as 'amazing and generous'. Generous it is not, but it is amazing in how well it is made to appear to promise so much while offering so little.

... Should the Storeys have read the material in the illustration of the formal guarantee that appeared in the brochure and so be bound by its words? I do not think so. This is not the situation that arose in *L'Estrange v F Graucob, Ltd*, [1934] 2 KB 394. Here the illustration of the formal guarantee, apart from its heading, is not really legible for most people, and the unusual step of reading it with a magnifying glass is a procedure that is not to be expected.

...

The simple fact is that Hallmark presented a document to the Storeys from which the average person would reasonably conclude that a Hallmark pool installed by a Hallmark dealer would have guaranteed durability for 15 years under Canadian climatic conditions. The ordinary person, whether the reasonable man on the Clapham bus or the average housewife on Hanwell Rd, would not think of reading the small print in an illustration in a brochure with a magnifying glass. What the legible language in the brochure conveyed was that a Hallmark pool installed as described was guaranteed for 15 years. That was the obvious meaning intended by that language and Hallmark cannot complain if we give effect to that meaning. Only the most suspicious, whether by nature or by legal training, would think of reading the very fine print in what is essentially a picture like those of the skating rink and magazines that surround it.

... This case may impose some pressure on Hallmark and other corporations to be more forthright in setting forth the precise nature of their undertakings to consumers. I see nothing wrong with that. On this matter, I share the view of Haines J in *Ranger v Herbert A Watts (Quebec) Ltd et al* (1970), 10 DLR (3d) 395 at p 405, [1970] 2 OR 225; affirmed 20 DLR (3d) 650, [1971] 3 OR 450 (Ont CA), where he stated:

> To allow a producer to evade the fair implication of his advertising is to permit him to reap a rich harvest of profit without obligation to the purchaser. ... By extraordinary skill the printed and spoken word together with the accompanying art form and

drama have become an alluring and attractive means of representation of quality and confidence. Honesty in advertising is a concept worthy of reexamination.

I might add that had there been no contract between Hallmark and the Storeys, Hallmark might well have been liable in tort within the principle enunciated in *Hedley Byrne & Co Ltd v Heller & Partners Ltd*, [1964] AC 465. ... The appeal should be dismissed with costs, which I hereby fix at $625. There should also be interest on the $9,000 damages awarded at the rate of 12% from the date of the trial judge's judgment to the date hereof. Appeal dismissed.

The *Hallmark* case may be related to UK regulation of guarantees. Under the Sale and Supply of Goods to Consumers Regulations 2002, where goods are sold or otherwise supplied to consumers with a consumer guarantee, the guarantee takes effect as a contractual obligation owed by the guarantor 'under the conditions set out in the guarantee statement and the associated advertising' (regulation 15). The regulations also address issues of transparency that arose in *Hallmark*, requiring that guarantees be in plain, intelligible language (regulation 15(2)). A guarantee is defined as 'any undertaking to a consumer by a person acting in the course of his business, given without extra charge'. Oughton and Willett speculate that the reference to advertising may increase the potential for English court to expand liability of manufacturers (Oughton and Willett, 2002: 322). The use of guarantees to exclude liability for negligence is limited by sections 2(1) and 5 of UCTA (see further below Chapter 6).

It has been argued that an idea underlying theories of recovery in this area is that of 'reasonable reliance'—whether it was reasonable for the plaintiff to rely on the representor's statement rather than on her own judgement. This idea is reflected in Commonwealth and US statutes which require that for a statement to be a term it must have 'a natural tendency' to induce the buyer to make the purchase. Section 74G of the Australian Trade Practices Act 1974 recognises the possibility of an action by an ultimate purchaser or user against a manufacturer where it makes an 'undertaking, assertion or representation in relation' to characteristics of the goods 'the natural tendency of which is to induce persons to acquire the goods' (see also Saskatchewan Consumer Protection Act, section 45(1)). It is obviously necessary to ask when it is reasonable for a consumer or purchaser to rely on manufacturers' advertising. The answer might vary depending on the standard of intelligence expected of the average consumer, the vagueness of the product claims, the nature of the product, the costs of obtaining accurate information and the underlying value judgements concerning the extent to which individuals ought to protect themselves in the marketplace. The value of these broader formulations of the doctrine of express warranties for advertising statements is that they raise the possibility of instituting a class action against a manufacturer.

---

3. Unfair Commercial Practices Regulation

Regulation of unfairness in consumer markets is accomplished primarily through two methods: antitrust and commercial practices regulation. This part is concerned with the latter category—deceptive and unfair commercial practices regulation. There are several central questions in the regulation of unfair commercial practices. First, what are the overall objectives of regulation—addressing market failures, protecting the vulnerable, enforcing community values of fairness? Second, how should this be achieved—through general clauses, specific regulation of individual sectors or a combination of specific and general provisions? Third, what should be the institutional structure of enforcement of regulation? Should public regulation be the exclusive method of enforcement or should private rights play a significant role? What should be the primary level of enforcement—local, national or regional?

Unfairness may occur in the formation, performance or enforcement of consumer transactions. Examples include deceptive and unfair advertising, high-pressure sales techniques, the use of unfair exclusion clauses in contracts, unfair debt-collection practices and the oppressive enforcement of contractual terms. The focus of consumer law regulation of these areas in the UK is on the protection of the consumer against unfair trade practices. This is also true of many Commonwealth statutes (eg the Australian Trade Practices Act, Canadian provincial Acts) which may provide higher levels of protection than the common law of misrepresentation and also sanction unconscionable acts and representations.

A different perspective on unfair trade practices is provided by the concept of 'unfair competition' where the focus is on practices that might damage competitors as well as consumers. Public regulation to protect consumers against, for example, false and misleading advertising has often originated in measures designed to protect businesses (often small businesses) from unfair competition (eg the US Federal Trade Commission, and the German Wettbewerb). This is particularly true of continental European countries, where unfair competition embraces such topics as misleading and comparative advertising, passing-off, loss leaders, special sales, and so on. In countries such as Germany businesses affected by these practices are often given a broad right to enforce these regulations. The concept of unfair competition draws attention to the fact that honest businesses as well as consumers may have an interest in fair trading, although this interest may not always coincide with those of consumers.

What are the objectives underlying the concept of fairness and 'fair trading'? This question is posed starkly by the introduction of the general clause under the Consumer Protection from Unfair Trading regulations 2008 and such concepts as 'treating customers fairly' (see below Chapter 7) or the 'unfair credit relationship' test that we will encounter under the Consumer Credit Act 1974. One conception of unfairness might reflect market values and be solely concerned with remedying imperfections in the neoclassical market model. The main thrust of policy would then be vigorous measures to maintain market competition, coupled with measures addressed to information imperfections that would undermine a rational consumers' ability to make effective choices, and failures in the private-law system. A broader equitable conception of substantive fairness might, however, identify its objectives as those of protecting the vulnerable and the poor, maintaining integrity in marketing and furthering values of risk-sharing and loss-distribution.

Unfairness might also include prohibitions on discrimination in advertising and the stereotyping of particular groups (see Ayres, 1991: 817). It might also be argued that certain types of advertising are unfair because they exploit human weakness, debase tastes or tempt individuals to over-commit themselves.

Economic losses from unfair or deceptive trade practices illustrate the classic enforcement problem of losses which are often small individually but large in aggregate. Where market pressures (eg reputation, repeat sales) fail to provide adequate redress, there may be limitations on the ability of the traditional legal processes (individual litigation) to provide either cost-effective redress or deterrence to unfair or deceptive trade practices. The diffuse nature of economic losses from unfair or deceptive trading (eg from misleading advertising) make individual action unlikely. A consumer may also face significant problems of proof, since oral sales patter will often be involved and unfairness or deception may arise from complex trading practices. In addition, the fact that the consumer may not have received a completely worthless product, the well-documented phenomenon of 'cognitive dissonance'—the rationalising of the benefits of a bad purchase—and the view of many consumers that selling is a 'game' may all create further barriers to individuals' taking action. These problems are magnified in the case of cross-border unfair practices.

It is sometimes argued that competitors, possessing larger resources than individual consumers, will have strong incentives to police unfair trading, to expose frauds and to bring private actions for redress. These actions may, therefore, act as a surrogate form of consumer protection. There are, however, limitations to this form of enforcement. Competitors are only likely to bring actions where there is a significant threat to their market share and may be unwilling to bring actions against the 'fly-by-night' trader. There is also the danger that the extensive use of private actions by competitors will dampen competition or be used to entrench a dominant market position at the expense of aggressive new entrants. This is one example of the general problem that traders may attempt to use 'fair trading' legislation as a method of trade protection, at the expense of consumers. This concern motivated the European Court of Justice to strike down strict controls on comparative advertising in Germany (see *Schutzverband gegen Unwesen in der Wiftschaft v Yves Rocher* (1993)). Finally, consumers receive no redress in the event of the successful suit of a competitor.

Enforcement costs are, therefore, a major rationale for public regulation which will protect consumers against the widely spread and diffuse losses caused by unfair trading. This rationale, coupled with the need for expertise, the need for co-ordinated enforcement and the need to monitor business activity has underlined arguments for the administrative regulation of competition law (Elzinga and Breit, 1976: 139) and consumer protection. However, the realisation that public enforcement may suffer from certain limitations (above Chapter 3) has led to greater interest in the role of private groups in enforcing public programmes.

Unfair trade practices may have a 'spill-over' effect on other transactions and areas of lifem and Ison argues that 'the standard of integrity observed in marketing can have spill-over effects in society at large and in public affairs, both directly through the participation of businessmen and indirectly through the imitation of their standards' (Ison, 1979: 432).

This view of legal regulation as shaping social values is also voiced by Sissela Bok:

> The very stress on individualism, on competition, on achieving material success which so marks our society also generates intense pressures to cut corners. … The more widespread[many] judge these practices to be, the stronger will be the pressures to join, even compete, in deviousness. The social incentives to deceit are at present very powerful; the controls, often

weak. Many individuals feel caught in practices they cannot change. It would be wishful thinking, therefore, to expect individuals to bring about major changes in the collective practices of deceit by themselves. Public and private institutions, with their enormous power to affect personal choice, must help alter the existing pressures and incentives. (Bok, 1978: 244)

Setting the ground rules for exchange in consumer markets cannot avoid distributional judgements on, for example, the extent to which one party may take advantage of special knowledge or the ignorance of his co-contractant. To permit aggressive marketing may benefit certain consumers but exact costs on others. Kronman has suggested as one distributional formulation the Rawlsian idea that advantage-taking may be justified if it benefits the disadvantaged party in the long run (Kronman, 1979–80: 483).This individualistic basis for fairness may be contrasted with more communitarian ideas of loss-spreading and risk-distribution.

Fair trading may also be associated with 'integrity in marketing' and with the ethical standards of business and marketing practices. For example, the UCPD refers to norms of 'professional diligence'. Embedding norms of trust and confidence may be important. A market riddled with unfair practices might forfeit consumer confidence.

Paternalism has also been an underlying motive for regulation, particularly in the area of consumer credit transactions. For example, although the Crowther Committee endorsed the 'first principle' that the users of consumer credit should be treated as adults 'fully capable of managing their own financial affairs', it also had considerable sympathy for the concept of a minimum deposit on credit terms as a means of 'protecting a great many fools from their folly'. More recently some scholars have advocated 'asymmetric paternalism' that justifies regulation where regulation (such as cooling-off periods) provides benefits for those who make mistakes or are subject to behavioural biases but have little impact on other consumers (Camerer et al, 2003: 1211) (see discussion below of cooling-off periods).

These introductory comments on fair trading underline the potentially conflicting values and ideologies at play in this area. They illustrate the tensions between different conceptions of the marketplace. The consumer marketplace is not a family relationship nor a commodity exchange (see Study Group on Social Justice, 2004).

3.1 Institutional framework of trade practices regulation

Much of UK policymaking on fair trading reflects incrementalism with a variety of approaches adopted towards unfair commercial practices. The Trade Descriptions Act 1968 and the Consumer Protection Act 1987 Part III were the central general controls of misleading practices. Both were criminal statutes. These were supplemented by the Control on Misleading Advertisements Regulations (1988, 2000) that involved co-regulation with the Advertising Standards Authority and injunctive enforcement by the OFT. In addition, certain practices were identified as particularly injurious (eg mock auctions and pyramid selling) and banned, or regulated (door-to-door selling) and certain industries were singled out for regulation (eg timeshares). The Fair Trading Act 1973 envisaged a more systematic approach to unfair commercial practices by conferring rule-making initiatives on the OFT so that it could respond to new forms of unfair practices. This proved to be a failure and much reliance was placed on the role of codes of conduct as a method of regulating trade practices. This also was not a particularly successful initiative. A more systematic approach was adopted towards consumer credit with the Consumer Credit Act 1974, which established an international benchmark in terms of the comprehensive regulation of consumer credit contracts.

The introduction of the UCPD by the EU—implemented by the Consumer Protection from Unfair Trading Regulations 2008—represents an ambitious attempt at comprehensive rationality in the field of unfair commercial practices regulation. There is an important relationship between the form of unfair trade practices legislation (detailed rules or broad standards) and the institutions of regulation (administrative agencies, courts). The inability of legislators to foresee all potential unfair trade practices, and the limitations on courts (eg the paucity of remedies available to them, their reactive nature, and their inability to monitor compliance and adjust for unintended consequences), have often made administrative regulation appear to be an attractive option in this area. This approach will generally entail the conferral on an agency of quasi-judicial powers to seek cease-and-desist orders, injunctions, levy civil fines and monitor a firm's behaviour, and quasi-legislative powers to make specific regulations for particular markets or practices.

The premier model of administrative regulation is the US Federal Trade Commission (FTC). The following extracts outline the rationale for the creation of this agency, with its broad powers to regulate 'unfair methods of competition' and, since 1938, 'unfair acts or practices'. It is suggested that the reader compare these rationales with those provided for the introduction of the UCPD.

Holloway v Bristol-Myers Corpn (1973) 485 F2d 986 at 990

Congress recognized that any attempt at an exhaustive catalogue of anti-competitive practices would only tempt those bent upon thwarting or circumventing the anti-trust laws to adopt new and different artifices to achieve the same ends. The legislature felt, moreover, that there was need for action of an early, preventive nature, to strike down devices and schemes in their incipiency, before they became entrenched in structure and industrial concentration. These factors suggested a statute whose prohibitions were couched in broad, generic terms, permitting application in a wide variety of commercial contexts and coping with evasive tactics. Yet this breadth of prohibition carried with it a danger that the statute might become a source of vexatious litigation. Expertise was called for, both to identify trade practices that posed the threat of monopoly and. to avoid using the statute as a vehicle for trivial or frivolous claims. There was, furthermore, a need to develop a central and coherent body of precedent, construing and applying the statute in a wide range of factual contexts, so as to define its operative reach. Finally, it would be of assistance to create a specialized forum where businessmen whose methods had been called into question could voluntarily revise their practices without the need to resort to the courts. It was in response to these needs that, on September 26, 1914, Congress passed the Federal Trade Commission Act and established the Federal Trade Commission.

FTC v Sperry & Hutchinson Co (1972) 405 US 233 at 239–40

When Congress created the Federal Trade Commission in 1914 and charted its power and responsibility under §5, it explicitly considered, and rejected, the notion that it reduce the ambiguity of the phrase 'unfair methods of competition' by tying the concept of unfairness to a common-law or statutory standard or by enumerating the particular practices to which it was intended to apply. It is impossible to frame definitions which embrace all unfair practices. There is no limit to human inventiveness in this field. Even if all known unfair practices were specifically defined and prohibited, it would be at once necessary to begin over again. If Congress were to adopt the method of definition, it would undertake an endless task.

The FTC model was one influence behind the creation in the United Kingdom of the Office of Director General of Fair Trading in 1973 and has been used as a benchmark by UK and European policymakers. The DTI noted in its comparative report on consumer policy regimes that the FTC had almost certainly 'the biggest concentration of … [consumer protection] expertise at the national level in the world' (DTI, 2003: 16) and the fact that the FTC operates with a broad brush mandate to police 'unfair acts or practices' was one reason for withdrawal of the opposition by the UK government to the general clause in the UCPD.

The recognition of potential sources of 'regulatory failure' have provoked renewed interest in the potential for private initiatives. We consider the role of private enforcement in Chapter 5.

---

4. A new start? The EU Unfair Commercial Practices Directive and its implementation

> The coming into force of the UCPD will mark a new era in UK fair trading law. (DTI, 2006: 3)

The UCPD is regarded by many commentators as one of the most significant EU consumer directives and there are already several specialist books and articles on its potential impact (eg Stuyck *et al*, 2005; Bernitz and Weatherill, 2006; Howells, Mickitz and Wilhelmsson, 2006). This section outlines the rationale for the Directive, the architecture and scope of the Directive and its potential effects on UK law

4.1 The rationale for the UCPD

Commission of the European Communities COM(2001) 531 final, Green Paper on European Union Consumer Protection

2. CONSUMER PROTECTION IN THE INTERNAL MARKET

… Existing EU consumer protection directives, when compared to national regulation, do not constitute a comprehensive regulatory framework for business-consumer commercial practices, the central aim of consumer protection.

Some of the directives, notably the sector-specific ones, have developed as a very detailed response to specific identifiable problems at a particular moment in time. This approach, combined with the long period between the proposal and implementation of EU measures (the distance selling directive was proposed in June 1992 but was not due to be implemented until June 2000), has guaranteed a certain level of obsolescence as market practices have moved on. This could make EU rules irrelevant, unnecessarily restrict innovation or allow rogue traders to keep one step ahead of the law. The time involved in modifying these directives to adapt them to technological development while maintaining the same level of consumer protection compounds such inflexibility.

3. THE FUTURE DIRECTION OF EU CONSUMER PROTECTION

3.1 The need for action

The cumulative impact of this situation is a 'consumer internal market' that has not achieved its potential nor matched the development of the internal market in business-to-business transactions. Consumers rarely participate directly in the internal market through cross-border shopping. For business, above all for SMEs, the differing treatment of identical commercial practices in each Member State is a daunting deterrent to developing cross-border sales and exploiting the internal market. At best, there is lack of certainty and clarity about fifteen sets of legal obligations. At worst, the sheer number of obligations is off-putting to nearly all businesses but those who can afford to establish in all Member States. For consumers, the lack of clarity and security over their rights is an important brake on their confidence and trust. The internal market, like all markets, depends on consumer confidence.

A fully functioning consumer internal market could make a substantial contribution to meeting the goals of the EU. The internal market's main asset is that it has the largest pool of consumer demand in the world—and this asset is not being fully exploited. Enabling businesses, especially SMEs, to access this potential, as easily as domestic markets would be a powerful stimulus to competitiveness. Simplifying existing rules and, where possible, deregulating would also help reduce disproportionate burdens on business. Consumers would have access to greater choice and better prices. Cross-border shopping would not supplant domestic shopping but would become a significant medium with a wider impact on markets than its share of retail sales.

This situation is not new. However, there is a case for further action to complete the consumer internal market now. The circulation of Euro notes and coins from 1 January 2002 will remove one major psychological obstacle to direct consumer participation in the internal market. E-commerce has the potential to remove many of the geographical and logistical barriers to the consumer internal market. SME's and consumers at different ends of the European continent can develop commercial relationships more easily than ever before. This potential remains unfulfilled, with e-commerce representing not only a small part of retail sales but also largely confined within national borders.

The prospect of enlargement also calls for further action, since without some reform, it could further complicate the legal picture. It is also an opportunity to endow candidate countries that do not always have a long history of consumer protection with simple and effective rules. The political case for reform has been recognised at the highest level. The Lisbon European Council set a new strategic goal for the Union 'to become the most competitive and dynamic knowledge-based economy in the world' by completing the internal market, developing predictable rules for e-commerce and simplifying and improving the regulatory environment . . .

Finally a fully functioning consumer internal market could play an important part in the strategy to bring the EU closer to its citizens, by dispelling the myth that internal market is a corporate business project and delivering tangible economic benefits to their daily life.

2 Overall approach

. . .

The central choice therefore revolves around the type of method needed to achieve greater harmonisation. There are essentially two options:

A specific approach based on the adoption of a series of further directives, or a mixed approach of a comprehensive framework directive, supplemented by targeted directives, where necessary.

3.3 Specific approach

Greater harmonisation could be achieved through a series of further specific directives. The number of directives needed is hard to estimate. Directives covering advertising (except the issues covered by the television without frontiers directive), marketing practices, payment and after sales services might be considered, together with certain sector-specific directives.

... There are clearly some doubts as to the effectiveness of relying exclusively on this approach in delivering a genuine internal market. The limited scope of existing consumer protection regulation at EU level has justified the need for the so-called minimum clauses in EU directives. Continuing with the approach of selective, specific legislation would require a clear commitment from the Member States to change this policy, both in respect of existing and new directives. In addition, many of the existing consumer protection directives will require amendment in order to address the obsolescence that has developed through new market developments or legislative requirements becoming outdated. Together this represents a formidable, if achievable, long-term programme.

3.4 Mixed approach

The alternative would be to develop a comprehensive, technology-neutral, EU framework directive to harmonise national fairness rules for business-consumer commercial practices.

This would be based on similar models to those seen in certain Member States and third countries for consumer protection and at EU level for product safety and that proposed for food safety. A framework directive would not override sector-specific directives. ... The framework directive would amount to a safety net to cover practices where cross-border restrictions are identified and which fall outside the coordinated fields of the sector-specific Directives. Where necessary, the framework directive would be accompanied in due course by a reform of existing consumer protection directives to ensure the overall coherence of the consumer protection system. Such a reform would be undertaken once the framework directive has been established and experience has been gained of its operation in practice.

To provide the required certainty and prevent differing legal interpretations by national courts, the framework directive would have to be more than simply a general principle regulating business-consumer commercial practices. It would address the main differences in national rules on commercial practices which affected the operation of the internal market, through establishing clear EU-wide rules through harmonisation.

The main advantage of a framework approach compared to a specific approach is that its comprehensive nature reduces the need for further detailed consumer protection regulation.

The existence of general benchmarks enable emerging commercial practices to be addressed without recourse to new regulation. Business can innovate in greater certainty and unfair practices can be tackled without further rule-making. A framework approach also permits simplification of existing rules. For example, the directives on misleading and comparative advertising could be subsumed into the framework directive. The flexibility of a framework directive would also eliminate the justification for minimum clauses in EU consumer protection directives.

A framework directive could also provide a firm basis for EU-wide self-regulation in the field of consumer protection and for the development of non-binding practical guidance. Both these tools can potentially reduce the need for detailed prescriptive regulation. Finally, a framework directive can provide the basis for some formal stakeholder participation in the regulatory process.

However, while a single framework directive is also in theory simpler and faster to negotiate than a series of directives, it would contain more issues of substance and therefore be harder to reach consensus.

Commission of the European Communities, 18.6.2003 COM(2003) 356 final, 2003/0134 (COD) Proposal for a Directive of the European Parliament and of the Council concerning unfair business-to-consumer commercial practices in the Internal Market and amending Directives 84/450/EEC, 97/7/EC and 98/27/EC Explanatory Memorandum

... A majority of respondents accepted the case for reform, and a majority of those who expressed a preference, including a majority of Member States, supported reform on the basis of a framework directive.

THE CASE FOR CHANGE

Potential benefits of the internal market.

10. Survey evidence suggests that the continued development of the internal market depends both on encouraging business to advertise and market across borders and on stimulating consumers, who are in principle willing to do so, to actually transact cross-border. ... Both the potential benefits, and the risks of allowing the present situation to continue, will be increased in an enlarged Union of 25 or more Member States.

Barriers and distortions.

13. The GFA study found that there are a number of barriers, some policy-induced, others not, which prevent traders and consumers from taking advantage of the internal market by shopping cross-border. These include tax, particularly VAT, time and distance (though these are also present in national markets and are being reduced by e-commerce), and language barriers. That said, 53% of Europeans say they can speak at least one European language in addition to their mother tongue and 26% can speak two.

14. However, even if all these other barriers were addressed, unfair commercial practices would in themselves constitute important barriers to the functioning of the internal market.

15. First, unfair commercial practices, if they are not addressed by effective consumer protection, can undermine consumer confidence. On average, 18% of consumers in a recent survey cited poor legal protection as a reason not to buy financial services cross-border, rising to 36% in one Member State. In another survey about cross-border shopping in general, consumers who felt less confident buying from another EU country than in their own country were asked why. 68% of those consumers cited lower standards of consumer protection laws as a very or fairly important reason for their lack of confidence while 76% cited as a very or fairly important factor a lack of trust in foreign sellers and a perceived greater risk of fraud or deception.

18. For consumers, the uncertainty of not knowing what consumer protection is provided by other EU countries' laws was a bigger barrier to cross-border shopping—with 79% of

respondents citing it as a very or fairly important obstacle—than their perception that the standards of protection were lower in other countries.

19. The impact of these barriers is exacerbated by the differences in the regulation of unfair commercial practices by Member States. The minimum clauses in existing consumer protection legislation, such as the misleading advertising directive perpetuate this problem by allowing Member States to add divergent requirements and provide differing degrees and types of protection.

22. The need for businesses to comply with a complex patchwork of different national requirements adds costs to those who market cross-border and for many is such a deterrent that they simply do not try:

—47% of businesses cited the need for compliance with different national regulations on commercial practices, advertising and other consumer protection regulations as very or fairly important obstacles to cross-border advertising and marketing.

—This obstacle was considered as significant as the need to comply with tax requirements(46%) and more important than language barriers (38%).

24. In addition, the differences in legislation increase the cost and complexity of enforcement, whether by public authorities or by self-regulatory bodies.

'The main debates during the adoption process concerned the unfairness standard (average consumer and transactional decision test); the maximum harmonization standard; the extent of the blacklist in the annex and the role of codes of conduct' (Howells, Micklitz and Wilhelmsson, 2006: 20).

4.2 Maximal harmonisation and the UCPD

A controversial aspect of the UCPD is its maximal nature, justified by the need to create a level playing field throughout the EU that will promote a competitive internal market with a high level of consumer protection. In a series of decisions the ECJ has confirmed the full harmonization nature of the Directive. In *VTB v Total Belgium and Galatea* C-261/07 and C-299/07, the Court indicated that:

[T]he Directive is intended to establish, in accordance with recitals 5 and 6 in the preamble thereto and Article 1 thereof, uniform rules on unfair business-to-consumer commercial practices in order to contribute to the proper functioning of the internal market and to achieve a high level of consumer protection.

52 Thus, the Directive fully harmonises those rules at the Community level. Accordingly, as Article 4 thereof expressly provides and contrary to the assertions of VTB and the French Government, Member States may not adopt stricter rules than those provided for in the Directive, even in order to achieve a higher level of consumer protection'

Advocate General Trstenjak expanded on this point in her opinion in *Plus WarenHandelsgesellschaft* (Case C-304/08):

As stated earlier in this Opinion, (43) Directive 2005/29 seeks to bring about the full harmonisation of the laws of the Member States concerning unfair commercial practices. In addition, contrary to what was previously the case in sector-specific measures for the harmonisation of consumer-protection law, Directive 2005/29 not only aims at minimum harmonisation, but also seeks to achieve maximum approximation of national provisions which prohibit the Member States, apart from certain exceptions, from retaining or introducing stricter rules, even in order to achieve a higher level of consumer protection. Both those aims are made clear in the preamble and in the general provisions of the Directive.

70. This follows, first, from recital 11 in the preamble to the Directive, which states that the convergence of national provisions through the Directive should create a high common level of consumer protection. Second, recital 12 speaks of consumers and business being able to rely on a single regulatory framework based on clearly defined legal concepts regulating all aspects of unfair commercial practices across the European Union. Article 1 of the Directive refers once again to the approximation of laws, the purpose of which is to contribute to the proper functioning of the internal market and to achieve a high level of consumer protection.

71. The objective of comprehensive maximum regulation at Community level within the area of life covered by Directive 2005/29 becomes clear yet again in recitals 14 and 15, which refer expressly to full harmonisation. This also follows from the internal market clause in Article 4 of the Directive, which provides that the Member States are neither to restrict the freedom to provide services nor to restrict the free movement of goods for reasons falling within the field approximated by the Directive.

72. By way of exception, Article 3(5) of the Directive provides that, for a period of six years from 12 June 2007, Member States may continue to apply national provisions within the field approximated by the Directive which are more restrictive or prescriptive than the Directive. However, this exception is confined to national provisions which are adopted to implement directives containing minimum harmonisation clauses. (45) Finally, there is a further exception to full harmonisation in Article 3(9) in relation to financial services, as defined in Directive 2002/65/EC of the European Parliament and of the Council of 23 September 2002 concerning the distance marketing of consumer financial services and amending Council Directive 90/619/EEC and Directives 97/7/EC and 98/27/EC (OJ 2002 L 271, p 16), and immovable property.

One consequence of full harmonisation is that measures which prohibit selling practices without requiring a demonstration that these practices affect consumer decision-making and which do not fall within the blacklist of schedule 1 will be struck down unless it can be shown that their sole rationale is to protect competitors. Many European states have laws which have per se prohibitions on a variety of selling practices, such as offering bonuses with sales, or prohibiting announcing sales outside fixed periods. These measures, which originate in unfair competition law, may be struck down. The *Total Galatea* case is a classic example: Total Belgium, a subsidiary of the Total group, the primary business of which is the sale of fuels at filling stations, offered free breakdown services for a period of three weeks to consumers who were Total Club cardholders with every purchase of at least 25 litres of fuel for a car or at least 10 litres for a motorcycle. An action was brought by a breakdown company that this practice contravened the Belgium law on combined offers which are prohibited per se subject to exceptions. In *Mediaprint Zeitungs- und Zeitschriftenverlag GmbH & Co KG* (Case C-540/08), *Wamo* (Case C-288/10) and *Zentrale zur Bekämpfung unlauteren Wettbewerbs v Plus Warenhandelsgesellschaft mbH* (Case C-304/08) the defendants offered a free chance to enter a lottery by collecting a certain number of points through shopping at the store. This was challenged under German law as an illegal coupling of a sale with a lottery. The ECJ struck down the relevant German regulation since it was a per se prohibition, not included within the blacklist. It also indicated that it might be difficult to escape the scope of the Directive by arguing that it protected competitors' interests, noting that 'national legislation relating to unfair commercial practices which harm "only" competitors' economic interests or which relate to a transaction between traders is thus excluded from that scope.'

Full harmonisation has already had some impact in the United Kingdom, where OFT proposals to ban certain forms of doorstep sales practices were rejected by the DTI partly on the basis that they would go beyond the protections in the UCPD. This example of doorstep sales also illustrates the relationship of the UCPD to more specific Directives such as the Doorstep Selling Directive. The latter Directive was a minimal harmonisation measure that relied on cooling-off periods. Under Article 3.4 of the UCPD in the case of conflict between these specific provisions and the provisions of the Directive, the specific provisions prevail. Some states, eg France, had, however, gone further than the minimal provisions and banned certain door-to-door sales. This protection beyond the minimal harmonisation level that currently exists may stay in place until 2013 (Article 3.5).

The extent to which the Directive will create a level playing field through maximal harmonisation depends partly on the uniform interpretation and application of the central concepts of market fairness in the Directive. Maximal harmonisation is justified in terms of the reduction of business costs for cross-border marketing and the creation of consumer confidence. Commentators (eg Wilhelmsson, 2004: 325) have expressed reservations about the strength of the consumer confidence argument (see discussion in Chapter 1). Many consumers are not aware of their own national consumer law. Consumers rely on many non-legal factors such as brand names and reputation in shopping decisions within their own countries, and often prefer to contract with individuals that they know or have been referred to by a friend or relative (Louch and Dimaggio, 1998). It is likely that similar dynamics will occur in foreign purchases. Consumers will be concerned about easily accessible remedies, should anything go wrong in a foreign or cross-border purchase. Almost no consumers wish to go to court. Provisions such as low-cost chargeback procedures operated by credit card companies or the ability to obtain redress from the local office of an international manufacturer are likely to be more attractive to customers. However, as we shall see (below Chapter 8) when discussing product quality, the EU has not imposed any direct liability between a manufacturer and a consumer for pure economic losses caused by products.

Wilhelmsson argues that consumer confidence is primarily a rhetorical tool to give the Directive a human face and that it is driven by the needs of business. There is probably some truth in this argument, which reflects the tendency we noted earlier to use the 'consumer interest' as a means of furthering the agenda of more powerful players and in the contemporary world—the agenda of neo-liberalism. However, not all business interests favoured the Directive. Multinational corporations supported it, but not all business groups. One might view the Directive as primarily embracing a liberal (neo-liberal) model of the consumer marketplace with its main target under full harmonisation being the German Unfair Competition Act that had protected small businesses through its application of a credulous person test in relation to misleading advertising and its strict controls on comparative advertising. Nordic countries may have feared that maximal harmonisation would reduce their level of consumer protection, including protection of vulnerable groups such as children, but only Denmark and Sweden in fact voted against maximal harmonisation.

4.3 The scope of the Directive

The Regulations apply to 'unfair business to consumer commercial practices before during and after a commercial transaction in relation to a product'. 'Commercial practices' are defined as 'any act, omission, course of conduct or representation, commercial communication including advertising and marketing by a trader directly connected with the promotion, sale, or supply of a product' (CPUT regulation 2). This is a comprehensive definition that goes beyond the pre-contractual focus of traditional rules on misrepresentation. It could include unfair and misleading debt collection practices, and the conduct of First National Bank discussed in relation to unfair terms in Chapter 6. Moreover, it is not limited to 'representations' but includes 'acts and omissions'. Products are defined to include 'goods and services including immoveable property, rights and obligations' (regulation 2(c)).

Article 3 of the UCPD contains a list of areas that are excluded from the Directive. Article 3.2 indicates that the Directive is without prejudice to contract law and in particular, to the rules on the validity, formation or effect of the contract. This raises the question of the relationship of the standards developed under the Directive and implementing regulations and those of common law misrepresentation (rules on the validity of the contract). The extent to which it will affect contract law will depend on whether private law enforcement is possible (see below Chapter 5). The Law Commission have proposed that private actions be permitted.

Whittaker argues that the directive may challenge existing national approaches through the influence of its paradigm of fair commercial behaviour (Whittaker, 2007). He suggests that the average consumer test adopted in the Directive might influence interpretation of the UTCC regulation in determining whether contractual clauses are intelligible to consumers. This prediction came true in the bank charges litigation (*OFT v Abbey National et al*) where the standard of the 'average consumer', with explicit reference to the UCPD, was adopted. The Directive though its use of the concept of good faith, might also influence conceptions of good faith in consumer contracts or that of 'unfair credit relationships' (see below Chapter 7) in consumer credit contracts.

The Directive does not affect national rules on health and safety although misleading statements about the health characteristics of a product are covered. It does not apply to the special rules applied under professional licensing schemes to uphold high standards of integrity in the professions. States may also apply more restrictive rules to financial services and immoveable property (Article 3(9)).

The Directive does not extend to legal requirements 'related to taste and decency' (see Recital 7). The example given in the Recital of a taste and decency requirement is regulation of commercial solicitation in the streets that 'may be undesirable in Member States for cultural reasons'. Sexism and the stereotyping of particular groups in advertising have often been conceptualised as issues of taste and decency. However, if these practices or other discriminatory practices directly affect consumers' economic interests and transactional decision-making, then they may constitute unfair commercial practices. The Commission Guidance on the scope of the Directive states:

> Article 1 of the Directive explicitly provides for the harmonisation of those practices 'harming consumers' economic interests.'

Therefore, national rules on commercial practices, including marketing and advertising, regulating the protection of human dignity, the prevention of sexual, racial and religious discrimination, or the depiction of nudity, violence, anti-social behaviour are not covered by the Directive.

4.3.1 The architecture of the Directive

The structure of the Directive follows the mixed approach outlined in the Green Paper, adopting a model of regulation with a 'grand' general unfairness clause (Article 5; regulation 3), two small general clauses addressing misleading (Articles 6, 7; regulations 5, 6) and aggressive commercial practices (Articles 8, 9; regulation 7) and a laundry list of specific prohibited practices (Annex 1) (see Stuyck, Terryn and Van Dyck, 2005: 124).

4.4 The role of the general clause

The grand general clause (Article 5; see CPUT regulation 3) prohibits a commercial practice that is contrary to the requirements of 'professional diligence' and that 'materially distorts or is likely to materially distort the economic behaviour with regard to the product of the average consumer or the average member of a targeted group'. 'Professional diligence' means the standard of special skill and care which a trader may reasonably be expected to exercise towards consumers, commensurate with honest market practice and/or the general principle of good faith in the trader's field of activity (see CPUT regulation 2.) It is a normative not a factual standard.

General clauses are well known in continental European systems. The Commission views Article 5 as a safety valve for practices not caught by more specific regulation in Articles 6–9 and as reducing the need for detailed regulatory responses to new problems. Giuseppe Abbamonte states that:

> The general prohibition has an autonomous regulatory function in the sense that a practice which is neither misleading nor aggressive can still be captured by the general prohibition if it meets its criteria. ... It serves as a safety net to catch any current or future practices that cannot be categorized as either misleading or aggressive. The primary motivation is to ensure that the Directive is future-proof. (Abbamonte, 2007: 20)

This statement mirrors the rationale for the development of the broad jurisdiction conferred on the US FTC to police 'unfair acts or practices'. General clauses pose questions rather than provide answers. A particular challenge is that of developing a European standard of fairness from the concepts of professional diligence: the standard of professional diligence represented a political compromise the political choices in elaborating fairness has been delegated to the ECJ. The US model envisages a central administrative agency that might develop the fairness standard, provide interpretive guidance or adopt rules based on the general prohibition. Within the EU the Commission provides guidance, but the development of fairness depends ultimately on judicial interpretation.

The Directive is described as a 'framework directive' but commentators are sceptical of this claim. Stuyck et al comment that:

> The mere fact that a framework fairness test—the grand general clause—is included does not make a directive a framework directive. On the contrary, especially in its black list

the UCPD embodies the extreme level of detail that is typical for the at times paternalistic directives in the consumer protection field together with the static and inflexible characteristics of the procedure of amending directives. (Stuyck et al, 2006: 144)

The concept of a framework directive is based on EU developments in areas such as product safety, where the Community establishes a general safety duty in relation to essential matters, but there is extensive delegation to hybrid public/private institutions in the development of rules, committees of experts play a significant role and under a 'safeguard clause' individual states may act against unsafe products. The UCPD does not establish any such structure. It is possible that the existence of ICPEN and the EU Regulation on Consumer Protection Cooperation (2006/2004) that creates a network of enforcers may promote opportunities for the development of a regional 'epistemic community' which will over time develop guidance on unfair commercial practices.

The introduction of a general clause into English law is not completely novel. UCTA provides broad standards for determining the validity of exclusion clauses and the UTCC regulations introduced the concept of good faith as a standard in consumer contracting. Amendments to the Consumer Credit Act 1974 confer discretion on the courts to strike down 'unfair credit relationships' and the Financial Services Authority has adopted a high-level regulatory principle of 'treating customers fairly'.

One might be sceptical of the impact of the general clause on English law. To the extent that it is dependent on public enforcement, English enforcement agencies usually view prosecution as a last resort and often look for clear violations of specific rules (see Chapter 5). They are likely to seek the certainty of regulations 5–7 and the prohibited practices in Annex 1. Experience under the Unfair Terms in Consumer Contracts Regulations indicate that the OFT generally bases its adjudications on the 'greylist' and procedural unfairness. However, the general clause may provide an opportunity for regulators to develop a dialogue with trade associations and industry over how to concretise this general standard and its implications for corporate dealings with consumers (see Scott, 2004).

---

5. Implementation: the CPUT Regulations 2008

The Consumer Protection from Unfair Trading Regulations 2008 implement the UCPD. The UK government originally opposed the concept of an unfair practices law with a broad general clause because of its perceived uncertainty and a belief that more specific rules could address any gaps in existing English law. However, the government ultimately viewed the Directive as an opportunity to achieve better regulation through simplification and to benchmark the UK against leading consumer protection models such as the US FTC, which also operates with a general clause. The UK government took the opportunity in implementing the UCPD directive to repeal many existing statutes and regulations including the substantive provisions of the Trade Descriptions Act 1968, Part III of the Consumer Protection Act 1987, and The Control of Misleading Advertisements Regulations 1988 (for a full list, see Schedule 2 of the Regulations).

The UK has adopted in general a 'copy-out' approach to the Directive, avoiding 'gold-plating'. The following extract outlines the approach adopted to implementation (see further Collins, 2010: 89).

DTI, Government Response to the Consultation Paper on Implementing the Unfair Commercial Practices Directive (2006)

The coming into force of the UCPD will mark a new era in UK fair trading history. The UCPD will allow enforcers to tackle those practices that are unfair but not currently unlawful, taking either civil or criminal enforcement action as appropriate. Simplification and modernisation of the existing framework will also make the law easier for its users—business, consumers and enforcers—to understand and apply. The Government is confident that the wide-ranging changes set out below will help it meet its objective of raising the UK's consumer protection regime to the level of the best in the world.

5.1 Interpreting the regulations

OFT v Purely Creative Industries [2011] EWHC 106

Briggs J: … The application of those provisions of the Regulations to the particular facts of the 2008 promotions has thrown up a number of issues and difficulties of interpretation. There was no dispute between counsel as to the correct approach to interpretation, which I can therefore summarise briefly as follows. Domestic regulations designed to implement EU directives, and in particular maximum harmonisation directives, must be construed as far as possible so as to implement the purposes and provisions of the directive. The interpretation of words and phrases is neither a matter of grammars nor dictionaries, nor even a matter of the use of those phrases (or of the underlying concepts) in national law. If similar words and phrases are used in the directive itself, then they must be interpreted both in the directive and in the implementing regulations by means of a process of interpretation which is independent of the member state's national law and, for that matter, independent of any other member state's national law. For that purpose the primary recourse of the national court is to the jurisprudence of the ECJ. The national court may also obtain assistance from, but is not bound by, guidance issued by the Commission, and by the decisions of other national courts as to the meaning of the relevant directive.

Note also the comments of Advocate General Trstenjak in *Plus WarenHandelsgesellschaft*.

5.2 The standard of protection: the average consumer and the transactional decision test under the UCPD

The average consumer is not defined in the Directive. Recitals 18 and 19 provide a guide as to its meaning:

In line with the principle of proportionality, and to permit the effective application of the protection the Directive takes as a benchmark the average consumer, who is reasonably well-informed and reasonably circumspect, taking into account social, cultural and linguistic factors, as interpreted by the Court of Justice, but also contains provisions aimed at preventing the exploitation of consumers whose characteristics make them particularly vulnerable to unfair commercial practices. Where a commercial practice is specifically aimed at a particular group of consumers, such as children, it is desirable that the impact of the commercial practice be assessed from the perspective of the average member of that group. ...The average consumer test is not a statistical test. National courts and authorities will have to exercise their own faculty of judgement, having regard to the case-law of the Court of Justice, to determine the typical reaction of the average consumer in a given case.

Where certain characteristics such as age, physical or mental infirmity or credulity make consumers particularly susceptible to a commercial practice or to the underlying product and the economic behaviour only of such consumers is likely to be distorted by the practice in a way that the trader can reasonably foresee, it is appropriate to ensure that they are adequately protected by assessing the practice from the perspective of the average member of that group.

CPUT Regulations 2(2)–(6) implement recitals 18 and 19. The standard of the average consumer developed in the Directive reflects a political compromise that emphasises the politically charged nature of the choice of standard. The standard of the 'reasonably well informed and reasonably circumspect consumer', based on the jurisprudence of the ECJ (see eg *Gut SpringenHeide*, 1998) was originally included in the definition section of the Directive. However, according to Micklitz,

the image of the average consumer as created by the European Court of Justice met strong opposition. The Scandinavian countries in particular argued against the normative concept of the informed and circumspect consumer, insofar as it would be a general yardstick which would endanger the protection of particularly vulnerable groups. (Howells, Micklitz and Wilhelmsson, 2006: 111)

Consumer groups also opposed the codification of the average consumer test. Recitals 18 and 19 therefore recognise this compromise which has been transposed in regulations 2(2)–(6) of the CPUT regulations. The inability of one group to secure its definition of average consumer in the Directive means that the inevitable political choice in determining the application of these standards is conferred on the courts

The normative issues involved in determining the concept of the average consumer are illustrated by the following examples provided in a paper by Christian Twigg Flesner, Geraint Howells and Deborah Parry (2005) in relation to false and misleading commercial practices.

1. Hand cream is sold in jars which have false bottoms and so the contents appear considerably greater than they actually are. Although the correct weight is marked on the jars, the containers are 30 per cent larger in volume than the amount of hand-cream.
2. Trader sells 'fake' Rolex watches at £10, with no indications given to say they are fakes.
3. Advertising a car as having had one 'owner' when it had been leased to several different people.
4. Salespersons visiting sheltered housing complexes selling Freeview television boxes, in an area where there is very poor Freeview reception.
5. A supermarket chain has a regular price for a particular product. The product is withdrawn for a short period and is reintroduced at more than double the previous

price. After a few weeks, the price is then halved and widely advertised as 'half-price' (though still above original selling price).
6. Seller of memorial headstones, aware that some cemeteries have restrictions on the types of memorials which can be installed, fails to check where headstone is to be located/fails to advise customers of possible restrictions before accepting orders.

The application of regulations 5 and 6 to these examples suggest that: (1) the average consumer is a contested concept whose meaning will depend on judicial constructions of the public; (2) it is difficult to separate actions from omissions; (3) the particular standard of deception chosen may have an impact on information provision in the market—for example, requiring a trader to indicate that a watch is 'fake', or to ensure, in example 1, that the correct weight is in large print, or to inquire of consumers where the headstone will be located. The issue of deception is not merely a factual inquiry; it is also normative.

5.2.1 The material distortion and transactional decision test

The Directive imposes two similar tests under Articles 5 and 6 to determine whether the practice is unfair or misleading. In Article 5 the commercial practice must be likely to 'materially distort the economic behaviour' of a consumer and under Articles 6, 8 and 9 be likely to 'cause him to take a transactional decision that he would not have taken otherwise'. The test of material distortion is defined in Article 2(c) as appreciably impairing 'the consumer's ability to make an informed decision, thereby causing the consumer to take a transactional decision that he would not have taken otherwise'; a 'transactional decision' is defined as 'any decision taken by a consumer concerning whether, how and on what terms to purchase, make payment in whole or in part for, retain, or dispose of a product or to exercise a contractual right in relation to a product, whether the consumer decides to act or refrain from acting' (Article 2(k); see CPUT regulation 2.1).

The terms of the Directive suggest that it does not require that the conduct be capable of inducing a purchase (the Directive applies also to post-contractual conduct).

EU Commission Guidance (2011)

There is a wide spectrum of transactional decisions which may be taken by the consumer in relation to a product or a service other than a decision to purchase (or not to do so). These transactional decisions may result in actions which have no legal consequences under national contract law and may be taken at any time between the moment the consumer is initially exposed to the marketing and the end of the a product's life or the final use of a service.

Pre-Purchase decisions

As shown in the example above, most common activities which consumers carry out in a 'pre-purchase' stage are to be considered transactional decisions. These include, for instance, a decision to travel to a sales outlet or shop, the decision to enter a shop (eg after reading a poster on the shop window or a billboard in the street), the decision to agree to a sales presentation by a trader or his or her representatives and the decision to continue with a web booking process. Further examples include a consumer's decision to agree to a 'free security survey' of his home, which is genuinely free, but whose sole purpose is to allow the trader to persuade the consumer to buy an alarm system.

Post-Purchase decisions

Decisions which consumers take after having purchased a product or contracted/subscribed for a service can also qualify as transactional decisions. The main category of post-purchase transactional decisions are those which relate to the exercise of consumers' contractual rights, such as the right of withdrawal, cancellation, the right to terminate a service contract or the right to change the product or switch to another trader.

For example, a consumer purchases a product and the trader makes him believe that he must purchase a warranty to have rights in case of defects.

The implications of having this broad concept of transactional decision are significant. It allows an extensive application of the Directive to a variety of cases where the impact of the unfairness of the trader's behaviour does not cause the consumer to enter a transaction or a service contract. Following this approach, a commercial practice may be considered unfair not only if it is likely to cause the average consumer to purchase or not to purchase a product but also if it is likely to cause the consumer to enter a shop, spend more time on the Internet engaged in a booking process or decide to not switch to another trader or product.

As such, the Directive does not limit the transactional decision test to the evaluation as to whether the consumer's economic behaviour (ie its transactional decisions) has actually been distorted. It requires an assessment of whether that commercial practice is capable (ie 'likely') to have such an impact on the average consumer.

Recital 6 indicates that the Directive does not 'affect accepted advertising and marketing practices, such as legitimate product placement, brand differentiation or the offering of incentives which may legitimately affect consumers' perceptions of products and influence their behaviour without impairing the consumer's ability to make an informed decision'. This comment seems to be based on a naïve view of the influence of commercial marketing. However, given the relatively broad definition of transactional decision it is unlikely in the great majority of cases to be a significant additional hurdle to a prosecution.

---

6. Judicial interpretation of the average consumer test

The average consumer test is based on the jurisprudence of the ECJ. The decision of the Court in *Estée Lauder* (2000) illustrates several aspects of the test. In this case the Court posed the question whether a cosmetic lifting cream marketed throughout Europe under the description 'Monteil Firming Action Lifting Extreme Creme' was misleading to German consumers because it gave consumers the impression that use of the product would obtain results which, in terms of their lasting effects, were comparable to surgical lifting. The Court held that this was a question for a national court (in this case a German court) to decide taking into account whether 'social, cultural or linguistic factors might have resulted in the term "lifting", used in connection with a firming cream, as meaning something different to the German consumer as opposed to consumers in other member states'. The Court outlined the test for determining whether the claim is misleading.

Estée Lauder Cosmetics GmbH & Co OHG v Lancaster Group GmbH, Case C-220/98, [2000] ECR I-117

27 It should be borne in mind that when it has fallen to the Court, in the context of the interpretation of Directive 84/450 (*misleading advertising*), to weigh the risk of misleading consumers against the requirements of the free movement of goods, it has held that, in order to determine whether a particular description, trade mark or promotional description or statement is misleading, it is necessary to take into account the presumed expectations of an average consumer who is reasonably well informed and reasonably observant and circumspect (see, in particular, Case C-210/96 *Gut Springenheide and Tusky* [1998] ECR I-4657, paragraph 31).

28 That test, based on the principle of proportionality, also applies in the context of the marketing of cosmetic products where, as in the case in the main proceedings, a mistake as to the product's characteristics cannot pose any risk to public health.

29 In order to apply that test to the present case, several considerations must be borne in mind. In particular, it must be determined whether social, cultural or linguistic factors may justify the term 'lifting', used in connection with a firming cream, meaning something different to the German consumer as opposed to consumers in other Member States, or whether the instructions for the use of the product are in themselves sufficient to make it quite clear that its effects are short-lived, thus neutralising any conclusion to the contrary that might be derived from the word 'lifting'.

30 Although, at first sight, the average consumer—reasonably well informed and reasonably observant and circumspect—ought not to expect a cream whose name incorporates the term 'lifting' to produce enduring effects, it nevertheless remains for the national court to determine, in the light of all the relevant factors, whether that is the position in this case.

31 In the absence of any provisions of Community law on this matter, it is for the national court—which may consider it necessary to commission an expert opinion or a survey of public opinion in order to clarify whether or not a promotional description or statement is misleading—to determine, in the light of its own national law, the percentage of consumers misled by that description or statement which would appear to it sufficiently significant to justify prohibiting its use (see *Gut Springenheide and Tusky* …).

The judgment in this case might be compared with the judgment of the ECJ in *Verein gegen Unwesen in Handel und Gewerbe Köln eV v Mars* (1995). In this case Mars had marketed ice-cream bars of the Mars, Snickers, Bounty and Milky Way brands with a coloured flash on the wrapper that indicated that the bars were 10% larger. The coloured flash of the wrapper was considerably more than 10% of the surface area. The issue was whether this presentation was misleading. The ECJ held that it was not and concluded that 'reasonably circumspect consumers may be deemed to know that there is not necessarily a link between the size of publicity markings relating to an increase in a product's quantity and the size of that increase'. A comment on the case raised the question whether the average consumer of ice-cream bars would include 'children and teenagers, who probably make up a large number of such customers' (Schulze, Schulte-Nolke and Jones, 2002: 115). Should the decision have been influenced by the fact that this is a low-cost product relatively frequently purchased and consumers are able to check at low cost the actual size of the product?

EU Commission Guidance (2011)

The Court of Justice and the General Court (formerly known as the Court of First Instance), in assessing the likelihood of confusion of certain trade marks, have given some indications as to the behaviour of the average consumer and the fact that his/her behaviour may be influenced by other factors. This can apply by analogy to the concept of the average consumer in the Directive.

According to the General Court, '[t]he average consumer normally perceives a mark as a whole and does not proceed to analyse its various details. … In addition, account should be taken of the fact that the average consumer only rarely has the chance to make a direct comparison between the different marks but has to place his trust in the imperfect image of them that he has retained in his mind. It should also be borne in mind that the average consumer's level of attention is likely to vary according to the category of goods and services in question.' [See eg Joined Cases T-183/02 and T184/02 *El Corte Inglés v Office for Harmonisation in the Internal Market (Trade Marks and Designs) ('Mundicolor')* [2004] ECR II-00965, para 68. See also case T-20/02 *Interquell GmbH v Office for Harmonisation in the Internal Market (Trade Marks and Designs) ('Happydog')* [2004] ECR II-1001, para 37.]

And, according to the Court of Justice, 'among the factors to be taken into account in order to assess whether the labelling at issue in the main proceedings may be misleading, the length of time for which a name has been used is an objective factor which might affect the expectations of the reasonable [average] consumer' (Case C-446/07 *Alberto Severi v Regione Emilia-Romagna*, judgement of the Court of Justice of 10 September 2009, para 62).

An example of this approach at a national level can be found in a recent judgment of an Italian administrative tribunal which, in relation to a decision of the Italian enforcement authority (ACGM), confirmed that:

the level of knowledge of the average consumer cannot be assessed in merely statistical terms … social, cultural and economic factors, including the economic context and market conditions in which the consumer operates must be taken into account…the relevance of the characteristics of the goods and/or services together with the specifics of the relevant market sector cannot be disregarded. (Tribunale Amministrativo Regionale del Lazio, Sezione I, Sentenza del 25 Marzo 2009, caso *Enel SpA contro Autorità Garante della Concorrenza e del Mercato*)

The case concerned misleading and aggressive commercial practices in the promotion and supply of electricity in Italy, after the liberalisation of the market. The Italian administrative court found that in the electricity market, the transition from a monopoly to a liberalized market not only altered the relationship between offer and demand, but had also increased the knowledge gap between consumers and traders. The court considered that, in such a context, the average consumer (ie somebody who is, in principle, reasonably well informed on the market conditions) could not be expected to have or gain the necessary knowledge or information to fill such a gap.

Essentially, the court took into account the fact that, in the electricity retail market, the average consumer had not yet adapted to the new market situation and that the reasonable level of knowledge one could expect from the average consumer had to be fixed accordingly.

All relevant factors must be taken into account, such as the circumstances in which products are sold, the information given to consumers, the clarity of such information, the presentation and content of advertising material, and the risk of error in relation to the group of consumers concerned.

The fact that a commercial practice is ordinarily employed in other countries without causing consumer protection concerns can be an element in assessing whether such a practice is unfair or not.

OFT v Creative Industries (2011) EWHC 106

This case concerned a number of promotions by Purely Creative Limited. The OFT argued that these were misleading under regulations 5, 6 and Article 31 of Schedule 1 to the regulations. The promotion was a personalized single-page letter with a logo UPR (unclaimed prize register) sent to just under 1,500,000 people obtained from a database of people who had responded to an earlier promotion. According to the judge, 'It was not targeted at any particular social or economic class.' The letter indicated that an individual had won a prize. Prizes ranged from £2500 to a 'Zurich Watch'. Ninety-nine per cent of individuals won a Zurich watch. The person could receive the prize either by telephone to receive a claim number and then sending in a claim form with a stamped addressed envelope, or by a written notification. At the foot of the page in much smaller but legible print it indicated that 'Calls cost £1.50 from a BT landline. Max time 6 minutes.' If you responded by letter you had to include a stamped addressed envelope and allow 28 days for delivery. All electrical items (eg watches) required a payment of £8.50 which included 'insurance and delivery'. On the reverse page of the promotion was the statement 'just call our Claims hotline now' and and an indication of the number of relevant prizes.

The pre-recorded phone response was structured so that responders stayed on the line for 5 minutes and 58 seconds before receiving notification. The overwhelming majority of consumers responded by telephone (at least 80%). As a consequence a consumer paid £8.95 in telephone charges, a delivery charge of £8.50, and the cost of two envelopes and stamps, approximately £18. The company received £1.21 for every £1.50 of the telephone revenue and so received £8.50 + £7.21 = £15.71.

Those who responded by telephone received a voucher which showed a picture of a watch face with 'Zurich' above a picture of Swiss flag and 'A GENUINE ZURICH WRIST WATCH'.

The unit cost of the watch was £9.36 (included acquisition, other costs, postage and packing).

Briggs J held that a misleading impression was created that consumers had won a prize when in fact they were being required to purchase a product. He also held that there was deception as to the geographical origin of product and a material omission as to the cost of the telephone that would have affected the transactional decision to respond by telephone. The misleading statement as to geographical origin would have affected the decision to proceed with the transaction rather than not proceed.

> Briggs J: ... Regulations 5 and 6 did not give rise to issues of interpretation which the parties raised in their cases or submissions. Nonetheless they do raise difficulties of interpretation and application in an English law context with which it is convenient to deal at this stage. Both these two regulations and their corresponding Articles in the UCPD rely heavily upon

the concept of the average consumer. I have already referred to the relevant part of the definition of that phrase in Regulation 2. The requirement to assume that the consumer is reasonably well informed, observant and circumspect reflects the commonsense proposition that the UCPD exists to protect from being misled consumers who take reasonable care of themselves, rather than the ignorant, the careless or the over-hasty consumer.

… It was common ground that, generally speaking, the EU jurisprudence encourages the court to conduct that exercise so far as possible without recourse to statistical or other expert evidence about typical consumer behaviour, or even the evidence of particular consumers. As Etherton J put it in OFT v Officers Club [2005] EWHC 1080 at paragraph 146:

'If the evidence is given by too few of them, their views will not be sufficiently representative of the entire range of such consumers; if a large number, intended to cover the full range, gives evidence, the adverse effect on the cost and duration of the trial may be disproportionate to the value of their evidence.'

In the present case neither of the parties has sought to adduce statistical or expert evidence, or the evidence of particular consumers, although some reference has been made to the presence or absence of consumer complaints about the 2008 promotions. Although they reminded me of the court's power to require such evidence to be made available, I have not considered it necessary to do so. The complaints were of such a varied nature that no reliable conclusions can be based on them.

Both Regulations 5 and 6 require it to be shown that the misleading act or omission:

'causes or is likely to cause the average consumer to take a transactional decision he would not have taken otherwise.'

I have already briefly identified the broad meaning of 'transactional decision', by reference to the definition of that phrase in Regulation 2(1). Although it may be debatable whether the Commission's guidance that this includes a decision to step into a shop after viewing an advertisement in the window goes too far, it was common ground that any decision with an economic consequence was a transactional decision, even if it was only a decision between doing nothing or responding to a promotion by posting a letter, making a premium rate telephone call or sending a text message.

More difficult, in particular to an English lawyer, is the question how high is the hurdle constituted by the causation requirement in each of Regulations 5 and 6. In English law the requirement that a misrepresentation is actionable only if it constitutes an inducement erects a relatively low hurdle, namely that the subsequent decision of the claimant was significantly influenced by the misrepresentation, rather than that the misrepresentation was the sole or even predominant cause. The requirement for an independent interpretation in the present context means that these deep-rooted conceptions must be put on one side.

Counsel could offer no guidance from European jurisprudence on the nature of the causation test imposed by Regulations 5 and 6 (based on substantially equivalent language in Articles 6 and 7 of the UCPD). Again, they left it to the court to identify the height of the hurdle. There is therefore little more than the language of the Directive, reflected in Regulations 5 and 6, upon which to form a view. Although it may be said that the general requirement to provide a 'high' level of consumer protection may properly incline the court towards a lower rather than higher hurdle in the causation test, it needs to be borne in mind that consumer protection is not to become so paternalistic in its extent as to constitute a barrier to the free movement of goods: see Commission v Republic of Austria Case-221/00 per Advocate General Geelhoed at paragraph 82 of his opinion.

It was common ground that the phrase 'causes or is likely to cause' is equivalent to the English standard of the balance of probabilities. The phrase 'to take a transactional decision he would not have taken otherwise' suggests a sine qua non test, namely, whether but for the relevant misleading action or omission of the trader, the average consumer would have made a different transactional decision from that which he did make. This may not mean that the misleading act or omission was the sole cause of the average consumer's decision, but it appears to mean that those Regulations will not have been infringed if the court concludes that, but for the misleading act or omission, the average consumer would nonetheless have decided as he did.

At first sight it might appear from the structure of Regulations 5 and 6 that, for the purposes of applying the causation test, misleading acts require to be assessed separately from misleading omissions. In my judgment that structure did not intentionally impose such an impracticable barrier, in particular because the causation test is the same under each regulation. I consider that the combined effect of all relevant misleading acts and omissions must first be ascertained, and then subjected to the test whether, taken in the aggregate, it would probably cause the average consumer to take a transactional decision which he would not otherwise have taken. Otherwise a communication which contained misleading acts and omissions, none of which would separately satisfy the causation test, may escape from classification as an infringement, even though (as may have been intended by the trader) their combined effect would satisfy the causation test.

The concept of the average consumer is not unfamiliar to UK courts faced with determining whether a misrepresentation is actionable at common law and establishing the standard of deception under the Trade Descriptions Act 1968.

6.1 The vulnerable consumer

Stephen Weatherill (2007) argues that the ECJ has developed a nuanced approach to the concept of the average consumer. He points out that the Court has been unwilling to adopt a glancing or credulous consumer test in cases relating to trade protection measures masquerading as consumer protection (see eg *Cassis de Dijon*) or cases where provisions seem to reflect public choice explanations based on trade protection rather than consumer interests (see *Rocher*, 1993; the ECJ strikes down German regulations that prohibit 'eye-catching' price comparisons even if they are true, and see *Pippig*, 2003). These decisions seem based partly on lifting barriers to consumer information by permitting comparative claims. They give effect to consumers' rights to information. On the other hand the court has recognised the validity of targeted measures to protect the vulnerable. For example, in *Buet* a ban on door-to-door selling of educational materials was upheld by the ECJ. The court commented:

Judgment of the Court (Fifth Chamber) of 16 May 1989—*R Buet and Educational Business Services (EBS) v Ministère public*—Reference for a preliminary ruling: Cour d'appel de Paris—France, Case 382/87

[C]anvassing at private dwellings exposes the potential customer to the risk of making an ill-considered purchase. To guard against that risk it is normally sufficient to ensure that purchasers have the right to cancel a contract concluded in their home.

13 It is necessary, however, to point out that there is greater risk of an ill-considered purchase when the canvassing is for enrolment for a course of instruction or the sale of educational material . The potential purchaser often belongs to a category of people who, for one reason or another, are behind with their education and are seeking to catch up. That makes them particularly vulnerable when faced with salesmen of educational material who attempt to persuade them that if they use that material they will have better employment prospects.

In cases under the Unfair Terms in Consumer Contracts Regulations the ECJ recognised the consumer as a 'weaker party' (see *Oceano Groups, Claro*). Much will depend on the extent to which the Court adopts a broad interpretation of vulnerability in Article 5(3) (Weatherill, 2007: 136). Weatherill argues that a 'broad view' should be taken of what constitutes credulity' to cover, for example, 'emotional foibles' and be 'receptive to the whole range of possible vulnerabilities and disadvantages with which particular groups of consumers are burdened' (Weatherill, 2007: 136).

Commission Guidance, *The Vulnerable Consumer* (2011)

Consumers who may be more vulnerable to certain practices because of their age are elderly people. Aggressive door-to-door selling methods is an example of a practice which may not affect the average consumer but which is likely to intimidate a certain group of consumers, in particular the elderly, who may be vulnerable to pressure selling. The Dutch and German enforcement authorities have also reported the practice of 'bus trips' organised by traders to market their products during the trip, which are particularly attractive to elderly people because of their entertaining nature. The elderly might also be particularly vulnerable to practices connected to certain products, such as burglar alarms.

Children might be particularly vulnerable to advertisements about videogames. Despite the fact that a substantial part of the target audience is constituted by adults, a trader could reasonably foresee that such advertisements may have an impact on a vulnerable category of consumers such as children. For example, the compatibility of a videogame with a specific device may be sufficiently clear to an adult consumer but, due to the way the information is provided, it may still confuse children.

Teenagers represent another category of consumers who are often targeted by rogue traders. An example of this is promoting products which are particularly appealing to teenagers in a way which exploits their lack of attention or reflection due to their immaturity. For example, an advertisement for mobile phone services conveying the message that by subscribing to a particular loyalty plan you can easily make and maintain friends is likely to be taken more literally by teenagers.

… credulity: this covers groups of consumers who may more readily believe specific claims. The term is neutral, so the effect is to protect members of a group who are for any reason open to be influenced by certain claims. An example might be members of a group who, because of particular circumstances, might believe certain claims more readily than others.

A dishonest trader may sell winning lottery number on his website which is open to the general public, although he knows that only the credulous consumers will be attracted to his site and lured into the scam.

Foreseeability

This criterion adds an element of proportionality in assessing the effects of a commercial practice on vulnerable consumers and the professional diligence which reasonably can be expected from a trader. It aims at holding traders responsible only if the negative impact of a commercial practice on a category of vulnerable consumers is foreseeable.

This means that traders are not required to do more than is reasonable, both in considering whether the practice would have an unfair impact on any clearly identifiable group of consumers and in taking steps to mitigate such impact.

...

The aim of the provision is to capture cases of dishonest market practices (e.g. outright frauds or scams) which reach the majority of consumers, but in reality are devised to exploit the weaknesses of certain specific consumer groups.

What should be the role of behavioural economics in assessing how the average or vulnerable consumer would understand statements?

Commission Guidance, *Misleading Actions*

It is then for the national courts and administrative authorities to assess the misleading character of commercial practices by reference, among other considerations, to the current state of scientific knowledge, including the most recent findings of behavioural economics. Thus, for example, the use of defaults (choices consumers are presumed to make unless they expressly indicate otherwise) or the provision of unnecessarily complex information may, according to the circumstances of the case, prove misleading.

The increasing acceptance in consumer policy of the behavioural literature on hyberbolic discounting, over-optimism, anchoring and framing outlined in Chapter 2 suggest that the context and framing of commercial practices may be important in determining whether consumers are likely to be vulnerable and that it may be difficult to make a priori judgements about the competence of the average consumer or the vulnerability of different groups (see also Stuyck, 2007: 167; Wilhelmsson, 2007: 211). Dating agencies, for example, may exploit the loneliness of recently separated individuals. It is possible that these practices may also fall under aggressive commercial practices (see below).

The following reasons suggest that the 'average consumer' test confers substantial discretion on national courts. First, the ECJ has drawn a distinction between the interpretation and the application of Community rules. It has indicated that the determination of whether an advertisement is in fact misleading under the average consumer test should be decided by national courts. Second, Article 13 of the preamble indicates that national courts, in applying the Directive, may take into account 'social, cultural or linguistic factors' in determining whether an advertisement would mislead a consumer in a particular country. Third, the Directive indicates in Recital 18 that 'the average consumer test is not a statistical test' and that national courts should exercise their own faculty of judgment. This approach might be situated against the background of German law that had at one time a test of determining an advertisement to be misleading if it misled 10–15 per cent of the intended audience. These factors all reinforce the open texture of the 'average' concept. Finally, since the ECJ has a crowded docket, it will only hear a few cases of principle (see *Freiburger Kommunalbauten Gmbh*, 2004).

Thomas Wilhelmsson, focusing on 'social, cultural and linguistic factors', argues that there are significant differences between national cultures within the EU in relation to how advertising and marketing may be perceived. Drawing on marketing literature, he argues that consumers have different levels of trust, rationality patterns (eg impulsiveness), decision-making behaviour, values and preferences (Wilhelmsson, 2006). One might well add class and gender to these cultural factors. In considering who is the average consumer it is worthwhile noting that in several celebrated cases, such as *Estée Lauder* or *Clinique* (1994), the consumer targeted by the advertising was female. This is also true in the United States where the 'credulous person' test was based on the marketing of a facial cream that promised 'rejuvenescence' (see *Charles of the Ritz v FTC* (1944)). Writers on consumer law have rarely attempted a feminist analysis of the average consumer in consumer law. Compare the approach of the ASA to cosmetic claims similar to those in *Estée Lauder* (see below, at 282).

If the interpretation of the 'average consumer' depends on so many contextual factors, are the arguments in favour of full harmonisation—such as certainty and lowering of transaction costs—undermined?

6.2 Material omissions

Article 7.1 of the UCPD (CPUT regulation 6) which addresses omissions to disclose material information is not framed as a duty to disclose but imposes indirectly a duty to disclose. Wilhelmsson comments that '[a] provision that deems pure omission to be unfair under certain conditions indirectly contains a duty to disclose. The Commission, however, has preferred not to describe the provision in such language.' The Explanatory memorandum (2003) to the initial version of the directive states that regulation of omissions avoids 'the need for a positive duty to disclose'. According to Wilhelmsson this 'met criticism for being unduly onerous and costly for traders' (Wilhelmsson, 2006: 148).

The material omission provision appears to represent a new development in English law by going beyond existing misrepresentation law and indirectly imposing a duty to disclose material information. However, this conclusion is misleading because under the Trade Descriptions Act, deception included cases where consumers draw incorrect inferences or information is true but incomplete. Deception may also arise from the appearance of a product (*R v Pears*, 1982: 142).

OFT v Purely Creative Industries (2011)

At first sight it might appear from the structure of Regulations 5 and 6 that, for the purposes of applying the causation test, misleading acts require to be assessed separately from misleading omissions. In my judgment that structure did not intentionally impose such an impracticable barrier, in particular because the causation test is the same under each regulation. I consider that the combined effect of all relevant misleading acts and omissions must first be ascertained, and then subjected to the test whether, taken in the aggregate, it would probably cause the average consumer to take a transactional decision which he would not otherwise have taken. Otherwise a communication which contained misleading acts and omissions, none of which would separately satisfy the causation test, may escape from classification as an infringement, even though (as may have been intended by the trader) their combined effect would satisfy the causation test.

The final question of interpretation, which arises only in relation to Regulation 6, relates to the provision in paragraph (3)(a) that 'material information' means inter alia:

'The information that the average consumer needs, according to the context, to take an informed transactional decision;'

The starting point under English common law in relation to pre-contractual negotiations is caveat emptor. That may be qualified both by statute and even by the common law in relation to particular types of transaction, such as the obligation to disclose latent defects when negotiating a sale of land, and the obligation of utmost good faith on an applicant for insurance. Again, these English law concepts must be put on one side, not least because in systems of civil law widely used in Europe there exist general obligations of good faith in contractual relationships which have no parallel in the common law.

A literal reading of Regulation 6(3)(a) and its equivalent in Article 7.1 of the UCPD might suggest that something approaching an utmost good faith obligation is imposed in relation not merely to the consumer's decision whether to contract, but also to every transactional decision, such as, in the present case, a decision whether to respond to a promotion by post, text message or premium rate telephone call. Although qualified by the causation requirement to which I have referred, I regard that analysis as imposing an excessively high hurdle, and counsel did not suggest otherwise. It cannot have been the intention of the framers of the UCPD to require that level of disclosure, and to do so would indeed cause barriers to the free movement of goods and services beyond that necessary to achieve a high degree of consumer protection. In my judgment the key to understanding this paragraph is the concept of 'need'. The question is not whether the omitted information would assist, or be relevant, but whether its provision is necessary to enable the average consumer to take an informed transactional decision.

Harrison & Another v Black Horse Ltd (2011) EWCA Civ 1128

Lord Justice Tomlinson: ...the suggestion that the charging of a high price for a product freely and readily available more cheaply elsewhere in the market is indicative of unfairness in the relationship between seller and buyer would be met with incomprehension.

6.3 What is at stake in the average consumer test? A comparative note

There continues to be conflict in the United States between protection of the rational consumer, reflected in the Federal Trade Commission Act and the protection of the credulous consumer, reflected in state court decisions and enforcement practices. The following is an extract from the FTC Policy Statement on Deception (1983) appended to *In Re Cliffdale Associates* (1984) (see www.ftc.gov/bcp/policystmt/ad-decept.htm). You should compare the analysis with the approach to the 'average consumer' under the UPCD.

II The Act or Practice Must be Considered from the Perspective of the Reasonable Consumer . . .

The Commission believes that to be deceptive the representation, omission or practice must be likely to mislead reasonable consumers under the circumstances. The test is whether the consumer's interpretation or reaction is reasonable. When representations or sales practices are targeted to a specific audience, the Commission determines the effect of the practice on a reasonable member of that group. In evaluating a particular practice, the Commission considers the totality of the practice in determining how reasonable consumers are likely to respond.

A company is not liable for every interpretation or action by a consumer. In an advertising context, this principle has been well-stated: An advertiser cannot be charged with liability with respect to every conceivable misconception, however outlandish, to which his representations might be subject among the foolish or feeble-minded. ..A representation does not become 'false and deceptive' merely because it will be unreasonably misunderstood by an insignificant and unrepresentative segment of the class of persons to whom the representation is addressed. (Heinz W Kirchner, 63 FTC 1282, 1290 (1963))

To be considered reasonable, the interpretation or reaction does not have to be the only one. When a seller's representation conveys more than one meaning to reasonable consumers, one of which is false, the seller is liable for the misleading interpretation. An interpretation will be presumed reasonable if it is the one the respondent intended to convey.

... When representations or sales practices are targeted to a specific audience, such as children, the elderly, or the terminally ill, the Commission determines the effect of the practice on a reasonable member of that group. For instance, if a company markets a cure to the terminally ill, the practice will be evaluated from the perspective of how it affects the ordinary member of that group. Thus, terminally ill consumers might be particularly susceptible to exaggerated cure claims...

As it has in the past, the Commission will evaluate the entire advertisement, transaction, or course of dealing in determining how reasonable consumers are likely to respond. Thus, in advertising the Commission will examine 'the entire mosaic, rather than each title separately.'

...

Pro forma statements or disclaimers may not cure otherwise deceptive messages or practices. Qualifying disclosures must be legible and understandable. In evaluating such disclosures, the Commission recognizes that in many circumstances, reasonable consumers do not read the entirety of an ad or are directed away from the importance of the qualifying phrase by the acts or statements of the seller. ...

Certain practices, however, are unlikely to deceive consumers acting reasonably. Thus, the Commission generally will not bring advertising cases based on subjective claims (taste, feel, appearance, smell) or on correctly stated opinion claims if consumers understand the source and limitations of the opinion. Claims phrased as opinions are actionable, however, if they are not honestly held, if they misrepresent the qualifications of the holder or the basis of his opinion or if the recipient reasonably interprets them as implied statements of fact.

The Commission generally will not pursue cases involving obviously exaggerated or puffing representations, ie, those that the ordinary consumers do not take seriously. Some exaggerated claims, however, may be taken seriously by consumers and are actionable. For instance, in rejecting a respondent's argument that use of the words 'electronic miracle' to describe a television antenna was puffery, the Commission stated:

Although not insensitive to respondent's concern that the term miracle is commonly used in situations short of changing water into wine, we must conclude that the use of 'electronic miracle' in the context of respondent's grossly exaggerated claims would lead consumers to give added credence to the overall suggestion that this device is superior to other types of antennae. (Jay Norris, 91 FTC 751, 847 n 20 (1978), aff'd, 598 F2d 1244 (2d Cir), cent denied, 444 US 980 (1979)) Finally, as a matter of policy, when consumers can easily evaluate the product or service, it is inexpensive, and it is frequently purchased, the Commission will examine the practice closely before issuing a complaint based on deception. There is little incentive for sellers to misrepresent (either by an explicit false statement or a deliberate false implied statement) in these circumstances since they normally would seek to encourage repeat purchases. Where, as here, market incentives place strong constraints on the likelihood of deception, the Commission will examine a practice closely before proceeding.

The FTC policy statement was influenced by neo-classical economists who argued that the protection of a few gullible people will result in lower levels of market information or put up the costs of advertisers that will ultimately be borne by consumers. The emphasis on the protection of 'the rational consumer' in the FTC definition was criticised by a dissenting commissioner as signalling a failure to protect unsophisticated consumers. In his opinion, there was a segment of American business which prospered by preying on vulnerable groups. The idea that FTC protection should be used to attain broader, equitable objectives has a relatively long pedigree, with Justice Learned Hand once commenting, for example, that (*FTC v Standard Education Society* (1937) 696):

> the Commission's duty, in part at any rate, is to discover and make explicit those unexamined standards of fair dealing which the conscience of the community may progressively develop.

Giuseppe Abbamonte (Director of the Health and Consumer Department of the European Commission dealing with regulation of unfair commercial practices) has written in his personal capacity that the average consumer standard assumes 'that consumers should behave like rational economic operators. They should inform themselves about the quality and price of products and make efficient choices' (Abbamonte, 2007: 24). The elasticity of the reasonable consumer test in the US has led commentators to question whether the new formulation has had a direct impact on agency practice. Michael Greenfield suggests that it only 'has a different flavour than the original' (Greenfield, 1993: 179). Ramsay has argued that:

> Determining whether the standard of deception should be that of protection of the reasonable or credulous consumer is a political battle over whose vision of market relations will be made to stick in society. It is about whether to view the law as fostering relationships of trust and interdependence or as promoting a Hobbesian world of self-interested distrust. Law, through its images of social behavior, affects the moral order of markets. It invites us, like the advertisement, to buy into and reproduce the legal images of behavior. If the law repeatedly produces images of the consumer as a rational person, carefully weighing alternatives, then those who are taken advantage of may simply blame themselves for their failures in the marketplace. A more appropriate understanding of the credulous person test is the assumption that consumers are entitled to trust settlers and manufacturers. Fostering trust focuses on the sales practices used in the market and the rationale for protection is the reinforcement of trust rather than protection for the week. (Ramsay, 1996: 85)

Norbert Reich, in a study of the FTC development of an unfairness standard has underlined the many influences on its development, concluding that 'there is indeed no concept of fairness, which depends so much on the circumstances of time, dominating legal theory … and the political attitudes which take precedence' (Reich, 2000).

6.4 Disclaimers, 'car clocking' and the CPUT regulations

Under the Trade Descriptions Act 1968 many prosecutions concerned odometer tampering and whether so-called 'disclaimers' of odometer readings were an effective defence to a prosecution. Prosecutions in relation to used car sales continue to constitute a substantial percentage of prosecutions under the CPUT regulations. Under the Trade Descriptions Act a frequent issue facing the courts was how 'arresting' a disclaimer must be in order for it to neutralise what would otherwise be a false trade description. The following OFT paper outlines the incentives for turning back odometers, and the extent of the practice:

OFT (2010)

Clocking

1.19 Car clocking—the practice of deliberately interfering with a vehicle's odometer so that a lower mileage is displayed—remains a persistent and damaging consumer crime, caught by both the CPRs and the Fraud Act 2006.

1.20 Clocking continues to cause significant consumer detriment, with HPI, a vehicle checking specialist, estimating that up to one in eight vehicles that it checks has a mileage discrepancy. Investigations by Trading Standards Services and the police have also uncovered major incidences of car clocking fraud, with one recent prosecution involving 320 cars with a total value of £1.5m.

1.21 We estimate the potential loss to consumers from the purchase of vehicles with false mileage would be up to £580 million a year, if all consumers were unaware of the false mileage.

1.22 Based on discussions with reputable garages we believe that occasions where there are legitimate reasons to correct a car's mileage are very rare…

OFT, *The Purchase of a Used Car* (1996)

3.8 The high unit value of cars, combined with the importance of mileage for value, makes clocking a highly remunerative crime. By the same token, the potential loss for individual consumers is also high.

The courts adopted a very stringent approach under the Trade Descriptions Act towards the use of odometer disclaimers. The requirement that a disclaimer must be 'as bold, precise and compelling as the trade description itself' and 'must be effectively brought to the notice of any person to whom the goods may be supplied' was adopted in *Norman v Bennett* (1974), and Lawton J in *R v Hammertons Cars* (1976). *Farrand v Lazarus* (2002) is of interest in discussing disclaimers and the approach that would be adopted to this case by the CPUT regulations. In this case an automobile dealer had purchased cars at auction that had warranted mileages of about 151,000, 105,000 and 115,000, respectively. Because the odometers on each car only showed five figures they displayed a mileage of 51,000 10,500 and 15,000 miles, respectively. When the dealer put the cars on sale it placed in the immediate vicinity of the odometer a sticker reading:

Code of Practice for the Motor Industry

1. We do not Guarantee the Accuracy of the Recorded mileage.

2. To the best of our knowledge and belief the reading is correct/incorrect. [On each vehicle the word 'correct' was deleted.]

According to Simon Brown J:

A similarly-worded disclaimer was affixed to every car in the garage. That form of disclaimer was (and we understand remains) in common use throughout the motor trade, having been produced by the Motor Agents Association (now called the Retail Motor Institute). The code of practice was written in consultation with the Office of Fair Trading. Part 3.8 of the code of practice reads: 'Reasonable steps will be taken to verify the recorded mileage of a used car and dealers will use their best endeavours to obtain a signed statement from the previous owner as to the car's mileage. Dealers should pass on any known facts about an odometer reading to a prospective customer.'

... Posters were visible within the garage which bore general disclaimers as to the mileages of vehicles on the premises.

This case was an appeal by prosecutors from an order of the Crown Court that had overturned convictions of the dealer in relation to the supply of the automobiles to which a false description had been applied.

Simon Brown J: ... The question ... is this: what is the position of the dealer who does not himself alter or replace the odometer, but who knows the vehicle's true mileage and knows that the odometer materially understates it? To neutralise the description by a sufficient disclaimer, must he disclose the true mileage, as the appellant authority's advice leaflet and the industry's code of practice suggest. ...

[20] ... was this particular disclaimer 'as bold, precise and compelling as the trade description itself ?' The answer must surely be No.

[21] To suggest merely that the reading on these odometers was incorrect to the best of the respondents' knowledge and belief seriously understated the fact that they knew perfectly well not only that the reading was incorrect, but that it was grossly and potentially misleadingly so. The pro forma nature of the disclaimer, moreover, and the fact that it is common to all cars sold at the respondents' garage again tend to depreciate its impact. Indeed, it could hardly be further from the sort of emphatic contradiction of the message sent by the odometer that to my mind was required to neutralise its effect. In my judgment, only disclosure of the known fact and extent of the falsity of the registered mileage figures would have achieved that here.

[28] I recognise, of course, that in the ordinary way dealers are under no positive duty to disclose the defects and disadvantages of their wares. Generally, they are entitled to be economical with the truth, although not, of course, to lie. With regard to inaccurate mileage readings, however, that, in my judgment, is not the law. In this limited respect they are required to volunteer the truth in so far as they know it.

[29] It follows that I, for my part, would answer the questions posed by the case stated in the negative and would allow this appeal.

Farrand v Lazarus is of interest because of its discussion of the positive obligation of disclosure on the dealer. This is relevant to how such cases will be handled under the CPUT regulations. The focus under the CPUT regulations may be conceptualised in terms of (a) the overall impression of the commercial practice on the average consumer and its impact on transactional behavior, and (b) the material omission to disclose.

Disclaimers are part of the information available to a consumer. The justification for the strict judicial approach, in these cases, may be the importance of the odometer as a 'signal' of the general condition and value of a motor car. In Chapter 2 we noted also the effect of 'anchoring' where the initial selection of a high price by a seller may affect a consumer's decision-making. Thus although a consumer is informed that a low odometer reading is incorrect, the odometer reading may still affect her judgement about the value of the car. Moreover, the power of sales patter and personal selling to neutralise written disclaimers, and the general pressure to 'clinch' the deal, suggest the need for a bold disclaimer notice.

Existing English common law often sanctioned 'half-truths' such as in *Dimmock v Hallett* (1866) where a statement that 'all the farms on the land were fully let' did not state that all the tenants had given notice to quit. It recognises misrepresentation by conduct when the Spice Girls gave the impression to potential sponsors that all were committed to the sponsorship contract when in fact Geri Halliwell had already indicated her intention to leave the group *Spice Girls v Aprilia World Services* (2002). It is therefore an overstatement that English law is based on caveat emptor in pre-contractual negotiations.

6.5 Material omissions and invitations to purchase

The triggering of the duty to disclose material information by an 'invitation to purchase' (regulation 6) is, according to commentators (see Busch, 2004: 94; Howells, Micklitz and Wilhelmsson, 2006: 154), not to be determined on the basis of contractual distinctions between offers and invitations to treat particularly since the UPCD is without effect on the rules on formation of contracts. Rather, it permits a distinction to be drawn between advertising that is merely concerned with brand awareness and more specific marketing which triggers the disclosure duty.

EU Commission Guidance (2011)

... The last part of the definition in Article 2(i) of the Directive ('thereby enables the consumer to make a purchase') does not require that the commercial communication provides the consumer with a mechanism to purchase (eg a phone number or a coupon). It means that the information given in the product marketing must be sufficient to enable the consumer to take a purchasing decision (ie to decide whether to purchase that product for that price or not).

The following will normally be considered invitations to purchase where the price and the characteristics of the product are given:

    an advertisement in a newspaper or on TV;
    an airline website displaying offers for flights and their prices;
    a menu in a restaurant;
    a leaflet from a supermarket advertising for discounted prices on certain products;

a radio advertisement for a mobile phone ring tone;
a product with a price on the shelf in a shop.

Based on Article 2 (i), a commercial communication or advertisement which does not include the price shall not be considered as an 'invitation to purchase' in the sense of the Directive.

A clear example of commercial communications which are not invitations to purchase would be advertisements promoting a trader's 'brand' rather than any particular product (ie brand advertising). Other examples include the promotion of a specific product or a service, through an exhaustive description of its nature, characteristics and benefits, without making reference to the price.

Konsumentombudsmannen v Ving Sverige, ECJ C-122/10 (2011)

Ving is a travel agency which arranges charter holidays and package holidays using scheduled flights. Ving also sells individual airline tickets and hotel accommodation to those who wish to travel independently. The holidays are sold via internet, by telephone, in their own agencies and in selected travel agencies throughout Sweden.

16 On 13 August 2008, Ving put a commercial communication in a daily Swedish newspaper offering trips to New York (United States of America) between September and December 2008. That advertisement contained certain information, namely, written in bold letters, 'New York from SEK 7 820', in smaller letters below that wording, 'Flight from Arlanda with British Airways and 2 nights in the Bedford Hotel – Price per person in double room including airport taxes. Extra nights from SEK 1 320. Applies to selected trips from September to December. Limited number of places' and, at the very bottom left side of the advertisement, 'Vingflex.se Tel. 0771-995995'.

17 On 27 February 2009, the Konsumentombudsmannen brought an action against Ving before the national court, the Marknadsdomstolen (Commercial Court), on the ground that that commercial communication was an invitation to purchase containing a misleading omission in so far as there was insufficient or no information on the main characteristics of the trip, inter alia the price. The Konsumentombudsmannen requested that Ving be ordered to state fixed prices in its advertisements and be prohibited, on pain of a penalty, from advertising an entry-level price. He furthermore requested that that travel agency be ordered to give more exact details of how and in what way the main characteristics of the trip such as, for example, the departure time, the consumer's options or corresponding characteristics, affect the entry-level price given in the commercial communication and of how that entry-level price is affected.

Ving disputes that the commercial communication in question constitutes an invitation to purchase. In the alternative, it submits that the main characteristics of the product were stated in an appropriate manner having regard to the medium of communication used and the product concerned and that the price was given in the manner provided for in Law 2004:347 on price information.

1. Is the requirement 'thereby enables the consumer to make a purchase' in Article 2(i) of Directive 2005/29 … to be interpreted as meaning that an invitation to purchase exists as soon as information on the advertised product and its price is available so that the consumer may make a decision to purchase, or is it necessary that the commercial communication also offer an actual opportunity to purchase the product (for example, an order form) or that it appears in connection with such an opportunity (for example, an advertisement outside a shop)?

…

3. Is Article 2(i) of … Directive [2005/29] to be interpreted as meaning that the requirement for a price is met if the commercial communication contains an entry-level price, that is to say, the lowest price for which the advertised product or category of products can be bought while the advertised product or category of products are available in other versions or with other content at prices which are not indicated?

4. Is Article 2(i) of … Directive [2005/29] to be interpreted as meaning that the requirement concerning a product's characteristics is met as soon as there is a verbal or visual reference to the product, that is to say, so that the product is identified but not further described?

5. If the answer to the … [fourth] question is affirmative, does that also apply where the advertised product is offered in many versions, but the commercial communication refers to them only by a common designation?

6. If there is an invitation to purchase, is Article 7(4)(a) of … Directive [2005/29] to be interpreted as meaning that it is sufficient for only certain of a product's main characteristics to be given and for the trader to refer in addition to its website, on the condition that on that site there is essential information on the product's main characteristics, price and other terms in accordance with the requirements in Article 7(4)?

7. Is Article 7(4)(c) of … Directive [2005/29] to be interpreted as meaning that it is sufficient to give an entry-level price for the price requirement to be met?'

…

A non-restrictive interpretation of the concept of invitation to purchase is the only one which is consistent with one of the objectives of that directive which, according to Article 1 thereof, is that of achieving a high level of consumer protection.

30 In the light of that information, the words 'thereby enables the consumer to make a purchase' must be analysed not as adding a further requisite condition to categorisation as an invitation to purchase, but as stating the purpose of the requirements set out with regard to the characteristics and the price of the product so that the consumer has sufficient information to enable him to make a purchase.

31 Such a finding is borne out by a literal interpretation based on the use of the adverb 'thereby' and is closely linked to the teleological interpretation of Article 2(i) of Directive 2005/29.

32 It follows that, for a commercial communication to be capable of being categorised as an invitation to purchase, it is not necessary for it to include an actual opportunity to purchase or for it to appear in proximity to and at the same time as such an opportunity.…

The third question

35 … third question ….

36 As Article 2(i) of Directive 2005/29 does not require the indication of a final price, it cannot automatically be ruled out that the requirement relating to the indication of the price of the product is met by a reference to an entry-level price.

37 That provision provides that an invitation to purchase must indicate the price of the product in a way appropriate to the means of the commercial communication used. That being the case, it is conceivable that, by virtue of the medium used, it might to difficult to state the price of the product corresponding to each of its versions.

38 Furthermore, Article 7(4)(c) of Directive 2005/29 itself concedes, as far as concerns misleading omissions, that, having regard to the nature of the product, a trader may not reasonably be able to communicate, in advance, the final price.

39 Furthermore, if a reference to an entry-level price had to be regarded as not meeting the requirement relating to the indication of the price referred to in Article 2(i) of Directive 2005/29, it would be easy for traders to indicate only an entry-level price in order to prevent the commercial communication in question from being categorised as an invitation to purchase and, therefore, from having to comply with the requirements of Article 7(4) of that directive. Such an interpretation would erode the practical effect of that directive, as pointed out in paragraphs 28 and 29 of this judgment.

40 It follows from the foregoing that an entry-level price may meet the requirement relating to the reference to the price of the product within the meaning of Article 2(i) of Directive 2005/29 if, on the basis of the nature and characteristics of the product and the commercial medium of communication used, that reference enables the consumer to take a transactional decision.

41 Consequently, the answer to the third question is that Article 2(i) of Directive 2005/29 must be interpreted as meaning that the requirement relating to the indication of the price of the product may be met if the commercial communication contains an entry-level price, that is to say the lowest price for which the advertised product or category of products can be bought, while the advertised product or category of products are available in other versions or with other content at prices which are not indicated. It is for the national court to ascertain, on the basis of the nature and characteristics of the product and the commercial medium of communication used, whether the reference to an entry-level price enables the consumer to take a transactional decision.

The fourth and fifth questions

49 The answer to the fourth and fifth questions is therefore that Article 2(i) of Directive 2005/29 must be interpreted as meaning that a verbal or visual reference to the product makes it possible to meet the requirement relating to the indication of the product's characteristics, and that includes a situation where such a verbal or visual reference is used to designate a product which is offered in a variety of forms. It is for the national court to ascertain, on a case-by-case basis, taking into account the nature and characteristics of the product and the medium of communication used, whether the consumer has sufficient information to identify and distinguish the product for the purpose of taking a transactional decision.

The sixth question

...

52 Article 7(4)(a) of Directive 2005/29 refers to the main characteristics of the product without however defining that notion or providing an exhaustive list. It is however stated that account must be taken, first, of the medium of communication used and, secondly, of the product.

55 It follows that the extent of the information relating to the main characteristics of a product which has to be communicated, by a trader, in an invitation to purchase, must be assessed on the basis of the context of that invitation, the nature and characteristics of the product and the medium of communication used.

56 It follows from the foregoing that Article 7(4)(a) of Directive 2005/29 does not preclude a reference to only certain of a product's main characteristics if the trader refers in addition to its website, on condition that on that site there is essential information on the product's

main characteristics, price and other terms in accordance with the requirements in Article 7 of that directive.

57 It must however be borne in mind that, according to Article 7(5) of Directive 2005/29, information requirements established by European Union law in relation to commercial communications, a non-exhaustive list of which is contained in Annex II to that directive, are to be regarded as material. Among the provisions referred to in that annex is Article 3 of Directive 90/314 on package travel, package holidays and package tours, paragraph 2 of which sets out a certain number of items of information which a brochure relating to that kind of travel and those kinds of holidays and tours must contain.

59 In the light of the foregoing, the answer to the sixth question is that Article 7(4)(a) of Directive 2005/29 must be interpreted as meaning that it may be sufficient for only certain of a product's main characteristics to be given and for the trader to refer in addition to its website, on condition that on that site there is essential information on the product's main characteristics, price and other terms in accordance with the requirements in Article 7 of that directive. It is for the national court to assess, on a case-by-case basis, taking into consideration the context of the invitation to purchase, the medium of communication used and the nature and characteristics of the product, whether a reference only to certain main characteristics of the product enables the consumer to take an informed transactional decision.

The seventh question

62 Whereas Article 2(i) of Directive 2005/29 seeks to set out the definition of an invitation to purchase, Article 7(4)(c) of that directive defines the information which, in the case of an invitation to purchase, must be regarded as material.

63 Although it is true that information regarding the price is regarded, in Article 7(4) of that directive, as being, as a rule, material, the fact remains that Article 7(4)(c) provides that, where the nature of the product means that the price cannot reasonably be calculated in advance, the information must include the manner in which the price is calculated, as well as, where appropriate, all additional freight, delivery or postal charges or, where these charges cannot reasonably be calculated in advance, the fact that such additional charges may be payable.

64 A reference only to an entry-level price may, therefore, be justified in situations where the price cannot reasonably be calculated in advance, having regard, inter alia, to the nature and characteristics of the product. It is apparent from the information in the documents before the court that, in order to establish the final price of a trip, a certain number of variable factors may be taken into consideration, inter alia the point at which a booking is made; the interest in the destination on account of the existence of religious, artistic or sports events; the particular characteristics of seasonal conditions; and the dates and times of travel.

72 ... Consequently, the answer to the seventh question is that Article 7(4)(c) of Directive 2005/29 must be interpreted as meaning that a reference only to an entry-level price in an invitation to purchase cannot be regarded, in itself, as constituting a misleading omission. It is for the national court to ascertain whether a reference to an entry-level price is sufficient for the requirements concerning the reference to a price, such as those set out in that provision, to be considered to be met. That court will have to ascertain, inter alia, whether the omission of the detailed rules for calculating the final price prevents the consumer from taking an informed transactional decision and, consequently, leads him to take a transactional decision which he would not otherwise have taken. It is also for the national court to take into consideration the limitations forming an integral part of the medium of communication used; the nature and the characteristics of the product and the other measures that the trader has actually taken to make the information available to consumers.

7. Misleading pricing: the search for market fairness

The regulation of false and misleading price claims has been an important topic of consumer law in the United Kingdom and elsewhere although the structure and rationales for regulation have generated continuing controversy. Four phases of regulation occurred in the UK. First the Trade Descriptions Act 1968 provided an under-inclusive list of prohibited pricing practices which were difficult to enforce. The second phase was more detailed regulation of so-called 'bargain offers'. This was intended to regulate comprehensively all bargain offers by specifying in detail the types of claims which a business might make and prescribing all others—even if they were not false. In addition, recommended retail prices were banned in relation to the sale of certain products such as beds and domestic electrical appliances. This detailed regulation created strong incentives for businesses to find loopholes and encourage the use of claims that were even more meaningless than those that had existed prior to its enactment. In addition, the detailed nature of the provisions increased their inaccessibility, raising compliance and enforcement costs. The costs of explaining the order to businesses and of providing for fair enforcement were high, particularly since the order did not appeal to common-sense ideas of fairness. The order, therefore undermined the moral authority of trading standards officers in their attempts to secure compliance. The third phase was therefore the introduction of a more general prohibition on misleading price claims in part III of the Consumer Protection Act 1987, which was, however, still limited to particular types of misleading claims. In order to reduce compliance and enforcement costs the prohibition was supplemented by a detailed code of practice, given statutory approval.

The CPUT regulations represent the fourth phase that includes a general prohibition on false or deceptive practices concerning the price or the manner in which the price is calculated, or the existence of a specific price advantage and also contains provisions that prohibit false or misleading 'liquidation sales' (schedule 1, 15), that a product will only be available at a special price for a very limited period (schedule 1, 7) and bait and switch price advertising (schedule 1, 5, 6). Price claims might also be attacked under the general unfairness clause as being contrary to professional diligence.

7.1 Why regulate misleading price claims?

Price advertising lowers consumer search costs, and aggressive price advertising might often be a sign of a competitive market. The importance of price advertising as a marketing strategy is underlined by the wide variety of such claims. For example: claimed reductions from a seller's actual price or future price; manufacturers' recommended prices; 'flash offers'; value or worth claims; 'ready assembled price'; and so on. Given the significance of price advertising, there may often be a temptation for businesses to exaggerate or make misleading claims in order to secure increased market shares, to enter a new market or simply to reap a short-term 'killing' before exiting from a market. Policymakers must attempt to assess the potential costs to competitors and consumers from such practices, along with the impact of regulation, which might discourage the socially valuable aspects of aggressive price advertising. In the following extract, Robert Pitofsky discusses these issues in the context of justifying the FTC's decision in the early 1970s to downgrade the enforcement of fictitious pricing claims and to reallocate the resources thus made available to the enforcement of product-quality claims.

R Pitofsky, 'Beyond Nader: Consumer Protection and the Regulation of Advertising' (1977), 90 *Harvard L Rev* 661, 667–69

When a seller deceptively asserts that [what he is selling] is selling at '20% off list' or 'free,' competitive or consumer injuries can result. Purchasers may be diverted from the more efficient low-price seller, and purchases may be executed that might not otherwise occur or at a time they would not otherwise occur. On the other hand, much alleged fictitious pricing is innocuous, either because consumers are in a position to check the validity of exaggerated claims (for example, where comparison shopping is relatively simple) or because the claims are so unlikely ('lowest price ever') or ambiguous ('10% off') that they will be ignored by almost all customers. Fictitious price claims that exaggerate the price against which the discount is compared may deny consumers the benefits of the bargain they thought they were receiving, but as long as consumers are accurately informed of the offering price, they can make sensible decisions, and the transactions may still be at prices lower than could be obtained at most other outlets in the marketing area.

Furthermore, much fictitious pricing enforcement entails considerable social and economic costs. A natural target for such enforcement has been discount houses, and the usual complainants have been nondiscounters who emphasize service and reliability rather than price. Aggressive enforcement against discounters that forces them to hew close to the line of accurate information may tend to dampen competitive activity. Often, 'cents-off,' free goods, couponing and other discount promotions are devices that assist new entrants in penetrating concentrated markets and that tend to unsettle stable and rigid pricing patterns. Couponing and free goods may be the only legal way that a seller can effectuate a price cut to consumers when intermediate distributors refuse to pass along a list price reduction. While the same procompetitive effects can be achieved by accurate price claims in connection with these promotions, the cost to sellers of ascertaining whether particular discount claims are accurate may deter them from making such claims at all. … Extreme examples of deceptive price claims might still be challenged, and fictitious price counts incorporated in omnibus complaints against clearly unethical sellers, but discontinuance of the effort to clear the market of ambiguous or exaggerated price claims seems justified.

Pitofsky underlines the competitive benefits of aggressive price advertising and the ability of consumers to protect themselves against misleading price claims. Richard Bragg has, however, commented that courts have underestimated the significance of misleading pricing. 'There is a distinct failure to understand that cumulatively, it can make large profits for the trader and leaves individual consumers with a grievance unrelated to the amount' (Bragg, 2006: 347).

The liberalisation of comparative advertising in Europe achieved partly through the ECJ (see eg *GB-Inno*, *Rocher*) and the Directive on Comparative Advertising (97/55) also recognises the importance of price comparisons.

Behavioural economics suggests a different interpretation of the effects of price claims than that adopted by Pitofsky. Willem van Boom recently described the impact of 'behavioural pricing' including framing, 'free gifts', bundling, and price partitioning (Van Boom, 2011: 359)

The OFT discusses some of these practices in the following material.

OFT Pricing Study, *Advertising of Prices*, OFT 1291, December 2010

Price framing occurs when a trader presents a price offer in a particular context that affects people's assessment of the value of the offer. Value is an abstract concept and so people use cues from the world around them to make sense of whether a particular offer is a good or bad deal. It is because of this that price framing has the power to influence, and sometimes mislead, consumers.

1.2 Clear, honest, upfront advertising of prices is beneficial to consumers and competition. Misleading advertising of prices, however, may lead to consumers spending more than they need to, buying a product which is not the best for them, wasting time or suffering annoyance, disappointment or regret. Fair dealing firms, sticking to the spirit of the consumer protection legislation, feel frustrated and disadvantaged when they observe their competitors pushing the boundaries too far.

...

1.6 We collected evidence about, and examined in detail, the following pricing practices:

- partitioned 'drip' pricing, where price increments 'drip' through during the buying process
- 'baiting sales', where only a very limited, or no, products are available at the discount price and consumers may ultimately purchase a full priced product
- 'reference prices', where there is a relatively high reference price compared to sale price, for example 'was £50, now £20', or '50% off'
- time-limited offers, such as sales which finish at the end of the month or special prices which are available for one day only
- volume offers, where it may be difficult for consumers to assess an individual price, for example 'three-for-two'
- complex offers, such as package prices with many separate elements to the price, and
- price comparison sites which may use some of the practices described above.

1.7 Such price framing practices can be extremely effective at altering people's perception of the value of an offer. For example, an experiment in the US found that consumers offered a car for $7,272 estimated the true value of the car to be considerably higher when they were also told 'Was $8,215' compared with when they were told 'Was $7,414'.

1.8 These effects are not restricted to sale pricing. Surcharges, for example, may also have a powerful influence on people's evaluation of a deal. For example, an online auction experiment found that consumers offered CDs with the 15 per cent auction surcharge excluded from the headline price were more likely to purchase compared with customers who were shown a single combined price.

Our findings

1.9 Some practices are more likely to lead to consumer harm than others, and harm is more likely in some circumstances than others. The following ranking of price frames represents, in general terms, our assessment of their potential to mislead:

- drip pricing
- time limited offers

- baiting sales and complex offers
- reference pricing
- volume offers.

1.10 This list represents our view about the potential for a certain pricing practice to mislead – it does not mean that all partitioned offers, for example, will mislead consumers. Whether any given offer is misleading depends on the specifics of the advert and a number of other factors. Furthermore, when deciding whether a particular advert is an enforcement priority we will also consider whether the advert leads to harm for consumers. In doing so, we will take into account the features of the market and the product to which the advert relates. Specifically:

- frequency of purchase: with more frequent purchases a consumer has greater opportunity to learn from their mistakes and become familiar with the offers in the market place
- ease of cross-market price comparisons: markets where like-for-like price comparisons are readily available, such as some of those characterised by good quality price comparison sites, are likely to assist consumers in verifying price claims
- the ease with which a consumer can independently verify quality: the easier it is for a consumer to identify whether a product is high or low quality prior to purchase the less likely they may be to rely on the price for information about quality
- the expense of the item: low value items, especially those bought frequently may present a learning opportunity with less financial harm than big ticket items bought less frequently
- reasonable consumer expectations: if the majority of consumers are aware of and understand the use of a particular practice, for example, whether there are charges for delivery or that time limited sales are often extended, it is less likely that a consumer will be misled by such a practice
- we would also take into account the size of the market and the overall level of harm likely to arise from the advert.

7.2 The regulation of hi-lo pricing

'Hi-lo' pricing describes the practices of retailers that offer a good at a high price for a short period of time in order to establish a regular price but generally sell the goods at a 'sale' price. Sales are a frequent occurrence. Recent cases in both the UK and Canada have addressed this issue.

In *Office of Fair Trading v Officers Club* (2005), The Officers Club was a discount clothes store that marketed clothes at '70% off' 'Red Star' prices. All goods were initially marketed at the higher price in a small number of stores for 28 days and then sold at a discount. The owner of the company had developed this scheme after being impressed by the use of this technique on a visit to the US. This strategy was used from 1993 until 2004. A representative in-store advertisement of a long-sleeved shirt stated 'Petroleum, Enzym' 'Was £29.0, You pay £9, 70% off everything'. There were also notices stating: 'All discounted goods have been for sale at the higher price at six or more of our branches for a minimum of 28 days in the preceding six months.' Only 19 out of the Officers Club 159 stores offered full-price items and 'None of those 19 stores offered more than 0.36% of its stock at the full price, none offered more than 3 styles at the full price, and none offered more than 2 sizes of a particular style at the full price.'

The OFT argued that 'an ordinary and reasonable consumer' would have drawn the inference that the discounts were genuine and that this would not have been removed by the disclaimer. The OFT submitted that 'in determining whether a discount is "genuine", it is relevant to take into account a number of factors, which overlap'. Those factors include, in particular, whether the higher prices were 'genuine', 'good faith' prices, at which the goods had been 'actively offered for sale' for a substantial period of time, or whether, by contrast, the higher prices were 'artificial' or 'inflated prices' and were set 'with the overriding purpose of claiming the subsequent discount'. The primary argument of The Officers Club was that its '70% off' strategy complied with the 28-day rule in the Code of Practice on Price Indications under Part 3 of the 1987 Act, ie it had been offered at the higher price for 28 days within the last six months and accordingly there could be no infringement.

Etherton J outlined the arguments of the The Officers Club:

> In support of its claim that TOC's notices were not misleading, and did not deceive, TOC relies on the fact that, notwithstanding the existence of the '70% off' strategy over many years, giving rise to millions of transactions each year and the sale of vast numbers of goods, there is no record of any member of the public ever having made a complaint to TOC about being misled, and only 9 complaints by members of the public to TSDs. Further, and finally, TOC claims that, even if its notices promoting the '70% off' strategy did make implied representations as to the discount being a genuine discount, and the higher prices being bona fide prices at which the goods were actively marketed for sale, such representations were true.

Etherton J concluded that:

> [T]aking into account all the notices typically to be found in one of TOCs stores when it was implementing the '70% off' strategy, those notices were representing to customers that the higher price was one at which TOC had offered for sale a significant number of the goods, for a period of not less than 28 days in the preceding 6 months, in the honest belief that they could be sold by TOC at that price. Those representations were, on the evidence, false and misleading within the meaning of the Regulations.

> The 'Red Star' items were not in fact offered for sale in significant quantities. As at 31 May 2003, by way of example, only 19 out of TOC's 159 stores offered higher price 'Red Star' items; none of those 19 stores offered more than 0.36% of its stock at the higher price; and the average proportion of 'Red Star' stock in the 19 stores was 0.14% ... usually a very small quantity of 'Red Star' items of a particular line were offered for sale. ... For example, typically between 24 and 36 shirts of a particular line would be offered for sale at the higher price; the actual numbers, sizes and colours would be entirely dependent on what the manufacturers supplied; and the 'Red Star' items would not be restocked for sale at the higher price ... over the period 1 September 2002 to 28 June 2003, only 0.15% of the total units sold by TOC were at the higher price.

> Further, I find that the higher price was not fixed by TOC in the honest belief that its goods could be sold by TOC at that price. ... Evidence was adduced, on behalf of TOC ... of the advertising practice of other retailers selling at discount prices... TOC... rely upon such evidence, at least in part, to support their contention that an ordinary reasonable consumer would not have regarded TOC's notices as making the implied representations which the OFT alleges, or, possibly, that even if the notices did make these implied representations the ordinary reasonable consumer would not have been deceived by the notices. I reject those arguments [paras 181–86]. In the first place, as I have already said, TOC itself accepts that the class of customers to whom the '70% off' advertisements were addressed would have included persons with little knowledge of the practices of such other retailers. ...

Second, there is no evidence before the Court that any retailers, or at any event any significant number of other retailers, use, or have used, a comparable strategy of a permanent large fixed percentage discount applicable to all or the vast majority of the retailer's goods.

Third, I can see no reason to assume, from the fact that other retailers operate and advertise price discount schemes involving a comparison between 'was' and 'now' prices, that consumers were not or were not likely to have been misled by TOC's notices promoting the '70% off' strategy. In some cases, the notices of other retailers, as well as TOC's notices, will have deceived and misled one or more consumers. In other cases, one or more consumers may not have been misled by the notices of other retailers, but may have been misled by TOC's notices. In short, I cannot see the basis for making any assumption in favour of TOC's notices by reason of the advertising practices of some other retailers.

...

It follows that TOC's notices promoting its '70% off' strategy were misleading advertisements within the meaning of the Regulations.

It is not in dispute that, if TOC's notices contravened the Regulations, they also constituted Community Infringements for the purposes of EA 2002, that is to say they harmed 'the collective interests of consumers'.

OFT research on the behavioural aspects of hi-lo pricing concluded that:

OFT, *Advertising of Prices* (2010), 35–36

Reference prices are frequently used by traders across a wide range of industries to demonstrate to consumers that they should visit a particular trader to save money; either compared with a different time or a different trader. Where reference prices are clearly presented to consumers and the reference price is accurate and in line with consumer expectations, it is an efficient way for a trader to demonstrate price offers which may be valued by consumers and helps reduce search costs associated with getting a good deal.

4.4 Including a reference price in an offer can create an anchor which consumers use as a starting point for estimating the real value of the product. Evidence set out in the psychology literature review shows that a reference price is very effective at encouraging consumers to make a purchase they may not otherwise have made by increasing consumers perceptions of the value of the product and the inferred saving. This change in perception arises because consumers do not fully adjust their perceptions of the offer away from the reference (or 'anchor') price.

4.5 The academic literature consistently finds that reference pricing influences people's perceptions of the value of the offer and reduces the effort consumers put into shopping around and comparing prices. Furthermore the evidence suggests that reference pricing can still influence consumers where reference prices are exaggerated or where consumers are sceptical about whether the references are genuine.

4.6 The psychology literature review shows that reference pricing affects consumers' intentions to purchase whether the reference price is genuine or not. As a result where the reference price is misleading and consumers are not able to easily identify or verify the reference price (and thereby verify the saving) there is considerable scope for consumer harm. It is important that references are genuine so they do not mislead consumers into making purchases they may not have made if the offer was communicated accurately.

In a Canadian judgment (*Sears*, 2005) a major department store offered tyres for automobiles at 45% off their regular price. These tyres were rarely sold at the regular price. As part of its defence Sears argued that consumers discounted the 'save 45%' and shopped around for tyres. These arguments were rejected by the Competition Tribunal who found that: (1) many consumers did not shop around when buying tyres; (2) it was difficult for consumers to compare prices because the brand of tyres were specially made for Sears and consumers would have difficulty in knowing *ex ante* whether the tyres were different in quality to branded tyres sold by other companies; (3) although individuals might discount the price to a certain extent they would probably think that they were still getting good value, particularly since the claim came from a credible source (a well-known retailer). They would therefore be less likely to continue searching for a better price.

This example of pricing suggests that there may be some overlap between Pitofsky's approach and the behavioural approach that stressed the 'anchoring' role of the regular price because the research found that discounts may be more significant in affecting purchase intentions in relation to higher-priced products. However, the behavioural literature suggests that repeat purchase behaviour may not always prevent consumers from believing in the plausibility of exaggerated reference prices and that the 'sceptical rational consumer' implied by the neo-classical model is belied in practice. Moreover, could the practice adopted by the The Officers Club be argued to be contrary to norms of professional diligence? To what extent does it undercut norms of consumer trust in the marketplace? Is the market more efficient if consumers are generally sceptical of price claims?

In 2010 the Department of Business, Innovation and Skills provided guidance on pricing that followed the approach of Etherton J. It also suggested some general guidance on pricing. The EU Commission has also provided guidance on the common UK pricing practice of 'buy one get one free'.

Department of Business Innovation and Skills, *Guidance on Pricing* (2010)

You should make the meaning of any price comparison clear to the consumer. ... If you make statements like 'sale price £5' or 'reduced to £39' you should quote the previous higher price to which you refer. You should not make a comparison with a price based on a different method of payment unless an unambiguous, easily identifiable and clearly legible explanation of the basis of the previous price is given.

1.1.5 You should make clear what sort of price the higher price is. Comparisons described by words like 'regular price', 'usual price' or 'normal price', which do not say whose regular, usual or normal price it is (for example 'our normal price') should not be used. You should avoid using descriptions like 'reduced from' and crossed out higher prices which do not refer to your own previous price. In general terms, words used other than with their normal everyday meanings should be avoided

EU Commission Guidance, *Free Offers*

'Free offers'

3.4.4. Basic criteria in relation to combined offers

The assessment is more complex when the word 'free' is used in the context of combined offers, which are commercial offers involving more than one product or service.

The following are the main principles which should be taken into account when assessing combined offers and which are already largely reflected in some advertising regulatory codes:

Traders must not try to recover their costs by reducing the quality or composition or by inflating the price of any product that must be bought as a pre-condition for obtaining the free item;

Traders should not describe an individual element of a package as 'free' if the cost of that element is included in the package price.

The two categories of combined offers are conditional-purchase promotions and package offers.

- 'free wall-chart when you buy Thursday's paper' is justified if the paper is sold without a wall-chart on other days for the same price;
- '25% extra free', for a bottle of shampoo, is justified if the bottle contains 25% more shampoo than is usually supplied at that price;
- 'free travel insurance for customers who book their holiday online' is justified if customers who book the same journey by telephone are offered the same price but not offered free insurance or if internet customers who choose to buy their insurance from a different provider pay the same for their holiday as those who choose to take advantage of the marketer's insurance offer;
- 'free delivery for customers who spend over £50 on groceries' is justified if the retailer does not offer free delivery when the grocery spend is less than £50;

A package is a pre-arranged combination of features offered for a long-term single, inclusive price where customers cannot exercise genuine choice on how many elements of the package they receive for that price.

... a mobile-phone subscription offers a certain amount of airtime, a certain number of text messages and a voicemail facility for one all-inclusive price. Each element is intrinsic to the quality and composition of the package being advertised for the package price. Because customers cannot exercise genuine choice over how many elements they receive for the price paid, the elements are all included in the package price and may not be described as 'free'.

What is the legal status of this guidance?

---

8. Aggressive commercial practices

The provisions in CPUT regulation 7 on aggressive commercial practices address the difficult question of elaborating ground rules for advantage-taking in consumer trans-actions, a question posed by the criterion of a 'significant impairment of a consumer's freedom of choice'. An important question is whether UPCD Articles 8 and 9 will develop norms that go beyond existing common law protections in the UK. One area is emotional exploitation in marketing. For example, dating agencies may engage in emo-tional exploitation of individuals who have had difficulties in establishing relationships or are lonely. The bereaved may be vulnerable to exploitation, as may new immigrants. Individuals subject to debt collection communications might be vulnerable. In the US some courts have applied the 'least sophisticated consumer' test under the Fair Debt Collection Practices Act (see *Wilson v Quadramed Corpn* (2000)). In North America there are many cases involving emotional exploitation of consumers. The FTC held to be unfair the sales practices of dance companies that included emotional exploitation as one technique to convince individuals to sign up for large numbers of dance lessons. In *Re Arthur Murray Studio of Washington Inc* 78 FTC 401 (affirmed 458 F2d 622) (5th cir 1972) the Commission described the following practice:

> The sales approach or technique used by respondent assumed that many of the people who come to dance studios do so for some more deep-seated reasons than simply a desire to learn to dance. …This factor could be loneliness, marital difficulties, or some unpleasant experience or unhappiness in the prospect's past which could be exploited for the purpose of selling dance instructions.

This was part of a practice of selling that included:

> awarding gift certificates for … instructions either through the use of so-called 'contests' in which all participants can win or by falsely representing that the person has been 'selected' to receive a free course of instruction: failing to provide the full number of free hours of dance instruction promised, but instead devoting much of the time to promoting the sale of dancing lessons; representing that certain clubs sponsored by respondents are bona fide adult social clubs when in fact such clubs are devices used to obtain leads to prospective students and to lure prospects into respondents' studios where a sales presentation could be made; using sham dance analysis tests where all prospective students are given passing grades, regardless of dancing ability, aptitude or proficiency; using 'relay salesmanship' which involves excessive efforts by a number of different salesman in a single day to persuade a prospective student to sign a contract for dancing instruction; and using 'intense, emotional and unrelenting' sales pressure to persuade a prospective student to sign a contract for a substantial number of dancing lessons without affording the prospect a reasonable opportunity to consider and comprehend the scope and extent of the contractual obligations involved.

English law has regulated this area through the doctrines of duress and undue influence. The common law of duress requires an illegitimate act that causes the other party to enter into the contract or otherwise take action. The illegitimate act was originally threats of physical violence, but was extended to duress of goods such as the wrongful seizure of goods followed by a demand for payment for their return to the rightful owner. For example, this might include a situation where an individual takes her car to the local garage for repairs. The garage takes the car apart, and then tells the consumer that it will have to charge an extra £300 and will not continue the repairs or put back the car together, unless the consumer agrees (see Bradgate, Brownsword and Twigg- Flesner, 2003: 70).

The English courts have more recently recognised a concept of economic duress in commercial contracts. This has often involved the situation where one party to a contract threatens to break the contract, unless more favourable terms are agreed. The courts have had difficulty in articulating a clear rationale for when economic duress will be applicable. They sometimes refer to a number of factors, for example, whether there was an illegitimate act, whether the innocent party had alternative options or access to independent legal advice or took steps to avoid the contract once the threat was removed (see eg Lord Scarman in *Universe Tankships* (1983)). The courts sometimes refer to the 'overborne will' theory to justify economic duress. This draws upon the contrast between a voluntary and involuntary choice (see *Pau On v Lin Yau*). However, this is not a very stable criterion. For example the law may invalidate a contract entered into by the captain of a ship in difficulty to pay a very high price to a tug, which will save it. One might say that the captain 'had no choice'. But as was pointed out in the following well-known US articles, voluntariness and an illegitimate act do not provide clear guidance.

Dalzell, 'Duress by Economic Pressure I' (1942) 20 *NCL Rev* 237

We have talked of contracts signed under duress as lacking 'real consent.' This seems to be a manner of speech rather than a reasoned conclusion. When I feel that I must choose between having a bullet lodged in my head and signing a contract, my desire to escape the bullet would hardly be described as unreal or merely apparent; and the signing of the contract is simply the expression of that fear of death. To call such a consent 'unreal' is to characterize the normal human desire to continue alive as mere pretence. The father who pays a ransom to his daughter's kidnappers does so because he fears he will lose his daughter. ...

What we meant by calling such consent unreal, was that it would not have been given except for the unpleasant alternative.

Dawson, 'Economic Duress—An Essay in Perspective' (1947) 45 *Mich LR* 253

If it can be assumed that the object of relief for duress is to cancel out advantages secured by superior bargaining power, the whole group of cases takes on a new perspective. The objective of ensuring the freedom of the individual will, so frequently proposed in the nineteenth century cases, becomes on this analysis an incidental or at most a subsidiary objective. More important, the concentration of the modern cases on the distinction between legal and illegal means seems misdirected. . . .

... Doctrines of duress are intended to raise precisely the question whether it is 'rightful' to use particular types of pressure for the purpose of extracting an excessive or disproportionate return.

The issue becomes therefore whether the choice is sufficiently unpleasant for the law to strike down the bargain. There is the extent to which the law will address structural inequalities, which result in limited choice. For example, should the law strike down a contract entered into by the poor consumer to pay a high price for credit because she 'has no choice'? Lord Denning provided a clear answer here in *Lloyds Bank Limited v Bundy* [1975] 1 QB 326:

No bargain will be upset which is the result of the ordinary interplay of forces. There are many hard cases which are caught by this rule. Take the case of a poor man who is homeless. He agrees to pay a high rent to a landlord just to get a roof over his head. The common law will not interfere. It is left to Parliament.

The concept of undue influence is broader than duress and recognises that certain relationships will be presumed to raise undue influence, while in other cases undue influence may be proved from all the circumstances of the case. This will usually require proof that there was a relationship of trust and confidence between the parties and that this relationship was used to bring about a particular transaction that would not be regarded as prudent. There is also the further category of the 'unconscionable bargain'. This involves situations where one party has exploited a weakness of the other party. These concerned sales of reversionary interests in land by 'poor and ignorant persons' or in more modern terms 'a member of the lower income group ... less highly educated' (*Cresswell v Potter* (1978)). Expectant heirs who borrowed money at high prices on security of their future inheritance were in the nineteenth century protected under the category of unconscionable bargains (*Earl of Aylesford v Morris* (1873)).

The English common law has rejected thus far Lord Denning's synthesis of these doctrines in *Lloyds Bank v Bundy* into an overarching doctrine of unconscionability that combined the idea of unfair terms and inequality of bargaining power, where one party took advantage of their bargaining power (see Lord Scarman in *National Westminster Bank Plc v Morgan* (1985)), although many commonwealth jurisdictions have adopted this doctrine (see Australia, *Commercial Bank of Australia v Amadio* (1983); Canada, *Harry v Kreutziger* (1978)). Thus in *Harry v Kreutziger* two formulations of unconscionability were proposed. The first was the *Bundy* test and the other was the following: 'The single question is whether the transaction, seen as a whole, is sufficiently divergent from community standards of commercial morality that it should be rescinded.' This formulation might be relevant to the application of Article 8 to aggressive commercial practices.

Although the concept of inequality of bargaining power in a consumer market might give content to the concept in the UCPD of conduct that leads to a 'significant impairment of consumer choice', further analysis is necessary to provide guidance for decision-making. Thus one might use the concept of a situational monopoly to rationalise cases such as the sinking ship which pays a high fee to a salvage tug, or in the consumer context the automobile repairer who will not return the car except on payment of a large amount.

The justification of the aggressive marketing sections may be located not only in economic rationales but also in theories of autonomy. Undoing aggressive and exploitative selling may protect the future autonomy of the consumer, particularly where there is likely to be a conflict between an individual's short-term and long-term preferences and the marketer often is aware of this fact (eg that an individual's appetite for dance lessons, fitness clubs, etc, are likely to decline significantly over the long run).

---

9. Prohibited practices: Schedule 1

Annex 1 (Schedule 1 regulations) contains a list of 31 commercial practices 'which are in all circumstances considered unfair'. The majority of these practices fall under the category of misleading practices. They include 'bait' and 'bait and switch' marketing (Articles 5, 6), pyramid selling (Article 14), false liquidation sales (Article 15), false health claims in relation to a product (Article 17), relying on emotional fears concerning risks to a consumers' security (Article 12), 'free' gifts that require the purchase of another product (Article 20), and creating the impression that one is not selling in the course of business (Article 22). Aggressive commercial practices include overly aggressive doorstep selling (Article 25) and telemarketing (Article 26), direct exhortations to children to buy an advertised product (Article 28), demanding payment for unsolicited products (Article 29) and misleading prize promotions (Article 31).

It is not necessary to establish a causal link between the practices and distortion of consumer behaviour, although in many cases such a consequence might be presumed. This list provides an exhaustive list of practices that are per se prohibited throughout the EU: Article 5(5) indicates that 'the same single list shall apply in all Member States and may only be modified by revision of this Directive' (see Wilhelmsson, 2006: 159). This 'laundry list' of prohibited practices may be an important source of prosecutions in the UK since it provides legal certainty for the prosecutor. Commentators have, however, criticised the list because of a lack of underlying logic 'coherence or policy priority in the selection and ordering of the examples' (Engelbrekt, quoted in Howells, Micklitz and Wilhelmsson, 2006: 160). Undoubtedly it is an eclectic list of practices chosen from the practices of different countries.

A more substantial criticism relates to the drafting of some clauses that are not precisely drafted, eg the provisions on pyramid selling and bait and switch marketing. The interpretation of regulation 31 has already resulted in a reference by an English court to the ECJ (see *OFT v Creative Industries*).

Stuyck et al also criticise the automatic presumption in the list as 'incompatible with the market-oriented philosophy of the UCPD (based on the informed decision paradigm)' and because 'certain practices will be absolutely prohibited even if in the circumstances of the case it is clear that at most a small minority of consumers would be affected' (Stuyck et al, 2006: 131). They also believe that the lack of clear drafting of some of the prohibitions will reduce legal certainty (an objective of the Directive) and because of the static nature of the list hold back 'innovation in harmless forms of competition'.

---

10. 'Cooling-off' periods in consumer transactions: a right to withdraw in consumer contracts?

A 'cooling-off' period is a limited period within which a consumer may cancel a contract which would otherwise have become binding on her. Cooling-off periods traditionally had two objectives: (i) to protect individuals against high-pressure sales; and (ii) to allow a consumer the opportunity to have access to more information concerning the proposed purchase. They were originally applied to door-to-door credit sales consummated away from business premises but have been extended to 'distance selling' (see below), including distance sales of financial services (Financial Services Distance Marketing Regulations 2004), the sale of timeshares, and the provision of extended warranties in relation to domestic electrical goods (The Supply of Extended Warranties on Domestic Electrical Goods Order 2005). The EU Directive on consumer credit introduced a general 14-day cooling-off period for all consumer credit transactions within the scope of the Directive (see now CCA 1974 section 66A). In other countries cooling-off rights exist in relation to individuals signing contracts for health clubs and other forms of personal development services (eg Ontario Consumer Protection Act 2002).

The proliferation of cooling-off periods resulted in regulatory complexity with differing cancellation periods for different transactions (see discussion in Hellwege, 2004: 712) and the need to regulate attempts to avoid the bite of the regulations. The Consumer Rights Directive (2011) will standardize the cooling-off period at 14 days for off-premises and distance selling. The former are defined as:

Off premises contract

'off-premises contract' means any contract between a trader and a consumer for the supply of a good or the provision of a service:

(a) which is any sales or service contract concluded away from business premises with the simultaneous physical presence of the trader and the consumer or any sales or service contract, or

(aa) for which an offer was made by the consumer with the simultaneous physical presence of the trader and the consumer away from business premises in the same circumstances, or

(b) whose main components have been determined in the course of an excursion, a leisure event or a sales demonstration organised by the trader or by a third party on behalf of the trader any sales or service contract concluded on business premises but negotiated away from business premises, with the simultaneous physical presence of the trader and the consumer, the aim of such excursion, leisure event or demonstration being to conclude a contract subsequently on business premises;

The Consumer Rights Directive (October 2011) Recitals 21 and 37 argue that:

In an off-premises context, consumers may be under potential psychological pressure or may be confronted with an element of surprise, irrespective of whether or not they have solicited the trader's visit. ... In the case of distance sales the consumer is not able to see the goods before concluding the contract, he should have a right of withdrawal. For the same reason, the consumer should be allowed to test and inspect the goods he wants to buy to the extent necessary to establish the nature, characteristics and functioning of the goods. Concerning off-premises contracts, the consumer should have the right of withdrawal because of the potential surprise element and/or psychological pressure.

Marco Loos suggests the objectives of cooling off periods to be:

protecting the buyer from aggressive commercial practices (doorstep selling, timeshare) ... to remove barriers for cross-border transactions and thus to stimulate the internal market (distance selling, distance marketing of financial services, life assurance). Finally, it may offer the consumer a possibility to obtain certain information or advice regarding the contract that he has concluded (sale of houses, and, to a lesser extent, financial services and life assurance). (Loos, 2009)

10.1 Doorstep selling

The regulation of doorstep selling has a relatively long history in consumer policy.

The Molony Committee in 1962 introduced the novel and 'radical' concept of a 'cooling-off' period in response to the many atrocity stories that they heard in relation to doorstep sales (see Sher, 1967–68: 717).

Final Report of the Committee on Consumer Protection, Cmnd 1781 (1962)

Door-to-door salesmen

741. The activities of some of these men have provoked a greater wrath and indignation among our representors than any other single subject. ... This condemnation ... is ... mainly confined to those ... who sell the more expensive types of goods by this method of approach; in particular vacuum cleaners, floor polishers, sewing machines, refrigerators and other major electrical appliances, and also educational publications. ...

742. We have received numerous and lurid accounts of the lengths to which some of these men are prepared to go in order to secure an order. We are told that they are known literally to force their way over the doorstep, to remain in the house for as long as six hours at a time—sometimes until midnight or later—keeping up a hypnotic flow of persuasive sales talk. It is alleged that their attitude and behaviour is sometimes such as to reduce householders—in particular women—to a state of acute physical fear. It is said that in persuading people to enter into heavy financial commitments, the terms of payment or of 'trade-in' allowances are deliberately misstated, and the figures on the order form or agreement concealed or omitted until the customer's signature has been obtained. ... By whatever proportion of door-to-door salesmen such practices are followed, and with whatever frequency, a considerable volume of evidence insisted that they are widespread (and successful) enough to amount to a serious social evil; resulting in homes labouring under an excessive burden of debt and sometimes torn by consequential domestic disharmony.

520 The third suggestion involved giving the hirer time for reflection and, if desired, retraction. It was proposed that ... for a definite period, say of 48 or 72 hours, the hirer would be entitled to withdraw from the agreement by giving notice of his decision. A variant of the proposal is that the right of withdrawal should be confined to agreements executed away from an established place of business. ... It would ensure that no-one assumed hire-purchase obligations without a full opportunity of understanding the nature of the bargain and weighing the transaction against his or her personal needs and resources. ... We have given close thought to this idea of a 'cooling-off' period because of its obvious value as a check on the excesses of salesmanship. We are concerned, if it is possible, to safeguard the hirer who is already to commit himself as well as those whose weak sales-resistance is overcome by practiced artifice. It is not in the true interest of any party (save the disreputable) that hirers should undertake obligations which they cannot reasonably discharge. ... We recommend a new requirement, namely that the copy of the agreement sent to the hirer must be headed by a notice in prescribed terms and print of minimum size informing the hirer that he is entitled to cancel the agreement by giving notice to the owner in writing within 72 hours of its receipt, and that if he gives such notice he will incur no liability whether or not the goods have been or are subsequently delivered; and that such should be the law. ... We have already referred to the novelty of a device such as we recommend. We make our recommendation with full appreciation that it is radical in conception.

Doorstep selling was traditionally more common in lower-income neighbourhoods in the UK (see OFT, 1977). In an extensive empirical study of credit practices (conducted in 1969), Ison discovered that 'those who bought from a salesman at home reported worse experiences than those who bought at retail premises or by mail order'

(Ison, 1979: 97). There was, however, a clear distinction between different types of door-to-door sale:

> The worst proportion of unfortunate experiences was reported in transactions involving salesmen without retail premises who sell only one type of item. A little better were the transactions involving a salesman from an area gas board, and better still were the transactions involving salesmen from other retail premises. The best experiences of all were reported by those who bought from a salesman who called regularly selling different types of items. These buyers reported experiences among the best in the total sample. (Ison, 1979: 97–98)

Experience with the regulations indicated the potential complexity of transforming the simple idea of 'cooling-off' into a legal regime and designing the optimal level of precision for a regulation. Detailed rules invited the Holmesian 'bad man' to circumvent the rule or restructure the transaction. For example, the OFT study extracted below indicates that some suppliers unnecessarily supplied goods or services before the cooling-off period expires to take advantage of a loophole in the regulations.

The introduction of the CPUT regulations will provide a potential safety net since practices that are not caught by specific cancellation rights may be contrary to professional diligence, or be misleading or aggressive commercial practices. Some techniques used by door-to-door sellers are blacklisted (eg the misleading door opener—'I'm conducting a survey'—known in the industry as 'sugging': see Annex 1) and high-pressure selling (Schedule 1, regulations 25, 26 and 29). Trade association codes of practice might assist here in maintaining standards. The Direct Marketing Association has a code of practice that provides consumers with a 14-day cooling-off period as well as a statement of best practices for direct marketing. These include requirements that companies maintain compliance officers and monitor the conduct of salespersons (see www.dma.org.uk/content/Pro-Code.asp).

In 2002 Citizens Advice made a supercomplaint to the OFT alleging the following problems with door-to-door sales: lack of awareness of consumer rights; consumers being misled by high-pressure sales techniques; the limitation of cancellation rights that were often ignored by salespersons; and goods being sold that were unsuitable for consumer needs or did not meet their requirements. In response the OFT conducted a market study of doorstep selling in 2004.

Office of Fair Trading, *Doorstep Selling: A Report on the Market Study* (2004) OFT 716

1 SUMMARY AND RECOMMENDATIONS

Introduction

… 1.3 As a sales channel doorstep selling covers a wide set of products ranging from household cleaning materials costing £1 or less to replacement double-glazing, costing many thousands of pounds. We have focussed on the biggest selling products by value and those which are targeted at more vulnerable consumers. This has given us an understanding of the way the sales channel works and our conclusions also apply to other products sold through this channel.

1.4 We estimate the overall value of those goods and services that we have focussed on, sold through doorstep selling, is at least £2.4 billion.

1.5 Given the wide range of products sold through this means we considered doorstep sales in three categories by value of transaction:

- • Low value purchases—goods or services under £35 per transaction;
- • Mid-value purchases—products or services valued between £35 and £500; and
- • High value purchases—purchases in excess of £500.

Characteristics of doorstep selling

1.7 Buying in the home represents a different experience from buying, for example, in a shop. Consumers can enter or leave shops as they wish, the transaction is more impersonal and, if they are unhappy with the way a product is being sold they can walk away. The home creates a very different environment. An academic study we commissioned identified a range of psychological influencing techniques that can be highly effective in inducing the consumer to buy. In our consumer survey, 85 per cent of consumers who said they would never buy through doorstep selling agreed that buying at home involves more pressure than buying in other settings.

1.8 Associated with this, many consumers have negative attitudes towards doorstep selling. Sixty-one per cent of consumers surveyed had never bought goods in this way, based partly on a dislike of certain features of doorstep selling, such as a lack of trust of salespersons, and partly on a preference for ordinary retail outlets. Of those consumers who had bought through doorstep selling a significant minority were dissatisfied with the product and the sales process. This is also reflected in the number of complaints made about doorstep selling which is high in relation to the money spent on these products—particularly for high value products.

1.9 Balanced against this, the views of consumers who had bought through doorstep selling was more positive. Although they may have experienced problems along the way, the vast majority (over 70 per cent) were happy overall with the sales process and products acquired. It is argued that doorstep selling can have a number of advantages for consumers:

- it avoids the need to travel. This is particularly useful if the product is a specialist one and retail outlets are scarce or if the consumer has mobility problems;
- if the product is complex and requires a time consuming discussion with the supplier, there may be more opportunity for this at home;
- there may potentially be scope for a home demonstration although the appropriateness of this will depend upon the product; and
- cold-calling may be a means of addressing consumer inertia, by actively presenting consumers with new options that may be to their advantage.

Solicited and unsolicited sales

1.10 Doorstep selling takes place in two ways:

- solicited, where the consumer actively initiates the visit by the salesperson, for example by specifically requesting a visit in response to an advert or mail shot; and
- unsolicited, where the visit does not take place at the express request of the consumer, for example where a salesperson makes a cold call.

Findings

1.13 ... we have identified a number of issues that cause concern. Many consumers find that they have made an inappropriate choice, often as a result of pressure selling, that the prices they have paid were too high and/or that the product they have bought is not suitable for the intended purpose. Subsequently they can find themselves inadvertently locked into a contract with no option to cancel. Added to this, we also have concerns about the effectiveness of current legislation and policy in tackling bogus trading.

1.14 The issues we have identified are most prevalent for high value goods (which attract more than 55 per cent of complaints) but we discuss them in relation to all value sectors below.

Consumer awareness

1.15 Across all categories of doorstep sales we found that consumers are generally unaware of their rights when buying through doorstep selling. The majority are unaware that they may enjoy a cooling off period when buying in the home (if the visit was unsolicited) and 34 per cent thought that they had more rights when purchasing in a shop. The survey also showed that consumers had some difficulty in making the distinction between solicited and unsolicited visits in accordance with the legal definition except for relatively simple examples.

Low value products

1.16 ... Our assessment is that doorstep sales of low value products do not merit any changes in existing consumer protection legislation or other initiatives.

This is because:

• the products are widely and easily available through other means, there is often a broad awareness of their prices in shops and consequently consumers are, by and large, better able to make an informed choice and to shop around if they wish;

• many suppliers are, for the most part, intent on securing repeated custom through offering convenience and value for money. Those consumers that do make regular repeat purchases are very satisfied with buying at home; and

• since the cost is small, the potential detriment from mis-selling is limited.

Medium value products

1.17 Gas and electricity sales (ie customers switching supplier) account for more than half (53 per cent) of sales. The remainder is accounted for by bulk buying of low value products (9 per cent), frozen food sales (5 per cent), telephone services (4 per cent) and sales of an assortment of products—domestic appliances, furniture, pictures and carpets—with no other individual product accounting for more than a few per cent. ...

High value products

1.21 The doorstep sales of key high value products are worth more than £2 billion annually. Home improvement products, particularly double-glazing and conservatories account for the majority of sales by value. This sector also includes a number of products targeted at the elderly or disabled such as stairlifts, mobility scooters and adjustable beds. Sales of these products alone are worth more than £200 million annually.

1.22 Most doorstep selling complaints relate to high value products. ..These complaints generally relate to consumers finding they have made an inappropriate choice, often as a result of pressure selling, that the prices they have paid were too high, that the product they have bought is not suitable for the intended purpose, or a combination of these reasons. Subsequently they find themselves locked into a contract with no option to cancel.

1.23 Our analysis bears out these claims:

• Our study by an academic psychologist shows that there can be intense pressure put on consumers buying in the home—both in solicited and unsolicited sales. The study identifies a range of sales tactics and influencing techniques that together are highly effective in securing sales, but can also lead the consumer to make inappropriate decisions. Evidence that these techniques are frequently employed was found in several pieces of research. Common ploys include: offering a high initial price followed by the offer of a discount, a discount on condition that the sale was agreed that day, telephoning a manager/colleague to secure a special deal;

- Prices can vary widely. In general high value products are infrequent purchases and consumers are unlikely to be familiar with prices or the availability of competing products and, such, are ill-equipped to make instant decisions on offers made. For example, in a tightly controlled comparison of similar double-glazing products we found prices paid by doorstep selling consumers varied by 45 per cent. For certain assistive products we found that consumers buying in the home are paying significantly more than if they bought through other sales channels. For example, for some rise and recliner chairs the price when purchasing in the home was 144 per cent more than the price in a high street store.

- Consumers can find themselves, often inadvertently, locked into contracts. While cooling off periods provide some flexibility for consumers to cancel contracts they regret making, under the current regulations they only apply to sales over £35 made during an unsolicited visit. Our analysis, however, found that:
  — consumers are often as likely to regret a purchase made from a solicited visit as from an unsolicited visit. ...
  — consumers are not sufficiently aware of their rights and the extent of protection they have under the law. Our survey found that only 6 per cent of consumers were aware that they may have additional rights when buying via doorstep selling.

The Cancellation of Contracts made in a Consumer's Home or Place of Work etc Regulations 2008 attempted to address these issues by extending the cooling-off period to solicited visits, requiring a separate notice to cancel, and rendering the contract unenforceable if a notice to cancel was not provided. The DTI rejected a ban on cold calling of property services because although

it is simple to understand and would reduce detriment caused by bogus traders, [it] removes a cost-effective sales method that can benefit consumers with a potentially severe impact on the property services industry, [the] activity of rogues may just be moved elsewhere and it would not comply with the UCPD.

This final reason shows the effect of the maximal harmonisation in the UCPD. The Consumer Rights Directive now requires full harmonisation (Article 4) of certain aspects of distance and off-premises contracts such as the formal requirements, the 14-day right of withdrawal (Article 9) and its expiry (12 months), a standard model withdrawal form (Article 11, Annex 1(B)), and exceptions to the right of withdrawal (Article 16).

The OFT study indicates that few consumers are aware of their rights in relation to doorstep selling. Research conducted by OFGEM shows that 25 per cent of consumers signing a fuel contract on the doorstep subsequently cancelled it (reported in OFT study at 57). Some consumers failed to cancel because of difficulties in exercising their cancellation rights and Citizens Advice argued that individuals experienced problems in attempting to cancel doorstep purchases for goods with prices over £1,000 (see Mori, 2005). Research in the US shortly after the introduction of cooling-off periods for door-to-door sales found a reduction in cancellation rates by consumers.

The authors explained this conclusion on the basis that the ability to cancel reduced consumers' doubts about the wisdom of the purchase (Shanklin and King, 1977: 105).

Economists hypothesise a number of costs and benefits that may arise from the introduction of a cooling-off period. There may be some costs to sellers in documentation and lost sales and in the need to recover merchandise. Rekaiti and Van den Bergh (2000) raise the possibility of opportunistic behaviour by consumers who use the product and then return it (moral hazard) and the uncertainty and delay caused by the cooling-off periods that might result in higher prices and reduced offerings by business. There is little empirical evidence, however, of these effects in doorstep sales. Potential benefits include a better allocation of consumer resources—away from purchases that are not really wanted—and stimulation of comparative shopping. It is also a potentially simple remedy for consumers who do not need to go to court or prove that they were misled by oral sales patter.

Although in theory these economic benefits may outweigh the costs, Ison is sceptical of the benefits in practice for the majority of consumers subject to doorstep selling. He argues that the requirement of sending a 'notice of cancellation' is likely to protect the more sophisticated consumer, and that those most vulnerable to door-to-door sales are unlikely to be familiar with the documentation necessary to establish their rights. Citizens Advice (2005: 4) did find that a greater proportion of those in social groups D and E found it difficult to exercise their cooling-off rights. One response is to reduce the costs of cancellation. Thus legislation in Ontario, Canada permits a cancellation to be made 'by any means that allows you to prove the date on which you gave notice'. Ison also argues that consumers may be induced to believe mistakenly, that they have lost the right to reject the goods after the expiration of the cooling-off period.

The studies by Ison and the OFT provide empirical substantiation for the economic hypothesis that there will be significant incentives for aggressive and fraudulent sales practices in markets where businesses are uninterested in repeat sales or in fostering goodwill. The efforts of the sales personnel of such businesses are devoted instead to aggressive sales practices designed to overcome consumer resistance (see also Sher, 1968: 717). Ison argued that the only effective regulation would be to ban the category of door-to-door selling which gives rise to abuse—itinerant salesmen selling one type of item on credit terms or who require part-payment in advance (Ison, 1979: 119). Ison's proposal was made almost 40 years ago. There continues to be significant problems with door-to-door sales of high-priced items.

10.2 Distance selling and cooling-off

Distance selling includes a variety of sales methods such as catalogue sales, telemarketing, videophone, television shopping, facsimile, the Internet or electronic mail. The current Distant Selling Regulations will be replaced by regulations implementing the EU Consumer Rights Directive which defines a 'distance contract' as any contract concluded between the trader and the consumer under an organised distance sales or service-provision scheme without the simultaneous physical presence of the trader and the consumer, with the exclusive use of one or more means of distance communication up to and including the time at which the contract is concluded.

It provides a 14-day cooling-off period. Several contracts are, however, excluded from the right to withdraw. What explains the following list of exceptions?

Member States shall not provide for the right of withdrawal set out in Articles 9 to 15 in respect of distance and off-premises contracts as regards the following:

(a) service contracts after the service has been fully performed if the performance has begun with the consumer's prior express consent, and with the acknowledgement that he will lose his right of withdrawal once the contract has been fully performed by the trader;

(b) the supply of goods or services for which the price is dependent on fluctuations in the financial market which cannot be controlled by the trader and which may occur within the withdrawal period;

(c) the supply of goods made to the consumer's specifications or clearly personalised;

(d) the supply of goods which are liable to deteriorate or expire rapidly;

(e) the supply of sealed goods which are not suitable for return due to health protection or hygiene reasons and were unsealed after delivery;

(f) the supply of goods which are, after delivery, according to their nature, inseparably mixed with other items;

(g) the supply of alcoholic beverages, the price of which has been agreed upon at the time of the conclusion of the sales contract, the delivery of which can only take place after 30 days and the actual value of which is dependent on fluctuations in the market which cannot be controlled by the trader;

(h) contracts where the consumer has specifically requested a visit from the trader for the purpose of carrying out urgent repairs or maintenance. If, on the occasion of such visit, the trader provides services in addition to those specifically requested by the consumer or goods other than replacement parts necessarily used in carrying out the maintenance or in making the repairs, the right of withdrawal shall apply to those additional services or goods;

(i) the supply of sealed audio or sealed video recordings or sealed computer software which were unsealed after delivery;

(j) the supply of a newspaper, periodical or magazine with the exception of subscription contracts for the supply of such publications;

(k) contracts concluded at a public auction;

(l) the provision of accommodation other than for residential purpose, transport of goods, car rental services, catering or services related to leisure activities if the contract provides for a specific date or period of performance;

(m) the supply of digital content which is not supplied on a tangible medium if the performance has begun with the consumer's prior express consent and his acknowledgment that he thereby loses his right of withdrawal.

10.3 Timeshares and cooling-off

The sale of timeshares has been associated with high-pressure selling. Potential buyers often will not have an opportunity to view their property before signing a contract. See now the Timeshare, Holiday Products Resale and Exchange Contracts Regulations 2010.

10.4 Cooling-off periods and stimulating competitive markets: extended warranties

Cooling-off periods originated in the protection of unwanted transactions entered into under pressure. Their extension to many transactions where there is not necessarily high-pressure selling suggests that they are also intended to function as a stimulant of competition. The European Commission justify the proposed 14-day cooling-off period for credit transactions in these terms:

> The delay allows consumers to shop around after conclusion of the agreement and possibly to find a better offer. This provision is intended to enhance competition.

Extended cooling-off periods to facilitate competition and reduce switching costs have been introduced in the extended warranty market for domestic electrical goods following an investigation by the Competition Commission. The Commission concluded that there was little competition on pricing of extended warranties.

Competition Commission, *Extended Warranties on Domestic Electrical Goods: A Report on the Supply of Extended Warranties on Domestic Electrical Goods within the UK*, vols 1, 2 and 3 at 3, 5, 6, 7

> The DEG [domestic electrical goods] retail market appears to be characterized by vigorous price competition. By contrast, there is relatively little competition on the pricing of EWs [extended warranties].
>
> Conclusions on monopoly situations.
>
> We identified a complex monopoly situation in the market for EWs sold at POS [point of sale], under section 7 of the Fair Trading Act. This complex monopoly situation results from the fact that those that sell EWs at POS have a competitive advantage, and so all those that are involved in selling EWs at POS are part of the complex monopoly situation. They comprise all retailers selling EWs at POS in stores, or through catalogues, mail order, telephone sales or the Internet, all manufacturers selling paid EWs with DEGs sold directly to consumers, all insurers underwriting paid EWs sold through retailers, and all service companies contracted with retailers, manufacturers, or insurers.
>
> Four overlapping characteristics of market behaviour suggested that, given the POS advantage, practices that might otherwise be unexceptionable could act to restrict or distort competition:
>
> (a) Almost all EWs are purchased at POS; few consumers seek information on EWs prior to their purchase; and consumers have little opportunity to consider alternatives to the EW on offer at POS.

(b) EWs on offer at POS are nearly always all from one provider, usually the retailer (or a third party which is the sole supplier to the retailer).

(c) There is generally no information available at POS on prices, or terms and conditions, of EWs available from alternative providers (such as manufacturers, insurers, credit card companies or others).

(d) There is generally no information available on DEG reliability, likely repair costs, or the probability of theft or accidental damage.

Conclusions on the public interest

In this context, we found that the practices of EW providers at POS restricted or distorted competition, in that the providers limited the choice of product, and limited the provision of relevant information about that product and alternatives (including price information). In the case of larger, and some medium-sized, retailers, and manufacturers selling direct to consumers, they were able to charge excessive prices, indicated by levels of profits significantly and persistently in excess of their cost of capital. Retailers at POS also limited the choice of cover and time periods, and required consumers to contract, and commit to paying for, EWs substantially in advance of receiving benefits. ...

Remedies

... We believe it appropriate to remedy the adverse effects by creating the conditions for more competition. In general terms, therefore, we favoured remedies designed to provide consumers with wider opportunities to assess their need for an EW and to choose between EWs, and to provide them with the information necessary to make well-informed decisions regarding their purchase of EWs.

The government introduced a statutory instrument to give effect to the recommendations of the Competition Commission. Regulation 8 of the Supply of Extended Warranties on Domestic Electrical Goods Order 2005 provides a 45-day period to cancel the extended warranty. The supplier must provide notice in writing to the consumer of this right at least 20 days before the end of this period. It also permits a consumer to cancel an extended warranty at any time and receive a pro-rata refund.

10.5 Rethinking cooling-off periods: a right to withdraw?

Cooling-off periods provide the right to withdraw from a contract. Some writers view them as an exception to the norm of *pacta sunt servanda* and therefore argue that they should be cabined within carefully circumscribed policy justifications. Economists draw attention to the costs and benefits of the right of withdrawal but differ on the conclusion to be drawn from this assessment.

Pamela Rekaiti and Roger van den Bergh, in an economic analysis of cooling-off periods, argue that cooling-off periods should be limited to situations where the consumer's rationality is likely to be undermined, the seller is likely to have superior knowledge about relevant market prices, and the consumer has difficulty in checking out a purchase before buying (Rekaiti and Van den Bergh, 2000: 371). On this basis a general cooling-off period for all credit transactions may be difficult to justify. In addition, if the objective is to stimulate competition, a right to make an early repayment of a loan without any charges or penalties for debtors might be a more effective method of stimulating switching by consumers (see discussion below Chapter 10 at 5.4). Rekaiti and Van den Bergh also raise questions about the effectiveness of a cooling-off period in curing some information problems. For example a 14-day cooling-off period in relation to a timeshare will often not permit an individual to inspect a property (but it may permit the consumer to check on the company offering the timeshare). Similarly a short cooling-off period may not be sufficient where an individual signs up to a long-term contract such as for a health or fitness club. The consumer may not realise until after a month or so that she will not make significant use of the facilities. An alternative form of regulation may be to require companies to offer a variety of contracts including monthly memberships. Rekaiti and Van den Bergh also recognise the limits of cooling-off periods if they are only used by a minority of marginal consumers.

Other writers argue that it is not necessary to impose a mandatory rule beyond the case of high-pressure door-to-door sales. A default rule might be introduced where consumers could be given the option of contracting out of the withdrawal regime on the theory that this option might be offered at a lower price.

G Wagner, 'Mandatory Contract Law: Functions and Principles in Light of the Proposal for a Directive on Consumer Rights' (2011) 3 *Erasmus Law Review* 47.

[T]he options approach would downgrade the current framework of the right of withdrawal, as set out in the Directive on Distance Contracts, to the status of an option that the parties may either accept or reject. A consumer surfing the internet for bargains could decide whether to purchase the item right away without a right of withdrawal or to preserve such a right and thus to preserve the option of 'having second thoughts'. Presumably, the price of packaging the good and including a right of withdrawal would be higher than the price charged just for the naked good, but such price differentials would only reflect the additional costs incurred by including a right of withdrawal. Such a solution would put an end to the cross-subsidisation of negligent consumer-buyers, who order goods without prior reflection, and diligent consumer-buyers, who take care to avoid ordering goods that do not suit their tastes and are thus less likely to exercise the right of withdrawal. By offering two different kinds of contract—one including a right of withdrawal and another one excluding it—the sellers could force the buyers to separate into two different groups. One group could be labelled the 'high-cost buyers,' since the frequency of withdrawal will be high, whereas the other group could be labelled the 'low-cost buyers,' as their the frequency of withdrawal will be low. At the same time, by allowing a choice between a definite purchase and a purchase that is revocable by the consumer ex post facto, the options approach would preserve the core of party autonomy, namely the right to choose between two meaningful alternatives.

Omri Ben-Shahar and Eric Posner, also adopting an economic approach, argue for a general right of withdrawal in terms of economic efficiency:

O Ben-Shahar and E Posner, The Right to Withdraw in Contract Law' (2011) 40 *Journal of Legal Studies* 115 at 121–22, 144.

[T]he optimal contract would balance the buyer's gain from the reduction of uncertainty, and the seller's loss in terms of depreciation. If the buyer gains a great deal of information from having the good in his house, and the good depreciates very little, the buyer would have the right to return the good. This right would benefit the seller ex ante, because buyers are more likely to buy a good if they have the right to return it if they do not like it. ... At some point depreciation costs will exceed the information benefits; at this point, the right to free withdrawal should end.

Another version of the optimal contract would give the buyer, rather than a free withdrawal right, the option to return the good and pay the depreciation loss to the seller. This contract forces the buyer to internalize the cost that the decision to withdraw imposes on the seller, and in this way gives the buyer the socially optimal incentive to keep or return the good. As long as the depreciation is priced accurately, this contract does not require an ex ante prediction of the point in time at which depreciation costs will exceed the information benefits.

Both of these contracts, however, may be impractical because they rely on accurate pricing of depreciation, either by the parties ex ante or by courts ex post. A third approach, one that overcomes this information problem, is to use time as a proxy for depreciation. If goods tend to depreciate slowly, while buyers can gain most of the information they need quickly, then the optimal right of withdrawal would extend for just a few days after the sale.

They argue that the right should be limited to distance contracts 'involving goods that (1) are complex and (2) do not readily depreciate or do depreciate in a way that can be easily measured so that compensation can be calculated'. To what extent do the exceptions in the Distance Selling Regulations mirror these criteria?

Our argument does not imply that the right to withdraw should be a mandatory rule, as it is in Europe. If the reason that European jurisdictions make the right mandatory is the concern that vendors would otherwise routinely contract around it, this concern is misguided. Vendors usually opt into the withdrawal regime—[A] return policy is not the type of fine print term that goes under the radar. ... Buyers seek information about sellers' return policies, because most buyers anticipate returns as a non-trivial contingency. Indeed return policies are regularly posted in a conspicuous manner. ... There are unique circumstances ... in which a mandatory right might be justified on the basis of asymmetric information or concerns about coercion. Door-to-door sales is perhaps one such context. ... A default rule would also allow heterogenous buyers to sort into the type of transaction desired. Some buyers value the right to withdraw less, either because they know they will not have an opportunity to return the goods or because they have better information about the goods.

eBay policies

A clear return policy can reassure buyers

If you have a clear return policy, chances are that you're more successful than other sellers on eBay. eBay's research shows that difficulty in returning items is the most common shopping barrier talked about by buyers. As a result, sellers who clearly spell out return policies in their listings have an edge on the competition. Typically they sell a higher percentage of their items.

eBay's research also shows that only a very small percentage of sold items are actually returned.

Jan Smits notes that many retailers voluntarily provide withdrawal rights even where they have no legal obligation to do so 'in order to create trust with their customers' (Smits, 2010–11: 671). Statutory withdrawal rights might 'crowd out' ideas of reciprocity between retailer and consumer. He cites research by Borges and Irlenbusch, who claimed that in Germany there was a high rate of return in mail order purchases

(35 per cent) apparently caused by a relatively small group of consumers with the highest return rate among women's clothes. Examples of 'borrowing' expensive television sets before soccer games were also mentioned. They also argue that there is some experimental evidence that the existence of a legal right may crowd out fairness norms of reciprocity between seller and buyer (Borges and Irlenbusch, 2007).

Examination of cooling-off periods illustrates the relationship of law to business practices and the potentially complex nature of the relationship between law and market norms (*cf* Internet case study in Chapter 3). Law reformers often lament the fact that consumers (and businesses) are unaware of their rights, but many consumers obtain more than their rights under generous return policies. The issue may not therefore be simply that of making individuals aware of their legal rights.

Cooling-off periods are attractive because they do not seem to interfere with consumer choice. Unlike bans or costly licensing procedures they protect individuals who wish to cancel without interfering with other individuals' choices. They are the favoured remedy of some behavioural economics scholars who label cooling-off as 'asymmetric paternalism' (Camerer et al, 2003: 1211). The authors argue that a regulation is asymmetrically paternalistic

> if it creates large benefits for those who make errors, while imposing little or no harm on those who are fully rational. Such regulations are relatively harmless to those who reliably make decisions in their best interest, while at the same time advantageous to those making suboptimal choices. … [Cooling-off periods] likely impose costs on sellers, but the greatest costs focus on those sellers who benefit from consumers making hasty, ill-conceived decisions in the heat of the moment. (ibid)

However, the limited empirical evidence suggests that those who may need them most (the infra-marginal consumer) are less likely to make use of them. Are cooling-off periods likely to be distributionally regressive in their benefits for consumers?

Do you agree that cooling-off periods are paternalistic? Freedom of contract includes the idea of freedom from contract. Do cooling-off periods in fact ensure a greater autonomy and freedom to the consumer by giving effect to freedom from contract? (see Rakoff, 2005: 437).

A different perspective on cooling-off periods is to view them from a political economy perspective in terms of the relevant interest groups. Are they an attractive political solution because they seem to be giving valuable rights to consumers with little substantial costs to large business enterprises?

5

Implementation and Enforcement of Unfair Commercial Practices Law

In the United Kingdom the institutional alternatives in this area have traditionally been:

1. markets and market institutions (reputation, the repeat purchase mechanism) and private law;
2. self-regulation and co-regulation;
3. public legislative standards enforced by local authorities using criminal sanctions; and
4. administrative regulation.

The UK model of regulation of unfair commercial practices reflects institutional history and traditions of government–industry relations. The reliance on strict criminal liability grew from the historical use of this technique in relation to adulterated food. The preference for detailed legislative regulation (eg Trade Descriptions Act 1968) rather than broad standards of unfairness represented concerns about the use of broad criminal standards, the historical relationship between the legislature and the courts in the UK, and a desire to limit judicial discretion. The use of self-regulation and soft law demonstrates both the influence of the generalist English administrative culture that draws on industry expertise and the power of particular industries as in the case of advertising self-regulation. The often overlapping nature of consumer regulation— laws, codes and guidance—raises issues of transparency and accountability.

There are several policy issues in the implementation and enforcement of unfair commercial practices. There is the choice between criminal and administrative sanctions, the role of local and national enforcement, and the balance between public and private enforcement. We consider the traditional form of UK regulation in this area, the regulatory offence, which combines strict liability with statutory defences, the critiques of this approach and the increasing use of administrative sanctions in consumer law—as reflected in Part 8 of the Enterprise Act 2002. A central contemporary question is the appropriate balance of public and private enforcement of consumer law. But as Colin Scott notes:

> [If] our interest lies in understanding the conditions under which businesses comply with their responsibilities, then it may be helpful to adopt a wider conception of enforcement which embraces both formal and informal mechanisms through which agencies (and others) seek to promote compliance. Novel enforcement mechanisms involve third parties—other businesses and non-governmental organisations—in processes of enforcement. Recognition of the limits of both governmental and private rights models of enforcement is likely to make such third party enforcement mechanisms increasingly important.' (Scott, 2010: 539).

Section 7 considers the role of industry self-regulation. Increasingly enforcement raises cross-border issues that are addressed in section 8.

---

1. The structure of public enforcement of unfair commercial practices law in the UK

UK trade practices law has historically been characterised by decentralised enforcement. Local trading standards offices had exclusive jurisdiction to enforce the Trade Descriptions Act 1968 and the OFT had limited enforcement powers. The DTI comparative report on consumer policy regimes (2003) noted that

> [T]he UK stands out in terms of the breadth of responsibilities which were dealt with at local levels ... enforcement of a large number of national statutes including weights and measures and product safety legislation are the responsibilities of local trading standards officers. It also appears unusual in delegating responsibilities to a relatively large number of authorities, given country size, including a large number of small local authorities. (DTI, 2003: 22–23)

The comparative advantages of local and national agencies in the United Kingdom may be profitably viewed in the light of: (i) enforcement costs; (ii) diversity versus uniformity; and (iii) citizen responsiveness (Tiebout, 1956; Mashaw and Rose-Ackerman, 1984).

Centralised enforcement may have advantages for enforcement directed towards national firms. One test case, or a communication directed to a head office, may secure countrywide compliance, avoiding a multiplicity of local actions. In addition, the national firm will face reduced compliance costs. A further argument for preferring central enforcement is that national agencies may have more bargaining power vis-à-vis national firms, although this must be balanced against the potential danger of agency 'capture'. National agencies may also take advantage of economies of scale in producing and collecting certain information—for example, in testing the safety of products, developing standards, and collecting information for licensing purposes. If consumer offences are committed mainly by the 'fly-by-night' or the small local operator, then local authorities will have a comparative advantage in terms of enforcement costs. For example, they will be able to collect, and process quickly, 'ground-level' information on offences. If information has to be transmitted up a long national bureaucratic chain, it may be lost or misinterpreted. In addition, it may be less costly (economically and psychologically) for local individuals to provide information on offences to local agencies.

Local agencies may be more responsive to the interests of local consumer and business interests. However, in so being, local agencies may court the danger of being 'captured' by these local interests. A more optimistic analysis might argue, however, that competition among enforcement authorities might stimulate innovations in enforcement.

It is not clear whether local or national agencies are more prone to 'capture'. National publicity may have a prophylactic effect on 'capture' at the national level. It may be questioned whether there is as much monitoring of bureaucratic activity (eg through the media, citizens groups) at the local level.

Concerns about inconsistency and the need for co-ordination in enforcement have existed for many years in the UK with a variety of responses, including co-ordinating bodies and the development of the principle of the 'home authority': in order to prevent national companies being presented with conflicting advice, they are requested to seek advice from the authority in the area in which their headquarters are based. However, prosecution policy is still very much a local matter. A 2003 DTI report concluded that 'resources are fragmented and the UK appears to benefit least from economies of scale'. The 2004 White Paper, *Expanding Competitive Markets: Empowered Consumers, Successful Business*, noted certain key problems: 'patchiness and variation in services delivered, the need for more strategic prioritization and effective joint working'. The Hampton Review (2005: 74) summarised contemporary criticisms:

THE RIGHT REGULATORY STRUCTURE

4.100 The local authority funding system is designed to allow authorities to set their own budgets across all local authority services, and variations are therefore an inevitable part of the system. In outer London trading standards departments, for example, the ratio of service staff to inspectable premises varied widely, averaging 400:1, but with a high of 748:1 (in Hillingdon), and a low of 219:1 (in Barking). The variations are not clearly attributable to mix of business, or to population types—it is notable that Hillingdon (highest) and Hounslow (fourth lowest at 279:1) are adjacent authorities. Similarly Brent and Harrow (256:1) is next to Barnet (687:1).

4.104 These inconsistencies also raise questions about the effectiveness of the Home Authority Principle. This principle is an informal agreement between local authorities that tries to correct the inevitable problems that arise from cross-boundary issues in trading standards and food. The principle requires local authorities to pay particular attention to goods and services originating in their area that are distributed or sold in different local authority areas. The home authority—the authority with the company's head office or main production centre in its area—is meant to act to as a focus for communication and liaison between the company and other local authorities. The operation of the principle is voluntary and therefore depends on communication between all parties involved.

4.105 Work arising from the Home Authority Principle is resource-intensive, unfunded, and unevenly spread around the country.

The Report concluded:

> 4.48 ... [T]he review recommends that a new body should be created at the centre of Government, to coordinate work on consumer protection and trading standards. This body would have lead policy responsibility for trading standards nationally. It would have the responsibility of overseeing the work of local authorities on trading standards issues, as the Food Standards Agency does in respect of food.
>
> Better coordination in local authorities' work
>
> 4.107 The review believes that consistency at local authority level requires better coordination of Departments and local authorities at national level. The review has already proposed the creation of a new Consumer and Trading Standards Agency, to bring greater coordination to the work of local authority trading standards departments.

The government did not introduce the proposed Consumer and Trading Standards Agency but rather established under the Regulatory Enforcement and Sanctions Act 2008 a Local Better Regulation Office that would be responsible for establishing national priorities to achieve consistency across authorities, while maintaining flexibility for local authorities and retaining the 'home authority' principle. The OFT would have a central role in acting as a champion for trading standards departments in government. However the National Audit Office reported in 2012 that there were continuing problems in the structure of enforcement:

Report by the Comptroller and Auditor General, *Protecting Consumers—The System for Enforcing Consumer Law*, HC 1087 (2012)

> The need to work collaboratively
>
> 6 The cost of detriment that needs to be tackled at the regional and national level is not routinely measured, but the data available suggests that it is in excess of £4.8 billion. It arises from large scams and intellectual property crime where offences occur across local authority boundaries . Doorstep crime perpetrated by itinerant traders is also a significant cause of consumer detriment but there are no reliable figures available to estimate the impact of this on consumers.
>
> 7 Although much detriment occurs at the regional and national level, incentives are weighted in favour of tackling local priorities. Eighty-nine per cent of respondents to our survey of Trading Standards Services have formal reporting arrangements with their local authority and 86 per cent of funding for enforcement is controlled by local authorities. Incentives and responsibilities for cross-border working are weaker. There can be strong cost and risk disincentives, especially for small Trading Standards Services.
>
> 8 Central government funding of £34 million for tackling cross-border detriment and coordinating local enforcement action is relatively low compared to the scale of the problem..
>
> 9 Despite the disincentives, we found that some larger Trading Standards Services do take on substantial cross-border cases, although there is a risk that the projected reductions in resourcing will reduce their willingness to do so.
>
> The Department estimates that annual funding for Trading Standards Services will reduce from its current level of £213 million to about £140 to £170 million by 2014, and some larger Trading Standards Services are likely to lose substantial resources. There is already considerable variation in the capacity and resourcing of Trading Standards Services, with some services having as few as two members of staff and others employing over eighty, but

there is no required minimum standard of service in place to guard against weaknesses in coverage.

In 2011 the coalition government, recognising that there would be cuts to the budgets of consumer enforcement agencies, proposed the following model to address issues of national, cross-boundary and local enforcement. This takes place in the context of the creation of the Consumer and Markets Authority, essentially a competition authority that will replace the OFT.

DBIS (2012) Empowering and Protecting Consumers: Government Response to the Consultation on Institutional Changes for Provision of Consumer Information, Advice, Education, Advocacy and Enforcement

The Government has decided that it will establish a National Trading Standards Board (NTSB) which will have responsibility for prioritising national and cross-local authority boundary enforcement in England and Wales. It will be created immediately and from that date have at its disposal the current BIS funding for enforcement to tackle national and cross-boundary cases. The NTSB will have discretion over how this money is used but will have to report regularly on its work, showing how it is meeting the requirements placed upon it and how it is securing maximum value for money.

55. From April 2013, the NTSB will receive additional funding from the current OFT enforcement budget and will take over the coordination and database-management functions currently undertaken by the OFT. This will ensure that there is better national data on Trading Standards to inform activity and measure impact on a national basis. Intelligence and coordination systems in England and Wales will come under the supervision of the heads of service who will make up the membership of the NTSB. The NTSB will establish a system to ensure effective intelligence can be used to set enforcement priorities for Trading Standards teams, appoint specialist lead authorities focusing on particular areas of legislation or policy and support those authorities and others to take action on larger and more complex cases in the national interest. Subject to transitional arrangements relating to live cases, the OFT will cease most of its work on 'pure' consumer enforcement cases.

56. Trading Standards officers from Scotland and Northern Ireland will attend NTSB meetings to advise on UK-wide enforcement issues and on the coordination of business education.

57. The CMA will have a primary objective to promote competition for the benefit of consumers. It will retain consumer enforcement powers as remedies for use in markets where competition is not working appropriately due to practices and market conditions that make it difficult for consumers to exercise choice. Linked to this, it will retain primary expertise in the enforcement of unfair contract terms legislation. The CMA should therefore be designated as the lead enforcement authority and source of business guidance in this one area, rather than seeking to duplicate this expertise in Trading Standards. Additionally, the CMA will retain most of the OFT's current role on international consumer law and policy liaison.

It is clear that the different bodies will need to work closely together to minimise duplication of effort and gaps in consumer detriment being addressed. The Government therefore believes that a mechanism is essential to share intelligence and information across the consumer and competition landscapes and to highlight potential cases or areas for study. In order to achieve this, the different organisations will need to be open about their priorities to ensure that gaps do not occur.

61. The NTSB will work with the CMA, the Regulated Industries Unit and the Citizens Advice service to share intelligence, identify future issues that could adversely affect consumers

and agree priorities for enforcement, information and education. A Strategic Intelligence, Prevention and Enforcement Partnership (SIPEP) of these bodies will be established which will report regularly to the Minister for Consumer Affairs to provide joint accountability on how the system as a whole is operating. There will also be a flow of information between the SIPEP and sectoral regulators

Important questions about this framework are whether it will provide the necessary expertise to develop priorities for enforcement. The political compromises involved in its establishment blur the lines of responsibility (eg on unfair contract terms enforcement).

2. Models of enforcement

Two approaches to enforcement might be initially identified: sanctioning and compliance. Sanctioning is where:

> the objective of enforcement is to detect and prosecute violations of the law and to use the legal penalties to punish lawbreakers. [This] … is a very legalistic approach … [which] employs prosecution and legal sanctions as the routine enforcement instruments. (Veljanovski, 1984: 172)

Bardach and Kagan claim that a sanctioning and legalistic approach was adopted by the US social regulatory agencies in the 1970s. By adopting this latter approach, these agencies would not, it was argued by reformers, suffer the 'capture' fate of the old agencies:

> [R]eformers believed that enforcement had to be tougher … because business enterprises were fundamentally amoral profit seekers, unwilling to abide by the law unless the prospect of legal punishment was swift, sure and severe. (Bardach and Kagan 1982: 44, 57)

Although this tougher enforcement strategy undoubtedly had benefits, particularly in stimulating greater self-regulation by firms, it had, as Bardach and Kagan have indicated, its costly side-effects. In their view, regulatory toughness undermined constructive co-operation and diverted energy into 'pointless and dispiriting legal routines and conflicts' (ibid: 119).

A contrasting approach is the compliance approach which has traditionally been adopted by English consumer protection agencies (Reiss in Hawkins and Thomas, 1984: 23; Hawkins, 1984; 2002). Prosecution is, according to Hawkins, 'a last resort', and the overall goal is to achieve the objectives of the legislation rather than sanction a breach. In introducing the Trade Descriptions Act 1968, George Darling outlined how he expected it to be enforced:

Official Reports HC, vol 759, cols 683–85, 22 February 1968

> [MR G DARLING:] … I am convinced that local authorities' consumer departments— whatever they care to call them—will establish friendly relations with the reputable traders in the area to get matters put right outside the courts, and I am equally convinced that these

departments and local traders will work together to put dishonest operators out of business by quickly reporting offences.

Against the background of these differing approaches in the early 1990s, Ian Ayres and John Braithwaite put forward the influential model of 'responsive regulation'. This organises compliance strategies in a pyramid with co-operative strategies at the base of the pyramid and more punitive strategies as one moves up the pyramid. There is a presumption in favour of starting at the bottom of the pyramid:

> [C]ompliance is most likely when the regulatory agency displays an explicit enforcement pyramid. … Most regulatory action occurs at the base of the pyramid where attempts are made initially to coax compliance by persuasion. The next phase of enforcement escalation is a warning letter; if this fails to secure compliance imposition of civil monetary penalties; if this fails, criminal prosecution; if this fails plant shut-down or a temporary suspension of a licence to operate; if this fails, permanent revocation of a licence. It is not the content of the enforcement pyramid on which we wish to focus … but its form. (Ayres and Braithwaite, 1992: 35–36)

Ayres and Braithwaite's model has influenced the approach of the UK, Australian and Canadian competition authorities to enforcement. The OFT adopted this 'enforcement pyramid' (OFT, 2008), with an emphasis on formal legal action as a last resort. The pyramid is based on the assumption that regulated entities may at different times act as 'virtuous actors, rational actors (amoral calculators) or incompetent or irrational actors'. Enforcement responds to these different models of behaviour with strategies that include deterrence and incapacitation.

The model is dynamic in that the regulator will move up or down the pyramid strategically: the overall goal is to achieve compliance. An effective enforcement pyramid depends on regulators having a range of enforcement mechanisms, from informal undertakings, to injunctions and criminal sanctions. The regulator needs to be able to be a 'benign big gun'.

Australian Law Reform Commission, *Principled Regulation: Federal Civil and Administrative Penalties in Australia* (2002)

> 3.34 On this model, the ideal approach of the regulator is described as 'the benign big gun'; that is, the regulator should have access to severe punishments but should rarely use them in practice. Using John Scholz's application of game theory to the arena of regulation, Ayres and Braithwaite's model requires the regulator to behave as though the organisations being regulated wish to cooperate, and ensure that it is economically rational for them to cooperate. Where breaches occur, the initial response should be to persuade and educate them as to the appropriate behaviour. Such an approach promotes self-regulation and the wish to preserve reputation.

> 3.35 However, once persuasion has failed, the issue of the use of penalties arises. This raises questions as to whether the penalties chosen both by legislators and by the regulator, if there is a choice, should be criminal or civil.

Nielsen and Parker outline some critiques of the presumption that one should start at the base of the pyramid:

But many other researchers of enforcement and compliance have doubted whether such a presumption is always, or indeed ever, likely to result in compliance success, or whether it is even possible for regulators to promote truly 'cooperative' compliance at the base of the pyramid when both regulator and regulate know that they can always escalate to punitive sanctions at the tip of the pyramid. (Nielsen and Parker, 2005: 23)

Baldwin (2004) suggests in a study based on interviews with senior officials of large UK corporations some limitations on the effectiveness of both punitive and meta-regulation approaches which attempt to harness internal compliance mechanisms. Although he notes one executive's comment that more punitive regulation 'concentrated our minds dramatically', he found irrationality and confusion in relation to risk management. He concluded that senior management might not be well placed to assess risk compliance within the organisation. Internal policies may not be closely aligned with corporate risk, but focused on short-term performance on the share price rather than good risk management. Internal incentives, such as bonuses or commissions for lower-level employees within a corporation, may not avert risks—'No one gets bonused on their management of regulatory risk.' Some firms might respond by 'creative compliance', 'bringing pressure on the regulator (to discourage prosecution) shifting risk or blame onto the shoulders of individuals or outsourced business partners; or evasion, non-cooperation with regulators and concealment' (Baldwin, 2004: 371). Given the limitations on risk management in larger firms, one might expect that small firms would be much less well informed about regulatory risks (see Hampton, 2005).

Baldwin also questions the effectiveness of strategies which attempt to change corporate culture (see discussion of FSA in Chapter 7 below). Two primary problems are identified. First, there is the difference in vision between regulators and corporate managers. Corporate managers view issues in terms of shareholder return balanced against regulatory risk. Second, given the large number of interests to be managed within a corporation, there is often more confusion and conflict than consensus on issues of risk. He is therefore sceptical of proposals that are intended to facilitate deliberative discussion within corporations and with their stakeholders in relation to corporate social and legal responsibilities.

---

3. Methods of public enforcement

Enforcement of unfair commercial practices law has traditionally been through the use of the criminal sanction, which we consider below. However, successive UK governments have indicated that administrative enforcement ought to play a significant role in the implementation of the UCPD under the CPUT regulations 2008, continuing the trend to administrative enforcement established under Part 8 of the Enterprise Act 2002. The Regulatory Enforcement and Sanctions Act 2008 envisages a broader range of enforcement tools, although these do not apply to enforcing the CPUT regulations.

**Government Response to the Consultation Paper on Implementing the
Unfair Commercial Practices Directive (2006) 4–5**

The UCPD will form the mainstay of fair trading legislation in future. This makes it even more important to set up an appropriate enforcement regime for the UCPD. The Government's aim is to establish an enforcement regime that is capable of tackling rogue and unfair practices effectively while minimising burdens on fair trading businesses. ... The Macrory Review emphasises the importance of providing enforcers with a wide range of enforcement tools so that they can deal effectively with the entire range of enforcement activities, from assisting compliance to prosecuting truly criminal or rogue operators. ...

This is also at the core of the Government's approach to implementing the UCPD. In a modern fair trading framework the main enforcement mechanism for non-serious breaches ought not to be criminal prosecutions; alternative tools, including civil sanctions, will normally be more appropriate and proportionate. The Government may therefore also consider whether adopting additional intermediate enforcement tools, such as administrative penalties, that may be recommended by the Macrory Review. Yet there continues to be a need for criminal sanctions and associated investigative powers to tackle truly rogue behaviour and unscrupulous trading activities. For these reasons, the UCPD will be enforceable both by civil injunctive action and by criminal prosecutions.

The current government follows this trend by proposing to make it simpler for trading standards officers to enforce legislation through civil action in the county courts.

At the outset one might identify several possible enforcement remedies:

1. Licence revocation (see below Chapter 7).
2. Imprisonment and/or fines.
3. Administrative orders: injunctions, cease and desist, undertakings of voluntary compliance that will be audited, civil penalties.
4. Corporate probation and enforced accountability.
5. Adverse publicity, ie 'naming and shaming'.
6. Restorative justice orders.
7. Restitution orders as part of criminal or administrative process.
8. Informal agreement to comply.
9. Warnings.
10. Education and advice.

Consumer law enforcement of trade practices in the UK has traditionally relied on criminal fines, with warnings and informal agreements also being used.

3.1 The old workhorse: the regulatory offence

The most common example of the use of the criminal law in the area of trade practices is the 'regulatory offence'. The characteristics of this are:

1. Over-inclusive statutory standards enforced by sanctions of strict criminal liability, generally tempered by certain statutory defences. The primary sanction is a fine rather than imprisonment.
2. A specialised bureaucracy is under a duty to enforce the Act. (In the United Kingdom this will generally be the local authority trading standards department.) This will, in

practice, involve the exercise of discretion by the agency in the implementation and enforcement of the standards (see below 3.1.5).

3. The courts most involved in day-to-day implementation of the Act are the lay bench of the magistrates' courts, although the higher courts also play a significant role in developing the text of the Act.

Criminal sanctions were traditionally used to protect consumers against hidden risks of physical injury and of other non-economic losses (Atiyah, 1979: 544–50). These sanctions were extended to economic losses—for example, from false and misleading advertising.

There is considerable debate as to the objectives which are furthered by the use of the criminal sanction and strict criminal liability in consumer protection; and their appropriateness compared with that of the enforcement methods of administrative systems of regulation (see further Cartwright, 2000). Positions on these normative issues are often been premised upon presumed distinctions between 'regulatory' and 'real' crimes, and on assumptions concerning the operation in practice of the criminal sanction. There is now a body of empirical literature on the actual operation of the criminal sanction in this area. (See discussion below and Richardson, 1987: 295–306; Croall, 1988; Rowan-Robinson, Watchman and Barker, 1988: 211; Hawkins, 2002.)

The materials in this section introduce these normative issues and explore the substantive and institutional characteristics of the regulatory offence. Given the central role of corporations as defendants in consumer offences, a theme running throughout concerns the effectiveness of the criminal sanction in controlling organisational behaviour. The initial extracts outline the arguments for distinguishing regulatory from real crime.

Law Reform Commission of Canada, 'Sanctioning the Corporate Offender' in *Criminal Responsibility for Group Action—Working Paper No 16* (1976) 11–12

'Real' crimes, we have suggested, should be primarily concerned with fundamental values in our society. By emphasizing and reinforcing values considered to be at the basis of our social system, 'real' criminal law promotes a society in which they are respected and are demonstrated in behaviour. It responds to social conduct that exhibits disrespect for values and is inextricably bound up with the notion of 'fault'. Intentional conduct that injures people, deprives them of their property, restricts their' freedom or subjects them to offensive interferences are examples of conduct that violates values regarded as so important to our society as to warrant the designation 'criminal' and the stigmatization that is associated with the use of the criminal justice system.

The kind of criminal law we classify as 'regulatory offences' involves a somewhat different objective. It is not primarily concerned with values, but with results. While values necessarily under-lie all legal prescriptions, the regulatory offence really gives expression to the view that it is expedient for the protection of society and for the orderly use and sharing of society's resources that people act in a prescribed manner in prescribed situations, or that people take prescribed standards of care to avoid risks of injury. The object is to induce compliance with rules for the overall benefit of society.

Because the primary concern in regulatory offences is not with reinforcing fundamental values, fault becomes less important. While in some cases it may be regarded as fair to impose responsibility only on those who intend to break a rule, it is generally regarded as acceptable to impose responsibility on people who have been negligent; i.e., on people who simply have failed to take reasonable care to ensure that a result or risk will not occur.

The Supreme Court of Canada, in considering a statute with similar strict liability and due diligence defences to the Trade Descriptions Act, commented that:

> Regulatory legislation involves a shift of emphasis from the protection of individual interests and the deterrence and punishment of acts involving moral fault to the protection of the public and society's interest. While criminal offences are usually designed to condemn and punish inherently wrong conduct, regulatory measures are generally directed to the prevention of future harm through the enforcement of minimum standards of conduct and care. (*R v Wholesale Travel Group Inc* [1991] 3 SCR 154 per Cory J)

This distinction between regulatory and real crime may be related to the general justifications for the use of the criminal sanction—rehabilitation, incapacitation, deterrence and retribution. The first three are concerned with bringing about certain socially desirable consequences, whereas retribution is less concerned with consequences than the idea of 'just deserts' for a morally culpable act. The following review article explores the application of these rationales to the use of the criminal sanction and strict criminal liability to regulate corporate crime.

'Developments in the Law: Corporate Crime' (1978–79), 92 *Harvard L Rev*, 1227 at 1231

II RATIONALE

A. The Rationale for Regulatory Crimes

… In justifying the imposition of criminal sanctions for illicit corporate activity, commentators most often cite deterrence as the primary rationale. They reason that retribution cannot be a concern of statutes dealing with activities which are not in and of themselves morally wrong; indeed, the activities proscribed may come very close to what is seen as good corporate practice in the competitive business world. Similarly, it is argued society is not concerned with incapacitating or rehabilitating those who might well be pillars of the community had they not violated a technical economic regulation. Furthermore … since corporate activity is normally undertaken in order to reap some economic benefit, corporate decision makers choose courses of action based on a calculation of potential costs and benefits. The calculating criminal is the one best deterred by punitive sanctions. Hence, commentators reason, deterrence plays a more significant role in the area of corporate crime than in other areas of the criminal law.

The absence of an element of retribution in some areas of corporate crime is substantiated by the existence of strict liability crimes.

Even though deterrence clearly plays a critical role in the justification of corporate criminal sanctions, the argument that retribution cannot be involved is unconvincing. It is not clear that the underlying activity is morally neutral in all cases. For example, while inadvertent leakage from a pollution control facility may be seen as morally blameless, the same would probably not be said of the intentional release of carcinogenic pollutants into a community's drinking water. Furthermore, even when the activity proscribed by law is not in itself morally wrong, the knowing violation of the law may be morally blameworthy. If a statute regulates and structures important social behavior and institutions, there is probably a moral duty to obey that law, at least in a reasonably just society. Thus even in the area of corporate crime, moral culpability could serve as a limitation upon the imposition of criminal penalties. If so, then the theory of corporate criminal liability mirrors the widely accepted view that criminal sanctions while aimed primarily at deterrence, incapacitation, and rehabilitation, may only be applied when the offender is morally culpable.

III STANDARDS OF LIABILITY

Standards of criminal liability for corporate offenses should be evaluated in light of the dual rationales for regulating corporate conduct through the criminal law—deterrence and just deserts (retribution). These two rationales frequently conflict in practice, so no standard of liability can fully achieve both goals. Standards which require no finding of wrongful intent or carelessness may effectively deter illegal behavior but do not comport with the moral principle of just deserts. At the other extreme, standards which require evidence that the crime was committed willfully or knowingly accord with the just deserts principle but make liability easy to evade and difficult to prove, thus providing inadequate deterrents to corporate crime. In designing standards of criminal liability for corporations and for individuals accused of regulatory offenses, the courts and legislatures must attempt to strike an appropriate balance between deterrence and just deserts.

The deterrence rationale has often been cited by English judges in cases involving consumer protection. The following comments are taken from a leading judgment on the Trade Descriptions Act 1968:

Tesco v Nattrass [1972] AC 153, 193

[LORD DIPLOCK:] Nowadays most business transactions for the supply of goods or services are not actually conducted by the person who in civil law is regarded as the party to any contracts made in the course of the business, but by servants or agents acting on his behalf. Thus, in the majority of cases the physical acts or omissions which constitute or result in an offence under the statute will be those of servants or agents of an employer or principal on whose behalf the business is carried on. That employer or principal is likely to be very often a corporate person as in the instant appeal. Consumer protection, which is the purpose of statutes of this kind, is achieved only if the occurrence of the prohibited acts or omissions is prevented. It is the deterrent effect of penal provisions which protects the consumer from the loss he would sustain if the offence were committed. ... Where, in the way that business is now conducted they are likely to be acts or omissions of employees of that party and subject to his orders, the most effective method of deterrence is to place on the employer the responsibility of doing everything which yes within his power to prevent his employees from doing anything which will result in the commission of an offence.

This, I apprehend, is the rational and moral justification for creating in the field of consumer protection, as also in the field of public health and safety, offences of 'strict liability' for which an employer or principal, in the course of whose business the offences were committed, is criminally liable, notwithstanding that they are due to acts or 'omissions of his servants or agents which were done without his knowledge or consent or even were contrary to his orders.

There were for many years calls for the 'decriminalisation' of consumer-law offences from both business and consumer interests (see, for example, Borrie, 1980: 318–21; Robin Young, 1980; Tench, 1981), with recommendations for greater reliance on administrative or self-regulatory measures (see Hampton, 2005: para 1.31).

A primary argument for decriminalisation is the limited range of criminal sanctions compared to the greater flexibility and range of administrative sanctions. For example, within an administrative regime, regulators might be authorised to close premises, impose administrative penalties, enter into enforceable undertakings with businesses in relation to their future activity, require publicity to 'name and shame' rule-breakers, or monitor conduct under a licensing regime. In the UK the Financial Services Authority may levy administrative penalties (see eg cases in Chapter 7). Undertakings might include corporate rehabilitation orders such as requiring corporations to run externally audited training schemes for employees. The opportunity to deploy a wider range of penalties has been thought to be a major advantage of decriminalisation.

Close attention should be paid to the question of the validity of these arguments when you read the material in section 3.1.5 below on the implementation in practice of strict liability in consumer-law offences. At this stage, it is worthwhile drawing attention to two points. First, the 'just deserts' argument is partly undermined by the fact that most consumer-law offences provide statutory defences which permit businesses to avoid liability if they have taken all reasonable care and if the offence was due to the default of another person. It has also been pointed out that it is often misleading to use the description 'no fault' in relation to the activity of corporations which make planned choices which it is known will inevitably result in a certain number of offences (Cranston, 1979: 115; Kelman, 1981: 591). Second, the advocates of decriminalisation assume that there is a moral consensus on, for example, 'conduct which is not by normal standards wicked'. Is it likely to be clear, for example, which consumer-law offences are the result of 'intentional conduct that injures people, deprives them of their property, restricts their freedom or subjects them to offensive interferences'? Harry Glasbeek comments that the scope of the protection of the principles of criminal law is often contested and that

> what is presented as a shared morality is that complex of values and beliefs dear to the hearts and minds of those who can exercise control over the political struggles that define the shared morality at any one moment of history. … [T]hose are the beliefs and values of the dominant capitalist class. (Glasbeek, 2002: 151).

3.1.1 The role of mens rea

The arguments in favour of *mens rea* offences in consumer law are that courts might be more willing to levy substantial fines or imprisonment against offenders. The availability of a wide range of administrative sanctions and the increased evidential burden would reduce the use by enforcers of criminal sanctions where they were not appropriate. On the other hand, with a *mens rea* offence it would be difficult to secure a conviction against a large corporation. The CPUT regulations retain strict criminal liability for almost all contraventions of the misleading and aggressive commercial practices provisions. However, the general prohibition (regulation 3) is a *mens rea* offence. This reflects a reluctance to impose strict criminal liability for breach of an open-textured provision.

3.1.2 Sanctions and deterrence

Much has been written on the effectiveness of criminal sanctions in deterring undesirable behaviour. While the general effectiveness of these sanctions has been questioned, it is often assumed that they may be effective in deterring business offences. This is premised on the economic assumption that businesses attempt to maximise profits and consequently will only violate the law if it is profitable to do so. Decisions to violate the law will therefore involve a cost–benefit calculation of the probable profit to be obtained through violation, the probability of prosecution and the amount of any punishment. If the costs of violation are likely to exceed the benefits, then the law will be obeyed. An optimal sanctioning policy would establish a fine that was at least marginally greater than the benefits from the illegal activity. The fine would have to take into account the fact that a corporation will discount the fine by the probability of being caught. The fine should reflect this fact, so that if there is a one in four chance of being apprehended for a crime that would reap $1,000 profit, then the fine should be set at a level greater than $4,000. The primary sanction used in consumer-law regulatory offences in the United Kingdom is the fine. It is also assumed that the stigma of criminal conviction, reflected in adverse publicity to an individual or organisation, may have a deterrent effect.

The economic approach to crime and punishment favours fines as the dominant sanction (Becker, 1968: 169; Breit and Elzinga, 1972–73: 693). This preference for fines rests on the fact that they are extremely flexible, allowing the punishment to 'fit' the crime, involve fewer social resources than alternatives (eg imprisonment) and might be used to compensate victims and to subsidise the public system of apprehension and enforcement. They may, in short, achieve maximum deterrence at minimum social cost.

In the real world, there are difficulties in this approach to the use of fines as a criminal sanction for consumer-law offences. First, in order to achieve optimal deterrence where enforcement resources are scarce, fines might have to be extremely high. Courts hesitate, however, to impose large fines for consumer-law offences. The Hampton Review in 2005 provides the following data on fines in regulatory offences.

Reducing Administrative Burdens: Effective Inspection and Enforcement (2005)

2.78 Although nearly 25,000 fines, formal cautions and prosecutions were brought against business in 2003–04, the resulting fines were very low. In 2004, there were 283 prosecutions by the Environment Agency; 272 cases resulted in conviction. The average fine handed down for companies in a magistrates' court was £6,680, and for the 17 cases in a crown court, £35,594. ... The deterrent effect of such fines is likely to be low. For any company other than the smallest, a £5,000 fine is likely to be an insignificant sum.

2.79 The infrequency of prosecutions means that magistrates rarely see regulatory offences. A magistrate will typically see a health and safety offence every 14 years, and an environmental case every 7 years. Infrequency of contact with regulatory cases, and the complex nature of the legislation and offences, can lead to inconsistent judgements, or fines that do not reflect the gain a business has taken from its illegal activity.

2.80 Regulators only prosecute the most serious cases, reflected in the small number of prosecutions, yet the average fines set out above are comparatively low, compared to the economic benefit companies can gain from illegal operation.

An OECD study of enforcement indicated an average fine of £675 for offences under section 1 of the Trade Descriptions Act (OECD, 2006: 42). The relatively low level of fines appears to be partly attributable to magistrates' intuitive belief that these offences are not 'true' crimes. (The use of civil penalties might address this problem, but it is highly unlikely that magistrates would levy fines large enough to achieve an optimal level of deterrence.)

Second, the economic approach assumes that individuals and organisations are 'amoral calculators' of the costs and benefits of compliance. However, Robert Kagan suggests that corporations might be divided into three types—'political citizens', 'amoral calculators' and the 'organisationally inept' (Kagan, 1984: 67)—and there is significant evidence that consumer-law offences often result from 'organisational failures' (Williamson, 1985: 148) and incompetence rather than from rational calculation. There is now a substantial literature that critiques the rational-actor model of corporations (see sources in Baldwin, 2004: n 55). There is also evidence that a large number of small businesses are unaware of regulatory requirements. Improvements in a company's compliance may often be achieved, therefore, through advice, persuasion and co-operation without the need for the sanctioning approach implicit in the economic analysis of the use of fines.

Third, the selective enforcement policy entailed by the economic approach would levy potentially severe sanctions only on those unfortunate enough to be caught. This might be regarded as unfair and inconsistent with notions of 'just deserts'. The primary reason for using the criminal sanction where equivalent civil penalties are available is to impose a moral censure on the offender. Braithwaite (1984) and others (Ball and Friedman, 1965) also stress the importance of the habit-forming function of the criminal law, and its consequent role in encouraging more-effective self-regulation. Braithwaite (1984: 319; and see also Schelling, 1984: ch 2) wrote:

> Do away with criminal punishment and you do away with much of the sense of morality which makes self-regulation possible. Self-regulation and positive regulation are therefore complementary rather than alternatives.

In a similar vein, Kadish has argued that a period of stringent enforcement of particular laws (eg those covering tax evasion or drunk driving) might have an important function in shaping the public conscience (Kadish, 1963: 211).

3.1.3 Statutory defences

According to Leigh, statutory defences 'usually stress two aspects of the defendant's conduct, namely whether the infraction was due to the act or default of another person, and whether the defendant exercised due diligence to prevent the infraction' (Leigh, 1983: 66). The particular defence in the CPUT regulations (regulation 17) is slightly wider than this and includes mistake, accident, reliance on information supplied or some other cause beyond the defendant's control in addition to the act or default of another person.

The most important issues under the heading 'statutory defences' have concerned the liability of corporations for acts of their employees. This topic introduces some of the difficulties involved in controlling corporate conduct by means of the criminal law (see Wells, 2001; Gobert and Punch, 2003). The leading case is *Tesco Supermarkets Ltd v Nattrass* (1972).

In this case, Tesco was charged with a mispricing offence contrary to section 11(2) of the Act. It pleaded in its defence that the offence was due to the act or default of its branch manager and that it had taken all reasonable precautions to avoid committing the offence. The justices convicted, fining Tesco £25. The Divisional Court dismissed its appeal. The House of Lords, however, upheld Tesco's appeal, holding that the branch manager was 'another person' within section 24. He was not an individual of sufficient status (director, manager, secretary, senior officer) to be identified with the company nor had senior management delegated their powers to him since he was controlled through the hierarchical chain of command. The company satisfied the due-diligence defence by having an adequate chain of command and an efficient working system of supervision to ensure that its shops were managed properly.

Tesco Supermarkets Ltd v Nattrass [1972] AC 153 at 169–71, 174–75 (HL)

[LORD REID:] … For the protection of purchasers or consumers Parliament in many cases made it an offence for a trader to do certain things. Normally those things were done on his behalf by his servants and cases arose where the doing of the forbidden thing was solely the fault of a servant, the master having done all he could to prevent it and being entirely ignorant of its having been done. The just course would have been to hold that once the facts constituting the offence had been proved, *mens rea* would be presumed unless the accused proved that he was blameless. The courts could not, or thought they could not, take that course. But they could and did hold in many such cases on a construction of the statutory provision that Parliament must be deemed to have intended to depart from the general rule and to make the offence absolute in the sense that mens rea was not to be constituent of the offence.

This has led to great difficulties. If the offence is not held to be absolute the requirement that the prosecutor must prove *mens rea* makes it impossible to enforce the enactment in very many cases. If the offence is held to be absolute that leads to the conviction of persons who are entirely blameless: an injustice which brings the law into disrepute. So Parliament has found it necessary to devise a method of avoiding this difficulty. But instead of passing a general enactment that it shall always be a defence for the accused to prove that he was no party to the offence and had done all he could to prevent it, Parliament has chosen to deal with the problem piecemeal, and has in an increasing number of cases enacted in various forms with regard to particular offences that it shall be a defence to prove various exculpatory circumstances.

In my judgment the main object of these provisions must have been to distinguish between those who are in some degree blameworthy and those who are not, and to enable the latter to escape from conviction if they can show that they were in no way to blame. …

Where a limited company is the employer difficult questions do arise in a wide variety of circumstances in deciding which of its officers or servants is to be identified with the company so that his guilt is the guilt of the company.

I must start by considering the nature of the personality which by a fiction the law attributes to a corporation. A living person has a mind which can have knowledge or intention or be negligent and he has hands to carry out his intentions. A corporation has none of these: it must act through living persons, though not always one or the same person. Then the person who acts is not speaking or acting for the company. He is acting as the company and his mind which directs his acts is the mind of the company. There is no question of the company being vicariously liable. He is not acting as a servant, representative, agent or delegate. He is an embodiment of the company or, one could say, he hears and speaks through the persona of the company, within his appropriate sphere, and his mind is the mind of the company. If it is a guilty mind then that guilt is the guilt of the company. It must be a question of law whether, once the facts have been ascertained, a person in doing particular things is to be regarded as the company or merely as the company's servant or agent. In that case any liability of the company can only be a statutory or vicarious liability. ...

Reference is frequently made to the judgment of Denning LJ in *HL Bolton (Engineering) Co Ltd v TJ Graham & Sons Ltd* [1957] I QB 159. He said, at p 172:

> 'A company may in many ways be likened to a human body. It has a brain and nerve centre which control what it does. It also has hands which hold the tools and act in accordance with directions from the centre. Some of the people in the company are mere servants and agents who are nothing more than hands to do the work and cannot be said to represent the mind or will. Others are directors and managers who represent the directing mind and will of the company, and control what it does. The state of mind of these managers is the state of mind of the company and is treated by the law as such.'

In that case the directors of the company only met once a year: they left the management of the business to others, and it was the intention of those managers which was imputed to the company. I think that was right. There have been attempts to apply Lord Denning's words to all servants of a company whose work is brain work, or who exercise some managerial discretion under the direction of superior officers of the company. I do not think that Lord Denning intended to refer to them. He only referred to those who 'represent the directing mind and will of the company, and control what it does.'

I think that is right for this reason. Normally the board of directors, the managing director and perhaps other superior officers of a company carry out the functions of management and speak and act as the company. Their subordinates do not. They carry out orders from above and it can make no difference that they are given some measure of discretion. But the board of directors may delegate some part of their functions of management giving to their delegate full discretion to act independently of instructions from them. I see no difficulty in holding that they have thereby put such a delegate in their place so that within the scope of the delegation he can act as the company. It may not always be easy to draw the line but there are cases in which the line must be drawn. ...

... [I]f I look to the purpose and apparent intention of Parliament in enacting this defence I think that it was plainly intended to make a just and reasonable distinction between the employer who is wholly blameless and ought to be acquitted and the employer who was in some way at fault, leaving it to the employer to prove that he was in no way to blame.

What good purpose could be served by making an employer criminally responsible for the misdeeds of some of his servants but not for those of others? It is sometimes argued—it was argued in the present case—that making an employer criminally responsible, even when he has done all that he could to prevent an offence, affords some additional protection to the public because this will induce him to do more. But if he has done all he can how can he do more? I think that what lies behind this argument is a suspicion that magistrates too readily accept evidence that an employer has done all he can to prevent offences. But if magistrates were to accept as sufficient a paper scheme and perfunctory efforts to enforce it they would not be doing their duty—that would not be 'due diligence' on the part of the employer.

Then it is said that this would involve discrimination in favour of a large employer like the appellants against a small shopkeeper. But that is not so. Mr Clement was the 'opposite number' of the small shopkeeper and he was liable to prosecution in this case. The purpose of this Act must have been to penalise those at fault, not those who were in no way to blame.

The Divisional Court decided this case on a theory of delegation. In that they were following some earlier authorities. But they gave far too wide a meaning to delegation. I have said that a board of directors can delegate part of their functions of management so as to make their delegate an embodiment of the company within the sphere of the delegation. But here the board never delegated any part of their functions. They set up a chain of command through regional and district supervisors, but they remained in control. The shop managers had to obey their general directions and also take orders from their superiors. The acts or omissions of shop managers were not acts of the company itself.

In my judgment the appellants established the statutory defence. I would therefore allow this appeal.

The *Tesco* decision has been criticised for its restriction of corporate criminal liability based on the 'directing mind' theory. The value of individual fault which underlies Lord Reid's interpretation of the statutory defences fits uncomfortably with the idea that many consumer-law offences are probably a result of 'organisational failures' (*Harvard Law Review*, 1979: 1243; Gobert, 1994):

[T]he criminal acts of a modern corporation result not from the isolated activity of a single agent, but from the complex interactions of many agents in a bureaucratic setting. Illegal conduct ... is the consequence of corporate processes such as standard operating procedures and hierarchical decisionmaking.

In addition, the lingering master–servant idea implicit in the top policymaking officials–subordinates distinction outlined by Lord Reid underestimates the organisational complexity of decision-making in large corporations. Gobert argues for a form of organisational responsibility where a company will be criminally liable if 'a crime is authorized, permitted or tolerated as a matter of company policy or *de facto* practice' (Gobert, 1994, quoted in Cartwright, 2000: 108). The company's mind is 'treated as a distinct organic entity whose mind is embodied in the policies it had adopted' (ibid: 108). On this basis it is not necessary to point to a particular individual who is responsible.

The ability of a corporation successfully to plead a statutory defence based on the actions of a lower-level employee has been questioned in later cases. Peter Cartwright argues that cases such as *Tesco Stores v Brent* (1993) and *R v British Steel* (1994), although based on different statutory provisions, demonstrate a change in attitude by the judiciary to statutory defences. He comments:

[The decision in Brent] contrasts sharply with that in Tesco Ltd. v Nattrass ... [Commenting on British Steel] there is difficulty in reconciling this decision with traditional conceptions of corporate criminality, just as there had been in Brent. ... The cases of British steel and Brent may suggest that the courts are increasingly reluctant to allow corporate employers to distance themselves from their employees for the purposes of statutory defenses. Although the wording of the defense in Brent was quite different from that in Nattrass the decision in Brent is significant in its rejection of the idea that only the knowledge of the senior officers can be that of the company. This reasoning could be seen as being taken a step further in British Steel, where it was applied to a defense which was similar to a due diligence defense, and which clearly was concerned with the steps taken by the company itself. ... It might be thought that, following Brent, when a corporate employer is charged with an offence under the trade descriptions Act and pleads a defence under section 24(1), the court will be concerned, not just with the actions of those who form the corporation's directing mind and will, but with the actions of the employee whose acts gave rise to the offense. If the employee has failed to exercise all reasonable precautions and all due diligence, perhaps, the company's defense will have to fail. (Cartwright, 2000: 100)

Cartwright also draws attention to *Meridian Global Funds Management Asia Ltd v Securities Commission* (1995), in which Lord Hoffmann indicated that it was a question of construction in each case as to whether a particular act should be attributed to the company and called into question of the 'directing mind' model adopted in *Nattrass*. Celia Wells argues that in these cases 'the courts are reflecting the general mood of reduced tolerance of corporate risk-taking in their decision-making' (Wells, 1995: 1327; Wells, 2001).

DSG Retail Ltd v Oxfordshire County Council (2001) illustrates an application of an unsuccessful pleading of the *Nattrass* defence and perhaps a more sceptical attitude by the judiciary to the due-diligence defence. In this case a large branch of Dixon's in Oxford displayed a notice indicating 'Price Check Price—We can't be beaten—We guarantee to match any local price—Dixon's.' A CD system was advertised at £299 and the same CD system was available for £189 at a local competitor. A trading standards officer visited the store on 12 April 1999 and asked if they would match the price. The assistant checked with his superior and stated that he had been told that they would not match the price. The officer returned to the store on 20 May 1999 and found the same offers being made and the same refusal by Dixon's to match the competitor's offer. On both occasions the assistants were acting on instructions of their superiors within the store. A successful prosecution was brought under section 20(1) of the Consumer Protection Act 1987 and the court rejected the application of the due-diligence defence since the refusal to match the price clearly reflected the 'policy approach' in this large branch of Dixon's. Dixon's appealed the conviction and the rejection of the due-diligence defence. It argued that the Crown Court failed sufficiently to distinguish between the individual assistants, their superiors at branch level and the defendant company. Kennedy LJ rejected this argument:

[H]e invited our attention to the well-known case of Tesco Supermarkets Ltd v Nattrass [1972] AC 153; 69 LGR 403.

I accept, of course, the proposition that was there established in the House of Lords, that there is a distinction to be made between the individual company and those who act on its behalf at local level. But here, as the Crown Court was at pains to point out, the evidence was such as to indicate that, at local level, there was a failure by the company properly to supervise and control the operation of their Oxford branch. That is something which, as it seems to me, the Crown Court and the justices were entitled to take into account in considering whether or not these defendants, who had raised a defence of due diligence, had indeed established such a defence. On the facts of this case, they had failed to do so. They demonstrated that they had sent out a notice (the terms of which are set out in the case stated) but when it came to what happened at local level, it was clear that on more that one occasion the terms of the general instruction were not complied with and the way in which those failures took place was such as to entitle the court, if so minded and it was so minded, to conclude that there was a lack of due diligence.

Accordingly, in relation to the second question posed: 'Does the defence of due diligence fail if the persons responsible for giving a misleading indication, in refusing to conform to a price match promise, are acting on instructions from their superiors?' I would give a qualified answer. The qualified answer being, that it may do as it was found to fail in the circumstances of this case.

Analysis of the cases on statutory defences suggests that courts look to the specific terms of the defence and the nature of the particular risk. Thus Deborah Parry notes that the courts have adopted a very demanding standard of due diligence for safety offences under section 39 of the Consumer Protection Act 1987 but a less demanding standard in relation to pricing offences (Parry, 1995). The courts have also set a high standard in relation to car dealers and 'clocked cars' (see eg *Wandsworth London Borough Council v Bentley* (1980); cf *Naish v Gore* (1971)) generally imposing an obligation on dealers to check the history of a car.

Suppliers in the distributor chain cannot meet the standard of due diligence by merely relying on guarantees provided by earlier suppliers but should conduct their own tests (*Taylor v Lawrence* (1977)). In *Sherratt v Geralds the American Jewellers* (1970) a retailer carried out no tests on watches supplied to them that were described as a 'diver's watch' and 'waterproof': the watch stopped after being in water for one hour. The suppliers relied on the wholesaler's reputation but this defence failed. The court indicated that the retailers had not taken 'elementary precautions of dipping the watch in a bowl of water [which] would have prevented the offense'. In safety cases suppliers should take random samples of products: simply making it a condition of an order from a wholesaler that goods should comply with regulations is not sufficient (*Garrett v Boots Chemists Ltd* (1980)). The nature and scale of a sample may depend on the nature of the goods (whether homogeneous or heterogeneous goods) but the burden of proof is on the defendant to show 'by independent statistical evidence or otherwise, that his testing system was adequate to the type of goods and the number of goods involved'. The supplier must also establish that 'the testing system was in practice carried out scrupulously' (*P&M Supplies Ltd v Devon Council* (1991); see also *Rotherham Metropolitan Borough Council v Raysun* (1988)). In *London Borough of Sutton v Halsall PLC* (1995), which concerned flammable Halloween capes that breached safety regulations, Kennedy LJ commented that:

> the authorities …show that an importer such as the respondent company in the present case, may be able to satisfy the burden of proof, if for example the importer buys from an established manufacturer who he has reason to trust, who is aware of his requirements, and in particular the safety requirements laid down by English law, and if the importer then subjects the goods to sampling. The sampling should however itself be properly organized random sampling, with a sufficient number of samples being properly tested to indicate compliance with the specifications.

Howells and Weatherill, after surveying the defences argue that 'For all the impression conveyed by this case law that the defence will be rarely made out, it is nonetheless not to be regarded as a dead letter' (Howells and Weatherill, 2005: 497).

There are issues of institutional competence concerning the ability of lower courts to assess the nature of sampling by a supplier. Thus Nolan J commented in *P & M Supplies* that:

[I]t seems to me that it is not practicable to decide that a given number of tests is inadequate without having a clear idea of what an adequate number of tests would be.

This case illustrates the need for benches of magistrates to be given help about these matters, preferably in the form of independent statistical evidence as to what should be done by a reasonable trader in these circumstances to avoid the sort of danger which the regulations are intended to prevent.

Application of the statutory defences requires the courts to assess the operating procedures and practices of the company to establish whether it exercised 'all reasonable precautions and due diligence'. Lord Diplock suggested in the *Tesco* case that for a large organisation such as Tesco's this required its taking all 'reasonable precautions in the selection and training of servants to perform supervisory duties', laying down 'an effective system of supervision' and 'using due diligence to see that it is observed'. These simple formulae conceal the formidable fact-finding and judgmental issues involved in deciding whether the requirements they state have been met by a large retailing organisation. Since the courts will have no comparative material on procedures operated by other retailers, they may have difficulty in determining standards for adjudicating this issue. Moreover, they may have great difficulty in determining whether there is, in practice, general adherence to these procedures and in assessing their operation over a period of time. Lord Reid counselled against accepting 'paper' schemes of supervision (see also *McGuire v Sittingbourne Cooperative Society* (1976)) but it may often be difficult in such cases to distinguish form from substance.

Since enforcement authorities are generally risk-averse in prosecution policy, the threat of such a defence, particularly by a large organisation, may induce them not to proceed. It might be argued, therefore, that corporations should be held strictly liable for the acts of their employees, leaving it to the corporations to take internal measures to correct their procedures and sanction culpable individuals. This would reduce the courts' fact-finding difficulties and increase the bargaining power of enforcement agencies in implementing the Act. (It would be necessary, if a social-welfare goal were in view, to estimate whether overall social costs—damage to consumers, enforcement and compliance costs—were minimised by such a strategy.)

Individual employees may be held liable under certain consumer protection offences (CPUT regulation 16) but not others. Thus in *R v Warwickshire County Council, ex p Johnson* the courts interpreted the words 'in the course of a business of his' in section 20 of the Consumer Protection Act 1987 as preventing the prosecution of an employee.

Cranston indicates there is generally little purpose served in prosecuting employees identified by the company as responsible for an offence. 'Why should they be blamed? They are locked into a system where they have to carry out a company's production or marketing scheme; in the case of junior employees, for low wages in what may be an uncreative environment' (Cranston, 2000: 330).

Senior management may be held liable under regulation 15 of the CPUT regulations. However, prosecutions of senior management are almost unknown in relation to consumer offences committed by large corporations. There is a large body of literature on the balance between individual and corporate liability (see eg Fisse, 1980; Kraakman, 1984; Wells, 2001; Glasbeek, 2002).

3.1.4 Statutory defences and meta-regulation

Does the existence of statutory defences stimulate companies to ensure that they have the proper organisational structure to avoid the risks of mistakes such as those made by DSG Retail? DSG Retail now has a 'Business Standards Department' that was created (2004) in response to anticipated regulation of the company by the Financial Services Authority in respect of the sale of insurance products. This department is also responsible for day-to-day contact with Trading Standards. According to the company:

> As well as responding to enquiries, an integral part of the work involves the Building Bridges programme which is designed to ensure the development of better links with the authorities and improved understanding on both sides.

> The department also has a brief to ensure that the company's systems, procedures and training ensure adequate levels of compliance with all relevant regulatory issues. As part of its philosophy it has adopted the company's 'Being The Best' policy and integrates those principles into its daily work. (http://www.dixonsretail.com/dixons/en/ourresponsibilities/marketplace/tradingstandards)

Parker (2007) argues that legal liabilities might create incentives for self-regulation by being calibrated to the effectiveness of self-regulation. The statutory defences are one method of doing this. Parker also argues that meta-regulation is not merely concerned with providing companies with a safe-harbour from prosecution by instituting internal compliance procedures but requires the development of the appropriate corporate culture. We do not have extensive knowledge of the effects of the regulatory offence on corporate decision-making. Parker and Nielsen, in their study of implementation of trade practices compliance systems in Australia, show that 'on the whole the implementation of trade practices compliance systems is partial, symbolic, and half hearted. Nevertheless, enforcement action by the Australian Competition and Consumer Enforcement Commission improves the level of implementation of compliance systems' (Parker and Nielsen 2006; see also Coglianese and Lazar, 2003).

3.1.5 Prosecuting the regulatory offence: the empirical data

The study of bureaucratic discretion is a vast topic, but we are concerned in this section only with the issue of discretion in enforcement. A major justification for the existence of discretion in this area is the over-inclusiveness of legislative standards. Although in the United Kingdom legislation has been relatively specific, the use of strict criminal liability will net many technical violations where the costs of prosecution would probably outweigh the social benefits. Selective enforcement is also justified by the limited resources—legal, budgetary and informational—of an agency. In addition, general legislative standards (eg those of the Unfair Commercial Practices Directive) will typically cover all sectors of trade, since there will be high rule-making costs in attempting to regulate individual trades. It is almost inevitable therefore that those entrusted with the enforcement of regulatory legislation will exercise significant discretion both in general policy choices and in individual decisions to prosecute. Trading Standards statistics indicate that in 2004, Trading Standards Offices carried out 203,697 inspections, sent 40,806 warning letters, 2,486 formal cautions and instituted 4,692 prosecutions (quoted in Regulatory Justice, 2006: 17). Approximately 10 per cent of these prosecutions were brought under the Trade Descriptions Act 1968. In 2010–11, 308 prosecutions were instituted under the Consumer Protection from Unfair Trading Regulations. Enforcement statistics indicate that the used-car and home-improvement sectors constitute substantial percentages of these prosecutions.

Although the conferring of a broad discretion on enforcement agencies is a typical characteristic of Anglo-Saxon legal systems, it has been criticised. Some critics stress the importance of clear rules and a consequent need to narrowly cabin and confine discretion (Davis, 1969: 28). On this approach, the dangers of discretion or 'selective enforcement' are equated with the dangers of arbitrary power. (Such views generally go hand in hand with a general distrust of government and public bureaucracies.) Other critics, less severe in tone, have drawn attention to the need to channel and structure discretion in order to achieve goals such as greater accountability in prosecution deci-sions, a clearer articulation of policies pursued and greater certainty and predictability in decision-making. Yeung argues that regulatory decisions should be: (i) authorised by law; (ii) certain and stable; (iii) accountable and transparent; (iv) procedurally fair; and (v) proportional, consistent and rational (Yeung, quoted in Parker, 2003: 227). Proposals to achieve these objectives include: (i) greater precision in statutory objec-tives; (ii) the use of public guidelines, statements of policy and rules of practice; and (iii) increased opportunities for private groups (eg public-interest groups) to monitor the enforcement process through, for example, access to agency records and judicial review. There are now several guidelines on the exercise of enforcement discretion (see below 3.1.6).

It is impossible to draw any useful conclusions on enforcement discretion without some understanding of the actual nature of the enforcement process. There are now a substantial number of studies of regulatory enforcement in the United Kingdom (see, for example, Carson, 1970; Gunningham, 1974; Cranston, 1979; Richardson, Ogus and Burrows, 1982; Hawkins, 1983, 2002; Hawkins and Thomas, 1984; Hutter, 1988; Peacock, 1985; for surveys, see Richardson, 1987: 295; Rowan-Robinson, Watchman and Barker, 1988: 211; Ogus, 1994: 89).

Several themes emerge from these studies.

First, there is the pervasiveness of discretion. Hawkins (2002) argues that dis-cretion is concentrated 'in the hands of those in the field who first encounter problems'. He also argues that 'the behaviour of a legal bureaucracy is shaped not simply by imperatives arising from its legal mandate, but by forces arising from the political, economic and social environment in which it is set'. In addition,

> [O]ther factors, acting on the decision- maker have their origins in features such as the current political setting, the state of the economy, governmental ideology about regulation, or the attitudes, values, and policy of the agency. ... [H]ow a case is framed is determined by a number of matters, including inspectors' personal values, their training, and the influence of colleagues (ibid: 434).

Enforcement is a continuing process involving repeated interactions between the enforcer and the regulated. This is a simple but crucial point for lawyers, used to studying the discrete individual case, to grasp. Regulatory enforcement involves a different time-frame and may be likened to a continuing 'game'. Prosecution decisions, for example, will involve a consideration of such issues as a violator's past conduct, the agency's 'typification' of a business, the prospect for securing future compliance and the effect of an individual prosecution on the agency's future bargaining power in relation to other firms. Prosecution decisions are clearly far more complex than simply deciding whether in an individual situation a business has breached relevant regulations or is 'at fault'. Both enforcer and regulated may often be 'repeat players', a fact which may have significance for those cases which either party is willing to argue through the higher courts (see, for example, below, *Tesco v Nattrass*). At this point it may be valuable to illustrate some of these themes by drawing on extracts from Ross Cranston's *Regulating Business* (1979), the only systematic account of the work of trading standards officers in enforcing consumer legislation in England and Wales. Cranston studied three consumer agencies during the period 1974–75. Although there have been several institutional changes since that time, the book continues to provide a fascinating description of the implementation of criminal regulation in this area.

Cranston indicated that consumer agencies acquired knowledge of violations through complaints and business inspections. Complaints were the dominant source for prosecutions, with 64 per cent of prosecutions resulting from this source. The following extract outlines his findings on the exercise by the agency of its discretion after detecting an offence and in making prosecution decisions:

> Consumer agencies which detect a consumer offence have four courses of action open to them—to overlook the matter, to advise the business how to avoid its recurrence, to warn it by issuing a caution, or to institute a prosecution. In many cases the distinction between advice and a caution is glossed over in practice, for a communication with a business will contain elements of both. The four possibilities do not constitute a hierarchy of responses, and businesses are not always dealt with progressively by advice, cautioning, and then finally legal proceedings. An offence is often sufficiently serious to justify a prosecution although a business has not been previously advised or cautioned about similar incidents. ...

> In essence, a caution involves drawing an offence to the attention of a business, requiring its correction and, depending on the circumstances, offering advice on how to avoid similar occurrences in the future. ... Consumer agencies deliberately manipulate the threat inherent in cautions to secure compliance with the law. ... Another technique in cautioning is to manipulate uncertainty. If a business is uncertain whether the consumer agency will prosecute it may prefer to avoid the risk by desisting from its objectionable practices. The approach of some officers is to give the impression that legal proceedings will be instituted, but eventually to caution, on the assumption that that will have a greater deterrent effect. With reputable firms, the technique is said by some enforcement officers to be particularly effective in securing compliance with law. 'When you send a caution when they expect a prosecution, then you get a lot of good will. They try harder for you because you didn't prosecute.' (Cranston, 1979: 101–03)

Cranston outlined the following factors as being relevant to a decision to prosecute:

R Cranston, *Regulating Business: Law and Consumer Agencies* (1979) 107–12, 116–18, 122–23, 130–31, 169

> [C]onsumer agencies regularly structure their discretionary decisions in accordance with definite criteria, although these are largely unwritten, sometimes unstated, and occasionally not recognised officially. ... [I]ndividual decisions are generally the outcome of an amalgamation of factors.

The setting of consumer agencies

Resources are an overriding limitation on the activity of consumer agencies. Breaches of consumer law which escape public attention can only be detected by consumer agencies on their own initiative if they have the resources. The magnitude of the substantive law and the volume of unlawful activity make it virtually impossible for consumer agencies with limited manpower and finance to enforce the whole range of legislation. The limitations inherent in the lack of resources cannot be overcome by the dedication of enforcement officers or the efficiency of consumer agencies. ...

The attitude which consumer agencies have to the courts (as bodies which are remote from the problems of protecting consumers) influences whether they initiate legal proceedings. Once a prosecution is commenced, a consumer agency forfeits controls over the matter to a court, and therefore it is reluctant to take action if it is uncertain about the outcome. ...

The attitude of enforcement officers

Variations between consumer agencies in the enforcement of identical consumer laws are partially explained by the interests and attitudes of the higher officials setting agency policy. If they adopt a particular policy (be it committed to advising businesses or be it more disposed to prosecuting wrongdoing) enforcement officers tend to adjust the way they exercise discretion. ...

Because enforcement officers exercise some discretion—whatever the prosecution policy of a consumer agency—their personal characteristics intrude to a varying extent on decisionmaking. ...

The need for certainty and success

Consumer agencies much prefer straightforward, successful prosecutions, a fact reflected in the high conviction rate for the prosecutions they bring. ... Straightforward cases are beneficial in conserving scarce resources which can be utilised in a variety of other ways to protect consumers. Successful cases maintain the prestige of consumer agencies and their officers and minimise the costs of controlling business wrongdoing. A series of unsuccessful prosecutions may encourage a greater number of businessmen to defend proceedings instead of pleading guilty, thus requiring an increase in the resources devoted to each prosecution. ...

Policy prosecutions are not unknown, however, where consumer agencies institute legal proceedings to bring home to a particular business or an area of commerce that certain practices are unacceptable. ... [C]onsumer agencies take an unadventurous view of novel legal claims. Law is surrounded with a mystique and is assumed to be largely unchallengeable and immutable. Most consumer agencies avoid the test case to overturn existing case law or to extend the meaning of the statutory language in consumer legislation. ...

The interest which consumer agencies have in straightforward, certain cases derives in part from their view of courts as remote from, and unsympathetic to, the practicalities of enforcing consumer law. There is no guarantee for consumer agencies that magistrates will take as serious a view of a prosecution as they do; the level of fines, which is regarded as too low, is taken as evidence of this. ...

The task of proving consumer offences is simplified because most consumer legislation creates offences of strict liability, which obviates the need to introduce any evidence about the state of mind of an offender. An exception is where services are falsely described, for intentional or reckless behaviour must be proved. The difficulty of establishing this means that under this head prosecutions are undertaken cautiously and consumer agencies usually confine themselves to obtaining redress for complainants. ...

Business and their offences

... In the decision whether to prosecute a business, its attributes, including its record and attitude, have particular salience for the master strategy adopted by consumer agencies of using persuasion, rather than force, to achieve compliance with consumer law. ...

The nature of businesses

The approach of consumer agencies to law enforcement draws on their typifications of businesses. ...

The assumption is that by their nature reputable businesses do not intend to commit offences and will take steps to prevent the recurrence of any which are the outcome of ignorance or mistake. Since they comply with the law if informed of their obligations or of defects in their trade practices, an effective alternative to the criminal sanction in most cases is advice or a caution. The additional assumption is that it is undesirable to prosecute those attempting to comply with the law for this can create resentment and perhaps a fall in standards. ...

... Offences of unscrupulous businesses are assumed to be committed intentionally and thus to deserve the application of formal sanctions. The essence of the following comments was repeated on many occasions by enforcement officers with respect to secondhand-car dealers: 'I could caution secondhand-car dealers until I am blue in the face. It's just so ludicrous to contemplate.' 'Even where I hadn't known of a car dealer before, I would prosecute, because it's possibly a symptom of something that's been going on for a long time'. ...

The nature of the offence

... Harm to the consumer, and whether it can be remedied, are other indices of the seriousness of an offence. This accords with the notion of strict liability—that it is irrelevant whether a business is at fault, for the aim is to prevent harm to the public. ...

The probability of a prosecution being brought is greater if an offence is detected by a consumer. To some extent a complaint is significant because consumer agencies tend to feel obliged to prosecute if they think that the public demands it. They attempt to reflect community preferences and to respond to most offences with independence and flexibility. ...

In practice, a business offering redress to a complainant can frequently avoid prosecution. ...

Conclusion

... Underpinning the prosecution policy of consumer agencies is the view, to which all adhere to varying degrees, that compliance with consumer law can be achieved more efficiently by advice and persuasion than by threats and court proceedings. Consumer agencies justify their approach by claiming that they are charged with implementing consumer law and not with prosecuting every breach of it.

Richard Bragg commented in 1991 that the normal attitude of enforcement officers 'is to see their major role as one of attempting to acquire compliance with legislation by information and persuasion ... in many authorities prosecution is seen as a last resort and, sometimes, even as an admission of failure' (Bragg, 1991: 202). Hawkins's more recent study confirms many of Cranston's findings: prosecution as a last resort; a preference for cases that are straightforward; prosecution as an unwelcome intrusion or even a loss of control; and finally prosecution as an expressive form declaring and affirming social ideals and values—a 'forceful and dramatic way of making a moral statement about the deliberate flouting of the law' (Hawkins, 2002). An exploratory study of early experience of enforcement of the CPUT regulations in Scotland identified the influence on prosecutions of limits on resources, and the particular approach of the local authority to business expressed in one comment that 'There is a reluctance to prosecute [within] this council. It's not really in this council's philosophy' (Williams and Hare, 2010: 395). They also noted similar typifications of businesses as those identified by Cranston.

Several issues concerning enforcement and prosecution policy arise from Cranston's description. First, consumer agencies appear generally to be concerned with enforcement rather than policy development. Court processes are used primarily as a method of establishing the agencies' authority in bargaining rather than to achieve rule development through possibly uncertain test cases

Second, it is clear that the sharp contrast drawn by some writers between regulation by the criminal law and administrative regulation does not exist. Cranston indicated that there is, in fact, a system of administrative regulation already in existence at the local level. Cautions, warnings and the threat of adverse publicity are an integral part of enforcement. Commentators on the role of the criminal sanction in administrative programmes of regulation have suggested that it ought to be a remedy of last resort (Belobaba, 1977: 51). Cranston's evidence indicates that it may already function in this manner.

Third, the difficulties in weighing the complex amalgam of factors involved in individual decisions to prosecute may lead to a policy of 'muddling through' or bureaucratic routinisation—a policy that focuses on tangible measures of success (compare the extract from Stigler above Chapter 3) without relating them to overall policy objectives. (Cranston, 1979: 171; see also Silbey, 1984: 147).

Cranston's critique of prosecution policy raises the question of how to reform it in order to make it more efficient and subject to greater accountability. A central question raised by Cranston's study is whether the contemporary changes to enforcement will change substantially the empirical picture painted by socio-legal scholars. We turn now to consider these changes.

3.1.6 Structuring enforcement discretion and risk-based enforcement

The Enforcement Concordat was drawn up in 1998 between local and national enforcement bodies. It was part of the search for 'better regulation' 'which recognizes the need for regulation but also recognizes that the burden on business should be kept to a minimum'. This code, which is now enacted under the Legislative and Regulatory Reform Act 2006, sets out the following principles of good enforcement.

The Principles of Good Enforcement: Policy and Procedures

87 The effectiveness of legislation in protecting consumers or sectors in society depends crucially on the compliance of those regulated. We recognise that most businesses want to comply with the law. We will, therefore, take care to help business and others meet their legal obligations without unnecessary expense, while taking firm action, including prosecution where appropriate, against those who flout the law or act irresponsibly. All citizens will reap the benefits of this policy through better information, choice, and safety.

Principles of Good Enforcement:

Policy

...

Openness

90 We will provide information and advice in plain language on the rules that we apply and will disseminate this as widely as possible.We will be open about how we set about our work, including any charges that we set, consulting business, voluntary organisations, charities, consumers and workforce representatives.

Helpfulness

91 We believe that prevention is better than cure and that our role therefore involves actively working with business, especially small and medium sized businesses, to advise on and assist with compliance. We will provide a courteous and efficient service and our staff will identify themselves by name. We will provide a contact point and telephone number for further dealings with us and we will encourage business to seek advice/information from us. ... We will ensure that, wherever practicable, our enforcement services are effectively co-ordinated to minimise unnecessary overlaps and time delays.

Proportionality

93 We will minimise the costs of compliance for business by ensuring that any action we require is proportionate to the risks. As far as the law allows, we will take account of the circumstances of the case and the attitude of the operator when considering action.

94 We will take particular care to work with small businesses and voluntary and community organisations so that they can meet their legal obligations without unnecessary expense, where practicable.

Consistency

95 We will carry out our duties in a fair, equitable and consistent manner. While inspectors are expected to exercise judgement in individual cases, we will have arrangements in place to promote consistency, including effective arrangements for liaison with other authorities and enforcement bodies through schemes such as those operated by the Local Authorities Co-ordinators of Regulatory Services (LACORS).

Many local authorities have prosecutorial guidelines. The significance of these guidelines for prosecution are illustrated in *R v Adaway* [2004] EWCA Crim 2831 where a home-improvement company successfully defended against a prosecution under the Trade Descriptions Act on the basis that the prosecution was an abuse of process since the authority had contravened prosecutorial guidelines. The authorities' Public Protection Enforcement Policy stated:

7.2. In order to take forward prosecution, the individual or organization must meet one or more of the following criteria:
— Engaged in fraudulent activity,
— Deliberately or persistently breached legal obligations.

The evidence showed that a trading standards officer had 'thought that [it] was a matter which should be resolved without recourse to the criminal law although he is recorded as telling the Byatts [the complainants] that "he had had previous problems with Quality Direct" and that "they had had a fair amount of court experience", matters which have not been elaborated before me as yet'. However, the court decided that it was clear that neither of the criteria identified in 7.2 were substantiated.

The court concluded:

It follows that this appeal must be allowed and the appellant's conviction quashed.

27. We add this. We have no information as to how much these proceedings have cost this local authority. We suspect that it must be many thousands of pounds. We cannot emphasize too strongly that before criminal proceedings are instituted by a local authority, acting in relation to the strict liability offences created by the Trade Descriptions Act, they must consider with care the terms of their own prosecuting policy. If they fail to do so, or if they reach a conclusion which is wholly unsupported, as the conclusion to prosecute in this case was, by material establishing the criteria for prosecution, it is unlikely that the courts will be sympathetic, in the face of the other demands upon their time at Crown Court and appellate level, to attempts to justify such prosecutions.

Trading Standards Offices use a risk-assessment methodology for enforcement that rates businesses as high, medium and low risk 'by reference to scores reflecting key variables, including for example, the probability of the risk occurring, the complexity of the activity, the number of consumers potentially affected, and local history management' (OECD, 2006b: 39). The risk assessment is intended to structure the monitoring role of trading standards officers. In 2005 the Hampton Review concluded that risk assessment should be a central aspect of enforcement and that regulators should provide greater advice to business on compliance with regulations:

2.28 … [I]nspection rates on trading standards overall show a balance of activity that does not seem to be informed by risk. In 2002–03, trading standards officers only inspected 60 per cent of high-risk premises, in 35,000 inspections, while still inspecting ten per cent of businesses classified as low-risk, in over 71,000 inspections. …

The unmet need for advice

2.53 Numerous surveys have found small businesses unaware of particular regulations—

… The review believes that this lack of knowledge is less a mark of failure by business, and more a failure by regulators to communicate their message. Advice reduces the risk of non-compliance, and the easier the advice is to access, and the more specific the advice is to the business, the more the risk of non-compliance is reduced.

2.54 Advice is needed because the regulatory environment is so complex, but the very complexity of the regulatory environment can cause business owners to give up on regulations and 'just do their best'. This is particularly true in respect of small businesses, many of whom, through pressure of time, take a conscious decision to avoid finding out about regulation.

2.68 The review believes that a more open and productive relationship between business and regulators can be achieved if regulators frame their interactions with lower-risk businesses around advice. Advice here means tailored, firm-specific advice to improve compliance. This could, in some cases, be more resource-intensive than a box-ticking inspection, but will bring benefits to the company, and by extension to the regulator's aim of achieving the goals of the regulation. (Hampton, 2005: 4, 29, 35–37).

The Hampton Review recommended that 'comprehensive risk assessment' be the foundation of all regulators' enforcement programmes. The risk assessment should:

(1) be open to scrutiny; (2) be balanced in including past performance and potential future risk (3) use all available good-quality data; (4) be implemented uniformly and impartially; (5) be expressed simply, preferably mathematically; (6) be dynamic not static; (7) be carried through into funding decisions; (8) incorporate deterrent effects; and (9) always include a small element of random inspection.

Risk-based approaches to regulation and its enforcement are responses to central government demands for more cost-effective implementation and better use of regulatory resources. Julia Black analysed the approach to risk assessment adopted by the FSA and raises several questions about this approach (Black, 2005). In many respects the FSA risk assessment and prioritisation model is unremarkable. It assesses the impact of the potential problem (number of consumers affected, nature and size of potential loss, effect on consumers as a whole, perceived importance of product, availability of compensation) multiplied by the probability of the problem occurring.

Black draws attention to the organisational and political dynamics that may affect risk assessments and their application. There is the danger that risk-assessment models may stimulate a 'tick the box' mentality within a bureaucracy or that decisions will be rationalised in terms of the criteria. Notwithstanding the apparent scientific and neutral outcome of a computer-generated risk-assessment model, the weighting of risks is done by individuals not machines and the weighting may be affected by organisational and external factors not directly related to the risk.

Black comments on this approach to regulation:

> [R]isk-based regulation requires us, in very clear and defined terms, to accept what we all know, but rarely admit: not only that regulators will not prevent every risk, will not find every breach, but that they consciously will decide not to try to do any of these things ... [this recognition requires] a new 'politics of accountability' ... a recognition and debate as to who should be making the decision as to what is important and what is not, in recognition that the decision is being made at all. For the decision may not be easy to see.

To the extent that allocation of priorities is a political as well as technical judgment should there be greater opportunity for public interest groups to shape enforcement policy? (See below 5.)

---

4. Administrative remedies

Administrative remedies include injunctions, undertakings, administrative penalties, licence revocation, adverse publicity, 'naming and shaming' and restorative justice orders. There is increasing recourse to injunctive powers in the enforcement of UK consumer legislation. Part 8 of the Enterprise Act 2002 includes this power as well as the power to seek an undertaking from a firm to comply and the possibility of seeking an interim enforcement order (see discussion below). These powers may be exercised by both the OFT and local Trading Standards Offices.

4.1 Enforcement orders

Part 8 of the Enterprise Act 2002 replaced Part III of the Fair Trading Act 1973 and the Stop Now Orders (EC Directive) Regulations 2001 (the 'SNORs') which gave effect to the EC Injunction Directive (1998). Part 8 confers power on both local Trading Standards Offices and the OFT to seek enforcement orders (similar to injunctions) or undertakings where businesses harm the 'collective interests' of consumers (section 211(1)). Part 8 confers a co-ordinating role on the OFT (and from 2013 the NTSB) in the use of the Part 8 enforcement powers.

In 2005 the OFT sought an interim enforcement order against a home-improvement company, MB Designs, and the case provided an opportunity for judicial consideration of several issues related to Part 8. MB Designs supplied windows, doors and conservatories to consumers. The company would measure the windows or doors and then install them or arrange for them to be installed. It offered the consumer a choice of contracts: 'Quick Fit', where the company carried out the survey, manufacture, delivery and installation of the product; 'Quick Trade', where the consumer chose an installer from a list provided by the company; and 'Quick Glass', where the consumer carried out the survey and the company manufactured the product. Many consumers chose the 'Quick Trade' contract which included a term indicating that the installer was independent of MB Designs and that responsibility in respect of installation lay with the installer. The company also included a term that

> The Customer should ensure that any representation or promise made before or at the time of signature to the contract not included in the printed form of the contract is added in writing to the face of the contract and signed by the Customer and the Company or its agent. In this way there will be no doubt as to the terms of the representation or promise. Any such statement not in written form must be agreed by the surveyor in writing.

The OFT led evidence provided by trading standards officers of serious problems with the quality of the products supplied by the company and in particular with the fitting of windows and conservatories. A local Trading Standards Office had received 299 complaints about MB Designs between 2001 and 2004. They were the second-most complained about double-glazing company in Scotland. Although the company was contacted on several occasions by trading standards officers it rarely accepted liability and indicated that it could exclude liability for defective installation through its contract terms. The OFT had been in correspondence with the company and had sought an undertaking under Part 8 of the Enterprise Act. The company refused to provide an undertaking. There were recurring patterns in the complaints: visible gaps around windows, scratches on windows, windows that could not open, doors that were not properly fixed in a very obvious way, and damage to surrounding parts of the customer's property. In a significant number of cases the complaints had been verified by independent tradespersons. Thirty consumers had completed questionnaires on the complaints for the OFT.

The OFT sought an interim enforcement order under section 218 of the Enterprise Act.

Office of Fair Trading v MB Designs (Scotland) Ltd [2005] Scot CS 85 (Court of Session)

Opinion of Lord Drummond Young

[1] … Part 8, which comprises sections 210–236 of the Act, deals with the enforcement of certain consumer legislation and other provisions of law designed to protect consumers. The relevant legislation has two sources, the domestic legislation of the United Kingdom, including such provisions as the Sale of Goods Act 1979 and the Supply of Goods and Services Act 1982, and directives and other legislation of the European Union. For Part 8 to apply, it is necessary that a person carrying on a business should have committed an 'infringement', as defined in the 2002 Act. Two categories of infringement are recognized, a domestic infringement, which involves a contravention of United Kingdom legislation or other provisions of the domestic law of contract within the United Kingdom, and a Community infringement, which involves a contravention of European Union legislation. For an infringement of either sort to occur, it is necessary that there should have been a contravention of the requirements imposed by the law on suppliers of goods and services, whether under United Kingdom or European legislation or at common law. In addition, it is necessary that such contravention should harm the collective interests of consumers. The latter expression is of fundamental importance; it makes clear that Part 8 is not concerned with individual breaches of contract or breaches of statutory provisions on the part of traders, but is rather concerned with the enforcement of general standards of trading.

…

[7] Section 217 is concerned with the making of an enforcement order after a full hearing of the case against the trader, including evidence if that should be necessary. The legislation contemplates, however, that it may be necessary for an enforcer to take action on a more urgent basis. Consequently section 218 authorises the court to make an interim enforcement order, and specifies the conditions that must be satisfied before such an order can be made. …

The present case involves an application made under section 218, and I discuss its provisions below at paragraphs [20] and [21].

[8] Part 8 also makes specific provision for bodies corporate, including limited liability companies. It is obvious that the separate legal personality of such bodies could be used as a device to evade the requirements of the 2002 Act. Consequently Part 8 allows corporate personality to be disregarded, by permitting enforcement orders to be made against persons such as directors and controlling shareholders who consent to or connive in conduct that amounts to a domestic or Community infringement. This power is relevant to the present case, because the first respondent is a limited company incorporated under the Companies Acts and the second and third respondents are directors of the first respondent. The general approach to construction of the legislation

[9] The provisions of Part 8 of the Enterprise Act 2002 dealing with Community infringements are intended to implement the obligations of the United Kingdom under European legislation dealing with consumer protection, notably the Injunctions Directive (Directive 98/27/EC of 19 May 1998 on injunctions for the protection of consumers' interests). Moreover the concepts used in those provisions are in large part derived from the Injunctions Directive. Consequently those provisions must be construed in the light of the wording and purpose of that Directive; that is in accordance with the principles laid down by the European Court of Justice. …Concepts derived from the Injunctions Directive are also used in Part 8 in respect of domestic infringements. That applies in particular to one of the fundamental concepts used in the legislation, the collective interests of consumers. It seems clear that such concepts must

be given the same meaning throughout Part 8; that is the obvious reason for using the same wording in relation to both Community and domestic infringements.

… [T]he orders contemplated by the Directive are designed to prohibit acts contrary to the consumer protection Directives set out in the Annex, to the extent that such acts harm the 'collective' interests of consumers. The Injunctions Directive is accordingly not concerned with the vindication of the rights of individual consumers, but rather the protection of consumer interests generally.

[13] The policy underlying the Injunctions Directive is found in the preamble.

'Whereas current mechanisms available both at national and at Community level for ensuring compliance with those Directives do not always allow infringements harmful to the collective interests of consumers to be terminated in good time; whereas collective interests mean interests which do not include the cumulation of interests of individuals who have been harmed by an infringement; whereas this is without prejudice to individual actions brought by individuals who have been harmed by an infringement'.

It is obvious that this provision is poorly expressed. Its second recital, defining 'collective interests', is a particularly bad case of drafting. If it is read literally, it suggests that 'collective' interests are something quite separate from the interests of individuals who have been harmed by an infringement, in such a way that the interests of those individuals form no part of the collective interests. In my view this does not make sense. It is difficult to see any other basis on which a court could rationally arrive at the conclusion that the collective interests of consumers had been or were likely to be harmed; without concrete instances of individual harm or the threat of harm any such conclusion would normally be mere speculation. This matter is clarified, however, by the French version of the Injunctions Directive.

The literal English translation of the crucial second part of this recital is as follows:

'[considering] that, by collective interests, one means interests which are not a *mere* accumulation of the interests of individuals to whom harm has been caused by an infringement'

This makes it clear that the expression 'collective interests' is not something wholly separate from the interests of individual consumers who have been harmed by infringements. That makes perfectly good sense; it means that the adjective 'collective' denotes the generality of consumers, considered as a body, but at the same time recognizes that the interests of individual consumers are part of those collective interests, and that harm to the collective interests will normally be inferred from a number of instances of harm to individual interests. The error in the English version is the failure to provide any equivalent for the French word 'simple'. This point is of some practical importance for reasons that are discussed below.

[14] The notion of the collective interests of consumers, therefore, indicates that there must be harm or a risk of harm to the public generally, or more precisely to members of the public who may buy the particular goods or services in question. This is distinct from the rights that any particular consumer may have against his or her supplier, whether under the general law of contract or under statutory provisions such as the Supply of Goods and Services Act 1982 or the European Directives listed in Schedule 13 to the 2002 Act. The collective interests of consumers, by contrast, are concerned not with the contractual rights of individual consumers but with general trading standards, and in particular with the general standard of goods or services supplied by a particular trader. Part 8 of the 2002 Act is designed to enforce such trading standards. In my opinion a statutory provision of this nature has two

important features. First, it is not designed to ensure that no defective product or service is ever supplied; it is rather designed to ensure that the incidence of defective products or services is kept at a low level, and that in cases where a defective product or service is supplied reasonable steps are taken to put matters right. Secondly, Part 8 is intended to deal with the overall incidence of defects in a trader's products or services, and it is immaterial for this purpose what the particular defects may be. It is accordingly immaterial that the defects may vary widely in their nature.

[15] The foregoing features of Part 8 have significant implications both for the evidence required to support an order under section 217 or section 218 and for the form of such an order. In relation to the evidence, harm to the collective interests of consumers will normally be inferred from an accumulation of individual instances. Evidence relating to those individual instances will generally be provided, however, by officials of the relevant enforcer, such as the present petitioner, or officials in the trading standards departments of local authorities. That is appropriate because it is the collective interests that are relevant, and the individual instances are only adminicles of evidence that go to establish harm to the collective interests. In the present case, the evidence for the petitioner is presented in the form of two affidavits, one from an officer of the petitioner's Consumer Regulation Enforcement Division and one from a Divisional Trading Standards Officer of one of the local authorities most directly concerned with the first respondent, South Lanarkshire Council. In my opinion the use of evidence of this sort is appropriate. Those affidavits are backed up by documentation relating to individual complaints about defective products or services supplied by the first respondent. In the present case, I am satisfied that the investigation of complaints relied on by the petitioner relates to a sufficiently large proportion to establish that those complaints are for the most part well-founded.

[16] In my opinion the features discussed at paragraph [14] above also have important implications for the form of order granted under section 217 or section 218. Counsel for the respondents submitted that the form of order available under those sections should conform to the requirements of an interdict at common law. ...

[17] I am ... of opinion that the standard of precision that is required in proceedings for interdict is not appropriate to an order under section 217 or section 218 and that it is not necessary, or indeed practicable, that such an order should be directed against specific acts. In any event, I am of opinion that rules of domestic law should not generally be imported into the construction of Part 8. Part 8 is essentially inspired by European legislation, in the form of the Injunctions Directive, and sections 217 and 218 are designed to enforce European legislation. Consequently the interpretation of Part 8 should aim at ensuring a uniform approach throughout the European Union. That interpretation should not be constrained by the detailed rules of procedure of any domestic legal system. Part 8 should rather be construed in a manner calculated to give effect to its underlying purposes, in particular the purposes disclosed in the Injunctions Directive. It follows that orders pronounced under sections 217 and 218 should be regarded as sui generis, and not as an example of interdicts or interim interdicts in Scots law.

[18] Section 220 permits enforcers, including the present petitioner, to apply to the court in respect of any failure to comply with an order, but says nothing more about enforcement procedures. Counsel for the respondents submitted that, unless such orders were framed with the same precision as an interim interdict, the person affected by the order would be uncertain what he had to do to avoid the penal consequences of breach of interdict. I do not agree. In the first place, it is clear that, before penal sanctions can be imposed, the existence of a breach of a court order must be clear. That is itself a major protection to the subject of an enforcement order. In the second place, it is important to bear in mind that a single instance

where defective products or services are supplied will not of itself amount to a breach of the order, because on the basis of a single instance it is normally impossible to say that there is harm to the collective interests of consumers. The need for more than one instance of defective supply means that a trader is likely to have clear advance notice that a breach of the order is possible. In the third place, the sanctions imposed for a contempt of court depend on such considerations as whether the breach is deliberate. Consequently, in the case of an inadvertent breach, the sanction is likely to amount to no more than a warning that a breach exists and should not be repeated. In the fourth place, the element of uncertainty as to whether or not a breach exists is something that frequently occurs in legal proceedings; it is inherent, for example, in concepts such as satisfactory quality and fitness for purpose as used in United Kingdom consumer protection legislation. In such cases the court must simply decide on which side of the line the facts lie. As I have said, in cases of doubt there will be no contempt of court, and in cases where the breach is inadvertent the sanction is unlikely to go beyond a warning.

The requirements of sections 217 and 218

[20] An enforcement order under section 217 clearly contemplates a full hearing of the application, with the leading of evidence if that should be necessary. Section 218 empowers the court to make an interim enforcement order at an earlier stage in proceedings. …The basic requirements if an interim enforcement order is to be made are set out in section 218(1) …it must appear to the court that, if the application had been for an enforcement order, it would be likely that the enforcement order would be granted. Thirdly, it must appear to the court to be expedient that the conduct in question should be prohibited or prevented immediately.

[21] The second of those requirements was the subject of dispute between the parties. Counsel for the respondents submitted that the expression 'likely to be granted' as used in section 218(1)(b) meant more likely than not; thus the court would have to reach the view that on a balance of probabilities an enforcement order would be granted. Counsel for the petitioner, on the other hand, submitted that the word 'likely' signified something less than probability. The legislation in question was concerned with the protection of consumers, and if there were doubt it should be resolved in favour of the interests of consumers. In my opinion the argument for the respondents is to be preferred. Section 218 involves a remedy that may have serious consequences for the person against whom it is used. If the petitioner's construction is correct, such an order could be imposed even if the court thought it less likely than not that a full enforcement order would be pronounced after a full hearing. That seems an improbable construction. I accordingly hold that the word 'likely' in section 218(1)(b) means more likely than not.

The application to the court

The petitioner goes on to aver that in fitting and installing the goods that it supplies to its customers the first respondent regularly failed, and continues regularly to fail, to exercise the requisite level of skill and care of a reasonably competent installer of windows, doors and conservatories. That involves of a breach of the common-law contractual term spondet peritiam artis et imperitia culpae enumeratur (a man is responsible for achieving the standard of skill of his profession, and lack of skill is counted a fault). In addition, it is averred that the first respondent had and has a practice of regularly supplying goods in breach of certain of the statutory terms implied by the Supply of Goods and Services Act 1982. The relevant terms are those in section 11D(2), that goods supplied should be of satisfactory quality, section 11D(6), that goods supplied should be fit for the purpose for which they are purchased, and section 11C(2), that goods supplied should correspond with the description attached to them. Various specific examples of breaches of the statutory terms are given.

... On the basis of the affidavits provided by Miss Parker and Mr. Templeton and the documentation produced along with those affidavits, I am satisfied that the conduct of the first respondent referred to in the petition was conduct in the course of a business; this point was not in dispute. I am further satisfied that that conduct involved repeated acts done or omissions made in breach of contract. This finding relates to the supply of both goods and services by the first respondent. In relation to the supply of goods, I am satisfied that in a substantial number of cases the goods supplied were defective, and that the defects involved breaches of contract, including breaches of terms of the Sale of Goods Act 1979 and the Supply of Goods and Services Act 1982. In relation to the supply of services, I am satisfied that the installation works carried out by or on the instructions of the first respondent were defective in a substantial number of cases, and that the defects amounted to breach of contract on the first respondent's part. I regard the first respondent's Quick Trade contracts as involving the supply of services by the first respondent in at least a substantial number of cases. That finding is sufficient in my opinion for me to take those contracts into account in considering whether there have been breaches of contract by the first respondent that are relevant for the purposes of Part 8.

[31] As I have already indicated, I am of opinion that harm to the collective interests of consumers will normally be inferred from the existence of a number of individual breaches of contract or other relevant defaults on the part of a trader. It must be possible, however, to conclude that something more exists than an accumulation of individual breaches. The extra element is harm to the public generally, in their capacity as consumers, or more precisely to the section of the public who are likely to buy or consider buying the first respondent's doors, windows or conservatories and to have those products installed by the first respondent or persons acting on behalf of the first respondent. In my opinion that extra element exists in the present case. The breaches of contract evidenced by the documents produced by the petitioner, which include breaches of the Sale of Goods Act 1979 and the Supply of Goods and Services Act 1982, are sufficiently extensive and sufficiently serious to enable me to draw the inference that there is indeed harm to the section of the public likely to buy the first respondent's products and services. On this basis I conclude that the first respondent's conduct has involved and continues to involve repeated domestic infringements in terms of section 211 of the 2002 Act.

[32] I am further satisfied that the second and third respondents have a special relationship with the first respondent in terms of section 222 of the 2002 Act, and that they have consented to or connived in the conduct of the first respondent that constitutes a domestic infringement as described in the last two paragraphs. It was not in dispute that a special relationship existed; the second and third respondents are both directors of the first respondent. It was clear from the documentation that they effectively directed the business of the first respondent ...

Unfair terms in contractual documentation

[41] The petitioner advances a further argument that the first respondent has, in its contractual documentation, included and relied upon a term which is unfair in terms of the Unfair Terms in Consumer Contracts Regulations 1999 (SI 1999 No 2083). This argument relates to a term, found in both the Quick Fit contracts and the Quick Trade contracts, to the following effect (clause 7 of the Quick Fit contract and clause 6 of the Quick Trade contract):

'The Customer should ensure that any representation or promise made before or at the time of signature to the contract not included in the printed form of the contract is added in writing to the face of the contract and signed by the Customer and the Company or its agent. In this way there will be no doubt as to the terms of the representation or promise. Any such statement not in written form must be agreed by the surveyor in writing.'

I should say that in both forms of contract this term is obscurely located; it is contained in the middle of detailed contractual provisions in small print which extend over one or two pages, and there is nothing to mark it out as a particularly important term. That is significant, because a term of this nature is of a different order from ordinary contractual terms. In particular, it regulates how alterations may be made to the substantive terms to meet the requirements of a particular contract. As such, it should in my opinion be placed in a prominent position, so that the customer who signs the contract is aware of what he must do to effect any necessary alterations to the printed form.

... It seems to me obvious that the main practical effect of terms of this nature will be to prevent the customer from relying on representations made by the first respondent's salesman. I accordingly reject the submission for the respondents that clause 7 and clause 6 should be regarded as essentially neutral terms. That is not how they operate in practice, and I am obliged by regulation 6(1) to take account of all the circumstances attending the conclusion of contracts between customers and the first respondent.

[44] I am of opinion that the petitioner's submissions on this matter are correct. The first respondent's contracts with their customers will normally be concluded between the customer and a representative of the first respondent who visits the customer's home; such a visit is required to enable the necessary measurements to be taken. It is obvious that the customer is likely to raise questions with the representative, and that the representative will reply. On the basis of the documentation produced by the petitioner, I conclude that those replies may frequently be at variance with the written terms and conditions. This applies in particular to the Quick Trade form of contract. ... On its face this form of contract involves a separate installation contract between the customer and an independent installer. It is clear from the documentation produced by the petitioner, however, that in many cases, possibly a majority, the customer gained the impression from the representative's statements that the first respondent was responsible for the installation.

[45] I am further of the opinion that the use of clauses such as clause 7 of the Quick Fit from of contract and clause 6 of the Quick Trade form of contract causes a significant imbalance in the parties' rights and obligations under the contract, to the detriment of the consumer, and that that is contrary to the requirement of good faith. The terms in question had clearly not been individually negotiated. In these circumstances I am satisfied that the requirements of regulation 5 of the 1999 Regulations are satisfied, and that the terms in question must be regarded as unfair in terms of those Regulations. That amounts to a Community infringement, in the following manner. Under section 212(3) of the 2002 Act the Secretary of State is empowered by order to specify the law in the United Kingdom which gives effect to the listed Directives of the European Union. The order in question is The Enterprise Act 2002 (Part 8 Community Infringements Specified UK Laws) Order 2003 (SI 2003 No 1374). In the Schedule to that Order, reference is made to one of the listed Directives, Council Directive 93/13/EEC of 5 April 1993 on unfair terms in consumer contracts. The corresponding United Kingdom legislation is specified as the 1999 Regulations. Thus a contravention of the 1999 Regulations is capable of giving rise to a Community infringement. If an act or omission is to constitute a Community infringement, it must harm the collective interests of consumers, in accordance with section 212(1) of the 2002 Act. I am satisfied that the use of terms such as clause 7 and clause 6 does harm the collective interests of consumers. Those terms appear, on the basis of the petitioner's documentary productions, to be used very widely by the first respondent, and they may accordingly have practical application in a substantial percentage of the first respondent's contracts. On that basis I am able to infer that there is harm to the section of the public likely to buy the petitioner's doors, windows and conservatories and to have those goods installed in their homes. On this

basis, therefore, I conclude that the first respondent has committed Community infringements through the use of terms in the form of clause 7 and clause 6.

[46] I should add that there had been correspondence between the petitioner and the first respondent and the latter's agents regarding those terms, but that the first respondent was not willing to give undertakings that the terms would not be used. An undertaking was offered that involved placing the term in question in a prominent place in a written contract and mentioning in it that any other representation or promise could be on a separate sheet of paper signed by the customer and the first respondent or its agent. While such an undertaking would clearly go some way to deal with the problems with the terms in question, I consider that in the particular types of contract under consideration, involving the supply of doors, windows and conservatories, the use of any term restricting liability for representations made by salesmen will normally be objectionable in itself. That is because it is of the nature of such contracts that the salesman will make statements about the product and its installation, and there is a very clear risk that such statements will not conform to the written terms. That risk is in my opinion sufficiently great to make it unfair and contrary to the requirement of good faith for a supplier of such products to make use of a term that restricts liability for such statements.

The orders sought by the petitioner

[47] On the basis of the foregoing information the petitioner seeks a number of orders against the respondents, on both a permanent and an interim basis. First, in relation to the first respondent, the principal order sought is:

'(1) To make against the said MB Designs (Scotland) Limited enforcement orders in the following terms:

(i) that the First Respondent shall not supply windows, doors and conservatories which are not of satisfactory quality, in breach of Section 11D(2) of the Supply of Goods and Services Act 1982 (as amended) (hereinafter referred to as "the Act of 1982"), such as to harm the collective interests of consumers;'

(similar orders were sought in relation to other legislation breached)

[48] Counsel for the petitioner moved me to grant interim enforcement orders in terms of paragraphs (1), (2) and (4) of the petition. I am satisfied for the reasons stated at paragraphs [30] and [31] above that the first respondent's conduct has involved repeated domestic infringements in terms of section 211 of the 2002 Act. I am further satisfied, for the reasons stated at paragraphs [44] and [45] above, that the first respondent's conduct in using terms such as clause 7 of the Quick Fit form of contract and clause 6 of the Quick Trade form of contract has constituted a Community infringement. It follows that the requirements of section 218(1)(a) are satisfied.

[49] Section 218(1)(b) requires that, if an interim enforcement order is to be made, it must appear to the court that if the application had been for an enforcement order such order would be likely to be granted. The requirements of an enforcement order, as set out in section 217, appear to me to be clearly satisfied, for the reasons stated at paragraphs [30], [31], [44] and [45] above, and in the light of the petitioner's documentary productions. I attach particular importance to the substantial number of examples of domestic and Community infringements that are evidenced by those productions, and to the fact that in a substantial number of cases there has been independent verification of complaints. The use of objectionable terms, which constitutes the Community infringement, is of course evidenced by the documents themselves.

[50] Section 218(1)(c) requires that it should appear to the court to be expedient that the conduct of the respondent that constitutes a domestic or Community infringement should be prohibited or prevented immediately. In my opinion this requirement is also satisfied in the present case. I think it clear that the supply of defective goods and services by the first respondents and the use of the objectionable contractual terms is continuing, and that it is appropriate that that should be prohibited in the manner contemplated by Part 8 of the 2002 Act. In this connection, I am of opinion that both the defects in the first respondent's products and services and the impact of the objectionable contractual terms is sufficiently serious to warrant action under Part 8.

[51] So far as the second and third respondents are concerned, I am satisfied for the reasons stated above at paragraph [32] that they are accessories in terms of section 222 of the 2002 Act, and that they have consented to or connived in the domestic and Community infringements committed by the first respondent. For that reason I consider that it is appropriate that interim enforcement orders should be made against the second and third respondents.

[52] Finally, I am satisfied that the orders sought by the petitioner are in appropriate terms. As indicated above at paragraph [16], I am of opinion that it is not necessary for the orders to specify the precise nature of the defects that are covered by it, nor that it should be directed to specific acts on the part of the respondents; a considerable degree of generality is acceptable. In addition, as indicated at paragraph [17] I do not regard it as objectionable that the orders in large part echo the statutory provisions; I do not think that any other course is practicable. Overall, I am of opinion that the terms of the orders sought are quite adequate to let the respondents know how they must regulate their future conduct. I will accordingly grant interim enforcement orders in the terms sought by the petitioner in heads (1), (2) and (4) of the petition as amended.

The Court of Appeal considered aspects of MB Designs in *Office of Fair Trading v Miller* [2009] EWCA concerning an application for contempt of an order made under the SNORs (now replaced by the Enterprise Act 2002) against a discount kitchen equipment supplier. The main judgment of the court (Lady Justice Arden) agreed with Lord Drummond Young's interpretation of the notion of 'collective interests of consumers' but disagreed with the conclusion that for a finding of contempt more than one instance of defective supply would be necessary. Rather

It must depend on the facts. A Community infringement is committed when harm is caused to the collective interests of consumers. It is possible that a single supply might be enough, as where a supplier put on to the market a large consignment of beverage stated to be a healthy drink for a baby that is wholly unsuitable for this purpose. For this reason, I do not consider that the expression 'Community infringement' requires a course of conduct.

Lord Justice Sedley commented that

while the material provisions do not demand proof of a course of conduct, they do envisage something more than a simple breach of contract. This legislation does not seek to supplant or supplement individual consumers' private law rights; it seeks to protect the body of consumers from commercial malpractice. Accordingly, as it seems to me, infringement envisages a situation such that (at least in a case such as the present) the public cannot safely or confidently deal with an alleged infringer. There is nothing to prevent such a situation arising from a single event.

The county court judge had commented on the practices of the defendant:

There is evidence that you are making efforts to comply with your obligations, but many of these efforts appear misguided. Your rule book is but one example: it is shambolic … you are an energetic entrepreneur and have rightly been described by your counsel as unorthodox. The problem you face is that an unorthodox approach may work perfectly well in a small organization, but it courts disaster in a company which has the avowed intention of being the largest independent kitchen retailer in the world.

The MB Designs case raises several issues in relation to public enforcement powers in consumer law.

First, the OFT does not have any power under Part 8 to levy civil penalties or obtain redress for consumers who suffer damage as a consequence of the breaches by the trader. The absence of an effective class action procedure in the UK means that consumers may face difficulties in achieving redress. Part 8 merely provides that an enforcement order is admissible as evidence in civil proceedings and shifts the burden of proof to the defendant to show that the act did not occur. It is possible that an enforcement agency in negotiating a voluntary undertaking under Part 8 will take into account an offer of redress in deciding whether to accept the undertaking under section 219.

Second, The powers and approach to Part 8 might be compared to those of other regulators. In Australia the Competition and Consumer Commission has power under section 87B of the Trade Practices Act to accept enforceable undertakings as an alternative to prosecution which provide compensation to affected parties.

Lord Drummond Young is dismissive of the idea that the collective interests of consumers is separate from the aggregation of individual interests. However, French law has adopted this position and this may account for the wording of the Directive. Howells and Weatherill argue against the adoption of the French position, noting that it has been difficult to apply in practice. (Howells and Weatherill, 2005: 594).

In the MB Designs case the enforcers gathered evidence over three years, although the OFT indicates that the average time from investigation to action under a Part 8 action is two months. Part 8 actions may clearly be resource intensive. This may deter local authorities from undertaking such civil enforcement. Assuming that this business would need a consumer credit licence, would the use of credit licensing powers have been any more effective in this context?

4.2 Administrative penalties

Administrative penalties may refer to two situations: the imposition of a civil penalty by an administrative tribunal and the ability of an agency to impose a penalty without a court order but subject to appeal by the regulatee. The following extract from the Macrory Report discusses the latter type of penalty.

Richard Macrory, *Making Sanctions Effective* (Cabinet Office, 2006) 41–42

Administrative penalties are widely used in countries such as the US, Australia and Canada. … The UK experience with administrative penalties is largely limited to the financial regulators. The Financial Services and Markets Act 2000 gives the Financial Services Authority a broad range of civil, administrative and criminal sanctioning powers, including the power to issue monetary administrative penalties. ... Since 2000 more than 70 cases have been concluded with an administrative penalty.

The competition commission can impose financial penalties under the Enterprise Act 2002 in relation to its investigation powers.

The Office of Fair Trading has access to financial penalties for noncompliance with competition law.

Administrative penalties can provide an intermediate step between the formal, costly and stigmatizing action of criminal prosecution and the more informal means of advice and persuasion to get firms back into compliance . . .

Well-designed administrative schemes can ... be flexible and take a more customized approach in dealing with regulatory noncompliance, especially in cases of variable penalties. For example, compliance history, the seriousness of the offense and its impact on the external environment or community can be taken into consideration. This flexibility can allow the regulator to ensure that the level of the MAP is appropriate to reflect the various aggravating and mitigating factors, encourage future compliance and be reflective and proportionate to the size of the business. Such a system could motivate defenders to take actions to move into compliance and provide a sanctioning option for those cases where it may not be appropriate to prosecute the offender and where previous advice or statutory notices have not been effective.

Appeal to an administrative agency from a decision of an agency to impose a penalty reduces the possibility of error costs by the regulator (OECD, 2006b: 7).

4.3 The enforceable undertaking

Section 219 of the Enterprise Act 2002 envisages the possibility of a person offering an undertaking. The OFT has suggested that it might use this to obtain consumer redress (see Smith, Director Competition Enforcement, 2006):

This approach could be used for both consumer and competition law breaches—for example, an unfair trading practice endemic in an industry could give rise to a compensation offer as part of an agreed set of Part 8 undertakings. We need to be creative and open to discussion on these alternative solutions.

The Macrory Report thought that:

EUs could be more effective in cases where a financial penalty or criminal conviction is likely to be absorbed by the business with a limited impact on the culture or management of the firm. They are also likely to be more effective in securing a change in businesses' behaviour when compared to warning letters or other means of persuasion currently available to the regulator. (Regulatory Justice, 2006: 65)

Enforceable undertakings have been used by the Australian Consumer and Competition Commission. Undertakings might include a clear commitment to cease the alleged misconduct, provisions for compensation, corrective advertising, the requirement to implement a compliance programme and to have it independently reviewed, and in a minority of cases a '"community service order" such as funding or implementing an industry or consumer compliance education program' (see Parker, 2004). These orders raise fairness or accountability issues to the extent that an enforcement body uses these undertakings to secure objectives that are not authorised by law.

Parker argues that there are three fundamental issues concerning enforceable under-takings: process; content; and accountability. She argues that they should involve face-to-face negotiations that have the aim of rectifying and preventing problems. Regulators should not accept undertakings, unless there is an admission of lia-bility. This addresses the critique that regulators 'twist the arm' of businesses to enter into undertakings that would not be available if it litigated the claim. The victims of alleged misconduct and other stakeholders affected should be present or represented in negotiations. Provided these process values are respected, there should be few controls on the content of the enforceable undertaking. However, she does believe that it is fundamental that there should be an apology to those affected by the conduct (Parker, 2004).

The OFT has used administrative powers such as credit licensing to obtain com-pensation for consumers and to extract promises from regulates, although the basis of the legal power to do so is not clear. The undertakings power under Part 8 is limited in scope although it does provide for the possibility of corrective advertising. Should it be extended to provide express powers for compensation and the types of remedies outlined in Australia?

4.4 Adverse publicity: naming and shaming

Adverse publicity can be a significant sanction. It is the primary sanction of the self-regulatory ASA (see below) and Australian research indicates that businesses are most concerned about the adverse publicity associated with an investigation ('The ACCC Enforcement and Compliance Survey: Report of Preliminary Findings' (December 2005)). The OECD report on UK enforcement suggested that the 'OFT policy on "naming and shaming" is not fully formed or agreed' (OECD, 2006b: 43). The OFT has published guidance on its use of publicity.

3.85 The OFT is committed to transparency and will usually put information on completed Part 8 cases into the public domain. Publicity will be accurate, balanced and fair. The factors that may be taken into account when considering publicity on Part 8 cases are:

• any legal restrictions on disclosure of information

• public accountability

• monitoring the future conduct of individual businesses

• deterring other businesses from engaging in the kind of conduct covered by the orders or undertakings obtained

• warning consumers about practices that are detrimental to their interests

• increasing consumers' awareness of their rights and how to exercise them

• facilitating complaints about further breaches, and

• educating the market.

3.86 In the case of undertakings to the OFT where no infringement is necessarily admitted, the OFT may still publish the undertakings. However, care will be taken to indicate accurately, the full circumstances and the basis upon which the undertaking was given. Information about completed cases will be publicised by placing it on the public part of the Consumer Regulations Website (see above Chapter 4) or by issue of a press release. Publicity will not be given to cases in which the OFT considers that no breach could properly be established and where no undertaking was obtained from the business.

The courts upheld the general power to publicise assurances under Part III of the Fair Trading Act in *R v Director General of Fair Trading, ex p FH Taylor & Co* (1981), but were careful to point out that the adverse publicity to the individual firm must not be purely sanctioning, but must be ancillary to the information and warning function that it serves.

In a study of the use of naming and shaming in the Dutch financial market, Van Erp found mixed results, concluding that 'In the field of financial regulation, publication of warnings, fines and penalties generally does not have strong effects in terms of damage to business interests' but in some cases 'had disproportionate impact.' It is 'a messy instrument' (quoting Posner) (Van Erp, 2011: 287)

4.5 Public power to obtain compensation and redress

The direct powers of public enforcement agencies in the United Kingdom to seek compensation for private individuals have traditionally been limited, and any redress is often achieved through indirect means. Trading standards officers might 'persuade' a trader to offer compensation or the OFT might use its licensing powers under the Consumer Credit Act 1974 to achieve a similar goal. A compensation order may be sought in criminal prosecution under sections 130–31 of the Powers of Criminal Courts (Sentencing) Act 2000. This procedure has the administrative advantage of settling both compensation and deterrence issues in one proceeding. In addition, it is not necessary that a potential civil liability exist in order for an order to be made (*R v Chappell* (1984)). However, in 2010–11, of 308 convictions under the CPUT regulations, only 13 defendants were asked to pay compensation. Research indicates that 'trading standards officers regard compensation claims as an additional burden' because

> Identifying the extent of harm caused to consumers sometimes requires additional investigation. … It places the investigator in the position of assessing the level of loss, harm and damage caused to a consumer which sometimes involves the use of additional experts to evaluate the 'value' of the consumer detriment and to prepare evidence of this for subsequent court proceedings. (Peysner and Nurse, 2008: para 7.4)

The Law Commission proposals to introduce simplified private remedies for breach of the CPUT regulations is intended also to facilitate an increase in compensation orders by trading standards officers.

Other jurisdictions permit a public agency to sue for damages on behalf of consumers affected by breaches of the law. In Alberta, Canada, the Director of Fair Trading may seek an injunction where there has been a contravention of the Fair Trading Act and at the same time seek any redress the court considers proper to those persons who suffered damage or loss arising from the contravention of the Act (see Fair Trading Act, section 159(2)(b)). The Director may also bring an action for compensation where there has been an unfair practice, on behalf of named consumers with their written consent if it is in the public interest to do so: the costs of this action are borne by the government (section 15 of the Fair Trading Act).

Achieving compensation for consumers is a valuable and tangible measure of success for an agency. This may, however, have the undesirable effect of excessive concentration on obtaining compensation, at the expense of the more routine but important role of achieving market-wide compliance.

4.6 Restorative justice orders

Restorative justice is defined as 'a process where all the parties with a stake in a particular offence come together to resolve collectively how to deal with the aftermath of the offence and its implications for the future' (Braithwaite, 2002)

Christine Parker argues that enforceable undertakings may provide an opportunity for restorative justice and she provides two examples from Australia: the mis-selling of insurance to Aboriginals, and abusive door-to-door selling of telecommunications. The mis-selling of insurance involved deceptive sales of insurance policies to relatively uneducated and often unemployed individuals. The resolution of this problem involved: (1) face-to-face meetings between the Australian Consumer and Competition Commission and senior company managers and the stakeholders and communities affected. Senior company managers were flown to remote Aboriginal communities and required to confront their victims; (2) meetings by the Commission with insurance regulators, industry associations and politicians concerning the underlying reasons for mis-selling and the development of methods to prevent such mis-selling in the future; (3) compensation being provided to consumers and a fund established to provide education in consumer rights to Aboriginals. Parker argues that if a criminal justice prosecution had been initiated it would not have been possible to achieve these results and many individual victims' claims would have been time barred.

Parker also argues that community service orders can be an important aspect of an enforceable undertaking:

> Community service undertakings can be seen as creative and restorative solutions to problems of remedying or preventing misconduct, not mere punishments. ... In some cases [they] have been used as a form of compensation where compensation would otherwise be difficult to accomplish [eg the provision of free ferry trips to aged pensioners on a journey where price fixing occurred]. ... These undertakings have in effect allowed businesses to voluntarily compensate the victims of their conduct where the narrower remedies available to a court would probably not have been able to provide meaningful compensation because the victims were too disparate. (Parker, 2004: 237)

Finally, a common aspect of undertakings in both Australia and elsewhere is the requirement on a corporation to adopt a corporate compliance programme that is independently audited.

---

5. The balance of public and private enforcement of unfair trading law

Chapter 3 discussed general issues in the balance of public and private enforcement.

The UK historically favoured a relatively sharp separation of public and private enforcement of trade practices law. Unless a public statute specifically indicates that its breach may give rise to a civil action as a breach of statutory duty (see eg section 41(1) of the Consumer Protection Act 1987), the courts have been unwilling to imply an action for breach of a statutory duty in consumer law (see eg *Square v Model Farm Dairies* (1939); Stanton, 2004: 324). The traditional formula for determining when a breach of a criminal statute will give rise to a civil action is that it does so when: (i) the statute imposes a standard of conduct for the special benefit of a particular class; (ii) the plaintiff was a member of the particular class protected by the statute; and (iii) the injury was caused by the statutory violation and was of a type that the statute was designed to prevent. Using this approach, the Court of Appeal in *Bulmer v Bollinger* (1978) refused to imply a civil action for breach of the Trade Descriptions Act 1968 since the Act was passed for the benefit of the general public and not for any particular class within it (compare *Garden Cottage Foods v Milk Marketing Board* (1983)).

The optimal role of private actions may be understood by relating them both to the general objectives of trade practices regulation in addressing market failures and to broader values, such as public participation in government decision-making. The judicial argument that private actions will not be implied where there is a wrong to the general public reflects the idea that public regulation in this area is often a response to diffuse harms spread widely throughout society. These diffuse harms, so the argument goes, necessitate the creation of public agencies with broad statutory powers which can attempt to achieve a socially optimal level of compliance. Within this conception, private actions will undermine the advantages of centralised and specialised administrative agencies in negotiating with regulated firms to achieve a workable and consistent regulatory system. The strongest statement of these policy rationales may be found in the judgment of Leventhal J in the US decision *Holloway v Bristol Myers Corpn* (1973). This case concerned a class action brought on behalf of consumers and advertising audiences for allegedly false, misleading and deceptive advertising by Bristol Myers for its pain reliever Excedrin. In rejecting the implication of private actions under section 5 of the FTC Act, Leventhal J drew attention to the values of administrative expertise, co-ordination, consistency and predictability which would be upset by allowing private enforcement:

> The Act gives the Commission a broad range of flexible enforcement powers available for use, as deemed necessary in the FTC's sound discretion and expert judgment. Inherent in the exercise of this discretion is the interplay of numerous factors: the relative seriousness of the departure from accepted trade practices, its probable effect on the public welfare, the disruption to settled commercial relationships that enforcement proceedings would entail, whether action is to be taken against a single party or on an industry-wide basis, the form such action should take, the most appropriate remedy, the precedential value of the rule of law sought to be established, and a host of other considerations. Above all, there is need to weigh each action against the Commission's broad range policy goals and to determine its place in the overall enforcement program. …

> Private litigants are not subject to the same constraints. They may institute piecemeal lawsuits, reflecting disparate concerns and not a coordinated enforcement program. The consequence would burden not only the defendants selected but also the judicial system. (997–98)

The major policy arguments in favour of the private enforcement of public programmes are those of regulatory failure and the limited resources of regulatory agencies, which make it difficult for them to achieve an optimal level of compliance. Public agencies in the United Kingdom regularly draw attention to the severe limitations on their resources. In addition, it may be questioned whether trade practices regulation requires the expertise which mandates exclusive public regulation. The existing, decentralised system of prosecution and enforcement suggests that greater incentives for private action are unlikely to disrupt any carefully co-ordinated enforcement programme. Private actors may be in a better position than public agencies to detect offences and private enforcement responds to the different intensities of consumer preferences. Private actions may respond also to the inevitable variations in the intensity of public enforcement which is affected by the changing political support for regulation. Private action may therefore be a valuable method for compensating for public under-enforcement (see further Yeung, in McCrudden, 1998: ch 3; Roach and Trebilcock, 1996: 461).

Under Part 8 of the Enterprise Act the Secretary of State may designate a body as an enforcement body if it 'has as one of its purposes the protection of the collective interests of consumers'. The criteria for designating a body under the Act are set out in the Enterprise Act 2002 (Part 8 Designated Enforcers: Criteria for Designation, Designation of Public Bodies as Designated Enforcers and Transitional Provisions) Order 2003, SI 2003/1399. These criteria are: the ability to act independent and impartially, demonstrated experience in promoting the collective interests of consumers, the capability to investigate infringements set out in Part 8 of the Act, and a willingness to follow best practices in enforcement and co-operate with the OFT including sharing information and co-ordinating enforcement. Which? has been designated under Part 8 but has not attempted to bring any actions.

Private rights of action may be divided into actions for damages and those seeking remedies such as injunctions or declarations. Undoubtedly, the existence of a viable class action procedure in the UK would increase the potential deterrent effect of private actions. The argument that such private rights of action should not be extended since consumers may have recourse to their existing civil law rights overlooks the doctrinal limitations on these rights. Private actions under public statutes may be a method of overcoming such limitations as privity of contract.

There may be dangers, however, in permitting private actions under broad, 'over-inclusive' statutes—for example, one requiring a 'duty to trade fairly'. Unrestricted private actions under such statutes might upset attempts by agencies to co-ordinate enforcement under a broad statutory mandate. Private enforcement may not screen out unmeritorious claims effectively, taxing judicial resources and may result in strike suits aimed at extorting settlements (Stephenson, 2005). The UK government has indicated that in implementing the UCPD, providing a private right of redress could clarify consumer rights and stimulate greater compliance. However it is concerned that 'adopting a private right of action for the whole of the Directive might have unintended and adverse consequences, by potentially providing consumers with undesirable latitude to sue traders and by impacting on the law of misrepresentation' (DTI, 2006: 7).

In many Commonwealth countries private groups and individuals are given a broad right of standing under unfair trade practices legislation. For example, section 172(1) of the Business Practices and Consumer Protection Act (formerly section 18 of the Trade

Practices Act) of British Columbia provides a broad standing provision that permits any person to bring an action for declaration or injunction where there is an actual or imminent contravention of the Act. There is also the possibility of monetary restitution for individuals of money paid to the supplier in contravention of the Act. This section seems to have been rarely used by consumer groups and has been used primarily by the public Director of Trade Practices seeking an injunction and occasionally monetary restitution for consumers. There is also the possibility of a class action for damages being brought under the Act.

The Law Commission has recently recommended a modest increase in private rights in relation to misleading and aggressive unfair practices under the CPUT regulations. The requirements for such actions would be as follows:

The Law Commission and The Scottish Law Commission, Law Com No 332, *Consumer Redress for Misleading and Aggressive Practices*, Cm 8323 (2012)

(1) There must be a contract between the parties or a payment made by the consumer. Thus consumers would not, for example, be entitled to compensation if they visited a shop in response to a misleading advertisement but did not buy anything. Nor would consumers have a separate right to compensation for being misled about their rights.

(2) The consumer would only have a right against the other party to the contract, usually the retailer or service provider. The legislation would not provide additional rights against others in the supply chain, such as producers or against individual directors.

(3) The list of banned practices under the Regulations would not give rise to automatic redress; they would only be covered by the new right if they would affect an 'average consumer'.

(4) The general prohibition against commercial practices which are 'contrary to the requirements of professional diligence' should not give rise to redress. It is too uncertain.

(5) Land transactions and financial services should not be covered. Instead the existing law should remain.

We are aware, however, that our proposed remedies will be enforced in a variety of settings: through compensation orders, ancillary to criminal proceedings; in negotiations between traders and consumers; and through court proceedings.

This means that remedies need to be simple and standardised. When facing choices between simplicity on the one hand and flexibility on the other, we have opted for simplicity. The law should be suited to the forum in which it is enforced.

THE ELEMENTS OF LIABILITY

We recommend a new statutory right of redress for a consumer against a trader. The consumer would need to show that:

(1) The trader carried out a misleading or aggressive practice;

(2) this was likely to cause the average consumer to take a decision to enter into a contract or make a payment they would not have taken otherwise;

(3) the misleading or aggressive practice was a significant factor in the consumer's own decision to enter into the contract or make the payment.

Where the consumer has entered into a contract, the consumer's right would lie against the other party to the contract. Where the consumer had made a payment, their right would lie against the party to whom the payment was made.

Defining a misleading practice

The new right would follow the substance of the definition of misleading practice in Regulation 5(2)(a). This approach moves away from the distinctions drawn under current law based on whether the misrepresentation is 'false' or 'factual'. It also moves away from the traditional language of acts or omissions, which is unhelpful, as much conduct does not fall clearly into either category.

No liability for 'pure omissions'

Under Regulation 6 it is a criminal offence for a trader to omit or hide material information. The most controversial issue was whether consumers should have a right of redress for a 'pure' omission, where the overall presentation was not misleading but material information was omitted. Views were mixed. Many consumer groups argued that the new legislation should mirror the Regulations. The OFT also said that it 'may confuse consumers as well as the courts' if Regulation 6 were not followed. By contrast, business groups argued that it would be too uncertain to introduce a private right of redress specifically for all material omissions; the scope would be difficult to define; and it would represent a departure from the current approach of UK law.

We have concluded that there should not be a private right of redress for 'pure' omissions. We would, however, welcome a review by BIS of the effect of the Regulations in five years time. If the test has proved too narrow, this decision could be reconsidered.

Defining an aggressive practice

The definition of aggressive practices would follow the substance of Regulation 7.

Defining the 'average consumer'

[The Commission adopts the test of the average consumer from the CPUT regulations]

A REPLACEMENT STATUTE

The recommended new right covers substantially the same ground as the Misrepresentation Act 1967 (in England and Wales) and section 10 of the Law Reform (Miscellaneous Provisions) (Scotland) Act 1985 (in Scotland). We think the new legislation should replace these provisions in so far as they cover business to consumer transactions within the ambit of the new Act.

Other common law and contractual remedies would remain. In particular, consumers would continue to be able to make claims under the Sale of Goods Act 1979 where goods are of unsatisfactory quality, though consumers would not be entitled to double recovery.

REMEDIES (Part 8)

Stakeholders told us that there was a need for certain, standardised remedies, even if these were sometimes 'rough and ready'. The most important remedy is the right to unwind the contract and obtain a refund. This fits with the primary aim of current private law, which is to restore the consumer to the position they were in before the misleading or aggressive practice took place.

S 40 Under the new legislation consumers would have two tiers of remedies. Tier 1 remedies would be the standard remedies and would apply on a strict liability basis. The amount would be based on the price paid and would not require evidence of loss. This means they could be used in both the civil courts and alongside enforcement action, for example in criminal compensation orders.

By contrast, Tier 2 remedies would apply only if the consumer proved additional loss; they would also be subject to the trader's due diligence defence.

The type of Tier 1 remedy would depend on how soon after the event the consumer complains and whether the consumer has fully consumed the product:

(1) The right to unwind. If the consumer raises a complaint within three months, and is able to reject some element of the goods or service, then the standard remedy is to unwind the contract. This means that the consumer can get a refund.

(2) Discount. If the consumer waits more than 3 months to sue or if the goods or services are fully consumed, then the consumer can claim a discount on the price.

Tier 2 remedies

Tier 2 remedies provide damages to compensate for indirect losses, including economic damage and distress and inconvenience.

They are provided only if the consumer can prove that the unfair practice caused actual loss, meeting a 'but for' test of causation. Furthermore, the trader can avoid this consequential liability if it can establish a due diligence defence.

UNFAIR PAYMENT COLLECTION (Part 9)

There is uncertainty about how far the Regulations cover misleading or aggressive demands for payment. They clearly include demands made following a sale but problems arise in other contexts. For example, consumers accused of copyright infringement or shoplifting, or those who have had their car towed, might be misled or pressured into paying significant sums of money.

We recommend that the Regulations should be amended to clarify that all commercial demands for payment are included within the definition of commercial practices. There was strong support for this, to protect consumers and to ensure consistency and clarity.

We also recommend that the new right to redress should include misleading or aggressive demands for payment. The many examples submitted by consumer groups illustrate that consumers would benefit from clearer and more certain rights to redress in these cases.

Where there has been an unfair demand for money and the money was not owed, the consumer would be entitled to a refund. Where it was owed, the consumer would not be entitled to a refund but would be able to claim for proven consequential losses, together with limited damages for proven distress and inconvenience.

IMPACT ASSESSMENT

Part 11. We anticipate three benefits from the proposals:

(1) Easier complaint handling. Legitimate traders would find it easier to deal with complaints of misleading practices. TSS and advice agencies would also benefit from simpler, easier ways of valuing consumer loss. This saving is estimated at around £5 million.

(2) Consumers who have suffered a misleading or aggressive practice would receive more compensation, estimated at between £2 million and £5 million.

(3) Combating aggressive practices more effectively would increase consumer confidence,

and therefore lead to increased sales. On a conservative estimate, improved protection might boost the market for doorstep sales by around £5 million.

---

6. Class and public-interest actions

A class action is a procedure which permits representatives of a group who have the same or a common interest in a claim to sue on behalf of the group for damages or an injunction. Several distinct justifications have been forwarded for class actions (for original rationales see Kalven and Rosenfeld, 1941: 684). From an economic viewpoint, they may be an effective method of requiring firms to internalise the costs of failures in contract performance, ensuring that private costs equal social costs. This may be achieved either through the judicial economy of a single damage decree for multiple claims or through a class settlement achieved between the representative plaintiff and the defendant. In the latter situation, the class action reduces the transaction costs, which Coase (1960) identified as the major obstacle to achieving an efficient solution to the problem of social cost (Wright, 1969: 383). If appropriate incentives are provided, a class action will overcome the problems of organising large groups of individuals.

Class actions may provide both compensation and deterrence. The latter role is dominant where such actions are brought for non-viable claims (*Harvard Law Review*, 1975–77: 1356). These are claims which are so small that 'the expenses an individual would incur in asserting a right to a share of a class judgment would be greater than his expected share of the recovery'.

This article drew a further distinction between individually recoverable and non-recoverable claims. A claim is individually recoverable if 'it warrants the costs of separate litigation'; it is non-recoverable if it would not justify the expense to an individual of independent litigation, but would justify the lesser expenditure required to obtain a share of a class judgment (*Harvard Law Review*, 1975–76: 1356). The greatest controversy is likely to be over the assertion of non-viable claims, since the sole justification here is deterrence, with private parties acting as surrogate public enforcers. Class actions may perform the important function of transforming 'private troubles' into 'public issues' (Wright Mills, 1959: 12) and creating pressure for public action or at least increased public engagement with an issue (see Starrs, 1969: 408). Class actions have also been justified as providing participation and self-determination to consumers, making up for the limitations of consumer representation in the political process and the failures of regulatory agencies. Class actions may also permit the development of substantive consumer law by exposing the courts to theories of recovery or legal arguments which would not otherwise have been advanced (*Harvard Law Review*, 1975–76: 1353; Ontario Law Reform Commission, 1982: 203). In addition to providing an opportunity for private groups to test the limits of substantive rights, class actions permit courts to see the true dimensions of consumer problems and the impact of alternative judicial policy choices (OLRC, 1982: 203).

Opponents of class actions have pointed to the dangers of their producing 'legalised blackmail', when unfair settlements are extorted from defendants afraid of the high costs of litigation. It is argued that the primary beneficiaries may be 'entre-preneurial lawyers' rather than consumers (see below 6.1). In addition, it has been argued that class actions might flood the courts, provide unmanageable administrative problems for judges and stir up unnecessary litigation of claims that otherwise would remain dormant. The filing of a class action might also generate adverse publicity for a defendant out of all proportion to the alleged infraction.

The Supreme Court of Canada elaborated on the rationales for class actions in *Western Canadian Shopping Centres Inc v Dutton* [2001] 2 SCR 534 McLachlin CJ:

> The class action plays an important role in today's world. The rise of mass production, the diversification of corporate ownership, the advent of the mega-corporation, and the recognition of environmental wrongs have all contributed to its growth. A faulty product may be sold to numerous consumers. Corporate mismanagement may bring loss to a large number of shareholders. Discriminatory policies may affect entire categories of employees. Environmental pollution may have consequences for citizens all over the country. Conflicts like these pit a large group of complainants against the alleged wrongdoer. Sometimes, the complainants are identically situated vis-à-vis the defendants. In other cases, an important aspect of their claim is common to all complainants. The class action offers a means of efficiently resolving such disputes in a manner that is fair to all parties. Class actions offer three important advantages over a multiplicity of individual suits. First, by aggregating similar individual actions, class actions serve judicial economy by avoiding unnecessary duplication in fact-finding and legal analysis. The efficiencies thus generated free judicial resources that can be directed at resolving other conflicts, and can also reduce the costs of litigation both for plaintiffs (who can share litigation costs) and for defendants (who need litigate the disputed issue only once, rather than numerous times. …

> Second, by allowing fixed litigation costs to be divided over a large number of plaintiffs, class actions improve access to justice by making economical the prosecution of claims that would otherwise be too costly to prosecute individually. Without class actions, the doors of justice remain closed to some plaintiffs, however strong their legal claims. Sharing costs ensures that injuries are not left unremedied. …

> Third, class actions serve efficiency and justice by ensuring that actual and potential wrongdoers do not ignore their obligations to the public. Without class actions, those who cause widespread but individually minimal harm might not take into account the full costs of their conduct, because for any one plaintiff the expense of bringing suit would far exceed the likely recovery. Cost-sharing decreases the expense of pursuing legal recourse and accordingly deters potential defendants who might otherwise assume that minor wrongs would not result in litigation

Although the modern class action developed in the United States, it has been introduced in several other Commonwealth countries, such as Canada and Australia, and also in some civil law jurisdictions, such as Quebec and Brazil. Debate over the merits of class actions has been skewed by a focus on US experience and a failure to understand the peculiar institutional characteristics of this action in the United States. These include: (1) the absence of limitations on damages for pain and suffering in personal injury cases; (2) the significant role of punitive damages; (3) the role of juries; (4) the absence of fee shifting rules (ie loser pays). The absence of a universal healthcare scheme or worker compensation plans that prevent an individual from suing for work-related injuries are also relevant. Lord Justice Steyn has expressed concerns that class actions might fuel the supposed compensation culture:

The question is sometimes raised whether this system should be replaced by the far more comprehensive and far-reaching system of class actions as it is known in the United States. There are marked cultural differences. First, the United States tort claims are tried by juries. Subject to narrow exceptions that is not so in England. Secondly, the scale of jury awards in the United States are far higher than awards made by judges in England. Massive awards for injuries, which are not of the most serious kind, would rightly not be tolerated by English public opinion. Thirdly, it is a feature of class actions in the United States that firms of lawyers earn billions of dollars in cases which do not even come to trial and often result in meagre recoveries by individual claimants. This too would be unacceptable in England. Finally, I would say that in England there is a general perception among judges, in this respect reflecting public opinion, that the tort system is becoming too expansive and wasteful. There is also an unarticulated but nevertheless real conviction among judges that we must not allow our social welfare state to become a society bent on litigation. The introduction of United States style class actions cannot but contribute to such unwelcome developments in our legal system. In my view the newly referred '2000' model of Group Litigation Orders is at present adequate for our purposes. (Steyn, quoted in Mulheron, 2005: 59)

Sinai Deutch documents three types of contemporary class action: (1) the private initiative model—this is the US model of class actions; (2) the consumer organisation claim model where consumer organisations have standing to apply to courts for an injunction or prohibition order in relation to unfair commercial practices—this is prevalent in countries such as Germany, Greece, Spain, France, Italy, Portugal; (3) the administrative authority model—this is where authorities have the power to sue for damage on behalf of consumers (Deutch, 2004).

The UK does not currently recognise the existence of class actions. Lord Woolf commented on the absence of class actions in 1995 and recommended that a modified group litigation order (GLO) be developed (Woolf, 1995: ch 17). The current GLO differs substantially from a class action procedure:

1. The GLO requires an individual to opt-in and actively participate in the action. It is therefore fundamentally different from the concept of the representative claimant who sues on behalf of all similarly situated individuals who may opt out of the litigation but are otherwise not required to actively participate. Opt-out regimes dominate in existing class action procedures throughout the world. Requiring a consumer to opt in at an early stage will trigger the many economic and psychological costs that are barriers to individual litigation. We know from behavioural economics that an opt-in requirement will result in few consumers joining the action.
2. The GLO provides skeletal regulation of the various issues that might arise in the course of the action.

The following are the current rules on representative parties and GLOs:

Representative parties with same interest

19.6(1) Where more than one person has the same interest in a claim—

(a) the claim may be begun; or

(b) the court may order that the claim be continued, by or against one or more of the persons who have the same interest as representatives of any other persons who have that interest.

(2) The court may direct that a person may not act as a representative.

(3) Any party may apply to the court for an order under paragraph (2).

(4) Unless the court otherwise directs any judgment or order given in a claim in which a party is acting as a representative under this rule—

(a) is binding on all persons represented in the claim; but

(b) may only be enforced by or against a person who is not a party to the claim with the permission of the court.

The notes to the rules state

r 19.6 is designed to allow representative proceedings to be treated, not as a rigid matter of principle, but as a flexible tool of convenience in the administration of justice, and should be applied, not in any strict or rigorous sense, but according to its wide and permissive scope. ...

III GROUP LITIGATION

Definition

19.10 A Group Litigation Order ('GLO') means an order made under rule 19.11 to provide for the case management of claims which give rise to common or related issues of fact or law (the 'GLO issues').

Group Litigation Order

19.11—(1) The court may make a GLO where there are or are likely to be a number of claims giving rise to the GLO issues.

(2) A GLO must—

(a) contain directions about the establishment of a register (the 'group register') on which the claims managed under the GLO will be entered;

(b) specify the GLO issues which will identify the claims to be managed as a group under the GLO; and

(c) specify the court (the 'management court') which will manage the claims on the group register.

(3) A GLO may—

(a) in relation to claims which raise one or more of the GLO issues—

    (i)   direct their transfer to the management court;

    (ii) order their stay until further order; and

    (iii) direct their entry on the group register;

(b) direct that from a specified date claims which raise one or more of the GLO issues should be started in the management court and entered on the group register; and

(c) give directions for publicising the GLO.

Effect of the GLO

19.12—(1) Where a judgment or order is given or made in a claim on the group register in relation to one or more GLO issues—

(a)   that judgment or order is binding on the parties to all other claims that are on the group register at the time the judgment is given or the order is made unless the court orders otherwise; and

(b)   the court may give directions as to the extent to which that judgment or order is binding on the parties to any claim which is subsequently entered on the group register.

(2) Unless paragraph (3) applies, any party who is adversely affected by a judgment or order which is binding on him may seek permission to appeal the order.

(3) A party to a claim which was entered on the group register after a judgment or order which is binding on him was given or made may not—

(a)   apply for the judgment or order to be set aside, varied or stayed; or

(b)   appeal the judgment or order,

but may apply to the court for an order that the judgment or order is not binding on him.

Case management

19.13 Directions given by the management court may include directions—

(a)   varying the GLO issues;

(b)   providing for one or more claims on the group register to proceed as test claims;

(c)   appointing the solicitor of one or more parties to be the lead solicitor for the claimants or defendants;

(d)   specifying the details to be included in a statement of case in order to show that the criteria for entry of the claim on the group register have been met;

(e)   specifying a date after which no claim may be added to the group register unless the court gives permission; and

(f)   for the entry of any particular claim which meets one or more of the GLO issues on the group register.

GLOs have been used primarily for high-value disputes and are not appropriate for cases where there are many small economic losses. Howells (2006) indicates that the vast majority of cases have involved personal injury and typically pharmaceutical product-liability claims. The opt-in requirement means that they are unlikely to be of use to cases involving mass consumer losses where individuals face significant barriers to 'opting in'. Moreover:

[O]pt-in procedures tend to stack the costs for those represented toward the beginning of the litigation (especially where individual proceedings have to be pleaded as under the GLO), and constitute one of the reasons why the procedure is generally considered to provide less favourable avenues for access to justice than an opt-out regime. A class action is both actually and potentially less cumbersome. A positive step to opt-in may well need to occur at some point under an opt-out regime, but that step will usually be deferred until either settlement or judgment has been approved or delivered. (Mulheron, 2005: 52)

Mulheron also notes that:

[T]he GLO schema has been drafted in a very light-handed manner, in comparison with the detailed legislative provisions governing the modern class action regimes of, say, the Australian federal and Canadian provincial jurisdictions. ... As a consequence, various important issues associated with the conduct of group litigation, such as judicial approval of settlement agreements, limitation periods, aggregate assessment of damages, and cy-près distribution of damages, are not covered by the terms of the GLO schema, in comparison with the class action regimes where such matters have received explicit attention by the drafters and legislators. (ibid)

Representative actions in the UK have suffered from the limitation going back to the decision of the English Court of Appeal in *Markt & Co Ltd v Knight Steamship Co Ltd* (1910) which required parties in representative actions to have the same interest, interpreted to mean that individuals with different contracts and individual damage claims could not be aggregated within a common representative action. While Mulheron argues that the English courts have relaxed these requirements in recent cases, she also concludes that the current 'muddling through' by the courts is not a substitute for modern class-action legislation that addresses the many issues necessary for implementation of such a procedure (Mulheron, 2005: 46). The Department of Constitutional Affairs consulted on representative actions in 2001, and in 2006 the DTI consulted on the possibility of representative actions in consumer protection legislation. The DBIS has been generally unsympathetic to class actions, wishing to restrict them to designated sectors and only available to designated groups.

DTI, *Representative Actions in Consumer Protection Legislation* (2006)

3. Where possible we are keen to avoid the use of the court system to resolve consumer complaints. However, sometimes court action is the only remaining recourse for a consumer seeking damages. … We believe that there may be a role for a consumer body, or similarly interested organisation, to bring a case on behalf of such a group in an attempt to win damages on their behalf.

5. Good traders have nothing to fear from this proposal. We support a broad range of complaint resolution methods to deal with disputes, without resorting to court action. We encourage companies to put systems in place to deal efficiently with consumer complaints inhouse. If complaints cannot be resolved internally, we would support the introduction of third party Alternative Dispute Resolution (ADR) schemes. …

6. While we are keen to increase consumer access to justice we want to avoid exposing business to spurious or vexatious claims or unwittingly creating a compensation culture. … We therefore propose that the following safeguards would have to be satisfied before a representative action could be brought to court

- Representative actions could only be brought by a body designated by the Secretary of State.
- Actions would only be brought on behalf of named consumers who could demonstrate loss and who wished to pursue a claim for damages, repair, or replacement of faulty goods.
- Permission would have to be sought from the court prior to bringing a case

14. In some jurisdictions designated consumer bodies can bring a claim for damages on behalf of consumers named and as yet unnamed as part of a representative action. If successful, damages can be awarded for named consumers who have suffered detriment and consumers who have yet to be identified. Damages for unnamed consumers are kept in a reserve and can be paid once consumers are identified.

15. This system also allows designated bodies to bring actions on behalf of consumers

at large on the basis that many people may have lost a small amount of money due to a breach of consumer law. In these cases the damages awarded are retained in a central fund, often used to promote consumer welfare in some way. This approach is designed to be punitive rather than returning what are often small amounts of money to many consumers, although sometimes vouchers are given, requiring consumers to spend more money before seeing any true financial benefit. A 'consumer as yet unnamed' may have already brought a private action against the company and hence the business may be doubly penalised.

16. We are keen to provide access to justice for consumers but are concerned that this method represents a scatter-gun approach, may be administratively cumbersome, and may leave businesses open to inappropriate claims. It would be unlikely to reflect actual loss, leading to unfairness, and could introduce punitive damages which would not reflect the Government's policy intentions. We therefore favour representative actions on behalf of named consumers.

Citizens Advice commented:

We can see from the case reports we receive from CABx that there is a clear need for action to be made available where consumers are not able or empowered to take action alone. … There is a huge opportunity to unlock the power of consumer organisations if they can act to deliver results for consumers with a common cause for action. This could also have the effect of filling some gaps in access to redress.

But, as we said in 2004, for this proposal to become a reality it will be necessary for consumer organisations to have access to their own in house salaried lawyers and for detailed discussions with DTI about how this activity might be funded. One proposal for possible case funding might be access to a Civil Legal Aid Contingency Fund.

… Citizens Advice is concerned that if these cases can only provide recourse to justice for a named group of consumers, those not in that group may be denied the opportunity for redress.We remain convinced that there is a need for representative actions to provide a gateway to redress for all consumers who have suffered detriment, perhaps employing the use of 'consumers as yet unnamed' in addition to named consumers, as explained in paragraph.

However, legal remedies in contract and tort law apply to individual consumers rather than consumers at large. Consumer groups should be able to access and benefit from other types of remedies—such as an apology, a single act of restitution or changes to policy and practice. We would suggest that the law of equity could intervene in such cases, by analogy to the 'Cy-pres doctrine' which enables courts to amend trusts and charitable companies practices to fulfil their original intentions; the same sort of remedy should be available where a group of consumers has suffered detriment. (Citizens Advice, 2006: 2–3)

A characteristic in recent years has been the 'unremedied systemic loss' associated with phenomena such as overdrafts and payment protection insurance. Mulheron noted in a research paper for the Civil Justice Council several aspects of unfair contract terms which involved small individual losses but large aggregate losses to consumer (Mulheron, 2009). The author describes the campaign on bank charges by Which? in 2006 that resulted in bank customers claiming en masse in the county courts. She documents the limits of individual litigation as a method of addressing this issue that resulted in a large rise in county court claims and the possibility of addressing it through an opt-out class action. Mulheron claims that approximately 53,000 claims were filed that plausibly related to bank charges between March 2006 and August 2007. The litigation strategies of the banks included:

**Rachael Mulheron, *Reform of Collective Redress in England and Wales:
A Perspective of Need* (2008) at 124, 125, 126, 128, 129 (internal references
omitted)**

[F]iling lengthy stock defences, and then awaited the listing for hearing by District judges
(who tended to list them in blocks as small claims hearings), only to settle with the claimant
either a few days before the hearing or on the morning of the hearing itself.

... where a plethora of individual litigation of this sort occurs, individual claimants cannot
always serve as 'torch bearers' for the general bank customer class in the absence of a
properly-constituted collective action, as Pitchford J recently noted in: *Brennan v National
Westminster Bank Plc* [2007] EWHC 2759 (QB) (27 Nov 2007), para 42 (the claimant bank
customer sought to amend his pleadings, which application was denied):

> The claimant made it quite clear in his witness statement what was his motivation for
> keeping the action alive at all costs. It was to enable him to act as standard bearer for other
> customers and to expose the unfairness of the bank's terms and conditions. This was not
> an adequate reason for permitting the action to proceed if the claimant's arguable claim
> had been fully satisfied by the bank, since consumer interests in general are the concern of
> OFT which is taking action to protect them and not the claimant. I accept that OFT would
> not, even if minded to seek a declaration, be able to bring surrogate proceedings on behalf
> of individual consumers. The fact is, however, that the public interest is represented by the
> OFT. On the other hand, if the claimant has reasonably arguable claims to a declaration,
> account, aggravated damages or exemplary damages he should not be prevented from
> pursuing them merely because he has a 'public interest' motive for doing so.

However, the claimant had no reasonable claims to those remedies.

Furthermore, any declaration in this claimant's favour, that the imposition of bank charges
levied on his account was unfair and/or a penalty, was to be judged by reference to all
the circumstances and terms of his contract—and in the circumstances, Justice Pitchford
considered that such a declaration would serve no useful purpose, at para 44:

> The claimant could not obtain a declaration in the terms sought because regulation 6
> required the court to assess the fairness of the term, amongst other things, in the
> circumstances attending the conclusion of the contract, that is the contract between the
> bank and the claimant. The trial judge could not make a declaration determinative of other
> contracts made with other consumers at other times.

The point about the non-utility of a declaration in the case of this particular customer is
interesting, for had this bank charges dispute been litigated under an opt-out collective action,
it may have been feasible for a variety of 'representative bank customers' to be chosen, to test
the efficacy of different terms used in standard bank–customer contracts as common issues,
and also to resolve some of the questions which, as Pitchford J mentioned, are not to be the
subject of the test case (para 21):

> OFT has not decided whether or not to litigate the fairness of historical terms and will
> not in any event be litigating the question whether consumers can establish liability in tort
> and/or are entitled to damages, interest, consequential loss, and exemplary and aggravated
> damages.

... The risk of inconsistent judgments

On 15 May 2007, District Judge Cooke handed down a decision on one bank charges case,
in *Berwick v Lloyds TSB Bank plc* (Birmingham County Court). Mr Berwick had sought
the recovery of £1,982.37 in bank charges levied on his account since 5 October 2000. The

judgment was largely favourable to the defendant bank. However, the risk of inconsistent judgments is evident from the facts that: the decision by Cooke DCJ is not a precedent which would bind any District or Circuit or High Court judge who hears a later case—later judges are obliged to have regard to previous decisions of the County Court, but are not obliged to follow them, and could reach a different decision on the same contract wording—only a High Court or further appellate judgment would be binding;

... Risk of delays in outcome

Significant delays have been incurred because of the way in which the bank charges disputes have evolved:

... it took a considerable period of litigation en masse before a test case was ordered to be heard, during which time many bank customers were enmeshed in a cycle of applications, holding defences, and stays, in the county courts;

(F) *Risk of adverse publicity.*

Individual actions requiring individual defences can put the defendant banks at risk of an embarrassing error. ...

(G) The potential extra-jurisdictional reach of an opt-out collective action. Were these bank charge cases to be litigated under an opt-out regime, where the opt-out regime was governed by a statute pertinent to England and Wales, one question which may arise is whether class members residing in another jurisdiction, and who allege that they were damaged by the same defendants, would have the scope to join the class (possibly as an opt-in class to thereby signify their submission to the court's jurisdiction) or otherwise fall within the class definition. ...

Capacity to be pursued under an opt-out regime

The recent certification decision in *Cassano v Toronto Dominion Bank* [2007] ONCA 781, in which the Ontario Court of Appeal certified an action brought on behalf of a class of credit-card holders (and overturned the trial judge's refusal of certification), provides an insight into how an opt-out action can serve to assist the resolution of the type of litigation that the bank charges customers have been attempting to pursue in English courts. The claim arose out of foreign currency transactions conducted with Visa credit cards issued by the Toronto-Dominion Bank. The card-holders claimed that the Bank breached its contract with them by charging undisclosed and unauthorised fees—a so-called 'conversion fee' and an 'issuer fee'—in respect of those foreign currency transactions, fees which were undisclosed under the standard cardholder agreement. The cardholders and the Bank disagreed over what, precisely, was covered within the ambit of the contractual phrase, *'Foreign currency transactions are converted to Canadian dollars at the exchange rate determined by the Bank'*, or whether such fees were covered as 'service fees'.

The class action was certified by the Court of Appeal on the basis that:

- whether the Bank had charged its card-holders an unauthorised fee when converting the debits and credits incurred in a foreign currency to Canadian dollars was an issue that could be resolved on a class-wide basis, because it depended on the interpretation of the standardised documents provided by the Bank to card-holders;

- the card-holders' damages for breach of contract (if such were proven) could be assessed on an aggregate, class-wide basis (the scenario fulfilled the precondition for aggregate assessment stipulated by s 24(1) of the Class Proceedings Act), and would not require proof of damages on an individualised basis, and thus, the class action would not be overwhelmed by the extent of individual issues;

- an opt-out class action was the preferable means of resolving the common issues because, at para 57: [t]he relatively small amounts of money that are likely to be at stake in individual claims and the disproportionately high costs associated with litigating claims on an individual basis overwhelmingly favour a class proceeding. Table 12 gives details of further decisions, arising out of similar overcharge scenarios, which have been certified in Ontario. In *Gilbert v Canadian Imperial Banks of Commerce* (2004), 3 CPC (6th) 35 (Ont SCJ) too, the relatively small amounts at issue was one of the key factors that prompted certification of the suit (at para 8):

> [t]he amounts of the individual settlements to class members is relatively small, from less than one dollar to almost $15, making it clear that a class proceeding advances the goals of the Act of access to justice and judicial economy.

Reforms to the Financial Services and Markest Act in 2010 would have introduced an opt-out class action in the field of financial services but the provisions were discarded in the 'wash up' to the general election of 2010.

Hensler (2010) provides a balanced view of the US experience of class actions. Hensler notes that there is potential for abuse in class actions where settlements reward lawyers primarily rather than the class, underlining the role of the judge in supervising fees. She comments that

> [P]olicy makers worry that increasing financial incentives to bring representative lawsuits and reducing the risk of adverse costs will fuel 'frivolous litigation'. But despite anecdotes about 'US style class actions', there is little evidence from the US that a large fraction of certified actions are 'frivolous'; indeed, recent evidence from Rand regarding consumer class actions against insurance companies suggests that the judiciary effectively screens out non-meritorious suits. (Hensler, 2010: 534).

6.1 Canadian experience of consumer class actions

The Canadian experience is relevant to the UK since it has a similar legal system without the characteristics associated with the 'excesses' of the US approach. Class actions are available in most Canadian provinces, including the three largest: Ontario, British Columbia and Quebec.

In Ontario, under the Class Proceedings Act 1992 a class action must be certified by the court. A court shall certify a class action where there is an identifiable class of two or more persons; the claims raise common issues; a class proceeding would be the preferable procedure; and there is a representative plaintiff who would fairly and adequately represent the interests of the class and who has produced a plan for the proceeding that sets out a workable method of advancing the proceeding on behalf of the class and of notifying members of the proceeding, and who does not have a conflict of interest on the common issues (section 5). Actions may be certified as class actions notwithstanding the fact that: (a) they relate to separate contracts; (b) they will require individualised assessment of damages; (c) the number of the class is not known; (d) different remedies are sought for different class members; or (e) the class includes a subclass of members with common issues not shared by all class members. These requirements address therefore the traditional restrictions on representative actions.

Members of the class are presumed to opt in and are bound by the court's decision unless they opt out within a time limit established by the court (section 9):

(a) Notice to class members is normally required and a variety of means may be used to establish notice. It may be dispensed with based on a cost/benefit analysis (section 17).
(b) Discovery is available against a representative plaintiff. It may also be made against other members of the class but is subject to control by the court (section 15).
(c) All settlements, even of actions that have not been certified, must be approved by the court (section 29) as must all fee arrangements (section 32).
(d) There is variation in jurisdictions concerning liability for costs. The traditional 'loser pays' principle only applies in Ontario, Quebec and Alberta. A representative plaintiff may only be liable for the other party's costs in British Columbia if the proceedings are 'frivolous or vexatious'. In Quebec only nominal costs may be awarded against a losing plaintiff. In Ontario the standard 'loser pays' rule applies. It is possible in Ontario to apply to the Class Proceedings Fund to relieve liability for costs. If an action is successful then the Fund receives 10 per cent of any settlement or judgment. In practice the Fund is cautious in funding actions (since it could be wiped out by a single large loss) and cases with the largest recoveries do not apply for funding.
(e) The court may aggregate damages in a fund to be shared proportionately by individual members of the class with distribution to each member of the class by reference to the records of the defendant. Statistical evidence may be admitted that would not otherwise be admissible relating to the distribution of the award.
(f) There is the possibility of cy-près recovery where it would be impracticable or impossible to distribute an award to members of the class.

A significant percentage of consumer rights class cases originated in Quebec, which has a liberal class-action regime, an active consumer group that seeks out potential class actions and a fund to aid financing of the litigation. Examples of consumer class actions include:

• several actions alleging undisclosed fees and illegal charges on credit cards;
• actions in relation to alleged illegal late charges on utilities;
• erroneous billing on mobile phones;
• actions claiming that products are defectively manufactured;
• misleading representations in relation to products;
• misleading selling practices in relation to life insurance;
• unfair practices by automobile insurance companies;
• price fixing;
• product liability actions (including tobacco actions).

Several of the above examples (eg the credit card overcharging cases) represent cases that are individually non-viable, ie that would not be brought but for the existence of the class action device. The price-fixing actions are of interest because they 'piggyback' on successful criminal prosecutions under the Federal Competition Act for price fixing which provides a private action for damages where there has been contravention of criminal provisions of the Act (see in UK section 47B of the Competition Act).

In Ontario the primary movers in many class actions are 'entrepreneurial lawyers' who seek out potentially viable class actions that are undertaken on a contingency fee basis. This model raises the potential problem of conflict between the interests of the agent (the lawyer) and the principal (the consumers). Lawyers may have an interest in maximising their fees from a case through a settlement that may not necessarily be in the best interests of consumers as a class. Alternatively they may refuse a reasonable settlement that would be in the best interests of their client. '[P]rivate attorneys generally may be too willing to bring non-meritorious suits, if these suits produce generous financial rewards for them' (Rand, 2000: 74).

A further problem is the possibility of collusion between lawyers for the plaintiff and defendant. A defendant may agree to a smaller settlement in return for a larger fee payable to plaintiff's counsel. One variation on this theme is the 'coupon settlement' where class members receive an award of coupons to purchase products from the defendant while the plaintiff's lawyer is paid in cash. Many consumers fail to apply for or redeem coupons, particularly where they are for small amounts, so that the plaintiff's lawyer and the defendant are the prime beneficiaries of the settlement. Moreover, there is something paradoxical in offering consumers the opportunity to purchase more product from a firm that is alleged in the class action to be exploiting consumers. The mechanism for controlling these practices is the requirement of judicial approval of all settlements and fees. Judges are rarely in favour of this form of settlement unless the coupons are exchangeable for cash.

In Quebec, consumer groups play an important role in developing class actions. Under the Quebec class-action legislation non-profit organisations may apply to a public fund (Le Fonds d'aide aux recours collectifs) to fund an action. These non-profit groups, as repeat players in class actions, are able to exercise greater control over their lawyers so that class actions are not solely 'une affaire aux avocats'. They are able to draw on the knowledge of their members to identify potential class actions while at the same time having a continuing responsibility to that membership.

The overwhelming majority of consumer economic loss cases are settled. Some of these settlements may include cy-près distributions (such as donations to charitable organisations). A leading academic authority in Canada on class actions concluded in 2001 that: '[T]here is little, if any evidence to date of the successful use of class actions as a form of litigation blackmail—bringing groundless class actions to extract unfounded settlements from defendants' (Watson, 2001: 285). Jasminka Kalajdzic in 2010 reviewed the role of consumer class actions in Canada. She concluded that consumers had benefited from class actions but pointed to a potential limitation in their use in cases of unfair trade practices where a successful defence might be raised that individual reliance must be proved. She notes attempts to circumvent this defence through waiver of tort, converting the claim to a restitutionary claim to disgorgement of profits and through the use of cy-près distribution (Kalajdzic, 2010:356).

Kalajdzic also notes the challenge to class actions through the use of mandatory arbitration clauses in individual contracts. Several provincial statutes nullify such clauses. In the UK mandatory arbitration clauses are prohibited in consumer contracts for claims under £5,000 (Arbitration Act, 1996 sections 89–91) and claims above that amount could be challenged under the utcc regulations. The cross-border sales proposal (COM(2011) 635 final) proposes to prohibit mandatory arbitration clauses (see Article 84(d)).

7. The role of self-regulatory organisations in enforcing unfair commercial practices law

The UCPD in Articles 10 and 11 envisages the encouragement of codes of practice and the possibility that an EU Member State may require 'prior recourse to other established means of dealing with complaints' before recourse to courts or to an administrative authority. CPUT regulation 19(4) implements Article 11. The OFT consulted on the approach to 'established means' in 2008–09 .

OFT 1043, *Compliance Partnerships: Response to Consultation* (July 2009)

The policy seeks to encourage bodies such as OFT Approved code sponsors and other trade associations to act as a first port of call for resolving compliance issues in addition to recognised statutory bodies such as the Advertising Standards Authority (ASA) and PhonepayPlus. It looks at alternative ways of bringing about compliance outside of the traditional statutory framework for enforcing the law. Rather than dealing with matters always through the criminal or civil courts, we will look to other bodies, which we refer to as our compliance partners, with tried and tested systems for dealing with non-compliance.

PRINCIPLES THE OFT WILL APPLY IN WORKING WITH COMPLIANCE PARTNERS

3.1 The OFT will use the following principles in identifying and working with appropriate compliance partners.

PRINCIPLE 1

In circumstances where the OFT is aware of or suspects non- compliance with the Regulations, it may deal with the matter itself, or seek to refer the matter to compliance partner(s), in line with its prioritisation principles.

3.2 The OFT targets its enforcement activity towards cases that are likely to deliver high impact results for consumers, in line with its prioritisation principles. The OFT will continue to intervene in those cases where it is appropriate for us to do so, but using appropriate 'established means' as a first port of call for resolving compliance issues will expand the reach of the Regulations and in so doing bring benefits to consumers, business and enforcers alike.

PRINCIPLE 2

The OFT will seek to refer a matter to the compliance partner best placed to resolve the problem. The OFT may consider it appropriate in some circumstances for different partners to tackle different elements of an issue.

3.3 When assessing which partner may be best placed to deal with the issue we will satisfy ourselves that the chosen partner has an effective way of bringing about the control of unfair commercial practices.

3.5 Factors we will take into account in referring to a compliance partner or partners may include:

• degree of detriment
• geographical location of detriment

- sector in which the detriment is arising
- nature and seriousness of the unfair commercial practice
- complexity of the issue
- history of the trader in dealing with compliance requests, and
- degree of compliance partner's alignment with the public interest.

3.6 The OFT will use its discretion to decide who is best placed meet the circumstances of each particular case. We may approach a different body or use a different set of arrangements from those used on a previous occasion. This is not to say we will be inconsistent in our referrals and in most cases it will be clear who is best placed to act.

PRINCIPLE 3

3.7 The characteristics that we expect to see in compliance partners are divided into sets of essential and desirable qualities/systems.

Essential qualities/systems

3.8 A body, or set of arrangements, will be able to demonstrate the following:

- it has adequate resources to address instances of non-compliance within its community
- it is law abiding in its own operation
- it is recognised by its community
- it is properly incentivised to act
- it has systems to place requirements on its community
- it has systems to enforce those requirements within its community
- there is an appropriate degree of independence in governance
- there is an appropriate degree of objectivity in governance
- it has regard for principles of better regulation and the Human Rights Act with regard to the rights of consumers and traders/businesses
- adequate controls in place for the safeguarding of confidential information, and • it is willing to report to the OFT on its compliance partnership activity.

Desirable qualities/systems

3.9 Compliance partners will also be able to display some or all of the following:
- systems for providing information/communication within markets
- a public facing element that may incorporate a complaint handling facility, and
- systems for staying abreast of developments in the law

Ultimately, the OFT continues to be under a duty to enforce the Regulations

Reporting to the OFT

4.13 A compliance partner should be willing to provide regular and timely reports to the OFT on its compliance partnership activity. The OFT will also explore the potential for publishing individual decisions where this would be in the public interest.

It is not clear how established means will operate if co-ordination of enforcement of consumer protection legislation is moved from the OFT to a trading standards co-ordinating body.

7.1 Mandated self-regulation and co-regulation: the Advertising Standards Authority

> On the whole we have tended to regard the law as such as perhaps too blunt an instrument for dealing effectively with false and misleading advertising... in our concept of the whole thing the law is not foremost; the law is almost a back up power if the administrative process of self regulation goes wrong. (Committee on European Communities (sub-committee D) HL, Wednesday 5 April 1978, Statement by Assistant Secretary, Department of Trade and Industry)

In contrast to its position in the United States and in several European countries, industry self-regulation in the United Kingdom is a primary instrument of control of deceptive and unfair advertising. Writing in 1986, Baggot and Harrison suggested that the persistence of self-regulation in advertising reflected three factors: the general preference of British governments for self-regulation and its 'compatibility with British administrative culture'; the considerable economic and political influence of the advertising industry and its ability to 'mobilize support throughout the media' and in Parliament where many MPs have advertising interests; and 'the low party political status of regulating advertising ... both Labour and Conservative MPs have represented advertising interests' (Baggot and Harrison, 1986: 143, 157).

The present UK system has developed in the continuing shadow of potential legal regulation of the advertising industry. It was the threat of legal controls being recommended by the Molony Committee which led to the formation of the Advertising Standards Authority (ASA) in the early 1960s. The Committee concluded that self-regulation 'should be given a chance to prove itself, not that it should be accepted come what may, as a certain and complete solution of the problem' (paragraph 794).

Self-regulation in advertising was to address primarily questions of taste and decency, cases where claims were not objectively true or false and advertising claims which play on emotional weaknesses. The Committee rejected the FTC as a regulatory model in this area because it distrusted the idea of a body with significant discretion creating and enforcing its own rules and with only limited accountability to Parliament (paragraph 794).

The ASA system was revised in 1974 after adverse comments on its operation by the Director General of Fair Trading, and after the Secretary of State for Trade and Industry again signalled the threat of legal regulation. After the DTI in 1980 criticised the reactive stance of the Authority in concentrating on complaint work, the ASA took a more 'proactive' stance, extending its monitoring work, conducting research on advertising directed to children, on alcohol advertising, and on sexism in advertising, and attempting to give greater publicity to its findings in cases involving national advertising campaigns. The fear that the EC Directive on Misleading Advertising would require the substitution of legal controls for self-regulation provided a strong incentive for the ASA to demonstrate its effectiveness to government. It appears to have succeeded.

The UK government, after lobbying successfully for recognition of self-regulation in the EC Directive, has complied with it by maintaining self-regulation, with a back-up injunctive power being conferred on the Director General of Fair Trading to prevent or sanction publication of misleading advertising. In 1990 decisions of the ASA were held to be subject to judicial review. In 1995 the ASA introduced the possibility of appeals against adjudications. These were initially handled by the Chair of the ASA, but in response to a concern that this created a conflict of interest, an independent reviewer was appointed in 1999.

The ASA's mandate now includes regulation of broadcast advertising under a co-regulatory contract with the Office of Communications under the Communications Act 2003 whereby the ASA will have primary responsibility for regulation with OFCOM having a similar backstop power to the OFT. This delegation is accomplished under the Delegation and Contracting Out Act 1994 that permits a minister or regulator to delegate specific functions to another person. In addition, a consumer panel, the Advertising Advisory Committee, was established for broadcast advertising; this Committee is composed of seven 'lay experts' and one industry representative. The role of this Committee is to 'ensure that the concerns of viewers and listeners are taken into account' when the broadcast advertising codes are revised or updated. The Broadcast Committee of Advertising Practice must provide a formal response to any advice provided by the Advisory Committee in relation to changes in the code. Since 2011 the ASA also regulates advertising on the Internet by owners of websites. Finally, the ASA is regarded as 'established means' under the CPUT regulations 2008.

In the late 1990s the Consumers Association, perhaps anticipating a more robust approach to consumer policy from the new Labour government (the Labour Party had indicated in 1986 that it would substitute regulation by the OFT for the present self-regulatory system (Consumer Charter, 1986)), criticised the lack of strong consumer representation on the ASA, the procedures for receiving complaints, the time-scale for adjudications, the transparency of decision-making processes, the lack of an independent appeals mechanism, and the limitations on sanctions (Parry, 2000: 137). The introduction of the independent assessor may have partly responded to this critique and its role as the frontline regulator of broadcast advertising will create further pressures to ensure that there are proper measures of accountability and performance.

The existence of judicial review, oversight mechanisms such as an independent reviewer of its adjudications, and an independent consumer panel to provide advice on the development of the advertising codes challenge simple dichotomies between public and private, state and market. It would be misleading to describe it as 'industry self-regulation'. It is more similar to 'mandated self-regulation' where an attempt is made to 'make associative, self-interested collective action contribute to the achievement of public policy objectives' (see Streeck and Schmitter, 1985: 17). The ASA administers, monitors and enforces a complex rulebook on advertising and now adopts many of the characteristics of the new public management in terms of transparency, accountability and the use of performance measures.

The UK model of advertising regulation is now being promoted by the European Association of Advertisers as a model for pan-European regulation of advertising under the EU Unfair Commercial Practices Directive.

Arguments in favour of the ASA focus particularly on the reduction it affords in rule-making and enforcement costs. Thus, the code, it is argued, will be less 'over-inclusive' than legislation and may be amended more quickly. In addition, the high costs of attempting to write precise rules in such areas as taste and decency (a topic not covered by the UCPD) may be avoided by delegating this task to the ASA on a case-by-case basis, and standards developed in self-regulation may provide the model for subsequent legal regulations. Enforcement through informal pressure, adverse publicity and the ultimate sanction of the denial of access to the media are claimed to be cheaper, quicker and more effective than legal procedures. It is also argued that, since the rules are interpreted in light of their spirit, the 'amoral calculator' is prevented from exploiting the literal wording of the code to serve her own interests. In addition, the peer pressure that is involved may induce a higher level of compliance than government regulation. If self-regulation handles the great majority of routine cases, government resources (courts, enforcement agencies) may be saved for more important cases or for other areas of regulation. The following extracts outline the structure of the ASA, and successive government views on the role of self-regulation.

The Present System in the United Kingdom, 38th Report, HL Committee on European Communities (1978) iv–v

> 7. The present system of advertising control in the United Kingdom is predominantly self-regulatory. Its central instruments are the Code of Advertising Practice Committee (CAP Committee) and the Advertising Standards Authority (ASA) which oversees its work. Two-thirds of the governing council of the Authority, including the Chairman, are independent of the advertising business. The budget of the ASA is raised by means of a 0.1% levy on display advertisements.

Department of Trade and Industry, Consultation Document, *EC Directive on Misleading Advertising* (1985)

> 3. … The Directive was adopted after many years of long and complex negotiations. These reflected a variety of attitudes among Member States towards the problems caused by misleading advertising and differing existing systems for dealing with it. In the UK the combination of a substantial body of legislation (for example on trade descriptions, consumer credit, medicines, broadcasting) and the well established self-regulatory system based on the British Code of Advertising Practice administered by the Advertising Standards Authority (ASA) appears to cope well with most problems which arise.

> GENERAL OBJECTIVES

> 7. The Government remain convinced that the present combination of statutory controls and self-regulation does not require a great deal of strengthening. It is sometimes suggested that self-regulation tends to give the benefit of the doubt to those whose activities are being scrutinised. The record of the ASA suggests that this is not the case in the field of advertising control. The Authority's constitution and system of financing means that it is remoter from industry influence than, for example, a trade association enforcing a Code of Practice upon its members. …

> 8. In those areas of advertising where the ASA currently provides the main control the Government see the new powers which the Directive require[s] to be introduced essentially as

a 'long stop'. The Government hope that the effect will be to strengthen rather than diminish the authority of the self-regulatory system.

11. In the vast majority of cases, however, the Government would expect complaints to continue to be dealt with satisfactorily either by the ASA.

Modern Markets, Confident Consumers (1998)

Advertising and claims

3.14 Advertising is important to the effectiveness of markets. It is the most visible way that companies promote their products and services. But consumer confidence depends on advertising claims being true. The Government strongly supports the self-regulatory controls on advertising in the United Kingdom run by the Advertising Standards Authority. These have gained world-wide recognition as a good example of how self regulation can work effectively to address consumer problems.

Director General of Fair Trading v Tobyward Ltd and another [1989] 1 WLR 517 (Ch)

HOFFMANN J: There is before the court a motion by the Director General of Fair Trading for an interlocutory injunction to restrain the publication of misleading advertisements. The first respondent is a company which markets and has extensively advertised a product called 'SpeedSlim'. The product is sold in the form of tablets and is claimed to cause loss of weight. The second respondent is the sole director of the first respondent.

The Director General applies under reg 5 of the Control of Misleading Advertisements Regulations 1988, SI 1988/915, which came into force on 20 June 1988. These regulations were made to implement Council Directive (EEC) 84/450. For the purposes of reg 2(2) of the 1988 regulations, an advertisement is misleading if—

'in any way, including its presentation, it deceives or is likely to deceive the persons to whom it is addressed or whom it reaches and if, by reason of its deceptive nature, it is likely to affect their economic behaviour or, for those reasons, injures or is likely to injure a competitor of the persons whose interests the advertisement seeks to promote.'

The director has a duty under reg 4(1) to consider any complaints that advertisements are misleading. A duty expressed in such broad terms might impose on the director's office an unacceptable volume of work but it is qualified in two respects. First, he need not consider complaints which appear to be frivolous or vexatious second, and much more important, he need not consider any complaint until the complainant has invoked what the regulations describe as 'such established means of dealing with such complaints as the Director may consider appropriate'.

The British advertising industry has a system of self-regulation which has been established under the auspices of its voluntary regulatory body, the Advertising Standards Authority (the ASA). There is a British Code of Advertising Practice which is administered by the code of advertising practice committee, and the committee and the ASA deal with complaints of breaches of the code. They are also willing to give guidance to advertisers on whether a proposed advertisement would be regarded as acceptable. So the proper working of the self-regulatory system is essential to the overall scheme of control, which contemplates that the director will deal only with exceptional cases in which for one reason or another self-regulation has proved inadequate.

… The making of the injunction is, however, a matter of discretion, and I must consider whether in this case it would be appropriate to do so. There are two reasons why I think I should. First, the regulations contemplate that there will only be intervention by the director when the voluntary system has failed. It is in my judgment desirable and in accordance with the public interest to which I must have regard that the courts should support the principle of self-regulation. I think that advertisers would be more inclined to accept the rulings of their self-regulatory bodies if it were generally known that in cases in which their procedures had been exhausted and the advertiser was still publishing an advertisement which appeared to the court to be prima facie misleading an injunction would ordinarily be granted.

The following are the current general rules and sanctions that may be applied by the ASA.

The central principle for all marketing communications is that they should be legal, decent, honest and truthful. All marketing communications should be prepared with a sense of responsibility to consumers and society and should reflect the spirit, not merely the letter, of the Code.

1.1 Marketing communications should be legal, decent, honest and truthful.

1.2 Marketing communications must reflect the spirit, not merely the letter, of the Code.

1.3 Marketing communications must be prepared with a sense of responsibility to consumers and to society.

1.4 Marketers must comply with all general rules and with relevant sector-specific rules.

1.5 No marketing communication should bring advertising into disrepute.

1.6 Marketing communications must respect the principles of fair competition generally accepted in business.

1.7 Any unreasonable delay in responding to the ASA's enquiries will normally be considered a breach of the Code.

1.7.1 The full name and geographical business address of the marketer must be given to the ASA or CAP without delay if requested.

1.8 Marketing communications must comply with the Code. Primary responsibility for observing the Code falls on marketers. Others involved in preparing or publishing marketing communications, such as agencies, publishers and other service suppliers, also accept an obligation to abide by the Code.

1.9 Marketers should deal fairly with consumers.

3.7 Before distributing or submitting a marketing communication for publication, marketers must hold documentary evidence to prove claims that consumers are likely to regard as objective and that are capable of objective substantiation. The ASA may regard claims as misleading in the absence of adequate substantiation.

4 Marketing communications must not contain anything that is likely to cause serious or widespread offence. Particular care must be taken to avoid causing offence on the grounds of race, religion, gender, sexual orientation, disability or age. Compliance will be judged on the context, medium, audience, product and prevailing standards.

Marketing communications may be distasteful without necessarily breaching this rule. Marketers are urged to consider public sensitivities before using potentially offensive material.

The fact that a product is offensive to some people is not grounds for finding a marketing communication in breach of the Code.

4.2 Marketing communications must not cause fear or distress without justifiable reason; if it can be justified, the fear or distress should not be excessive. Marketers must not use a shocking claim or image merely to attract attention.

The sanctions available to the ASA include adverse publicity through the media, advising the media to deny advertising space to a contravening party, in exceptional cases expulsion of a member's trading privileges by a member of ASA, and requiring persistent offenders to have their copy pre-vetted. Deborah Parry suggests that because the ASA is not able to control the extent to which adverse rulings receive publicity, it is a somewhat 'unreliable form of sanction' (cf comments above concerning naming and shaming) (Parry, 2000: 146).

The current role of the ASA involves the investigation of complaints concerning advertisements and the carrying out of a monitoring programme to check compliance with the Code of Advertising Practice, the objective of which is to ensure that advertisements are 'legal, decent, honest and truthful'. The Code of Advertising practice contains a combination of general rules, which apply to advertisements of all kinds, and specialised rules for particular types of claims—for example, those concerning alcohol, tobacco and vitamins, health claims, and those in advertisements directed at children.

An important aspect of the work of the ASA is responding to individual complaints concerning advertising messages. In 2010 the ASA received 25,124 complaints about 13,074 advertisements. Complaints from the public (rather than the industry) represented 96 per cent of complaints. Misleading advertisements were the largest category of complaint for non-broadcast advertisements, and offensiveness the largest category for broadcast advertisements. As a consequence of ASA action 2,226 advertisements were changed or withdrawn (ASA, Annual Report, 2010). The ASA considers significant numbers of complaints concerning misleading and unsubstantiated advertisements rather than taste and decency, which Molony had viewed as the primary topics for consideration by the ASA. The results of the complaint work are published in monthly case reports. The ASA may settle cases informally or open a formal investigation. According to the 2010 Annual Report, 'We prefer to work by persuasion and consensus and, where appropriate, we will resolve issues informally. For example, where a minor or clear cut breach of the Advertising Codes has been made and the advertiser agrees to change or withdraw their ad straightaway.'

There is, in general, no right to redress for a complainant to the ASA, and one might wonder, therefore, why consumers bring complaints to the ASA. The ASA may be acting as a safety valve for consumer dissatisfaction with advertising, allowing consumers to 'let off steam' (Hirschman, 1970: 124). This may be valuable for industry, but should it be described as 'access to justice'?

The ASA initially reacted 'grudgingly and slowly' to issues concerning sex stereotyping and the representation of minorities (Boddewyn, 1986:39), thus questioning the efficacy of self-regulation on these issues. It was only through continued and sometimes co-ordinated external pressure that it made a significant response to gender issues in advertising. Dee Amy-Chinn has criticised its performance in addressing the representation of women in advertising. She argues that the 'non-representative nature of complainants, the inadequacy of after-the fact adjudication, the difficulty of judging against "soft" criteria and the inability of the ASA to heed its own research' have resulted in flawed regulation (Amy-Chinn, 2007: 1036–37). She notes a 2001 study of those complaining to the ASA that concluded that the demographic makeup was not 'far removed from a mixture of university lecturers and the legendary "Disgusted of Tunbridge Wells"'. The ASA primarily regulates for 'offence' rather than 'harm' although the two are distinct and may 'limit progressive images and ideas' (ibid: 1047). She notes that 'legitimizing claims of offence on the grounds of emotional upset or affront … without requiring any concrete demonstration of harm is particularly problematic at a time when claiming offence seems to be the fashion of the day' (ibid: 1040). Her argument is that although regulation of advertisements which cause genuine harm should be regulated, the current ASA system does not achieve this goal.

The ASA introduced the idea of claim substantiation, requiring an advertiser to provide objective support for claims in its advertising. A court may now require this in actions brought under Part 8 of the Enterprise Act 2002. Claims substantiation drew on US innovations in advertising regulation in the early 1970s. In Re Pfizer Inc 81 FTC 23 claim substantiation requirements by the FTC were upheld based primarily on the asymmetry of knowledge between consumers and producers in relation to complex products and their performance characteristics. The court concluded that it was more rational for the 'manufacturer to confirm his affirmative product claims rather than impose a burden on the individual consumer to test, investigate or experiment for himself. … In addition fairness to competitors requires that the vendor have a reasonable basis for making performance claims.' Cosmetic products that claim to have similar effects to facelifts have been sanctioned by the ASA for failure to provide adequate substantiation. Claim substantiation also substantially reduces enforcement costs by reversing the burden of proof.

The ASA has, however, always opposed another US innovation from the 1970s, namely corrective advertising—requiring an advertiser to correct lingering consumer misimpressions and to correct market shares illegally achieved through false advertising. Corrective advertisements have the short-term goal of correcting misimpressions and the longer-term goal of deterring misleading claims. Section 217(8) of the Enterprise Act 2002 does confer power to order corrective advertising but UK authorities demonstrate little enthusiasm for this remedy. The ASA 'is generally skeptical of the value of the publication of corrective statements by advertisers; in our view they tend to harm overall trust in advertising and could be confusing for consumers' (ASA, 2006: 4). Do you agree with this assessment? Certainly (a) corrective advertisement remedies in the US were hotly contested by advertisers (why?); (b) advertisers could undercut the effects of corrective notices by placing them in the context of more positive statements; and (c) it did not always correct the lingering misimpression. Thus after a corrective advertising remedy was imposed on Listerine to counteract the misleading impression that it prevented colds and sore throats 39 per cent of users still used Listerine on the grounds that it prevented colds and sore throats!

The following extracts represent cases where ASA adjudications were subject to (unsuccessful) judicial review. The cases are of interest on several grounds. First, there is the substantive issue of assessing substantiation in advertising claims. Second, you will see that the issue of the right to commercial speech under the European Convention on Human Rights is raised (see further below) and there is the approach of the courts to judicial review of hybrid bodies such as the ASA (compare with approach to judicial review of the Financial Ombudsman Service below at 457).

Queen on application of Matthias Rath BV The Advertising Standards Authority and the Independent Reviewer [2000] EWHC Admin 428

Turner J

1. The relevant parts of the leaflet of which complaint was made were as follows:

Heart attacks and strokes are not diseases, but—similar to scurvy—the consequence of vitamin deficiency and they are preventable by optimum intake of vitamins. ... The results of vitamin research leave no doubt that such other widespread diseases as high blood pressure, heart failure, diabetic circulatory problems, osteoporosis and even cancer can also be controlled by optimum intake of essential nutrients. ...

[T]he British Government was about to forbid forever the dissemination of natural health information in relation to vitamins and other natural therapies. What forced the Government to withdraw this unconscionable legislation was our previous health news ... that had been distributed during the first weeks of August. ...

The complaints and the adjudication were as follows:

1. Whether the advertisers could substantiate the efficacy of their treatments in preventing heart disease and high blood pressure

1 and 2. The (ASA) considered that the advertisers had not substantiated that their products had the claimed benefits and had presented their opinion in a way that could be confused with medical fact. It considered that the leaflet was misleading

2. Whether it was clear that it was merely the advertisers opinion that heart attacks and strokes were not diseases and were preventable by optimum vitamin intake

3. Whether the advertisers could substantiate the claims about legislation and political influence

3. The Authority considered that the advertisers had not justified their interpretation of the legislation and had not shown that they had influenced the change to the legislation.

4. Whether the testimonials were genuine.

4. The Authority noted that the testimonials were in German and had informed them that all evidence must be submitted in English. The Authority considered that the advertisers had not proved that the testimonials were genuine.

5. Whether the advertisement discourages sufferers of serious medical conditions from seeking medical treatment.

5. The Authority noted that although the newsletter mentioned serious medical conditions it did not state the need for recipients to seek medical advice. Furthermore, the Authority noted that respondents could order three other products, about which the advertisers had not commented.

The Regulatory framework

12. There exist The British Codes of Advertising and Sales Promotion the tenth edition of which came into force on 1 October 1999. ...

¶8.1 Advertisers may give a view about any matter, including the qualities and desirability of their products, provided it is clear that they are expressing their own opinion rather than stating a fact.

¶14.1 Advertisers should hold signed and dated proof for any testimonial they use. ...

¶50.1 Medical and scientific claims made about ... health-related products should be backed by evidence, where appropriate by trials conducted on people.

¶50.2 Advertisers inviting customers to diagnose their own minor ailments should not make claims that might lead to a mistaken diagnosis.

¶50.3 Advertisers should not discourage essential treatment.

¶68.4 ... (The chief tasks of the ASA) are to promote and enforce high standards in advertisements, to investigate complaints. ...

¶68.36 In exceptional circumstances, Council can be asked to reconsider its adjudication. Written requests for a review should be sent to the Independent Reviewer. ... There are two grounds on which such a request can be made:

* Where additional evidence becomes available.
* Where a substantial flaw in Council's adjudication can be demonstrated.

The Independent Reviewer will decide whether there are grounds to proceed:

* The Independent Reviewer will evaluate the substance of the request with advice from two Assessors. ...
* If it is decided to proceed, the Independent Reviewer will conduct an investigation of the file and will compile a report and recommendation for the ASA Council.

¶68.39 A number of sanctions exist to counteract advertisements ...that conflict with the Codes: ... adverse publicity, which acts as a deterrent may result from rulings published in the ASA's monthly report.

The decisions challenged

13. These are

1. the decision of the ASA to publish in its monthly report the adjudication into the complaint by the Health Authority and

2. The decision of the Independent Reviewer refusing the request of the claimants for reconsideration of the decision of the ASA in relation to the complaints.

Nature of the challenges

14. It is convenient first to give consideration to the challenge as it affects the Independent Reviewer. In concluding that his letter had stated that the (late) supply of the translations of the testimonials did not undermine the truth of the adjudication, it was submitted that the Independent Reviewer had misapplied or misinterpreted the Code as he had not expressly referred to the (now) translated testimonials or to evidence of patent and other experimental material from the United States. The submission was that the Independent Reviewer had considered the evidence as it existed at the time of the original adjudication, rather than the evidence as it was at the time at which he was asked to review the decision. It was

submitted that the existence of the new evidence meant that there had been a substantial flaw in the original decision. It was submitted that without indication that the Independent Reviewer had actually considered the fresh material, his decision was liable to be struck down. It was further submitted that if the report were to be published by the first defendants without amendment, which reflected the new evidence, it would have an adverse effect on the claimants' reputation and their business.

15. The Code itself recognises that a part of the self-regulatory sanction is that there will be adverse publicity. As originally drafted, the skeleton argument suggested that to the extent that the report will state that the testimonials had not been proved to be genuine, that would suggest that the claimants had published false information.

16. The defendants' response on this point was both short and cogent. There was no substance in the suggestion that, by publishing the report in the terms of its draft, the first defendant was accusing the claimants of publishing false information. All it was doing was pointing out that the claimants had not justified the testimonials within the time limited by the first defendants. This is clearly right. The testimonials had not been translated into English at the date of the determination by the ASA Council, so the Independent Reviewer was entitled to comment entirely factually, as he had done. As to the remainder of the complaint against him, it was submitted that under the provisions of clause 68.36 of the Code, it was a matter for the exercise of the Independent Reviewer's discretion whether he should embark on a review in the light of any new evidence placed before him.

17. In support of the complaint which concerned the efficacy of the treatments advocated by the claimants, it was pointed out that evidence in relation to US patents and pilot studies had been before the ASA Council at the time of its adjudication. Evidence in regard to a pilot study which had been conducted was exiguous on its face and contained results in respect of nine patients only.

18. It could not therefore sensibly be said that the Independent Reviewer had exercised his discretion in such a manner that it was judicially reviewable. But there was the additional point that he had not adverted sufficiently to the reasons for his decision.

19. In my judgment, the position is clear. Given the material which was already before the Council of the ASA when it made its decision which the claimants wished to be reviewed by the Independent Reviewer, it was not incumbent on him to do more than to say that the new material did not cause him to embark on a review. In short, the claimants had only themselves to thank that there were no translations of the testimonials available when the Council made its adjudication, the Independent Reviewer's comments on this were factual. There was not in respect of this so-called new evidence anything new which should have persuaded the Independent Reviewer that the original decision was flawed or that there was new evidence which he should review.

20. The basis of the claim for prior restraint was that the effect of publishing the report of the adjudication was to infringe the claimants' right to freedom of expression contrary to the provisions of Article 10.1 of the European Convention on Human Rights (ECHR). The contention was that the adjudication would have an adverse impact on the reputation of the claimants and their business, that it would interfere with their right to express their political views in relation to the withdrawal of the proposed MLX 249.

21. The complaint is focussed on the impact on their reputation if publication were to take place. Even in its modified form, the submission that publication of the report would question the integrity of the claimants, is not plausible as invoking infringement of the asserted Convention right. It was submitted that the first defendants could not rely upon the exceptions contained in Article 10.2 because the provisions of the Code were not 'prescribed by law'

even if they were 'necessary in a democratic society' and 'intended' for the 'protection of health'.

22. It was submitted that the first defendant was a public authority, for the purposes of the Convention. Without conceding this point, the first defendants did not argue to the contrary.

23. The claimants' argument proceeded along the following lines. A public authority acts unlawfully if its actions are incompatible with a Convention right. The ASA, is amenable to judicial review and is thus a public authority; see *R v Advertising Standards Authority ex parte The Insurance Service* [1990] COD 42. If the monthly report were to be published by the first defendants as proposed, it would interfere with the claimants' right to freedom of expression. For Convention purposes, political speech and commercial advertising are both activities which are embraced by the phrase 'freedom of expression'. For the purposes of this judgment, I am content to assume, but do not have to decide, that the sales literature of the claimants contains matter which is both advertising and political by nature. On the authority of *Casado Coca v Spain* (1994) 18 EHRR 1 at p 20, it was submitted that interference, for the purposes of Article 10.1, was capable of occurring when publication of an adjudication took place after the original material had been published. ...

26. In my judgment, the application for permission to bring proceedings for judicial review has to fail, just as the application for an order of prior restraint has already failed. I entertain no doubt that the Code of Practice, which has an underpinning of subordinate legislation and which is readily accessible is 'prescribed by law'. The Code of Practice is readily accessible and its provisions are sufficiently clear and precise to enable any person who is minded to place advertisements to know within what limits they are likely to prove acceptable and will also know what are the consequences if he were to infringe its provisions. In these circumstances, given the statutory underpinning, albeit short of direct statutory effect, the Code of Practice meets the purposive intentions of Article 10.2. Moreover, the advertisements themselves were explicitly concerned with matters of health as a consequence the requirement that the challenged rulings were 'necessary for the protection of health', in the sense that the advertisements were capable of conveying misleading information, was fully met.

28. It remains to consider the first defendants' submission to the effect that what the claimants were seeking to protect was not the right to assert that they had been effective in obtaining the withdrawal of the proposed AMX249, as constituting an expression of political opinion, but their reputation. Such an objective was plainly outside the protection afforded by Article 10.1. On a proper reading of the claim that the claimants' had been effective in obtaining the withdrawal or abandonment of the proposed MLX249, the claim was not one which asserted any political opinion. It was a claim based on the proposition that the claimants had been effective in persuading the Government, or the relevant governmental agency to change its mind. I have not been persuaded that such an activity, even if the underlying factual proposition had been proved (which it has not), was the expression of political opinion. It was an attempt to persuade a governmental agency to change its mind. As to the right to freedom of expression it has been said

In my judgment, the public interest is served by the publication of the ASA monthly report, one of the objects of which is to notify the media world of advertising which is not of an acceptable standard. In the instances of which the claimants complain the ASA was clearly entitled to reach the conclusions which it did.

29. It remains to consider the reasons why I refused the application for prior restraint. The first is that the claimants had not satisfied me that they had grounds for bringing proceedings for judicial review, see above. Secondly, there can be no doubt but that they had been guilty of extreme delay in making their application for permission. Despite the attempts made by

their counsel to satisfy me that the first defendants, as a public body, were remiss in sending the material for publication to the printers and arranging distribution when they had been told, I eschew the use of the word `knew', that the claimants intended to bring proceedings for judicial review, the reality is that the claimants had threatened that they would be making an application, but they never responded to the first defendants' requests for information as to the grounds upon which they would be seeking relief. The first defendant was, in my judgment, entirely correct in their decision to continue with printing and distribution of the report while leaving it to the claimants, who had been given early warning of the intended date of publication, to start such proceedings if they thought fit.

...The whole basis of the claimants' application is that this is a public law matter. In my judgment, it would be wrong for the court to apply a private law response to such a claim. That would be unjust to the first defendants as well as the public who have an expectation that a body the first defendants will publish its opinions in a manner and time that is appropriate. They should only be prevented from doing that on pressing grounds. None have been suggested in the present case.

31. For the above reasons, the application for permission must be refused.

In 2007 Debt Free Direct, a company offering a variety of 'debt solutions', brought a judicial review application to prevent the publication of an adjudication by the ASA. The court concluded that it would require compelling reasons to prevent a 'public body' such as the ASA from publishing its adjudications which were in the public interest. See *Debt Free Direct Ltd, R (on the application of) v Advertising Standards Authority Ltd* [2007] EWHC 1337 (Admin) (Administrative Court).

In the following case Ribena had made the claim that 'Ribena ToothKind No Added Sugar does not encourage tooth decay'. This was held to be an absolute claim and unsubstantiated because it was less likely to encourage tooth decay but only if compared with drinks that contained a greater concentration of carbohydrate. Smith Kline challenged this finding on, among other grounds, the basis that it contravened Article 10 of the European Convention on Human Rights.

Smith Kline Beecham and ASA [2000] EWHC Admin 442 (21 December 2000) (QB)

14. The Margin of Reasonable Claims Point.

It is said that the ASA should have recognised a range of claims which could reasonably be made and asked whether the claim 'does not encourage tooth decay' was within that margin. It is further said that this is especially important as it impacts on the exercise of commercial free speech where a requirement of justification or pressing need arises in relation to any interference, see *R v Secretary of State for the Home Dept ex parte Simms* 2000 2 AC 115 and *R v Advertising Standards Authority ex parte Robertson* 4.11.99. Mr Pannick argues that if this was an objectively reasonable claim it should not have been regarded as misleading.

Article 10 of the European Convention for the Protection of Human Rights is no different from English law on the subject. I find that the Code under which the ASA acts, which is indeed a restriction on advertising but one designed to restrict misleading claims, is entirely consistent with Article 10 to which the ASA does have regard. Under the Code requirements for substantiation the more stark, categorical or absolute the claim the greater the degree of substantiation required. With an absolute claim there can be no margin. Following the test in *Casado Coca v Spain* 18 EHRR 1 at page 24 I ask myself whether the measures taken at national level are justifiable in principle and proportionate. I find they are and that the interference in question is properly limited. I find that the ASA approached this claim appropriately within the application of their Code and asked themselves whether the absolute claim being made was substantiated. When they found that it was not there was no room for any margin of reasonable claims argument.

15. It follows from the totality of the above that this challenge fails and that the adjudication of the ASA in this matter is upheld.

It is difficult to measure the success of a body such as the ASA. From the advertisers' viewpoint, a major objective of the ASA is to promote confidence in advertising and deflect pressure for further regulation. The ASA is well financed and its performance compares favourably with advertising self-regulation in countries such as Canada or the United States. The 'high visibility' of advertising and the continuing controversy over its power to shape social goals mean that there will be many individuals and groups monitoring it and that monitoring costs will not be high. Second, the continuing threat of national or EU regulation has provided a strong incentive for self-regulation to demonstrate that it is effective. The code is limited now by the UCPD that establishes maximal harmonisation. The code can probably not go beyond the Directive in its prohibitions in those areas within the scope of the Directive. The interests of governments are served by being able to avoid the costs of direct regulation by transferring any dissatisfaction with regulation to a third party. Thirdly, the independent nature of the ASA council, which includes consumer representatives and a balance between the sexes, political persuasions, religions, philosophies and social attitudes, appears to provide a degree of objectivity in code development and application.

7.2 Codes of practice

The OFT has promoted codes of practice as a method of consumer protection for many years, originally under the Fair Trading Act 1973 where codes were a major output of the agency. The coalition government propose the termination of OFT-supported codes of practice, inviting the Trading Standards Institute to propose a self-funded successor.

The major economic justification for codes of practice as an alternative to government regulation is that they reduce rule-making and enforcement costs. Other major benefits that accrue from the use of such codes are that with them there is no need to engage parliamentary time, their rules may be more specific and may be fine-tuned to particular industries, and by their use trade associations may secure a higher level of voluntary compliance and may help to speed up the diffusion of consumer policy to their members. A perceived cost is the danger of increased cartelisation (particularly in the light of its history among trade associations in the United Kingdom). It is worth noting again that the conditions thought to be favourable to successful self-regulation are similar to those which economists view as potentially leading to industry cartelisation. The danger of cartelisation, and of the consumer-welfare losses that may follow from it, made the OFT economists and its competition branch sceptical of the value of such codes. Consumer lawyers are often sceptical about the effectiveness of codes. To the argument that codes are easier to adopt than legislation their response is that this is not always in fact true, particularly if the code is to be of value to consumers. Industries often accept codes only to avoid legislation so that without the threat of legislation codes are not likely to be beneficial to consumers. Although recognising that businesses are more likely to obey codes that they have negotiated and accepted, consumer lawyers point to the limits of enforcement of a code against those businesses who do not subscribe to the code (see European Consumer Law Group, 1983: 211–12). Codes of practice were adopted in most of the sectors where consumer complaints were prevalent. There were a number of common features of such codes. These are: the specification of the legal rights and obligations of firms and consumers; procedures for the resolution of complaints; controls on the form of advertising and the provision of adequate and clear information; the specification of performance levels, eg in relation to service calls; the promotion of good business management, eg proper staff training; the provision of publicity through an association symbol; and provisions for investigation and enforcement (Pickering and Cousins, 1980).

From 1973 to 2001 the OFT encouraged the development of codes under the Fair Trading Act 1973 and a substantial number were developed. However, academic research indicated that codes had only a marginal impact on consumer and trader behavior, engaged substantial OFT resources in negotiation and monitoring their impact, and seemed to be a method in some cases of associations using codes to head off regulation and increase the status of the trade association

The OFT withdrew support from all existing codes of practice in 2001 at the same time as the announcement of a new approach to the approval of codes. A key aspect of the new procedures is that codes which successfully meet the new two-stage criteria may use a logo on the code indicating that it is approved by the OFT. In addition, the OFT will engage in a marketing campaign to support the logo. Given the need to ensure that the logo 'signal' is not misleading, the process for approving and monitoring codes is more formal and rigorous. The OFT states that the objectives of the new codes are to 'help customers identify trustworthy businesses to buy from ... provide a powerful marketing tool for participating businesses ... [and] sharpen competitive edge by developing best practice within a sector and helping businesses to respond to market change' (OFT, 2006: 1).

There is a two-stage process for approval of a code. In the first stage the code sponsor promises that the code will meet the OFT core criteria (see below) and the OFT assesses whether the code criteria are met in principle. Assuming that the code meets the core criteria, it proceeds to the second stage where the sponsors of the code must provide evidence that the code is operating effectively in order to be permitted to use the OFT seal of approval. This includes evidence that 'members' compliance with the code is being effectively monitored and that their compliance level is high: customer satisfaction is being regularly assessed and the results ...show a high level of satisfaction; complaints are being handled in accordance with the procedures' (OFT, 2006: 2). Code sponsors must develop performance indicators (eg mystery shopping exercises and independent compliance audits) for the code and commit to publishing the results of testing of performance indicators. Consumer organisations, enforcement agencies and advisory services must be adequately consulted both in the development and operation of the code. The OFT will also draw on its own monitoring in assessing a Part 2 application. The OFT would withdraw approval from codes that are not effective. Section 8 of the Enterprise Act confers power on the OFT to 'make arrangements for approving consumer codes' and provide the official symbol of an approved code (section 8(4)(b)).

The OFT launched the code scheme by inviting applications from sponsors in seven sectors where it felt codes of practice would deliver significant benefits to consumers, for instance because complex products or services were involved, high-risk transactions were commonplace or consumers' awareness of their rights was low. The priority sectors were: used cars, car repairs and servicing, credit, funerals, travel, estate agents and direct marketing. Two further sectors, domestic appliance repair and furniture, were added in 2002 (OFT, 2003).

In its 2002–03 Annual Report, the OFT notes that:

> We believe the new scheme is far more robust than the previous system. It helps consumers identify trustworthy traders with confidence. It also offers considerable benefits to businesses which, in return for the costs of achieving high standards of customer service, can use their membership of an OFT-approved code to attract customers. (OFT, 2003: 45)

Although the OFT received a substantial number of applications for codes, only a modest number have been approved under stage 2 (ten over the ten years of the scheme). The OFT promoted those codes that pass both stages of the approval process with a major publicity campaign in 2005. In 2006 ABTA withdrew from the codes scheme because it had reduced its financial protection for consumers of fraudulent tour operators and thus could not meet the criteria for approval.

The new approach to codes of practice differs from earlier 1991 guidelines in requiring greater objective evidence of the performance of codes as a condition of approval and more clearly defined requirements for continuing consultation with external groups. The more rigorous evidence requirements are one reason for the slow development of the new codes initiative. It will usually take at least two years for a code to reach stage 2 status. Trade associations may have difficulties in selling the benefits of codes to their members, particularly given the more onerous requirements of the new process.

The OFT evaluated the effects of codes on business behaviour (OFT, 2006). The review concluded that businesses that are subject to codes perceived the benefits of codes to exceed the costs. However, the costs of implementing and maintaining an OFT-approved code for member businesses were low. There was evidence of fewer complaints against code members than non-member firms in the same industry (although there may have been a self-selection bias here) and code members had more structured approaches to redress. There was little measurable benefit in turnover or profits or costs to businesses from being a member of a code. Trade associations enhanced their reputation as sponsors of codes and increased demands for membership —the OFT scheme provided them with leverage to convince members to improve their code. However, many respondents thought that the tougher criteria in the new code scheme, eg the requirements of independent redress, protection of prepayments and monitoring, were too prescriptive and discouraged applications. Some respondents also thought that the time taken for approval of the code was too long, the process should be more transparent and the OFT should be more knowledgeable about the particular industry.

In 2010 the OFT evaluated consumer experience of codes:

[T]here are two primary roles associated with codes: signalling quality and raising standards across an entire sector. Whilst our research did not evaluate the second role, evidence on the first one was not consistent across the three codes, a fact that might reflect the different stages of development and differences between the sectors themselves.

1.8 In the carpet sector, where there has been an OFT Approved code since March 2007, customers of businesses who were Carpet Foundation members tended to be more satisfied—across a number of measures—than customers of businesses who were not.

1.9 There was less consistency in the findings for the assistive products sector, where the code had completed Stage One but was not yet approved during the period covered by this research. There was, however, some indication that customers of member businesses were more satisfied overall than customers of non-member businesses, especially purchasers of mobility access products.

1.10 By contrast, in the motor vehicle service and repair sector, application of the garage to join the code is associated with lower levels of customer satisfaction, although we cannot conclude that there is a causal link.

1.11 Our analysis is based on three key measures of consumer confidence and satisfaction: the extent to which customers were satisfied with the way the product or service was sold to them, the extent to which they agreed that it provided value for money, and their confidence that they had been fairly treated by their supplier.

The mixed experience of codes of practice may have resulted in current proposals to terminate the OFT scheme.

Why have codes of practice not lived up to their expectations? The government currently supports 'non-regulatory' alternatives such as codes, but the premier code scheme operated by the OFT is being terminated.

The OFT described codes of practice as an alternative to 'classic regulation' (OFT, Annual Report, 2005–06), perhaps suggesting that they are a new departure in regulation, fitting the 'decentred' approach to regulation, where government attempts to harness the resources of private actors to achieve higher levels of consumer satisfaction. But the OFT has always attempted to harness the resources of private actors and there is certainly continuity with the past in the new approach to codes. The core criteria are a modified version of 1991 guidelines on codes and the new codes have been proposed and adopted in areas where there was significant potential consumer detriment—similar to the initiatives in the 1970s. Indeed several sectors targeted are the same as those from the 1970s. Perhaps organisations such as the Direct Selling Association, whose code has been approved, hope to stave of further regulation of doorstep selling through an industry code.

The new approach to codes placed increased emphasis on evidence and monitoring, and requirements for consultation with consumer groups. The paradox is that this increased rigour made it more difficult to achieve approval for codes. There was also emphasis in the new initiative on codes contributing to the competitiveness of UK industries and the commercial benefits of a code to an industry. This represents the influence of Michael Porter's conception of a regulatory agency driving national firms to achieve higher standards of quality which will make them competitive in a global economy. But this does not seem to have transpired in practice with codes.

Although codes of practice are informal sets of rules, they may have an effect on liability under the legal system. The terms of a code might be incorporated into an individual contract, and a false statement as to membership of a trade association or adherence to a code of conduct will give rise to liability under the provisions of the CPUT regulation 5(3)(b). One question is the effect of codes on small businesses (Hutter, 2006: 5). Small businesses are less likely to be members of trade associations or have the ability to meet the more rigorous standards in codes.

8. Cross-border enforcement of unfair commercial practices law

Cross-border enforcement is increasingly important given the existence of the Internet and the possibility of cross-border malpractices. Two measures are relevant here. First, the OFT has powers as a 'general enforcer' under Part 8 of the Enterprise Act to take action in foreign courts against businesses located in other EU countries that are infringing the collective interests of consumers under EU consumer protection directives.

The first case under these provisions was brought by the OFT against a home shopping firm based in Belgium that targeted UK consumers with misleading mail shots that led consumers to believe that they had won £10,000. To receive the prize the consumer had to make a purchase from the accompanying catalogue. Consumers were to send their order to a PO box number in Hampshire. The OFT was successful in arguing before Belgian courts that this practice contravened both English and Belgian implementation of the Control of Misleading Advertisements Directive (see *OFT v Duchesne*, www.oft.gov.uk/news-and-updates/press/2008/86-08). Hans Micklitz argues that this case was costly in terms of resources for the OFT (Micklitz, 2007: 244).

The OFT argues that the 'most significant hurdle to effective cross-border public enforcement of consumer law has been the lack of a fully effective network of enforcers' (Kaye, 2006: 420). Thus in the Duschesne case the OFT would normally ask the relevant authority in the state where the trader was located to take action. However, the relevant body was a private consumers association which could not justify the risk of taking the case, particularly since the company did not target consumers in Belgium. This second issue is addressed by the adoption of the EU Regulation on consumer protection co-operation (Regulation No 2006/2004). This creates a network of enforcers in the EU with responsibilities to provide mutual assistance in the case of trans-border violations of community law (defined in Article 3(b) as 'intra community infringements') and also a framework for wider co-operation and exchange of information. The extract below from the explanatory memorandum to the regulation outlines its rationale.

The regulation requires Member States to designate competent public authorities (Article 3(c)), with a required minimum set of enforcement powers (Article 4) who will co-operate with other authorities through the exchange of information (Article 6), and also take appropriate enforcement measures (Article 8). The OFT is the designated authority in the UK. The regulation also provides for the co-ordination of market surveillance and enforcement activities (Article 9). The Commission will maintain an electronic database of information that may be consulted by enforcement authorities (Article 10) and Member States shall regularly provide the Commission with statistics on consumer complaints received by competent authorities (Article 15.1). Article 16 provides for exchange of information, the development of a common approach to classification of complaints and for the exchange of personnel. Article 19 establishes a committee to oversee the application of the regulation composed of representatives of the member states and chaired by the Commission.

The regulation is important for several reasons. First, the network provides an institution that might play a co-ordinating role in relation to the development of the UCPD directive similar to that of the FTC in the United States. Second, it underscores the role of public enforcement rather than private enforcement by consumer organisations (the model adopted in Germany).

The Commission outlines in the explanatory memorandum its reasons for preferring public enforcement. Consider these rationales in relation to arguments concerning the balance of public and private enforcement.

34. There are several reasons why an EU network of public authorities is required.

—Only public authorities can have the investigation powers necessary to obtain evidence of an infringement.

—Only public authorities can provide sufficient guarantee of the confidentiality and professional secrecy concerning information exchanged. A guarantee of confidentiality and secrecy is essential to ensure the trader's reputation is not unfairly harmed and to prevent investigations being compromised.

The public authorities in the large majority of Member States where they exist have demonstrated the efficiency and effectiveness of a public dimension to enforcement. The threat of speedy action from public authorities is an important deterrent to rogue traders, especially those taking advantage of the opportunities of the internet. The credibility of this deterrent at EU level would be harmed if there were gaps in the network.

—Public authorities are both impartial and accountable in the way that they operate to defend the public interest. This is an important reassurance for traders. Private bodies are not so accountable. In order to ensure the accountable operation of the regulation, the mutual assistance rights provided in the regulation should therefore only be entrusted to public authorities. In addition, private bodies are primarily concerned, given their organisation along national lines, with consumers in their own country rather than other consumers in the EU

—The effectiveness of the enforcement network established in the proposal depends upon the reciprocal rights and obligations of mutual assistance. ... This reciprocity can only be guaranteed by equivalent public authorities in each Member State.

—Given that a large majority of the Member States recognise the value of a public dimension to their enforcement systems, the creation of a network of public authorities at EU level is an important element in overcoming reluctance to apply the principles of maximum harmonisation to consumer protection laws. Reassuring the Member States that consumers will be protected by equally effective public authorities when shopping cross-border will make inclusion of maximum harmonisation in a directive on unfair commercial practices and future consumer legislation more acceptable.

—The prospect of enlargement demands action to safeguard consumer interests in an enlarged internal market. Most of the new Member States do not have a long tradition of consumer protection enforcement, although they have established public authorities. The proposed regulation is therefore an opportunity to ensure that effective enforcement is in place throughout the new internal market.

Cristina Poncibo discusses the experience of the co-operation network (Poncibo, 2012). The network has not realised its potential partly because of fragmentation among EU 'networks of consumer protection, namely: the European Consumer Centres Network (ECC-Net), Fin-net' … and because member states often allocate a number of bodies as competent authorities. National authorities may not devote sufficient resources to the network and in some cases do not actively use the system (see EU, 2009) and although the network 'has been given lofty tasks', it has 'few powers and resources'. She also notes that the activities of the CPC and the Competition network are 'not well controlled within the EU democratic and political framework, nor are their activities subject to legal review by the EU courts'. The EU reported in 2012 on the operation of the networks

Report from the Commission to the European Parliament and the Council on the application of Regulation (EC) 2006/2004 of the European Parliament and of the Council of 27 October 2004 on cooperation between national authorities responsible for the enforcement of consumer protection laws (the Regulation on consumer protection cooperation) COM(2012) 100 final

The national reports … give some evidence that the efficiency (and thus also the effectiveness) of the Network may be suffering from resource constraints in authorities.

2.5. The CPC Committee

During the reference period the Committee met between 3 and 4 times per year. … The Committee plays a central role for the CPC Network. It provides in particular, a platform for discussion of trends in consumer protection; contributes to developing a common approach in enforcement within the CPC Network through the endorsement of common standards and guidelines … and gives operational orientations to the CPC Network in the form of annual Enforcement Action Plans. The Enforcement Action Plans focuses on the common activities carried out by the Network, such as its annual internet checks, the 'sweeps'.

3. THE CPC NETWORK: MANY IMPROVEMENTS BUT STILL A LONG WAY AHEAD

Overall the Network has handled an amount of cases that is comparable to the previous reference period, ie roughly 540 requests for either information or to take enforcement measures in order to stop a detected infringement. The number of alerts however significantly decreased, ie the number of unilateral messages that are sent by one authority to other concerned authorities to warn about an infringement to consumer laws that was detected or which it has reasonable grounds to suspect.

In terms of the directives infringed, breaches to the provisions on misleading and/or other deceptive advertising practices, covered by Directive 2005/29/EC on unfair commercial practices are the most common type of breaches handled by the Network, followed by breaches to the provisions of the e-commerce Directive.

Since the beginning, most of cases handled by the Network relate to practices that use on-line means of advertising: in 2010 45% of the information requests referred to messages targeting consumers by e-mail, text messages or the internet. The equivalent figure for enforcement requests increases to 77%. This is partially due to the annual "sweeps" carried out by the CPC-Network. ...

3.2. General assessment

The reference period of the present report can be summarised as one of stabilisation and consolidation of the Network's activities, despite the constraints reported by authorities due to the difficult economic and financial environment in which they had to operate. This is the general conclusion that derives from the Member States' Biennial reports and the Commission's own experience in monitoring the Network.

... The CPC Network has moreover developed a solid core of joint activities in addition to the bilateral enforcement cooperation. This joint work aims at giving a new EU- wide dimension to enforcement and ultimately at enhancing consumer protection in the internal market. In the past two years, this common enforcement work has become an integral part of the Network's activities. The internet inquiries the Network carries out every year, ie the 'sweeps', are the central element of this work. They produce concrete results for consumers through the common enforcement phase during which the authorities follow up on detected breaches to ensure compliance. ... The Network's recent evolution can partly be explained by the fact that authorities have learnt in the past two years to cooperate through the Network, i.e. become (more) familiar with the cooperation mechanisms introduced by the CPC Regulation and the IT-tool developed by the Commission for the information exchanges of the Network.

The trend however also shows, as highlighted in many of the national Biennial reports, that the measures undertaken to address the shortcomings identified in 2009 in the first Biennial Report have produced positive results.

Training needs have been met more effectively since a training plan is established every year with the authorities. ...

The planning of common activities (and thus of resources) through the adoption of annual Enforcement Action Plans provides a sound, structured and transparent programming process. These plans contribute to identifying the areas of common interest and comprise all the common activities carried out by the Network in addition to the hard core (generally bilateral) enforcement cooperation.

The production of guidance documents has helped to develop more of a common understanding about how to cooperate within the CPC Network. ... The workshops that have been regularly organised since 2009 offer an additional opportunity for authorities to exchange views, best practise and so work towards reaching a common understanding and/or approach to enforcement. ...

Whilst the CPC Network has undeniably consolidated its activities in the past two years, there is also clear evidence that the network has yet to reach its full potential. There are still a few Member States that have never issued a request for mutual assistant (or only an alert) and a non negligible number that has dealt with fewer than 5 requests all types comprised. As things stand, a maximum of 9 Member States can be considered to have been using the system actively since the beginning.

3.3. The CPC-Network: further efforts needed

More work is in particular needed in the areas described below.

The number of authorities that do not actively use the cooperation mechanisms established by the CPC Regulation remains significant. This applies in particular to the enforcement of the sectoral legislation listed in the CPC Regulation's annex but not exclusively. As highlighted in the first Biennial Report, the existence of parallel networks in these areas may have had an impact on the CPC Network effectiveness but this still needs to be confirmed. Moreover many consumer authorities in Member States seldom use the CPC Network. ...

There is no uniform understanding about how to use the cooperation tools established by the Regulation despite the development of commonly agreed rules and guidance documents. Partial knowledge of the rules and a certain lack of discipline in applying them are factors in this context (eg few authorities provide regular feedback on the progress made in their investigative and enforcement activities as established) but there are also more fundamental divergences that stand in the way of a more efficient use of the CPC mechanisms. In particular for the alerts, where there no common approach among authorities about how and when to use them, as well as the requests for enforcement measures, for which authorities have (very) different standards of legal analysis and evidence.

There is no common approach to the Network's enforcement priorities. ... The Network has not succeeded in developing a "corporate identity" and remains mostly a virtual network linked by a common IT-tool. Contacts between case- handlers if not related to the dealings of a given case remain the exception and could perhaps explain why the Network has never used the forum in the CPC-System. Language barriers are likely to play a role in this context but do not suffice to explain the absence of exchanges between authorities.

Some horizontal issues, many of them already identified in the 2009 Biennial report, also continue to affect the CPC Network:

- The differences in national consumer legislation in the EU contribute to lengthening the proceedings and add complexities to cooperation as authorities must first verify whether cooperation can be envisaged and to what extent.
- The issue of applicable law continues to split the Network; new questions have now arisen in the framework of the workshops dedicated to this topic in terms of the applicable law and the national procedural rules.
- Little is communicated about the Network's successful cases, even inside the Network and this might be generating the perception that the network may not be meeting expectations. At the same time authorities are reluctant to share this type of information: only a couple of national biennial reports include examples of successful cases although this was part of the agreed common structure.
- Different views have emerged regarding the role the Commission should have in the framework of enforcement cooperation.

6

Standard Form Consumer Contracts and the Search for Fairness

> I think we all start with a general predisposition in favour of freedom of contract. (Lord Morris of Borth-y-Gest, *Official Reports* HL, vol 383 col II 10, 23 May 1976 (debate on the Unfair Contract Terms Act))

> The freedom was all on the side of the big concern. ... The big concern said, 'Take it or leave it'. The little man had no option but to take it. (Lord Denning MR in *George Mitchell v Finney Lock Seeds Ltd* [1983] 1 AER 109 at 113)

A central issue in consumer law has concerned the regulation of the fairness of the terms of consumer contracts—which are often standard form contracts. This chapter outlines the rationales for such regulation, and discusses judicial and administrative regulation of consumer contracts. I discuss and evaluate the performance of the OFT in regulating unfair terms under the Unfair Terms in Consumer Contracts Regulations 1999 that implement the EU Directive on Unfair Terms in Consumer Contracts (Directive 93/13). This chapter pursues general themes in the regulation of fairness that are explored in further detail concerning credit relationships in Chapter 7.

---

1. Rationales for regulation

1.1 Inequality of bargaining power

'Inequality of bargaining power' was during the 1960s and 1970s a recurring justification for the regulation of unfair terms. This seemed often to reflect the 'exploitation thesis'—the thesis that well-organised businesses impose take-it-or-leave-it terms upon individual consumers, and that consumers are unable to protect themselves against this power. The ECJ has argued that this approach underlies the system of protection introduced under the Unfair Terms in Consumer Contracts Directive:

> [T]he system of protection introduced by the Directive is based on the idea that the consumer is in a weak bargaining position vis-à-vis the seller or supplier, as regards both his bargaining power and his level of knowledge. This leads to the consumer agreeing to terms drawn up in advance by the seller or supplier without being able to influence the content of the terms. (*Oceano Grupo Editorial SA v Rocio Murciano Qintero* C-240 to C244/98, ECJ 2000)

This theme could be found in academic writings and policy documents, and often formed the inarticulate major premise for judicial decisions striking at unfair terms. An influential source for this theme was Friedrich Kessler's 'Contracts of Adhesion: Some Thoughts about Freedom of Contract' (1943). Although this article pre-dated the growth of the consumer movement, it expressed clearly the fears of later writers concerning the use of private contract as an instrument of corporate power. Kessler's article was influenced by Weber's writings on bureaucratic domination in modern society and by the Frankfurt School's vision of a new authoritarianism, implicit in the growth of large and impersonal private and public bureaucracies (Priest 1985: 484).

F Kessler, 'Contracts of Adhesion: Some Thoughts about Freedom of Contract' (1943), 43 *Columbia L Rev* 629 at 631–32, 640

> The development of large scale enterprise with its mass production and mass distribution made a new type of contract inevitable—the standardized mass contract. A standardized contract, once its contents have been formulated by a business firm, is used in every bargain dealing with the same product or service. The individuality of the parties which so frequently gave color to the old type contract has disappeared. The stereotyped contract of today reflects the impersonality of the market. ... It is to be noted that uniformity of terms of contracts typically recurring in a business enterprise is an important factor in the exact calculation of risks. Risks which are difficult to calculate can be excluded altogether. Unfor[e]seeable contingencies affecting performance, such as strikes, fire, and transportation difficulties can be taken care of. ... Standardized contracts have thus become an important means of excluding or controlling the 'irrational factor' in litigation. In this respect they are a true reflection of the spirit of our time with its hostility to irrational factors in the judicial process, and they belong in the same category as codifications and restatements.

> In so far as the reduction of costs of production and distribution thus achieved is reflected in reduced prices, society as a whole ultimately benefits from the use of standard contracts. And there can be no doubt that this has been the case to a considerable extent. The use of standard contracts has, however, another aspect which has become increasingly important. Standard contracts are typically used by enterprises with strong bargaining power. The weaker party, in need of the goods or services, is frequently not in a position to shop around for better terms, either because the author of the standard contract has a monopoly (natural or artificial) or because all competitors use the same clauses. His contractual intention is but a subjection more or less voluntary to terms dictated by the stronger party, terms whose consequences are often understood only in a vague way, if at all. Thus, standardized contracts are frequently contracts of adhesion; they are *a prendre ou a laisser*. ... [S]tandardized contracts have also been used to control and regulate the distribution of goods from producer all the way down to

the ultimate consumer. They have become one of the many devices to build up and strengthen industrial empires. ...

... Freedom of contract enables enterprisers to legislate by contract and, what is even more important, to legislate in a substantially authoritarian manner without using the appearance of authoritarian forms.

The image of the lone consumer subject to the power of the large corporation was reinforced by an article by David Slawson. He argued that the standard-form consumer contract is essentially undemocratic 'private legislation', imposed upon consumers by large private organisations. After noting that 'standard form contracts probably account for more than ninety-nine percent of all the contracts now made', he concluded (Slawson, 1971: 529) that the overwhelming proportion of standard forms are 'not democratic because they are not, under any reasonable test, the agreement of the consumer ... recipient to whom they are delivered. ... The form may be part of an offer which the consumer has no reasonable alternative but to accept.'

This was reflected in judicial attitudes toward standard form consumer contracts. For example, Lord Reid commented in 1967 as follows on terms in standard-form consumer contracts:

> In the ordinary way the customer has no time to read them, and if he did read them he would probably not understand them. And if he did understand and object to any of them, he would generally be told he could take it or leave it. And if he then went to another supplier the result would be the same. Freedom to contract must surely imply some choice or room for bargaining. (*Suisse Atlantique Societe d'Armement Maritime SA v Rotterdamshce Kolen Zentrale* [1967] 1 AC 361)

It appeared from these views that the freedom of consumers to negotiate contracts was dead in consumer transactions and that the law must ensure an optimal level of risk allocation between consumer, retailer and manufacturer. This was the theme of Jolowicz, writing in 1970:

> Regulation must not depend on the niceties of privity of contract or contract and tort. ... [I]t is impossible for the contract between buyer and seller, or for the rules of law which regard the consumer transaction as falling essentially within the law of contract, to produce a satisfactory allocation of the risks involved ... it is necessary ... that the law itself, not the contract between buyer and seller, should regulate the allocation of risk between the parties. (Jolowicz, 1970: 8)

The concept of inequality of bargaining power influenced the Molony Committee (above Chapter 1 at 1) and the Crowther Report on consumer credit (see below Chapter 7) which justified its consumer-protection proposals in terms of this concept, and the Molony Committee recommended a prohibition on 'contracting out' of the implied obligations under the Sale of Goods Act in terms of that concept.

Contracts of adhesion were objectionable because they seemed to reflect an underlying distribution of power and resources that 'offended our conception of distributive fairness' (Kronman, 1983: 771).

1.2 Neo-classical economic analysis and standard-form contracts

Economic analysis challenged the apparent pervasiveness of unfairness in standard-form consumer contracts. Michael Trebilcock, a noted law and economics scholar, comments that 'standard form contracts have suffered a bad press from both judicial and academic members of the legal fraternity over many years' (Trebilcock, 2003: 93). Neo-classical economists conceptualise inequality of bargaining power as attributable to two potential failures in the market for contract terms: monopoly or information failure. Thus Richard Posner argues that:

> [I]f one seller offers unattractive terms, a competing seller, wanting sales for himself, will offer more attractive terms. The process will continue until the terms are optimal. ... What is important is not whether there is haggling in every transaction but whether competition forces sellers to incorporate in their standard contracts terms that protect purchasers. (Posner, 2003: 116)

To substantiate these failures it is necessary to investigate the market for product terms rather than focusing on the individual transaction. This conclusion suggests that the issue of unfairness in standard form consumer contracts is an issue of market regulation and the focus of analysis the extent of competition in the market for product terms. This approach has implications for the approach to regulation since it raises questions about the capability of courts to conduct a market-wide analysis.

MJ Trebilcock, 'Rethinking Consumer Protection Policy' in Rickett and Telfer (eds), *International Perspectives on Consumers' Access to Justice* (Cambridge, Cambridge University Press, 2003) 93–94

> I have argued ... that problems of unfairness, resulting from imperfect information, are not as severe as they might seem at first sight. To the extent that there is a margin of informed sophisticated and aggressive consumers in any given market, who understand the terms of the standard form contracts on offer and who either negotiate over these terms or switch their business readily to competing suppliers offering more favourable terms, this margin of sophisticated competitive shoppers may effectively discipline the entire market, so that inframarginal (less well informed, sophisticated or mobile) consumers can effectively free-ride on the discipline brought to the market by the marginal consumers. However, where suppliers are able either to term or performance discriminate between marginal and infra-marginal consumers, this generalized discipline will be undermined, and there is a clear risk that the inframarginal consumers will be exploited on account of their imperfect information as to the contract terms.

V Goldberg, 'Institutional Change and the Quasi-Invisible Hand' (1974) 17 *Journal of Law & Economics* 461, 483–87

> Suppose, however, that rather than view the standard form contract as a voluntary agreement, we view it instead as private legislation; the legislature in effect delegates the lawmaking process to private parties. The previous analysis suggests the bias that this 'legislation' might have. We will first stipulate that we are interested here only in the 'hidden' terms of the contract—those beside the basic price and quantity terms. While such terms could be tailor made for each contract, there are substantial economies to be gained by spreading the costs of producing (and analyzing the impact of) these terms over a large number of contracts.

The firm, which regularly enters into the same type of transactions, will be able to achieve these economies (either by itself or by purchasing the service from specialists—lawyers); the consumer, generally, will not. The standard form contract therefore will be legislation produced in an arena which rewards the resources held by one party—the firm. The result, in Llewellyn's words 'has seemed even in such highly competitive spheres as installment sales, residence leases, investments, and commercial banking to be … [the] accumulation of seller protective instead of customer-protective clauses.'

We might expect competition in the market to constrain the firm's power in this arena. After all, the firm makes its price in this arena too, and if the industry is reasonably competitive we would expect that this competition would shield the price taker from the firm's power. Why will not competition among producers protect the contract term taker as well? The answer is twofold. On the one hand the cost of acquiring and processing information on contract terms is much greater than for price; unless the firm intentionally makes the particular term an important selling point—as is sometimes the case with the length or inclusiveness of the warranty —few, if any, customers will perceive the existence of variations in terms. Any movement toward contractual equilibrium due to the aggressive bargain-seeking of a few customers will be slow indeed due to both (1) the fewness of customers who will find it worthwhile to pay the costs of acquiring information, and (2) the ease with which a producer can 'contract term discriminate'—renegotiate the terms for the few aggressive customers while keeping the high information barrier for other customers virtually intact. The second answer is that the 'aggressive bargain-seeking customer' is usually just a minor figure in the equilibrating process. More important, in general, is the role of new entry (or exit) of producers. If the firms in an industry are making profits because they have written standardized contract terms that are very favorable to them, they will attract new entrants into the industry. The entry will continue until excess profits are bid away. The benefits to the firms of the standardized terms will be capitalized into the firms' value. Thus, while competition between producers will in the long run yield zero profits, the firm will be able to attain a capital gain (or prevent a capital loss) by choosing the appropriate standard contract terms.

This does not necessarily mean, however, that the industry as a whole will be better off or that the industry's gains will come at the expense of the consumer. It might well be that the equilibrium terms arrived at are optimal for both producers and consumers, but there is no reason to presume this to be true. Consider, for example, the following scenario. Assume a competitive insurance industry with minimal government intervention. Firms in the industry compete by lowering their price and then compensate for this by decreasing the coverage (in as hidden a way as possible) with other firms being forced to cut also in order to remain competitive. A sort of 'Gresham's Law' of bad policies driving out good would ensue. Both the quality of insurance contracts and the total sales of the industry are likely to fall.

This is not the end of the story. Both producers and consumers will have incentives to search for methods for improving upon this result. Ignoring solutions relying on an active government … a number of solutions might arise. Brand names and advertising might be used as indicators of product quality in general (including the terms of the contract); consumers might take price as an indicator of quality; or private producers of information might appear. While such private marker solutions will, to some extent, ameliorate the Gresham's Law problem considered in the previous paragraph, there is no reason to believe that the market will negate the standard form contract problem.

If the government's role is restricted to passive enforcement of private contracts, then there will be many standard form contract terms produced which are, in effect, legislation produced by a single party. The consumer need not necessarily suffer as a result, but his protection by market forces will in many instances be weak. Indeed, if we could argue that standard forms inevitably led to the enrichment of producers at the expense of consumers, the task of our social engineer would be considerably simplified. But this is not the case. In some instances all parties will benefit from the standard forms while in others all parties will be hurt. In many instances some consumers will benefit while others will be harmed. ... Thus, the social engineer faces problems in identifying situations in which parties are likely to be helped by intervention and a further set of problems in balancing the anticipated benefits to some groups against the losses of others.

1.3 Behavioural economics and standard-form contracts

Goldberg's argument that competition may not necessarily result in a mix of terms that match consumer preferences is reinforced by the literature on behavioural economics (see above Chapter 2) (see further Faure and Luth, 2011: 357). Consumers may be limited in their ability to process information (information overload), and only pay attention to 'salient' terms such as price and warranty terms. Behavioural economics confirms the limits of consumer search in relation to subsidiary terms in consumer contracts (see Korobkin, 2003: 1203). Consumers are also over-optimistic and may underestimate certain risks (such as the probability of defaulting on their obligations). These biases exist throughout the population and are not restricted to conventional classifications of vulnerable consumers in law ('widows and orphans'). For example, Stefano Della Vigna and Ulrike Malmender in an empirical study of health-club attendance found that consumers joining health clubs chose a contract that was suboptimal given their subsequent attendance frequency. Consumers could choose between a monthly contract, an annual contract and a pay-per-visit option. The monthly contract was automatically renewed from month to month, whereas the annual contract expired unless the consumer renewed. The researchers found that consumers who chose a monthly membership paid 70 per cent more than if they had chosen the pay-per-visit option. In addition, those on monthly contracts were more likely to stay enrolled for more than one year than those choosing the annual contract. They explained their findings as based on overconfidence. 'Consumers overestimate, for example, their future self-control or their future efficiency in pursuing costly activities. This leads to overestimation of attendance and of cancellation in automatically renewed contracts' (Della Vigna and Malmender, 2006: 695). This finding also suggests that offering consumers a choice of term will not always lead to the optimal contract being chosen. This behavioural approach was adopted in *OFT v Ashbourne Investments* (see below).

The health-club example illustrates the nature of many consumer service contracts. Individuals may have different preferences and have to predict their future use of the service. Sellers offer a variety of packages but this choice does not reduce the possibility that consumers may choose suboptimal packages and that sellers may be able to exploit consumers' misperceptions. This type of contract differs from the standardised consumer product where we might expect marginal consumers to police the market and the possibility of significant interpersonal learning by consumers (Bar-Gill, 2008). The ability of sellers to exploit consumer misperceptions about their use of a service will be higher in relation to non-standardised products. Because consumers may have behavioural biases about their use of a service (eg a credit card) new entrants to an industry that do not exploit biases may face high costs in securing a significant market share.

The market may not therefore necessarily correct itself . The potential detriment caused by this is illustrated in Bar-Gill's analysis of credit card pricing (above Chapter 2).

Behavioural economics underlines the difficulties of establishing what counts as an 'autonomous choice' and the existence of time-inconsistent preferences. Recognising that we may often be 'multiple selves', the preservation of the future autonomy of a consumer may often provide a reason for regulation.

The extreme case of *Horwoods v Millar's Timber and Trading* (1917), where a contract of loan was struck down because an individual was shackled to a moneylender and not permitted to move house, change job, deal with any of his unencumbered furniture or raise money for the medical treatment of his family—so that Warrington J commented that: 'The man has put himself ... almost body and soul in the power of this money-lender ... even in the most trivial incidents of life'—illustrates the argument that mandatory rules in relation to credit default may be justified in protecting the future freedom or autonomy of the consumer (see discussion below on consumer credit). The difficulties of addressing present biases through the provision of pre-contractual information or cooling off periods may justify substantive regulation of terms. For example, the ability to declare bankruptcy in the event of over-indebtedness is a mandatory term of all consumer credit contracts which responds to problems of overoptimism and underestimation of risk.

1.4 Understanding the role of standard-form contracts in corporate relationships with consumers

A final strand in the debate on standard-form consumer contracts has been their link to the growth of bureaucracy in modern life. Some implications of this were noted by Rakoff.

T Rakoff, 'Contracts of Adhesion: An Essay in Reconstruction' (1983) 96 *Harvard L Rev* 1174 at 1222

> The Form and the Firm—The use of standard form documents to govern relations with the external market is only one aspect of the institutional dynamic. Modern business firms are typically organized by departments and through hierarchies. The characteristics of such firms counsel the adoption of standard forms and rigidify allegiance to them.

> Form documents promote efficiency within a complex organizational structure. First, the standardization of terms, and of the very forms on which they are recorded, facilitates co-ordination among departments. The costs of communicating special understandings rise rapidly when one department makes the sale, another delivers the goods, a third-handles collections, and a fourth fields complaints. Standard terms make it possible to process transactions as a matter of routine; standard forms, with standard blank spaces, make it possible to locate rapidly whatever deal has been struck on the few customized items. Second, standardization makes possible the efficient use of expensive managerial and legal talent. Standard forms facilitate the diffusion to underlings of management's decisions regarding the risks the organization is prepared to bear, or make it unnecessary to explain these matters to subordinates at all. Third, the use of form contracts serves as an automatic check on the consequences of the acts of wayward sales personnel. The pressure to produce may tempt salesmen to make bargains into which the organization is unwilling to enter; the use of

standard form contracts to state the terms of the deal obviates much of the need for, and expense of internal control and discipline in this regard.

No less importantly, form documents help to solidify the organization's internal power structure. In private organizations, as in public bureaucracies, discretion is power—and this is true of discretion at the bottom of the hierarchy as well as at the top. As subordinates are given wider discretion, they become more difficult to discipline, because standards of performance are less clear. From the point of view of an organization that desires to maintain internal hierarchy, the most desirable salespeople are nearly interchangeable: they sell a standard product at a standard price on standard terms. When price is negotiable, the employee's status increases somewhat. If all terms were negotiable, a much greater degree of training and ability —and consequently of status and reward—would be required. Instead, the routinization of transactions through the use of standard forms reserves discretion for positions further up the organizational hierarchy.

Many of the terms often included in contracts of adhesion bear out this analysis. The flavor of hierarchy suffuses the common provisions disavowing an agent's authority to vary the terms of the document or stipulating that acceptance will occur only on approval by a superior or the home office. Clauses requiring that modifications be written or that notices be given in a specified manner seem designed in good part to accommodate bureaucratic office procedures. Even terms that appear to have quite independent purposes may have latent organizational functions as well. Apart from its obvious role in litigation, a clause transforming a vague legally implied term ('a reasonable time') into a precise one ('ten days') may simultaneously serve to inform subordinates of the decision made by managerial and legal personnel. Similarly, it has been suggested that one reason enterprises routinely disclaim liability for consequential damages is the difficulty of keeping track of the commercial special needs of the customer that are made relevant by the test of *Hadley v Baxendale*.

Socio-legal studies of consumer markets indicate that firms do not always in practice follow the literal terms of their standard form contracts. For example, many companies will offer 'no questions asked' refunds or exchanges. Firms may, as Rakoff argues, use standard-form contracts to retain discretion to distinguish between consumers in complaint handling. Indeed, some recent economic analysis argues that standard-form consumer contracts are best understood as two-part contracts: 'clear standard-form terms plus managerial discretion to renegotiate' (Johnston, 2006: 857). The fear of the 'opportunistic' consumer was reflected in Kessler's general argument that form contracts are a method of controlling risk. Firms also retain discretion in contracts to modify unilaterally the terms of consumer contracts. Given the existence of many long-term service contracts (credit card, utilities, mobile phones, etc) there are good reasons for the necessity of terms adjustment. However, the power to alter terms raises issues of fairness for consumers (Bar-Gill and Davis, 2010) and the appropriate technique for achieving fairness given the potential heterogeneity of consumer preferences. You should consider to what extent the role of the OFT (see discussion below) addresses the issues raised by corporate discretion in the application by corporations of their standard form consumer contracts.

2. Regulatory techniques

There are several approaches that might be adopted to regulate the supply and demand for contract terms. These include:

1. Information remedies: suppliers might be required to disclose relevant contract terms (see, for example, truth in lending, below Chapter 7), to present terms in a comprehensible manner (plain language legislation and see regulation 7 of the Unfair Terms in Consumer Contracts Regulations and the Consumer Protection from Unfair Trading Regulations 2008) or to provide consumers with opportunities to search for better terms (cooling-off legislation). Terminology might be standardized (eg the use of APR). Organisations might be subsidised to provide consumers with comparative price and term information and to educate consumers concerning their rights.
2. Default terms might be altered, for example, requiring consumers to affirmatively opt in to particular contract terms.
3. The detailed regulation of terms through administrative regulation, or the creation of inalienable rights (see sections 6–7 of the Unfair Contract Terms Act 1977) through bans on the use of particular types of terms.
4. The control of the supply of terms, directly through administrative pre-clearance (see Israeli Standard Form Contracts Act), or indirectly by licensing entry into a particular market (see Consumer Credit Act 1974, sections 21–25).
5. Negotiation of standard terms by a private or public consumer bargaining agent. (See below the role of the OFT.) This might include the development of model contracts.

The choice of approach must obviously depend on a mixture of factual and value judgements. For example, do studies of lower-income credit markets and buying behaviour suggest that required disclosures will lead to more competitive terms? Are there distributional reasons for banning the use of certain terms in these markets? Ought low-income credit consumers be permitted to contract on certain terms such as high levels of interest rates? These questions are pursued in the context of regulation of credit practices. In this section, I wish to address basic institutional choices in regulation: (1) Judicial control might be a central feature. This could be either through the application of common law or through legislative standards. (2) Administrative agencies, eg the OFT, might concretise general unfairness standards and act as a bargaining agent for consumers in the promotion of reasonable terms.

2.1 Judicial control

2.1.1 Consumer law and the materialisation of contract law

The development of control of unfair consumer terms in English law illustrates the materialisation and differentiation of contract law in the twentieth century (see Wieäcker, trans Weir, 1995: 431–41). Materialisation refers to the breakdown of the formal system of contract law as an autonomous system of law that assumed a basis of formal equality between contracting parties. The rise of the doctrine of 'fundamental breach' of contract as a method of addressing exemption clauses in consumer contracts illustrates this process of breakdown. Courts used the doctrine to strike down unfair terms but (apart from Lord Denning) maintained the myth of a freely bargained contract by justifying their decisions on the basis of the parties' intentions, namely that they had not intended the exemption clause to cover the particular breach. The result orientation in many of these cases provided little coherent doctrine and resulted in inappropriate use of the doctrine in situations where there was no unfairness (see eg *Harbutt's 'Plasticine' v Wayne Tank & Pump Co Ltd* (1970)).

Courts also used the doctrine of reasonable notice to police unfair terms, requiring that in unsigned contracts a consumer be given reasonable notice of terms in tickets or other contractual documents before entering the contract. This was based on the fiction that the consumer might then bargain over the terms. In a restatement of this doctrine the Court of Appeal in *Interfoto Picture Library Ltd v Stiletto Visual Programmes Ltd* (1989) indicated that onerous or unusual clauses would require very explicit notice such as a 'big red hand' as suggested by Lord Denning in *J Spurling Ltd v Bradshaw* (1956). The doctrine of reasonable notice did not apply to signed documents under the rule in *L'Estrange v Graucob* which states that in the absence misrepresentation, fraud or *non est factum*, an individual is bound by her signature and it is immaterial whether she has read the document. This rule has been rejected in some Commonwealth jurisdictions where reasonable notice is required in relation to onerous clauses in signed standard-term contracts (see *Tilden Rent-a-Car v Clendenning* (1978)). The use of the doctrine of reasonable notice was often a covert approach to addressing the issue of the unreasonableness of terms.

The English courts failed to develop a substantive theory of unreasonableness or unconscionability at common law. Lord Denning's articulation in *Lloyds Bank Ltd v Bundy* (1975) of a general concept of unconscionability representing a combination of unequal bargaining power and unfair terms was not taken up by later English cases although it has had substantial influence in Commonwealth countries.

The reluctance of the UK judiciary to articulate a general theory of unfairness in contract law may be explained partly by the power of the classical conception of freedom of contract as providing the organising framework for contracts and also a belief that regulation of contracts on the basis of fairness was a political decision that was most appropriately undertaken by the legislature. In contrast, in the US and Canada, the courts developed conceptions of unreasonableness and unfairness in contract law, partly because of the limited scope of legislative intervention (see eg Wilson J in *Hunter v Syncrude* (1989)). Bill Whitford notes that in the US there is 'far less legislation about contract law than is desirable … and [t]he principal relevance of the lack of significant American legislation in contract law is to justify a tradition of judicial activism in formulating rules of law' (Whitford, in Campbell, Collins and Wightman, 2003: 197).

The development of current legislative controls is outlined in the following Law Commission consultation document:

The Law Commission, *Unfair Terms in Contracts: A Consultation Paper* **(2002) 10–11**

The principal control over unfair terms has been legislative. Until 1994 these controls centred on exclusion and limitation of liability clauses.

2.11 The first statute invalidating such clauses in contracts is said to have been the Railways and Canal Traffic Act 1854. Over the years various other controls were also put in place, for example by the Hire Purchase Act 1938. Wider controls, even of exclusion and limitation of liability clauses, did not come until the 1970s. ... [T]he Supply of Goods (Implied Terms) Act 1973 ('SOGITA') prevented any sellers from excluding or restricting liability under section 12 of the SGA 1893 (seller's implied obligation as to title). In consumer sales sellers were prevented from excluding or restricting their liability under sections 13–15 of the SGA 1893 (merchantability, fitness for particular purpose and correspondence with description or sample); in other sales those liabilities could be excluded or restricted, but only to the extent that it could be shown to be fair and reasonable to allow reliance on the exclusion or restriction. [In 1977] UCTA ... incorporated, in slightly modified form, the controls in SOGITA. It also imposed wider controls over exclusions and limitations of 'business' liability both for breach of contract and for negligence in tort [delict]. Certain exclusions or restrictions are made absolutely ineffective and others are subjected to a test of reasonableness. The protection of UCTA applies both to transactions between a business and a consumer and to many business-to-business transactions, particularly where a business deals on its own written standard terms. Despite its title, UCTA applies only to exclusion and limitation of liability clauses, broadly defined, and to indemnity clauses in consumer contracts. Thus other types of term were not subject to any statutory control. Some types of contract, for example contracts of insurance, were exempted from the operation of UCTA. ... In 1993 the European Council of Ministers passed the Directive. This was implemented in the UK by the Unfair Terms in Consumer Contracts Regulations 1994 ('the 1994 Regulations'), now superseded by UTCCR [1999 and 2001].

2.1.2 Judicial control under UCTA

The Unfair Contract Terms Act 1977 (UCTA) introduced bright-line rules that voided exclusion clauses in relation to liability for physical injuries caused by negligence and consolidated the prohibition on contracting out of the implied terms in the supply of goods in sale and near-sale agreements. It also introduced a broad standard of unreasonableness to police exclusion and limitation of liability clauses in other consumer contracts (eg services) and business contracts.

Two cases illustrate judicial development of standards under the reasonableness test of UCTA. These are *Woodman v Photo Trade Processing Ltd* (1981) and *Smith v Eric Bush* (1990). *Woodman* was a case brought by an individual assisted and represented by the Consumers' Association. The arguments addressed to the court were, therefore, more comprehensive than in ordinary litigation. The plaintiff alleged that Photo Trade Processing Ltd (PTP) had negligently lost certain films which he had entrusted to Dixons, their agent, for processing. These included negatives of a friend's wedding which he had intended to present to his friend and which were, therefore, of some sentimental value. PTP did not dispute the loss but sought a defence to the breach of their implied obligation to exercise reasonable care by relying upon a clause in their contract which limited liability to the replacement of the lost film. The clause was contained in a notice, 4 inches square, exhibited on Dixons' shop-counter. It read:

All photographic materials are accepted on the basis that their value does not exceed the cost of the material itself. Responsibility is limited to the replacement of films. No liability will be accepted, consequential or otherwise, however caused.

PTP argued that this clause was reasonable. They pointed out that similar exclusion clauses were 'standard practice throughout the trade'. There were some specialist firms who would accept liability but the judge indicated that Mr Woodman had 'no realistic alternative'. The action was brought under section 2(2) of UCTA.

The judge held that the exclusion clause was unreasonable and awarded the consumer £75 damages for distress and disappointment. He relied on three arguments:

1. PTP, by adopting the same terms as the rest of the trade, offers its customers no choice;
2. Mr Woodman's attention was not drawn to the exclusion clause nor was he advised to insure; and
3. the exclusion clause was not reasonably necessary to protect PTP's competitive position in the trade. In addition, much was made of the fact that PTP should have operated a 'two-tier' system offering the consumer the alternative of extended coverage for a higher price.

Consider the evidence (market data, etc) used to establish the 'no choice' argument and the relevance of the nineteenth-century railway monopoly case. Are there questions of political legitimacy involved in judges' setting the trading terms for an industry?

Woodman v Photo Trade Processing Ltd (1981), Exeter County Court (unreported)

His Honour Judge Clarke … I now turn to consider the 'requirement of reasonableness' in relation to the clause in question. I was asked, particularly by Mr Meeke and to some extent by Mr Tench, if I found this particular clause to be unreasonable, to go further and suggest what type of clause would be reasonable. To some extent I must consider the reasonableness of alternatives in order to throw light upon the reasonableness of the clause in question. But I must stress that it is no part of my function to lay down what type of clause PTP should use. That must be for them to decide.

PTP argue that the clause they use is reasonable, and for the benefit of the public themselves, because it enable[s] them to operate a cheap mass-production technique. No evidence was adduced as to the extent of their cost savings as a result of the absence of claims and the absence of checking mechanisms to prevent loss, but I suspect that it amounts to more than the 'few pence' on every film suggested by Mr Tench. In these cost-conscious days I accept that a cheap mass-production service is desirable, and it is probably good enough for the vast majority of ordinary photographers who could well complain if they have to pay more in order to protect the interests of a minority whose pictures are of greater value.

The Act, however, does not require me to consider only what is reasonable for the majority of the public. I have to consider whether the term in this particular contract is fair and reasonable 'having regard to the circumstances which were, or ought reasonably to have been, known to or in the contemplation of the parties when the contract was made.' Dixons did not know what I would call the 'picture value' of Mr Woodman's photographs, but I conclude that it ought reasonably have been within their contemplation that:—

(1) His photographs might have a high 'picture value', and

(2) He might be entrusting the film to them because he had no alternative.

I was told that there are, as yet, no reported authorities on the Unfair Contract Terms Act itself; but I was referred to three cases which provide some guidance.

Firstly there is Peek v North Staffordshire Railway (1863 10 HLC 493), a decision on Section 7 of Railways and Canal Traffic Act 1854 which permitted transport undertakings to impose conditions limiting their liability if adjudged by a Court to be just and reasonable. The clause under scrutiny in that case excluded all liability for loss or injury to various categories of fragile goods 'unless declared and insured according to their value.' It is a clause less onerous to the customer than that in the present case to the extent that PTP excluded liability without any option of declaring and insuring a special risk. And yet the House of Lords found the North Staffordshire Railway clause to be unreasonable.

Three main reasons emerge for the decision in Peek's case;

1 because it excluded liability for the consequences of negligence as well as mere accident,

2 because the railway was in a monopoly situation which realistically forced the customer to agree to their terms of business, and

3 because the only alternatives offered to the customer were either total exclusion of liability or insurance at a fixed rate which the Court regarded as so exorbitant as to compel customers to accept exclusion of liability.

Peek[']s case is complicated, by the obligation laid upon common carriers to carry for reasonable remuneration; but it has strong bearing upon the present case because PTP, by adopting the same terms as the rest of the trade, also offers its customers no choice. The present case is also similar because of the exclusion of liability for negligence as well as accident, but I do not regard this feature with the same degree of horror as did the House of Lords in Peek's case. The mischief is the same in that the trader is enabled to drop his standards with impunity, but the pressures of public opinion upon traders to maintain standards are stronger than they were in 1863. Furthermore it must be less objectionable to exclude liability for negligence where the items are comparatively small in value. A common carrier may handle cargoes of immensely greater value than any photograph.

The exclusion clause in the present case is marginally more reasonable than that in Peek's case because it at least preserves liability for the 'tangible value' of the films. But it is less reasonable in that it offers no insurance facility whatever. Insurance is a matter that I am specifically required to consider by Section 11 (4) of the Act. No doubt PTP could insure, but in the circumstances of this particular trade where no claims are likely to be really heavy, it would be more reasonable to satisfy claims out of their resources boosted by increased charges to their customers.

If there is to be insurance, it would have to be remembered that only the customer knows the 'intangible value' of his films. A system could be devised whereby a customer discloses the insurance value of his films when he hands them in for processing, but I do not regard insurance as a requirement of reasonableness in the film processing trade. The customer cannot buy a replacement photograph with his insurance moneys. What he really wants is some assurance that the processor will take extra care not to lose his more precious pictures.

Next I was referred to Levison v Patent Steam Carpet Cleaning Co Ltd (1977) 3 AER 498, where Lord Denning, MR, anticipating the introduction of the Unfair Contract Terms Act, held that a limitation of liability clause was unreasonable because the cleaning company had not specifically drawn it to the attention of the customer and advised him to insure. Comparing that with the present case, Mr Woodman's attention was not specifically drawn to the exclusion clause, nor was he advised to procure his own insurance (not that insurance would readily be available to him in such circumstances).

Thirdly I was referred to Schroeder Music Publishing Co Ltd v Macauley (1974) 1 WLR 1308 where Lord Diplock, dealing with a contract alleged to be an unreasonable restraint of trade, posed as a test of fairness the question of 'whether the restrictions are both reasonably necessary for the protection of the legitimate interests of the promisee and commensurate with the benefits secured to the promisor under the contract.'

Applying that test to the present case, I think that PTP do have a legitimate interest in keeping their costs down in order to remain competitive in that trade. But it cannot be regarded as reasonably necessary to protect that interest by compelling everybody, including the few who have high value photographs, to take their chance with the PTP mass-production system. For the majority of customers the lower prices resulting from excluded liability may be a commensurate benefit, but even then the balance is uncertain because he does not know the extent of the risk he runs to get those lower prices.

No evidence was offered as to the frequency with which films are lost during the PTP process. However, on this particular contract with Mr Woodman the balance must be to his disadvantage because of the importance of his particular photographs.

I conclude therefore that the clause in question is unreasonable having regard to almost all the criteria mentioned in the three authorities I have referred to. I have also considered the criteria set out in Schedule 2 of the Act, but in the circumstances of this case they seem to add nothing new, except only to the extent that account should be taken of 'alternative means by which the customers' requirements could have been met.' It is the feasibility of those alternatives which I must now consider.

Mr Tench suggested three possible alternatives, one of which was that PTP should accept all liability for negligence but exclude it for 'mishap.' This would certainly be reasonable from the customer's point of view, provided that the burden of proving 'mishap' falls upon PTP once the customer has proved the loss of films entrusted to them. But there would be few such 'mishaps' and in practice it would be virtually equivalent to the acceptance of full liability. As such I think it leans unreasonably against PTP.

A further suggestion by Mr Tench was that there should be some standardised level of compensation for the loss of 'picture-value' in every case. For example, 10 times the film cost or processing cost. I was referred to the 'Code of Practice for the Photographic Industry', and paragraph 47 of that code states 'The Consumer may be informed of the reasonable compensation offered in the event of a film being lost or damaged by the processor or retailer.' This appears to envisage some sort of pre-arranged formula for compensation (another example of which is paragraph 76 which suggests a 'refund' as appropriate where developing and printing work is considered unsatisfactory because of an irreparable defect). However, I do not think that such a sy[s]tem, by itself, can be fair and reasonable in this trade because of the degree of uniformity in film costs and processing charges. In some industries servicing charges vary widely according to the delicacy or amount of work needing to be done, and in those instances compensation calculated as a multiple of servicing charges would achieve a sort of rough justice. But photographic film is reasonably uniform in price, and the developing and printing process is more or less uniform in cost. Compensation as a multiple of either figure would therefore also fall within a narrow range, and what is fair to the bulk of customers would be less than fair to a minority.

The Code of Practice appears to recognise this difficulty in that paragraph 49 adds a further recommendation for the benefit of that minority. This paragraph reads:

'The Retailer will advise the laboratory if an order being placed for processing is of exceptional value or importance, before the order is accepted, provided he has been informed by the consumer. There may be a special service combined with a higher price.'

The authors of the Code therefore do envisage the need for additional care in some cases, and it is that element that is totally lacking in the PTP terms of business. The so-called 'Special Service' was Mr Tench's third suggestion. He called it a 'two-tier System' of a normal service with total exclusion of liability and a special service at a higher charge with full acceptance of liability.

Even if such a special service were to provide for a standardised level of compensation at an appropriately high level to suit the needs of the minority, such a system has all the benefits to the customer of giving him a choice. It presents him with an alternative where he can reasonably expect more than normal care to be taken of his photographs.

But it is not necessarily the case that PTP should have to set up such a special service for themselves. If Mr Meeke is right and specialised laboratories do exist who accept liability and who are accessible to the general public, then PTP only have to refer their customers who want it to that laboratory. Such a system would certainly require that the choice be brought to the attention of all customers. Furthermore the Special Service option would have to be identified (ie name and address) and made convenient so that the customer is not indirectly compelled to accept the normal service.

Not many customers would opt for such a special service at a higher price (although MrWoodman might well have been among that few if he had had the option) and I conclude that it would still leave ample scope for PTP to continue its low-cost mass production technique for ordinary holiday photography.

In the light of the Code of Practice I reach the conclusion that some such form of two-tier system is not only reasonable but practicable. Accordingly PTP (on whom the burden lies under Section 11(5) of the Act) have failed to persuade me that the clause which they applied to Mr Woodman's contract satisfies the statutory test of reasonableness. It remains for me to consider the question of damages.

It seems to me that the disappointment and distress suffered by Mr Woodman was quite exceptional and yet well within the range of what was foreseeable to PTP. I would not differ from the view of the Learned Registrar that the sum of £75 is appropriate.

The photo-processing industry is very competitive. Is it clear, therefore, why retailers should be under an obligation to make available particular facilities for the occasional situation such as Mr Woodman's? Do most consumers assume that photo-processors are not liable for sentimental losses, so that it is difficult to see this case as one of 'unfair surprise'? The argument that the customer had 'no choice' seems contradicted by the fact that Mr Woodman could have used a firm subscribing to the photographic industry's code of practice. Hugh Beale argues that:

[T]his case seems an example of the court attempting to impose its view of what would be reasonable, rather than striking down what is unreasonable. It is entirely appropriate for the Office of Fair Trading to negotiate such an improvement, but is it appropriate for a court to decide that a business ought to offer two levels of service with the higher costs that this will entail, given the relatively minor nature of the plaintiff's loss? It seems particularly odd for a court to do this when the clause is well-known and easy to understand and where there is fierce competition in the relevant industry. (Beale, 1986: 136)

However, two further points may be made. Individuals may underestimate the risk that a photo-processing company may lose the film and not focus on this issue at the time of contracting. In addition, the photo-processing company is a repeat player and has better knowledge of the risks than the consumer. These considerations weigh in favour of some obligation being placed on the business to either offer two levels of service or to provide prominent warnings. You should compare the approach of the court with that of the OFT below in relation to limitation of liability clauses (see below 3.1).

Smith v Eric Bush (a firm) **[1990] 1 AC 831**

This case concerned the liability in negligence of a valuer appointed by a building society to value a house in the situation where the valuer knows that the valuation will be relied on by the prospective purchaser and mortgagor. In this case the prospective purchasers had applied to the Abbey National for a mortgage. Abbey National were required by statute to obtain a report and valuation of the property and the purchasers paid an inspection fee of £36.89. The application form contained the following notice:

> I accept that the society will provide me with a copy of the report and mortgage valuation which the society will obtain in relation to this application. I understand that the society is not the agent of the surveyor or firm of surveyors and that I am making no agreement with the surveyor or firm of surveyors. I understand that neither the society nor the surveyor or the firm of surveyors will warrant, represent or give any assurance to me that the statements, conclusions and opinions expressed or implied in the report and mortgage evaluation will be accurate or valid and the surveyor's report will be supplied without any acceptance of responsibility on their part to me.

The report indicated that 'no essential repairs' were required. In reliance on the report the purchasers obtained an advance of £3,500 and purchased the property for £18,000. Eighteen months later, bricks from the chimney collapsed and fell through the roof, causing substantial damage assessed at £4,379.97 to the first floor of the house. The House of Lords upheld the findings of the lower courts that the valuer was liable to the purchasers in negligence. The further issues were whether the UCTA applied to the disclaimer clause, and, if so, whether the disclaimer satisfied the test of reasonableness under the Act. The House of Lords concluded that the UCTA did apply and that the disclaimer was unreasonable.

> Lord Griffiths: [The] facts [of this case] are similar to hundreds of thousands of house purchases that take place every year. It concerns the purchase of a house at the lower end of the market with the assistance of finance provided by a building society. The purchaser applies for finance to the building society. The building society is required by statute to obtain a valuation of the property before it advances any money (see s 13 of the Building Societies Act 1986). This requirement is to protect the depositors who entrust their savings to the building society. The building society therefore requires the purchaser to pay a valuation fee to cover or, at least, to defray the cost of obtaining a valuation. This is a modest sum and certainly much less than the cost of a full structural survey, in the present case it was £36.89. If the purchaser pays the valuation fee, the building society instructs a valuer who inspects the property and prepares a report for the building society giving his valuation of the property. The inspection carried out is a visual one designed to reveal any obvious defects in the property which must be taken into account when comparing the value of the property with other similar properties in the neighbourhood. If the valuation shows that the property

provides adequate security for the loan, the building society will lend the money necessary for the purchaser to go ahead, but prior to its repeal by the Building Societies Act 1986 would send to the purchaser a statutory notice pursuant to s 30 of the Building Societies Act 1962 to make clear that by making the loan it did not warrant that the purchase price of the property was reasonable.

Mrs Smith did not obtain a structural survey of the property. She relied upon the valuer's report to reveal any obvious serious defects in the house she was purchasing. It is common ground that she was behaving in the same way as the vast majority of purchasers of modest houses. They do not go to the expense of obtaining their own structural survey, they rely on the valuation to reveal any obvious serious defects and take a chance that there are no hidden defects that might be revealed by a more detailed structural survey.

The valuer's report said 'the property has been modernised to a fair standard ... no essential repairs are required' and it valued the property at £16,500. If reasonable skill and care had been employed when the inspection took place, it would have revealed that as a result of removing the chimney breasts in the rooms the chimneys had been left dangerously unsupported. Unaware of this defect and relying on the valuer's report, Mrs. Smith bought the house for £18,000 with the assistance of a loan of £3,500 from the building society.

After she had been living in the house for about 18 months, one of the chimney flues collapsed and crashed through the bedroom ceiling and floor causing damage for which Mrs. Smith was awarded £4,379.97 against the surveyors who had carried out the valuation.

Mr Hague, on behalf of the surveyors, conceded that on the facts of this case the surveyors owed a duty of care to Mrs. Smith unless they were protected by the disclaimer of liability. ...

At common law, whether the duty to exercise reasonable care and skill is founded in contract or tort, a party is as a general rule free, by the use of appropriate wording, to exclude liability for negligence in discharge of the duty. The disclaimer of liability in the present case is prominent and clearly worded and on the authority of *Hedley Byrne & Co Ltd v Heller & Partners Ltd*, [1964] AC 465, insofar as the common law is concerned effective to exclude the surveyors' liability for negligence. The question then is whether the Unfair Contract Terms Act 1977 bites upon such a disclaimer. In my view it does.

The Court of Appeal, however, accepted an argument based upon the definition of negligence contained in s 1(1) of the Act of 1977 which provides:

> 'For the purposes of this part of this Act, "negligence" means the breach—(a) of any obligation, arising from the express or implied terms of a contract, to take reasonable care or exercise reasonable skill in the performance of the contract; (b) of any common law duty to take reasonable care or exercise reasonable skill (but not any stricter duty); (c) of the common duty of care imposed by the Occupiers' Liability Act 1957 or the Occupiers' Liability Act (Northern Ireland) 1957.'

They held that, as the disclaimer of liability would at common law have prevented any duty to take reasonable care arising between the parties, the Act had no application. In my view this construction fails to give due weight to the provisions of two further sections of the Act. Section 11(3) provides:

> 'In relation to a notice (not being a notice having contractual effect), the requirement of reasonableness under this Act is that it should be fair and reasonable to allow reliance on it, having regard to all the circumstances obtaining when the liability arose or (but for the notice) would have arisen.'

And s 13(1):

'To the extent that this part of this Act prevents the exclusion or restriction of any liability it also prevents—(a) making the liability or its enforcement subject to restrictive or onerous conditions; (b) excluding or restricting any right or remedy in respect of the liability, or subjecting a person to any prejudice in consequence of his pursuing any such right or remedy; (c) excluding or restricting rules of evidence or procedure; and (to that extent) ss 2 and 5 to 7 also prevent excluding or restricting liability by reference to terms and notices which exclude or restrict the relevant obligation or duty.'

I read these provisions as introducing a 'but for' test in relation to the notice excluding liability. They indicate that the existence of the common law duty to take reasonable care, referred to in s 1(1)(b), is to be judged by considering whether it would exist 'but for' the notice excluding liability. The result of taking the notice into account when assessing the existence of a duty of care would result in removing all liability for negligent misstatements from the protection of the Act. It is permissible to have regard to the second report of the Law Commission on Exemption Clauses (Law Com No 69) which is the genesis of the Unfair Contract Terms Act 1977 as an aid to the construction of the Act. Paragraph 127 of that report reads:

'Our recommendations in this part of the report are intended to apply to exclusions of liability for negligence where the liability is incurred in the course of a person's business. We consider that they should apply even in cases where the person seeking to rely on the exemption clause was under no legal obligation (such as a contractual obligation) to carry out the activities. This means that, for example, conditions attached to a licence to enter on to land, and disclaimers of liability made where information or advice is given, should be subject to control. ...'

I have no reason to think that Parliament did not intend to follow this advice and the wording of the Act is, in my opinion, apt to give effect to that intention. This view of the construction of the Act is also supported by the judgment of Slade, LJ, in *Phillips Products Ltd v Hyland (Note)*, [1987] 1 WLR 659, when he rejected a similar argument in relation to the construction of a contractual term excluding negligence.

Finally, the question is whether the exclusion of liability contained in the disclaimer satisfies the requirement of reasonableness provided by s 2(2) of the Act of 1977. The meaning of reasonableness and the burden of proof are both dealt with in s 11(3) which provides:

'In relation to a notice (not being a notice having contractual effect), the requirement of reasonableness under this Act is that it should be fair and reasonable to allow reliance on it, having regard to all the circumstances obtaining when the liability arose or (but for the notice) would have arisen.'

It is clear, then, that the burden is upon the surveyor to establish that in all the circumstances it is fair and reasonable that he should be allowed to rely upon his disclaimer of liability.

I believe that it is impossible to draw up an exhaustive list of the factors that must be taken into account when a judge is faced with this very difficult decision. Nevertheless, the following matters should, in my view, always be considered.

1. Were the parties of equal bargaining power. If the court is dealing with a one-off situation between parties of equal bargaining power the requirement of reasonableness would be more easily discharged than in a case such as the present where the disclaimer is imposed upon the purchaser who has no effective power to object.

2. In the case of advice would it have been reasonably practicable to obtain the advice from an alternative source taking into account considerations of costs and time. In the present case

it is urged on behalf of the surveyor that it would have been easy for the purchaser to have obtained his own report on the condition of the house, to which the purchaser replies, that he would then be required to pay twice for the same advice and that people buying at the bottom end of the market, many of whom will be young first-time buyers, are likely to be under considerable financial pressure without the money to go paying twice for the same service.

3. How difficult is the task being undertaken for which liability is being excluded. When a very difficult or dangerous undertaking is involved there may be a high risk of failure which would certainly be a pointer towards the reasonableness of excluding liability as a condition of doing the work. A valuation, on the other hand, should present no difficulty if the work is undertaken with reasonable skill and care. It is only defects which are observable by a careful visual examination that have to be taken into account and I cannot see that it places any unreasonable burden on the valuer to require him to accept responsibility for the fairly elementary degree of skill and care involved in observing, following-up and reporting on such defects. Surely it is work at the lower end of the surveyor's field of professional expertise.

4. What are the practical consequences of the decision on the question of reasonableness. This must involve the sums of money potentially at stake and the ability of the parties to bear the loss involved, which, in its turn, raises the question of insurance. There was once a time when it was considered improper even to mention the possible existence of insurance cover in a lawsuit. But those days are long past. Everyone knows that all prudent, professional men carry insurance, and the availability and cost of insurance must be a relevant factor when considering which of two parties should be required to bear the risk of a loss. We are dealing in this case with a loss which will be limited to the value of a modest house and against which it can be expected that the surveyor will be insured. Bearing the loss will be unlikely to cause significant hardship if it has to be borne by the surveyor but it is, on the other hand, quite possible that it will be a financial catastrophe for the purchaser who may be left with a valueless house and no money to buy another. If the law in these circumstances denies the surveyor the right to exclude his liability, it may result in a few more claims but I do not think so poorly of the surveyor's profession as to believe that the floodgates will be opened. There may be some increase in surveyor's insurance premiums which will be passed on to the public, but I cannot think that it will be anything approaching the figures involved in the difference between the Abbey National's offer of a valuation without liability and a valuation with liability discussed in the speech of my noble and learned friend, Lord Templeman. The result of denying a surveyor, in the circumstances of this case, the right to exclude liability, will result in distributing the risk of his negligence among all house purchasers through an increase in his fees to cover insurance, rather than allowing the whole of the risk to fall upon the one unfortunate purchaser.

I would not, however, wish it to be thought that I would consider it unreasonable for professional men in all circumstances to seek to exclude or limit their liability for negligence. Sometimes breathtaking sums of money may turn on professional advice against which it would be impossible for the adviser to obtain adequate insurance cover and which would ruin him if he were to be held personally liable. In these circumstances it may indeed be reasonable to give the advice upon a basis of no liability or possibly of liability limited to the extent of the adviser's insurance cover.

In addition to the foregoing four factors, which will always have to be considered, there is in this case the additional feature that the surveyor is only employed in the first place because the purchaser wishes to buy the house and the purchaser in fact provides or contributes to the surveyor's fees. No one has argued that if the purchaser had employed and paid the surveyor himself, it would have been reasonable for the surveyor to exclude liability for negligence, and the present situation is not far removed from that of a direct contract between the surveyor and the purchaser. The evaluation of the foregoing matters leads me to the clear conclusion that it would not be fair and reasonable for the surveyor to be permitted to exclude liability in the circumstances of this case. I would therefore dismiss this appeal.

It must, however, be remembered that this is a decision in respect of a dwelling house of modest value in which it is widely recognised by surveyors that purchasers are in fact relying on their care and skill. It will obviously be of general application in broadly similar circumstances. But I expressly reserve my position in respect of valuations of quite different types of property for mortgage purposes, such as industrial property, large blocks of flats or very expensive houses. In such cases it may well be that the general expectation of the behaviour of the purchaser is quite different. With very large sums of money at stake prudence would seem to demand that the purchaser obtain his own structural survey to guide him in his purchase and, in such circumstances with very much larger sums of money at stake, it may be reasonable for the surveyors valuing on behalf of those who are providing the finance either to exclude or limit their liability to the purchaser.

Counsel for the valuers had argued that: (1) the exclusion clause is clear and understandable and reiterated and is forcefully drawn to the attention of the purchaser; (2) the purchaser's solicitors should reinforce the warning and should urge the purchaser to appreciate that he cannot rely on a mortgage valuation and should obtain and pay for his own survey; (3) if valuers cannot disclaim liability they will be faced with more claims from purchasers some of which will be unmeritorious but difficult and expensive to resist; (4) a valuer will become more cautious, take more time and produce more gloomy reports which will make house transactions more difficult; and (5) if a duty of care cannot be disclaimed the cost of negligence insurance for valuers and therefore the cost of valuation fees to the public will be increased. Lord Templeman commented on these arguments as follows:

> [A]ll these submissions are, in my view, inconsistent with the ambit and thrust of the Act of 1977. The valuer is a professional man who offers his services for reward. He is paid for those services. The valuer knows that 90 percent of purchasers in fact rely on the mortgage valuation. If a purchaser obtains a second valuation the sale may go off and then both valuation fees will be wasted. Moreover, he knows that mortgagees such as building societies ... are trustworthy and that they appoint careful and competent valuers and he trusts the professional man so appointed. Finally, the valuer knows full well that failure on his part to exercise reasonable care and skill may be disastrous to the purchaser.

In an early analysis of the Unfair Terms in Consumer Contracts Directive, Hugh Collins argued that the directive embodies ideas of a social market model:

> Individuals may be prepared to buy and sell inferior goods and services so an unregulated market system will not achieve this public good. Legal regulation can aim towards this public good by imposing compulsory terms in contracts, and invalidating contrary agreements. The objective is to achieve a particular kind of market. (Collins, 1994: 229)

He argues that the reasoning of the House of Lords in *Smith v Bush* supports this interpretation because the House of Lords would have prevented contracting out of liability by the surveyor even if the consumer had paid a trivial price. He also argues that the exclusion of liability for negligently inflicted death or injury reflects a social market policy concerning risk distribution that is also enshrined in the Products Liability Directive.

Smith v Bush may be described as articulating a new set of ground rules for consumer markets that limit the risks to which a consumer may be exposed. In this case any costs caused by the protection of a potentially catastrophic risk for an individual are spread among all consumers. The goal is to ensure the future autonomy of the consumer. *Smith v Bush* articulates general standards for future development. Statutes and regulations in areas such as consumer credit (see below Chapter 7) and consumer safety (Chapter 9) represent specific applications of these standards. Why do you think these were not referred to by Lord Griffiths?

---

3. The OFT: developing an approach to unfair contract terms regulation: negotiation, litigation and 'high-impact cases'

Many of the cases developing the jurisprudence under the Unfair Terms in Consumer Contracts Regulations have been brought by the OFT (formerly Director General of Fair Trading) which was given power to bring injunctions under these Regulations in 1995. The limits of courts and private litigation in regulating standard-form consumer contracts was articulated clearly by Arthur Leff in 1970.

AA Leff, 'Unconscionability and the Crowd: Consumers and the Common Law Tradition' (1970) 31 *University of Pittsburgh L Rev* 349 at 356–57

[T]he problem is … with … the common-law tradition itself when sought to be used to regulate the quality of transactions on a case-by-case basis, each one of which is economically trivial (so that you need free legal help for the consumer, and the seller can almost always avoid nasty precedent by an early surrender or settlement), and each one of which depends upon several doses of 'the total context of the fact situation' and 'copious examination of the manifestations of the parties and the surrounding circumstances' followed by a balancing effort. One cannot think of a more expensive and frustrating course than to seek to regulate goods or 'contract' quality through repeated lawsuits against inventive 'wrongdoers'. … I suppose there is some marginal need for some provision to deal with particularly egregious consumer-contract horrors not yet reached by any statute. The key factor I suppose, is that in dealing with mass vices in mass contracts, administration by way of the litigation bureaucracy is likely to have only trivial impact, for good or evil. One does not cure any serious breakdown in a theoretically competitive market system by case-to-case sniping, but one doesn't do much harm either.

In 2000 the European Commission reported on the implementation of the Directive on Unfair Terms in Consumer Contracts. It found that terms contravening the Directive continued to be common throughout the community. It also commented on some disadvantages of court regulation of terms and the need for a 'positive' system of eliminating unfair terms.

Commission of the European Communities, *Report from the Commission on the Implementation of Council Directive 93/13 EEC of 5 April 1993 on Unfair Terms in Consumer Contract***s, COM(2000) 248 final**

> The civil penalties provided for by the Member States do not seem sufficient to protect consumers and to effectively oblige professionals to refrain from using unfair terms.
>
> Indeed the only risk (and it is a minor one) run by the professional when a consumer challenges a term before the courts is that this term may be declared invalid. Besides, when an action for an injunction is brought against a professional the only risk he runs is that he may have to replace the offending term by another one. In both cases the professional is ultimately in a situation pretty similar to the one which would have existed if he had never used the unfair term. However, he can make the most of the term in respect of all consumers who do not have the information or wherewithal to react. In the case of injunctions the penalty is not dissuasive enough to the extent that it does not penalise the prior use of the unfair term, but simply means that the professional may not use it in future.
>
> ... It is interesting to note that, although the courts play a predominant role, many systems have a substantial 'administrative' admixture. In some Member States it is not only consumer associations that are entitled to seek injunctions against unfair terms: the initiative may be taken by a person responsible for upholding the public interest. This is notably the case of the Director of the Office of Fair Trading in the United Kingdom, the Director of Consumer Affairs in Ireland, the consumer ombudsman in the Nordic countries, and the Verbraucherschutzvereine in Germany.
>
> ... At the level of collective negotiations, certain national systems provide for a priori control of contractual conditions. This control begins with the very drafting of the contractual terms in the context of collective agreements. Standard-form contracts are drafted in the framework of negotiations between the consumer associations (the Netherlands is a typical case) or bodies Experience with these collective agreements has been mixed. For example, although these agreements have not had much impact in France (mainly because their effects were limited to the signatory organisations and valid only at local level), experience in Sweden has shown that, following negotiations in the individual sectors, the number of judgments handed down by the courts in the field of unfair terms dropped significantly. Likewise in the Netherlands the professional organisations and consumer associations have concluded fullfledged sectoral-level agreements.

Goldberg outlines the advantages and disadvantages of administrative regulation:

V Goldberg, 'Institutional Change and the Quasi-Invisible hand' (1974) 17 *Journal of Law & Economics* **461 at 487–90**

> One possible response to the standard form contract problem would be to provide consumers with an agent who would aid in the production of standardized terms ... the legislature might choose to delegate the task to a regulatory agency (or other nonlegislative body). This arrangement permits an ongoing review of contract terms; the agency can adjust terms in light of past experience and can bargain with the producers concerning possible innovations.
>
> Not all consumers will benefit equally from the agent's efforts. Indeed, in most instances some consumers are likely to be worse off, receiving protection from a clause that affected them little or not at all in exchange for a higher price. Given that the agent's costs must be spread over a large number of consumers with different preferences, it is inevitable that the agent must regularly engage in making interpersonal comparisons in producing contract

terms. To be sure, the same is true without government intervention where the firm (or the market) in effect plays the role of agent in producing and modifying standard form contract terms.

It should come as no surprise that the agent will be at least in part a 'double agent.' Producers will seek a voice in determining who plays the role of agent and will ultimately try to influence the nature of the terms produced, the penalties for noncompliance, and the extent of public enforcement. …

If we confine our analysis to the relative political power of the parties, then it is by no means clear that the consumer has less power in the governmental solution; indeed, it is quite likely that the opposite is the case.

Article 10 of the UTCCR imposes a duty on the OFT to consider any complaint made to it that a contract term drawn up for general use is unfair. This model initially gave no role to private groups to challenge terms (see critique in Rott, 2001) and the Consumers' Association brought an action against the government on the basis that it had failed properly to implement the requirements of the Directive. The 1999 Regulations extends the power to seek undertakings or an injunction to other qualified bodies which include the Consumers' Association and sectoral regulators.

The OFT assumed responsibility for administering the UTCCR in 1995. In 1996 the Office commented: 'Our experience in these first months leads us to believe that the use of unfair terms is widespread and amounts to a serious problem in the United Kingdom. This was contrary to our expectations' (OFT, Bulletin 2). In 1997 it stated that

despite developments such as the introduction of the Unfair Contract Terms Act 1977—20 years ago—the use of unfair terms remains a serious problem in the United Kingdom. … contracts tend to incorporate far more defensive material than traders legitimate interests require, and are often couched in impenetrable, jargon-ridden terms which may baffle or even mislead consumers.

These findings are not surprising. Businesses had continued to use exclusion clauses after the introduction of the UCTA in the 1970s, viewing them primarily in terms of the psychological bargaining power that they conferred in negotiations with consumers who were often unaware of their rights (see Yates, 1982: 29, quoted in Collins, 1999: 229). The Consumer Transactions (Restrictions on Statements Order) 1976 made it a criminal offence for businesses to include statements in documents that excluded the implied terms in the supply of goods, but few prosecutions were brought under the Order (now repealed) (see Bradgate, 1999: 43). There seemed to be limited awareness of the UTCCR among businesses, particularly small businesses.

A characteristic of the review of unfair terms by the OFT is that it is an abstract review. It assesses the terms outside the context of their use in an individual case and differs therefore from the individualised judicial approach. According to the Law Commission in its consultation paper (above 2.1), this means that the regulations must cover both substantive and procedural unfairness.

3.63 It is submitted that, whichever approach is followed, it must be the case that substantive unfairness alone can make a term unfair under UTCCR. This is because the Director General of Fair Trading ('DGFT') and the bodies listed in Schedule 1 have power to prevent the use of unfair terms and this may be done 'in the abstract', in the sense that the precise way in which the clause is presented to the consumer may not be known. If there had to be procedural unfairness this preventive power could only be used when the procedure was known to the DGFT or other body. Equally, the indicative list would lose much of its force. It is clearly aimed at terms which, for the most part, are thought to be unfair in substance. It makes separate provision for terms which have been incorporated by an unfair procedure, such as 'irrevocably binding the consumer to terms with which he had no real opportunity of becoming acquainted before the conclusion of the contract'.

3.1 Phase 1: change through negotiation

The OFT initially implemented the UTCCR by negotiating changes of terms with individual firms and trade associations. The following extracts provide material from Bulletins that the OFT publish in relation to actions taken against unfair terms. Regulation 15 requires the OFT to publish details of any undertakings and confers a discretion in regulation 15(3) to disseminate information and advice concerning the operation of the regulations. The interpretations in the Bulletins by the OFT do not have authoritative legal effect: the UTCC reserves this role for the courts. However, they are an important source of soft law and may be influential in shaping the outcome of negotiations.

OFT, *Unfair Contract Terms Bulletin No 1* (1996)

1.7 The Director General's sanction against unfair terms is to apply to the courts for an injunction …to stop them being used in the future. This is the last resort

1.8 The Director General may 'have regard' to undertakings about the use of unfair terms. But … we seek voluntary change. While we aim to be robust in applying the regulations we are not inflexible in our dealings with suppliers. We pursue a fair administrative process of negotiation. We open a dialogue with the business involved and only when this proves unsuccessful and unconstructive will we move to the formal legal process. …

1.9 When we identify unfair terms in consumer contracts we invite the supplier to modify or drop them. We may ask for more information before making a decision about unfairness. Where the supplier belongs to a trade association, we may find it appropriate to approach that body as well. It is to the credit of suppliers that most, to date, have been willing to cooperate with us to improve their standard trading terms and conditions. While we have no authority to draft terms for individual suppliers (a task for which, in any event, we do not have the resources), we assist as much as we can by pointing them in the right direction.

1.10 The process of negotiation produces change by voluntary agreement.

OFT, *Unfair Contract Terms Bulletin No 4* (1997)
This and the following extract outline the approach of the OFT to issues of transparency and unfairness under the regulations.

We challenge any term where the obscurity of the language used could put a significant number of consumers at a disadvantage … consumers should have the chance to see and understand terms before they agree to them … the Regulations and the underlying EC Directive present a fundamental challenge to a precedent based, buyer beware approach to drafting. In a sense they represent the death of freedom of contract, because they turn on its head the general duty of lawyers to draft wholly and exclusively in the interests of their clients, in whatever language is best adapted to preserve and enhance the clients' legal position. Those who draft standard form consumer contracts will not comply with the Regulations—and consequently will not serve the best interests of their clients—if they do not now also take into account and respect the interests of consumers.

OFT, *Unfair Contract Terms Guidance* (2008)

The requirement of 'good' faith embodies a general 'principle of fair and open dealing'. It means that terms should be expressed fully, clearly and legibly and that terms that might disadvantage the consumer should be given appropriate prominence—see below. However transparency is not enough on its own, as good faith relates to the substance of terms as well as the way they are expressed and used. It requires a supplier not to take advantage of consumers' weaker bargaining position, or lack of experience, in deciding what their rights and obligations shall be. Contracts should be drawn up in a way that respects consumers' legitimate interests.

In assessing fairness, we take note of how a term could be used. A term is open to challenge if it is drafted so widely that it could cause consumer detriment. It may be considered unfair if it could have an unfair effect, even if it is not at present being used unfairly in practice and there is no current intention to use it unfairly. In such cases fairness can generally be achieved by redrafting the term more precisely, so that it reflects the practice and current intentions of the supplier.

The OFT's starting point in assessing the fairness of a term is, therefore, normally to ask what would be the position for the consumer if it did not appear in the contract. The principle of freedom of contract can no longer be said to justify using standard terms to take away protection consumers would otherwise enjoy. The Regulations recognise that contractual small print is in no real sense freely agreed with consumers. Where a term changes the normal position seen by the law as striking a fair balance it is regarded with suspicion.

Transparency is also fundamental to fairness.

The OFT in this extract seems to follow the approach adopted in *Smith v Bush*. It asks the 'but for' question—what would be the position of the consumer if the term did not appear in the contract?—and assumes that the common law default rule generally represents a fair allocation of risk.

The following extracts outline the OFT's views on some of the terms covered by the 'grey list' in Schedule 2. It also contains example of decisions where contract terms have been held to be unfair. They illustrate how terms may be deleted, withdrawn, clarified, given heightened prominence in the contract, or redrafted to restrict the unfettered discretion of the supplier.

Exclusion and Limitation of Liability Clauses

Consider the approach of the OFT to exclusion and limitation of liability clauses which might be caught by both the UTCC and UCTA. The paragraph references are to those in Schedule 2 of the Regulations.

Paragraphs 1(a) and (b) Exclusion and limitation clauses

1.3 A disclaimer will often exclude or limit liability for breach of the 'implied' terms that the law presumes are included in a contract when nothing is expressly agreed on the issues involved. These help ensure agreements are workable, and generally reflect what the law considers a reasonable person would have agreed. Excluding them can have the effect of allowing one party to act unreasonably or negligently to the other with impunity. Any term which can have that effect in a consumer contract is particularly likely to be considered unfair.

1.5 Certain other arguments cannot be used to justify an over-extensive disclaimer.

That it is intended only to deal with unjustified demands. If a disclaimer could be used to defeat legitimate claims it is likely to be unfair. The Regulations are concerned with the effect terms can have, not just with the intentions behind them. If the potential effect of a term goes further than is intended, it may be possible to make it fair by cutting back its scope

… **That the customer's statutory rights are said not to be affected.** An unfair disclaimer is not made acceptable by being partially contradicted by an unexplained legal technicality whose effect only a lawyer is likely to understand.

… Disclaimers sometimes say that liability is excluded to the extent permitted by the Regulations. That is open to objection, because it is unclear and uncertain in its effect.

Original term

The support provided hereunder shall be substantially as described. This warranty is exclusive and is in lieu of all other warranties and Microsoft disclaims all other warranties, express or implied, including but not limited to warranties of merchantability and fitness for a particular purpose.

Action taken

New term: *Microsoft warrants that it will provide Support with reasonable care and skill, within a reasonable time, and substantially as described in this Agreement. Microsoft does not make any other promises or warranties about Support service.*

Consequential loss exclusions

Terms excluding claims for consequential loss are supposed to protect the supplier from remote or unforeseeable liability. But the OFT considers they can bar the consumer from seeking redress in certain circumstances when it ought to be available. Such a term effectively disclaims liability for any loss or damage resulting from any breach of contract by the supplier unless it would have been generally obvious to anyone that the breach in question would cause that loss or damage.

2.3.8 Under the ordinary rules of law, compensation is awarded for loss or damage that the parties themselves could reasonably have been expected to foresee, at the time of entering the contract, even if no-one else could have foreseen it. The OFT considers consumers should not be deprived of the right to claim for damages on that basis.

2.3.9 In any case the technical meaning of "consequential loss" is unknown to most people. Its use in standard contracts can lead to consumers thinking—and being told—that they have no claim for any loss consequent on a supplier's breach of contract. This may effectively deprive them of any compensation at all. But, for the reasons just given, the OFT does not accept that this sort of term is fair even if it is put in plainer language.

Original term

Nor shall Lessor be liable for any indirect or consequential loss or damage.

Action taken

New term: *We are also responsible for losses you suffer as a result of us breaking this agreement if the losses are a foreseeable consequence of us breaking the agreement. Losses are foreseeable where they could be contemplated by you and us at the time the vehicle is rented. We are not responsible for indirect losses which happen as a side effect of the main loss or damage and which are not foreseeable by you and us (such as loss of profits or loss of opportunity).*

Reference

British Vehicle Rental & Leasing Association Bulletin 6

Exclusion of liability for delay

2.6.3 The fact that delays can be caused by circumstances genuinely beyond the supplier's control does not make it fair to exclude liability for all delays however caused. Such terms protect the supplier indiscriminately, whether or not he is at fault.

2.6.4 Contracts sometimes say that "every effort" will be made to honour agreed deadlines, yet still exclude all liability for any delay. This leaves the consumer with no right to redress if no effort is actually made. Guarantees of this kind are largely valueless.

2.6.5 Clauses excluding liability for delay may be acceptable where they are restricted in scope to delays unavoidably cause by factors beyond the supplier's control.

Original term

The Company will make all reasonable endeavours to start and complete the works by the dates given but will not accept liability for delays.

Action taken

New term: *The Company will do all that it reasonably can to meet the date given for delivery and/or installation. In the case of unforeseen circumstances, beyond the reasonable control of the company the Company will contact the Customer and agree an alternative date.*

Reference

Casewell Ltd, t/a Homecare Windows—Bulletin 4

Supplier rights to vary terms, cancel performance and exercise discretion in performance

Cancellation Clauses paragraph 1(f)

Excessive Notice Periods for consumer cancellation

Paragraph 1(h) of Schedule 2

8.2 Particular suspicion attaches to a term in a contract for a fixed period which, if early notice to cancel is not given, automatically commits the consumer to a renewed fixed term.

8.3 The OFT considers that an over-long cancellation notice term may also be unfair in a contract which continues indefinitely rather than for a fixed term. Consumers entering such contracts normally expect to be able to end it a reasonable time after they decide they no longer want or can no longer afford what is provided under it. If they are required to make a cancellation decision too far ahead of time, they are liable either to forget to do so when they need to, or wrongly to anticipate their future needs. In either case, the effect of the term is the same as that of an automatic renewal clause—they experience an unintended extension of their payment obligations

Original term

This agreement shall commence on the connection date and shall continue for the minimum period of 12 months and thereafter until terminated by no less than three months notice in writing given by either party to the other. Such notice to be given not before the expiry of the minimum period.

Action taken

New term: *This agreement is for a minimum period of 12 months it may be terminated by giving one month's notice, which commences on or after the end of the initial 11 months.*

Reference

Singlepoint (4U) Ltd—Bulletin 9

Supplier's right to vary terms generally Schedule 2 paragraph 1(j)

Original term

Sky may at any time vary or add to these Conditions as it deems necessary.

Action taken

New term: *[Sky may] change or add to Conditions—for security, legal or regulatory reasons— We will give you at least one month's notice of any changes or additions. We will not use this right to vary the terms of any special offer which applies to you you may end this contract at any time by giving one month's notice, if we tell you we are going to change these conditions.*

Reference

British Sky Broadcasting Ltd—Bulletin 5

Right to change what is supplied Schedule 2 para 1(k)

Original term

… a reduction or other variation in the number or identity of the channels included in the Sky Multi-Channels Package will not vary the Subscription Payments payable by the Subscriber: bonus Channels will be supplied to Subscribers at no additional cost. … Sky may at any time without notice vary the terms on which these Channels are supplied including but … not limited to introducing or otherwise making a charge …

Action taken

New term: *You may end this contract at any time … we … withdraw any Sky Premium Channel or reduce significantly the level of service of the Sky Multi-Channels Package.*

Reference

British Sky Broadcasting Ltd—Bulletin 5

OFT, Unfair Contract Terms Bulletin No 5 (1998)

[T]he OFT's position on variation clauses is this: any term in any kind of contract that effectively gives an unrestricted power to vary significant terms for captive consumers creates a contractual imbalance that is likely to be considered unfair.

Supplier's right of final decision, paragraph 1(m)

Original term

The Company will repair or replace any part as it deems necessary and where a part which is a replacement is defective then the Company will issue a further part.

Action taken

New term: *The Company shall use all reasonable endeavours to supply minor spare parts and replacement components required to maintain the equipment in good working order and no extra charge will be made for the supplies. If, however, the equipment is damaged otherwise than by fair wear and tear, the Company reserves the right to charge the Subscriber for supplying the same.*

Reference

European Environmental Controls Ltd—Bulletin 4

Entire agreement clauses Schedule 2(1)(n)

Entire agreement ... clauses, paragraph 1(n)

14.1.1 Good faith demands that each party to a contract is bound by his or her promises and by any other statements which help secure the other party's agreement. If a standard-form contract excludes liability for words that do not appear in it, there is scope for consumers to be misled with impunity.

14.1.2 These objections apply equally to other types of wording which have the same effect, for instance clauses saying that employees or agents have no authority to make binding statements or amendments to the contract. They also enable the supplier to disclaim liability for oral promises even when they have been relied on by the consumer reasonably and in good faith.

14.1.3 Consumers commonly and naturally rely on what is said to them when they are entering a contract. If they can be induced to part with money by claims and promises, and the seller can then simply disclaim responsibility on the basis of such a legal technicality, the scope for bad faith is clear. Even if such a term is not deliberately abused, it weakens the seller's incentive to take care in what he says, and to ensure that his employees and agents do so.

Original term: Vacation 2000 (Holiday Club Anglian) Limited takes no responsibility for any verbal claims, or other offers made in conjunction with this offer by its distributors, agents which are not included in this promotion.

Action taken

New term: *Vacation 2000 accepts responsibility under these Terms and Conditions for its commitments to you. It also accepts responsibility by its duly authorised agents.*

Reference

Vacation 2000 (Holiday Club Anglian) Ltd

Transferring inappropriate risks to consumers

Original term

You will be still be liable for the minimum charge and all call charges [if] you lose the apparatus or it is stolen.

Action taken

New term: *You will still be liable to pay these sums if the apparatus is lost or stolen. When we receive notice from you confirming the genuine loss or theft and that matter has been reported to the police, you will not be liable for call charges from that date.*

Reference

Advance Mobile Communications—Bulletin 8

Plain and intelligible language

Regulation 7 Plain and intelligible language

19.2 ... In line with their purpose of protecting consumers from one-sided agreements, and the requirement of the underlying Directive that 'consumers should actually be given an opportunity to examine all the terms' (Recital 20), they have to be understood as demanding 'transparency' in the full sense.

19.3 It follows that what is required is that terms are intelligible to ordinary members of the public, not just lawyers. It is not sufficient for terms to be clear and precise for legal purposes, except in contract normally entered only on legal advice.

Original term

The masculine includes the feminine gender and the singular shall include the plural and vice versa and a reference to a statutory provision will be interpreted as a reference to the provision as amended or re-enacted from time to time including any regulation or statutory instrument issued pursuant to such provision at any time.

Action taken

Term deleted.

Reference

Stirling Security Group Ltd—Bulletin

Hans Micklitz argues that the OFT decides cases primarily on the combination of the grey list in Schedule 2 and the plain and intelligible language provision. 'Very seldom are terms declared unfair without reference to these sections' (Micklitz, 2005: 396–97). In addition he makes the important observation that the UTCC has provided the opportunity for administrative enforcement of the prohibitions on exclusion clauses in the UCTA. To what extent may the cases on the control of the supplier's discretion (eg boat rental) be compared to public law norms controlling the exercise of discretion by public bureaucracies and norms of non-discrimination?

3.2 Assessing the initial performance of the OFT

In 1999 and again in 2003 the National Audit Office reviewed the work of the OFT in protecting consumers from unfair trading practices. It commented in 1999 on the performance of the agency in addressing unfair contract terms:

National Audit Office Report by the Comptroller and Auditor General, *The Office of Fair Trading: Protecting the Consumer from Unfair Trading Practices* (HC 57 1999/00)

3.37 The OFT seek to persuade businesses to comply with the Regulations and use their powers to seek an injunction only where negotiations are unsuccessful. They seek to help businesses to comply by explaining fully their reasons where they believe terms are unfair, and by publishing regular Bulletins which include examples of terms they consider unfair alongside revised versions they have negotiated with businesses. Almost all of the cases requiring action by the OFT have been settled through advice or undertakings [59% advice or warning, 41 % undertakings] although the OFT usually warn businesses that they will be taken to court if they do not comply with the Regulations. The OFT have found it necessary to take only one company to court (in July 1999) …

3.38 Where similar terms are used across whole business sectors, the OFT sometimes group less urgent cases and work with trade associations to deal with as many traders as possible together. For example, the British Vehicle Rental and Leasing Association, which represents 85 per cent of car rental companies, introduced a model car-hire contract in line with the Regulations in November 1998 at the instigation of the OFT.

3.39 The OFT have secured substantial financial benefits for consumers by acting under the Unfair Terms in Consumer Contracts Regulations. They identified two cases in 1998 where the financial benefits for consumers secured through changes in contract terms amounted to over £100 million a year [removal of unfair penalties in mortgage loans, savings £65.2 million; eight mobile phone companies agreed to amend mobile telephone contracts to reduce the notice period from three to one month, savings between £60 and £80 million a year]. The financial benefits realised by consumers from the OFT's unfair contracts work are likely to be greater than this, however, since the OFT do not routinely seek this information from the businesses they negotiate with on unfair contracts.

3.40 We talked to 11 businesses who had amended their contracts following action by the OFT. They told us that the OFT's intervention had led to revised contracts that are easier for consumers to read and understand. One mobile phone company told us that they expected the revised contract to make their services more attractive to consumers. A mobile phone company agreed to revise their mobile telephone contracts in March 1999 following extensive negotiations with the OFT. They changed their three-month notice period to one month and revised a term that gave them the right to increase prices. The company told us the work of the OFT had led to a better deal for customers and changes to mobile telephone industry contracts earlier than would have occurred due to market forces alone. The company also said that the changes in contracts had made them easier to understand and that this might attract consumers to their services.

3.41 The number of unfair contracts cases dealt with by the OFT has not kept pace with the number of complaints which are increasing at an annual rate of some 17 per cent (Figure 33). In an attempt to keep up with their workload, the OFT have increased the staff devoted to unfair contracts work, from the equivalent of 12.5 staff years in 1998–99 to 17.7 staff years in 1999–2000.

3.42 The OFT completed 85 per cent of cases within nine months in 1998–99 (against a target of 80 per cent), and 91 per cent of cases within 15 months (against a target of 95 per cent). At the end of May 1999, the OFT were considering 788 unfair contract cases. Some 72 of these cases (nine per cent) had been open for between two and three years and 24 cases (three per cent) had been open for more than three years. Forty-eight of the total of 96 complaints which had been with the OFT for more than two years were package holiday contracts. Negotiations were not opened with the companies until the OFT had received complaints about all the major players in the industry and had sufficient resources to mount concerted sectoral action. In most cases the negotiations with these companies had been active for less than a year.

…

3.43 We examined an illustrative sample of 12 cases where the OFT acted to secure amendments to contracts between 1997 and 1999.We identified how long the OFT had taken to negotiate amendments to contracts, and calculated how much of the elapsed time was attributable to the business, and how much was attributable to the OFT. We did not find a consistent pattern. For example, in one case, which took nearly two and a half years to complete, three-quarters of this time the OFT were waiting for the company to respond to their letters. In another case, which took four and a half months to complete, a fifth of the elapsed time was attributable to the company.

3.44 We found that in four cases the OFT had not contacted the businesses concerned until more than five months after they had received the first complaint. This delay was partly due to the difficulty the OFT have experienced in keeping up with the growing number of complaints. The OFT told us that where complaints do not pose an immediate threat to consumers they are accorded a lower priority and dealt with when resources allow, and that they always advise consumers who complain to them how they can help themselves.

3.45 In the 12 cases we examined in detail, we also talked to the businesses concerned. Nine of the 11 businesses who responded told us that they felt that the OFT had handled negotiations well; and all said that they had taken the approach from the OFT seriously.

3.46 Most businesses want to comply with their obligations and, since the Unfair Contracts Regulations came into force in 1995, the OFT have focused on explaining to businesses how the Regulations apply and helping them to comply. In their negotiations with businesses the OFT rely on their interpretation of the Regulations, which have been tested in the Courts only once and are therefore open to challenge by businesses legal advisers.

In 2003 the National Audit Office outlined the conclusions of the House of Commons Public Accounts Committee on their 1999 Report on the OFT and the response of the government to the committee's conclusions.

National Audit Office Report by the Comptroller and Auditor General, *The Office of Fair Trading: Progress in Protecting Consumers' Interests* (HC 430 2002–03)

PAC conclusion on investigating Unfair Contract Terms

… The OFT told us that their approach of grouping cases to take an industry by industry view contributed to delays in settling cases. Grouping cases may produce benefits, but the delay in settling cases are unsatisfactory, and we recommend that the OFT should set and achieve target dates for settling complaints and reducing the backlog.

The OFT accepts the Committee's analysis. The number of complaints continues to rise steeply. The OFT received 25 per cent more complaints in 1999–2000 than in 1998–99, and it is believed that there is considerable additional pent-up demand for enforcement activity since complaints recorded by trading standards services about unfair terms numbered over 1,200 in the period October–December 1999. The scale of the problem could not have been predicted and is the main reason for the delays in dealing with a significant proportion of cases. The OFT has sought and received funding for 10 more staff (a 55 per cent increase in staffing levels) and recruitment is underway. The OFT has set a target for 2000–01 to close the oldest third of the 756 cases on hand in April 2000. The OFT approach of dealing with entire sectors and changing a trade association's recommended or model terms promotes the adoption of fairer terms through an entire business sector. The OFT has found that unless an entire sector moves at the same time, individual business will not make the necessary changes because they fear a loss of competitiveness … it was necessary to take action against the

International Air Transport Association (IATA) recommended airline conditions rather than an individual company such as British Airways or Air France. IATA has now agreed new airline conditions, which it will recommend for adoption by all its members.

Public Accounts Committee

Although the Regulations empower the OFT to obtain a court injunction to stop businesses using unfair court terms, almost all of the unfair contracts cases the OFT have settled since the Regulations came into force have been resolved through advice or businesses giving undertakings that they would comply with the Regulations. The OFT have taken only one company to court, in July 1999. Taking cases to court is costly, but the OFT acknowledge that their success in court should demonstrate to businesses that OFT legal action is not an empty threat. Despite the OFT's emphasis on the need for strengthened fair trading legislation, they have made little use of their existing powers. They should be less restrained from taking cases to court under these Regulations in future.

The Government's response

The OFT has made effective use of its administrative powers so that companies have, in every case but one, responded to enforcement action by agreeing to remove unfair terms. The OFT has no power to take businesses to court if they agree to make the necessary changes. Businesses are told at the outset that they risk court action if they refuse to revise their contracts. They are left in no doubt that the OFT will take legal action where it is necessary. Not all are willing to co-operate initially, but only one has refused to improve its terms following threats of legal action. All others have accepted that they were, despite their initial reluctance, able to remove unfair terms from their contracts.

As part of its five-year review of the underlying Council Directive on unfair terms the EC commissioned a report on its implementation in each member state. The report on UK enforcement noted that the Director General of Fair Trading had combated the use of unfair terms with 'outstanding success'. The subsequent Commission report agreed, and attributed this success to the OFT's policy of initiating negotiation with businesses and trade associations. But, to repeat, court action will be used where necessary.

In 2000 Susan Bright provided a favourable review of the performance of the OFT under the UTCCR (see Bright, 2000: 331). She argues that the OFT has

energetically pursued complaints and has been able to secure the alteration of contracts in several business sectors through a process of rigorous negotiations, with almost no need to resort to legal actions ... the Unfair Contract Terms Unit has been overtly 'pro-consumer' unhampered by doubts expressed in other quarters about the proper interpretation of, in particular, the unfairness provisions.

She notes that about half of complaints come from local trading standards departments and consumer advice organisations. Bright speculates why the approach through negotiation has, in her view, been so successful and suggests the following factors:

[T]he fear of bad publicity ... the fact that many of the terms are fair in part: by rewriting them the trader can still secure the protection needed whilst also being fair to the consumer; if left unamended, the terms may be wholly unenforceable against the consumer. Dealing with trade associations is also an efficient way of reaching businesses; as representative figures within that sectoral activity, associations will often be anxious to present a positive public image and to maintain good working relationships with the Office of Fair Trading. (Bright, 2000: 335)

The Law Commission comments in 2002 in its consultation document on unfair terms that:

> the work of the OFT's Unfair Contract Terms Unit has had a major impact on the market. The OFT has secured the removal of many unfair terms which were almost certainly invalid under UCTA; and this shows that allowing parties to challenge terms in their individual contracts, while invaluable to them, has a limited impact on contracting practices generally.

The experience of the OFT in implementing the UTCCR indicates the potential ability of an administrative agency to bring about broad-scale changes in industry terms (eg mobile phones). This may be more effective than relying on individual consumers bringing actions in court as suggested by Leff. It may be distributionally progressive since evidence suggests that the majority of plaintiffs who use the county courts as plaintiffs are drawn from middle-class and professional groups. Could the OFT interventions reduce the complaint costs of consumers with firms? Studies on complaint handling indicate that many consumers handle consumer problems without the intervention of a third party, so that much consumer disputing takes place at the level of two-party negotiation. Pleasance et al (2004) claim that courts and ombudsmen play a minimal role in the resolution of consumer disputes. They note that in 40 per cent of cases consumers took no further action if the complaint was unsuccessful. However, this conclusion should be placed in the perspective of the argument by Geraint Howells that there has been an 'explosion' in consumer credit litigation since the mid-2000s (Howells, 2010). The reduction in clauses that confer broad discretion on a supplier may also alter the bargaining power of consumer and supplier by outlining more clearly the exact scope of the rights of the parties.

4. A new approach? Greater use of test and high-impact cases

The OFT seemed to change its approach to unfair terms in the mid-2000s with a greater focus on test cases which might have a 'high impact'. These include *OFT v Abbey National et al*, *OFT v Foxtons* and *OFT v Ashbourne Investments*. The OFT closed the unfair terms unit which had negotiated the changes outlined above.

The first case in the OFT's litigation against unfair terms pre-dated this policy shift but is useful as illustrating the use of litigation as a test case strategy by the OFT.

Director General of Fair Trading v First National Bank plc [2002] 1 AC 481

This case concerned a standard term used by First National Bank, the largest provider of home-improvement financing in the UK. Much of its lending was in the sub-prime lending market. The relevant term, condition 8 of the agreement (see judgment of Lord Bingham) stated that, in the event of default by the consumer on repayment of the loan, interest would continue to accrue at the contractual rate on the unpaid balance both before and after any judgment entered against the consumer by the lender. The rationale for this clause was that county court regulations prohibited a court from awarding statutory interest on any judgment debt given on a regulated consumer credit agreement under the Consumer Credit Act 1974. There was no prohibition on the lender inserting such a term in a contract.

One consequence of this term was that where an instalment payment order was made by a court it was possible for an individual to repay the instalments but still be left with a substantial liability, represented by accrued interest. The OFT had received many complaints about this practice in relation to First National Bank (but not other lenders) although similar terms were included by many other lenders. A central concern in the complaints was that individuals were not aware that there would be a liability for accrued interest and the instalment payments often reflected offers of repayment that had been accepted by the bank and that reflected what individuals could afford to pay.

Sections 129–36 of the Consumer Credit Act 1974 empower the county court to make a time order for payment by instalments that could include a reduction or elimination of the interest payable. However, evidence presented to the court of first instance indicated that 'in the vast majority of cases … there is no real hearing in the course of which the terms of the agreement are brought to the attention of the court or submissions made in respect of them. In practice in most cases the borrower will consent in writing to an instalment order which will be accepted by the lender and the court will automatically make an order without such consideration. The borrower will remain unaware of the provisions of clause 8, notwithstanding that it appears to be the current practice of the bank to draw attention to the provisions of clause 8', and the presence of a statement on the county court forms that the claimant may be entitled to further interest (see [2000] 1 WLR 98 at 106). Enforcement of the accrued interest would require a further county court proceedings and, in practice, the debtor would usually pay the interest or the bank would waive it. The OFT claimed that the clause caused uncertainty and confusion among borrowers.

The trial judge held that the term was not unfair since the term was not expressly invalidated under any statutory provision, and would not at the time of entering into the loan strike a potential borrower as unfair. Nor, given the powers of the court under sections 129–36 was there any procedural unfairness.

The Court of Appeal, in contrast, held that the term resulted in unfair surprise for the borrower, constituting procedural unfairness and also resulted in a significant imbalance between the parties since it allowed the bank to obtain interest when it would not normally be permitted to under the default rules of county court judgments under the Consumer Credit Act 1974 and without any compensating benefit to the borrower. The House of Lords upheld the appeal of First National Bank.

Their Lordships took time for consideration:

Lord Bingham of Cornhill [outlining the relevant term]: '… Time is of the essence for making all repayments to FNB as they fall due. If any repayment instalment is unpaid for more than seven days after it became due, FNB may serve a notice on the customer requiring payment before a specified date not less than seven days later. If the repayment instalment is not paid in full by that date, FNB will be entitled to demand payment of the balance on the customer's account and interest then outstanding together with all reasonable legal and other costs charges and expenses claimed or incurred by FNB in trying to obtain the repayment of the unpaid instalment of such balance and interest. Interest on the amount which becomes payable shall be charged in accordance with condition 4, at the rate stated in paragraph D overleaf (subject to variation) until payment after as well as before any judgment (such obligation to be independent of and not to merge with the judgment).'

Emphasis has been added to the last sentence of this condition, since it is to that sentence alone that the Director's objection relates. I shall refer to this sentence as 'the term'.

[A] lender under a regulated credit agreement who obtains judgment against a defaulting borrower in the county court will be entitled to recover the principal outstanding at the date of judgment and interest accrued up to that date but will not be entitled to an order for statutory interest after that date, and even if the court had power to award statutory postjudgment interest it could not do so, in any case where an instalment order had been made, unless there had been a default in the due payment of any instalment. The lender may recover post-judgment interest only if he has the benefit of an independent covenant by the borrower entitling him to recover such interest. There is nothing to preclude inclusion of such a covenant in a regulated credit agreement, unless it falls foul of the fairness requirement in the Regulations.

7 Section 71 of the County Courts Act 1984 conferred a general power on the county court, where any judgment was given or order made for payment of a money sum, to order that the money might be paid 'by such instalments payable at such times as the court may fix'. The 1974 Act also conferred on the county court three powers relevant for present purposes. First, the court was empowered to make a time order ... [see ss 129–36] ... the Director's challenge, although addressed only to the bank's use of and reliance on the term, if upheld, may well invalidate any similar term in any other regulated agreement made by any other lender with any borrower. The questions at issue are accordingly of general public importance.

(1) The applicability of the Regulations

10 In reliance on regulation 3(2)(b) Lord Goodhart, on behalf of the bank, submitted that no assessment might be made of the fairness of the term because it concerns the adequacy of the bank's remuneration as against the services supplied, namely the loan of money. A bank's remuneration under a credit agreement is the receipt of interest. The term, by entitling the bank to post-judgment interest, concerns the quantum and thus the adequacy of that remuneration. This was the more obviously true if, as Lord Goodhart submitted, the merger rule as commonly understood is unsound. ...

11 To this submission Mr Crow, representing the Director [argued] ... condition 8, of which the term forms part, is a default provision. Its purpose, and its only purpose, is to prescribe the consequences of a default by the borrower. It does not lay down the rate of interest which the bank is entitled to receive and the borrower bound to pay. It is an ancillary term, well outside the bounds of regulation 3(2)(b).

12 In agreement with the judge and the Court of Appeal, I do not accept the bank's submission on this issue. The Regulations, as Professor Sir Guenter Treitel QC has aptly observed (Treitel The Law of Contract, 10th ed (1999), p 248), 'are not intended to operate as a mechanism of quality or price control' and regulation 3(2) is of 'crucial importance in recognising the parties' freedom of contract with respect to the essential features of their bargain': p 249. But there is an important 'distinction between the term or terms which express the substance of the bargain and "incidental" (if important) terms which surround them' (Chitty on Contracts, 28th ed (1999), vol 1, ch 15 'Unfair Terms in Consumer Contracts', p 747, para 15-025). The object of the Regulations and the Directive is to protect consumers against the inclusion of unfair and prejudicial terms in standard-form contracts into which they enter, and that object would plainly be frustrated if regulation 3(2)(b) were so broadly interpreted as to cover any terms other than those falling squarely within it. In my opinion the term, as part of a provision prescribing the consequences of default, plainly does not fall within it. It does not concern the adequacy of the interest earned by the bank as its remuneration but is designed to ensure that the bank's entitlement to interest does not come to an end on the entry of judgment. ...

(2) Unfairness

… 17 The test laid down by regulation 4(1), deriving as it does from article 3(1) of the Directive, has understandably attracted much discussion in academic and professional circles and helpful submissions were made to the House on it. It is plain from the recitals to the Directive that one of its objectives was partially to harmonise the law in this important field among all member states of the European Union. The member states have no common concept of fairness or good faith, and the Directive does not purport to state the law of any single member state. It lays down a test to be applied, whatever their pre-existing law, by all member states. If the meaning of the test were doubtful, or vulnerable to the possibility of differing interpretations in differing member states, it might be desirable or necessary to seek a ruling from the European Court of Justice on its interpretation. But the language used in expressing the test, so far as applicable in this case, is in my opinion clear and not reasonably capable of differing interpretations. A term falling within the scope of the Regulations is unfair if it causes a significant imbalance in the parties' rights and obligations under the contract to the detriment of the consumer in a manner or to an extent which is contrary to the requirement of good faith. The requirement of significant imbalance is met if a term is so weighted in favour of the supplier as to tilt the parties' rights and obligations under the contract significantly in his favour. This may be by the granting to the supplier of a beneficial option or discretion or power, or by the imposing on the consumer of a disadvantageous burden or risk or duty. The illustrative terms set out in Schedule 3 to the Regulations provide very good examples of terms which may be regarded as unfair; whether a given term is or is not to be so regarded depends on whether it causes a significant imbalance in the parties' rights and obligations under the contract. This involves looking at the contract as a whole. But the imbalance must be to the detriment of the consumer; a significant imbalance to the detriment of the supplier, assumed to be the stronger party, is not a mischief which the Regulations seek to address. The requirement of good faith in this context is one of fair and open dealing. Openness requires that the terms should be expressed fully, clearly and legibly, containing no concealed pitfalls or traps. Appropriate prominence should be given to terms which might operate disadvantageously to the customer. Fair dealing requires that a supplier should not, whether deliberately or unconsciously, take advantage of the consumer's necessity, indigence, lack of experience, unfamiliarity with the subject matter of the contract, weak bargaining position or any other factor listed in or analogous to those listed in Schedule 2 to the Regulations. Good faith in this context is not an artificial or technical concept; nor, since Lord Mansfield was its champion, is it a concept wholly unfamiliar to British lawyers. It looks to good standards of commercial morality and practice. Regulation 4(1) lays down a composite test, covering both the making and the substance of the contract, and must be applied bearing clearly in mind the objective which the Regulations are designed to promote.

18 In support of his contention that the term is unfair the Director adduced evidence of complaints made to him by a number of borrowers. Some of these disclose a very highly unsatisfactory state of affairs. In one case a husband and wife borrowed £3,000 plus £443.70 for insurance to finance improvements to their home. The principal was repayable over a five year term by instalments of £84.89 plus £8.98 insurance. The borrowers fell into arrear and judgment was given for £3,953.11. The court ordered this sum to be paid by monthly instalments of £4.18, at which rate (it was calculated) the judgment debt would take 78 years to clear. Meanwhile, under the contract, interest would continue to accrue even if the instalments were fully and punctually paid. The bank's deponent described these borrowers as ;a good example of customers who demonstrated an ability easily to pay the instalments for home improvements when the credit was granted but thereafter appeared to have undertaken many other financial commitments which seriously prejudiced their ability to pay; the bank.

A financial statement prepared on these borrowers some months before the county court judgment is consistent with that assertion.

19 For the Director, reliance was placed on the provisions in the 1991 Order which denied the court power to order payment of statutory interest on money judgments given under regulated agreements and precluded entitlement to interest in any case where payment by instalments had been ordered and the instalments had been fully and punctually paid. It was argued that the term was unfair because it denied the borrower the protection which those provisions afforded. It was argued, in the alternative, that the term was unfair for the more limited reason upheld by the Court of Appeal.

20 In judging the fairness of the term it is necessary to consider the position of typical parties when the contract is made. The borrower wants to borrow a sum of money, often quite a modest sum, often for purposes of improving his home. He discloses an income sufficient to finance repayment by instalments over the contract term. If he cannot do that, the bank will be unwilling to lend. The essential bargain is that the bank will make funds available to the borrower which the borrower will repay, over a period, with interest. Neither party could suppose that the bank would willingly forgo any part of its principal or interest. If the bank thought that outcome at all likely, it would not lend. If there were any room for doubt about the borrower's obligation to repay the principal in full with interest, that obligation is very clearly and unambiguously expressed in the conditions of contract. There is nothing unbalanced or detrimental to the consumer in that obligation; the absence of such a term would unbalance the contract to the detriment of the lender.

21 It seems clear, as the judge pointed out [2000] 1 WLR 98 at 111 that a secured lender who does not obtain a money judgment but instead proceeds for possession and sale under the mortgage may obtain interest at the contract rate provided for in the mortgage down to the date when he is actually repaid, and in my opinion there is nothing unbalanced or detrimental to the consumer in that result either.

22 Should it then be said that the provisions of the 1991 Order render the term unfair, providing as it does for a continuing obligation to pay interest after judgment notwithstanding the payment of instalments by the borrower in accordance with a court order? It is, I think, pertinent that the 1974 Act, which laid down a number of stipulations with which regulated agreements must comply, did not prohibit terms providing for post-judgment interest even though it required claims to enforce regulated agreements to be brought in the county court which could not at the time award statutory interest in any circumstances. The 1974 Act was passed to protect consumers and such a prohibition would no doubt have been enacted had it been recognised as a necessary or desirable form of protection. The Crowther Committee, on whose report (Cmnd 4596, March 1971) the Act was based, did not recommend such a prohibition; indeed, it contemplated the recovery of contractual interest: see paragraphs 5.4.3, 6.6.33, 6.6.44(iv) and 6.7.16. ... I do not think that the term can be stigmatised as unfair on the ground that it violates or undermines a statutory regime enacted for the protection of consumers.

23 It is of course foreseeable that a borrower, no matter how honourable and realistic his intentions when entering into a credit agreement, may fall on hard times and find himself unable to honour his obligations. The bank's standard conditions recognise that possibility by providing for the contingency of default. The 1974 Act even more fully recognises that possibility, by providing for time orders to be made and providing that when a time order is made the terms of the underlying agreement may also be amended. These provisions are clearly framed for the relief not of the borrower who, having the means to meet his contractual obligations, chooses not to do so, but for the relief of those who cannot pay or cannot pay without more time. Properly applied, these provisions enable the undeserving

borrower to be distinguished from the deserving and for the contractual obligations of the deserving to be re-drawn in terms which reasonably reflect such ability, if any, as he may then have to repay within a reasonable period. Where problems arise in practice, it appears to be because borrowers do not know of the effect of sections 129 and 136; neither the procedure for giving notice of default to the borrower nor the prescribed county court forms draw attention to them; and judgments will routinely be entered in the county court without the court considering whether to exercise its power under the sections.

24 I have no hesitation in accepting the proposition, inherent in the Director's submissions, that this situation is unacceptable. I have much greater difficulty in deciding whether the difficulties derive, as the Court of Appeal concluded, from the unfairness of the term or from the absence of procedural safeguards for the consumer at the stage of default. When the contract is made, default is a foreseeable contingency, not an expected outcome. It is not customary, even in consumer contracts, for notice to be given to the consumer of statutory reliefs open to him if he defaults. The 1974 Act does not require that notice of the effect of sections 129 and 136 be given. The evidence contains examples of clauses used by over 30 other lenders providing for the payment of interest after judgment, and none alerts the borrower to these potential grounds of relief. Regulation 4 is directed to the unfairness of a contract term, not the use which a supplier may make of a term which is in itself fair. It is readily understandable that a borrower may be disagreeably surprised if he finds that his contractual interest obligation continues to mount despite his duly paying the instalments ordered by the court, but it appears that the bank seeks to prevent that surprise by sending what is described in the evidence as a standard form of letter:

> 'You need only pay the amount ordered by the court under the terms of the judgment but you should be aware that under the terms of the agreement interest continues to accrue on your account. It is therefore in your interest to increase the instalment paid as soon as possible otherwise a much greater balance than the judgment debt may quickly build up.'

On balance, I do not consider that the term can properly be said to cause a significant imbalance in the parties' rights and obligations under the contract to the detriment of the consumer in a manner or to an extent which is contrary to the requirement of good faith.

25 I do not think that the issues raised in this appeal raise any question on which the House requires a ruling from the European Court of Justice to enable it to give judgment and I would not accordingly order a reference to be made.

26 For the reasons I have given, and those given by each of my noble and learned friends, I would allow the bank's appeal with costs in the House and the Court of Appeal and restore the order of the judge.

...

Lord Steyn

30 My Lords, this is the first occasion on which the House has had the opportunity to examine an important branch of consumer law. It is therefore appropriate to consider the framework in which the questions before the House must be considered.

31 As between the Directive and the domestic implementing Regulations, the former is the dominant text. Fortunately, the 1994 Regulations, and even more so the Unfair Terms in Consumer Contracts Regulations 1999, appear to have implemented the Directive in domestic law in a manner which ought not to cause serious difficulty. The purpose of the Directive is twofold, viz the promotion of fair standard contract forms to improve the functioning of the European market place and the protection of consumers throughout the European

Community. The Directive is aimed at contracts of adhesion, viz 'take it or leave it' contracts. It treats consumers as presumptively weaker parties and therefore fit for protection from abuses by stronger contracting parties. This is an objective which must throughout guide the interpretation of the Directive as well as the implementing Regulations. If contracting parties were able to avoid the application of the Directive and Regulations by exclusionary stipulations the regulatory scheme would be ineffective. The conclusion that the Directive and Regulations are mandatory is inescapable.

32 The Directive is not an altogether harmonious text. It reflects the pragmatic compromises which were necessary to arrive at practical solutions between member states with divergent legal systems. But, despite some inelegance and untidiness in the text, the general principle that the construction must be adopted which promotes the effectiveness and practical value of the system ought to overcome difficulties. And the concepts of the Directive must be given autonomous meanings so that there will be uniform application of the Directive so far as is possible.

33 The Directive made provision for a dual system of ex casu challenges and pre-emptive or collective challenges by appropriate bodies. ... The Directive and the Regulations do not always distinguish between the two situations. This point is illustrated by the emphasis in article 4.1 of the Directive and regulation 4(2) on the relevance of particular circumstances affecting a contractual relationship. The Directive and the Regulations must be made to work sensibly and effectively and this can only be done by taking into account the effects of contemplated or typical relationships between the contracting parties. Inevitably, the primary focus of such a pre-emptive challenge is on issues of substantive unfairness.

... Clause 8 of the contract, the only provision in dispute, is a default provision. It prescribes remedies which only become available to the lender upon the default of the consumer. For this reason the escape route of regulation 3(2) is not available to the bank. So far as the description of terms covered by regulation 3(2) as core terms is helpful at all, I would say that clause 8 of the contract is a subsidiary term. In any event, regulation 3(2) must be given a restrictive interpretation. Unless that is done regulation 3(2)(a) will enable the main purpose of the scheme to be frustrated by endless formalistic arguments as to whether a provision is a definitional or an exclusionary provision. Similarly, regulation 3(2)(b) dealing with 'the adequacy of the price or remuneration' must be given a restrictive interpretation. After all, in a broad sense all terms of the contract are in some way related to the price or remuneration. That is not what is intended. Even price escalation clauses have been treated by the Director as subject to the fairness provision. ... It would be a gaping hole in the system if such clauses were not subject to the fairness requirement. For these further reasons I would reject the argument of the bank that regulation 3(2), and in particular 3(2)(b), take clause 8 outside the scope of the Regulations.

35 Given these conclusions the attack on the merger principle mounted by the bank was misplaced. ...

36 It is now necessary to refer to the provisions which prescribe how it should be determined whether a term is unfair. Implementing article 3(1) of the Directive regulation 4(1) provides ...

There are three independent requirements. But the element of detriment to the consumer may not add much. But it serves to make clear that the Directive is aimed at significant imbalance against the consumer, rather than the seller or supplier. The twin requirements of good faith and significant imbalance will in practice be determinative. Schedule 2 to the Regulations, which explains the concept of good faith, provides that regard must be had, amongst other things, to the extent to which the seller or supplier has dealt fairly and equitably with the consumer. It is an objective criterion. Good faith imports, as Lord Bingham of Cornhill has observed in his opinion, the notion of open and fair dealing: see also *Interfoto Picture Library Ltd v Stiletto Visual Programmes Ltd* [1989] QB 433. And helpfully the commentary to the 2000 edition of Principles of European Contract Law, prepared by the Commission of European Contract Law, explains that the purpose of the provision of good faith and fair dealing is 'to enforce community standards of decency, fairness and reasonableness in commercial transactions'; a fortiori that is true of consumer transactions. Schedule 3 to the Regulations (which corresponds to the annex to the Directive) is best regarded as a check list of terms which must be regarded as potentially vulnerable. The examples given in Schedule 3 convincingly demonstrate that the argument of the bank that good faith is predominantly concerned with procedural defects in negotiating procedures cannot be sustained. Any purely procedural or even predominantly procedural interpretation of the requirement of good faith must be rejected.

37 That brings me to the element of significant imbalance. It has been pointed out by Hugh Collins that the test 'of a significant imbalance of the obligations obviously directs attention to the substantive unfairness of the contract': 'Good Faith in European Contract Law' (1994) 14 Oxford Journal of Legal Studies 229, 249. It is however, also right to say that there is a large area of overlap between the concepts of good faith and significant imbalance.

38 It is now necessary to turn to the application of these requirements to the facts of the present case. The point is a relatively narrow one. I agree that the starting point is that a lender ought to be able to recover interest at the contractual rate until the date of payment, and this applies both before and after judgment. On the other hand, counsel for the Director advanced a contrary argument. Adopting the test of asking what the position of a consumer is in the contract under consideration with or without clause 8, he said that the consumer is in a significantly worse position than he would have been if there had been no such provision. Certainly, the consumer is worse off. The difficulty facing counsel, however, is that this disadvantage to the consumer appears to be the consequence not of clause 8 but of the County Courts (Interest on Judgment Debts) Order 1991. Under this Order no statutory interest is payable on a county court judgment given in proceedings to recover money due under a regulated agreement. … Counsel said that for policy reasons it was decided that in such a case no interest may be recovered after judgment. He said that it is not open to the House to criticise directly or indirectly this legal context. In these circumstances he submitted that it is not legitimate for a court to conclude that fairness requires that a lender must be able to insist on a stipulation designed to avoid the statutory regime under the 1991 Order. Initially I was inclined to uphold this policy argument. On reflection, however, I have been persuaded that this argument cannot prevail in circumstances where the legislature has neither expressly nor by necessary implication barred a stipulation that interest may continue to accrue after judgment until payment in full.

39 For these reasons as well as the reasons given by Lord Bingham I agree that clause 8 is not unfair and I would also make the order which Lord Bingham proposes.

The 2006 amendments to the Consumer Credit Act 1974 contain provisions relevant to the *First National* case. The unfair relationships provision (section 140A) permits the court to examine the way in which a term operates in the context of the relationship between the parties, not merely at the time of entering into the contract (see below Chapter 7 at 10.1) and greater disclosure obligations are placed on creditors who wish to recover interest after judgment (see below Chapter 7).

To what extent do the judges in *First National* share a common conception of 'good faith'?—as including both procedural and substantive aspects?

Law Commission Consultation Paper No 166, Scottish Law Commission Discussion Paper No 119, *Unfair Terms in Contracts* (2002) 42–43

(a) 'Contrary to the requirement of good faith' and 'significant imbalance'

3.57 There has been considerable debate in the legal literature as to the correct interpretation of the words of regulation 5(1). One view is that 'contrary to the requirement of good faith' and 'significant imbalance' are two separate but equal requirements, the first addressing issues of procedural fairness and the other of substantive fairness. Thus a term would be unfair only if it is shown both that in substance the term produced an imbalance between the rights and obligations of the parties to the consumer's detriment; and that the process by which the contract was made was contrary to good faith.

3.58 This approach would suggest a possible difference between UTCCR and UCTA. It suggests that a term will be unfair under UTCCR only if both substantive and procedural unfairness are present. In contrast, under UCTA it would appear permissible for the court to conclude that a clause is unreasonable simply because of its content ('substantive' unfairness) without there having been anything unreasonable in the way in which the contract was made or the term included in it ('procedural' unfairness). For example, it seems open to a court to conclude that it was not reasonable for a business to exclude its liability for negligence causing loss or damage to property even though the business had taken care to point out the clause to the consumer and the consumer had not raised any protest.

3.59 A second view of UTCCR is that 'significant imbalance ... to the detriment of the consumer' is in the nature of a threshold requirement: the clause cannot be regarded as unfair if any imbalance is either insignificant or is actually in the consumer's favour. This leaves the main test of whether or not a term is unfair resting on the concept of 'contrary to ... good faith'. The question then arises of the meaning of 'good faith' in this context. Can it consist entirely of substantive elements, not requiring any procedural impropriety?

3.60 A third and converse approach is to say that the reference to good faith is no more than a 'bow in the direction of [the] origins' of the German law on unfair terms which was so influential on the Directive, and which in turn was a development from the initial case law on the good faith article of the German Civil Code. German law is said now to pay scant regard to good faith when dealing with unfair clauses. On this view, the critical question is whether there is a significant imbalance to the detriment of the consumer. This view is supported by the fact that the French legislature decided not to incorporate the good faith criterion in its legislation implementing the Directive. It is also a view that seems to be supported by the European Commission.

3.61 However, the Recitals to the Directive seem to consider good faith to be an operative criterion, as they refer to the requirement of good faith being 'satisfied by the seller or supplier where he deals fairly and equitably with the other party whose legitimate interests he has to take into account'. The omission from the French legislation is partly explicable by the facts that French law already has a general requirement of performance in good faith, and that it would regard a supplier who sought to enjoy a disproportionate advantage to the detriment of the consumer as not acting in good faith.

3.62 A final approach is to say that there are two routes to unfairness within UTCCR. A term which in itself causes a significant imbalance will be contrary to 'good faith' and hence unfair. A term which appears in its substance not to have such an effect may in fact also be unfair if there has been a lack of procedural good faith. This approach allows for both procedure and substance to be considered, but allows certain terms to be ruled unfair per se.

The Law Commission in its proposals for unification of the UTCCR and UCTA propose a single test of whether a term is 'fair and reasonable' that would include both substantive and procedural unfairness and contain guidelines for assessing the issue of fairness and reasonableness (Law Commission, 2005: 44–45).

Several writers have suggested that 'reasonable expectations' of the consumer is the key to understanding the UTCCR. For example, Collins argues:

> In the context of ancillary terms in consumer contracts, the criterion of reasonable expectations may prove the most useful guide to the interpretation of the concept of good faith, for it describes what the consumer might reasonably expect to be contained in the small print of the contract: if the terms differ significantly in favour of the supplier, this could be described as inflicting an unfair surprise on the consumer and evidence of a lack of good faith on the part of the supplier. (Collins, 2003: 290)

This approach echoes Llewellyn's comment that:

> Free contract supposes free bargain ... where free bargaining is absent in fact, the conditions and clauses to be read into a bargain are not those which happen to be printed on the unread paper, but those which a sane man might reasonably expect to find on that paper. (Llewellyn, 1960: 370).

And Lord Steyn has stated that 'a theme that runs through our law of contract is that the reasonable expectations of honest men must be protected. It is not a rule or principle of law. It is the objective which has been and still is the principle [*sic*] moulding force of our law of contract' (*First Energy (UK) Ltd v Hungarian International Bank Ltd* 1993).

The concept of reasonable expectations is a vague criterion (see discussion in Stapleton, 1999; Yee, 2001; Mitchell, 2003). It could be subject to quite differing interpretations. Baron Bramwell argued for reasonable expectations in contract in the nineteenth century in *Parker v The South Eastern Railway* (1877) but his application of this concept would undoubtedly differ from that of Lord Steyn. In the context of UCTA and the UTCCR, where the courts may strike down express terms of the contract, it needs to be connected to a broader theory of autonomy and risk-taking in consumer markets. Do the economic theories outlined in the introduction to this chapter concerning information failure and bounded rationality suggest any clearer guidance?

In *First National* is it likely that the consumers affected by the practice of First National Bank would assume that they would still owe substantial amounts after they had repaid the debt by instalments? First National Bank was a sub-prime lender, that is to say, it lends to individuals with blemished credit records. These are generally lower-income and less-well-educated consumers. Although the House of Lords undertook an abstract review of the contract, it would have to make assumptions about the average consumer's understanding or reasonable expectations of the term.

4.1 Threatening action: credit card penalty charges

During the early 2000s substantial concern was expressed about the late fees charged by credit card companies. The OFT threatened legal action against financial institutions on the basis that the charges, generally about £25, were both penalties and contraventions of the UTCCR. It prepared a substantial document to justify its conclusions (see OFT, Calculating Fair Default Charges, 2006).

OFT press release, 26 July 2005

The OFT has written to eight major credit card companies to consult on its provisional conclusion that the levels of default charges they impose (eg for late payments) are excessive.

The OFT believes that it is unfair for the purposes of contract terms regulation to require a consumer who defaults in one of these ways to pay a disproportionately high charge. The OFT considers that, in a consumer contract, a default charge is likely to be disproportionately high if it is more than a genuine pre-estimate of the damages that the card issuer would win in court if it sued the cardholder for breach of contract.

… The OFT's provisional view is that the levels of the default charges imposed by the credit card companies need to be reduced in order to be fair.

The credit card companies have cooperated with the OFT's investigation into default charges. They have stated that they consider their default charge provisions are fair. The OFT has now explained to them why it does not accept their view and has given them three months in which to provide suitable undertakings or otherwise to address the concerns it has raised. The OFT has powers to take enforcement action in the courts if necessary to protect consumers.

OFT Board Meeting Minutes, Thursday, 6 April 2006

Credit Card Default Charges

There has been close dialogue with the banks and APACS prior to and following the recent announcement on unlawful penalty charges. The announcement has produced a large amount of positive press coverage.

The *Financial Times* reported on 24 August 2006 that all 36 main credit card issuers had reduced their penalty fees to £12 or less and that the OFT was going to insist that the principles in their report should be followed in relation to other charges, such as overdraft fees.

The following factors may have led to the success of the default charges initiative: the technical analysis of default charges by the OFT, the political support from consumer groups and presumably the government (one minister described them as 'outrageous'), and the ability to deal with a relatively small number of industry players. Compare the approach here with that taken to the applicability of section 75 of the Consumer Credit Act to purchases outside the UK. (See below at 556.) In the latter case the OFT used test case litigation.

4.2 Bank charges

Since the mid-1980s the major banks in the UK operated a 'free if in credit' policy, but with substantial charges for those who used overdraft facilities. By 2008, 30 per cent of these banks' income on current accounts resulted from a variety of authorised and unauthorised overdraft charges. The OFT study of this market indicated significant cross-subsidisation of generally older, more affluent consumers by younger, lower-income consumers. The increased focus on this issue by regulators, Which? and the media in the context of stories of 'rip-off' credit stimulated a groundswell of small claims against the banks that the overdraft charges were unfair (see extract by Rachael

Mulheron above at 269). In June 2007 a test case was proposed by the banks, with each party taking liability for its costs. The Supreme Court decided the case on the narrow issue of whether the overdraft charges were exempt from assessment because they formed part of the price of the agreement under regulation 6(2).

OFT v Abbey National [2009] UKSC 6

Lord Walker

3. The question for the court is … limited, and … technical. It is whether as a matter of law the fairness of bank charges levied on personal current account customers in respect of unauthorized overdrafts (including unpaid items charges and other related charges) … can be challenged by the … Office of Fair Trading … as excessive in relation to the services supplied to the customers.

6. The Directive in its final form applies only to contractual terms which have not been individually negotiated. That is the effect of Article 3, which sets a fairly high threshold for meeting that test. The Council's original proposals had been more far-reaching but they attracted a lot of criticism, especially from commentators in France and Germany, who were concerned at such extensive inroads into freedom of contract. An article by Professor Brandner and Professor Ulmer of the University of Heidelberg ((1991) 28 CML Rev 647) was particularly influential. In September 1992 the Council brought forward new proposals which can be described as a compromise solution balancing the need for consumer protection against residual freedom of contract.

38. The issue is a very important one, but it is essentially quite a short point, even when all the elements relevant to a purposive approach to construction are taken into account. …

43. This House's decision in First National Bank shows that not every term that is in some way linked to monetary consideration falls within Regulation 6(2)(b). Paras (d), (e), (f) and (l) of the 'greylist' in Schedule 2 to the 1999 Regulations are an illustration of that. But the relevant term in First National Bank was a default provision. Traders ought not to be able to outflank consumers by 'drafting themselves' into a position where they can take advantage of a default provision. But Bairstow Eves London Central Ltd v Smith [2004] 2 EGLR 25 shows that the Court can and will be astute to prevent that. In First National Bank Lord Steyn indicated that what is now Regulation 6(2) should be construed restrictively, and Lord Bingham said that it should be limited to terms 'falling squarely within it'. I respectfully agree. But in my opinion the Relevant Terms and the Relevant Charges do fall squarely within Regulation 6(2)(b).

47. … Charges for unauthorised overdrafts are monetary consideration for the package of banking services supplied to personal current account customers. They are an important part of the banks' charging structure, amounting to over 30 per cent of their revenue stream from all personal current account customers. The facts that the charges are contingent, and that the majority of customers do not incur them, are irrelevant. On the view that I take of the construction of Regulation 6(2), the fairness of the charges would be exempt from review in point of appropriateness under Regulation 6(2)(b) even if fewer customers paid them, and they formed a smaller part of the banks' revenue stream. Even if the Court of Appeal's interpretation had been correct, I do not see how it could have come to the conclusion that charges amounting to over 30 per cent of the revenue stream were (para 111) 'not part of the core or essential bargain.'

50. The correct construction of article 4(2) of the Directive is not essential for the determination

of this appeal. The correct construction ... is a question of community law, but the application of the Article, properly construed to the facts is a question for national law. Even if the Court of Appeal was not clearly wrong on the issue of construction, it was in my respectful opinion clearly wrong in applying its construction to the facts. In other circumstances it might be regarded as rather unprincipled to take that means of avoiding an important issue of Community law, but in the special circumstances of this case I would regard it as the lesser of two evils. There is a strong public interest in resolving the matter without further delay.

Lord Phillips

60. This agreement between the parties reflects acceptance by the Banks in the Court of Appeal of a finding by Andrew Smith J that was contrary to one of their submissions. The Banks had submitted that a term of a contract that provided the 'price or remuneration' for 'goods or services supplied' was absolutely exempt from assessment for fairness by reason of Regulation 6(2). This was described as the 'excluded term' construction of the Regulation. Andrew Smith J held that this was not correct. Regulation 6(2) precluded assessing a price term for fairness by reference to its adequacy as payment for the goods or services provided in exchange. It did not, however, preclude assessing a price term for fairness according to other criteria. This has been described as the 'excluded assessment' construction of the Regulation.

61. Mr Sumption submitted that the difference between the 'excluded term' and the 'excluded assessment' constructions was 'a distraction from the real issues'. It is certainly a distraction from the narrow issue that the parties are now agreed is before the court. But it is only because the 'excluded assessment' construction has prevailed that the issue has been narrowed from that in the Agreed Statement of Facts and Issue. Had the 'excluded term' construction prevailed, a finding in favour of the Banks that the Relevant Terms were included within the meaning of the word 'price' in Regulation 6(2) would have precluded any challenge to those terms on the ground of fairness. As it is, if the Banks succeed on the narrow issue, this will not close the door on the OFT's investigations and may well not resolve the myriad cases that are currently stayed in which customers have challenged Relevant Charges.

72. This raises the questions by what criteria do you decide whether the charges are payment for services, if so, whether individual charges are payments for individual services or part payment for a package of services, and from whose viewpoint do you decide those questions? So far as the latter question is concerned, the choice would appear to be between the viewpoint of the customer, having regard to the facts that he would reasonably be expected to know, the viewpoint of the Banks, having regard to the more extensive knowledge held by the Banks, or no viewpoint at all, on the basis that these questions have to be answered by application of an objective test to all the material facts. There is an allied question of whether the language used to describe the obligations imposed by the terms is relevant or whether one looks simply at the nature and effect of those obligations.

Lord Mance

101. [I]t is common ground that not every provision for payment contained in a contract for the supply of goods or services is rendered immune from scrutiny under Regulation 6(2). There can be payments which do not constitute either 'price or remuneration' of goods or services supplied in exchange. Further, payments which do constitute price or remuneration in this sense can be challenged as unfair on grounds which do not relate to their appropriateness in amount as against the goods or services supplied in exchange. Heads (d), (e), (f) and (l) in the grey list of terms set out in Schedule 2 to the Regulations fall within one or both categories. Director-General of Fair Trading v First National Bank plc [2002] 1 AC 481 provides another example.

113. In my opinion, the identification of the price or remuneration for the purposes of article 4(2) and regulation 6(2) is a matter of objective interpretation for the court. The court should no doubt read and interpret the contract in the usual manner, that is having regard to the view which the hypothetical reasonable person would take of its nature and terms. But there is no basis for requiring it to do so by attempting to identify a 'typical consumer' or by confining the focus to matters on which it might conjecture that he or she would be likely to focus. The consumer's protection under the Directive and Regulations is the requirement of transparency on which both insist. That being present, the consumer is to be assumed to be capable of reading the relevant terms and identifying whatever is objectively the price and remuneration under the contract into which he or she enters. A contract may of course require ancillary payments to be made which are not part of the price or remuneration for goods or services to be supplied under its terms. The First National Bank and Bairstow Eves cases illustrate the distinction by reference to default terms.

117. ...There is no reason why the price or remuneration payable for a package of services should not consist of a contingent liability. ... Like Lord Walker, I would therefore disagree with the Court of Appeal's application of its test, even had I considered that test to be correct so far as it focused on what was or was not 'ancillary' to the main bargain.

The Supreme Court did not address the issue whether the terms were in plain intelligible language, with both parties accepting the findings of the trial judge that the terms met the test. The trial court judgment will therefore be influential in any future decision on this issue. Andrew Smith J concluded that the test was whether the terms were plain and intelligible to 'the average consumer who is reasonably well-informed and reasonably observant and circumspect'. The terms should be sufficiently clear 'to enable the typical consumer to have a proper understanding of them for sensible and practical purposes ... [and] understand the effects of the terms'. Note the influence of the 'average consumer' test in the UCPD.

Simon Whittaker provides a severe critique of the reasoning of the Supreme Court (Whittaker, 2011: 106). First, he argues that the 'excluded term' rather than 'excluded assessment' approach is more justified by the terms of Recital 19 and the decision of the ECJ in *Caja de Madrid* (Case C-484-08) (decided after the bank charges case) which concluded that:

31. Article 4(2) of the Directive provides only that the 'assessment of the unfair nature is not to apply to the terms to which that provision relates, on condition that they are drafted in plain intelligible language. ...

32. ...The terms referred to in Article 4(2) ... escape the assessment as to whether they are unfair only in so far as the national court having jurisdiction should form the view, following a case-by-case examination, that they were drafted by the seller in plain, intelligible language.

34. ... Art 4(2) of the Directive is concerned ... solely with establishing the detailed rules and the scope of the substantive assessment of contract terms which have not been individually negotiated and which describe the essential obligations of contracts concluded between a seller or supplier and a consumer.

Second, he rejected the objective interpretation approach in favour of an interpretation based on the understanding of the average consumer. This would further the Directive's purpose of protecting the weaker party 'except where those terms reflect a true exercise of their contractual autonomy, that is a genuine choice'. This purpose lends support to an approach to Article 4(2) which adopts the viewpoint of the average consumer as to the price because that is likely to form the basis of that consumer's genuine choice. The average consumer is also a well-known concept in European law, adopted in the UTCCR. Using this concept in relation to unfair terms would harmonise the approach under both regulations. (For further commentary on the bank charges case, see: Brown, 2011; Devenney, 2011; Willett, 2011; Smith and Kenny, 2011; Micklitz, 2010; De Muynck, 2010.)

The *Abbey National* case saved the banks billions of pounds. They have responded to the judgment by altering their practices on overdrafts. The 2011 Treasury and DBIS response to the consultation on consumer credit and insolvency outlines these measures:

BIS/HMT Consumer Credit and Personal Insolvency Review: Formal Response (2011)

The evidence provided in response to the Review showed that there have been significant developments in the personal current account market in recent years. Working with the OFT, banks have committed to introduce measures to improve the transparency of unarranged overdraft charges. Through The Lending Code, they have also agreed to act sympathetically, positively and proactively if they have reason to believe that one of their customers is in financial difficulty. Many have also revised their charging structures in the last two years and, overall, charges have fallen. Recent figures from the OFT, for example, show that the average unpaid item charge fell by more than half from £34 in 2007 to £14 in March this year. However, responses to the Review also showed that there were still concerns about how charges—including the new charging structures—affect consumers, particularly where charges may not be clear or transparent enough.

6. The Government has been working with the British Bankers' Association and key current account providers to agree further commitments to improve transparency and control of charges for consumers. These commitments will apply to all full-facility accounts offered by the major current account providers including Barclays, HSBC, Lloyds Banking Group, Royal Bank of Scotland and Santander, representing 85 per cent of the personal current account market in the UK.

As a result of these further commitments all customers of the major current account providers will:

(i) have the option to receive a text or email alert from their bank when their balance falls below a certain level, giving them the opportunity to manage their spending so as to avoid going into an unarranged overdraft. Many will also be able to receive an alert if they do go into an unarranged overdraft, enabling them to take action to put their account right and avoid or minimise charges.

(ii) be made aware of a 'grace period' within which they can credit funds to put their account back within their limit and avoid a charge being applied.

(iii) benefit from a small buffer zone within which unarranged overdraft charges will not be levied. This will prevent consumers from incurring a substantial charge as a result of going into unarranged overdraft by a very small amount.

7. Banks have committed to offer text alerts to all full-facility current account holders by March 2012 and to deliver the other two commitments by March 2013 at the very latest. However, it is our understanding that for most consumers, these services will be available significantly earlier. Many banks will also be taking this opportunity to refresh their communications with

their customers to ensure that there is better understanding of the charges they could face and how they can be avoided.

8. These additional commitments complement enhanced transparency measures which have already been agreed between the industry and the OFT and which all current account providers are implementing. These include making charges clearer on monthly statements and providing indicative charging scenarios on their websites to enable consumers to compare how different banks charge for different patterns of unarranged overdraft use.

9. In particular, from the end of this year, all personal current account customers will receive an annual statement detailing how much they have paid for their bank account over the previous twelve months. The annual statement will act as a trigger point for consumers to stand back and consider whether they are getting good value for money from their current account and, if not, to consider switching to another provider.

10. Consumers need to know that they are able to switch current accounts quickly and easily, without fear of errors. In response to the recommendation made by the Independent Commission on Banking, the industry will introduce a new guaranteed 7-day switching service by September 2013. With the new service (which will be free of charge), consumers will be able to be confident that their account will be switched within 7 working days, without any risk of their payments going astray.

4.2.1 Paying not to go to the gym?

OFT v Ashbourne Management Services [2011] EWCA 1237

Kitchin J: The defendants' activities first came to the attention of the OFT in the spring of 2000 following a series of complaints from consumers. Since that time the OFT and the defendants have engaged in a dialogue as a result of which the defendants have made a series of amendments and revisions to the terms of Ashbourne's standard form agreements. This process has been so extensive that I now have before me no fewer than 13 versions of those agreements. Despite the offer of an undertaking by the defendants that henceforth they will only use the final version, it seems that each of the earlier versions may still be in use and so I am required to consider them all.

The practices of which the OFT complains may be summarised as follows:

(i) recommending that gym clubs enter into membership agreements which are regulated consumer credit agreements, as defined in section 8 of the CCA, on standard form agreements that do not meet the form and content requirements of section 61(1)(a) of the CCA;

(ii) recommending that gym clubs enter into membership agreements on standard terms which are unfair within the meaning of the UTCCR;

(iii) adopting unfair commercial practices contrary to the CPR.

Background

The claim is supported by three witness statements by Mr Jason Freeman, a projects director within the OFT's Consumer Markets Group. He explains that the OFT decided to investigate Ashbourne because it has received numerous complaints from consumers; the company operates nationally; it has apparently entered into some 300,000 agreements on behalf of around 700 gym clubs; it has shown a reluctance to amend its agreements in line with the

OFT's recommendations and there is evidence to suggest that it has persisted in certain practices notwithstanding assurances that they would cease.

Ashbourne's business has been advertised on a website which reveals details of its business model. A section headed 'Gym Membership Management Recruitment & Retention' describes its general nature:

'Ashbourne provides gym membership management, recruitment and retention services for hundreds of gyms and health & fitness clubs.

We manage your monthly membership payments. By dealing directly with defaulters on your behalf, we ensure you maintain positive customer relations with your members in the club.

Members making enquiries in the gym regarding payments or contracts can be referred to us and you are able to contact us with any special instructions regarding your members.

The advantages of using Ashbourne Membership Management:

- Improve and simplify your membership management by receiving regular monthly payments

- Give your customers access to a secure online payment system, making it easy for members to sign up and pay online

- Minimise bad debts through the use of Default Registration as a sanction. Obtain active help for those with debt problems through our alliance with Debt Dr

- Improve your membership retention and loyalty through automatic renewal and our excellent customer service

- Recruit new members using our membership recruitment service

- Utilise our experienced, professional customer service team to handle queries, freeing up your time to develop your business'

An important feature of the model appears from another section entitled 'Freedom to tailor your fees and your contract terms' which reads:

'Ashbourne can advise on the best membership contract strategy. We can help you decide on the fee structure of the membership contract and on the inclusion of any special terms.

We then tailor an agreement to suit your needs. For example, if your gym or health club is a "high end" facility that rivals the national chains, it is likely that a contract similar to theirs, commonly a 90-day rolling contract, will be most suitable.

However, if your club has a low monthly subscription, it is better to adopt a longer minimum term contract of 12, 24 or 36 months.'

Ashbourne does not deal with clubs at what it describes as the 'high end' of the market but rather with clubs with a 'low monthly subscription'; and it advises them to adopt agreements with minimum membership periods of 12, 24 or 36 months. This is a matter which has caused the OFT particular concern.

Another aspect of the business model which has caused the OFT great concern is the approach Ashbourne adopts to those members who have fallen behind with their payments or who wish to terminate their agreements before the end of the minimum membership period. The website describes such members as defaulters and they are dealt with by registration of their defaults with a credit reference agency, as the following passage reveals:

'The Power of Default Registration

Taking defaulters through the court process is adversarial, costly and provides no guarantee of success. Our approach is different; we register defaults with Experian and other Credit Agencies.

Default registration is more effective than a County Court Judgment as it seriously affects an individual's credit status, prevents the opening of a new bank account or credit card, and any existing borrowing is subject to review. People's credit record is being scrutinised by financial institutions more than ever before, so this is a powerful sanction. A default registration remains on a member's file for six years.

Benefits

Default registration removes the adversarial nature and cost of a legal process. ...'

A little later the website continues by way of amplification:

'Prompt Payment Resolution

For a minority of members, keeping up with payments can become a problem. Our approach is to identify issues as quickly as possible and provide a path for payment to resume. Our "firm but fair" approach produces a 98% payment collection rate while minimising confrontation. In all correspondence we emphasise the health and lifestyle benefits of gym membership.

Step-by-step approach

From the first day of non-payment onwards, regular letters are sent, giving members current details of their arrears and ways in which payment can be brought back up to date. This usually prompts a phone call, which then allows us to enter into a dialogue to reconcile the situation and retain the member.

If membership payment resumes, this is forwarded to you on the next remittance date. In the case of persistent defaulters, after a series of letters has been sent providing clear membership payment options, we register a bad debt with a credit reference agency as a Default Registration for the total outstanding balance on the membership.'

Ashbourne emphasises the success of this strategy with the following observation:

'Just the threat of Default Registration brings the vast majority of defaulters back on track.'

...

Para 116

1. **Unfair terms—general**

2. The OFT contends that various terms in Ashbourne's standard form agreements are unfair within the meaning of regulation 5 of the UTCCR. In particular it relies on those terms which:

3. (i) impose minimum membership periods of 12, 24 or 36 months;

(ii) make prompt payment by the member of each monthly subscription a condition of the agreement;

(iii) provide that in the event of termination before the end of the minimum period, the member is to become liable to pay the full amount payable in respect of the whole minimum period, or the full amount with a discount for accelerated payment;

(iv) purport to exclude the consumer's right to terminate for the gym club's breach; alternatively, purport to impose an obligation on the consumer to make payments in respect of the period after termination when the consumer has terminated for the gym club's breach;

(v) require notice of cancellation to be given to Ashbourne rather than the gym club;

(vi) fail to state in plain intelligible language the responsibility of a clearly identified supplier to provide gym facilities.

4. The OFT therefore invites me to make orders under regulation 12 of the UTCCR restraining Ashbourne from using any of its standard form agreements or any similar agreements which contravene the UTCCR and from relying on any unfair terms in existing agreements.

5. The OFT further submits that Ashbourne's activities are also unfair practices contrary to the CPR and amount to Community infringements within section 212 of the EA 2002 for at least the following reasons:

(i) Ashbourne's use or recommendation of the terms is contrary to regulation 3(3) of the CPR in that it does not meet the standard of honest market practice or good faith that may reasonably be expected;

(ii) Ashbourne's presentation of the terms is contrary to regulations 3(4)(a) and 5 of the CPR in that it is likely to deceive the average consumer in relation to the rights of the gym club or the consumer's own rights or the risks he may face;

(iii) and in either case Ashbourne's activities are likely to cause the average consumer to take the transactional decision of entering into the agreement or making a payment which he is not obliged to make; (iv) Ashbourne's reliance on the terms in chasing payment is contrary to regulation 3(3) or regulations 3(4)(c) and 7 of the CPR in that it does not meet the standard of honest market practice or good faith that may reasonably be expected; is likely significantly to impair the average consumer's freedom of choice through harassment, coercion or undue influence; and is likely to cause the average consumer to take the transactional decision of making a payment that he would not otherwise take.

Minimum Terms

Unfair terms—minimum term

Clause 2 of each of Ashbourne's standard form agreements sets a minimum membership period of 12, 24 or 36 months. Agreement 9 introduces, in clause 5, the qualification that the member may terminate in the event that the facilities and services provided by the gym club fall well below the standard the member might reasonably expect it to provide. This qualification is retained in all later versions of the agreements.

Agreement 10 spells out in capitals, in clause 2, that the member is liable to pay the monthly membership subscription for the minimum membership period and may be obliged to do so even if the member would prefer to cancel the agreement. As a result of observations made by the OFT, it also introduces provision for transfer, suspension and termination.

A member may transfer his membership to another person if that person agrees to become a member for the balance of the minimum period. He may suspend his membership in the event of loss of livelihood or medical advice not to use the gym due to injury or illness. The position will be reviewed after two months and, if the circumstances have not changed, the membership may be cancelled after a further two months. In the meantime, the obligation to pay monthly subscriptions continues. The agreement may also be cancelled in the event of change of principal place of work; or a move to a new home which is more than 15 miles away.

Agreements 11 to 13 confer upon the member additional rights to suspend or terminate. As I have mentioned, the OFT does not suggest there is any material difference between them in this respect so I need only refer to Agreement 13. This again spells out in capitals the obligation upon the member to pay the monthly membership subscription for the minimum membership period unless the membership is 'terminated without liability, suspended or transferred'. Each of these is then explained, together with the right to cancel. These extend the rights of the member to suspend or bring the agreement to an end so as to include loss of livelihood by the member or the member's spouse or partner; and an inability to use the gym for any medical reason including pregnancy or because the member has recently given birth. In the event of suspension, the member is now relieved of the obligation to pay monthly subscriptions.

The OFT is concerned about these terms because it has received many complaints which demonstrate that consumers tend to overestimate the use they will make of their gym club memberships, that unforeseen circumstances often make it impractical for members to use the gym facilities, and that often a monthly payment that may have been affordable at the beginning of the agreement ceases to be affordable before the end of the minimum membership period. Mr Jason Freeman has exhibited to his witness statements many such complaints. They also reveal that consumers often do not appreciate that they have entered into an agreement which requires them to remain a member for a minimum period until they seek to bring it to an end. Indeed statements have sometimes been made to them which have positively misled them into believing that they have a right to terminate under their agreements when in truth they do not.

… The OFT also points to that part of Ashbourne's website to which I have referred at paragraph [7] above. Here it advises gym clubs which have what it refers to as 'high end' facilities that a 90 day rolling contract similar to that of the national chains will be the best option. But if a gym club has a 'low monthly subscription' then, Ashbourne advises, it is better to adopt a longer minimum term contract of 12, 24 or 36 months.

It is therefore apparent that the standard form agreements the subject of these proceedings are directed at the lower end of the market.

The parties have identified three issues … : first, whether the term imposing a minimum membership period falls within the scope of regulation 6(2)(a); second, whether the term is in plain intelligible language; and third, whether the term is fair. I will address them in turn.

Does the term imposing a minimum membership period fall within the scope of regulation 6(2)(a) UTCCR?

…

The OFT contends that the term in each of Ashbourne's standard form agreements which requires the customer to remain a member for a minimum period does not fall within regulation 6(2)(a) because the main subject matter of each agreement is membership of the gym club and the right to use the club which is conferred by that membership. The period of time for which that right is conferred is an ancillary or subsidiary provision. The OFT also contends that even if the minimum period term is part of the main subject matter of the agreement it may still be assessed for fairness by reference to the consequences of earlier termination.

The defendants respond that there is nothing incidental, ancillary or subsidiary about a term which defines the period during which the benefits are to be conferred. It is quite literally a defining feature of the obligation assumed by the gym club.

... [After discussing the *First National Bank* case and the *OFT v Abbey National*] ... Turning now to the application of these principles in the context of this case, I believe that the main subject matter of each of Ashbourne's standard form agreements involves, on the one hand, the agreement by the gym club that a consumer may become a member of the club and use and access its facilities for the minimum period and, on other hand, the payment by the member of a monthly subscription of a certain sum, again for that minimum period. I do not accept that a term providing for the minimum period is not a 'core term' but is merely a 'subsidiary provision', as the OFT urged upon me. There is a danger in using these expressions as shorthand for the words of regulation 6(2) as the Supreme Court explained in the Abbey National case. However, in so far as it is helpful to use them, I believe that clause 2 of each of the agreements is a core term rather than a subsidiary provision because it defines the period during which the member is entitled to use the facilities of the gym club and, in return, must pay a particular monthly subscription. Nor do I believe the OFT gains any assistance from paragraphs 1(b), (e) or (o) of the indicative list of terms. These all concern terms dealing in one way or another with default or non-performance. I therefore believe that clause 2 of each of the agreements does fall within the scope of regulation 6(2).

That is not the end of the analysis, however, because the question then arises as to whether regulation 6(2)(a) precludes any assessment of the fairness of clause 2 of each of the agreements or whether the regulation only precludes an assessment relating to the definition of the main subject matter of the contract, that is to say its meaning, description and clarity. ... [R]egulation 6(2)(a) only precludes the assessment of the fairness of a term by reference to the definition of the main subject matter of the contract. This is not only the natural meaning of the words used in regulation 6(2) but also gives effect to the purpose of its two paragraphs as explained by Lord Walker JSC. Moreover, as the House of Lords explained in the First National Bank case, this regulation should be given no wider an interpretation than necessary. This is a matter to which I must return in addressing the third issue, namely fairness.

Is the term expressed in plain intelligible language?

...

The question whether a particular term is expressed in plain intelligible language must be considered from the perspective of an average consumer. Here such a consumer is a member of the public interested in using a gym club which is not a high end facility and who may be attracted by the relatively low monthly subscriptions.

[Kitchin J concluded that the terms were in plain intelligible language]

Fairness

I must now turn to the issue of fairness and consider whether the terms in Ashbourne's standard form agreements which provide for a minimum membership period are so weighted as to cause a significant imbalance in the parties' rights and obligations to the detriment of the consumer in a manner or to an extent which is contrary to good faith. As has been seen, Ashbourne recommends minimum periods of 12, 24 or 36 months for each of them. In assessing their fairness, it is, I think, important to have firmly in mind the average consumer to whom these agreements are targeted.

At the outset I recognise that the gym clubs set their own price structures but, as Mr Clayton-Wright says, the subscriptions they charge for agreements with minimum membership periods are invariably lower than those for rolling monthly membership agreements. Moreover, it is this lower charge which induces the average consumer to enter into such an agreement rather than taking one of the other tariff options or, perhaps, not joining the gym club at all.

This average consumer tends to overestimate how often he will use the gym once he has become a member and further, unforeseen circumstances may make continued use of its facilities impractical or unaffordable. Indeed, it is, as the defendants say, a notorious fact that many people join such gym clubs having resolved to exercise regularly but fail to attend at all after two or three months. Yet, having entered into the agreement, they are locked into paying monthly subscriptions for the full minimum period.

The defendants recognise the potential for unfairness the clauses providing for minimum membership periods have in circumstances such as these but say it is addressed by the qualifications introduced into Agreement 10 which expressly provide for termination in the event of a repudiatory breach by the gym club; permit the transfer of a membership; and provide for suspension or termination in the event of loss of livelihood, injury or illness, change of principal place of work or a move to a new home.

Mr Freeman explained why these qualifications are inadequate in his second witness statement and, as a result, the defendants have produced Agreement 13 which confers upon the member additional rights to suspend or terminate in the circumstances I have described. This agreement also relieves the member of the obligation to pay monthly subscriptions during the period of any permitted suspension.

I accept that these amendments go some way to reduce the burden on members but they do not remove it because it is not possible to anticipate all events which may render continued use of a gym impractical or unaffordable and they provide fertile ground for dispute as to their proper interpretation, as the letters of complaint show. Further, and most importantly, they do not begin to address the tendency of the average consumer to overestimate the use he will make of the gym facilities and, indeed, that he is likely not to attend at all after two or three months.

It is of course true that members have the benefit of a relatively low monthly subscription. But an analysis of the tariffs of three sample gym clubs conducted by Dr Mathew Bennett, the Director of Economics within the OFT, shows that a member wishing to terminate an annual agreement after three months would face a termination charge which is significantly higher than the discount he has received. The same applies after six months. The termination charge only equals the discount the member has received if he terminates after 10 or 11 months.

So far as the gym clubs are concerned, the terms providing for a minimum membership period are highly advantageous because clubs of this kind are rarely so oversubscribed that they cannot take on new members, particularly members who have overestimated the use they are going to make of the gym facilities.

I must also consider whether this imbalance in the parties' rights and obligations arises in a manner or to an extent which is contrary to good faith.

In this regard, the defendants know that the average consumer overestimates the use he will make of the gym and that frequently unforeseen circumstances make its continued use impossible or his continued membership unaffordable. They are also well aware that the average consumer is induced to enter into one of their agreements because of the relatively low monthly subscriptions associated with them but that if he ceases to use the gym after between three and six months he would be better off joining on a pay per month basis. Yet the defendants take no steps to have these matters brought to the attention of consumers. Nor do the defendants ensure that consumers are made clearly aware of their overall liability at the outset which might alert them to the risks associated with early termination and the likely benefits of entering into an agreement for a shorter term.

Moreover, I do not believe the defendants have ever offered a satisfactory explanation for the different advice they give on their website to what they describe as 'high end' gym clubs. For these, they say, a contract similar to those of the national chains, commonly a 90 day rolling contract, will be most suitable.

In all these circumstances I believe that the defendants' business model is designed and calculated to take advantage of the naivety and inexperience of the average consumer using gym clubs at the lower end of the market. As the many complaints received by the OFT show, the defendants' standard form agreements contain a trap into which the average consumer is likely to fall.

I must of course give weight to the requirement that there must be a significant imbalance. Taking this and all the other matters to which I have referred into account I have reached the conclusion that the terms of Agreements 1-10 setting minimum membership periods of 12, 24 or 36 months are so weighted as to cause a significant imbalance in the parties' rights and obligations in a manner and to an extent which is contrary to good faith. The position in relation to Agreements 11–13 is, I believe, different because they do extend the circumstances in which members may terminate before the end of the minimum period. In the case of these agreements I have come to the conclusion that the threshold is higher and that a significant imbalance in the parties' rights and obligations in a manner or to an extent which is contrary to good faith only arises in those cases in which the minimum term exceeds 12 months, that is to say those which provide for a minimum membership period of 24 or 36 months. My conclusion in relation to these later agreements might well have been different had they permitted the member to terminate after 12 months on, say, 30 days notice, perhaps with a provision requiring the member to pay the difference between the agreed subscription and that for a rolling monthly membership for the period prior to the date of termination.

This brings me to the final part of the analysis, namely whether this assessment of fairness relates to the definition of the main subject matter of the agreements. In my judgment it does not. The assessment does not relate to the meaning or description of the length of the minimum period, the facilities to which the member gains access or the monthly subscription which he has to pay; nor does it relate to the adequacy of the price as against the facilities provided. Instead it relates to the obligation upon members to pay monthly subscriptions for the minimum period when they have overestimated the use they will make of their memberships and failed to appreciate that unforeseen circumstances may make their continued use of a gym impractical or their memberships unaffordable. Put another way, it relates to the consequences to members of early termination in light of the minimum membership period. Accordingly I believe the assessment is not precluded by regulation 6(2).

Unfair commercial practices

The OFT contends Ashbourne has engaged in four categories of behaviour which amount to unfair commercial practices. I will deal with them in turn. In so doing it should be understood that I am only concerned with activities since the CPR came into force on 26 May 2008. I should also note that the OFT's case developed as the hearing progressed.

Unfair terms

The OFT also submits that the activities of the defendants in recommending and using Ashbourne's standard form agreements which contain terms which contravene the UTCCR constitute unfair business practices contrary to the CPR and amount to Community infringements within section 212 of the EA 2002 for the reasons set forth in paragraph [118] above.

This submission turns on the various allegations of unfairness I have considered in paragraphs [129] to [221] of this judgment. I have found that Ashbourne's standard form agreements or their particular terms are unfair in various respects. A trader may reasonably be expected not to include unfair terms in standard form agreements which he recommends; not to present standard terms in such agreements which are likely to deceive the consumer in relation to the rights of the gym club or his rights as consumer or the risks he may face; not to omit material information or provide information which is unclear; and not to demand payments which the consumer is not bound to pay. In recommending the use of these agreements which are unfair or contain unfair terms and in seeking payment of subscriptions under them which members are not bound to pay, the defendants have done all of the foregoing and have not acted in accordance with the standard commensurate with honest market practice and have caused consumers to take transactional decisions they would not otherwise have taken, namely to enter into such agreements and to make payments under them. In so far as the defendants have carried out such activities since 26 May 2008 they have therefore engaged in unfair commercial practices which have harmed the collective interests of consumers.

Credit reference agency reporting

The complaint about the defendants' activities in reporting information about members to credit reference agencies has a number of aspects.

... Third, the OFT says that if the agreements are not regulated credit agreements, the information the defendants are reporting or threatening to report to credit reference agencies will nonetheless be inaccurate if it is claimed under a term which is unfair or if it is nothing more than an amount that the defendants consider the gym club is entitled to in damages. I agree and I do not understand the defendants to suggest otherwise.

Fourth, the OFT contends that reporting or threatening to report to credit reference agencies the fact that an individual owes a debt which is, in reality, no more than a claim for unliquidated damages, or which, for any other reason, including the proper construction of the agreement in question, is not owed is an unfair commercial practice contrary to regulations 3(3), 3(4) (a), 3(4)(c), 5 and 7. This, it seems to me, overlaps with the OFT's third point, and is, in principle, another valid complaint. Once again, I do not understand this to be disputed by the defendants.

Fifth, the OFT says that demanding payment of a sum when the liability to pay that sum is disputed by reference to representations made by the defendants or by the gym club or by reference to express contract terms, whether made orally or in writing, is an unfair commercial practice contrary to regulations 3(3), 3(4)(a), 3(4)(c), 5 and 7. If made good on the facts, this too is a sound complaint.

In my judgment, the third, fourth and fifth contentions of the OFT are well founded and are justified on the facts of this case. In large measure they follow from my findings in relation to unfair terms. So far as the OFT's fifth point is concerned and notwithstanding assurances by the defendants as to their future conduct, which assurances were reiterated by Mr Clayton-Wright in his witness statement, Mr Freeman has provided instances of continued misuse of credit reference agency reporting by the defendants in his third witness statement.

Mrs Dorothy Francis entered into gym club membership agreements for herself and her daughter, aged 14, on 26 March 2010. She says was told by the sales representative that she could cancel at any time. She rapidly found that the gym was unsuitable for her and that her daughter was unable to use most of the equipment because of her age. So she tried to cancel the agreements. She then received from Ashbourne a series of letters refusing to let her cancel, demanding payment and threatening to instigate default registration with a credit reference agency. Eventually Mrs Francis succumbed to Ashbourne's threats because she did not want her credit rating to be affected.

... Mrs Nicola Edwards entered into a gym club membership agreement on 1 April 2010 for a minimum period of 36 months. She attempted to cancel the agreement on 1 July 2010 because she found the club was providing an unsatisfactory service. On 6 September 2010 she received a letter from Ashbourne's 'Litigation Department' stating that it had instigated default registration with a credit reference agency and that this would affect 'every aspect of her life'. However, if she paid the balance of the monthly subscriptions for the whole minimum period the default registration would be erased. If she did not, it would be confirmed. Following a complaint by Mrs Edwards the gym club in issue offered to settle the dispute by accepting a payment of a sum being the difference between the sum she would have paid for monthly membership and the sum she contracted to pay per month under the agreement, for the three months for which she used the gym facilities. This, the OFT recognises, was a fair approach for the gym club to have adopted.

In all these circumstances I am satisfied that, in so far as the defendants have carried out these activities since 26 May 2008, they have engaged in unfair commercial practices which have harmed the collective interests of consumers.

Unwanted letters and aggressive tactics

The OFT has drawn attention in its evidence to further activities of Ashbourne which, it says, constitute misleading and aggressive commercial practices contrary to regulations 3(4)(a), (b) and (c), 5, 6 and 7. These have been addressed by the offer by Ashbourne to give undertakings in terms sought by the OFT not to do any of the following acts, namely: exaggerate the significance and consequences of the reporting of information to a credit reference agency; threaten to inform and/or inform any credit reference agency that individuals have failed to make payments without informing the individuals of their right to access records kept about them by credit reference agencies and to have incorrect entries corrected; and send letters which purport to be from a 'litigation department' which does not exist, or otherwise threaten legal proceedings when it has no intention to issue such proceedings.

Conclusion

I have found that various aspects of Ashbourne's standard form agreements are unfair contrary to the UTCCR and that the defendants have recommended the use of these agreements; that the defendants have engaged in unfair commercial practices contrary to the CPR; and that the defendants have engaged in activities which constitute Community infringements under the EA 2002. The OFT is entitled to declarations and injunctions to reflect my findings. I will hear further argument as to the precise form of order if it cannot be agreed.

Are you convinced by Kitchin J's arguments on regulation 6(2) in the light of the *Abbey National* analysis? According to a study on the fitness industry, approximately 12 per cent of the UK population are registered as members of health and fitness clubs or publicly owned fitness facilities. The majority of the members of gym clubs are 'typically young, affluent and single'. The OFT gave wide publicity to the judgment in *Ashbourne*, warning other gyms about the possibility of contravening the UTCC and the CPUT regulations. In January 2012 it opened an investigation under the Enterprise Act 2002 'into a number of companies that operate gym and fitness club chains or who provide management services to gyms. It is considering whether these companies are using or recommending unfair contract terms in breach of the Unfair Terms in Consumer Contracts Regulations 1999 and/or are engaging in any unfair business practices under the Consumer Protection from Unfair Trading Regulations 2008' (OFT, 2012: http://www.oft.gov.uk/OFTwork/consumer-enforcement/consumer-enforcement-current/health-contracts/).

Evaluating the impact of the OFT litigation in a case like *Ashbourne* must take into account the direct effects on the parties and the indirect effects on consumer awareness and other businesses. In *OFT v Foxtons* the OFT successfully challenged terms used by Foxtons concerning renewal commissions and sales commissions paid by consumer landlords to Foxtons (see *OFT v Foxtons Limited* [2009] EWHC 1681 (Ch)). It commissioned an evaluation of the impact of its intervention. The survey concluded that although the Foxtons case resulted in an estimated £4.4 million in benefits for consumer landlords of Foxtons through a reduction in renewal commissions and the abolition of sales commissions (when the landlord sells the property to the tenant), it was difficult to quantify the indirect benefits of the case. However, awareness of the decision was low among consumer landlords and relatively low among other letting agents. The OFT concluded that 'it may take time for consumers and businesses to become aware of changes to or clarifications of the law as a result of a court ruling and for businesses to change their behaviour in response. Such changes are also likely to need re-enforcing over time' (OFT1346eval, 2011: 8). The £4.4 million in benefits also does not take into account what are termed potential 'waterbed effects' where the supplier claws back lost income through a different term or price adjustment.

Would it be more effective to regulate the industry directly? This is the approach adopted in several Canadian and US jurisdictions. These statutes provide specific rules on the length of contracts, the possibility of cancellation, etc. Consider the costs and benefits of this approach. The following extract is legislation in Ontario Canada.

Ontario (Canada) Consumer Protection Act 2002 SO 2002, Chapter 30 Schedule A

'personal development services' means,

(a) services provided for,

(i)   health, fitness, diet or matters of a similar nature,

(ii) modelling and talent, including photo shoots relating to modelling and talent, or matters of a similar nature,

(iii) martial arts, sports, dance or similar activities, and

(iv) other matters as may be prescribed, and

(b) facilities provided for or instruction on the services referred to in clause (a) and any goods that are incidentally provided in addition to the provision of the services;

Application

29. (1) Sections 30 to 36 apply in respect of personal development services or proposed personal development services for which,

(a) payment in advance is required; and

(b)   the consumer's total potential payment obligation, excluding cost of borrowing, exceeds a prescribed amount.

Exceptions

... 30. (1) Every personal development services agreement shall be in writing, shall be delivered to the consumer and shall be made in accordance with the prescribed requirements. ...

Agreements for one year only

31. (1) No personal development services agreement may be made for a term longer than one year after the day that all the services are made available to the consumer.

Deemed separate agreement

(2) Any personal development services agreement that provides for a renewal or an extension of the agreement beyond one year shall be deemed to create a separate agreement for each renewal or extension of one year or less.

Renewal provision

(3) A personal development services agreement that provides for the renewal or extension of the agreement is not valid unless the supplier complies with the prescribed requirements.

Deemed non-renewal of agreement

(4) A personal development services agreement that provides for a renewal or extension of the agreement shall be deemed not to be renewed or extended if the consumer notifies the supplier, before the time for renewal or extension, that the consumer does not want to renew or extend.

Only one agreement

32. (1) No supplier shall enter into a new agreement for personal development services with a consumer with whom the supplier has an existing agreement for personal development services unless the new agreement is for personal development services that are distinctly different from the services provided under the existing agreement.

... (3) For the purposes of subsection (1), a different term or a different commencement date does not constitute a distinct difference in the personal development services to be provided.

Renewals exempted

(4) Nothing in this section prevents a personal development services agreement from being renewed during the term of the agreement provided that the renewal meets the requirements under section 31.

Initiation fee

33. No supplier of personal development services shall,

(a)   charge a consumer more than one initiation fee; or

(b)   charge an initiation fee that is greater than twice the annual membership fee.

Instalment plans

34. (1) Every supplier of personal development services shall make available to consumers at least one plan for instalment payments of membership fees and initiation fees, if applicable,

that allow consumers to make equal monthly payments over the term of the personal development services agreement.

(2) No supplier shall provide an instalment payment plan through which the total amount paid by instalments exceeds the membership or initiation fee, if applicable, by more than 25 per cent.

Cancellation: cooling-off period

35. (1) A consumer may, without any reason, cancel a personal development services agreement at any time within 10 days after the later of receiving the written copy of the agreement and the day all the services are available.

Cancellation: failure to meet requirements

(2) In addition to the right under subsection (1), a consumer may cancel a personal development services agreement within one year after the date of entering into the agreement if the consumer does not receive a copy of the agreement that meets the requirements under section 30.

Would this form of regulation be possible in the UK since it might be challenged as going beyond the total harmonisation in the UCPD?

4.3 The OFT as bargaining agent for consumers

The OFT may viewed as a bargaining agent for consumers, changing the ground rules of contracting in consumer markets. As a bargaining agent for consumers the OFT may reduce the discretionary power of business (eg 'Sky may at any time without notice vary terms') and require firms to live up to oral promises made by suppliers (see, for example, the prohibition on entire agreement clauses and the *Vacation 2000* case). It is possible that the greater clarity in contract terms may have a progressive distributional impact. Another alternative, however, could be that businesses will provide less information on contract terms in the documents that they provide to consumers.

John Wightman argues that in business contracting there will often be relatively well-known customary understandings that a firm will not insist on the full or literal enforcement of a term. He refers to such customary understandings as one method of 'taming' standard-form contract terms which appear on their face to be one sided. He argues that the absence of widely known and accepted customary practices in consumer transactions means that a supplier will often be able to exercise discretion in determining whether to provide a concession to a consumer. In a study of retailer complaint handling practices, Ramsay found that 'many retailers perceived themselves as exercising a discretionary power, applying reasonable standards of the marketplace for the privilege of reasonable customers as interpreted by store personnel' (Ramsay, 1981: 131–32). The possibility of market discrimination in favour of the more articulate, middle-class consumer tracks concern about economic discrimination between marginal and infra-marginal consumers, with the latter being exploited by businesses. Wightman argues that the absence of shared understandings in consumer transactions sets the stage for giving effect to the expectations of consumers (Wightman, 2003: 175–77) through a bargaining agent such as the OFT.

Several questions arise concerning this role of the OFT as a bargaining agent.

First, if the OFT is an agent for consumers, then principal–agent issues arise, ie ensuring that the regulator is not captured or shirks its role. There are two major controls here: monitoring by other regulators such as the National Audit Office and the possibility of public interest groups taking action in relation to unfair terms.

Second, Goldberg raises the question whether all consumers will benefit from an administrative bargaining agent, arguing that 'some consumers are likely to be worse off, receiving protection from a clause that affected them little or not at all in exchange for a higher price' (for a similar criticism, see Gillette, 2005). Could this analysis be applied to the prohibition on contracting out of liability for consequential loss? Is it likely that this prohibition would result in higher prices? Is this risk spreading appropriate? Or is the better approach that of Hugh Beale who argues that there may be structural imbalance if 'the supplier reduces the price slightly and thereby gains a few extra sales, but at the price of placing a very large potential loss on the small number of consumers for whom the risk will materialize' (Beale, in Beatson and Friedmann, 1995: 243).

Third, negotiation was the dominant mode of regulation under the UTCCR and this carries on the traditional informal approach of the OFT to regulation . However, the more recent approach has favoured 'high-impact' cases. Lawyers may favour litigation, particularly high-impact litigation, but whether this is the best method of regulation is a difficult issue to assess. The evaluation of the *Foxtons* case indicates that there was a mixed impact: unfair terms were still being used by a relatively large number of letting agents. In contrast, the high profile of the bank charges case meant that although the OFT lost the litigation, continuing pressure for change has had an effect on the banks' terms. The bank charge litigation was only one act in a continuing political battle.

Bargaining between an agency and business takes place within the shadow of the law, traditions of regulation (adversarial/co-operative) and the particular political climate. The National Audit Office drew attention to the limited resources of the OFT in the late 1990s in combating unfair contract terms. This provided a justification for the Labour government to increase resources to the OFT as part of its rejuvenation of the agency, embracing consumer empowerment as part of the Third Way strategy. The Conservative government had shown little enthusiasm for implementation of the UTCC directive, and it was not until after a Labour government came to power in 1997, with a commitment to promote the consumer interest, that there was more financial and political support for the work of the OFT.

The UTCC powers should also be seen in the context of other OFT powers to address industry-wide problems. For example, it might encourage codes of practice, or initiate a market investigation in response to a 'supercomplaint'. The approach under the UTCCR was often used for negotiated rule-making in relation to a particular sector. The OFT believe that this approach is superior to individual negotiations:

> We maximized the impact of our work by targeting sectors where we felt there were significant problems with unfair contract terms. We did this by working with organizations that provide model contracts for their sectors and by issuing guidelines to businesses.We reached many more businesses this way than would have been possible through taking regulatory action only against individual businesses.

The sectors targeted included used-car warranties and glazing contracts. (OFT Annual Report and Resource Accounts 2003–04)

To what extent does the OFT approach to unfair contract terms fit the 'responsive' or 'decentred' model of regulation outlined in Chapter 3? Could we view the OFT as playing the role suggested by Michael Porter in his book *The Competitive Advantage of Nations*—encouraging best practices that will make businesses more competitive internationally? For example, one of the mobile phone companies interviewed by the National Audit Office indicated that the work of the OFT 'had led to a better deal for customers and changes to mobile telephone industry contracts earlier than would have occurred due to market forces alone'. This seems to contradict Posner's argument that competition will solve the problem of consumer standard-form terms.

7

Regulation of Consumer Credit Markets

'No inquiry fees. Money at 5 per cent, to be obtained at a moment's notice, or nearly so'. I have a volume of advertisements of that character.

Do you know any case in which only 5 per cent is charged for the loan of money on those bills of sale?

—No it is a myth.

(Evidence of Charles Edward Ward, Nottingham accountant to the Select Committee on Bills of Sale Act (1878) Amendment Bill at 45)

The process of persuading people to incur debt, and the arrangements for them to do so, are as much a part of modern production as the making of the goods and the nurturing of the wants. … [O]ne wonders, inevitably, about the tensions associated with debt creation on such a massive scale. The legacy of wants, which are themselves inspired, are the bills which descend like winter snow on those who are buying on the installment plan. By millions of hearths throughout the land, it is known that when these harbingers arrive, the repossession man cannot be far behind. Can the bill collector be the central figure in the good society? (JK Galbraith, *The Affluent Society* (3rd edn 1976) 148, 149)

I do not borrow on credit cards; it is too expensive. (Mr Barrett, Chairman, Barclaycard, Select Committee on Treasury, Minutes on Evidence, 2003)

Credit is central to contemporary consumer economies. It is not surprising, therefore, that governments should be closely concerned with promoting and regulating its use. Credit for consumption is not a modern invention and there is a long history of regulation, through methods such as usury laws. The period from 1980 until the global financial crisis of 2008, was characterised by a substantial growth in both consumer and mortgage credit. Deregulation of credit markets, securitisation, the application of sophisticated computer technology to develop predictive credit scores and risk-based pricing, and the spread of all-purpose credit cards, facilitated the extension of consumer and mortgage credit. The period since the late 1990s has also been remarkable for national, regional and international initiatives to reform consumer credit regulation, and the global financial crash followed by the 'great recession' challenges assumptions about the role of consumer credit in the economy and the appropriate approach to regulation.

The internationalisation of consumer credit raises issues of economic and social policy for both developed and developing countries. International principles and best practices for consumer finance regulation are proposed in the wake of the global financial crisis. This chapter provides a case study for examining distinct approaches to regulation and a variety of regulatory techniques. These include: detailed disclosure requirements throughout the life of a credit agreement; price and terms control; the role of open-texture standards, eg the standard of 'unfair credit relationships', and broad discretionary powers conferred on courts to modify relationships; harnessing of market incentives by placing liability on gatekeepers (see below discussion of section 75 of the CCA); the alteration of default rules; screening access of suppliers to the credit market through licensing. Consumer credit contracts are often long-term relationships with the possibility of changes in the situations of the parties over the life of the contract. They therefore provide tests for the extent to which the law will recognise the relational nature of these contracts and develop distinct principles for them.

The institutional structure of regulation in the UK is in flux. The UK has experience of two regulators, the Office of Fair Trading (OFT) and the Financial Services Authority (FSA). Current legislative proposals (2012) introduce a new Financial Conduct Authority that will take over the existing jurisdiction of the OFT. The US has recently established a Federal Consumer Financial Protection Bureau, reviving the 'New Deal' model of the administrative agency. A key question is the extent to which greater *ex ante* product and supplier regulation is desirable rather than reliance on controls on point-of-sale practices.

---

1. The role of consumer credit in the economy

I Ramsay, 'Consumer Credit Regulation After the Fall: International Dimensions' (2011) 1 *Zeitschrift für Europäisches Unternehmens- und Verbraucherrecht* 24

Consumer credit and the lifecycle model of consumption

An influential approach in economics argues that consumer credit plays an important role in lifecycle budgeting, balancing saving and spending and income smoothing. Households may commit future income to present consumption needs based on their lifetime income expectations. If income in the future is expected to increase then it is optimal to borrow to finance present consumption. ... Since earnings are generally 'hump shaped', younger consumers may be expected to borrow more. Consumer credit permits the accumulation of capital assets such as homes but also depreciating assets (washing machines, etc) which provide immediate services which might substitute for more expensive external services (such as a commercial laundry). Borrowers might however be constrained in access to credit particularly when they are younger. The deregulation of the 1980s permitted consumers to achieve a more desirable balance of consumption and saving. ... Consumers may underuse credit because of uncertainty as to the future so that one role of regulation is to stimulate trust and confidence in credit markets. A well functioning consumer credit market could therefore enhance consumers' capabilities—to use Sen's phrase. Even the poor may benefit from credit through the use of consumer credit for income smoothing.

The arguments summarized above were made by the Crowther Committee (1971) in the UK ... when consumer credit was in its infancy in the UK. These arguments were important legitimators for the development of consumer credit to an increasingly banked population. The EU repeated them in an early draft of the Consumer Credit Directive stating that 'credit is the lubricant of economic life'. ...

Similar arguments are made in relation to credit for developing countries, that consumer credit permits income smoothing and that it may be beneficial to poorer consumers. The lifecycle model of consumer behaviour remains influential in policy making and financial literacy strategies, and in explaining patterns of indebtedness at different stages of the lifecycle. Critics do point to anomalies in savings behavior between countries, cross cultural differences, and evidence of increased debt, over-indebted ness and bankruptcy among older consumers which pose questions about the model. The increased availability of credit without fixed repayment schedules—the credit card being the classic example—also loosens the discipline of the traditional instalment plan.

Consumer credit: loans for wages?

Barba/Pivettti challenge the lifecycle model as a description of the growth in household debt in the US and UK economies since the 1980s. They argue that the role of credit in these economies should rather be characterised as 'loans for wages'. Consumer debt compensated for relatively stagnant disposable incomes and reductions in the welfare state as globalization, with the abolition in barriers to the mobility of capital, permitted capital to be increasingly free of labour power. Consumer debt was an 'effort by low and middle income households to maintain as long as possible their relative standards of consumption in the face of persistent changes in income distribution in favour of households with higher incomes'. Within this model, the male breadwinner model of the family was replaced by a model where families rely on two incomes for survival, creating increased dangers of downward mobility in the event of sickness, accident or unemployment occurring to one income earner.

The growth in inequality during the period since 1979 was masked therefore by the ability of individuals to use credit to purchase a 'taste' if not an equal share of the economic pie. However, credit was often offered on terms which reflected regressive cross-subsidisation between consumers, further increasing inequalities. Given these facts it is not surprising that the rise in formal measures of over-indebtedness in countries such as the UK and US has been concentrated in lower middle-class and lower-income populations which have the highest ratio of debt to income and assets as well as the highest debt-service ratio. A characteristic of those countries with this model of economy has been relatively 'high' levels of bankruptcy and insolvency. The loans for wages model may not fit easily all European countries. Its implications are a higher level of default on debts, which may vary from one or two missed payments to bankruptcy, with a continuing need to reintegrate individuals within the credit system. This was achieved in the US by a generous consumer bankruptcy system and European countries have since the 1980s made debt adjustment and personal insolvency more accessible. There is evidence in the wake of the crisis of an attempt to return to the loans for wages model in the US and UK with the associated idea that empowered consumers drive productivity. ...

Institutional patterning and consumer credit markets

[An] individualistic focus obscures the collective issues raised by behavioural analysis of financial crises, namely the 'herd' nature of both the supply and demand side of the market—described in the 1930s by Keynes as 'animal spirits'—captured more recently by the concept of 'irrational exuberance. It draws attention to the 'social habit structure' of credit markets. This 'habit- structure' is partly constituted by the institutional structure of regulation—the ground rules of the market. This institutional approach stresses the long term patterning effects of market ground rules. John Kenneth Galbraith originally described this effect when he outlined the twin roles of permitting extensive advertising and consumer credit in 'want creation' in the US during the post- second-world-war era and in creating a culture of private consumption—a Consumers' Republic—promising increased welfare and equality through private consumption. Galbraith's thesis of 'want creation' became unfashionable among neo-classical economists partly because it was difficult to model but it now has some empirical support.

1.1 Consumer credit in the UK

Valuable historical accounts now exist of consumer credit in the UK. (See eg O'Connell, 2009; Johnson, 1998; Finn, 2003; Brown, 2006. A useful survey of historical development of consumer credit in Europe and North America is Goode, 1979. For the US, see Calder, 1999; Cohen, 2003.)

The Crowther Committee (1971) provides much information on the state of consumer credit in the late 1960s. In 1967 the UK consumer debt to disposable income ratio was 4.2 compared with 11.8 in Canada and 9.6 in the United States. Table 1 indicates the forms of credit used in 1969. The Committee concluded that 'without being complacent … we in this country are as yet a long way from the point where the volume of consumer credit outstanding is likely to reach dangerous proportions'. Hire-purchase was used most frequently by those in social groups C1 and C2. Bank overdrafts were the province of groups AB.

Table 1. Forms of consumer credit, 1969 (Crowther Committee Table 3.7)

Credit form	Percentage of population ever using	Percentage of population using in 1969
Hire-purchase	49	7
Television rental	37	3
Mail order on credit	28	10
Check trading	12	2
Credit sale	8	2
Bank overdraft	6	
Personal loan from bank	5	
Personal loan finance coy	4	1
Loan from insurance coy	2	
Loan from a moneylender	1	
Second mortgage	1	

Personal sector indebtedness in the United Kingdom increased significantly from the early 1980s (Social Trends, 1988: 109). This reflected deregulation of controls on lending to consumers in 1982, the abolition of 'terms control' on hire-purchase, deregulation of mortgage lending and increased financial services competition. The debt to disposable income ratio grew from 25 per cent in 1981 to 68 per cent in 1988, with much of this debt representing home mortgages. After a downturn in borrowing

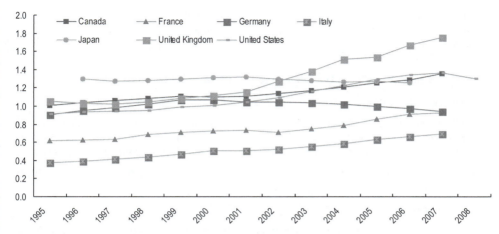

Figure 1 Household indebtedness to gross disposable income, 1995–2008 (OECD Factbook, 2010)

during the recession of the early 1990s there were large increases in borrowing during the New Labour era, particularly through housing equity withdrawal (Engelen et al, 2011). In 1975 there were only 3.3 million Visa cards and 3.1 Access cards, whereas by 2003 APACS (Association for Payment and Clearing Services) estimated that there were 66.8 million credit and charge cards in issue with an average of 2.2 cards per person (APACS, 2004: 5). A pre-crash assumption was that growth in borrowing is not necessarily bad if it is accompanied by growth in income and assets (Bank of England, 2006: 16).

Figure 1 indicates the increase in outstanding household debt to disposable income in several OECD countries since the mid-1990s. Much of this is constituted by secured mortage debt.

In 2003 the DTI described the contemporary consumer credit market:

DTI, *Fair Clear and Competitive: The Consumer Credit Market in the 21st Century*, Cm 6040 (2003) 13–17

The consumer credit market has changed fundamentally since the introduction of the Consumer Credit Act 1974. September 2003 figures from the Bank of England show the total level of outstanding debt to individuals in the UK is £906bn—of which £737bn is secured lending and £168bn is, largely, unsecured. In real terms, this compares with a level of outstanding debt of £521bn (£454bn secured) ten years ago.

1.9 The following table shows how the composition of consumer debt, between different types of credit products, has changed over time.

Proportion of households with current commitments (%)		Average amount owed per household (£, adjusted to 2002 prices)	
2002	1989	2002	1989
Credit Cards 19	15	1,570	565
Mail Order 17	23	240	Na
Loans 15	16	5,000	*2,190

HP/Credit Sale	13	17	3,800	*
Overdraft	19	12	450	1,676
Store Cards	8	7	210	197

* either loan or hire purchase

Source: Kempson E (2002) Household Survey of Over-Indebtedness, DTI

Consumer Credit Products

1.13 Personal loans secured by way of a second charge over the consumer's home, remain a popular way of raising finance. These loans are usually sold through brokers and are heavily marketed in the press and on television, often for debt consolidation purposes.

1.14 … A number concentrate on making loans available to consumers with debt problems or who have difficulty in proving their income.

Credit Cards

1.16 According to the Cruickshank Report, the credit card market in the UK is the most developed in Europe, accounting for about a third of all EU transactions, with many consumers now using credit cards as their preferred payment medium. …

Loans

1.17 The market for non-mortgage loans includes unsecured loans, as well as loans secured on personal assets other than residential property. The market as a whole is not concentrated.

1.18 Unsecured loans are usually sold direct to consumers, either at bank branches, by telephone, post or the internet. …

Small Short Term Loans

1.20 There are several forms of small-value, short-term loans that feature in today's credit market, for example, doorstep lenders, cheque cashers and pawnbrokers, along with other companies linking credit to the possession of goods. A feature of this type of lending is that the term of the loan is normally taken over a period of less than 12 months.

1.21 There are around 30,000 agents working in the home credit industry, mostly women, with an estimated 3 million customers. The sums advanced are usually small, typically between £100 to £300, with a repayment period in the range of 26 to 52 weeks. The charges are fixed and all-in (even if the customer misses a payment there is nothing extra to pay).

1.22 Pawnbroking is a form of secured lending. The average size of loans provided by pawnbroker is around £100, 85% of which are redeemed within the statutory, 6-month redemption period. Mail Order, Hire Purchase and Store Cards

1.23 Mail order credit provides a convenient method of shopping, allowing consumers to make purchases that can be paid off weekly, over an agreed period of time. Agency mail order has about 20.8 million users, of which somewhere between 8 and 10 million are drawn from the same socio-economic groups as the home credit customer-base.

1.24 Hire purchase agreements are often used by individuals to finance the purchase of expensive assets, such as a car. The finance is usually structured so the consumer pays a deposit, a number of monthly instalments and then a final payment to secure ownership of the asset.

1.25 Store cards allow consumers a form of running-account credit to purchase goods from a particular store. The cards are normally store-branded, but the credit will usually be provided by a finance company. Often, there are incentives attached, such as exclusive promotions and discounts.

1.26 Overdrafts are a feature of current account products and offer consumers a more short-term form of credit. Some accounts have a fixed limit, while others are negotiated on a month-by-month basis. Invariably, overdrafts are repaid more quickly than unsecured loans.

1.27 Credit unions have been in existence for about 40 years, in the UK. The first credit union was started in Northern Ireland in 1960, arriving on mainland Britain in 1964. There are about 200,000 borrowing members and a total membership of around 400,000. The credit union movement is more developed in Scotland, which has 139 unions holding 45% of the movement's assets, in the UK compared with 547 throughout the whole of England and Wales.

Elaine Kempson outlines different patterns of credit use:

> Levels of credit use were highest among householders in their twenties, two thirds of whom had an average of 2.6 commitments. Householders in their thirties or forties made only slightly less use but then use declined steeply with age. Consequently only a quarter of householders aged over 60 had a current credit commitment. Credit use was highest among families with children, and especially among lone parents, three quarters of whom had current commitments. The arrival of a new baby was clearly linked to higher than average levels of use. At the other end of the scale, few single pensioners had any credit commitments currently.

In other words, credit is used most when people set up home and when they have young children. (Kempson, 2002: 10)

1.2 Sub-prime and high-cost credit

A broad distinction may be drawn between the *prime* and *sub-prime* (sometimes referred to as non-status) lending market. Collard and Kempson argue that:

> there are two groups of lender in the subprime credit market. The first tends to offer credit products that cater specifically to the needs of low income borrowers. It includes ... home credit companies and pawnbrokers ... and rental purchase shops. ... The second group comprises companies that offer similar credit products to ... prime lenders such as banks. The difference is that they are targeted at people who have difficulty gaining access to the mainstream credit market, because they have a poor credit record or a history of bad debt. (Collard and Kempson, 2005: 1)

Munro et al argue that the second group represent those who may be excluded by credit-scoring systems operated by high-street prime lenders. They suggest that sub-prime products are 'sold as being for those with county court judgments against them, or who have been bankrupt; for those who have had in arrears in the past: and for those who have been refused credit elsewhere or who have an impaired credit record'. Self-employed individuals who are unable to prove their income may also be excluded (Munro et al 2005: 2). Stephens & Quilgars estimated that in 2005 approximately 9.5 per cent of mortgages were 'non-prime' lending (Stephens and Quilgars, 2008: 203). This is significantly lower than in the United States. They also concluded that a pre-dominant role for second mortgages was that of credit repair, ie debt consolidation. It was not being used to 'access home-ownership [but] much more extensively to recover from previous difficulties' (Pannell, 2006: 6) According to research by the Council of Mortgage Lenders (2006), 'adverse credit lending offers individuals who have suffered debt problems a valuable "last chance" opportunity to sort out their finances, and so helps to limit the overall extent of arrears and possessions'.

The sub-prime market was more profitable than prime credit, and mainstream lenders entered the market through subsidiaries. Part of the reason for this is the reluctance of mainstream lenders to be associated with sub-prime lending. The form of lending might often by through brokers and the lenders financed the loans through securitisation. The more risky nature of these loans resulted in higher levels of arrears and repossessions and the structure of selling (through brokers and securitisation) reduced incentives to take care in selling. The OFT in 2004 outlined some of the potential dangers associated with debt consolidation that included consumers assuming that the broker was providing independent advice, being unaware that brokers were often on commission from lenders, the inappropriate sale of payment protection insurance and 'churning' where loans were repeatedly renegotiated to earn more fees.

Many higher court decisions under the Consumer Credit Act 1974 arose from cases involving sub-prime mortgage lending. Some of the concerns raised by these cases include: (1) high interest charges (generally over 30 per cent APR); (2) dual interest rate clauses intended to circumvent the CCA 1974 prohibition on lenders increasing interest rates on default; (3) high broker's fees and non-disclosure of brokerage fees (*Wilson v Hurstanger*, 2007); (4) high payment protection insurance fees which are payable in a single premium and attract interest; (5) the existence of fees such as 'legal fees' which are not required to be repaid until the loan is repaid but which accumulate compound interest and result ultimately in a large payment. Finally, if an individual fell into arrears on the agreement, then the acceleration clause made the total loan recoverable with accrued interest and an individual could only redeem by repaying the full amount.

The issues associated with sub-prime mortgages were highlighted in the early 2000s by the case of Tony and Michelle Meadows. They bought a home in 1986 for £22,500. At that time they had one daughter. When another child arrived in 1987 they decided to renovate their home to include another bedroom and to install central heating. Tony was between jobs, expecting to find employment. They wanted to borrow £2,000 in 1989 for renovations but were in arrears on their existing mortgages (by approximately £21,000 and £1,250) so needed to find a new lender and responded to an advertisement by Phoenix Finance, a credit broker which passed the application to Home Loans (Northern), who assigned the mortgage to London North Securities. The loan purpose was given as home improvements. The amount of the loan was changed to £5,000 to pay off arrears on existing mortgages and the property was valued at £47,000. The ultimate loan was for £5,750 at 34.9% per annum, with £750 charged for insurance and added to the loan. The loan envisaged 180 payments of approximately £146 a month, resulting in interest of about £20,000 on the loan. They confirmed in the contract that 'once the first mortgage arrears have been cleared I will be able to afford monthly payments of £146'. The contract also included in bold capitals:

THE BORROWER CONFIRMS THAT HE HAS READ AND UNDERSTOOD THIS AGREEMENT. IN PARTICULAR THE BORROWER CONFIRMS THAT HE HAS BEEN RECOMMENDED BY THE LENDER TO TAKE INDEPENDENT LEGAL OR OTHER

APPROPRIATE PROFESSIONAL ADVICE ON THE CONTENTS HEREOF AND IN RESPECT OF THE TRANSACTION GENERALLY.

The couple were relatively quickly in arrears and interest was payable at the contract rate, compounded on a monthly basis, with the result that by 2004 the amount out-standing was over £300,000. Possession proceedings had been brought in the early 1990s but a suspended order made. In 2003 the Meadows realised they might have a defence against a repossession order. The lower court held the agreement both to be extortionate under sections 137–40 of the CCA and also on technical issues concerning formalities under the CCA.

The Meadows case dramatically illustrated the effects of compound interest on an unpaid debt. Compound interest was prohibited under the Moneylenders Acts, until these acts were abolished in 1974. The agreement was attacked on technical grounds, namely: (1) it misstated the amount of credit by including items for paying off the earlier mortgages and insurance that should have been included as a charge for credit rather than credit; (2) the agreement was extortionate because of the compounding of interest on arrears. The Court of Appeal struck down the bargain on the technical basis related to the classification of the insurance and did not address the extortionate bargain issue. An expert witness for the claimant indicated that compounding arrears 'is standard practice in business and commerce'. (See *London North Securities v Meadows* [2005] EWCA Civ 956.)

The case was covered extensively in the media with headlines such as 'Court frees Merseyside couple from debt that soared from £5,750 to £384,000' (*Guardian*, 29 October 2004): 'Lender loses appeal over couple's £5,750 loan that ballooned to £384,000. Money lender's trail of misery' (*Daily Telegraph*, 28 July 2005).

Other cases involving sub-prime mortgages include *McGinn v Grangewood Securities* (2002), where legal fees of £250 at the time of the transaction had with compounding of interest increased to over £80,000 by the time the loan would be repaid, prompting the judicial understatement that 'it is to my mind a somewhat disturbing feature of the case that that fact was not spelled out to Mrs Mcginn'; and *Broadwick Financial Services v Spencer* (2002), where an initial loan of £1,000 had grown to over £18,000 with accumulated arrears.

The sub-prime cases raise the question of the effectiveness of protections at the point of sale (eg information) compared with changing the structure of selling or regulating in greater detail the terms of contracts within the sub-prime market (see discussion below at 5).

In 2010 the OFT analysed the unsecured 'high-cost' credit market.

OFT, *Review of High-Cost Credit* (2010)

Gross advances of consumer credit in 2008 accounted for some £200 billion, with most borrowers having access to mainstream credit, which is credit used by a wide range of consumers and typically supplied by suppliers involved in other mainstream financial markets, such as banking or insurance.

… [T] here is no formal and accepted definition of the term 'high-cost credit'. Our research has covered a number of different products, and we have concluded that there is no single economic market for high-cost credit. Rather we have found that markets for high-cost credit include the following products:

- home credit

- short-term small-sum lending including payday loans

- pawnbroking, and

- rent-to-buy retail credit

Our research and internal analysis suggests that the value of loans made in 2008–9 by specialist high-cost credit suppliers is around £7.5 billion. This estimate can be disaggregated by type of loan product:

- around £900 million of payday loans

- around £600 million of pawnbroking loans

- around £1.26 billion of home collected credit

- around £340 million of loans from credit unions, and

- around £4.25 billion of sub-prime retail credit.

What is high-cost credit?

2.4 High cost credit products are typically small loans borrowed over short periods—while the cost expressed as a total charge (in pounds) may seem reasonable, the annual percentage rate (APR) is often high because of the short time over which the loan is taken and the high charge relative to the loan value.

...

2.6 Some credit products (payday loans, pawnbroking, home credit) are high-cost because they incur significant charges relative to the amount borrowed. However, other credit products (credit cards, store cards and retail credit) may often be high-cost where the borrower makes extended use of the credit facilities offered. ...

2.10 Mainstream lenders do not offer high-cost credit but many of them provide wholesale funding for companies in this sector.

2.11 Many borrowers of high-cost credit are unable to borrow from mainstream lenders because they are on low incomes or because they have poor credit ratings. ... Consumers' choice of loan may depend on their circumstances and employment status: payday loans are only available to employed people whereas pawnbroking and home credit are not so restricted.

The new demand landscape for credit provision to those on low incomes and the implications for the provision of affordable credit

12 On the one hand, overdraft, credit card (used to buy goods and services) and personal loans from banks are the three most widely used products by mainstream credit users (respectively by slightly less than 50 per cent, 40 per cent and 30 per cent of the sample). On the other hand, non-standard credit users are more likely to use catalogue credit (more than 50 per cent of the sample) and informal borrowing from friends and family (more than 35 per cent) than overdrafts (less than 30 per cent). The Social Fund, home credit (both more than 25 per cent) and home credit vouchers (almost 20 per cent) are more used than credit cards to buy goods or services or personal loans from bank (slightly more than 15 per cent).

Economic markets within the high cost credit sector

2.12 We have found that the high-cost credit products that are the focus of this review represent distinct product markets.

...

2.14 On the supply side, substitutability opportunities appear to be limited, since different products require different business models (for example, a network of local agents for home collected loans, compared to more traditional high-street business premises) and skills (for example, a pawnbroker must possess skills related to evaluating the value of items pawned, which are not required for other high cost credit products).

2.15 As a result, most suppliers specialise in offering one of these specialist high cost products. The most notable exception is the joint provision of payday lending and pawnbroking, which are frequently offered by the same suppliers who take advantage of economies of scope by better utilising their high-street premises to attract a broader range of customers.

2.17 For the above reasons, we consider that each of the specialist high-cost products within the scope of the review constitutes a separate economic market.

Polly Toynbee in her book, *Hard Work Life in Low-Pay Britain* (2003), describes her experience of buying a bed and visiting a rental purchase shop called Crazy George (now rebranded Brighthouse):

Polly Toynbee, *Hard Work Life in Low-Pay Britain* (2003) 43–45, 53–54

On the counter are the Crazy George catalogues with this message: 'Discover Affordable Shopping Made Easy!' Inside it promises, 'All our products are available with NO DEPOSIT AND NO CREDIT CHECKS'. Unlike discount stores such as Argos or Ikea, everything here is extraordinarily expensive, way beyond ordinary department store prices for things that looked bright but shoddy. All the prices are quoted at the per week higher purchase price in bold letters. The total cash price is in small letters underneath, because people don't come here to pay cash. The cheapest double bed they offered, the 'Nicole', was a basic metal number. It cost £4.99 a week for 156 weeks—3 years. I was not convinced the Nicole would last that long. Even smaller print said 'mattress available separately' with no mention of what the mattress cost extra. The APR was 29.9 percent. The small print underneath the picture said the Nicole cost an astounding £432.38 cash, without mattress. Checking around locally, I saw a bed that looked much the same in MFI in Clapham High Street for £189 with mattress. ...

But I could see why it was tempting to shop this way. However much better value it would be for me to buy the MFI bed from the remnants of my social fund loan, I just haven't got £199 to buy it and I could not borrow that money from anywhere else. If I really needed a double bed I could see how easy it would be to persuade myself that a mere £4.99 a week was more affordable, in my circumstances. Crazy George would give me the bed on production of nothing more than a pay slip, a tenancy agreement and two Ids, even though I was penniless. Like most of the well-off I had never heard of Crazy George, because the well-off never need credit at these usurious rates when every bank is tripping over itself to lend cash to the rich at good rates. ...

Wherever there is a Starbucks, a Waterstones, a Jigsaw or a Habitat you can bet there isn't a Crazy George's nearby. We who own cars can drive out to vast department stores like Ikea and pay cash for a houseful of good bargains. Those who have no cars and no cash end up paying 29.9 percent APR. Who knows what the repossession rate must be? … Thinking about borrowing and the way the poor cripple themselves with debt, I could see why once you had no money, borrowing no longer seemed much of a problem. There is no further to fall, so why not? If you are living hand-to-mouth anyway, debt does not seem to aggravate matters much. With 4p in your pocket and £70 of rent and other arrears already, nothing could be worse, so why not?

An example of the alternative credit market is the home credit market where suppliers provide credit on a weekly basis. In 2006 the Competition Commission concluded that profits substantially in excess of the cost of capital were persistently earned by those firms in the home credit market which represented a substantial part of the market. Price competition was weak, partly because of the insensitivity of consumers to price and limited incentives for lenders to compete on price. Most home credit customers paid most attention to the availability and the affordability of credit, ie the level of the weekly payment rather than the APR. Consumers' insensitivity to price was reinforced by their difficulty in assessing and comparing prices of competing home credit products. Consumers faced high costs in switching to another lender since there were no centralised data on borrowers' creditworthiness, eg in a credit bureau. It was difficult for new lenders to assess the creditworthiness of a borrower:

> Home credit customers were more likely than the population as a whole to be female, to be under 35, to have young families, to fall into socio-economic groups D and E, to live in a low-income household and to live in housing rented from a local council or housing association. We did not find that these characteristics had changed much in recent years. Home credit customers had at least one other credit option, though for some, home credit was the only available source of credit. …

> We found that the prices of home credit loans, however measured, were high by comparison with the prices of other credit products (though, given the differences in the product offerings, that does not necessarily imply that a home credit loan represents worse value for money). We found that APRs generally exceeded 100 per cent, and for loans of around six months often exceeded 300 per cent. TCCs (Total Cost of Credit) varied from around £30 per £100 borrowed for the shortest loans to over £100 per £100 borrowed for some of the longest. (Competition Commission, 2006: 7)

The top two reasons for using home credit were borrowing for a special occasion, eg Christmas or a birthday, and crisis borrowing, because the consumer had an urgent need for money. This might be because of delays in receiving benefit money or the need to replace household goods (Competition Commission, 2006: 2–42). Research for the Competition Commission suggested the following types of home credit user:

> [A] *novices* were unsophisticated borrowers, who needed a loan for various reasons, for example for a car, and accepted the offer of home credit, which came across as more approachable than other sources of credit. They had probably not really considered alternative sources.

> [B] *impulse borrowers* were using home credit to finance the 'live now, pay later' lifestyle and using loans for nonessential items, where the impulse to buy might come at certain times of the year. Some have access to other forms of credit.

> [C] *crisis borrowers* were rather hard pressed and used home credit to tide them over financial crises, for example delays in receiving benefit money or the need to replace household goods.

They often had a regular or low incomes and used home credit to help them get through lean times. They often had or felt they had no alternatives to home credit.

[D] *occasional borrowers* used home credit in a fairly disciplined way to finance specific needs. They made a point of paying off loans rather than renewing them, and some were using home credit to complement other sources of credit such as shop credit, credit cards, etc.

[E] *home credit habitues* originally started using home credit in hard times. They now seem to be keeping up home credit loans, whether or not they were needed, apparently to keep up a relationship with their agent.

[F] *secret borrowers* were a relatively small segment of those interviewed. Other family members were not aware that they had taken out home credit loans. For various reasons or motivations, it was important to them to hide the fact and purpose of the loan from their partner are family.

[G] *home credit leavers* have managed to reestablish their access to mainstream credit sources, credit union, etc. They were in the process of winding down their home credit borrowing. (Competition Commission, 2006: 2–27)

The above extract indicates the intersection of gender and class issues in the use of high-cost credit. It confirms other research which has noted the high level of risk of serious debt for low-income lone mothers. What policies should be adopted to regulate this market? Is the behaviour of consumers in this market rational? Or any less rational than middle-class behaviour?

1.3 Financial exclusion

The high costs of access to credit for some consumers raises the issue of financial exclusion.

HM Treasury, *Promoting Financial Inclusion* (December 2004)

THE NATURE OF FINANCIAL EXCLUSION

Defining financial exclusion

1.6 The term 'financial exclusion' is used in different ways. It can be a broad concept related to a lack of access to a range of financial services or a narrow concept reflecting particular circumstances such as: geographical exclusion; exclusion on the grounds that charges and prices are prohibitively high; or exclusion from marketing efforts. Self exclusion is also important—where an individual believes there is little point in applying for a financial product because they expect to be refused, sometimes because of a previous experience of refusal, because they know someone else who has been refused, or because of a belief that 'they don't accept people who live round here, or who are like me'.

1.7 These aspects of exclusion are not mutually exclusive. They will overlap and reinforce each other, resulting in individuals, households and communities having little or no connection to mainstream banking and financial services.

The costs of financial exclusion

1.8 Financial exclusion imposes significant costs on individuals, their wider neighbourhood, and on society as a whole.

1.9 For the individual, some of the most important costs associated with financial exclusion include:

- higher charges for basic financial transactions and credit—lack of access to a bank account means that certain financial transactions such as money transfer and cheque cashing may be more expensive;

- no access to certain products or services—a range of services, such as contract mobile telephones, require a bank account for regular Direct Debits;

- lack of security in holding and storing money—operating solely on a cash budget leaves people more vulnerable to loss or theft;

- barriers to employment—a bank account for receipt of wages is a basic requirement for most employers; and

- entrenching exclusion—having no formal banking or credit history at all can be as much of a disadvantage as an impaired credit history in accessing certain financial services.

1.10 For the wider community, there are further additional costs:

- contributor to child poverty. The Child Poverty Review, published in July 2004, highlighted the links between financial exclusion and child poverty.

Paying more for certain financial services and the impact of debt on family life can exacerbate the harm caused by child poverty:

- costs to the benefit system. The benefit system aims to provide a minimum standard of living for claimants. If benefit claimants are forced to use high cost credit, less benefit is available for other essentials; and

- link to social exclusion. The 1998 report of the Social Exclusion Unit noted interactions between social and financial exclusion, and put particular emphasis on access to banking services, insurance 'red-lining' (where financial institutions refuse to provide a product or service in a particular area) and the problems of expensive credit.

James Devlin found that financial exclusion (defined as exclusion from a current account, savings account, home contents insurance, life assurance and a pension) was most significantly influenced by employment status, household income and housing tenure, closely followed by marital status, age and the level of academic qualification attained (Devlin, 2005: 105). He argues that these findings highlight 'the importance of tackling poverty and social exclusion more generally when attempting to solve the problem of financial exclusion' (ibid: 101).

Finally, in the first edition of this book (1989) I described illegal moneylending rackets in Glasgow in the early 1980s and posed the question of the most effective method of addressing this issue. It would seem that the problem has not diminished since that time. The DTI in its White Paper in 2003 indicates that in the Strathclyde area alone there were some 60 rings of illegal lenders operating in the early 1990s with one resident of a hostel for the homeless being charged 1.3 million per cent interest (DTI, 2003: 89). In 2006 a survey of illegal lending in the UK estimated that there were approximately 165,000 households using illegal moneylenders in the UK. Some of illegal lending was not dissimilar to legal lending but much of it involved potential violence in enforcement. The authors concluded that the most appropriate alternative source was an expanded Social Fund (see below). Some of the problems faced by those using illegal lenders were multi-dimensional (DTI, 2006).

---

2. The costs and benefits of consumer credit

The Crowther Committee (1970), adopting the economic assumption of the 'rational consumer', indicated that a person:

> will be using credit in a rational and economically efficient manner if the monetary and nonmonetary returns are at least equal to the costs within the constraints imposed upon him by his income and net worth. ... It should be the objective of policy to enable as many consumers as possible to employ credit in this way. (paragraph 3.8.2)

The major social cost of credit identified by the Crowther Committee was over-commitment and default. Over-indebtedness became a significant public policy issue in the UK in the late 1990s and the media regularly reported on 'debt explosions', 'credit binges' and 'a ticking time bomb of debt' (see eg Bien, 2004).

Credit card marketing practices were often the target for criticism and the First House of Commons Treasury Select Committee on Credit Cards in 2003 commented that:

> Irresponsible marketing can give an impression that taking on debt is painless. Lenders must take particular care when marketing cards to young people, vulnerable consumers and those on low incomes. (2003: 3)

There are different approaches to measuring over-indebtedness, including both subjective and objective measures (for a review, see Oxera, 2004). The House of Commons Treasury Committee report on the Transparency of Credit Card Charges (2003–04, HC 125) indicated that:

> 74. There is no generally accepted definition of over-indebtedness. ... The DTI Task Force on Overindebtedness ... suggested the following definitions for households that indicated a high risk of getting into financial difficulty, if not already in difficulty:
>
> • having four or more current credit commitments (7% of all households)
>
> • spending more than 25% of gross income (excluding mortgages) on consumer credit (5% of all households)
>
> • spending more than 50% of gross income (including mortgages) on consumer credit (6% of all households)

The Griffiths Commission concluded in 2005 that

> there is a serious debt problem for a small proportion of our society, roughly 3 million people. It is spread throughout the population as a whole, but disproportionately affects low income families, loan payments and people in their 20s and early 30s. Although debt is a serious problem for only a small proportion of society, the evidence suggests that up to 12 million more people struggle to repay their credit commitments from time to time. (Griffiths, 2005: 14)

A review of studies of over-indebtedness by Oxera in 2004 noted that individuals tend to under-report outstanding debt in survey responses. The Money Advice Service indicates that in 2011 'There are 4.3 million "over-indebted" households in the UK, of which 2.1 million will actively seek debt advice while 2.2 million would benefit from debt advice but will not proactively seek it.' The Labour government established a task force (2000) and subsequently introduced an ambitious over-indebtedness strategy that included:

- Development of a national strategy for financial capability.
- Increases in affordable credit through development of credit unions and alternative models of affordable credit.
- Introduction of a stakeholder suite of financial products to promote asset saving.
- Investigation of the role of interest-rate ceilings.
- Strengthening of credit licensing and attacks on unfair lending practices.
- Attacks on illegal money-lending.
- Improved data sharing to underpin responsible lending decisions.
- Increases in the funding of free and available debt advice
- Alternative dispute resolution for debt disputes.
- The improvement of insolvency, the introduction of a debt relief order.
- Improvements in housing benefits and the administration of council benefits.

The policies were intended both to regulate credit markets and expand credit choices—addressing problems of financial exclusion. The government has also established access to affordable credit as an important policy goal (see Treasury, 2004: 24) through, for example, greater access to credit unions (see below 13). Reforms to credit disclosure legislation (see below) are also intended to make credit more transparent. Throughout this chapter you should consider the effectiveness of these *ex ante* and *ex post* approaches to the problem of over-indebtedness. In 2010 the National Audit Office concluded, however, that the over-indebtedness task force was badly managed and did not have sufficiently clear benchmarks for assessing its success (National Audit Office, 2011).

---

3. Rationales for regulation of consumer credit markets

UK policy documents since the early 1970s assume that consumer credit is in general beneficial, and that policy should maximise informed choice subject to protections against abusive and unfair practices. The report of the Crowther Committee in 1971 legitimated consumer credit by drawing attention to its economic and social benefits and providing a blueprint for a modernised regulatory statute, the Consumer Credit Act 1974. The Committee concluded that the social benefits of consumer credit outweigh its costs and recommended the expansion of the market for credit, subject to certain protective measures, particularly for those who default on their obligations. The Committee summarised its views on the social role of consumer credit thus:

3.9.1 … [O]ur general view is that the state should interfere as little as possible with the consumer's freedom to use his knowledge of the consumer credit market to the best of his ability and according to his judgement of what constitutes his best interests. While it is understandable and proper for the state to be concerned about the things on which people spend their money and even to use persuasion to influence the scale of values implied by their expenditure patterns, it remains a basic tenet of a free society that people themselves must be the judge of what contributes to their material welfare.

3.9.2 Our examination of the social effects of consumer credit has not uncovered any strong social reasons for departing significantly from this view. Since the vast majority of consumers use credit wisely and derive considerable benefit from it, the right policy is not to restrict their freedom of access by administrative and legal measures but to help the minority who innocently get into trouble to manage. their financial affairs more successfully—without, however, also making conditions easier for the fraudulent borrower. The basic principle of social policy must, therefore, be to reduce the number of defaulting debtors. This is in everybody's interest.

The White Paper on Consumer Credit in 2003 (Fair, Clear and Competitive: the Consumer Credit Market in the 21st Century) notes that:

Consumer credit is central to the UK economy. ... For most, credit cards and other secured and unsecured lending provide people with greater control and flexibility when managing their finances—collectively benefiting the economy. ... But credit, of course can also introduce risks of its own. Some consumers take out loans that are inappropriate and expensive. Others are tipped into debt by a sudden change of circumstance. But there are also consumers that are preyed upon by loansharks, whose activities often exploit the socially deprived sections of the community. ...

1.69 We want to encourage an open and fair credit market, where consumers can make fully informed decisions and businesses can compete aggressively on a fair and even basis. Vigorous competition provides a spur for business to be more productive, innovative and efficient, which will provide benefits to consumers in terms of lower prices, higher quality, and more choice and innovation. ...

1.70 ... Promoting a fair and open credit market enables consumers and business to interact in a more efficient way. However it is not an end in itself. Consumers circumstances can change rapidly, and there can be undue surprises post purchase. We can contribute to social justice and create prosperity for all by tackling the problems associated with over indebtedness and improving financial inclusion. We want to educate consumers and provide easier access to help and advice for those in financial difficulty. And we want low-income consumers to have access to affordable credit.

And in 2011 the Coalition government stated:

Consumer Credit and Personal Insolvency Review (2011)

First, we want all consumers to be empowered to make better choices for themselves. Consumers should be free to borrow if that is what they decide is in their best interest. It is not for the Government to pass judgement on whether a particular product is good or bad but, in line with the Coalition principles of freedom, fairness and responsibility, we want to provide consumers with the tools they need to make informed decisions. Second, we want to ensure there is a safe and fair regulatory framework for both credit and personal insolvency. These frameworks must protect vulnerable consumers, particularly those at risk of falling into or those already in financial difficulty, and drive rogue companies out of the market

The Crowther Committee assumed that the most effective and fair method of addressing the needs of lower-income individuals was through the social welfare system, which would address directly what was perceived as the basic problem, insufficiency of resources, and not place the burdens of redistribution solely on those who supply services to lower income consumers.

Report of the Committee on Consumer Credit (Crowther Committee), Cmnd 4596/1971

Part 6. The Protection of the Consumer in Credit Transactions

Inadequate Income

6.1.8 Many families, through no fault of their own, find their income quite insufficient for their needs, even with such supplementary benefits as are available. ...

6.1.9 To persons in this position the need to borrow may become acute. There is little point in talking of thrift to one who needs money to keep warm or to buy the minimum of food and clothing necessary for subsistence. Such people are therefore peculiarly vulnerable to harsh and oppressive terms. They will pay any rate of interest necessary to procure a loan for their immediate use. ...

6.1.10 These facts raise serious questions of social policy. The most that protective legislation can hope to achieve for consumers in this situation is the alleviation of hardship by judicial control over the enforcement of judgement debts and over the repossession and realization of goods or other property held by the debtor under a security agreement.

Changes in the social welfare system since that report have increased the extent to which those at risk of poverty use credit to meet regular expenses.

A major potential source of failure in the credit market is imperfect consumer information and imperfect processing of information. Consumer credit often involves commitments over a substantial period of time. Individuals may either overestimate or underestimate the probability of defaulting on their obligations. Overestimation would lead to an undersupply and underestimation to an oversupply of credit. The behavioural literature in consumer decision-making (above Chapter 2) has drawn attention to individuals' misestimation of risk and overoptimism. The National Consumer Council in a survey of credit decisions by consumers commented:

Most of our respondents suppressed the risks involved, and felt confident (possibly overconfident ...) in their ability to stay out of trouble ... consumers were aware that unexpected events could seriously affect their ability to pay but felt that this was something that happens to others. Most felt losing their jobs, suffering a serious accident or illness were remote possibilities. (National Consumer Council, 2002: 4)

The problem of hyperbolic discounting illustrated in the credit card example in Chapter 2 suggests that there may be a conflict between individuals' short-term and long-term preferences. Remedies might include not only greater information but also, for example, greater access to insurance against the consequences of default. This may protect an individual's future autonomy against short-term myopia. This might be provided by the market or through government restrictions on the consequences of default (eg on forms of harassment or on the enforcement of harsh contract terms, or the availability of bankruptcy). The costs of the latter proposal would then be borne by creditors, who would in turn distribute these costs among their customers.

Neo-classical models assume the virtues of competition and disclosure in credit markets but behavioural analysis indicates that competition in credit markets may be systematically skewed to taking advantage of the behavioural biases of consumers. Firms that do not adopt this strategy may not prosper. Competition does not necessarily result in new entrants offering choices which might be more welfare enhancing. Adair Turner, chair of the FSA, recently mused that 'it is notable that some of our greatest concerns about high distribution margins and inappropriate advice have arisen in activities … characterised by huge numbers of competitive firms' and the FSA concludes that 'it is inherently more difficult for competition in retail financial services to be as effective as it is in other consumer services'. This is partly because in the case of credit, consumers are primarily interested in price and there is less opportunity for quality differentiation as is possible with products. True transparency in credit pricing reduces substantially the profitability of companies so that profits must come from obscuring additional costs such as insurance, etc.

Imperfect creditor information may also be a source of market failure. Without adequate information, creditors may be unable to differentiate between low- and high-risk borrowers. This is the problem of adverse selection noted in Chapter 2. If creditors had perfect information on borrowers' likelihood of repayment, the only problem would be pricing the initial transaction. The development of technology increasingly permits creditors to reduce the costs of this risk assessment. However, the collection of such information clearly raises issues concerning privacy and individual autonomy (see below). We also noted how information asymmetry on the part of mainstream lenders may be one reason for their reluctance to enter the sub-prime lending market or develop products for low -income consumers (above Chapter 2). The Crowther Committee's generally favourable conclusions on the social role of consumer credit were tempered by the view that there was a need for consumer-protection regulations. In addition to imperfect consumer information as a cause of market failure, they drew attention to the role of cultural and social factors in the use of credit, factors suggesting certain limitations of consumer legislation in this area.

The Committee was also concerned to maintain a 'fair balance' between creditor and debtor, and it proposed a variety of measures to control trading malpractices and regulate terms and remedies on default. Many of these protections were contained in existing legislation on hire-purchase and money lending; the proposals represented continuity rather than innovation. The Committee did, however, articulate clearly the distributional values of risk and loss-spreading which underpinned its consumer protection proposals:

> In setting out in the chapters which follow our proposals for the content of a revised consumer credit law we have continually borne in mind the following:
>
> (i) In considering which of two relatively innocent parties should bear the greater loss, it is much easier for the business creditor to do so than the individual debtor. The former can, in the light of his business experience, take account of certain loss risks in his charges and thus spread the burden over the public at large. The impact of one item of loss upon an individual debtor may be extremely severe.

(ii) At the same time the concept of risk spreading must not be taken too far. Every restriction on a creditor's remedy has to be paid for. To the extent to which the creditor is not himself willing or able to absorb the loss or expense in which he is involved by the restrictions imposed on him, this must be passed on to his customers. Hence the good customer is made to subsidise the bad. Moreover, the burden of bad debts bears particularly harshly on the small trader, who may be ill-able to afford to write them off and may be in no position—because of competition—to pass them on to his customers in the form of increased prices. Hence the law must recognise that creditors too have rights and are entitled to legal protection. (paragraphs 6.1.16(i), (ii))

---

4. The Consumer Credit Act 1974

The findings of the Crowther Committee have been warmly welcomed by the credit industry. (*The Times*, 21 November 1971)

The Consumer Credit Act 1974 is the primary source of protection for consumers of credit. The main provisions of the Act are based on the recommendations of the Crowther Committee. The Committee's objectives had been to provide a framework which would encourage the development of a competitive credit market while ensuring that there would be a fair balance in that market between business and consumers.

Existing legislation at the time of the Committee's report regulated according to form rather than substance and discriminated between different types of transaction. Hire-purchase and moneylending were subject to different forms of regulation whereas loans made by banks and large finance houses were exempt from these controls. The Committee proposed, therefore, regulation according to substance and the uniform treatment of all credit grantors. A major goal was the rationalisation of the regulatory framework, and this was reflected in the proposed comprehensive licensing regime, which would also, it was hoped, promote consumer confidence in the credit market. Within this licensing framework, artificial restrictions on credit-granting were to be abolished in order to expand the market for credit and promote competition. The functional model of Article 9 of the US Uniform Commercial Code provided a model for general reform. Proposals would expand the pool of assets which a consumer might make available as security, and required standardised disclosures of the cost of borrowing would stimulate competition.

Given the general thrust of the Crowther Committee's proposals, it is not surprising that the majority of large credit grantors openly welcomed them, since they ensured future growth while proposing to eliminate the fly-by-night from the market (McManus, 1975: 73–75). Regulation was a precondition for the development of a mass consumer credit market. The government did not implement all the recommendations of the Committee (see Cmnd 5427/1973). In particular, it rejected on fairness grounds the abolition of restrictions on the taking of security in personal property (thus retaining in force the Bills of Sales Acts of 1878 and 1882) and retained the artificial concept of hire-purchase.

The original scope of the Act regulated credit, defined in section 9 as including 'a cash loan or any other form of financial accommodation', provided to individuals, or hire payments that did not exceed £25,000. This financial limit was abolished by the 2006 amendments (see section 8(1)(a)). However, financial limits on certain sections have been reintroduced by those provisions giving effect to the 2008 EU Consumer Credit Directive (see eg section 55A). The main transactions which are exempt from regulation under the Act are first charge mortgages, which are now regulated by the FSA under the Financial Services and Markets Act of 2000 (see section 16 CCA); certain transactions involving 'high net worth individuals' (section 16A); and lending to individuals for business purposes above £25,000. The Act does not use a general 'purpose of use' definition to distinguish consumer credit. Roy Goode indicates that this was rejected because 'of the difficulty that a lender would face in knowing the purpose for which the loan was intended' and that the purpose of use test was 'too vague and subjective to form an acceptable basis for defining the limits of the … legislation' (Goode, 1989: 88).

The main regulatory techniques are:

- control of supplier access to the consumer credit market through licensing;
- required disclosures of information by credit grantors;
- regulation of the terms and conditions of credit contracts; and
- restrictions on the remedies available to a creditor in the event of default.

The Act introduced a battery of new concepts and definitions (see section 189). Some of the significant distinctions within the Act are:

1. The distinction between fixed and running account credit (section 10). Running account credit would include borrowing on a credit card and is more common now than when the Act was passed. The distinction is of significance in relation to determining whether an agreement is exempt and the disclosure of the cost of borrowing.
2. Restricted and unrestricted use credit (section 11). The latter describes a situation where a debtor may use the credit for any purpose.
3. Debtor–creditor–supplier and debtor–creditor agreements (sections 12–13). This distinction is relevant to whether an agreement is exempt and is the key to determining the scope of connected lender liability under section 75 (see below, Chapter 8 at 4).

The Act is implemented by detailed regulations and contains several anti-avoidance provisions. One reason for this detailed regulation is that the history of consumer credit law is often a history of creditors acting as amoral calculators, evading and 'outflanking' protective legislation (Nicol, 1981) by altering the form of a transaction particularly in relation to protections for low-income groups. The CCA is sensitive to these issues. Thus the 'small agreements' exemption in section 17 cannot be avoided by creating two agreements (section 17(3)). Section 18 applies to what are termed 'multiple agreements' where there may be a combination of categories of agreement. The Act requires that the agreement must meet the requirements of all the categories and this was 'to ensure that the Act (and in particular the … ceiling on its application is not avoided by artificially combining distinct bargains' (Goode, 1989: 153).

The 2006 amendments reformed truth in lending regulations and disclosure in contractual documents and forms; expanded credit licensing powers; replaced the 'extortionate credit' test by an unfair relationship test; introduced an alternative dispute resolution scheme, to reduce the costs of consumer redress; and reformed the rules relating to an early settlement of a loan. These gave effect to the Labour government's promise to modernise the Act and attack loan-sharks. The most recent 2010 amendments implement the EU 2008 Directive on Consumer Credit which modifies disclosure requirements and introduces 'responsible lending' obligations under a duty to explain (section 55A) and assess creditworthiness (section 55B). The 2012 Act will alter the institutional framework of regulation (see below 4.1). The institutional framework of control initially adopted in the CCA 1974 placed overall administrative responsibility for licensing and monitoring the consumer credit market with the Director General of Fair Trading (now the OFT) and gave him and local trading standards officers joint responsibility for enforcement (sections 1, 161(1)). In addition, the county courts were given wide discretionary powers to modify the terms of enforcement and to reopen extortionate bargains.

Many of the provisions of the Act provided a framework which has now been fleshed out by detailed regulations and a specialised bureaucracy (currently the OFT, to be replaced by the Financial Conduct Authority) provides extensive guidance on its interpretation to businesses and to local enforcement agencies. Its complexity led to criticisms of the cost-effectiveness of various aspects of the Act, in particular of the licensing regime and advertising provisions. Some argue, therefore, that a more 'principled' approach to regulation would be desirable, based on the FSA's approach to regulation. We analyse below the approach of the FSA in its 'treating customers fairly' initiative as a potential future approach.

4.1 Institutional structure of credit regulation

The global financial crisis stimulated reflection internationally on the optimal institutions of regulation of consumer credit and finance.

Financial Stability Board, *Consumer Finance Protection with Particular Focus on Credit* (2011) at 5–8

In the wake of the financial crisis, FSB members explored a number of different options for strengthening consumer protection, including establishment of consumer protection authorities, implementation of responsible mortgage lending practices, and product intervention, including product design. Examples of substantial reforms underway in each of these areas are set out below.

Establishment of consumer protection authorities

The crisis in the US subprime mortgage market highlighted that weaknesses in the US regulatory and supervisory framework allowed financial firms to offer risky products to consumers with inadequate disclosure of the risks, use third party agents (mortgage brokers) that lacked appropriate oversight, and repackage the resulting debt into poorly understood structured securities. The crisis highlighted the fact that weaknesses or regulatory gaps with respect to non-bank entities within a financial system can significantly impact consumer protections. These weaknesses, in part, reflected the lack of ability to substantially regulate in the area of individual and household borrowing by some agencies. The US enacted the

Dodd–Frank Wall Street Reform and Consumer Protection Act of 2010 (Dodd–Frank Act) to address many of the weaknesses identified. ...

The Dodd–Frank Act substantially consolidated core consumer protection functions from seven banking and financial regulators into one agency, the Consumer Finance Protection Bureau (CFPB).

Implementation of responsible mortgage lending practices

The most common reforms are taking place in the area of responsible mortgage lending practices. The global financial crisis brought into focus how the effects of irresponsible lending practices can quickly spread beyond national borders through the global distribution of securitised risks particularly in mortgage loans. Changes in this area are occurring across the European Union and in the US with particular focus on assessing a borrower's ability to repay the mortgage loan.

Since 2005, the UK FSA has been analysing the UK mortgage market and released its Mortgage Market Review in 2009 which was followed by a consultation document in 2010 on responsible lending. The mortgage market review identified a number of issues, many of which have been highlighted by the financial crisis and involves enhancements to regulatory requirements intended to ensure responsible lending. And in the US, CFPB will take up a proposal from the Federal Reserve Board to implement a statutory mandate to require creditors assess a borrower's ability to repay a mortgage before making the loan and establish minimum mortgage underwriting standards.

Product intervention

A transformation is underway in the UK supervisory and regulatory framework for consumer finance protection. Reforms of the UK system of financial regulation are planned and the

Financial Services Authority (FSA) will be disbanded and a new system will be established comprised of more specialised and focused regulators:

- the Financial Policy Committee (FPC): a macro-prudential regulator within the Bank of England to monitor and respond to systemic risks.

- the Prudential Regulation Authority (PRA): a subsidiary of the Bank of England, supervising deposit takers, insurers and a small number of significant investment firms.

- the Financial Conduct Authority (FCA), responsible for regulating conduct in retail and wholesale markets, supervising the trading infrastructure that supports those markets, and for the prudential regulation of firms not prudentially regulated by the PRA.

The FCA will take over the FSA's responsibility for consumer protection in relation to first- charge mortgage lending and, in future, second-charge mortgage lending. ... Some of the FCA's focus will be on developing a new, more proactive and interventionist approach to retail conduct regulation with a focus on preventing consumer detriment. The previous approach of relying solely on disclosure of information and supervision at the point of sale was seen as having limited effectiveness. In particular, when poor conduct is discovered, significant detriment can already have occurred, causing losses to consumers and damage to confidence. The new proactive approach is intended to address the 'root causes' of consumer detriment such as poor products or inappropriate business models and incentive structures within firms. This will include earlier intervention in the product lifecycle, with a greater willingness to challenge the way that firms design and distribute products and services aimed at retail customers, although consumer protection around the point of sale will remain essential. The FCA's approach was set out by the FSA in a document published in June 2011.

2.3 Consumer advocacy

In order to maintain effective and robust consumer protection frameworks, national authorities need to understand the consumer perspective. Maintaining strong links with consumer groups can also help support a proactive approach to regulation by offering an early warning of potential risks to consumer protection. To achieve this, many FSB members have established a formal process for engaging consumer groups. In these jurisdictions, organisational bodies are established to advise government agencies on financial policies from a consumer and user perspective. Such advisory bodies are generally comprised of representatives from both consumer and investor organisations and individual members, and advise on policies and activities as well as consumer research and education projects. How governments engage with consumer groups varies across the membership. For instance, the French Autorité de Controle Prudential (ACP) must officially consult Comité Consultatif du Secteur Financier (CCSF), which is comprised of consumer organisations representatives in France, before it can adopt recommendations and positions in the consumer protection field. ...

In the UK, the Enterprise Act of 2002 allows designated consumer bodies to submit 'super complaints' to the Office of Fair Trading (OFT). ...

And in the US, consumer advocacy organisations have a formal advisory role in at least three ways. First, under federal rulemaking procedures, proposed regulations issued by the CFPB, as well as those issued by other federal agencies, are published in the Federal Register for a formal comment period. Consumer organisations and individuals, as well as business, may provide comments in that process. Second, the CFPB has established an Office of Community Affairs. This office meets regularly with consumer groups, civil rights organisations, and other stakeholders to discuss the spectrum of relevant consumer financial protection issues. The Office of Community Affairs works to create a feedback loop between consumer advocacy organisations and the CFPB, sharing all input and perspectives from the field with appropriate CFPB policy teams. Third, the CFPB will establish a Consumer Advisory Board, which will include consumer protection experts, to advise, consult with, and provide information to the CFPB. In addition to these formal channels, the CFPB will have multiple outreach and program initiatives to reach consumers and those who assist them, including offices focusing on military service members and their families, older Americans, students, and lower income consumers.

HM Treasury, *A New Approach to Financial Regulation*, Cm 8268 (2012)

The Government believes that fundamental change is necessary to ensure that regulation is able to keep up with a rapidly changing market and to tackle detrimental practices more swiftly. The Government also believes that this change can best be achieved by bringing consumer credit into the same regulatory regime as other financial services (FSMA), while retaining the existing consumer rights and protections in the CCA.

4.19 Respondents to the Government's consultation on the credit regime generally supported the proposal for a single regulator for all retail financial services, and a stronger, more flexible regime than is currently possible under the CCA. However, respondents also emphasised the diversity of firms and activities covered by CCA and the need for a proportionate, risk-based approach. They also noted that the consumer credit industry has only recently had to adapt to changes to the CCA.

4.20 Further engagement with stakeholders in recent months has made clear that many would welcome an outcome that brings consumer credit firms, particularly providers of high-cost credit, within FCA regulation, while maintaining the core rights and protections provided by the CCA.

4.21 Therefore, the Government is now working to develop a model that will ensure that regulation does more to protect consumers, but also reflects the particular characteristics of the consumer credit market, and remains proportionate.

4.22 The Financial Services Bill therefore includes provisions enabling a full transfer of consumer credit regulation to the FCA, with retention of substantive CCA provisions. The Government will exercise these powers if and when it has identified a model of FCA regulation that is proportionate for the different segments of the consumer credit market. The exercise of these powers will be subject to impact assessment and the approval of both Houses of Parliament.

4.23 The Government is confident that a proportionate and effective consumer credit regime in the FCA will be deliverable. However, the Government retains the option to improve consumer protection by enhancing the regulatory powers and approach under CCA, should it conclude that a model for consumer credit regulation under FSMA and the FCA cannot be delivered in a way that improves consumer protection while delivering good regulatory proportionality and value.

Martin Wheatley (Head of FCA), 'My Vision for the FCA' (2012) www.fsa.gov.uk

We need … a new approach to getting the right outcomes for consumers…The regulatory model had failed. The standard orthodoxy was that…people make rational decisions when given sufficient information: that market are self-correcting and ..that if you oversee the distribution channels—the right products get to the right people. All three orthodoxies failed.

---

5. *Ex ante* regulation: a safety model for credit regulation?

The world financial crisis has stimulated greater interest in *ex ante* product regulation to prevent systemic problems such as the mis-selling of payment protection insurance, endowment mortgages or the sub-prime mortgage debacle in the Unites States. Elizabeth Warren argues for a consumer safety model of credit.

Elizabeth Warren, 'Unsafe at Any Rate' (Summer 2007) *Democracy Journal* 8–9.

It is impossible to buy a toaster that has a one-in-five chance of bursting into flames and burning down your house. But it is possible to refinance an existing home with a mortgage that has the same one-in-five chance of putting the family out on the street—and the mortgage won't even carry a disclosure of that fact to the homeowner. Similarly, it's impossible to change the price on a toaster once it has been purchased. But long after the papers have been signed, it is possible to triple the price of the credit used to finance the purchase of that appliance, even if the customer meets all the credit terms, in full and on time. Why are consumers safe when they purchase tangible consumer products with cash, but when they sign up for routine financial products like mortgages and credit cards they are left at the mercy of their creditors?

The difference between the two markets is regulation. … Nearly every product sold in America has passed basic safety regulations well in advance of reaching store shelves. Credit products, by comparison, are regulated by a tattered patchwork of federal and state laws that have failed to adapt to changing markets. Moreover, thanks to effective regulation, innovation in the market for physical products has led to more safety and cutting-edge features. By comparison, innovation in financial products has produced incomprehensible terms and sharp practices that have left families at the mercy of those who write the contracts.

Sometimes consumer trust in a creditor is well-placed. Indeed, credit has provided real value for millions of households, permitting the purchase of homes that can add to family wealth accumulation and cars that can expand job opportunities. Credit can also provide a critical safety net and a chance for a family to borrow against a better tomorrow when they hit job layoffs, medical problems, or family break-ups today. … But for a growing number of families who are steered into over-priced credit products, risky subprime mortgages, and misleading insurance plans, trust in a creditor turns out to be costly. And for families who get tangled up with truly dangerous financial products, the result can be wiped-out savings, lost homes, higher costs for car insurance, denial of jobs, troubled marriages, bleak retirements, and broken lives.

Consumers can enter the market to buy physical products confident that they won't be tricked into buying exploding toasters and other unreasonably dangerous products. They can concentrate their shopping efforts in other directions, helping to drive a competitive market that keeps costs low and encourages innovation in convenience, durability, and style. Consumers entering the market to buy financial products should enjoy the same protection. Just as the Consumer Product Safety Commission (CPSC) protects buyers of goods and supports a competitive market, we need the same for consumers of financial products—a new regulatory regime, and even a new regulatory body, to protect consumers who use credit cards, home mortgages, car loans, and a host of other products.

The time has come to put scaremongering to rest and to recognize that regulation can often support and advance efficient and more dynamic markets.

The UK has experience of *ex ante* regulation of consumer finance products by both the OFT and since 2004 the FSA.

5.1 *Ex ante* regulation: the evolving experience of credit licensing

The rationales for the introduction in section 25 of the Consumer Credit Act 1974 of comprehensive credit licensing by an administrative agency were the failures of private law to protect individual rights or deter unscrupulous practices and the limited scope of existing licensing regimes. There was a path-dependency to this approach in the UK. Moneylenders had been required to be licensed under earlier legislation, which had entrusted the licensing function to the local magistrates' courts. The absence of an agency to monitor compliance and enforce the legislation meant that it was, in practice, ineffective. Moreover, the limitation of its scope to moneylenders caused unnecessary market distortions. Administrative licensing was therefore proposed to provide uni- form treatment for all credit grantors by an expert body which could monitor market activity. Members of the Crowther Committee had been impressed by the US practice of licensing and also the idea of an administrative regulator of the credit market. There was also an important fairness goal. The Crowther Committee had drawn attention to the fact that:

6.1.19 The basic problem is that the law protects least those whom it is designed to serve most. The low-income consumer is particularly open to oppression, yet he is usually unable—through ignorance, fear or sheer inability to manage his affairs—to avail himself of the protection which is offered to him by the process of litigation. Such a person will rarely take the initiative in instituting proceedings for the redress of his grievance, since apart from the factors just mentioned the expense is likely to be out of proportion to the resulting benefit.

6.3.3 ... [W]e have reached the conclusion that there should be an effective licensing system covering all types of institution concerned with the granting of consumer credit. The protective methods listed ... above [information and so on] are all concerned with individual transactions. Hence, though they are important, their efficacy is in practice limited by the fact that, for reasons we have already given, a single individual may be unaware of his legal rights or unable or unwilling to exercise them; and the more unscrupulous type of credit grantor may well take' the view that the occasional check on his malpractices by a determined consumer in an isolated transaction is not a serious deterrent, and is outweighed by the financial advantages he may derive from evading the law. There is thus a need for an agency entrusted with the continuing supervision of consumer credit grantors, with power to investigate trading practices, require production of accounts and records and, in the case of serious malpractice, suspend or revoke the offender's licence.

...

7.2.2 [I]n respect of licensing everyone should likewise be treated in the same way. This might, of course, mean that there should be no licensing for anyone. This would be possible; the law could simply lay down what could and what could not be done within the defined field of consumer credit, and provide that anyone who offended would be subject to a penalty, enforced in the courts. Firm as is our attachment to the general principle that legitimate trade should be left alone as much as possible, we think that, in the particular field with which we are concerned, this would be going too far. Parliament found it necessary, in an age of universal belief in laisser faire, to require the licensing of pawnbrokers and later the registration and then the licensing of moneylenders, with specific exemption order for bodies which were to be exempt from such registration or licensing, and we do not think it would be right simply to abolish these provisions without putting anything else in their place. We therefore propose a licensing system—though much less complex than either of the two just mentioned—for the whole field. ...

7.4.2 Without wishing to see any abatement in the individual's right to appeal to the courts, we think it is clear that, in the particular field of consumer credit, there must also, and primarily, be provision for administrative supervision and enforcement. It will be one of the duties of the Commissioner to keep a watch on the activities of those to whom he has issued licences. ...

7.4.3 He will have several methods of enforcement available to him. His power to revoke a licence, or to refuse to renew it, will be by itself a powerful weapon, and will no doubt prove to be the one that he most frequently uses. But it will not by itself do more than stop an abuse or transgression. It cannot put right what has already been done, and though the withdrawal of a licence will put the offender out of business, this may not, in particular cases, be thought to be the appropriate remedy or retribution. We think the Commissioner should therefore be empowered to apply to the courts for injunctions and to initiate criminal prosecutions. We have considered whether he should also have the power, such as has been given to the corresponding officials in some other countries, to initiate civil proceedings on behalf of private individuals and others who may not wish to proceed themselves but whose cases raise issues of importance. In the particular field with which we are concerned, such a power could be of great value, since the consumer who has suffered injustice or damage is often unable or unwilling to act for himself.

The wide scope of the licensing 'net' means that it is a general weapon in the regulation of unfair practices in relation to areas such as the motor trade or home improvements. Since licences may be revoked or refused where a person has 'engaged in business practices appearing to the Director to be deceitful or oppressive, or otherwise unfair or improper (whether unlawful or not)' (section 25(2A)(e) of the Consumer Credit Act 1974), the licensing power is effective over a wide range of harmful activities. In addition, the licensing sanction—the denial of the ability to carry on business—is a potentially powerful bargaining lever in the securing of compliance with a wide variety of consumer legislation, in the 'chilling' of potentially unfair behaviour, in the deterring of unscrupulous operators from entering the legal consumer credit market, and in the securing of compensation for consumers (notwithstanding the absence of statutory authorisation to use it for this purpose, see below). It may also provide valuable information on market practices.

On the other hand licensing of a whole industry is costly: it will be over-inclusive and does not attack unfairness directly since attacking unlicensed activity is a proxy for attacking unfair trading. Licensing could result in 'capture' of the agency but given the minimum standards for entry, and the fact that licensing covers a wide range of credit grantors, this does not seem a serious danger. It is possible, however, that later prospective entrants may face higher standards for entry than those faced by traders already licensed. Revoking a licence will be subject to significant due process protections which will increase the costs of assembling an individual case and reduce its effectiveness as a deterrent to the 'fly-by-night' trader (see Ogus and Rowley, 1981). The broad discretion to issue and revoke licences (eg under section 25(2)(e)) creates the dangers of abuse.

During the 1980s the OFT regarded licensing as a valuable regulatory instrument. Lord Borrie (then Director General of Fair Trading) argued in 1983 that the effectiveness of licensing should not be measured by the number of licences revoked or refused but through its use as a bargaining lever in persuading businesses to draw 'up fairer agreements and [provide] compensation to members of the public who have been overcharged and unfairly treated'. Licensing might also deter firms from launching schemes that might endanger their licence and encourage them to 'tighten up' their procedures and instructions to employees. The possible non-enforceability of an agreement entered into by an unlicensed credit broker might also encourage greater internal policing by credit grantors (Borrie, 1983: 91, 100–01).

The traders involved in licensing decisions (eg minded to refuse, revoke) during this period can be divided into six groups: motor dealers, debt collectors and investigators, home-improvement companies, finance companies, mortgage and secured credit, and sale and lease of commercial equipment (see eg OFT Annual Report, 2004–05: statistical annex). Over the years motor dealers generally represent the largest number of cases. The Annual Report of 1980 provided initial guidance on the practices that the OFT would regard as calling into question a licensee's fitness to hold a licence.

Director General of Fair Trading, Annual Report (1980) 31–33

Over-charged consumers benefit from licensing

In 1980, in order to give guidance to traders, the Director General made the first public statements about unfair practices revealed by the licensing process—those, in the words of the Act, which appear deceitful, oppressive, unfair or improper (whether unlawful or not). Such announcements are expected to become a feature of the licensing process. In statements in March and July, he announced refunds in excess of £1 million and £1/2million respectively by certain credit and hire companies. In demonstrating their fitness, these companies gave assurances that the practices had been stopped and steps taken to reimburse customers who had suffered. The Director General cited the following unfair practices:

Charging interest on money not advanced …

Variation of rates of interest in breach of contract …

Failure to check accounts after company error …

Failure to give satisfactory information for consumers …

Unfair practices connected with the voluntary termination of car credit agreements— some finance companies had been encouraging customers to sign a car over to them when they could not keep up the payments on it. The customers believed that the debt would be satisfied by the sale of the car. But sales took place at auctions where very low prices were returned, and the customers then received a demand for the balance still outstanding. The companies concerned stopped this practice and customers were compensated.

Other practices on which the Director General has acted

… Moneylending—for many households, borrowing from a doorstep moneylender becomes an important part of the budget. With the lack of security and the cost of the agent's weekly visits, such lending is bound to be expensive. Large sums are often borrowed, both in single amounts and as a series of small loans, and the opportunities for abuse are considerable. The Office found instances where the prohibition on canvassing cash loans in the home had been circumvented: moneylenders had taken advantage of visits made for other purposes, asked the customer to sign a card requesting a visit—though he had not expressed interest in a loan—or secured his unwitting invitation in other documents.

… Investigation revealed practices, many proscribed by the Moneylenders Act 1927, which could easily lead to severe financial difficulties for borrowers. No memorandum of the loan agreement was supplied; agreements were left blank, omitted vital details such as the true rate of interest, or stated a false rate; the first repayment was deducted from the loan immediately. … Another practice examined by the Office, 're-loaning', is widespread. A large part of each new loan is used to payoff an existing loan, usually without any rebate for early settlement. The Office thinks the practice may be unfair and could lead to extortionate credit bargains, because the proportion of money paid in interest steadily increases the longer the re-loaning continues.

Other areas identified include debt collection practices (see OFT Annual Report, 1981 and 1982), mortgaging and insurance business (1982), high-pressure sales of double glazing (1981) and the marketing of orthopaedic appliances by preying on consumer anxieties about their future health (1981). During the 1990s the OFT set out guidance for potentially problematic areas such as the sub-prime lending market (1997) and in 2001 the debt-management sector.

In 1999 the National Audit Office investigated the credit licensing powers of the OFT, in a political context where the New Labour government wished to rejuvenate the agency.

Report by the Comptroller and Auditor-General, *The Office of Fair Trading: Protecting the Consumer from Unfair Trading Practices*, HC57 session 1999–00

2.17 The OFT have warned traders that they risk losing their consumer credit licences if they do not comply with published guidelines tailored to combat specific unfair practices. This approach has helped to counter problems arising from the automatic charging of credit protection insurance. ...

The OFT's action against unfair practices in the non-status lending market

Non-status borrowers are those with a poor credit rating who often find it difficult to obtain finance from traditional sources on normal terms and conditions. In 1996, the OFT received many complaints about the treatment of non-status borrowers, including:

• consumers being persuaded to take out loans beyond their ability to repay high up-front fees and commissions which were not properly disclosed or explained;

• dual interest rates—a mortgage or loan is often sold at a concessionary rate but a much higher standard rate becomes payable in cases of default.

In February 1997 an OFT news release warned of unfair practices in the non-status lending market. Complaints continued and in July 1997 the OFT published guidance warning of unfair practices which, if they continued, would put brokers and lenders credit licences at risk.

Following requests for clarification, the OFT published revised guidelines in November 1997. They also wrote to lenders and brokers repeating their earlier warning and enclosing a questionnaire asking them to report how far they now complied with the OFT's guidance. Some 93 per cent of the 244 lenders and 99 per cent of the 914 brokers who replied confirmed compliance.

The OFT's action to end negative option selling of credit protection insurance

The OFT acted to eliminate the sale of credit protection insurance by the negative option method in which the consumer has to take positive action to avoid being charged a premium. The OFT consider this an unfair business practice because consumers do not have a genuinely free and informed choice about the product.

In 1992, following complaints by consumers to trading standards services, the OFT notified two mail order companies that they were considering revoking their credit licences because of this practice.

The OFT then warned the mail order industry as a whole so that other companies could take steps to avoid similar proceedings. In 1994, the OFT wrote to the banking and consumer credit trade associations and asked them to ensure that those of their members who used negative option selling would cease to do so. All the associations undertook to eliminate the practice.

The individual licensing process was used therefore both as a form of rule-making by providing guidance on unfair practices as well as a mechanism for obtaining consumer redress. This process may have provided a partial substitute for the rule-making power that existed in Part II of the Fair Trading Act 1973. Licensing, it may be remembered, allows the Director General to proscribe practices which are not breaches of existing laws. If licensing is used to develop rules on unfair practices, then should there be the opportunity for notice and comment by third parties?

The due process controls on revoking licences make it difficult to exercise this power, and the OFT (see below) often had difficulties in accessing information on an applicant. The Consumer Credit Act 1974 provided no intermediate sanctions that could be exercised by the OFT. It was difficult for the Office to revoke a licence based solely on a pattern of complaints (Borrie, 1982: 95–96). In the late 1990s the administration of the licensing process was investigated by the Comptroller and Auditor General and this resulted in a critical report by the Committee of Public Accounts. The Comptroller and Auditor General concluded:

> (a) refusing or revoking a trader's consumer credit licence is a powerful sanction (b) few consumer credit licences are refused or revoked, but many more traders withdraw their applications following queries from the OFT (c) the OFT do not always obtain in good time information relevant to traders' fitness to hold a licence (d) the OFT are not working as effectively as they could with trading standards services. (Comptroller and Auditor-General, 1999: 36)

It often took several years between the events giving rise to licence revocation and the actual revocation. The Public Accounts Committee echoed these criticisms of the performance of the OFT in the use of its licensing powers. It also noted that the OFT was unable to access information from the Police National Computer unless they have cause to believe that a trader has previous convictions and that the OFT has only belatedly started to gather information on discrimination (discrimination on grounds of sex, colour, race or ethnic or national origins is a ground for refusing a licence under section 25(2A)(d)).

During the early 2000s the OFT was compared unfavourably with the FSA which had a much broader toolkit of sanctions than the OFT. The 2006 amendments to the 1974 Act extended the powers of the OFT.

First, the criteria in section 25 of the Act for denying the granting of a licence was extended to include the ability of the trader to carry on its business in a fit manner in the future (eg through ensuring an adequate managerial structure) and the inclusion of 'irresponsible lending' as a criterion for refusing a license. Second, under section 33A the OFT may exercise the intermediate power of imposing conditions on licensees. Section 39A confers a power on the OFT to impose civil penalties up to £50,000 on persons who do not comply with the conditions imposed under section 33A. Finally, the OFT is given greater power to require information from licensees, and gain access to premises (section 36B–D). The power to obtain information includes situations where acts or omissions have occurred that cast doubt on whether a person is a fit person to hold a licence. These powers brought the OFT regime somewhat closer to the model of licensing operated by the FSA under the Financial Services and Markets Act 2000.

The OFT outlined the development of a two-track licensing process linked to the risks posed by particular forms of credit.

OFT, Evidence to House of Commons Business, Innovation and Skills Committee Debt Management Session 2010–12 (2012) HC 1649

The issues currently facing the OFT in discharging its responsibilities under the CCA are dominated by four broad themes:

- The unfair treatment of consumers in financial difficulties who are no longer able to service their debts.

- The unfair treatment of consumers who are otherwise vulnerable, for example through age, mental capacity limitation, or poor financial literacy.

- The irresponsible treatment of consumers seeking credit, often where they have limited access to mainstream provision as a result of impaired credit records or low incomes.

- Preventing entry into credit markets of individuals with a history of violent or fraudulent behaviour or firms which simply lack the competence to meet expected standards.

Since the introduction of new powers in April 2008, the OFT has operated a risk-based strategy based on:

- A strong gateway to exclude violent, fraudulent or otherwise unfit traders from the market.

- Developing clear, practical guidance and driving up standards of behaviour.

- Credible deterrence through targeted high impact intelligence-led enforcement, particularly focused on issues of wider market significance.

8. Our gateway risk model treats debt collection, debt management, secured sub-prime lending and lending in the home as high risk activities. We have subjected these businesses to a greater degree of scrutiny at the application stage and have conducted a rolling programme of thematic compliance reviews and enforcement work in these sectors. More detail on our approach to debt management and high cost lending is set out in sections 2 and 3 of this note.

9. Our enforcement work is complemented by active engagement with industry to drive up standards. We work closely with trade associations and other forums to ensure firms are aware of their responsibilities under the Act and the OFT's expectations. We have produced a suite of sectoral and cross-cutting guidance setting out the standards we expect of businesses engaging in particular regulated credit activities and making clear the behaviours which the OFT considers will call a firm's fitness into question and may trigger enforcement action.

10. This guidance does not have the status of rules or legislation. It does not place positive obligations on firms, but rather sets out the behaviours or omissions which may be likely to lead to OFT enforcement action. Statutory obligations on firms are set out in the Act. A significant portion of these are governed by the maximum harmonisation European Consumer Credit Directive..

11. Where firms fail to meet the standards set out in legislation or guidance, or engage in activities which the OFT considers to be otherwise unfair or improper (whether lawful or not) the OFT can take enforcement action.

… Between April 2009 and March 2011 the OFT revoked or refused the licences of 104 firms and placed requirements on a further 53.

14. The regime is fully funded through industry fees. Our budgeted income for 2011/12 is approximately £10 million. This is raised by a fee of £435 for sole trader or £1075 for other firms when applying for or renewing a licence. As the fee is collected on a five year cycle this is equivalent to an annual fee of £87 or £215 respectively. In addition, allfirms pay a flat

levy of £150 to fund the Financial Ombudsman Service, which we collect on their behalf alongside the fee. ... [A]s at November 2011 there were approximately 84,000 consumer credit licenceholders, of whom 50,500 have obtained or renewed their licences under the new standards introduced in April 2008 by the Consumer Credit Act 2006 (CCA06). An estimated 53% of consumer credit licenceholders describe their primary activity as some form of financial services provision (including debt related services). The remainder engage in wider retail activities, mostly introducing consumers to credit to finance the purchase of goods and services.

32% of licensed firms are sole traders, 8% partnerships, around 58% corporates, and 2% others such as charities and clubs. An estimated 70% of licenceholders are micro-enterprises, employing fewer than 10 people. The number of credit licence applications has been steadily declining over a number of years.

5.2 FSA approaches to regulation: the 'treating customers fairly' initiative

The new Financial Conduct Authority will take over the conduct of business aspects of the existing FSA regime. The FSA operates under 'high-level principles' and 'conduct of business' rules (see rule-making power under section 138 and conduct principles section 64 FSMA). It can amend rules without the intervention of Parliament, and licences those carrying on regulated activity. It has extensive information-gathering and investigative powers and a wide range of flexible enforcement powers. It may publicly censure licensees, has broad powers to impose penalties 'of such amount as it considers appropriate' (section 206(1)), may vary or revoke permission, and require firms to make restitution (sections 382 and 384) as well as having the ability to seek injunctive and other court orders. Breach of most conduct of business rules are actionable as a breach of statutory duty. However, contraventions do not make any transaction void or unenforceable (section 151) or criminal.

The FSA may require a firm to establish a consumer redress scheme (under section 404 FSMA) when

(a) ... there may have been a widespread or regular failure by relevant firms to comply with requirements applicable to the carrying on by them of any activity;

(b) it appears to it that, as a result, consumers have suffered (or may suffer) loss or damage in respect of which, if they brought legal proceedings, a remedy or relief would be available in the proceedings; and

(c) it considers that it is desirable to make rules for the purpose of securing that redress is made to the consumers in respect of the failure (having regard to other ways in which consumers may obtain redress).

The FSA 'treating customers fairly' initiative is a useful example of attempts to change the culture of organisations by embedding norms of fairness within organisations. The rationale for 'high-level principles' was that they were 'regarded as more likely to advance consumers' interests in fair treatment than would reliance on detailed pre-scriptive rules for each sector and financial product. Firms too were thought to benefit from basing the new fairness requirements on principles, specifically through the construction of a less intrusive regulatory order than a rule-based system would require (Williams, 2010: 233).

FSA, *Treating Customers Fairly—Towards Fair Outcomes for Consumers* (2006) 4, 5, 7, 11, 12, 19, 20, 24, 27, 29, 31, 40

The requirement on firms to treat their customers fairly is not new: it is part of the existing regulatory requirements and is firmly rooted in our principles for business.

Principle six states: a firm must pay due regard to the interests of its customers and treat them fairly. ... The TCF [Treating Customers Fairly] initiative is a core part of our move to a more principles-based approach to regulation.

We see real benefits for consumers in tipping the balance of our regulation more towards principle and away from prescription. As part of the move towards a more principles-based approach we are keen to avoid introducing new detailed rules. ...

We recognize that some firms may prefer the clarity and certainty associated with a rules based approach. As part of our initiatives we have used a range of approaches, for example, the publication of case studies and the statements of good and poor practice, to help firms to interpret the meaning of relevant principles and to challenge firms to review their practices and to facilitate change. And we believe that trade associations and other organizations can have a significant role in helping firms in different sectors to develop acceptable practices within a more principles-based regime, for example through industry codes and other guidance materials.

The principles are themselves rules. And some aspects of what is meant by the principles have been fleshed out in our more detailed rules. So, despite our move to simplify rules where possible, some detailed rules will remain and compliance with them will remain an important aspect of treating customers fairly. ...

The TCF initiative starts from the position that the vast majority of firms intend to treat their customers fairly. Indeed, what is required of firms varies considerably depending on their starting point. ... Overall, however, we believe that the current picture on TCF implementation is mixed.

We have developed six consumer outcomes which explain what we want the TCF initiative to achieve.

Outcome one: consumers can be confident that they are dealing with firms where the fair treatment of customers is central to the corporate culture.

TCF is a cultural issue. As such, we expect it to be driven from the top, and from all firms. We expect demonstrable commitment from senior management. ... TCF should be reflected in the approach taken to human resources and reward within an organization as well as the frontline business areas. It should be taken into account when corporate strategy is determined and when standard form consumer contracts are drafted. Senior management and the board should receive management information that enables them to assess whether customers are being treated fairly. Putting consumers at the center of the corporate culture means that TCF, rather than simply being about process, should translate into practical outputs in the shape of fair outcomes for consumers.

Outcome two: products and services marketed and sold in the retail market that are designed to meet the needs of identified consumer groups and are targeted accordingly. ...

Outcome three: consumers are provided with clear information and are kept appropriately informed before, during and after the point-of-sale. ...

Outcome four: where consumers receive advice, the advice is suitable and takes account of their circumstances. ...

Outcome five, consumers are provided with products that perform as firms have led them to expect, and the associated service is both of an acceptable standard and as they have been led to expect. ...

Outcome six: consumers do not face unreasonable post sale barriers imposed by firms to change product, switch provider, submit a claim or make a complaint. ...

In our July 2005 report 'Treating customers fairly—building on progress' we suggested that firms might be categorized into four groups when assessing progress on the TCF—those that are simply aware of the initiative: those involved in strategy and planning, including conducting a gap analysis to establish what areas might need to be tackled: those implementing change: and those embedding TCF into their business. ...

During the year, we have particularly thought more about what a firm that is successfully embedding looks like. We believe that the embedding phase, and achieving a step change in behavior is characterized by the following:

- The fair treatment of consumers is established throughout the firm—not just in systems and controls but in business culture including strategy, training, remuneration and staff behaviors.

- Recognition that the firm is engaged in a continuous process—rather than being a shortterm project that can be completed and then put to one side, TCF should be built into processes and strategies so that it is automatically taken into account in all relevant business decisions [eg when new products or services are launched].

- Adequate management information available for firms management to monitor TCF; and

- Improvement in the quality of the outcomes experienced by the firm's customers.

Having determined the program for achieving TCF senior management will need to use appropriate management information to measure whether they are treating customers fairly and whether their aspirations for change are being realized throughout the business. Identifying appropriate management information continues to be a challenge for many firms. In particular, it is essential that firms use measures that distinguish between customer satisfaction and fair treatment of customers ... fairness and satisfaction are unlikely to be synonymous. A customer can, for example, be satisfied with an unsuitable product or dissatisfied with an entirely fairly adjudicated general insurance claim. Until senior management are able to judge the firm's performance against appropriate management information. It will not be possible for them to assess their TCF performance adequately or to conclude they are embedding.

... There is some way to go before senior management commitment and the work invested in the TCF initiative overall reaches the frontline of all firms activities and translates to significant improvements across the full range of outcomes for consumers.

... The development of appropriate management information, including information from mystery shopping and customer surveys, will enable firms to monitor how they are performing against the defined outcomes and to determine when they have reached the embedding phase.

Under the Unfair Terms in Consumer Contracts Regulations 1999 we have seen many examples of significant deficiencies in firms standard form consumer contracts. We see this as an example of how the General TCF agenda has failed to take hold in a specific area.

... We have not surveyed smaller firms to establish what stage of the TCF process they have reached. But with regard to the adoption of the fair treatment of customers as part of a firm's corporate culture, we note that:

- Unsurprisingly, many smaller firms do not tend to approach TCF by looking at processes, carrying out gap analyses and developing a formal strategy.

- Smaller firms tend to invest less upfront on new initiatives like TCF and generally have significant fewer resources to devote to such activities.

- The shorter lines of communication inherent in small firms between management and customer facing staff have made it easier for good practice to be implemented across the business once management have embraced TCF. In many cases senior management are the customer facing staff, or at least are much closer to them.

Firms need to be open with customers about their fees and whether they will be receiving commission when selling particular products.

Treating customers fairly maps out a division of responsibilities between financial firms and the regulator for fair treatment of financial consumers. ... Firms are responsible for demonstrating fair treatment of customers and the FSA for ensuring that firms establish and maintain systems and controls that not only deliver fair treatment to customers but also allows regulators to observe firms' practices and thus assess how firms organize their dealings with customers and how they perform their contracts. The FSA provides extensive guidance to firms, but refuses to publish a formal 'definition' on the basis that a formal definition is likely to be overly rigid, inappropriately prescriptive and may be treated, at least by some firms as representing a 'ceiling' on firms' obligations towards consumers or an invitation simply to add another factor to existing internal compliance processes. (Williams, 2010: 234)

5.2.1 Payment protection insurance and approaches to regulation

Many recent actions under the FSA principles have related to payment protection insurance. This insurance protects a borrower against being unable to keep up their repayments due to accident, sickness or involuntary unemployment. It is sold with a variety of unsecured and mortgage credit as well as credit cards. It is usually purchased at the same time as the consumer enters into the credit agreement. The OFT conducted a market study of payment protection insurance in 2006 and referred this market to the Competition Commission. Some of the identified concerns included the following:

[T]he complex nature of payment protection insurance make comparisons between different policies difficult and suppliers do little to inform consumers adequately off the details off the cover. Payment protection insurance, has a low claims ratio when compared to other insurance products, and it seems reasonable to assume that distributor profitability is sizable, with little evidence of substantial competition. Some unsecured personal loan providers and possibly some credit card providers appeared to be offsetting low margins on credit offerings with profits generated from the sale of payment protection insurance.

Insurance that is sold in relation to second mortgages and unsecured loans is generally single premium insurance. This is charged at the outset of the loan. The consumer does not usually pay at that time. It is added to the loan, and repaid over the period of the loan. A consumer may not be aware that she is paying interest on the insurance. Insurers compete to provide policies to distributors who then sell them to consumers. Given the profitability of payment protection insurance there may be little incentive on distributors to purchase the cheapest insurance and distributors may be offered commissions or some form of profit sharing in the sale of the policies. This may create incentives for overselling. (OFT, 2006: 2)

The FSA also investigated payment protection insurance in 2005 and 2006 (FSA, 2005, 2006). It was particularly concerned about selling practices relating to single premium policies where information on interest was not disclosed and consumers were not given information on the lack of refunds for such insurance. It also found that the structure of incentives and targets for sale staff could encourage misselling in some firms and that there was not adequate training and competence of sales staff in around half the firms that they investigated. The amendments to the Consumer Credit Act Agreements Regulations in 2004 uses a formality to regulate payment protection insurance by requiring a separate signature to a prescribed form of consent.

GE Capital Bank Limited (FSA ref 2045721) (2007)

1. THE PENALTY

1.1 ... [T]he FSA imposes on the firm a financial penalty of £610,000.

1.3 The penalty is imposed for breaches by the firm of the following Principles for Businesses in relation to general insurance:

(a) failing to conduct its business with due skill, care and diligence (Principle 2);

(b) failing to take reasonable care to organise and control its affairs responsibly and effectively, with adequate risk management systems (Principle 3); and

(c) failing to pay due regard to the interests of its customers and failing to treat them fairly (Principle 6).

2. REASONS FOR THE PENALTY

2.1 The primary business of GECB is the provision of credit finance through loans, credit cards and store cards. The firm is the credit provider for store cards offered by many of the UK's high street retailers. For a number of years the firm has sold insurance products, mainly the Account Cover product sold in relation to its store cards. This includes payment protection insurance (PPI), purchase protection insurance and price protection insurance. Account Cover is a monthly renewable cover.

2.2 In the period from Q2 2005 (the relevant period) in relation to its general insurance business the firm breached Principles 2, 3, and 6, in the following areas:

(a) Sales: the firm failed, where appropriate, to review, amend and then operate its sales procedures to ensure that all customers received adequate information about the policy before they made a decision on whether to take the insurance.

(b) Training: in light of evidence that sales staff were not complying consistently with its sales procedures, the firm failed to amend its training procedures.

(c) Monitoring and Management Information: the firm failed, where appropriate, to review, amend and then operate its monitoring procedures to ensure that the monitoring for training, sales, commission incentives, penetration rates, complaints, cancellations, and claims, was effective and appropriate for its business. The firm failed adequately to act in response to the management information which was collected and available. By Q2 2005 this ought to have alerted the firm to the fact that its procedures were not working as intended and were not resulting in sales which were consistently compliant with FSA requirements.

(d) Customers: the firm failed to implement any procedure to contact customers to remedy the non-compliant sales which were identified by its monitoring procedures.

(e) Compliance: the firm failed to resource its compliance function adequately and in proportion to the sales distribution model adopted by the firm.

The breaches by GECB stem from a failure to review and amend its systems and controls for the sale of insurance in light of the evidence emerging from Q2 2005 that its procedures were not in practice delivering consistently compliant sales. The insurance could be sold on behalf of GECB by store staff employed by high street retailers across the UK and therefore the firm operated an unusually large sales distribution model. The failures had the potential to impact upon a very large number of customers. The FSA expects firms to review their systems and controls and to change them quickly if they are not operating as intended.

2.3 The FSA considers that the breaches have been mitigated by the changes made or proposed by the firm following the commencement of the FSA investigation. In particular:

(a) The firm has paid in full all previously excluded claims made by customers who were sold a policy on or after 14 January 2005.

(b) The sales process, and in particular the documentation used at point-of-sale has been redesigned to make it more likely that the firm's procedures will be adhered to . . .

(c) The firm has developed and is implementing a risk-based approach to monitoring using a wide range of tools including mystery shopping, observation, customer contact and desk-based analysis of data on sales. The firm has appointed 50 new 'field' compliance and training staff to visit stores to monitor sales and training. Importantly, the system for reporting and escalating management information (MI) is being enhanced. Additional controls are being implemented to enable senior management to respond to MI by suspending insurance sales by individuals or stores which fail to meet the appropriate standards.

(d) The firm has developed and is implementing a procedure to ensure that non-compliant sales will be followed-up with the customer. ...

(e) To reduce the risk that any customer may have suffered detriment as a result of the breaches outlined above the firm will be undertaking a comprehensive customer contact exercise. Until that process is complete the firm has undertaken that it will not seek to rely on any policy exclusions for new claims made. ...

2.4 The FSA considers that the substantial changes to the firm's systems and controls for selling insurance and the proposals to conduct a comprehensive customer contact exercise and to pay redress where appropriate are significant steps in demonstrating the firm's commitment to treating customers fairly (TCF). These are important mitigating factors. ...

2.5 In addition, the FSA has had regard to the nature of the insurance being sold and the likely financial impact on the customer. For most consumers this type of insurance will not be as significant a transaction as some other types of general insurance. The financial impact on most customers was likely to have been modest.

The firm has received full credit for settlement of the disciplinary case at an early stage; it has received a 30% discount for settling the case at stage one. Were it not for this discount the penalty would have been £871,000. Without the firm's commitment to remedial action and appropriate redress the financial penalty would have been substantially higher.

HFC Bank Limited Final Notice (2008)

FINAL NOTICE

1. THE PENALTY

1.3 … [T]he FSA imposes a financial penalty on HFC in the amount of £1,085,000.

3. BACKGROUND

3.2 HFC's branch business is as a provider of unsecured and secured loans. It has a secondary focus on general insurance business, mostly through the sale of PPI. The FSA regulates HFC's general insurance business but not its lending activity, which is outside the scope of the FSA's activities. Over the Relevant Period HFC traded under the 'Household Bank' and 'Beneficial Finance' names.

3.3 The FSA's investigation has focused solely upon sales made by HFC's branch network.

The PPI products sold

3.4 HFC sells PPI through its branch network when arranging personal loans for customers. It offers a bundled policy which provides cover for accident, sickness and involuntary unemployment. It also offers a life policy which can be purchased for joint or single lives. The life policy can be sold on its own or in conjunction with the bundled accident, sickness and involuntary unemployment policy.

3.5 HFC sells single premium PPI policies with unsecured loans. It also sells a limited amount of regular premium PPI with other types of loan. The sales process for regular premium PPI is substantially the same as that for single premium PPI. In the event that a customer claims against the PPI policy, any benefits due are directly payable to HFC to cover the customer's loan repayments. A full refund is given if the customer cancels within 30 days of the start of the policy. A partial, less than pro rata refund is given if the policy is cancelled after that period (eg a quarter of the premium is returned if the policy is cancelled half way through its term).

3.6 HFC also offers critical illness and personal accident cover. These policies provide more limited cover than PPI at a lower cost. Benefits under these insurances are paid to the customer, rather than to HFC.

3.7 PPI was sold in conjunction with 75% of all loans sold by HFC's branch network in the Relevant Period. Out of all PPI sold, 86% of policies covered life, accident, sickness and involuntary unemployment, 6% accident, sickness and involuntary unemployment, and 8% life alone.

The sales process

3.8 HFC sells PPI on an advised basis. It receives leads from retailers who have arranged credit with HFC for customers in respect of their retail purchases. These customers' credit arrangements are typically nearing the end of an interest free period. HFC sales staff contact some of these customers to discuss further loans or refinancing existing loans.

3.9 If the customer is interested in a new loan, an appointment is made for the customer to visit an HFC branch. At that meeting the sales adviser will discuss the loan, PPI and other insurance options with the customer and make recommendations.

FSA work within the Relevant Period

3.10 During the Relevant Period the FSA has highlighted to firms the importance of having in place robust systems and controls and treating customers fairly when selling PPI and has highlighted various areas where firms are not complying with the FSA's requirements. These concerns have been expressed in reports published by the FSA, individual feedback to firms, a Dear CEO letter and Enforcement actions.

3.11 In November 2005 the FSA published the results of the first phase of its thematic work on PPI and wrote a Dear CEO letter to the industry outlining the findings of the thematic project and highlighting a number of key areas where firms were not treating their customers fairly.

3.12 This letter stressed that if a firm gives advice it should review how the suitability assessment is made to ensure the adviser fully assesses the customer's needs for PPI...

3.13 A second phase of PPI themed work was reported on in October 2006. The FSA highlighted in its report some key areas of widespread concern. These included the FSA's concern that some firms were still failing to establish that the PPI policies they recommended were suitable because they were not collecting sufficient information from the customer.

3.14 In July 2006, between the first two phases of the FSA's thematic work on PPI, the FSA visited HFC and identified a number of concerns relating to the firm's sale of PPI.

... 5. BREACHES OF THE FSA'S PRINCIPLES FOR BUSINESSES AND RULES

5.1 Principle 9 (suitability) provides that:

A firm must take reasonable care to ensure the suitability of its advice and discretionary decisions for any customer who is entitled to rely upon its judgement.

...The suitability assessment

5.4 Throughout the Relevant Period, HFC's documented procedures (including process guides for sales advisers and training material) and monitoring did not require adequate information to be collected and then properly used when recommending PPI. These failings created an unacceptable risk that advisers might make unsuitable sales. HFC failed, in particular, to require advisers to gather and analyse sufficient information about the following matters:

(1) A customer's future needs and circumstances: HFC did not ensure that the customer's intentions regarding the term of the loan and the PPI policy would be taken into account in the suitability recommendation when selling single premium PPI (which accounted for approximately 75% of sales). In the event of early settlement or cancellation of the policy after the initial 30 day period, the customer would receive a refund which was substantially less than pro rata (eg if the policy was cancelled at mid-term, a rebate was given of approximately one quarter of the premium). Likewise, the terms of the financing used to pay for the single premium resulted in the customer paying substantially more than a pro rata amount of interest if the policy was terminated early. Therefore, HFC's single premium product may not have met the needs of customers who expected (or were likely to want) to refinance the loan from HFC (eg to get a lower interest rate or a larger loan).

HFC's failings were serious given that HFC's business model anticipated refinancing the loans of existing customers (over half the loans sold by HFC were to existing HFC customers).

HFC also did not ensure that any foreseeable alteration in customers' circumstances in relation to the PPI eligibility criteria would be taken into account. This meant that a customer could potentially have been sold a product for which he was eligible at the point of sale but would not be able to claim on later during the life of the loan (eg if a customer was likely to start working less than 16 hours a week).

(2) Alternative means to protect the loan: HFC failed to ensure that advisers properly took into account any existing means the customer may have had to protect some or all of the loan. This might have been from another insurer, the customer's employer, or a product which HFC had itself previously sold. When advisers established that the customer had existing means (which they were trained to do), HFC required that the advisers ask customers whether they wanted to rely on them, instead of training and requiring the adviser to take the alternative means into account in making a personal recommendation.

(3) The type and level of cover required: HFC's sales procedures did not provide guidance to advisers as to the factors (such as individual circumstances and cost) to be taken into account in assessing whether to recommend life cover on its own, accident, sickness and involuntary unemployment cover on its own or both together or whether another insurance product offered by HFC (see paragraphs 3.4 to 3.6 above) may have been suitable. Further, in respect of life cover, whilst advisers recorded details of how many dependants a customer had, HFC failed to ensure that advisers had regard to how this information might impact on a customer's need for life cover, or the relative benefits (including affordability) of taking the standalone single/joint life cover.

(4) Pre-existing medical conditions: Whilst HFC required advisers to make customers aware of the exclusion relating to pre-existing medical conditions, it did not require advisers to explain the meaning of the exclusion. HFC proceeded on the basis that it was the customer's responsibility to understand the limitations attached to PPI and to take account of any pre-existing medical conditions when considering purchasing PPI.

The impact of this failing is potentially serious. Approximately 27% of the claims rejected by HFC (3% of the total claims made by HFC's customers) were as a result of pre-existing medical conditions.

5.5 HFC's failings partially stemmed from an assumption that, provided the customer was eligible, PPI was suitable unless the customer indicated that he wished to use any alternative means he already had. It did not therefore put in place adequate systems and controls to gather and to analyse sufficiently information on its customers' personal circumstances and objectives.

Communication to the customer of the basis for the personal recommendation

5.6 HFC used a generic SODAN rather than one tailored for each customer. This failed to:

(1) adequately set out an individual customer's demands and needs;

(2) confirm whether HFC personally recommended the contract;

(3) explain the reasons for the personal recommendation for the PPI policy and why it was suitable; and

(4) record any demands and needs of the customer that the personal recommendation did not meet (nor did HFC require that advisers communicate this in any other way).

5.7 As a result of this failure customers could not see and review the rationale for the recommendation, check its accuracy and give proper consideration to the recommendation and whether they wished to purchase the policy.

5.8 A SODAN is particularly important when PPI is sold as a secondary product where, at the point of sale, the customer may be more focussed on the loan rather than on the associated insurance. The failing undermined the customer's ability to consider fully whether to accept the firm's PPI recommendation and, following the sale, whether it should keep or cancel the policy in the 30 day cancellation period.

The need for robust procedures to ensure suitability

5.9 Firms selling PPI must have adequate processes in place to ensure suitable and compliant sales. There were a number of additional factors in respect of the sale of PPI by HFC during the Relevant Period which increased the importance of particularly robust systems and controls to ensure that PPI was only sold when suitable:

(1) Over the Relevant Period HFC's sales force was spread over 235 branch sites in total (136 by the end of the period). This required a significant degree of coordination and monitoring to ensure consistency of standards; and

(2) HFC advisers and branch managers were eligible for bonuses which were, in part, based on reaching a target of selling PPI with 80% of the loans (calculated by loan value, rather than numerical loan sales). For example, during the early part of the Relevant Period (up to June 2005) the attainment of the PPI target penetration rate had a potentially significant impact on bonuses (i.e. it could double and potentially quadruple the value of the bonus). Until August 2006, there were significant disincentives (up to 33% of bonuses) attached to failing to meet certain targets and compliance standards which included PPI sales targets. After August 2006, there was a potential 12–18% uplift to sales advisers' bonuses for reaching PPI targets (although in fact HFC estimates that the PPI element of advisers' bonuses then averaged approximately £19 per month). Whilst there is nothing inherently wrong with a remuneration policy which recognises and rewards sales, HFC's remuneration structure increased the risk that advisers might make, and branch managers approve, unsuitable sales of PPI to achieve those bonuses. The total amount of bonus available was significant compared to an adviser's basic salary (in 2005 and 2006 an adviser's monthly salary could be increased by up to 25%).

Compliance monitoring

5.10 HFC's Compliance department was responsible during the Relevant Period for the design and execution of a programme of compliance monitoring. Whilst the compliance monitoring visits and subsequent reports may have indicated general trends in relation to the sale of PPI, the reports did not contain sufficient detail to enable Compliance and/or senior management to obtain a sufficient understanding of the risk of potentially unsuitable sales in the branches. The application of weightings to the areas covered on the monitoring visits meant that a branch could fail "suitability" and/or 'fact finding' in relation to PPI sales and still receive a satisfactory rating for insurance compliance and overall. Given that only unsatisfactory reports were escalated to senior management, potentially unsuitable PPI sales or potentially less compliant branches were not escalated, although they were made the subject of mandatory or targeted action for which the branch manager would be responsible. There were also insufficient systems and controls for ensuring that any training needs identified in the reports were followed up properly.

5.11 Even where the monitoring reports did highlight the risk that customers might not have been treated fairly (eg where it was unclear if a customer had existing cover when purchasing PPI), there was no adequate system in place to ensure that such cases were investigated further and customers remediated if appropriate.

Management information

5.12 During the Relevant Period senior management did receive certain management information, both orally and in writing. However, the principal management information received by senior management in relation to PPI was the statistical summary of the compliance monitoring visit reports described at paragraphs 5.10 and 5.11 above. There was little commentary to accompany the statistics, effectively limiting senior management's oversight of compliance to a review of compliance trends. Where specific risks were identified by Compliance, there was no procedure by which HFC's senior management would be informed of these or how they were to be followed up (if at all) by the Compliance team.

5.13 The monthly management information produced in relation to complaints was not reviewed by Compliance and was not broken down specifically into complaints relating to PPI. In the majority of cases there was no information about the reason for the complaint. A report on the root cause of complaints was available but most complaints relating to advice fell within the wide category of 'point of sale issues' which covered a range of issues including identifying existing benefits, eligibility and affordability. Therefore, senior management were unable to identify any trends or relevant remedial action (eg additional training of sales staff).

5.14 Neither HFC's senior management nor Compliance received or considered claims information in respect of PPI. Consequently, whilst approximately 27% of rejected claims were as a result of pre-existing medical conditions, neither HFC senior management nor Compliance investigated whether the rejections might have been as a result of potential deficiencies in the sales process.

Principle 3

5.15 Principle 3 (Management & Control) provides that:

A firm must take reasonable care to organise and control its affairs responsibly and effectively, with adequate risk management systems.

... 5.18 HFC was under an obligation throughout the Relevant Period to take reasonable care to organise and control its affairs responsibly and effectively and, in particular, to take reasonable care to establish and maintain effective systems and controls for compliance with applicable requirements and standards under the regulatory system.

5.19 The matters set out in paragraphs 5.1 to 5.14 above illustrate a failure by HFC to take reasonable steps through its sales process and its procedures for training, manager oversight, compliance monitoring and management information to ensure the suitability of the advice given by its advisers. Consequently, HFC breached Principle 9 of the FSA's Principles for Business (as detailed above). The design and form of HFC's principal risk management systems in relation to PPI, namely the mandated sales process, compliance monitoring and management information, also show that HFC failed to take reasonable care to organise and control its affairs responsibly and effectively.

5.20 These matters show that, in establishing and maintaining its systems and controls, HFC failed to have proper regard to the nature, scale and complexity of HFC's PPI branch business, its high PPI penetration rate (both targeted and achieved), its customer base, and the nature of the single-premium policy.

5.21 In particular, in determining how frequently branches needed to be visited, the monitoring process was not designed to take account of risk factors in individual branches such as the proportion of customers purchasing PPI, complaints and cancellations when deciding where to target resources. This meant that branches where there were more potentially serious problems were treated in the same way as other branches where there may have been potentially less serious issues, although a risk based approach to a review of files within branches was applied. Similarly, as noted above, HFC's principal management information in relation to PPI comprised a statistical summary of the compliance monitoring visits, with little commentary to accompany the statistics, effectively limiting senior management's oversight of compliance to a review of compliance trends.

5.22 These failings therefore constitute a breach of Principle 3 (in addition to Principle 9).

Record keeping

5.23 HFC's record keeping was also inadequate and in breach of Principle 3. Its failure to generate proper SODANs, which were the only record of advice given to its customers, impacted on HFC's ability to monitor its sales force.

5.24 In addition, out of 139,144 sales of all types of PPI policy between 14 January 2005 and 31 December 2006, HFC estimates on the basis of its own sampling that there were some 10,000 cases where no soft or hard copy SODAN was retained (7% of such sales). This was caused by the loss of data from local servers which were not centrally backed up at the time of the merger of two separate strands of HFC's branch network in 2006. While the information itself was retained, this failing prevents HFC (or the FSA) from being able to review sales transactions quickly and effectively.

5.25 Moreover, during the Relevant Period, when an adviser entered information about a customer during the sales process, if that customer was an existing customer, any information previously contained on the system about them was overwritten.

5.26 As a consequence of the above failings HFC is unable to demonstrate the suitability of its sales of PPI during the Relevant Period.

6. RELEVANT GUIDANCE ON PENALTY

Deterrence

6.2 A financial penalty is required to strengthen the message to the industry that it is vital to take proper steps to ensure in advised sales that the advice a firm gives customers is suitable and that a firm has in place adequate systems and controls in relation to the sale of PPI...

6.4 The FSA has had regard to the seriousness of the breaches, including the nature of the requirements breached, the number and duration of the breaches, the number of customers who were exposed to risk of loss and whether the breaches revealed serious or systemic weaknesses of the management systems or internal controls. For the reasons set out at paragraph 2.7 above and having regard to the impact on HFC's customers, the FSA considers that the breaches are of a particularly serious nature. The seriousness is further increased by the fact that the breaches occurred over a period of 28 months.

The extent to which the breach was deliberate or reckless

6.5 The FSA does not consider that HFC acted in a deliberate or reckless manner.

The size, financial resources and other circumstances of the firm

6.6 HFC has a prominent position in the consumer finance market with a significant degree of public recognition. During the Relevant Period approximately 163,000 PPI policies were sold (including approximately 124,000 single premium policies) on approximately 216,000 loans.

6.7 There is no evidence to suggest that HFC is unable to pay the penalty.

The amount of profits accrued or the loss avoided

6.8 HFC derived considerable revenues through sales of PPI through its branch network, both through profit on the sale of the PPI product and from giving customers a larger loan to pay for the single premium policy. Further, since the policies were underwritten by subsidiary companies of HFC, further group profits were derived from HFC's sales.

Conduct following the breach

6.9 In June 2007 HFC instructed external reporting accountants to conduct a third party review of HFC's PPI sales processes.

6.10 As a result of the review HFC is in the process of making a significant number of changes to its sales processes. It has also agreed to strengthen its compliance monitoring and oversight arrangements. HFC has also committed to a robust remedial action plan, overseen by third party accountants, involving a programme of customer contact and, if appropriate, steps to ensure that its customers are not disadvantaged.

7. CONCLUSION

7.1 Having regard to the seriousness of the breaches and the risk they posed to the FSA's statutory objectives of maintaining confidence in the financial system and securing the appropriate degree of protection for consumers, the FSA has imposed a financial penalty of £1,085,000 on HFC.

FSA, *The Financial Conduct Authority Approach to Regulation* (June 2011)

Payment Protection Insurance

The FSA's actions taken in the PPI market illustrate the type of intervention that the FCA will make. PPI was a major retail market, with sales of over 5 million policies a year during 2000 to 2005, with premiums in the region of £7 billion a year. It was very profitable for firms. Often the underlying loan served as a loss leader on which to sell PPI. It was targeted at consumers taking on debt, many of whom were financially vulnerable, as their focus was typically on securing the loan with the insurance incidental to the transaction.

The FCA can build on and use some of the techniques which the FSA used to correct and prevent future problems. These included mystery shopping and examination of consumer outcomes which highlighted failures in firms' practices that were causing consumer detriment. Firms were asked to stop selling single premium policies, which they agreed to do, and the FSA introduced new rules backed by evidence of market failures and cost benefit analysis. It adopted a proportionate approach to redress for consumers, tailored to the range of PPI products available in the market and the range of identified failures. Tough enforcement action was taken against 24 firms. The FSA cooperated closely with the ombudsman service, the FSCS, the Office of Fair Trading (OFT) and the Competition Commission throughout.

The FSA was ready to defend its judgement in Court and did so. The strategy has led to the likely pay-out of billions of pounds in compensation to consumers who suffered misselling. The decision of the High Court supported the FSA's reliance on Principles, as well as rules and guidance, in setting the standards for firms' treatment of consumers.

5.16 The FSA recognises that, overall, its response to the misselling of PPI should have been stronger. Stronger action sooner could have limited the growth of the problem. The PPI market shows cultural challenges that the FCA will need to address if it is to prevent the crystallisation of large-scale risks and widespread consumer detriment. In particular, the FCA will need to: spot issues earlier; be willing to intervene early to improve standards either in specific firms or wider; take robust action designed to address weaknesses in competition revealed by economic analysis; give greater recognition, sooner, to the importance of securing redress (and not leave this solely to the ombudsman service); and, improve cooperation and working arrangements with the ombudsman service to ensure regulatory issues which complaints are revealing are dealt with sooner.

The provision of single premium PPI at point of sale is now prohibited under the Payment Protection Insurance Market Investigation Order 2011.

The approach to regulation adopted by the FSA raises several issues. First, it may be difficult to change corporate culture. Sharon Gilad's empirical study of 'treating customers fairly' found that many firms could not see the need for change since they viewed themselves as successful firms that treated customers fairly, notwithstanding the prevalence of widespread misselling (Gilad, 2011: 309). Baldwin (2004) has drawn attention to the difficulties in changing internal corporate behaviour. The TCF initiative may create relatively high initial compliance costs for firms. Small firms may have difficulty in achieving the appropriate level of compliance and this might lead to fewer such firms in the market.

The *HFC* case concerned Household Finance, a US finance company that was taken over by HSBC bank in the early 2000s and subsequently sold. In 2003 it paid $484 million to settle consumer claims in the US (Engel and Mcoy, 2011: 62). The business model outlined in the *HFC* case has a relatively long history, raising the question of whether it may be easy to change this model. In 1999 an ex-employee of a major US finance company provided the following evidence to a Senate Committee.

Equity Predators: Stripping, Flipping and Packing their Way to Profits, Hearings before the Special Committee on Aging United States Senate (105th Congress) (2d Session) (16 March 1998) Serial No 105-18 at 30

I have worked for finance companies for more than 7 years, and my testimony is based on my experience as an employee of three of this country's largest finance companies. ...

Finance companies try to do business with blue-collar workers, people who have not gone to college, older people who are on fixed incomes, non English-speaking people, and people who have significant equity in their homes. In fact, my perfect customer would be an uneducated widow who is on a fixed income, hopefully from her deceased husband's pension and Social Security, who has her house paid off, is living off of credit cards, but having a difficult time keeping up with her payments and who must make a car payment in addition to her credit card payments.

The finance companies I have worked for use three primary methods to obtain new customers. First, they often send guaranteed loan vouchers to potential customers. ... Second, finance companies often run different types of pro motions using the mail to seek business from new customers.Third, finance companies obtain many of their customers by participating in retail sales installment loans. The finance companies arrange to do installment financing with local retail dealers. When a retail customer wants to finance the purchase of a stereo, for example, the finance company, rather than the retail dealer, actually makes the loan and gains a new customer. When a finance company obtains a new customer through one of the methods I have just described, it receives information about the customer's credit history, employment, income, home ownership and debts. As soon as the finance company makes that retail loan, for example, a branch employee reviews information about the customer, works up a financial plan and contacts the customer. Although we would tell customers that we were calling to see if they got their merchandise, the real purpose of the call was to solicit the customer into converting the retail installment loan into a more profitable personal loan or home equity loan. Going into the call, since you already have all the information on the customer, you can go ahead and work out a payment plan, payment options, bill consolidation plans, or home equity plans. We call this the 'up-sell', and our goal was always to up-sell to the biggest loan possible.

The conversion of a retail installment loan, live check or other small loan into a personal or home equity loan is also known as a 'flip.' To flip one of these small loans into a personal or home equity loan, we were trained to sell the monthly 'savings'—that is, how much less per month the customer would be paying off if we flipped the loan. In reality, the 'savings' that we were trained to sell to the customers were just an illusion. The uneducated customer would jump for the 'savings,' thinking that he would have more money to buy other things. What the customer would not figure out, and what we would not tell him, is that he would be paying for a longer period of time and, in the end, would pay a whole lot more.

Finance companies require branch employees to make contact every 3 months with customers to prevent payoffs and up-sell to bigger loans. At some of my branches, we tried to call every one of our real estate customers at least once a month. The purpose of these contacts was to slip as many loans as possible. Our tactic was to try to gain the trust and confidence of the customer.

We typically began a telephone solicitation by asking if there were new events in the customer's life that called for additional money. We were trained that we should always ask the customer if he or she needed more money. For our home equity customers, we stressed that the interest on the loan was tax-deductible. Because the terms of those loans did not usually exceed 15 years, we told customers that they could retire earlier, because their house would be paid off sooner. For our debt consolidation customers, we stressed that they could take the money that they were saving in their monthly payments and invest it in a mutual fund. …

When I served as a branch manager, increasing the number of refinance loans was a frequent topic at branch manager, district and statewide meetings. Among the things we were taught at these meetings was to target blue-collar workers for loan flips. We were also told to target present customers who were delinquent on their loan payments. Delinquent customers made good flipping candidates, because we could put additional pressure on them. We were instructed to tell those customers that they could either bring their account balance current or refinance their loan. We knew that these customers would almost always agree to refinance, because they did not have the money to pay on their current loan and did not want the finance company to institute foreclosure or collection proceedings.

In 2011 the FSA outlined in a consultation document its thoughts on a new regulatory approach in the area of consumer finance.

FSA, *Product Intervention*, DP 11/2011

Issues for discussion

1.9 As our Chairman, Adair Turner, noted at the British Bankers' Association Conference in July 2010, our new regulatory approach represents:

'…a major shift in philosophy and I believe a necessary one. But also one which carries risks—the risk that we swing to the other extreme, restricting consumer choice where we do not need to, and imposing regulatory costs which are disproportionate to what we can realistically achieve. We need to strike a balance, and to get that balance right, we need to debate it openly and explicitly: with the industry, with the press, with the politicians, with society.'

1.10 This DP contributes to that debate. The key theme is how improved consumer protection should be balanced with a healthy level of choice and competition in the market. A more intrusive approach may lead to a reduction in the number of products available to consumers. But limiting consumer choice may be acceptable when the resulting benefits to the majority of consumers from not being missold a product outweigh the costs to the minority who might benefit from being able to access it.

1.12 We still want to see innovation, but only where it is in the interests of consumers. It is not our intention to create a 'zero failure' regime where consumer detriment is impossible—this is likely to be unattainable in practice and would require a huge increase in our resources— but we aim to reduce the frequency with which large-scale market problems occur and, if possible, to stop them from happening at all. ...

1.15 The discussion in this paper relates to a broad range of financial products used by retail consumers: deposits, insurance policies, investment products and mortgages.

1.16 We recognise that there are significant differences among the sectors we regulate. This DP covers a broad range of issues, but the approach adopted in practice would vary to take account of market differences. For example, the Mortgage Market Review (MMR) is already considering the appropriate use of specific product interventions relevant to the mortgage market.

1.17 We also recognise that consumers are not a homogenous group and there are varied levels of financial sophistication among them that may warrant different treatment. We draw this out in a number of places in the DP where it is particularly relevant.

... In this chapter we discuss our aim to 'intervene, earlier in the product chain if necessary, to anticipate consumer detriment and choke it off before it occurs'. We are more willing than previously to target products when specific problems emerge, rather than focusing so much on selling practices as we have in the past. We aim to take rapid action to stop problems from growing and affecting large numbers of consumers, and to deter the creation of products likely to lead to consumer detriment.

2.2 We expect benefits to consumers, firms and the regulator:

- consumers should be more certain that they are able to purchase financial products designed in their interests and that will work in the way they expect them to;

- firms should benefit from growing confidence in the market and fewer product failures that result in reputational damage and large amounts of redress; and

- we should be able to meet our objectives of consumer protection and market confidence more efficiently.

Background

2.3 Previously, our regulatory approach focused on transactions at the point-of-sale; that is, the interaction between the consumer and the firm selling them a financial services product. We have, however, seen many episodes of significant consumer detriment in the financial services industry—for example:

- on pensions and investment products—pension mis-selling, large-scale mis-selling of endowments and, more recently, problems with split capital investment trusts and structured products;

- on general insurance—both the FSA and the competition authorities have had to take action over payment protection insurance (PPI) sales; and

- on mortgages—charging practices for customers in arrears have prompted regulatory intervention to protect consumers.

As our Chairman noted:

> 'looking back over the last 20 years, what we see is a series of waves of major customer detriment—products missold, huge and rising numbers of complaints, and then Financial Ombudsman Service (the Ombudsman Service) and FSA intervention to require compensation against specific complaints, and then full reviews; with huge payments made in compensation—around £3bn for mortgage endowments—£11.8bn for pension misselling—£195m for split capital investment trusts.

> And as the waves followed one after another it became increasingly obvious that there are problems in retail financial services which were not going to be solved simply by demanding fair disclosure in the sales processes—that there are deep reasons why retail financial services markets do not work smoothly and can produce adverse effects for consumers.'

...The issue therefore arises whether still more interventionist policies might be justified. This chapter describes what such policies might be, and the circumstances in which they might be appropriate, while also highlighting some of the arguments against their use.

6.4 Starting with the most radical interventions and moving to less intrusive, we explore the following options in this chapter:

- product pre-approval;
- banning products;
- banning or mandating product features (including setting minimum standards for products);
- price interventions;
- increasing the prudential requirements on providers;
- consumer and industry warnings;
- preventing non-advised sales; and
- additional competence requirements for advisers.

6.5 We have not sought to make this a comprehensive list of all the options. We welcome views on what other interventions might be appropriate. ...

6.7 We recognise that regulatory failure is a real risk. In considering the solutions to underlying causes of persistent problems, the regulator must always be aware of the possibility of unintended consequences. In broad terms, regulatory failure refers to situations in which regulation has economic costs higher (or economic benefits lower) than were originally expected, so that the net effect is harmful or less beneficial than it might have been. We need to be mindful of this risk and welcome this debate on the degree to which we ought to pursue the options discussed.

6.8 While we aim to restrict the market for products likely to lead to detriment for customers, we may not always hold the necessary expertise to dictate the best solution to the market. There is a risk that consumer choice for acceptable products may be reduced. However, as part of a new financial services regulatory philosophy that tolerates fewer product failures, this might be inevitable. It is important for the industry and society to offer views and expectations on how the market should be regulated and where the correct balance lies between choice and consumer protection.

The Financial Services Bill 2010–12 confers power on the FCA to ban or require conditions on the supply of a product (section 137A).

---

6. Empowering the demand side of the market? Information remedies

6.1 Required disclosures: truth in lending

Required disclosures by credit providers are a central aspect of the Consumer Credit Act 1974. These disclosures may be required in advertising (section 44), before a contract is executed (section 55), in the contract document (sections 60–61), during performance (section 77A) or on default (section 87). Similar comprehensive regulations were enacted in the United States in the early 1970s and have been adopted in many European and Commonwealth jurisdictions. Most interest has focused on precontractual disclosures, their rationale and impact, and in particular on the requirement that the costs of borrowing be stated as a standardised annual percentage rate (APR).

A primary objective of truth in lending was to provide consumers with the information necessary to make a 'rational' credit purchase. Standardised price disclosures would, it was argued, reduce consumer search costs, facilitate price comparisons and stimulate a more competitive market. The failure of credit grantors to agree on an industry-wide standard, and the lack of incentive for an individual credit grantor to develop a standard were deemed to justify a role for government in standard-setting.

The Crowther Committee noted that existing barriers to consumer search had resulted in significant price dispersions for similar types of credit—a signal of an uncompetitive market (paragraph 3.3.3).

The following extract, from the Crowther Committee report, outlines these rationales.

Report of the Committee on Consumer Credit (Crowther Committee), Cmnd 4596/1971

3.8.3 There are various reasons why in our view the debtor should be told the inclusive cost of borrowing in terms of a rate per cent per annum. The first of these is that it will enable him to 'shop around' and ascertain the cost of borrowing from one type of financing institution as opposed to another and to compare the costs quoted by two or more members of the same type of financing institution. Without a rate per cent disclosure such comparisons are impossible for all but the most sophisticated consumer, since so many variables are involved. ... Secondly, since interest on savings is currently quoted in terms of a rate per cent the consumer will be able to compare the charge he would incur on a prospective credit transaction with the interest he received on his savings, and this may influence his decision whether to obtain credit or to realise his savings and utilise them for the expenditure in question. Equally, a prospective cash purchaser will be better equipped to know whether it is to his advantage, in terms of cost, to pay cash or to borrow on credit and invest his own funds in savings. Thirdly, the disclosure of the cost of borrowing in terms of an effective rate per cent will make credit grantors themselves more conscious of the level of their charges compared with those of other credit grantors and may thus stimulate competition in rate quotation and to some degree influence the level of credit charges customarily imposed in various types of transaction.

3.8.1. [F]aced with the temptation to spend people need to be made fully aware of the limits of their own capacity to make repayments, the cost and availability of borrowing and the rules and regulations surrounding credit trading, so that they do not over-extend their financial resources by ill-informed and rash use of credit facilities

The 2003 White Paper *Fair, Clear and Competitive: the Consumer Credit Market in the 21st Century* echoed these sentiments, arguing that 'consumers are confused by the complexity of modern credit products, and a lack of transparency in the way they are sold' and it proposed a more 'modern, transparent and, as a result competitive credit market' through reforms to consumer credit advertising, the form and content of agreements, online agreements and early settlement of consumer credit transactions (DTI, 2003: 30–31). Similar rationales appear in the rationale for standardised information disclosure in the EU Consumer Credit Directive (2008).

Credit disclosures have therefore a number of functions. Standardised disclosures may perform a market-perfecting function by providing a low-cost, reliable signal for individuals wishing to compare different credit products. If sufficient individuals search by using this signal, then this will induce competition in the market and reduce price dispersions. In addition, it should facilitate new entrants to the credit market. Standardised disclosures may prevent market discrimination by credit providers between marginal (active searchers) and infra-marginal consumers. Disclosures may perform a warning function, alerting a consumer to particularly high costs of credit or the severe consequences, such as loss of a home, for a consumer who defaults on the agreement. They also provide a standardised synopsis of credit terms for future reference by the consumer in the event of a dispute (Landers and Rohner, 1979: 740–44). It is important to keep these different functions in mind in assessing its effectiveness.

6.1.1 Credit advertising

The regulation of credit advertising under the Consumer Credit Act (sections 43–47) is a useful example of the difficulties involved in fashioning an information remedy (Beales, Craswell and Salop, 1981). In addition to a general prohibition on misleading advertising in section 46, there are detailed regulations which set out specified information which must be included in credit advertisements. The objectives of the regulations are to prevent incomplete and potentially misleading advertising while at the same time preserving flexibility for advertisers. Advertisements were originally divided into three categories—simple, intermediate and full—and disclosures required if a specific 'trigger' is advertised. Thus, an advertiser may simply be interested in reminding consumers that he provides credit. An example of such a 'simple' advertisement would be 'X Credit, Finance for car purchase'. However, if she then quotes a price for credit, this will trigger disclosures under the intermediate or full category.

Experience of these regulations suggests some of the potential costs involved in detailed regulation of information. The complexity of the regulations resulted in high enforcement and compliance costs. Moreover, since only certain advertising claims were subject to disclosure requirements, there may be incentives for businesses to avoid the 'trigger', with a consequent shift to unregulated claims. This may result in a reduction in the amount of consumer information available. The case of *Jenkins v Lombard North Central plc* (1984) provides an example of this unintended effect of regulations intended to increase the amount of consumer information available. In this case, the finance company, in order to avoid the costs and potential difficulties in complying with the Act, decided to concentrate on 'corporate advertising', ie on merely reminding the public of its existence. The court held that this type of advertising escapes the net of the Act. A similar shift from regulated to unregulated claims has been documented in the United States (Thain, 1976: 257).

The current 2010 advertising regulations (Consumer Credit (Advertisements) Regulations 2010) apply triggered disclosures (see regulation 4) and require a representative example to be provided including the APR. The 'representative APR' must be one which the lender reasonably expects to offer in 51 per cent of agreements entered into as a result of the advertisement. Advertisements to persons 'who might otherwise consider their access to credit restricted' must always provide a representative APR and this shall be given greater prominence than any other statement concerning credit (regulation 6). Regulation 10 regulates the use of certain expressions such as 'interest free', and 'pre-approved' credit.

6.1.2 Pre-contractual information

Contemporary disclosures are now contained in the 2010 Consumer Credit (Disclosure of Information) regulations that apply to those credit agreements under £60,260 (the monetary limit in the EU Directive). The disclosures must be made 'in good time' before the agreement is made. There is a standardised European Consumer Credit Information sheet which must be provided to consumers. The required information is set out in regulation 3(4) and includes a 'warning regarding the consequences of missing payments' and the existence of a right of withdrawal (now 14 days for all consumer credit contracts).

6.1.3 The impact of credit-cost disclosure

Most interest in the impact of information remedies has focused on the impact of the standardised credit-cost disclosures (APR). Like any form of standard, the APR has both costs and benefits. The main potential benefits are outlined in the extracts above from the Crowther Committee's report. A primary economic attraction is that it attempts to harness market incentives to police the price of credit, obviating the need to rely on government regulation of interest rates. In addition to the costs of devising and enforcing the standard, there is the cost that lies in the danger that focus on the APR may provide a misleading 'signal' concerning the add-on cost of credit, particularly on small amounts, eg payday loans. In these cases, small differences in repayment periods and weekly charges will be translated into large differences in APR. Sellers might also attempt to exploit the APR 'signal' by burying the credit charge in an inflated cash price, although this is unlikely to occur in a competitive market. Section 45 of the Consumer Credit Act partly addressed this problem by prohibiting advertising of goods or services for sale on credit if at the time they are not also available for cash purchase.

One issue concerns what is included in the calculation of the 'total charge for credit' that must be disclosed as a monetary amount and calculated as the APR. Firms could undercut the impact of the APR by charging 'administration fees' and presenting a consumer with a lower APR than their competitors. See now the Consumer Credit (Total Charge for Credit) Regulations 2010. What appears to be the rationale for the inclusion and exclusion of a particular charge from the total charge for credit?

There are some complexities involved in calculating the APR. Most credit is now 'running-account credit' (CCA, section 10) such as credit card debt where it is not clear at the outset how much will be borrowed by the consumer nor at what rate the consumer will pay off the credit each month. How do the Consumer Credit Act regulations address this issue? (See the Consumer Credit (Advertisements) Regulations, 2010 Regulation 1(2) Schedule.)

Opinions differ on the effects of truth in lending on the consumer credit market. The National Consumer Council conducted a survey of consumers' attitudes and behaviour in relation to consumer credit before the introduction in 1980 of the truth-in-lending regulations under the Consumer Credit Act. It found that, although most people had some idea of whether one type of credit was 'expensive' compared to other types of credit, over two-thirds were vague concerning the actual interest rate which they would pay (see National Consumer Council, 1980: 70–71).

Research conducted in 1994 concluded that 64 per cent of consumers surveyed would 'generally draw the right conclusions from using the APRs, even though they might not fully appreciate precisely what the APR represented' (OFT, 1994: 70) and in 2003 43 per cent of consumers in a survey chose correctly the best value credit card based on the APR (OFT, 2004b: 28). However, a majority did not choose correctly and a study by the National Consumer Council indicates that although the APR is used as a signal of the cost of credit, other important factors in consumer credit decision-making are the monthly cost and the length of repayment period rather than the APR (National Consumer Council, 2002). A study conducted by the DTI in 2003 drew the following conclusions:

> When considering which loan or credit card to apply for the foremost factor in people's minds is the reputation of the lender. Next comes perhaps surprisingly given the relatively little awareness of this term the APR [83%] then any additional charges, simplicity and ease of the process. ... Three quarters of those polled say that the language used in advertisements for consumer credit is confusing and 84% claimed that the language used in the paperwork is confusing. (DTI, 2003: 2)

In another study (DTI, 2004: 5, 7, 19), the DTI found that the first things that consumers check on a credit card agreement are the credit limit and the APR. The majority of consumers indicated that they rarely studied the detail of the terms and conditions. A qualitative study in 2005 after the introduction of new disclosure regulations concluded that

> respondents did not understand the exact definition of APR. However, they ... felt that they could compare between lenders without knowing how the exact figure was calculated ... consumers did not understand the exact definition of 'typical APR' ... only a very few

consumers read credit agreements. ... They do however, check key details such as the monthly payment amount and the number of payments. (Michaelis, Mackey and Smith, 2006: 2).

The increased focus on APR may have increased incentives among lenders to include costs that may not be included in the APR (eg insurance), to 'backload' costs through high default or late-payment fees or to make it more difficult to compare fees through variable credit costs and the use of 'teaser rates'.

Ben-Shahar and Schneider present a sceptical approach to mandated disclosure.

O Ben-Shahar and C Schneider, 'The Failure of Mandated Disclosure' (2011) 159 *U Penn L Rev* 647 at 654, 655, 666–67, 681–82, 684, 730, 738, 739, 740.

TILA was a prototype consumer-protection statute and became the template for most consumer-credit legislation, legislation which now mandates detailed disclosures for credit generally, credit cards, automobile loans, student loans, mortgages, and other home-secured loans. ... Attempts to protect poor borrowers often recruit disclosure requirements.

Disclosure requirements dominate regulation of another kind of credit—mortgages, including high-risk mortgages. ... Lenders must even say that defaulting can lead to foreclosure and that it is prudent to shop for low rates.

Truth-in-lending legislation is a crown jewel of the Disclosure Empire, and if mandated disclosure works anywhere, it should work here. Unlike some disclosure regimes, TILA (Truth in Lending Act) was actually given thought. Congress spent eight years debating it. The bill's proponents largely got the law they wanted. They expected disclosure of APRs to produce sensible shopping for credit. Administrative agencies have repeatedly labored and issued regulations intended to make TILA work.

Consumers are more aware of APRs, but they remain confused about using them.

> One leading study, for example, showed that as knowledge of the APR increased, knowledge of the finance charge itself (expressed in dollars) declined. Apparently, most consumers (mistakenly) believe that the disclosed rate is a percentage of the initial balance, rather than [the] average or declining balance. As a result they miscalculate the finance charges to be twice the actual amount. In other words, [truth-in-lending] legislation succeeded in making consumers increasingly aware but it has not managed to explain to them what it is they have been made aware of.

... Worse, only well-educated and well-off consumers seem to have enjoyed whatever increased awareness of credit terms TILA brought.

More fundamentally, there is little reason to think disclosure statutes improved the terms borrowers pay. For example, one study suggests that the Credit and Charge Card Disclosure Act of 1988 did not increase competition in the credit card industry. Interest rates and funding costs did not exhibit any measurable improvement following the act.

Mandated disclosure is a Lorelei, luring law-makers onto the rocks of regulatory failure. It is alluring because it resonates with two fundamental American ideologies. The first is free-market principles. While mandated disclosure constrains unfettered rapacity and counteracts caveat emptor, the intervention is soft and leaves everything substantive alone: prices, quality, entry. Instead of specifying the outcomes of transactions or dictating choices, it proffers information for making better decisions. Second, mandated disclosure serves the autonomy principle. It implements the belief that people make better decisions for themselves than anyone can make for them and that people are presumptively entitled to freedom in making decisions. The more-information-is-better mantra seems to serve both the free-market and autonomy principles.

Mandated disclosure appeals to law-makers for other reasons. First, it looks cheap. It requires almost no government expenditures, and its costs seem to be imposed on the villain of the story, the stronger party who withholds information.

Second, mandated disclosure looks easy. It only requires more communication between parties who are already communicating. In hindsight, one can usually identify the information that could have led the disclosee to a better conclusion.

Third, mandated disclosure looks effective. Mandated information often seems relevant to a difficult decision. If asked, consumers often say they want the information.

Mandated disclosure's appeal to law-makers and the allure of the more-is-better mantra lead law-makers to mandate disclosure too often and too broadly. ...

An influential law-and-economics argument maintains that a few sophisticated readers of disclosures can discipline disclosers and force them to offer better term, eschew hidden traps, and behave efficiently. Mandated disclosure can be regarded as a way to inform these sophisticated readers, whose presence would benefit all disclosees. We doubt, however, that sophisticated disclosees are 'reading agents' for other disclosees.

First, this theory conflicts with the premise of mandatory disclosure. The sophisticated readers are supposed to induce businesses voluntarily to disclose information and avoid self-serving behavior. That is, recognizing the presence of sophisticated consumers and seeking to please them, businesses voluntarily disclose information and make it useful. Failure to do so would either drive the sophisticates away or reduce their willingness to pay. Mandated disclosure, by contrast, assumes that without a mandate, there will be no disclosure. It thus assumes that there are not enough sophisticated consumers who know to demand and are able to scrutinize the information. And this assumption is ordinarily correct. The factors that discourage disclosees from scrutinizing disclosures apply to even sophisticated disclosees. If nobody reads disclosures, it matters not that some non-readers are sophisticated.

Even if there were enough readers, they cannot be good agents for other consumers unless they are reasonably typical. But the eccentric with the time, knowledge, skill, and determination—not to mention paranoia—to plow through these disclosures is atypical. ... Furthermore, businesses can try to identify and segregate these readers, so that the benefits they know to insist on will not leak to the non-reading majority. Sophisticated readers may selectively enjoy the 'good' terms in the contract because they are buried in the fine print. And even if agency readers were subject to the same oppressive terms as everybody else, they might negotiate ad hoc accommodations. Therefore, the agency account works only for a market in which disclosers cannot distinguish readers from nonreaders and must give all consumers the better deal readers insist on. ...

[M]andated disclosure can undermine other consumer-protections. For example, the doctrine of unconscionability and many anti-fraud principles allow courts to strike oppressive terms from contracts. Usually courts direct their scrutiny against substantively intolerable terms but only if there was some procedural unfairness in making the contract. Often the latter requirement is met by a finding that an oppressive term was 'hidden,' or that it surprised the consumer. If, however, the discloser performs as mandated—if the discloser can point to a form that was handed to the consumer in a way that complied with regulatory requirements and which the consumer received and signed—the 'hidden' element is not satisfied. ... Thus, an empty but formally correct disclosure can keep the contract from being unconscionable, however problematic its terms.

[M]andated disclosure can lead to inequity. Mandated disclosure helps most those who need help least and helps least those who need help most. Information is most useful to well-educated and well-off people who have the resources and sophistication to locate, interpret, and use the revealed information.

Policymakers have attempted to address criticisms of extended information disclosures. The FSA developed the summary 'Key Facts' document for mortgages and found that consumers viewed its 'Key Facts Documentation' as 'a useful information source, a legal record for the mortgage firm and . . . a means of comparing mortgage products' (FSA, 2006: 7). The FSA also found significant differences in comprehension of key facts between consumers with different levels of financial literacy.

Finally, some writers, drawing on the apparently modest impact of disclosures, have questioned the APR's rationale. They argue that the decision to place emphasis on the APR reflected a normative judgement of government that consumers ought to purchase credit by using the APR (Whitford, 1973: 423–25).

A further objective of information policies has been to reduce the number of defaulting debtors. This policy is reflected in 'wealth warnings' such as the following:

'YOUR HOME MAY BE REPOSSESSED IF YOU DO NOT KEEP UP REPAYMENTS ON A MORTGAGE OR ANY OTHER DEBT SECURED ON IT'

or in relation to consolidation loans:

'THINK CAREFULLY BEFORE SECURING OTHER DEBTS AGAINST YOUR HOME.'

The former disclosure was introduced in response to concerns about borrowers losing their homes after using them as security for a loan (NCC, 1987). But how effective are such disclosures at the time of entering into the contract in preventing default given the implications of the literature on overoptimism and underestimation of certain risks? Undoubtedly they exploit consumers' loss aversion and might therefore have some effect. But one must have some scepticism about their influence on consumer behaviour.

6.2 Post-contractual information

The criticism that disclosure results in information overload may not be applicable to information that is relevant to post-contractual events. Individuals may have a strong interest in obtaining information at this time and may turn to the contract as a source of information. Whitford has argued that post-contractual disclosures may have greater impact than pre-contractual ones. Post-contractual disclosures may be directed towards situations in which consumers are likely to have a strong interest in obtaining information (eg default), and are less distracted by other point-of-sale distractions. Such disclosures may contain substantial detail (Whitford, 1973: 466–67). An interesting example of a post-contractual disclosure is the notice of default required under the Consumer Credit Act 1974, which must contain the following conspicuous statement:

IF YOU ARE NOT SURE WHAT TO DO YOU SHOULD GET HELP AS SOON AS POSSIBLE. FOR EXAMPLE YOU SHOULD CONTACT A SOLICITOR, YOUR LOCAL TRADING STANDARDS DEPARTMENT OR YOUR NEAREST CITIZENS' ADVICE BUREAU.

These disclosures may facilitate communication and an agreed rescheduling of a debt, thus avoiding the further costs of default (see Whitford, 1973: 466–68).

The 2006 amendments to the Consumer Credit Act 1974 extend post-contractual disclosures to require annual statements in relation to fixed sum agreements (see section 77A) to include the following statement:

> If you have a problem with your agreement, please try to settle it with your lender in the first instance. If you are not happy with the way in which your complaint was handled or the result, you may be eligible to make a complaint to the Financial Ombudsman Service. You can contact the Financial Ombudsman Service on [0845 080 1800] or at www.financialombudsman.org.uk

Under further amendments (section 78(4)(A)) introduced in 2006), regulations require information to be provided to consumers in running account credit (eg credit cards) of the consequences of failing to make a minimum payment or only making a minimum payment (see case study Credit Cards). There are also the requirements of information sheets if a consumer is in arrears.

Consumer Credit (Information Requirements and Duration of Licences and Charges) Regulations 2007

> The following form of wording shall be contained in a statement under this Part—
>
> 'Minimum payments
>
> 'If you make only the minimum payment each month, it will take you longer and cost you more to clear your balance.'

Where an agreement makes provision for the charging of post-judgment interest in connection with a judgment sum, a statement in the following form must be included:

> You should be aware that if we take you to court and get a judgment against you requiring you to pay us the money you owe us under the agreement, you may have to pay us both the amount of the judgment and interest under the agreement on all the sums owed by you at the date of the judgment until you have paid these in full. This means that even if you pay off the whole amount of the judgment, you may still have a further sum to pay.

and

> This notice should include a copy of the current Office of Fair Trading information sheet on default. This contains important information about your rights and where to go for support and advice. If it is not included, you should contact us to get one.

Behavioural analysis has drawn attention to the difficulties of devising effective disclosures. For example, the reference to a minimum payment on a credit card bill may have an anchoring effect and cause individuals to make lower payments (Stewart, 2009).

The FSA claims to follow a 'principled' basis to regulation that focuses on outcomes rather than using detailed prescriptions. However, its regulation of mortgage disclosure reveals that it also uses detailed rules. In reviewing its financial promotions regulation it did find that generally senior management did not have direct involvement in 'the systems and controls relating to the creation of financial promotions' (FSA, 2006: 4).

6.3 Formalities and the sanction of nullity: attacking agreements through heightened formalism

The requirements for a formal written document and required information in consumer credit contracts perform cautionary and evidential functions. Formalities protect against fraud in consumer transactions and reduce the potential for subsequent disputes. In order to provide an adequate incentive for firms to comply, legislation may impose a sanction of non-enforcement of the credit obligation if the formalities are not complied with. This 'self-enforcement' approach is based partly on the limits of private enforcement in markets with a high potential for consumer detriment.

Section 61 of the Consumer Credit Act 1974 requires that contract terms be legible, in the prescribed form as required by the regulations made under the section, and signed by the debtor. If the requirements of section 61 are not met the contract is 'improperly executed'.

Prior to the 2006 amendments to the Act improperly executed agreements fell into two categories: those that were completely unenforceable (section 127(3); section 65) and those which might be enforceable with leave of the court. In the latter case the court may take into account the degree of culpability of the lender and the prejudice caused to the debtor in determining whether to enforce an agreement (section 127). A consumer credit agreement which did not disclose the amount of credit correctly or the credit limit or how debtors might discharge their obligations was completely unenforceable. In *Wilson v First County Trust Ltd* (2003), the House of Lords upheld the enforceability of this sanction of nullity notwithstanding the argument that this section contravened the Human Rights Act 1998 and Part I of Article 6 and Part II of Article 1 of the European Convention on Human Rights. The Consumer Credit Act 2006 altered section 127 so that all improperly executed agreements may be enforced with leave of the court. The reasoning of Lord Nicholls in Wilson is useful in outlining clearly the rationale for a 'bright-line' sanction of nullity even though it might seem to be unfair on the lender in the particular circumstance of the individual case.

Wilson and others v Secretary of State for Trade and Industry (Appellant) [2003] UKHL 40

Lord Nicholls of Birkenhead

[73] The unattractive feature of this approach is that it will sometimes involve punishing the blameless pour encourager les autres. On its face, considered in the context of one particular case, a sanction having this effect is difficult to justify.

[74] Despite this criticism I have no difficulty in accepting that in suitable instances it is open to Parliament, when Parliament considers the public interest so requires, to decide that compliance with certain formalities is an essential prerequisite to enforcement of certain types of agreements. This course is open to Parliament even though this will sometimes yield a seemingly unreasonable result in a particular case. Considered overall, this course may well be a proportionate response in practice to a perceived social problem. Parliament may consider the response should be a uniform solution across the board. A tailor-made response, fitting the facts of each case as decided in an application to the court, may not be appropriate.

This may be considered an insufficient incentive and insufficient deterrent. And it may fail to protect consumers adequately. Persons most in need of protection are perhaps the least likely to participate in court proceedings. They may well let proceedings go by default (see, in relation to moneylending agreements, the Crowther Report, p 236 (para 6.1.19)).

The abolition of the automatic sanction of nullity in the 2006 amendments may have been partly because of the abolition of the £25,000 credit limit and the lobbying of credit providers. Attacking agreements based on the failure to meet formalities has been a central strategy of litigants in the UK in recent years (see eg *Carey v HSBC* [2009] EWHC 3417 on sections 77 and 78 CCA, and cases on the determination of the 'total charge for credit'). Howells (2010) discusses these cases. This use of formalism as a strategy is not, however, restricted to the UK. It was a common tactic in the United States, Canada and Australia, and was adopted by some judges in France (see *Époux X v Credit Foncier de France*, Cass civ 1e, 29 October 2002 Bull civ no 1513; *Cofinoga Merignac SA v Sylvain Sachitanathan*, ECJ Case C-264/02 [2004] ECR I-02157]). It was a tactic adopted under the Moneylenders Acts 1927, much criticised by the Crowther Committee which noted the excessive technicality of the Acts and the fact that 'the lender who makes even a technical slip in a moneylending transaction within the Moneylenders Acts is disabled from recovering any part of the loan' (paragraph 4.2.13). Thus in *Eldridge v Taylor* [1931] KB 416 (CA) Greer J commented that 'Acts of Parliament which are intended to protect borrowers against fraudulent or harsh and unconscionable money-lending contracts sometimes result in protecting fraudulent and dishonest borrowers. But if the statute has that effect we must follow its words without regard to its consequences. This is one of these exceptional cases.'

The use of heightened formalism often results in a backlash because it seems that businesses are unable to enforce agreements because of the failure of a 'technical' formality and the sanction is disproportionate to the breach. Analogies might be drawn with the fate of the original Statute of Frauds, which became a trap for the unwary.

6.4 Early settlement and promoting competition

The ability to settle a credit agreement early without penalty is a valuable consumer right. It may reinforce competition in the credit market, because the ability of the consumer to switch to a lender offering better terms may have a competitive effect. Combined with truth in lending which reduces search costs through the standardised APR, this may reduce switching costs.

The DTI indicates that 70 per cent of unsecured loans were settled early in 2002. The 2010 amendments implementing the Consumer Credit Directive permit part repayment as well as full settlement of consumer credit obligations. Section 95A sets out the circumstances and formula by which a creditor may recover compensation for early settlement

6.5 Reducing creditor costs: credit information, credit scoring and credit bureaux

Lenders face information costs in making credit offers since they must assess the likelihood of an individual repaying the debt. Reliable information on a debtor's creditworthiness may be valuable in the initial lending decision and in reducing subsequent enforcement costs.

During the past 25 years there has been a large growth of interest by economists in the problems of asymmetric information in credit markets. Stiglitz and Weiss (1981: 71) argue that in any lending pool there will be both good and bad risks and it may be difficult for a lender *ex ante* to distinguish whether borrowers will repay or how much effort they will make to repay in the event of changed circumstances and low-risk borrowers may not be able to distinguish themselves *ex ante* from high-risk borrowers. A fixed interest rate will therefore be a bargain for some borrowers but not for others. If a lender increases interest rates to compensate for increased risk, then it will attract more higher-risk borrowers. It may be more profitable, therefore, to lend at a lower rate with the result that certain borrowers will not receive a loan. The consequence is therefore that credit is rationed rather than the price continuing to increase to reflect the increased risk.

Borrowers might signal to creditors their willingness to pay by providing security over their goods. This is limited in relation to personal property in the UK by the Bills of Sale Acts. However, a major antidote to adverse selection in consumer credit markets has been the development of credit scoring and credit bureaux. Developments in computer technology have substantially reduced creditors' costs of storing and using credit information on an individual's creditworthiness. Standardised 'credit-scoring' systems for assessing creditworthiness have been developed by many major creditors, and credit bureaux specialise in the collection and dissemination of credit information. These techniques reduce the costs of assessing and monitoring credit risk and have facilitated the management of large numbers of small credit accounts—such as credit cards. Credit scoring has also facilitated 'risk-based pricing' in the credit card market where credit card companies differentiate more finely between customers in relation to the level of interest payable on outstanding balances. The Competition Commission in its Report on Home Credit outlined the benefits of credit scoring:

Competition Commission, *Home Credit Inquiry* **(2006)**

APPENDIX 2.1

Credit scoring, data sharing and home credit

(a) Increases the mobility of customers. A portable credit record allows customers to move more easily—there is less risk associated with the severing of old relationships and starting new ones as accurate/transparent information is avail-able which helps the new provider establish and build trust more quickly.

(b) Reduces the cost of borrowing to lenders

(i)   Reduces bad debts. Past payment performance is a good predictor of likely future non-payment and hence a system that uses a credit record can reduce the amount of bad debt and cost of missed payments. ...

(ii) Significant cost and time savings. A recent presentation from the World Bank suggests that there may be significant cost and time savings from having a reliable credit scoring system based on shared data. ... Evidence from mainstream lenders has also suggested that individual/ manual assessment, the alternative to an automated credit scoring system, is seen as too costly an option.

(c) Provides an unbiased analytical assessment. Experian stated that individual scorecards provided an unbiased analytical assessment that was not reliant on an individual's judgement and allowed the provider to have consistent decision rules.

(d) Increases the likelihood of customers repaying. Customers will be more likely to repay if credit-scoring systems are in place—to boost their own ratings and give themselves access to cheaper credit. In general, the more providers a credit record is shared with the greater the inducement to repay as the more severe is the penalty for non-payment.

(e) Reduces the level of overindebtedness. According to the Financial Times, the Bank of England has called for high street banks to increase the amount of positive and negative data they share with CRAs. In addition, Which? states that it believes that poor credit data sharing is one of the chief culprits behind the UK's credit card serial borrowing crisis. ...

(f) Makes pricing mirror cost. As other creditors can more accurately assess the risk of default they are able to price credit products in line with customers' risk profile and hence the price paid by 'good' customers is likely to fall. ...

(g) Reduces the market power of incumbents. It has been suggested that creditors can use their information advantage over their existing borrowers to increase their rents. In addition, a credit provider taking on a new customer or a group of customers with no information about the likelihood of default will be at a disadvantage compared with an incumbent provider that has information about the likelihood of default. The Treasury Select Committee also noted that with the increased prevalence of risk-based pricing, non-sharing of positive information may preclude consumers from being eligible for lower rates elsewhere as competition for these customers is prevented.

(h) Increases credit penetration among 'higher risk' groups. Evidence from the USA suggests that credit scoring has enabled a significant penetration of lending into lower socioeconomic groups.

Credit bureaux now exist in many countries throughout the world. A basic distinction exists between registries that contain only negative information, such as judgments against a consumer, and those that contain positive information, such as the amount of current balances and payment patterns of consumers. Private credit reporting agencies in the US and the UK contain positive and negative information on consumers, whereas in France and Australia, in response to concerns about privacy, only negative information is maintained on files (see further Miller, 2003; Jappelli and Pagano, 2006; Ferretti, 2010). In the UK, credit bureaux reports include electoral roll information, public record information such as bankruptcies and county court judgments (held on file for six years) as well as credit and mortgage account information and the number of searches of the report by other credit grantors. The UK finance industry has developed 'principles of reciprocity' which state that data are shared 'only for the prevention of over-commitment, bad debt, fraud and money laundering' and 'subscribers must never use shared data to target any customers of other specific subscribers'.

The effects of credit reporting are slightly more complex than outlined in the Competition Commission report. A negative reporting system may be predicted to produce greater incentives to repay than a system that includes positive information. In the latter system a borrower who knows that a financial institution will also release positive information may have a higher incentive to default since she knows that one default may be discounted by lenders who have access to other positive information on the credit file (see Padilla and Pagano, 2000) Extensive information sharing may facilitate a deeper consumer credit market but not necessarily result in lower levels of indebtedness or even default. The development of 'sub-prime' or 'non-status' credit markets in North America, where there are higher risks of default, were facilitated partly by sophisticated positive credit-scoring systems. Increased credit information might facilitate a 'sweatbox model' of lending (Mann, 2008) whereby lenders maximise profits from sub-prime borrowers. A negative information system might dampen the development of this form of market as well as preventing individuals with a history of negative information from 'graduating' into the mainstream consumer market. These comments suggest some ambiguity about the overall effects of more creditor information: greater competition that could create incentives to 'over-sell', more access to credit but greater indebtedness among a more risky borrower pool.

Information sharing in credit markets raises issues of privacy rights and concerns about invasion of privacy (see Information Commissioner, 2006). The Data Protection Act 1998, which gives effect to the European Data Protection Directive 1995, requires that credit-grantors and credit-reference agencies follow the principles for data collection outlined in Schedule 1 to the Act. These require in turn that one of the principles in Schedule 2 should be applicable. One of these is that an individual has consented to the disclosure of the processing of personal data. In addition to data protection law the law of banking confidentiality (see *Tournier v National and Provincial Bank of England* (1924)) permits disclosure by a bank of a customer's personal information to a third party in only a limited number of situations, including where the consumer has agreed to the information being disclosed. The effects of these laws are that in many cases data on accounts opened before the enactment of the Data Protection Act 1998 when financial institutions introduced 'fair processing notices' may not be shared. The DTI estimates that data on approximately 40 million non-consensual accounts is not shared (DTI, 2006: 10).

It is possible that disclosure to credit-reference agencies could be justified under Schedule 2 of the Data Protection Act 1998 which permits processing for the legitimate interests of the processor and third parties to whom the information is disclosed. Surveys indicate that consumers demonstrate a high level of concern about the privacy of their financial information (DTI, 2006: 15–16) but it is difficult to know to what extent some of the fear reflects Ison's argument concerning fear of the unknown. Legislation to permit the sharing of non-consensual data might be challenged under Article 8 of the European Convention on Human Rights (right to privacy).

The rights of a consumer to obtain access to any records that a credit reference agency holds on her are governed by the Data Protection Act 1998. Sections 7–9 of the Act, and the accompanying regulations (see Data Protection (Subject Access) (Fees and

Miscellaneous Provisions) Regulations 2000) permit consumers to access information held on them (for a fee of £2) by a credit reference agency, and the agency must inform the consumer of her right under section 159 of the Consumer Credit Act to have a corrective statement added to the file (section 159(3)) and, if an entry is deleted or modified, to notify each person to whom it furnished financial information relating to the consumer within the past six months. Section 10 of the Data Protection Act 1998 also permits an individual to serve a notice requiring the credit reference agency not to process any data on the grounds that this would cause the consumer unwarranted damage or distress. Section 13 of the Act permits an individual to seek damages that may include damages for distress suffered because of a contravention of the Act by an agency (see also Chapter 3 on identity theft).

The use of credit scoring permits greater segmentation and discrimination between consumers. One author argues that systems such as credit scoring represent 'a pan-optic sort'—a form of disciplinary surveillance similar to Bentham's vision of the panopticon prison where individuals would always be in view of the authorities and would organise their behaviour in the knowledge that they are being watched (Gandy, 1993: 2). Thus credit ratings would become a new form of morality within this system where individuals adjust their behaviour in the light of the norms of proper credit use. This might be analogous to the new forms of governance in neo-liberalism discussed in Chapter 3. Credit reference agencies are therefore important institutions of regulation and governance, admitting some and excluding others. Given the importance of these 'private' systems in sorting consumers into increasingly segmented markets, it is essential that such systems be accountable.

Many jurisdictions have regulations to prevent unjustified discrimination in credit granting. In the UK these include the Sex Discrimination Act 1975, section 29, the Race Relations Act 1976, section 20, and the Disability Discrimination Act 1995. In addition, section 25(2)(c) of the Consumer Credit Act 1974 directs the OFT to have regard to whether an applicant has practised discrimination on grounds of sex, colour, race or ethnic or national origins in deciding whether to grant a credit licence. Discrimination in credit granting may be direct or indirect. Direct discrimination describes the situation where an individual is treated differently based on a prohibited ground (sex, race, disability) from a similarly situated individual. Indirect discrimination occurs where a similar standard is applied to all groups applying for credit but the application of the standard places individuals from a particular race, ethnic or national origin at a particular disadvantage and it cannot be shown that the provision, criterion or practice is a proportionate means of achieving a legitimate aim (see the Race Relations Act 1976, section 1 as amended by the Race Relations Act 1976 (Amendment) Regulations 2003, section 3).

Indirect discrimination could be a basis for challenging a credit-scoring system that placed particular racial groups at a disadvantage. In the United States the use of stability of home ownership has been argued to be a discriminatory characteristic on the basis that minorities may have to move more often than other groups in order to seek employment and progress in their careers (see Taibi, 1994). Credit scores are increasingly used as a screening device for insurance sales and renting property. In Canada the use of credit ratings as a screening device for renting property has been attacked as discriminating against new immigrants (see *Ontario (Human Rights Commission) v Shelter Corporation* (2001)).

---

7. Responsibilising the consumer: financial literacy

Many regulatory initiatives such as truth in lending depend on active, responsible borrowers. In recent years regulators have taken much greater interest in attempting to ensure that consumers are financially literate. In 2006 the FSA published the results of a major survey to assess the ability of the UK population to manage their money.

FSA, *Financial Capability in the UK: Establishing a Baseline* (2006), 3

Four main themes stand out:

Large numbers of people from all sections of society, are not taking basic steps to plan ahead, such as saving sufficiently for their retirement or putting money aside for a rainy day.

The problem of overindebtedness is not but its effects of large proportion of the population, but that when it strikes it is often severe, and that many more people may find themselves in trouble in an economic downturn.

Many people are taking on financial risks without realizing it, because they struggle to choose products that truly meet their needs.

The under 40s, on whom some of the greatest demands are now placed, are typically much less financially capable than their elders, even allowing for their generally lower levels of income and experience in dealing with financial institutions.

Richard Hecklinger, Deputy Secretary General OECD, *New Statesman*, Special Supplement on Financial Literacy, 9 January 2006

There are three main reasons why financial education has become so important. One is that an increasing number of workers will have to rely on the defined contribution pension plans and their personal savings to finance their retirement. This is because governments are beginning to scale back the benefits of state-supported social security programs, and the number of employers offering defined benefit plans is decreasing. The second is that consumer debt is at a record level, and the deregulation off financial markets has led to increased competition for new credit card holders. As a result, many young people have been burdened with high debts at a time when they are trying to start a family and buy a home. And the third is that with the growth in the number of financial transactions taking place in electronically, it is increasingly important that individuals have, at least, a bank account. Yet, in a number of countries, a significant percentage of consumers do not participate in the financial system. This percentage is even higher for minority consumers.

Williams (2007) surveys the rise of financial literacy as a significant aspect of government policy with many agencies (eg FSA until 2010) being given mandates to promote financial literacy. Williams notes that although it is justified by consumer empowerment, a more critical explanation is that it shifts responsibility from the state to the 'responsibilised' consumer—a form of regulation by which the state holds individuals accountable for aspects of market governance ... that it used to provide'. William also notes the practical difficulties facing financial literacy initiatives given the findings of behavioural economics.

The UK established in 2010 the Consumer Financial Education Body (CFEB) under section 2 of the Financial Services Act 2010 with a general remit to enhance the understanding and knowledge of members of the public of financial matters and the ability to manage their own financial affairs. This remit has been carried forward in the 2012 legislation (the CFEB is now the Money Advice Service) with the additional duty to assist members of the public with the management of debt.

There remains controversy over the effects of financial literacy initiatives.

I Ramsay and T Williams, 'The Crash that Launched a Thousand Fixes: Regulation of Consumer Credit after the Lending Revolution and the Credit Crunch' in K Alexander and N Moloney (eds), *Law Reform and Financial Markets* (2011) 221

In 2003, the OECD launched an international 'Financial Education Project', sponsored by Prudential plc's corporate responsibility program. This project is based on a belief that 'financially illiterate' consumers cannot cope with the proliferation of consumer financial products that has resulted from neo-liberalism's expansion of financial markets; and by concerns about the long-term implications for public policy of consumers making unwise financial choices. Identifying financial education as an important aspect of the solution to the problem of consumers spending too much and saving too little, the OECD project encourages countries to develop effective regulatory policies to enhance financial literacy within their populations. The OECD project's early policy documents, published before the recent crisis erupted, make bold claims to the effect that financially literate consumers will improve economic growth, help to reduce poverty and potentially moderate the volatility of financial markets in emerging economies. These publications characterise financial illiteracy as an urgent and pervasive problem for financial markets, and represent literate financial consumers as 'regulatory subjects' whose decisions will increase price competition among suppliers, stimulate innovation and may ultimately reduce the need for regulatory action in consumer financial markets. The OECD has continued to promote the improvement of consumer financial literacy as an important policy initiative after the crash, and other international organisations and development institutions—including the World Bank and the UK's Department for International Development—have become advocates of financial literacy programmes.

Since 2003, several countries have launched high profile national programmes to promote financial literacy (sometimes termed financial capability), and the OECD's International Gateway for Financial Education reports that more countries are developing such programmes every year. ... Although the particular mandates and specific goals of these initiatives vary, it is common for their work to be characterised as 'empowering consumers' at a minimum through the provision of information, the development of financial skills and the activation of a consumers' sense of financial responsibility. These policy initiatives link the enhancement of consumers' financial capabilities to their responsibilization, through the idea that financial literacy improves the capacity of consumers to protect themselves against risks of 'mis-buying' and mis-selling of financial products. A second important linkage is the idea that financial literacy generates demand for financial products as consumers become more active and more self-reliant—that is, more self-regulating—about how they manage income smoothing and their future economic security. As consumers become more capable and therefore responsible they in turn are supposed to reduce the need for regulatory intervention.

... [I]t is difficult to find balanced discussion of its role in financial services regulation. The idea of 'responsibilizing' consumers by upgrading their financial capabilities fits neatly into strategies of governance in neo-liberalism where suitably upgraded consumers in the credit market will become part of the supposed virtuous circle of driving competition, innovation and productivity in financial services. Consumers will also, it is argued, be able to avoid the problems of over-indebtedness through better financial management. Financial literacy has become part of the professional discourse of policy makers and the helping professions. There remains however much that is untested in the financial literacy literature. The World Bank comments that 'improving financial literacy is a long term process for which little is clearly understood as to what works (and what does not) in improving financial behaviour'. A review of behavioural finance suggests that it is not absence of information but behavioural biases which cause consumers to make repeated mistakes in credit markets .

Saul Schwartz, in a recent review of the effectiveness of education in improving financial capability in the context of retirement planning, found

mixed results at best. However, research suggests that incorporating some principles of behavioural economics into the design of retirement programs—for example, making increases in the contribution rates of defined-contribution pension plans automatic—would have a far greater impact on individuals' retirement income prospects. This would counter people's decision-making biases, such as favouring the status quo when better alternatives are available and the inability to commit to saving. (Schwartz, 2010: 1)

---

8. Responsible lending

An emerging international concept in consumer credit regulation is the principle of 'responsible lending'. The EU Consumer Credit Directive introduced a duty on lenders to provide adequate explanations to consumers about the characteristics of the credit product and to check the 'creditworthiness' of borrowers, where appropriate by reference to credit bureaux data: the proposed EU mortgage directive also contains a responsible lending obligation. The UK government, representing UK financial interests, originally objected to the responsible lending provision in the early draft of the Consumer Credit Directive which would have imposed a 'suitability' obligation on creditors.The government argued that the introduction of the unfair relationship test and greater pre-contractual information was an adequate substitute for a responsible lending obligation. It also bracketed over-indebtedness initiatives such as information sharing, the use of 'health warnings' on credit card statements, a strengthened credit licensing scheme and a 'crack down' on illegal lending under the heading of responsible lending (see DWP, 2004: 33–34).

Three areas of consumer credit law now reflect the influence of responsible lending in the UK: (1) the duty to explain the nature and consequences of different forms of credit (section 55A); (2) the duty to make a creditworthiness assessment; and (3) irresponsible lending as a factor in determining the fitness of a consumer credit licence holder. The following extract outlines the OFT guidance on irresponsible lending and in particular its understanding of section 55A and B of the Act.

OFT, *Guidance on Irresponsible Lending* (2011)

- fair treatment of borrowers. Borrowers should not be targeted with credit products that are clearly unsuitable for them, subjected to high pressure selling, aggressive or oppressive behaviour or inappropriate coercion, or conduct which is deceitful, oppressive, unfair or improper, whether unlawful or not. Borrowers who may be particularly vulnerable by virtue of their current indebtedness, poor credit history, or by reason of age or health, or disability, or for any other reason, should, in particular, not be targeted or exploited.

- forbearance and consideration towards borrowers experiencing difficulty. We would expect creditors to work with such borrowers with a view to providing them with reasonable time and opportunity to meet repayments

- proportionality in dealings between creditors and borrowers. Actions taken in respect of arrears or default should give proper consideration to available options with repossession of a borrower's home only being used as a last resort.

ASSESSMENT OF AFFORDABILITY

4.1 In the OFT's view, all assessments of affordability should involve a consideration of the potential for the credit commitment to adversely impact on the borrower's financial situation, taking account of information that the creditor is aware of at the time the credit is granted. The extent and scope of any assessment of affordability, in any particular circumstance, should be dependent upon—and proportionate to—a number of factors.

4.2 Whatever means and sources of information creditors employ as part of an assessment of affordability should be sufficient to make an assessment of the risk of the credit sought being unsustainable for the borrower in question. In our view this is likely to involve more than solely assessing the likelihood of the borrower being able to repay the credit in question. We consider that before granting credit, significantly increasing the amount of credit, or significantly increasing the credit limit under an agreement for running account credit, creditors should take reasonable steps to assess a borrower's likely ability to be able to meet repayments under the credit agreement in a sustainable manner.

'Assessing affordability', in the context of this guidance, is a 'borrower-focussed test' which involves a creditor assessing a borrower's ability to undertake a specific credit commitment, or specific additional credit commitment, in a sustainable manner, without the borrower incurring (further) financial difficulties and/or experiencing adverse consequences.

Borrowers are encouraged to always undertake their own assessment of affordability concurrent with that undertaken by the creditor.

4.3 The OFT regards 'in a sustainable manner' in this context as meaning credit that can be repaid by the borrower:

a without undue difficulty—in particular without incurring or increasing problem indebtedness

b over the life of the credit agreement or, in the case of open-end agreements, within a reasonable period of time

c out of income and/or available savings, without having to realise security or assets.

4.4 The OFT would regard 'without undue difficulty' in this context as meaning the borrower being able to make repayments (in the absence of changes in personal circumstances that were not reasonably foreseeable at the time the credit was granted):

- while also meeting other debt repayments and other normal/reasonable outgoings and

- without having to borrow further to meet these repayments.

4.5 We consider that all assessments of affordability should be based on the premise that the borrower should be able to repay the credit over the term. It is accepted that providers of open-end credit, where there is no fixed term, will be limited in their ability to be able to make an assessment of whether repayments might be met in a sustainable manner over the whole life of the credit agreement—but they should be able to make a reasonable assessment of sustainability at the time the credit agreement is entered into (and on the basis of reasonable assumptions regarding the likely duration of any drawdown). The creditor's assessment should have regard to the borrower's ability to pay off the maximum amount of credit available (equivalent to the credit limit) over a reasonable period of time.

4.6 The OFT cannot stipulate exactly what will constitute a 'reasonable period of time' for this purpose as this will vary from case to case depending on the circumstances of the borrower and the amount of the credit. However, in the OFT's view, in the case of running account credit, the borrower should be able to repay the credit on a timeline at least akin to that used for other forms of unsecured lending such as fixed sum personal loans, made for an amount equivalent to the credit limit. If there was no realistic likelihood, based on an affordability assessment, that a borrower would have been capable of paying off an outstanding balance within a reasonable period of time if he spent up to his credit limit, then we are likely to consider this to constitute irresponsible lending on the grounds that the borrower has been provided with clearly inappropriate credit. The fact that a borrower may be able to 'service a debt' over many years simply by making minimum repayments does not, in our view, equate to being able to pay off a debt in a reasonable period of time.

We consider that the credit limit should have been set by the creditor (presumably aware of the borrower's current disposable income and any reasonably foreseeable future changes in the level of his disposable income—for example, if the borrower is close to retirement age and facing a significant fall in disposable income) on the basis of having undertaken an appropriate affordability assessment.

4.7 The OFT would not necessarily consider repayments to be unsustainable simply because the borrower may miss an occasional payment as it falls due. However, under such circumstances, we would not expect creditors to:

- extend formally the duration of the agreement i.e. we would expect creditors to allow for missed repayments to be made up at a later date (within the original term of the loan or otherwise accommodated) or

- where the duration of the agreement is formally extended, increase the total amount payable to unsustainable levels or otherwise cause an adverse impact on the borrower's overall financial situation.

4.8 Where the assessment of affordability suggests that a borrower is unlikely be able to meet repayments under a credit agreement in a sustainable manner over the life of the agreement, in our view, it should not be made available for that amount and duration. However, a smaller amount of credit, for example, may be sustainable (based on the assessment of affordability).

A senior member of the OFT recently commented on the status of OFT guidance.

HC Business, Innovation and Skills Committee, Debt Management, Fourteenth Report of Session 2010–12

… David Fisher, OFT told us:

I sometimes find that people perhaps think the name 'guidance' is a bit of a misnomer. We call it guidance because that is what the Consumer Credit Act calls it.

It is more than guidance. It is not soft law, as some people call it. It is not a rule, as the FSA are capable of doing, but it is effectively setting out to businesses the minimum standards that we expect of them, and we illustrate it with examples of business practices that we would regard as irresponsible and that go to the question of whether they are fit to hold a consumer credit licence.

So we make it very clear to industry that we expect them to comply both with the letter and the spirit of the guidance. If they do not, and we have good evidence that they do not, we will take that into consideration when we are considering asking ourselves the question, 'Does this company remain fit to hold a consumer credit licence?' be it as a debt management company or any other in the sector.

Australia introduced a responsible lending obligation under the National Consumer Credit Act 2009. Consider how it differs from section 55A and B.

National Consumer Credit Protection Act 2009

129 Assessment of unsuitability of the credit contract

For the purposes of paragraph 128(1)(c), the licensee must make an assessment that:

(a) specifies the period the assessment covers; and

(b) assesses whether the credit contract will be unsuitable for the consumer if the contract is entered or the credit limit is increased in that period.

130 Reasonable inquiries etc. about the consumer

Requirement to make inquiries and take steps to verify

(1) For the purposes of paragraph 128(1)(d), the licensee must, before making the assessment:

(a) make reasonable inquiries about the consumer's requirements and objectives in relation to the credit contract; and

(b) make reasonable inquiries about the consumer's financial situation; and

(c) take reasonable steps to verify the consumer's financial situation; and

(d) make any inquiries prescribed by the regulations about any matter prescribed by the regulations; and

(e) take any steps prescribed by the regulations to verify any matter prescribed by the regulations.

(2) The regulations may prescribe particular inquiries or steps that must be made or taken, or do not need to be made or taken, for the purposes of paragraph (1)(a), (b) or (c).

131 When credit contract must be assessed as unsuitable

... (2) The contract will be unsuitable for the consumer if, at the time of the assessment, it is likely that:

(a)   the consumer will be unable to comply with the consumer's financial obligations under the contract, or could only comply with substantial hardship, if the contract is entered or the credit limit is increased in the period covered by the assessment; or

(b)   the contract will not meet the consumer's requirements or objectives if the contract is entered or the credit limit is increased in the period covered by the assessment; or

(c)   if the regulations prescribe circumstances in which a credit contract is unsuitable—those circumstances will apply to the contract if the contract is entered or the credit limit is increased in the period covered by the assessment.

(3) For the purposes of paragraph (2)(a), it is presumed that, if the consumer could only comply with the consumer's financial obligations under the contract by selling the consumer's principal place of residence, the consumer could only comply with those obligations with substantial hardship, unless the contrary is proved.

Information to be used to determine if contract will be unsuitable

(4) For the purposes of determining under subsection (2) whether the contract will be unsuitable, only information that satisfies both of the following paragraphs is to be taken into account:

(a)   the information is about the consumer's financial situation, requirements or objectives, or any other matter prescribed by the regulations under paragraph 130(1)(d) or (e);

(b)   at the time of the assessment:

    (i)   the licensee had reason to believe that the information was true; or

    (ii)   the licensee would have had reason to believe that the information was true if the licensee had made the inquiries or verification under section 130.

In 2011 the FSA outlined its proposals for good mortgage underwriting:

FSA Mortgage Proposals (2011)

At the core of the proposals are three principles of good mortgage underwriting:

Mortgages and loans should only be advanced where there is a reasonable expectation that the customer can repay without relying on uncertain future house price rises. Lenders should assess affordability;

This affordability assessment should allow for the possibility that interest rates might rise in future: borrowers should not enter contracts which are only affordable on the assumption that low initial interest rates will last forever; and

Interest-only mortgages should be assessed on a repayment basis unless there is a believable strategy for repaying out of capital resources that does not rely on the assumption that house prices will rise.

The FSA believes it is important to have the rules well established long before any future upturns in the economy.

Key features of the proposed future regime include:

•   Income will have to be verified in every mortgage application;

- Lenders do not have to consider in detail what borrowers spend but cannot ignore unavoidable bills, such as heating and council tax;

- Interest-only mortgages can still be offered as long as borrowers have a credible plan to repay the capital. But relying on hopes of rising property values is not enough;

- Lenders will have to consider the impact of increases in interest rates in line with current market expectations;

- Some applicants, such as those trying to consolidate debts with a mortgage, will have to get advice to ensure they understand the full implications and costs; and

- Existing borrowers will be unaffected and lenders will have the flexibility to provide new mortgages to some existing customers even where they do not meet the new affordability requirements.

The FSA is also calling for feedback on developing a specific approach for entrepreneurs who borrow against their home to fund their business.

The FSA estimated the impact of its mortgage affordability proposals on those who might most be affected, ie first-time buyers, credit-impaired consumers, debt consolidators, and the self-employed, and concluded that the effects would be modest in terms of exclusion (see FSA CP11/31). A responsible lending duty may be justified economically by the existence of superior credit information and ability to assess risk. Given the existence of behavioural biases, it may protect an individual's future self against the myopia of her present self. More positively, it may ensure that a product is not unsuitable for an individual's needs. It represents a collective 'hands tying' by creditors against engaging in the 'irrational exuberance' associated with certain periods in market cycles and reduces pressure on firms to follow practices that are unfair or that exploit consumers' behavioural biases because firms may fear losing a competitive edge.

The perceived disadvantages of broad responsible lending requirements are that they will raise compliance costs, make creditors more risk averse, and result in a denial of access to credit for some consumers. Denial of access for some consumers may of course be the objective of a responsible lending requirement . The EU mortgage lending proposals, for example, are intended to exclude higher-risk consumers.

Responsible lending may suggest a greater duty of care owed by a lender to a borrower (see Pottow, 2007): that a lender must not merely promote her own interest, but take into account the interests of the borrower, recognising that the credit contract is a joint undertaking. This conception of good faith (see also Unfair Terms in Consumer Contracts Regulations) represents a middle ground between the classical conception of self-interested actors and the conception of a fiduciary relationship where one party must act in the interests of the other party. These ideas could infuse the development of the 'unfair relationships' test introduced to the Consumer Credit Act 1974. In France the Court of Cassation has held that a credit granter that does not check properly the financial capacity of ordinary borrowers and lends an excessive amount will have breached its duty of care to warn a debtor (see Calais-Auloy and Steinmetz, 2006: 608). English law did not develop such a duty at common law. It has imposed a modest duty on the banks to ensure that spouses who may be unduly influenced by their partners receive independent legal advice (see *Royal Bank of Scotland v Etridge* (2001)).

9. Regulating contract terms and credit relationships: relational contracting

9.1 Controlling discretion and reacting to changed circumstance

Many consumer credit agreements are long-term contracts, such as a credit card agreement, with the possibility of changes in the situation of the parties as well as the external environment, such as interest rate changes. One response by lenders is to include a broad discretion within their standard-form contracts to change contract terms. This may include an alteration in the interest rate based on risk-based pricing, the credit limit, the minimum payment, rewards associated with the contract or a decision to terminate the contract. How should this be regulated? Chapter 5 discussed the application of the UTCCR to discretionary modifications. This section considers how the law might shape or regulate the governance mechanisms of credit contracts. Should new forms of default rules be adopted—for example, requiring affirmative opt-in of consumers to changes in contracts such as increases in credit limits? This topic is a subset of issues raised by relational contracting literature and the study of discretion in contract law (see further the discussion in Campbell, Collins and Wightman, 2003: 219; and Collins, 2003b).

Bar-Gill and Davis outline this problem of unilateral modification

O Bar-Gill and K Davis, 'Empty Promises' (2010) 84 *So Cal L Rev* 1

The root of the problem is that when sellers impose modifications unilaterally there is no guarantee that the modifications will be mutually beneficial; sellers are likely to propose unilateral modifications that serve their own interests, but not necessarily those of consumers. This reality raises three main concerns. First, many consumers will fail to appreciate the risk that sellers will impose self-serving modifications. Thus, consumers may enter into welfare-reducing contracts (that is to say, contracts that leave them worse off than if they had not contracted at all). Second, even if the contracts they sign are not welfare reducing (that is, contracting is still better for the consumer than not contracting), consumers in many cases would be better off if sellers offered contracts that set some constraints on unilateral modification. Third, sellers' unchecked power to modify contracts prevents the efficient operation of markets for consumer products. Comparison shopping becomes meaningless when the product or contract can be changed easily soon after the purchase is complete. This fact in turn undermines competition.

English law approached these issues of unilateral modification traditionally through the covert technique of the implied term. In *Paragon Finance v Nash* (2001) consumers had entered into a contract with a lender one of whose terms conferred a broad discretion to change interest rates. The Court of Appeal concluded that this was not an unfettered power. Note the extent to which Dyson LJ considered the extent to which the market and regulation would protect an individual against arbitrary increases in credit and the extent to which standards of reasonableness are imported from public law.

Paragon Finance plc (formerly National Home Loans Corp) v Nash; Paragon Finance plc v Staunton, **Court of Appeal (Civil Division) [2001] EWCA Civ 1466**

Until April 1997 the claimant was called 'The National Home Loans Corpn plc'. It first entered the mortgage market in the mid-1970s. The attraction of the claimant to would-be borrowers was that it was willing to make self-certification loans, ie loans to borrowers who vouched for their income. The company was badly affected by rising interest rates in the late 1980s, and got into serious financial difficulties. It was forced to withdraw from further lending in 1991. It was refinanced by a consortium of banks in 1992, and re-entered the market in 1994 via a new subsidiary company, Home Loans Direct Ltd, which in 1997 changed its name to Paragon Mortgages Ltd ('Paragon'). At the heart of both actions is the complaint that the claimant has consistently charged interest rates which are significantly higher than those of other mortgage lenders, and has done so in order to cover the cost of its refinancing or to retrieve its financial position.

3 Mr and Mrs Nash live at 75 Clifton Road, South Norwood, London SE25. On 5 February 1987 they received an offer of loan from the claimant in a sum of £45,000 by way of remortgage of their property. The offer specified that the loan was to be for 25 years. The capital was to be secured by an endowment policy. The interest was to be payable monthly at a variable rate. The starting rate was stated to be 12.75%. The offer of loan incorporated certain special conditions as well as the printed general conditions of the claimant then current. These latter incorporated the claimant's mortgage conditions (1986 ed).

4 On 30 March 1987 Mr and Mrs Nash entered into a loan agreement on the terms of the offer and the loan was secured by a legal charge on their property. They paid the interest as required. In December 1992 they surrendered the endowment policy. They paid the surrender value to the claimant, and converted the loan to a repayment basis, so that each monthly payment covered both interest and capital. Their financial circumstances took a turn for the worse, and they fell into arrears. By March 1999 the arrears exceeded £5,000. The claimant started proceedings on 5 May 1999.

[The term states]

> 'Interest shall be charged at such rates as the Company shall from time to time apply to the category of business to which the Company shall consider the mortgage belongs and may accordingly be increased or decreased by the Company at any time and with effect from such date or dates as the company shall determine provided that the company will take such steps as it considers to be reasonable and appropriate to bring any such increase or decrease to the attention of the borrower ...'

19 It was also pleaded that, upon the true construction of the variation of rate clause, the claimant was bound to exercise its discretion to vary the interest rate 'fairly as between both parties to the contract, and not arbitrarily, capriciously or unreasonably'. The recorder rejected this construction of the contract, but said (paragraph 121) that his decision would be different if the defendants had sought to achieve the same result by way of an implied term. Encouraged by this remark, the defendants in both proceedings applied to the recorder for permission to amend their defences and counterclaims. The implied term was formulated in accordance with the recorder's suggestion.

Was there an implied term in the terms pleaded?

30 I cannot accept the submission of Mr Malek that the power given to the claimant by these loan agreements to set the interest rates from time to time is completely unfettered. If that were so, it would mean that the claimant would be completely free, in theory at least, to specify interest rates at the most exorbitant level. ...

31 ... [Discussing the Staunton agreement] In the absence of an implied term, there would be nothing to prevent the claimant from raising the rate demanded of the Stauntons to exorbitant levels, or raising the rate to a level higher than that required of other similar borrowers for some improper purpose or capricious reason. An example of an improper purpose would be where the lender decided that the borrower was a nuisance (but had not been in breach of the terms of the agreement) and, wishing to get rid of him, raised the rate of interest to a level that it knew he could not afford to pay. An example of a capricious reason would be where the lender decided to raise the rate of interest because its manager did not like the colour of the borrower's hair.

32 It seems to me that the commercial considerations relied on by Mr Malek are not sufficient to exclude an implied term that the discretion to vary interest rates should not be exercised dishonestly, for an improper purpose, capriciously or arbitrarily. ... I should explain in a little more detail why I would reject Mr Malek's submission that there is no need for an implied term at all.

33 Of course I accept as a general proposition that a lender must have an eye to the market when it sets its rates of interest. To do otherwise is bound ultimately to lead to commercial disaster. But commercial considerations of that kind will not necessarily deter a lender from acting improperly in all situations. They may not deter a lender from unfair discrimination against an individual borrower. They may not even avail a class of borrowers. Take the present cases. The defendants borrowed from the claimant, which withdrew from the lending business in 1991. The rates of interest offered by Paragon are highly competitive. But the history of the interest rates demanded by the claimant in the late 1990s demonstrates how limited the deterrent argument is. The proof of the pudding is in the eating. Between 1989 and 1992 the difference between the claimant's standard rate and the rate demanded by the Halifax Building Society was approximately two percentage points. By 1997 the gap was in excess of four points. In March 1999 it rose to 5.14%, when the claimant's rate was 12.09% and the Halifax rate was 6.95%.

34 The argument based on the existence of the regulatory powers of the Director General of Fair Trading is in my view not sufficient to deny the implied term. I note that in the Lombard case [1989] 1 All ER 918, 923 the court said that if a lender capriciously treated old borrowers unfavourably 'one would *hope* that the Director General of Fair Trading would consider whether he should still have a licence under the 1974 Act' (my emphasis). One would indeed have such a hope, but that does not seem to me to be a secure basis on which to decide that there is no need for an implied term that a lender will not exercise the discretion to set rates of interest capriciously. ...

35 Finally, I must consider whether the fact that the borrowers can redeem their mortgages and seek loans from another source if the rates are set capriciously etc is a sufficient reason for acceding to Mr Malek's argument. In my view, it is not. As with the last point, this is not so much an argument against the need to imply a term as an argument that it is unlikely to be broken because the lender will be aware that it is open to the borrower to go elsewhere. But it seems to me to be obvious that there may be circumstances in which the lender will act capriciously towards an individual borrower knowing that it might compel the borrower to redeem the mortgage and go elsewhere. Indeed, the lender may have decided to increase the rate of interest for that very reason. But why should the lender be able capriciously to compel the borrower to find another lender with impunity? The borrower may find it difficult to find another lender, especially if he has fallen into arrears with the first lender as a result of that lender's interest rate policy. His employment status may have changed adversely since he entered into the first loan agreement. The process of remortgaging is costly. The new lender

will probably require a survey. There will be lawyer's fees. And there may be a penalty for early redemption.

36 ... I would hold that there were terms to be implied in both agreements that the rates of interest would not be set dishonestly, for an improper purpose, capriciously or arbitrarily. I have no doubt that such an implied term is necessary in order to give effect to the reasonable expectations of the parties. I am equally in no doubt that such an implied term is one of which it could be said that 'it goes without saying'. If asked at the time of the making of the agreements whether it accepted that the discretion to fix rates of interest could be exercised dishonestly, for an improper purpose, capriciously or arbitrarily, I have no doubt that the claimant would have said 'of course not'.

37 I come, therefore, to the question whether the implied term should also extend to 'unreasonably'. The first difficulty is to define what one means by "unreasonably". Mr Bannister was at pains to emphasise that he was not saying that the rates of interest had to be reasonable rates in the sense of closely and consistently tracking LIBOR or the rates charged by the Halifax Building Society. He said that what he meant by the unreasonable exercise of the discretionary power to set the rate of interest was something very close to the capricious or arbitrary exercise of that power.

41 So here ...we find a somewhat reluctant extension of the implied term to include unreasonableness that is analogous to Wednesbury unreasonableness. I entirely accept that the scope of an implied term will depend on the circumstances of the particular contract. ... It is one thing to imply a term that a lender will not exercise his discretion in a way that no reasonable lender, acting reasonably, would do. It is unlikely that a lender who was acting in that way would not also be acting either dishonestly, for an improper purpose, capriciously or arbitrarily. It is quite another matter to imply a term that the lender would not impose unreasonable rates. It could be said that as soon as the difference between the claimant's standard rates and the Halifax rates started to exceed about two percentage points the claimant was charging unreasonable rates. From the defendant's point of view, that was undoubtedly true. But, from the claimant's point of view, it charged these rates because it was commercially necessary, and therefore reasonable, for it to do so.

42 I conclude therefore that there was an implied term of both agreements that the claimant would not set rates of interest unreasonably in the limited sense that I have described. Such an implied term is necessary in order to give effect to the reasonable expectations of the parties.

... [I]n my view, there is no real prospect that the defendants would be able to prove at trial that the claimant acted in breach of the implied term in relation to either of these defendants. Accordingly, I would uphold the decision of the recorder to refuse permission to amend.

In 2010 the government agreed a protocol with the credit and store card companies that included:

- Right to control: consumers will have the right to choose not to receive credit limit increases in future and the right to reduce their limit at any time; and consumers will have better automated payment options. Consumers will have access to these options online.

- Right to reject: consumers will be given more time to reject increases in their interest rate or their credit limit.

...consumers who are at risk of financial difficulties will be protected through a ban on increases in their credit limit as well as the ban on increases in their interest rate, and card companies will work with debt advice agencies to agree new ways they will provide targeted support to consumers at risk to help improve their situation before they get in too deep. ...

- Consumers will have the right to tell their card company at any time that they want to reduce their current limit. This will be available online or through an automated telephone system so consumers can do so without having to speak to an adviser.

Right to reject

Consumers will be given more time to reject increases in their interest rate or their credit limit.

- Consumers will now have 60 days to tell their card company they want to reject an interest rate increase, close the account, and pay down the outstanding balance at the existing rate. This doubles the time consumers have to consider an interest rate increase and take action. In addition, consumers will be notified at least twice during the 60 days that they have the right to reject and card companies will tell them how much their borrowing will cost at the higher rate so they are able to see the real impact of an interest rate increase when making their decision.

- Consumers will be able to reject any increase in their credit limit at any time. Card companies will make it as easy as possible for people to do so, in particular by automating this process.

Right to information

- A new, separate, interest rate increase communication will be sent to consumers facing an interest rate increase at least 30 days before the change. Previously, some lenders only notified consumers through their monthly statement. Consumers will also be reminded after this that they can reject the interest rate increase within 60 days, close the account and pay down the outstanding balance at the existing rate. These communications will explain in clear and simple language how their rate is changing, what it will cost them and that they have a right to reject the new interest rate.

- A new credit limit increase communication will be sent to consumers offered an increase in their credit limit at least 30 days before the change. This will explain in clear and simple language how their limit is changing and what they can do if they wish to reject the new limit. The communication will reassure consumers that their card company will not treat them any differently simply because they have exercised their right to reject a limit increase or reduce their limit.

- Card companies will work with debt advice agencies to agree how they will identify consumers at risk and to ensure that the communications they send out are clear and easy to understand.

The Government is also making a longer term commitment to place these principles on a statutory footing, taking account of the effectiveness of these voluntary arrangements. This will lock in good practice, and give these new rights the full force of the law.

To what extent does the above protocol draw a fair balance between the rights of creditor and borrower? What is the legal status of this protocol? Could it be invoked before the FOS (see below) or taken into account in a licensing case? Would a default rule requiring affirmative consent by a consumer to an increase in credit have been desirable? In the United States, see the Credit Card Accountability Responsibility and Disclosure Act of 2009.

10. Regulation of the price of credit: usury

Controls on the price of credit have a long historical pedigree—their origins may be traced to the medieval prohibition on usury (see further Tawney, 1947; Wilson, 1963: Atiyah, 1979: 65–67, 550–51; Glaeser and Scheinkman, 1998). Many countries (eg France, the Netherlands, Germany, some US and Australian states) employ interest-rate ceilings as a method of consumer protection. France has different interest-rate ceilings depending on the nature and amount of the credit (see Articles L313-3–L313-6 Code de la consommation). The German Supreme Court has enforced an interest-rate ceiling of double the average interest rate. Islamic finance prohibits interest. There is continuing controversy and disagreement concerning the value of interest-rate ceilings. They are often justified as a means of protecting low-income consumers and of providing credit at fair prices. However, as the following extract illustrates, there is significant scepticism among economists as to the effectiveness and fairness of such measures as an instrument of consumer protection.

Iain Ramsay, 'To Heap Distress upon Distress: Comparative Reflections on Interest Rate Ceilings (2010) 60 *UTLJ* 707 at 710–11, 715–16

Interest-rate ceilings may take many forms and may be premised on a variety of rationales. There may be a single ceiling or a range of ceilings for different types of loans, as currently exists in France. Ceilings may be linked to market prices or may be established as a fixed rate. They may be based on the total cost of credit (eg, £17 per £100) or a percentage rate. Some ceilings include only interest charges, while others, as an anti-avoidance strategy, include all costs. The latter approach will inevitably result in a high interest rate for small short-term loans. Ceilings are sometimes established at a level intended to mimic the market; in other cases they are established at a much higher rate than the market, as a method of policing the outlier transaction.

There are several rationales for ceilings, including (1) responding to behavioural mistakes where individuals are perceived to underestimate the risks of high-cost credit; (2) providing a bright-line rule substantially above the market rate, reducing the high costs of proving fraud or exploitation in credit markets; (3) addressing problems in competition in a market that leads to supra-normal prices; (4) preventing externalities from high-cost credit, such as state costs of support for individuals who become over-indebted;and (5) ensuring a 'fair' price in transactions.

The economic criticisms of interest-rate ceilings are well known. They are a 'blunt instrument,' since not all high-interest loans are necessarily unfair or result in over-indebtedness, and not all consumers may under-estimate the risks of high-cost credit. Ceilings may be circumvented through the charging of 'fees' or insurance and may have undesirable substitution effects where individuals are forced into less convenient, more costly, and less transparent forms of credit. They may result in cross-subsidization or credit exclusion for some consumers where suppliers withdraw from the market. Ceilings may hurt most low-income consumers, who are often the intended beneficiaries of the ceilings. … For these reasons, other policy instruments, such as more competition, better information, more warnings, de-biasing interventions, or product term regulation, are proposed. More focused interventions might be used to respond to behavioural mistakes, such as restrictions on cash advances at gambling casinos. Better social programs, rather than attempted market redistribution, might reduce the extent to which the poor pay more.

The variety of types of ceilings and their distinct rationales suggest caution in making broad statements about their effects, recognizing that studies of the effects of one type of ceiling may not be applicable to other types. Many issues concerning the effects of ceilings are empirical. The extent of circumvention, market substitution, and exclusion depends on the level of the ceiling and the elasticity of supply and demand.

... English economic opinion since Bentham has generally opposed ceilings. John Stuart Mill thought that the usury law reflected religious prejudice and had 'been condemned by all enlightened persons since the triumphant onslaught made upon it by Bentham in his Letters on Usury.' The general usury laws were abolished in 1854, although controls remained on the price of pawns, described as 'the poor man's bank.' By the 1870s there was concern about high-cost moneylending and the use of bills of sale. The 1898 Select Committee on Moneylenders considered but rejected the idea of ceilings, based partly on analysis of US experience with ceilings. The arguments outlined by the committee against ceilings are remarkably modern: (1) high interest rates do not necessarily equate to unfairness; (2) different conditions are applicable to different types of loans, and interest rates may not be the best measure of the cost of small loans; (3) the ceiling would become the norm; and (4) ceilings would be circumvented. Instead it proposed conferring almost unlimited discretion on judges to hold a bargain to be unconscionable. In 1927 there was substituted the presumption that an interest rate above 48 per cent was unconscionable. However, the courts did not use this as a price ceiling and upheld higher charges unless there was evidence of advantage taking. During the twentieth century, the main working-class form of credit in the United Kingdom was hire-purchase, which was not subject to the usury laws. Consumers often paid high interest rates and were unable to obtain the tax deductions available to wealthier consumers, who had access to loans and overdrafts.

The Crowther Committee was ambivalent about interest rate ceilings.

Report of the Committee on Consumer Credit (Crowther Committee), Cmnd 4596/1971

6:6.6 We have found the question of statutory control of interest rates extremely difficult to resolve. ... There may be cases where, in view of the poor financial standing of the borrower, interest of 100 per cent would not yield an excessive profit to the lender; but if the borrower falls into a risk category as low as this, then we feel he ought not to be eligible for loans from the private sector. We recognise that such a borrower has to live; he has to have money from somewhere. But we feel that this is a problem which, assuming it to be capable of solution at all, must be solved through social welfare services rather than by the granting of loans at enormous interest rates.

The Committee concluded that, given the difficulties in administering rate ceilings, fixing an inflexible ceiling for interest rates was not an answer to the problems of low-income debtors, but they would have maintained the presumption that interest-rate ceilings over 48% were prima facie harsh and unconscionable. However the Conservative government did not introduce ceilings in the Consumer Credit Act 1974, substituting the open-textured 'extortionate credit bargain' provisions (see below).

During discussion of reforms of the Consumer Credit Act 1974 in 2005–06 and the problem of over-indebtedness, some politicians and interest groups (eg Debt on our Doorstep) proposed the introduction of interest-rate ceilings in the UK. The government, as part of its over-indebtedness strategy, commissioned comparative research which concluded that the existence of interest-rate ceilings in France and Germany resulted in consumers using either more expensive forms of credit (eg mail order) or being excluded from the credit market, and being required to seek credit in the illegal market (see DTI/Policis, 2005). The assumptions and conclusions in the DTI commissioned report have been challenged by groups concerned about over-indebtedness (see Debt on our Doorstep, 2005; Consumer Focus, 2009) and the issue of interest-rate ceilings has again emerged recently in the context of high-cost credit and payday loans. The OFT recommended against the introduction of ceilings in its report, *High-Cost Credit*.

The Competition Commission, in its study of home credit, ultimately concluded against the introduction of interest-rate ceilings: it concluded 'that there was a risk that price caps would contribute to a reduction in access to credit for some customers (and thus to a possible increase in financial exclusion)' (Competition Commission, Final Report, 2006: 11).

Select Committee House of Commons Business, Innovation and Skills Committee, Debt Management, Fourteenth Report of Session 2010–12

Cap on total cost of credit

49. Various consumer groups have been campaigning for a cap on the total cost of credit to prevent payday loans from spiralling out of control especially through rollovers. Martin Lewis argued: If I were doing this, I would put a total cost cap on. I would talk to the decent players out there about what the total cost cap should be. I would make them portray total cost, which includes all possible fees, which they do not do right now.

As a concept, if you borrow £100, you should never have to pay back more than £150. That is roughly how I would do it; I would base it on cost. Do not take the £50 as my limit—that is conceptual. That would incorporate any number of rollovers, which would be effectively a ban on the number of rollovers going on.

...

50. Despite a large number of responses to the Government's consumer credit review calling for a cap on the total credit that could be charged, the Government said that there was a lack of hard evidence about the impact that the proposal would have. It has therefore commissioned the University of Bristol to carry out research into this area. The Government highlighted that other research had shown that price controls, such as a limit on APR, could restrict availability of legal credit to low income consumers and push them to loan sharks.

51. However, there is already positive research available for the Government on the total cost of credit cap. A report by the Centre for Responsible Credit highlighted the situation in Ontario, Canada where there is a cap of $21 per $100. The Ontarian Government carried out huge amounts of research before putting this into place—through the Maximum Total Cost of Borrowing Advisory Board. It consulted with industry, social, poverty, consumer and financial groups and other experts. It also considered the experience of other jurisdictions with a payday lending marketplace including the review of materials on payday lending across Canada, in the United States and overseas. In addition, the Board commissioned its own research from Ernst & Young.

10.1 Judicial control of credit terms: unfair credit relationships

I am very confident that the unfairness test and the ADR will work and that there will be no need for interest rate caps, but we will always keep that option open. (UK HC, Parliamentary Debates, 6th ser, vol 434, col 1412, 9 June 2005, Gerry Sutcliffe, Undersecretary of State, DTI)

The government did not introduce rate ceilings in the Consumer Credit Act 1974. However, it allowed the possibility of judicial price control by extending the power of the courts to reopen extortionate credit bargains (see sections 137–40). Under the Moneylenders Acts, a loan had been presumed to be extortionate if the interest rate was more than 48 per cent. The new provisions made no reference to this presumption and extended the power to reopen transactions to any credit agreement, whatever the amount of credit extended, provided that the debtor was an individual. It was clear from the outset, in the parliamentary discussion on these provisions, that they would provide little regulatory bite.

A modest number of cases were brought under this provision. One of the contributing factors to this absence of litigation was that 'uncertainty about the likely outcome will significantly undermine a borrower's willingness to engage with the legal process' (DTI, 2001: 41–42). Howells and Weatherill argue (2005: 43) that the DTI analysis may underestimate the significance of these provisions as a bargaining tool, since, given the vagueness of the provision, it is always possible to argue that a bargain might be extortionate.

The 2006 amendments to the Consumer Credit Act 1974 replaced the extortionate credit bargain provisions with a new 'unfair relationship' provision (section 140A). The section applies to any agreement which involves the extension of credit to an individual whether or not it is a regulated agreement under the Act (eg includes a high-net-worth exception). A credit relationship may be unfair because of the terms of the agreement, the way in which the creditor has exercised or enforced any of his rights under the agreement, or any other things done or not done by or on behalf of the creditor, whether before or after the making of the agreement or any related agreement.

The unfair relationship test is more extensive than controls under the UTCCR. These regulations do not apply to core terms and the unfair relationship test permits the court to focus not only on the terms themselves at the time of entering into the contract, but also how they are invoked during the course of the agreement. For example, it is possible that the type of practice in the *First National Bank* case (above Chapter 4) might have been attacked under the unfair relationship test. It is also possible that, given its broad scope, the unfair relationship test could be used as a private law method of attacking irresponsible lending practices.

Some of the practices that might be addressed by the unfair relationship test include:

1. Excessive security.
2. Dual interest rates, with a very high default rate being applied immediately a payment is late. Under existing law it was difficult to strike down so-called dual interest rate clauses, because it was not clear from the outset, of the agreement whether they would operate unfairly (see *Paragon Finance plc v Nash* and *Broadwick Financial Services v Spencer*).

3. Conversion from unsecured to secured loans following default through the use of charging orders.
4. Unfair practices connected with debt consolidation such as 'churning'.

The unfair relationship test seems to be an advance over the extortionate credit bargain provisions. However, Roy Goode is critical of the test, commenting that 'the criteria to be applied by the courts are so vague that everything is left to the court, and an impossibly uncertain provision. It is guaranteed to generate thousands of lawsuits, leaving it to the Court of Appeal to establish authoritative criteria to produce consistency' (Goode, 2005: 96). The Unfair Commercial Practices Directive may also be relevant to the conduct of the creditor during the agreement.

Section 140D of the Consumer Credit Act 2006 requires the OFT to provide advice and information on the relationship between the unfair relationship clauses and Part 8 of the Enterprise Act 2002. This guidance recognises that it is difficult to provide sharp guidelines on the application of the test. It suggests that irresponsible lending might be included within the conception of unfairness. It also recognises that the FSA's approach, based on 'treating customers fairly' may be relevant (OFT, Unfair Relationships, Consultation Paper, 2006).

The following cases illustrate early judicial approaches to the unfair relationships test.

Harrison v Black Horse [2011] EWCA Civ 1128 (Court of Appeal Civil Division)

This case concerned the failure by a lender to disclose the 'handsome commission' that it would make on the sale of single-premium PPI. 87 per cent of the premium went in a commission to the associated company of the lender. It represented 677 per cent of the cost of the insurance. One argument raised was that the failure to disclose such a large commission represented an unfair relationship between the parties. This was a test case: many cases were stayed pending the decision.

The Harrisons, a couple in their early fifties, had borrowed £46,000 in 2003 paying £11,500 in PPI. In 2006 they renegotiated a further loan of £60,000, with £54,800 to pay off the previous loan, cancel its PPI and take out a further PPI policy of £10,200. The balance of the loan was for home improvements and a holiday. In 2009 they discharged the loan through further refinancing, cancelling the PPI . They had paid about £10,000 on PPI by 2009 when they started a debt-management plan and subsequently an individual voluntary arrangement. The lenders, selling as an agent of the associated company Lloyds TSB insurance, earned a commission of £8,887.

The policy was sold by a telephone script, followed up by a package of information on the contract with key facts including a 'secured lending policy summary' and two-page document containing the terms. They were sold joint life, disability and redundancy cover that expired after five years, although they would continue to pay the premiums for the balance of the loan. The maximum possible benefit under the non-life insurance was £18,705, less than the potential cost of the PPI over the 23 years of the loan. A stand-alone insurance policy would have cost approximately £2,000.

The consumers thought that the insurance was compulsory but the script made clear that it was not. 'He just thought that he had to have it because he had had it with previous loans.' Mr Harrison did no more than scan the paperwork. Lord Justice Tomlinson commented that: 'I do not approach the case on the basis that they were sophisticated in financial matters, but it would be both patronizing and unwarranted on the evidence to suggest that they would have any difficulty in understanding the essential features of the transaction.'

[Tomlinson LJ:] This appeal is brought by two of many borrowers who seek to recover, in whole or in part, the cost of payment protection insurance, 'PPI', which they were sold by a lender, typically although not here a bank, at the same time as they negotiated a loan from that lender. On this appeal redress is sought under sections 140A and B of the Consumer Credit Act 1974, 'the Act', which gives to the court wide-ranging powers in circumstances where the relationship between a creditor and a debtor has been determined to be unfair to the debtor.

… We are concerned with a loan advanced and associated PPI sold in 2006. Our decision will be relevant to many who seek redress in respect of transactions entered into at around that time. But since April 2011 the sale of PPI has been prohibited at the point of sale of credit, as has the sale of PPI within seven days before the sale of credit and indeed the sale of single premium PPI policies—see The Payment Protection Insurance Market Investigation Order 2011 issued by the Competition Commission in exercise of its powers under the Enterprise Act 2002.

In view of the wide-ranging nature of complaints concerning the 'mis-selling' of PPI, it is worth emphasising at the outset how very narrow is the ambit of this appeal. It traverses very little if any of the terrain illuminated by the market investigations to which I have just referred, in the latter of which there were identified fifteen common types of failings in PPI sales. Rather it focuses upon a single aspect of the typical transaction which has not attracted direct regulatory comment, the failure by the lender to disclose to the borrower that it would receive from the insurer a handsome commission upon the sale of the PPI. Indeed, given that typically the cost of the PPI premium was itself advanced to the borrower under the same credit agreement as the principal loan, repayment of which it ostensibly protected, the reality was that the commission simply became a debt payable by the borrower to the lender at the expiry of the term of the loan, on which interest was payable in the interim for so long as the loan remained outstanding. It should furthermore be noted that it is not the mere non-disclosure of the receipt of commission which is here alleged to provide an avenue to redress. The argument depends upon the size of the commission. Whilst in broad terms the borrowers rely upon various aspects of the relationship between themselves and the lender as giving rise to unfairness, what is said to be critical is the circumstance that typically the commission was disproportionate to the actual cost of the insurance. Here the borrowers were told that the Payment Protection Plan premium was £10,200. Of that, 87% was retained by the lender. Put another way, the commission was 677% of the apparent cost of the insurance, although these figures may in truth be misleading as concealing a cross-subsidy between the cost of the PPI and the annual percentage rate or cost of the loan. In the present case, and presumably it is typical, the PPI insurance was principally provided by an associated company within the same group of companies as the lender.

After considering the applicability of an action for negligence (rejected because of an absence of a duty of care) and the application of the ICOB rules (potentially a breach but no damages because no evidence as to how the Harrisons would have changed their actions), or conflict of interest (not applicable because the commission was not payable directly to the sales agent), Lord Justice Tomlinson considered the applicability of section 140A and the approach of Judge Waksman in the lower court.

Finally the judge turned to unfair relationship. He noted rightly that the process of assessment of facts and the balancing and weighing of different factors is classically an exercise for the judge at first instance, with which an appellate court should be reluctant to interfere unless the judge below has proceeded upon an erroneous view of the law, taken into account immaterial factors or failed to take into account material factors or simply reached a conclusion not open to him on the facts—cf *Aldi Stores Limted v WSP Group plc* [2008] 1 WLR 748 at paragraph 16 per Thomas LJ and *George Mitchell (Chesterhall) v Finney Lock Seeds Limited* [1983] 2 AC 803 at 816 per Lord Bridge of Harwich. The latter is a case particularly in point since there the House of Lords upheld a decision that certain conditions of sale did not satisfy the requirement of reasonableness under s.55 of the Sale of Goods Act 1979 or s.11 of the Unfair Contract Terms Act 1977.

This notwithstanding, the judge addressed the argument in the light of two recent decisions of the County Court and the circumstance that, as already noted above, the District Judge had not in fact dealt with the large commission and its non-disclosure. Like the District Judge, Judge Waksman rejected the assertion of an unfair relationship. The cost of the PPI and the features of the cover had been known and accepted. There had been no pressure to accept PPI. The Harrisons had a real opportunity to consider whether or not to take it. They might have been interested to learn of the size of the commission but there was no evidence as to how they might have reacted to that knowledge. Again, the size of the commission was irrelevant given that there was no likelihood of a conflict of interest arising.

I turn then to the principal argument in the case, and that which was addressed at the hearing. Mr Doctor had many criticisms of the sales process, pointing out that questions 3 and 4 in the questionnaire were questions to which anyone would be likely to answer 'yes', whilst question 7 could only ever be answered in the negative since no-one could have cover in place specifically linked to a loan agreement which had not yet been concluded. He also made the point that the effort involved in selling the PPI seems hardly to justify so large a commission, and that Black Horse had made no effort to justify it as in fact involving some element of cross-subsidy or anything of that sort. Telling though points of this nature are, they do not to my mind point to unfairness in the relationship. At bottom Mr Doctor's argument really resolves to a single point that, in the absence of an explanation, the commission is so egregious that it gives rise to a conflict of interest which it was the lender's duty to disclose. Only disclosure could give the borrowers the opportunity to decide whether they wished to purchase a product in circumstances where the lender derived so significant a benefit from the purchase.

In the absence of an explanation such as an element of cross-subsidy the commission here is on any view quite startling and there will be many who regard it as unacceptable conduct on the part of lending institutions to have profited in this way. I struggle however to spell out of the mere size of the undisclosed commission an unfairness in the relationship between lender and borrower. Moreover the touchstone must in my view be the standard imposed by the regulatory authorities pursuant to their statutory duties, not resort to a visceral instinct that the relevant conduct is beyond the Pale. In that regard it is clear that the ICOB regime after due consultation and consideration does not require the disclosure of the receipt of commission. It would be an anomalous result if a lender was obliged to disclose receipt of a commission in order to escape a finding of unfairness under s.140A of the Act but yet not obliged to disclose it pursuant to the statutorily imposed regulatory framework under which it operates. Mr Doctor had no answer to this point.

Nor do I think that the circle can be squared by arguing that a recommendation of suitability cannot be objective if given by a lender in receipt of a large commission. The judge rejected that submission on the facts of this case. There is also the obvious difficulty in deciding where the line is to be drawn. How large must the commission be before there is held to be a conflict of duty and interest? The cover was expensive but the lender was in the circumstances for the reasons I have given under no obligation to advise that the same cover could have been obtained more cheaply elsewhere. A seller is not ordinarily obliged to warn his buyer that his product is expensive when compared to other similar products and in my judgement it is telling that in this heavily regulated market no such obligation has been imposed. It was irrelevant to the Harrisons that the high price they were paying contained a substantial element of reward for Black Horse. For the reasons given by the judge the extent of that reward could not have influenced the recommendation given, notwithstanding the perhaps unattractive feature of the prescribed procedure that the Black Horse sales force was exhorted to advise the customer of the applicable features, benefits and exclusions relevant to each of the features of the PPI cover and to 'attempt to overcome any objections'. In any other context the suggestion that the charging of a high price for a product freely and readily available more cheaply elsewhere in the market is indicative of unfairness in the relationship between seller and buyer would be met with incomprehension. I can see no principled basis upon which the suggestion can succeed here, notwithstanding the high price can properly be characterised as involving the non-disclosure of the receipt of a large commission.

This decision raises several issues. First, the existence of section 140A recognises that even though there is compliance with specific rules (such as ICOB), the regime might not be exhaustive. Second, is it so difficult to draw a line on the question of fairness? Is this not what judges are for—making difficult decisions? Third, in determining unfairness, to what extent is Tomlinson LJ focusing on the immediate circumstances surrounding the transaction rather than the general structure of selling PPI where many consumers (44 per cent) assume that they have to take out PPI. Fourth, does this decision illustrate the concerns expressed by Ben-Shahar and Schneider about information disclosure, namely that the formal disclosure protects firms against claims of unconscionability? It is an effective shield against liability although it may have little effect on consumer decision-making. Fifth, compare the approach of the court to that adopted by the FOS (below) and the FSA (below) to issues of PPI. Finally, this decision concerned events before 2008. Would the application of the CPUT regulations to this case result in a different decision?

Robert Shaw v Nine Regions [2009] EWHC 3514 (QB)

Evans J

The Background

4. The defendant is a company which lends money in the sub prime market. The service it provides is characterised by the ease with which a loan can be obtained. Money is available immediately upon completion of the Loan Agreement. No credit checks are carried out upon the borrower and the borrower is able to retain possession of the item, usually a car or in this case a motorcycle, upon which the loan is secured by bill of sale. There was evidence before the lower court that loans of this type are intended for early repayment in that they suit customers who require short-term loans. However, this ease of borrowing does not come cheap and the interest charged on these loans is high.

5. On 4th July 2009, the claimant entered into a Loan Agreement with the defendant, by which the claimant borrowed £3,000 from the defendant. The Loan Agreement sets out important financial information relating to the loan. The term of the Agreement is given as 36 months

or 156 weeks and the total amount payable under the Agreement is £13,724.88, made up of the £3,000 capital loan and £10,724.88 interest on that loan. That amount was repayable in 156 weekly installments of £87.98. The interest rate is given as 119.16 per cent per annum.

6. The total amount repayable could be increased if various charges were applied to the loan, such as a £12.00 charge for sending the borrower a reminder that an instalment had not been paid on time, or for sending a default notice.

8. When he entered this agreement the claimant was given a document headed 'Pre-contract Information' in which the terms of the loan were clearly set out and he was also required to fill in a Customer Income and Expenditure Form, setting out details of his income and expenditure to establish that he was able to afford to repay the loan. There is no doubt that the claimant fully understood the terms of the Loan Agreement into which he entered. Not only did he sign the statement when he entered the agreement saying that he had read and understood the Terms and Conditions of the Agreement, (and also stating that he found them to be fair and reasonable, a matter upon which the Recorder ultimately placed no weight), but the claimant had also, wisely, carried out research in the sub prime market before he took out this loan.

9. The claimant wanted the money immediately so that he could go on holiday. It was the ease by which the money could be obtained which attracted him to this kind of agreement, and before taking out the loan he had already formed the intention to repay it as soon as possible from the proceeds of an insurance claim which he anticipated would be settled in the near future.

10. Unfortunately, the insurance claim was not settled as promptly as the claimant had hoped. On 21st July 2008 there is a £12.00 charge applied to the account for a letter telling the claimant that an instalment payment was overdue. Thereafter, there were several further such charges applied to the account. However, the claimant did make payments into the account. On 23rd July 2008 he paid £87.98 and on 12th August 2008 £293.27.

11. In the absence of further payments the defendant sent a default notice to the claimant and on 12th September 2008 the defendant wrote to the claimant explaining that if he did not comply with the default notice that had been sent, he would be liable for the total amount due under the Agreement, and the defendant would be entitled to seize his motorcycle and the Agreement would be terminated.

12. In telephone conversations between the parties, the claimant said that he would challenge the loan and he complained about the validity of the bill of sale, the high interest rate on the loan and the charge of £12.00 per reminder letter. It is clear from the evidence that was before the Recorder that prior to 29th September 2008 the claimant had decided to repay the loan in total.

... 22. The claimant's witness statement was ordered to stand as his Particulars of Claim. In it he sets out a large number of complaints, but the nub of his case was contained in paragraph 41; that reads as follows:

'The applicant further avers that his relationship with the respondent is unfair within the meaning of section 140A of the Consumer Credit Act 1974 (as amended) because: (i) the terms of the credit agreement are unfair because the interest rate of 341.9 per cent APR is extortionate; (ii) the terms of the related bill of sale are unfair as submitted above passim (sic); (iii) of the way in which the respondent has enforced the agreement with respect to applying charges and with respect to defaulting the loan and moving to repossession; (iv) the respondent did not explain the nature and implications of the related bill of sale clearly, or at all, prior to offering it and the Loan Agreement for signature.'

23. In its Defence and Counterclaim the defendant denied the alleged unfairness and counterclaimed for the sum of £10,856.88 together with interest and costs.

24. A significant part of the evidence in the county court focused on the fairness or unfairness of the interest rate charged by the defendant. The claimant contended that 341.79 per cent APR was an extortionate rate and at the second day's hearing he produced details of the interest rates charged on what he said were comparable Loan Agreements. The first was an interest rate of 19.1 per cent APR charged on non-status loans by the Hackney Credit Union. Three further examples were all from mainland Europe: pawn brokers in Germany who charge 4 per cent per month (that is 48 per cent annually); Mont-de-Piêté in Brussels, which acts under the same conditions as pawn brokers but charges 6.5 per cent annually: and Credit Municipal in Paris (and many other French cities), which charges between 8 per cent and 12 per cent annually on pawns.

25. The defendant argued that its interest rate as distinct from its APR of 119.16 per cent (that is 9.93 per cent per month) was not high in comparison with lending in the sub prime market generally, which is a high risk lending market. Examples were given, which included a typical pawn brokers rate of 10 per cent per month (that is 120 per cent annually), which is charged despite the fact that a pawn broker retains possession and control of the security throughout the term of the loan and does not have to suffer the fragility of the security under agreements such as that under which this loan was made. Other examples included monthly rates of 10 per cent and 9.25 per cent for loans similar to those provided by the defendant.

26. As for the examples given by the claimant, the defendant pointed out that a credit union was a completely different model from that in the sub prime market with which this court was dealing, and that each of the other examples quoted were outside the jurisdiction.

29. In paragraphs 5 and 6 of the judgment, the Recorder addresses the question of whether the relationship created by the agreement was unfair. From the opening words of paragraph 6, it is clear that the Recorder applied the correct burden of proof. He then sets out in sub-paragraphs the matters upon which the creditor relied as showing that the relationship created by the agreement was fair. The Recorder accepted that the claimant was prone to very bad financial judgment, but concluded, also, that he was a sophisticated, articulate and intelligent man who knew exactly what the terms of the Agreement were after having given them careful consideration. He accepted the loan was for the purpose of going on holiday, rather than because of any financial pressure upon the claimant and that the claimant could afford this loan.

32. Surprisingly, in view of the evidence he had heard and the importance of the issue, the judgment contains no explicit finding on the fairness or unfairness of the defendant's rate of interest. However, both parties agree that it is implicit in the findings the Recorder did make and also in the way he approached the order he made that he found that the interest rate charged under the Loan Agreement was fair. I agree with the parties that this finding is implicit in the judgment and I am also satisfied that the Recorder was entitled on the basis of the evidence before him to come to that conclusion.

Mrs Sharon Morrison & Mr Kenneth Morrison v Betterpace Ltd (t/a Log Book Loans), 1 September 2009 (County Court at Lowestoft) Case No 9 LO 00559

Claim: The borrowers sought an order under section 140B(1)(b) of the Consumer Credit Act to require the creditor not to recover Mrs Morrison's vehicle; an order under section 140B(1)(c) to discharge the sum of £5,420 payable by the debtor; and an order under section 140B(1)

(f) to alter the terms of a related agreement to enable the applicant to settle the arrears of £2,340 by affordable instalments.

Type of agreement: Two log book loans secured by bill of sale (the second loan was taken out to pay off the first loan but was secured on a different vehicle). The first agreement (with Mr Morrison) was dated 17 November 2007 and was for £1,500 repayable over 58 weeks at 343.4% APR. The second agreement (with Mrs Morrison) was dated 8 April 2009 and was for £2,340 repayable over 58 weeks at 485.25% APR, although the creditor subsequently agreed to accept monthly payments.

Judgment: The judge found that:

- The two agreements were related transactions and so any matters which might be deemed to be unfair to Mr Morrison could be deemed to be unfair to Mrs Morrison.

- It was fair that the bailiffs should be instructed to recover Mr Morrison's car as he had made no payments for about 10 months and had not contacted Betterpace at all during that time. For that reason too, it was not oppressive or unfair for Betterpace to insist on repossession that day or full payment.

- The actions of the bailiffs were not oppressive so as to put Mrs Morrison under duress, and they did not employ tactics which rendered the relationship between Mrs Morrison and Betterpace unfair.

- The interest rate on the first agreement was high but so too were the risks to the creditor. The courts had upheld agreements which included very high APRs in circumstances where the risks to the lender were high.

- The Morrisons read the documents carefully. They were clear, were not in small print and were relatively short. The language was understandable.

- The terms of the first agreement were not unfair and immediate possession was not unfair because of the history of default.

However, the judge found that the circumstances of the second agreement were out of the ordinary in this marketplace. Betterpace was not advancing any new money, as Mrs Morrison was essentially taking over the responsibilities to pay the balance of the loan owed by Mr Morrison. The creditor did not explain to Mrs Morrison that the interest charged on her loan would not be 343.3%, as charged to Mr Morrison, but 485.3%, which was the rate applicable to new loans at that time. The judge found that that was a significant increase and one that appeared unfair in the very particular circumstances of the transaction. He concluded therefore that the interest rate should be reduced to 343.3%. He added that he was not called upon to determine whether the larger rate of 485.3% was unfair and so he made no finding on this point.

The judge also found that the computer model which worked out the charges to be attributable to Mrs Morrison's account was not changed after the creditor agreed to accept monthly payments. It was excessive that a monthly payer could be liable for up to four or five default letters every month at £12 per time. It was fair and appropriate that default letters were limited to one per month at £12 per time.

Result: Unfair relationship under section 140A. The judge ordered the interest rate on the second agreement to be reduced to that of the first, and the number of default letters to be limited to one per month at £12 each. The parties to agree a schedule of repayments.

Logbook loans Co subsequently lost their credit licence because of deceptive and aggressive debt-collection activity. The higher English courts have generally held that whether the interest is too high must be determined by reference to the relevant market. Sub-prime rates are inevitably higher than mainstream rates. Thus Lord Justice Dyson held in *Broadwick* that in determining whether the interest rate in the sub-prime market was extortionate, it was necessary to compare it with interest rates in that market.

> I cannot accept that the judge was in error in failing to compare the rates of pure interest charged by Broadwick with those charged by leading banks and building societies. The primary lending market is so different from the non-status vendors market that such a comparison is of no relevance.

Will the introduction of the creditworthiness test in the Consumer Credit Act 1974 along with the unfair relationships test mean that situation such as *Meadows* will not occur in the future? The Council of Mortage Lenders concluded that 'adverse credit' lending offered consumers a last chance opportunity to sort out their finances. Is it better to have a safer market that may restrict some choices at the margin?

---

11. Ombudsmen: The Financial Ombudsman Service

Ombudsmen have become an important form of grievance mechanism in financial services markets and a model for redress in other consumer markets. (See Morris, 1987: 131, 199; 2008: 785; Morris and Little, 1999; Rawlings and Willett, 1994: 307. See generally James, 1997. On the background to the current Financial Ombudsman Service, see James, 2002: 191; James and Morris, 2003). The rationale for the establishment of these schemes is outlined in the National Consumer Council study *Banking Services and the Consumer* (1983), which stimulated the development of consumer services ombudsmen.

National Consumer Council, *Banking Services and the Consumer* (1983) 105–08

> The volume of business transacted by banks and other financial institutions inevitably generates customer grievances. ...

> The great majority of banker/customer disputes are resolved simply and at an early stage. But there are occasions when customers feel that there has been no satisfactory response to their complaint. Even when a complaint is referred to a bank's head office where it may well be reviewed anew, as far as the aggrieved consumer is concerned, no independent judgment has been brought to bear on the issues. It is not unnatural, therefore, that those who remain dissatisfied after making a complaint should feel rightly or wrongly—that the bank's main concern has been to defend its own interests. The only satisfactory means of resolving intractable and genuine disputes is through an independent third party.

> Many disputes between customer and bank could, in principle, be brought before a court. This will be so where issues of law are in dispute and in most—but not all cases of disputed fact. We do not wish to see any reduced recourse to the courts. It is important that banks should not be seen as being above the law and that the courts should continue to be able to apply the law to them. We have also seen how court judgments have been instrumental in developing the law of banking in a way which is fair to all concerned.

However, very few individuals ever take a dispute with a bank to court. ... We recognise the danger that the establishment of alternative or supplementary systems may deflect attention away from the deficiencies of the court system. ...

Nevertheless, there are positive advantages in privately organised schemes. They obviously avoid the real and imagined psychological obstacles that surround the courts. They provide additional choice to consumers. They offer wide scope for innovation and are more likely than the courts to adopt 'active' styles of fact-finding and informal, simple and flexible means of decision-making. They can also reap the benefits of a 'specialist' approach—a scheme which deals with just one industry will know far more about that industry than the courts. A privately organised scheme can also be set up to deal with more than the strict issues of law and fact, to which the courts are confined. Such a scheme can, for example, be authorised to deal with complaints that there has been maladministration or a failure to observe the proper standard of professional behaviour. Finally—and this is important—a scheme can observe and comment on (for example in an annual report) the wider trends and practices revealed by individual disputes.

Our general conclusion is, therefore, that privately organised schemes can bring positive advantages for both consumers and businesses. But it is vital that any scheme incorporate a number of safeguards; that recourse to the ordinary courts should remain available; and that attention should not be diverted away from overdue reforms in the courts themselves. ...

... The advantages do not lie only with customers. The banks have much to gain as well. Such a scheme would be an effective means' of improving and maintaining public confidence. It could provide banks with valuable information about the causes of dissatisfaction amongst their customers. It could enable them to improve their services. And it could reduce the risks of the bad publicity for a bank which surrounds the occasional case which does get to court.

These public law 'transplants' may provide both a readily accessible process for dealing with specific grievances and a means of identifying patterns of misconduct (see Harlow, 1978: 446). They may also develop consumer norms of fairness. The Financial Ombudsman Service is now constituted by statute under the Financial Services and Markets Act 2000 and the 2006 amendments to the Act confer jurisdiction on the service in relation to consumer credit disputes. The service is free to consumers (it may also be used by small businesses). Firms subject to the jurisdiction of the Financial Ombudsman Service must submit disputes to the Ombudsman and are bound by the Ombudsman's decision. His award may include compensation of up to £150,000. There is no substantive appeal to the courts although firms may seek judicial review. Complainants, however, are not bound by the decision of the Ombudsman and may pursue their case in court. Given the costs of such action this is likely to be a rare occurrence.

Rhoda James outlines certain characteristics of the current Financial Ombudsman Service:

Rhoda James, 'The New Dispute Resolution System in the UK Financial Services Industry' (2002) *Journal of International Financial Markets* 191

Decision-making on grounds of fairness

A feature of ombudsman schemes is that decisions may be made on grounds of substantive fairness, which may in some cases override the legal rules. ... The ability to make decisions according to a standard of fairness is an important feature of most ombudsmen systems, since it is this which is largely responsible for allowing an ombudsman to 'do justice' in the individual case—a feature which has been seen as a central characteristic of an Ombudsman-type remedy. In framing the legislation to include this discretionary power, the Government clearly felt it was a necessary power in the consumer interest in a field where there is often inequality of bargaining power between the parties, in addition to a body of legal rules weighted against the consumer (notably in the insurance sector). At the same time, the FOS is acutely aware that the exercise of such a discretionary power needs to be structured and based on transparent principles. ... The FOS is developing a body of informal precedents to ensure broad consistency and predictability for firms, and it publishes divisional case digests.

Sections 228–29 of FSMA 2000 outline the basis for decision making by the Ombudsman who must provide written reasons to the parties. 'Fair and reasonable' requires the Ombudsman to take 'into account the relevant law, regulations, regulators' rules and guidance and standards, relevant codes of practice and, where appropriate, what he considers to have been good industry practice at the relevant time'. Remedies might include a money award that may take into account mental distress and a direction to the financial institution, for example, to remove a note on a credit file. The award is enforceable in the county courts. The complainant cannot be required to bear the respondent's costs (section 230) but may have an award made against her if the complainant's conduct was unreasonable or improper. The Ombudsman may operate on more informal rules of evidence than a court.

The following data are taken from the FOS 2010–11 Annual Report

- We handled 1,012,371 initial enquiries and complaints from consumers—around 4,000 each working day.

- Around 1 in 5 of the initial consumer enquiries we received turned into a formal dispute requiring the involvement of our adjudicators and ombudsmen—a record 206,121 new cases, up 26% on the previous year.

- 51% of new cases were about the sale of payment protection insurance (PPI), with the number more than doubling to 104,597—the highest number ever received in a year about a single financial product.

- The number of investment-related complaints dropped by 30% and banking complaints fell by 9%.

- 51% of the total number of cases we dealt with related to 4 financial services groups— while 3,592 businesses accounted for just 5% of our caseload.

- We resolved 164,899 cases—fewer than planned, because of the legal action taken against us on PPI complaints.

- Our involvement resulted in compensation for consumers in 51% of complaints.

- We resolved almost half of all disputes (apart from PPI) within three months and three quarters within six months.

- We operated on a cost-base of £106 million with an average staff of 1,300.

- We provided information and handled enquiries in 49 different languages and formats— from British Sign Language to Sinhala, mpeg to Braille.

- We handled 675 parliamentary enquiries and 16,706 calls to our technical advice desk.

- We featured in 5,500 articles in the media—and 78% of adults in the UK said they were aware of the Financial Ombudsman Service.

Who uses the Financial Ombudsman Service? The 2010–11 Annual Report indicates:

Two thirds of consumers who use our service are between the ages of 35 and 65. This reflects the fact that they are more likely to own a wider range of financial products. Our research also shows that people in these age groups are generally also more likely to know about their consumer rights, including their right to complain to the ombudsman.

However, during the year the proportion of complaints we received from consumers over 65 increased by a record 42%. This reflects the significantly larger number of older people who have referred complaints to us about payment protection insurance (PPI). It may also reflect our outreach work with older and retired people over the last few years—with more consumers in the older age groups now showing increased confidence in complaining. ...

Men continue to complain more to the ombudsman service than women. Theses figures have remained unchanged for several years. However, many complaints relate to accounts and policies that are held jointly, where conventionally the first-named account-holder (the name our system records) is generally a male partner.

More women contact us initially on our consumer helpline than subsequently pursue complaints with us formally. This is something we have been monitoring closely.

Our research suggests that women are more likely to be satisfied than men with the way a financial business handles their complaint. This may explain why fewer women return to us with a formal complaint, after our helpline has explained the complaints procedure and the importance of complaining first to the business they are unhappy with.

The main way that most consumers who refer complaints to us hear about the ombudsman continues to be through the media (although this figure fell by 9% year-on-year). ...

Our analysis of the occupations of people who refer complaints to the ombudsman shows a steady socio-economic shift among the consumers who use our service. In recent years, the proportion of complaints to the ombudsman from skilled, semi-skilled and unskilled workers has risen by 60%, while complaints from people from professional and managerial backgrounds have fallen proportionately by over 40%. ... This shift may reflect the type of complaints that consumers refer to the ombudsman service—and the financial products and services involved. Between 2004 to 2007, up to two thirds of the complaints we handled related to mortgage endowments and were brought by mainly middle-aged homeowners.

But since 2007 we have seen significant increases in complaints involving current accounts, overdrafts, credit and payment protection insurance (PPI)—products which are held extensively by a broader socio-economic range of consumers [39 percent of complaints about PPI came from social classes DE compared with only 27 percent from class AB]. Over the last three years we have seen a steady increase in the proportion of consumers using our service who define themselves as belonging to a non-white ethnic group. 12% of people who brought complaints to the ombudsman service said they had a non-white ethnic background (10.5% in the previous year).

The following table indicates cases resolved since 2002.

31 March	Cases resolved
2011	164,899
2010	166,321

2009	113,949
2008	99,699
2007	111,673
2006	119,432
2005	90,908
2004	76,704
2003	56,459
2002	39,194

The Hunt Review in 2008 concluded that the Financial Ombudsman Service 'looks too much like a middle class service for middle-class people' (Hunt, 2009: 2) and recommended a higher profile for the institution, as well as outreach to lower-income and more vulnerable consumers. It also recommended greater publicity through greater publication of decisions (anonymised) in full, more publicity on the opportunity for an internal appeal from the initial provisional adjudication to an Ombudsman, a scorecard of firms against whom complaints are made and improvement of the wider implications process (see further Morris, 2008). These reforms have now been implemented.

The Annual Report 2010–11 outlines the current approach taken to dispute settlement:

> Our preference is to resolve complaints informally—getting both sides to agree at an early stage to the views or informal settlements that our adjudicators may suggest.

> But more complex or sensitive disputes may require detailed investigations and lengthy reviews, including an appeal to one of our panel of 71 ombudsmen for a final decision.

> *cases requiring an ombudsman's final decision*

> During the year, the number of cases requiring the direct involvement of an ombudsman—and a formal ombudsman decision—increased significantly. 10,730 cases had a final decision by an ombudsman in the financial year 2009/2010—rising 63% to 17,465 cases in 2010/2011 (following a 24% rise in the previous year).

> This increase in the number of cases where a complaint is pursued to an ombudsman decision appears to continue a trend highlighted in last year's annual review. This is the shift towards more entrenched disputes—with businesses increasingly taking a harder-fought and legalistic approach, and consumers becoming more demanding and less willing to concede.

> Of the final decisions made by ombudsmen during the year, 38% of requests were made by financial businesses and 62% by consumers. In over eight out of ten final decisions, ombudsmen reached the same basic conclusions as the adjudicators who handled the cases in the earlier stages. Where they did not do so, there was usually a finely-balanced judgement call or, more often, new facts came to light only at that very late stage.

> hearings

> … During the year we again held fewer than 20 hearings in cases where the ombudsman considered that it would help them get to the bottom of a case. We hold hearings only where the ombudsman believes a case cannot be fairly decided on the basis of the documentary evidence and the material that the two sides have already provided.

> If we are asked for a hearing by either a consumer or a business, we consider carefully what value it will add. We do not believe that hearings should be held just to allow either side to confront the other in person—and neither side is given a private meeting with the ombudsman deciding the case.

... In total we upheld 51% of the complaints we settled in the financial year 2010/2011—compared with 50% of cases in the previous year.

... In many cases it is poor communication between a financial business and its customer that leads to a simple misunderstanding escalating to the stage where the ombudsman service has to get involved.

Consumers can sometimes pursue complaints in an unfocused way that may make them appear unreasonable to the business they complain to. On the other hand, businesses sometimes respond to customer concerns unhelpfully and defensively—aggravating problems that a clear, helpful and sympathetic explanation might have resolved.

A consumer's failure to present a reasoned argument does not automatically mean that a case has no merit—or that the complaint should be categorised as 'frivolous and vexatious'.

Of the 164,899 complaints we settled during the financial year 2010/2011, we concluded that 1,447 cases (0.9% of the total) could be categorised in this way (0.4% in the previous year). We do not charge a case fee to the business complained about where we decide that a complaint is frivolous and vexatious.

Timeliness

We resolved 41% of all complaints within three months and 70% within six months—both improvements on the previous year. However, reducing the time it takes us to settle cases remains a key priority for us in terms of improving our customer service—and we aim to further improve timeliness next year.

In the financial year 2010/2011, we handled 2,489 complaints about our service—including complaints subsequently referred to the independent assessor. These related to 1.2% of our total caseload. 5% of these complaints were made by businesses and the others were all from consumers or their representatives.

We upheld 33% of these complaints. This involved paying compensation in 271 cases, in recognition of the inconvenience caused by delays or administrative errors on our part. The average payment—including compensation recommended by the independent assessor—was £258.

Where we are unable to resolve a complaint about our service, it can be referred to the independent assessor—for a formal independent review of the level of service we have provided.

Discrete rules were enacted for the handling of payment protection insurance. These include a requirement on firms to undertake a root cause analysis.

DISP App 3.4 Root cause analysis

DISP 1.3.3 R requires the firm to put in place appropriate management controls and take reasonable steps to ensure that in handling complaints it identifies and remedies any recurring or systemic problems. If a firm receives complaints about its sales of payment protection contracts it should analyse the root causes of those complaints including, but not limited to, the consideration of:

(1) the concerns raised by complainants (both at the time of the sale and subsequently);

(2) the reasons for both rejected claims and complaints;

(3) the firm's stated sales practice(s) at the relevant time(s);

(4) evidence available to the firm about the actual sales practice(s) at the relevant time(s) (this might include recollections of staff and complainants, compliance records, and other material produced at the time about specific transactions, for example call recordings and incentives given to advisers);

(5) relevant regulatory findings; and

(6) relevant decisions by the Financial Ombudsman Service.

Where consideration of the root causes of complaints suggests recurring or systemic problems in the firm's sales practices for payment protection contracts, the firm should, in assessing an individual complaint, consider whether the problems were likely to have contributed to a breach or failing in the individual case, even if those problems were not referred to specifically by the complainant.

Where a firm identifies (from its complaints or otherwise) recurring or systemic problems in its sales practices for a particular type of payment protection contract, either for its sales in general or for those from a particular location or sales channel, it should (in accordance with Principle 6 (Customers' interests) and to the extent that it applies), consider whether it ought to act with regard to the position of customers who may have suffered detriment from, or been potentially disadvantaged by such problems but who have not complained and, if so, take appropriate and proportionate measures to ensure that those customers are given appropriate redress or a proper opportunity to obtain it. In particular, the firm should:

(1) ascertain the scope and severity of the consumer detriment that might have arisen; and

(2) consider whether it is fair and reasonable for the firm to undertake proactively a redress or remediation exercise, which may include contacting customers who have not complained.

11.1 Ombudsmen, the rule of law and norm development

The following are examples of cases decided by the ombudsmen, primarily in relation to consumer credit. You should compare them with how a court might approach the issues (eg *Harrison v Black Horse*) and the role of the ombudsmen in policing unfair terms.

Payment Protection Insurance Cases

A trainee chef, Mr A, complained about the way in which he was sold a payment protection policy when he applied for a credit card. He said he had understood he was being insured, but had not been told that the policy was optional.

He said he was not given any information about the cost or benefits of the policy. And he stated that a representative of the credit card company had simply filled in the application form for him, written a small 'x' at the bottom of the form, and then asked him to sign his name next to the 'x'.

The credit card company rejected his complaint. It said it was clear from the application form that the insurance policy was optional and that Mr A had chosen to take it. The company also said that the insurance premiums were itemised on Mr A's credit card statement each month, so he must have been aware that he was paying for an additional—optional—product.

complaint upheld

We asked the credit card company to send us Mr A's application form. We noted that on the final page, close to the space for the customers signature, there was a 'tick box' next to a statement that the customer wanted payment protection insurance. This had been ticked.

The tick in the box, the written details entered on the form, and the small 'x' placed next to the signature all appeared to have been written in the same handwriting, using a ballpoint pen. However, the signature itself looked markedly different and had been written with a thick, felt-tipped pen. This tended to support Mr A's account of events.

We also noted that Mr A had been 19 years of age at the time of the sale. This was the first time he had applied for any financial product or service other than a basic bank account.

We did not agree with the credit card company that it was clear from the application form that the insurance cover was optional. Nor did we agree that, by signing the form, Mr A had clearly indicated his wish to buy the policy. There was no evidence that he had been told anything about the cover at the time of the sale. And the fact that Mr A's statement showed that the premium was collected monthly did not mean he must have been aware the insurance was optional.

We upheld the complaint and told the company to return to Mr A all the premiums he had paid to date, plus interest.

71/02

A couple in financial difficulties take out a succession of loans and are sold a new single-premium payment protection policy each time, adding to their outstanding debt

Mr and Mrs J had been experiencing financial difficulties for some while and their situation worsened in early 2005, after Mrs J gave up work to look after their children. Finding it difficult to meet the monthly repayments on their loan, they approached a different lender to see if it could help.

The lender offered them a new loan of £18,000. This allowed them not only to settle their existing loan (for around £11,000) but also to clear the overdraft on their current account and settle several credit card debts and sizeable bills. In order to keep their monthly repayments as low as possible, the couple chose to take the new loan over 10 years.

Unfortunately, Mr and Mrs J's financial problems did not resolve themselves and within 18 months they again approached the lender for help. It agreed a new and higher loan. This was spread over 15 years and was secured by a second mortgage on the couple's home.

Some time later, a friend pointed out to them that each time they had obtained a new loan they had also been sold a new payment protection policy. So they asked the lender if it would refund their insurance premiums, as part of a wider settlement of their continuing debt problems. The lender said it would arrange a small, partial refund if the couple cancelled their policy. Unhappy with this, the couple referred their dispute to us.

complaint upheld

We noted that each time Mr and Mrs J had taken out a loan they had been asked to pay for the insurance by means of a single premium. This was added to the underlying loan and repaid (plus interest) over the entire length of the loan, even though—in each case—the policy itself only provided cover for 5 years.

There was nothing to suggest that the lender had explained to Mr and Mrs J the significance of this arrangement—particularly the fact that that they would still be paying for the policy for some time after the cover had ended.

Although the lender told us it did not offer advice, it was clear that it had actively encouraged the couple to buy the policies. In view of the couple's financial circumstances, we did not consider the sale of these policies to have been appropriate.

Flexibility was an important consideration, as it seemed likely the couple would need to restructure the loan at a later date. They would not wish to incur significant costs in doing this.

However, the policies they were sold lacked flexibility and, because of the limitations on the refund of premiums, were particularly costly if they were cancelled after a relatively short period.

In our view, the lender should not have encouraged the couple to buy these policies, and the couple would not have wanted the policies if the business had explained matters more fully.

We said the lender should re-calculate the amount outstanding on the couple's loan account, putting them in the position they would have been in if they had not bought the policies. We said the business should also pay the couple back the amount they had paid for the policies, plus interest on these amounts.

We had some concerns about the way in which the lender had dealt with Mr and Mrs J, given their overall financial difficulties. We therefore suggested it should look at ways of assisting them with a wider settlement of the debt, including waiving the fees it had levied in recent months in connection with several overdue loan repayments.

consumer argues with loan provider that her debt is 'unenforceable'

Mrs A was being pursued by a loan provider for a debt that she did not think she should be required to pay.

After reading on an online forum that debts could be written-off if the loan provider could not supply a 'true copy ' of the original loan agreement, she asked the loan provider to send her a photocopy of the original agreement containing her signature.

The loan provider said it was unable to do this as it no longer had the original agreement. It sent her instead a reconstituted agreement containing all the original terms and conditions. Mrs A responded by saying the loan provider should stop making demands for repayment as the debt was 'now unenforceable in law '.

The loan provider said that Mrs A was mistaken about this. She therefore referred the dispute to us and asked us to confirm that the debt was 'legally unenforceable'.

complaint not upheld

We told Mrs A that we did not have the power to declare whether or not credit agreements are legally enforceable, as that is something for a court to decide. However, we said we were able to look into her complaint on the basis of whether the loan provider had treated her in a way that was fair and reasonable.

After obtaining evidence from Mrs A and the loan provider, we established that she had taken out the loan nearly ten years earlier, to pay for some computer equipment. She had been in arrears with her repayments for most of that time. At one stage she had tried to persuade the loan provider to accept a 'partial payment in final settlement of the total amount outstanding'. And for nearly three years before that she had been paying the loan provider just £1 per month.

When Mrs A had first contacted us, she told us there had 'always been considerable doubt ' about whether the debt was hers at all. So we asked her to tell us why she thought the debt might not be hers. We also asked why she had continued making payments for some years—and had made an offer to settle the debt—if she did not believe she owed any money. All she told us in response was that she had not known what else to do.

It was clear from the evidence that Mrs A had taken out the loan and we thought it was fair and reasonable for the loan provider to seek repayment of the debt. We also thought that the loan provider had fully complied with its responsibility to deal with Mrs A's situation sympathetically, in view of her financial difficulties.

We explained this to Mrs A and gave her details of free money advice organisations that she could contact for help in managing her debts. We did not uphold her complaint.

The role of the Financial Ombudsman Service in developing consumer norms based on fairness and good banking practice is illustrated by the case of *Norwich and Peterborough Building Society v The Financial Ombudsman Service* (2002). This case concerns an application for judicial review of the decision by the Financial Ombudsman Service concerning superseded savings accounts. In 1998, Mr Jones had a variable-rate TESSA account of £3,000 with the building society. In April 1999, the government superseded the TESSA with an ISA and in May 1999 Jones opened an ISA. This account was so attractive to savers that the building society closed it to further applicants in June 1999. The building society also offered a TOISA which was available to individuals with TESSAs that had matured. This was not available to Mr Jones. In June 2000 Mr Jones complained that he was receiving a lower rate of interest on his TESSA compared to his ISA. The ombudsman upheld the complaint, holding that it was unfair for the building society to pay less interest on its TESSAs than TOISAs and ordered that Mr Jones should be paid the difference in interest rates for the period between April 1999 and 11 September 2000 which was when the building society communicated to Mr Jones that he could move his TESSA to another TESSA provider without penalty. Mr Jones did not do this because the building society paid better rates than its competitors.

The ombudsman based his decision on two grounds: (1) interpretation of rules 2.17 and 2.18 of the banking code; and (2) a 'relative onerousness' test, based on its fairness jurisdiction. This latter test states that it is unfair treatment for a building society to pay a lower rate of interest on an investment account to which it has attached more onerous terms than another investment account to which the society has attached less onerous terms. The court concluded that interpretation of the banking code was an issue for the court and that the ombudsman had interpreted the code incorrectly. However, the court held that the ombudsman was justified in basing his decision on the 'relative onerousness' test.

Norwich and Peterborough Building Society v The Financial Ombudsman Service [2002] EWHC 2379

Mr Justice Ouseley:

'Superseded accounts:

2.17 From time to time, we offer new savings and investments accounts. If you have any type of savings and investment account, other than a fixed rate account, which has been "superseded" because:

New accounts are no longer opened; or

The account is not actively promoted:

We will either:

(a) keep the interest rate on the superseded account at the same level as an account with similar features from the current range: or

(b) switch the superseded account to an account with similar features from the current range.

Examples of similar features include notice periods, types of withdrawals, numbers of free withdrawals, how deposits and withdrawals from the account are made.

This means that the interest rate on your account will always be at least as good as the interest rate on an account with similar features from the current range.'

'2.18 Where there is no account with "similar features" we will, within 30 days of your account becoming superseded, contact you to:

Tell you that the account is superseded:

Tell you about our other accounts: and

Help you switch accounts without any notice period and without any additional charges.'

Mr Justice Ouseley, concluding that the ombudsman had misinterpreted the banking code, then turned to the 'relative onerousness' test.

I do not consider that the attack on the 'relative onerousness' test as an irrational or arbitrary measure of fairness is sustainable. Mr Boswood's submission elevates it into an altogether more sophisticated analytical tool than it is. It is but a very simple test incapable of making fine distinctions or doing more than provide a broad comparison between accounts, which will often not be able to provide an answer to the question of whether one account is less onerous than another. It may provide no answer at all to Mr Boswood's simple example, let alone to a more elaborate package, but that does not make it an irrational tool of comparison. It does permit of subjectivity in application but it is necessary for the Ombudsman to be able to exercise his own judgment as to what is fair.

The Ombudsman is entitled ... to adopt a test, or several tests, to assist him in reaching a view as to what is unfair. The very breadth of that word, and the fact that reasonable people can differ very strongly about what is or is not fair, necessitates the development by the Ombudsman of some guide or criteria which he can apply in his task. It also makes for consistency in decision-making.

If the Ombudsman treated this guide or 'relative onerousness' test as a surrogate for unfairness so that factors obviously relevant to fairness were ignored because they did not fit within the framework of 'relative onerousness', that would constitute an error of law. I do not consider that the Ombudsman has used the concept as a surrogate for unfairness in that way. True it is that his test is the focus of his analysis of unfairness but even were it the exclusive focus, which to my mind would be too exacting a reading of his decision, it is not the adoption of the test which has caused him to regard certain matters as immaterial but his view as to what is fair. The legal effect of his disregarding various contentious matters can and should be considered against the true scope of 'fairness'.

I reject also Mr Boswood's submission that the 'relative onerousness' test has caused the Ombudsman to fetter his discretion, and to pay lipservice only to particular circumstances. It is inevitable that a test or criterion will be of general application and will produce similar results in similar cases; that involves no fetter. ... The refusal to disclose earlier decisions on 'relative onerousness' does not support any argument as to the fettering of discretion or the inability of the Ombudsman to explain his test. The test is very simple and does not require disclosure of other decisions for its inscrutable workings to be unmasked.

Although the Ombudsman correctly disclaimed any regulatory role, the impact of a decision that Mr Jones had been treated unfairly will inevitably constitute a decision that in such circumstances, which must be very widespread, a TESSA holder should receive the same interest as an ISA holder, if that account is still available or as a TOISA holder, in the alternative. More precisely, the account holder should do so until informed that the account can be transferred without notice or penalty to another account. But I do not consider that the general application of the conclusion means that the Ombudsman should be seen as having moved from a consistent adjudicator to industry regulator.

I turn to deal with those factors which Mr Boswood submitted were obviously relevant on a rational view as to the scope of 'fairness' but which he said the Ombudsman had set aside.

The question of whether Mr Jones would have been better off moving to a TESSA with another institution goes solely to the question of loss and compensation. The Ombudsman is entitled to conclude that it was unfair for the notice or penalty restriction to be maintained, and Mr Jones not to be told that he could move freely elsewhere, regardless of whether the opportunity thus afforded would actually benefit Mr Jones or not.

The fact, which I regard as established by the various graphs which N&P produced, that its TESSA and other rates were better than those of its competitors, was legitimately regarded by the Ombudsman as irrelevant to fairness. The Ombudsman was entitled and, to avoid being a regulator, probably obliged, to examine fairness as between account holders of the one institution. Those at N&P all benefited from its competitive rates, but not all were so restricted as its TESSA holders. The Ombudsman is entitled to conclude, within the broad scope of the judgment as to unfairness which it is for him to make, that it is not for him to make the assessment as to whether Mr Jones would be better off transferring his TESSA to another TESSA provider. That is for Mr Jones once he has the necessary opportunity. Were it otherwise, the Ombudsman's decisions on unfairness would involve a view on comparative terms and interest rates as between institutions. It could lead to a conclusion that it was fair for Mr Jones to be prevented from some transfers but perhaps not others, which would be a considerable extension of his role and could easily shade into a regulatory function.

...

What undoubtedly irks N&P, and it is easy to see why the finding would cause resentment and annoyance, is that the Ombudsman concluded that fair treatment required that it tell Mr Jones and its other TESSA holders that they could move freely to competitors, (especially when they were not so competitive), which was not something required by the Banking Code. As I have said, the Banking Code does not provide for all situations, and should not be interpreted so that it does when clearly it does not. But that also means that what is fair or unfair cannot be judged exclusively by reference to it. It is the very fact that a TESSA holder has no real choice, if he is to retain his tax benefits but to stick with a TESSA, that makes the opportunity of a move elsewhere, without penalty, so important. There are powerful arguments as to what is fair or unfair or both sides, but I cannot conclude that in these respects the Ombudsman's approach is irrational. He deals with that consideration in a lawful manner within the broad scope of fairness.

... The Ombudsman was not acting retrospectively in the sense of changing established rules or guidance, and applying it to earlier decisions of the institutions. He is entitled to reach a conclusion that treatment is unfair based on his analysis of the material presented; he does not have to have signalled in advance that treatment of a particular type would be unfair. Whilst there might be some ground for complaint that the Banking Code was being stretched beyond its previous known confines on the Ombudsman's approach, that would not have prevented it being applied in that way if the proper interpretation of the Code permitted it. It would be unfair on complainants to do otherwise. A common misunderstanding as to the position cannot fairly make the position other than what it is. Even less can it be said that the Ombudsman must forewarn institutions of his approach. There is also force in Mr Pannick's point that it had been well known that there was a strong public concern that TESSA holders were being unfairly treated and the fact that they were locked in for 5 years meant at least that they were being taken for granted and not actively courted. The institutions were effectively on notice that they had to be actively looking to ensure that they were not being unfair.

I found more problematic the question of whether it was rational for the Ombudsman to use the TOISA as a comparator account when Mr Jones was not eligible for it and indeed not eligible for it as a matter of law rather than as the result of a decision by N&P. ...

The Ombudsman is correctly looking at fair treatment as between the various account holders at the institution in question, and in my judgment, the fact that a complainant may not be eligible for an account does not preclude a reasonable view that his treatment has been unfair by reference to it. Ineligibility is not by itself a sufficient answer preventing a comparison being made with another account, and a conclusion drawn that the complainant is being unfairly treated. The answer from the institution's point of view must lie in the justification for the difference rather than in the simple fact of ineligibility. There will often be no difficulty in an institution explaining that one type of account is treated more favourably than another for commercial reasons, to attract and retain accounts in the best ways it can, to compete in the market. But it is for the institution to explain why the ineligibility means that the other differences in treatment are fair.

At all events, whilst many would reasonably take N & P's side on this point, and agree that it was fair to exclude from comparison accounts for which the complainant was ineligible, I do not consider that the alternative approach is outside the scope of a rational approach to fairness. ...

To my mind it follows that in substance the Ombudsman is saying that fair treatment did not simply require the equalisation of rates; fair treatment required either the equalisation of rates or the removal of the restriction on movement of the funds. Until the latter step was taken, it was unfair for the rates to be different. If the Ombudsman had concluded that the unfairness continued after notification to Mr Jones that he could move freely but caused no loss, I would have expected that to be spelt out, for in this context it would be an odd conclusion that the treatment had been unfair but had caused no loss; the concept of a technical unfairness is not a sound one to a lawyer's mind and should be even less so to the Ombudsman. If he had intended his test to be that the interest rates should be equalised and the other terms equalised as well, I would have expected him to say so, because of its farreaching implications. The 'relative onerousness' test, as explained in paragraphs 33 and 37 of the Decision Letter is concerned to prevent a lower interest rate being paid on the account with the more onerous terms. So unfairness can be removed either by reference to rates or terms. The interest rates could have been equalised and the notice restriction maintained, in which case the loss caused by unfair treatment would have ceased upon equalisation of rates. Or, as here, the restrictions were removed so that the unfair interest rate treatment ceased to be unfair.

But it would also be consistent with the expressed reasoning of the Ombudsman as clarified by Mr Pannick for discriminatory interest rates as between TESSAs and TOISAs to be reinstated, provided that the restrictions do not remain. This makes sense of the fact that the Ombudsman appears to require, not a window of opportunity for a transfer but a permanent change either in the interest rate relative to the TOISA rate or in the restrictions imposed. If within 30 days of the TESSA being superseded, Mr Jones had received the notification which he received only on 11th September 2000, the Ombudsman would have found neither unfairness nor any loss. I also find in this conclusion support for the Ombudsman's view in relation to fairness, though not in relation to paragraph 2.18 of the Banking Code, that it is legitimate and not irrational to require the institution to notify an account holder that he can move freely to another institution. Differential rates are seen as fair with free movement.

His reasoning is thus all of a piece and internally consistent, as between fair treatment and loss. The reasoning and decision of the Ombudsman does not rationally support a conclusion that his test meant equality of terms and of interest rates, and that he required both. That would not be an application of the 'relative onerousness' test, that more onerous accounts should not receive lower interest rates than less onerous accounts, but a requirement of equality as between account types which is not his professed test. Once N & P removed its restrictions, the TESSA is no longer more onerous at N & P's hands, ignoring the statutory restrictions as the Ombudsman did.

Conclusion

At root, the Ombudsman's view is simply that it is unfair for Mr Jones to be paid less interest on his TESSA than on a TOISA because the TESSA has the greater restrictions. Whether seen as removing unfairness (which is in my view what the Ombudsman means) or as going to loss, the unfairness can be remedied either by equalising the rates or by removing the restrictions, even though the latter may not produce substantial benefits. One can of course sensibly argue that to compare Mr Jones' account with one for which he is not eligible, is itself unreasonable and that N&P is being put in a position in which it has to pay more interest or reduce restrictions to bring the TESSA in to line with an account for which he is not eligible. I see much force in those points. But I cannot conclude that the Ombudsman's view of unfairness goes beyond the scope of the broad concept of 'unfair treatment', of which statute has made him the judge.

Is an ombudsman exercising strong or weak discretion in application of the fairness criteria? Ronald Dworkin argues that weak discretion is like the hole in the doughnut, ie that there are legal standards for determining whether a discretionary decision is correct or incorrect. Strong discretion describes the situation where one may criticise the discretionary decisionmaker, but not say that he or she was wrong in making the decision. The concept of fairness is clearly dynamic and complex taking into account norms of best industry practice (see comment by Nobles, 2003; O'Shea and Rickett, 2006). It does not seem to be a justice that varies with 'each ombudsman's foot' (Lightman, quoted in Nobles, 2003: 781). In this context commentators have noted the equitable and variable nature of decision making in small claims proceedings in the County Court. How different are the standards applied in the small claims procedure to those applied by the ombudsman?

The judgment in *Norwich* shows deference to the norms developed within the ombudsman system, and Richard Nobles argues that 'when decisions about fairness need to be made in the context of complex and specialist activities such as are dealt with in this case, constructing those principles is better left by the courts to ombudsman, who have a closer relationship with, and better knowledge of, the industry in question'.

Nobles is critical of the approach of the court's treatment of the code as 'a collection of rules rather than a series of examples illustrating a general principle of unfairness' (Nobles, 2003: 781 at 785). The code does state that 'subscribers should ensure that they abide by the spirit, as encompassed by the key commitments, as well as the letter of the code'. You should compare the approach of the court in this case to codes with that in the case of The Officers' Club (see above Chapter 6 at 4.7)

In *Heather Moor & Edgecomb Ltd* [2008] EWCA Civ 642 an investment advisor sought judicial review of the decision of the ombudsman on the basis that the decision contravened Article 6 and Article 1 of protocol 1 of the European Convention on Human Rights . The ombudsman had decided that the advisor had contravened good industry practice. The appellant had argued that the ombudsman was bound to determine complaints solely based on the law and that the scope for subjectivity in Financial Ombudsman Service decisions was such as to make them unpredictable and arbitrary. These arguments were rejected by the Administrative Court and the Court of Appeal. In the Court of Appeal Stanley Burnton J observed:

> 45. A statutory provision is only incompatible with a Convention right if and to the extent that it necessarily involves infringing that right. It is not suggested that the ombudsman is not an independent and impartial tribunal. The scheme does not preclude the ombudsman from hearing cases in public, or from pronouncing his decision in public: whether and to what extent he may decide not to do so I consider below. And so the only question is whether the ombudsman scheme satisfies the requirements of the Convention as to the law to be applied to a dispute and as to the fairness of the applicable procedure.

He then referred to the criteria of accessibility and precision set down in *Sunday Times v United Kingdom* (1979–80) 2 EHRR 245, and continued:

> 47. Does the scheme established under the 2000 Act, interpreted in accordance with its natural meaning, comply with these requirements? In my judgment, it can and does. The Ombudsman is required by DISP 3.8.1 to take into account the relevant law, regulations, regulators' rules and guidance and standards, relevant codes of practice and, where appropriate, what he considers to have been good industry practice at the relevant time. He is free to depart from the relevant law, but if he does so he should say so in his decision and explain why. The other matters referred to in this rule are matters that a court would take into account in determining whether a professional financial adviser had been guilty of negligence or breach of his contract with his client. Again, if the Ombudsman is to find an advisor liable to his client notwithstanding his compliance with all those matters, the Ombudsman would have to so state in his decision and explain why, in such circumstances, assuming it to be possible, he came to the conclusion that it was fair and reasonable to hold the adviser liable. In these circumstances, I consider that the rules applied by the Ombudsman are sufficiently predictable. All the matters listed in DISP 3.8.1 are formulated or ascertainable with sufficient precision. So far as guiding the conduct of financial advisers are concerned, provided that they comply with 'the relevant law, regulations, regulators' rules and guidance and standards, relevant codes of practice and, where appropriate, … good industry practice', they can be assured that they will not be liable to their client in the absence of some exceptional factor requiring a different decision. Lastly, the common law requires consistency: that like cases are treated alike. Arbitrariness on the part of the Ombudsman, including an unreasoned and unjustified failure to treat like cases alike, would be a ground for judicial review.

Rix J agreed with Burnton J, adding some comments on the rule of law and publicity:

> 90. Finally, I would like to say something about the matter of the FOS 'register'. This has been the subject of written submissions, but has not figured in oral argument, no doubt because the parties appreciated that it would not affect the outcome of this appeal. Nevertheless, it remains the case that the Act's Schedule 17, at para 16, in providing for the enforcement of

an Ombudsman's money award in the county courts of England and Wales and by similar means in Northern Ireland and Scotland speaks of such an award 'which has been registered in accordance with scheme rules'. Thus it is a statutory requirement that the scheme rules provide for the registration of money awards. Accordingly, DISP 3.9.15 R requires the Ombudsman to keep a register: 'The Ombudsman must maintain a register of each money award and direction made.' In referring to directions, the scheme rules go beyond the statute. FOS seeks to comply with its rule by keeping an internal data base. It is not available to public inspection. I have my doubts as to whether such an internal data base amounts to a 'register' properly so called. A register is an official list or record. It may be that it can be kept in any form, but I suspect that it needs to be open to public inspection. Since we have not heard oral argument on this matter, I merely refer to this point in passing.

An application was made to the European Court of Human Rights.

Heather Moor & Edgecomb Ltd v United Kingdom Application (2011) ECHR 1019

Admissibility decision

The applicant argued that the procedure followed by FOS in dealing with the complaint against it was contrary to art.6 of the Convention since: (i) FOS was neither independent nor impartial; (ii) it refused to hold a hearing; (iii) it failed to deliver its decision publicly; and (iv) it did not take decisions based on law, which was also contrary to art 1 of Protocol No 1.

(i) *The complaint of lack of independence and impartiality*

35 The Court notes from the judgment of Stanley Burnton LJ that the applicant did not raise this complaint before the Court of Appeal. Domestic remedies have therefore not been exhausted in this respect. Consequently, this part of the application must be rejected in accordance with art 35 § 1 and 4 of the Convention.

(ii) *The complaint about the lack of an oral hearing*

(b) The Court's assessment

The parties accepted that art 6, under its civil head, is applicable to the facts of this case. The Court agrees. In deciding the complaint against the applicant and ordering it to pay compensation to L, the Ombudsman determined the applicant's civil rights and obligations. The procedure must therefore conform to the standards set down in art 6.

According to the Court's well-established case law, an oral and public hearing constitutes a fundamental principle enshrined in art 6(1). As the Court recognised in that and other cases, however, the holding of a hearing is not an absolute obligation. There may be proceedings in which it is not required, where the courts, or other deciding authority, may fairly and reasonably decide the case on the basis of the parties' written submissions and other written materials. Considerations of efficiency and economy may also be relevant in certain contexts, one example being social security law. The present context is of protection for consumers in the domain of financial services and investment advice. Parliament's intention, clearly stated in the legislation, was to provide for the resolution of certain disputes quickly and with minimum formality. It notes in this respect the very high number of disputes that FOS deals with annually, which the Government put at 150,000. The Court does not find such a legislative policy inappropriate. It notes, moreover, that the existence of FOS does not preclude access to the courts; the complainant may reject an Ombudsman's decision and take legal proceedings instead against a firm, while it is open to a firm to seek judicial review of an Ombudsman's decision in a particular case. In the present case, this led to oral argument in the Court of Appeal over three days, and resulted in a lengthy judgment that considered, inter alia, whether the circumstances of this case called for an oral hearing before the Ombudsman.

The applicant has alleged that FOS operates a policy of not holding hearings. The Court considers that the general practice of FOS, whatever it may be, is beyond the scope of this application, which must be decided on its particular facts. It notes from the rules governing the complaints procedure that it is open to the parties to a complaint to seek a hearing, and that the Ombudsman considers any such request in the light of the Convention. That is what in fact happened in the present case. HME's request was initially considered by an adjudicator and then by two ombudsmen at different stages of the procedure. Each of these gave reasons why they considered a hearing unnecessary. Their view was endorsed by the Court of Appeal. At each stage the view was taken that the contemporaneous written evidence provided a sufficient factual basis for determining the complaint, there being no contradiction in it. Before this Court the applicant has sought to question the whole approach that was taken by the Ombudsman, whose findings of fact were subsequently accepted by the Court of Appeal. The Court recalls that it is not its function to deal with errors of fact or law allegedly committed by a national court, or other competent authority, unless and insofar as they may have infringed rights and freedoms protected by the Convention. Moreover, while art 6 of the Convention guarantees the right to a fair hearing, it does not lay down any rules on the admissibility of evidence or the way it should be assessed, which are therefore primarily matters for regulation by national law and the national courts .

As the Court has indicated previously, the key consideration is the overarching principle of fairness embodied in article 6. The fact that proceedings are of considerable significance for an applicant, as is the case here, is not decisive for the necessity of a hearing. The applicant was afforded ample opportunities to present its case and to know and respond to the arguments put forward by L, and to make final representations on the basis of the Ombudsman's provisional decision. The Court therefore accepts the Government's argument that the relevant issues of fact and law could be adequately addressed in, and decided on the basis of, written submissions. It finds that the requirements of fairness were complied with and did not necessitate an oral hearing before the Ombudsman.

The Court would observe, moreover, that contrary to the applicant's criticisms about the scope of judicial review in this case, in its judgment the Court of Appeal did in fact consider on their merits each of the grounds raised by HME without ever having to decline jurisdiction in replying to them (see *Zumtobel v Austria*, 21 September 1993). This can only reinforce the Court's conclusion that the absence of an oral hearing before the Ombudsman was not contrary to art.6 of the Convention. This complaint is therefore manifestly ill-founded and must be rejected in accordance with art 35 § 3 and 4 of the Convention.

(iii) *The complaint about the non-publication of the Ombudsman's decision*

The Court recalls that the publicity of legal proceedings, which renders the administration of justice visible, contributes to the achievement of the aim of art 6(1), namely a fair trial (see *Ryakib Biryukov v Russia* ECHR 2008, with further references). With respect to the requirement of the public pronouncement of judgments, the Court has held that in each case the form of publicity must be assessed in the light of the special features of the proceedings in question, having regard to their entirety, and by reference to the object and purpose of art 6 § 1. The Court observes that, in contrast to certain types of case such as those involving children (eg *KS v United Kingdom* (45035/98) September 25, 2001), there was no compelling reason to withhold the Ombudsman's decision from publication. The considerations of quickness and informality that are relevant to the holding of an oral hearing are not relevant to the public pronouncement of 'judgment'. However, looking at the domestic proceedings in this case in their entirety, the Court cannot but agree with Stanley Burnton LJ that the Court of Appeal's judgment on the case, which quoted at length from the Ombudsman's final decision, achieved the purpose of art 6(1). Consequently, the Court finds that this complaint too is manifestly ill-founded and must be rejected in accordance with art 35(3) and (4) of the Convention.

(iv) *The complaint about the legal basis of the Ombudsman's decision*

The Court's assessment

As noted above, Stanley Burnton LJ found that the applicable statutory provisions (s 228 and DISP 3.8.1) conveyed the clear intention of Parliament that the Ombudsman's decision was not limited to the rules of common law, but allow for a subjective appraisal of what is "fair and reasonable in all of the circumstances of the case". He observed that the many guiding factors set out in DISP 3.8.1(2) were matters that a court would take into account in the context of an action in negligence or breach on contract, ie were typical legal considerations. The Court considers that the scope of the Ombudsman's discretion is not so broad as to automatically contravene the principle of foreseeability that is an integral part of the rule of law. Moreover, as can be seen from the lengthy extracts set out in the judgment of the Court of Appeal, the Ombudsman explained in detail the basis for upholding the complaint against the applicant. While the applicant has challenged the findings made against it, the Court detects no sign of any arbitrariness in the decision of the Ombudsman. It has already found that the procedure conducted by the Ombudsman provided sufficient opportunity to the applicant to know the details of L's complaint and to respond to it. It was also enabled to respond in detail to the provisional decision of the Ombudsman. It cannot therefore be said that the final decision or the manner in which the Ombudsman dealt with the complaint were unforeseeable. In sum, the Court is persuaded by the reasoning on this point of Stanley Burnton LJ (at para 47 of the Court of Appeal judgment, see above). The applicant's complaint in this respect is manifestly ill-founded and therefore inadmissible under art 35 § 3 and 4 of the Convention.

For these reasons, the Court, by a majority, declares the application inadmissible.

Although the *Heather* case upheld the approach of the Financial Ombudsman Service, the 2012 amendments to the FSMA impose a duty on the Financial Ombudsman Service to publish a report of any determination made by an ombudsman unless in the ombudsman's opinion it is deemed inappropriate (section 230A FSMA) The Financial Ombudsman Service has now developed proposals for greater publication of its decisions. The complainant would not be identified in the public document. Which groups will benefit from this increased legalisation of the ombudsman procedure?

The *Norwich* case recognises that decisions by the financial ombudsman service may have broad implications and that there is an implicit regulatory role in these decisions. The Financial Ombudsman Service and FSA have drawn up protocols for addressing cases 'with wider implications'. These may involve consultations with expert groups.

Disp 3.5.5: The Ombudsman may, where he considers it appropriate, take into account evidence from third parties; including, but not limited to, the FSA, other regulators, experts in industry matters and experts in consumer matters.

The wider-implications process was reviewed in 2010 when it was suggested that such a case was:

... whether it involves (or is likely to involve):

- a number of firms;

- 5,000 or more complaints referred (or likely to be referred) to the ombudsman service; and
- the underlying cause of complaints is very similar.

Amendments to the Financial Services and Markets Act in 2010 conferred power under section 404 for the FSA to require firms to establish a consumer redress scheme where there 'may have been widespread or regular failure by relevant firms to comply with requirements', and consumers have suffered or may suffer loss or damage recoverable in legal proceedings. The FSA did not act under this power in establishing the consumer redress scheme for PPI (see DISP App 3.3 Handling of Payment Protection Insurance)

> DISP 1.3.3R requires the firm to put in place appropriate management controls and take reasonable steps to ensure that in handling complaints it identifies and remedies any recurring or systemic problems. If a firm receives complaints about its sales of payment protection contracts it should analyse the root causes of those complaints including, but not limited to, the consideration of:
>
> (1) the concerns raised by complainants (both at the time of the sale and subsequently);
>
> (2) the reasons for both rejected claims and complaints;
>
> (3) the firm's stated sales practice(s) at the relevant time(s);
>
> (4) evidence available to the firm about the actual sales practice(s) at the relevant time(s) (this might include recollections of staff and complainants, compliance records, and other material produced at the time about specific transactions, for example call recordings and incentives given to advisers);
>
> (5) relevant regulatory findings; and
>
> (6) relevant decisions by the Financial Ombudsman Service.
>
> Where consideration of the root causes of complaints suggests recurring or systemic problems in the firm's sales practices for payment protection contracts, the firm should, in assessing an individual complaint, consider whether the problems were likely to have contributed to a breach or failing in the individual case, even if those problems were not referred to specifically by the complainant.
>
> Where a firm identifies (from its complaints or otherwise) recurring or systemic problems in its sales practices for a particular type of payment protection contract, either for its sales in general or for those from a particular location or sales channel, it should (in accordance with Principle 6 (Customers' interests) and to the extent that it applies), consider whether it ought to act with regard to the position of customers who may have suffered detriment from, or been potentially disadvantaged by such problems but who have not complained and, if so, take appropriate and proportionate measures to ensure that those customers are given appropriate redress or a proper opportunity to obtain it. In particular, the firm should:
>
> (1) ascertain the scope and severity of the consumer detriment that might have arisen; and
>
> (2) consider whether it is fair and reasonable for the firm to undertake proactively a redress or remediation exercise, which may include contacting customers who have not complained.

The introduction of an ombudsman recognises that private power, like public power, can often be a source of maladministration and injustice and should be subject to accountability: mechanisms such as the market (exit) and the courts may not be adequate or appropriate when an individual faces a large bureaucracy. The Financial

Ombudsman Service may therefore achieve the goals of dispute settlement, compensation, and behaviour modification as well as developing a dialogue on norms within the financial services industry. It is probably misleading to describe it as alternative dispute resolution since, given the difficulties that an individual faces in suing a large financial institution, ombudsmen are often the only option for the consumer.

12. Over-indebtedness and regulation of credit default

Since the late 1960s, there has been a growing body of empirical literature on the phenomenon of credit breakdown and debt default. The earliest, and best-known, US works are *The Poor Pay More* (1969) and *Consumers in Trouble: A Study of Debtors in Default* (1974) by David Caplovitz. In the latter, Caplovitz provided detailed evidence of what he termed the new social problem of 'debt entanglement' in the United States. Debtors in default were generally drawn from the lower-middle range of income, were in the early stages of the family lifecycle and were more prone than other debtors to occupational instability and unemployment. The major cause of default was loss of income through unemployment. He also found that creditors who made significant use of the courts and harsh collection measures were also most likely to use high-pressure and deceptive sales techniques. These findings are important in drawing attention to the influence of creditors' remedies on the perimeters of consumer credit and on integrity in marketing (Ison, 1979: ch 10). There is evidence that a minority of those individuals who were sued for debt refused to pay because they felt they had been cheated (Caplovitz, 1974; Ison, 1979; Ramsay, 1986; Civil Justice Review, 1988: 111).

Empirical studies of credit breakdown in the United Kingdom since the late 1970s suggest a similar profile of the default debtor to that drawn by Caplovitz. In 1980 Adler and Wozniak studied individuals subject to formal debt-collection procedures in Scotland. The typical consumer goods debtor was a 'young married person or single parent aged between 30 and 40 with two or more dependent children and employed in a manual occupation'. The reasons for default were similar to Caplovitz's study with loss of income the primary reason (Adler and Wozniak, 1980: table 7).

The Civil Justice Review in 1988 found that nearly 40 per cent of debtors in the county courts were unemployed at the start of the proceedings (Civil Justice Review, 1988: para 590). In 1989 the OFT concluded that unemployment was the major source of over-indebtedness and that problems with debt were a function of social class and income with much higher levels among lower-income working-class consumers (OFT, 1989). Richard Berthoud and Elaine Kempson found in 1992 that chronic debt troubles were not a consequence of consumerism defined as consumer overspending but rather the situation where limited income made it difficult for families to make ends meet (see Berthoud and Kempson, 1992). In 2002 Kempson compared the findings from this earlier study with contemporary reasons for over-indebtedness:

Table 2. UK reasons for financial difficulties (% of households, primary reason)

	1989	2002
Loss of income	26	45
—redundancy	-	19
—relationship breakdown	-	5
—sickness or disability	-	7
—other loss of income	-	14
Other change of circumstances	7	-
— Insufficient (1989) low (2002) Income	25	14
Overcommitment	21	10
Increased/unexpected expenses	10	12
Overlooked or withheld payment	12	8
Third-party error	–	5
Debts left by former partner	–	4
Other reasons	12	3

Source: 1989 Figures quoted in Berthoud and Kempson, 1992; Kempson, 2002.

Default debtors appear generally to be 'unfortunate' rather than 'inadequate' or 'amoral calculators' (Adler and Wozniak, 1980). The significance of loss of income and unemployment as a primary reason for default has been highlighted by many studies (Adler and Wozniak, 1980; Hoerman, 1986; Sullivan, Warren & Westbrook, 2000; Niemi, Ramsay and Whitford, 2003, 2009). More recent small-scale studies (Elliott, 2005) suggest that financial mismanagement was a cause of debtors misfortunes and that individuals continued to borrow even after a change in life circumstances. Data from the Insolvency Service (2008) indicate that the ambiguous category of 'living beyond means' may be a significant reason for insolvency (see Table 3).

Table 3. Insolvency Service, England and Wales (2008), study of reasons for individual bankruptcy 2006–07 as recorded by Official Receiver

Living beyond means	30%
Unplanned change of circumstance[a]	43%
Business failure	16%

[a]This includes '"life events", such as illness, an accident or a relationship breakdown, and the loss or reduction of income (either of the bankrupt or his/her household)'.

Over-indebtedness may be associated with lost productivity, family breakdown and financial exclusion. Nigel Balmer, Pascoe Pleasence, Alexy Buck and Heather Walker recently examined the relationship between debt and health (2005: 48):

Associations have been found between debt and various aspects of ill-health. For example, studies have shown a relationship between debt and maternal depression among lone parents and credit card debt and ill health. There is also evidence of increased anxiety as the ratio of credit card debt to income increases. Moreover, analysis of the British Household Panel Survey has suggested that mortgage indebtedness not only adversely impacts on health, but also increases the likelihood that men will visit general practitioners, with the stress caused by mortgage arrears and repossession highlighted elsewhere as a major health issue. Similarly, in a recent study of those seeking debt advice from Citizens Advice Bureaux, 62 per cent of respondents reported that their problem led to stress, anxiety or depression. Twenty seven per cent said they had consequently sought treatment or counselling from a general practitioner (although half of these had received prior treatment; the debt problem having then compounded their situation). (Balmer et al, 2005: 48)

This study found that debt overlapped with other problems such as relationship break-down, domestic violence and personal injury. Age (25–34) and long-term illness or disability were significant predictors of long-term debt. Balmer et al concluded that the 'frequent occurrence of debt problems alongside other civil justice problems, and the association of debt problems with social problems such as unemployment, sug-gests the importance of dealing with problems together rather than in isolation'.

Given behavioural tendencies, such as status quo bias, there may be a tendency to continue to use credit and credit cards to maintain a lifestyle until it is 'too late'. A major challenge for policy is to attempt early intervention or encourage an indi-vidual to take action before they are over-indebted (see below).

In a qualitative study of debtors and creditors in 2003, entitled *Can't Pay or Won't Pay*, Nicola Dominy and Elaine Kempson concluded that the great majority of people who fall into arrears with credit or household commitments have every inten-tion to pay on time, but simply lack the money to do so. Only a minority of people might be considered as 'won't pay'. The archetypal 'can't pay' fall into three catego-ries: people on low income who face unexpected expenditure; people who have had a substantial fall in income, leaving them unable to meet all their commitments; and people with mental health problems.

12.1 Creditors' remedies and consumer protection

The recovery of 'delinquent' debts is a complex process which ranges from the polite reminder notice to the devastation of bankruptcy proceedings. There is a high level of attrition at each stage of the collection process. Creditors may use the threat of the formal remedy system, therefore, as a means of persuading debtors to enter into a voluntary settlement or they may abandon collection attempts. In addition, since debt recovery is an integral part of the larger economic system of credit and market behaviour it cannot be viewed in isolation from the credit market. An enforcement system that does not protect debtors' rights may result in an over-extension of credit or create incentives for irresponsible or fraudulent marketing. An effective credit-reporting system may be a more certain and effective sanction against non-payment than enforce-ment through the courts, but may be abused as in *OFT v Ashbourne Investments*.

The rules and procedures governing the formal and informal collection of debts have been subject to criticism from all sides. Creditors view many of the procedures as ineffective, drawing attention, for example, to the low recovery rate through the warrant of execution procedure in the county courts (see eg Baldwin, 2003). Other critics have highlighted the unnecessarily harsh effects of remedies upon debtors and their depend-ants, pointing out that many debtors are unable rather than unwilling to repay their debts. The modernisation of the system of formal procedures of debt enforcement has been a government priority (see eg Department of Constitutional Affairs, 2003).

The Crowther Committee justified its proposals for restrictions on the enforce-ment of security and default remedies, in terms primarily of loss distribution. In its view, creditors are generally in a better position than consumers to assess the risks and bear the costs of default. They can spread these costs among all debtors through a small increase in price.

12.2 The regulation of default

An important object of the regulation of default should be the promotion of fair settlements between creditor and debtor, preferably at an early stage after default. In a typical case, a debtor may be at a disadvantage on default. Unless she is a repeat defaulter, she is unlikely to be knowledgeable about her rights or choices. While she has the power to refuse to respond to creditor action, in the long run this may result in extra financial and psychological costs. The DTI, in its 'Over-indebtedness Action Plan' (DTI, 2004: 36) indicates that the government aims to 'ensure that where possible, debt problems and disputes can be resolved without the stress and additional expense of court proceedings (to borrowers, lenders and society as a whole). The courts should only be used in the last resort'.

12.2.1 The growth of the UK over-indebtedness industry

Free money advice centres developed in the early 1970s in England when legal advice workers recognised that their clients increasingly required financial advice, which was 'time-consuming and required expertise not necessarily associated with lawyers'. An influential model of free independent money advice was developed by the Birmingham settlement money advice centre. This model uses specialist lay advisers to advise debtors, represent them in court and negotiate with creditors on their behalf. The adviser will attempt to maximise the income and benefits of the client, address priority debts (such as mortgage and fuel arrears) and then deal with consumer credit obligations. This is sometimes described as a holistic approach to debt problems.

This model of debt advice is adopted by Citizens Advice. Consumer debt problems are the second largest area of problems dealt with by Citizens Advice Bureaux with 1.1 million new consumer and debt problems in 2004–05. In a survey of their debt clients in 2006 they noted:

> Nearly two in five households in this survey depended entirely on benefit income. The average total household debt was £13,153, an increase of approximately 30 per cent between 2003 and 2006. On average, debts were 17.5 times the client's total monthly household income. This is a significant increase from 2001 when average debts were 14 times a client's average total monthly household income. Half of the clients in the survey had less than £20 per month to offer to all of their creditors, and over half of those had nothing to offer creditors at all.

> On average it would take CAB debt clients who were able to make a repayment to their nonpriority creditors 77 years to repay the debts at the amount offered. Only 10 per cent had a positive balance in a bank or building society account and the average amount held was only £404. Forty four per cent had other assets, such as a vehicle, their home or a life insurance policy. However, in many cases the value of these assets may not be realisable. Twenty three per cent of CAB debt clients in this survey had a disability or long-term illness. (Citizens Advice, 2006: 1–2)

Given the inability of this group to make realistic repayments, Citizens Advice argued that many of these clients would benefit from the proposed Debt Relief Order (see below). Citizens Advice Bureaux are a primary source of legal advice on debt problems for many lower-income consumers. Reviews comparing the performance of lawyers and non-lawyer debt advice agencies such as Citizens Advice found that 'it was non-lawyers who were operating at the higher levels of quality in social welfare law (debt, welfare benefits, and employment in particular)' (Moorhead et al, 2003: 765, 796). There was also a difference in style between lawyers and debt advice agencies. In debt matters, 'non-lawyers adopt a more holistic, less court centred approach, and … may be avoiding litigation-based strategies'. Debt advice agencies are more likely than lawyers to address the possibility of rescheduling all debts rather than limiting advice to debts that might be challenged in court. Lawyers were far more likely than advice agencies to challenge the validity of debts (see Moorehead, 2003: 796).

Iain Ramsay, A Tale of Two Debtors: Responding to the Shock of Over-indebtedness in France and England—A Story from the Trente Piteuses (2012) 75 *MLR* 212 at 246

A central difference between France and England is the role of the private over-indebtedness industry in England and Wales which includes 'one-stop shops' offering a range of debt repayment options and international debt-buying companies to whom creditors sell their debts. … From the mid 1990s creditor-financed and for-profit debt management companies grew. The growth of this industry can be measured by the fact that a major study of debt advice in 1995 hardly discusses private debt management services, although recognising a large unmet need for debt advice, perhaps reaching one million people. By 2009 there were approximately 150 fee-charging debt management companies although the market is dominated by a few 'one stop shops'. These private intermediaries play an important role in sorting and processing debtors. Given their profit making status there is the danger of inappropriate steering or refusal to treat debtors who do not offer significant profit. Some individuals may fail to obtain any relief either from the private or public sector. Widespread malpractices in this industry were identified by the OFT, resulting in both regulatory action and new regulatory proposals. The pressure on public costs suggests that the private sector will continue to play a significant role in the treatment of over-indebtedness.

House of Commons Business, Innovation and Skills Committee, Debt Management, Fourteenth Report of Session 2010–12

96. According to the Government there are in excess of a million consumers each year seeking advice on how best to deal with the financial difficulties they face. These consumers access that advice through a wide variety of providers but two distinct approaches are available, the free to client debt advice and paid-for debt management:

Free to client debt advice

i. Charities: for example the Money Advice Trust (MAT) which runs the National Debtline, and Citizens Advice (and their local bureaux). Some of these charities receive central government and/or local authority funding. For example MAT operates a funding model in which a tenth of its income is 'self-generated' and the remainder is funded 70% by private sector voluntary contributions and 30% by central government contributions. Funding ratios vary significantly across organisations; some charities, particularly local ones, may receive a majority of their funding from government via their local authority. Charities which operate this model tend to provide holistic debt advice, and often very detailed support to individuals, for example by explaining options, ways of negotiating with creditors, writing letters to creditors, helping clients create personal budgets) but they do not provide formal debt management plans or individual voluntary arrangements (IVAs).

ii. Direct government advice: from the housing or welfare department of a local authority.

iii. Fair share advice: this model is operated by Consumer Credit Counselling Service (CCCS) and Payplan. They provide debt management plans, individual voluntary arrangements (IVAs) and other formal debt solutions to individuals. These plans, and the associated debt advice, is free to the individual at every stage. Funding is received from creditors on a pro-rata basis according to the amount of debt repaid through these formal plans.

Paid-for debt management

iv. Commercial debt management companies: provide formal debt management solutions such as debt management plans and individual voluntary arrangements (IVAs). They charge their clients through upfront fees and ongoing management charges. Such companies include Gregory Pennington, MoneyPlus Group, Debt Advisory Line, ClearDebt and Baines & Ernst. It is this form of debt advice that is of particular concern to us. ...

... While the provision of debt advice can have a positive influence on individuals, commercial debt management companies are categorised by the Office of Fair Trading (OFT) as one of the 'high risk' industries it regulates. This is because debt management services are a 'distress' purchase; consumers seeking debt management help tend to be over-indebted, vulnerable and desperate for help. Research by the Money Advice Trust has shown that consumers do not shop around for debt management services. Consumers are potentially committing themselves to a debt solution which can affect their lives for years. The risks if things go wrong can be significant, potentially leaving consumers in a worse financial position, which in some cases can include the loss of the consumers' home.

... It was estimated in a review of the sector by the OFT that commercial debt management companies (DMCs) make £250 million a year from over-indebted clients. Following our call for evidence on consumer credit and debt management we received many submissions criticising DMCs. Which? accused the industry of 'mis-selling, cold- calling, mis-leading advertisements and inflated claims'.

The OFT has published new guidance on debt management practices and the industry has developed a code of practice.

Regulation of informal debt collection includes: information provision; licensing by the OFT; CPUT regulations on unfair, misleading and aggressive debt-collection practices (provided they lead to an individual taking a transactional decision to his detriment); unfair credit relationships; common law of defamation: the Protection of Harassment Act 1997; and treating customers fairly. Individuals might complain to the Financial Ombudsman Service about debt collection practices.

The OFT has published guidance on debt-collection practices. The debt collection guidance is 'not designed to be a comprehensive checklist of behaviour ... [it] outlines unfair practices with illustrative examples'. Categories of unfair collection practices include communicating with consumers in an unclear, inaccurate or misleading manner (eg through the use of official looking documents likely to mislead debtors as to their status), falsely implying or claiming authority (eg claiming to work on instructions from the courts), or misrepresenting the status of the collector, suggesting falsely that the collector has government backing. Others include contacting debtors at unreasonable times and at unreasonable intervals, ignoring or disregarding claims that the debts have been settled or disputed and continuing to make unjustified demands for payment, visiting debtors at inappropriate locations such as work or hospital and claiming collection costs from a debtor in the absence of express contractual authority. The OFT has also indicated that credit companies that 'do business or continue to do business with third parties engaged in questionable fitness behaviour' will have their fitness called into question. This is important because one reason for companies subcontracting debt collection is to externalise spite, ie aggressive actions are taken by a third party that will not sully the reputation of the credit grantor since the consumer will direct their annoyance, upset or anger at the third party rather than the credit grantor (OFT, *Debt Collection Guidance Response to the Consultation Paper and Final Guidance on Unfair Business Practices*, July 2003, updated October 2011).

The OFT has used its licensing powers to impose conditions on debt-collection agencies.

OFT imposes requirements on 1st Credit over debt collection practices

25 February 2009

The OFT has taken action against 1st Credit Ltd requiring the company to improve its debt collection practices.

The OFT has imposed 'requirements' on 1st Credit using consumer credit powers, after an investigation found that some of its business processes and procedures failed to meet satisfactory standards. As a result, 1st Credit Ltd and its associated companies must:

- refrain from issuing statutory demands warning of bankruptcy where it is unlikely that proceedings will be initiated

- not discuss legal action with consumers unless it is likely that such action will be taken

- ensure that sensitive cases involving vulnerable individuals, for example those with mental health or medical problems, are dealt with appropriately, and

- ensure that all matters of concern raised with them by the free advice sector and other third parties are dealt with appropriately.

- 1st Credit must also report back to the OFT every six months providing statistics regarding the number of enforcement actions it has taken against debtors.

Failure to comply with the requirements could lead to a fine of up to £50,000 for each occurence and/or possible revocation of 1st Credit's consumer credit licence.

Reforms to the Consumer Credit Act in 2006 promote early intervention in cases of over-indebtedness. Extensive disclosure obligations on creditors exist in relation to arrears, on default, and concerning the ability of a creditor to recover interest after judgment. The Act now requires a creditor to send a debtor a notice of sums in arrears (see section 86C) where, for example, a debtor is at least two payments in arrears on a running account agreement such as a credit card. An arrears information sheet must be provided by the lender to the debtor. The general purpose of these provisions is to facilitate the possibility of a debtor and creditor working out an agreement on their own or with the assistance of a Citizens Advice Bureau, lawyer or credit counselling agency.

A debtor might also make an application to court to obtain a time order (section 129) to reschedule payments (see below 11.2.1) in response to an arrears notice. An arrears notice must communicate this option to a debtor.

Creditors must provide debtors with notices before they terminate an agreement or recover possession of any goods or enforce any security (see sections 76, 87, 88). Section 87 applies where there has been a breach of the agreement by the debtor or hirer. Under the 2006 amendments section 87 provides the debtor with 14 rather than the current 7 days to cure the breach. A default notice must be strictly complied with otherwise it is invalid. There is, however, no private remedy under the Consumer Credit Act 1974 for failure by the creditor to follow section 87 and any remedy would be based on a common law cause of action such as conversion or wrongful taking of possession. There is a good argument here for a minimum damage provision for breach of the section.

The effectiveness of the notices above may depend on the extent to which they counter debtor inertia in response to a formal notice. Behavioural analysis suggests that notices should point out the dangers of inaction while also holding out the positive benefits of contacting a third party.

Many jurisdictions regulate default charges, which can add large amounts to a debt. The Consumer Credit Act 1974 stipulates that default interest may not exceed the contract rate (section 93). Section 86(e) now regulates 'default sums' which includes any sums other then interest that are payable on breach but not including accrued arrears. A creditor must provide the debtor with notice of the default sums and may only charge simple interest on the sum.

Debt collection practices may be sanctioned under the CPUT regulations. The following case provides an example of persistent aggressive collection practices.

Ferguson v British Gas [2009] EWCA Civ 46 (Court of Appeal)

1. It is one of the glories of this country that every now and then one of its citizens is prepared to take a stand against the big battalions of government or industry. Such a person is Lisa Ferguson, the claimant in this case. Because she funds the claim out of her personal resources, she does so at considerable risk: were she ultimately to lose she would probably have to pay British Gas's considerable costs. I call the defendant 'British Gas', its full name being 'British Gas Trading Limited.'

2. Ms Ferguson used to be a customer of British Gas. She says she ceased to be so on 25th May 2006, on the same day becoming a customer of nPower. In her Particulars of Claim she sets out what she says British Gas did to her thereafter. Because the detail is lengthy I set out the relevant part of the Particulars in full in the Annex to this judgment rather than burden the reader with it here.

3. To summarise, starting on 21st August 2006 and continuing until at least late January the next year, British Gas sent Ms Ferguson bill after bill and threatening letter after threatening letter. Nothing she could do would stop it. The threats were threefold in nature: those to cut off her gas supply, to start legal proceedings and, a matter most important to her as a businesswoman, to report her to credit rating agencies. She wrote letter after letter pointing out that she had no account with British Gas, she made phone calls (with all the difficulty of getting through), but to no avail. Mainly her letters received no response. Sometimes she received apologies and assurances that the matter would be dealt with. But then the bills and

threats continued. She complained to Energy Watch. She wrote to the Chairman of British Gas twice with no response. She says she wasted many hours, and, more importantly, was brought to a state of considerable anxiety, not knowing whether the gas man would come at any time to cut her off, whether she would have legal proceedings served upon her or whether she would be or had already been reported to a credit rating agency. Even when her solicitor wrote on her behalf about an unjustified bill of 18th January, no response was received.

4. Ms Ferguson claims that British Gas's course of conduct amounts to unlawful harassment contrary to the Protection from Harassment Act 1997. She claims £5,000 for distress and anxiety and £5,000 for financial loss due to time lost and expenses in dealing with British Gas. She is open about her reason for bringing these proceedings. It is mainly not to claim damages for herself—she says she will give a substantial proportion of any sum awarded to charity. Ms Ferguson's principal object is to bring British Gas to book. In her words they should 'not simply blame information technology. They should instead start taking responsibility for the running of their company in a competent, honest and ethical manner.'

5. British Gas says it has done nothing wrong; that it is perfectly all right for it to treat consumers in this way, at least if it is all just done by computer. It goes so far as to say that the claim is so weak that Ms Ferguson's Particulars of Claim disclose no reasonable ground for bringing it. So the claim should be struck out and not even allowed to go to trial.

…

The Gravity test

Mr Porter accepted that what British Gas did to Ms Ferguson amounted to 'a course of conduct.' But, he submitted, it was not enough even arguably to amount to 'harassment'. No reasonable court could so conclude and hence the claim was without reasonable foundation. …

1. I accept that a course of conduct must be grave before the offence or tort of harassment is proved. And that, as Mr Porter accepted after some discussion, the only real difference between the crime of s 2 and the tort of s 3 is standard of proof. To prove the civil wrong of harassment it is necessary to prove the case on a balance of probabilities, to prove the crime, the standard is the usual criminal one of beyond a reasonable doubt.

…

3. Having accepted Mr Porter's submission about the legal test requiring gravity, I apply it here. I am quite unable to conclude that the impugned conduct is incapable of satisfying the test. On the contrary I think, at the very least, that it is strongly arguable that it does. I ask myself whether a jury or bench of magistrates could reasonably conclude that the persistent and continued conduct here pleaded was on the wrong side of the line, as amounting to 'oppressive and unacceptable conduct'. I am bound to say that I think they could. And, in contrast to the Sunderland case, for instance, I would think it entirely proper for a prosecutor such as a Trading Standards Officer, to bring criminal proceedings in respect of a case where there has been such a period of persistent conduct and such threats as are pleaded here.

4. What British Gas was threatening was undoubtedly serious. Mr Porter sought to downgrade it by saying that Ms Ferguson knew the claims and threats were unjustified. That is absurd: a victim of harassment will almost always know that it is unjustified. The Act is there to protect people against unjustified harassment. Indeed if the impugned conduct is justified it is unlikely to amount to harassment at all.

5. Mr Porter also made the point that the correspondence was computer generated and so, for some reason which I do not really follow, Ms Ferguson should not have taken it as seriously as if it had come from an individual. But real people are responsible for programming and

entering material into the computer. It is British Gas's system which, at the very least, allowed the impugned conduct to happen.

6. Moreover the threats and demands were to be read by a real person, not by a computer. A real person is likely to suffer real anxiety and distress if threatened in the way which Ms Ferguson was. And a real person is unlikely to take comfort from knowing that the claims and threats are unjustified or that they were sent by a computer system: that will not necessarily allay the fear that the threats will not be carried out. How is a consumer such as Ms Ferguson to know whether or not, for instance, a threat such as 'we will tell a credit reference agency in the next 10 days that you have not paid' (letter of 2nd January) will not be carried out by the same computer system which sent the unjustified letter and all its predecessor bills and threats? After all no amount of writing and telephoning had stopped the system so far—at times it must have seemed like a monster machine out of control moving relentlessly forward—a million miles from the 'world class level of service' (letter of 9th January) which British Gas says it aims to offer.

... [I]t seems to me that all the Act requires of the victim is to identify the course of conduct and what passed between the victim and the alleged harasser. The court is then notionally to put knowledge of that and of any other relevant information into the mind of this reasonable person. The court then decides whether that person would consider that the course of conduct amounts to harassment. Mr Porter suggested that there might be what I would call a defence of incompetence or the right hand not knowing what the left hand was doing. I am doubtful as to this as a matter of construction of the statute. The 'reasonable person' is given the 'same information' which, as I say, seems to be of the entire course of conduct plus the victim's responses. It is the point of view of the victim in the light of these facts which the reasonable person is to consider. The perpetrator's private reasons or excuses or explanations for the conduct do not come into it.

Could the conduct in this case be sanctioned now under the Consumer Protection from Unfair Trading Regulations 2008? If the UCPD is a full harmonisation measure, can the Prevention of Harassment Act 1997 continue to be applicable to the topic of financial services? For further discussion see Osuji (2011).

12.2.2 Regulating the collection bureaucracy

FSA Final Notice GMAC–RFC (2009)

1. THE PENALTY

1.1. The FSA gave GMAC-RFC Limited ('GMAC'/'the firm') a Decision Notice on 26 October 2009 which notified the firm that pursuant to section 206 of the Financial Services and Markets Act 2000 ('the Act'), the FSA had decided to impose a financial penalty of £2.8 million on the firm. This penalty is imposed for breaches of Principle 3 (Management and control) and Principle 6 (Customers' interests) of the Principles for Businesses ('the Principles') and Rules 12.4.1 R and 13.3.1 R in the Mortgages and Home Finance: Conduct of Business sourcebook ('MCOB') in the period between 31 October 2004 and 30 November 2008 ('the Relevant Period').

...

1.3 GMAC will also carry out a customer redress programme with a view to providing redress to those customers who were charged specific excessive and unfair charges (i.e. charges that were not a reasonable estimate of the costs of the additional administration required as a result of the customer being in arrears) in respect of their mortgage account. The estimated cost of redress for the period 1 November 2004 to 31 August 2009 is up to £7.7 million, plus interest, for both regulated mortgage contracts and buy-to-let contracts.

2. REASONS FOR THE ACTION

2.1 The breaches of the Principles and MCOB Rules, which are described in more detail in section 4 below, relate to a number of serious and sustained failings by GMAC in its dealings with some of its customers in arrears or facing repossession, in relation to their mortgage with GMAC.

3. RELEVANT STATUTORY PROVISIONS AND GUIDANCE

3.5 Principle 6 provides that:

… A firm must pay due regard to the interests of its customers and treat them fairly.

3.6 MCOB 12.4.1R provides:

(1) A firm must ensure that any regulated mortgage contract that it enters into does not impose, and cannot be used to impose, a charge for arrears on a customer except where that charge is a reasonable estimate of the cost of the additional administration required as a result of the customer being in arrears.

3.7 MCOB 13.3.1R provides:

(1) A firm must deal fairly with any customer who: is in arrears on a regulated mortgage contract or home purchase plan; has a sale shortfall; or is otherwise in breach of a home purchase plan.

(2) A firm must put in place, and operate in accordance with, a written policy (agreed by its respective governing body) and procedures for complying with (1).

2 Arrears fee where there is a performing arrangement to pay ('ATP'). 5

4. FACTS AND MATTERS RELIED ON

4.1 … GMAC operated as a non-bank lender in the prime, sub-prime and buy-to-let mortgage sectors. GMAC reduced its loan originations from August 2007 and stopped all originations in May 2008; since then it has concentrated on the management of its loan book. It has around £3.9 billion of regulated mortgage contracts under its administration. During the Relevant Period, GMAC administered 188,543 regulated mortgage contracts with a total balance of approximately £24.6 billion.

4.2 GMAC was one of the firms that took part in the FSA's thematic work in connection with its Arrears Handling and Repossessions Thematic Review which started in 2008.

Mortgage account servicing

4.3 Field counsellors were engaged by GMAC to visit customers to discuss their mortgage arrears and to consider available options. GMAC regularly reviewed mortgage account servicing, but outcomes in arrears and repossessions focussed on quantitative measurements, such as the average number of days to get to court order, and did not provide any qualitative assessments of performance or TCF.

4.4 GMAC carried out a gap analysis of the training provided to mortgage servicing staff and noted that as at October 2008, the staff only received a limited amount of generic TCF training, which was not tailored to how mortgage servicing and arrears handling was carried out. Mortgage servicing staff were given limited guidance on how to implement TCF on a day to day basis in their work.

4.5 Not all new mortgage servicing staff within the arrears department were given sufficient information about the application of TCF and temporary staff did not attend any induction process and so were unaware of TCF initiatives. There was inadequate measurement of the mortgage servicing staff's TCF knowledge or on-going assessment through performance of the staff's application of TCF in arrears handling.

4.6 An FSA review of audits carried out by GMAC showed that few TCF and customer outcome measures were included or commented on in those audits. For example, there was no analysis of why 'Arrangements to Pay' ('ATPs') failed or why GMAC's applications within repossession proceedings had an average success rate of only 33.2%. As a result, there was insufficient management information to measure whether customers were being treated fairly.

4.7 GMAC commissioned a report on arrears policy, practices and procedures by an independent firm of management consultants who reported in draft in January 2009. The report observed that there was not a clear view of the end to end operations within mortgage servicing which prevented a complete understanding by GMAC of actual procedures, associated risks, required management information or staff capabilities in respect of its mortgage account servicing. This in turn generated a risk of weak compliance and governance. This was demonstrated by an issue raised earlier in September 2008 by GMAC's own audit, which identified the failure to consistently grant the proper authorisation to execute arrears amendment transactions.

Arrears handling

4.8 GMAC's Collections Policy applied to customers who were in arrears with their mortgage or who had incurred a mortgage shortfall debt. Mortgage servicing staff applied that policy with the assistance of guidance. However, the guidance concentrated on information provision and establishing the reason for arrears in dealings with customers rather than a consideration of all appropriate arrears rehabilitation tools.

4.9 Options available to GMAC included alterations to the payment date, repayment type, extension to the term of the mortgage, capitalisation of arrears or a switch to a different mortgage product. These were considered if requested by the customer, but would not be routinely offered as an option by GMAC. A review of training programmes for mortgage servicing staff indicated that, prior to changes introduced in November 2008, arrears resolution centred on collecting payments via an ATP, with insufficient assessment of the viability of the ATP or whether there were other options to resolve the arrears situation that would produce a better outcome for the customer.

3 An arrangement to pay is an agreement with the customer to effect a monthly payment over an agreed term in order to clear the customer's arrears.

4.10 The thematic review identified that some letters were sent to customers that were misleading or did not accurately reflect the status of the mortgage account. Insufficient control or monitoring of these letters meant that letters were sent to customers that:

(1) in one instance, quoted two different arrears amounts in the same letter;

(2) continued to threaten legal action where there had been a decision to suspend the application for repossession;

(3) when letters before action were issued, demanded full repayment of arrears where there was no evidence that this was a demand that the customer could meet; and

(4) explained the procedure for applying for a suspended possession order but did not explain the effect of an immediate order for possession. GMAC's practice was to apply for an order for possession suspended for a fixed period only if the customer agreed, prior to the hearing, to a repayment plan that was acceptable to GMAC. If no agreement was made, GMAC would apply for an immediate order for possession, but the effect and consequences of this were not explained clearly to the customer.

4.11 A review of GMAC's Collections Policy confirmed that staff were required to draw attention to the Citizens Advice Bureau National Debt Line, provide guidance on income maximisation and confirm that field counsellor visits were available and that those visits were to establish facts. However, the thematic review of file notes and call recordings did not demonstrate that this information was always being given to customers.

4.12 The Collections Policy in force in 2006 and 2007 was structured to focus on the collection of arrears payments, rather than reaching a flexible arrangement that took into account individual customer's circumstances. It instructed:

(1) 'where possible collect full payment of the arrears immediately, preferably by direct debit;

(2) if full payment is not possible, collect a part payment of the arrears;

(3) if no payment is immediately possible following point two above, obtain agreement to pay in instalments any arrears that might remain'.

4.13 Applications for immediate repossession orders were frequently made by GMAC without evidence that all other viable options had been considered and that repossession was being used only as a last resort.

4.14 GMAC's Collections Policy also required that each account that was two or more months in arrears was to be reviewed every 60 days. However, an internal audit review of 30 accounts in arrears demonstrated that 6 of those accounts were not reviewed in accordance with its own policy.

4.15 GMAC had management information which showed that an application by the customer to postpone or dismiss an eviction was often successful and GMAC was not always successful in securing the order it had applied for. However, prior to 2008, GMAC did not analyse or take further action in relation to that information.

Arrears charges

4.16 GMAC imposed certain charges related to activities carried out whilst the customer was in arrears, in circumstances that resulted in the unfair treatment of customers.

4.17 These unfair charges were:

(1) charges for non-payment of the monthly mortgage payment by direct debit, when the account was in arrears and no monthly payment was being made;

(2) calculation and imposition of the Early Repayment Charge on mortgage balances which included arrears fees and charges within that balance; and

(3) the proportion of the solicitors' instruction fee that exceeded the actual cost.

4.18 The above charges were unfair because they did not accurately reflect the additional administration work to the mortgage account caused by the fact that the customer was in arrears.

5. ANALYSIS OF BREACHES AND SANCTION

5.1 Principle 3 requires that a firm takes reasonable care to organise and control its affairs responsibly and effectively, with adequate risk management systems. In failing to ensure the mortgage servicing staff were given sufficient training in treating customers fairly and failing to obtain and use appropriate management information, GMAC failed to put in place adequate oversight of the mortgage servicing function and failed to properly consider and act on management information it obtained in relation to TCF and arrears handling.

5.2 This led to a risk that the firm's systems and controls were insufficient in relation to the handling and oversight of mortgage arrears to ensure the fair treatment of customers, and accordingly, the firm was in breach of Principle 3.

5.3 Principle 6 requires that a firm must pay due regard to the interests of its customers and treat them fairly. In doing so, firms should ensure that customers are treated fairly if they are in arrears with their mortgage by being flexible in considering a customer's individual circumstances to ensure that the firm uses court action for repossession of a customer's home only as a last resort.

5.4 In focussing mainly on the collection of payment of arrears rather than always considering what may be a more suitable arrangement based on the customer's circumstances and in issuing proceedings for repossession before all alternatives to repossession had been considered, the firm failed to pay due regard to the interests of some of its customers.

5.5 In addition, GMAC did not treat its customers fairly as a result of applying certain charges and fees to customers' accounts that were unfair as they did not accurately reflect the additional cost of administering an account in arrears in breach of MCOB 12.4.1R and 13.3.1 R.

5.6 This resulted in some customers incurring excessive and unfair charges (i.e. charges that were not a reasonable estimate of the costs of the additional administration required as a result of the customer being in arrears) and accruing additional costs that could have been avoided had GMAC adopted a more flexible and fairer approach to arrears management tailored to the customer's individual circumstances.

5.7 As a result of the above, GMAC failed to pay due regard to the interests of its customers and treat them fairly in breach of Principle 6.

5.8 When exercising its powers the FSA seeks to act in a way which it considers most appropriate for the purpose of meeting its regulatory objectives as set out in section 2(2) of the Act. The FSA considers that imposing a financial penalty in respect of the Firm meets the regulatory objectives of market confidence and protection of consumers.

Deterrence

5.11 In determining the appropriate sanction, the FSA has had regard to the seriousness of the contraventions, including the nature of the requirements breached, the number and duration of the breaches, and the number of customers who suffered financial loss.

5.12 The FSA considers GMAC's failings to be serious because:

(1) the failings persisted over a significant period of time and impacted a large number of customers some of whom already had an adverse credit status;

(2) a portion of GMAC's lending was to the sub-prime sector and arrears rates in this sector are higher than those in the rest of the mortgage market; and

(3) the FSA has published a considerable amount of material on the importance of regulated firms treating customers fairly ('TCF') to communicate to firms the FSA's expectations in relation to a firm's obligation in respect of TCF.

...The amount of benefit gained or loss avoided as a result of the breaches

Conduct following the breaches

5.17 GMAC implemented significant changes to its systems and controls and practices as detailed above and will implement a customer redress programme.

5.18 GMAC has been given full credit for co-operating with the FSA by agreeing a substantial customer contact and redress package detailed at para 1.3 above to ensure timely redress for consumers.

Disciplinary record and compliance history of the Firm

5.19 GMAC has not been the subject of previous disciplinary action.

6. CONCLUSION

6.1 Taking into account the seriousness of the breaches and the risks they posed to the FSA's statutory objectives of market confidence and the protection of consumers, the FSA has imposed a financial penalty of £2.8 million on the firm

12.3 Controls on repossession

Roy Goode argues that a characteristic of English commercial law is the facilitation of self-help by creditors and traditionally there were few controls on secured creditors' ability to repossess a security without a court order. However, in consumer law the unequal bargaining position of the consumer has led to significant controls on repossession by creditors. The contemporary provisions in the Consumer Credit Act 1974 are updated versions of the original 1938 provisions that responded to abusive practices in relation to hire-purchase transactions. Because the law conceptualised the hirer as having no property right or equity in the goods, the goods could be immediately repossessed on the slightest breach and this resulted in the abusive practice of the 'snatch back'. Peter Scott describes this phenomenon:

> [W]hile most firms wanted payment in full rather than repossession, there was a significant proportion—including some who engaged in considerable advertising—that specialized in repossessing goods after most payments were made ... many cases were reported of debtors who had almost completed contracts having their goods snatched within hours of missing a single payment. (Scott, 2002: 195, 215)

The 1938 Hire Purchase Act represented the influence of consumer and responsible trade interests as well as a government that was under pressure to respond to a 'major social evil'.

The current provisions in the Consumer Credit Act 1974 prevent repossession of goods without a court order if one-third of the price has been paid (section 90). The sanction for contravention of the Act under section 91 is that the agreement is terminated and the debtor is released from all further liability and can recover all sums paid under the agreement. Moreover a creditor or owner cannot enter any premises to repossess goods without a court order (section 92(1)). Breach of this section is actionable as a breach of statutory duty (section 92(3)). A debtor may, however, consent to a repossession order at the time of repossession (section 173(3)). It is not known how many such 'voluntary surrenders' are made and whether debtors are fully aware that they may still be liable for damages to the creditor. Ison (1979) argued that it was prevalent and that creditors often did not obtain the best price on resale of the goods. The requirement of 'informed consent' was discussed in *Mercantile Credit v Cross* (1963) concerning a debtor 'in humble circumstances' who had received a notice of termination from the hire-purchase company after being in default, although he had paid more than one-third of the purchase price:

> It is said, however, that a hirer's consent has to be looked at as though it were in the nature of a waiver or acquiescence, and therefore is of no effect unless it is given with full knowledge of the legal rights of the party whose consent is in question. It seems to me that that is going much too far. I agree that consent has to be a free and voluntary consent, and I am disposed to agree that it must be an informed consent. Here the fact is that the hirer has been informed, in language about as simple as could be devised, of exactly what his rights are, and what the rights of the owner of the goods are. If a hirer chooses not to read what the notice required to be inserted in his hire-purchase agreement says, he himself is, to my mind, the only sufferer. It cannot be said that if, having failed to ascertain what his rights are, he then gives a consent which he might not otherwise have given, his consent is any the less a real consent. I take the same view as the county court judge took on this part of the case. It appears to me that the consent which the hirer (the defendant) gave in this case was a full and free consent, given after he had received full information as to what his rights were, and that it is a consent to which effect must be given in pursuance of the provisions of the Act of 1938. On the main part of the case, therefore, I entertain no doubt whatsoever that this appeal must fail.

The values underlying these sections on repossession include those of protecting the equity that a consumer may have built up against arbitrary seizure. The due process requirements recognise that individuals might be subject to unreasonable search and seizure of their property by private as well as public institutions and it also perhaps recognise a duty of good faith in termination. The requirements may also facilitate more settlements between creditor and debtor. In some cases a consumer may have complaints about the goods but her remedy of withholding payment may be of little use if the goods can be arbitrarily seized. An empirical study of the impact of a similar provision in Wisconsin that required a court order for all repossessions irrespective of the amount paid concluded that the provision had resulted in more consensual workouts (Whitford and Grau, 1978: 983).

After a creditor has repossessed goods of a debtor, sale of the repossessed goods may not cover its losses. The creditor may wish to sue a debtor for the 'deficiency' between the resale price and the price agreed to be paid by the debtor. In English law the concept of hire-purchase complicates the issue, since technically the transaction is not a credit sale or a security agreement, and consumers were able to return the goods at any time during the agreement. Creditors inserted 'minimum payment clauses'—a charge for depreciation in hire purchase and conditional sales as a method of capturing the deficiency—but the courts subject this to the rule against penalties and Goode suggests that they would be unlikely to award damages that exceed the amount a debtor is liable for if she voluntarily terminates the agreement (see sections 99–100). These provisions represent a legislative compromise between the interests of creditors and debtors and permit creditors to recover under section 100:

> 100—(1) Where a regulated hire-purchase or regulated conditional sale agreement is terminated under section 99 the debtor shall be liable, unless the agreement provides for a

smaller payment, or does not provide for any payment, to pay to the creditor the amount (if any) by which one-half of the total price exceeds the aggregate of the sums paid and the sums due in respect of the total price immediately before the termination.

Goode's argument that a similar rule would be applied to a creditor's termination of the agreement is supported by the following county court decision *Rover Finance Ltd v Peter Siddons* (2002). In this case the defendant had paid £4,596.47 before defaulting on a conditional sale agreement to purchase an automobile and the finance company was claiming the balance of payment on the agreement. The District Court judge held that section 100 must be taken into account even where the finance company has terminated for breach. A 'minimum payment' clause which entitled the finance company to recover more than would be recovered under section 100 would be a penalty. Since the consumer had paid more than was required under section 100, the finance company's claim was dismissed.

The 50 per cent rule was intended to provide a form of rough justice between hirer and owner. During the current reforms of the Consumer Credit Act the DTI raised the question whether this should be raised to 75 per cent. No consensus was achieved and the status quo was preserved.

Some companies attempt to avoid the penalty doctrine by inserting clauses that indicate that time of payment is a condition. Such a clause is not a clause relating to damages (and therefore subject to the penalty doctrine) but breach of it permits the innocent party to claim damages for loss of bargain. This was a consequence of the decision in *Lombard North Central plc v Butterworth* (1987). However, such a clause would be subject now to challenge under the Unfair Terms in Consumer Contracts Regulations.

The provisions in relation to protected goods and section 100 apply only to regulated hire-purchase and conditional sales agreement and do not apply to a loan that is secured against the personal property of the debtor. In practice this form of loan was rare in England because it would need to conform to the Bills of Sale Acts of 1878 and 1882, which are relatively complex. The Law Commission indicated that in 2001 only 2,840 Bills of Sale were registered and this would include both business and consumer debtors. However, in recent years the use of bills of sale has grown significantly, the Law Commission indicating that 11,000 were registered in the first six months of 2005 (Law Commission, 2005: 15) with consumer bills generally registered against cars. By 2009 'there were about 38,200 registered bills of sale. ... During the first six months of 2010, more than 19,000 new bills of sale were registered, which represents a similar level of use seen in the first half of 2008 and 2009. It is difficult to assess accurately the overall value of consumer loans secured through bills of sale, but we estimate that the size of the market in 2010 to be in the region of £38m–40m' (DBIS, 2011: 4). Eighteen per cent were made to small businesses but it is primarily the 'log-book loan' business, described in *Shaw v Nine Regions* above.

Concerns about practices in this industry and the absence of protections for borrowers from seizure prompted calls for reform. In 2011 the government rejected the possibility of banning bills of sale for consumer lending on the basis that:

> [T]he evidence received in response to the consultation did not indicate that the problems identified were sufficient to justify a ban on using bills of sale for consumer lending. There are certainly examples of bad practice by lenders and of consumers experiencing problems with bills of sale loans. But the size of the problem is comparatively small. The value of bills

of sale lending is estimated at £38–£40m, compared to £7.5bn for high cost credit generally. It is estimated that a secured vehicle is repossessed as a result of default in only 2%–3% of cases (800–1200 loans out of about 38,000).

40. We also recognise that bills of sale are an important source of credit for some consumers and small businesses and we do not feel that at this time it would be right to cut off this particular supply of credit. This is especially so at a time when mainstream sources of credit are becoming more difficult to access. (DBIS, 2011, paras 39–40)

The Bills of Sale Act was an early form of consumer protection 'designed to prevent persons of modest means from improvident arrangements by, amongst other things, mortgaging goods they do not yet own' (Law Commission, 2002: para 9.10). This policy is reflected in many modern personal property security statutes that prohibit 'after acquired property' clauses and also control the extent to which individuals may create broad security interests over their household goods and permit an individual to cure arrears.

The strictures of the Bills of Sale Acts are one reason for the development of hire-purchase in the UK as the primary form of security for selling consumer goods. Hire-purchase is a legal fiction. It is in substance the creation of what is known as a purchase money security interest in consumer sales, achieving the same result as if an individual had borrowed funds from a financial institution and given the financial institution a security over the goods purchased. The Law Commission (2002) thought that consumers should be able to enter into the latter type of transaction subject to safeguards since it would extend consumers' ability to raise funds and might obviate the need to use their home as security, a potentially more dangerous form of security. If this were permitted, then it would be necessary to regulate the process of enforcement of such security. For example, legislation in a number of Canadian provinces that dates from the Depression era requires a creditor to choose between seizing consumer goods subject to a security interest and suing on the debt. A creditor may not do both. There is little evidence of its impact on credit granting within the provinces.

12.3.1 Time orders

A court has a relatively broad discretion in relation to applications by a creditor to enforce a regulated credit agreement. A suspended return order is a common order (under sections 133, 135 and 136) in hire-purchase cases. Time orders for repayment may be made under section 129 as the court considers 'just' and debtors may now apply for a time order after receiving a notice of arrears as well as a notice of default. In *Southern District Finance v Barnes* the Court of Appeal outlined the following guidelines for the application of a time order:

Southern and District Finance plc v Barnes and another; J & J Securities Ltd v Ewart and another; Equity Home Loans Ltd v Lewis [1996] 1 FCR 679, 27 HLR 691, [1995] CCLR 62, (1995) *Times* 19 April (transcript: John Larking)

Leggatt J

Enforcement of regulated agreements

These appeals, which have been heard together, concern the powers of the County Court in relation to applications for time orders under ss 129 and 136 of the Consumer Credit Act 1974. In this judgment references to sections are to sections of that Act. So far as material s 129 provides that—

"(1)… if it appears to the court just to do so—

…

(b) on an application made by a debtor or hirer under this paragraph after service on him of—

(i) a default notice …

(c) in an action brought by a creditor or owner to enforce a regulated agreement or any security, or recover possession of any goods or land to which a regulated agreement relates,

the court may make an order under this section (a 'time order').

(2) A time order shall provide for one or both of the following, as the court considers just

(a) the payment by the debtor or hirer or any surety of any sum owed under a regulated agreement or a security by such instalments, payable at such times, as the court, having regard to the means of the debtor or hirer and any surety, considers reasonable …"

Section 136 says—

"The court may in an order made by it under this Act include such provision as it considers just for amending any agreement or security in consequence of a term of the order."

It follows that in an action by a lender for an order for possession of property on which the loan was secured, if the conditions are fulfilled for the making of an order, the Court must before doing so consider whether it is just to make a time order.

It is common ground that each of the agreements, the subject of the present appeals, is a 'regulated agreement'. Section 130(6) gives the Court power to vary or revoke a time order on the application of any person affected by it. Most regulated agreements contain an accelerated payments clause whereby if the borrower fails to pay an instalment on its due date, the lender shall be entitled after giving a default notice, to require payment at once of the balance of the total indebtedness. Most regulated agreements also contain a provision that if any instalment is not paid on its due date, interest may be charged on it from then until the date of payment at the rate of interest applicable to the loan.

Time orders

The first of the main issues argued before us has been as to the meaning of 'any sum owed' within the scope of a time order. Mr Michael Beloff QC argued for the borrowers in the first appeal that to be 'owed' a sum does not have to be immediately payable … Mr Beloff relies on the principle of real property law that if a mortgagee (with immaterial qualifications) takes proceedings to realise his security, his doing so amounts to a demand for the whole of the outstanding balance. … An application for an order of possession is an exercise by the creditor of the right to realise the total indebtedness secured by the charge on the property. As a matter of law as well as of common sense, when a creditor brings a possession action he demands payment of the whole of the sum outstanding under the charge.

Power to vary agreements

The second main issue in this Court is as to the scope of the power given by s 136 to include in a time order 'such provision as it considers just for amending any agreement or security in consequence of a term of the order.'

In my judgment the key phrase in s 136 is 'in consequence of a term.' Unless the contemplated amendment is truly a consequence of a term of the time order, and the making of it is also just, there is no power to make it. It is a provision of limited scope.

Judicial control

(1) When a time order is applied for, or a possession order sought of land to which a regulated agreement applies, the Court must first consider whether it is just to make a time order. That will involve consideration of all the circumstances of the case, and of the position of the creditor as well as the debtor.

(2) When a time order is made, it should normally be made for a stipulated period on account of temporary financial difficulty. If, despite the giving of time, the debtor is unlikely to be able to resume repayment of the total indebtedness by at least the amount of the contractual instalments, no time order should be made. In such circumstances it will be more equitable to allow the regulated agreement to be enforced.

(3) When a time order is made relating to the non-payment of money: (a) The 'sum owed' means every sum which is due and owing under the agreement, but where possession proceedings have been brought by the creditor that will normally comprise the total indebtedness; and (b) The Court must consider what instalments would be reasonable both as to amount and timing, having regard to the debtor's means.

(4) The Court may include in a time order any amendment of the agreement, which it considers just to both parties, and which is a consequence of a term of the order. If the rate of interest is amended, it is relevant that smaller instalments will result both in a liability to pay interest on accumulated arrears and, on the other hand, in an extended period of repayment. But to some extent the high rate of interest usually payable under regulated agreements already takes account of the risk that difficulties in repayment may occur.

(5) If a time order is made when the sum owed is the whole of the outstanding balance due under the loan, there will inevitably be consequences for the term of the loan or for the rate of interest or both.

(6) If justice requires the making of a time order, the Court should suspend any possession order that it also makes, so long as the terms of the time order are complied with.

Against that background each of these appeals must be considered in turn.

Barnes v Southern & District Finance plc

The defendants Mr and Mrs Barnes purchased the freehold of 98 Poplar Avenue, Bedford, and thereafter granted a first charge in respect of the property. On 22 April 1992 an agreement was made with the plaintiffs Southern & District Finance plc for a regulated loan of £12,000, repayable over ten years by 120 instalments of £260 pm. About £1,300 was then outstanding to the first mortgagees. On 2 February 1993 a default notice was served on the defendants seeking payment of arrears of £1,300 by 17 February 1993. As soon as that period had expired without the arrears having been discharged, mortgage possession proceedings were brought in the Bedford County Court. The defendants applied for a time order on 1 March 1993. On 27 September 1993 in a comprehensive judgment reviewing all the County Court authorities Mr Assistant Recorder Crampin QC gave judgment for the plaintiffs, dismissed the defendants' application for a time order, and adjourned the proceedings. No default notice had been served for any sum other than arrears. On the adjourned hearing date the Assistant Recorder made an order for possession in 28 days suspended for one year, conditional on payment of £150 pm., and ordered the matter to be re-listed before 8 November 1994 for reconsideration of the instalment order. He gave to the defendants leave to appeal to this Court. ... In my judgment the Assistant Recorder applied s 129 incorrectly in finding that the 'sum owed' for the purpose of the time order he was considering could relate only to the unpaid instalments, and he was wrong to conclude that s 136 did not empower him to alter the rate of interest payable on the unpaid instalments. It would have been a proper exercise of discretion, in order to mitigate the impact of the interest charged on the unpaid instalments, to reduce the monthly rate of interest from 1.952% to 1% during the period of suspension of the possession order. Accordingly, I would allow the appeal and remit the matter to the Bedford County Court.

Equity Home Loans Ltd v Lewis

In 1984 the defendant Mrs Lewis purchased the freehold of a house at 39 Cwmdare Street, Cardiff, South Glamorgan. She then borrowed first from a bank and then from a building society. On 22 April 1991 she entered into a credit agreement with the plaintiffs Equity Home Loans Ltd for a regulated loan of £4,000 repayable over 15 years by 180 monthly instalments of £105.56 at a monthly rate of interest of 2.72%, or an APR of 44.1%. The loan was secured by a second legal charge. On 29 June 1993 a default notice was served on the defendant. This sum not having been paid on 22 October 1993 mortgage possession proceedings were begun in the Cardiff County Court. The arrears then amounted to £680.49. On 16 December 1993 the defendant applied for a time order. On 11 January 1994 Deputy District Judge Nicholson made an order for possession against the defendant and dismissed her application for a time order. But on 14 March 1994 Judge Hywel Roberts allowed an appeal by the defendant and made a time order substituting for the contractual monthly payments an order for the payment of the outstanding balance of £16,994.92 by six monthly payments of £25 and 174 monthly payments of £96.81. He considered that, although the balance of the total indebtedness had not been called in, he 'could by no means take the view that the only sums which could be the subject of a time order are those which had accrued by way of arrears.' He also ordered that 'the regulated agreement is to be varied so that there shall be no further interest due under the agreement', and made an order for possession suspended so long as the instalments were paid. By 'no further interest' the judge evidently meant 'no additional interest'.

The facts of this case are extreme. The loan must have bordered on the extortionate, although that has not been alleged. The total sum payable was £19,000. So the borrower was to pay £15,000 over 15 years in order to borrow £4,000. Since on average, if the capital is assumed to have been repayable by equal instalments, not much more than half of the sum borrowed would have been outstanding at any stage, she would in effect have been paying £1,000 a year in order to borrow an average sum of little over £2,000.

When the judge rescheduled the instalments due under the agreement, he did so over a fresh period of 15 years. Since nearly 3 years had passed since the agreement was made, this had the effect of extending the total of the agreement to nearly 18 years. The judge reduced the rate of interest to nil, since otherwise throughout the extended period of the loan interest would have been payable on the arrears at the exorbitant rate prescribed, and that would have defeated the purpose of giving time. In effect as a sanction for non-payment of instalments a suspended possession order was substituted for a penal rate of interest. The court gave the plaintiff leave to appeal against his order. Though the judge's methods were robust and his reasoning economical, his instincts were sound and his order just. I would dismiss the appeal.

Southern District Finance v Barnes represents a relatively cautious approach to the broad provisions in sections 129–36 and a general unwillingness to adjust the terms of the contract. Mcmurtry comments that of the 'admittedly few cases in which the courts have used a time order to relieve a borrower in financial difficulties , only very tentative steps have been taken to unleash the full potential of the provisions' (Mcmurtry, 2010: 122). Notwithstanding the potential of sections 129–36, few applications appear to be made for time orders. A study in 2009 by Citizens Advice, Shelter and Advice UK found that time orders were applied for in only 1 out of 31 Consumer Credit Act repossessions and no time order was granted (Turning the Tide, 2009). One commentator conjectured that 'borrowers do not know or are uncertain about the time order procedure and non-legally qualified money and housing advisors are nervous of suggesting applications' because of the complexity of the law (Lord, 2012: 8).

There is also the disparity between the protection afforded by sections 129–36 of the CCA 1974 and section 36 of the Administration of Justice Act 1970 in relation to mortgagors where the jurisdiction of the Consumer Credit Act is not applicable. Section 36 is more limited and the court will not extend the term of the agreement. Amendments to the Consumer Credit Act 1974 now permit an application to court at an earlier time than under section 36 which are only applicable when proceedings are before the court. Moreover under section 126 of the Consumer Credit Act 1974 mortgages are only enforceable by court order.

The global financial crisis and its consequences on the UK housing market stimulated interest in further protection for homeowners facing repossession. Several initiatives include: income support for mortgage interest available to individuals claiming a variety of forms of income support; homeowners' mortgage support which permits deferral of payments; mortgage rescue, involving either housing associations or mortgage to rent; and a mortgage protocol requiring repossession to be treated as a last resort and 'such a claim must not normally be started unless all other reasonable attempts to resolve the position have failed'. The protocol does not, however , 'alter the parties' rights and obligations'. Whitehouse argues that the mortgage arrears protocol was a lost opportunity to modernise mortgage law in relation to consumers (Whitehouse, 2009: 793).

Home ownership has been a major objective of successive UK governments. Its extension to more risky borrowers since the 1970s raises the issue of an appropriate safety net, particularly given the volatility of the English housing market with four major boom and bust cycles since the 1970s. Loss of a home is not merely an economic loss, entailing loss of status and self-esteem, with potentially severe impacts on a family and children. Stephens et al have proposed an insurance safety net funded partly by government and by all borrowers. The proposal is outlined as follows:

[T]he cover provided by private insurance products and their suitability have been called into question. The state funded safety net has weakened over time, not least with the reduction in the standard interest rate payable to SMI claimants, and the introduction of time-limited support. Temporary concessions introduced during the current downturn are soon to expire and require a consistent long-term alternative. There is therefore an urgent need for reform of the current combination of partial safety nets. A partnership insurance scheme in which borrowers, lenders and the government join together to purchase block insurance providing borrowers with protection against income loss arising from designated risk events is also an option. ... It is noted that partnership insurance can be structured to avoid making it compulsory for all borrowers or creating incentives for bad borrowing or lending. (Stephens, 2011: 68)

12.3.2 Unsecured remedies

The primary enforcement remedies for a court judgment in England and Wales are attachment of earnings orders, charging orders and warrants of execution. Attachment of earnings orders are attractive to creditors because individual debtors rarely have assets worth seizing. There is a danger, however, that an individual may lose her job because employers dislike attachment of earnings orders. While dismissal on such a ground would constitute unfair dismissal there is no specific provision in England and Wales similar to those countries that prohibit dismissal because an individual's wages are being attached. The Tribunals Courts and Enforcement Act 2007 facilitates attachment of earnings orders by introducing fixed-rate deductions for orders rather than individualised assessments and permits the tracing of debtors who change their employment by permitting HM Revenue to provide the court with details of the new employment.

Charging orders under the Charging Orders Act 1979 (see also Civil Procedure Rules Part 73) turn an unsecured debt into a secured debt by permitting a creditor to place a charge against a debtor's home and subsequently to seek an order for sale of the charged property. While there are significant judicial controls on the sale of a charged property and the *White Book* indicates that 'to order a sale of the judgment debtor's property ... would be an extreme sanction' (White Book, 2006: 1863), a charging order creates significant bargaining leverage for a creditor over the debtor and consumer groups have criticised their use in relation to relatively small debts.

OFT Acts on Concerns about Charging Orders, www.oft.gov.uk/news-and-updates/press/2010/119-10

The OFT has imposed requirements on Alliance and Leicester Personal Finance Limited, American Express Services Europe Limited, HFC Bank Limited (part of the HSBC Group) and Welcome Financial Services Limited (part of Cattles plc) to address concerns about the way some consumer debts are enforced.

Charging orders are a legitimate way to secure and ultimately recoup unpaid debts, however, a recent investigation by the OFT found problems with the way some lenders use them.

Problems uncovered by the OFT's investigation were specific to each business, as set out in the individual requirements, but across the sector they include a failure to consider the customer's circumstances or proportionality before asking the court to put a charging order in place; not building adequate checks into the lender's decision-making process; and also applying substantial charges for referring cases to a debt collection agency. In a minority of cases, lenders sent oppressive and/or misleading correspondence.

The four companies subject to today's announcement have co-operated fully with the OFT during the investigation and have each made changes to address the specific problems identified within their business, as set out in the requirements. The OFT is working to ensure that the whole banking industry uses charging orders and other debt enforcement tools responsibly.

Ray Watson, the OFT's Director of Consumer Credit, said:

Our investigation uncovered instances of charging orders being used to secure debts of less than £600. Lenders are entitled to use charging orders but must do so proportionately. Where we consider the use of charging orders to be unfair or oppressive we will take action to protect consumers.

---

13. Restructuring and writing down consumer debts

In many cases an individual may have multiple debts that she is unable to repay. The following section outlines the current formal alternatives available (see further Ramsay, 2003, 2012; Walters and Skene, 2006): bankruptcy, individual voluntary arrangements, debt-relief orders and administration orders. Table 4 indicates the current use of these remedies and Figure 2 places the UK in the context of other common law systems.

Table 4. English insolvency alternatives, 2010

Individual bankruptcy	59,173
Individual voluntary arrangement	50,693
Debt-relief order	25,179
Administration order	1,100
Debt-management plan	100,000-150,000 (estimate)

Sources: Insolvency Service; Ministry of Justice, Judicial and Court Statistics 2010.

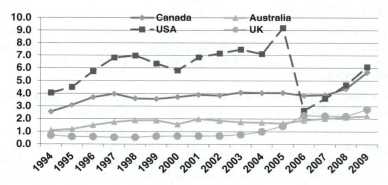

Figure 2. Individual insolvency filings, per 1,000 population 18+ 'Anglo Origins', 1994–2009.
Source: Office of Superintendent of Bankruptcy Canada.

The government reviewed the existing options in 2011 and concluded that 'while the current range of debt solutions is not seen as perfect, little strong evidence has been offered to suggest a complete overhaul is required or would bring substantive benefit' (DBIS: HM Treasury, 2011). Citizens Advice in its parliamentary brief to the DBIS Select Committee on Debt Management took a different position:

Citizens Advice, *Debt Management and Debt Advice Briefing* **(December 2011)**

The current 'system' of debt remedies is really a group of voluntary and statutory schemes that have developed over time. It is not a coherent, planned whole and as a system suffers from a number of significant flaws. The experience of CAB clients raises the follows issues:

- The statutory debt remedies have explicit or implicit boundary criteria that exclude people from the debt relief they need. As a result people can 'fall into the gaps' between these boundaries leaving them without a suitable option This produces the bizarre result that a person with significant disposable income can get both debt relief and protection from their creditors (through an IVA) while some of the most vulnerable debtors cannot.

- There is currently no debt solution that provides support and protection for people experiencing an extended period of financial difficulty. In other words, there is no effective statutory 'breathing space' scheme, even though this is what many people in financial difficulties need.

- As the solutions do not articulate into a coherent system, there is no easy way for people to move between remedies if their circumstances change. For instance people who have paid for an IVA can find themselves back at square one if the remedy fails.

- The gaps, limitations and failures of the system to support and protect people in financial difficulties creates an opportunity for unscrupulous traders to exploit financially vulnerable people.

13.1 Individual voluntary arrangements

Individual voluntary arrangements (IVAs) were modernised in 1986 (see Part VIII Insolvency Act 1986) as an alternative to bankruptcy, permitting individuals to reach an arrangement with their creditors. The Cork Committee (1982) envisaged that this mechanism would be used by company directors who had guaranteed debt to the company, professionals who would lose their status if they resorted to bankruptcy and self-employed business persons. They were not intended for use by consumer debtors.

An IVA permits a debtor, through a nominee (an insolvency practitioner) to make a binding composition with her creditors. It may involve the sale of assets or income repayments. Approval of a proposal requires a majority in excess of 75 per cent in the value of unsecured creditors present or voting by proxy (see Insolvency Act 1986, sections 257–58). The rights of secured (eg a mortgagee of the home) or preferential creditors cannot be affected without the consent of these creditors. Under an IVA, a debtor will normally obtain a qualified private insolvency practitioner to act as nominee and supervisor of the arrangement. The role of the nominee is to submit a report to the court as to whether a meeting of creditors should be held to consider the proposal. The supervisor will supervise a proposal that is accepted. The costs and complexity of an IVA were presumed to make them unavailable to consumers. However, in recent years there has been increased specialisation by a small number of insolvency practitioners in providing streamlined IVAs to consumers. Michael Green, in research on individual voluntary arrangements, concludes that the great majority of IVAs now represent consumer debts (Green, 2002).

A study of individuals using IVAs indicates that the typical debtor owes £40,000 to 10 creditors. Over 56 per cent of debtors are under 40 years old. Forty-five per cent of individuals were in unskilled employment, over half earned less than £20,000 and over 80 per cent less than £30,000. Under 30 per cent of debtors owned a property. Eighty-three per cent indicated that 'expenditure in excess of income' was the cause of failure. The study suggested that there were three types of individuals who used an IVA: a single woman in her twenties with a university education; a self-employed builder in his forties who had problems with tax; and a working-class couple in their thirties with heavy housing debt and credit card bills (see Boyden et al, 2006). These arrangements will usually last for three–five years and result in a dividend to creditors of approximately 36–41 pence.

The large providers of IVAs are now quoted on the AIM exchange. There have been criticisms of fees taken and quality of advice provided by some insolvency practitioners in relation to IVAs (see Insolvency Practices Council, 2003 Annual Report: 3). Other debt advice agencies such as Citizens Advice have questioned the insolvency practitioners' monopoly on providing IVAs.

In 2005, an insolvency service working group recommended the introduction of a 'streamlined, lower-cost simple IVA regime, which is more suited to the needs of those experiencing financial difficulty today'. This regime would apply to individuals with unsecured debts below £75,000. The majority required for approval would be reduced from 75 per cent of creditors to a simple majority in value. The default period for an arrangement would be five years. There would be greater transparency in fees and the reduction in costs should make the arrangement more accessible to individuals. These reforms have not been implemented by law although a simple IVA 'protocol' now exists.

13.2 Administration orders

The administration order has been described as the 'poor person's bankruptcy' since its introduction in the Bankruptcy Act of 1883. It was intended to avoid the difficulties of recovering small debts among the 'wage-earning classes' where it would be too costly to apply the machinery of the Bankruptcy Act, and to provide a middle way between immunity from liability for the debtor and imprisonment for debt. Both the Payne Committee in 1970 and Cork Committee in 1982 envisaged a significant role for a modified form of administration order, which would address the needs of the consumer debtor, who would be provided with the opportunity to repay all or a portion of his debts. There was no limitation on the time period for which an administration order could be made (see County Court Act 1984, sections 112–17 and Order 39 of the County Court Rules 1981). Creditors included in the order are prevented from taking proceedings against a debtor while the order is in force. There is no entry fee payable by a debtor for an administration order and court fees for the implementation of the order, which may not exceed 10 per cent of the total amount of the debts, are deducted from the repayments.

The operation of the Administration Order has been severely criticised for many years. The rules limited the total indebtedness to £5,000, and there appears to be some uncertainty in practice as to whether debts may be written off at the end of the order. Most orders are unsuccessful and courts do not monitor them closely. Seventy-five per cent of users receive unemployment benefits and 65 per cent are young females (Civil Justice Division and Information Management Division, Department of Constitutional Affairs, 2003; Kempson and Collard, 2004). The Ministry of Justice has demonstrated little interest in its reform and the government in 2011 proposed the abolition of the administration order.

13.3 Bankruptcy as a consumer remedy

Bankruptcy permits an individual to discharge the great majority of her unsecured debts in return for giving up most of her assets (see Insolvency Act 1986, sections 283, 307–08A). An individual who wishes to use the bankruptcy procedure under the Insolvency Act 1986 must petition the court for a bankruptcy order on the grounds that she is unable to pay her debts (Insolvency Act 1986, Chapter 45, section 273). The great majority of consumer bankruptcies are processed by the Official Receiver, an official within the insolvency service, rather than a private insolvency practitioner, since there will rarely be any assets to make the bankruptcy attractive to a private practitioner. An individual must pay an initial upfront fee of £525 to cover the costs of administration and must also pay court fees. The deposit fee may not be waived and this fee has been upheld as not contravening the European Convention on Human Rights and Fundamental Freedoms as restricting a fundamental right of access to the courts (Article 6) (see *R v Lord Chancellor, ex p Lightfoot* (2000)).

Significant changes were introduced to the bankruptcy regime in England and Wales by Part 10 of the Enterprise Act 2002. These provisions liberalise the discharge process so that an individual is normally discharged from her debts after 12 months. These changes were not introduced as a response to concerns about consumer over-indebtedness but were intended to promote entrepreneurialism by reducing the risks of business failure. Individuals with discretionary income may be required to make an income payment order of up to 3 years (section 310). There is also the possibility of a Bankruptcy Restriction Order, which may last from 2 to 15 years. The introduction of this order responds partly to the practical difficulties which the Official Receiver encountered in instituting criminal actions against practices such as credit card fraud and is intended to provide a lower-cost and more effective method of sanctioning reckless, irresponsible and fraudulent debtors. This order may be applied for by the Official Receiver, where, for example, an individual had incurred a bankruptcy debt without reasonable expectation of being able to pay it, demonstrated unjustifiable extravagance in living, or had filed a previous bankruptcy within 6 years (Schedule 20, section 2) (see *Official Receiver v Southey* [2009] BPIR 89). The main effect of an order in relation to consumer debtors is that credit over £500 may not be obtained without disclosing the existence of the order to a creditor and publicity will be given to these orders through the existence of a public register, which will provide a signal to creditors so that they can distinguish between the honest and responsible debtor.

It is often stated that the purpose of personal insolvency is to provide the debtor with the possibility of a *fresh start* free from debt. The extent of the fresh start will partly depend on the extent to which he or she may retain assets or be subject to requirements to make substantial income payments to her creditor. Policy in England and Wales has traditionally been reluctant to make insolvency widely accessible, perhaps because of concerns about the impact on commercial morality. The changes in 2002 were preceded by several White Papers and the Insolvency Service outlined the changing ideas about the goals of insolvency in its Consultation Paper, *Bankruptcy: A Fresh Start* (2000):

> The idea that bankruptcy might represent an easy solution for those who can bear with equanimity the stigma of their own failure seems at considerable odds with present-day reality. Despite that, it is clearly one that any proposal for reform of the law relating to personal insolvency must ensure does not become reality. Nor should any changes to the system serve to encourage individuals not pay their debts when, with a little effort, payment, in full or in part, could be made. However the experience of official receivers is that the last majority of people who become bankrupt become so from necessity not choice, that they will have made very considerable efforts to avoid becoming bankrupt and that they will have dealt responsibly with their creditors. For many individuals bankruptcy represents a personal tragedy, the last act in a series of events that have led to financial disaster. For many others there is still an element of shame in being unable to pay their debts. Bankruptcy, whilst an unpleasant experience, offers the prospect of financial rehabilitation.

In England and Wales the primary disincentive to bankruptcy is that an individual may lose her home since secured debts such as mortgages are not discharged. In addition, a bankruptcy will be registered on a credit bureau file for several years and empirical research suggests that banks may be unwilling to open accounts for bankrupts.

There is little systematic empirical analysis in England and Wales on the different remedies. Ramsay provides an overview.

Iain Ramsay, 'A Tale of Two Debtors: Responding to the Shock of Over-Indebtedness in France and England—A Story from the Trente Piteuses' (2012) 75 *MLR* 212 at 237–39, 240–41

> By 1999 the majority of English bankruptcies were related to consumer debt rather than the carrying on of a business. In 2005, consumer bankruptcies represented 76 per cent of bankruptcies compared with 39 per cent during the height of the early 1990s recession. They currently represent over 80 per cent of bankruptcies, with the great majority being debtor rather than creditor petitions. ... Bankruptcy is in theory a court process with a debtor submitting a bankruptcy petition to the court and creditors appointing a trustee to administer the bankruptcy. Bankruptcy also engages the state through the Insolvency Service, a government executive agency, which administers and supervises the system of official receivers and has overall responsibility for the regulation of insolvency practitioners. ... The large numbers of consumer debtors with few assets had led to greater 'routinisation' of the bankruptcy process. The court process was increasingly a brief formality, the debtor interviewed briefly (or not at all) by the Official Receiver (OR) and then waiting out the discharge period. This routinisation does not mean that the court process was not experienced as stigmatising by bankrupts nor that the OR is not an effective gatekeeper against fraud. The contemporary administrative routinisation is symbolised by the elimination of court procedures for the Debt Relief Order, and proposals to eliminate the court from making bankruptcy orders in debtor petitions, as a means of reducing costs and delays and 'ensuring that capacity and resources within HMCS (Her Majesty's Court Service) are not wasted on activities that could better be done elsewhere.'

> Paradoxically, in a country associated with neo-liberalism, there is a substantial public service role, through the office of the Official Receiver, in investigating and processing

consumer bankruptcies. ... Private trustees are appointed in less than 10 per cent of individual bankruptcies. However, as part of the new public management where public institutions operate more like businesses, the service is operated on a cost recovery basis. ... The personal insolvency regime 'must be funded by those who benefit from its operation and must not form a burden on the public purse.'

... Subsequent government policy making has embraced the idea of the IndividualVoluntary Arrangement (IVA) as the central mechanism for consumer insolvents, balancing the 'need to maximise returns to creditors' and providing a realistic repayment of a portion of debts which would responsibilise consumers—and reduce public costs.

... It was not anticipated [in 1986] that the IVA would be transformed by entrepreneurial insolvency practitioners to develop a consumer market for compositions through high volume processing by IVA 'factories'. These developed in the late 1990s, advertised widely, and provided relatively substantial fees for the professional intermediaries which were deducted from the monthly repayments to creditors. The growth of this industry in the mid 2000s was temporarily halted by a backlash of major institutional creditors who, acting through their nominees, rejected many proposed plans by setting high required dividends. Since these institutions would often have more than 25 per cent of the voting rights (an IVA requires acceptance by 75 per cent in value of creditors) they could effectively block proposals, and possibly steer individuals to other 'creditor friendly' form of repayment. Some individuals however would be denied access to any form of relief. The political solution to this conflict within the market was mediated through a working group chaired by the Insolvency Service which resulted in an IVA Protocol intended to address some of the creditor concerns.

The absence of systematic and reliable empirical studies on personal bankrupts in England makes it difficult to provide authoritative pictures of the different types and classes of bankrupt. ...

The limited empirical data on bankruptcy (which do not distinguish between individual business and consumer bankrupts, and which would include individuals now using Debt Relief Orders) in the mid to late 2000s indicate high levels of unemployment, low homeownership (less than 10 per cent) and significantly larger percentages of divorced individuals than in the general population. Individuals aged between 30–49 are over-represented, reflecting the lifecycle period of high consumption needs. Males are over-represented (56 per cent compared to 47 per cent in the population). The mean average of debt is £54,360 in 2007–08, but over 60 per cent of debtors have liabilities under £40,000. Almost fifty per cent of bankrupts have no assets: eleven per cent have assets over £5,000. Approximately 20 per cent of bankrupts make income payments of up to three years (with a mean average total amount paid of approx £2,000 in 2009–10). Early data on the users of the Debt Relief Order, intended for the 'No Income No Asset' bankrupt highlights the marginal nature of this group, dominated by women (63 per cent) with eighty per cent not in employment (including retired and home carers) fifty four per cent unemployed and 45 per cent single.

13.4 The role of bankruptcy in contemporary society

Since the 1980s many continental European countries have introduced debt adjustment and personal insolvency systems, sometimes using the US model of the 'fresh start' as an inspiration (Niemi, Ramsay and Whitford, 2003, 2009). The right to access bankruptcy or debt adjustment is therefore a mandatory term in all consumer lending contracts. Thomas Jackson justifies this non-waivable right in a society premised on the values of autonomy and the maintenance of a credit economy. Jackson argues that consumers systematically misjudge risk and are subject to over-optimism and under-estimation in relation to the risks of borrowing. In his view 'individuals systematically misjudge [or ignore] their own interests. And ... this bias leads them to consume too much and save too little' (Jackson, 1984–85: 1393). The non-waivable right to a dis-charge protects the future autonomy of the consumer as well as protecting third parties who may depend on the debtor.

Bankruptcy functions for an individual in a similar manner to limited liability for businesses or an insurance policy. The protection of bankruptcy, however, like insur-ance, creates moral hazard problems with the possibility of individuals over-consuming credit, because the full social costs of this activity are not going to be borne by the individual. Conceptualised as insurance, it is necessary to model the effects of different levels of protection of income and assets on credit granting, interest rates and the substitution of secured for unsecured credit. Jackson suggests some limitations on the extent of the discharge in order to protect against moral hazard but thinks that there is a good reason for the US position of strong protection of income in bankruptcy, because this protects human capital, which is the least diversifiable of an individual's assets. Moreover, the existence of a right to bankruptcy creates incentives for creditors to monitor debtor behaviour and lending practices, with the inevitable costs of bankruptcy in a credit society internalised in the price and availability of credit.

Jackson makes two further conclusions. First, information remedies such as cooling-off periods are unlikely to address the behavioural problems which concern future risks that will occur long after the cooling-off period. Second, there should be a general rule permitting a discharge, because it would not be easy for individualised decision making in bankruptcy to sort out individuals who had suffered from bounded ration-ality and those who were calculating gamblers (Jackson, 1984–85: 1393). English law does require individualised decision-making in determining whether a debtor ought to be subject to a bankruptcy restriction order.

The statistics in Figure 2 indicate that England and Wales does not have a high rate of personal insolvency compared with the US and Canada. The UK government dis-cussed the growing use of personal insolvency in its 2006 report on over-indebtedness.

DWP/DCA, *Tackling Over-indebtedness*, Annual Report (2006)

[T]he Bank of England principally attributes the increasing number of personal insolvencies to the rise in household indebtedness and goes on to say that it is unlikely that the recent rise in bankruptcies are due to the changes introduced by the Enterprise Act 2002, given that the upward trend in insolvencies was established before the change to legislation.

3.9 The increase in bankruptcies in England and Wales needs to be considered alongside the increase in Northern Ireland and sequestrations and protected trust deeds in Scotland where, in both cases, they are increasing at a greater rate than in England and Wales but where there has been no equivalent change to their insolvency legislation until very recently. Similarly, there has been no significant change to the law relating to IVAs, but the increase in such arrangements is greater than the increase in bankruptcies

3.16 There is currently no evidence to suggest that bankruptcy is a lifestyle choice despite early press coverage and anecdotal evidence suggesting that due to the Enterprise Act changes, bankruptcy is now perceived as an easy option.

There has been little systematic reflection on the role of consumer bankruptcy within consumer credit policy and social policy in England and Wales (see Ramsay, 2003; 2006: 663). This contrasts with the large US literature where high levels of consumer credit, a modest social safety net and no universal healthcare result in bankruptcy being an important 'safety net' for primarily middle-class (defined by home-ownership, education and occupation) individuals who are over-indebted (Porter, 2012). Bankruptcy provides an opportunity for individuals to return to the credit economy. Bankruptcy in the US is, according to Teresa Sullivan, Elizabeth Warren and Jay Westbrook, 'the ultimate free market solution to bad debt. It forces individual creditors who made voluntary lending decisions to bear the costs of their bad credit decisions out of the profits from their good loans' (Sullivan,Warren and Westbrook, 2000: 260). Even with the recent reforms to US bankruptcy law (see Bankruptcy Abuse Prevention and Consumer Protection Act 2005) that introduce a 'means test' for access to bankruptcy, US law still provides a relatively generous fresh start.

However, there is increasing evidence for the failure of bankruptcy to provide a fresh start in the US with bankrupts facing continuing financial problems after bankruptcy and being unable to save a home, an objective of Chapter 13 , the repayment chapter in US bankruptcy (Porter, 2012). Porter and Thorne (2006) conclude that one-third of bankrupts face continuing financial problems one year after their discharge and that lenders viewed recently discharged bankrupts as profitable sources for high-cost lending. A study by the Insolvency Service indicates that 90 per cent of debtors thought that bankruptcy had given them a fresh start. However, this study was conducted shortly after the bankruptcy process (May/June following bankruptcy petitions in previous August) and had a relatively low response rate. Further longitudinal research would be desirable. Banks often close individuals' accounts on bankruptcy and the UK government in a 2011 paper recognised that 'financial rehabilitation following bankruptcy can be an unduly lengthy process, and a number of stakeholders commented on the difficulties a bankrupt can experience in operating even a basic bank account facility' (DBIS, Treasury, 2011: para 5.50).

13.3.1 Debt Relief Orders

Debt relief orders were introduced in 2009 based on a New Zealand model to address the problem of the NINA (no income/no asset) debtor.

Regulatory Impact Assessment

... There is a category of person for whom none of the current remedies for those with serious debt problems apply: this group has insufficient disposable income to make monthly payments, no assets that can be sold to defray even some of the debt and they cannot afford the petition deposit required to go bankrupt. We think there is a need to plug this gap, and provide a form of relief for people who have fallen into debt, who do not owe a great a deal but who have no reasonable prospect of ever being able to pay off even part of the debt. The government is committed to contributing to social justice and working to create the conditions for business success by tackling over-indebtedness and financial exclusion. Part of this commitment includes access to help for those in financial difficulty, and improving the support and processes for those who have fallen into debt.

In order to keep costs as low as possible, approved intermediaries from the debt advice sector assist an applicant to decide if the debt relief order procedure is right for her before she applies to the Official Receiver, and will assist the debtor in making an application. Again to reduce costs, the facility to apply for a debt relief order will be available only online. An individual is still required to pay an entry fee of £90 to cover the administration costs. The government rejected the possibility of removing the deposit for individuals using the debt relief order. The English approach contrasts with Australia, where the great majority of consumer bankrupts are processed by a public agency, which does not charge a fee. The Australian government rejected proposals to introduce a fee after research indicated that the cost to the government of processing bankrupts was $250. The government indicated that 'charging people seeking protection of the insolvency system would be inconsistent with personal insolvency policy … the personal insolvency system provides an overriding general community benefit, not just relief for the debtor, so the cost of processing the petitions … should be met by taxpayers, not individual debtors' (Insolvency and Trustee Service Australia Cost Recovery Impact Statement, 2005: 7–18).

Reflecting on these reforms, as well as on the role of time orders under the Consumer Credit Act 1974, one might ask to what extent they give effect to the principle of social *force majeure* in contract law. Thomas Wilhelmsson argued that this principle applies where a consumer is affected by a special occurrence such as illness or unemployment or family life (divorce, death of family member) and there is a causal connection between this and the consumer's difficulty in paying. These factors should lead to a mitigation of the sanctions that would be imposed on the consumer. Wilhelmsson views this as a social principle that brings social influences into private law doctrine (Wilhelmsson, 1990: 1).

---

14. Institutional alternatives: expanding choice and access to affordable credit

Addressing financial exclusion is an important UK European objective, an aspect of reducing social exclusion embodied in the Treaty of Lisbon. Access to affordable and appropriate credit is one aspect of financial inclusion and this includes improving the coverage and capacity of a third-sector lenders such as credit unions and community finance development initiatives.

14.1 Credit unions

Members of credit unions in the mid-2000s were mostly women, middle-aged with a relatively high proportion in paid employment. Those who were members of community-based credit unions and 'new model' credit unions tended to be social housing tenants and to be unbanked, characteristics of financial exclusion. In addition, new model credit unions had the largest proportion of non-white members, predominantly black British (Collard and Smith, 2006: 6–8).

The Griffiths Commission outlined the following limitations of credit unions:

> The majority of credit unions are small with less than 200 members and an average of only 36 loans on their books. Christine Moore, of the East Manchester credit Union, told the commission that 'our average loan is about £500, and we cannot make enough money from these deals'.

> Members must repay their loans at the credit union's premises. The savings this creates helps explain why the charges for credit union loans are less than for home credit However, there is a wealth of evidence to show both that customers of home credit consider the convenience of weekly collection highly, and that these collections substantially reduce the risk of default. For these reasons, representatives of community finance initiatives freely acknowledged that they do not compete fully with home credit providers

> The management in small credit unions is often voluntary and lacking in the management skills to build the organization. Professor Paul Jones told the commission that one of the greatest challenges facing the credit union movement was "the modernization and transformation of credit unions into a more entrepreneurial movement", with a change from a traditional social welfare model, relying on volunteers, to a more professional business and market oriented organization, with full-time staff.

> Credit unions suffer from the brand image of being 'the poor man's bank'. (Griffiths Commission, 2004: 62–64)

Efforts have been made to 'modernise' credit unions and loosen the 'common bond' requirement that limited the scope of membership. The Legislative Reform (Industrial and Provident Societies and Credit Unions) Order 2011 implements this objective by loosening the strictness of the 'common bond'. (For further discussion of the role of credit unions, see Ryder, 2009; O'Connell, 2009: ch 7.)

House of Commons, Business, Innovation and Skills Committee, Debt Management, Fourteenth Report of Session 2010–12 (2012)

Credit Unions and the Post Office

80. Credit Unions in Britain are small, co-operative financial institutions. There are currently approximately 400 credit unions in the UK serving about 900,000 people. The Credit Union Act 1979 sets down the Credit Union operating principles in law:

- The promotion of thrift among members;
- The creation of sources of credit for the benefit of members at a fair and reasonable rate of interest;
- The use and control of their members' savings for their mutual benefit; and
- The training and education of members' in the wise use of money and in the management of their financial affairs.

81. In the past decade, British credit unions have trebled their membership and assets have expanded four-fold. The Association of British Credit Unions Ltd (ABCUL) informed us that

the sector has made over half a million loans in the last four or five years, all in the £200 to £400 area.

82. As this growth has taken place, the role that credit unions can play—both in providing equitable financial services to the whole of their communities and providing diversity in the financial services sector—has been increasingly recognised by government and policy-makers. The Coalition's Programme for Government committed to promoting mutuals as part of a diverse financial services system. The Department for Work and Pensions is currently conducting a feasibility study, the outcome of which will determine whether and how an earmarked £73 million credit union modernisation and expansion fund will be invested in the credit union sector. In addition, the Government recently introduced a Legislative Reform Order to amend the Credit Unions Act 1979 intended to enable credit unions to reach out to more people.

84. Professor Iain Ramsay of the University of Kent also noted that credit unions were 'a tiny part of the UK market at the moment' and that whilst he was in favour of encouraging them to grow in terms of providing an alternative form of competition in the market he believed that 'they can only be one part of the solution to high-cost credit.'

85. Mark Lyonette, Chief Executive of ABCUL was also of the view that credit unions were not in the best position to compete with the 'high-tech, payday-lending Wonga model' because they were not able to match the 'sophisticated automation and credit scoring behind the scenes' which were deployed by those companies. However he highlighted the situation in the United States where credit unions have now successfully entered the payday loan market:

> I should say that about 90 million people use credit unions in the States. They angsted for a long time over whether they should offer an alternative to the payday lending product. In the end, a number of them did at a much lower cost with the same features—for example, eight days, ten days or the end of the month.

86. The Minister was encouraging on the role of the credit unions, in particular on the potential for them to work within the Post Office network. He highlighted the work currently being done by the Department for Work and Pensions on credit unions and the fund made available by Government to invest in the credit union sector over the spending review. He was of the view that:

> If you could access credit union payments over the Post Office network, and they were there and able to advertise credit union products, I think it would be the biggest shot in the arm imaginable for the credit union sector.

87. There was a suggestion that Credit Unions should be signposted from payday lenders so that people are aware that there is a lower cost alternative. ABCUL explained:

> In the same way that there is an obligation in the debt management industry to make people aware that there might be cheaper or free alternatives available, it might be something that is worth thinking of in this area. You would not be able to recommend any particular institution; it would be more like a wealth warning where you actually suggest that there might be cheaper ways to do this.

88. Credit Unions have a valuable role to play in this market and their role needs to be highlighted by Government. We support the argument that the Post Office network has huge potential to work with the Credit Unions to provide short-term loans at a lower cost than commercial payday lenders. We recommend that the Government set out in its response, how it proposes to use Post Offices as a vehicle to expand the Credit Union market.

Credit union loans are subject to an interest rate cap of 2 per cent a month (26.8% APR). ABCUL data based partly on FSA returns indicates the size of the credit union sector in July 2011:

Membership, assets, savings and loans have all at least doubled recently, laying the foundations for British credit unions to emulate their international counterparts.

Around 420 credit unions across England, Scotland and Wales

952,000 people are credit union members, including over 115,000 junior savers

£703m is saved in British credit unions

£570m is out on loan to members

25 credit unions across the UK now offer current accounts

More than 34,000 people have their current account with a credit union

Some credit unions offer mortgages, cash ISAs and insurance products.

Table 5. Breakdown of high-cost credit market and social fund

Social Fund	£670 m	0% APR
Home credit	£4 bn	300–400
Payday loans	£1–2bn	2,500
Pawnbroking	£1–2 bn	100
Bills of sale	£30–40 m	400–500

Source: House of Commons Business, Innovation and Skills Committee, Fourteenth Report (2012).

14.2 The Social Fund

The Social Fund was introduced in the 1988 to replace social grants by loans.

HM Treasury, *Promoting Financial Inclusion* (2004)

The Social Fund

73. The Social Fund was introduced in 1988 as a flexible means of assisting benefit claimants and people on low incomes with expenses that they could not meet from their regular income. Loans are interest-free and are generally repaid by deductions from benefits. ... Budgeting loans are interest-free and available to people who have been in receipt of one of the main income-related benefits for at least six months.

75. We received evidence drawing attention to a variety of problems with the Social Fund. ... [T]here are many (especially elderly) eligible people who are completely unaware of the Social Fund. The funding for both Budgeting loans and Community Care Grants is inadequate to meet the needs that exist, so that eligible applicants generally only get some of the money they apply for, if they get any financial help at all. Constraints on the Budgeting Loan scheme budget also mean that repayment rates are generally much higher than in the commercial sector, which causes financial difficulties for some users and deters others from applying at all.

81. The Social Fund plays a vital role in helping those on low incomes to access affordable loans to meet one-off items of expenditure. ... The funding for the Social Fund should more clearly match the needs of those on low incomes. We have received evidence to suggest that the Social Fund is failing in its mission to assist those most in need of credit. It is essential that the Social Fund becomes more fully integrated with other provision of affordable credit for people on low incomes. Given that many people rejected by the Social Fund turn to unlicensed lenders, we recommend that the Government instigate arrangements to refer unsuccessful applicants to local credit unions and CDFIs where appropriate or other providers of affordable credit.

House of Commons, Business, Innovation and Skills Committee, *Debt Management*, Fourteenth Report of Session 2010–12

Social fund

89. The current welfare system provides grants and interest-free loans from the discretionary part of the Social Fund to help people on low incomes with costs which are difficult for them to meet from their regular income; for example to buy school uniforms or to replace white goods. Grants and loans are currently administered by Jobcentre Plus. The budget for the discretionary Social Fund in 2011–12 was £732 million.

90. Under the Welfare Reform Bill, the discretionary Social Fund will be abolished in April 2013. Instead, in England, a new system of Local Welfare Assistance will be introduced, to be administered and provided by local authorities.

91. Loans will be replaced by 'payments on account'. These will be recoverable payments intended to help towards meeting the expenses which are difficult to budget for out of normal benefit income or for which the claimant has been unable to save, or to deal with fluctuations in expenditure throughout the year, for example where children in the household who would normally have free school meals are on summer holidays.

92. The Government says that the reasons for the change include the increase in the cost of loans and the need to focus discretionary payments on the most vulnerable people. The Government also believes that a discretionary system is likely to be more effective if it is administered locally and 'linked to other support services' rather than being centrally administered.

93. Martin Lewis described what was happening to the social fund as 'just horrendous' and highlighted what he saw as serious problems with the Government's approach:

> It is going to become discretionary for local councils going forward, and I do not see, with the budget cuts at the moment, that they are going to be offering them. What we used to do is have a state-funded social fund that was there to supply short-term lending for people in emergencies, and in the midst of the payday loan boom, we are taking it away. I do not get that.

94. However, the Minister said that the argument that the inability of the benefits system to deliver loans was driving people towards payday loans had not been raised with him. However, he undertook to 'talk to DWP colleagues' about this matter.

95. We are concerned by anecdotal evidence which suggests that the removal of the Social Fund will push people towards payday and other high cost lenders. In its response to this Report, we will expect the Department to set out what meetings—at Ministerial and Official level—have already taken place on this issue; and to set out what joint plans Ministers from BIS and the DWP have put in place to ensure that the Social Fund and the proposed 'local

welfare assistance' will protect the most vulnerable from payday and other high cost lenders or loan sharks.

14.3 Harnessing the resources of mainstream finance

House of Commons Treasury Committee, *'Banking the Unbanked': Banking Services, the Post Office Card Account, and Financial Inclusion*, Thirteenth Report of Session 2005–06 Report

Lessons from the US Community Reinvestment Act

16. Another possible legislative approach that was frequently referred to in evidence was one based on the United States Community Reinvestment Act (CRA). The CRA was enacted in 1977 to prevent so-called 'red-lining'—the practice of banks explicitly choosing not to offer lending services to people identified as living in certain districts—and to encourage banks and thrifts to help meet the credit needs of all segments of their communities, including low and moderate-income neighbourhoods. The CRA and its implementing regulations require federal financial institution regulators to assess the record of each bank and thrift in helping to fulfil their obligations to the community and to consider that record in evaluating applications for charters or for approval of bank mergers, acquisitions and branch openings. We were told that the CRA is part of a 'three legged stool' that encourages banks to serve the needs of low-income communities, the other two legs being made up of fair lending and other anti-discrimination laws, and reporting laws such as the mortgage disclosure acts. Banks are evaluated in several areas and receive a rating based on their activities in low-income communities. Ratings are based on loan provision, branch and cash services and community development activity. The CRA is principally concerned with lending rather than the provision of current accounts. Banks can comply with the CRA and improve their rating through direct provision of financial products and services or by investing in organisations embedded in local communities such as Community Development Finance Institutions or local community banks. We learnt that banks increasingly view CRA activity as activity that could yield profitable business opportunities or attract tax relief.

A key lesson from our visit to the USA was that, over time, the CRA has become less important in forcing banks into investment and other decisions that it might not wish to make than in enhancing transparency about bank activities in deprived communities.

One of the key recommendations of the Social Investment Taskforce, which was established by the Chancellor of the Exchequer to consider ways in which increased investment could be made in the poorest communities, was that United Kingdom banks disclose their lending data in respect of low-income areas. A recent report assessing progress in relation to the Taskforce's recommendations concluded that, 'while a number of banks have disclosed some information about their activities, not all have done so. The current regime of voluntary disclosure leaves an environment where banks are providing information that makes helpful comparison problematic.'

20. One of the strengths of the CRA in the USA lies in the requirements it imposed on banks to report information on activities in low-income areas and the culture that helped to establish where banks were more conscious both of their activities in such areas and of the profitable business opportunities such activities created. Although we do not see a case at present for the introduction of legislation comparable to the US Community Reinvestment Act, we recommend that the Government, the banks and the Financial Inclusion Taskforce work together to prepare and then publish measures of engagement by the individual banks

with the socially excluded, provided on a standard basis no later than the middle of 2007. More generally, the adequacy of the provision by banks of information which enables full and effective monitoring to be carried out will be an important criterion in determining the overall success of the voluntary partnership approach to combating financial exclusion in banking services.

Chapter 2 outlined some of the market failures that might cause mainstream lenders to be reluctant to provide services such as short-term loans to lower-income consumers and how the CRA responds to these failures. Michael Barr in a comprehensive review of the CRA (Barr, 2005) argues that the Act has been on balance beneficial. The CRA permits community groups to intervene at hearings on a bank's performance and since 1989 have been able to access data on the race and income of applicants for home mortgage loans. The CRA ratings of 'need to improve', 'satisfactory' and 'outstanding' are made public and some government agencies and states will only bank with institutions that receive a higher than satisfactory rating. We might view the CRA as a form of 'meta-regulation'. It is a strategy that harnesses legal powers, reputational incentives and social pressures (through community activists) to achieve its objectives. It does not require the making of unprofitable loans or result in significant cross-subsidisation by shareholders or middle-income consumers. It has undoubtedly promoted reflection within the banks on how best to serve lower-income consumers and may have helped to change some cultural perceptions of the profitability of lower-income markets. It has the potential for achieving what Parker describes as 'open self-regulation' that brings together management responsibility and the law and increases democratic social responsibility. There is little evidence that the CRA contributed to the sub-prime mortgage crisis. Mortgage loans associated with the CRA have a low foreclosure rate. (For further discussion of the possibilities of harnessing mainstream lenders to serve low-income areas, see Wilson, 2011).

A theme throughout this chapter has been that of ensuring individuals get the 'right' rather than the 'wrong' type of credit. What are the central policies and institutions that will ensure such an outcome?

8

Quality Regulation and Post-purchase Quality Problems

The objectives of this chapter are to explore different techniques of achieving product and service quality in consumer markets and providing redress for consumers where products and services do not meet consumers' reasonable expectations. We introduce different techniques for addressing quality problems and then consider the role of the classic private law standards in the Sale of Goods Act 1979, exploring their underlying rationale and application to the purchase of high-value consumer products such as automobiles. After considering the responsibilities of retailer and manufacturer, we analyse the possibility of establishing more detailed quality standards that reduce consumer redress costs and hopefully the number of unresolved disputes between consumer and supplier. The different techniques for regulating quality—information, standards, licensing—are illustrated in the context of the market for the sale of used cars and car servicing. The chapter raises the relative role of overlapping general rules, detailed standards and industry codes in regulation and the appropriate institutional structure for their development. It suggests that consumer 'law' is a continuing process of experimentation and that the relationship of legal norms to market norms is not simple.

1. Sources of quality problems: an economic perspective

Two kinds of market failure are likely to account for the quality problems of products causing economic loss to consumers. First, consumers may often lack adequate information on the reliability, durability and running costs of products, and sellers will generally have superior information on these matters (see above Chapter 2, at 2). In addition, consumers may often be unclear as to the exact nature of their post-purchase rights and the relative rights and responsibilities of buyer and seller. This lack of adequate information will be exacerbated if warranty coverage is contained in complex legal terms or buried in fine print. Consumers may also lack easily accessible information comparing the relative performance of different sellers. Consumers may focus on the purchase price, seriously underestimating the after-purchase costs associated with product use; the literature on bounded rationality discussed in Chapter 2 indicates that consumers may misperceive the costs and benefits of services. The Competition Commission found in its investigation of extended warranties that consumers in the UK focused on the price rather than the long-term costs of products.

Extended Warranties on Domestic Electrical Goods: A Report on the Supply of Extended Warranties on Domestic Electrical Goods within the UK, vol 1 (2003) 178

> In the NOP quantitative survey, reliability was only mentioned by 6 per cent of consumers as the most important reason why they chose a particular model of electrical product, and durability by 2 per cent. It also emerged from the NOP qualitative survey that consumers did not gather information about repair costs when shopping around for a DEG unless volunteered by word of mouth (for example, when discussing experiences with friends or family). Consumers in the NOP qualitative survey reported that no information was available in-store about repair costs.

Different aspects of a good or service—eg diagnosis and treatment—may be 'bundled' together (see above Chapter 2 at 2). Bundling is not necessarily detrimental to consumers since it may reduce the overall cost of the product, but it is also an area where consumers may make mistaken assumptions about the costs of the 'bundle' because of behavioural biases. And the market may not respond through competition (see above Chapter 2 at 4). Professional and financial services may often have credence characteristics, that is to say, experience of the service may not be a reliable guide as to whether the consumer has received the appropriate quality. Complex products that are infrequently purchased and that have credence or experience characteristics are likely to be areas of quality problems. Markets such as life insurance, building and plumbing services, and funerals may fall within this category.

We noted in Chapter 2 Akerlof's argument that the inability to signal quality reliability could result in a 'market for lemons'. While consumers may adapt to this level of quality, they would be willing to pay a higher price if quality was more easy to observe. This problem of 'adverse selection' gave rise to interest in two mechanisms to address information asymmetry: signalling by the better-informed party and screening by the uninformed party. A better-informed party could signal the quality of their product or service through a variety of mechanisms such as generous return policies, product guarantees, trade marks and advertising. However, these signals might in turn be manipulated by suppliers—for example, by offering guarantees but making it difficult for individuals to exercise their guarantee rights or by placing small print conditions on their exercise. Mechanisms such as product guarantees may also raise moral hazard problems. This refers to the fact that individuals who are protected by a guarantee may have less incentive to take care of a product.

1.1 The repeat-purchase mechanism, reputation and product quality

The repeat-purchase mechanism (Klein and Leffler, 1981: 615) may provide incentives for maintaining appropriate levels of product quality. Many stores which view consumers as repeat purchasers provide 'satisfaction guaranteed or money refunded' and generous return policies (Ross and Littlefield, 1977–78: 199; Ramsay, 1981: 117: Bhatia, 2004), thereby significantly reducing enforcement costs. Third-party information brokers (eg Which?) and testing agencies may also provide information.

Di Maggio and Louch found that in high-cost, infrequent transactions consumers often preferred to deal within social networks of friends and relatives and that those who purchased services such as home maintenance services from within these networks expressed higher levels of satisfaction than those who did not. These findings suggest that many consumer transactions are, like commercial contracts, embedded within social networks of reciprocal obligations. Social networks may partly account for price heterogeneity in markets (see Di Maggio and Louch, 1998: 619). They may also account for the failure of codes of practice as signals of quality. Consumers may prefer information from a social network to the more abstract signal of a code.

A variety of information remedies may be used to address quality problems (see above Chapter 3, at 3.1) For example, labelling, grading systems or information standards ('natural' for particular types of food, for example), such as the use of the British Standards Institute (BSI) 'Kitemark' symbol to signal quality, reduce consumers' costs in processing complex information and stimulate competition around the particular attribute. In addition, encouragement of comparative testing and quality certification by voluntary groups may be provided by state subsidies. 'Trial periods' may be introduced and product standards be written. The existence of the Internet can facilitate at low cost reliable comparative quality information.

Trademark protection is a valuable form of quality assurance since it protects brand names—an important source of market reputation. There are, however, potential dangers for consumers associated with trademarks. Dangers lie where trademarks become generic (eg aspirin), are deceptive (eg through a lowering in quality over time) or, through heavy advertising, contribute to artificial product differentiation. The essential issue in trademark policy is, therefore, that of imperfect information.

The second major cause of such economic loss is the market failure that results from the high enforcement costs of using the private-law system. Enforcement failures may be caused by procedural hurdles—for example, the high costs of the existing legal system or the need for technical expertise. They may also be attributable to the vagueness of existing standards, which raises the costs of negotiation and settlement. For example, a major criticism of the standard of 'merchantability' (now 'satisfactory quality') in English law was the uncertainty of its application in consumer markets (see discussion below, 3.2–3.4). A consequence of enforcement failures will be a reduction in incentives for producers to maintain an optimal level of quality control.

Where issues of health and safety are not involved, it has been relatively rare for UK governments to write quality standards. This has reflected the difficulties facing governments in accurately reflecting the potential variety of consumer tastes and the danger that lies in stifling variety and innovation.

Porter, however, argues for the important role of quality standards in contributing to global competitiveness. In *The Competitive Advantage of Nations* (1990) he argues for tough regulatory standards because

> tough regulatory standards are ... an opportunity to move early to upgrade products and processes ... firms like governments are often prone to see the short-term cost of dealing with tough standards and not their longer term benefits in terms of innovation ... selling poorly performing, unsafe or environmentally damaging products is not a route to real competitive advantage ... sophisticated buyers will usually appreciate safer, cleaner quieter products before governments do. (Porter, quoted in Braithwaite and Drahos, 2000: 616)

Braithwaite and Drahos argue that location in a state with tough environmental standards does 'confer a long-run competitive advantage' (ibid). Private standard-setting groups such as the BSI or the International Standards Organization, a federation of national standards organisations, may play a role here in promoting 'continuous improvement' and 'total quality management standards'. ISO 9000, for example, contains a model consumer complaint handling standard which provides for the possibility of independent auditing of performance. These standards may be important in the distribution chain since retailers may require suppliers to meet these standards as a condition of supply. Retailers can therefore play a role in quality control. Given the growth of international quality standards a central question is the role of consumer participation in the development of standards, a topic we explore in relation to safety standards in Chapter 9.

1.2 Complaints, legal rights and problem solving

In 1983, the National Consumer Council conducted a survey of consumers' buying problems. The study was restricted to those consumers visiting Consumer Advice Centres (CACs) and Citizens' Advice Bureaux (CABx). Although this study is now somewhat dated, its conclusions remain important for policy on consumer redress:

National Consumer Council, *Buying Problems: Consumers, Unsatisfactory Goods and the Law* (1984) 18–20, 22, 25

THE NATURE OF THE PROBLEMS

We wanted to find out when the goods were purchased and how quickly the products had caused problems after they had been bought or first used (the two are not necessarily the same). Ninety per cent or more of the products had been bought new—the major exception was cars—and used with[in] the week. ...

Respondents were asked to note the type of fault. ... One in five of the products did not work, but this figure rose to 45 per cent with electrical goods. Two particular points of importance for the legal arguments later in the paper came through: first the popularity of the phrase 'not fit for its intended purpose' which was quoted by half the sample: secondly, the incidence of minor faults, defined as the items being scratched, dented or faulty in appearance. ...

One particular problem which was highlighted by the comments of many of the consumer advisers is the difficulty of assembling hard evidence needed to substantiate (or repudiate) complaints about goods. The right sort of independent expertise is clearly both rare and expensive. The general picture, however, is that all too often the necessary expertise is simply unobtainable, or is only available at disproportionate expense.

WHAT DO CONSUMERS WANT?

Our research gave us useful information about what consumers wanted by way of redress . . . refund of full price or replacement of product predominate. Just over half the total sample said that their preferred solution would be a full refund price. A slightly smaller number said that they wanted the product replaced by a new one. ...

... [T]he most vivid impression left by the survey is that aggrieved consumers want their original purchasing decision to be fulfilled. They want what they first wanted something that works and fulfills its promise. They do not want long-running sagas where faults take months to repair; or where new faults emerge. They do not want to be deprived of both product and money for long periods.

In 2010 the Law Commission commissioned consumer research as part of its inquiry into remedies for faulty goods. The Commission argued that:

4.3 The most striking finding of the research was the extent to which participants were unaware of their legal rights. This was illustrated by reactions to the phrase 'this does not affect your statutory rights'. Participants were familiar with the words, but almost universally unaware as to what their rights were.

4.4 Participants had a flawed understanding of their legal rights. Some mistakenly believed they had a good understanding of the law, whilst others freely admitted their lack of knowledge. Some consumers underestimated their legal rights whilst others overestimated their legal rights.

4.5 Participants' lack of knowledge was also illustrated by their perceptions of how long rights last:

(1) Participants believed that they had a legal right to a full refund for 30 days (two-thirds of responses) or for one year (one-third of responses). Virtually no one was aware that they must reject goods within a 'reasonable period'.

(2) One-third of people thought that the right to a replacement lasted for 30 days, whilst one-half believed that it lasted for one year. A few participants chose a different period, but it appeared that no one identified the six-month reverse burden of proof.

(3) Participants tended to think that they had a longer right to repairs, with most answers stating that it lasted for one year (one-half) or that it depended on the guarantee (one-third).'

OTHER FINDINGS

4.22 Consumers were highly influenced by the policies set out by retailers and manufacturers. Participants also thought that market reputations would help them when they faced a problem. In their opinion, the second tier remedy of rescission with partial refund was unlikely to be used, as it would damage a retailer's reputation. In parallel, many participants said that one of the reasons for choosing a shop is that shop's returns policy.

4.23 Consumers may benefit from retailers' efforts to retain their goodwill. However, they may also accept what a retailer tells them their policy is, even if this is less generous to the consumers than their legal rights.

4.24 It appears from our research that retailers' and manufacturers' guarantees influence consumers' views of their rights. In some situations they encourage a belief that remedies can last for a long time, such as those who thought that they can get a refund for faulty products for a full year. On the other hand, some shops' policies may have led some consumers to underestimate their rights, for example to believe that all consumer rights are limited to 30 days.

4.25 Participants suggested that consumer rights should be publicised and that key rights should be posted in prominent positions in stores.

The research concluded that, notwithstanding the absence of knowledge of legal rights:

[T]he impression from these focus groups was that only rarely did lack of understanding of their legal rights really work against these particular consumers. While most were sympathetic to the principle of simplifying the law, confusion surrounding current laws and consumer rights coupled with the policies of retailers to please and appease customers means the current situation can sometimes work to the benefit of consumers.

The EU Commission carried out in 2009 research on European consumers' experiences and expectations in relation to remedies for defective products.

Eurobarometer Sales Remedies (2009)

In the study it was found that, in the case of consumables purchased in their home country, consumers usually seek replacement or a refund if a product is faulty. While replacement seems to be the preferred option in most situations, a refund is sometimes felt to be more appropriate; for example, when there is no exact replacement available, when the consumer expects a replacement product to be also faulty, or when they have lost faith in the product, brand or vendor. Repair does not appear to be a remedy that is requested or desirable in the case of most consumable items (with occasional exceptions for items of clothing) and neither is a discount. For foodstuffs and consumable items of lower value, citizens do not always seek a remedy. This is often because of the low value of the product and the effort that would be involved in returning it to the store.

• In the case of cross-border consumable purchases consumers' also tend to seek either immediate replacement or a refund if a product is faulty. The main difference between cross-border and domestic situations is that more consumers seem to opt for a refund, or opt for a refund earlier in the process in cross-border cases. This is because they tend to view obtaining a replacement as a potentially complicated, costly or time-consuming process in a cross-border context and do not feel the result would be worth the effort involved. Another difference noted was that some consumers appear to be willing to accept a discount on the purchase price, when it is offered by the vendor for such products in a cross-border context.

• When considering faults with durable goods, particularly larger or more expensive items, consumers tend to express greater levels of concern about the impact of these faults and the need to obtain a satisfactory sales remedy.

In these cases there is often a higher level of emotional investment in the purchase, alongside the higher product price. The remedies sought for faulty durable items bought in the home country appear to depend on the age of the product (ie how long it is since the product was initially purchased). Consumers appear to seek replacement for a newly purchased item that is faulty, while repair is sought for items that have been used 'for a while' (generally defined as more than 6 months) before the fault occurs or is identified. However, if an older product continues to malfunction even after repair, consumers would then opt for the replacement of such a product.

- There are few differences in consumers' general mindsets about sales remedies for domestic versus cross-border durable purchases. The preferred remedy for the majority of cross-border faulty durable purchases was replacement or, if replacement was not possible, a refund was the second most desired remedy.

1.4 Responses to legal rights

- It appears that the majority of respondents were not aware of all of their rights. Most notably the majority were unaware of the statutory time period in which remedies can be sought. There were also some areas where clarification was needed; most notably, consumers were unsure about what would constitute a 'reasonable period of time'.

IDC Ramsay, 'Consumer Redress Mechanisms for Defective and Poor-quality Products' (1981) 31 *University of Toronto LJ* 17 at 25–26

Two-party negotiation was therefore the most important institution for the solution of a consumer's problems with poor quality and defective products. How useful is this institution to the consumer, what are its dynamics, and what sort of norms are applied at this level of complaint handling? A number of studies have attempted to provide partial answers to these important questions and also to document in greater detail the nature of two-party negotiation between consumer and retailer.

Ross and Littlefield conducted a study of the complaint-handling practices of a major appliance store in Denver, Colorado. The most significant finding of their study was that complaint to a retailer was both a cheap and an effective form of redress for consumers. Consumer-satisfaction was achieved most commonly by repair, but if a consumer insisted on replacement or refund then this was granted. Indeed, a consumer often obtained more than the law required under the sales provisions (Article 2) of the Uniform Commercial Code. For example, retailers accepted back goods notwithstanding that the consumer's decision to return them was arbitrary. This policy was also followed by other large firms operating in the home appliance field in Denver.

The study also indicated that middle-class individuals who complained (the bulk of retailers' customers were described as middle class) seemed to be well served by retail enterprises but that 'the factors producing generous responses to their complaints may be absent for economically disadvantaged consumers and other special groups.' These factors included willingness and ability to complain, and the important fact that customers for appliances in the mass market are likely to be repeat players.

The authors concluded by questioning the conventional wisdom of consumer reform which placed emphasis on providing consumers with greater access to legal remedies. While recognizing that this policy was of some importance, they nevertheless argued that the energies of consumer activists ought to be channelled into fostering conditions under which complaint is likely to be effective. They concluded: 'Two-party negotiation is generally simpler, quicker, and less costly than any third-party institution even when the latter is modified to handle small claims. Similarly, changing the substantive law of sales is unlikely to produce outcomes as favorable to consumers as those they can obtain through the complaint mechanisms.'

All the extracts indicate that, notwithstanding the absence of knowledge of legal rights, consumers often obtained what they expected on complaining, sometimes more than their legal rights. What is the relationship of these findings to those on 'return policies' of retailers which were discussed under the right of withdrawal (above Chapter

4)? What should be the role and relationship of state law to these market norms and practices?

---

2. Consumer product warranties

An analysis of consumers' post-purchase problems should begin with a discussion of express product warranties. Product warranties are a commonplace in the consumer market. Almost all new consumer durables and motor cars are sold with some sort of product warranty. Consumer product warranties will usually contain explicit repair and replacement obligations as well as indicating the procedures for complaint and making claims.

Warranties play a central role in allocating the risks of post-purchase defects between producer and consumer. It is important, therefore, to understand the explanation for their existence and content. Do they exist, for example, in order to exploit consumers by depriving them of their legal rights under the implied terms of the Sale of Goods Act 1979. During the 1960s and 1970s, warranties seem to have been primarily viewed in this manner. Lord Denning, for example, was of the view that many guarantees should be headed in bold 'NON GUARANTEE'. Section 5 of the Unfair Contract Terms Act prevents manufacturers from using guarantees to contract out of their liability in negligence. The famous US case of *Henningsen v Bloomfield Motors* (1960) seemed to confirm this view of warranties as exploitative devices. In this case, Francis J struck down Chrysler's warranty, which the company had attempted to rely on to exclude liability for breach of the implied warranty of merchantable quality:

> The terms of the warranty are a sad commentary upon the automobile manufacturers' marketing practices. Warranties developed in the law in the interest of and to protect the ordinary consumer who cannot be expected to have the knowledge or capacity or even the opportunity to make adequate inspection of mechanical instrumentalities, like automobiles, and to decide for himself whether they are reasonably fit for the designed purpose. But the ingenuity of the Automobile Manufacturers Association, by means of its standardized form, has metamorphosed the warranty into a device to limit the makers' liability. (78–80)

In contrast, economists often view warranties as a response to market pressures, and the warranty as providing a low-cost means of redress against a manufacturer. The debate over warranties reflects the earlier discussion on standard-form contracts (see above Chapter 6). Priest has argued that three theories might be used to explain the existence and content of product warranties: (i) the exploitation theory; (ii) the signalling theory; and (iii) the investment theory (Priest, 1981: 1299).

The exploitation theory views warranties as devices imposed upon consumers by sellers and producers. Warranties are a reflection of consumers' inequality of bargaining power. Producers will attempt to limit or exclude liability to consumers as much as possible, and are able to do so through their superior bargaining power. The signalling theory stresses the high costs facing consumers in assessing the reliability and durability of products. Warranties, therefore, may be used as a signal of product reliability: the more reliable the product, the lower the costs of warranty coverage for the manufacturer and the more extensive the coverage for the consumer. However, since signals only reduce consumer information costs and do not remove them, there will still be some consumer misperceptions of risk. Thus, while manufacturers will have incentives to offer extensive protection on certain central terms where consumers face low information-processing costs, subordinate terms relating to issues such as exclusion of liability will be defined in a manner favourable to the producer. The signalling theory of warranties has influenced policymakers. Twigg- Flesner notes that the European Commission appeals to this theory as a basis for regulation of guarantees in the Sale of Goods and Associated Guarantees Directive (Directive 99/44) (Twigg-Flesner, in Howells, 2005: 150). Thus in the Green Paper on Guarantees for Consumer Goods and After-Sales Services (COM(93) final) it states:

> Guarantees are steadily becoming a preferred method of competition between firms and one of the most widespread arguments used in advertising

And recital 21 of the Directive on the Sale of Consumer Goods and Associated Guarantees states:

> Whereas for certain categories of goods, it is current practice for sellers and producers to offer guarantees of goods against any defect which becomes apparent within a certain period: whereas this practice can stimulate competition; whereas, while such guarantees are legitimate marketing tools, they should not mislead the consumer; whereas, to ensure that consumers are not misled, guarantees should contain certain information, including a statement that the guarantee does not affect the consumer's legal rights.

The Regulations implementing the Directive in the UK contain provisions that require the contents of the guarantee to be set out in 'plain intelligible language'. They also create a contractual obligation between the guarantor and consumer. The definition of guarantee applies to guarantees given 'without extra charge', thus excluding the extended warranties sold by retailers (see Sale and Supply of Goods to Consumers Regulations 2002, regulations 2, 15).

Twigg-Flesner draws attention to a significant body of literature that questions the independent role of guarantees as a signal of quality (Twigg-Flesner, in Howells, 2005: 148–49). He cites evidence that there is no clear relationship between guarantees and quality and that consumers in the UK 'generally rely on other sources to obtain information about product quality … guarantees do not always and certainly not consistently provide information about the quality of goods'. Consumers seem to be more interested in the reputation of a retailer than in the availability of a warranty.

The signalling theory underpinned the US Magnusson–Moss Warranty Act. A central feature of the Act is disclosure. The Act does not require that a product be warranted but regulates the content of the warranties that are offered. In order to make warranties more intelligible, manufacturers must 'clearly and conspicuously designate their warranties as either "FULL" or "LIMITED"'. A 'full' warranty must, for example, not impose any limitation on the duration of any implied warranty, not exclude or limit consequential damages unless this conspicuously appears on the face of the warranty.

The Act adopted the signal theory of warranties. The 'full' or 'limited' warranty would provide a signal to the consumer of the reliability of a product and focus competition on reliability (see the extract from Beales et al in Chapter 3 at 3.1). This might counteract the tendencies of consumers to focus on more immediate issues, such as price. It was hoped that, by reducing consumers' information-processing costs and by stimulating competition, the Act might ultimately lead to the manufacture of products of higher quality. The Act also attempts to reduce the costs of consumers' pursuing remedies under a warranty, by the introduction of informal dispute-settlement procedures. If dispute-settlement procedures meet the required standards, the consumers are required to use these procedures before going to court. The objective of these programmes is to avoid costly and time-consuming litigation (see Ervine, 1985).

An initial Federal Trade Commission study of the impact of the Act found that there were more full warranties after its enactment than before, and concluded that the increase was probably attributable to the enactment of the disclosure requirement (FTC, 1979; Wisdom, 1979: 1117). However, later studies suggest that warranties remain not readable or easy to understand and that the Act may have increased the number of limited warranties which 'tend to have difficult reading levels' (Moore and Shuptrine, 1993: 33). More easily available comparative information on warranties might be a more effective policy in driving competition for better warranty coverage.

The investment theory reflects the comparative advantage of consumers and producers to insure against product defects and prolong product life. This theory has been developed at length by Priest (1981). The following extract from an article by William Whitford outlines the basic elements of his theory.

W Whitford, 'Comment on a Theory of the Consumer Product Warranty' (1982) 91 *Yale LJ* 1371

Professor Priest's 'investment theory' predicts that warranties will contain the same terms that they would contain in a nearly perfect market. According to his investment theory, there are two principal determinants of warranty content in such a market.

First, if the losses from product defects are avoidable through appropriate actions, the warranty will allocate the loss to the party who can avoid it at least cost. Sometimes losses are best avoided through preventive investments—by the manufacturer through investments in product design or quality control, or by the consumer through investments in a search for the product best adapted to the intended use and investments in proper care and maintenance of the product after purchase. In other instances, losses are best avoided through the repair of a malfunctioning product, and either the manufacturer or the consumer can be the least-cost repairer. Whatever the cheapest method of loss avoidance, the investment theory predicts that warranty terms will allocate losses to induce efficient loss avoidance by the efficient loss avoider.

If losses from product defects are not totally avoidable, then the second determinant of warranty content under the investment theory is the effectiveness of the manufacturer as an insurer against losses. For example, if the risk of loss from product defects varies greatly among consumers, due to important differences in the circumstances of each consumer, Priest believes that the manufacturer is a relatively poor insurer because it usually cannot segregate consumers into risk classes as cheaply and effectively as alternative insurers. In these circumstances, the investment theory predicts that manufacturers will limit warranty coverage to those risks that virtually all consumers share, forcing consumers that face greater risks to self-insure or to obtain alternative insurance. Thus, low risk consumers will not pay for more insurance than their circumstances require. Warranties are likely to exclude consequential damages on this basis, for example, if the potential magnitude of consequential damages varies dramatically among consumers.

A major part of the article in which Priest set out the three theories of warranty content was an empirical testing of the three theories. Priest argued that this testing indicated that the contents of warranties were more consistent with the investment theory than with the other two theories. He noted, for example, that manufacturers of automobiles, recreational vehicles and coaches, but not those of 'washers, televisions, ranges, and mobile homes', disclaimed the implied warranty of merchantability and excluded consequential damages. He explained these differences by the wider range in potential use for vehicular products, differences in the potential magnitude of consequential losses and the greater ability of individuals to self-insure against vehicular accident and collision damage.

G Priest, 'A Theory of the Consumer Product Warranty' (1980–81) 90 *Yale LJ* 1297 at 1343–46

6. The Disclaimer of the Implied Warranty of Merchantability and the Exclusion of Consequential Damages

The disclaimer of the warranty of merchantability has always appeared suspect. ... The disclaimer of a warranty of no greater than ordinary product quality appears quintessentially exploitative. Similarly, such a disclaimer displayed conspicuously in a product warranty seems to corroborate the signal theory's assumption that consumers are ignorant of warranty terms at the time of purchase.

The exploitation theory implies that all manufacturers will both disclaim the implied warranty of merchantability and exclude coverage of consequential damages. The implication of the signal theory is similar, except that the disclaimer and exclusion derive from consumer ignorance rather than more typical sources of monopoly power. The investment theory, however, suggests different interpretations of the two provisions. The effect of the legal implication of the warranty of merchantability is to delegate to a jury the judgment of what are the 'ordinary' purposes to which a product may be put. A jury may appreciate the class of consumers and uses for which the product is designed. But if the jury errs, its verdict will charge a manufacturer for the failure of a product to satisfy a use not preferred by the dominant class of consumers, making both the class of consumers and the manufacturer worse off. Manufacturers whose products have a wide range of potential uses are exposed to greater risk from this delegation and will be more likely to disclaim the implied warranty of merchantability. On the other hand, manufacturers will exclude consequential damages where the expected differences among consumers in consequential losses are high. ...

The disclaimers and exclusions are far from universal. Of sixty-two warranties, only twenty-four disclaim merchantability and only twenty-three exclude consequential damages.

Furthermore, none of the manufacturers within six of the sixteen product groups disclaims merchantability and none within seven of the sixteen groups excludes consequential damages. These figures, of course, are inconsistent with both the exploitation and signal theories. Moreover, the data tend to refute the exploitation and signal hypotheses in other ways. We have seen that there is little apparent relation between firm market power and disclaimers or exclusions. Furthermore, the distribution of disclaimers and exclusions does not seem to correspond to coherent estimates of the level of consumer information. Why should purchasers of dryers, automobiles, recreational vehicles, and coaches be systematically less informed about disclaimers and exclusions than purchasers of washers, televisions, ranges, and mobile homes?

Upon closer examination of the data, it is warranties of the vehicular products that most frequently disclaim the warranty of merchantability and exclude consequential damages. The warranty of merchantability is disclaimed in sixteen of twenty-three vehicular product warranties, as compared with only six of thirty-four appliance warranties and two of four mobile home warranties. Similarly, consequential damages are excluded in seventeen of twenty-three vehicular product warranties, but in only five of thirty-four appliance warranties and in one of four mobile home warranties. With respect to the disclaimer, the range of potential uses may be greater for vehicular products than for appliances such as ranges, washers, and televisions. Moreover, the vehicular product warranties are those which most frequently incorporate exclusions of specific uses, such as racing, towing, or hauling heavy loads.

Similarly, differences among consumers in the potential magnitude of consequential damages may be greater for vehicular than for other products. Many vehicular warranties enumerate several elements of loss stemming from the incapacity of the vehicle—loss of time, meals, lodging, the cost of a rental car—that are specifically excluded from coverage. The magnitude of these losses, of course, varies with the driving patterns of each consumer. A more significant element of consequential loss is damage to property where a defect leads to a traffic accident. The exclusion of recovery for this loss, however, is likely to reflect only the relative superiority of consumer self-insurance—by means of an accident or collision policy more carefully designed to the individual's needs. These explanations of the data, however, are only suppositions. They cannot be confirmed or refuted from the warranty sample.

On the basis of the investment theory, Priest argued that extending manufacturer liability beyond the warranty contract is likely to reduce consumer incentives to repair or self-insure. As a consequence, the rate of product defects 'will increase and this extension will also have a regressive distributional effect, that is, consumers who are more careless or earn higher than average incomes are those for whom the warranty premium is less than the level of risk that they introduce into the pool'.

Priest's explanation remains controversial (Whitford, 1982; Schwartz and Wilde, 1983: 1398). Hugh Collins, for example, argues that Priest's argument is unconvincing because the warranty of quality only applies to ordinary uses of goods and that the purpose of excluding the warranty of satisfactory quality 'must be to evade the quality standard even where this is the efficient standard' (Collins, 1999: 291).

Priest's argument questions the whole thrust of legislation which extends the liability of producers and sellers. In relation to the economic losses by consumers from product defects, are there policy arguments for extending producer liability? Given the differences in consumer tastes, should the goal rather be that of encouraging greater choice in warranties and of providing consumers with comparative information on these choices? For example, consumers might be given the opportunity to buy products with no warranty, a limited warranty or full coverage. At present, this is impossible since warranties are tied in with the sale of the product. Wagner argues, following Priest, that suppliers should be able to deviate from the norms of the Sale of Goods Act, subject to the case-by-case control of the UTCCR (Wagner, 2010: 34). Do you agree? Should we distinguish between economic losses and physical injuries from products? Are loss- and risk-spreading policies as relevant in the case of economic losses?

3. Private liability law

Lawyers have traditionally viewed private-law remedies as an important guarantee of the appropriate quality of products and services. Litigation or the mere threat of litigation may provide compensation for consumers and incentives to businesses to maintain quality control. Private law might be said to have the advantages of decentralised enforcement where standards of quality are contractually tailored to the individual circumstances of the plaintiff. It provides a tailor-made remedy.

Consumer rights concerning the identity and quality of goods in the United Kingdom are primarily contained in the common law of contract, sections 13–14 of the Sale of Goods Act 1979 (as amended by the Sale and Supply of Goods Act 1994 and the Sale and Supply of Goods to Consumers Regulations 2002), the Supply of Goods (Implied Terms) Act 1973, the Supply of Goods and Services Act 1982, the Unfair Contract Terms Act 1977, the Unfair Terms in Consumer Contracts Regulations 1999, the Consumer Credit Act 1974, the Consumer Protection Act 1987 and the common law tort of negligence.

Retailers, rather than manufacturers have the primary liability for defective goods under sections 13–14 of the Sale of Goods Act 1979. Often regarded as central topics in sales law, and certainly the area of greatest litigation, the implied conditions of description and quality impose obligations of strict liability that may not be contracted out of in sales by businesses to consumers. An attempt to do so would constitute a contravention of the CPUT regulations 2008. The implied conditions in sales contracts also provide the model for description and quality obligations for goods in other supply contracts such as hire-purchase, work and materials, and contracts of hire.

This area of sales law is not easy to rationalise at a doctrinal level because the sections are applicable to many differing fact situations with correspondingly distinct policy rationales. The open texture of the standards of 'merchantable', 'reasonable fitness for purpose' and 'satisfactory quality' confer a broad discretion on judges to particularise the broad standard to the facts of the case and their perception of the appropriate allocation of risk. This may differ in the context of a case of personal injuries caused by product defects, a claim for pure economic loss by a commercial business against a retailer, a claim by a consumer for having received a 'lemon' automobile, or breach of an international commodity contract. Although, as we shall see, there are some significant differences in the treatment of consumer and commercial sales, there is not a self-contained consumer code so that decisions in commercial cases are treated as relevant to the interpretation of a consumer case. These distinctions suggest that it may be desirable to enact a separate consumer sales code (see Bridge 2003: 173–77).

Discussion of the substantive obligations of description and quality is further complicated by the fact that since these implied terms are conditions, an individual is prima facie entitled to reject the goods for breach of the condition. It is probably the case that judicial interpretation of the standard (eg is this car 'satisfactory quality') has been affected by concern for the remedial consequences of a conclusion that goods are not of satisfactory quality. The English courts often concealed their attempts to allocate risks between the parties under extensive semantic analysis (see eg *Ashington Piggeries v Christopher Hill* (1972); *Kendall v Lillico* (1969)). Finally, the model of strict liability in the sale of goods is of importance in relation to product liability. Jane Stapleton claims that the implied terms as to quality

> have been the single most potent aspect of the development of the law of product liability. It made commercial sellers accustomed to strict obligations with respect to quality long before they were exposed to a fault standard in tort in this regard, and long before pressures developed to convert that standard into a strict standard. (Stapleton, 1994: 14)

Since these obligations arise from the contract of sale, the doctrine of privity of contract means that a third-party user may not in general claim under these protections. While this finding has been mitigated by statute (see Contracts (Rights of Third Parties) Act 1999), it is still a hurdle for a litigant (see below). Unless a manufacturer contracts directly with a consumer, a manufacturer in the UK will not be liable in negligence to a consumer in tort for pure economic loss. This legal position differs from general consumer expectations that manufacturers are primarily responsible for defective products. In addition, third parties such as family members who did not contract with the seller would not be in privity of contract with the seller.

During the past three decades, there have been many criticisms and reforms of these private-law protections. The deficiencies of the Sale of Goods Act were summarised by the Ontario Law Reform Commission in 1972, in particular that the remedies are unrelated to practical realities and that it ignores the powerful position of the manufacturer in the distribution chain (Ontario Law Reform Commission, 1972: 23, 166). After working through this chapter you should assess the extent to which reforms since the date of that report have addressed the problems identified by the Ontario Law Reform Commission.

European developments have had an impact on this area of law through the Unfair Terms in Consumer Contracts Regulations and the EC Directive 1999/44/EC that harmonises certain aspects of the sale and supply of goods and consumer guarantees. The primary effect of the latter directive on UK law is on the remedies available to a buyer (see below 3.5). The Directive requires that goods should be conforming, regulates guarantees (see above) and adds the following factor to be taken into account in assessing the sales standard of satisfactory quality, namely 'any public statements on the specific characteristics of the goods made about them by the seller, the producer or his representative, particularly in advertising or on labelling'. The Directive is implemented in UK law by the Sale and Supply of Goods to Consumers Regulations 2002 (SI 2002/3045) (see Oughton and Willett, 2002: 299). Under the implementing regulations a consumer is 'any natural person who, in the contracts covered by the Regulations, is acting for purposes which are outside his trade, business or profession'. The implementing regulations define a non-conforming good as one which breaches an express term or the implied terms of sections 13–15. The recent proposal for a common European sales regulation also contains provisions on implied quality terms (see Articles 100-101), extending them to contracts for digital content (see below) and imposing an obligation of strict liability for installation of goods carried out by a seller.

3.1 Correspondence with description

The implied condition in section 13 of the Sale of Goods Act 1979 is perhaps less important than that of satisfactory quality but it includes a private sale, whereas section 14 liability applies only to professional sellers. There are two issues under section 13: (1) when is there a sale by description? And (2) what constitutes the extent of the description condition?

A 'sale by description' was originally restricted in the nineteenth century to a sale of unascertained goods, eg a commodity sale of '500 tons of Oregon Grade A Wheat', where the description identified the goods. The restriction of this condition and the implied term of merchantable quality to sales by description was an exception to caveat emptor because the buyer could not inspect the goods and was relying on the description. This contrasted with a sale of specific goods (see definition in Sale of Goods Act) where caveat emptor would apply. However, after the passage of the Sale of Goods Act 1893 English judges interpreted the concept of a sale by description broadly in order to provide protection to buyers. This reflected therefore a consumerist orientation by the courts towards interpretation of the Act.

Almost all sales will be sales by description. Reference is often made to the judgment of Lord Wright in *Grant v Australian Knitting Mills* (1936) where he stated that

> there is a sale by description even though the buyer is buying something displayed before him on the counter; a thing is sold by description, though it is specific, so long as it is sold not merely as the specific thing but as a thing corresponding to a description eg woollen undergarments, a hot-water bottle.

Section 13(3) of the Act, added in 1973, clarifies a doubt raised by the Molony Committee (1962: paragraph 441) as to whether a sale by description extends to self-service stores such as supermarkets.

The second issue concerns the scope of characteristics covered by the description. The courts have suggested that the concept of description goes to the issue of the identity rather than the quality of the goods (see Lord Wilberforce in *Ashington Piggeries Ltd v Christopher Hill* (1972)) which are addressed by the section 14 obligations of satisfactory quality and reasonable fitness for purpose. It may not always be easy to distinguish 'identity' from 'quality'. Suppose one bought a car with the description 'Blue, Ford Focus 2004, one owner, leather seats'. If the car did not have leather seats would this be a breach of section 13? The interpretation of this question has often arisen in commercial cases where buyers have not always had good reasons for rejecting goods but have latched on to small deviations from the contractual description to successfully claim that they are entitled to reject the goods (see eg *Arcos Ltd v EA Ronaasen & Son* (1933); *Moore & Co v Landauer & Co* (1921)). The courts have in later commercial cases disapproved of this strict approach to the description term, suggesting that the description must relate to 'a substantial ingredient of the identity of the thing sold' (Lord Wilberforce in *Reardon Smith Line Ltd v Hansen Tangsen* (1976)), and section 15A of the Sale of Goods Act 1979 now reduces the problem of opportunistic breach by a buyer in commercial sales. However, the arguments for a strict default rule that the goods must correspond with their description, interpreted broadly, may be stronger in consumer sales conferring greater bargaining power on the consumer. It would create incentives for sellers to ensure that the description was correct.

Varley v Whipp [1900] 1 QB 513

In this case the plaintiff had sold a second-hand self-binding reaping machine to the defendant. The defendant did not see the machine before purchasing it. It was described to him as being new the previous year and having only been used to cut 50–60 acres. An issue in this case was whether the sale was by description. Channell J concluded that it was:

> The term 'sale of goods by description' must apply to all cases where the purchaser has not seen the goods, but is relying on the description alone. It applies in a case like the present, where the buyer has never seen the article sold, but has bought by the description. In that case, by the Sale of Goods Act, 1893, s 13, there is an implied condition that the goods shall correspond with the description which is a different thing from a warranty. The most-usual application of that section no doubt is to the case of unascertained goods, but I think it must also be applied to cases such as this where there is no identification otherwise than by description.

Harlingdon & Leinster Enterprises Ltd v Christopher Hull [1991] 1 QB 629, [1991] 1 QB (CA) 564, [1990] 1 All ER 737

This case concerned two London art dealers. Christopher Hull wished to dispose of two oil paintings by the German expressionist painter Gabrielle Münter. Hull was not a specialist in German expressionism and did not have any training in determining whether the paintings were or were not by Münter. Hull found out that the plaintiffs had a good reputation as dealers in German art and had a special interest in buying and selling expressionist paintings. Hull telephoned them and stated that 'he had come across and was in a position to sell two paintings by Gabrielle Münter'. An employee of the plaintiffs visited the gallery. During their conversation Hull stated that he did not know much about the paintings, that he had never heard of Gabrielle Münter and thought little of her painting. Mr Hull to a certain extent indicated that he was relying on the plaintiff. Neither the employee nor the principal of the buyer had special training in the assessment of German expressionist painting and did not ask Hull about the provenance of the painting. The plaintiffs did look at a Christie's auction catalogue which described it as being the work of Gabriele Münter. The plaintiffs bought the painting for £6,000 subject to the condition of finding a buyer. Both plaintiff and defendant believed that the painting was by Münter. The third-party buyer made an examination of the painting and found that it was a forgery. The plaintiff refunded the money to the third party and was now suing for the return of the price from the original seller or alternatively damages. Several theories of liability were argued including breach of the condition of description, merchantable quality, and misrepresentation. The following extract discusses whether the sale was one by description.

> *Cur Adv vult*

> Nourse LJ: The sales to which the subsection is expressed to apply are sales 'by description'. Authority apart, those words would suggest that the description must be influential in the sale, not necessarily alone, but so as to become an essential term, ie a

condition, of the contract. Without such influence a description cannot be said to be one by which the contract for the sale of the goods is made.

I think that the authorities to which we were referred are consistent with this view of s 13(1). In *Varley v Whipp* [1900] 1 QB 513 … [after outlining the decision in this case].

Other authorities show that s 13(1) may apply to a contract for the sale of specific goods which have been seen by the buyer, provided that their deviation from the description is not apparent on a reasonable examination … [and referring to the case of *Couchman v Hill*] Scott LJ, with whose judgment Tucker and Bucknill LJJ agreed, said ([1947] 1 All ER 103 at 105, [1947] KB 554 at 559):

> '… as a matter of law I think every item in a description which constitutes a substantial ingredient in the "identity" of the thing sold is a condition …'

It is suggested that the significance which some of these authorities attribute to the buyer's reliance on the description is misconceived. I think that that criticism is theoretically correct. In theory it is no doubt possible for a description of goods which is not relied on by the buyer to become an essential term of a contract for their sale. But in practice it is very difficult, and perhaps impossible, to think of facts where that would be so. The description must have a sufficient influence in the sale to become an essential term of the contract and the correlative of influence is reliance. Indeed, reliance by the buyer is the natural index of a sale by description. It is true that the question must, as always, be judged objectively and it may be said that previous judicial references have been to subjective or actual reliance. But each of those decisions, including that of Judge Oddie in the present case, can be justified on an objective basis. For all practical purposes, I would say that there cannot be a contract for the sale of goods by description where it is not within the reasonable contemplation of the parties that the buyer is relying on the description. … On a view of their words and deeds as a whole the parties could not reasonably have contemplated that the defendants were relying on the plaintiffs' statement that the painting was by Gabriele Münter. On the facts which he found the judge could not, by a correct application of the law, have come to any other decision.

Stuart-Smith LJ (dissenting): For my part I have great difficulty in understanding how the concept of reliance fits into a sale by description. If it is a term of the contract that the painting is by Münter the purchaser does not have to prove that he entered into the contract in reliance on this statement. This distinguishes a contractual term or condition from a mere representation which induces a purchaser to enter into a contract. In the latter case the person to whom the representation is made must prove that he relied on it as a matter of fact.

In a comment approving the majority judgment in this case Paul Robson and John Adams argue that 'the modern approach to the warranties in sections 13–15 of the Sale of Goods Act is arguably to ask the question 'What qualities ought this seller, as a reasonable person, to have expected this buyer, as a reasonable person, to rely on him to provide?' (Robson and Adams, 1990: 433). This case is probably an extreme case and the decision may be partly explained by the general understanding (though not a trade custom) in the London art world that sales between dealers are caveat emptor.

3.2 Satisfactory quality and fitness for particular purpose

Section 14 of the Sale of Goods Act requires that the sale be made in the course of a business. In *Stevenson v Rogers* (1999) the Court of Appeal was faced with determining whether the sale by a fisher of his fishing boat was in the course of a business and therefore triggered the application of the implied conditions. The court concluded that the sale was in the course of a business.

> Lord Justice Potter: It seems to me clear that, free of any constraints imposed by the decisions to which we have been referred, this court, making use of the tools of construction now available to it, should construe the words of s 14(2) of the SGA 1979 at their wide face value. In my view, it is not necessary to do more than to turn to the statutory change of wording in s 14(2) as between the 1893 Act and s 3 of the SG(IT)A 1973 (which s 14(2) of SGA 1979 simply re-enacted) to see that it was the intention of the SG(IT)A 1973 to widen the protection afforded to a purchaser by s 14(2) from a situation where the seller was a dealer in the type of goods sold, to one where he simply made a sale 'in the course of a business'; the requirement for regularity of dealing, or indeed any dealing, in the goods was removed. Given the removal of that requirement, there is on the face of it no reason or warrant (at any rate in a civil rather than a criminal context) to re-introduce some implied qualification, difficult to define, in order to narrow what appears to be the wide scope and apparent purpose of the words, which is to distinguish between a sale made in the course of a seller's business and a purely private sale of goods outside the confines of the business (if any) carried on by the seller.
>
> That said, I acknowledge the argument that, because of the varied approach of the courts in differing areas of the law to the question of what is or is not done in the course of a trade or business, an ambiguity or real doubt arises as to whether or not the words of s 14(2) should be taken at face value or whether they should be interpreted to connote at least some degree of regularity and so as to exclude sporadic sales which are no more than incidental to the seller's business. In the light of that argument, this seems to me a case where it is appropriate and proper under the rule in Pepper v Hart to refer to Hansard and in particular to the statement of Sir Geoffrey Howe when introducing the Bill. ... Reference to Hansard makes clear that the mischief which parliament intended to rectify in relation to s 14(2) was that s 14(2) of the 1893 Act had a restrictive effect and was inadequate to impose on every business seller (whether or not habitually dealing in goods of the type sold) the implied condition as to merchantable quality. It was in that context that the draft clause annexed to the First Report was enacted without modification in s 3 of SG(IT)A 1973. Thus, resort to the mischief rule confirms my view formed at first impression that the changed wording of s 14(2) should not be read so as to bear the limitation for which Mr Norris argues.

The Sale and Supply of Goods Act 1994 substituted the standard 'satisfactory quality' for the standard of 'merchantable quality' that had existed in the original 1893 Sale of Goods Act. Satisfactory quality is the requirement that 'goods are of a satisfactory quality if they meet the standard that a reasonable person would regard as satisfactory, taking account of any description of the goods, the price (if relevant) and all other relevant circumstances (section 14(2A)). The 'satisfactory quality' definition was intended to clarify several issues in relation to consumer sales that were unclear under the old definition of 'merchantable quality'. In a series of cases in the late 1960s and early 1970s the House of Lords attempted to clarify the doctrine of merchantable quality. There were two approaches evident in these cases to the concept of merchantable quality. The first was based on the idea of commercial acceptability. This asks the question whether a reasonable buyer, acquainted with knowledge of the defects, would be willing to purchase the goods under the contract description without substantial abatement of price. If the goods are multi-purpose goods, then provided some buyers would be willing to buy for one of purposes, then the goods will be merchantable. This formulation emerged from Lord Reid's opinion in *Henry Kendall v William Lillico* (1969) and *BS*

Brown v Craiks (1970). A second approach evident in *Henry Kendall* is to ask whether the goods are usable for any purpose for which such goods would normally be used. If they are fit for one of the purposes, then they are merchantable. This definition tracks closely the idea of 'fitness for purpose' in section 14(3) and there were often overlaps between the two sections.

It was argued that these definitions were not clear on issues relating to the purchase of consumer goods for use. The appearance of goods may be important to consumers who do not buy goods merely for their use value. Durability and freedom from minor defects are also important to consumers although for how long a good should be durable remains a question of fact. Since 'merchantability' was decided at the time of delivery of the goods, two possible arguments about durability were that that the defect which has subsequently arisen is evidence of the fact that the good was defective at the time of the original sale or that there is a continuing warranty that the goods shall be merchantable or reasonably fit for a reasonable period or time (see Lord Diplock in *Lambert v Lewis* (1981)). Minor defects may also render a good unsatisfactory. Thus Cowan Ervine quotes the Law Commission's report that:

> dents, scratches, minor blemishes and discolorations, and small malfunctions will, in appropriate cases be breaches of the implied term as to quality, provided they are not so trifling as to fall within the principle that matters which are quite negligible are not breaches of contract at all. (Ervine, 2004: 699)

Section 14(2B) therefore indicates that the quality of goods includes in appropriate cases 'fitness for all purposes for which goods of the kind in question are commonly supplied, appearance and finish, freedom from minor defects, safety and durability'. The clarification of the meaning of satisfactory quality also has an educational objective since it communicates to consumers the relevant factors that they may refer to when determining whether a product is unsatisfactory. This may be useful in bargaining with suppliers (see below discussion of remedies).

The Sale and Supply of Goods to Consumers Regulations 2002 adds new subsections 14(2D) and (2E) which state that public statements (eg advertising) on the specific characteristics of the goods made by the seller, the producer or his representative may be taken into account in determining satisfactory quality. It was accepted law that labels on a product are adopted by the retailer as part of the description of the product. The addition of subsection (2D) permits a court to take into account both seller and manufacturer statements about the goods. While these statements may have been taken into account under the previous law, Willett et al suggest two potential changes by this section. First, by referring specifically to these statements it will be easier for a consumer to bargain with a supplier in a situation where such statements have been made. Second, the inclusion of manufacturers' statements that have not necessarily been repeated by the seller may expand liability for manufacturers' statements in English law (Willett et al, 2004: 97–98; and see above Chapter 4). The case of *Jewson v Kelly* below is an example where the courts took into account statements in a brochure in determining the scope of the description of goods.

Jewson v Kelly, Jewson Limited v Leanne Teresa Boyhan as Personal Representative of the Estate of Thomas Michael Kelly [2003] Court of Appeal (Civil Division) EWCA Civ 1030

Mr Kelly was an entrepreneur who wished to convert a former convent school building into 13 self-contained flats that he would then sell to the public. He decided that it would be necessary to replace the existing oil-fired heating boiler with individual heating units for each flat. He decided that the only feasible heating method was electricity and he contacted Jewson, a builders' contractors, to find out if there were any electric boilers which could be used at the building. A representative of Jewsons made extensive inquiries and told Kelly that he thought he had found what Kelly was looking for. This was the Amptec boiler. At a subsequent meeting on site with the Amptec representative present Kelly was told that the boilers 'were perfect for [his] requirements as they were more efficient and cost less to run than gas boilers'. He was also told that the boilers complied with all relevant regulations and legislation and Kelly was provided with a copy of Amptec's promotional literature. Kelly bought the boilers in reliance upon what he had been told at this meeting. The boilers worked satisfactorily. However, the allegation was that they were not of satisfactory quality or reasonably fit for their purpose because they reduced the Standardised Assessment Procedure (SAP) ratings on the flats. SAP ratings are an energy rating that informs householders of the overall energy efficiency of a home: it takes into account several characteristics including the thermal insulation, other characteristics of the building, and the efficiency and control of the heating system. SAP ratings would normally be looked at by surveyors for intending purchasers. Because of the conversion to electricity a new SAP rating was required and this was considerably lower than the previous rating and the range normally achieved by converted flats. Kelly brought an action against Jewson for breach of the implied conditions of satisfactory quality and reasonable fitness for purpose, arguing that the SAP ratings deterred purchasers and caused him significant loss of profit of £213,450 or alternatively a difference in value of £450,000 between flats with the 'appropriate' boiler and the flats with an Amptec boiler. The judge had held that the boilers were not of satisfactory quality and not reasonably fit for their purpose. The Court of Appeal upheld Jewson's appeal.

Before: Lord Justice Clarke, Lord Justice Sedley and Mr Justice Cresswell

On Appeal from the High Court of Justice Queen's Bench Division

Lord Justice Clarke: ... The question which must be asked under section 14(2) is thus whether the boilers were of satisfactory quality. I will return below to the extent to which the 'other relevant circumstances' to be taken into account extend to circumstances peculiar to the buyer or his purposes.

15. Under section 14(3) the questions are these:

i) whether Mr Kelly, expressly or by implication, made known to Jewsons the purpose for which the boilers were being bought;

ii) if so, whether they were reasonably fit for that purpose;

iii) if they were not reasonably fit for that purpose, whether Jewsons have shown

   a) that Mr Kelly did not rely upon their skill and judgment or,

b) if he did, that it was unreasonable of him to do so.

51. The third question [iii above] divides into two parts, namely whether Jewsons have shown that Mr Kelly did not rely upon their skill and judgment and whether, if he did, it was unreasonable to do so . . .

55. As I see it, the problem in the instant case is that too little (if any) attention was paid at the trial to the possibility that there might be only partial reliance on a seller's skill and judgment. The principle of partial reliance is well settled. For example in the *Ashington Piggeries* case Lord Wilberforce said at p 490B:

'Equally I think it is clear (as both courts have found) that there was reliance on the respondents' skill and judgment. Although the Act [ie section 14(1) of the Sale of Goods Act 1893] makes no reference to partial reliance, it was settled, well before the *Cammell Laird* case [1934] AC 402 was decided in this House, that there may be cases where the buyer relies on his own skill or judgment for some purposes and on that of the seller for others. This House gave that principle emphatic endorsement.'

56. In the same case Lord Diplock made a speech which was dissenting in part but contained a number of statements to similar effect which are not affected by the fact of his dissent. For example he said this at p 506E with regard to section 14(1) and (2) of the Sale of Goods Act 1893:

'The key to both subsections is reliance—the reasonable reliance of the buyer upon the seller's ability to make or select goods which are reasonably fit for the buyer's purpose coupled with the seller's acceptance of responsibility to do so. The seller has a choice whether or not to accept that responsibility. To enable him to exercise it he must be supplied by the buyer with sufficient information to acquaint him with what he is being relied upon to do and to enable him to appreciate what exercise of skill or judgment is called for in order to make or select goods which will be fit for the purpose for which the buyer requires them.'

57. A little later Lord Diplock said this with regard to partial reliance at pp 507H to 508F:

'I turn next to "partial reliance." The actual words of subsection (1) appear to contemplate two classes of contracts only; one, where the buyer does not rely at all upon the skill or judgment of the seller to see to it that the goods supplied are reasonably fit for a particular purpose; the other where the buyer does so rely and the other requirements of the subsection are satisfied. As a matter of linguistics it is possible to construe the expression "so as to show that the buyer relies" as referring to a reliance which was only partial, in the sense that the reliance was not the only or even the determinative factor which induced the buyer to enter into the contract. But it is not possible to extract from the language of the subsection any qualification upon the implied undertaking by the seller, if there is such reliance, that the goods supplied by him shall be reasonably fit for the particular purpose for which they are required by the buyer. Yet as a result of technological advances since 1893 there are an increasing number of cases where the preparation of goods fit for a particular purpose calls for the exercise of more than one kind of expertise. The buyer may himself possess one of the kinds of expertise needed but lack another and may choose a seller who has led him to believe that he, the seller, possesses it. The only reliance by the buyer upon the skill or judgment of the seller is that in the preparation or selection of the goods he will exercise that kind of expertise which he has led the buyer reasonably to believe that he possesses. The goods supplied may then be unfit for the particular purpose for which both parties knew they were required, either because of a defect which lay within the sphere of expertise of the seller or because of a defect which lay within the sphere of expertise of the buyer himself.

The way in which the principle of reliance which underlies subsections (1) and (2) should be applied to a more complex contract of this kind, which was not in the immediate contemplation of the draftsman of the code, poses another stark question of legal policy. In large part this decision was made by your Lordships' House in 1934 in the *Cammell Laird* case [1934] AC 402. It was there laid down that if the defect in the goods which rendered them unfit for their purpose was due to a characteristic which it lay within the sphere of expertise of the seller to detect and avoid, the responsibility for their unfitness lay with the seller. The ratio decidendi leads ineluctably to the corollary that if the defect was due to a characteristic which it lay within the sphere of the expertise of the buyer to detect and avoid, the seller was not contractually responsible for it. It did not attract the implied condition under subsection (1). The field of the seller's undertaking as to the fitness of the goods for the purpose corresponded with the field of the buyer's reliance upon the skill and judgment of the seller.

My Lords, this seems to me to be consistent with common sense and business honesty. It was accepted as the correct principle by both courts below and by all parties to the appeals in this House.'

58. Those principles are to my mind of particular importance to the facts of this case. There is, I think, no doubt that they apply to the 1979 Act: see eg paragraph 11-076 of the 6th edition of Benjamin's Sale of Goods. Thus, as the editors put it, there may be reliance in one area or respect but not in others. The principles expressed by Lord Diplock must of course now be read subject to the express provision of section 14(3) that the burden is on the seller to show that the buyer did not rely upon his skill or judgment or, if he did, that it was unreasonable of him to do so.

59. Mr de Garr Robinson submits that this is at best a case of partial reliance, namely reliance only that the Amptec boilers were fit for their purpose as boilers. His submissions may be summarised thus. While Mr Kelly made it clear to Jewsons (and indeed Amptec) that he wanted to buy the boilers in order to instal them in flats for sale, he gave them no information about the nature of the building being converted. He thus gave them no or insufficient information upon which they could form a view as to the effect which the boilers would or might have on the flats' SAP ratings. In order to form a view on that question so as to exercise relevant skill and judgment, it would be necessary for Jewsons (and indeed Amptec) to have considerably more information than Mr Kelly made available to them.

60. I would accept those submissions. I do not think that it could properly be held on the facts that Mr Kelly relied upon the skill and judgment of Jewsons save as to the intrinsic qualities of the boilers. He did not rely upon them in relation to the question whether the boilers were suitable for installation in flats with the particular characteristics of these flats, having regard to their effect on the flats' SAP ratings. ... In short this was a case of partial reliance

Satisfactory Quality

67. The above analysis seems to me to lead clearly to the conclusion that there was equally no breach of the term as to satisfactory quality implied by section 14(2) of the 1979 Act. As indicated above, the problem in this class of case is the overlap between subsections (2) and (3). In particular the problem is what circumstances can properly be regarded as relevant to the question whether the goods were of satisfactory quality. Subsection (2A) requires the goods to meet the standard that a reasonable person would regard as satisfactory. It thus seems to me that a circumstance would be relevant if a reasonable person would regard it as relevant to the question whether the goods were of satisfactory quality.

68. The judge held in paragraph 82, applying his conclusions in paragraphs 73 to 75, that a reasonable man would regard the boilers as of unsatisfactory quality if their installation

in the flats led to SAP ratings which were so low that a proposed purchaser might delay purchasing the flats or pulling out of a purchase. For my part, I would not accept that conclusion. As already stated, the function of section 14(2), by contrast with section 14(3), is to establish a general standard of quality which goods are required to reach. It is not designed to ensure that goods are fit for a particular purpose made known to the seller. That is the function of section 14(3).

69. I recognise that there is scope for debate as to how far it is appropriate to have regard to the purposes for which goods are wanted by the purchaser in deciding what circumstances are relevant for the purposes of subsections (2) and (2A). There may be exceptions, but in general a particular purpose which is not one of the ordinary uses for which goods of the relevant type are generally supplied seems to me to be irrelevant. The question in most cases will be whether the goods are intrinsically satisfactory and fit for all purposes for which goods of the kind in question are supplied. In my opinion these boilers satisfied that criterion. They were satisfactory as boilers.

Lord Justice Sedley: I agree that this appeal succeeds for the reasons given by Lord Justice Clarke. I nevertheless take the liberty of setting out my own reasoning about section 14(2) and (3) of the Sale of Goods Act 1979 as amended, since we are to some extent surveying new ground.

Substandard Goods: Section 14(2)

77. Section 14(2) is directed principally to the sale of substandard goods. This means that the court's principal concern is to look at their intrinsic quality, using the tests indicated in subsection (2A)(2B) and (2C). Of these, it can be seen that the tests postulated in paragraphs (a) and (d) of subsection (2B), and perhaps others too, may well require regard to be had to extrinsic factors. These will typically have to do with the predictable use of the goods. But the issue is still their quality: neither these provisions nor the residual category of 'all the other relevant circumstances' at the end of subsection (2A), make it legitimate, as a general rule, to introduce factors peculiar to the purposes of the particular buyer. It is section 14(3) which is concerned with these.

78. By parity of reasoning I am unable to accept Mr McGuire's submission that the reasonable person who features in subsection (2A) is a reasonable person equipped with the buyer's personal agenda—so long, Mr McGuire is constrained to add, as he has communicated it to the seller. That too is in general a section 14(3) matter. The reasonable person in section 14(2A) is a construct by whose standards the judge is required to evaluate the quality of the goods. So, for example, the safety and durability of a soft toy would ordinarily need to be judged in relation to how a toddler may handle it—not in relation to the possibility of its being given to the dog. If it gets into a toddler's mouth and causes harm, it may well have been sold in breach of section 14(2). If the dog chokes on it, the claim must probably be brought under section 14(3) or fail—unless, say, the toy was bought in a pet shop, for that might well be a relevant circumstance within section 14(2A). ...

79. Here Mr Kelly bought some Amptec electric boilers from Jewsons. He got exactly what he had bargained for: twelve boilers which worked perfectly well. A reasonable person knowing what we now know would have said that they were of satisfactory quality—adding that it might nevertheless have been a mistake to install them because their dependence on peak-rate electricity made them expensive to run and (assuming that the reasonable person knew about it) depressed the flats' SAP ratings. The extrinsic factors relied on by Mr McGuire for the contrary argument are not of the kind which, being general, affect the quality of the goods. They go to the marketability of the flats in which the goods were to be installed. It might arguably have been otherwise if, for example, the boilers could only ever function at

a impossible cost in fuel; but there may well be flats in which space is at a premium and usage intermittent, making an Amptec boiler an acceptable option. The material extrinsic factors, therefore, were of a kind which, being peculiar to the buyer and his needs, had to be introduced under section 14(3). In reaching this view I have been helped, but not finally persuaded, by Mr McGuire's supplementary written submission on the meaning of section 14 as amended.

Unfitness for Known Purpose: Section 14(3)

80. For the rest, I agree with Lord Justice Clarke about the case made for Mr Kelly under section 14(3). With or without clause 8.7 of the printed terms, it is not possible to accept, on the facts found by the judge in his careful judgment, either that Mr Kelly made it known to Jewsons that he needed boilers which would produce acceptable SAP ratings, or that he relied, or could reasonably have relied, on Jewsons' skill and judgment in selecting boilers with this in mind. It is now apparent that Mr Kelly would probably have done better to pay the steep price quoted to him for bringing gas into the twelve flats which lacked it. It worked out at a little under £3,000 a flat, and in retrospect he should perhaps have incurred the extra expense and passed it on, so far as possible, to the purchasers. But there is no way in which he—or now, sadly, his personal representatives—can translate such a business misjudgment (itself largely the product of hindsight) into a seller's liability under section 14 of the Sale of Goods Act. The conscientious judgment of the deputy High Court judge has, if I may say so with respect, become so closely focused upon the detail of the counterclaim that it has lost this essential perspective.

Do you think that this decision was affected by the fact that the original plaintiff in this case was an entrepreneur rather than a consumer?

3.2.1 Limits of liability: allergies and idiosyncrasies

In this case the problem in the operation of the goods (a camshaft for a marine engine) was traceable to an idiosyncrasy in the vessel.

Slater v Finning [1997] AC 473

Lord Steyn: ... Mr CM Campbell QC for the appellants ... emphasized that the buyers were unaware of any unusual feature of the particular vessel. He argued that under section 14(3) a seller who undertakes to supply equipment suitable for use in a particular vessel takes the risk that performance of the goods may be adversely affected by an unanticipated and unusual feature of the vessel.

[para 30] One is entitled to assess the submission of counsel in the light of the results which would follow from its adoption. In argument illustrations of various far-reaching consequences were given. I thought the most telling was the example given by my noble and learned friend, Lord Griffiths. Postulate a firm specialising in the supply of motor car tyres. A customer walks in and asks for a tyre suitable for his car which is parked on the forecourt. The firm supplies a tyre. The car breaks down due to the collapse of the tyre. There was nothing wrong with the tyre. But a defect in the steering mechanism caused the problem. Is the supplier, who was ignorant of the steering problem, liable to the customer because the tyre was unfit for the particular vehicle? If the answer is in the affirmative, such a supplier (if he is unable to disclaim liability) may be forced to resort to time-consuming and expensive investigations of cars to which tyres are to be fitted. Such a view of the law would therefore tend to complicate commonplace transactions. Considerations of everyday

commerce militate against the adoption of the argument, It also seems to lead to an unjust result. The submission of counsel generates an initial and provisional sense of incredulity.

[para 31] What then is the correct analysis? One must first turn to the words of section 14(3) of the Act of 1979. ...

[para 32] But section 14(3), and indeed 14(1) and (2), are not to be construed as a virginal text. Substantially the same statutory principles have been judicially interpreted over the last hundred years. About those principles as they appeared in section 14 of the Sale of Goods Act 1893, it was observed that the old rule of caveat emptor has become the rule of caveat venditor in order to meet the requirements of modern commerce and trade. ...

[para 34] That brings me to the interpretation of the words in section 14(3), which are of critical importance in the present case, namely that 'the buyer, expressly or by implication, makes known ... to the seller ... any particular purpose for which the goods are being bought.' The courts have consistently given a broad and liberal interpretation to these words, consistent with the reasonable and effective protection of the buyer. Thus the courts have refused to hold that the word 'particular' purpose conveys the opposite of general: instead they have construed 'particular' as signifying a specified purpose, which may be very general, eg a bicycle to ride on the road. Similarly, the courts have adopted a non technical approach to the manner in which the buyer must communicate the purpose to the seller. No conceptual difficulty arises in cases of express communication, but usually there will not be an express communication. One then turns to the process of implication. In the context a practical and flexible approach has prevailed. That is best demonstrated by the observations of Lord Wright in *Grant v Australian Knitting Mills Ltd* [1936] AC 85. In dealing with the implication of the purpose for which the goods are bought, Lord Wright in giving the judgment of their Lordships said, at p 99:

> 'It will usually arise by implication from the circumstances: thus to take a case like that in question, of a purchase from a retailer, the reliance will be in general inferred from the fact that a buyer goes to the shop in the confidence that the tradesman has selected his stock with skill and judgment: the retailer need know nothing about the process of manufacture: it is immaterial whether he be manufacturer or not: the main inducement to deal with a good retail shop is the expectation that the tradesman will have bought the right goods of a good make: the goods sold must be, as they were in the present case, goods of a description which it is in the course of the seller's business to supply: there is no need to specify in terms the particular purpose for which the buyer requires the goods, which is none the less the particular purpose within the meaning of the section, because it is the only purpose for which any one would ordinarily want the goods. In this case the garments were naturally intended, and only intended, to be worn next the skin.'

[para 35] It is sufficient that the seller was aware of the buyer's purpose. On the other hand, it must be borne in mind that our law generally subscribes to an objective theory of contract. What matters in this context is how a reasonable person, circumstanced as the seller was, would have understood the buyer's purpose at the time of the making of the contract. ...

...

The implication will normally be that the goods are fit for the purpose for which the goods would ordinarily be used. Applying this approach to the facts of the present case, the seller was entitled to assume that the camshafts would be used in a Caterpillar engine in an ordinary vessel. And the implied condition must be so limited in scope. The particular purpose for which the buyers ordered the new camshafts was for installation in a vessel which was in fact afflicted by an abnormal tendency to resonate excessively. It follows that on the facts found by the Lord Ordinary there was no breach of the implied condition.

[para 38] While the application of first principles persuades me that the buyers' claim is unsustainable, that conclusion is reinforced by the decision of the Court of Appeal in *Griffiths v Peter Conway Ltd* [1939] 1 All ER 685. The plaintiff contracted dermatitis from a Harris Tweed coat which she had bought from the defendant. The judge found that the plaintiff had an unusually sensitive skin and that the coat would not have harmed an ordinary person. The Court of Appeal dismissed an appeal by the plaintiff against the judge's dismissal of her claim. Sir Wilfrid Greene, M.R., explained that if a person suffering from such an abnormality desires to obtain the protection of the implied condition, at p 691:

> The essential matter for the seller to know … consists in the particular abnormality or idiosyncrasy from which the buyer suffers. It is only when he has that knowledge that he is in a position to exercise his skill or judgment. … The fact that those essential characteristics are not known … to the buyer does not seem to me to affect the question.

[para 39] Contrary to the submission of counsel for the appellants on the present case, the Court of Appeal held that it is no answer to argue that the buyer was unaware of the abnormality. Given that the enquiry is as to what the buyer made known to the seller in order to enable the seller to use his skill or judgment to select suitable goods, that holding must be right. Counsel for the appellants accepted that *Griffiths v Peter Conway Ltd.* was correctly decided but he said that the reasoning was wrong. He said the Court of Appeal should have decided the case on the ground of lack of reliance by the plaintiff. I disagree. The particular purpose for which the plaintiff required the coat was for wear by a person with an abnormally sensitive skin: failure to make this known to the seller was fatal to the claim. This decision fits in exactly with the approach indicated by first principles. And I would hold without hesitation that the reasoning of Sir Wilfrid Greene, MR, was correct.

[para 40] Outside the field of private sales the shift from caveat emptor to caveat venditor in relation to the implied condition of fitness for purpose has been a notable feature of the development of our commercial law. But to uphold the present claim would be to allow caveat venditor to run riot.

Is Steyn J's analysis of section 14(3) similar to that adopted by Lord Justice Clarke in *Jewson*?

3.2.2 Conceptualising the implied term of satisfactory quality

There has been much written on the best method of conceptualising the implied terms of quality in sale and supply contracts. Prosser suggested the following scheme:

William Prosser, 'The Implied Warranty of Merchantable Quality' (1943) 27 Minn L Rev 117 at 122–25

> 1. The warranty is a misrepresentation of fact. The seller has asserted, whether expressly or by his conduct, that the goods are of a particular kind, quality or character, and the buyer has purchased in reliance upon that assertion. This is obviously a tort theory, closely allied to the cases of deceit; and it differs from deceit only in that it imposes strict liability for innocent misrepresentations, in the absence of any 'scienter' in the form of knowledge of their falsity or lack of belief in their truth. Logically, however, it does require reasonable reliance on the part of the buyer upon some supposed information of the seller concerning the truth of the assertion; and if the seller does not purport to have such information it should follow that the buyer does not reasonably rely upon it, and no implied warranty is to be found. …

2. The warranty has in fact been agreed upon by the parties as an unexpressed term of the contract of sale. The seller has contracted to deliver described goods, and it is understood that they are to have certain qualities; but that understanding has not been embodied in the agreement. Nevertheless the court, by interpreting the language used, the conduct of the parties and the circumstances of the case, finds that it is there. Such a contract term 'implied in fact' differs from an express agreement only in that it is circumstantially proved. ...

Obviously this theory is pure contract. It arose only after warranties had been held to be enforceable in a contract action; and the first case in which it appeared was one in which the seller did not know what the goods were, and the buyer knew that he did not know and never had seen them. It does not rest upon any belief on the part of the buyer that the seller has superior information, or any information at all about the goods; and the seller's innocence or ignorance or inability to deliver what he has contracted to deliver will no more excuse him than in any other breach of contract. Any "reliance" of the buyer upon the seller becomes important only in so far as it bears upon his actual understanding of what the latter has undertaken to deliver.

3. The warranty is imposed by the law. It is read into the contract by the law without regard to whether the parties intended it in fact; it arises merely because the goods have been sold at all. This theory is of course one of policy. The loss due to defective goods is placed upon the seller because he is best able to bear it and distribute it to the public, and because it is considered that the buyer is entitled to protection at the seller's expense. It is perhaps idle to inquire whether the basis of such a liability is contract or tort. It partakes of the nature of both, and in either case it is liability without fault. It is not often that 'implication of law' is differentiated clearly from 'implied in fact;' but the question of the policy involved is seldom absent from warranty cases, and there are a respectable number in which it appears to have controlled the decision.

If it be asked which of these three theories is the basis of the law of implied warranties in general, it can only be answered: all three. It is seldom that it makes any difference which is adopted; but when the occasion arises, the courts have flitted cheerfully from one to another as the facts may demand, always tending to an increasing extent to favour the buyer and find the warranty.

The first theory underlines the informational role of the implied conditions (see further Hedley, 2001: 114). The possibility of liability for breach of an implied condition based on a consumer's reasonable expectations about the performance of a product creates incentives for a supplier to provide accurate information where the product will not meet these expectations. This is reinforced by the information disclosure requirements of the UCPD.

It is not possible to exclude the implied conditions in consumer sales but there may still be the question of *defining* what are the implied conditions in a particular sale. For example, suppose a seller were to offer a product with a prominent statement on the goods that they are sold 'with all faults' or 'as is', would this be relevant to determining the substance of the obligation undertaken by the supplier? See in this context section 13(1) of the UCTA, the UTCCR and note the relevance of section 14(2)(c) of the Sale of Goods Act and the 'but for' test applied in *Smith v Bush* above Chapter 4 at 2.1.)

In the case of a sale 'with all faults' a court might be influenced by the nature of the bargain (theory 2) the price that was paid by a consumer, the conspicuousness of the disclosure and a consumer's understanding of the statement. A court might also, however, be influenced by theory 3. The third theory appears most relevant to consumer sales since it is not possible to contract out of the implied conditions of description and quality. However, it would be misleading to think that the courts do not also take into account the first two theories in determining liability (see further Mitchell, 2001: 645; Hedley, 2001: 114–25). A German court has held that a general description intended 'to lower expectations' will not be given effect to if it conflicts with 'all the relevant circumstances of the sale' (OLG (Court of Appeal) Oldenburg, 22 September 2003, (2004) DAR 92). In the particular case the car had been described as being only suitable for parts but this was contradicted by the price paid and other surrounding circumstances. The description was categorised as a subterfuge to exclude the implied conditions.

3.3 Judicial standards in relation to high-value consumer products—automobiles and yachts

Most reported consumer litigation under the Sale of Goods Act 1979 has concerned motor cars. The following cases provide examples of defective automobiles as well as other high-value consumer products. Consider in each case why it was necessary to litigate the claims and what guidance the case provides to future litigants. In 1975, Whincup wrote in regard to the requirements of merchantability and reasonable fitness for purpose that:

> there is surprisingly little guidance as to what they actually mean in the context of one of the most common and yet most important consumer transactions, the purchase of a car. Tales of defective cars, both new and second-hand are legion—but how serious do the defects have to be before the buyer can reject the car and demand his money back? (Whincup, 1975: 660)

The first case *Bernstein v Pamson Motors* has been criticised (see Reynolds, 2003) as inconsistent with the approach adopted in the same year by the Court of Appeal in *Rogers v Parish* and its views on rejection must be read in the light of *Clegg v Anderson*. In addition section 35 of the Sale of Goods Act has been subsequently changed to clarify that requesting a repair by a seller does not constitute acceptance and making the opportunity to examine the goods relevant to whether there was a lapse of a reasonable time. The Law Commission in its report *Consumer Remedies for Faulty Goods* (2009) commented that:

> 2.12 In the well known case of Bernstein v Pamson Motors (Golders Green) Limited it was held that a reasonable time for rejection of a new car had lapsed after three weeks and 142 miles. There are two major problems with this case. First of all, the interpretation of a reasonable time in Bernstein was generally considered by commentators to be too strict. In the event, the case was settled out of court, prior to appeal, with the consumer receiving full payment. Secondly, it is doubtful whether it is still good law. In Clegg v Andersson T/A Nordic Marine, speaking of Bernstein, Sir Andrew Morritt VC said: 'In my view it does not represent the law now'. It is unlikely that Bernstein would be decided in the same way following the 1994 amendments to SoGA. These amendments made the time for examination only one issue relevant to the reasonable time for rejection...

A short extract is retained from this case on the topic of the definition of merchantable quality as applied to motor cars.

Bernstein v Pamson Motors [1987] 2 AER 220 (QBD)

Rougier J: ... In *Bartlett v Sidney Marcus Ltd* (1965) it was decided that the two attributes of, to use an ugly word, driveability and safety were the only ones which the buyer of a secondhand motor car was entitled to expect. Undoubtedly, however, the buyer of a new car is entitled to something more, how much more depending on the various considerations of description, price and all other relevant circumstances.

In *Crowther v Shannon Motors* [1975] 1 WLR 30 a second-hand Jaguar, eight years old, that had done 80,000 miles, seized up after it had been driven 2,300 miles. Lord Denning, who had also given judgment in *Bartlett v Sidney Marcus*, commented that:

> Mr Rudd, who put the case very cogently before us, submitted that a car which had covered 2,354 miles must have been reasonably fit for the purpose of driving along the road. He drew attention to a case some years ago in this court of Bartlett v Sidney Marcus Ltd. [1965] 1 WLR 1013. We emphasised then that a buyer, when he buys a secondhand car, should realise that defects may appear sooner or later. In that particular case a defect did appear in the clutch. It was more expensive to repair than had been anticipated. It was held by this court that the fact that the defect was more expensive than had been anticipated did not mean that there had been any breach of the implied condition. But that case seems to me to be entirely distinguishable from the present case. In that case it was a minor repair costing £45 after 300 miles. Here we have a very different case. On the dealers' own evidence, a buyer could reasonably expect to get 100,000 miles life out of a Jaguar engine. Here the Jaguar had only done 80,000 miles. Yet it was in such a bad condition that it was 'clapped out' and after some 2,300 miles it failed altogether. That is very different from a minor repair. The dealers themselves said that if they had known that the engine would blow up after 2,000 miles, they would not have sold it. The reason obviously was because it would not have been reasonably fit for the purpose.

> Some criticism was made of a phrase used by the judge. He said 'What does "fit for the purpose" mean?' He answered: 'To go as a car for a reasonable time.' I am not quite sure that that is entirely accurate. The relevant time is the time of sale. But there is no doubt what the judge meant. If the car does not go for a reasonable time but the engine breaks up within a short time, that is evidence which goes to show it was not reasonably fit for the purpose at the time it was sold

In *Thain v Anniesland Trade Centre* (1997) a Sheriff Court in Scotland decided that a five-year-old Renault 19 that had covered 80,000 miles, and required a new gearbox after a few weeks was still of satisfactory quality. The judge seemed to reason that in the light of the price paid (£2,995) the buyer took the risk of expensive repairs.

Rogers v Parish (Scarborough) Ltd [1987] 2 WLR 353 (CA)

The plaintiffs purchased a Range Rover under a conditional sale agreement from the defendants for more than £14,000. This vehicle was defective and the plaintiffs agreed to the substitution of another new Range Rover. At the time of delivery, this vehicle had several defects: oil seals at vital junctions were no longer sound and the engine and gearbox had defects. It had, in fact, been standing on the defendants' forecourt for 18 months. There were also substantial defects in the bodywork. The plaintiffs drove the car upwards of 5,500 miles for 6 months. Notwithstanding a series of inspections and repairs, the car remained unsatisfactory and the plaintiffs gave notice that the car was rejected. In the Queen's Bench Division, the car was found to be of merchantable quality and fit for its purpose. The plaintiffs appealed. The plaintiffs had commenced their action in October 1982. The case was heard in the Court of Appeal on 4 and 5 November 1986. As you read the report, note the discussion of the significance of the manufacturer's warranty to the issue of merchantable quality.

Mustill LJ ... It is convenient to deal first with the contention that the goods were unmerchantable at the time of delivery and that the plaintiffs were accordingly entitled to reject them.

The language of section 14(6) is clear and free from technicality, and it should be sufficient in the great majority of cases to enable the fact-finding judge to arrive at a decision without exploring the intricacies of the prior law. In my judgment the present is not one of those exceptional cases where it may be necessary to have recourse to the former decisions in order to give a full meaning to the words of the subsection.

... [T]he judge applied the test of whether the defects had destroyed the workable character of the car. No doubt this echoed an argument similar to the one developed before us that if a vehicle is capable of starting and being driven in safety from one point to the next on public roads and on whatever other surfaces the car is supposed to be able to negotiate, it must necessarily be merchantable. I can only say that this proposition appears to have no relation to the broad test propounded by section 14(6) even if, in certain particular circumstances, the correct inference would be that no more could be expected of the goods sold.

This being so, I think it legitimate to look at the whole issue afresh with direct reference to the words of section 14(6). Starting with the purpose for which 'goods of that kind' are commonly bought, one would include in respect of any passenger vehicle not merely the buyer's purpose of driving the car from one place to another but of doing so with the appropriate degree of comfort, ease of handling and reliability and, one might add, of pride in the vehicle's outward and interior appearance. What is the appropriate degree and what relative weight is to be attached to one characteristic of the car rather than another will depend on the market at which the car is aimed.

To identify the relevant expectation one must look at the factors listed in the subsection. The first is the description applied to the goods. In the present case the vehicle was sold as new. Deficiencies which might be acceptable in a second-hand vehicle were not to be expected in one purchased as new. Next, the description 'Range Rover' would conjure up a particular set of expectations, not the same as those relating to an ordinary saloon car, as to the balance between performance, handling, comfort and resilience. The factor of price was also significant. At more than £14,000 this vehicle was, if not at the top end of the scale, well above the level of the ordinary family saloon. The buyer was entitled to value for his money.

With these factors in mind, can it be said that the Range Rover as delivered was as fit for the purpose as the buyer could reasonably expect? The point does not admit of elaborate discussion. I can only say that to my mind the defects in engine, gearbox and bodywork, the existence of which is no longer in dispute, clearly demand a negative answer.

It is however also necessary to deal with an argument based on the fact that the vehicle was sold with the benefit of a manufacturer's warranty, a fact which was relied upon to show that the buyer was required to take in his stride to a certain degree at least the type of defects which would otherwise have amounted to a breach of contract. Speaking for myself, I am far from satisfied that this argument is open to the defendants at all, having regard to the express disclaimer in the contract of sale, and also in the warranty, of any intention to vary the buyer's rights at common law, and also having regard to section 6 of the Unfair Contract Terms Act 1977. Nor am I convinced that this objection can satisfactorily be answered by saying that the argument founded on the warranty operates not to deprive the buyer of his common law rights but rather as a relevant circumstance for the purposes of section 14(6) operating simply to diminish the reasonable expectation of the buyer.

Moreover, I am not clear about the logic underlying the argument. Assume that on an accurate balancing of all the relevant circumstances it could be said that the buyer of a new Range Rover could reasonably expect it to have certain qualities and that accordingly he has a contractual right to receive a vehicle possessing those qualities and to recover damages, including damages for any consequential loss, if it does not possess them. Can it really be right to say that the reasonable buyer would expect less of his new Range Rover with a warranty than without one? Surely the warranty is an addition to the buyer's rights, not a subtraction from them, and, it may be noted, only a circumscribed addition since it lasts for a limited period and does not compensate the buyer for consequential loss and inconvenience.

If the defendants are right a buyer would be well advised to leave his guarantee behind in the showroom. This cannot be what the manufacturers and dealers intend or what their customers reasonably understand.

Assume, however, that I am wrong in all this and that the presence of the warranty did in some degree have the effect of diminishing the standard of expectation and hence the vendor's required standard of performance. Even so, I can only say that, after re-balancing the relevant circumstances, I would again conclude that these defects lie well outside the range of expectation and that the vehicle was not merchantable.

In the light of this conclusion the question whether the vehicle was 'new' when delivered becomes academic. Since the general issue may be of some importance to the motor trade and was not fully explored in argument before us I would say only that on the particular facts of this case I would not differ from the conclusion of the judge that the vehicle was properly described as 'new.'

Clegg v Olle Andersson (t/a Nordic Marine) **[2003] EWCA Civ 320**

In this case the claimant Mr Clegg, who was a skilled yachtsman, purchased a £236,000 Malo yacht from Andersson, a Malo dealer, in December 1999. In the contract of sale the keel was described as being in accordance with the manufacturer's standard specifications that prescribed 'draught of 1.95 m, displacement of 13.8 t and ballast (encapsulated lead keel) 5.5 t'. However, on delivery of the yacht in August 2000 the dealer found that the keel was substantially heavier than the manufacturer's specifications and Mr Clegg was informed of this fact at this time. Two weeks after taking delivery the claimant sent a letter to Andersson drawing attention to several problems with the yacht including that of the overweight keel. Between then and February 2001 Clegg and Anderson corresponded about the keel and its potential impact on the stability and safety of the vessel. The dealers also discussed the problem with the manufacturers, who indicated that they could adjust the weight of the keel. The claimant did not want to be rushed into accepting this option until he had taken independent professional and legal advice. In correspondence in September Mr Clegg stated that 'It is highly commendable that Malo have reacted so quickly but I didn't request it and most certainly do not wish them to carry out any remedial work without my Advisors having approved [it].' Stability tests on the vessel were not carried out until the end of January 2001. The tests showed that the overweight keel compromised the boat's performance in relation to 'sea-keeping, dryness, rolling, speed etc'. The report on the tests suggested a number of modifications but the option of reducing the keel weight by 800 kg was recommended. At the beginning of March Andersson sent Clegg drawings of the proposed alterations. On 6 March solicitors for Clegg sent a letter to Andersson rejecting the boat.

The Cleggs claimed the return of the cost of the yacht, put at £251,718, and damages of £37,750. In addition to bringing the legal action, at a boat show in 2001 Mr Clegg and five of his supporters wore T-shirts emblazoned with disparaging comments concerning Malo and Mr Andersson.

There were two issues for the court. First, was there a breach of condition under sections 13 or 14 of the Sale of Goods Act? Second, had the Cleggs lost their right to reject because of the lapse of a reasonable time?

Sir Andrew Morritt

WAS THERE A BREACH OF CONDITION?

The Cleggs contended that there was. They relied on ss 13 and 14(2) of the Sale of Goods Act 1979 as amended by the Sale and Supply of Goods Act 1994. They claimed that the yacht as supplied was (a) not as described in the contract (s 13) and (b) not of satisfactory quality (s 14(2)). The judge rejected both submissions.

[29] Section 14, so far as material, is in the following terms:

...

On the basis of all the evidence to which I have referred I conclude that a reasonable person would consider that the yacht as delivered was not of satisfactory quality because of the overweight keel, the adverse effect it had on rig safety and the need for more than minimal remedial work. It follows that in my view the Cleggs have established a breach of condition under s 14(2) of the 1979 Act. In those circumstances it is unnecessary to consider the claim for breach of condition under s 13(1).

... DID THE CLEGGS LOSE THEIR RIGHT TO REJECT THE YACHT BEFORE 6 MARCH 2001?

[50] It is not disputed that the result of my conclusion in respect of s 14(2) is that the Cleggs were, initially, entitled to reject the yacht. The question is whether by their subsequent conduct they lost that right on or before 6 March 2001. This issue depends on the proper application to the facts of this case of s 35 of the Sale of Goods Act 1979 as amended by the Sale and Supply of Goods Act 1994. The material provisions are:

[51] The terms of s 35 pose three questions, namely: (1) did the Cleggs intimate to Mr Andersson that they accepted the yacht; (2) did the Cleggs do any act in relation to the yacht which was inconsistent with the ownership of Mr Andersson; and (3) had a reasonable time elapsed by 5 March 2001 in which the Cleggs retained the yacht without intimating to Mr Andersson that they had rejected it? The judge answered each of the first two questions in the affirmative. He indicated that had it arisen he would have answered the third question in the affirmative too.

[54] The intimations on which the judge relied in relation to the first question were (a) Mr Clegg, with knowledge and experience of the overweight keel, telling Mr Andersson in late August 2000 that he liked the yacht, (b) Mr Clegg's letter of 28 August 2000 indicating that the decision whether any and, if so, what remedial work should be done was for Mr Clegg, (c) Mr Clegg's letter of 13 January 2001 informing Mr Andersson that the Cleggs intended to

move the yacht to Portugal or Gibraltar in early May 2001 and (d) the action of the Cleggs in leaving personal possessions on the yacht from August 2000 until March 2001.

... In my view intimations (a) and (b) should be considered together, not least because the terms of the letter of 28 August 2000 (see [11], above) show the sense in which Mr Clegg's statement should be regarded. He refers to the overweight keel as a fundamental point. He asks for a revised specification and measurements. He questions the effect on EU weight requirements and on a resale and asks for the appointment of an independent surveyor because he does not have the relevant expertise. I do not read this as an intimation of acceptance; rather Mr Clegg was asking for information so that he might then determine whether or not he should accept the yacht. That this was his position is, in my view, made plain by the correspondence passing between him and Mr Andersson between 28 August and 8 September 2000 (see [12]–[16], above). The information he sought was not in fact supplied until 15 February 2001.

[56] Mr Clegg's letter of 13 January 2001... cannot be read as an intimation that Mr Clegg had, or then, accepted the yacht. He was concerned to get the information for which he had previously asked. Had it proved to be satisfactory then, no doubt, he would wish to move the yacht to Portugal or Gibraltar in early May. That would depend on the sailing/ testing he wished to carry out in March/April. I do not read that letter as intimating an intention to move the yacht to Portugal if the information or the result of the testing was not satisfactory. Until at least the information was received Mr Clegg was not in a position to decide whether to accept the yacht or not. No doubt the Cleggs had left personal effects in the yacht but, given the outstanding request for further information, that action cannot be regarded as an intimation of acceptance either.

[57] The inconsistent acts on which the judge relied in relation to the second question were (a) the letter dated 5 September 2000 from Mr Clegg to Mr Andersson directing him that remedial work should not be done, (b) insuring the yacht and (c) attempting to register the yacht. I am unable to agree with the judge in respect of any or all of these acts either.

[58] By s 35(6)(a) a buyer is not deemed to have accepted goods if he asks for or agrees to their repair by the seller. The circumstances existing on 5 September 2000 were that Mr Clegg had sought but had not yet been provided with the information required by him to decide whether or not to accept remedial works to the yacht. If he had agreed to their repair that would not have amounted to acceptance. In my view Mr Clegg's indication that he did not agree to any remedial works unless and until he had been provided with the information he sought is also incapable of amounting to acceptance of the yacht. . . .

The third act on which the judge relied was Mr Clegg's attempt to register the yacht in the name of his wife and himself. In cross-examination Mr Clegg said that he had applied through an agent to register the yacht in Guernsey. From the context I infer that this was done before or at the time of delivery in August 2000. In para 7 of his supplemental witness statement he indicated that he was required to do so by the terms of the loan agreement. I am unable to see how this act can amount to an act inconsistent with the reversionary interest of Mr Andersson to which I have referred.

Accordingly I am unable to accept that the three acts relied on by the judge, either alone or together, are capable of amounting to acts inconsistent with the ownership of Mr Andersson. With regard to the third question [Morritt V-C then discussed *Bernstein v Pamson Motors*].

... [S]ub-s (5) provides that whether or not the buyer has had a reasonable time to inspect the goods is only one of the questions to be answered in ascertaining whether there has been acceptance in accordance with sub-s (4). Subsection (6)(a) shows that time taken merely in requesting or agreeing to repairs, and, I would hold, for carrying them out, is not to be counted.

[64] In these circumstances I consider that time taken to ascertain what would be required to effect modification or repair is to be taken into account in resolving the question of fact which arises under sub-s (4). In the light of the undisputed fact that Mr Clegg did not receive the information he had sought in August and September 2000 until 15 February 2001 I consider that the three weeks which elapsed thereafter until the letter of rejection dated 6 March 2001 did not exceed a reasonable time for the purposes of s 35(4) of the 1979 Act.

[65] ... [T]he judge speculated on why Mr Clegg determined to reject the yacht when he did. He rejected the evidence of Mr Clegg and considered that he sought to manoeuvre his wife and himself into a better bargaining position with regard to Mr Andersson. In my view the reason why the Cleggs rejected the yacht when they did is irrelevant if, as I consider, they had the right to do so.

HALE LJ: I agree and would only add that at times the argument before us seemed to lose sight of the real issues in the English law of sale of goods. These are not whether either party has behaved reasonably. The defendant may well feel that he and the manufacturers Malo did their best to put right what had gone wrong and that the claimant purchaser should have taken up one of the options which they advised. If it is established that the seller is in breach of a condition of the contract, however, the choice does not lie with him.

[71] ... Mr Andersson only thought the boat acceptable because they could put it right. That is not the point. Seller and buyer often agree to try and put defects right but neither is obliged to do so. The fact that the remedy supplied by English law may be thought disproportionate by some is irrelevant to a consideration of whether the implied term has been broken.

[72] The test is whether a reasonable person would think the goods satisfactory, taking into account their description, the price (if relevant) and all other relevant circumstances: see s 14(2A). The question, as the joint Report of the Law Commission and the Scottish Law Commission explained, is 'not whether the reasonable person would find the goods acceptable; it is an objective comparison of the state of the goods with the standard which a reasonable person would find acceptable' (Sale and Supply of Goods (Law Com No 160) (1987) para 3.25).

[74] In English law ... the customer has a right to reject goods which are not of satisfactory quality. He does not have to act reasonably in choosing rejection rather than damages or cure. He can reject for whatever reason he chooses. The only question is whether he has lost that right by accepting the goods: s 11(4). Once again, amendments made in the 1994 Act were designed to strengthen the buyer's right to reject by restricting the circumstances in which he might be held to have lost it. In particular, the Commissions (see [72], above) thought that informal attempts at cure should be encouraged: para 5.28.

[75] The buyer loses the right to reject if he informs the seller that he has accepted the goods, or if he acts inconsistently with the seller's reversionary interest in the goods, or if he leaves it too long before telling the seller that he rejects them: s 35(1), (4). The first two of these are subject to his having a reasonable opportunity of examining the goods to ascertain whether they conform to the contract, including the implied terms in s 14; whether he has had such an opportunity is also relevant to the third: s 35(2), (5). And a buyer does not accept the goods simply because he asks for or agrees to their repair: s 35(6). It follows that if a buyer is seeking information which the seller has agreed to supply which will enable the buyer to make a properly informed choice between acceptance, rejection or cure, and if cure in what way, he cannot have lost his right to reject.

[76] This was a buyer who was told very early on that something was not right with his brand new boat and given one suggestion for curing it. When he sought time and information to reflect upon the best way forward the sellers agreed to supply the information required. When they eventually produced this, they not only made it clear that there was no 'do nothing' option, but presented two very different options for putting it right, each different from the one they had originally proposed. In my view, time only began to run then and the three weeks it took the buyer to inform the seller that he was rejecting the boat were not more than a reasonable time.

See also *Lammara v Capital Bank Plc* (2004) (Sheriff Court) where the pursuer was entitled to reject a Land Rover in June 2001 that he had purchased in March 2001 for £51,550; and *Jones v Gallagher* (2004) where an installed kitchen had a colour mismatch. Although there was a breach of the implied condition of satisfactory quality, the plaintiffs lost their right to reject because of a three-month lapse between delivery and intimation of rejection.

The Law Commission in its report on Consumer Remedies for Faulty Goods (Law Commission No 317, Scottish Law Commission No 216, 2009) canvassed the different approaches adopted by courts to the question of the lapse of a reasonable time.

A reasonable time for rejection: the case law

2.11 Early cases tended to require the buyer to inspect the goods immediately, at the place of delivery. However, over the years, as goods have become more complex, courts have allowed buyers more time to inspect goods. ...

[After discussion of *Bernstein v Pamson Motors*]

2.14 In *Truk (UK) Limited v Tokmakidis GmbH* it was held that a commercial buyer was entitled to reject goods over a year after the sale. An important factor in the court's decision was that the vehicle had been sold with the intention it should be resold. The reasonable period was said to take into account the amount of time it was likely to take to find a sub-buyer and then a period for the sub-buyer to test the goods. Another important factor was that there was a prolonged period of negotiation as to the proper course of action once the fault was discovered.

2.15 The buyer in *Bowes v Richardson & Son Ltd* was held to be entitled to reject a new car seven months after delivery. There were several problems with the car, some of which had occurred immediately after delivery, others months later. The seller had carried out repairs, but had never properly completed them. As such, the court held that the buyer had never had the opportunity to fully assess the repairs and so could not be held to have accepted the goods.

2.16 *Fiat Auto Financial Services v Connelly* concerned a buyer who rejected a car after nine months and more than 40,000 miles. This was held to be a reasonable time. The sellers had attempted but failed to rectify several faults. Sheriff Deutsch said the right to reject is not lost during any period where the purchaser is waiting for information to make an informed judgement as to whether to accept or reject the goods and the actions of a seller in dealing with defects and attempts to cure defects may postpone deemed acceptance.

2.17 In *Hurst v Grange Motors*, the buyer rejected a second-hand Rolls Royce after three months. This was held to be a valid rejection, since in the three months between purchase and learning of the seriousness of the defect the buyer had not had an opportunity to ascertain whether the car had conformed to the contract, and so had not accepted it.

2.18 *J & H Ritchie Limited v Lloyd Limited* concerned a combination seed drill and harrow, purchased as a single item. The harrow had vibrated when used and the seller repaired it to 'factory gate standard' but refused to tell the buyer what had been wrong with it. The buyer discovered, through informal means, what the fault had been. Due to the nature of the fault, the buyer was concerned that it could have caused other problems in the harrow and so decided to reject it eleven weeks after purchase.

2.19 The House of Lords held that the buyer had been entitled to reject the harrow, based on two different strands of reasoning. Lord Hope said that, given the facts of the case, a term should be implied into the contract of sale to the effect that the seller was required to inform the buyer as to the nature of the repairs carried out. Lord Rodger reasoned that there was a separate contract for repair between the two parties and that the term should be implied as part of the latter contract.

Conclusion

2.20 The length of the reasonable period is not easy to predict. It depends on the facts of the individual case, including the nature of the goods. In addition, the period may be extended by repairs and any negotiations as to repairs.

3.3.1 Computer software

St Albans City and District Council v International Computers Ltd [1996] EWCA Civ 1296

A computer software company supplied a program to the Council that was defective because it overstated the tax base of the Council, resulting in significant losses to the Council. The Court of Appeal held the company liable based on an express term in the contract. Glidewell LJ went on to consider the nature of a supply contract for computer software.

Glidewell LJ. If a disc carrying a program is transferred, by way of sale or hire, and the program is in some way defective, so that it will not instruct or enable the computer to achieve the intended purpose, is this a defect in the disc? Put more precisely, would the seller or hirer of the disc be in breach of the terms as to quality and fitness for purpose implied by s 14 of the Sale of Goods Act and s 9 of the Act of 1982? Mr Dehn, for ICL, argues that they would not. He submits that the defective program in my example would be distinct from the tangible disc, and thus that the 'goods'—the disc—would not be defective.

There is no English authority on this question, and indeed we have been referred to none from any Common Law jurisdiction. The only reference I have found is an article published in 1994 by Dr Jane Stapleton. This is to a decision in Advent Systems Ltd v Unisys Corporation 925 F 2d 670 that software is a 'good'; Dr Stapleton notes the decision as being reached 'on the basis of policy arguments.' We were referred, as was Scott Baker J, to a decision of Rogers J in the Supreme Court of New South Wales, Toby Construction Ltd v Computa Bar (Sales) Pty Ltd (1983) 2 NSWJR 48. The decision in that case was that the sale of a whole computer system, including both hardware and software, was a sale of 'goods' within the New South Wales legislation, which defines goods in similar terms to those in the English statute. That decision was in my respectful view clearly correct, but it does not answer the present question. Indeed Rogers J specifically did not answer it. In expressing an opinion I am therefore venturing where others have, no doubt wisely, not trodden.

Suppose I buy an instruction manual on the maintenance and repair of a particular make of car. The instructions are wrong in an important respect. Anybody who follows them is likely to cause serious damage to the engine of his car. In my view the instructions are an integral part of the manual. The manual including the instructions, whether in a book or a video cassette, would in my opinion be 'goods' within the meaning of the Sale of Goods Act, and the defective instructions would result in a breach of the implied terms in s 14.

If this is correct, I can see no logical reason why it should not also be correct in relation to a computer disc onto which a program designed and intended to instruct or enable a computer to achieve particular functions has been encoded. If the disc is sold or hired by the computer manufacturer, but the program is defective, in my opinion there would prima facie be a breach of the terms as to quality and fitness for purpose implied by the Sale of Goods Act or the Act of 1982.

However, in the present case, it is clear that the defective program 2020 was not sold, and it seems probable that it was not hired. The evidence is that in relation to many of the program releases an employee of ICL went to St. Albans' premises where the computer was installed taking with him a disc on which the new program was encoded, and himself performed the exercise of transferring the program into the computer.

As I have already said, the program itself is not 'goods' within the statutory definition. Thus a transfer of the program in the way I have described does not, in my view, constitute a transfer of goods. It follows that in such circumstances there is no statutory implication of terms as to quality or fitness for purpose.

Would the contract then contain no such implied terms? The answer must be sought in the Common Law. The terms implied by the Sale of Goods Act and the Act of 1982 were originally evolved by the Courts of Common Law and have since by analogy been implied by the courts into other types of contract. Should such a term be implied in a contract of the kind I am now considering, for the transfer of a computer program into the computer without any transfer of a disc or any other tangible thing on which the program is encoded?

The basis upon which a court is justified in implying a term into a contract in which it has not been expressed is strict. Lord Pearson summarised it in his speech in *Trollope & Colls Ltd v NW Metropolitan Regional Hospital Board* 1973 1 WLR 601 at 609 when he said:

> 'An unexpressed term can be implied if and only if the court finds that the parties must have intended that term to form part of their contract; it is not enough for the court to find that such a term would have been adopted by the parties as reasonable men if it had been suggested to them; it must have been a term that went without saying, a term which, though tacit, formed part of the contract which the parties made for themselves.'

[para 64] In my judgment a contract for the transfer into a computer of a program intended by both parties to instruct or enable the computer to achieve specified functions is one to which Lord Pearson's words apply. In the absence of any express term as to quality or fitness for purpose, or of any term to the contrary, such a contract is subject to an implied term that the program will be reasonably fit for ie reasonably capable of achieving the intended purpose.

In the present case if, contrary to my view, the matter were not covered by express terms of the contract, I would hold that the contract was subject to an implied term that COMCIS was reasonably fit for, that is, reasonably capable of achieving the purpose specified in the 'Statement of User Requirements' in Chapter 5 of St Albans' Invitation to Tender, and that as a result of the defect in release 2020 ICL were in breach of that implied term.

Some commentators have argued that Glidewell's analysis is incorrect. The supply of a computer disk is similar to a book with the disk substituting for the cover of a book. On this analysis the information in the disk would be analogous to a service with an obligation to take reasonable care (a negligence standard) rather than the strict liability of the 'reasonable fitness for purpose' test. The central question, however, is whether there should be strict or negligence liability for software defects. To the extent that software is a mass-produced product, then traditional arguments of loss and risk spreading (see *Morrow v New Homes* below) justify a strict liability standard.

At the beginning of the twentieth century when the automobile was being developed, automobile manufacturers sold cars before they had perfected the technology of car manufacturing and consequently significant numbers of defects occurred during this developmental stage. They attempted to transfer these costs of innovation to consumers by exploiting privity and structuring the distribution chain as a franchise so that the dealers were not agents of the manufacturers. In *Macpherson v Buick* (1916), where a wheel came off a car injuring the consumer, Cardozo J imposed a duty on manufacturers to make a reasonable inspection of component parts before putting the product on the market. The liability rule was not the only factor in increasing greater quality control but it was one factor (see Clarke, 2005: 1).

Can we draw an analogy to the development of the computer software industry where innovation is promoted at the expense of consumers? Would it be appropriate therefore to impose strict liability as a mechanism to create incentives for greater quality control? The proposal for a common European sales regulation (COM (2011) 635 final) states in Article 100 that digital content must inter alia:

(a) be fit for any particular purpose made known to the seller at the time of the conclusion of the contract, except where the circumstances show that the buyer did not rely, or that it was unreasonable for the buyer to rely, on the seller's skill and judgement;
(b) be fit for the purposes for which goods or digital content of the same description would ordinarily be used;
(c) possess the qualities of goods or digital content which the seller held out to the buyer as a sample or model.

3.4 The structure of consumer remedies: designed for adjudication or bargaining?

The great majority of consumer disputes are settled by bargaining between the parties or in the shadow of the law. It is therefore relevant to ask whether the existing remedies in the Sale of Goods Act 1979, as recently modified by the Sale and Supply of Consumer Goods Regulations 2002, facilitate fair settlements between retailer and purchaser. The potentially powerful remedy of rejection has often been viewed as a consumer remedy—increasing the bargaining power of the consumer who does not have to accept a cure by the supplier. In 1987 the Law Commission and Scottish Law Commission concluded that a right to cure should not be introduced because it might reduce the bargaining power of the consumer.

The Law Commission and the Scottish Law Commission, *The Sale and Supply of Goods* (1987) 36–8

[T]he remedy of termination of the contract and rejection of the goods has obvious attractions for the consumer buyer: it is easy to understand; it places him in a strong bargaining position; he need not be left with defective goods in. his hands; and he can purchase goods of the same description from someone else if he has lost confidence in the original seller. …

In legal theory the consumer has the absolute right to reject for any defect. True, he may seldom exercise that right, almost always being prepared to accept repair or replacement. However, if the seller is unreasonable it is against that legal background that the discussion takes place. Any legal ground upon which rejection might arguably be resisted, however weak such ground might be on the facts, gives the seller a potential weapon with which to undermine the position of the ordinary consumer. Sometimes, moreover, what' the law is believed to be is more important than what it is. There should be no ambiguity or misunderstanding about the rights of the consumer buyer.

K Llewellyn, 'On Warranty of Quality and Society II' (1937) 37 *Columbia L Rev* 341 at 388

Rescission, properly handled, is a needed remedy. … Rescission for minor defects is, however, essentially an ultimate consumer's remedy: it fits the case of the wallpaper which is just enough off-color, or the radio which is just enough off-true, to edge the nerves. It goes back to the horse; it is the proper remedy for horses, or for things with horse-effect on the user.

Assume that automobiles are the modern equivalent of the horse. Implementation of the EU Directive on certain aspects of the sale of goods and associated guarantees has introduced greater complexity into the UK system of remedies. The EU remedies are based on a commercial model, the Convention on International Sale of Goods, and introduce a hierarchy of remedies in addition to the existing English system of rejection and damages that are retained. In consumer cases section 48A–F provides the possibility of the remedies of repair, replacement, price reduction or rescission. Section 48A(3) provides that goods which do not conform to the contract of sale up to six months after the date of delivery of the goods are presumed to have been non-conforming at the date of delivery. Section 48C of the Act provides the new remedy of rescission. This section permits the court to adjust the positions of the parties to take account of any benefit that the consumer has received from the goods. It contemplates the possibility that rescission may be exercised more than six months after the sale or supply of goods and confers on the consumer the possibility of a long-term right to reject (rescind). However, the court would have to be satisfied that the goods were not of satisfactory quality at the time of delivery.

Under section 48(D) the buyer may not reject the goods after he has requested a repair or replacement until he has given the seller a 'reasonable time' to repair or replace the goods. Section 48(E) permits a court to make an order of specific perform-ance to repair or replace the goods. This extension of the right to specific performance is not dependent on the traditional 'inadequacy of damages' formula in English law but rather the possibility of substituting another remedy from Part VA. One writer has sug-gested that this extension of specific performance to ordinary goods is revolutionary

(Harris, 2003). However, the remedy of replacement may often be in line with consumer expectations and market practices. In addition, Schwartz argues that there is often significant product differentiation in modern consumer goods so that damages as a substitute remedy may be inadequate because 'the supply of products that will substitute precisely for the promisor's performance is reduced' (Schwartz, 1979: 271). For further analysis see Willett et al (2004). Given the complex overlaps between the EU Directive and English law, and the existing uncertainties in the law on rejection, the Law Commission proposed the following structure of rights.

The Law Commission No 317 and the Scottish Law Commission No 216, *Consumer Remedies for Faulty Goods* (2009)

CLARIFYING THE RIGHT TO REJECT: A NORMAL PERIOD OF 30 DAYS

1.20 Consultees told us that the problem with the right to reject is uncertainty over how long it lasts. This uncertainty brings complexity to what is intended to be a simple and certain tool. We recommend that in normal circumstances, a consumer should exercise the right to reject within 30 days from the date of purchase, delivery or completion of contract, whichever is later. This would give a reasonable opportunity to inspect the goods and to test them for a short period in actual use.

1.21 We think that the introduction of a normal 30-day period for the right to reject will benefit the average consumer by simplifying the law. It is rare for consumers to obtain legal advice for consumer disputes, so the law should be capable of being understood, remembered and asserted by consumers.

1.22 At present, consumer advisers are often concerned about advising consumers that they can exercise the right to reject after two weeks. If consumer advisers were able to tell consumers that the standard period was 30 days, it would give consumers greater confidence and reduce the need to rely on ambiguous case law. We also think that our recommendation will assist retailers by providing a simple standard for their staff.

1.23 Most consultees agreed that the 30-day normal period should apply with limited exceptions, in order to strike an acceptable balance between flexibility and certainty. We recommend that the 30-day period should have some flexibility in limited circumstances. A shorter period would be appropriate where goods are of a type expected to perish within 30 days. A longer period would be appropriate where it was reasonably foreseeable at the time of the sale that the consumer would not be able to test the goods within 30 days (for example, where a consumer buys a Christmas present in October, or a lawnmower in November).

'MINOR' DEFECTS (paras 3.98–3.110)

1.24 We recommend that legal protection for consumers who purchase goods with 'minor' defects should not be reduced with regard to the right to reject and also to the proposed directive.

1.25 Under the current law, once a consumer has shown that one of the implied terms has been breached, they may exercise the right to reject, provided they have not accepted the goods. There is no exclusion for minor defects, such as imperfections in appearance, finish or small malfunctions.

1.26 Under the European Commission's proposed directive, this would change. Not only would the right to reject be abolished, but in addition under the European remedies consumers would not be entitled to rescind a contract for minor defects. If the retailer were unable to repair the defect or replace the goods, the consumer would be required to accept a reduction in price.

1.27 Consumers generally care a great deal about the appearance of new goods, such as cars, furniture and white goods. They often spend a long time selecting goods for their appearance, and pay extra for a specific appearance. In these cases, if a repair or replacement is not practical or possible, the consumer will only have the remedy of price reduction. Furthermore, the trader will not be bound by clear rules about how price reduction should be calculated.

1.28 Another risk is that traders might argue that any fault is minor, so that rescission will no longer be offered in practice. Consultees felt strongly that removing the right to a refund for minor defects would be a retrograde step, leading to unnecessary disputes over whether a fault was minor.

THE RIGHT TO REJECT IN OTHER SUPPLY OF GOODS CONTRACTS (paras 5.1–5.33)

1.29 The law makes distinctions between sales and other contracts to supply goods (such as hire, hire purchase, exchange and work and materials contracts). For other supply of goods contracts, consumers do not lose the right to reject after the lapse of a reasonable time. Instead they may reject goods even for latent defects, provided they have not acted to 'affirm' the contract or (in Scotland) to 'waive' their rights.

1.30 We recommend that the normal period of 30 days should apply to other supply contracts involving the transfer of property, such as work and materials and exchange contracts. We also recommend that it should apply to hire purchase contracts. The argument for a uniform regime is that it would simplify the law, removing a complexity that few consumers or retailers understand.

1.31 Some consultees were concerned that the 30-day normal period might operate harshly in work and materials contracts (such as double-glazing or conservatories). However, the period will not start to run until the date of purchase, delivery or completion of contract, whichever is later. So, where the goods are under the control and in the possession of the trader for a prolonged period, or where the trader takes some time to finish the job, so that the consumer is unable to examine the goods, the 30-day period will not begin to run until work is complete.

1.32 In addition, the 30-day period is a standard period and not an absolute fixed period, so that account can be taken of circumstances rendering it reasonably foreseeable that the consumer will need longer than 30 days to test the goods in use. A typical example would be double-glazing fitted in summer. The consumer would need longer than 30 days to check that it was watertight in storm conditions.

1.33 Where a fault arises in a hire contract, the law allows the consumer to terminate the contract, paying for past hire but not future hire. We recommend this should be preserved.

REFORMING THE CONSUMER SALES DIRECTIVE—MOVING TO A SECOND TIER REMEDY

1.34 Under the scheme of remedies set out in the CSD, it is often difficult to know when a consumer can move from a first to a second tier remedy. When can they give up on a series of failed repairs or replacements, and rescind instead?

1.35 This proves to be a problem in practice, as consumers suffer detriment as a result of failed repairs and replacements. They fear becoming locked in a cycle of failed repairs.

1.36 The European Commission has attempted to address the problem by proposing a new provision, allowing a second tier remedy where 'the same defect has reappeared more than once within a short period of time'. We are concerned, however, that this provides scope for disputes over whether a fault is the same as a previous fault and what constitutes a short period of time.

1.37 We recommend that a consumer should be able to proceed to a second tier remedy after one failed repair or replacement. We think it would be beneficial if the proposed directive provided this level of clarity, which would be easy for consumers and traders to understand.

THE PROPOSED TWO-YEAR CUT-OFF PERIOD

1.38 The European Commission has proposed that consumers should not be entitled to pursue a retailer for any fault which becomes apparent more than two years after delivery. Currently, in the UK, the limits which apply are those set in general contract law. In England and Wales, there is a limitation period of six years, and in Scotland a prescriptive period of five years.

1.39 Our concern is that the European Commission's proposed two-year cut-off might not be suitable for some goods which are intended to be long-lasting and where faults take time to come to light: for example, a boiler which breaks down after 26 months, or water pipes which burst during the first hard frost. Similarly, where a consumer buys a fake antique, it may take time for the problem to be discovered.

1.40 Consultees felt strongly that introducing this proposed time limit to claims would add complexity to the law, and would lead to an undesirable reduction of consumer rights. We recommend that the time limits for bringing claims should continue to be those applying to general contractual claims in England, Wales and Scotland.

1.44 We recommend that the domestic remedy of damages should be retained.

How will these proposals affect cases concerning automobiles, the staple of litigation concerning satisfactory quality? Is the 30-day rule likely to be confused with return policies? What is the likely impact on two-party disputes between suppliers and consumers? The coalition government has adopted the '30-day rule' in a proposed Consumer Bill of Rights (DBIS, 2012).

If a buyer rejects goods or rescinds the contract the seller may refuse to accept the rejection. In these circumstances may the buyer continue to use the goods until her claim to reject is finally adjudicated or will continued use be deemed to constitute acceptance? This is an important issue for consumers since, in the case of an item like an automobile, they will rarely have income to purchase or rent a second car during the period of the dispute.

In the US some courts have permitted a reasonable use of goods by a consumer after rejection based on the following factors:

(1) Whether seller, after receiving the buyer's notice of rejection … cooperated in taking back the goods

(2) whether buyer or seller acted in bad faith

(3) the degree of hardship that the buyer would have suffered by discontinuing use of the goods

(4) the reasonableness of buyer's use after revocation as a method of mitigating damages

(5) whether seller was unduly prejudiced by the use

(6) whether, during the period of use, seller persisted in assuring buyer that all non

conformities would be cured or that provision would otherwise be made to recompense buyer for the dissatisfaction and inconvenience caused by the non conformities

... A primary reason for the move away from a no-use rule by some courts has been the belief that the buyer should not lose a vital code remedy because of circumstances beyond the buyers control. Particularly, the buyer should not lose remedies because of the seller's breach and subsequent refusal to take back the goods. Consequently, many courts have considered the seller's failure to take back the goods to be a major factor in *determining* that the buyer's post-rejection or post revocation use was justified. (Bates, 1993: 43–44)

To what extent do the legal remedies discussed above reduce the need for consumers to purchase extended warranties from retailers (see above the discussion at 2)? The media reports that many retailers claim that they have no liability to a consumer beyond the one year guarantee that is typically offered by manufacturers on electrical goods.

Shoppers are being sold short when expensive electrical goods break down. If a TV or fridge packs up just one day after an initial one-year guarantee, customers are told they have to pay for the repair. (Inman, 2006)

There is a durability requirement under the Sale of Goods Act. In a survey conducted by Which? all manufacturers of white goods indicated that their goods should last 5–10 years, televisions 8–10 years and videocassette recorders 6–9 years. The durability requirement does not impose a legal obligation that goods should last for this period but a presumption might be applied that if they break down after 18 months, then they were defective at the time of delivery. The EU Directive on certain aspects of the sale of consumer goods and associated guarantees enacted (Article 5) that a seller be liable for lack of conformity where this becomes apparent 'within two years of delivery'. This was a minimum protection and not enacted into English law. UK protection is limited by the six-year limitation period.

Which? argues that the unwillingness of the retailer to shoulder liability is because retailers want to sell extended warranties to consumers uncertain of their legal rights. The absence of any legal liability on a manufacturer for pure economic loss to a consumer (see below) results in a consumer being unable to hold a manufacturer legally liable beyond any guarantee period.

3.5 Rejection rights outside the Sale of Goods Act

Farnworth Finance Facilities Ltd v Attryde and another [1970] 1 WLR 1053 (CA)

Lord Denning MR: The first defendant is a civil servant employed by the Ministry of Aviation at Aberporth in Cardiganshire. In 1964, when he was aged 23, he wanted a new motor cycle. He read an advertisement issued by the Enfield Cycle Co Ltd and decided to get a Royal Enfield Interceptor. He went to dealers, the second defendants, King's Motors (Oxford) Ltd of Wolverhampton. They got a machine from the makers and supplied it to him on hire-purchase terms. The finance company was Farnworth Finance Facilities Ltd of Cardiff, the plaintiffs. The second defendants had the forms in their office at Wolverhampton. The first defendant signed them and took delivery of the machine. The cash price was £427 5s 10d. The finance charges were £89 16s. Add £1 option to purchase. Thus making a total hire-purchase price of £518 1s 10d. The first defendant paid £155 5s 10d down, with instalments payable over the next three years of £10 1s a month.

The first defendant took delivery of the machine on 11th July 1964. But he had a lot of trouble with it. He took it back to the second defendants. They tried to correct the faults, but did not succeed. So he took it back to the makers, the Enfield Cycle Co Ltd at Redditch. They had it for nine days—from 21st to 31st July 1964. They remedied some defects, but they did not succeed in remedying all the faults. On 13th August, the first defendant took it back again to the Enfield Cycle Co Ltd. They had it this time for some weeks. He did not get it back until 15th October 1964. They had remedied some defects, but not all. He used it for five weeks, from 15th October to 23rd November. But he found that there were still serious faults. The last straw was on Saturday, 2ust November 1964. As he was turning out from a drive, the rear chain broke. The broken chain knocked a hole in the crank case and caused considerable damage. It would be a very expensive repair. He decided that he would not go on with it any further. He wrote on Monday, 23rd November 1964: 'I am not making any further effort to get Enfields or things to put things right. I have tried hard enough and got nowhere. Obviously I will not continue to pay hire charges for a machine I cannot use and which has been a troublesome burden ever since I've had it. Please come and repossess the bike you will find it at the address given at the start of this letter.' That was his address in Cardiganshire. So being utterly disappointed, he rejected the machine.

It was a big loss to him: for he had paid £155 10s down. He had paid four instalments of £10 1s. So he had paid £195 14s. The plaintiffs, or someone on their behalf, came and took possession of the machine. They sold it for £142 5s. They then sued the first defendant for a further £149 1s. He no longer had the motor cycle, and he was now being sued for a further £149 1s. He resisted the claim on the ground that the plaintiffs had been guilty of a fundamental breach of their obligations under the contract. He put in a counterclaim for his own loss. The plaintiffs said that, if they were in breach, they could claim indemnity from the second defendants. So they joined them as defendants.

[Lord Denning held the plaintiffs liable to the defendant customer based on the doctrine of fundamental breach which precluded them from relying on their exclusion of the implied term of reasonable fitness for purpose]

The next question is whether the first defendant affirmed the contract. Counsel for the second defendants points out that the first defendant had ridden this bicycle for 4,000 miles. Even after he got it back from the makers on 15th October he had used it for five or six weeks till 23rd November and had ridden 3,000 miles on it. Counsel said that by using it all that time the first defendant had affirmed the contract and it was too late for him to repudiate it. But as the argument proceeded, I think that counsel for the first defendant gave the right answer. He pointed out that affirmation is a matter of election. A man only affirms a contract when he knows of the defects and by his conduct elects to go on with the contract despite them. In this case the first defendant complained from the beginning of the defects and sent the machine back for them to be remedied. He did not elect to accept it unless they were remedied. But the defects were never satisfactorily remedied. When the rear chain broke, it was the last straw. It showed that the machine could not be relied on. This knowledge was not brought home to him until this last final incident. The first defendant was entitled to say then: 'I am not going on with this machine any longer. I have tried it long enough.' After all, it was a contract of hiring. The machine was not his until the three years had been completed—and the price paid. Owing to the defects, the first defendant was entitled to throw up the hiring; to say he would have no more to do with it; and to claim damages. The judge found that the first defendant did not affirm the contract and I agree with him.

I may add that, even if the first defendant had affirmed the contract (so that he would be liable to pay the instalments), nevertheless counsel for the second defendants conceded quite rightly that the first defendant would still have been able to claim damages for the fundamental breach. The exception clauses would not protect the plaintiffs. But I need not go into that question because in my view there has been no affirmation. The first defendant was entitled to reject the machine and claim damages against the plaintiffs. I may say that the plaintiffs supported the first defendant. They were quite ready to admit that this machine was unroadworthy, but they claimed to be indemnified by the second defendants.

There is one other point, and that is on damages. Counsel for the second defendants said that the first defendant ought to give credit for the use which he had of the motor cycle for some 4,000 miles. He relied on Charterhouse Credit Co Ltd v Tolly when such a credit was allowed. But it seems to me that the value of any use had by the first defendant is offset by the great amount of trouble he had. So no credit need be given for the use. I see no reason for interfering with the award of the judge on damages.

So the plaintiffs are liable to the first defendant. But they are entitled to claim over against the second defendants on the express promise that the machine was in a roadworthy condition. They can recover against them the full amount of £149 1s, and for the £195 9s 10d that they have to pay the first defendant. The judge so ordered. I find that there is no fault to be found with the judgment of the judge in this case, and I would dismiss the appeal.

Several points are raised by the *Farnworth* case. First, the implied terms in hire-purchase contracts may now not be excluded so that the doctrine of fundamental breach is not necessary. Second, where a finance company (or credit card) is involved as a third-party financier they will be subject to the same liabilities as the supplier of the goods (see section 75 of the Consumer Credit Act below). Finally, note that Mr Attryde was in court as defendant rather than plaintiff. Note, too, the proposal of the Law Commission to extend the 30-day rule to hire-purchase contracts.

3.6 Manufacturers' legal liability to consumers for economic loss

Manufacturers may be directly liable to an ultimate purchaser for a shoddy product if they make express claims in advertising that are relied upon by the purchaser. English courts have been unwilling to impose liability on manufacturers for advertising statements. Guarantees explicitly provided by a manufacturer also create a direct contractual relationship between consumer and manufacturer under the EC Regulations. However, English courts have held that manufacturers will not be liable in negligence to a consumer where the consumer suffers only pure economic loss. The case of *Junior Books Ltd v Veitchi* (1983) opened up the possibility of a manufacturers' liability for negligently inflicted economic loss. However, subsequent cases (see *Murphy v Brentwood District Council* (1991); *Bellefield Computer Services Ltd v E Turner and Sons Ltd* (2000); and see generally Miller and Goldberg, 2004) have denied liability in commercial settings and there has been no systematic analysis of the relevant policies in a consumer setting. The EC Directive on sale of consumer goods and guarantees rejected the concept of direct producer liability to the ultimate purchaser for economic loss. The original Green Paper in 1993 proposed a regime of joint and several liability to the end consumer for the quality of goods supplied, but this proposal was abandoned in the Directive. The Consumer Protection Act 1987 that implements the EU Directive on Products Liability excludes liability in section 5(2) in relation to defects in the product that do not cause personal injury or damage to the other products.

The UK position contrasts with Commonwealth jurisdictions and the United States. The Supreme Court of Canada has recognised in *Winnipeg Condominium Corpn No 6 v Bird Construction* (1995) the liability in negligence of a builder to a subsequent owner where the owner was required to repair cladding on a negligently constructed building which was potentially dangerous. The builder was liable for the cost of repair and the Supreme Court of Canada declined to follow the decision of the House of Lords in *Murphy*. The Court followed the minority judgment of Laskin J in *Rivtow Marine Ltd v Washington Iron Works* (1973). While the decision dealt with real property rather than chattels, the arguments may be transferable to litigation over defective products. In a case based on the Quebec Civil Code the Supreme Court of Canada held a manufacturer directly liable to a consumer for a latent defect in a new automobile purchased by the consumer from one of the manufacturers' dealers. Recovery was based on the theory of the warranty running with the product to the ultimate purchaser (see *General Motors v Kravitz* (1979)). This decision was inspired by the *action directe* in French law that permits a buyer to sue anyone in the distribution chain for a manufacturing defect or hidden defect in the product (see Calais-Auloy and Steinmetz, 2006).

Legislators in other Commonwealth jurisdictions (Saskatchewan, Australia, New Zealand) have also imposed direct liability for breach of quality obligations by manufacturers to the ultimate user of a product The Saskatchewan Consumer Protection Act 1996 was based on the assumptions of the Ontario Law Reform Commission, outlined above (518) (see further Romero, 1978–79: 83). The primary concern of the Act is product quality rather than personal injury, and both manufacturer and retailer are made liable for breach of the implied warranties, although the manufacturer is only liable for his breaches and not those where the retailer has applied his own description to a product. The warranties protect not merely the purchaser but also subsequent owners.

There has been no empirical study of the impact of the Saskatchewan Act. An early study by Romero (1983–84: 288) indicates that of the modest number of cases litigated under the Act the great majority have concerned economic losses from defective motor cars and have been brought against the retailer rather than the manufacturer. This raises the issue of whether the imposition of liability on a manufacturer is likely to have much impact on consumer redress. The National Consumer Council study quoted from above (508) found that, although consumers believe that manufacturers are directly liable to consumers for the quality of their products, few complainants make direct contact with the manufacturer (NCC, 1984: 122). The retailer remains the primary conduit for channelling manufacturers' liability.

In addition to the issue of vertical privity (manufacturer–retailer–purchaser), there is also horizontal privity where non-purchasing consumers such as family members are prevented by privity from suing the retailer in contract. While courts have sometimes circumvented this rule by, for example, arguing that where an individual contracts on behalf of a family in relation to a spoiled holiday he may recover damages on behalf of the family members (*Jackson v Horizon Holidays Ltd* (1975)), this approach has been disapproved in later cases (see *Woodar Investments v Wimpey Construction* (1980)). In the UK the Contracts (Rights of Third Parties Act) 1999, section 1 provides a limited protection for third parties where the contract expressly provides that a third party may enforce a term in his own right or the term purports to confer a benefit on him and it appears that the parties intended the term to be enforceable by the third party. Cranston provides the example of 'goods made to order by a manufacturer and sold through a retailer, as often happens with furniture such as sofas and beds' (Scott and Black, 2000: 175). The provisions of the Act are limited by the fact that the third party must be expressly identified in the contract either by name, as a member of a class or as answering a particular description.

In the United States courts have held manufacturers liable to ultimate consumers for economic loss based on a theory of the warranty running with the product. In *Morrow v New Moon Homes, Inc* (1977) 548 P 2d 279 (SC, Alaska), the plaintiffs had bought a mobile home in October 1969 from a retailer in Fairbanks, Alaska that was manufactured by New Moon Homes in Oregon. The mobile home was defective: the furnace malfunctioned; the doors did not close properly; the bathtub leaked water; and the roof leaked. The retailer subsequently went out of business. After attempting to contact New Moon and receiving no response, the plaintiffs finally brought an action against them for breach of implied warranties of merchantability and fitness for purpose in manufacturing and selling an improperly constructed mobile home. The Supreme Court of Alaska permitted the action by the buyers against the manufacturer based on a a theory of implied warranty running with the product. The court outlined the following policy arguments in favour of recovery

> Robinowitz CJ: The principal theory of liability advocated by the Morrows at trial was that New Moon had breached statutory warranties which arose by operation of law with the manufacture and distribution of this mobile home.

> The critical question in this case is whether the Morrows, as remote purchasers, can invoke the warranties attributable to the manufacturer which arose when New Moon passed title of the mobile home to the next party in the chain of distribution. In other words, do the implied warranties of merchantability and fitness run from a manufacturer only to those with whom the manufacturer is in privity of contract?

> … The policy considerations which dictate the abolition of privity are largely those which also warranted imposing strict tort liability on the manufacturer: the consumer's inability to protect himself adequately from defectively manufactured goods, the implied assurance of the maker when he puts his goods on the market that they are safe, and the superior risk bearing ability of the manufacturer. In addition, limiting a consumer under the Code to an implied warranty action against his immediate seller in those instances when the product defect is attributable to the manufacturer would effectively promote circularity of litigation and waste of judicial resources. Therefore, we decide that a manufacturer may be held liable for a breach of the implied warranties of AS 45.05.096 and AS 45.05.098 without regard to privity of contract between the manufacturer and the consumer.

> The more difficult question before this court is whether we should extend this abolition of privity to embrace not only warranty actions for personal injuries and property damage but also those for economic loss. … In considering this issue we note that economic loss may be categorized into direct economic loss and consequential economic loss. …

> The claim of the Morrows in this case is one for direct economic loss.

> A number of courts recently confronting this issue have declined to overturn the privity requirement in warranty actions for economic loss. One principal factor seems to be that these courts simply do not find the social and economic reasons which justify extending enterprise liability to the victims of personal injury or property damage equally compelling in the case of a disappointed buyer suffering 'only' economic loss. There is an apparent fear that economic

losses may be of a far greater magnitude in value than personal injuries, and being somehow less foreseeable these losses would be less insurable, undermining the risk spreading theory of enterprise liability.

... Several of the courts which have recently considered this aspect of the privity issue have found those arguments unpersuasive. We are in agreement and hold that there is no satisfactory justification for a remedial scheme which extends the warranty action to a consumer suffering personal injury or property damage but denies similar relief to the consumer 'fortunate' enough to suffer only direct economic loss. Justice Peter's separate opinion in *Seely v White Motor Co.*, 63 Cal 2d 9, 45 Cal Rptr 17, 24, 403 P 2d 145, 152 (1965), persuasively establishes that the cleavage between economic loss and other types of harm is a false one, that each species of harm can constitute the 'overwhelming misfortune' in one's life which warrants judicial redress. The Supreme Court of New Jersey is also in complete agreement with this view:

> 'From the standpoint of principle, we perceive no sound reason why the implication of reasonable fitness should be attached to the transaction and be actionable against the manufacturer where the defectively made product has caused personal injury and not actionable when inadequate manufacture has put a worthless article in the hands of an innocent purchaser who has paid the required price for it. In such situations considerations of justice require a court to interest itself in originating causes and to apply the principle of implied warranty on that basis, rather than to test its application by whether personal injury or simply loss of bargain resulted in the breach of the warranty. True, the rule of implied warranty had its gestative stirrings because of the greater appeal of the personal injury claim. But once in existence, the field of operation of the remedy should not be fenced in by such a factor.'

The fear that if the implied warranty action is extended to direct economic loss, manufacturers will be subjected to liability for damages of unknown and unlimited scope would seem unfounded. The manufacturer may possibly delimit the scope of his potential liability by use of a disclaimer in compliance with AS 45.05. 100 or by resort to the limitations authorized in AS 45.05.230. These statutory rights not only preclude extending the theory of strict liability in tort, *supra*, but also make highly appropriate this extension of the theory of implied warranties. Further, by expanding warranty rights to redress this form of harm, we preserve '... the well developed notion that the law of contract should control actions for purely economic losses and that the law of tort should control actions for personal injuries.' We therefore hold that a manufacturer can be held liable for direct economic loss attributable to a breach of his implied warranties, without regard to privity of contract between the manufacturer and the ultimate purchaser. It was therefore error for the trial court to dismiss the Morrow's action against New Moon for want of privity.

... Our decision today preserves the statutory rights of the manufacturer to define his potential liability to the ultimate consumer, by means of express disclaimers and limitations, while protecting the legitimate expectation of the consumer that goods distributed on a wide scale by the use of conduit retailers are fit for their intended use.

Within the European Union the advantage of producer liability to a consumer for pure economic loss could be that it may encourage cross-border shopping since manufacturers may often have branches throughout the Union where an individual could seek redress. Liability would increase the bargaining power of the consumer. However, the EU did not include producer liability in the Sale of Goods Directive.

3.7 Reducing consumer costs in quality disputes? Lemon Laws

Given the limitations of private-law litigation for consumers in the area of quality (eg the need for expertise, the economic and psychological costs) some jurisdictions have introduced more specific rules. Many US states have introduced 'lemon laws' that attempt to reduce the costs of a consumer settling a dispute in relation to new and used car warranties. Thus if the same non-conformity in a car has been subject to repair three or more times under an express warranty, then it is presumed to be a 'lemon', entitling the consumer to replacement (see eg Ohio lemon law). However lemon laws do not reduce all uncertainty. Thus, non-conformity is defined in the Ohio statute a relatively open-textured manner as 'any defect or condition that substantially impairs the use, value or safety of a motor vehicle'. In the UK the trade association, the Society of Motor Manufacturers and Traders, has established a conciliation and arbitration programme that has a modest caseload and in Canada there is also an arbitration programme.

4. Harnessing market gate-keepers for redress: connected-lenders' liability

The supply of goods and services on credit often involves a third party as financier. For example, a purchaser of a car may sign a loan agreement with a finance company. The dealer may often have continuing arrangements with the finance company to whom she introduces customers, or to whom she assigns her contracts for the supply of goods or services. A more recent development is the use of credit cards and other payment intermediaries to pay for purchases.

A consumer in these situations may have separate contracts with the supplier and financier of the goods or services. This separation might, unfortunately, reduce seller incentives to respond to complaints concerning product defects and create incentives for fraud. For example, sellers who are not dependent on repeat purchases and market goodwill may have little incentive to maintain market performance or deal adequately with consumer complaints if they can obtain immediate and full payment from a third party (eg a finance company or credit-card company). In addition, if the finance company is shielded from liability for defects, then it may have little incentive to monitor the seller's performance. This lack of incentive will be reinforced by the fact that finance companies are more likely to be concerned with maintaining goodwill with dealers upon whom they rely for their flow of business than with consumers.

The source of the problem in these situations appears to be the economic and psychological costs which a consumer might face in attempting to hold a seller accountable for defective products or poor service. An argument might be made, therefore, for placing responsibility for defects upon a third-party creditor who deals repeatedly with the seller and is consequently better able than individual consumers to hold the seller accountable for these problems. If consumers are entitled to invoke against a third-party creditor the same legal rights and defences which they have against the seller, then this would be a strong incentive for creditors to monitor the behaviour of the sellers with whom they deal. There is also a risk-spreading argument: that the financier is in a better position than the consumer to spread the costs of defective performance amongst all consumers.

The Crowther Committee's proposals for 'connected-lender' liability' formed the basis for connected-lender liability under section 75 of the Consumer Credit Act 1974. The Committee developed the rationale for these proposals that, in substance, seller and financier are often engaged in a joint venture, with the finance company as the dominant partner. Discussing the situation where the retailer introduces a customer to the finance house, the Committee stated:

Report of the Committee on Consumer Credit (Crowther Committee), Cmnd 4596/1971

6.6.22 [T]he finance company is not in the position of a purely independent lender to whom the borrower comes for a loan. To a considerable extent the finance house and the dealer are engaged in a joint venture. The finance house controls the contract documents used by the dealer in his instalment credit business. It competes keenly with other' finance houses for the privilege of obtaining the dealer's credit business. On motor vehicle business it pays the dealer a substantial commission. ... for introducing a hire-purchase contract, thus giving the dealer a positive incentive to procure the customer's signature to a hire-purchase agreement instead of selling for cash. It provides general financial support for the dealer, the cost of which may be materially influenced by the volume of retail instalment credit business introduced to it by the dealer. ... [T]he finance house relies on the dealer as a medium for promoting its own business and it cannot be equated with a wholly independent lender such as a bank approached by the borrower himself.

Obligations of the Connected Lender

6.6.24 We think that once more a distinction has to be drawn between a lender who is completely independent and one whose relationship with the seller makes him a connected lender. ... We consider that there is no ground for making an independent lender answerable for defects in goods supplied with the aid of the loan, or for giving a borrower a right to set off loss or damage suffered in respect of defective goods against a claim for sums due under the loan contract. But where the lender is a connected lender, then for the reasons we have indicated different considerations apply. If with all the pressure for business exerted by the lender and the financial inducements the lender offers, the seller seeks to boost sales by making false representations, or supplies goods which are defective, is it right that the lender should be able to disclaim all responsibility and insist on repayments of the loan being punctually maintained? We do not think so. We accept that the person who should bear ultimate responsibility is the seller who made the misrepresentation or supplied the defective goods, but we do not consider that it is sufficient to leave the borrower with his remedy against the seller, even assuming that with a changed legal structure the sale is made direct to the customer, so answering the problem . . . of the absence of a contractual nexus.

6.6.25 There are many reasons why in practice a legal right which the buyer may have against his seller is not sufficient protection. Where the seller is reputable he will usually be prepared to deal with justified complaints and rectify the matters complained of. The majority of the cases in which the buyer is likely to suffer are those where a seller is of doubtful repute and is able to continue in business only because of the financial support he receives from the lender. The buyer supplied with defective goods may find that to secure redress from such a seller he has to incur the worry and expense of litigation, in which the burden of taking the initiative lies on him; and that in some cases the seller's financial position is so poor that it is doubtful whether he will be able to meet the judgment even if the buyer is successful. The buyer's difficulties of pursuing a claim against the seller are enhanced if, whilst wrestling with the financial problems of litigation, he has to go on paying the lender under the loan agreement.

A further issue concerned the extent of the 'connected-lenders' liability. The Crowther Committee set out the alternatives and recorded its preferred choice, which was subsequently adopted in section 75 of the Consumer Credit Act.

Liability of Connected Lenders

6.6.26 There are three different ways in which the borrower might be given relief against a connected lender. The first is to make the lender answerable in damages for misrepresentations made by the seller in antecedent negotiations and for breaches of any term of the agreement relating to title, fitness or quality of the goods. An alternative and intermediate measure is to provide that, while the lender shall not incur a positive liability in damages, the borrower shall, by way of defence to a claim for sums due under the loan agreement, be entitled to set off any claim that he has for such a misrepresentation or breach. The third approach is to require the borrower to pursue his remedies against the seller in the first instance, the lender becoming liable to the consumer only if the latter is unable to obtain redress from the seller because of his insolvency. ...

6.6.27 We have reached the conclusion that the first of these approaches is that which should be adopted. If the borrower's claim does not arise, or is not made, until after he has repaid a substantial part of the loan a mere right of set-off will not give him adequate protection. Indeed, the borrower who pays his loan instalments promptly will be worse off than one who has been dilatory and thus has a substantial accrued indebtedness against which to exercise his right of set-off when the nature and extent of his own claim become clear. The third alternative would not in our view adequately protect the borrower. It imposes on him what is for the average consumer the heavy burden of initiating litigation instead of merely defending an action and exercising a right of set-off and counterclaim. Moreover, the obligation to pay the loan instalments while pursuing his claim against the seller may substantially diminish his ability to prosecute his claim.

The relevant provisions of the Consumer Credit Act 1974 are sections 75, 12 and 187, which together spell out the conditions for when a connected-lending situation will exist. Section 75 does not apply to hire-purchase, conditional-sales or credit-sale agreements where the supplier and creditor are the same person. (Section 75 is interesting to lawyers since it is a clear breach of the traditional doctrine of privity of contract.)

The approach adopted by the Crowther Committee and section 75 results in a lender's being liable for potentially large consequential damages (eg for personal injuries and property damage from defective products and services) and has led to criticism from lenders. They have argued that this liability may require them to increase their reserves with a consequent effect on the price of credit. The Wisconsin Consumer Act, perhaps the most pro-consumer of US state legislation, limits such liability to the amount owed at the time the defence is raised, and determines that if a consumer is unable to receive satisfaction from judgment against the supplier, the creditor will be liable up to the total amount of the finance. Section 75 does not protect consumers merely against the 'fly-by-night' creditor. It may be conceptualised as an insurance contract for consumers, justified in terms of the loss-spreading principles outlined by the Crowther Committee (above Chapter 7). The costs of this protection are spread widely among users. In 1994, the OFT proposed to limit the liability of credit card issuers to the amount charged to the credit card, introducing a liability similar to that in the United States (OFT, 1995). The DTI ultimately proposed no change in liability under section 75.

The major area where section 75 does apply is in relation to credit cards. The ability of the consumer to hold a credit card company liable for problems associated with the supply of goods and services is clearly a very important protection in cross-border and Internet transactions, given the difficulties of using the court system (see above Chapter 3).

Several issues have arisen in the application of section 75 to credit cards. These include: does section 75 apply when a credit card is used outside the UK? Is a bank that issues a credit card company liable where the defaulting supplier is recruited into the credit card network by another bank? And does the protection extend to a second card-holder (eg a spouse) since the protection only extends to a 'debtor'?

The OFT brought a declaratory action to clarify the application of credit card liability to purchases abroad, and to so-called four-party liability. The Supreme Court clarified these issues in the following case

Lloyds TSB Bank plc and others v The Office of Fair Trading [2007] UK HL 48

LORD HOPE OF CRAIGHEAD

My Lords,

9. I have had the advantage of reading in draft the speeches of my noble and learned friends Lord Hoffmann and Lord Mance. I agree with them, and for the reasons they give I would dismiss the appeal.

13. The simple and unqualified statement of the right that is expressed in section 75(1) is consistent with the policy that lies behind the Act, informed by recommendations by the Crowther Committee. Its long title states that the new system which it lays down is 'for the protection of consumers'. That policy applies to debtors and creditors within the territorial reach of the Act generally. Transactions of that kind are to the commercial advantage of the supplier and the creditor. The creditor is in a better position than the debtor, in a question with a foreign supplier, to obtain redress. It is not to be assumed that the creditor will always get his money back. But, if he does not, the loss must lie with him as he has the broader back. He is in a better position, if redress is not readily obtainable, to spread the cost. He is in a better position to argue for sanctions against a supplier who is not reliable. For his part, the debtor is entitled to assume that he can trust suppliers who are authorised to accept his credit card. These considerations, which support the right of recourse in relation to tripartite arrangements, are just as powerful in the case of four-party transactions.

LORD MANCE

17. Credit cards have become a worldwide convenience. For many they have superseded cheques. Consumers often use them to pay for goods or services where formerly cash would have been tendered. Consumers may know that their use carries the advantage of a potential right of recourse against the card issuer should the supplier breach his obligations relating to

the supply contract. This advantage arises under section 75(1) of the Consumer Credit Act 1974. The question now is whether it extends to the use of credit cards in relation to foreign transactions. ...

22. The Committee in chapter 6.12 applied its reasoning regarding connected lending to the liability of credit card issuers for defective goods and services, explaining that:

> '6.12.9 ... there is in fact a close business relationship between an issuer and the suppliers who have agreed to accept that issuer's credit cards. The issuer, through provision of the card, swells the turnover of the supplier, and for conferring this benefit usually receives by way of discount an agreed percentage of the invoice price of the goods or services supplied. Moreover, a cardholder dealing with a reputable issuer has every reason to assume that the issuer will list only reputable suppliers.'

Further, the card issuer was 'much better placed than the cardholder to secure redress from the offending supplier' and agreements between issuers and suppliers would usually impose an express obligation on the supplier to deal promptly with legitimate complaints by cardholders (para 6.12.10). The consideration that a card issuer might be unwilling to make a claim on a particular supplier for fear of losing that supplier's goodwill was 'a commercial matter which the issuer or other lender has to decide for itself'; it did not justify depriving the consumer of the protection which the Committee believed he should otherwise have (para 6.12.11).

23. As appears from these passages, the Crowther Report was issued and the 1974 Act enacted in an era when credit cards involved tri-partite arrangements—between a card issuer and card holder, between the card issuer and suppliers authorised by the card issuer to accept its cards and between the card holder and a particular supplier in relation to a particular supply. American Express and Diners Club continue to operate on this basis. But the position with most other cards is now more complex. Large-scale consolidation has led to card issuers becoming members of one of the two main international credit card networks, VISA and MasterCard. Under the rules of these networks, certain card issuers are authorised to act as 'merchant acquirers', in practice only within their home jurisdictions. They contract with suppliers ('merchants') to process all such suppliers' supply transactions made with cards of the relevant network, by paying to such suppliers the price involved, less a 'Merchant Service Charge'. Suppliers do not become members of the network, but contract with merchant acquirers to honour the cards of the network (ie to accept them in payment of supplies). Where the merchant acquirer is itself the issuer of the card used in a particular transaction, the transaction is tripartite and the merchant acquirer looks direct to its card holder (debtor) for reimbursement of the price. But in the more common (and in the case of a foreign transaction inevitable) case of use of a card issued by a card issuer other than the merchant acquirer who acquired the particular supplier, the network operates as a clearing system, through which the merchant acquirer is reimbursed by the card issuer, less an 'Interchange Fee'. This is a fee less than the Merchant Service Charge, so that both the merchant acquirer and the card issuer receive a commission on the transaction. The House was told that there are some 700,000 credit card outlets within the United Kingdom, and some 29 million worldwide. The value of foreign transactions in which United Kingdom credit card issuers are involved is, however, presently less than 10% of that of domestic transactions.

24. In the courts below, the appellant card issuers contended that the consequence of the development of four-party schemes—whereby a credit card can be used to pay a supplier not recruited into the network by, and not in a contractual relationship with, the relevant card issuer—was that there were no 'arrangements', pre-existing or in contemplation, between that card issuer and supplier within the meaning of s 12(b) of the 1974 Act. So, they submitted, section 75(1) could have no application. Both Gloster J [2005] 1 All ER 843 and the Court of Appeal (Waller, Smith and Moore-Bick LJJ) [2007] QB 1 rejected that submission, and the

House refused permission to appeal on the point. The Crowther Committee and Parliament when enacting the 1974 Act did not know how the credit card market would develop. But the language of 'arrangements' used in the Act is well capable of embracing the modern relationships between card issuers and suppliers under networks like VISA and MasterCard…

25. … Legislation is primarily territorial. It is now common ground that section 75(1) is subject to some territorial limitation.

26. The precise delimitation of a United Kingdom credit agreement is open to debate, on lines explored in Goode's Consumer Credit Law and Practice (1999) paras 49.82–49.90 (suggesting that the relevant nexus depends upon the co-location in the United Kingdom both of the debtor or hirer's residence or place of business and of the negotiation or making of the credit agreement, or, in other cases, upon an evaluation of all the factors connecting that agreement with the United Kingdom) and Guest and Lloyd's Encylopaedia of Consumer Credit Law para 2-194/2-9 (tentatively advancing as the test whether the relevant debtor or hirer dealt as part of the United Kingdom market—eg resided and negotiated the agreement here).

27. No party to this appeal invites the House to engage in that debate. What matters is that there is nothing in sections 11, 12 or 75(1) purporting to legislate extra-territorially in relation to the supplier or the supply transaction financed by the credit agreement. To impose on United Kingdom card issuers a liability to United Kingdom card holders by reference to liabilities arising under a foreign supply transaction is not axiomatically to legislate extra-territorially. It is not uncommon for domestic contractual relationships to involve obligations defined by reference to foreign contracts or events. In these circumstances, I agree with the OFT's submission that, if there is any limitation on the transactions to which section 75(1) applies, it must be found in ordinary principles of construction and implication.

28. [The appellants] submit that the implications, if section 75(1) applies to overseas transactions, are 'startling and readily apparent', in that it would make United Kingdom card issuers the potential guarantors of some 29 million foreign suppliers, with whom they would not have any direct contractual relations. Gloster J in a clearly reasoned judgment accepted this among other of the appellants' submissions. But it is one which depends on today's market. The 1974 Act falls to be construed against the background of the market as it existed and was understood and foreseen at the time of the Crowther Report and the passing of the Act.

29. Further, the general factors outlined in paragraphs [4] to [6], which led the Crowther Committee to recommend the imposition on card issuers of a liability reflecting suppliers' liability to debtors, all apply as much to overseas as to domestic supply transactions—if not more so. In relation to overseas transactions, there would be likely to be an even greater discrepancy between the card holder's ability to pursue suppliers on the one hand and the ease with which card issuers could obtain redress through the contractual and commercial ties which Crowther contemplated would link them and suppliers. Card issuers' ability to bear irrecoverable losses and so 'spread the burden' exists in relation to both overseas and domestic transactions.

30. That, in today's market, arrangements between card issuers and overseas suppliers under schemes such as VISA and MasterCard are indirect (rather than pursuant to a direct contract as is still the case with American Express and Diners Club) is a consequence of the way in which the VISA and MasterCard networks have developed and operate. Likewise, the fact that the rules of these networks give card issuers no direct choice as to the suppliers in relation to whom their cards will be used. The choice of suppliers is, in effect, delegated to the merchant acquirers in each country in which these networks operate, and provision

is made, as one would expect, to ensure and monitor the reliability of such suppliers in the interests of all network members. That network rules may not provide all the protections that they might, eg by way of indemnity and/or jurisdiction agreements, is neither here nor there. They could in theory do so, and it is apparent that there are some differences in this respect between different networks. The Crowther Report and 1974 Act proceed on the basis of a relatively simple model which contemplated that card issuers would have direct control of such matters. A more sophisticated worldwide network, like VISA or MasterCard, offers both card issuers and card holders considerable countervailing benefits. Card issuers make a choice, commercially inevitable though it may have become, to join one of these networks, for better or worse.

31. Mr Hapgood QC for the appellants drew attention to features of the present legal and commercial situation which they as card issuers regard as anomalous. Liability under section 75 only arises where the cash price of the supply is over £100 but not more than £30,000 (section 75(3)). It arises even if the credit only relates to part of the price (as where the consumer pays part in cash or by cheque). It is potentially unlimited, a source of repeated complaint by card issuers. It arises even where the card holder in practice uses his credit card like a charge card, paying off the entire balance in one instalment at once. Charge cards which, by contract, operate on this basis have been excluded from the operation of the 1974 Act by regulations made under section 16(5)(a). None of these anomalies is special to, or can be determinative of, the application of section 75(1) to overseas transactions. Their effects could be exacerbated if overseas transactions are covered, but, if so, only as a matter of degree and not in any way which provides a reason in principle for a different construction of section 75 to that which would otherwise apply.

32. As a matter of fact, it is accepted that, even in 1974, there was some limited use of credit cards (in particular Barclaycard) for overseas transactions. Further, the 1974 Act itself contemplated that credit agreements might have overseas aspects which could require special attention. Thus, section 16(5)(c) enables the Secretary of State by order to provide that the Act should not regulate consumer credit agreements with 'a connection with a country outside the United Kingdom'. Section 9(2) provides that 'Where credit is provided otherwise than in sterling, it shall be treated for the purposes of this Act as provided in sterling of an equivalent amount'. These provisions are directed at the nature of the credit agreement and of the credit provided under it, rather than directly at the supply transaction in a debtor-creditor-supplier context. But they militate nonetheless against the appellants' submission that the 1974 Act is incapable of affecting any form of credit to support an overseas transaction.

34. At the forefront of the appellants' case is the submission that the 1974 Act contains provisions showing that it cannot have been intended to apply to overseas transactions. First among those relied upon is section 75(2):

> "Subject to any agreement between them, the creditor shall be entitled to be indemnified by the supplier for loss suffered by the creditor in satisfying his liability under subsection (1), including costs reasonably incurred by him in defending proceedings instituted by the debtor."

This is supplemented in section 75(5) by a provision entitling the creditor 'in accordance with rules of court' to have the supplier made a party to any proceedings brought against the creditor under section 75(1). The appellants submit, and Gloster J accepted, that the 'whole premise' of these provisions is that a United Kingdom court will have jurisdiction over the supply transaction and the supplier.

35. Mr Sumption QC for the OFT accepts that the statutory indemnity provided by section 75(2) cannot operate worldwide. He submits that it is limited to contractual or restitutionary

relationships subject to the law of one of the parts of the United Kingdom. It does not have either the mandatory quality or the background in social policy of section 75(1) to give it any wider application. Rather, it was designed to reflect that which it was assumed would anyway exist: see the Crowther Report para 6.6.31; and it is subject to any contrary agreement. ... Under the 1974 Act, section 173(1) voids any term to the extent that it is inconsistent with a provision of the Act for the debtor or hirer or his relative or any surety. Section 75(1) is such a term, s.75(2) is not.

36. The appellant card issuers submit that, if section 75(2) is limited to relationships between a card issuer and supplier subject to a domestic law of the United Kingdom, this confirms that section 75(1) cannot extend to overseas supply transactions. But that does not follow. First, the relationship of a United Kingdom card issuer and an overseas supplier may be subject to (say) English law. At the time of the Crowther Report and the 1974 Act, it would have been envisaged that such a relationship would in all likelihood involve a direct contract, and a United Kingdom card issuer would on that basis have been quite likely to stipulate for English law. Even now, network rules and the contractual agreements made by merchant acquirers with overseas suppliers could select a United Kingdom law to govern the relationship between United Kingdom card issuers and overseas suppliers, and they could no doubt also be structured to make the relationship directly contractual for at least indemnity purposes. The characteristics of an overseas supply transaction between a debtor and a supplier for which the appellants contend (cf paragraph 28 above) determine neither the nature nor the governing law of the relationship between a United Kingdom card issuer and an overseas supplier. Yet, on the appellants' case, section 75(1) and (2) cease to apply if an overseas supply transaction has at least those characteristics, even if the relevant card issuer could and would otherwise have the statutory indemnity provided by section 75(2) because his relationship with the supplier was governed by United Kingdom law. Mr Hapgood submits that subsections (1) and (2) of section 75 cannot be 'disconnected'. But the appellants' own case involves a disconnection, since it seeks to derive, from an indemnity provision capable on its face of applying to all creditor-supplier relationships subject to United Kingdom law, a limitation in the scope of liability under s 75(1) based on characteristics relating to the supply-debtor transaction which have no necessary connection with the creditor-supplier relationship.

37. Secondly, whatever the law applicable to the relationship between the United Kingdom card issuer and the relevant supplier, the card issuer may very well have a right to indemnity in respect of sums paid compulsorily under section 75(1). Section 75(2) does no more than reflect a well-recognised restitutionary right at English common law. Other developed legal systems are likely to recognise a similar right. ... It cannot in these circumstances be assumed that Parliament envisaged that section 75(2) would be the only route to indemnity. Take the example of a tripartite situation which could have been foreseen at the time of the Act—a relationship between a United Kingdom card issuer and a French supplier subject to French law and to an express indemnity mirroring section 75(2). It is hard to think that Parliament would have intended the card holder to lose the benefits of section 75(1) merely because the indemnity arose contractually rather than statutorily.

38. Thirdly, the Crowther Report does not suggest that liability under section 75(1) depends on the existence of an effective indemnity. Section 75(2) is itself subject to any contrary agreement. More relevantly, Crowther recognised that the effect of section 75(1) would be to impose on card issuers irrecoverable losses, but took the view that card issuers were better able to bear them than card holders: see paragraph 19 above. Again, this militates against treating the existence of a statutory indemnity under section 75(2) as critical to liability under section 75(1).

39. As to section 75(5), it is true that, whatever rules of court may provide, an overseas supplier will be less easily brought before a United Kingdom court than a domestic supplier, and may simply ignore any attempt to join him, in which case any United Kingdom judgment may not be enforceable against him here or anywhere. But again it was a principal theme of the Crowther Report that creditors would have a strong contractual and commercial influence over their suppliers and that, where resort could not be had to such suppliers, losses were better borne by creditors, who could spread them over the public at large, than by debtors.

...

43. The ineffectiveness of the provisions for cancellation in relation to overseas supply transactions (eg made with a foreign supplier for supply overseas subject to a foreign law) is more problematic. But the Court of Appeal was in my view right to hold that it is insufficient to affect the apparently unqualified application of sections 11, 12 and 75(1) to any supply transaction. The cancellation provisions of section 67 et seq are ancillary to the main purpose of the Act. ... The right to cancel can ... only arise in limited circumstances, and can then only impact on linked transactions in the case of a debtor–creditor–supplier agreement where credit is advanced within the very short cancellation period provided by section 68. That means, in the case of a credit card, that the card was issued and used and cancellation then took place within that period—probably a very rare occurrence. Be that as it may, it remains true that the cancellation provisions could in law be ineffective or inapplicable in certain situations which may be envisaged at least theoretically. But that possibility, arising in the ancillary context of cancellation within the cooling-off period, is in my view quite inadequate to shape or change the construction otherwise attaching to the separate and much more central provisions of section 75(1).

44. For the reasons I have given, which substantially coincide with those given by Waller LJ in the Court of Appeal, I consider that there is nothing in the 1974 Act to introduce or require any further limitation in the territorial scope of section 75(1), other than that the credit agreement must be a United Kingdom credit agreement. I therefore reject the appellant card issuers' submission that section 75(1) is limited in application to domestic supply transactions and so inapplicable to overseas supply transactions, however defined. I would accordingly dismiss this appeal.

The liability of the credit card companies may be conceptualised as a form of 'network liability' (Teubner, 1998). This requires a different perspective than one that regards the various contracts in credit card transactions as discrete contracts. The financial network that is the credit card system is not merely an intermediary: it is often driving the development of consumer markets and is in a strong bargaining position in relation to merchants. The credit card associations are an international 'private government network'. Their rules are enforced through contracts with banks, and merchants may be 'fined' if they do not follow the association rules. The card payment networks have developed internal policies imposing obligations on their issuers that in some cases exceed legal obligations. Credit card networks will generally take the power to chargeback transactions to acquiring banks, who in turn chargeback merchants. According to Ronald Mann:

> Visa and MasterCard also impose fees [generally about $25] for each chargeback processed through their networks. Merchants that have a large number of chargebacks often are obligated to deposit funds with their acquirers as a reserve to cover anticipated future chargebacks. Merchants with too many chargebacks eventually are evicted from the networks. (Mann, 2006: 28)

Arnold Rosenberg argues that there should be greater transparency in the credit card chargeback system. Currently, the chargeback experience of individual merchants is regarded as confidential information. The card systems such as Visa will code a chargeback under a variety of sub-codes including 'merchandise not as described or defective'. This information could be valuable to a consumer who is interested in identifying merchants by their chargeback records. He argues that 'the provision of chargeback data could be restricted to consumers who own or use payment cards, increasing consumer goodwill. Indeed, the data could be offered for a fee, with the fee waived for consumers who use their cards regularly' (Rosenberg, 2006: 573). He also argues that greater transparency would deter seller misconduct and analogises this form of disclosure to the current ratings that are maintained by eBay in relation to online merchants. Section 75 will not apply to an individual who is an additional account-holder on a credit card. The protection under section 75 only applies to a 'debtor' and Goode argues that 'a person is not a debtor unless he is liable as a party to the credit agreement' and that in this situation 'the person liable on the credit card is not the cardholder but the account holder' (1989: para 7.12). Whether an individual might succeed in avoiding this limitation through the use of agency principles is not clear.

Finally, section 75 does not apply to debit cards (see section 187(3A) of the Consumer Credit Act 1974, added to the Act by the Banking Act 1987, section 89; and see discussion above Chapter 3, case study). Section 56 of the CCA 1974 is also relevant since a debtor may hold a third-party financier liable (in misrepresentation or breach of an express promise) for statements made by the supplier in antecedent negotiations.

A final provision, section 84, relates to lost and stolen cards and caps the liability of the consumer to a maximum of £50 before notification of the lost card to the credit card company. This protection was developed when credit cards were a nascent industry and consumer confidence was needed by the industry to develop the spread of the card. It is a useful example of distributional risk spreading which has provided strong incentives to credit card companies to develop security measures. Do you think that this level of liability could create moral hazard problems?

The first edition of this text in 1989 raised the question of the distributional impact of section 75 and whether it benefited primarily middle-income consumers who used credit cards for high-value transactions. As a form of insurance it may create incentives for individuals to enter into more risky transactions. The costs of failures in these transactions will be passed on to consumers through increases in the costs of using a card reflected in the UK primarily in interest charges. Since these charges are generally not paid by more affluent consumers, the overall structure could be regressive. However, companies often do charge for payment by a credit card, supposedly reflecting the section 75 risk. The concept of a 'risky' transaction is somewhat ambiguous. The EU wishes to encourage confidence in consumers undertaking more transactions online—this could be viewed as encouraging taking greater risks. See further for arguments against section 75 liability, Bisping (2011). Article 14 of the Consumer Rights Directive prohibits traders from charging consumers fees in respect of the use of a given means of payment that exceed the cost borne by the trader for the use of such means.

5. The regulation of product market quality: the case of used cars

Much consumer litigation has concerned the problems of new and used cars. While the amount of such litigation is not necessarily a reliable guide to underlying problems in a market, it appears from other complaint data that motor cars are a continuing source of problems for consumers. The previous section indicated some specific measures taken in relation to this market; this section focuses on alternative methods of regulating the used-car market. Methods of regulation might include: specific pre-contract information; statutory guarantees; negative and positive licensing. Currently almost all dealers will be licensed under the Consumer Credit Act 1974. Regulation 6 of the Consumer Protection from Unfair Trading Regulations 2008 which may sanction misleading omissions and imposes information obligations where there is an invitation to purchase, as well as the information obligations in the Consumer Rights directive, create general obligations on dealers to provide pre-contractual information.

In 1979, the OFT published a consultative paper on the problems a consumer faces in buying a used car. The report noted the high number of trade descriptions cases associated with the motor trade. None of the recommendations in the subsequent 1980 report (presales information reports; redesign of vehicle registration documents to show previous keepers; tamper-proof odometers) were adopted. In response to continuing high levels of complaints the OFT again reported on the purchase of used cars in 1996 and 1997 (OFT, 1996, 1997). In 2002 the OFT once again raised concerns about the used car trade, noting that 'the used-car trade continues to be a source of concern to consumers and enforcement officers. In 2002 the OFT in a discussion of credit licensing noted that the motor trade accounted for nearly a third of all licensing action in 2002.'

In the used-car trade in the United Kingdom a substantial proportion of the businesses are small (perhaps, it is suggested, because increased size brings few economies), and the majority of used-car retailers are single-establishment firms. The OFT indicated in 1979 that 69 per cent of sales were made by main dealers (franchised distributors whose main business is the sale of new cars) and 26 per cent by used-car retailers. There are also a small percentage of back-street dealers who are not established retailers and who often deal in cars in very poor condition—those which ordinary retailers decline to carry. Auctions also dispose of a small percentage of used cars, the quality and history of which are often suspect. New entry to the used-car trade is relatively easy and competition is fairly intense. The 1996 Report states that dealers in major manufacturers such as Ford and Vauxhall had increased the status of used cars by selling them with packages akin to new ones in order to differentiate themselves from the 'rogue' used-car dealer. In the light of these rough data, consider the potential impact of the alternative policies canvassed in the extracts (for example, required disclosures, mandatory guarantees, etc). You might also wish to reflect on the advantages and disadvantages of market regulation as against those of the broad, general standards of legislation such as the Sale of Goods Act 1979.

OFT, *Buying a Used Car: Consumers' Problems—A Consultative Paper* **(1979)**

CHAPTER VI: STRENGTHENING THE CONSUMER'S POSITION

6.1 ... [T]he consumer's main problems in buying a used car were identified as:

(a) inadequate (and often inaccurate) information about a car's history and mileage;

(b) inadequate information about the actual condition of the vehicle;

(c) the offer for sale of unroadworthy vehicles; and

(d) difficulty in gaining redress when things go wrong.

Potential responses to these problems:

B. A PRE-PURCHASE INSPECTION REPORT OR FAULT LIST

6.3 This is perhaps the most significant single piece of information the consumer requires to make a sensible purchasing decision. However, much would depend on the accuracy and scope of the inspection. The main option appears to be an inspection and report by the retailer.

6.7 The proposal that all retailers should carry out a standard detailed inspection and make available to consumers prior to sale a report in standard form (ideally including estimates of outstanding repair costs) warrants more detailed consideration.

Costs

6.8 This proposal would involve two types of cost: the cost of the inspection and the subsequent cost involved in remedying defects. ... The cost relating to remedial work is more difficult to quantify. Reputable retailers already often carry out remedial work and although a more extensive test might result in more work, and thus increase price levels, the market would still be capable of offering the consumer a choice. Some consumers might wish to purchase a cheaper vehicle and be prepared to accept certain defects or items requiring repair.

C. GUARANTEES

6.10 The introduction of statutory inspections and reports would go some way to reducing the area of doubt but the inevitably general nature of such reports would leave plenty of scope for argument over, for example, whether given the car's previous mileage and the price paid, the clutch should have become defective six weeks and 900 miles later.

Statutory guarantees

6. 18 Given the vagueness of the consumer's rights against the seller of a car which proves to be defective and the many disputes which arise, it is for consideration whether legislation should be introduced to assure the consumer of a clear, minimum standard of protection. It would be possible to lay down by statute certain minimum rights against the seller which would assure the consumer of repair-cost-free motoring for a specific period after purchase. Such rights would be without prejudice to the consumer's general rights under the Sale of Goods Act. The standard, minimum rights would apply to all transactions in the course of a trade or business, including those by back-street retailers; and their wide application would make them generally known to consumers. It must be accepted of course that action of this kind would not remove all scope for disputes about defective cars. Inevitably there would have to be an exemption for defects resulting from misuse or negligence by the consumer and this would be bound to cause argument in some cases. Nevertheless, a standard set of minimum rights would bring a good deal more certainty into the situation than exists at present.

6.20 [Referring to Australian legislation which requires statutory guarantees] We understand that the main result of this Australian legislation has been that retailers have generally carried out additional work to vehicles prior to sale. This has increased initial costs and prices but has also reduced the number of vehicles returned for repairs. The legislation has also apparently severely reduced the retail trade in vehicles costing less than $500 (ie where the trader can opt out). There seems to be no reason why similar legislation in the UK should have different results.

OFT, *Selling Second-hand Cars* (1997)

Licensing schemes

2.10 The consultation paper discussed the suggestion of establishing some kind of licensing scheme for motor dealers, and the idea drew significant support. The basic aim would be to enable enforcement authorities to remove from the market those traders with the worst record for abusing consumer trust.

2.11 There are two main types of licensing scheme: negative licensing, where traders do not require to be licensed before setting up in business, but can be banned if they transgress clearly defined rules of conduct; and positive licensing, where they have to demonstrate their 'fitness' before they can start trading. Many respondents favoured a positive licensing system but there was also support for a negative scheme.

2.13 Partly because of the need to screen all applicants, positive licensing schemes are likely to be more costly to administer than negative ones. To a large extent, however, the cost of a negative scheme will depend on the scale of the monitoring activity undertaken by the licensing authority. If a negative scheme involves intensive monitoring, supported by a database of all relevant traders, the overall costs to the authority and to the trade may not be very different. A positive scheme clearly has the advantage of vetting those who wish to enter the trade and ensuring a significant degree of preventive supervision by the licensing authority.

2.14 But positive schemes do have disadvantages. Very substantial resources would be needed at a local level to police a positive motor dealer licensing scheme fully, particularly if it were to lay down detailed standards of conduct.

2.15 A positive licensing scheme may also constitute a barrier to entry to the market by involving a degree of cost or bureaucracy. This may reduce competition. A further disadvantage of such a scheme is its potential for disputes about demarcation. Clearly, the question of who must, and who need not, have a licence is a fundamental consideration—and, with it, the issue of whether regulatory control is being evaded. A dealer might find it all too easy to redefine himself as a motor mechanic who sells second-hand vehicles as a side-line.

2.17 Some Scottish local authorities operate licensing schemes for car dealers in their area under the Civic Government (Scotland) Act 1982.

2.18 Among respondents generally, there was considerable support for the idea of introducing a statutory licensing scheme for the motor trade in order to modify behaviour through licence conditions—with the ultimate sanction of being able to remove the licences of unsatisfactory traders.

In 2001 the Society of Motor Manufacturers and Traders called for a compulsory licensing system for motor traders ('SMMT calls for motor traders to be licensed', press release 17 September 2001). It proposed that 'any company selling, repairing or servicing cars would have to show it works to a set of minimum standards before being granted a licence to trade'.

The OFT paper mentions the Scottish licensing of used-car dealers by local authorities. There is little systemic evidence of the performance of this scheme. The licensing authorities in Scotland did however require used-car dealers to provide a pre-sale information sheet to purchasers. This was challenged successfully as being ultra vires the power of a local licensing power in *Stewart (AP)(Respondent) v Perth and Kinross Council (Appellants)(Scotland)* (2004). Other jurisdictions have regulated the used-car market through the use of detailed disclosure provisions (see eg Quebec Consumer Protection Act RSQ, chapter P40.1 sections 155–63). Study of the impact of this type of disclosure regulation in the United States, in the state of Wisconsin, suggests that it has enhanced consumers' bargaining power in subsequent disputes with dealers and had resulted in more thorough inspections by dealers (Bardach and Kagan, 1982: 245). McNeil et al suggested, however, that this disclosure legislation had benefited primarily middle-income consumers, perhaps because they were more effective at complaining (McNeil et al, 1978–79: 696).

Detailed regulation of information disclosure in the used-car market may now be constrained by the maximal nature of harmonisation under the UCPD, and the introduction of statutory pre-sale information requirements might be challenged by business. Detailed regulation of information on used cars highlights the issue of the optimal precision of rules. The general norms in the UCPD are unlikely to result in as high compliance as detailed regulation and self-regulatory measure will not affect those who are not members of trade associations (often small firms). Given the deregulatory thrust of the UCPD it is unlikely that further detailed regulation will be enacted.

Several Commonwealth jurisdictions have a licensing system for motor vehicle dealers (eg several provinces in Canada, and several Australian states). These schemes require businesses and salespersons to meet honesty and competence standards, regulate pre-contractual information and terms and provide a compensation scheme. The Ontario model delegates enforcement of licensing under the Motor Vehicle Dealers Act to an industry body, the Ontario Motor Vehicle Industry Council, but requires annual reporting and accountability to the relevant government department. Regulation is financed through registration fees. Many of the registrar's actions are brought against 'curbsiders' (individuals selling automobiles without an established business location and who may be posing as private sellers). The Council operates a risk management approach to enforcement and attempts to develop dealer professionalism through required courses for dealers and salespersons.

6. Services

Contracts of services cover a wide variety of transactions from the relatively straightforward installation of a product to complex medical procedures. There may be particular aspects of information asymmetry related to the provision of services (see above Chapter 2 at 2).

6.1 Civil liability and service quality

In 1981 the National Consumer Council identified three areas of concern with consumer services: quality, the time it took to complete the service and the cost of the service (see National Consumer Council, 1981). This report resulted in the passage of the Supply of Goods and Services Act 1982 which primarily codifies the common law obligations in relation to contracts where goods and services are provided or where services are provided.

The common law traditionally uses a default rule that service providers have an obligation of reasonable care in the provision of services in contrast to the strict liability in relation to the sale and supply of goods. This was codified in section 13 of the Supply of Goods and Services Act 1982. Section 12(3) of the Act indicates that this obligation applies to the service element in a contract of work and materials or hire of goods. However, section 16(3) also provides that:

(3) Nothing in this Part of this Act prejudices—

(a) any rule of law which imposes on the supplier a duty stricter than that imposed by section 13 or 14 above; or

The distinction between the default rules of negligence for services and strict liability for goods was based on the presumption that services may be more complex and that it is difficult to guarantee a result. Presumably a consumer might bargain for a strict liability standard. While certain services, such as complex medical or legal services, may justify such a distinction, it is difficult to apply this distinction to all services. Many services are straightforward and would justify an obligation of result. These could include building services or car repairs. Consumers may often be led by service providers to reasonably expect the desired result.

One technique available to the courts to protect consumers is to classify a transaction as a sale of goods in order to impose strict liability. The English courts developed two tests for distinguishing sales of goods from contracts for work and materials: a substantial value test based on whether the purchaser was essentially contracting for the skills of a service provider (*Robinson v Graves* (1935)—painting of portrait not a sale contract) and a test of whether the ultimate aim of the contract was the transfer of property in goods (*Lee v Griffin* (1861)—provision of dentures a sale). The original importance of classification of these contracts related to the application of the Statute of Frauds which required a writing in a contract of sale but not if it was a contract of work and materials. Although this distinction is no longer of importance the courts may still use these classifications as a method of imposing or denying liability.

The classification of the sale of food in a restaurant as a sale of goods (see *Lockett v A & M Charles* (1938)—where an individual suffered food poisoning) was undoubtedly influenced by the fact that such a classification imposed strict liability on the restaurateur in a situation where the restaurateur had shown that he had taken all reasonable care. Conversely, the unwillingness of the Canadian Supreme Court to impose liability on medical practitioners for the supply of contaminated semen resulted in their refusal to classify the contract as one of a sale of goods (*Kobe Ter Neuzen v Korn* (1995)). Another technique used by the courts is to reverse the burden of proof. For example, in the case of a dry-cleaning contract where the goods are lost the courts have imposed a duty on the service provider to provide an explanation for the loss. If she is unable to do so then she will be presumed to be negligent (*Levison v Patent Steam Carpet Cleaning* (1977)).

In the following case Lord Denning uses the classic English technique of implying a term in the particular circumstance of the case to justify a higher level of liability on a service provider. The case concerned the liability of a consultant structural engineer for the design of a warehouse floor.

Greaves & Co (Contractors) Ltd v Baynham Meikle and Partners [1975] 1 WLR 1095

Lord Denning MR. This case arises out of a new kind of building contract called a 'package deal'. The building owners were Alexander Duckham & Co Ltd. They wanted a new factory, warehouse and offices to be constructed at Aldridge in Staffordshire. The warehouse was needed as a store in which barrels of oil could be kept until they were needed and despatched, and in which they could be moved safely from one point to another. The 'package deal' meant that the building owners did not employ their own architects or engineers. They employed one firm of contractors, the plaintiffs, to do everything for them. It was the task of the contractors not only to provide the labour and materials in the usual way but also to employ the architects and engineers as sub-contractors. The contractors were to do everything as a 'package deal' for the owners.

Now, as between the owners and the contractors, it is plain that the owners made known to the contractors the purpose for which the building was required, so as to show that they relied on the contractors' skill and judgment. It was therefore the duty of the contractors to see that the finished work was reasonably fit for the purpose for which they knew it was required. It was not merely an obligation to use reasonable care. The contractors were obliged to ensure that the finished work was reasonably fit for the purpose. ... In order to get the warehouse built, the contractors found they needed expert skilled assistance, particularly in regard to the structural steel work. The warehouse was to be built according to a new system which was just coming into use. ...

The contractors employed a firm of experts, the defendants, Messrs Baynham Meikle and Partners, structural engineers, to design the structure of the building and, in particular, the first floor of it. There were discussions with them about it. It was made known to them—and this is important—that the floors had to take the weight of stacker trucks—sometimes called fork-lift trucks. These were to run to and fro over the floors carrying the drums of oil. The structural engineers, Baynham Meikle, were given the task of designing the floors for that purpose.

Mr Baynham made his designs; the warehouse was built and put into use. It was used for the transport of these oil drums with the stacker trucks. But, after a little time, there was a lot of trouble. The floors began to crack. The men took strong objection to working there. They thought it was dangerous. The cracks seemed to be getting worse. So much so that the experts were called in. Attempts were made to cure the trouble, but without success. The position now is that the warehouse is of very limited use. It is anticipated that remedial works will have to take place at great expense. The damages are said to come to £100,000.

What was the cause of this cracking of the floors? The structural engineers said that it was due to the shrinkage of the concrete for which they were not responsible. There was nothing wrong, they said, with the design which they produced. But the judge did not accept that view. He found that the majority of the cracks were caused by vibration and not by shrinkage. He held that the floors were not designed with sufficient strength to withstand the vibration which was produced by the stacker trucks.

On those findings the first question is: what was the duty of the structural engineers towards the contractors? The judge found that there was an implied term that the design should be fit for the use of loaded stacker trucks; and that it was broken. Alternatively, that the structural engineers owed a duty of care in their design, which was a higher duty than the law in general imposes on a professional man; and that there was a breach of that duty.

To resolve this question, it is necessary to distinguish between a term which is implied by law and a term which is implied in fact. A term implied by law is said to rest on the presumed intention of both parties; whereas, a term implied in fact rests on their actual intention.

It has often been stated that the law will only imply a term when it is reasonable and necessary to do so in order to give business efficacy to the transaction; and, indeed, so obvious that both parties must have intended it. But those statements must be taken with considerable qualification. In the great majority of cases it is no use looking for the intention of both parties. If you asked the parties what they intended, they would say that they never gave it a thought; or, if they did, the one would say that he intended something different from the other. So the courts imply—or, as I would say, impose—a term such as is just and reasonable in the circumstances. Take some of the most familiar of implied terms in the authorities cited to us. Such as the implied condition of fitness on a sale of goods at first implied by the common law and afterwards embodied in the Sale of Goods Act 1893. Or the implied warranty of fitness on a contract for work and materials: *Young & Marten Ltd v McManus Childs Ltd*. Or the implied warranty that a house should be reasonably fit for human habitation: see *Hancock v B W Brazier*. And dozens of other implied terms. If you should read the discussions in the cases, you will find that the judges are not looking for the intention of both parties; nor are they considering what the parties would answer to an officious bystander. They are only seeking to do what is 'in all the circumstances reasonable'. That is how Lord Reid put it in *Young & Marten Ltd v McManus Childs Ltd*; and Lord Upjohn said quite clearly that the implied warranty is 'imposed by law'.

Apply this to the employment of a professional man. The law does not usually imply a warranty that he will achieve the desired result, but only a term that he will use reasonable care and skill. The surgeon does not warrant that he will cure the patient. Nor does the solicitor warrant that he will win the case. But, when a dentist agrees to make a set of false teeth for a patient, there is an implied warranty that they will fit his gums see *Samuels v Davis*.

What then is the position when an architect or an engineer is employed to design a house or a bridge? Is he under an implied warranty that, if the work is carried out to his design, it will be reasonably fit for the purpose? Or is he only under a duty to use reasonable care and skill? This question may require to be answered some day as matter of law. But in the present case I do not think we need answer it. For the evidence shows that both parties were of one mind on the matter. Their common intention was that the engineer should design a warehouse which would be fit for the purpose for which it was required. That common intention gives rise to a term implied in fact.

In the light of that evidence it seems to me that there was implied in fact a term that, if the work was completed in accordance with the design, it would be reasonably fit for the use of loaded stacker trucks. The engineers failed to make such a design and are, therefore, liable.

If there was, however, no such absolute warranty of fitness, but only an obligation to use reasonable care and skill, the question arises: what is the degree of care required? ... It seems

> to me that in the ordinary employment of a professional man, whether it is a medical man, a lawyer, or an accountant, an architect or an engineer, his duty is to use reasonable care and skill in the course of his employment. ...
>
> It seems to me that ... Mr Baynham did not take the matters sufficiently into account which he ought to have done. That amounts to a finding of breach of the duty to use reasonable care and kill. On each of the grounds, therefore, I think the contractors are entitled to succeeded. They are entitled to a declaration of liability and indemnity. I would, accordingly, dismiss the appeal.

Willett and Oughton argue that in cases where service providers install goods the EC Directive on Sale of Goods and Associated Guarantees (Article 2(5)) assumes a strict liability standard but the implementation by the UK of the Directive is not clear as to the nature of the installer's obligations (see Sale and Supply of Goods to Consumers Regulations 2002 (SI 2002/3045) regulation 9). Willett and Oughton argue that there is authority for implying a strict standard and that in 'design and build' cases such as *Greaves* it will often not be difficult to establish the standard of performance where the end product is goods. Where services are applied to goods, as in the case of car repairs, liability should, in their view, be based on an obligation of result with a defence available where the goods repaired have a latent defect making them not amenable to repair (eg as in *Slater v Finning* above) (Willett and Oughton, 2007: 211). Article 101 of the proposal for a common European sales regulation imposes a strict obligation for installation carried out by the supplier or her agent or by the consumer following a supplier's instructions.

The Australian Trade Practices Act has adopted a default rule of strict liability in relation to services in section 74(2):

> Where a corporation supplies services (other than services of a professional nature provided by a qualified architect or engineer) to a consumer in the course of a business and the consumer, expressly or by implication, makes known to the corporation any particular purpose for which the services are required or the result that he or she desires the services to achieve, there is an implied warranty that the services supplied under the contract for the supply of the services and any materials supplied in connexion with those services will be reasonably fit for that purpose or are of such a nature and quality that they might reasonably be expected to achieve that result, except where the circumstances show that the consumer does not rely, or that it is unreasonable for him or her to rely, on the corporation's skill or judgment.

The Supply of Goods and Services Act 1982 codifies the common law obligation that a service must be provided within a reasonable time which is a question of fact (section 14). Thus in a case where a reasonable time in the trade for repairing an automobile would have been five weeks and the repair took eight weeks, there was a breach of this term (*Charnock v Liverpool Corporation* (1968)). Clearly this vague standard is not of great use to a consumer and more detailed standards developed through codes of practice would be desirable for standard services such as car repairs.

Utility providers in privatised industries have developed specific performance targets as a response to concerns about service quality. These measures in regulated industries such as gas and telecommunications reflect a concern that quality degradation may occur where there are price caps. Publication of comparative quality data and encouraging providers to offer a variety of packages may be one approach to quality regulation. Another is to provide detailed performance measures. For example, the BT code of practice contains a tariff of a 'daily rate rental credit' for a consumer if BT fails to repair or supply a service on time and a one-off fixed rate payment if they fail to keep an appointment.

A third concern in relation to services is the cost of the service. The Supply of Goods and Services Act 1982 again codifies the common law by requiring that a reasonable price be paid if there is no express term as to price (section 15). In many service contracts such as home improvements or car repairs the price may not be determined at the outset and this can result in subsequent disputes.

The National Consumer Council noted that:

> with some jobs the contractor may be reluctant to give a firm quotation because he has little idea until he starts work of what the job will entail. … A consumer who has been given no idea of what the price will be is clearly in a vary vulnerable position. And those who need work carried out in an emergency are especially at risk … even if the consumer suspects that the charge is exorbitant, it takes courage to refuse to pay for work already done. … Once the job is completed he is likely to pay the bill either because he wants his goods back (as in the case of cars and small electrical repairs) or because he fears retaliatory action by the contractor, in the form of a county court summons. (NCC, 1981)

Individuals may be provided with an estimate or quotation. Whether either is binding depends on the intention of the parties. Most writers on this topic state that an estimate may be exceeded whereas quotations are binding. An estimate that was significantly below the actual price could be a misleading or unfair commercial practice under the UCPD. In Canada the Ontario Consumer Protection Act 2002 provides that the price of a service may not exceed the estimate by 10 per cent.

6.2 Service performance and consumer bargaining power

A primary remedy of a consumer is to withhold payment of the price of services. The following case illustrates the common law approach to this issue.

Bolton v Mahadeva **[1972] 1 WLR 1009 (CA)**
In this case the defendants had central heating installed at a price of £560. Because of alleged deficiencies the defendant withheld payment after completion of the work. The judge at first instance held that because of a defective flue there were fumes which affected the condition of the air in the living rooms. He also found that the house was on the average 10 per cent less warm than it should have been with the heating system. Because of these deficiencies the judge held that the defendant was entitled to set off £174.50 against the contract price, leaving a balance of £385.50. The defendant appealed.

> Cairns LJ … The main question in the case is whether the defects in workmanship found by the judge to be such as to cost £ 174 to repair—ie between one-third and one-quarter of the contract price—were of such a character and amount that the plaintiff could not be said to have substantially performed his contract. That is, in my view, clearly the legal principle which has to be applied to cases of this kind.
>
> The rule which was laid down many years ago in *Cutter v Powell* in relation to lump sum contracts was that, unless the contracting party had performed the whole of his contract, he

was not entitled to recover anything. That strong rule must now be read in the light o certain more recent cases to which I shall briefly refer. The first of those cases is *H Dakin & Co Ltd v Lee*, a decision of the Court of Appeal, in which it was held that, where the amount of work which had not been carried out under a lump sum contract was very minor in relation to the contract as a whole, the contractor was entitled to be paid the lump sum, subject to such deduction as might be proper in respect of the un-completed work. ...

... Perhaps the most helpful case is the most recent one of *Hoenig v Isaacs*. That was a case where the plaintiff was an interior decorator and designer of furniture who had entered into a contract to decorate and furnish the defendant's flat for a sum of £750; and, as appears from the statement of facts, the Official Referee who tried the case at first instance found that the door of a wardrobe required replacing, that a bookshelf which was too short would have to be remade, which would require alterations being made to a bookcase, and that the cost of remedying the defects was £55 18s 2d. That is on a £750 contract. The ground on which the Court of Appeal in that case held that the plaintiff was entitled to succeed, notwithstanding that there was not complete performance of the contract, was that there was substantial performance of the contract and that the defects in the work which there existed were not sufficient to amount to a substantial degree of non-performance.

In considering whether there was substantial performance I am of opinion that it is relevant to take into account both the nature of the defects and the proportion between the cost of rectifying them and the contract price. It would be wrong to say that the contractor is only entitled to payment if the defects are so trifling as to be covered by the de minimis rule.

The main matters that were complained of in this case were that, when the heating system was put on, fumes were given out which made some of the living rooms (to put it at the lowest) extremely uncomfortable and inconvenient to use; secondly, that by reason of there being insufficient radiators and insufficient insulation, the heating obtained by the central heating system was far below what it should have been. There was conflicting evidence about those matters. The judge came to the conclusion that, because of a defective flue, there were fumes which affected the condition of the air in the living rooms, and he further held that the amount of heat given out was such that, on the average, the house was less warm than it should have been with the heating system on, to the extent of 10 per cent. But, while that was the average over the house as a whole, the deficiency in warmth varied very much as between one room and another. The figures that were given in evidence and, insofar as we heard, were not contradicted, were such as to indicate that in some rooms the heat was less than it should have been by something between 26 and 30 per cent.

The learned judge, having made those findings, came to the conclusion that the defects were not sufficient in degree to enable him to hold that there was not substantial performance of the contract. ...

Now, certainly it appears to me that the nature and amount of the defects in this case were far different from those which the court had to consider in *H Dakin & Co Ltd v Lee* and *Hoening v Isaacs*. For my part, I find it impossible to say that the judge was right in reaching the conclusion that in those circumstances the contract had been substantially performed. The contract was a contract to install a central heating system. If a central heating system when installed is such that it does not heat the house adequately and is such, further, that fumes are given out, so as to make living rooms uncomfortable, and if the putting right of those defects is not something which can be done by some slight amendment of the system, then I think that the contract is not substantially performed.

The actual amounts of expenditure which the judge assessed as being necessary to cure those particular defects were £40 in each case. Taking those matters into account and the other matters making up the total of £174, I have reached the conclusion that the judge was wrong in saying that this contract had been substantially completed; and, on my view of the law, it follows that the plaintiff was not entitled to recover under that contract.

It appears to me that the result should be this, that the appeal should be allowed and the judgment in favour of the plaintiff should be set aside

Contractors may require significant up-front payments in home improvement contracts. The effects of these clauses on consumer bargaining power and the possibility that they might fall within the UTCCR are considered in the following OFT Bulletin.

The OFT had expressed concerns about home-improvement companies requiring consumers to pay the whole or nearly the whole contract price for a job in advance of delivery and installation (see OFT, *Unfair Contract Terms*, Bulletin 5) as restricting a consumer's right of set-off and therefore inappropriately excluding or limiting the legal rights of a consumer under para 1(b) of Schedule 2 of the UTCC regulations.

The OFT commented:

The OFT has made it clear that it considers that, in order to assist suppliers' cash-flow and to reduce the risk of unfair retention to an acceptable level, the use of 'stage' payments is reasonable. But, at the same time, it also takes the view that the concept of fairness requires that a significant proportion of the total price payable must be left outstanding until completion. If the right of set-off is to have any value either as a deterrent or a means of compensation for breach of contract, it must allow retention of a sum that adequately reflects what the victim of a defective installation could expect to sue for. It cannot properly be a mere token figure, nor a percentage of the price no greater than the discounts that suppliers commonly offer by way of sales promotion or other incentive.

The OFT is discussing with a relevant trade association the feasibility of a scheme whereby a fair final stage payment is held not by the consumer but an independent third party.

OFT, *Guidance on Home Improvement Contracts* (2005) 11, 62–63

In the late 1990s, the OFT took action against use of 'full payment in advance' clauses, as used by a number of major home improvement companies. … The companies proposed to join the Qualitas payment protection scheme. … Under this scheme, in the event of any dispute arising over quality of goods or service, a substantial proportion of the purchase price is removed from the control of the company, and is held in deposit until the consumer's complaint is dealt with through an independent dispute resolution procedure. If the consumer's complaint is upheld then he or she is reimbursed or compensated. OFT agreed in return to discontinue enforcement action.

6.3 Consumer damages

Consumers often buy goods and services for personal enjoyment. John Wightman argues that such personal contracts deserve separate treatment from where an individual is contracting for exchange. Losses may be experiential and are hard to put in monetary terms. 'Experiences such as being threatened with the sack or eviction, or having nightmare experiences with defective cars, holidays, utilities services, pensions or endowment mortgages may vary in the sympathy they evoke but all have the capacity to rupture lives beyond the impact on the pocket' (Wightman,1996: 97). He also argues that, unlike commercial corporations, individuals do not have the ability to shift or spread the loss. The question may be raised whether traditional remedies such as damages and specific performance should be affected by these considerations.

In *Farley v Skinner* the plaintiff employed a surveyor for a property that he was interested in purchasing and requested that the surveyor investigate the possibility of the property being affected by aircraft noise. The surveyor breached his obligation to take reasonable care in investigating this issue. The noise from aircraft did not affect the market value of the property. Could the plaintiff recover for the discomfort, inconvenience and distress which he experienced because of the aircraft noise?

Farley v Skinner [2001] UKHL 49

Lord Steyn

V. Recovery of non-pecuniary damages

In contract law distinctions are made about the kind of harm which resulted from the breach of contract. The general principle is that compensation is only awarded for financial loss resulting from the breach of contract. ... There are, however, limited exceptions to this rule ... the two exceptions mentioned by Bingham LJ, namely where the very object of the contract is to provide pleasure (proposition (2)) and recovery for physical inconvenience caused by the breach (proposition (3)), are pertinent. The scope of these exceptions is in issue in the present case. It is, however, correct, as counsel for the surveyor submitted, that the entitlement to damages for mental distress caused by a breach of contract is not established by mere foreseeability: the right to recovery is dependent on the case falling fairly within the principles governing the special exceptions.

VI. The very object of the contract: the framework

18. It is necessary to examine the case on a correct characterisation of the plaintiff's claim. ... The case must be approached on the basis that the surveyor's obligation to investigate aircraft noise was a major or important part of the contract between him and the plaintiff ... it is a claim for damages flowing from the surveyor's failure to investigate and report, thereby depriving the buyer of the chance of making an informed choice whether or not to buy resulting in mental distress and disappointment.

19. The exceptional category of cases where the very object of a contract is to provide pleasure, relaxation, peace of mind or freedom from molestation is not the product of Victorian contract theory but the result of evolutionary developments in case law from the 1970s. Several decided cases informed the description given by Bingham LJ of this category. The first was the decision of the sheriff court in *Diesen v Samson* 1971 SLT (Sh Ct) 49. A photographer failed to turn up at a wedding, thereby leaving the couple without a photographic record of an important and happy day. The bride was awarded damages for her distress and disappointment. In the celebrated case of *Jarvis v Swans Tours Ltd* [1973] 1 All ER 71, [1973] QB 233, the plaintiff recovered damages for mental distress flowing from a disastrous holiday resulting from a travel agent's negligent representations (compare also *Jackson v Horizon Holidays Ltd* [1975] 3 All ER 92, [1975] 1 WLR 1468). In *Heywood v Wellers* (a firm) [1976] 1 All ER 300, [1976] QB 446, the plaintiff instructed solicitors to bring proceedings to restrain a man from molesting her. The solicitors negligently failed to take appropriate action with the result that the molestation continued. The Court of Appeal allowed the plaintiff damages for mental distress and upset. While apparently not cited in *Watts v Morrow*, *Jackson v Chrysler Acceptances Ltd* [1978] RTR 474 was decided before

Watts v Morrow. In the Chrysler Acceptances case the claim was for damages in respect of a motor car which did not meet the implied condition of merchantability in s 14 of the Sale of Goods Act 1893. The buyer communicated to the seller that one of his reasons for buying the car was a forthcoming touring holiday in France. Problems with the car spoilt the holiday. The disappointment of a spoilt holiday was a substantial element in the award sanctioned by the Court of Appeal.

20. At their Lordships' request counsel for the plaintiff produced a memorandum based on various publications which showed the impact of the developments already described on litigation in the county courts. ... I am satisfied that in the real life of our lower courts non-pecuniary damages are regularly awarded on the basis that the defendant's breach of contract deprived the plaintiff of the very object of the contract, viz pleasure, relaxation, and peace of mind. The cases arise in diverse contractual contexts, eg the supply of a wedding dress or double glazing, hire purchase transactions, landlord and tenant, building contracts, and engagements of estate agents and solicitors. The awards in such cases seem modest. ... But the problem persists of the precise scope of the exceptional category of case involving awards of non-pecuniary damages for breach of contract where the very object of the contract was to ensure a party's pleasure, relaxation or peace of mind.

21. An important development for this branch of the law was *Ruxley Electronics and Construction Ltd v Forsyth, Laddingford Enclosures Ltd v Forsyth* [1995] 3 All ER 268, [1996] AC 344. ...

VII. The very object of the contract: the arguments against the plaintiff's claim

[23] The first argument fastened onto a narrow reading of the words 'the very object of [the] contract' as employed by Bingham LJ in *Watts v Morrow* [1991] 4 All ER 937 at 960, [1991] 1 WLR 1421 at 1445. Cases where a major or important part of the contract was to secure pleasure, relaxation and peace of mind were not under consideration in *Watts v Morrow*. It is difficult to see what the principled justification for such a limitation might be. ... There is no reason in principle or policy why the scope of recovery in the exceptional category should depend on the object of the contract as ascertained from all its constituent parts. It is sufficient if a major or important object of the contract is to give pleasure, relaxation or peace of mind.

...

VIII. Quantum

28. In the surveyor's written case it was submitted that the award of £10,000 was excessive. It was certainly high. Given that the plaintiff is stuck indefinitely with a position which he sought to avoid by the terms of his contract with the surveyor I am not prepared to interfere with the judge's evaluation on the special facts of the case. On the other hand, I have to say that the size of the award appears to be at the very top end of what could possibly be regarded as appropriate damages. Like Bingham LJ in *Watts v Morrow* [1991] 4 All ER 937 at 960, [1991] 1 WLR 1421 at 1445 I consider that awards in this area should be restrained and modest. It is important that logical and beneficial developments in this corner of the law should not contribute to the creation of a society bent on litigation.

IX. Conclusion

29. In agreement with the reasoning of Clarke LJ I would therefore hold that the decision of the majority in the Court of Appeal was wrong.

X. Inconvenience and discomfort

30. It is strictly unnecessary to discuss the question whether the judge's decision can

be justified on the ground that the breach of contract resulted in inconvenience and discomfort ... aircraft noise is capable of causing inconvenience and discomfort within the meaning of Bingham LJ's relevant proposition. It is a matter of degree whether the case passes the threshold. It is sufficient to say that I have not been persuaded that the judge's decision on this point was not open to him on the evidence which he accepted. For this further reason, in general agreement with Clarke LJ, I would rule that the decision of the Court of Appeal was wrong.

The ECJ decided in *Simone Leitner v TUI Deutschland* (2002) ECR I-2631 under the Package Holiday Directive that a consumer was entitled to recover damages from a travel agent for non-material loss. In this particular case the holidaymaker contracted salmonella poisoning while on holiday in Turkey. The Austrian court had disallowed this claim for loss of enjoyment on the basis that Austrian law did not permit the recovery of non-material damages. The Court interpreted clause 5 of the Package Travel Directive in light of the Community objectives of prevention of distortion of competition and consumer protection. It concluded that the existence in some Member States but not others of an obligation to provide compensation for non-material damage would cause significant distortions of competition since non-material damage frequently occur in spoiled holidays. The Court noted the growing tendency among many states to award damages for non-material loss and the opinion of the Advocate General indicated a 'widespread trend' towards a wider concept of liability.

> This trend is linked to ... the rapid development of tourism and to the fact that holidays, travel and leisure breaks are no longer the privilege of a limited sector of society, but are a consumer product for a growing number of people to which they devote part of their savings and their holidays from work or school. The very fact that holidays have assumed a specific socio-economic role and have become so important for an individual's quality of life, means that their full and effective enjoyment represents in itself an asset worth protecting.

There is also detailed regulation of package travel contracts. The EU Directive on Package Travel was implemented in the UK by the Package Travel, Package Holidays and Package Tours Regulations 1992, SI 1992/3288. In addition there is a code of practice operated by ABTA.

---

7. Car servicing

Car servicing is an area where services (diagnosis and service) are bundled together and there may be significant information asymmetry between supplier and consumer.

OFT, *Car Servicing and Repairs*, The Report of the Director General's Inquiry into Car Servicing and Repairs (2000) OFT307 at I, 1

> As a nation we rely heavily on our cars. We own 24 million of them, and the number continues to rise. Over £9 billion per annum is spent on car servicing and repairs.
>
> On analysing this market, I have found that car servicing and repair is often of an unacceptably poor quality and consumers lack the information, the experience and the

expertise to make the best use of what information is available. Consumers rightly demand greater safety and better value for money. But as cars become more complex, fewer and fewer consumers can judge whether work has been properly carried out.

… We also found that garages could often be vague about costs or the precise details of what was included in a service. Such shortcomings were experienced in every part of the market, including that served by franchised dealers. Our findings indicate widespread consumer detriment, a lack of confidence in the industry and an inability on the part of consumers to judge when service is satisfactory. In consequence, as our survey confirmed, consumers tend to change garages only when a problem is encountered.

1.4 Several factors have contributed to this unsatisfactory state of affairs. The lack of any nation-wide system for rating quality and customer satisfaction inhibits shopping around for the best deal. Although there is a vast amount of data on customer satisfaction, complaints and convictions, it is not generally accessible to consumers. In addition, most new car buyers incorrectly believe that servicing is tied in by warranty terms to the franchised dealer who sold the car, or to franchised dealers selling the same marque. Clearer guidance from the industry is needed to remove this misconception.

1.5 We attribute many of these shortcomings to inadequately trained staff.

DTI, *Car Servicing and Repairs Mystery Shopping Exercise* (2002)

Only 5% of garages surveyed were rated very good, indicating they had carried out a thorough service, according to the manufacturer's service schedule, rectified all the introduced faults and other defects found prior to service.

51% were rated either poor or very poor. A poor rating indicated that the garage had omitted more than two minor items, or the vehicle had a minor safety defect that the garage had failed to rectify or report. 'Very poor' indicated that the garage had missed one or more serious safety related faults, or a major service item that should have been carried out or a part replaced had not been conducted.

There was no significant difference in overall ratings between the types of garage—53% of independent garages and 50% of franchise dealers were rated either poor or very poor with 6% of independents and 4% of dealers being rated as very good.

There was no significant difference in overall ratings between trade association members and non-members.

Additional notable points from the research are as follows:

Overall, 17% of garages carried out unnecessary work. This was particularly so in London and the South where 28% of garages carried out unnecessary work.

Overall, 40% of garages missed or did not replace at least one item on the service schedule. This was particularly so for female car owners—58%.

Overall, 86% of garages missed at least one of the introduced faults. 17% missed all four introduced faults.

43% of garages did not provide customers with an accurate quote prior to the service.

71% of garages did not show the customer the original parts that had been replaced.

8% of garages carried out work that had not been agreed with the customer prior to the work being undertaken. This percentage was higher among independent garages—12%.

- Services were most expensive in London and the South and cheapest in Scotland.

National Consumer Council, *At a Crossroads: Getting the UK Car Servicing and Repair Sector Back on Track* (2005) 2–3, 11

The car servicing and repair sector causes significant consumer detriment. The government's own mystery shopping research indicates that half of garages offer a poor standard of service. In financial terms this may cost consumers as much as a staggering £4 billion a year, or nearly £11 million every day. More serious still, shoddy workmanship on a vehicle carries obvious risks to public safety. Information asymmetries—or imbalances of information that typically occur when the trader has better or more information than the buyer—mean that consumers are ill equipped to choose a reliable garage, or to spot mistakes or dishonesty.

Self-regulation has failed time and again to tackle these problems; indeed there have been eleven different schemes over the last 30 years. This approach has failed so far because the ingredients for credible self-regulation were missing; and the market is complex, fragmented and includes many small traders. The smaller trade associations have made some progress by gaining approval from the Office of Fair Trading (OFT) for their codes of practice. But this progress has been seriously compromised by the withdrawal of the two largest trade associations —the Retail Motor Industry Federation and Scottish Motor Trade Association—from this scheme.We are clear that this same system of self-regulation must apply across the whole sector if it is to have any chance of making the impact that is needed.

… If self-regulation ultimately fails, there is a range of possible regulatory solutions. One is to enable dedicated enforcement activity through regional compliance centres, which could be supervised by the proposed Consumer and Trading Standards Agency. This could be supported by a system of registration funded by an industry levy. Another possibility is to licence technicians or outlets, or both. Useful models include the authorisation system in place for MOT test stations, the accreditation system being developed by the Institute of the Motor Industry, and the CORGI registration system.

In addition, measures to create informed consumer choice, and a single independent redress scheme for the whole sector, should also form part of any package of solutions.

Government and industry are at a crossroads. For now, the industry has control of the steering wheel, but time is fast running out for self-regulation to deliver real improvement to consumers. Unless the industry collectively can quickly obtain and maintain full OFT approval for their codes, policy-makers will have no choice but to impose regulatory solutions …

The car servicing and repair sector is consistently one of the most complained-about markets in the UK economy.

In 2004 the OFT convinced car manufacturers not to require servicing ties as part of their warranties so that consumers could choose where they have their new cars serviced. This was to aid consumer choice and foster competition. In response to criticisms the motor trade developed a code of practice for service and repairs under the OFT code scheme. This ultimately received full OFT approval in 2011. The code promises:

- comprehensive monitoring of member garages, including inspection visits by independent RAC engineers
- quotes or estimates for work include a written breakdown of costs, detailing the charges for labour and parts

- where further work is required, the member garage must get customer permission before proceeding with this

- member garages do not take upfront deposits

- independent disciplinary procedures are in place, with a range of sanctions including warnings and termination of membership, to deal with garages that breach the Code

- a low-cost independent redress scheme is available to customers

- all customers can give online feedback about the garage on the Motor Codes website. (www.oft.gov.uk/news-and-updates/press/2011/126-11)

In several Commonwealth jurisdictions legislators have enacted specific legislation to regulate motor vehicle repairs. For example, the Ontario Consumer Protection Act 2002 requires written estimates to be provided, and evidence of authorisation of any subsequent repairs. Failure to do so may result in a consumer obtaining a free repair under a sanction of nullity (see Ontario Consumer Protection Act 2002, c 30 sections 56–64).

9

Product Safety Regulation

> Salmonella, listeria, BSE in beef, botulism, dichlorvos in farmed salmon, alar in apple juice, anti-freeze in wine, insecticide residues in bran and fruit, the adulteration of cooking oil in Spain, aluminium sulfate in water, flammable furniture and children's nightclothes, dangerous toys, swimming buoyancy aids that deflate, models of car and gardening equipment that lack well-known safety devices, IUD-induced injuries, opren, thalidomide. ... The market, it seems, offers us a rich choice of harming ourselves using products that are widely available. (Burrows, 1992)

One might add genetically modified food to Burrows's list. Consumer health and safety is a large topic, including health and safety in the area of food and drugs (see, for example, the Food Standards Act 1999, Medicines Act 1968), general product safety and the health and safety implications of particular products such as motor vehicles. This chapter focuses on the regulation of unsafe products under the Consumer Protection Act 1987 and the General Product Safety Regulations 2005 (SI 1803) which implement the 2001 EU Directive on general product safety (Directive 2001/95).

Consumer safety regulation illustrates several themes in the study of regulation of risk in consumer markets: (1) the tension between economic and ethical values; (2) expert and lay risk assessment; (3) technocratic and democratic decision-making; (4) the demise of the public/private distinction given the central role of private groups in policy implementation; (5) the internationalisation of regulation: consumer safety within the EU illustrates the attempt to develop transnational ground rules for the internal market. Finally, safety regulation—and its balance of *ex ante* and *ex post* regulation—has provided a model in recent years for regulation in other areas such as credit.

Since the late 1980s there have been several influences on regulatory approaches to risk management in the EU. Scandals and crises have often driven the development of product safety. David Vogel argues that 'the most important factor contributing to the increased stringency of health, safety and environmental regulation in Europe has been a series of regulatory failures and crises that placed new regulatory issues on the political agenda and pressured policy makers to adopt more risk averse or precautionary policies' and European-wide issues such as 'mad cow disease' and 'dramatically exposed the gap between the single market—which exposes all European consumers to goods produced anywhere within the EU—and the inability of European institutions to assure the safety of the products sold within that market' (Vogel, 2003: 568, 570). In 2007, a substantial influx from China of potentially dangerous toys into the EU and US created a regulatory scare and a reassessment of the effectiveness of the EU system at identifying and addressing swiftly safety problems in consumer products. Nottage (2010) provides further comparative analysis of safety regimes.

---

1. Rationales and objectives: defining an acceptable social risk

A primary economic reason for regulating product safety is inadequate consumer information. Consumers may be unaware of hidden or long-term risks, eg from carcinogens, and market pressures may fail to provide producers with incentives to disclose this information (see above Chapter 2). The need for regulation may also be justified by the difficulties individuals face in processing complex health and safety data—for example, concerning the composition of pharmaceutical drugs or of food additives, or by the fact that consumers may act irrationally or misperceive risk (or do both). Adam Smith believed that 'the chance of loss is by most men undervalued' (quoted in Rea, 1983: 112), and there is evidence that, since the perception of risk is often based on personal experience, individuals may often underestimate the (low) probabilities of relatively rare accidents occurring (Tversky and Kahneman, 1974). There may also be significant externalities—third-party effects—which will be used to justify regulation. A product may injure persons other than the purchaser, and the price paid may, therefore, not reflect the true social cost of the product.

An economic approach to safety regulation assumes that regulation is desirable where the economic benefits of regulation outweigh the economic costs. However, many might feel uncomfortable with such an approach to product safety, where injury and death may be involved. Many regard the value of life as fundamental and consequently reject the idea of subjecting it to calculations of economic costs and benefits. The development of consumer-protection regulation may partly represent a quest for security from harm from new technology. These ideas underlie ethical approaches which postulate a right to protection from certain risks to life or health—irrespective of calculations of economic costs and benefits. These approaches reflect an underlying conception of personal autonomy in which individuals may not be used as a means to social ends. Sagoff, for example, argues that the principal value informing safety legislation may be autonomy not efficiency: '[Safety legislation] may represent an attempt … to control the conditions under which we pursue happiness—the conditions under which we lead our lives' (Sagoff 1982: 10). On one interpretation, valuing autonomy means that an unequal distribution of risks in society is only acceptable if all affected parties acting rationally freely consent to it. One possible outcome of this consensual process would be the principle that individuals would submit to an unequal distribution of risks only if this will make the least-advantaged better off in the long run (Rawls, 1971). This approach emphasises the importance of the right to equal participation of all affected interests in social decisions on safety and the importance of democratic dialogue (see Habermas, 1998). The process of determining the distribution of risk becomes central within this conception of autonomy.

Finally, paternalism, based on a mistrust of individuals' abilities to assess or protect themselves against product risks, may also often be an important motive in the advocacy and provision of safety regulation. A variation on this is the idea of self-paternalism. Individuals may wish to protect themselves against mistakes caused by their own impulsive behaviour or by their failure to think through risks (Schelling, 1984: ch 3).

Safety regulation is likely to be both more and less sensitive to political pressures than to pressures deriving from an assessment of economic loss (see Viscusi, 1998; Hood, Rothstein and Baldwin, 2001). The highly visible and perhaps tragic consequences of safety errors may create powerful political pressures for regulatory action. The media can engage public attention at low cost through dramatic headlines. In the United States, Ralph Nader's claim that the Corvair was 'unsafe at any speed' was a powerful stimulant of a great upsurge of consumerism, as were the Thalidomide and the Spanish oil disasters in England and Spain. Given the pressure for action, politicians may respond by making highly symbolic gestures—for example, by banning products or taking strong regulatory measures. These may be preferred to measures such as information policies or taxes, even if the latter would be more effective in the long run. Yet the highly symbolic commitment may be undercut at the low-visibility, day-to-day process of enforcement. On the other hand, the complexity of the scientific issues associated with food and drug technology makes it difficult for consumers to have a continuing and sustained input to the process of formulating and enforcing safety standards. Before the advent of BSE, food standards were largely agreed 'between civil servants and business officials' (Grant, 1987: 43), and others have argued that expert committees in this area were dominated by the food interests (Cannon, 1987; Fallows, 1987). The Food Standards Agency was established in 2000 partly to restore confidence in the way food safety decisions are made.

These comments suggest that current policy on product safety is not necessarily the outcome of a rational assessment of the economic costs and benefits of particular products. But we have already questioned whether policy on product safety should follow this kind of rational path, and it is clear that decisions on product safety involve both technical and political judgment. This is illustrated by any attempt to define a socially acceptable level of safety. For example, what do we mean when we say that a product is safe? One response might be 'free from risk'. But almost nothing can be absolutely free from risk. 'Safe' must, therefore, mean free from an unacceptable risk. Lowrance has drawn attention to a distinction between '*measuring risk*, an objective but probabilistic pursuit, and *judging the acceptability of that risk* (*judging safety*), a matter of personal and social value judgment' (Lowrance, 1976: 8; and see Douglas, 1985: ch 1). What is viewed as an acceptable risk may vary over time and depend on differing individual and social 'tastes' for risk. As Western societies have become less vulnerable to disease and natural hazards, greater political concern has been shown concerning hazards from man-made products. This has occurred even if historically the risks from these products are actually declining (Lowrance, 1976: 3; Beck, 1992;

Giddens, 1994; above Chapter 1). However, risk assessment is itself conducted within a context of scientific uncertainty. Fisher (2000: 115) points out that this uncertainty is not simply due to 'a simple need to do more research'. There may be epistemological uncertainties because 'we don't know what we don't know'. The EU in its communication on the 'precautionary principle' notes that 'Judging what is an "acceptable" level of risk for society is an eminently political responsibility. Decision-makers faced with an unacceptable risk, scientific uncertainty and public concerns have a duty to find answers.'

Communication from the Commission on the Precautionary Principle, COM(2000) 1

At Community level the only explicit reference to the precautionary principle is to be found in the environment title of the EC Treaty. ... However, in practice, the scope of this principle is far wider and also covers consumer policy, European legislation concerning food and human, animal and plant health.

Recourse to the precautionary principle

According to the Commission the precautionary principle may be invoked when a phenomenon, product or process may have a dangerous effect, identified by a scientific and objective evaluation, if this evaluation does not allow the risk to be determined with sufficient certainty.

Recourse to the principle belongs in the general framework of risk analysis (which, besides risk evaluation, includes risk management and risk communication), and more particularly in the context of risk management which corresponds to the decision-making phase.

The Commission stresses that the precautionary principle may only be invoked in the event of a potential risk and that it can never justify arbitrary decisions.

The precautionary principle may only be invoked when the three preliminary conditions are met:

- identification of potentially adverse effects;
- evaluation of the scientific data available;
- the extent of scientific uncertainty.

Precautionary measures

The authorities responsible for risk management may decide to act or not to act, depending on the level of risk. If the risk is high, several categories of measures can be adopted. This may involve proportionate legal acts, financing of research programmes, public information measures, etc.

Common guidelines

The precautionary principle shall be informed by three specific principles:

- the fullest possible scientific evaluation, the determination, as far as possible, of the degree of scientific uncertainty;
- a risk evaluation and an evaluation of the potential consequences of inaction;
- the participation of all interested parties in the study of precautionary measures, once the results of the scientific evaluation and/or the risk evaluation are available.

In addition, the general principles of risk management remain applicable when the precautionary principle is invoked. These are the following five principles:

- proportionality between the measures taken and the chosen level of protection;

- non-discrimination in application of the measures;

- consistency of the measures with similar measures already taken in similar situations or using similar approaches;

- examination of the benefits and costs of action or lack of action; This is not simply an economic cost-benefit analysis: its scope is much broader, and includes non-economic considerations, such as the efficacy of possible options and their acceptability to the public

- review of the measures in the light of scientific developments.

The burden of proof

In most cases, European consumers and the associations which represent them must demonstrate the danger associated with a procedure or a product placed on the market, except for medicines, pesticides and food additives.

However, in the case of an action being taken under the precautionary principle, the producer, manufacturer or importer may be required to prove the absence of danger. This possibility shall be examined on a case-by-case basis. It cannot be extended generally to all products and procedures placed on the market.

The potential tensions between democratic and technocratic decision-making where scientific assessment of risk takes precedence over politics suggests that there may be a substantial discrepancy between scientific and lay assessments of risk. Loewenstein et al, in a study of discrepancies between emotional and cognitive reactions to risks, comment:

> Individuals' emotional reactions to risk not only often differ from their cognitive evaluations of those risks; they also often diverge from the evaluations of experts. Public perception of the risks of silicone implants in causing autoimmune diseases, for example, led Dow Corning to stop production of implants in 1992 and file for bankruptcy in 1995, despite two major medical reports that revealed no evidence of silicone related illnesses and a clean bill of health from the American College of Rheumatology. ... The divergence between the emotional reactions of the public to risks and professionals appraisals of risks creates a significant dilemma for policymakers. On the one hand, many policymakers would like to be responsive to public attitudes and opinions. On the other hand, there is a strong rationale for basing public policy on the best scientific assessment of risk severity. (Loewenstein et al, 2001: 281)

Behavioural economists suggest that individual perceptions of risk in society are affected by the availability heuristic and that this can trigger 'availability cascades'. This is where individuals with 'little personal information base their own beliefs on the apparent beliefs of others'. Availability entrepreneurs, such as government, media and business, may attempt to raise the salience of particular information so that individuals become reluctant to oppose beliefs that become spread widely. While recognising that these campaigns produce social benefits by stimulating debates on issues that had traditionally been regarded as private troubles, the campaigns may also fuel collective misperceptions and 'populist firestorms' so that 'apparently democratic outcomes will rest on misinformation' (Kumar and Sunstein, 2000: 387). Consider, for example, the myth of the 'compensation culture' that is stoked by (misleading) stories about seemingly outrageous product-liability claims. Kumar and Sunstein suggest that policies that protect against availability cascades include cost–benefit analysis and risk-information sites on the Internet.

In the first edition of the book I described the background to the Scented Erasers (Safety) Order 1984, suggesting that policymaking in this area did not seem to be based on rational analysis. There are now at both national and European level the requirement for impact assessments and for better and smarter regulation (eg EU, 2010) that are not be driven by 'atrocity stories'. Contrast, however, the comments of Braithwaite and Drahos in reviewing the history of global business regulation. They argue that:

> in all the regimes we have studied, during the twentieth century anxiety among mass publics, triggered mostly by reading stories of disasters in the mass media, had substantial effects in globalizing new forms of regulation (Braithwaite and Drahos, 2000: 500)

and they cite examples such as Bhopal, stock market crashes, *Unsafe at any Speed*—and one might add Thalidomide, BSE, genetically modified organisms and the global financial crisis of 2008. These events resulted in a shift in power relations between corporations and citizens and in their view enriched democracy by stimulating public dialogue.

Distributional issues are particularly significant when one is dealing with potential inequalities in risk. The methodology of cost–benefit analysis may bias outcomes in favour of certain groups. For example, valuing life in terms of forgone earnings places a higher value on the lives of high-income earners. In addition, if social preferences for safety are measured by consumers' willingness to pay, then, given that those with higher incomes will be willing to pay more, a cost–benefit analysis would be likely to support a proposal to increase the safety of a product at the cost of an associated increase in price that might deny poorer consumers access to the product.

The problem of valuing intangible benefits is acute. This is reflected in the extensive literature concerning 'the value of life' (see eg Jones-Lee, 1980). Behavioural literature is relevant here since the endowment effect indicates that individuals are loss averse and want to be paid much more to avoid a loss than to forgo a gain. Thus individuals wish to be paid much more to accept an increase in risk rather than they would pay to eliminate the identical risk (Guria et al, 2005: 113; Knetsch, 2005: 32;). In addition, prevention of injury may be preferable to compensation. This may be partly justified by economists' findings that in general individuals are far more willing to pay large amounts to reduce risks to themselves rather than pay large insurance premiums to provide compensation after an injury has occurred.

A stark example of different evaluations of life is provided by the Ford Pinto litigation in the United States. This car had a fuel tank which tended to rupture in rear-end collisions. Ford management were aware of the problem but decided not to change the design. The modification was rejected on the basis of a cost–benefit calculation which assumed that the added protection would save 180 lives and 180 injuries. Each life saved was valued at $200,000 and each injury saved at $67,000. The costs of modification were $11 × 12.5 million vehicles. In a subsequent court case, the jury awarded a person injured in a fire resulting from the ruptured fuel tank of a Ford Pinto $128 million. This was reduced to $6 million on appeal (Adams, 1985: 12).

There is the further objection to the use of cost–benefit analysis in making decisions about consumer safety that certain values ought not to be subject to such an analysis. This objection reflects the ethical argument that there is a special value to life—that there is a 'right' to safety which can only be reconciled with other values through moral judgement.

The limits of cost–benefit analysis as a decision-making procedure, and the political nature of safety decisions, shift attention from the question of how to decide safety levels to that of who should decide and the *processes* for decision making. A similar conclusion has been drawn by many writers in relation to the ability of scientific expertise, on its own, to provide clear guidance in the area of new technology. Regulation of consumer safety poses therefore the issue of developing optimal public administration or governance that respects values of efficiency, effectiveness, legitimacy and accountability.

UK consumer safety policy documents have often stressed the concept of balancing the social benefits of higher standards against costs (see eg DTI, 1976, 1984). The General Product Safety Regulations 2005 (SI 2005/1803) that implement Directive 2001/95/EC of the European Parliament and of the Council on general product safety require producers to supply a safe product (regulation 5); 'safe' is not equated with 'free from risk':

> s 2. ... 'safe product' means a product which, under normal or reasonably foreseeable conditions of use including duration and, where applicable, putting into service, installation and maintenance requirements, does not present any risk or only the minimum risks compatible with the product's use, considered to be acceptable and consistent with a high level of protection for the safety and health of persons. In determining the foregoing, the following shall be taken into account in particular—
>
> (a) the characteristics of the product, including its composition, packaging, instructions for assembly and, where applicable, instructions for installation and maintenance,
>
> (b) the effect of the product on other products, where it is reasonably foreseeable that it will be used with other products,
>
> (c) the presentation of the product, the labelling, any warnings and instructions for its use and disposal and any other indication or information regarding the product, and
>
> (d) the categories of consumers at risk when using the product, in particular children and the elderly.
>
> The feasibility of obtaining higher levels of safety or the availability of other products presenting a lesser degree of risk shall not constitute grounds for considering a product to be a dangerous product.

The standard of safety adopted in the EU General Product Safety Directive contrasts with the Products Liability Directive which adopts a 'consumer expectations' test of safety. Consider the potential differences between these tests and see the discussion below in *A and others v National Blood Authority.*

Consumer-safety regulation involves several stages: problem identification; policy instrument choice (eg information requirement, standard, individual licensing, ban, product recall or moral suasion); and implementation and enforcement.

1.1 Identification of product risks

Product faults alone, rather than the environment in which they occurred or the behaviour of the user, are a relatively minor cause of injuries in the home (DTI, 2002). A primary source of information in the UK on product dangers is the Home Accident Surveillance System (HASS). This was established in 1979 in response to criticisms of the reactive approach taken to the administration of the Consumer Protection Act 1961. It collects data on accidents from the accident and emergency departments of hospitals. Its goals are to provide reliable, comprehensive and nationally representative information on home accidents, to identify new hazards, to allocate priorities for action and to provide a basis for estimating the costs of different types of home accident. Detailed studies of particular topics are undertaken consequent on identification of issues by HASS. There are, however, limitations on these data: fatal accidents are, for example, not included; the database is relatively small; and it is often difficult to gain clear information on the background to the accidents. These data must be related to the intensity and frequency of the use of the products that caused the harm in order to provide a picture of the probability of injury from those products. Gathering this information from HASS is, therefore, merely a first step in attempting to provide a ranking of priorities for intervention. The DBIS has now ceased to collect HASS and LASS (the Leisure Accident Surveillance System) data, and Hodges argues that in the UK there is currently 'little or no systematic attempt to collect safety data' which could be used to evaluate

> the prevailing level of safety of products, the efficiency of the regulatory systems or of particular measure: whether a particular measure is justified on a cost–benefit test, such that the marginal increase in safety that it produces can be compared with the marginal increase in cost; whether particular initiatives should be launched or are successful. (Hodges, 2005: 235)

Ranking of safety issues should be related to consumers' ability to protect themselves. This appears to be reflected in existing regulations in the United Kingdom, the United States and Canada, that have focused on products with hidden risks (eg from flammability or composition) and children's products. Children may be particularly vulnerable, in part because of their physical characteristics, but also because it is third parties, ie parents, who generally buy the toys; they are not the users and may overlook or underestimate any risks involved in playing with them.

---

2. The development of consumer product safety regulation in the United Kingdom

Until 1961 there was no general regulation of consumer safety (Molony Committee, Interim Report, 1960: para 40; see Howells, 1998). The growth of consumer safety policy during the 1960s and 1970s coincided both with greater consumer concern about, and greater scientific awareness of, the hidden and long-term risks from products. The Thalidomide disaster occurred in the 1960s, and the protection provided in successive

Consumer Safety Acts must be seen along with, for example, the regulation of drugs under the Medicines Act 1968.

The Consumer Protection Act 1961 was essentially framework legislation which permitted the Secretary of State for Trade and Industry to make safety regulations. Subsequent experience of regulation under this Act revealed several deficiencies, which were catalogued in a Green Paper published in 1976 (*Consumer Safety—A Consultative Document*, Cmnd 6398). In response to these criticisms, the Consumer Safety Act 1978 was passed. This Act extended powers to ban (but not recall) products temporarily through prohibition notices and orders. Manufacturers and producers could also be required to publish warning notices. Standard-setting, however, remained generally a relatively slow and cumbersome process. In addition, trading standards officers experienced difficulties in enforcing the Act against small importers and in taking swift action where no safety regulations existed. These issues were addressed in the Consumer Safety (Amendment) Act 1986, which extended enforcement powers by introducing suspension powers (section 3) and forfeiture powers (section 6) and permitted customs and excise authorities to transmit information to trading standards officers. The Consumer Protection Act 1987 continued the general power to establish product safety standards (section 11) and require information disclosures and re-enacts the extension of enforcement powers in the 1986 Act. A significant addition was, however, its introduction of a general duty to supply goods which are 'reasonably safe' (section 10(2)). 'Safe' was defined as 'such that there is no risk, or no risk apart from one reduced to a minimum' (section 19(1)).

This general safety duty provided a model for European developments and the Consumer Protection Act 1987 must now be read in the light of the General Product Safety Regulations 2005 which implement the 2001 Directive of the European Parliament and Council on general product safety (Directive 2001/95/EC) and replace the 1994 Regulations. The main innovations in the 2005 Regulations are:

(a) a broader definition of product than earlier regulations;
(b) substitution of a general safety obligation in regulation 5 for the existing obligation under section 10 of the 1987 Act;
(c) greater safety obligations on distributors of products;
(d) significant post-marketing surveillance obligations on producers;
(e) introduction of a legal obligation on producers in specified circumstances to recall products; and
(f) greater structuring of enforcement discretion (see further Cartwright, 2007: 309).

The basis of the EU rules are those of market integration while maintaining a high level of consumer protection (see below 3). The regulations apply to a wide range of products, new and second hand, including products provided in the course of a service.

Regulation 5 of the 2005 regulations establishes a general obligation to supply safe goods. Regulation 6 presumes conformity with regulation 5 in certain situations and is intended to create incentives for the adoption by businesses of specific standards such as ISO 9000 which address quality control (see below). However, these standards do not provide a complete 'safe harbour' since regulation 6(4) provides a safeguard clause that permits enforcement authorities to exercise powers against a product where there is evidence, notwithstanding the conformity to regulation 6(1)–6(3), that the product is dangerous. Thus in *Whirlpool (UK) Ltd v Gloucestershire County Council* (1993) a cooker hood that melted when used with a gas cooker (but not with an electrical cooker) was held to be dangerous notwithstanding that it conformed to British Standards. The judge held that in determining safety one must have regard to all the circumstances. 'In my view, this contemplates not the goods themselves viewed in isolation, but the use to which they are put; in this case the use which must have been contemplated by all concerned, namely use over a gas cooker. It [the standard] is concerned with the goods themselves taken in isolation.' Similarly, notwithstanding that a 'Tipper Trike', a toy intended to be used by very young children, complied with a British Standard, this Standard did not extend to all issues covered by the essential safety requirements in the relevant Toy Safety regulations and was not a defence to a prosecution for contravention of the regulations (*Balding v Lew-Ways Ltd* (1995)).

2.1 Product safety standards

The establishment of product safety standards is often viewed as the major output of government agencies concerned with consumer safety. A continuing concern in policymaking has been the length of time taken to produce standards (see eg Molony Committee, 1962, para 62; 1976, 1984 White Papers). The general duty in the Consumer Protection Act 1987 was intended to create incentives for private standard-setting. This will occur, it is argued, because large private, bureaucracies will wish to have detailed standards in order to be sure of complying with the general legislation. For example, powerful middlemen (retailers, wholesalers) in the market may put pressure on suppliers to develop standards. The Act (and the earlier White Paper) says little about the important issue of consumer participation in the process of standard setting beyond a duty to consult under section 11(5) such organisations as appear to him to be representative of interests substantially affected by the proposal and to consult such other persons as he considers appropriate (Weatherill, 1987: 81). There is the continuing concern that, without proper consumer representation, product safety standards will reflect, in the main, private industry interests or practices. Similar concerns have been expressed about European developments on the technical harmonisation of standards—where private groups play an important role.

Standard-setting is both a technical and political process, and the difficulties involved are a reflection of the need to respond to technical and political factors. There is the need for high-quality information and analysis of the social impact and the costs and benefits of any proposed standard. It is also important, given the uncertainty of technical judgements on such issues as cost–benefit analysis and the controversial nature of choices involved in establishing the appropriate level of safety, to ensure the participation of those affected. The legitimacy of the standard-setting process is therefore a central issue.

A pervasive problem facing a standard-setting agency is that of obtaining enough accurate and reliable information to enable it to write an effective standard (Breyer, 1982: 109). This is true both at the stage of problem diagnosis and at the stage of standard formulation. The most comprehensive source of information will be in the hands of the regulated industry. However, that industry will have incentives to provide information favourable to its position and may use it as a bargaining chip. Other affected groups in standard setting, eg consumers, are unlikely to have access to similar levels of expert information. The importance of industry information, and the general desirability of securing voluntary compliance with standards, explain the often co-operative approach adopted towards industry and the central role which these private groups play in standard-setting. In the United Kingdom, in practice, the consultation process takes place through the British Standards Institution (BSI), a 'private' body financed partly by government and partly by industry. This body plays a key role in standard-setting nationally and internationally. The government has long indicated the desirability of close co-operation between government and the BSI, stating in 1984 that 'in future regulatory bodies should wherever it is necessary to express technical requirements in regulations, do this as far as possible by reference to British Standards' (DTI, *Standards, Quality and International Competitiveness*, 1982: 3.5). The BSI is not, however, concerned primarily with safety but with promoting standards as competitive devices for British industry. The following extract outlines relevant sections of the current memorandum of understanding between the government and the BSI:

Memorandum of Understanding between the United Kingdom government and the British Standards Institution in respect of its activities as the United Kingdom's national standards body

'British Standards' means formal consensus standards as set out in BS 0-12 paragraph 3.2 and based on the principles of standardisation recognized inter alia in European standardisation policy

Article 3 Recognition by the Government of BSI as the NSB (National Standards Body)

3.1 The Government recognises BSI as the NSB. This includes recognition of BSI as the United Kingdom member of ISO (International Organisation for Standardisation) and CEN (European Committee for Standardisation). ...

3.2 The Government will support BSI's efforts to achieve harmonisation of relevant standards through these international and European standards organisations, international agreements and other arrangements in the interests of the UK.

3.3 The Government will keep BSI informed of any intergovernmental discussions concerned with standards or associated technical regulations, unless there are reasons of confidentiality for not doing so. It will invite BSI where appropriate to participate in such discussions, especially those which may lead to intergovernmental agreements concerning standards, and will fully take into account BSI's views on the best means of implementing such agreements.

Article 4

Commitments of BSI (as NSB) and the Government

4.1 BSI will ensure:

...

(ii) that it provides the Government with information about any of its standards or standards activities when required to do so;

(iii) that it achieves the requirements of membership of the major European and international standards organisations and, by means of participation in such organisations, the optimal promotion of UK interests through their policies and standards;

(iv) that it fulfils the requirements for being cited as the UK NSB for the purposes of Directive 98/34/EC (or any successor Community act to that Directive), carrying out efficiently and effectively the responsibilities of the UK NSB laid down in that Directive, and the requirements of any other EC legal instruments which may refer to national standards bodies.;

(v) through appropriate facilitation, the production and maintenance of any standard required by the Government for legislation (whether referenced in the legal instrument or otherwise indirectly required) or for public procurement purposes;

(vi) the provision and maintenance of a portfolio of formal consensus standards and other standardisation products which will meet the requirements of UK business and, as appropriate, other stakeholders including the Government, consumers, and small businesses; and a means of identifying, evaluating, prioritising and acting on proposals for standardisation projects; (vii) that, within the portfolio described in Article 4.1

(vi), formal consensus standards are provided and maintained whenever there is a requirement that the criteria for such standards be met;

(viii) that it contributes to strategic planning of the national standardization infrastructure, including maintaining its own strategic standardization planning and evaluation facility with the involvement of the Government and business;

(ix) co-operation with the Government to use standardisation to support policy; ...

Article 8 Standards development

8.1 In the preparation of British Standards, BSI will ensure that its committees adhere to the guidance and recommendations of BS 0: 1997 'A Standard for Standards' and any subsequent amendment or revision thereof. ...

8.3 BSI will seek a fair and acceptable balance of all relevant interests in its work and will encourage their full participation in producing British Standards and in formulating the UK position on proposed European and international standards which not only reflect sound and modern technical practice but also take fully into account the commercial needs of both manufacturers and users. If work on standards or other standardization products is funded or partly funded by participants, BSI will take care that opportunities for participation are available to other stakeholders as appropriate.

The BSI 'Standard for Standards' BS 0-2 recognises the need for 'fairness in the representation on any committee' and that the 'quality of standards and their acceptance, particularly by the courts, depends largely upon the widest and most authoritative representation available' (BS 0-2 Article 6.3.1: see further Schepel, 2005: 122–30). The BSI plays a key role in national, regional and international standard-setting. Government, industry and consumer groups are represented on the BSI safety committees. The BSI thus provides a focus for technical expertise and interest participation. The principle of consensus which operates within these committees inevitably means that the standard-setting process is relatively drawn out and reflects a political compromise. Consumer representatives may find it difficult to match the expertise of business (see further Ogus, 1994: 200).

3. Consumer safety and transnational market governance within the EU

3.1 The EU 'new approach' to standards and consumer product safety standardisation: free movement in a safe market

The EU is increasingly the source of product standards and the EU model of safety standards, implemented in the UK by the General Product Safety Regulations 2005 follows the 'new approach' to technical standardisation (see generally Pelkmans, 1987: 49; McGee and Weatherill, 1990; Ogus, 1994: 174–79; Howells, 2000: 305; Hodges, 2004: ch 5; Schepel, 2005: ch 7; Cartwright, 2007).

The EU in 2000 described the new approach as one of the successes of the Union.

***Guide to the Implementation of Directives Based on the New Approach and the Global Approach*, Brussels (2000) 3, 7**

> The European Union has developed original and innovative instruments to remove the barriers to free circulation of goods. Among these, the New Approach to product regulation and the Global Approach to conformity assessment take pride of place. The common thread between these complementary approaches is that they limit public intervention to what is essential and leave business and industry the greatest possible choice on how to meet their public obligations. Since 1987 some 20 directives, adopted on the basis of the New Approach and the Global Approach, have progressively come into force. ...
>
> New barriers to trade, which result from the adoption of diverging national technical standards and regulations, can be prevented through a procedure laid down by Directive 98/34/ EC. Member States are obliged to notify draft technical regulations and standards to the Commission and to the other Member States. During a standstill period these may not be adopted, which leaves the Commission and the other Member States the possibility to react. In the absence of reactions within the initial standstill period of three months, the draft technical regulations may then be adopted. Otherwise, where objections are raised, a further three months standstill is imposed. The standstill period is 12 months where there is a proposal for a directive. However, the standstill period does not apply where, for urgent reasons, a Member State is obliged to introduce technical regulations in a very short space of time in order to protect public health or safety, animals or plants. Directive 98/34/EC also gives the Commission the possibility of inviting, after consultation with the Member States, the European standards organizations to elaborate European standards.
>
> 1.2. Legal Background
>
> On 7 May 1985, the Council adopted a Resolution on A New Approach to technical harmonization and standards, providing a new framework for the harmonisation of national regulations for industrial products. The New Approach was devised to facilitate the achievement of the Internal Market and to develop flexible and technology-neutral legislation by moving from detailed product specific technical requirements to defining the essential requirements for types of products, thus promoting innovation and competitiveness.
>
> This was complemented in 1989 by the Council Resolution on a Global Approach to conformity

assessment, followed by two other Council Decisions setting out more detailed specifications on testing and certification procedures and providing guidelines for the use of the CE marking, which are intended to be used in the harmonisation directives. There are provisions for the Commission to 'report periodically whether conformity assessment and CE marking procedures are working satisfactorily or need to be modified.'

Council Resolution of 7 May 1985 on a New Approach to Technical Harmonization and Standards [1985] OJ C136

The following are the four fundamental principles on which the new approach is based:

— legislative harmonization is limited to the adoption, by means of Directives based on Article 100 of the EEC Treaty, of the essential safety requirements (or other requirements in the general interest) with which products put on the market must conform, and which should therefore enjoy free movement throughout the Community,

— the task of drawing up the technical specifications needed for the production and placing on the market of products conforming to the essential requirements established by the Directives, while taking into account the current stage of technology, is entrusted to organizations competent in the standardization area,

— these technical specifications are not mandatory and maintain their status of voluntary standards,

— but at the same time national authorities are obliged to recognize that products manufactured in conformity with harmonized standards (or, provisionally, with national standards) are presumed to conform to the 'essential requirements' established by the Directive. (This signifies that the producer has the choice of not manufacturing in conformity with the standards but that in this event he has an obligation to prove that his products conform to the essential requirements of the Directive.)

In order that this system may operate it is necessary:—on the one hand that the standards offer a guarantee of quality with regard to the 'essential requirements' established by the Directives,

— on the other hand that the public authorities keep intact their responsibility for the protection of safety (or other requirements envisaged) on their territory.

The quality of harmonized standards must be ensured by standardization mandates, conferred by the Commission, the execution of which must conform to the general guidelines which have been the subject of agreement between the Commission and the European standardization organizations. In so far as national standards are concerned their quality must be verified by a procedure at Community level managed by the Commission, assisted by a standing committee composed of officials from national administrations.

At the same time safeguard procedures must be provided for, under the management of the Commission assisted by the same committee, in order to allow the competent public authorities the possibility of contesting the conformity of a product, the validity of a certificate or the quality of a standard.

In following this system of legislative harmonization in each area in which it is feasible, the Commission intends to be able to halt the proliferation of excessively technical separate Directives for each product. The scope of Directives according to the 'general reference to standards' formula should encompass wide product categories and types of risk.

. . .

IX. Standing committee

A standing committee shall be set up chaired by a representative of the Commission and consisting of representatives appointed by the Member States who may avail themselves of the help of experts or advisers.

... The tasks of the committee shall be concerned with the implementation of the Directive.

The central characteristics of the new approach are therefore:

1. the delegation to private standard-setting bodies to establish standards (CEN);
2. the possibility of greater use of performance standards that leave manufacturers free to adopt the most effective method of achieving safety;
3. the ability of a manufacturer to self-certify either through using a third-party recognised standard or receiving approval of its design through a 'notified body';
4. the existence of the safeguard clause that permits states to act against goods that are unsafe notwithstanding the existence of a product standard;
5. the creation of a standing committee of national representatives and expert advisers chaired by the Commission to oversee the implementation of the directive;
6. the requirement of surveillance by national authorities of product safety.

The EU approach is designed to create incentives for the development of private standards and the use of performance rather than design standards. This follows the UK approach in the Consumer Protection Act 1987 reflecting the UK influence on the EU Directive. Performance standards state the required performance of a product (eg that a ladder be able to withstand a certain amount of force); design standards specify the detailed design of a product (eg that a ladder must have at least four rungs). Economists generally prefer performance standards, since they do not hamper innovation and directly address the problem, rather than the indirect method of design specifications. Design specifications may, however, be less costly to enforce. Thus, in the ladder example the inspector need only check that it has at least four rungs. The trend in British standard-making is towards the use of performance standards.

A central aspect of the EU Commission is addressing issues of information, ensuring that information about dangerous products can be rapidly disseminated throughout the EU.

Guidelines for the management of the Community Rapid Information System (RAPEX) and for notifications presented in accordance with Article 11 of Directive 2001/95/EC

1.1 Background and Objectives of the guidelines

The objectives of the RAPEX system are:

(a) to provide a rapid exchange of information between Member States and the Commission about measures and actions taken in relation to consumer products because of a serious risk to the health and safety of consumers;

(b) to inform Member States and the Commission about the existence of a serious risk even before measures are adopted or actions taken;

(c) to obtain and circulate to all Member States information on the follow-up given to the information exchanged by the Member States receiving it;

with the aim of:

(a) preventing the supply to consumers of products which pose a serious risk to their health and safety, and where necessary withdrawing them from the market or recalling them from consumers;

(b) facilitating the monitoring of the effectiveness and consistency of market surveillance and enforcement activities in the Member States;

(c) identifying the need and providing a basis for action at Community level, where necessary;

(d) contributing to the consistent enforcement of Community product safety requirements and to the proper functioning of the internal market. The notification mechanism of Article 11 of the GPSD also facilitates prevention of the supply to consumers of dangerous products (not presenting a serious risk) and monitoring of market surveillance activities in the Member States.

The 2001 regulations increased the potential for information flows about potentially dangerous products by imposing greater obligations on markets actors (producers, distributors) to maintain records and notify the relevant authority in a member state of products posing a serious risk (see below).

The new approach to standards was reviewed by the Commission (DG Sanco) in 2003. The Commission stated that the new approach had been a successful tool for the development of the internal market but identified a number of areas for improvement. These included:

1. The appropriate balance between pre- and post market controls. Some items such as toys or electrical appliances are not easy to check and trace once they are in circulation.

2. The criteria and procedures applied by individual states in certifying 'notified bodies'. The Commission noted that:

> it is the individual directives which provide the legal basis for notification and contain the legally binding criteria that Member states must apply when assessing notified bodies. Nevertheless the directives do not include detailed provisions on how these principles should be implemented. This situation reflects a political decision that the designation of national bodies should remain a national competence. ... There has been no systematic exchange of information between Member States concerning the criteria and procedures applied at national level for the assessment and surveillance of notified bodies. This lack of transparency has encouraged suspicions about uneven levels of implementation which, in turn, undermine the confidence that is essential if the mutual recognition and acceptance of certificates issued by notified bodies is to function smoothly.

The Commission concluded that it was important to develop greater transparency to ensure that there were no restrictions on the free movement of goods because of shortcomings of notified bodies and to demonstrate to third countries such as the US with whom the EU had trade agreements that there was a consistent approach to implementation of legislation in the EU.

3. The public may be misled by the CE marking as a signal of quality.

The legal status of the CE marking ... is not a commercial quality mark but should be seen as a declaration by the manufacturer, or his authorized representative, that the product conforms to all applicable harmonized provisions. Although this distinction is quite clear to authorities, it is not so to the public which, while it increasingly recognizes the mark, often mistakes its meaning. In particular, there is a tendency to add elements to the understanding of this marking that were never the intention of the directives. (para 2.4)

4. The need for effective market surveillance through the commitment of adequate resources by states, increased strategic information through accident data analysis, greater cooperation between safety authorities and other authorities such as customs, and more effective cross border cooperation.

The identification of substantial numbers of hazardous toys imported from China in 2007 resulted in a re-evaluation of the effectiveness of the EU system in monitoring and responding swiftly to potential safety risks. This took place at the same time as the EU was reforming the ground rules for the circulation of products within the EU—rules on accreditation and market surveillance (see COM(2007) 35 final, The Internal Market for Goods: A Cornerstone of Europe's Competitiveness, Regulation 765/2008: Decision No 768/2008). The EU also acted under Article 13 of the General Product Safety Directive that permits it to take action where there is a serious risk and there are inconsistent actions taken by Member States. This concerned the risk of injury to children from toys with powerful magnets that if swallowed could cause serious internal injury. According to the Commission 'Over 18 million magnetic toys were recalled worldwide during the summer of 2007, and a significant proportion of these toys were on the European market.' The Commission enacted a decision that required a warning to be attached to the toy. In 2010 the Commission reported on the operation of the Product Safety Directive.

DG Health and Consumer Report on the Consultation on the Product Safety Directive (DG Sanco, 2010)

The Commission report on the implementation of the General Product Safety Directive (the 'GPSD') published in January 2009 revealed a certain number of shortcomings in the application of this Directive.

... four main areas for improvement were identified: (i) procedures for mandating standards under the GPSD, (ii) harmonisation of safety evaluations, (iii) market surveillance cooperation and coordination and (iv) alignment with the Free Movement of Goods Package. (DG Health and Consumer, 2010).

Procedures for mandating standards under the GPSD

The great majority of respondents consider that the absence of referenced European standards for many products covered by the GPSD makes conformity assessment and enforcement more costly. There is also strong support for directly referencing existing European standards even where they are not based on a prior Commission mandate, as long as they provide a high level of consumer safety.

The speed of standardisation procedures under the GPSD is not satisfactory for a majority of responding stakeholders. The idea that the safety requirements formulated in Commission decisions should become mandatory and directly applicable is also strongly supported as the current method under the GPSD is perceived to leave too much margin of manoeuvre to the European standardisation organisations.

Harmonisation of diverging safety evaluations

Compliance with EU product safety 'emergency' measures adopted under Article 13 of the GPSD would be easier (i) if these measures were directly applicable to economic operators and/or (ii) if they were linked to a clearly defined permanent solution (eg adoption of a standard or of primary legislation) or if their validity could be extended to a fixed period of up to three years (with equal subsequent prolongation periods). Inconsistent application of EU 'emergency' measures on product safety by national market surveillance authorities ('NMSAs') was viewed as a problem by economic operators.

Diverging test results as well as diverging interpretation of standards and the risk assessment guidelines, have occasionally caused safety evaluations by one Member State to be contested (whether formally or informally) by another Member State(s). To overcome these divergences, which create barriers to the internal market, all groups of stakeholders favour setting product safety requirements at the EU level. In addition, the creation of a database for risk assessments and the establishment of an EU risk assessment agency were suggested.

Market surveillance coordination and cooperation (including the functioning of the RAPEX system and the safety of products marketed online)

A majority of Member States consider that they undertake sufficient market surveillance. Nevertheless a lack of resources for inspections and training are mentioned as reasons for not doing more. Member States cooperate with each other and consider such cooperation to be very beneficial, although they encounter problems linked mainly to differences in enforcement practices or, again, a lack of resources. Actions to improve cooperation in this area supported by over half of the respondents include providing more financial support to joint surveillance actions and exchanges of officials, and establishing a coordination forum at EU level.

While economic operators and other stakeholders are divided as to whether Member States undertake sufficient market surveillance or whether the cooperation with customs authorities works well, a majority considers that differences between Member States in enforcing product safety legislation are causing problems for businesses. They also believe that cooperation between NMSAs of different Member States needs to be improved. Respondents are overwhelmingly of the opinion that more intensive information sharing and/or cooperation between Member States would enhance the safety of consumers throughout the EU.

The results of the public consultation also show that many Member States still have difficulties complying fully with their obligations under the RAPEX system; in particular, they have problems notifying the Commission of preventive and restrictive measures and ensuring follow-up action to notifications distributed through the RAPEX system. The main reasons are insufficient human and financial resources, an overly complex notification procedure and insufficiently detailed data provided in RAPEX notifications. Other stakeholders overwhelmingly see the positive role of the RAPEX system in the product safety area and consider that it contributes to better protecting the consumers throughout the EU.

Economic operators and other stakeholders do not think that national authorities pay as much attention to products sold online as they do to products sold through other distribution channels. If NMSAs perform market surveillance on products marketed online, they do so in an incidental, fragmented and uncoordinated manner. A large majority of NMSAs would find it easier to enforce product safety rules if harmonised rules concerning products sold online were introduced at the EU level.

Alignment with the Free Movement of Goods Package

Stakeholders voiced a uniform call for a single market surveillance regime by simplifying and consolidating the two existing market surveillance systems established under the GPSD and the Free Movement of Goods Package. [The main legislative pieces of the Free Movement of Goods Package are: (i) Regulation 765/2008/EC setting out the requirements for accreditation and market surveillance relating to the marketing of products and repealing Regulation (EEC) No 339/93 ([2008] OJ L218, 82) and (ii) Decision 768/2008/EC of 9 July 2008 on a common framework for the marketing of products and repealing Council Decision 93/465/EEC ([2008] OJ L218, 82).]

Traceability of manufacturers and importers is a problem for market surveillance authorities. Harmonisation of the obligations of economic operators in the non-harmonised area with those in the harmonised area, including traceability requirements and the obligation to establish technical documentation, would make enforcement activities more effective. In addition, economic operators and other stakeholders, including consumer organisations and a number of business associations, see more benefits than disadvantages if the obligations of economic operators with regard to harmonised products were applied uniformly to all products.

The Australian Productivity Commission reviewed the new approach adopted in the EU through the introduction of a general safety standard.

Review of the Australian Consumer Product Safety System Productivity Commission Research Report (2006) 105

There is surprisingly limited evidence regarding the actual impacts [costs and benefits] of the general safety provision in Europe. Experience with the GPSD however does not suggest that has resulted in a clear improvement in safety outcomes, and there is some evidence of increased costs (although as noted above, the GPSD includes ancillary obligations which would create additional costs for businesses and governments).

The Commission then referred to a study conducted by a UK law firm, CMS Cameron McKenna, of manufacturing industry on the implications of the new European GPSD:

While most manufacturers think the GPSD stands to benefit consumers, they view it as unnecessary additional regulation based on little evidence of a lack of safety of European products. Few respondents (19 per cent) … felt it would benefit the manufacturers 'a lot'. In contrast, 42 per cent felt that it would benefit consumers 'a lot'. Enforcement statistics show that consumer products in Europe are safe, the only small problem being some third world electrical imports.

Howells considers that the most likely benefit of the introduction of the general safety obligation in Europe is allowing 'enforcement authorities to take swift remedial action in the face of newly identified dangerous products'. Further consultation since the release of the Discussion Draft, including with the DTI in the United Kingdom, did not generate any additional 'hard evidence' of the impacts of the GPSD. While the Commission did not uncover new formal assessments/evaluations indicating net benefits there was also no clear evidence that the GPSD had failed to meet its objectives. Given the costs imposed, the 'jury is still out' in terms of the net benefits associated with the basic general safety obligation

The new approach was intended to deregulate while at the same time maintaining safety standards, blending neo-liberalism and the social market. Ogus, writing in 1994, argues that it contributed to the general deregulation movement (Ogus, 1994: 178). Indeed some commentators thought that it was too liberalising. Yet business—not-withstanding the fact that some of the above comments are self-serving—views it as increasing regulation. The Cameron McKenna survey above found that one-third of respondents have no risk-assessment system in place for their products. The absence of internal risk-assessment procedures among many companies poses once again the problem of regulating corporate decision-making. For consumers a general safety standard provides a relatively transparent signal that they can expect products which they purchase to be safe avoiding any difficult decision making trade-off between price and safety.

3.2 Representation of consumer interests on standardisation bodies

The 'new approach' to standards is an experiment in transnational governance. While it is not possible to explore all aspects raised by this form of governance (see further Joerges, 2005; Schepel, 2005), consider the role of consumer participation in 'private' standard bodies such as CEN. CEN is a standards-setting body established in 1961 by national standards bodies. The new approach envisages a central role for CEN in establishing standards. Howells comments that several criticisms have been levelled against CEN. 'These involve suggestions that its procedures are too slow, that it fails to promote the European dimension to standardization, and that it does not fully integrate social partners, such as consumers, into its structure and working methods' (Howells, 2000: 316).

Why should consumer groups be represented on standard setting bodies? Rothstein describes three types of rationale:

> Normative rationales hold that risk regulation is not a value-free enterprise and that, therefore, broadening participation within risk regulation is important for moral, democratic and enlightenment reasons. Greater openness and participation, so it is argued, can: (1) help inform a wide range of social and ethical judgements throughout the regulatory process; (2) confer democratic legitimacy to regulatory processes and outcomes; and (3) strengthen general public knowledge about risk governance. ...
>
> Epistemic rationales, in contrast, hold that regulatory decision-makers are often hampered by uncertainties and information asymmetries. Sources of knowledge outside the traditional regulatory structures can, therefore, help reduce the chance of policy error. ...
>
> Finally, instrumental rationales hold that broadening participation is a useful tool for ensuring the political viability of regulatory processes, particularly in the context of declining levels of trust in political institutions . Greater openness and participation is argued by many to increase public confidence in the legitimacy and integrity of risk regulation. (Rothstein, 2004: 858–59)

Rothstein notes however that 'participative reforms, however, may promise more than they can deliver ... [a]s participation is widened to meet democratic goals, so such proc-esses can become resource-intensive, unpredictable and hard to fit with the institutional and legal constraints of policy-making'. In addition, although 'widening participation can make for more robust policy, such processes can also present problems for deci-sionmaking. Such processes can be disproportionately resource-intensive. …Moreover, outcomes of participative processes are likely to be highly dependent on who actually participates or is invited to participate' (ibid).

A central question in relation to standard-setting relates to the ability of con-sumer groups to effectively participate in the process. In 1995 ANEC (l'Association européenne pour la coordination de la représentation des consommateurs dans la nor-malisation) was established with representation from all EU countries nominated by national consumer organisations. ANEC is funded by the European Commission and EFTA, with contributions from national consumer organisations. The following extracts outline the role of ANEC and also provide arguments for improving public interest stakeholder participation in CEN and CENELEC (European Committee for Electrical Standardisation).

> ANEC provides technical expertise and advice based on a network of more than 200 consumer representatives across Europe. Our experts contribute directly to the work of more than 60 technical committees, working groups and new deliverables of the European Standards Organisations (ESOs). We have standing Europe-wide working groups on a number of priority areas: Child Safety, Design for All, Domestic Appliances, the Environment, the Information Society, Services and Traffic Safety.

> Research and testing projects underpin ANEC's activities at a technical level. Consumer representatives need scientific information to back up their arguments in the standardization committees and working groups—and this is particularly important when they have to argue against strong industry interests.

> Why is consumer representation important?

> Consumer participation in the standardisation process is important for many reasons: firstly, because consumer representation counterbalances the industry view; secondly, goods and services based on standards developed with consumer participation may be more easily accepted in the marketplace; thirdly, consumers are the ones that are most affected by the standards at the end of the process and finally, in the EU context, consumers ensure that the public interest is represented in standardisation work that complements European legislation under the New Approach to Technical Regulation.

ANEC proposals for improving public interest stakeholder participation in CEN and CENELEC (10 March 2006)

> The New Approach to Technical Harmonisation entrusted the European standardization organisations with the task of defining European safety standards. This delegation of powers from the legislator to private organisations simplified legislation and law-making on the one hand, and induced a democratic deficit on the other hand. Therefore the European Commission, politicians and consumer organisations in the aftermath of the introduction of the New Approach called for an independent consumer body in standardisation to ensure the legitimacy of the New Approach and to organise consumer representation in standardisation. They referred to existing structures in the bigger Member States, in particular France, Germany and the United Kingdom, where the standardisation process had been opened for consumer participation in the 1970s or even earlier.

> Consumer participation is indeed important to counterbalance the industry view. The opening-up of the standardisation process for public interest stakeholders, meanwhile also

for environmental groups, as a compensation for the delegation of legislative powers to private bodies has become an indispensable element of the New Approach.

However, public interests stakeholders remain a minority and a typical European standardization committee dealing with product specifications (eg toys, electrical appliances, packaging) consists of approx. 60–80% of members representing corporate interests. Therefore, ANEC believes that rules or rights for public interest stakeholders, such as consumer representatives, need to be reinforced, in particular in standardization work related to the public interest and when extending New Approach principles to new policy areas. Standardisation plays a prominent role in the 2005 re-launch of the Lisbon objectives and is considered one of the key factors to enhance Europe's competitiveness. The intention to use standardisation instead of legislation in the services area will have a direct impact on consumers and it is vital that the consumer view is an integral part of this concept. The challenge here is two-fold. First, there is no overarching legislative framework, in which standards could operate, as is the case in the product area. Second, there is a need to innovate the European standardization system so as to ensure that it is equipped to cope with these future tasks.

An EC questionnaire on consumer representation in standardisation activities at national, European and international level in 2004 concluded that 'a lack of public funding is considered to be a clear obstacle to the representation of consumers' interests in standardisation'. The Commission quoted the following submission from a Consumer Committee within a standardisation body which 'provides a picture of the current situation':

EC Questionnaire on Consumer Representation in Standardisation Activities at National, Regional, European and International Level: Evaluation Report (2004)

The burden of consumer representation in Europe is carried by two–three countries with very little support from other countries. The situation is worse proportionately at international level. ... Other countries need significant funding and support from their national standards bodies and government if true representation is to be achieved at national level. ... Funding at the international level is, in practice, so limited that consumer interests are rarely represented and, when they are, it is almost always by those from developed countries. This does not help to develop international standards which will create a level playing field for developing and developed countries and contribute to reducing barriers to international trade. Furthermore, most 'new' Member States experience a lack of resources, a lack of technical expertise and a lack of interest in standardisation issues on the part of public authorities. Where interest is shown, it is usually at national level and rarely at European level. Also, most of the 'new' Member States responding to the questionnaire indicate a lack of information from their European counterparts. Many express the need for the European Union to find a way to reduce these national differences in order to develop an integrated approach to standardisation issues, and to promote harmonised European standards.

Christopher Hodges, in contrast, argues that there is no empirical evidence that the 'undoubtedly strong involvement of industry, and weaker involvement of consumer representatives, in the production of standards has led to a safety deficit' (Hodges, 2005: 220).

In 2005 Consumers International documented the role of consumer participation in international standard-setting bodies. The following extract describes its view on the International Standards Organisation. ISO standards may be incorporated in EU standards and many large organisations adopt ISO 9000 standards on quality control as a method of addressing risks and achieving regulatory compliance with the general product safety regulations. For example, according to Cavaliere, 'a product is traceable and can easily be recalled ... when firms are organized along the lines of the ISO 9004 standard' (Cavaliere, 2004: 311).

Consumers International, *Decision Making in the Global Market: Trade, Standards and the Consumer* (2005) 5, 45–47, 48

International Standards

Food and products standards are set at national and international levels to protect consumers, but there is evidence that this positive aim is being compromised by the 'capture' of standards by trade interests.

World Trade Organization (WTO) agreements are intended to remove barriers to trade between countries. It has raised the status of international standards from being voluntary, to the level of obligations on national governments. WTO Members are required to use them as a basis for their own technical regulations and product standards. Failure to do so leaves governments vulnerable to accusations of maintaining trade barriers, and to trade disputes.

The effect is that standards are being set with the objective of increasing trade, or avoiding trade disputes, instead of protecting the interests of consumers. National governments are also obliged to review their regulations and standards to ensure that they comply with new international standards.

The problem of standards 'capture' is further compounded by the decision making processes of the WTO, and international standard-setting bodies such as Codex, where the consumer voice has little opportunity to make itself heard.

Increasingly, business interests dominate international standard setting. This has implications for consumer protection and the influence consumer advocates have on standard setting at national and international level . . .

The ISO and IEC are two of the best-known international standards organisations. IEC's objective is to promote understanding and international cooperation on all matters of standardisation and related matters such as the verification of conformity to standards in the fields of electricity, electronics and related technologies. ISO's aim is to promote the development of standardisation to facilitate international exchange of goods and services and cooperation in the spheres of intellectual, scientific, technological and economic activity.

The relative importance of the work of both has increased in recent years due to reliance on standards as a means of avoiding technical barriers to trade and achieving the goals of regulatory reform. The World Trade Organization's Technical Barriers to Trade (TBT) Agreement directs governments to use international standards as 'a basis for' domestic regulations except when such standards would not fulfil legitimate objectives. The TBT committee has adopted a set of criteria to which international standards should conform. These include transparency, openness, impartiality and consensus, effectiveness and relevance, coherence, and a development dimension.

The use of international standards has also been promoted through the adoption of extensive standards policies at national and regional levels. The European Union (EU) has placed considerable emphasis on the use of standards in the establishment of the internal market in Europe. The adoption of the so-called 'New Approach' to technical harmonization was one of the major implementing actions of the single market programme. As a result, European standards now account for some 90% of the output of national standards development organisations (SDOs) in Europe with only 10% being exclusively national standards. This is the reverse of the same proportions at the beginning of the 1980s. So as not to create new barriers to trade the European standards bodies' concluded co-operation agreements with their international counterparts. As a result approximately 40% of the 10,000 standards under the control of the European Committee for Standardisation/Comité Européen de Normalisation (CEN) are based on international standards and approximately 90% of those standards under the control of the European Committee for Electro-Technical Standardisation/Comité Européen de Normalisation Electrotechnique (CENELEC).

The membership of ISO consists of national standards bodies most broadly representative of standardisation in their respective countries. National bodies in countries without a Member body can be registered as either a correspondent or subscriber Member with no voting rights. Only one body in each country may be admitted to membership.

ISO and IEC issued a joint statement on consumer participation in standardisation work in 1979. This statement recognised the basic principle that all interests should be taken into account in the international standardisation process including that of consumers. Specific recommendations were made to ISO and IEC national Members.

The ISO has also adopted a Code of Ethics which commits Members to take appropriate measures to facilitate the participation of consumers and other affected parties from civil society, SMEs and public authorities. The Code also commits ISO parties to contribute to help Members from developing countries improve their capacity and their participation in international standardisation.

The issues

ISO has formed its own Committee on Consumer Policy (COPOLCO). The Membership of COPOLCO is, however, still nominally the national Members of ISO. The presence of consumer representatives on national delegations to the annual COPOLCO meeting is dependant on the national Members who determine the composition of the delegation.

National delegations are appointed by the national standards bodies and under ISO rules consumer representatives do not have a right to be included on the delegation. Other organisations attend the COPOLCO meetings as observers. These include Consumers International and ANEC, the European consumer voice in standardisation.

Scrutiny of the attendance lists at past ISO meetings reveals that not all delegations include consumer representatives. Some are simply made up of officials from the national standards bodies or only include government officials.

The influence of COPOLCO has increased through the 1990s and it often takes the lead in proposing new avenues of work that are eventually taken up within ISO. Improvements in the workings of COPOLCO, and the attitude to consumer issues in ISO, have occurred gradually over time and some issues that have been raised have not been resolved. The work of the Technical Management Board (TMB), policy setting and governance bodies of ISO are not open to the public.

Measures have been introduced recently to provide financial support for participation by representatives from developing and least developed countries (LDCs) in the work of ISO. This aid has been extended to consumer representatives.

...

Management body documents from ISO and IEC are not publicly available. Documents from specific technical bodies are available to organisations that have a liaison with them. They should also be available to NGOs who participate in national mirror committees (committees that are established within national SDOs to follow work at international level, and who decide on the positions national delegations will take to international meetings and how national votes will be cast during the international standards development process).

The fundamental issue is whether there should be direct stakeholder participation at international level. It should be relatively easy to make a case in the specific instance of disadvantaged groups such as consumer groups, development NGOs, trade unions or environmental groups. They are invariably a minority interest at the national level so it is too easy for their voice to be lost in the drive for national consensus and a national line to present at international standards meetings. Direct participation gives voice to their concerns. This principle has been accepted in many other arenas such as the Codex Alimentarius Commission and in the United Nations Economic Commission for Europe (UNECE) where global technical regulations for vehicle safety are being developed.

---

4. Post-marketing surveillance and the enforcement of product safety standards

The 2005 safety regulations make significant changes in post-marketing surveillance obligations and enforcement. The primary innovations are:

(1) An obligation on producers and distributors to notify enforcement authorities where a product that he has placed on the market poses risks that are incompatible with the general safety requirement, including the action taken to prevent the risk (which might include a recall) and identification of other countries in the EU where the product has been marketed. This notification will normally be made to trading standards officers (regulation 9). Regulation 9(4) stipulates:

> [A] person who is a producer or a distributor shall co-operate with an enforcement authority (at the enforcement authority's request) in action taken to avoid the risks posed by a product which he supplies or has supplied. Every enforcement authority shall maintain procedures for such co-operation, including procedures for dialogue with the producers and distributors concerned on issues related to product safety.

Fairgrieve and Howells argue that 'The potential breadth of this reporting obligation (in regulation 9) could place an intolerable burden on businesses and regulators' (Fairgrieve and Howells, 2006: 64). The EC has developed guidelines on when notification is necessary and how it should be made, and the following guidance is provided by the DTI about this obligation in their guidance on the regulations:

> 6.4 The authorities will advise on actions aimed at removal of the risk and work with the producer or distributor on completing the notification. The authorities will then forward this to the appropriate national contact point for further action, and to the DTI where there is a serious risk requiring notification under the rapid exchange of information scheme (RAPEX) (DTI. 2006: 14).

This suggests significant cooperation between enforcement authorities and business and Cartwright suggests that regulation 9(4) reflects the development of 'an ever closer relationship between producers, distributors, and enforcement authorities' (Cartwright, 2006: 317).

(2) The introduction of legal powers for enforcement authorities to recall a product if they have reasonable grounds for believing that a product is dangerous (regulation 15) (see Fairgrieve and Howells, 2006: 59). Previously, recalls were made on a voluntary basis. A recall notice may only be issued where other action under the regulations would not prevent the risk and the action being undertaken by the producer or distributor is insufficient (regulation 15(4)(a)(b)). There is also the possibility of the trader requiring the authority to seek independent advice for an arbitrator before instituting the recall. An immediate recall may be instituted in the case of a product posing a serious risk requiring urgent action. The DTI in its advice on the regulations emphasises that a legal recall should be used as a last resort (DTI, 2006: 21). Fairgrieve and Howells comment that:

> During the consultation process, there was a concerted effort to down-play the impact of the new remedy. The DTI noted that producers had a 'good track record of carrying out voluntary recalls of dangerous products in a timely and appropriate way' and that, 'where a producer can show that it acted responsibly, to the extent that it is reasonable to expect of it and, in respect of a voluntary product recall, in accordance with industry practice, it is improbable that any enforcement authority could claim that the action has been insufficient or unsatisfactory.' Indeed the DTI, CBI and British Retail Consortium have developed a Good Practice Guide to Consumer Product Recall. Consequently, compulsory recalls are unlikely to be a frequent occurrence, on the (reasonable) assumption that industry will continue to accept voluntary recalls where appropriate. (Fairgrieve and Howells, 2006: 66)

The regulations confer enforcement powers on enforcement authorities to serve a variety of safety notices. These include: suspension notices (regulation 11); requirements to mark (regulation 12); requirements to warn (regulation 13); withdrawal notices (regulation 14); and recall notices (regulation 15). There are some innovations here. First, the enforcement powers may all be exercised by local as well as central government (regulation 10). Previously, issues such as prohibition notices could only be exercised by central government. Cartwright suggests that this change will 'likely lead to an increase in enforcement activity' (Cartwright, 2006: 526). Second, there are the recall powers outlined above.

Much enforcement of product safety was traditionally informal, involving moral suasion and negotiation with trade associations and retailers (Weatherill, 1987: 88; Cartwright, 2006: 533) following the UK compliance model of enforcement. Large retailers may agree to withdraw products which involve unacceptable risks but are not covered by regulations. The following comment is from Prosafe, a European forum for product safety enforcers:

> The emphasis is placed on preventative methods to ensure safety requirements are being observed. Local authority departments and businesses operating within their area, particularly those for whom they have established a 'Home Authority' responsibility, usually work closely together to ensure compliance with the law. Inspection visits are made and informative guidance notes issued to assist manufacturers and suppliers of goods. (www.prosafe.org/uk/ep.htm)

Regulation 10(5) specifically outlines the approach which an enforcement agency should adopt to enforcement.

> 10. … (5) An enforcement authority shall in enforcing these Regulations act in a manner proportionate to the seriousness of the risk and shall take due account of the precautionary principle. In this context, it shall encourage and promote voluntary action by producers and distributors. Notwithstanding the foregoing, an enforcement authority may take any action under these Regulations urgently and without first encouraging and promoting voluntary action if a product poses a serious risk.

And regulation 16 indicates that:

> 16.—(1) Whenever feasible, prior to serving a safety notice the authority shall give an opportunity to the person on whom the notice is to be served to submit his views to the authority. Where, due to the urgency of the situation, this is not feasible the person shall be given an opportunity to submit his views to the authority after service of the notice.

Cartwright suggests that this section indicates that there is 'greater emphasis on enforcement authorities giving notice of their intention to act than was the case under previous legislation' (Cartwright, 2006: 531).

The DTI outlines the approach to enforcement in its guidance on the product safety regulation.

DTI Guidance to the General Product Safety Regulations (2005)

> Measures available to enforcement authorities
>
> 7.10 Dialogue and the encouragement of voluntary action is specifically encouraged as an alternative to formal enforcement. …
>
> 7.11 Generally, it is assumed that where the producer or distributor is already taking the action necessary to remove the risk to consumers it will not be necessary for the enforcement authorities to serve a safety notice.
>
> 7.12 Other than in the case of urgency resulting from the identification of a serious risk the parties concerned must, whenever feasible, be given an opportunity to submit their views before the adoption of a measure. In other cases they must be given the opportunity to comment following implementation of the measure.
>
> 7.13 The measure chosen must be proportionate to the seriousness of the risk: Precautionary Principle
>
> 7.16 The Precautionary Principle applies where there are threats of substantial, serious or irreversible harm to consumers but there is clear scientific uncertainty over the extent of the threats posed.
>
> 7.17 Judgements handed down by the Court of Justice (C-434/02 and C-210/03) presuppose that for the Principle to apply the risk should be plausible and realistic based on the identification of potentially negative effects on health and safety and a comprehensive assessment of the risks based on the most reliable scientific data available (including international research). Where it proves to be impossible to determine with certainty the existence or extent of the alleged risk because of the insufficiency, inconclusiveness or imprecision of the results of the scientific study into the risk, but the likelihood of real harm to public health and safety persists should the risk materialise, the Precautionary Principle justifies the adoption of measures under the Regulations.

7.18 A measure adopted under the Precautionary Principle must recognise that it is not appropriate to seek to reduce the risk to zero. It should also be proportionate to the expected risk and appropriate for attaining a high level of public health in accordance with the definition of a safe product in the Regulations. The enforcement authority taking the measure must keep it under regular review in the light of new scientific evidence.

Cartwright comments on the DTI's interpretation of the principle.

> The DTI offers a fairly narrow interpretation of the principle, stating that it applies 'where there are threats of substantial, serious or irreversible harm to consumers, but there is clear scientific uncertainty over the extent of the threats posed'. ... If a narrow interpretation is followed, the principle will have relatively little impact upon enforcement authorities' decisions.

> A broader interpretation of the precautionary principle might have required enforcement authorities to take action whenever there is a reasonable chance that a product be judged unsafe. The precautionary principle would then amount to 'erring on the side of caution'. However, such an interpretation might be difficult to square with the requirement that action be proportionate. (Cartwright, 2006: 535)

A significant factor in enforcement decisions is regulation 16(4) which requires an enforcement authority to pay compensation to a person having an interest in the product if a suspension notice is served and there has been no contravention of any requirements of these regulations. Similar liability may arise in relation to withdrawal and recall notices. This liability was introduced by the Conservative government in 1987. Cartwright comments:

> The powers to award compensation have been criticized by Howells, who argues that the risk of authorities having to pay compensation is 'a real restraint on the freedom of officers to act as they see best'. There is a danger that authorities could be dissuaded from taking formal action except in the most serious and clear-cut circumstances. (Cartwright, 2006: 538)

Enforcement is least costly in markets where there are a small number of manufacturers, or an established trade association, and a small, stable selection of products. Manufacturers in these markets may be sensitive to the negative publicity of being associated with unsafe products. Enforcement problems have been most significant in relation to imported products and the products of small producers. Importers and small producers are likely to face higher costs of compliance and to have a lower probability of being detected than large national producers. Moreover, the adverse publicity from a product seizure is likely to be of less concern to an importer or small producer than to a large, brand-name manufacturer or retailer. For example, toys have posed a continuing problem for enforcement agencies, since there are many small companies involved in the market, foreign imports constitute a significant part of the market and there is a large annual turnover of new toys entering the market.

The Consumer Protection Act 1987 attempts to address these problems by restricting the statutory defences available to first suppliers (regulation 10(4)) and by giving wider suspension and forfeiture powers to trading standards officers (see regulations 14 and 15). As noted in Chapter 7, the courts have interpreted the due-diligence defence strictly in safety offences.

There has been little study of the impact in the United Kingdom of consumer safety standards on accident levels or on consumers' and producers' behaviour. US empirical studies differ in their assessment of the effectiveness of consumer safety standards (see eg Grabowski and Vernon, 1978; Linneman, 1980; Viscusi, 1984: 85–6; Zick et al, 1986: 36; Kelman, 1988).

There is some evidence that the distribution of the burdens and benefits of safety standards may vary between different groups of consumers and producers. Relatively careless consumers appear to benefit considerably more than others from, for example, flammability standards on mattresses and furniture (Department of Trade, 1980; Linneman, 1980). In fact, many product regulations probably eliminate products which consumers would not have purchased if they had had full information (eg balloons made of potentially carcinogenic substances).

Economists have also indicated the subtle impact of product safety regulations on consumer behaviour. Peltzman argued that safety measures may actually increase accidents, by reducing consumer incentives to take care. He substantiates this argument by reference to data on the pattern of accidents following the introduction of seat-belt legislation (Peltzman, 1975: 526; see also Adams, 1985). Later studies have, however, questioned the validity of this hypothesis (see Crandall and Lave, 1986: Kelman, 1988: Ogus, 1994: 201). A review of the evidence on behavioural adaptation by individuals to safety measures concluded that there probably is some adaptation but that it was difficult to identify and measure distinct from other factors (Hedlund, 2000: 82).

---

5. Private liability law: product liability

There is a large literature on the topic of product liability (see eg Stapleton, 1994; Miller and Goldberg, 2004; for a useful recent comparison of the US and Europe, see Howells and Owen, 2010) and there has been much general interest in the implementation of the EC Product Liability Directive. Geraint Howells suggests that in Europe the 'academic interest is out of proportion with the extent to which product liability figures into actual practice' (Howells, 2000: 305). Product liability is a topic broader than consumer protection and we briefly consider the role of private liability law in the provision of compensation and deterrence in the context of the EC Product Liability Directive (85/374/EEC), implemented in the UK by the Consumer Protection Act 1987

The Pearson Commission in 1978 found that the number of injuries caused by products was relatively small and the risk of death lower than for other categories of injury. They also drew a distinction between two distinct types of defect.

Royal Commission on Civil Liability and Compensation for Personal Injury (Pearson Commission) (1978), Cmnd 7054, paragraph 1204

The importance of products liability

1204 Potentially dangerous defects in manufactured goods are commonly divided into two categories. First, there is the 'manufacturing defect'—the defective manufacture of a single item in an otherwise normal production run. This may be due to a material weakness, for example, a flaw in the steel used to make a particular bicycle. An EEC Commission working document pointed out that it may be possible to discover such weaknesses only at disproportionately high cost, such as by an X-ray examination of all the steel used to make all the bicycles. Secondly, there is the 'design defect'—a basic flaw common to a whole product type. For an illustration, one need look no further than the thalidomide disaster. Products liability claims may be comparatively few in number, but the range of risk extends from minor harm to major catastrophe.

Private liability law has the twin goals of compensation and deterrence. The former places it within the general context of accident compensation, the latter within the general social objective of achieving an optimal level of safety. The basic question is whether the individualistic system of private law can contribute significantly to the achievement of these social goals in a society of mass consumption—with the potential of mass catastrophe. Many lawyers, consumer advocates and official reform bodies seem to believe so.

There are several possible private-law theories of liability in relation to defective products that cause physical injury. It may be possible to frame an action in contract or under the implied conditions of the Sale of Goods Act 1979. Liability here is strict in the sense that it is not a defence to an action that the seller took all possible care in the manufacture or supply of the product. Although courts do import into sales law ideas of reasonableness through techniques such as 'reasonable fitness' and non-liability to the allergic consumer, the strict liability of sales law provided the historical precedent for the concept of strict liability for defective products (see Stapleton, 2002: 1228).

A second theory is through tort law. In the UK this may be pursued at common law and under Part 1 of the Consumer Protection Act 1987 which introduces a system of strict liability. Wiegand argues that the development of strict liability for defective products in US law was influential on European developments in consumer protection (Wiegand, 1991: 229). US ideas certainly influenced English judges' interpretation of the Sale of Goods Act in the 1960s and early 1970s. In a series of cases they implicitly adopted ideas of channelling liability to a manufacturer for physical injuries (albeit to animals not humans) caused by their products (see *Ashington Piggeries* and *Hardwicke Game Farm*).

5.1 Liability under the Consumer Protection Act 1987

Part 1 of the Consumer Protection Act 1987 implements in the UK the EU Product Liability Directive (85/374/EEC and 1999/34/EC). The 1999 Directive extends the directive to food sold in its direct state. The Directives were implemented in England and Wales by the Consumer Protection Act 1987 and the Product Liability (Modification) Order 2000. The development of EU product liability regulation was driven by two factors: the first was the general public concern and outrage driven by the disaster caused by the Thalidomide tragedy where 8,000–10,000 children were born seriously deformed after their mothers had taken the sedative Thalidomide during pregnancy to counter morning sickness. The Thalidomide tragedy resulted in the creation of the Pearson Commission as well as exposing the limits on the pre-marketing controls on the supply of pharmaceuticals. A second driver was the interest of the European Commission during the 1970s to promote a market for citizens and not merely business interests.

Notwithstanding these consumerist pressures, Stapleton argues that:

> there remained intense concern within the European Parliament and the Council that substantial exculpatory provisions be included in any future Directive. As a result the Directive is one of the high watermarks of Euro-fudge and textual vagueness. It used a cryptic 'definition' of defect in Article 6: 'A product is defective when it does not provide the safety which a person is entitled to expect, taking all circumstances into account ...' It also allows a Member State discretion on a number of critical matters including the exculpatory Article 7 (e), which became known as the 'development risk defence' ... the Directive tries to square a circle: it uses the rhetoric of 'strict liability', and yet, in Articles 6(2) and 7(e) it seems to provide solid protections for reasonable businesses, a compromise demanded by the U.K. Government of Margaret Thatcher. (Stapleton, 2002: 1231).

The Consumer Protection Act 1987 represents modest change from a negligence regime for injuries caused by the 'one-off' manufacturing defect where liability, is, in practice, almost the equivalent of strict liability (see eg *Hill v James Crowe (Cases) Ltd* (1978)). An extensive discussion of central issues under the Consumer Protection Act occurred in the case of *A and others v National Blood Authority and others*.

A and others v National Blood Authority and others [2001] EWHC QB 446 [2001] 3 All ER 289

Burton J

THE CLAIMANTS

1. This trial has concerned the claims of 114 claimants for recovery of damages arising out of their infection with Hepatitis C from blood and blood products through blood transfusions from 1 March 1988. The 114 claimants received blood transfusions or blood products usually in the course of undergoing surgery, whether consequent upon having suffered an accident or otherwise, or immediately after childbirth or in the course of treatment for a blood disorder. The earliest date of infection in respect of which claimants can make such claims is 1 March 1988, being the date when the CPA was brought into effect.

THE DEFENDANTS

3. The National Health Service bodies responsible for the production and supply of blood and blood products prior to 1 April 1993 in England (and also covering northern Wales) were 14 regional blood transfusion centres (RTCs), controlled and administered by regional health authorities. From that date, by the National Blood Authority (Establishment and Constitution) Order 1993, SI 1993/583, the National Blood Authority (NBA) was established, with responsibility for the RTCs and both central blood laboratories (the Central Blood Laboratory Authority (CBLA), which itself had responsibility for the Blood Products (later Bio Products) Laboratory (BPL), and the Blood Groups Research Laboratory (BGRL)). Subsequently the National Blood Authority (Establishment and Constitution) Amendment Order 1994, SI 1994/589 provided that all rights enforceable by or against a regional health authority in respect of the exercise of functions which became exercisable by the NBA were to be exercisable against the NBA.

THE CLAIMS

12. The claims in this trial have been that, pursuant to the CPA, those who received blood

or blood products infected by Hepatitis C subsequent to 1 March 1988, when the Act came into effect, are entitled to recover damages: that is notwithstanding that: (i) the Hepatitis C virus itself had not been discovered or identified at the date when the claims commence on 1 March 1988; (ii) no screening test to discover the presence of such virus in a donor's blood was even known of, certainly not available, until Ortho's assay, first publicised in spring/summer 1989; and (iii) it is not sought to be alleged (at least not in this trial) that the United Kingdom blood authorities for whom the defendants are responsible were negligent in not introducing the screening tests until they did on 1 September 1991 (or now, as a result of the agreed concession, 1 April 1991) nor that they were negligent in not having introduced surrogate tests. The case which is put is that they are liable irrespective of the absence of any fault, under the directive and the CPA.

THE DIRECTIVE

13. The directive, resolved by the Council on 25 July 1985, had taken a long time in coming. In the first instance this was because discussion of it, which had begun in 1969/1970 in the light of the Thalidomide scandal, was held up largely due to the impending arrival of a number of new members of the Community, including the United Kingdom; but then because of the very lengthy processes of discussion and negotiation, and of intergovernmental and parliamentary discussion, which then took place. A number of matters appear to be common ground between the parties to these proceedings: (i) that its purpose was to increase consumer protection; (ii) that it introduced an obligation on producers which was irrespective of fault, by way of objective or strict liability, but not absolute liability; (iii) that its aim was to render compensation of the injured consumer easier, by removing the concept of negligence as an element of liability and thus of the proof of liability; and (iv) that it left an escape clause (in those Community jurisdictions, like the United Kingdom, where such provision was desired) for products otherwise found pursuant to the directive to be defective, if the producer could bring himself within what was, in the course of the 'travaux preparatoires', described as a 'development risks' defence.

16. The relevant Articles are as follows:

4. *The injured person shall be required to prove the damage, the defect and the causal relationship between defect and damage:*

6.1. *A product is defective when it does not provide the safety which a person is entitled to expect, taking all circumstances into account, including:*

(a) *the presentation of the product;*

(b) *the use to which it could reasonably be expected that the product would be put;*

(c) *the time when the product was put into circulation.*

6.2. *A product shall not be considered defective for the sole reason that a better product is subsequently put into circulation.*

7. *The producer shall not be liable as a result of this Directive if he proves:*

(a) *that he did not put the product into circulation; or*

(b) *that, having regard to the circumstances, it is probable that the defect which caused the damage did not exist at the time when the product was put into circulation by him or that this defect came into being afterwards; or ...*

(d) t*hat the defect is due to compliance of the product with mandatory regulations issued by the public authorities; or*

(e) *that the state of scientific and technical knowledge at the time when he put the product into circulation was not such as to enable the existence of the defect to be discovered.*

THE CPA

18. The most authoritative consideration of the CPA has of course been in the case of *European Commission v UK*, to which I have referred and that was consideration in principle, not by reference to the facts of any case, and directed specifically to art 7(e) (and s 4(1)(e)). As I have set out the Commission contended that the section did not properly or lawfully reflect the article as it should.

19. Whatever the content of a unilateral declaration may be, a Community government is obliged in law to enact the directive, and the Commission contended before the Court of Justice that the United Kingdom Government had not done so. The Court of Justice concluded that, notwithstanding that there was a difference of wording, it could not be satisfied that it was intended by the United Kingdom to interpret its statute differently from the directive, nor was the United Kingdom entitled to do so.

21. Although the United Kingdom Government has not amended s 4(1)(e) of the CPA so as to bring it in line with the wording of the directive, there is thus binding authority of the Court of Justice that it must be so construed. Hence, although I shall in certain respects require to consider sections of the CPA, when dealing with the issues raised before me of causation and/ or quantum of loss, to which I shall refer, the major discussions in this case, and all the areas of most live dispute, have concentrated entirely upon the wording of arts 6 and 7(e) of the directive, and not upon the equivalent sections of the CPA, to which I shall make little or no further reference.

ARTICLE 6

The common ground

31. I turn then to consideration of art 6. There is a foundation of common ground.

i. Article 6 defines '*defective*', and hence a defect. A harmful characteristic in a product, which has led to injury or damage, may or may not be a defect as so defined, and thus within the meaning of the directive. It is common ground that the liability is 'defect-based' and not 'fault-based', ie that a producer's liability is irrespective of fault (Recitals 2, 6).

ii. The purpose of the directive is to achieve a higher and consistent level of consumer protection throughout the Community and render recovery of compensation easier, and uncomplicated by the need for proof of negligence. ...

iii. The onus of proof is upon the claimants to prove the product to be defective.

iv. The question to be resolved is the safety or the degree or level of safety or safeness which persons generally are entitled to expect. The test is not that of an absolute level of safety, nor an absolute liability for any injury caused by the harmful characteristic.

v. In the assessment of that question the expectation is that of persons generally, or the public at large.

vi. The safety is not what is actually expected by the public at large, but what they are entitled to expect. The common ground is that the question is what the legitimate expectation is of persons generally, ie what is legitimately to be expected, arrived at objectively. 'Legitimate expectation', rather than 'entitled expectation', appeared to all of us to be a more happy formulation (and is analogous to the formulation in other languages in which the directive is published); the use of that expression is not intended to import any administrative law concepts.

vii. The court decides what the public is entitled to expect: Dr Harald Bartl in *Produkthaftung nach neuem EG-Recht* (1989) described the judge (as translated from the German) as '*an informed representative of the public at large*' ...

viii. There are some products, which have harmful characteristics in whole or in part, about which no complaint can be made. The examples that were used of products which have obviously dangerous characteristics by virtue of their very nature or intended use, were, on the one hand knives, guns and poisons and on the other hand alcohol, tobacco, perhaps foie gras.

The differences between the parties

32. Having set out what is common ground, I now summarise briefly the difference between the two parties, some of which is already apparent from my setting in context of the factual common ground.

i. As to art 6, the claimants assert that, with the need for proof of negligence eliminated, consideration of the conduct of the producer, or of a reasonable or legitimately expectable producer, is inadmissible or irrelevant. Therefore questions of avoidability cannot and do not arise: what the defendants could or should have done differently; whether there were any steps or precautions reasonably available; and whether it was impossible to take any steps by way of prevention or avoidance, or impracticable or economically unreasonable. Such are not '*circumstances*' falling to be considered within art 6. In so far as the risk was known to blood producers and the medical profession, it was not known to the public at large (save for those few patients who might ask their doctor, or read the occasional article about blood in a newspaper) and no risk that any percentage of transfused blood would be infected was accepted by them.

ii. The defendants assert that the risk was known to those who mattered, namely the medical profession, through whom blood was supplied. Avoiding the risk was impossible and unattainable, and it is not and cannot be legitimate to expect the unattainable. Avoidability or unavoidability is a circumstance to be taken into account within art 6. The public did not and/or was not entitled to expect 100% clean blood. The most they could legitimately expect was that all legitimately expectable (reasonably available) precautions—or in this case tests—had been taken or carried out. The claimants must therefore prove that they were legitimately entitled to expect more, and/or must disprove the unavoidability of the harmful characteristic. There would need to be an investigation as to whether it was impossible to avoid the risk and/or whether the producers had taken all legitimately expectable steps. In so far as there was thus an investigation analogous to, or involving similar facts to, an investigation into negligence, it was not an investigation of negligence by the individual producer and was necessary and, because it was not an investigation of fault, permissible. If, notwithstanding the known and unavoidable risk, the blood was nevertheless defective within art 6, then it is all the more necessary to construe art 7(e) so as to avail those who could not, in the then state of scientific and technical knowledge, identify the defect in a particular product so as to prevent its supply.

iii. The claimants respond that art 7(e) does not apply to risks which are known before the supply of the product, whether or not the defect can be identified in the particular product; and there are a number of other issues between the parties in respect of art 7(e) to which I shall return later.

All circumstances

33. Article 6 must then be considered against the background of this summary of the issues. In the establishment of the level of safety, art 6 provides that the court (on behalf of the public at large) takes into account all circumstances, including the following.

i. *Presentation*, ie the way in which the product is presented, eg warnings and price. As set out above, the expanded wording of s 3(2)(a) of the CPA is helpful.

ii. The use to which the product could reasonably be expected to be put, eg:

a. if the product is not a familiar or usual one, such as a scrid, it will be necessary to find out what its expected or foreseeable use is;

b. if it is expected and required to be dangerous in respect of its expected use, eg a gun, then complaint cannot be made of that dangerousness; but complaint could still be made of a different dangerousness, such as if it exploded on the trigger being pulled; and

c. if it is not expected to be dangerous in respect of its expected use, but the use to which it is put is unexpected, then it may not be defective.

iii. The *time* when the product is circulated, for example when the product is out of date or stale.

35. The dispute therefore is as to what further, if anything, falls to be considered within '*all circumstances*'. There is no dispute between the parties, as set out in para 31(i) and (ii) above, that consideration of the fault of the producer is excluded; but does consideration of 'all circumstances' include consideration of the conduct to be expected from the producer, the level of safety to be expected from a producer of that product? ... The defendants themselves accept that the risk/utility model adopted in the United States cannot be applied in its entirety, because of the express exclusion, so far as the directive is concerned, of any question of liability for negligence. Nevertheless the defendants assert that there is a 'basket' of considerations: the likelihood of injury resulting and the seriousness of it if it results, the cost and the quality of the product, the efficacy of the product (with and without safety precautions), none of which would necessarily be contentious from the claimants' point of view. What would, on any basis, be contentious would be the further contents of the defendants' basket, namely the avoidability or unavoidability of the danger, and the availability or unavailability of alternatives.

The contentions proceed as follows:

The defendants assert that, in looking at the product, it is essential to consider, in deciding what level of safety could reasonably have been expected, what more if anything could have been done: what precautions or tests could be used/should have been used/were available to be used/can legitimately be expected to have been used. If, the defendants contend, the producer did not use obviously available safety processes or precautions, then that itself must be a factor to be taken into account against him, just as it would be in his favour if all available safety precautions were adopted. ... The claimants, however, assert that, given that it is common ground that the article imposes liability irrespective of fault, the exercise of considering what could or should have been done by the producer is an impermissible and irrelevant exercise, which lets questions of fault back in by the back door. ... The claimants contend that any consideration of the method or processes of production, including the safety precautions taken or not taken, is irrelevant. ... They assert that it is necessary only to look at the product itself (including comparison with similar or identical products on the market), which would involve its expected or intended use, without considering what more could have been done (and how easy or difficult or cheap or expensive it would have been to have done it). ...

ARTICLE 7(e)

Once again there is a great deal of common ground, not least because in relation to this article there is in certain respects binding authority and guidance from the Court of Justice (*European Commission v UK*).

49. Such common ground is as follows. (i) The *state of scientific and technical knowledge* referred to is the most advanced available (to anyone, not simply to the producer in question), but it must be 'accessible'. In response to a more extreme position being taken by the Commission, the Advocate General answered as follows, in his opinion in *European Commission v UK* at paras 22–24, which, although not expressly approved in the judgment of the Court of Justice, is taken to be the state of the law:

> '22. ... *Where in the whole gamut of scientific opinion at a particular time there is also one isolated opinion (which, as the history of science shows, might become with the passage of time opinio communis) as to the potentially defective and/or hazardous nature of the product, the manufacturer is no longer faced with an unforeseeable risk, since, as such, it is outside the scope of the rules imposed by the directive.* ...
>
> *More generally, the "state of knowledge" must be construed so as to include all data in the information circuit of the scientific community as a whole, bearing in mind, however, on the basis of a reasonableness test the actual opportunities for the information to circulate.*'

The article is not concerned with the conduct or knowledge of individual producers. As the court made clear (at 495 (para 29)):

> '... *the producer of a defective product must prove that the objective state of scientific and technical knowledge, including the most advanced level of such knowledge, at the time when the product in question was put into circulation was not such as to enable the existence of the defect to be discovered.*'

The issues between the parties

50. Must the producer prove that the defect had not been and could not be discovered in the product in question, as the defendants contend, or must the producer prove that the defect had not been and could not be discovered generally, ie in the population of products? If it be the latter, it is common ground here that the existence of the defect in blood generally, ie of the infection of blood in some cases by Hepatitis virus notwithstanding screening, was known, and indeed known to the defendants. The question is thus whether, in order to take advantage of the escape clause, the producer must show that no objectively assessable scientific or technical information existed anywhere in the world which had identified, and thus put producers potentially on notice of, the problem; or whether it is enough for the producer to show that, although the existence of the defect in such product was or should have been known, there was no objectively accessible information available anywhere in the world which would have enabled a producer to discover the existence of that known defect in the particular product in question. The crux of the dispute therefore is as follows.

i. The claimants say that once the defect in blood is known about, as it was, it is a known risk. A known but unavoidable risk does not qualify for art 7(e). It may qualify for art 6, not because it was unavoidable (see their contentions set out in [35] above) but if it could be shown that, because the risk is known, it was accepted, and lowered public expectations—like poison and alcohol. But otherwise once it is known, then the product cannot be supplied, or is supplied at the producer's risk and has no protection from art 7(e). Hence an art 7(e) defence is, as was intended, a development risks defence; for if it is not known that a particular product, perhaps a pioneering such product (such as a scrid), has or can have a harmful characteristic, whether by virtue of its inherent nature, its raw materials, its design or its method of manufacture, and then the defect materialises, or is published about, for the first time, it has prior to that time been a true development risk, and protection is available under art 7(e). However, once the risk is known, then if the product is supplied, and if the defect recurs, by then it is a known risk, and, even if undiscoverable in a particular example of the product, there is no escape. There is only one stage of consideration, and if there be 'non-Manchurianly accessible' knowledge about the product's susceptibility to a defect, be it a manufacturing or design defect, there is no availability of art 7(e). As it is common ground in this case that there was such knowledge, the defendants cannot avail themselves of art 7(e).

ii. The defendants say that if a risk is unavoidable, it falls within art 6 (see their contentions in paragraph 35 above) but, if not, then it can still qualify for protection under art 7(e), if non-Manchurianly accessible information cannot enable a producer to discover the defect in the particular product. There may be no 'stage one'—ie knowledge of the risk-but, even if there is, there is a 'stage two'-namely consideration as to whether any accessible knowledge could have availed the producer to take any steps which he did not take

51. Nothing much can be gained by simply looking at the words of art 7(e). The following points should be recorded.

i. The claimants rely heavily upon purposive construction, that is that the directive and this article must be construed in order to further the purpose of the directive, namely consumer protection and ease of recovery of compensation.

ii The defendants counter that this is an express escape clause, specifically so as to allow a level of protection for producers who are non-negligent. There is provision for a member state to exclude art 7(e) from its legislation if (Recital 16) it was *'felt . . . to restrict unduly the protection of the consumer'*, so this is what the clause was aimed at: and they refer also to Recital 7, whereby a *'fair apportionment of risk between the injured person and the producer implies that the producer should be able to free himself from liability if he furnishes proof as to the existence of certain exonerating circumstances'.*

iii. The claimants contend that it is clearly apparent from *European Commission v UK* (to which I shall refer further below) that art 7(e) is intended to be construed restrictively: and in any event there is as much a concept of Community law as of the common law that a proviso, exception or escape clause should be construed restrictively.

iv. The defendants rely on the fact that in art 7(b), another of the exonerating circumstances, namely whereby a producer can show that the defect did not exist when the product left his factory etc, the defect being there referred to must be a defect in the product in question, rather than in the population of products. They assert that, at least by reference to English rules of construction, such a usage in a neighbouring sub-clause throws light on the meaning of art 7(e).

v. The knowledge in art 7(e) must be such as to 'enable' the existence of the defect to be discovered. The claimants submit (and refer to other languages of the directive to support the proposition) that this simply means 'permit' or 'give the opportunity for' this to occur: and that this is less consistent with knowledge leading to the discovery of the defect in a particular product than with knowledge enabling the existence of the defect to be discovered generally, so that the risk of its being in the particular product is thus known of, as opposed to being an unknown development risk for which the producer could be excused. The claimants also rely on the fact that the passive voice is used: 'to enable the existence of the defect to be discovered' generally, rather than the issue being whether it enables 'the producer to discover' the defect in a particular product. ...

CONCLUSIONS ON ARTICLE 6

55. I do not consider it to be arguable that the consumer had an actual expectation that blood being supplied to him was not 100% clean, nor do I conclude that he had knowledge that it was, or was likely to be, infected with Hepatitis C. It is not seriously argued by the defendants, notwithstanding some few newspaper cuttings which were referred to, that there was any public understanding or acceptance of the infection of transfused blood by Hepatitis C. Doctors and surgeons knew, but did not tell their patients unless asked, and were very rarely asked. It was certainly, in my judgment, not known and accepted by society that there was such a risk, which was thus not 'sozialadaquat' (socially acceptable), as Professor Taschner and Count von Westphalen would describe such risks: Taschner and Riesch *Produkthaftungsgesetz und EG Produkthaftungsrichtlinie* (1990) at p 291 and von Westphalen Produkthaftungshandbuch at 27. Thus blood was not, in my judgment, the kind of product referred to in the Flesch/Davenant question and answer in the European Parliament ie '*a product which by its very nature carries a risk and which has been presented as such (instructions for use, labelling, publicity, etc.)*', '*risks which are .... inherent in [a] product and generally known*': nor as referred to by Professor Howells at para 1.17 as being risks which '*consumers can be taken to have chosen to expose themselves to in order to benefit from the product*'.

56. I do not consider that the legitimate expectation of the public at large is that legitimately expectable tests will have been carried out or precautions adopted. Their legitimate expectation is as to the safeness of the product (or not). The court will act as what Dr Bartl called the appointed representative of the public at large, but in my judgment it is impossible to inject into the consumer's legitimate expectation matters which would not by any stretch of the imagination be in his actual expectation. He will assume perhaps that there are tests, but his expectations will be as to the safeness of the blood. In my judgment it is as inappropriate to propose that the public should not 'expect the unattainable'—in the sense of tests or precautions which are impossible—at least unless it is informed as to what is unattainable or impossible, as it is to reformulate the expectation as one that the producer will not have been negligent or will have taken all reasonable steps.

57. In this context I turn to consider what is intended to be included within '*all circumstances*' in art 6. I am satisfied that this means all relevant circumstances. It is quite plain to me that (albeit that Professor Stapleton has been pessimistic about its success) the directive was intended to eliminate proof of fault or negligence. I am satisfied that this was not simply a legal consequence, but that it was also intended to make it easier for claimants to prove their case, such that not only would a consumer not have to prove that the producer did not take reasonable steps, or all reasonable steps, to comply with his duty of care, but also that the producer did not take all legitimately expectable steps either. ...

63. I conclude therefore that *avoidability* is not one of the *circumstances* to be taken into account within art 6. I am satisfied that it is not a relevant circumstance, because it is outwith the purpose of the directive, and indeed that, had it been intended that it would be included as a derogation from, or at any rate a palliation of, its purpose, then it would certainly have been mentioned; for it would have been an important circumstance, and I am clear that, irrespective of the absence of any word such as '*notamment*' in the English-language version of the directive, it was intended that the most significant circumstances were those listed.

64. This brings me to a consideration of art 7(e) in the context of consideration of art 6. Article 7(e) provides a very restricted escape route, and producers are, as emphasised in *Commission v UK*, unable to take advantage of it, unless they come within its very restricted conditions, whereby a producer who has taken all possible precautions (certainly

all legitimately expectable precautions, if the terms of art 6, as construed by Mr Underhill, are to be cross-referred) remains liable unless that producer can show that '*the state of scientific and technical knowledge [anywhere and anyone's in the world, provided reasonably accessible] was not such as to enable the existence of the defect to be discovered*'. The significance seems to be as follows. Article 7(e) is the escape route (if available at all) for the producer who has done all he could reasonably be expected to do (and more); and yet that route is emphatically very restricted, because of the purpose and effect of the directive. This must suggest a similarly restricted view of art 6, indeed one that is even more restricted, given the availability of the (restricted) art 7(e) escape route.

CONCLUSIONS ON ARTICLE 7(e)

74. As to construction:

i. I note (without resolving the question) the force of the argument that the defect in art 7(b) falls to be construed as the defect in the particular product; but I do not consider that to be determinative of the construction of art 7(e), and indeed I am firmly of the view that such is not the case in art 7(e);

ii. the analysis of art 7(e), with the guidance of European Commission v UK, seems to me to be entirely clear. If there is a known risk, ie the existence of the defect is known or should have been known in the light of non-Manchurianly accessible information, then the producer continues to produce and supply at his own risk. It would, in my judgment, be inconsistent with the purpose of the directive if a producer, in the case of a known risk, continues to supply products simply because, and despite the fact that, he is unable to identify in which if any of his products that defect will occur or recur, or, more relevantly in a case such as this, where the producer is obliged to supply, continues to supply without accepting the responsibility for any injuries resulting, by insurance or otherwise;

iii. the *existence of the defect* is in my judgment clearly generic. Once *the existence of the defect* is known, then there is then the risk of that defect materialising in any particular product.

75. The purpose of the directive, from which art 7(e) should obviously not derogate more than is necessary (see Recital 16) is to prevent injury, and facilitate compensation for injury. The defendants submit that this means that art 7(e) must be construed so as to give the opportunity to the producer to do all he can in order to avoid injury: thus concentrating on what can be done in relation to the particular product. The claimants submit that this will rather be achieved by imposing obligation in respect of a known risk irrespective of the chances of finding the defect in the particular product, and I agree. ...

THE RESULT IN LAW ON ISSUE 1

78. Unknown risks are unlikely to qualify by way of defence within art 6. They may, however, qualify for art 7(e). Known risks do not qualify within art 7(e), even if unavoidable in the particular product. They may qualify within art 6 if fully known and socially acceptable.

79. The blood products in this case were non-standard products, and were unsafe by virtue of the harmful characteristics which they had and which the standard products did not have.

80. They were not *ipso facto* defective (an expression used from time to time by the claimants) but were defective because I am satisfied that the public at large was entitled to expect that the blood transfused to them would be free from infection. There were no warnings and no material publicity, certainly none officially initiated by or for the benefit of the defendants, and the knowledge of the medical profession, not materially or at all shared with the consumer, is of no relevance. It is not material to consider whether any steps or

any further steps could have been taken to avoid or palliate the risk that the blood would be infected.

The consequence

82. In those circumstances the claimants recover against the defendants because their claim succeeds within art 4, the blood bags being concluded to be defective within art 6, and art 7(e) does not avail.

Consider the significance of the directive to the next action and also place it within the context of the supposed compensation culture.

Bogle and others v McDonald's Restaurants Ltd and McDonald's Restaurants Limited Defendant **[2002] EWHC 490 (QB)**

Mr Justice Field:

Introduction

This is the trial of a set of preliminary issues ordered to be determined by Master Turner, with the approval of the Lord Chief Justice. The issues are generic issues arising from the pleaded cases of a group of claimants suing for personal injuries caused by the spillage of hot drinks (in two cases hot water) served by the defendant ("McDonald's"). The claims are all separate and distinct, but they share a number of common features and allegations. They were therefore made the subject of a Group Litigation Order on 21 February 2001. There are presently 36 claimants in the group. The majority are children; at least 16 were aged 4 or under at the time the injury was sustained.

The period during which most of the injuries were suffered is 1996 to 1998; one claim dates from 1986, another from 1994 and a third from 1991. In all of the cases the hot drink had been purchased by an adult and in all except one it is alleged that a lidded cup containing a hot drink fell over either on or from a tray, or on or from a table, the lid came off and part at least of the hot contents poured over the claimant. A fairly typical set of alleged facts is afforded by the case of Lamar Bartley who, aged almost 10 months, was taken by his mother, Gail McDonald, to a McDonald's restaurant in Nottingham. Ms. McDonald had her four other children with her as well as Lamar and was in the company of four other adults with seven other children. Ms. McDonald bought three hot drinks and five cold drinks and carried them to a table. It is alleged that another customer put his tray on the same table and in so doing pushed Ms. McDonald's tray off the table spilling hot coffee onto Lamar who suffered serious scalding injuries requiring a skin graft under general anaesthetic.

The exceptional case is that of Sam Bogle who, aged 15 months, was taken by his child minder to the McDonald's at Hinkley Town Centre. It is alleged that Sam went to a drink a cup of hot coffee which had been left on a table with its lid removed, and in doing so spilled the contents onto himself, sustaining scalding injuries to his face, neck, chest, shoulders and back.

The generic issues

The generic issues ordered to be tried on a preliminary basis (with a few grammatical amendments) are:

(1) Whether the Defendant was negligent in dispensing and serving hot drinks at the temperature at which in fact it did in these cases.

(2) Whether it was necessary for the Defendant in order properly to discharge any duty

of care owed towards the Claimants, to dispense and serve the hot drinks at some lower temperature than in fact it did, and, if so, at what maximum temperature.

(3) Whether the cups used by the Defendant were of such unsound and/or inadequate construction as to render the Defendant's use of them for the service of hot drinks to its customers, negligent.

(4) Whether the lids used by the Defendant for such purposes were of such poor fit or otherwise so inappropriate as to render the Defendant's use of them for the service of hot drinks to its customers, negligent.

(5) Whether there was a duty upon the defendant to warn its customers as to the risk of scalding from hot drinks.

(6) If there was such a duty, whether the defendant was in breach of it.

(7) As regards the hot drinks which it produced for sale to customers, whether the Defendant was in breach of the Consumer Protection Act 1987 because those hot drinks were "defective".

The background facts

McDonald's restaurants sell meals and drinks to eat in or take away at over 1200 locations across the UK. Most of the restaurants are owned and operated by McDonald's but some are operated by franchisees. For the purpose of these proceedings McDonald's accepts responsibility for the operation of all McDonald's restaurants. In 1999, the average number of transactions carried out by McDonald's each day in the U.K. was in excess of 1.1 million, involving 2.5 visitors. The restaurants are family restaurants: children constitute a significant proportion of the total number of visitors. Amongst the products sold are hot coffee and tea. At the material time these were served in polystyrene cups, known as foam hot cups. From 1995 coffee was served in cups of two sizes, an 8 oz regular and a 12 oz large. Tea was only served in regular sized cups. Once filled with black coffee or hot water and a tea bag the cups had a plastic lid fitted on them and were then presented to the customer on a plastic tray if the drink was to be consumed on the premises; if the purchase was made in a drive thru outlet, the cup was placed in preformed inserts in a fibre tray. Neither milk (creamer) nor sugar was added prior to the lid being fitted. If the customer wanted either or both of these additions he had to remove the lid; they were available in pre-packed form. If tea was purchased the tea bag had a string which passed under the lid. If a tea customer wished to remove the tea bag the lid first had to be taken off. The lids had a small vent hole to prevent pressure building up. Prior to 1996 the lids had a tear-off tab to allow the drink to be consumed without removing the lid. After 1996, the tab was tear-back rather than tear-off. However, whether tear-off or tear-back, the tab did not allow milk and/or sugar to be added or a tea bag to be removed with the lid still on. If there were to be additions to the drink or a tea bag removed, the lid had to be taken off. In September 2001 McDonald's changed the way they brewed and served coffee. This followed a review conducted towards the end of 1999. The cups now used are manufactured from fibroboard and the lids do not have a tear-off or tear-back tab but have instead a slot through which the drink can be consumed without the lid having to be removed. These changes occurred after the period relevant to the claims in this case. There is no evidence that the changes were brought about because of a concern within McDonald's that the previous cups and lids were unsafe. At all material times, McDonald's were aware that there was a risk that a visitor might be badly scalded and suffer a deep thickness burn by a hot drink that is spilled or knocked over after it has been served.

[Field J held that McDonald's was not negligent. He then turned to the claim under the Consumer Protection Act 1987.]

(7) As regards the hot drinks which it produced for sale to customers, whether the Defendant was in breach of the Consumer Protection Act 1987 because those hot drinks were 'defective'. …

I gratefully adopt the analysis of Burton J of sections 3 and 4 of the CPA and Articles 6 and 7 of the Directive in *A and others v The National Blood Authority and another* [2001] 3 All ER 289. Accordingly, I proceed on the following basis:

(a) the burden of proving that a product is defective is on the party who so asserts (here the claimants);

(b) in determining whether the safety of the product is not such as persons generally are entitled to expect, the court, acting as an informed representative of the public at large, must objectively assess the legitimate expectations of persons generally and whilst those expectations may accord with actual expectation, they may be more than what the public actually expect;

(c) in determining the safety of the product the court should take into account all the relevant circumstances including in particular the matters recited in s. 3(2) of the CPA; (d) however, the avoidability of the risk of harm is not a relevant circumstance;

(d) products that are obviously dangerous (such as a knife) are not defective: the consumer has a free choice whether to expose himself to the risk, but that choice must be an informed choice.

McDonald's accept that in adding hot water to coffee grounds and tea bags it is a 'producer' of hot drinks to whom s 2(2) applies. The issue to be decided therefore is whether the claimants have proved that during the relevant period the safety of the tea and coffee served by McDonald's was not such as persons generally were entitled to expect.

The claimants submit:

(1) the expectations of persons generally will be affected by the potential seriousness of injury that the tea and coffee served by McDonald's ('the product') can cause;

(2) the temperature at which the product was served was such that serious injury would result from the briefest contact;

(3) the product was served in containers and in circumstances in which they were liable to tip or be knocked over with ease;

(4) clear and unambiguous warnings of the risk of injury could have been given to customers but were not;

(5) the size of McDonald's organisation and the resources available to it were such that the public was entitled to expect that the subject of the safety of adult and child customers had been fully researched, considered and assessed and that appropriate reasonable measures were in place to safeguard them against risks of serious injury. This was not done. There had been no research. The risks had not been assessed. In reality and in contrast to the safety of employees, safety of customers was not considered;

(6) drinks were served to customers in restaurants which were crowded and busy with excited children; and

(7) the safety of customers was dependent on three unwarranted assumptions made by McDonald's:

(i) the lid would be placed securely on the cup; this could not be guaranteed particularly since it was a task likely to be performed by youthful employees and, in the case of tea, if the string from the tea bag was between the lid and the cup, security of the lid was less likely to be achieved;

(ii) the cup would not be knocked over with sufficient force or in circumstances such that its contents would be spilled;

(iii) adult customers and child customers would be aware of the nature and extent of the risk of scalding injury from contact.

It is clear on the evidence that hot coffee or tea spilled if:

(a) a lidded cup was dropped to the floor from a tray or table;

(b) a lidded cup was violently knocked over;

(c) a cup was tipped over after the lid had been removed to allow the drink to be consumed;

(d) a lidded cup whose tab had been torn/pulled back was tipped over, in which case the drink would escape through the resulting gap in the lid, but much less quickly than if the lid were off.

In the nature of things spills onto a visitor were occasionally bound to occur causing a deep thickness burn. There were no warnings given to customers until 1995 after which the words 'Caution: Hot!' and 'Caution: Contents Hot!' were printed on the cup.

However, I hold that the safety of the hot drinks met the legitimate expectations of persons generally. I do so for the following reasons. The serving staff were trained and one of the matters included in the training was the capping of hot drinks securely. This training took place as soon as an employee started his employment. On his first day there was an orientation class followed over the next three weeks by on-the-job training. At the end of this and before the end of the fourth week a probationary review had to be successfully passed before continuous employment was offered. Within the first three weeks every new employee had to complete an Observation Check List ('OCL') which included the procedure of capping hot drinks securely. By using OCLs and on-the-job training a full time employee was fully trained after five months at a standard restaurant, six months at a drive-thru restaurant. After full training the employee had to complete ten OCLs in each succeeding six month period and the results were discussed between the manager and the employee. Further, a Performance Appraisal was conducted every six months at which OCL scores were considered. The staff were also warned in McDonald's Health & Safety Manual that hot drinks could be very dangerous, especially to young children and instructed, inter alia, tactfully to advise customers if they thought drinks could be a hazard. The training was thorough so that the fact that 70% of the serving staff were between the ages of 16 and 20 did not mean that visitors were subjected to greater risk than if the staff had been older.

I accept Mr Hathaway's evidence that he carried out a risk assessment of hot drinks causing serious burns and that the conclusion resulted in the warning and instruction in the Health & Safety Manual mentioned above. But even if this step had not been taken, the omission in itself would not be relevant, since in my opinion what the court is concerned with is the ultimate safety of the product and not what considerations the producer gave to its safety.

The drinks were served in polystyrene cups that were amply strong enough to hold their contents. The serving staff were trained to place lids securely on the cups before they were handed to customers. The insulation efficiency of the cups meant that purchasers could not tell by holding the cup just how hot the contents were. However, the great majority of those who bought tea and coffee would be of teenage years or older and they could be expected to know that the tea and coffee served by McDonald's was hot and would cause a serious scalding injury if spilled on someone. The angle at which full cups tipped over was 20 degrees in the case of a regular cup and 18 degrees in the case of a large cup. However, having been designed and manufactured to do so, the lids stayed on the cups if they were tipped over. This was so, in my judgement, even if the lid had been removed and then put on again. If the tab had been torn back or off, the lid would stay on but the contents would come out of the resulting gap in the lid but much less slowly than if the lid had been removed.

Persons generally expect tea or coffee purchased to be consumed on the premises to be hot. Many prefer to consume a hot drink from an unlidded cup rather than through a spout in the lid. Persons generally know that if a hot drink is spilled onto someone, a serious scalding injury can result. They accordingly know that care must be taken to avoid such spills, especially if they are with young children. They expect precautions to be taken to guard against this risk but not to the point that they are denied the basic utility of being able to buy hot drinks to be consumed on the premises from a cup with the lid off. Given that the staff were trained to cap the drinks securely and given the capabilities of the cups and lids used, I am satisfied that the safety of the hot drinks served by McDonald's was such as persons generally are entitled to expect. Accordingly, I hold that in serving hot drinks in the manner in which they did McDonald's was not in breach of the CPA.

Conclusion

The burns suffered by many of the claimants were serious, involving severe pain and skin grafts. I have taken this carefully into account whilst considering the issues I have to determine. However, for the reasons given above, I answer 'No' to all of the preliminary issues; the allegations contained in those issues that McDonald's are legally liable for these unfortunate injuries have not been made out.

Few cases have been brought under the Directive. The ECJ has interpreted the Directive as a maximal harmonisation measure so that several cases have examined the extent to which it precludes existing private-law actions in Member States. The rationale for this maximal interpretation is based on the argument that the Directive was adopted by unanimous consent and that consequently the balance between the competing interests in the Directive should not be upset. Article 13 has been interpreted to permit existing contractual or non-contractual liability that is not based on the defectiveness of the product, for example negligence or a contractual warranty (see *Maria Victoria Gonzalez Sanchez v Medicina Asturiana SA*, Case 183/00).

The extension of group actions, as used in *Bogle*, could increase the number of claims. However, the limits on liability in many states, the absence of punitive damages, the exclusion of small cases of property damage and the provision of compensation through the welfare state mean that the Product Liability Directive has had a modest effect on access to justice for consumers and does not in itself play a significant regulatory role in deterring the production of unsafe products. A review of the impact of the Product Liability Directive in 2003 concluded that although there has been a 'noticeable increase in product liability claims in the EU over the past ten years', this was primarily attributed not to the Directive but to 'increased awareness of consumer rights, increased consumer access to information and media activity'. The Directive may also have increased the willingness of producers to settle claims out of court. Most respondents to the review thought that the Directive had contributed 'a little' to an increase in the level of safety of products in the EU, with one-third of respondents thinking the Directive had not contributed to the level of safety of products marketed in the EU (Lovells, 2003: 26). There is little evidence of a rise in insurance rates (see Cavaliere, 2005: 299). A subsequent review by the Commission in 2006 concluded that 'stakeholders and experts are generally in favour of maintaining the balance struck by the Directive between competing interests' (COM (2006) 496 final). Mathhias Reiman comments that 'in Western Europe, the EC Directive has had little impact on product liability law in action. ... Actions for damages caused by defective products were rather infrequent in Europe. ... and the introduction of strict liability appears to have done almost nothing to change that picture' (Reimann, 2003: 146–47). Apparently many claims continue to be brought in negligence on the continent of Europe (Micklitz et al 2010: 444).

If strict liability is relatively unimportant, why did its introduction generate such heated controversy? Perhaps the product liability debate illustrates the general argument that it is easier for consumer groups to mobilise public opinion on highly visible issues, and that diffuse groups such as consumers tend to receive through the political process merely symbolic benefits.

The recital to the Directive claims that:

> Whereas liability without fault on the part of the producer is the sole means of adequately solving the problem, peculiar to our age of increasing technicality, of a fair apportionment of the risks inherent in modern technological production;

Several writers view the movement to strict liability as a misconceived law reform, based on false assumptions about the ability of the private-law system to perform the compensation and deterrence functions the promotion of which was sought by the reform (see eg Ison, 1967; Glasbeek and Hasson, 1977). Belobaba summarises the arguments against the effectiveness of tort as an effective compensation system:

> The deficiencies of tort litigation as a vehicle for universal product injury compensation are apparent to anyone after only a moment's reflection. The arbitrary exclusion of those victims who can't find or can't 'fault' a defendant; the inequities of the lawsuit 'lottery'; the inordinate delay in obtaining compensation; the horrific expense of the litigation mechanism: each of these points, and others, have now been amply documented in the literature. And everyone agrees: if the only rationale for retaining tort litigation was compensation, then tort would have been abolished decades ago. (Belobaba, 1983: 77)

The most appropriate response to the failure of tort in respect of compensation and deterrence may be a universal accident-compensation scheme with product safety regulations (eg information requirements and product standards) enforced by fines fulfilling the deterrent role. Such a scheme exists in New Zealand but it is beyond the scope of this text to analyse further the role of compensation schemes (see further Howells and Weatherill, 2005: 259, and sources cited therein).

References

Abbamonte G (2007) 'The Unfair Commercial Practices Directive and its General Prohibition' in S Weatherill and U Bernitz (eds), *The Regulation of Unfair Commercial Practices under EC Directive 2005/29 New Rules and New Techniques* (Oxford, Hart Publishing).

Akerlof G (1970) 'The Market for "Lemons": Qualitative Uncertainty and the Market Mechanism', 84 *Quarterly Journal of Economics* 488.

Adler M and Wozniak E (1980) *The Origins and Consequences of Default—An Examination of the Impact of Diligence*, Research Report No 6 (Edinburgh, Scottish Law Commission).

Advertising Standards Authority (2006) 'Response to the DTI's Consultation on Implementing the EU Directive on Unfair Commercial Practices and Amending Existing Consumer Legislation', www.asaorguk/asa/search/searchhtm?xsearch=corrective%20advertising.

Alwitt LF and Donley TT (1998) 'The Low-income Consumer: Adjusting the Balance of Exchange', 21 *Journal of Consumer Policy* 231.

Amy-Chinn D (2007) 'Regulating Against Offence: Lessons from the Field of UK Advertising', 29 *Media & Critical Theory* 1036.

Andreasen A (1975) *The Disadvantaged Consumer* (New York, Free Press).

Arrow KJ (1974) *The Limits of Organization* (New York, Norton).

Atiyah P (1979) *The Rise and Fall of Freedom of Contract* (Oxford, Clarendon Press).

Australian Competition and Consumer Commission (2005) *Enforcement and Compliance Survey: Report of Preliminary Findings* (Canberra).

Australian Law Reform Commission (2003) *ALRC 95: Principled Regulation: Federal Civil and Administrative Penalties in Australia* (Canberra, ALRC).

Ausubel L (1991) 'The Failure of Competition in the Credit Card Market', 81 *American Economic Review* 50.

—— (1999) 'Adverse Selection in the Credit Card Market', Working Paper, Department of Economics, University of Maryland.

Ayres I (1991) 'Fair Driving: Gender and Race Discrimination in Retail Car Negotiations', 104 *Harvard Law Review* 817.

Ayres I and Braithwaite J (1992) *Responsive Regulation: Transcending the Deregulation Debate* (Oxford, Oxford University Press).

Baggot R and Harrison L (1986) 'The Politics of Self Regulation The Case of Advertising Control', 14 *Review of Politics* 143.

Bagwell K (2005) 'The Economic Analysis of Advertising', www.columbia.edu/~kwb8/papers.html.

Baker E (1975–76) 'The Ideology of the Economic Analysis of Law', 5 *Philosphy and Public Affairs* 1.

Baldwin R (2004) 'The New Punitive Regulation', 67 *MLR* 351.

—— (2005) 'Is Better Regulation Smarter Regulation', *Public Law* 485.

Baldwin R and Cave M (1999) *Understanding Regulation: Theory, Strategy, and Practice* (Oxford, Oxford University Press).

Ball, H and Friedman, L (1965) 'Use of Criminal Sanctions in the Enforcement of Economic Legislation: A Sociological View', 17 *Stanford Law Review* 97.

Balmer NJ, Pleasence P, Buck A and Walker H (2006) 'Worried Sick: The Experience of Debt

Problems and their Relationship with Health, Illness and Disability', 5 *Social Policy and Society* 39.

Bank of England (2006) *Financial Stability Review.*

Bardach E and Kagan R (1982) *Going by the Book: The Problem of Regulatory Unreasonableness* (Philadelphia, Temple Univeristy Press).

Bar-Gill O (2004) 'Seduction by Plastic', 98 *Northwestern University Law Review* 1373.

—— (2006) 'Bundling and Consumer Misperception', 73 *University of Chicago Law Review* 33.

—— (2008) 'The Behavioral Economics of Consumer Contracts', 92 *Minnesota Law Review* 749.

—— (2009) 'The Law, Economics and Psychology of Subprime Mortgage Contracts', 94 *Cornell Law Review* 1073.

Bar-Gill O and Davis K (2010) 'Empty Promises', 84 *Southern California Law Review* 1.

Barr M (2005) 'Credit Where it Counts: The Community Reinvestment Act and its Critics', 80 *New York University Law Review* 513.

Barr, N (1987) *The Economics of The Welfare State* (London, Weidenfeld & Nicolson).

Barron A (2007) 'Reasonable Expectations, Good Faith and Self-Regulatory Codes', *Yearbook of Consumer Law* 3.

Bates JR (1993) 'Continued Use of Goods After Rejection or Revocation of Acceptance: The UCC Rules Revealed, Reviewed and Revised', 24 *Rutgers Law Journal* 1.

Bauman Z (2011) 'The London Riots—On Consumerism Coming Home to Roost', *Social Europe* www.social-europe.eu/2011/08/the-london-riots-on-consumerism-coming-home-to-roost

Beales H, Craswell R and Salop S (1981) 'The Efficient Regulation of Consumer Information', 24 *Journal of Law and Economy* 49.

Beck U (1992) *Risk Society: Towards a New Modernity* (London, Sage).

—— (2006) 'Living in the World Risk Society', 35 *Economy and Society* 329.

Becker GS (1968) 'Crime and Punishment: An Economic Approach', 76 *Journal of Political Economy* 169.

Ben-Shahar O and Posner E (2011) 'The Right to Withdraw in Contract Law', 40 *Journal of Legal Studies* 115.

Ben-Shahar O and Schneider C (2011) 'The Failure of Mandated Disclosure', 159 *University of Pennsylvania Law Review* 647.

Benjamin A (1997) 'Consumer Protection in Less-developed Countries: The Latin American Experience' in I Ramsay (ed), *Consumer Law in the Global Economy:National and International Dimensions* (Aldershot, Ashgate).

Bell J (1983) *Policy Arguments in Judicial Decision* (Oxford, Oxford University Press).

Belobaba E (1983) *Consumer Product Warranty Reform, Vol II: Products Liability* (Ottawa, Consumer and Corporate Affairs, Canada).

Benson J (1994) *The Rise of Consumer Society in Britain, 1880–1980* (London, Longman).

Bentham J (1962) 'In Defence of Usury' [1816] in J Bowring (ed), *The Works of Jeremy Bentham* (New York, Russell and Russell) vol 3 pp 1–29.

Bernstein, M (1955) *Regulating Business by Independent Commission* (Princeton, Princeton University Press).

Berthoud R and Kempson E (1992) *Credit and Debt: The PSI Report* (London, PSI).

Berzein M (2005) 'Emotions and the Economy' in N Smelser and R Swedberg (eds), *The Handbook of Economic Sociology*, 2nd edn 6 (Princeton, Princeton University Press) ch 6.

Best A and Andreasen A (1976–77) 'Consumer Response to Unsatisfactory Purchases: A Survey of Perceiving Defects, Voicing Complaints, and Obtaining Redress', 1 *Law and Society Review* 701.

Better Regulation Commission (2006) *Risk, Responsibility and Regulation: Whose Risk Is it Anyway?* (London, Better Regulation Commission).

Better Regulation Task Force (2003) *Imaginative Thinking for Better Regulation* (London, Better Regulation Commission).

—— (2006) *Principles of Good Regulation (revised)* London.

Bhatia N (2004) *Return Policies for Customer Purchases*, PhD thesis, University of California.

Bien M 'How to Get Down from the Credit Mountain', *Independent on Sunday* 25 April 2004.

Bisping C 'The Case Against S 75 of the Consumer Credit Act 1974 in Credit Card Transactions' (2011) *Journal of Business Law* 457.

Black J (2001) 'Decentring Regulation: Understanding the Role of Regulation and Self-regulation in a "Post-Regulatory" World' 54 *Current Legal Problems* 103.

—— (2002) 'Critical Reflections on Regulation', Discussion Paper Centre for the Analysis of Risk and Regulation LSE 4 London: Centre for Analysis of Risk and Regulation.

—— (2005) 'The Emergence of Risk Based Regulation and the New Public Management in the UK' *Public Law* 512.

Blankenburg E (1986) 'The Poverty of Evolutionism: A Critique of Teubner's Case for "Reflexive Law"', 18 *Law and Society Review* 273.

Board of Trade (1962) *Final Report of the Committee on Consumer Protection* (The Molony Committee), Cmnd I 781 (London, HMSO).

Boddewyn JJ (1986) 'Advertising Self-regulation: Organization Structures in Belgium, Canada, France and The United Kingdom' in W Streeck and P Schmitter (eds), *Private Interest Government* (London, Sage).

Bok S (1978) *Lying: Moral Choice in Public and Private Life* (New York, Pantheon).

Boltanski L. and Chiapello È (2011) *Le nouvel esprit du capitalisme* (Paris, Gallimard).

Boorstin D (1962) *The Image: A guide to Pseudo-Events in America* (New York, Harper).

Borrie G (1980) 'Laws and Codes for Consumers' *Journal of Business Law* 315.

—— (1982) 'Licensing Practice Under the Consumer Credit Act' *Journal of Business Law* 1.

—— (1984) *The Development of Consumer Law and Policy—Bold Spirits and Timorous Souls* (London, Sweet & Maxwell).

—— (1984) 'A Duty to Trade Fairly' 7 *Journal of Consumer Policy* 197.

Boyden P (2006) *Living on Tick: The 21st Century Debtor* (London: PriceWaterhouseCoopers).

Bragg R (1991) *Trade Descriptions* (Oxford, Oxford University Pres).

—— (2006) 'Consumer Protection Act 1987—New Code of Practice on Pricing' *2007 Yearbook of Consumer Law* 345.

Braithwaite J (1981–82) 'The Limits of Economism in Controlling Harmful Corporate Conduct', 6 *Law and Society Review* 481.

—— (2000) 'The New Regulatory State and the Transformation of Criminology', 40 *British Journal of Criminology* 222.

—— (2003) '"Meta-Regulation" for Access to Justice', www.law. berkeley.edu/centers/Kadish/gala03/Braithwaite%20Kent.pdf.

Braithwaite J and Drahos P (2000) *Global Business Regulation* (Cambridge, Cambridge University Press).

Braucher J (1988) 'Defining Unfairness: Empathy and Economic Analysis at the Federal Trade Commission 68 *Boston University Law Review* 349.

—— (2001) 'Rent Seeking and Risk-Fixing in the New Statutory Law of Electronic Commerce: Difficulties in Moving Consumer Protection Online' *Wisconsin Law Review* 527.

—— (2001) 'Delayed Disclosure in Consumer E-Commerce as an Unfair and Deceptive Practice' 46 *Wayne Law Rev* 1805.

Breit W and Elzinga KG (1976) *The Antitrust Penalties, A Study in Law and Economics* (New Haven, Yale University Press).

Breyer S (1982) *Regulation and its Reform* (Cambridge, MA, Harvard University Press).

—— (1995) *Breaking the Vicious Circle: Towards Effective Risk Regulation* (Cambridge, MA, Harvard University Pres).

Bridge M (2003) 'What Is to Be Done about Sale of Goods?' 119 *Law Quarterly Review* 173.

Bright S (2000) 'Winning the Battle Against Unfair Contract Terms' 20 *Legal Studies* 331.

Brito DL and Hartley P (1995) 'Consumer Rationality and Credit Cards' 103 *Journal of Political Economy* 400.

Brown, S (2006) *Consumer Credit and Over-indebtedness: Past Present and Future*, PhD thesis, Leeds University.

—— (2011) 'Using the Law as a Usury Law: Definitions of Usury and Recent Developments in the Regulation of Unfair Charges in Consumer Credit Transactions', *Journal of Business Law* 91.

Brownsword R and Howells G (1999) 'When Surfers Start to Shop: Internet Commerce and Contract Law' 19 *Legal Studies* 287.

Brynjolfsson ED and Smith M (2003) 'Search and Product Differentiation at an Internet Shopbot' (Cambridge, MA, Center for ebusiness@MIT).

Burgess A (2001) 'Flattering Consumption: Creating a Europe of the Consumer', 1 *Journal of Consumer Culture* 93.

Burrows P (1992) 'Consumer Safety under Products Liability and Duty to Disclose', 12 *International Review of Law and Economy* 457.

Bush J (2004) *Consumer Empowerment and Competitiveness* (London, NCC).

Calais-Auloy J and Steinmetz F (2006) *Droit de la Consommation* (7th edn) (Paris, Dalloz).

Cafaggi F (2010) 'New Foundations of Transnational Private Regulation', WP RSCAS 2010/53, Private Regulation series no 04.

Cafaggi F and Micklitz H-W (2010) *European Private Law after the Common Frame of Reference* (Cheltenham, Edward Elgar).

Calder L (1999) *Financing the American Dream: A Cultural History of Consumer Credit* (Princeton, NJ, Princeton University Press).

Callies G-P (2006) 'Online Dispute Resolution: Consumer Redress in a Global Market Place', 7 *German Law Journal* no 8 (1 August).

—— and Zumbansen P (2010) *Rough Consensus and Running Code* (Oxford, Hart Publishing).

Campbell D, Collins H and Wightman J (eds) (2003) *Implicit Dimensions of Contract: Discrete, Relational and Network Contracts* (Oxford, Hart Publishing).

Camerer C, Issacharoff S, Loewenstein G, O'Donoghue T, Rabin M (2003) 'Regulation for Conservatives: Behavioral Economics and the Case for 'Asymmetric Paternalism', 151 *University of Pennsylvania Law Review* 1211.

Cannon G (1987) *The Politics of Food* (London, Century Publishing).

Caplovitz D (1974) *Consumers in Trouble: A Study of Debtors in Default* (New York, Free Press).

—— (1963) *The Poor Pay More: Consumer Practices of Low Income Families* (New York, Free Press).

Carson WG (1970) 'Some Sociological Aspects of Strict Liability and the Enforcement of Factory Legislation' 30 *MLR* 396.

Cartwright P (2000) *Consumer Protection and the Criminal Law Law, Theory, and Policy in the UK* (Cambridge, Cambridge University Press).

—— (2007) 'The General Product Safety Regulations 2005: Implementing Directive 2001/95/EC in the UK', *Yearbook of Consumer Law* 309.

—— (2006) 'Enforcement, Risk and Discretion: the Case of Dangerous Consumer Products', 26 *Legal Studies* 524.

Castells, M (1997) *The Power of Identity, The Information Age: Economy, Society and Culture*, vol II (Oxford, Blackwell)

Cavaliere A (2004) 'Product Liability in the European Union: Compensation and Deterrence Issues' 18 *European Journal of Law and Economics* 299.

Caves RE and Greene DP (1996), 'Brands' Quality Levels, Prices, and Advertising Outlays:

Empirical Evidence on Signals and Information Costs' 14 *International Journal of Industrial Organization* 29.

Cayne DJ and Trebilcock MJ (1973) 'Market Considerations in the Formulation of Consumer Protection Policy' 23 *University of Toronto Law Journal* 396.

Chamberlin, E (1950) *The Theory of Monopolistic Competition* (6th edn) (Cambridge, MA, Harvard University Press).

Chen Y and Sudhir K (2004) ' When Shopbots Meet Emails: Implications for Price Competition on the Internet', 2 *Journal Quantitative Marketing and Economics* 233.

Chitty on Contracts (2004) (28th edn) (London, Sweet & Maxwell).

Choi S and Pritchard AC (2003) 'Behavioral Economics and the SEC', 56 *Stanford Law Review* 1.

Citizens Advice (2006) *Deeper in Debt* (London, Citizens Advice).

—— (2006) *Representative Actions in Consumer Protection Legislation: Response to DTI from Citizens Advice* (London, Citizens Advice).

Civil Justice Review (1988) *Report of the Review Body on Civil Justice*, Cmnd 394 (London, HMSO).

Clarke, S (2005) 'Unmanageable Risks: MacPherson v Buick and the Emergence of a Mass Consumer Market', 23 *Law and History Review* 1.

Coase R (1960) 'The Problem of Social Cost', 3 *Journal of Law and Economy* 1.

—— (1977) 'Advertising and Free Speech' in A Hyman and B Johnson (eds), *Advertising and Free Speech* (Levington, MA, DC Heath and Co).

Cohen D (1980) 'The FTC Advertising Substantiation Program' 44 *Journal of Marketing* 26.

Cohen, L (2003) *A Consumers' Republic: The Politics of Mass-Consumption in Postwar America* (New York, Knopf).

Collard S and Kempson E (2005) *Affordable Credit: The Way Forward* (Bristol, The Policy Press).

—— and Smith N (2006) *Membership Counts: Who Uses Credit Unions?* (Bristol, Personal Finance Research Centre).

Collins H (1994) 'Good Faith in European Contract Law', 14 *OJLS* 229.

—— (1999) *Regulating Contracts* (Oxford, Oxford University Press).

—— (2003a) *The Law of Contract* (4th edn) (London, Lexis).

—— (2003b) 'Discretionary Powers in Contracts', in Campbell, Collins and Wightman (2003) ch 8.

—— (2004) 'Regulating Contract' in C Parker, C Scott, N Lacey and J Braithwaite (eds), *Regulating Law* (Oxford, Oxford University Press).

—— (2010) 'Harmonization by Example: European Laws against Unfair Commercial Practices, 73 *MLR* 89.

Comanor W and Wilson TA (1974) *Advertising and Market Power* (Cambridge, MA, Harvard University Press).

Commission of the European Communities (1999) *Consumer Policy Action Plan* Brussels.

—— (2000) *Report from the Commission on the Implementation of Council Directive 93/13 on Unfair Terms in Consumer Contracts* COM 248.

—— (2001) *Green Paper on European Union Consumer Protection* COM 531.

—— (2002) *Proposal for a Directive of the European Parliament and of the Council on the harmonization of the laws regulations and administrative provisions of the Member States concerning credit for consumers* COM(2002) 443 final.

—— (2003) *Green Paper on Services of General Interest* COM(2003) 270 final.

—— (2003) *Proposal for a Directive of the European Parliament and of the Council concerning Unfair Business-to-Consumer Commercial Practices in the Internal Market* COM 356.

—— (2004) *Consumer Confidence in E-Commerce: Lessons learned from the EConfidence Initiative* Brussels.

—— (2005) *Directive of the European Parliament and Council concerning unfair business-to-consumer commercial practices in the internal market and amending Council Directive 84/450/EEC, Directives 97/7/EC, 98/27/EC and 2002/65/EC of the European Parliament and of the Council and Regulation (EC) No 2006/2004 of the European Parliament and of the Council.*

—— (2007) *EU Consumer Policy Strategy 2007–2013 Empowering consumers, enhancing their welfare, effectively protecting them.*

—— (2008) *Directive 2008/48 EC of the European Parliament and of the Council on credit agreements for consumers and repealing Council Directive 87/102/EEC.*

—— (2009) *Report from the Commission to the Parliament and Council on the implementation of Directive 2001/95/EC of the European Parliament and of the Council of 3 December 2001 on general product safety* COM 905.

—— (2011) *Report from the Commission to the European Parliament and Council on the application of Regulation (EC) 2006/2004 of the European Parliament and of the Council of 27 October 2004 on cooperation between national authorities responsible for the enforcement of consumer protection laws (the Regulation on consumer protection cooperation).*

—— (2011) *Proposal for a Directive of the European Parliament and Council on alternative dispute resolution for consumer disputes and amending Regulation (EC) No 2006/2004 and Directive 2009/22/EC (Directive on consumer ADR).*

—— (2011) *Proposal for a Regulation of the European Parliament and of the Council on online dispute resolution for consumer disputes.*

—— (2011) *Proposal for a Regulation of the European Parliament and Council on a common European Sales Law.*

Competition Commission (2003) *Extended Warranties on Domestic Electrical Goods: A Report on the Supply of Extended Warranties on Domestic Electrical Goods within the UK*, vols 1–3 (London, Competition Commission).

—— (2006) *Store Cards Market Investigation* (London, OFT).

—— (2006) *Home Credit Market Investigation* (London, OFT).

—— (2009) *Market Investigation into Payment Protection Insurance*

Comptroller and Auditor-General (2003–04) Regulatory Impact Assessments, Compendium Report 2003–04, Report by the Comptroller and Auditor General, HC 358 (London, HMSO).

Consumer Council (1971) *Justice Out of Reach: A Case for Small Claims Courts* (London, HMSO).

Consumer Credit (1970) Report of the Committee (The Crowther Committee), Cmnd 4596 (London, HMSO).

Consumer Focus (2011) *Making Ends Meet: The Costs and Implications of Money Management for Low Income Consumers* (London, Consumer Focus).

Consumers International (2005) *Decision Making in the Global Market: Trade, Standards and the Consumer* (London, Consumers International).

—— (2006) *From Bean to Cup: How Consumer Choice Impacts upon Coffee Producers and the Environment* (London, Consumers International).

Coteanu C (2005) *CyberConsumer Law and Unfair Trade Practices* (Aldershot, Ashgate).

Cooper J and Dhavan R (eds) (1986) *Public Interest Law* (Oxford, Blackwell).

Cornish W (1981) *Intellectual Property* (London, Sweet & Maxwell).

Cousins DC and Pickering JF (1981) 'Codes of Practice as an Element in Consumer Policy Research into the British Experience' in MJ Baker and D Tixier (eds), *Consumerism, Public Policy and Consumer Protection* (Cergy, ESSEC).

Cranston R (1979) *Regulating Business: Law and Consumer Agencies* (London, Macmillan).

Craswell R (1981) 'Identification of Unfair Acts and Practices by the Federal Trade Commission' *Wisconsin Law Review* 107.

—— (1982) 'Tying Requirements in Competitive Markets: The Consumer Protection Issues', 62 *Boston University Law Review* 661.

—— (1985) 'Interpreting Deceptive Advertising', 65 *Boston University Law Review* 657.

Croall H (1988) 'Mistakes, Accidents and Someone Else's Fault: The Trading Offender in Court' 15 *Journal of Law and Society* 293.

Crosland CAR (1956) *The Future of Socialism* (London, Jonathan Cape).

Cseres K (2005) *Competition Law and Consumer Protection* (The Hague, Kluwer).

Dalzell J (1942) 'Duress by Economic Pressure', 20 *North Carolina Law Review* 237.

Davis J (1977) 'Protecting Consumers from Overdisclosure and Gobbledygook: An Empirical Look at the Simplification of Consumer-Credit Contracts', 63 *Virginia Law Review* 841.

Davis KC (1969) *Discretionary Justice: A Preliminary Inquiry* (Baton Rouge, Louisiana State University Press).

Dawson, JP (1947) 'Economic Duress—An Essay in Perspective', 45 *Michigan Law Review* 253.

—— (1976) 'Unconscionable Coercion: The German Version', 89 *Harvard Law Review* 1041.

De Muynck M 'Credit Cards, Overdraft Facilities and European Consumer Protection: A Blank Cheque for Unfairness?' (2010) 18 *European Review of Private Law* 1181.

Della Vigna S and Malmendier U (2004) 'Contract Design and Self-Control: Theory and Evidence', CXIX *Quarterly Journal of Economics* 353.

—— (2006) 'Paying Not to Go to the Gym', 96 *American Economic Review* 694.

Department of Environment, Food and Rural Affairs (2005) *Securing the Future: Delivering UK Sustainable Development Strategy* (London, The Stationery Office).

Department of Business Innovation and Skills (2011) *Consumer Credit and Personal Insolvency Review* (London, DBIS).

—— (2011) *Better Choices: Better Deals Consumers Powering Growth* (London, DBIS).

——(2012) *Empowering and Protecting Consumers: Government Response to the Consultation on Institutional Reform* (London, 2012).

—— (2011) *A New Approach to Financial Regulation: Consultation on Reforming the Consumer Credit Regime* (London, DBIS/Treasury).

—— (2012) *Simpler Laws, Stronger Rights: Consultation on the Supply of Goods, Services and Digital Content.*

Department of Prices and Consumer Protection (1974) *A National Consumers' Agency*, Cmnd 5726 (London, HMSO).

—— (1976) *Consumer Safety: A Consultative Document* Cmnd 6398 (London, HMSO).

Department of Trade and Industry (1982) *Standards, Quality and International Competitiveness* Cmnd 8621 (London, HMSO).

—— (1999) *Modern Markets: Confident Consumers*, Cm 4410.

—— (2002) *Research on the Proportion of Home Accidents involving Product Fault or Contributory Behaviour, Consumer and Competition Policy Directorate* (London, DTI).

—— (2003) *Fair, Clear and Competitive: The Consumer Credit Market in the 21st Century* Cm 6040 (London, TSO).

—— (2003) *Consumer Awareness of Credit Issues: Research Study conducted for DTI by MORI* (London, DTI).

—— (2003) *Comparative Report on Consumer Policy Regimes* (London, DTI).

—— (2004) *Qualitative Research into Consumer Understanding of the Form and Content of Credit Product Documents: MORI* (London, DTI).

—— (2005) *A Fair Deal for All: Extending Competitive Markets: Empowered Consumers, Successful Business (Consumer Strategy)* (London, TSO).

—— (2005) *Tackling Overindebtedness: Annual Report* (London, DTI/DWP/DCA).

—— (2006*) Government Response to the Consultation Paper on Implementing the Unfair Commercial Practices Directive* URN 06/2121 (London, DTI).

—— (2006) *Consultation on the Removal of Barriers to the Sharing of Non-consensual Credit Data*, URN 06/1357 (London, DTI).

—— (2007) *Consultation on the Draft Consumer Protection from Unfair Trading Regulations 2007*.

Deutch S (1994) 'Are Consumer Rights Human Rights?', 32 *Osgoode Hall Law Journal* 537.

—— (2004) 'Consumer Class Actions: Are They a Solution for Enforcing Consumer Rights? The Israeli Model' 27 *Journal of Consumer Policy* 179.

Devenney J (2011)'Gordian Knots in Europeanised Private Law: Unfair Terms, Bank Charges and Political Compromises', 62 *Northern Ireland Legal Quarterly* 33.

Devlin J (2005) 'A detailed Study of Financial Exclusion in the UK' 28 *Journal of Consumer Policies* 75.

DTI/Policis (2005) *The Effect of Interest Rate Controls in Other Countries* (London, DTI).

DTI (2006) *Illegal Lending in the UK*.

Dimaggio P and Louch H (1998) 'Socially Embedded Consumer Transactions: For What Kinds of Purchases Do People Most Often use Networks?', 63 *American Sociological Review* 619.

Dominy N and Kempson E (2003) *Can't Pay or Won't Pay? A Review of Creditor and Debtor Approaches to the Non-payment of Bills* (London, DCA).

Doorey D (2005) 'Who Made That? Influencing Foreign Labour Practices through Reflexive Domestic Disclosure Regulation', 43 *Osgoode Hall Law Journal* 1.

Drexl J (1998) *Die wirtschaftliche Selbstbestimmung des Verbrauchers* (Tubingen, JCB Mohr).

Duggan A and Ramsay I (2012) 'Front End Approaches to Access to Justice: The Case of Consumer Credit' in Trebilcock M, Duggan A and Sossin L (eds), *Improving Access to Justice for the Middle Class* (Toronto, University of Toronto Press).

Duffy K (1995) *Social Exclusion and Human Dignity in Europe* (Strasbourg, Council of Europe).

Durkin T (2002) 'Consumers and Credit Disclosures: Credit Cards and Credit Insurance', *Federal Reserve Bulletin* (April) 201.

DWP, Over-indebtedness Action Plan, 2004

Ehrlich I and Posner R (1974) 'An Economic Analysis of Legal Rulemaking, 3 *Journal of Legal Studies* 257.

Elliott A (2005) *Not Waving but Drowning: Over-indebtedness by Misjudgement* (London, CSFI).

Ellison G and Ellison S (2004) *Search Obfuscation, and Price Elasticities on the Internet* (Cambridge, MA, NBER).

Elster J (1983), *Sour Grapes: Studies in the Subversion of Rationality* (Cambridge, Cambridge University Press).

Engel K and Mcoy P (2011) *The Subprime Virus: Reckless Credit, Regulation Failure and Next Steps* (Oxford, Oxford University Press).

Engelen E, Ertürk I, Froud J, Johal S, Leaver A, Moran M, Nilsson A and Williams K (2011) *After the Great Complacence: Financial Crisis and the Politics of Reform* (Oxford, Oxford University Press).

Ervine C (1987) 'Protecting New Car Purchasers: Recent United States and English Development Compared' 34 *International and Comparative Law* 342.

Ervine C (2004) 'Satisfactory Quality: What Does it Mean?' *Journal of Business Law* 684.

European Consumer Law Group (1983) 'Non-legislative Means of Consumer Protection', 6 *Journal of Consumer Policy* 209.

Everson M (2006) 'Legal Constructions of the Consumer' in F Trentmann (ed) *The Making of the Consumer: Knowledge Power and Identity in the Modern World* (Oxford, Berg).

Everson M and Joerges C (2006) 'Consumer Citizenship in Postnational Constellations?', European University Institute Working Paper no 2006/47.

Ewen S (1976) *Captains of Consciousness: Advertising and the Social Roots of the Consumer Culture* (New York, McGraw-Hill).

Fairgrieve D and Howells G (2006) 'General Product Safety—A Revolution through Reform', 69 *MLR* 50.

Farrell J and Klemperer P (2006) 'Coordination and Lock-in: Competition with Switching Costs and Network Effects', http://ssrncom/abstract=917785.

Faure M and Luth H (2011) 'Behavioural Economics in Unfair Contract Terms: Cautions and Considerations', 34 *Journal of Consumer Policy* 337.

Federal Trade Commission (1968) *Economic Report on Installment Credit and Retail Sales Practices of District of Columbia Retailers* (Washington DC, FTC).

—— (1979) *Consumer Information Remedies* (Washington DC, FTC).

—— (1980) 'Letter from the Federal Trade Commission to Senators Ford and Danforth' (Unfairness Policy Statement) HR Rep No I 56, 98th Congress, 1st Sess, Pt I, at 33 (1983).

—— (2006) *The FTC in 2006: Committed to Consumers and Competition* (Washington DC, FTC).

Federal Trade Commission Staff Report (1979) *Impact of the Magnusson-Moss Warranty Act: A Comparison of Forty Major Consumer Product Warranties from Before and After the Act.*

Financial Services Authority (2000) *In or Out? Financial Exclusion: A Literature and Research Review* (London, FSA).

—— (2005) *The Sale of Payment Protection Insurance –Results of Thematic Work* (London, FSA).

—— (2006) *Consumers and Mortgage Disclosure Documentation* Consumer Research 54 (London, FSA).

—— (2006) *Financial Promotions: Progress Update and Future Direction* (London, FSA).

—— (2006) *The Sale of Payment Protection Insurance – Results of Follow-up Thematic Work* (London, FSA).

—— (2010) *Mortgage Market Review: Responsible Lending*, CP10/16 (London, FSA).

—— (2010) *The Assessment and Redress of Payment Protection Insurance Complaints: Feedback on the Further consuLtation in CP10/6 and Final Handbook Text* (London, FSA).

—— (2011)*The Financial Conduct Authority Approach to Regulation* (London, FSA).

—— (2011) *Product Intervention* DP11 (London, FSA).

—— (2011) *Mortgage Market Review: Proposed package of reforms* CP11/31 (London, FSA).

Financial Stability Board (2011) *Consumer Finance Protection with Particular Focus on Credit.*

Finn, M (2003) *The Character of Credit* (Cambridge, Cambridge University Press).

Fisher E (2000) 'Drowning by Numbers: Standard Setting in Risk Regulation and the Pursuit of Accountable Public Administration', 20 *OJLS* 109.

Fisse B and Braithwaite J (1983), *The Impact of Publicity on Corporate Offenders* (Albany, State University of New York).

Frederick S, Loewenstein G and O'Donoghue T (2002) 'Time Discounting and Time Preference: A Critical Review', XL *Journal of Economic Literature* 351.

Freiberg A and O'Malley P (1984) 'State Intervention and the Civil Offense' 18 *Law and Society Review* 373.

Friedan B (1963) *The Feminine Mystique* (New York, Norton).

Friedman M (1962) *Capitalism and Freedom* (Chicago, University of Chicago Press).

Friedman M and Friedman R (1980) *Free to Choose* (Harmondsworth, Penguin).

Fuchs D and Lorek S (2005) 'Sustainable Consumption Governance: A History of Promises and Failures' 28 *Journal of Consumer Policy* 261.

Gabaix X and Laibson D (2006) 'Shrouded Attributes, Consumer Myopia, and Information Suppression in Competitive Markets' 121 *Quarterly Journal of Economics* 505.

Gabriel Y and Lang T (2006) *The Unmanageable Consumer* (2nd edn) (London, Sage).

Galanter M (1974) 'Why the "Haves" Come Out Ahead: Speculation on the Limits of Legal Change', 9 *Law and Society Review* 95.

Galbraith JK (1955) *The Great Crash* (Boston, MA, Houghton Mifflin).

—— (1967) *The New Industrial State* (Boston, MA, Houghton Mifflin).

—— (1973) *Economics and the Public Purpose* (Boston, MA, Houghton Mifflin).

—— (1984) *The Affluent Society* (4th edn) (London, André Deutsch).

Gandy OH (1993) *The Panoptic Sort: A Political Economy of Personal Information* (Boulder CO, Westview).

Gans J (2005) 'Protecting Consumers by Protecting Competition: Does Behavioural Economics Support this Contention?' 13 *Competition and Consumer Law Journal* 1.

Gellhorn E (1973) 'Adverse Publicity by Administrative Agencies', 86 *Harvard Law Review* 1380.

Giddens A (1994) *Beyond Left and Right: The Future of Radical Politics* (Cambridge, Polity).

—— (2000) *The Third Way and its Critics* (Cambridge, Polity).

—— (2007) *Europe in the Global Age* (Cambridge, Polity).

Gilad S (2011) 'Institutionalizing Fairness in Financial Markets: Mission Impossible?', 5 *Regulation & Governance* 309.

Gillette C (2002) 'Reputation and Intermediaries in Electronic Commerce', 62 *Louisiana Law Review* 1165.

—— (2005) 'Pre-approved Contracts for Internet Commerce' 42 *Houston Law Review* 975.

Giulietti M, Waddams-Price C and Waterson M (2005) 'Consumer Choice and Competition Policy: A Study of UK Energy Markets' *The Economic Journal* 949.

Glaeser EL and Scheinkman J (1998) 'Neither a Borrower nor a Lender Be: An Economic Analysis of Interest Restrictions and Usury Laws', 41 *Journal of Law and Economics* 1.

Glasbeek H (1984) 'Why Corporate Deviance Is not Treated as a Crime—The Need to Make "Profits" a Dirty Word', 22 *Osgoode Hall Law Journal* 393.

Glasbeek H (2002) *Wealth by Stealth: Corporate Crime, Corporate Law, and the Perversion of Democracy* (Toronto, Between the Lines).

Glasbeek H and Hasson R (1977) 'Fault—The Great Hoax' in Klar L (ed) *Studies in Canadian Tort Law* (Toronto, Butterworths).

Gobert J (1994) 'Corporate Criminality: New Crimes for the Times', *Criminal Law Review* 722.

Goffman E (1969) *The Presentation of Self in Everyday Life* (Harmondsworth, Penguin).

Golding P (ed) (1986) *Excluding the Poor* (London, Child Poverty Action Group).

Goldthorpe JH, Lockwood D, Beckhofer F and Platt J, (1969) *The Affluent Worker in the Class Structure* (Cambridge, Cambridge University Press).

Goldthorpe, J et al (1961, 1987) *Social Mobility and Class Structure* (New York, Oxford University Press).

Goode R (1979) *Consumer Credit* (Leyden, Sijthoff).

—— (1989) *Consumer Credit Law* (London, Butterworths).

—— (2005) Evidence to HL on Proposed Consumer Credit Harmonization Directive.

Goodin RE (1989) 'Theories of Compensation', 9 *Oxford Journal of Legal Studies* 56.

Gordon R (1987) 'Unfreezing Legal Reality: Critical Approaches to Law', 15 *University of Florida Law Review* 195.

Grabowski H and Vernon J (1978) 'Consumer Product Safety Regulation' 67 *American Economics Review* 284.

Grady M (1981) 'Regulating Information: Advertising Overview' in K Clarkson and T Muris (eds), *The Federal Trade Commission Since 1970: Economic Regulation and Bureaucratic Behavior* (Cambridge, Cambridge University Press).

Graham C (2006) 'The Politics of Necessity: Electricity and Water in Great Britain', 29 *Journal of Consumer Policy* 435.

Granovetter M (1985) 'Economic Action and Social Structure: The Problem of Embeddedness', 91 *American Journal of Sociology* 481.

Grant W (2000) *Pressure Groups and British Politics* (London, Macmillan).

—— (2002) *Economic Policy in Britain* (London, Palgrave-Macmillan).

—— and Nath S (1984) *The Politics of Economic Policy Making* (Oxford, Blackwell).

Gray J (1978) 'Unsolicited Goods and Services Acts 1971 and 1975: A Case Study of the Process Leading to the Enactment of Private Members' Bills', *Public Law* 242.

Green M (2002) *Individual Voluntary Arrangements, Over-indebtedness and the Insolvency Regime* (Bangor, University of Wales).

Greenfield M (1983) *Consumer Transactions* (Westbury NY, Foundation).

—— (1993) *Consumer Law* (Boston, Little Brown).

Grether D, Schwartz A and Wilde L (1985–86) 'The Irrelevance of Information Overload: An Analysis of Search and Disclosure' 59 *Southern California Law Review* 277.

Griffith JAG (1985) *The Politics of the Judiciary* (London, Fontana Press).

The Griffiths Commission (2005) *What Price Credit?* (London, Centre for Social Justice).

Grundmann S, Kerber W and Weatherill S (eds) (2001) *Party Autonomy and the Role of Information in the Internal Market* (Berlin, de Gruyter).

Gunningham N (1974) *Pollution, Social Interest and the Law* (London, Martin Robertson).

Guria J, Leung J, Jones-Lee M and Loomes G (2005) 'The Willingness to Accept Value of Statistical Life Relative to the Willingness to Pay Value: Evidence and Policy Implications', 32 *Environmental and Resource Economics* 113.

Haas P (1989) 'Do Regimes Matter? Epistemic Communities and Mediterranean Pollution Control', 43 *International Organization* 377.

Habermas J (1975) *Legitimation Crisis*, trans T McCarthy (Boston, MA, Beacon Press).

—— (1998) *Between Facts and Norms: Contributions to a Discourse Theory of Law and Democracy*, trans W Rehg (Cambridge, MA, MIT Press).

Hadfield G, Howse R and Trebilcock M (1998) 'Information Based Principles for Rethinking Consumer Protection Policy', 21 *Journal of Consumer Policy* 131.

Halligan L (2005) 'The Debt Pandemic', *The New Statesman* 24 October.

Halsey AH (1986) *Change in British Society* (3rd edn) (Oxford, Oxford University Press).

Hampton P (2005) *Reducing Administrative Burdens: Effective Inspection and Enforcement* (London, Treasury).

Handler J (1980) *Social Movements and The Legal System* (New York, Academic Press).

Hannah L (1976) *The Rise of the Corporate Economy: The British Experience* (Baltimore, MD, John Hopkins University Press).

Hanson J and Kysar D (1999) 'Taking Behavioralism Seriously: Some Evidence of Market Manipulation' 112 *Harvard Law Review* 1420.

Harford T (2006) *The Undercover Economist* (London, Penguin).

Harland D (1999) 'The Consumer in the Globalized Information Society—The Impact of the International Organizations' in T Wilhelmsson, S. Tuominen and H Tuomola (eds), *Consumer Law in the Information Society* (The Hague, Kluwer).

Harlow C (1978) 'Ombudsmen in Search of a Role', 41 *Modern Law Review* 446.

—— (1986) 'Public Interest Litigation in England: The State of the Art' in I Cooper and R Dhavan (eds), *Public Interest Law* (Oxford, Blackwell).

Harris D 'Specific Performance—A Regular Remedy for Consumers', 119 *LQR* 541.

Hart HLA (1963) *Law, Liberty and Morality* (Stanford, CA, Stanford University Press).

Harvard Law Review (1967) 'Developments in the Law: Deceptive Advertising', 80 *Harvard Law Review* 1005.

——(1975–76) 'Developments in the Law: Class Actions', 89 *Harvard Law Review* 1319.

—— (1978–79) 'Developments in the Law: Corporate Crime' 92 *Harvard Law Review* 1227.

Harvey D (2005) *A Brief History of Neoliberalism* (Oxford, Oxford University Press).

Hawkins K (1984) *Environment and Enforcement: Regulation and the Social Definition of Pollution* (Oxford, Clarendon Press).

—— (2002) *Law as Last Resort: Prosecution Decision-making in a Regulatory Agency* (Oxford, Oxford University Press).

—— and Thomas J (eds) (1984) *Enforcing Regulation* (Boston, MA, Kluwer-Nijhoff).

Hayek, F von (1945) 'The Use of Knowledge in Society', 35 *American Economic Review* 519.

—— (1961) 'The Non Sequitur of the 'Dependence Effect', 27 *Southern Economic Journal* 346.

Hedlund J (2000) 'Risky Business: Safety Regulations, Risk Compensation, and Individual Behavior', 6 *Injury Prevention* 82.

Hellwege P 'Consumer Protection in Britain in Need of Reform', 63 *Cambridge Law Journal* 712.

Hensler D (2010) Using Class Actions to Enforce Consumer Protection Law' in Howells, Ramsay and Wilhelmsson (eds), *Handbook of Research on International Consumer Law* (Cheltenham, Edward Elgar).

——, Dombey-Moore B, Giddens E, Gross J, Moller P and Pace N (2000) *Pursuing Public Goals for Private Gain* (Santa Monica CA, Rand).

Hillman R (2002) 'The Rhetoric of Legal Backfire', 43 *Boston College Law Review* 819.

—— (2006) 'Online Consumer Standard Form Contracting Practices: A Survey and Discussion of Legal Implications' in JK Winn (ed), *Consumer Protection in the Age of the 'Information Economy'* (Aldershot, Ashgate).

Hilton M (2003) *Consumerism in Twentieth-century Britain* (Cambridge, Cambridge University Press).

Hinton T and Berthoud R (1988) *Money Advice Services* (London, PSI).

Hirsch F (1976) *The Social Limits to Growth* (Cambridge, MA, Harvard University Press).

Hirschman AO (1970) *Exit, Voice and Loyalty* (Cambridge, MA, Harvard University Press).

Hirshhorn R (1983) 'The Administration of The Hazardous Products Act' in D Dewees (ed), *The Regulation of Quality* (Toronto, Butterworths).

Hodges C (2005) *European Regulation of Consumer Product Safety* (Oxford, Oxford University Press).

Hodgson, G (1984) *The Democratic Economy: A New Look at Planning, Markets and Power* (Harmondsworth, Penguin).

Hoermann G (ed) (1986) *Consumer Credit and Consumer Insolvency: Perspectives for Legal Policy from Europe and the USA* (Bremen, ZERP).

Holder J (1991) 'Regulating Green Advertising in the Motor Car Industry', 18 *Journal of Law and Society* 323.

Hood C, James O, Scott C, Jones GW and Travers T (1999) *Regulation Inside Government* (Oxford, Oxford University Press).

Hood C, Rothstein H Baldwin R (2001) *The Government of Risk* (Oxford, Oxford University Press).

Horowitz DL (1977) *The Courts and Social Policy* (Washington DC, Brookings).

House of Commons Constitutional Affairs Committee (2005–06) *Compensation Culture*, HC 754-I (London, TSO).

House of Commons Treasury Committee (2003–04) *Transparency of Credit Card Charges: First Report*, HC 125 (London, TSO).

—— (2006–07) *Financial Inclusion: The Roles of the Government and the FSA, and Financial Capability*, HC 53 (London, TSO).

House of Commons, Select Committee Business Innovation and Skills (2012) *Debt Management* (London TSO).

House of Lords European Union Committee (2005–06) *Consumer Credit Harmonization Directive Interim Report*, HL 37 (London,TSO).

Howell N and Wilson T (2005) 'Access to Consumer Credit: The Problem of Financial Exclusion in Australia and the Current Regulatory Framework', 5 *Macquarie Law Journal* 127.

Howells G (2000) 'The Relationship between Product Liability and Product Safety—Understanding a Necessary Element in European Product Liability through a Comparison with the US Position', 39 *Washburn Law Journal* 305.

—— (2005) 'The Potential and Limits of Consumer Empowerment by Information', 32 *Journal of Law and Society* 349.

—— (2006) 'The Rise of European Consumer Law—Whither National Consumer Law?' 28 *Sydney Law Review* 63.

—— (2007) 'England and Wales' in Stuyck et al (eds), *An Analysis and Evaluation of Alternative Means of Consumer Redress other than Redress through Ordinary Judicial Proceedings* (Leuven, KUL).

—— (2010) 'The Consumer Credit Litigation Explosion', 126 *LQR* 617.

—— and Owen (2010) 'Products Liability Law in America and Europe', in Howells, Ramsay and Wilhelmsson, *Handbook of Research on International Consumer Law* (Cheltenham, Edward Elgar).

—— and Weatherill S (2005) *Consumer Protection Law* (Aldershot, Ashgate).

—— and Wilhelmsson T (2003) 'EC Consumer Law: Has it Come of Age?', 28 *European Law Review* 370.

——, Micklitz H-W and Wilhelmsson T, (2006) *European Fair Trading Law: The Unfair Commercial Practices Directive* (Aldershot, Ashgate).

Hutter BM (2006) 'The Role of Non-state Actors in Regulation' in F Schuppert (ed), *Global Governance and the Role of Non State Actors* Nomos 63.

—— and O'Mahony J (2004) 'Business Regulation: Reviewing the Regulatory Potential of Civil Society Organisations', CARR Discussion Paper Centre for Analysis of Risk and Regulation at the London School of Economics and Political Science 26.

Information Commissioner (2006) *A Report on the Surveillance Society for the Information Commissioner by the Surveillance Studies Network.*

Inman P (2006) 'Faulty Goods? You've Still Got Rights when the Guarantee Runs Out.', *Guardian* 25 March.

The Insolvency Service (2000) *Bankruptcy: A Fresh Start* (London, The Insolvency Service).

—— (2006) *Causes of Failure in Bankruptcy and Compulsory Liquidation: A Report* (London, The Insolvency Service).

—— (2007) *Survey of Debtors Petitioning for Bankruptcy* (London, Insolvency Service).

—— (2010) *Debt Relief Orders Initial Evaluation Report* (London, Insolvency Service).

Ippolito PM and Mathios A (1990) 'Information, Advertising and Health Choices: A Study of the Cereal Market', 21 *RAND Journal of Economics* 459.

—— (1991) 'Health Claims in Food Marketing: Evidence on Knowledge and Behavior in the Cereal Market' 10 *Journal of Public Policy and Marketing* 15.

Ireland N (2004) 'Firms' Strategies for Reducing the Effectiveness of Consumer Price Search', Warwick Economic Research Papers no 627.

Ison TG (1967) *The Forensic Lottery* (London, Staples Press).

—— (1972) 'Small Claims', 35 *Modern Law Review* 18.

—— (1977) 'Expand Rejection Rights not Remedies', *Proceedings of 7th Annual Workshop on Commercial and Consumer Law.*

—— (1979) *Credit Marketing and Consumer Protection* (London, Croom Helm).

Jacoby J, Speller D and Berning C (1974) 'Brand Choice Behaviour as a Function of Information Load – Replication and Extension', 1 *Journal of Consumer Research* 33.

Jackson TH (1984–85) 'The Fresh Start Policy in Bankruptcy Law', 98 *Harvard Law Review* 1393.

Jaffe, L (1956) 'Review', 65 *Yale Law Journal* 1068.

—— (1972–73) 'The Illusion of an Ideal Administration', 86 *Harvard Law Review* 1183.

James R (1997) *Private Ombudsmen and Public Law* (Aldershot, Ashgate).

—— (2002) 'The New Dispute Resolution System in the UK Financial Services Industry', 1 *Journal of International Financial Markets* 191.

—— and Morris, P (2003) 'The New Financial Ombudsman Service in the United Kingdom:

Has the Second Generation Got it Right?' in C Rickett and T Telfer (eds), *International Perspectives on Consumers' Access to Justice* (Cambridge, Cambridge University Press).

Japelli T and Pagano M (2006) 'The Role and Effects of Credit Information Sharing' in G Bertola, R Disney, and C Grant (eds), *The Economics of Consumer Credit* (Cambridge, MA, MIT Press).

Jarrell G and Peltzman S (1985) 'The Impact of Product Recalls on the Wealth of Sellers', 93 *Journal of Political Economy* 512.

Johnson P (1985) *Saving and Spending: The Working-class Economy in Britain, 1870–1939* (Oxford, Oxford University Press).

Johnston A and Unberath H (2007) 'The Double-Headed Approach of the ECJ Concerning Consumer Protection', 44 *Common Market Law Review* 1237.

Johnston J (2006) 'The Return of Bargain: An Economic Theory of How Standard Form Contracts Enable Cooperative Negotiation between Businesses and Consumers', 104 *Michigan Law Review* 857.

Jolls C (2005) 'Behavioral Economics', wwwlawyaleedu/faculty/CJollshtm.

Jordan EH and Rubin PH (1979) 'Economic Analysis of the Law of False Advertising', 8 *Journal of Legal Studies* 527.

Justice (1980) *Breaking the Rules: The Problems of Crimes and Contraventions* (London, Justice).

Kadish S (1963) 'Some Observations of the Use of Criminal Sanctions in Enforcing Economic Regulations', 30 *University of Chicago Law Review* 423.

Kahneman D, Knetsch J and Thaler R (1986a) 'Fairness as a Constraint on Profit Seeking: Entitlements in the Market', 76 *American Economic Review* 728.

—— (1986) 'Fairness and the Assumptions of Economics', 59 *Journal of Business* S285.

—— (1990) 'Experimental Tests of the Endowment Effect and the Coase Theorem', 98 *Journal of Political Economy* 98.

Kalajdzic J (2010) 'Consumer (In)justice: Reflections on Canadian Consumer Class Actions', 50 *Canadian Business Law Journal* 356.

Kalven H Jr and Rosenfield M (1941) 'Contemporary Function of the Class Suit', 8 *University of Chicago Law Review* 684.

Kelman M (1981) 'Interpretive Construction in the Substantive Criminal Law', 33 *Stanford Law Review* 591.

—— (1988) 'On Democracy Bashing: A Skeptical Look at the Theoretical and "Empirical" Practice of the Public Choice Movement', 74 *Virginia Law Review* 199.

Kempson E (2002) *Over-indebtedness in Britain* (London, Department of Trade and Industry).

—— and Collard S (2004) *Managing Multiple Debts: Experiences of County Court Administration Orders among debtors, creditors and advisors* (London, Department for Constitutional Affairs).

——, Collard S and Moore N (2004) *Fair and Reasonable: An Assessment of the Financial Ombudsman Service* (London, FOS).

Kennedy D (1976) 'Form and Substance in Private Law Adjudication', 89 *Harvard Law Review* 1685.

—— (1982) 'Distributive and Paternalist Motives in Contract and Tort Law, with Special Reference to Compulsory Terms and Unequal Bargaining Power', 41 *Maryland Law Review* 563.

Kennedy I (1981) *The Unmasking of Medicine* (London, Allen and Unwin).

Kessler F (1943) 'Contracts of Adhesion: Some Thoughts About Freedom of Contract', 43 *Columbia Law Review* 620.

King D and Narliker A (2003) 'The New Risk Regulators? International Organisations and Globalisation', 74 *Political Quarterly* 337.

Klein B and Leffler K (1981) 'The Role of Market Forces in Assuring Contractual Performance', *J Political Economy* 615.

Kleinig J (1984) *Paternalism* (Totawa, NJ, Rowman and Allanheld).

Klemperer P (1995) 'Competition when Consumers Have Switching Costs: An Overview with Applications to Industrial Organization, Macroeconomics, and International Trade', 62 *Review of Economic Studies* 515.

Knetch J (2005) 'Gains, Losses and the US-EPA Economic Analyses Guidelines: A Hazardous Product?', 32 *Environmental and Resource Economics* 91.

Koetz H (1982) 'Civil Litigation and the Public Interest', 1 *Civil Justice Quarterly* 237.

Kolko G (1963) *The Triumph of Conservatism* (New York, Free Press).

Komesar NK (1981) 'In Search of a General Approach to Legal Analysis: A Comparative Institutional Alternative', 79 *Michigan Law Review* 1350.

Korobkin R (2003) 'Bounded Rationality, Standard-Form Contracts and Unconscionability', 70 *University of Chicago Law Review* 1203.

Kronman A (1980) 'Contract Law and Distributive Justice', 89 *Yale Law Journal* 472.

—— (1983) 'Paternalism and the Law of Contracts', 92 *Yale Law Journal* 763.

Kysar D (2005) 'Preferences for Processes: The Process/Product Distinction', 118 *Harvard Law Review* 525.

Laibson D, Andrea R and Tobacman J (2003) 'A Debt Puzzle' in P Aghion, R Frydman, J Stiglitz and M Woodward (eds), *Knowledge, Information and Expectations in Modern Microeconomics: Essays in Honor of Edmund S Phelps* (Princeton, NJ, Princeton University Press) 228.

Laing AW, Newholm T and Hogg G (2005) 'Crisis of Confidence: Re-narrating the Consumer–Professional Discourse', 32(1) *Advances in Consumer Research* 514.

Lancaster K (1975) 'Socially Optimal Product Differentiation', 65 *American Economic Review* 567.

Landers JM and Rohner RJ (1979) 'Functional Analysis of Truth in Lending', 26 *UCLA Law Review* 711.

Landis JM (1938) *The Administrative Process* (New Haven, CT, Yale University Press).

Larson MS (1977) *The Rise of Professionalism: A Sociological Analysis* (Berkeley, University of California Press).

Lasch C (1979) *The Culture of Narcissism* (New York, WW Norton & Co).

—— (1984) *The Minimal Self: Psychic Survival in Troubled Times* (New York, WW Norton & Co).

Law Commission (2002) *Unfair Terms in Contracts*, Consultation Paper No 119 (London, TSO).

—— (2002) *Registration of Security Interests: Company Charges and Property other than Land Consultation*, Paper No 164 (London, TSO).

—— (2005) *Company Security Interests*, Cm 6654 (London, TSO).

—— and Scottish Law Commission No 69 (1975) *Exemption Clauses: Second Report* (London, HMSO).

—— and —— (1987) *The Sale and Supply of Goods* London: HMSO.

—— and —— (2005) *Unfair Terms in Contracts*, Cm 6464 (London, TSO).

—— and —— (2009) *Consumer Remedies for Faulty Goods* (Law Com No 317/ Scot Law ComNo 216) Cm 7725.

—— and —— (2012) *Consumer Redress for Misleading and Aggressive Practices* (Law Com 332, Scot Law Com 226)

Law Reform Commission of Canada (1976) 'Sanctioning the Corporate Offender in Criminal Responsibility for Group Action', Working Paper no 16 (Ottawa, Queen's Printer).

—— (1986) 'Policy Implementation, Compliance and Administrative Law', Working Paper no 51.

Law School, University of Adelaide (1969) *Report to the Standing Committee of State and Commonwealth Attorneys-General on the Law Relating to Consumer Credit and Money Lending* (The Rogerson Report) (Adelaide, Government Printer).

LeGrand J (1982) *The Strategy of Equality* (London, Allen & Unwin).

—— and Robinson, R (1984) *Privatisation and the Welfare State* (London, Allen & Unwin).

Leff AA (1970) 'Injury, Ignorance and Spite—The Dynamics of Coercive Collection', 80 *Yale Law Journal* 1.

—— (1970) 'Contract as Thing', 19 *American University Law Review* 131.

—— (1970) 'Unconscionability and the Crowd: Consumers and the Common Law Tradition', 31 *University of Pittsburgh Law Review* 349.

—— (1976) *Swindling and Selling* (New York, Free Press).

Leibenstein H (1950) 'Bandwagon, Snob, and Veblen Effects in the Theory of Consumers' Demand', 64 *Quarterly Journal of Economics* 183.

Leigh LH (1982) *Strict and Vicarious Liability: A Study in Administrative Criminal Law* (London, Sweet & Maxwell).

Leiss W (2001) *In the Chamber of Risks: Understanding Risk Controversies* (Montreal, McGill–Queen's University Press).

Lennard D, Mitchell W, McGoldrick P and Betts E (2001) 'Why Consumers Under Use Food Quantity Indicators', 11 *International Review of Retail Distribution and Consumer Research* 177.

Levi-Faur D (2005) 'The Global Diffusion of Regulatory Capitalism', 598 *Annals of the American Academy of Political and Social Science* 12.

Lindblom CE (1977) *Politics and Markets: the World's Political Economic Systems* (New York, Basic Books).

Linneman P (1980) 'The Effects of Consumer Safety Standards: The 1973 Mattress Flammability Standard', 23 *Journal of Law and Economy* 461.

Llewellyn K (1937) 'On Warranty of Quality and Society II', 37 *Columbia Law Review* 341.

—— (1960) *The Common Law Tradition: Deciding Appeals* (Boston, MA, Little Brown).

Loewenstein G, Hsee C, Weber E and Welch N (2001) 'Risk as Feelings', 127 *Psychological Bulletin* 267.

Lomnicka E (2004) 'The Reform of Consumer Credit in the UK', *Journal of Business Law* 129.

London Economics (1997) 'Consumer Detriment under Conditions of Imperfect Information', OFT Research Paper 11.

Lovells (2003) *Product Liability in the European Union: A Report for the European Commission* Markt/2001/11D Brussels.

Lowi T (1987) 'The Welfare State, The New Regulation and the Rule of Law' in AC Hutchinson and P Monahan, *The Rule of Law: Ideal or Ideology?* (Toronto, Carswell).

Lowrance W (1976) *Of Acceptable Risk: Science and the Determination of Safety* (Los Altos, CA, W Kaufman).

Lunt P (2006) *The Psychology of Consumer Detriment: A Conceptual Review* (London, OFT) 792.

Macaulay S (1963) 'Non-contractual Relations in Business: A Preliminary Study', 28 *American Sociological Review* 55.

—— (1979) 'Lawyers and Consumer Protection Laws', 14 *Law and Society Review* 115.

Machan T and Den Uyl J (1987) 'Recent Work in Business Ethics: A Survey and Critique', 24 *American Philosophical Quarterly* 107.

Mack J and Lansley S (1985) *Poor Britain* (London, Allen & Unwin).

MacLachlan P and Trentmann F (2004) 'Civilising Markets: Traditions of Consumer Politics in Twentieth-century Britain, Japan, and the United States' in M Bevir and F Trentmann (eds), *Markets in Historical Context: Ideas & Politics in the Modern World* (Cambridge, Cambridge University Press).

MacNeil I (1980) *The New Social Contract* (New Haven, CT, Yale University Press).

Macrory R (2006) *Regulatory Justice—Making Sanctions Effective* (London, Cabinet Office).

Maher I (2002) 'Competition Law in the International Domain: Networks as a New Form of Governance', 29 *Journal of Law and Society* 111.

Majone G (1993) 'Controlling Regulatory Bureaucracies: Lessons from the American Experience', EUI Working Paper (Fiesole, EUI).

—— (1996) *Regulating Europe* (London, Routledge).

Mann R (2006) *Charging Ahead: The Growth and Regulation of Payment Card Markets* (Cambridge, Cambridge University Press).

Marschak TA (1978) 'On The Study of Taste Changing Policies', 68 *American Economics Review* 386.

Martin R (2002) *The Financialization of Daily Life* (Philadelphia, Temple University Press).

Mashaw J and Rose-Ackerman S (1984) 'Federalism and Regulation' in Eads and Fix (eds), *The Reagan Regulatory Strategy* (Washington DC, Brookings).

Matthews R (2006) 'The Agonies of Too Much Choice', *Financial Times* 6 January.

McBarnet D (1981) *Conviction: Law, The State and the Construction of Justice* (London, Macmillan).

McCrudden C (ed) (1998) *Regulation and Deregulation* (Oxford, Oxford University Press).

McGee A and Weatherill S (1990) 'The Evolution of the Single Market—Harmonisation or Liberalisation', 53 *MLR* 578.

McGuire S and Macdonald R (1996) 'Small Claims Court Cant', 34 *Osgoode Hall Law Journal* 509.

McManus J (1975) 'The Consumer Credit Act 1974', 2 *British Journal of Law and Society* 66.

McMeel G (1997) 'Comment', 113 *Law Quarterly Review* 47.

McMurtry L (2010) 'Consumer Credit Act Mortgages: Unfair Terms, Time Orders and Judicial Discretion', *Journal of Business Law* 107.

McNeil I, Nevin K, Trubek D and Miller R (1979) 'Market Discrimination against the Poor and the Impact of Consumer Disclosure Law: The Used Car Industry', 13 *Law and Society Review* 695.

Mcvea H (2005) 'Financial Services Regulation Under the Financial Services Authority: A Reassertion of the Market Failure Thesis?' 64 *Cambridge Law Journal* 413.

Michaelis S, Mackey S and Smith K (2005) 'Measuring the Effectiveness of Consumer Credit Reform' (London, DTI).

Micklitz H-W (1986) 'Perspectives of a European Directive on the Safety of Technical Consumer Goods', 23 *Common Market Law Review* 617.

—— (2003) 'The Necessity of a New Concept for the Further Development of the Consumer Law in the EU' 4 *German Law Journal* No 10 (1 October 2003).

—— (2005) *The Politics of Judicial Co-operation in the EU: Sunday Trading, Equal Treatment and Good Faith* (Cambridge, Cambridge University Press).

—— (2007) 'Transborder Law Enforcement—Does it Exist? In Weatherill and Bernitz (eds), *The Regulation of Unfair Commercial Practices under EC Directive 2005/29 New Rules and Techniques* (Oxford, Hart Publishing).

—— (2010) 'Reforming European Unfair Terms legislation in consumer contracts', 6 *European Review of Contract Law* 347.

——, Reich N and Rott P (2009) *Understanding EU Consumer Law* (Antwerp, Intersentia).

——, Stuyck J and Terryn E (2010) *Cases Materials and Text on Consumer Law* (Oxford, Hart Publishing).

Mill JS (1974) *On Liberty* (Harmondsworth, Penguin).

Miller GA (1956) 'The Magical Number Seven, Plus or Minus Two: Some Limits on Our Capacity for Processing Information', 63 *Psychological Review* 81.

Mills CW (1961) *The Sociological Imagination* (Oxford, Oxford University Press).

Miller J and Goldberg R (2004) *Product Liability* (2nd edn) (Oxford, Oxford University Press).

Miller MJ (ed) (2003) *Credit Reporting Systems and the International Economy* (Cambridge, MA, MIT Press).

Mitchell CE (2003) 'Leading a Life of it's Own? The Roles of Reasonable Expectations in Contract Law', 23 *OJLS* 639.

Moran M (2003) *The British Regulatory State: High Modernism and Hyper Innovation* (Oxford, Oxford University Press).

Morgan B (2003) *Social Citizenship in the Shadow of Competition: The Bureaucratic Politics of Regulatory Justification* (Andover, Ashgate).

—— (2006) 'The North–South Politics of Necessity: Regulating for Basic Rights between National and International Levels', 29 *Journal of Consumer Policy* 465.

Morris P (1987a) 'The Banking Ombudsman—I', *Journal of Business Law* 131.

—— (1987b) 'The Banking Ombudsman—II', *Journal of Business Law* 199.

—— (2008) 'The Financial Ombudsman Service and the Hunt Review: Continuing Evolution in Dispute Resolution', *Journal of Business Laws* 785.

—— and Little G (1999) 'The Ombudsman and Consumer Protection' in P Cartwright (ed), *Consumer Protection in Financial Services* (The Hague, Kluwer).

Morton FS and Zettlemeyer, S-RJ (2003) 'Consumer Information and Discrimination: Does the Internet Affect the Pricing of New Cars to Women and Minorities', *Quantitative Marketing and Economics* 65.

—— (2005) 'How The Internet Lowers Prices: Evidence From Matched Survey and Auto Transaction Data' (Cambridge, MA, National Bureau of Economic Research).

Mulheron R (2005) 'Some Difficulties with Group Litigation Orders—And Why a Class Action Is Superior', 24 *Civil Justice Quarterly* 40.

—— (2009) *Reform of Collective Redress in England and Wales: A Perspective of Need* (London, Civil Justice Council).

Mullainathan S and Thaler RH (2000) 'Behavioral Economics', MIT Department of of Economics Working Paper no 00-27, http://ssrncom/abstract=245828

Munro C (2003) 'The Value of Commercial Speech', *Cambridge Law Journal* 134.

Munro M, Ford J, Leishman C and Noah KK (2005) *Lending to Higher Risk Borrowers: Subprime Credit and Sustainable Home Ownership* (York, Rowntree).

Munyck M (2010)'Credit Cards, Overdraft facilitiEs and European Consumer Protection: A Blank Cheque for Unfairness?', 18 *European Review of Private Law* 1181.

Nadel MV (1971) *The Politics of Consumer Protection* (Indianapolis, Bobbs Merill).

Nader L (1980) *No Access to Law: Alternatives to the American Judicial System* (New York, Academic Press).

Nader R (1965) *Unsafe at any Speed: The Designed-in Dangers of the American Automobile* (New York, Grossman Publishers).

National Audit Office, Report by the Comptroller and Auditor General (1999) *The Office of Fair Trading: Protecting the Consumer From Unfair Trading Practices*, HC57 (London, Stationery Office).

—— (2002) *The Office of Fair Trading—Progress in Protecting Consumers' Interests*, HC 430 (London, Stationery Office).

—— (2006) *Enforcing Competition in Markets* (London, TSO).

—— (2011) *Protecting Consumers: The System for Enforcing Consumer Law*, HC 1087.

National Commission on Consumer Finance (1972) *Consumer Credit in the United States* (Washington DC, NCCF).

National Consumer Council (1980) *Consumers and Credit* (London, NCC).

—— (1981) *Service Please* (London, NCC).

—— (1983) *Banking Services and the Consumer: A Report by the National Consumer Council* (London, Methuen).

—— (1984) *Buying Problems: Consumers, Unsatisfactory Goods and the Law* (London, NCC).

—— (1984) *Plain Language for Consumers* (London, NCC).

—— (1987) *Security Risks: Personal Loans Secured on Homes* (London, NCC).

—— (1987) *Measuring Up* (London, NCC).

—— (1989) *Ordinary Justice* (London, HMSO).

—— (2002) *Credit-Choice or Chance* (London, NCC).

—— (2004) *Paying More: Getting Less* (London, NCC).

—— and Welsh Consumer Council (1983) *Consumers and Debt* (London, NCC).

Nava M (1987) 'Consumerism and its Contradictions', 1 *Cultural Studies* 204.

Nelson P (1974) 'Advertising as Information', 82 *Journal of Political Economy* 729.

Nobles R (2003) 'Rules, Principles and Ombudsmen: *Norwich and Peterborough Building Society v The Financial Ombudsman Service*', 66 *MLR* 781.

Nottage L (2004) *Product Safety and Liability Law in Japan: From Minamata to Mad Cows* (London, Routledge).

—— (2010) 'Product Safety Regulation' in Howells G, Ramsay I and Wilhelmsson T, *Handbook of Research on International Consumer Law* (Cheltenham, Edwar Elgar).

—— and Kozuka S (2011) 'Lessons from Product Safety Regulation for Reforming Consumer Credit Markets in Japan and Beyond', 34 *Sydney Law Review* 129.

Nozick R (1974) *Anarchy, State and Utopia* (New York, Basic Books).

O'Connell S (2009) *Credit and Community: Working Class Debt in the UK since 1880* (Oxford, Oxford University Press).

O'Grady, KJ (1982) 'Consumer Remedies', 60 *Canadian Bar Review* 549.

O'Shea P and Rickett C (2006) 'In Defence of Consumer Law: The Resolution of Consumer Disputes', 28 *Sydney Law Review* 139.

OECD (1983) *Product Safety: Risk Management and Cost-Benefit Analysis* (Paris, OECD).

—— (2002) *Regulatory Reform in the United Kingdom: Government Capacity to Assure High Quality Regulation* (Paris, OECD).

—— (2006a) *Consumer Dispute Resolution and Redress in the Global Marketplace* (Paris, OECD).

—— (2006b) *Report on the Effectiveness of Enforcement Regimes* (Anthony Ogus and Michael Faure) DSTI/CP (Paris, OECD).

OFCOM (2006) *Television Advertising of Food and Drink Products to Children—Statement and Further Consultation.*

—— (2006) *Television Advertising of Food and Drink to Children.*

—— (2007) *Television Advertising of Food and Drink Products to Children: Final Statement.*

Offe C (1984) *Contradictions of the Welfare State* (London, Hutchinson).

Offer A (2006) *The Challenge of Affluence: Self-control and Well-being in the United States and Britain since 1950* (Oxford, Oxford University Press).

Office of Fair Trading (1974) 'The Purported Exclusion of Inalienable Rights', Dossier 22 (London, OFT).

—— (1975) *Bargain Offer Claim: A Consultative Document* (London, OFT).

—— (1978) *Review of The United Kingdom Self-regulating System of Advertising Control* (London, OFT).

—— (1979) *Consumer Problems with Used Cars—A Consultative Document* (London, OFT).

—— (1980) *Opticians and Competition* (London, HMSO).

—— (1981) *Review of the Price Marking (Bargain Offers) Orders 1979: A Report by the Director General of Fair Trading* (London, OFT).

—— (1989) *Overindebtedness* (London, OFT).

—— (1994) *Consumer Credit Deregulation* (London, OFT).

—— (1995) *Connected Lender Liability* (London, OFT).

—— (1996) *The Purchase of a Used Car* (London, OFT).

—— (1997) *Selling Second Hand Cars* (London, OFT).

—— (1999) *Vulnerable Consumers and Financial Services The Report of the Director General's Inquiry* (London, OFT) 255.

—— (2000) *Consumer Detriment* (London, OFT) 296.

—— (1996, 2001) *Unfair Contract Terms Bulletins* (London, OFT).

—— (2001, 2008) *Unfair Contract Terms Guidance* (London, OFT).

—— (2001) *Consumer Codes of Practice: The OFT's Response to the Consultation* (London, OFT) 344.

—— (2003) *Inspiring Consumer Confidence: The OFT's Consumer Codes Approval Scheme* (London, OFT).

—— (2004a) *Doorstep Selling: A Report on the Market Study* (London, OFT) 716.

—— (2004b) *Credit Card Survey* (London, OFT) 709.

—— (2005) *Research into misleading price comparisons Prepared for the OFT by Nottingham University Business School* (London, OFT) 790

—— (2006) *Review of impact on business of the Consumer Codes Approval Scheme: A report for the Office of Fair Trading by the Centre for Economics and Business Research Ltd (CEBR) with Opinion Research Business* (London, OFT) 870.

—— (2006) *Evaluating the Impact of the Car Warranties Market: Study Prepared for the Office of Fair Trading by Europe Economics* (London, OFT) 852.

—— (2006) *Calculating Fair Default Charges in Credit Card Contracts A Statement of the OFT's Position* (London, OFT) 842.

—— (2006) *Payment Protection Insurance: Report on the Market Study and Proposed Decision to Make a Market Investigation Reference* (London, OFT) 869.

—— (2010) *Review of High Cost Credit: Final Report* (London, OFT) 1232.

—— (2011) *Evaluating the Impact of the OFT's Consumer Enforcement Case against Foxtons in Respect of Commission Terms in Letting Agreements* (London, OFT) 1346eval

—— (2012) *Investigations into Health and Fitness Club Contracts*.

Office of Fair Trading NOP Surveys Ltd (1979) *Consumer Credit Survey* (London, OFT).

Ogus A (1994) *Regulation: Legal Form and Economic Theory* (Oxford, Oxford University Press).

—— (2005) 'Regulatory Paternalism:When Is it Justified?' in K Hopt, E Wymeersch, H Kanda and H Baum (eds), *Corporate Governance in Context: Corporations, States and Markets in Europe , Japan and the US* (Oxford, Oxford University Press).

—— and Rowley C (1981) 'The Costs and Benefits of Part XI1 of the Fair Trading Act 1973 and Licensing under the Consumer Credit Act 1974' (unpublished research paper for OFT).

Okun A (1975) *Equality and Efficiency: the Big Tradeoff* (Washington DC, Brookings).

Oliver R (1979) 'An Interpretation of the Attitudinal and Behavioural Effects of Puffery' 13 *Journal of Consumer Affairs* 8.

Ontario Law Reform Commission (1972) *Report on Consumer Warranties and Guarantees in the Sale of Goods* (Toronto, Department of Justice).

—— (1979) *Report on Products Liability* (Toronto, Ministry of the Attorney General).

—— (1982) *Report on Class Actions* (Toronto, Ministry of the Attorney General).

Osuji O (2011) 'Business-to-Consumer Harassment, Unfair Commercial Practices Directive and the UK—A Distorted Picture of Uniform Harmonization?' 34 *Journal of Consumer Policy* 437.

Oughton D and Willett C (2002) 'Quality Regulation in European Private Law' 25 *Journal of Consumer Policy* 299.

Oxera (2004) *Are UK Households Over-indebted?* (Oxford, Oxera).

Padilla A and Pagano M (2000) 'Sharing Default Information as a Borrower Discipline Device', 44 *European Economic Review* 1951.

Page AC (1986) 'Self-regulation: The Constitutional Dimension', 49 *MLR* 141.

Parker C (2004) 'Restorative Justice in Business Regulation? The Australian Competition and Consumer Commission's Use of Enforceable Undertakings' 67 *MLR* 209.

—— (2006) 'The "Compliance" Trap: The Moral Message in Responsive Regulatory Enforcement', 40 *Law & Society Review* 591.

—— (2007) 'Meta-regulation: Legal Accountability for Corporate Social Responsibility' in D McBarnet, A Voiculescu and T Campbell (eds), *The New Corporate Accountability: Corporate Social Responsibility and the Law* (Cambridge, Cambridge University Press).

Parker CE and Nielsen VL (2006) 'Do Businesses Take Compliance Seriously?', University of Melbourne Legal Studies Research Paper no 197: http://ssrncom/abstract=946850.

Parry D (2000) 'The Future of Voluntary Regulation of Advertising', 8 *Consumer Law Journal* 137.

Paterson A, Moorehead R and Sherr A (2003) 'Contesting Professionalism: Legal Aid and Non lawyers in England and Wales', 37 *Law & Society Review* 765.

Paulus I (1974) *The Search for Pure Food* (London, Martin Robertson).

Peacock A (ed) (1985) *The Regulation Game: How British and West German Companies Bargain with Government* (Oxford, Blackwell).

Pelkmans J (1987) 'The New Approach to Technical Harmonization and Standardization', 25 *Journal of Commmon Market Studies* 249.

Peltzman S (1975) The Effects of Automobile Safety Regulation', 83 *Journal of Political Economy* 667.

—— (1976) 'Towards a More General Theory of Regulation', 19 *Journal of Law and Economy* 211.

—— (1981) 'The Effects of FTC Advertising Regulation', 24 *Journal of Law and Economy* 403.

Perrow C (1986) *Complex Organisations: A Critical Essay* (3rd edn) (New York, Random House).

Pertschuk M (1982) *Revolt Against Regulation: The Rise and Pause of the Consumer Movement* (Berkeley, University of California Press).

Pickering JF and Cousins DC (1980) *The Economic Implications of Codes of Practice* (Manchester, UMIST).

—— (1982) 'The Benefits and Costs of voluntary Codes of Practice', 16 *European Journal of Marketing* 31.

Pitofsky R (1977) 'Beyond Nader: Consumer Protection and the Regulation of Advertising', 90 *Harvard Law Review* 661.

Pleasence P, Buck A, Balmer NJ, O'Grady A and Genn H (2004) 'Causes of Action: Civil Law and Social Justice', LSRC Research Paper no 11 (Norwich, TSO).

Polanyi K (1957) *The Great Transformation* (Boston, MA, Beacon Press).

Pollay RW (1986) 'The Distorted Mirror: Reflections on the Unintended Consequences of Advertising', 50 *Journal of Marketing* 18.

Poncibo C (2012) 'Networks to Enforce European Law: The Case of the Consumer Protection Cooperation Network', 35 *Journal of Consumer Policy* 175.

—— and Incardona R ,(2007) 'The Average Consumer, the Unfair Directive , and the Cognitive Revolution' 30 *Journal of Consumer Policy* 21.

Porter K and Thorne D (2006) 'The Failure of Bankruptcy's Fresh Start', 92 *Cornell Law Review* 67.

Porter M (1990) *The Competitive Advantage of Nations* (New York, The Free Press).

—— and Ketel, C (2003) *UK Competitiveness: Moving to the Next Stage* (DTI, ESRC).

Posner, R (1974) 'Theories of Economic Regulation', 5 *Bell Journal of Economics* 335.

—— (1969–70) 'The Federal Trade Commission', 37 *University of Chicago Law Review* 47.

—— (2003) *Economic Analysis of Law* (6th edn) (Boston, MA, Little Brown).

Pottow J (2007) 'Private Liability for Reckless Consumer Lending', *University of Illinois Law Review* 405.

Preston I (1975) *The Great American Blow-Up* (Wisconsin, University of Wisconsin Press).

Price Commission (1978) *The Pricing of Beds*, HC 650 (London, HMSO).

—— (1978) *Lever Brothers Ltd: Soaps, Detergents and Related Products*, HC657 (London, HMSO).

Priest G (1981) 'A Theory of the Consumer Product Warranty', 90 *Yale Law Journal* 1297.

—— (1986) 'The Invention of Enterprise Liability: A Critical History of the Intellectual Foundations of Modern Tort Law', 14 *Journal of Legal Studies* 461.

Productivity Commission (2006) *Review of the Australian Consumer Product Safety System* (Canberra, Commonwealth of Australia).

Prosser WL (1943) 'The Implied Warranty of Merchantable Quality', 27 *Minnesota Law Review* 117.

Prosser T (1983) *Test Cases for the Poor: Legal Techniques in the Politics of Social Welfare* (London, Child Poverty Action Group).

—— (1986) *Nationalised Industries and Public Control: Legal, Constitutional and Political Issues* (Oxford, Blackwell).

—— (1999) 'Theorising Utility Regulation', 62 *MLR* 196.

—— (2005)*The Limits of Competition Law: Markets and Public Services* (Oxford, Oxford University Press).

Public Accounts Select Committee (2000) *The Office of Fair Trading: Protecting the Consumer from Unfair Trading Practices*, HC 501 (London, TSO).

Rachlinski J (2003) 'The Uncertain Psychological Case for Paternalism', 97 *Northwestern University Law Review* 1165.

Rakoff TD (1983) 'Contracts of Adhesion: An Essay in Reconstruction', 96 *Harvard Law Review* 1174.

—— (2004) 'Is "Freedom From Contract" Necessarily a Libertarian Freedom?' *Wisconsin Law Review* 477.

Ramsay IDC (1981) 'Consumer Redress Mechanisms for Defective and Poor Quality Products', 31 *University of Toronton Law Journal* 117.

—— (1984) *Rationales for Intervention in the Consumer Market Place* (London, OFT).

—— (1985) 'Framework for Regulation of the Consumer Marketplace', 8 *Journal of Consumer Policy* 353.

—— (ed) (1986) *Debtors and Creditors: A Socio-legal Perspective* (Abingdon, Professional Books).

—— (1991) 'Consumer Law and the Search for Empowerment', 19 *Canadian Business Law Journal* 397.

—— (1995) 'Consumer Law, Distributive Justice and the Welfare State', 15 *OJLS* 177.

—— (1996) 'Small Claims Courts' in Ontario Law Reform Commission, *Civil Justice Review*, vol 2 (Toronto, Ministry of the Attorney General).

—— (1996) *Advertising Culture and the Law: Beyond Lies, Ignorance and Manipulation* (London, Sweet & Maxwell).

—— (1997) (ed) *Consumer Law in the Global Economy: National and International Dimensions* (Aldershot, Ashgate).

—— (2003) 'Bankruptcy in Transition: The Case of England and Wales—The Neo-liberal Cuckoo in the European Bankruptcy Nest' in Niemi-Kiesiläinen, Ramsay and Whitford (eds), *Consumer Bankruptcy in Global Perspective* (Oxford, Hart Publishing).

—— (2006) 'Consumer Law, Regulatory Capitalism and the New Regulation', 28 *Sydney Law Review* 9.

—— (2010) 'To Heap Distress upon Distress? Comparative Reflections on Interest Rate Ceilings', 60 *University of Toronto Law Journal* 707.

—— (2010) 'Regulation and the Constitution of the Single Market: The role of Consumer law' 50 *Canadian Business Law Journal* 322.

—— (2011) 'Consumer Credit Regulation After the Fall: International Dimensions I' *Zeitschrift für Europäisches Unternehmens- und Verbraucherrecht* 24.

—— (2012) 'A Tale of Two Debtors: Responding to the Shock of Over-indebtedness in France and England—A Story from the *Trente Piteuses*', 75 *MLR* 212.

—— and Williams T (2011) 'The Crash that Launched a Thousand Fixes: Regulation of Consumer Credit after the Lending Revolution and the Credit Crunch' in K Alexander and N Moloney (eds), *Law Reform and Financial Markets* (Cheltenham, Edward Elgar).

——, Salloum J, Hortox N and Mowatt G (eds) (2007) *Risk and Choice in Consumer Society* (Athens, Sakkoulas).

Randall M (2006) 'Commercial Speech under the European Convention on Human Rights: Subordinate but Equal?', 6 *Human Rights Law Review* 53.

Rawlings P and Willett C (1994) 'Ombudsman Schemes in the United Kingdom's Financial Sector: the Insurance Ombudsman, the Banking Ombudsman and the Building Societies Ombudsman', 17 *Journal of Consumer Policy* 307.

Rawls J (1971) *A Theory of Justice* (Cambridge, MA, Harvard University Press).

Reich N (1992) 'Protection of Consumers' Economic Interests by the EC' 14 *Sydney Law Review* 23.

—— (2000) 'Fair Trading with Consumers – Can the American Federal Trade Commission (FTC) Be a Model for Effective Consumer Protection in a Single European Market?' Bremen, http://eceuropaeu/dgs/health_consumer/events/event32_wrks2-1_enhtml.

—— (2006) 'Protection of Consumers' Economic Interests by the EC', 28 *Sydney Law Review* 37.

—— and Micklitz HW (1980) *Consumer Legislation in the EC Countries: A Comparative Analysis* (New York, Van Nostrand Reinhold).

Reich RB (1979) 'Toward a New Consumer Protection', 128 *University of Pennsylvania Law Review* 1.

Reiss, A Jr (1984) 'Selecting Strategies of Social Control Over Organizational Life' in K Hawkins and J Thomas (eds), *Enforcing Regulation* (Dordrecht, Kluwer).

Report of the Royal Commission on Legal Services (1979) Cmnd 7648 (The Benson Commission) (London, HMSO).

Rekaiti P and Van den Bergh R (2000) 'Cooling-off Periods in the Consumer Laws of the EC Member States: A Comparative Law and Economics Approach', 23 *Journal of Consumer Policy* 371.

Report of the Review Committee (1982) *Insolvency Law and Practice* (The Cork Committee) Cmnd 8558 (London, HMSO).

Report of the Advisory Council on the Penal System (1970) *Reparation by the Offender* (London, Home Office).

Report of the Committee on the Enforcement of Judgement Debts (1969) (The Payne Committee) Cmnd 3909 (London, HMSO).

Reynolds FMB (2003) 'Loss of the Right to Reject', 119 *LQR* 544.

Richardson G, Ogus A and Burrows P (1986) *Policing Pollution: A Study of Regulation and Enforcement* (Oxford, Clarendon Press).

Richardson G (1987) 'Strict Liability for Regulatory Crime: The Empirical Research' *Criminal Law Review* 295.

Richardson J and Jordan G (1979) *Governing Under Pressure* (Oxford, Martin Robertson).

Roach K and Trebilcock M (1996) 'Private Enforcement of Competition Laws', 34 *Osgoode Hall Law Journal* 461.

Roberts W (1975) *The Formation of Consumer Protection Policy in Britain 1945–73*, PhD thesis, Kent University.

Romano R (1985–86) 'A Comment on Information Overload, Cognitive Illusions, and their Implications for Public Policy', 59 *Southern California Law Review* 313.

Romero L (1978–79) 'The Consumer Products Warranties Act', 43 *Saskatchewan Law Review* 91.

Rose N (1999) *Powers of Freedom: Reframing Political Thought* (Cambridge, Cambridge University Press).

Rosenberg A (2006) 'Better than Cash? Global Proliferation of Debit and Prepaid Cards and Consumer Protection Policy', 44 *Columbia Journal of Transnational Law* 520.

Ross L and Littlefield N (1977–78) 'Complaint as a Problem Solving Mechanism', 11 *Law and Society Review* 199.

Rothstein H (2004) 'Precautionary Bans or Sacrificial Lambs? Participative Risk Regulation and the Reform of the UK Food Safety Regime', 82 *Public Administration* 857.

Rott P (2001) 'The Protection of Consumers' Interests after the Implementation of the EC Injunctions Directive into German and English Law' 24 *Journal of Consumer Policy* 401.

Rowan-Robinson, J et al (1988) 'Crime and Regulation', *Criminal Law Review* 220.

Rowbotham S (1999) *Threads through Time: Writings on History and Autobiography* (Harmondsworth, Penguin).

Royal Commission on Criminal Procedure (1980) *Prosecutions by Private Individuals and non-Police Agencies* Research Study No 10.

Royal Commission on Civil Liability and Compensation for Personal Injury (The Pearson Commission) (1978) Cmnd 7050 (London: HMSO).

Ryder N (2009) 'The Credit Crunch: The Right Time for Credit Unions to Strike?', 29 *Legal Studies* 75.

Sagoff M (1982) 'On Markets for Risk', 41 *Maryland Law Review* 755.

Salop S and Stiglitz J (1977) 'Bargains and Ripoffs: A Model of Monopolistically Competitive Price', 44 *Review of Economic Studies* 493.

Sandrock D (2005) *Never Had it So Good: A History of Britain from Suez to the Beatles* (London, Abacus).

Scheingold SA (1974) *The Politics of Rights: Lawyers, Public Policy and Political Change* (New Haven, CT, Yale University Press).

Schelling T (1984) *Choice and Consequence* (Cambridge, MA, Harvard University Press).

Schepel H (2005) *The Constitution of Private Governance: Product Standards in the Regulation of Integrating Markets* (Oxford, Hart Publishing).

Schmitter PC (1974) 'Still the Century of Corporatism?', 36 *Review of Politics* 85.

Schulze R, Schulte-Nolke H and Jones J (2003) *A Casebook on European Consumer Law* (Oxford, Hart Publishing).

Schumpeter J (1947) *Capitalism, Socialism and Democracy* (New York, Harper).

Schwartz A and Wilde L (1979) 'Intervening in Markets on the Basis of Imperfect Information: A Legal and Economic Analysis', 127 *University of Pennsylvania Law Review* 630.

Schwartz A (1979) 'The Case for Specific Performance', 89 *Yale Law Journal* 271.

—— (1983) Enforcement of Security Interests in Consumer Goods', 26 *Journal of Law and Economics* 117.

—— (1983) Imperfect Information in Markets for Contract Terms: The Examples of Warranties and Security Interests', 69 *Virginia Law Review* 1387.

—— (1995) 'Legal Implications of Imperfect Information in Consumer Markets', 151 *Journal of Institutional and Theoretical Economics* 31.

Schwartz A and Scott R (1991) *Commercial Transactions: Principles and Policies* (2nd edn) (Thomson, West).

Schwartz S (2010) 'Can Financial Education Improve Financial Literacy and Retirement Planning?', IRPP Study no 12, Montreal, 1

Scitovsky T (1976) *The Joyless Economy: An Inquiry into Human Satisfaction and Dissatisfaction* (New York, Oxford University Press).

Scott C (2000) 'Accountability in the Regulatory State', 27 *Journal of Law and Society* 38.

—— (2004) 'Regulatory Innovation and the Online Consumer', 26 *Law and Policy* 476.

—— and Black J (2000) *Cranston's Consumers and the Law* (3rd edn) (London, Lexis).

Scott, H (1978) 'The Risk Fixers', 91 *Harvard Law Review* 737.

Scott J and Trubek D (2002) 'Mind the Gap: Law and New Approaches to Governance in the European Union', 8 *European Law Journal* 1.

Scott, P (2002) 'The Twilight World of Interwar British Hire Purchase' *Past and Present* 195.

Scott RE (1985–86) 'Error and Rationality in Individual Decision making: An Essay on the Relationship between Cognitive Illusions and the Management of Choice', 59 *Southern California Law Review* 329.

Selwyn N (2004) 'Reconsidering Political and Popular Understandings of the Digital Divide', 6 *New Media and Society* 341.

Seiter E (1993) *Sold Separately: Parents and Children in Consumer Culture* (New Brunswick, NJ, Rutgers University Press).

Sen A (1999) *Development as Freedom* (New York, Knopf).

Seyfang G (2004) 'Consuming Values and Contested Cultures: A Critical Analysis of the UK Strategy for Sustainable Consumption and Production', 623 *Review of Social Economy* 323.

Shanklin W and King H (1977) 'Evaluating the FTC Cooling-Off Rule', 11 *Journal of Consumer Affairs* 101.

Shanks M (1983) 'The Consumer as Stakeholder and the Implications for Consumer Organisations', 6 *Journal of Consumer Policy* 133.

Sher BD (1968) 'The "Cooling-Off" Period in Door-to-Door Sales', 15 *UCLA Law Review* 717.

Shiner R (2003) *Freedom of Commercial Expression* (Oxford, Oxford University Press).

Shonfield A (1965) *Modern Capitalism: The Changing Balance of Public and Private Power* (Oxford, Oxford University Press).

Silbey S (1980–81) 'Case Processing: Consumer Protection in an Attorney-General's Office', 15*Law and Society Review* 849.

Simon H (1982) *Models of Bounded Rationality* (Cambridge, MA, MT Press).

Slaughter A-M (2004) *A New World Order* (Princeton, Princeton University Press).

Slawson D (1971) 'Standard Form Contracts and Democratic Control of Lawmaking Power', 84 *Harvard Law Review* 529.

Smith M and Pearson A (1969) 'The Value of Strict Liability', *Criminal Law Review* 5.

Smith A (1904) *An Inquiry into the Nature and Causes of the Wealth of Nations* (London, Methuen).

Smith R and Kenny M (2011) 'Orchestrating Sub-prime Consumer Protection in Retail Banking: Abbey National in the Context of Europeanised Private Law', 19 *European Review of Private Law* 43.

Smits J (2011) 'The Right to Change Your Mind? Rethinking the Usefulness of Mandatory Rights of Withdrawal in Consumer Contract Law', 29 *Penn State International Law Review* 671.

Snow A and Weisbrod BA, (1978) 'Consumerism, Consumers and Public Interest Law' in Weisbrod, Handler and Komesar (eds), *Public Interest Law: An Economic and Institutional Analysis* (Berkeley, University of California Press).

Social Trends (1988) (London, HMSO).

Spence M (1974) *Market Signalling* (Cambridge, MA, Harvard University Press).

Stanton K (2004) 'New Forms of the Tort of Breach of Statutory Duty', 120 *LQR* 324.

Stapleton J (1994) *Products Liability* (London, Weidenfeld).

—— (1999) 'Good Faith in Private Law', 52 *Current Legal Problems* 1.

—— (2002) 'Bugs in Anglo-American Products Liability' *South Carolina Law Rev* 1225.

Starrs, JE (1969) 'Consumer Class Actions' 49 *Boston University Law Review* 211.

Stearns P (1997)'Stages of Consumerism: Recent Work on the Issues of Periodization', 69 *Journal of Modern History* 102.

Stephens M (2011) *Tackling Housing Market Volatility in the UK* (Joseph Rowntree).

—— and Quilgar D (2008) 'Sub-prime Mortgage Lending in the UK', 8 *European Journal of Housing Policy* 197.

Stephenson G (1983) *The Criminal Law and Consumer Protection* (Ashford, Middx, Barry Rose).

Stevenson J (1984) *British Society 1919–45* (Harmondsworth, Penguin).

Stewart R (1975)' The Reformation of American Administrative Law', 88 *Harvard Law Review* 1667.

—— and Sunstein CR (1982)' Public Programs and Private Rights', 95 *Harvard Law Review* 1193.

Stigler GJ (1961) 'Private Vice and Public Virtue', 4 *Journal of Law and Economics* 1.

—— (1971) 'The Theory of Economic Regulation', 2 *Bell Journal of Economics and Management Science* 3.

—— (1975) *The Citizen and the State: Essays on Regulation* (Chicago, University of Chicago Press).

—— and Becker, G (1977) *'De Gustibus non est disputandum'*, 67 *American Economic Review* 76.

Stiglitz J (2000) 'The Contributions of the Economics of Information to Twentieth Century Economics', 115 *Quarterly Journal of Economics* 1441.

—— and Weiss A (1981) 'Credit Rationing in Markets with Imperfect Information', 71 *American Economic Review* 393.

Streeck W and Schmitter PC (1985) *Private Interest Government* (London, Sage).

Certain Other Consumer Goods (Deventer, Kluwer).

Study Group on Social Justice (2004) 'Social Justice in European Contract Law: A Manifesto', 10 *European Law Journal* 653.

Stuyck J (2000) 'European Consumer Law After the Treaty of Amsterdam: Consumer Policy Beyond the Internal Market?', 37 *Common Market Law Review* 367.

—— (2005) 'EC Competition Law after Modernisation: More than Ever in the Interest of Consumers', 28 *Journal of Consumer Policy* 1.

Stuyck J, Terryn E and Van Dyck T (2006) 'Confidence Through Fairness? The New Directive on Unfair Business-to-Consumer Commercial Practices in the Internal Market', 43 *Common Market Law Review* 107.

Sullivan TA, Warren W and Westbrook JL (2000) *The Fragile Middle Class: Americans in Debt* (New Haven, Yale University Press).

Sunstein C (1990) *After the Rights Revolution: Reconceiving the Regulatory State* (Cambridge, MA, Harvard University Press).

—— (2002) *The Cost–Benefit State: The Future of Regulatory Protection* (Chicago, American Bar Association).

—— (2011) 'Empirically Informed Regulation', 78 *University of Chicago Law Review* 1349.

—— and Thaler R (2003) 'Libertarian Paternalism Is Not an Oxymoron', 70 *University of Chicago Law Review* 1159.

—— (2008) *Nudge* (New Haven, Yale University Press).

Sutherland M and Sylvester A (1993) *Advertising and the Mind of the Consumer* (St Leonards, NSW, Allen and Unwin).

Sylvan L (2005) 'Social Movements and their Influence', 64 *Australian Journal of Public Administration* 83.

—— (2005) 'Comments: Activating competition: The Consumer–Competition Interface', 12 *Competition and Consumer law Journal* 191.

Taibi A (1992) 'Banking Finance and Community Economic Empowerment: Structural Economic Theory, Procedural Civil Rights and Substantive Racial Justice', 107 *Harvard Law Review* 1463.

Tawney RH (1947) *Religion and the Rise of Capitalism: A Historical Study* (New York, New American Library).

Telser LG (1965) *Advertising and Competition* (London, Institute for Economic Affairs).

Tench D (1981) *Toward a Middle System of Law* (London, Consumers' Association).

Teubner G (1983) 'Substantive and Reflexive Elements in Modern Law', 17 *Law and Society Review* 239.

—— (1987) 'Juridification, Concepts, Aspects, Limits, Solutions' in G Teubner (ed), *Juridification of Social Spheres: A Comparative Analysis of the Areas of Labor, Corporate Antitrust and Social Welfare Law* (Berlin, Walter de Gruyter).

—— (1993) *Law as an Autopoietic System* (London, Blackwells).

Thain, G (1976) 'Credit Advertising and the Law: Truth in Lending and related matters', *Washington University Law Quarterly* 257.

Thaler RH (1981) 'Some Empirical Evidence on Dynamic Inconsistency', 8 *Economics Letters* 201.

Thomas R (1988) 'Alternative Dispute Resolution—Consumer Disputes', 7 *Civil Justice Quarterly* 206.

Tiebout C (1956) 'A Pure Theory of Local Expenditures', 64 *Journal of Political Economy* 416.

Tilly C (2004) *Social Movements, 1768–2004* (Boulder, CI, Paradigm Publishers).

Touraine A (1971) *The Post-industrial Society* (New York, Random House).

Toynbee P (2003) *Hard Work: Life in Low-pay Britain* (London, Bloomsbury).

Treasury (2004) *Promoting Financial Inclusion* (London, TSO).

—— (2006) *Releasing the Resources to Meet the Challenges Ahead: Value for Money in the 2007 Comprehensive Spending Review* (London, TSO).

—— (2007) *Financial Inclusion: The Way Forward* (London, TSO).

—— (2012) *A New Approach to Financial Regulation*, Cmd 8268 (London, TSO).

Trebilcock MJ (1969) 'Consumer Protection in the Affluent Society', 16 *McGill Law Journal* 263.

—— (1972) 'Private Law Remedies for Misleading Advertising', 22 *University of Toronto Law Journal* 1.

—— (1975) 'Winners and Losers in the Modern Regulatory System: Must the Consumer always Lose?', 13 *Osgoode Hall Law Journal* 618.

—— (1985) 'Regulating Service Quality in Professional Markets' in D Dewees (ed), *The Regulation of Quality: Products, Services, Workplaces and the Environment* (Toronto, Butterworths).

—— (2003) 'Rethinking Consumer Protection Policy' in C Rickett and T Telfer (eds), *International Perspectives on Consumers' Access to Justice* (Cambridge, Cambridge University Press).

—— et al (1977) *Study on Consumer Misleading and Unfair Trade Practices in Canada* (prepared for the Department of Consumer and Corporate Affairs in Ottawa).

—— et al (eds) (1982) *The Choice of Governing Instrument* (Ottawa, Economic Council of Canada).

Trentmann F (2006) 'Knowing Consumers-Histories, Identities, Practices' in F Trentmann (ed), *The Making of the Consumer: Knowledge, Power and Identity in the Modern World* (Oxford, Berg).

Tribe J (2006) *Bankruptcy Courts Survey 2005—A Pilot Study Final Report* (London, Centre for Insolvency Law).

Trumbull G (2006) *Consumer Capitalism: Politics, Product Markets, and Firm Strategy in France and Germany* (Ithaca, NY, Cornell University Press).

—— (2010) 'Consumer Policy' in D Coen, W Grant and G Wilson (eds), *The Oxford Handbook on Business and Government* (Oxford, Oxford University Press,).

—— (2012) 'Credit Access and Social Welfare: The Rise of Consumer Lending in the United States and France', 40 *Politics and Society* no 1.

Trzaskowski J (2011) 'Behavioural Economics, Neuroscience and the Unfair Commercial Practices Directive' 34 *Journal of Consumer Policy* 377.

Tversky A and Kahneman D (1974) 'Judgment under Uncertainty: Heuristics and Biases', 185 *Science* 1124.

—— and —— (1991) 'Loss Aversion in Riskless Choice: A Reference-dependent Model', 106 *Quarterly Journal of Economics* 1039.

Twigg-Flesner C (2005) 'Information Disclosure about the Quality of Goods—Duty or Encouragement?' in Howells, Jansen and Schulze (eds), *Information Rights and Obligations* (Aldershot, Ashgate).

—— (2003) *Consumer Product Guarantees* (Aldershot, Ashgate).

——, Parry D, Howells G and Nordhausen A (2005) *An Analysis of the Application and Scope of the Unfair Commercial Practices Directive: A Report Prepared for the DTI* (London, DTI).

Van Boom W (2011) 'Price Intransparency, Consumer Decision Making and European Consumer Law', 34 *Journal of Consumer Policy* 359.

van Erp J (2011) 'Naming without Shaming: The Publication of Sanctions in the Dutch Financial Market', 5 *Regulation & Governance* 287.

Veblen T (1899) *The Theory of the Leisure Class: An Economic Study of Institutions* (New York, Macmillan).

Veljanovski C (1984) 'The Economics of Regulatory Enforcement' in K Hawkins and J Thomas (eds), *Enforcing Regulation* (Dordrecht, Kluwer).

—— (1983) 'Regulatory Enforcement—An Economic Study of the British Factory Inspectorate', 5 *Law and Policy Quarterly* 75.

Viscusi WK (1984) *Regulating Consumer Product Safety* (Washington DC, American Enterprise Institute).

—— (1985) 'Consumer Behavior and The Safety Effects of Product Safety Regulations', 28 *Journal of Law and Economics* 527.

—— (1998) *Rational Risk Policy* (Oxford, Clarendon Press).

Vogel D (2003) 'The Hare and the Tortoise Revisited: The New Politics of Consumer and Environmental Regulation in Europe', 33 *British Journal of Political Science* 557.

Wagner G (2010) 'Mandatory Contract Law: Functions and Principles in the light of the proposal for a Directive on Consumer Rights' in A Ogus and W van Boom (eds), *Juxtaposing Autonomy and Paternalism in Private Law* (Oxford, Hart Publishing).

Wallace GJ (1976) 'The Uses of Usury: Low Rate Ceilings Re-examined', 56 *Boston University Law Review* 451.

Walters A, McKenzie S and Donna W (2007) 'Consumer Bankruptcy Law Reform in Scotland, England and Wales', 80 *American Bankruptcy Law Journal* 477.

Warren E and Tyagi AW (2003) *The Two-income Trap: Why Middle-class Mothers and Fathers Are Going Broke* (New York, Basic).

Warren E (2007) 'Unsafe at Any Rate' *Democracy Journal*, Summer, 8.

Waterson M (2003) 'The Role of Consumers in Competition and Competition Policy', 21 *International Journal of Industrial Organization* 129.

Watson GD (2001) 'Class Actions: the Canadian Experience', 11 *Duke Journal of Comparative & International Law* 269.

Weatherill S (1987) 'Consumer Safety Legislation in the United Kingdom', 2 *European Consumer Law Journal* 81.

—— (1999) 'Consumer Policy' in P Craig and G de Burca (eds), *The Evolution of EU Law* (Oxford, Oxford University Press).

—— (2005) *EU Consumer Law and Policy* (Cheltenham, Edward Elgar).

—— (2007) 'Who Is the "Average Consumer"?' in S Weatherill and U Bernitz (eds) *The Regulation of Unfair Commercial Practices under EC Directive 2005/29 New Rules and New Techniques* (Oxford, Hart Publishing).

—— and Bernitz U (2007) *The Regulation of Unfair Commercial Practices under EC Directive 2005/29 New Rules and Techniques* (Oxford, Hart Publishing).

Weber R and Dawes R (2005) 'Behavioral Economics' in NJ Smelser and R Swedberg (eds), *The Handbook of Economic Sociology* (2nd edn) (Princeton, Princeton University Press) 90.

Wells C (1995) 'A Quiet Revolution in Corporate Liability for Crime', 145 *New Law Journal* 1326.

—— (2001) *Corporations and Criminal Responsibility* (2nd edn) (Oxford, Oxford University Press).

Wheatley M (2012) *My Vision for the FCA*, http://www.fsa.gov.uk/library/communication/speeches/2012/0125-mw.shtml.

Whelan C (1990) *Small Claims: An International and Comparative Analysis* (Oxford, Oxford University Press).

Whincup M (1975) 'Reasonable Fitness of Cars', 38 *MLR* 660.

White AR (1985) *Grounds of Liability: An Introduction to the Philosophy of Law* (Oxford, Clarendon Press).

Whish R (2003) *Competition Law* (London, LexisNexis).

Whitehouse L (2009) 'The Mortgage Arrears Pre-action Protocol: An Opportunity Lost', 72 *MLR* 793.

Whitford WC (1973) 'The Functions of Disclosure Regulation in Consumer Transactions', *Wisconsin Law Review* 400.

—— (1981) 'Structuring Consumer Protection Legislation to Maximise Effectiveness', *Wisconsin Law Review* 1018.

—— (1982) 'Comment on a Theory of the Consumer Product Warranty', 91 *Yale Law Journal* 1371.

—— (2003) 'A Comparison of British and American Attitudes Towards the Exercise of Judicial Discretion in Contract Law' in D Campbell, H Collins and J Wightman (eds) (2003), *Implicit Dimensions of Contract : Discrete, Relational and Network Contracts* (Oxford, Hart Publishing) ch 6.

Whitman JQ (2007) 'Consumerism Versus Producerism: A Study in Comparative Law', 117 *Yale Law Journal* 340.

Whittaker S (2007) 'The Relationship of the Unfair Commercial Practices Directive to European and National Contract Laws' in Weatherill and Bernitz (eds), *The Regulation of Unfair Commercial Practices under The EC Directive* (Oxford, Hart).

Wiegand W (1991) 'Reception of American Law in Europe', 39 *American Journal of Comparative Law* 229.

Wieäcker F (1995) *A History of PrivateLaw in Europe: With particular Reference to Germany*, trans T Weir (Oxford, Clarendon Press).

Wightman J (2003) 'Beyond Custom: Contract, Contexts and the Recognition of Implicit Understandings' in D Campbell, H Collins and J Wightman (eds) (2003), *Implicit Dimensions of Contract: Discrete, Relational and Network Contracts* (Oxford, Hart Publishing).

Wilhelmsson T (1990) 'Social Force Majeure'–A New Concept in Nordic Consumer Law', 13 *Journal of Consumer Policy* 1.

—— (1992)'Administrative Procedures for the Control of Marketing Practices—Theoretical Rationale and Perspectives', 15 *Journal of Consumer Policy* 159.

—— (2003) 'Services of General Interest and European Private Law' in C Rickett and T Telfer (eds) ,*Consumers' Access to Justice* (Cambridge, Cambridge University Press) 149.

—— (2004) 'The Abuse of the "Confident Consumer" as a Justification for EC Consumer Law', 27 *Journal of Consumer Policy* 317.

—— (2007) 'The Paradox of the Risk Society and the Fragmentation of Consumer Law' in I Ramsay et al (eds), *Choice and Risk in Consumer Society* (Athens, Sakkoulas).

Willett C (2007) *Fairness in Consumer Contracts* (Aldershot, Ashgate)

——, Morgan-Taylor M and Naidoo A (2004) 'The Sale and Supply of Goods to Consumers Regulations', *Journal of Business Law* 94.

—— (2011) 'The Functions of Transparency in Regulating Contract Terms: UK and Australian Approaches', 60 *International & Comparative Law Quarterly* 355.

—— and Oughton D (2007) 'Liability for Incorrect Installation and Other Services Associated with Consumer Goods' in G Howells, A Nordhausen, D Parry and C Twigg-Flesner (eds), *The Yearbook of Consumer Law* (Aldershot, Ashgate).

Williams C and Windebank J (2002) 'The 'Excluded Consumer': A Neglected Aspect of Social Exclusion', 30 *Policy and Politics* 501.

Williams F (ed) (1977) *Why the Poor Pay More* (London, NCC).

Williams GA (2007) 'Empowerment of Whom and for What? Financial Literacy Education and the New Regulation of Consumer Financial Services', 29 *Law & Policy* 226.

—— (2010) 'Open the Box: An Exploration of the Financial Services Authority's Model of Fairness in Consumer Financial Transactions' in M Kenny, J Devenney and F O'Mahony (eds), *Unconscionability in European Private Financial Transactions* (Cambridge, Cambridge University Press).

Williams J and Hare C (2010) 'Early Experiences of the Enforcement of the Unfair Commercial Practices Directive in Scotland', 33 *Journal of Consumer Policy* 377.

Williamson OE (1985) *The Economic Institutions of Capitalism: Firms, Markets, Relational Contracting* (New York, Free Press).

Wilson C and Waddams Price C (2005) 'Irrationality in Consumers' Switching Decisions: When More Firms May Mean Less Benefit' (ESRC Centre for Competition Policy).

Wilson GK (1984) 'Social Regulation and Explanations of Regulatory Failure', 32 *Political Studies* 203.

Wilson J (ed) (1980) *The Politics of Regulation* (New York, Basic Books).

Wilson T (1963) *A Discourse Upon Usury* [1572] (New York, AM Kelley).

—— (2004) 'The Inadequacy of the Current Regulatory Response to Payday Lending', 32 *Australian Business Law Review* 193.

Wilson T (2012) 'Supporting Social Enterprises to Support Vulnerable Consumers: The Example of Community Development Finance Institutions and Financial Exclusion', 35 *Journal of Consumer Policy* 197.

Winkler J (1975) 'Law State and Economy: The Industry Act 1975 in Context', 2 *British Journal of Law and Society* 103.

Wintrobe R (1997) 'Modern Bureaucratic Theory' in D Mueller (ed) *Perspectives on Public Choice* (Cambridge, Cambridge University Press).

Wisdom M (1979) 'An Empirical Study of the Magnusson–Moss Warranty Act', 31 *Stanford Law Review* 1117.

Wolf C (1979) 'Theory of Non-market Failure—Framework for Implementation Analysis', 22 *Journal of Law and Economics* 107.

Wolff H (1996) *Access to Justice, Final Report to the Lord Chancellor on the Civil Justice System in England and Wales* (London, Lord Chancellor's Office).

Wolff K (ed) (1950) *The Sociology of Georg Simmel* (New York, Free Press).

World Health Organization (2005) *The Challenge of Obesity in the WHO European Region*, Fact Sheet EURO/13/05.

Worswick G and Ady PM (eds) (1962) *The British Economy in the Nineteen-fifties* (Oxford, Clarendon Press).

Wright GA (1969) 'The Cost-internalization Case for Class Actions', 21 *Stanford Law Review* 383.

Yee WP (2001) 'Good Faith: Protecting Parties' Reasonable Expectations', 1 *Oxford University Commonwealth Law Journal* 195.

Yeung K (1999) 'Private Enforcement of Competition Law' in C McCrudden (ed), *Regulation and Deregulation* (Oxford, Oxford University Press).

—— (2003) *Securing Compliance: A Principled Approach* (Oxford, Hart Publishing).

—— (2005) 'Government by Publicity Management: Sunlight or Spin?' *Public Law* 360.

Yngvesson B and Hennessey P (1975) 'Small Claims, Complex Disputes: A Review of the Small Claims Literature', 9 *Law and Society Review* 219.

Ziegel J (1973) 'The Future of Canadian Consumerism', 51 *Canadian Bar Review* 190.

Index

Introductory Note

References such as '138–9' indicate (not necessarily continuous) discussion of a topic across a range of pages. Wherever possible in the case of topics with many references (but not in the case of cited authors), these have either been divided into sub-topics or only the most significant discussions of the topic are listed. Because the entire volume is about 'consumer law', the use of this term (and certain others occurring throughout the work) as an entry point has been restricted. Information will be found under the corresponding detailed topics.